EASA Professional Pilot Studies

Phil Croucher

"Never allow your ego, self-confidence, love of flying, pressure from a customer, boss or co-pilot, or economic need to interfere with your good judgement during any stage of a flight. There is no amount of pride, no thrill, pleasure, schedule or job that is worth your licence or your life and the lives of your passengers. Complacency kills, and so does being a cowboy." John Bulmer

This book is for Sue

Legal Bit

These notes are sold as is without warranty of any kind, either express or implied, including but not limited to the implied warranties of merchantability and fitness for a particular purpose. Neither the Author, the Publisher nor their dealers or distributors assume liability for any alleged or actual damages arising from its use. **In other words**: *These notes are for private study, and contains interpretations of official documentation, which changes, so there could be technical inaccuracies through no fault of the author or publisher. As a result, alterations will be made without reference to anyone, and they are not guaranteed to suit your purposes. The author, publisher, and their distributors or dealers are not responsible for situations arising from their use.*

Copyrights, etc.

This book copyright © 2018 Phil Croucher ISBN 0-9268332-2-8/978-1-92-683322-4

Notice is hereby given that the name PHILIP ANDREW CROUCHER, in capital letters, or any variation thereof, is claimed by Phil Croucher, which name may not be used without permission.

Graphics copyright © Steve Sparrow, Phil Croucher (with help from Corel Corporation). Special thanks to David Webb. Charts in this publication are not to be used for navigation purposes.

All Rights Reserved

Our staff of Witches, Weird Hags and Assorted Familiars are prepared to cause Visitations of a most Irritating and Embarrassing nature upon anyone foolish enough to copy parts of this work without the permission of the author.

Seriously, no part of this publication may be reproduced, stored in a retrieval system or transmitted by any means, electronic, mechanical, photocopying, recording or otherwise, or used in any other form than originally supplied, without prior written permission from the author.

Table Of Contents

0	**Introduction**	**0-1**
1	**Human Performance & Limitations**	**1-1**
	Accidents	1-1
	The Human Factor	1-2
	Evolution	1-3
	Decisions, Decisions	1-6
	Decision Making Models	1-13
	Learning & Performance	1-17
	Threat & Error Management	1-18
	Risk Management	1-21
	The Body	1-23
	Stress	1-51
	Communication	1-56
	Judgment	1-61
	Flight Deck Management	1-64
2	**Airframes**	**2-1**
	Forces Involved	2-1
	Fatigue & Stress	2-2
	Flight Controls	2-19
3	**Principles of Flight**	**3-1**
	Definitions	3-1
	Newton's Laws	3-4
	Airflow	3-5
	The Aerofoil	3-10
	Stalling	3-14
	Forces In Flight	3-30
	Stability & Equilibrium	3-47
	Propellers	3-54
	High Speed Flight	3-60
	Wake Turbulence	3-71
4	**Systems**	**4-1**
	Fuel Supply	4-1
	Hydraulics	4-5
	Electricity & Magnetism	4-18
	Computers, Etc	4-53

TABLE OF CONTENTS

Fire Detection	4-60
Fire Protection	4-63
Oxygen Systems	4-64
Pneumatics	4-66
Air Conditioning	4-70
Automatic Flight Control	4-73
Icing & Protection	4-83

5 Engines — 5-1

Engine Power	5-1
Reciprocating Engines	5-3
Turbines	5-17
Fuel	5-36
Engine Instruments	5-42
Lubrication	5-45

6 Instruments — 6-1

Pressure	6-1
Temperature	6-3
Flight Instruments	6-5
Pitot-Static System	6-6
The Altimeter	6-8
Airspeed Indicator	6-14
The Machmeter	6-17
Vertical Speed Indicator	6-18
The Compass	6-19
Gyroscopes	6-24
Artificial Horizon	6-27
Heading Indicator (DGI)	6-29
Turn Coordinator	6-33
Flight Management Systems	6-35
Inertial Navigation	6-45
Warning & Recording	6-51
Flight Recording	6-55

7 Air Law — 7-1

International Air Law	7-1
1 - Licences & Ratings	7-8
2 - Rules Of The Air	7-11
3 - Meteorological Services	7-22
4 - Aeronautical Charts	7-22
7 - Registration Marks	7-22
8 - Airworthiness	7-22
9 - Facilitation	7-25
10 - Telecommunications	7-26
11 - Air Traffic Services	7-26
12 - Search & Rescue	7-38
13 - Accident Investigation	7-39
14 - Aerodromes & Airports	7-40
15 - Aeronautical Information	7-47
17 - Security	7-49
PANS-OPS (DOC 8168)	7-50

TABLE OF CONTENTS

8 Operational Procedures — 8-1
regulations — 8-1
Commercial Air Transport — 8-1
Operations Manual Part A — 8-3
Operations Manual Part B — 8-31
Operations Manual Part C — 8-31
Operations Manual Part D — 8-32
Emergencies & Equipment — 8-34
Performance — 8-43
Planning Minima — 8-44
Maintenance — 8-46
Noise Abatement — 8-47
Wake Turbulence — 8-47
Bird & Wildlife Hazards — 8-47
Long Range Operations — 8-48

9 Flight Performance & Planning — 9-1
Regulations & Compliance — 9-1
Powerplants — 9-2
Aircraft Weight — 9-4
Types Of Performance — 9-4
Factors Involved — 9-5
V-Speeds — 9-16
Charts — 9-20
Single Engine Piston — 9-21
Multi-Engine Piston — 9-25
Medium Range Jet Transport — 9-28

10 Mass & Balance — 10-1
Units & Conversions — 10-1
The Centre Of Gravity — 10-1
SEP 1 — 10-12
MEP1 — 10-14
MRJT — 10-15
LRJT — 10-21

11 Radio Navigation — 11-1
Wave Motion — 11-1
How It All Works — 11-2
Radio Navigation — 11-13
VOR — 11-13
ADF/NDB — 11-19
Airways — 11-23
TACAN — 11-23
FANS — 11-24
RNAV — 11-24
Direction Finding — 11-35
Radar — 11-36
DME — 11-44
ILS — 11-45

TABLE OF CONTENTS

12 Communications — 12-1
- Definitions — 12-2
- Q Codes — 12-5
- Categories Of Message — 12-6
- Operating Procedures — 12-6
- Radio Failure — 12-12
- Distress & Urgency — 12-12
- Propagation & Frequencies — 12-14
- Interception — 12-14
- IFR Stuff — 12-14

13 Navigation (General) — 13-1
- The Earth — 13-1
- Positional Reference — 13-1
- Speed & Distance — 13-4
- Convergency — 13-5
- Maps & Charts — 13-10
- Time & Time Zones — 13-17
- The Triangle of Velocities — 13-22
- The Flight Computer — 13-26
- Miscellaneous — 13-26

14 Meteorology — 14-1
- The Sun — 14-1
- The Atmosphere — 14-3
- Thermodynamics — 14-5
- Clouds — 14-10
- Air Masses — 14-14
- Frontal Systems — 14-15
- Wind — 14-19
- Pressure — 14-36
- Precipitation — 14-43
- Turbulence — 14-44
- Thunderstorms — 14-44
- Icing — 14-48
- Visibility — 14-50
- Met Services & Information — 14-52
- Charts — 14-59

15 Flight Planning & Monitoring — 15-1
- ATS Flight Plan — 15-1
- European Airways — 15-1
- Jeppesen Manual — 15-2
- Fuel — 15-6
- Charts — 15-16

Introduction

This book is based on the modular self-study program for the EASA ATPL(A) examinations provided by Caledonian Advanced Pilot Training. However, due to book size restrictions, it does not contain basic maths & physics information - this can be downloaded from www.captonline.com/samplenotes.pdf.

Proper pilot performance is based on knowledge, planning, and anticipation of what the aircraft will do - and you will not be able to achieve that without studying properly. Your real training starts in your first job, and what you learn before then can be very important.

For example, most pilots gain licences from several countries over their careers - if you have a good core knowledge, you will be in and out of the exam rooms a lot quicker. In addition, if you do the minimum work for your exams, by learning the answers rather than the material ☺, it will be painfully obvious to the interview panel when you go for a job.

DIFFERENCES

> "The book certainly approaches the ATPL subjects from a rather different angle than I have ever encountered. The humour, wit and undoubted flight experience of the writer come through when discussing the various ATPL exam subjects. My impressions of the book are vary favourable. Having read it twice, it struck me as being very well researched, informative and well laid out."
>
> Rod Parker, BALPA

For people coming to the EASA world from North America, some differences are immediately apparent. First of all, although there are areas where you don't need to speak to anyone on the radio, they are few and far between, and at low level, as almost all airspace is controlled in some way or another (bush pilots take note!) The transition level is also very low, at 3,000 feet in most countries, so get used to those low flight levels.

Next, another barometer setting is typically used for takeoffs, landings and operations within the circuit, called QFE, which is simply one that gives you a reading of zero feet when on the ground at an aerodrome. It isn't used in North America because many aerodromes are at high elevations and the readings would be off the scale. The setting you are used to, the aerodrome setting against mean sea level, is called QNH.

And what about all those Q codes? They are a hangover from the old wireless telegraphy days, and are not officially supposed to be used, although everyone does (the idea was to use short codes instead of commonly used expressions to reduce transmission times. QSY, for example, is "changing frequency"). Flight duty times are much shorter, too, and are not part of the exam. You should also join the circuit overhead and there is no UNICOM.

With regard to examinations, it may seem that you are learning a lot of stuff that will not be useful to you. That's certainly true to a certain extent, but the EASA system makes you learn everything you might need for your career before you start, rather than as you go along - in North America, you will likely be exposed to the same material over the years, but from company ground school and various other type rating courses. In Canada, for example, and most other countries, even though it's not part of the pilot exams, you will have to do a Dangerous Goods exam before you start flying for your company. It's just that the Europeans have no guarantee that this will happen and expect you to be a seasoned professional from the start - the original intention behind the EASA exams was to be the equivalent of a BA degree, since people were regarded as joining a profession. As with many other degrees, a lot of the subject matter was included as padding for credibility purposes, and the main purpose was all lost somewhere along the way. Currently, the EASA ATPL, according to Bristol University, has the same standing as two years of a degree-level course.

However, some of the content is there for third party reasons - Human Factors training is an international requirement, and radio theory must be learnt because you have a cut-down version of the amateur radio licence, and you need to know how not to screw up the airwaves.

EQUIPMENT REQUIRED

For the UK exams, you will also need:

- The **Jeppesen Student Pilot Route Manual**, used in Flight Planning and Navigation. Random copies of this are exchanged at exam time, so don't write notes on them!
- **Flight computer**. Must be:
    - Jeppesen CR-3
    - Pooleys CRP-5
    - AFE ARC 2
- **Chart plotting gear**, including a clear ruler marked in mm/cm and inches, 18 ins long at least, dividers, square protractor
- Calculator. Must be:
    - Texas Instrument TI-30XS
    - Sharp EL-W531
    - Citizen SR-260
    - Casio FX-83/85 series (available from most supermarkets)
    - Casio FX-300

Tip: The hours, minutes, secs functions can save loads of time and avoid (

The above can be obtained from:

- Transair (www.transair.co.uk)
- Pooleys (www.pooleys.com) - mention CAPT for a discount!
- Airplan Flight Equipment (www.afeonline.com)
- The Flight & Model Store (www.flightstore.co.uk)

"Pure book knowledge should be impeccable - every second of doubt about "what do I do now?" is worth 30% of workload. Mostly because the self-doubt and second-guessing are real time and mental capacity wasters. The more you know flat cold, the easier it is to fly under the gauges"

Nick Lappos

Everyone **is responsible for flight safety!**

Human Performance & Limitations

The essential problem is that our bodies are not made to cope with the conditions imposed by aviation. In the air, physical and psychological stresses occur on top of the normal stuff of everyday life that should be taken note of in order to do our jobs properly. Minor illnesses, stress, fatigue, alcohol and caffeine can affect your performance, and there are even regulations to cover their use, all discussed later.

Amendment 159 of Annex 1 to the Chicago Convention (see *Air Law*) makes the study of Human Factors a mandatory part of obtaining a professional pilot's licence. Such training is all about the **safety and efficiency of the operation** and the **well-being of the individual**.

Competence is based on the knowledge, skills and attitudes of the pilots involved. ICAO lists 8 core competencies to be mastered by professional pilots:

- Communication
- Aircraft Flight Path Management - Manual Control
- Aircraft Flight Path Management - Automation
- Leadership and teamwork
- Problem solving and decision making
- Application of procedures
- Workload management
- Situational Awareness

Thus, amongst other things, competent pilots must be motivated, team players, good communicators, and be able to manage crews and stress.

As humans are part of the system, they must be medically fit and be certified as such by a physician at regular intervals. Your professional licence is not valid without a Class 1 medical certificate, which is valid for 12 months if you are under 40 and 6 months if you are over, except when multi-crew, when it goes back up to 12 months.

You may not act as flight crew if you know or suspect that your physical or mental condition renders you unfit so to do. In other words, you may not exercise licence privileges once you are aware of a decrease in your medical fitness that makes you unable to safely execute your duties.

EASA Rule **CAT.GEN.MPA.100** (see *Operational Procedures*) states that crew members must not perform duties:

- when under the influence of psychoactive substances or alcohol or when unfit due to injury, fatigue, medication, sickness or similar causes.
- until a reasonable time has elapsed after deep water diving or following blood donation (**due to possible fainting** or **hypoxia** in the latter case).
- if applicable medical requirements are not fulfilled.
- if they are in any doubt of being able to accomplish their assigned duties.
- if they know or suspect that they are suffering from fatigue (see 7.f of Annex IV to Regulation (EC) No 216/2008)* or feel otherwise unfit, to the extent that the flight may be endangered.

No crew member must allow task achievement/ decision making to deteriorate to the extent that flight safety is endangered because of the effects of fatigue, taking into account, inter alia, fatigue accumulation, sleep deprivation, number of sectors flown, night duties or time zone changes. Rest periods must provide sufficient time to enable crew members to overcome the effects of the previous duties and to be well rested by the start of the following flight duty period.

Medicals are only valid if you meet the initial issuing requirements. A Board of Inquiry or insurance company may interpret the words "medically fit" a little differently than you think if you fly with a cold or under the influence of alcohol or drugs. In any case, you should talk to a medical examiner as soon as possible in the case of:

- admission to a hospital or clinic for over 12 hours
- surgery or other invasive procedures
- regular use of medication
- regular use of correcting lenses

You should also inform the authorities in writing of significant personal injuries involving your capacity to act as a member of a flight crew, or illness that lasts for more than 21 days (after that period has elapsed), or pregnancy. In these cases, your medical is suspended, but it can be reinstated after an examination, or if you are exempt. It can be given back directly after giving birth.

ACCIDENTS

A *reportable* accident occurs when:

- anyone is killed or seriously injured from contact with an aircraft, including jet blast or rotor downwash.
- an aircraft sustains damage or structural failure.
- an aircraft is missing or inaccessible.

between the time any person boards it *with the intention of flight*, and all persons have disembarked. This does not include injuries from natural causes, which are self-inflicted or inflicted by other people, or any to stowaways hiding in places not normally accessible to passengers and crew.

HUMAN PERFORMANCE & LIMITATIONS
The Human Factor

Significant or *Substantial Damage* means damage or failure affecting structure or performance, normally needing major repairs - essentially, anything that may involve an insurance claim.

Under ICAO, a *fatal injury* involves death within 30 days. A *serious injury* involves:

- more than 48 hours in hospital within 7 days
- more than *simple fractures* of *fingers*, *toes* and *nose*
- lacerations causing nerve or muscle damage or severe haemorrhage
- injury to any internal organ
- 2nd or 3rd degree burns or any over 5% of the body
- exposure to infectious substances or radiation

An **incident** is any happening, other than an accident, which hazards or, if not corrected, would hazard any aircraft, its occupants or anyone else, *not* resulting in substantial damage to the aircraft or third parties, crew or passengers. In other words, a dangerous event, but not as serious as an accident.

An accident is the end product of a chain of events so, in theory, if you can recognise the sequence it should be possible to stop one before it happens. A common saying is that "the well oiled nut behind the wheel is the most dangerous part of any car". Not necessarily true for aviation, perhaps but, in looking for causes other than the hardware when it comes to accidents, it's hard not to focus on the pilot (or other people - e.g. the human factor) as the weak link in the chain - around 75% (between 70-80%) of accidents can be attributed to this, although it's also true to say that the *situations* some aircraft (and people) are put into make them liable to misfortune, particularly with helicopters - if you continually land on slippery logs, something untoward is bound to happen sometime!

The current teaching is that the human factor is the weak link at the root of most accidents, so if you remove the bad apple the problem should go away, but it isn't the whole story. Circumstances can also be involved, and even experienced pilots can get caught out. Take, for example, one who is tasked to do two flights in an afternoon, the first one with a light load of two people and the second with four. It would seem logical to fill the machine up with enough fuel to cover both flights, since the loads allow it and the schedule is tight between them, so you can save time by not refuelling. But what if the first passengers are late, or don't even turn up? You are then faced with doing the second trip with more fuel than you would normally plan for to allow for safety margins, even though you might be within the weight limits. Of course, you could defuel, but that can be a major inconvenience when you are the only one there and the passengers are waiting in the usual car-park-as-a-passenger-lounge! Thus, it is not necessarily a person's character, but their circumstances that can be at the root of an accident, as has been proven by many psychological studies involving prison guards.

The "safety record" of an airline can also be nothing but a numbers game. Take a flight from Los Angeles to New York with two hundred passengers on board - the distance is 3000 miles, so they have flown 600,000 passenger-seat miles. With 150 on the flight back, you get 1,050,000, for being in the air for only 9 hours! If they have 20 aircraft doing that five days a week, and injure one passenger, they can say it happened only once in 105,000,000 passenger-seat-miles, which is still only 900 hours! Having said that, when flying, you are still safer by over 9:1 against driving or 300:1 over riding a bicycle on the road! Currently, the accident rate is *around 1 per million aircraft movements*.

However, it is impossible to design all errors out, so no system is safe - it still depends on people for its operation, and safety is not the only goal they have to achieve (Transport Canada's statement that a safety management system is a "businesslike approach to safety" does not mean that company profits, etc. should be taken into account, but that safety procedures should be integrated into the company's normal business practice). Granted, some people in any system may have an "attitude" problem, as discussed later, but it is definitely not the only factor! Thus, there is hardly ever a single cause responsible.

And if you are thinking that safety procedures might be expensive, review the consequences of an accident:

- Fatalities and/or injuries
- Customer relations & company reputation suffer
- You need another aircraft ....
- .....while still paying for the one you crashed
- Any schedule gets screwed up
- The insurance is increased
- You end up with unwanted attention from the media and the authorities - the strongest economic pressure to improve safety is often the need to avoid negative publicity.

Even if you don't get that far, it's safe to say that, for every accident, there are thousands of incidents - it costs $15,000 for an airliner to return to the gate, or $500,000 to shut down an engine in flight in terms of lost revenue and other indirect costs, such as hotels for passengers. It even costs $100 or so just to start a turbine engine! Such losses are uninsured and cost the airline industry over $36 billion in 2001.

THE HUMAN FACTOR

There are two broad aspects to Human Factors:

- **Engineering**, which includes:
    - **Ergonomics**, or human capabilities and limitations in the design of machines and objects, work processes and environments. In World War II, many problems were caused by mismatches between machines and operators.
    - **Anthropometry**, the study of human body measurements (from the whole population except the lowest and highest 5%).
- **Cognitive Psychology**. The study of human behaviour and the mental processes that drive it. That is, how mental processes interact with each other to help us understand and use objects.

The emphasis on the human element in relation to accidents was first recognised in '79 and '80, where over 500 incidents relating to shipping were analysed, and 55% were found to be related to human factors. Did you think that was *1979 & 80*? It was actually in *1879* and 80! In fact, as well as the iceberg, the *Titanic* had to dodge the *Deutschland*, which was floating around the shipping lanes, having run out of coal (it also nearly collided with the *New York* on its way out of Southampton). Since then, through the *1980s* and 90s, aviation accidents in the USA were analysed in depth, and it was found that *crew interaction* was a major factor in them since, nearly 75% of the time, it was the first time they had flown together, and nearly half were on the first leg, in situations where there was pressure from the schedule (over 50%) and late on in the duty cycle, so fatigue was significant (doesn't everything happen late on Friday afternoon?)

The Captain was also flying 80% of the time. The problem is, that it's not much different now - 70% of aircraft accidents in the USA in 2000 were pilot-related, based on mistakes that could easily be avoided with a little forethought, and it was more or less the same figure way back in 1940. Now, the figure worldwide is around 80%.

The accident rate is highest during takeoff and landing, but it is also high in the cruise, usually because the machine hits something in the way - one major cause of accidents is *Controlled Flight Into Terrain*, or CFIT, where a serviceable aircraft under the positive control of the crew interacts with something solid. Despite that, though, the phase of flight most prone to accidents (and subject to human error) is intermediate and final approach.

In other words, 60% of accidents occur during the 4% of time spent nearer the ground.

If air traffic continues to grow at the present rate, we will be losing 1 airliner per week and even more GA aircraft - the Australian authorities are looking at 1 helicopter per week, which is why Human Factors training is now an ICAO requirement, with the syllabus drawn from many sources, including Psychology, Engineering, Physiology, Medicine, Sociology, Biology and others.

One problem is that the sort of mistakes that cause accidents arise from within individual pilots - if you want to be technical, they arise from *intrapersonal* (inside oneself) rather than *interpersonal* (between people) causes. A good example of an intrapersonal cause is an internal conflict, such as the one faced by a First Officer who must challenge the Captain.

Modern life is stressful enough - we are all hostages to other peoples' expectations and attitudes, and it often seems that, within an hour of waking up, we have a mix of attitudes all of our own, by the time the toast has been dropped (face down) and everyone's had their bite out of you. However, what happens outside should not be brought into the cockpit - one function that checklists perform is to help keep your mind on the job and exclude outside influences. *Using a checklist before starting is a contribution to safety because the concentration required reduces distraction from personal stress.*

It has also (finally) been realised that traditional methods of flight instruction have been missing something - the assumption has always been that, just because you have a licence, you know what you are doing, or that good, technically qualified pilots (or doctors, for example) make good decisions as a matter of course (I know many stupid doctors!) Naturally, everybody on the shop floor has always known that this is not necessarily so, and a lot of experienced pilots make mistakes, so experience is not the answer, either. In fact, experience can be a harsh teacher*, assuming you heed its lessons anyway, so ways have had to be found to use training instead, hence the ICAO requirements for Human Performance training. This means that manipulating the flying controls is less than half of the training required to be a competent pilot.

*Good judgment is based on experience, which is based on bad judgment......

Currently, aeronautical decision making is seen as a function that comes under standard psychological theory and practice (*Brecke*, 1982; *Stokes and Kite*, 1994). In fact, research into the human factors related to aircraft accidents and incidents has highlighted decision making as a crucial element (*Jensen*, 1982; *O'Hare, Wiggins, Batt, and Morrison*, 1994). The irony is that people who are aware that such training is a Good Thing do not need the courses - the sort that should most benefit are like the Enstrom owner who mentioned to his shocked engineer that he didn't like the look of two bolts in the tail rotor assembly, so he turned them round and shortened one of them, since it was longer than the other. After patiently explaining during wall-to-wall counselling that the reason why one bolt was longer was for balance purposes, and that they were inserted one way round for a reason, the engineer suggested he take his custom elsewhere.

As with most other things, aviation is more of a mental process than a physical one. For example, it takes much longer to become a captain than it does to become a pilot, and CRM/PDM/Human Factors training aims to shorten the gap by substituting training for experience (the terms are used interchangeably here).

It (CRM) is mostly concerned with the cognitive* and interpersonal skills needed to manage flights within an organised aviation system, being intended to develop the effectiveness of crew performance by improving attitudes towards flight safety and human relationships. Almost the first thing you have to take on board is that not everyone does things the same way as you do, as a result of which, compromises have to be made in order to get the job done. Another is that, when operating by yourself, feedback is missing, which is useful for making decisions. The only real replacement for this is reviewing your flights and discussing them with colleagues, which is more difficult for helicopter pilots, because of the lack of meeting places (but licensed premises are good).

*The mental processes used for situational awareness, solving problems and taking decisions.

EVOLUTION

As the problem of crew co-operation needed to be addressed, management principles from other industries, such as Quality Assurance and Risk Management, were distilled into what is mostly called *Crew Resource Management*, prompted, in Canada, at least, by three accidents, one of which was at Dryden, which was also instrumental in new Canadian icing laws being passed.

On the day concerned, the weather was forecast for generally unsettled and deteriorating conditions, with lowering cloud and freezing precipitation. The Fokker F-28 landed late in the day, and behind schedule, which sounds like a typical day in aviation, especially with the crew having been 6 days away from home.

Because the Auxiliary Power Unit wasn't working, they had to keep one engine running, as there was no external start facility at Dryden. After refuelling, and when the passengers had been loaded, another 10 turned up, which meant that fuel had to be taken off. Since the engine had to be kept running for another 35 minutes, once all that was over, they needed more fuel, so there was another short delay to take more on. No de-icing was available, because one engine had to be kept running.

For up to 2 months before, and within the previous five days, the aircraft had been subject to multiple unserviceabilities, including smoke in the cabin and oily smells. It could have been grounded, but there was pressure to keep to the schedule and getting another would have involved a delay. Maintenance deferred the repair of the fire detection system and a red placard, reading *APU unserviceable*, was placed on the APU panel.

The flight crew had also recently converted from Convairs, which are very forgiving when it comes to taking ice, so perhaps they thought they could use that experience on the super-critical wing of the F-28.

By now it was snowing heavily, and the F-28 had to wait at the holding point while a Cessna in distress landed. The takeoff roll began 70 minutes behind schedule. After a slower than normal acceleration, the aircraft rotated and took off briefly, to settle back down on the runway. After a second attempt, it managed to get off the ground, passing the end of runway at only 15 ft. The whole exercise ended in a fireball of orange flames.

Thus, although he bears the final responsibility, the Captain sure didn't get much help from elsewhere (it didn't help that there was no ATC either - clearances at Dryden are given from Winnipeg, which is a four-hour drive away, aside from the fact that the airport authority was trying to cut down on the firefighting equipment, so there was chaos at the incident itself).

Dryden Crash - Photographer Unknown

As it happens, most weather-based accidents in small aircraft involve inadvertent entry into cloud by people with only the basic instrument training required for the commercial licence. Next in line is icing. With regard to jet transports and executive jets, it's CFIT (*Controlled Flight Into Terrain*), and the figures are 50% and 72%, respectively. Although it was introduced too early, and is prone to false alarms, GPWS marked a substantial decrease in hull loss rates in the 80s, after a TWA 727 hit a mountain near Washington DC in 1974, killing 92 people only two months after another plane nearly hit the same mountain.

From 33 such accidents in 1964, the figure fell to just 8 in 1984, although this is still too high. Around 40% of fatal accidents were in aircraft without GPWS.

CRM was actually developed from the insights gained from installing Flight Data and Cockpit Voice Recorders, when crews were not considered to be assertive enough, and Captains not receptive enough. CRM back then could probably best be summed up in the phrase "I'm the Captain - you're not!", which leads to situations where, although it's part of the First Officer's job to monitor and challenge the Captain, a failure to do so could be down to the Captain's management methods, because that's where the rest of the crew take their lead from.

Prompted by a NASA workshop in 1979, United Airlines started to include the training, and not just for pilots. The goal was *synergism*, meaning that the total performance of a crew should be greater than the sum of its parts, or each crew member (like Simon & Garfunkel, or Lennon & McCartney, who are talented enough by themselves, but so much better as a group).

For example, when you combine two radio frequencies, you get one more above and below. If you combine two singers, there is a third voice in there somewhere. It's all a matter of vibration, and it's the same with people, or flight crews. There is an extra buzz when a team is working well together, or when 2 + 2 = 5.

As an example, until the mid 1960s, the French night mail crews routinely made landings at night in dense fog using standard instruments. Their regularity of service was 98%. A British journalist (*Flight International*) wrote in 1964 that one night they got down to 70 feet and saw only one light. At 100 feet they had seen nothing, but crew sympathy was such that no word was necessary to agree on a change of plan and go down further. The crew knew what the Captain had in mind. To achieve such synergy, members of any team must feel that they and their opinions are valued, and understand their roles. As, in most companies, the teams change from day to day (or flight to flight), the whole organisation must therefore foster teamwork, *from the top down*, and attempt to reduce the effects of jagged edges between people. In other words, the relatively simple concept of learning to live with others and allowing for their differences, which involves sharing power on the flight deck, at the very least, as *multi-crew* means what it says - the real point is that *everyone* should know what's going on. The behaviour of people in a company is very much a reflection of the management, in our case the commander, so there is an obligation to foster a positive working environment which, essentially, means not being surly or miserable - the cockpit culture should allow anyone on board to speak up if they feel they have to.

Referring back to the Dryden accident, the significant amounts of snow on the wings were noticed by a flight attendant and two captains who were travelling as passengers, but who did not communicate the problem to the pilots. The flight attendant later said that she was concerned by the snow but, because she had been put off by company pilots in similar situations in the past, she decided not to go to the cockpit. Although the immediate cause of the Dryden accident was accumulation of snow and ice on the wings during a delay in obtaining takeoff clearance, it was determined that the event was triggered by no less than 17 inadequate corporate processes.

HUMAN PERFORMANCE & LIMITATIONS
Evolution

A reading of the accident report on the Air Florida flight that hit a bridge and ended up in the Potomac would also be instructive - the FO was clearly sure that something was wrong (icing) but didn't like to say so.

Like it or not, you are part of a team, even if you are the only one in the cockpit, and *you* have to fit into an established system, especially when IFR.

The CRM concept evolved from the original *Cockpit* Resource Management, through *Crew* Resource Management, where Decision Making became more important, into a third generation, which involved cabin crews, etc., and introduced aviation-specific training, as a lot of what served previously was very much psychology-based, but it is very difficult to escape psychology in just about every walk of life these days, and now aviation is no exception - all airlines use selection tests, as do many corporate employers. In fact, 90% of aviation casualties in World War I were down to human factors (50% during training), and in World War II they started testing to weed out people who had questionable decision-making skills, so it's not really new.

CRM then became integrated into all flight training, and an element is now met on nearly all check rides, with a complete syllabus cycle taking place over three years. In the US, the fourth generation can take the form of an *Advanced Qualification Program* (AQP) tailored specifically to individual company needs. Now we are in the sixth generation, which concentrates more on cockpit behaviour, and which is called *Threat & Error Management*, discussed later. A further development could be to change the name (yet again) to *Company* Resource Management, where other departments get involved in the same training. The benefit of this for Air Aurigny (in the Channel Islands) has been improved communication between departments and a sharpening up of the whole operation once people saw what everybody else had to cope with - turnaround times became shorter, which made a direct contribution to the bottom line.

However, as mentioned above, the general principles of CRM have been around for some time - Field-Marshal Montgomery wrote that the best way to gain a cohesive fighting force was efficient *management* of its components, and he certainly succeeded in getting the Army, Navy and Air Force to work together. However, as far as definitions go, you could call it *Cockpit* Resource Management when you're single pilot, and *Crew* Resource Management when you're not. Previously, you might have been introduced to the concept of *Airmanship*, which involved many things, such as looking out for fellow pilots, doing a professional job, not flying directly over aircraft, always doing pre-flight inspections, doing a clearing turn before taking off, etc. In other words, actions relating to being the "gentleman aviator", or exhibiting professional behaviour as an airman, which involves discipline, skill, knowledge (of yourself and the aircraft), risk management, etc.

These days, especially when multi-crew, there are new concepts to consider, such as *delegation, communication, monitoring* and *prioritisation*, although they will have varying degrees of importance in a single-pilot environment. In fact, the term "pilot error" is probably only accurate about a third of the time as all it really does is indicate where a breakdown occurred. There may have been just too much input for one person to cope with, which is not necessarily error, because no identifiable mistakes were made. Perhaps we need a new phrase that occupies the same position that "not proven" does in the Scottish Legal System (somewhere between Guilty and Not Guilty).

STOP Airmanship is still a valid concept, and should be treated with as much respect as the regulations!

Anyhow, the aim of this sort of training is to increase flight safety by showing you how to make the best use of any resources available to you, which include your own body (physical and psychological factors), information, equipment and other people (including passengers and ATC), whether in flight or on the ground, even engine handling or using the humble map - copilots are trained for emergencies, for example, so they can be used instead of automatically taking over yourself when something happens - like a human autopilot, in fact. Using a GPS for navigation, and ignoring the other navigation aids or the map, is bad CRM.

You should be able to make better decisions after being introduced to the concepts, principles and practices of CRM, or Decision Making, with the intention of reducing the accident rate even further. That is to say, we know all about the hardware, now it's time to take a look at ourselves. Aircraft have limitations, and so do you! An accident-prone person, officially, is somebody to whom things happen at a higher rate than could be statistically expected by chance alone. Taking calculated risks is completely different from taking chances. Know your capabilities, and your limits. Things that can help, particularly with single-pilot operations, are:

- **Knowledge** - know the flight manual
- **Preparation** - do as much as you can before the flight - is that runway *really* large enough to stop in if one engine fails? Has all the servicing been done? Is the paperwork correct? Visualise the route from the map - and fold it as best you can for the route. Got enough batteries for the GPS? Do you know the Minimum Safe Altitude if you get caught in cloud? And who to call? An hour's preparation on the ground is worth two in the air.

Pilots who receive decision-making training outperform others in flight tests and make 10-15% fewer bad decisions, and the results improve with the comprehensiveness of the training. Your training cannot cover everything - instead, you are given enough training to be able to make decisions for yourself, hence the importance of decision making training.

CRM courses are supposed to be discussion-based, which means that you are expected to participate, with the intention that your experiences will be spread around to other crews. This is because it's quite possible never to see people from one year to the next in a lot of organisations, particularly large ones, and helicopter pilots in particular have no flying clubs, so experience is not being passed on. In fact, if you operate in the bush, you might see some of your colleagues during training at the start of the season, and not see them till the end, if at all. Even when single-pilot, you still have to talk to management and engineers, and to people even more important - the customers!

In short, CRM/PDM is the effective utilisation of all available resources (such as crew members, aircraft systems and supporting facilities) to achieve safe and efficient operation, by enhancing your communication and management skills. In other words, the emphasis is placed on the non-technical aspects of flight crew performance (the so-called *softer skills*) which are not part of the flying course but which are also needed to do your job properly - those associated with teamwork, and smoothing the interfaces between members of a team, loosely based on the four NOTECHS (non-technical skills) categories of:

- Co-operation
- Leadership
- Situational Awareness
- Decision Making

EU regulations (Part Ops ORO.FC.115) state the requirements. CRM training encountered on check rides, etc. will be given by TRIs/TREs, who will have base privileges attached to their licences, but the kind of stuff that is done in a classroom must be done by a fully accredited person.

Captaincy

As we said before, you could loosely call this airmanship, with an element of common sense, but a newer term is *Captaincy*, as flying is a lot more complex now than when the original term was more appropriate. Both are transforming into *Threat & Error Management*, which is discussed later.

The elusive quality of Captaincy is probably best illustrated with an example, using the subject of the Point Of Equal Time. If you refer to *Flight Planning*, you will find that it is a position where it takes as much time to go to your destination as it does to return to where you came from, so you can deal with emergencies in the quickest time. In a typical pilot's exam, you will be given the departure and destination points, the wind velocity and other relevant information and be asked to calculate the PET along with the PSR (*Point of Safe Return*), which is OK as far as it goes, but tells you nothing about your qualities as a Captain, however much it may demonstrate your technical abilities as a pilot.

Now take the same question, but introduce a flight across the Atlantic, during which you are told that a passenger has appendicitis. First of all, you have to know that you need the PET. Then you find out that you are only 5 minutes away - technically, you should turn back, but is that really such a good decision? (Actually, it might not be, since it will take a few minutes to turn the old girl around anyway). Commercially, turning back could be disastrous, and here you find the difference between being a pilot and a Captain, or the men and the boys, and why CRM training is becoming so important.

A Captain is supposed to exhibit qualities of loyalty to those above and below, courage, initiative and integrity, which are all part of the right personality - people have to *trust* you, so character is an important part of being a pilot. This, unfortunately, means being patient and cheerful in the most trying of circumstances, and even changing your own personality to provide harmony within the crew, since it's the objective of the whole crew (as a team) to get the passengers to their destination safely. As single crew, of course, there is only you in your cockpit, but you still have to talk to others, and we all work in the air transport industry - it just happens that your company is paying your wages at the moment. In this context, the word "crew" includes anybody else who can help you deliver the end product, which is - safe arrival!

Safety Management Systems

A safe arrival is only as good as the system behind it - this would include the pilot who doesn't abuse the machine, the engineers who take pride in their work, the support staff in the operations office who don't overload the pilot with work they should be doing, and a management culture that allows people to approach their jobs in a manner that fosters safety and professionalism over short term customer satisfaction, and who are proactive (trying to stop the next accident) rather than reactive (wiping up the mess after the last one). To do this, various layers of paperwork have been developed over the years, culminating in the Safety Management Systems that each company is required to have. Although certain systems should be in place anyway, such as operations manuals or compliance systems (see *Operational Procedures*), they don't go far enough. The ops manual, for one thing, is a one-way document, and readers are simply expected to comply with its requirements.

A compliance system goes a step further by having someone monitor the system and produce a slight amount of feedback to management (and occasionally from staff), but this has limitations before it starts, because the system on which it is based was originally for manufacturing, which does not lend itself well to a service industry such as aviation. It is a generic management system standard which doesn't have much to do with the end product, except for ensuring its production under sound management procedures, "leading to efficiency and consistency, and, ultimately, cost reductions".

However, to allocate resources to improve safety, management needs timely information. For this, you need a system that starts at the bottom, allows information to flow both ways, and is non-punitive (a just culture). The goal of an SMS is "to develop the tools and skills that allow organisations to manage and mitigate risk to a level beyond the capability of normal regulatory oversight." In short, as with the compliance system, the Authority keeps an eye on your company by assessing the effectiveness of the Safety Management System. In theory, if this is well managed and proactive, they can assume the rest of the company runs just as well and their involvement can be reduced without compromising safety. This involves a change in approach from management, and the skill of the auditor.

So Is It Working?

A study that examined 558 airline mishaps between 1983-2002 was conducted by the Johns Hopkins Bloomberg School of Public Health in the United States. It revealed that there were 40% less incidents involving pilot error, which was attributable to better training and technology that aids pilot decision making.

DECISIONS, DECISIONS

The best way out of trouble is not to get into it, which is easier said than done. You, the pilot, are the decision-maker - in fact, under the Chicago Convention, your word is law when in flight, but you are also responsible for what goes on.

Aviation is noticeable for its almost constant decision-making. As you fly, particularly in a helicopter, you're probably updating your next engine-off landing point every minute or so. Or maybe you're keeping an eye on your fuel and continually calculating your endurance. It all adds to the tasks with which you're meant to keep up to date., because the situation is always changing. In fact, a decision *not* to make a decision (or await developments) is also a decision, being aware that we don't want indecision. To drive a car 1 mile, you must process 12,000 pieces of information - that's 200 per second at 60 mph! It has to be worse with flying, and possibly over our limits - human capabilities are actually quite marginal, being able to deal with only one thing at a time, and vulnerable to fatigue and stress - the most demands are at the beginning and end of a flight, but the latter is when you are most tired and your heart rate is highest.

Decision making provides a structured, systematic approach to the analysis of changes during flight and how they may affect its safe outcome, of which risk management (discussed later) is an important component. It involves the generation of alternative courses of action based on several factors, which may include available knowledge, past experience, stress, etc. It can be supported by written information, like checklists or SOPs (Standard Operating Procedures). In emergencies, decision making requires the distribution of tasks (i.e. delegation) and crew coordination, and it is generally most efficient if the crew adapts their management style to meet the demand.

However, a good decision depends in the first place on proper analysis of a situation........

Information Processing

The way we interpret the information on which we base decisions can be complex. With the eyes and ears, which are the main ways of receiving information, *the processing is done in the brain*, which uses past experience to interpret what it senses - it therefore has expectations, and can pre-judge a situation. In fact, as accident reports routinely show, in high stress conditions, the brain may even blank out information not directly concerned with the task in hand. Certainly, the processing of information before it is brought to our attention is done in such a way as to protect our self-esteem and confidence. In other words, when people act contrary to their self-identity, anything that doesn't pass through that filter is either rejected or made to fit.

Information processing usually means the interpretation of signals from the sensory organs by the brain, which can be selective. It is the process of receiving information through the senses, analysing it and making it meaningful. This is represented by the diagram below.

In the process, physical stimuli, such as sound and sight, are given attention and must be perceived as important before being received into sensory memory for final interpretation by the Central Decision Maker (the thinking and reasoning area inside the brain), in conjunction with *Short Term* (STM) or *Long Term Memory* (LTM). Some processes can bypass all that completely, such as motor programs, which operate subconsciously., but such automatic decision making only comes with experience. In short, the brain processes information in four stages:

- Sensation
- Perception
- Decision
- Response

Although there may be lots of input, there is only one channel out of the Central Decision Maker (the thinking and reasoning area in the brain), which must be shared when things are busy. Anything not currently being attended to is held in short term memory. The system works also in reverse, in that feedback on results can be used to improve knowledge and future judgment.

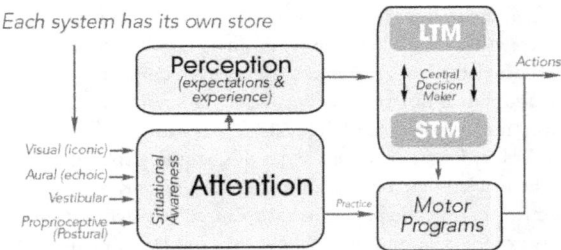

Perception at this point means converting that information into something that is immediately meaningful, or realising that it's relevant to what you're doing (you only perceive what you can conceive). What comes out depends on past experience of those events, your expectations, and whether you're able to cope with the information at that time (or are even paying attention). Good examples are radio transmissions, which you can understand, even if you can't hear them properly, because you expect certain items to be included, and you know from experience that they're bad anyway. One danger is that you may hear what you want to hear and not what is actually sent. Another is seeking information to confirm your mental model (making the ground fit the map).

In flight, however, as a "Central Decision Maker", you take on the role of an information processor - in this, you have a unique talent, in that decisions can be made without having all the relevant information to hand. If you were to ask a computer to choose between a clock that was gaining five minutes a day, and one that had stopped completely, it would probably choose the one that had stopped, because it was accurate twice a day, as opposed to once every 60 days or so. Machines cannot discriminate, and they need *all* relevant information, which is good if you just want them to report facts, as with instruments, but not if you want them to make decisions. Thus, *the human information processing system is highly efficient when compared to computers because it is flexible.* On the other hand, human performance degrades in more subtle ways than with machines, which either work or they don't.

Memory

Sensations and perception come before learning (discussed later), and memory is the result. The word can mean either a storage place, a means of moving data in and out of it, and the data itself. It describes the ability to recall or recognise information or events that have been previously learnt or experienced (*Ormrod*, 2001). How long information is stored depends on its level of processing.

Memory is a feature in human information processing. We need it to learn new things - without it, we could not capture information, or draw on past experience to apply it in new situations (i.e. remembering). Thus, there are three processes involved in using memory:

- input *(or encoding)*
- storage
- retrieval

any one of which can fail and make you think you're losing your memory, though this can depend on whether the items are placed in short or long term memory. However, to encode something in the first place, it must be given *attention*, before it can be *perceived* against all the other stuff going on. This means that much of what we are exposed to never even enters the memory, and thus is not available for recall. As a result, what are often called memory problems are really lapses in attention. In 1951, Dr. Wilder Penfield began a series of scientific experiments in which he proved that, by touching the temporal cortex with a weak electrical probe, the brain could be caused to play back some past experiences, and the feelings associated with them, despite the patients not normally being able to recall them.

He came to the following widely accepted conclusions:

- The brain acts like a tape recorder. We may forget experiences, but they are recorded somewhere.
- The brain also records the feelings associated with the experiences, and they stay locked together.
- People can exist in two states simultaneously (patients replaying hidden events and feelings could talk about them at the same time).
- Hidden experiences when replayed are vivid, and affect how we feel at the time of replaying.
- There is a connection between mind and body, or a link between the biological and the psychological.

Anyhow, most psychologists (by no means all!) agree that there are 3 types of memory:

INSTINCT (SENSORY MEMORY)

What Jung called "race memory" gives an immediate (gut reaction) response to a stimulus, like being hard-wired. Some psychologists call this *sensory memory*, as it provides a raw reaction to sensory input (a knee jerk*).

*A stereotypical and involuntary reaction of the organism on stimulation of its receptors is called a *reflex*.

That is, it can retain information long enough to allow you to decide whether a stimulus is important or not, or whether it is for the eyes or ears. It allows us to pay attention to one thing whilst being aware of and able to process events in wider surroundings (the *Cocktail Party Effect*, discussed below, is a good example). *Iconic Store* is where visual images are kept for about half a second. *Echoic memory* (for the ears) might last for between 250 milliseconds up to a few seconds. The *Haptic Store* retains physical senses of touch and internal muscle tensions. The slight delay allows you to string connected events together and remember a series of words as a structured sentence until the Central Decision Maker can cope with the input. There are as many sensory registers as there are senses.

Information that is not lost from sensory memory is passed on to..........

SHORT TERM MEMORY (STM)

Otherwise known as *working*, or *active*, memory by later theorists, this is for data that is used and forgotten almost instantly, or is used for current information (actually, nothing is ever forgotten, but the point is that Short Term Memory is for "on the spot" work, such as fuel calculations or ATC clearances, and figures greatly with situational awareness, which can follow short term memory's limitations). STM involves information from the present or immediate past, and can only handle somewhere between 5-9 items at a time (that is, 7 ± 2), unless some tricks are used, such as grouping or association (*chunking*), meaning that what can be held in short term memory depends on the rules used for its organisation, which are in long-term memory. Mnemonics are also good (such as HASELL), since STM appears to like words, albeit taking things rather literally - words will be recalled exactly, and in the order they were processed, unlike in long term memory, which may recall their *meaning* instead. Thus, short term memory stores information as sounds, rather than pictures, and it is almost error-free.

Data in short term memory typically lasts between 20-30 seconds, and is highly sensitive to distraction. It is probably what Einstein was referring to when he thought that, as soon as one fact was absorbed, one was discarded.

 As short term memory tends to hold information for immediate use, don't expect to remember short term information - *always write clearances down*!

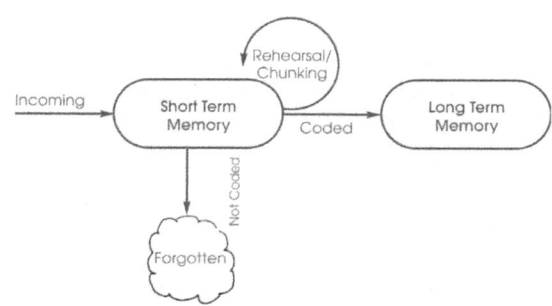

Because the capacity of short-term memory is so limited, items must clamour for attention, which may be based on *emotion*, *personal interest*, or the *unusual*. As mentioned, you can extend working memory's capabilities, either by *rehearsal* (mental repetition), or *chunking* (associating items with each other), or breaking up the information into sequences, as you might with a telephone number. The sequence of letters ZNEBSEDECREM becomes a lot easier to remember once you realise it is MERCEDES BENZ backwards, and suddenly your short term memory has space for more data. Information is therefore often modified as it is stored, being encoded for easier recall.

 Some say that it is not working memory's capacity that is lacking, but its *processing ability*. Short term memory usually starts failing at 12 000 feet (due to hypoxic hypoxia), but its onset may occur as low as 8 000 feet.

Unfortunately, you cannot do any chunking or association without ....

HUMAN PERFORMANCE & LIMITATIONS
Decisions, Decisions

LONG TERM MEMORY (LTM)

This is where all our basic knowledge (memories of childhood, training, etc.) is kept, with more capacity and ability to retain information than short-term memory - its storage capacity is regarded as unlimited, and possibly consists of several interlaced systems, such as **semantic** memory (for facts and figures, and basic knowledge of the world), **episodic** memory (specific events), **procedural** memory (for skills) and **generic** (general) memory, according to some sources. Semantic and episodic memory together are **Declarative Memory**. Episodic memory is influenced by our expectations of what should have happened. It is affected the most by amnesia.

LTM works better when dealing with information that has special relevance or meaning, whereas short-term memory is more meaning-free. Where training is concerned, many processes can be carried out automatically in LTM, with little thinking. Repetition (or *rehearsing*) is used to get information into it, combined with organising it, placing it into some sort of context or associating it with an emotion (when studying, concentrate on the *meaning* rather than the subject matter).

The nervous system has a rhythm of arousal that peaks around 20:00 hours, and long-term memory improves as arousal is heightened, reaching a peak late in the day. Short term memory, however, reaches its zenith around 10:00-11:00 hours - it's about 15% more efficient in the morning and 15% less in the evening.

The reason why long term memory is needed for association purposes is because it contains the rules that give the items meaning. For example, chess players can have extraordinary short term memory for positioning of pieces, *if the rules in long-term memory are obeyed*. Upon random positioning, short term recall reverts to normality. People with brain damage (after accidents, etc.) can often remember only one type of information, which supports the idea that the above types of memory are quite distinct, and that data can go directly into long term memory.

Knowledge stored in long-term memory should be pre-activated (with *planning* and *anticipation*) so it can be available when required and have the access time reduced. This is the purpose of a briefing before a flight (LTM's main limitation is that, **unless the information in it is accessed from time to time**, its retrieval can be difficult).

If an input is similar to something in long term memory, there is a tendency to assume they are the same. This is *mindset*, where you believe what you want to believe, rather than what is true.

Sensation & Perception

This is the process of giving meaning to what is sensed, or *interpreting*, *organising* and *elaborating* on the input, discarding anything that is not relevant. It is the other end of a process involving sensation which uses a set of cognitive processes to organise, make sense of, store, retrieve and apply the data you get from your senses. Without cognitive processing, the data received by your senses is useless. So, sensation is the physical side and perception is the psychological side of what we do.

To collect data with your senses, you need:

- A stimulus.
- A sensory organ to convert it into a nerve impulse.
- A nerve pathway to carry the impulse to the brain.
- An area within the brain to receive and process the impulse.

Much of our sensory and perceptual processing is automatic and unconscious. In fact, the brain is constantly receiving and processing data, but only so much of it gets through because it is below a certain threshold of attention, discussed elsewhere.

Variations on the perception theme could come from:

- The **stimulus** itself. The Moon on the horizon appears larger than it does when it is overhead, even though the size of the image on the retina might be the same (this is because you are viewing it through many layers of the atmosphere, which is denser at low level).
- The **situation**, or the context in which an image is viewed. The figures 1 and 3 could be perceived as the letter B if they are together in a list of letters.
- The **state of the perceiver** regarding motivation or emotion, or memories and expectations. If you are hungry, pictures of food can appear to be brighter, and the colour of a drink can has been shown to affect the taste of its contents.

Perception therefore happens in the brain, after a stimulus has been detected. The process by which information gets to the brain is called *transduction*. The brain distinguishes between stimuli by paying attention to the part that is activated. The *Gestalt Theory** relates to *perception* and *organisation*.

*A system of thought that regards mental phenomena as arranged in patterns or structures (gestalts) perceived as a whole and not as the sum of their parts. The Gestalt laws are the basic principles governing how objects are organised and perceived.

Subcutaneous (under the skin) pressure receptors are stimulated by pressure on the corresponding body parts when sitting, standing or lying down. Proprioceptors ("seat-of-the-pants sense") do not orientate you to your surroundings, but inform you of the relative motion and relative position of your body parts. *They can give false inputs to body orientation when visual reference is lost, so cross check and believe your instruments.*

DATA FILTERS

The minimum level of stimulation that must occur before anything is noticed for most humans in ideal conditions is:

- **Sight** - A candle flame seen from 17 miles away
- **Touch** - a bee's wing on your cheek from 1 cm away
- **Taste** - 1 teaspoon of sugar in 2 gallons of water
- **Smell** - 1 drop of perfume in a 3-roomed house
- **Hearing** - The ticking of a watch 20 feet away

A shark, on the other hand, can sense one drop of blood in thousands of gallons of water!

HUMAN PERFORMANCE & LIMITATIONS
Decisions, Decisions

ADAPTATION
Sensory receptors are quick to adapt to their surroundings, which is an effect commonly found when with instrument flying. Adaptation occurs when the response to a stimulus decreases after being exposed to it continually - in other words, the senses get used to it (as when sleeping through traffic noise, or turning slowly). The sense of smell is quickest to adapt, but IFR pilots know this happens with the sense of balance as well (the *leans*).

THRESHOLDS
Sensory stimulation is the first stage of information processing, and the basis of perception is the intensity of the stimulus.

- The **absolute threshold** is the minimum level (for a sensor) at which a stimulus is noticed, for 50% of the time. It depends not only on the data sensed, but also our psychological state, including experience, expectations and motivation, so the same stimulus can produce different responses at different times. For example, you will notice a lower stimulus if you are looking for it.

- The increase in stimulation required for us to notice a change between two stimuli (for 50% of the time) is the *difference threshold* or the **Just Noticeable Difference** (JND). The JND involves *Weber's Law*, which states that, as the strength of an original stimulus increases, the magnitude of the change must also increase for a JND to be perceived. The JND threshold is therefore variable, in that it depends on the background against which changes are detected, and the strength of the original stimulus. If a sensory threshold *increases*, sensitivity *decreases*.

THE COCKTAIL PARTY EFFECT
This is an early term used in attention research, which is now sometimes referred to as the lunch-queue effect (cocktail parties are so old-fashioned). It helps shield us from too much sensory input, being *the ability to pick up relevant information unintentionally*, allowing us to zero in on what is important to us while filtering out unimportant data, like focussing attention on a single talker amongst the background noise, ignoring other conversations (*Arons*, 1992; "The Cocktail").

According to *Clifford* (2005), the effect can occur when we are either paying attention to one of the sounds around us, or when it is invoked by a stimulus which grabs our attention suddenly. For example, if someone the other side of a party calls out your name, you notice that sound and respond to it immediately, while still paying some attention to the original group. Or, during a conversation in the cockpit, you respond to your callsign over the RT. As it happens, much of the early work about this can be traced to problems faced by air traffic controllers in the early 1950s, when they received many messages simultaneously over loudspeakers - it was very difficult to distinguish single voices from the many. Colin Cherry, at MIT in 1953, conducted perception experiments in which subjects were asked to listen to two different messages from speakers at the same time, and try to separate them.

It was revealed that our ability to separate sounds from the background is based on the *characteristics* of the sounds, like the gender of the speaker, or the direction from which the sound is coming, pitch, or the speaking speed, although spatial differences in the location of the sources greatly assists this ability. "Our minds can be conceived as a radio receiving many channels at once"; each channel perceives a kind of sound, but we can pay attention to only one channel at a time because of our limited capacity, so there is an audio filter in our brain which selects the channel to which we should pay attention from many kinds of sounds perceived. This is *Broadbend's Filter Theory*.

Attention
Sensory receptors are quick to adapt to their surroundings, which is an effect commonly found when with instrument flying. Adaptation occurs when the response to a stimulus decreases after being exposed to it continually - in other words, the senses get used to it (as when sleeping through traffic noise, or turning slowly). The sense of smell is quickest to adapt, but IFR pilots know this happens with the sense of balance as well (the *leans*).

*Distraction is the divided attention of an individual from a chosen object of attention onto the source of the distraction, often suffered by engineers.

As mentioned above, the human body is not a good multi-tasker, and to keep the various balls in the air over a typical flight, we must learn to *prioritise* and switch rapidly between tasks, which depends on how much attention the primary task is demanding. This can be reduced by using standard operating procedures, as with R/T and SOPs - the less thought secondary tasks require, the less attention they take up, especially when an external event happens to upset those well-made plans and flood the system.

There are several types of attention

- **Divided Attention**. The highest level, referring to the alternative management of several matters of interest at (almost) the same time and being able to respond simultaneously to multiple tasks or task demands. Some tasks may suffer at the expense of others, especially if they are similar in nature.

- **Alternating attention**. The mental flexibility that allows you to shift your focus and move between tasks with different cognitive requirements.

- **Selective Attention**. Here, you give greater attention to one or more sources of input out of several (the cocktail party effect is a good example). Such a selective mechanism is required because the resources of the Central Decision Maker and short-term memory are limited. It is the process during which information is sampled to see if it is relevant, which makes you able to detect information meant for you, even if you are not specifically monitoring the source. Officially, it is the ability to maintain a behavioral or cognitive set in the face of distracting or competing stimuli.

- **Focussed Attention**. Responding discretely (separately and individually) to specific stimuli.

- **Sustained Attention**. Otherwise called *vigilance*, the ability to stay alert over long periods of time, often on one task, or to maintain a consistent behavioral response during continuous and repetitive activity.

VIGILANCE

The amount of attention given to a task is directly influenced by the amount of vigilance, which is defined as the degree of activation of the Central Nervous System.

When humans get involved in monitoring tasks, such as making sure the autopilot doesn't misbehave, there is a noticeable decline in performance after about 30 minutes. After this time, problems are identified more slowly.

What Is A Decision?

In simple terms, the mental processes used in determining a course of action. It is supposed to be the end result of a chain of events involving judgment, after which you choose between alternatives. The process involves not only our eyes and ears which gather data, but our attention, which should not be preoccupied all the time. To keep track of what's going on, you must split your attention for a short period between everything, typically a split second at a time, having prioritised all the tasks that need to be completed. Risk assessment, discussed at the end of this section, is part of the process, as is timing, as a good decision that is made too late is useless*, although this does not mean that you should become impulsive.

*It's a good decision to avoid the mountain in front of you, but not 30 seconds before you hit it!

Although decision making is a *systematic and analytical process* involving several steps, things often seem to happen all at once, so it's important not to get fixated on one thing at the expense of another, which is typically what happens when flying under pressure. Gather all the information you can in the time available or, better still, get in the habit of updating information you're likely to need in an emergency as the flight progresses, especially when single-pilot, because then you will have much of the information you need in place. For example, when faced with time pressure, as when starting an instrument approach, prepare for it by getting the weather in advance, considering alternatives, etc. This also helps to activate the relevant information in long-term memory.

There are three elements to the evaluation process. *Diagnosis* comes first (which is more of a skill than is thought), followed by the *generating of possible solutions* and the *assessment of any risks*. When evaluating a situation, you should stay cool and not let emotions cloud your decision (within the limits of short term memory) - that is, do not let false hopes affect your thinking, as they might if your engine fails over trees - you first have to get over the idea that you will hit something! Once you have all the information, of course, there is no point in delaying the making of the decision, which must be followed by action! When other crew members are involved, time should always be taken to explain the reasons for a decision, even if it is after landing.

A poor decision is often attributed to faulty reasoning. For example, from the fact that cats and dogs both have four legs, you might conclude that a cat is a dog. Alternatively, if a pilot comes from a broken home, and you know that people who come from broken homes are social misfits, you might also conclude that the pilot concerned is a social misfit. In this case, your faulty conclusion arises from a *false premise*, because not all people from broken homes are social misfits.

Some steps involved with making a decision are to:

- **G**ather all relevant information - using your senses (which may be wrong).
- **R**eview it.
- **A**nalyze alternatives, keeping situational awareness and using risk assessment. When you are in a hurry, correct analysis may be bypassed in favour of a decision prepared beforehand.
- **D**ecide and Do - make your choice and act on it, although other factors may affect the quality of your decision and your ability to implement it.
- **E**valuate the outcome - and be prepared to start all over again (know when to fold 'em).

 CRM's function, in the guise of better crew interaction, is actually to facilitate the decision making process, but the popular conception is the opposite, i.e. that CRM is part of DM. The problem solving comes first and the decision making comes late in the process, at the *Decide & Do* stage.

The above decision making steps are not rigid, but may be merged or even repeated in a situation. For example, when adverse weather is ahead, you might get the updated weather, then vary the route or land to wait it out. Then you might get airborne and find you have to do it all over again, but this time land for refuelling, before getting airborne once more. The whole thing can be a continuously evolving process, which can be made quicker if some experience has already been gained, hence the value of training.

However, in normal life, what usually happens is that the thinking comes afterwards. When shopping for a house, for example, you might look at the outside and decide you like it there and then, until you discover that there is a factory around the corner that works all night, or the shops are too far away to walk to, or the neighbours are nasty. Or you take the line of least resistance and follow the actions that seem to work as far as you can - only when you have bought some time, or see that your actions are not leading anywhere, do you think about changing anything - this is often what happens in an emergency. You are more decisive when you can make sense of the selections available, which includes cutting the list to manageable proportions, as the more choice you have, the more you tend to take the easiest path, and too much choice affects decision making, as you cannot handle too much information (try ordering a sandwich in Subway).

The result is that people faced with too much choice may not make a decision at all. Decisions requiring creativity often benefit from being left to incubate below the level of awareness, as is done when sleeping on a problem.

Two circumstances where past experience can hinder decision making include *mental set** (or *rigidity*), where an older solution is used, even when more efficient ones exist (which could be called *reproductive* thinking, rather than *productive* thinking), and *functional fixedness*, where we fail to see other solutions than the normal ones (in other words, think out of the box).

**Set*, or the tendency for mental processes to be channelled in one direction under expectations based on past experience, is a characteristic of the survival mechanism which allows you to blank out unwanted stimuli while you get on with an emergency.

Thus, you can put yourself into a set that sees the world in a certain way and be so fixated on a bulb in a gear down light that isn't working that you forget to put the gear down! This happened on a TriStar in Florida.

Under stress, or high states of arousal, there is a tendency to stereotype, your attention narrows and the quality of your decisions becomes less. You become more liable to problems with set and reversion to previous training - this can become infectious if the Captain is affected, due to the Authority Gradient. *Mental Set* is a cognitive banana skin, which describes the frame of mind we are in when we are coasting along on mental autopilot. It occurs when there is very little time to process information and have to take certain things for granted.

Perceptual set relates this to the perception process, meaning that you see what you want to see. For example, *top-down perception* comes into play when you make a scene fit what you expect it to be, rather than perceive reality (making the ground fit the map). One example is expecting to see landing gear down lights as green and basing your actions on that premise.

Training can reduce the need for making decisions - after all, the reaction to engine failure is pretty much cut and dried, and you only need a decision when there is an element of confusion. However, many decisions can be made before that point to reduce the after effects, such as choosing a good position if something happens. Although the options chosen should lead to the most favourable expected outcome with the least risk (or cost!), this is often not possible. Sometimes there are only two choices, one risky, the other not. It should be noted that humans tend to risk more to prevent a loss.

Influences on making choices can include *randomness* (flip a coin), *routine* (helps with small decisions), *rules* (start No 1 engine on odd days) and *outside influences*, say from spouses or friends. The trouble is that our brains were designed for a more simple life, with decision making taken out of the loop. With the vast amount of choices available to us these days we have to think as well - either rationalise our decisions or risk making bad ones. The result is that we choose not to choose, or rationalise a decision afterwards, based on our prejudices and expectations.

The subconscious mind, using the information it can gather outside our conscious awareness, filters the choices available and presents the options to the conscious mind via the thalamus*, in less than 0.2 seconds, which can be further reduced in a state of flow, or the zone - this skill based mode, under Rasmussen's SRK Model, is the fastest form of "decision making".

*In presenting the choices to your conscious mind, the thalamus actually says something like:

> *"The choice of going to the pub will involve a huge burst of dopamine whereas, if you study for your exams, the dopamine level will be so low that you won't feel good at all...."*

Most sensible people would go down to the pub. This is where willpower comes in, and the learning of new habits because, once you get used to studying, and the thalamus finally gets the idea, the exam choice will gain a higher priority for the dopamine.

Analysing decision-making steps in detail is inappropriate in an emergency, which is why you need *distribution of tasks* and *crew coordination* first. Sometimes we have to make rapid-fire decisions under high pressure and with little information, but you may be surprised to hear that you might not actually need that much, especially with proper training, rules and rehearsal.

To summarise, good decision making has 4 elements:

- Proper definition of the question or problems.
- Intelligence gathering, but not to confirm biases.
- Following systematic rules.
- Learning from feedback or reviewing past performance.

The above steps may not follow that sequence and may even influence the others - for example, gathered intelligence may lead to a redefinition of the problem.

Decisions that can have far-reaching effects are actually quite small. Say you have just landed in twilight, and it is reported that your port and starboard navigation lights are not working. These, of course, are required equipment when flying at night. Do you shut down and wait for an engineer to fix them, or stay overnight (at great expense) and try again in the morning? Or do you take off in what is still officially daylight and pretend that they stopped working while you were in flight, relying on ATC to tell you about other traffic, and put the landing light on, figuring that, if things were normal, people wouldn't see the navigation lights anyway? Or do you take off in what is still daylight and pretend to yourself that they stopped working while you were in flight, relying on ATC radar to tell you about other traffic, and *vice versa*, and put the landing light on, figuring that if things were normal, people wouldn't see the navigation lights anyway?

Anyhow, the normal process is to recognise a change, assess alternative actions, make a decision and monitor the results. This can be enhanced with *awareness of undesirable attitudes*, learning to *find relevant information*, and *motivation* to act in a timely fashion.

Each decision you make eliminates the choice of another so, once you make a poor one, a chain of them usually follows. In fact, a decision-making chain can often be traced back up to and over fifty years, depending on whether the original cause was a design flaw (the F-15 and F-16, for example, are functionally identical to fly, except that the speed bands go the opposite ways). Another factor is the data itself; if it's incomplete, or altered through some emotional process, you can't base a proper decision on it, so:

- Don't make a decision unless you have to.
- Keep it under review once you've made it.
- No decision can be a decision (but no indecision!)

Most important, though, is to be prepared to *change* a decision!

Group Decision Making

Many decisions are made collectively, particularly in families. In theory, therefore, a more cautious element should be built in to the process, with a greater chance of all information being recognised and considered, for more consistency. As it happens, group decisions are *more extreme* than those of the individual, meaning that an inclination to be cautious or risky will be increased. This is the *group polarisation effect*.

Primary groups play an important role in the development of personal identity, being those in which one exchanges implicit items, such as love, caring, concern, animosity and support, like in a family. Relationships formed in primary groups are often long-lasting and goals in themselves. They also are often psychologically comforting to the individuals involved and provide a source of support.

People in **secondary groups** interact on a less personal level, and their relationships tend to be temporary, such as a flight crew, where choice is involved. As such groups are established to perform certain functions, people's roles in them are more interchangeable.

A unanimous group will exert strong pressure to conform - if even one person dissents, the conformity is much less marked, so a minority can influence a group if it maintains a consistent position without appearing to be rigid, arrogant or dogmatic. Even if you are working single-pilot, you are still part of a group - a *peer group* of other pilots, and the effects are just the same. Many accidents have occurred because people have worried more about how they look to their colleagues than taking the right actions. *Differences of opinion should be regarded as helpful.*

During the early stages of an incident, for example, it may not be easy to determine exactly what is going on, and what should be done. People look to someone in authority (i.e. the Captain) for such information. If there is no one, people often feel unable to make their own decisions as they do not wish to stand out from the crowd. In fact, one of the ways a situation can be regarded as dangerous or not is by other peoples' reactions to it. If they are maintaining a calm exterior, as is done in some cultures, a situation could be seen as less dangerous than it really is, as people don't want to be seen to be over-reacting. People will try to live up to group norms (e.g. teenagers), which can be set quite quickly, even in a group that hasn't met much before.

NORMS

A norm is an unwritten rule that is followed by the majority of a group. Norms are therefore codes of behaviour (or cultures) that can be very powerful, and rejection is a danger if you don't conform to them. For example, it may be the norm in your company that people who make mistakes are ridiculed. Airmanship is a norm. A *positive norm* is one where expected behaviour is condoned and contributes to the betterment of the group. Washing down an aircraft after a flight, even if it isn't your job, is one example. A *neutral norm* is one that is neither positive or negative, which does not detract nor enhance an accepted standard, so there is no great impact. A *negative norm* (or a violation) is a short cut or accepted practice that detracts from safety, which is why Chernobyl exploded - the engineers left out most of the safety procedures when they were trying an experiment. Drinking and driving used to be a good example, and in the days of the *Titanic* it was normal practice to steam straight ahead at high speed, even though the rules said they shouldn't.

Responses

After a decision based on a stimulus, there is a response, but one due to excessive pressure is more likely to be based on insufficient data and be wrong than a more considered one, assuming time permits. If you make a rushed decision, you are more likely to overlook the current situation and apply a decision prepared earlier, although a previously made one based on sound thinking is more likely to work than one cooked up on the spur of the moment, provided, of course that the situation is the same or similar. A correct, rather than rapid, reaction is appropriate.

DECISION MAKING MODELS

Effective decision making involves the accurate understanding of a situation, an appreciation of its implications, the formulation of plans and contingencies, followed by the best course of action. Equally important is a crew's ability to recognise changes and to start over if necessary. Increased stress levels can adversely impact the ability to perceive and evaluate cues from the environment and may result in the narrowing of attention, which can lead to confirmation bias, so worst-case scenarios should specifically be included so that all aspects are considered.

Another important aspect is the concept of shared mental models, which largely depend on the understanding of the circumstances, expectations about the future, and past experience (a mental model is what is *believed* about a situation*). The more experience an individual has, the more accurate their mental model is likely to be.

*That is, models of what people know (or think they know) about a system or situation. They should naturally be closely related to reality because future actions are based on how that model predicts an appropriate course. *Schemata* can be defined as a set of linked mental representations of the world, which are used to understand and to respond to situations. While allowing humans to plan future actions based on past experience, they can also lead to rigid ways of thinking.

People have their own mental models, which are internal to them, so there may be different ideas about a particular situation. For example, the mental models (and therefore expectations) of pilots and passengers are likely to be wildly different.

A large part of the mental model a pilot may have of a particular aircraft will be influenced by experience from other types.

Rasmussen's SRK Model

Rasmussen isolated three types of information processing demands, or behaviour, and hence the likely errors, in his *SRK (Decision Making) Model,* which refers to the conscious control exercised by people doing their thing. Put another way, the model is directed at those in supervisory positions, particularly during emergencies, having originated from a study of technicians involved in electronic troubleshooting.

AUTOMATIC

SKILL-BASED

Human performance at this level is governed by stored patterns of preprogrammed instructions, meaning that it is based on practice and prior learning, to become part of the "muscle memory", or *motor programs,* of your body, so reactions are largely unconscious and automatic, or routine, and are not consciously monitored once selected. An example is a pilot knowing how much power is being used by the positioning of an arm, and not by looking at the instruments.

Automatic or skill-based behaviour can be considered to be less prone to error or, put another way, the most reliable, because you get early feedback to correct things. It is when you are very familiar with a task, and are tired or interrupted (a major problem for engineers!) and you have to start thinking in a way you are not used to when the task is resumed, that errors might rear their ugly heads. The classic example of out-of-sequence behaviour concerns the rotor blades on a Bell 206 - if the passengers are late, you typically tie the blades down while you wait for them and forget to undo them again!

Because motor programs are not continuously monitored, skill-based behaviour can lead to **environmental capture**, that is, doing something because it's always done and not because it's the right thing to do. You could also end up with the right skill in the wrong situation (**action slip),** meaning pulling the flap lever instead of that for the gear. As well, you might not catch new stimuli, and one other disadvantage is that it is difficult to explain (and thus pass on) to other people. Modification of skill-based learning requires it to be relearnt at a deep level, so experienced pilots are the most affected.

In summary, you are prone to errors here when you are preoccupied, tired, or otherwise distracted, so you must be consciously aware of your actions, and more deliberate. Keep alert enough to sustain your attention, and maintain currency - Wiegman & Shappell have shown that over 80% of general aviation accidents can be put down to skill-based errors, where pilots are not flying properly, and currency is an issue. Skill-based errors concern the way that highly practised actions can become so automatic that we don't need to think about them, so we fall back on habitual routines when we really mean to do something else (driving home when you should be going to the supermarket), so you must keep your mind on what you are doing and the choices you make. Thus, automation does not help! In a co-ordinated turn, most of your activity is skill-based, as is the choice of the moment you select the gear down.

Associated errors include:

- Errors of Routine
- Environmental Capture
- **Action Slips**. Otherwise called absent-mindedness, these are attentional failures, such as not completing a sequence of events through lack of monitoring, or inserting or omitting parts of a checklist. They appear during highly practised activities where you would expect to make fewer mistakes. This is because, in the early stages of an activity, you pay more attention - when you get more skilled and the process becomes more automatic, the control and monitoring is lost.

CONSCIOUS

RULE-BASED

This relies on previously considered courses of action, or stored rules, and follows procedures, like checklists and SOPs, so it is a slower process, and more sequential. If you approach an airfield under VFR, at a prescribed altitude, exactly following the approach procedure, you would appear to show rule-based behaviour. The mental processing is still internalised (it is in long term memory) but it is event driven, such as "if the nose pitches up, apply forward control." That is, there is little anticipation.

What usually happens when an accident occurs is that the brain goes smartly into neutral whilst everything around you goes pear-shaped. Checklists can help to bridge the gap of inactivity by giving you something more or less correct to do whilst psyching yourself up and evaluating information ready for a decision. The US Navy, for example, trains pilots to stop in emergencies, and reset the clock on the instrument panel, which forces them to relax or, at least, not to panic. Rule-based behaviour is generally robust, which is why procedures and rules are important, but it is possible to use the wrong procedure due to misdiagnosis, or even forget it.

Associated errors include:

- **Errors of Technical Knowledge**
- Commission (most common), such as taxying out to the wrong runway.
- Departure from SOPs
- Interruptions
- Violations

It follows that the rules should be precise and not assume a minimum level of knowledge to be used properly!

KNOWLEDGE-BASED

Knowledge-based tasks are those for which there is no external guidance, so there is almost complete conscious control. Such thinking on your feet requires considerable mental effort, and your responses will be correspondingly slower, aside from needing to review them constantly to assess their impact. Humans do not perform very well in such situations, but they do perform better than machines, which are more suited to the other two modes. People who apply previous experience from an outside source to cope with a current task are good examples, such as an aeroplane pilot caught in Vortex Ring on a helicopter who instinctively pulls power to get out of trouble, unaware, without special training, that that will only make things worse. This is the sort of thinking you apply if you need to think things through, or maybe work on the *why* so the *how* becomes apparent, because there are no applicable rules. As your primary weapons are *thinking* and *reasoning*, this is probably the only area that machines cannot cope with, and why we still need humans in the cockpit to make proper decisions. For example, the captaincy example involving a decision to return to base or carry on that is used previously is knowledge based. Errors at this level might arise from making diagnoses without full knowledge of a system.

Associated errors arise from resource limitations and incomplete or incorrect knowledge. They include:

- **Confirmation Bias**, which is the tendency to search for information to confirm a theory, while overlooking contradictory information. It can be likened to making the ground fit the map, rather than accepting the fact that we are lost, because we are more likely to disregard a negative idea. You could also look upon it as a tendency to *ignore information that confirms a decision is a poor one*. You should therefore look for things that are wrong to help confirm your decision.
- **Frequency Bias**, where a previously prepared response for another emergency may be used instead, leading to errors of commission.

The SHEL Model

Human factors concerns the interaction between people and machines, procedures, and the environment.

HUMAN PERFORMANCE & LIMITATIONS
Decision Making Models

The SHEL Model is one factor of decision making that was originally presented by a psychologist called Edwards. It is a framework that describes the components and interfaces between the various subsystems to do with aviation. Its proper application can help prevent errors, and is a particular factor in the design of flight decks.

The letters of the word *SHEL* stand for *Software, Hardware, Environment* and *Liveware*, which represent influences on the typical pilot. *Hardware*, naturally enough, is the mechanical environment, *Environment* covers such things as hypoxia, temperature, etc., whilst *Software* covers checklists, etc. *Liveware* copes with interactions between the pilot (in the centre) and other people.

LIVEWARE-HARDWARE

This is the first area that needs attention. Adjustable seats and controls are a good start (*ergonomics*, mentioned overleaf), but displays are important as well. As an example, the 3-needle altimeter was a classic example of poor design that led to accidents, where people confused the hundred- and thousand-foot needles (see right). EFIS/ECAS displays are also not entirely satisfactory because, although they present a lot of information in a small space, they fail to show patterns and trends, and it is harder to read digits than it is to read analogue dials, where you get used to a picture of needle positions, and any misplaced are easily noticed. When you have to read numbers, it takes a second or two to interpret the information. *Analogue presentation is most suitable for qualitative or comparative information.*

LIVEWARE-SOFTWARE

Liveware-software problems occur when documentation is poorly written and presented (this also includes warning systems). Below is an example of the sort of checklist that comes from a typical Chief Pilot's office. It would appear to do the job quite well, but closer inspection reveals that it could do with a little work here and there. For example, it is not obvious what are headings and what are not.

FIRE

Immediate Actions
ON GROUND:
Respective EMER OFF sw¹   Open switch guard, press and release
Fuel Prime Pumps   Both OFF
Engines   OFF
Rotor Brake   ON
Battery   OFF
Passengers   Evacuate

IN FLIGHT:
OEI flight condition   Establish
Respective EMER OFF sw¹   Open switch guard, press and release
Affected engine   Identify, then OFF
Passengers   Alert
Check for signs of fire
Warning light off   LAND AS SOON AS POSSIBLE
Warning light on   LAND IMMEDIATELY

Considerations
1. Respective engine will be automatically cut off. ACTIVE will illuminate on the EMER OFF sw panel and F VALVE CL will illuminate on the CAD.

Here is the same checklist, suitably tweaked:

FIRE

Immediate Actions

On Ground
1. Switch guard   Open, press and release
2. Fuel Prime Pumps   Both OFF
3. Engines   OFF
4. Rotor Brake   ON
5. Battery   OFF
6. Passengers   Evacuate

In Flight
1. OEI flight condition Establish
2. Switch guard   Open, press and release
3. Affected engine   Identify, then OFF
4. Passengers   Alert
5. Fire   Check for signs
6. LAND AS SOON AS POSSIBLE

Considerations
1. Respective engine will be automatically cut off. ACTIVE will illuminate on the EMER OFF sw panel and F VALVE CL will illuminate on the CAD.

It didn't take much effort to improve things, with a little spacing and layout, in keeping with the SHEL model. Contrast the above with this example from an airline, which violates almost every rule of technical writing:

LIVEWARE-ENVIRONMENT

In the early days of aviation, humans were matched to the environment, with special suits and the like. Now, technology allows the environment to be better matched to the human to provide the optimum working environment. Noise, vibration, temperature, air quality and heat all need to be carefully controlled, as do work patterns and shifts that fail to take account of sleep disturbance and jet lag.

Prolonged amounts of noise, vibration or turbulence is fatiguing and annoying - noise is particularly prevalent in helicopters, especially with the doors off. Vibration at the right frequency (8-12 Hz) causes back pain.

The others include:

- **1-4 Hz** - Affects breathing ($^1/_{10}$-2 Hz affects the vestibular apparatus)
- **4-10 Hz** - Chest and abdominal pain
- **8-12 Hz** - Backache
- **10-20 Hz** - Headaches, eye strain, throat pain, speech disturbance & muscular tension
- **30-40 Hz** - Interference with vision

Otherwise, resonance of body parts can result from vibrations between 1-100 Hz.

Flicker occurs when light is interrupted by rotor blades or propellers. Military helicopter pilots are tested for *Flicker Vertigo* during selection, as the Sun flashing through them can be a real problem (turn them off in cloud). A steady light flickering at around 4-20 Hz can produce unpleasant and dangerous reactions, including nausea, vertigo, convulsions or unconsciousness, which are possibly worse when you are fatigued, frustrated, or in a state of mild hypoxia. Flicker certainly modifies certain neuro-physiological processes; 3-30 a second appears to be a critical range, while 6-8 will diminish your depth perception (the Germans set their searchlights to flicker during World War II, to get up the nose of bomber pilots). Hangovers make you particularly susceptible. When being affected by flicker, you should turn off the strobe lights.

LIVEWARE-LIVEWARE

Poor relationships or communication between crew members, outside workers and even management have led to disasters, so group dynamics are important in getting people to work together in teams. See *Communication*.

AUTOMATION

The brain's limitations, in terms of speed of computation and the ability to multi-task (i.e. none!) began to be recognised as early as 1959, with the Boeing 707, when it was realised that pilots could soon exceed their design capabilities, and that the help of various black boxes was needed. Many **routine tasks** can be done by computers, which are just electronic machines - the man-machine system is meant to *relieve pilot workload and increase time for supervision*. To avoid wrong decisions, *a system should at least be able to report malfunctions*. But how much control should be given to black boxes? If they have too much, the cockpit becomes boring and errors can go unnoticed amongst the monotony (hypovigilance). Pilots can also become less confident in their basic airmanship and flying skills (improved training, especially CRM, reduces these negative effects).

Although automation can conserve resources and attention, and generally improve the safety record, it can result in routine errors, or *slips*, such as when programming waypoints into the system or keeping track of the aircraft status and position. Machines can wait for infrequent information without getting bored, and can perform long-term control and set values, again, without getting bored, but people can exercise judgment, make better decisions and detect unusual conditions (smells, noises), while getting bored very easily. So, on the one hand, automation is good, because it can take a lot of routine work away from you, and flight management systems can operate an aircraft very fuel-efficiently. A FADEC (fuel control thingy) has many monitoring functions, so the chances for human error are reduced and reliability is better.

On the other hand, automation can induce a feeling of *automation complacency* (too much reliance on the machine) and lead you not to check things as often as you should (*reduced vigilance*), or push the envelope, as when using a GPS in bad weather - with much of the navigation task taken away from you, it is tempting to fly in worse weather than you can really cope with (flying in bad weather is like sex - the further you get into it, the harder it is to stop). As your visual clues decrease, your mental processes focus more on trying to see where you're going and less on flying until you lose control, when flying on instruments is no help because you are not mentally prepared for it.

You can avoid automation complacency by regarding systems as *one more crew member that needs to be cross-checked* - that is, you have to make sure that the autopilot is actually taking you in the right direction. You can cope with low error tolerant situations (where errors could have serious consequences) by *constantly complying with cross-over verification procedures* (i.e. cross monitoring).

A high degree of automation may alter traditional tasks so much that your attention and competence is reduced once you are out of the loop. Thus, communication and coordination call for a greater effort from the crew. The trouble is that we rely on machines so much, and their rapidity of change adds to our stress, as described by Alvin Toffler in his book, *Future Shock*.

However, one major benefit is the integration of many sources of information and its presentation in a clear and concise manner (sometimes!), as with the glass cockpit, and providing a major contribution towards situational awareness, as long as you keep a mental plot going, as the information presented can be highly filtered.

Put more in exam language, *the use of modern technology in glass cockpits facilitates feedback from the machine via more concise data for communication on the flight deck*. So there. What it doesn't help with is the fact that one knob used to have one function in older systems - now several functions may be hidden at different levels, for which there is no substitute for knowing the menu system.

MODES

Modes represent a system's behaviours, or functions so, the more functions there are, the more modes you have, and the potential for error. Instead of using unique displays and controls for each mode, one set can be made to perform different functions depending on the mode selected - a good example is the menu system of the average Flight Management System (FMS), discussed in *Instruments*.

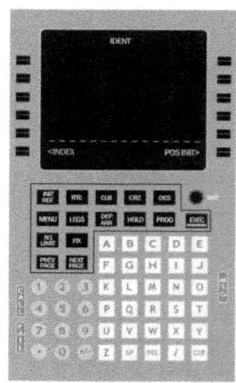

In the Display Unit shown above, the Line Select Keys, or the buttons on either side of the screen, change their functions according to the mode selected but, however good this many-to-one mapping may be, it can involve mode errors from insufficient knowledge of the system.

Mode awareness means being aware of the active modes and understanding the relevant actions and responses to use the system properly. It involves knowledge* of the configurations of an aircraft and their interactions with the modes of the automatic flight system in use, which include such items as current and target speed, altitude, heading, AP/FD armed/engaged modes and the state of the FMS, to name but a few.

*The role of the pilot has changed from flying to being a systems or flight-deck manager, or an outer-loop controller (a setter of high level goals), rather than an inner-loop controller (a mere manipulator of the controls).

Mode errors are one kind of breakdown in human-computer interaction, from word processors up. When a device does something in one way in one mode and another way in another mode, there is an increased potential for error. The lack of understanding of what an automatic system is doing is called **mode confusion**.

Call-outs are what crewmembers say to others in particular situations. They are intended to ensure effective crew communication, promote situational awareness, and ensure crew understanding of systems and their use (*Airbus Industrie*, 2006). In an attempt to reduce the risk of mode confusion (*Sarter & Woods*, 1997) some manufacturers have required flight crews to callout all flight guidance automation mode changes to force pilots into monitoring the flight mode annunciator. The idea is that pilots need to know the actual flight guidance mode at all times and that, by requiring all mode changes be called out, the pilots will spend more time on the FMA and, presumably, their mode awareness will increase.

In order to maintain mode awareness, you must be continuously vigilant for indications from several locations within the cockpit.

Recent studies of automation in the cockpit have suggested that after over a year of experience on type:

- 55% of pilots indicated that occasionally the FMS did things that surprised them (especially VNAV!)
- 20% of pilots did not understand all the modes or features available to them (although an examiner I know suggested that the figure is way higher).
- The most common questions on the flight deck are:
  - 'What is it doing?'
  - 'Why did it do that?'
  - 'What will it do next?'
  - 'I wonder if it will do that again?'

Airbus has a low level of pilot input - the system will look after the aircraft with minimal help from the crew (which is discouraged). Boeing has a slightly greater pilot input.

ERGONOMICS

Under this heading comes cockpit design and automated systems, being associated with the human/workplace interface. How many times have you jumped into the cockpit of a different machine, to find the switches you need in a totally different place? This doesn't help you if you rely on previous experience to find what you need (in emergencies you tend to fall back to previous training), so the trick is to know what you need at all times, and take the time to find out where it is (*read the switches*).

LEARNING & PERFORMANCE

The types of learning include:

- **Classical/Operant Conditioning**, such as an experienced pilot's reaction to a fire warning.
- **Insight**, or a pilot setting up on-board navigation equipment.
- **Observational Learning**/Imitation. A student pilot following the instructor then doing it solo.
- **Experience**. Learning from our mistakes.
- **Skill Learning**. Observational learning, along with practice, plays an important role in the learning of skills (*Motor Programs*).

You are *skilled* when you:

- Train or practice regularly.
- Know how to manage yourself.
- Know how to keep resources in reserve for the unexpected.

Factors That Affect Learning

People store information in long term memory best when they understand it, and can integrate it with what they already know. Learning by rote does not encode information in long term memory very strongly, as it is not as well understood, organised or integrated. In addition, it is relatively isolated, and therefore harder to recall. Meaningful learning, on the other hand, allows you to apply your knowledge to new situations because it involves understanding (*transfer* is the name given to the ability to use what has been learnt to solve new problems).

Motor programs (see *Information Processing*, above) are stored routines that enable patterns of behaviour to be executed without continuous conscious control. According to *Anderson*, the acquisition of such expertise has three stages, namely:

- **Cognitive**, where you think about what is being done (*Declarative Knowledge*).
- **Associative**, concerning the integration of the various aspects of the subject to be learned (*Knowledge Compilation*). You may slip back to this level in a non-routine situation (official language for an emergency!) Stress and lack of practice make it more likely.
- **Autonomous**, or **Automatic** (depends on which book you read). You operate with no conscious control (*Procedural Knowledge*).

In other words, you start with a theoretical knowledge of what needs to be done, move through practice, to where the knowledge is completely in memory (although I have never felt that learning the complete alphabet was necessary before learning to read). In aviation terms, in the first (or *cognitive*) phase, an instructor might talk about skills you will acquire, including the task, typical errors and target performance. Next comes the *associative phase*, where techniques are demonstrated and learned, and errors are gradually reduced. The *Autonomous* or *Automatic* stage is where you have it down pat.

The *quality* of learning is promoted by *feedback*.

Performance

The effect of experience and habit (see *Judgment*) on performance can be positive or negative. Your performance is better when you are relaxed, regardless of the time of day. As far as the average influence of age on pilot performance is concerned, it has little impact when it can be compensated for with flight experience.

Having said that, human performance varies according to the time of day and often according to body temperature. Poorest performance can be expected around 03:00 hours.

THREAT & ERROR MANAGEMENT

Human error is the largest contributing factor in aviation accidents and incidents today. Understanding and accepting that human error is natural and inevitable is a significant step in mitigating the risk of an accident or incident. Error prevention & error protection is only possible with a dynamic and open self awareness.

The assumption is that, because you have a qualification, you know what you are doing, but the truth is, we are surrounded by incompetence and people make mistakes all the time. Even the simplest jobs can be plagued with them, and they are not performed by idiots, but normal, otherwise intelligent people. Take flat pack instructions and exam questions! If these jobs are so simple, it's not surprising that a number of the people involved in aviation will also make mistakes, especially under the typical pressures involved.

Threat and Error Management (TEM) is a new framework (largely sponsored by the University of Texas) for what used to be called Airmanship, or simply common sense. Although this could also be a definition of CRM, TEM is more concerned with particular flights than aviation in general. It is a way of flying that either minimizes risk or maximizes safety margins, allowing pilots to recognize and counter everyday problems that may result in accidents or incidents with non-technical skills (NOTECHS), based on the analysis of incidents and accidents in high capacity airlines. Defensive flying, if you like. Sadly, the ICAO definition means hardly anything:

> *"The TEM framework is a conceptual model that assists in understanding, from an operational perspective, the inter-relationship between safety and human performance in dynamic and challenging operational contexts."*

We could probably improve on that:

> *"Detecting and responding to threats and errors so that the outcome does not involve further errors, threats or undesired states."*

Threats are events or hazards that:

- are outside the control of pilots, for which good situational awareness is one antidote.
- increase the operational complexity of the flight.
- need crew attention and management, which takes up resources, especially when they are already busy.

Examples include situations that could be avoided, such as looking for a fuel cache when down to your reserves, when you didn't check (before you took off) that the fuel cache was where it is supposed to be in the first place. You could also have landed your helicopter after a slinging job and not disconnected the sling after you shut down (there is now a danger that you could take off again and forget that it is there).

Most threats can be anticipated, especially with experience, but how one is perceived is the basis of any stress experienced. The difference is that threats come *at* pilots, whereas errors come *from* pilots. Resisting threats is managing the future and resisting errors, the past.

The accepted progression is that unmanaged *threats* can lead to *errors*, and to *undesirable aircraft states*, the severity of which can depend on whether the pilot is experienced or under training, as the same error can have different consequences. Undesired aircraft states are deviations from flight paths or configurations that reduce safety margins, which are considered to be the last stages before an accident or incident. In short, threats, errors and undesired aircraft states are everyday events that must be managed to maintain safety margins. As such, it offers a flexible approach to risk management. Thus, the importance lies not in the fact that threats and errors exist, but how they are managed (they are assumed to be handled sequentially).

Countermeasures can be grouped into 4 main categories:

- **Crew**—active leadership, communication, and crew participation, for an environment that encourages open communication, briefings, workload management and a crew acting together as active threat managers.
- **Planning**—briefings, planning, preparation, managing anticipated and unanticipated (unexpected) threats, contingency management.
- **Execution**—pilot monitoring, scanning, cross-checking, workload management, automation management.
- **Review**—evaluation of planning, inquiry, what-if planning. Existing plans should be reviewed and modified when necessary, and crew members should be able and willing to ask questions, investigate discrepancies, & clarify any plans.

You should also treat interruptions and breaks in the workflow pattern with caution, because they can change your behaviour. For example, you could miss out an entire checklist. As experience is gained, you can move through them with little mental engagement, and it is easy to assume that, because you are on item C, that item B has already been dealt with. However, once started, a jump to another checklist to deal with an emergency may mean that the one you were going to do before you were rudely interrupted gets completely forgotten. This is called *prospective memory failure*, and is a symptom of the fact that humans are not good remembering tasks that have been deferred for future execution. The remedy is, if you are not sure, to *slow down* and re-run the entire checklist.

Threat Management

A threat is a situation or event that may have a negative impact on the safety of a flight, or any influence that provides an opportunity for pilot error, such as:

- **Environmental threats**, that could include bad weather, aerodrome conditions, terrain, other traffic, ATC requirements, etc.
- **Organisational or operational threats, that** could include pressure from management, aircraft malfunctions, maintenance errors, etc.
- **Other errors**, such as stress, fatigue or distractions

Threats can also be expected (anticipated) or unexpected (unanticipated). Expected threats can be pre-handled, but unexpected ones need use of your skill and knowledge.

Error Management

> *"Knowledge and error flow from the same mental sources - only success can tell one from the other." Ernst Mach, 1905*

In other words, correct performance and systematic errors are two sides of the same coin.

One working definition of human error is *"where planned sequences of mental or physical activity fail to achieve intended outcomes, not attributable to chance."* Another is *"the mismatch between the intention and the result of an action."* The ICAO definition is: *"An action or inaction by a flight crew that leads to deviations from organisational or crew intentions or expectations".*

Studies of human error rates during simple repetitive tasks have shown that errors can normally be expected on about *1 in 100* occasions. After methodical training, a rate of *1 in 1000* is realistic and pretty good. A system can be *tolerant of error* when the consequences will *not seriously jeopardize safety*. If an error is allowed to affect a system, the system is described as *vulnerable*.

Given that there is usually only one correct way of performing a task, we are lucky that errors only manifest themselves in a limited number of ways, which are linked to the ability of long term memory to retrieve stored knowledge to suit the situation. This is one advantage that humans have over computers - namely, the ability to simplify complex informational tasks.

After James Reason, human error is neither as abundant nor as varied as its vast potential might suggest. Not only are errors much rarer than correct actions, they also tend to take a surprisingly limited number of forms. Also, those that appear do so in a similar manner, which makes them easier to identify. Having said that, the element of predictability in relation to errors is difficult. The accuracy of error prediction depends on the nature of the task, the mechanisms governing performance, and the nature of the people involved, so we have probabilities that certain errors will arise, rather than precision. On January 1st, many people will use the last year when writing the date down, but we won't know how many.

Latent errors, like unnoticed waypoint errors in a GPS database, have consequences that lie dormant, and are difficult to recognise (or foresee) because of the time lag between their generation and occurrence. They may also only be found in certain circumstances, so they can lull pilots into a false sense of security. Their consequences could be serious. Latent errors are hard to prevent, but should be made visible by a Safety Management System. **Active errors**, on the other hand, are committed *at the human/system interface*, and have immediate consequences, which is how they can be detected (for example, overspeeding the engine). They can also be corrected relatively quickly, with fewer consequences.

PROCEDURAL ERRORS   040 01 03

When looking at errors, we must also look at what is to be achieved and how it will be achieved. In other words, there is a distinction between *prior intentions* and *intentions in action* (*Searle*, 1980) - you can do something on the spur of the moment without intending to, as you will find by reading any court report. Indeed, the law requires that there should be intent behind the act for there to be a crime.

Actions that deviate from intention either achieve the intended goal, or they do not (*slips*), but even intended actions can be regarded as erroneous if the plan is not adequate - errors of this kind are called *mistakes*.

Mistakes involve a mismatch between the prior intention and the intended consequences. For slips and lapses, the problem lies with the difference between the intended actions and those that were actually executed.

In short, a mistake is a *planning* failure, and   040 03 02 03
a slip or lapse is an *execution* failure
(someone might write down the wrong GPS coordinates). That is, there is a substitution or insertion of an inappropriate action into a sequence that was otherwise good. *Slips do not satisfy the operator's intent*. A lapse is an *omission* of one or more steps of a sequence. As mentioned previously, it is possible to miss out entire checklists.

MISTAKES & VIOLATIONS

The majority of fatal crashes are not down to errors in execution (35%) or perception (23%), but in the original decision-making process (43%), because decision errors are not typically slips or lapses, but *mistakes*, which arise where the *planned actions* are incorrect. This may be the result of incorrect knowledge or diagnosis, like shutting down the wrong engine after incorrectly identifying the failed one. Whereas slips are mostly found in skill-based mode, mistakes happen more often in rule- or knowledge based modes (see *The SRK Model*).

Violations are more deliberate acts, usually done for speed or convenience, however well-meaning. For example, if the takeoff path is obstacle free and you decide to take off anyway with a tailwind that is above limits, that is a violation. Technically, violations are *deliberate deviations from rules, procedures or regulations*, although unintentional ones can occur.

- *Routine violations* eventually become normal practice.
- *Situational violations* arise out of particular circumstances, including time pressure, workload, inadequate tools or facilities.
- *Optimising violations* concern breaking the rules for the hell of it (couldn't they think of a better name?)
- *Exceptional violations* are inevitable, when the normal rules no longer apply.

Whether violations occur is down to the attitudes, beliefs, norms and culture of the company. Aside from ignoring safety rules on a particular task, they put the rest of the system in jeopardy because other people assume that the rules will be followed.

Pilots can make mistakes within five basic categories:

- **non-compliance**, like failure to follow checklists, or official guidance, or good safety practices.
- **procedural errors**, where you do something incorrectly, or in a different order - an example is a checklist item out of sequence.
- **faulty communication**, such as readback errors and miscommunication with ATC.
- **lack of proficiency** - airmanship (TEM) skills.
- **decision making**. These errors improve with situational awareness.

Ways of allowing for better error detection include:

- Improvement of the man-machine interface.
- Development of systems for checking the consistency of situations.
- Compliance with crossover redundant procedures by the crew (cross monitoring).

MANAGEMENT

Errors need management in order not to affect safety. They are cumulative! Officially, errors are actions or inactions that:

- lead to deviations from intentions or expectations.
- reduce safety margins.
- increase the probability of adverse operational events on the ground and during flight.

Error Management could be regarded as *a counter-measure against bad decisions*. New pilots naturally make mistakes - experienced pilots tend to have monitoring errors, and are more likely to think they are flying an older type.

There are three lines of defence against errors:

- **Avoiding** them in the first place (that is, not getting into a position that requires your superior skills to get out of). This needs situational awareness and, by implication, active monitoring of the situation.
- If they happen, **detecting** and trapping errors before they are significant.
- Sorting out the mess afterwards (error **recovery**).

Error management accepts that mistakes happen, and adopts a non-punitive approach to minimise the effects (which does not mean that you should break the rules on purpose!) Evidence of this can be seen in anonymous reporting procedures, such as CHIRP in the UK and the *Aviation Safety Action Program* (ASAP) in the US.

There have also been attempts to remove the human from the system altogether (although someone still has to program the computer!) However, it is impossible to eliminate mistakes, so clearing up the mess is important. Professor James Reason, in his book, *Human Error*, points out that the barriers against accidents (or the sequence of human events) consist of a trajectory of opportunity originating at the higher levels of a system, passing through *preconditions* and *unsafe acts* and on to three successive layers of in-depth defence, which may include atypical conditions at any point.

You could liken them to several slices of Swiss cheese, with the holes as windows of opportunity in continual flux.   040 01 04

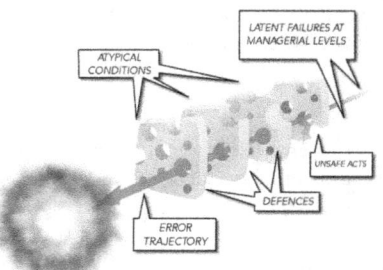

Although the slices represent layers between management decision making and the incident concerned, it does not mean that all accidents stem from management! In addition, the chances of something actually happening are quite small.

On the day the holes line up, something will happen so, if you can recognise the sequence, you should, in theory, be able to pull some of the holes out of line, and prevent an accident. One Australian fire fighting pilot went to transmit, pushed the wrong button and dropped his water bucket instead. He landed, picked it up and went home for a couple of days, figuring that he must be tired and was better off out of it. Unfortunately, the chain can sometimes not be broken in time.

Recognising an error chain will not necessarily mean that an accident will actually occur, but detecting the holes in the cheese slices lining up should be cause for concern and spark off an investigation (the purpose of a Safety Management System). However, the events in a chain may not happen one after the other, and may not even depend on each other, with months between incidents.

The 4-7 links in the average chain means you have up to seven opportunities to stop an accident.

SITUATIONAL AWARENESS

Being aware of what's going on is your biggest weapon against errors.   040 03 02 02

SAFETY CULTURE

A safety culture is formed from the shared beliefs, values, behaviours and attitudes of an organisation, and describes how safety is managed within it (i.e. what happens when nobody is looking!) It is relatively enduring, stable and resistant to change, and a subpart of national culture. In Japanese companies, junior people must do exactly as they are told, which could lead to an accident if a pilot is ordered to fly in bad weather (by the company chairman, for example), and cannot refuse.

The non-punitive approach to errors was developed to encourage people to report them. There's no point, for example, in introducing penalties into a reporting system (so that if you report yourself, you get punished!), because no errors will be reported and the Safety Officer is the only one that looks good! Compared to the largely punitive cultures that the no-blame culture sought to replace, it was at least a step in the right direction, in recognising that most unsafe acts were just errors, or the kinds of mistakes that anyone can make. However, there are people who wilfully participate in unsafe acts or violations, for which it was not suitable. An active Safety Culture is vital to the continuing success of any Safety Management System.

According to Professor James Reason, it includes:

- A **Just Culture**, or an atmosphere of trust in which people are encouraged (or even rewarded) for providing essential safety-related information commensurate with their experience and training. However, there is also a clear line between acceptable and unacceptable behaviour. In essence, it is a non-punitive safety system that facilitates open communication within an organisation, that promotes a questioning attitude, is resistant to complacency, committed to excellence, and fosters both personal accountability and corporate self-regulation in safety matters.
- A **Reporting Culture** is an organisational climate in which people are prepared to report their errors and near-misses.
- An **Informed Culture** exists where those who manage and operate the system have current knowledge about the human, technical, organisational and environmental factors that determine the safety of the system as a whole, so risk management will be more effective. An organisation that collects and analyses relevant data relates to an informed culture.
- A **Flexible Culture** exists where an organisation is able to reconfigure themselves in the face of high tempo operations or certain kinds of danger.
- In order to have a **Learning Culture**, an organisation must possess the willingness and the competence to draw the right conclusions from its safety information system and the will to implement major reforms.

Factors that promote a good safety culture include *leadership*, *commitment* and *good examples*. Where a good safety culture is predominant, the accountability rests largely with management, the highest levels of which must make necessary resources available. Other types of culture are:

- A **Punitive Culture** exists where fear accounts for any decisions that are made, to avoid disciplinary action or losing a job.
- **Open Cultures** have open channels between the workforce and management.
- **Closed Cultures** are the opposite.

RISK MANAGEMENT

Risk management is an important part of decision making because, when good procedures are followed, risk is reduced. For pilots, managing risk is a balance between completing a task against the prospect of harm, damage or loss whilst doing so.

Whether a risk is small enough to accept in order to complete a task is a matter of judgment. When the links in an error chain start to come together, the risk starts building, as error is one source of risk, and occupies the largest share of the total. Uncertainty about a situation can often indicate its presence.

One definition of risk is the chance that a situation, or the consequences of one, will be hazardous enough to cause harm, injury or loss. Another is that a *risk arises every time a person is in the presence of a hazard*. Health & Safety legislation defines a **hazard** as a condition, event or circumstance that has the potential to cause harm or damage to people or aircraft, equipment and structures (associated with the present, in that a hazard is always there). A **risk** is the potential outcome from that hazard, expressed in terms of the likelihood of anything happening and its severity (and therefore associated with the future). In other words, the risk is a value judgment based upon the hazard. The EASA requirement for an Acceptable Level of Safety is 10^{-6}* which, for an airline the size of, say, Lufthansa, would represent the loss of one hull every ten years.

*Safety management textbooks (e.g. Reason, *Managing the Risks of Organizational Accidents*) describe four approaches to risk management. Taking Helicopter Emergency Medical Services (or HEMS, the *immediate* and *rapid transportation* of medical personnel, supplies or ill or injured persons and anyone else directly involved) as an example, we get:

- **zero risk**, i.e. no risk of an accident that may have harmful consequences, using the highest standard of equipment, although, with helicopters, there are many parts such as the tail rotor or main rotor gearbox that do not have redundancy.
- **de minimis** - minimised to an acceptable safety target. This would normally be 10^{-6} (remote probability), but can be 10^{-8} (extremely remote) for some helipads at hospitals in congested hostile environments (see *AGK* for more details).
- **comparative risk**, to other types of exposure, such as carrying a patient with a spinal or respiratory injury in an ambulance instead
- **as low as is reasonably practicable**, where additional controls are not economically or reasonably practicable. The risks encountered in aviation do not always arise from being airborne. Ground operations pose their own problems. It's also worth pointing out that hazards need not be technical - there are business risks, too, such as when a company is growing quickly and can be exposed to cash flow problems, where safety might get a lower priority against simply surviving. There may be a high staff turnover, or you may have a disproportionate amount of inexperienced pilots that need proper supervision. A proactive safety manager will be looking for such problems before they start. Commercial viability is important, so there comes a point where the cost of reducing a small risk is uneconomic, particularly when there may be a lag of up to 20 years between management/board decisions and an accident with roots in that decision. People balancing the safety decisions have often retired by the time the effect of their decisions are felt.

To have absolutely no risk, of course, we shouldn't take off at all, but that's not what we're here for (some communities in remote places *depend* on pilots taking risks, hence commuter airlines), so we need some way of evaluating risk against a yardstick to get the job done, or balance profitability with safety. *Risk management* is the key, best used in an ample-time decision-making situation, where time is not critical. For example, in a helicopter, it can be more dangerous to avoid the height/velocity curve (say when coming out of a confined area) than to be in it for a few seconds. Part of a captain's job is to decide which of the risks presents the least hazard - that is, is there a greater risk of colliding with something when coming out of the clearing than having an engine failure? Is it better to take off downwind into a clear area, or into wind with a lot of obstructions where the fire trucks can't get to you? Risk Management means measuring the degree of harm against that of exposure - the more you have to lose, the less risks you want to take.

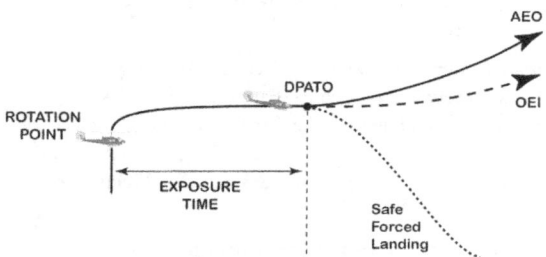

As a further example, in Performance Class 2 helicopter operations, you can get away with not having an assured safe-forced landing area in the takeoff or landing phase, on the assumption that turbine engines would have a failure rate of about 1:100,000 per flying hour, which would allow an exposure time of about 9 seconds during take-off or landing.

This has been established as an acceptable Residual Risk, which is what remains when all mitigating procedures are applied. Risk is minimised by ensuring that the helicopter is operated within the exposed region for the minimum time, and procedures are followed to minimise the consequences if an engine fails. For example, there are three areas in HEMS operations where risk, beyond those allowed in the regulations, are identified and related risks accepted:

- in the en-route phase, where alleviation is given from height and visibility rules
- at the accident site, where alleviation is given from the performance and size requirement
- at an elevated hospital site in a congested hostile environment, where alleviation is given from the deck edge strike, provided other elements are satisfied.

This is why specialist training may be required, such as instrument training to compensate for the increased risk of inadvertent entry into cloud, or operation with two crewmembers, which can be two pilots, or one pilot and a HEMS technical crew member.

Anyhow, the goal of whoever operates a Safety Management System is to:

- Identify any hazards that may be encountered (e.g. wet helidecks).
- Identify the risks associated with them (spinning helicopters).
- The level of risk for each scenario.
- Apply rules or design SOPs to minimise the risks.

Risk Management, therefore, is a decision-making tool that can be applied to either eliminate risk, or reduce it to an acceptable level, preferably before takeoff (things that stop you eliminating risk entirely would either be impracticality, or money). With it, you have to first identify a hazard, analyse any associated risks, make a decision and implement it (with a *risk strategy*) and monitor the results, with a view to changing things if need be. However, this depends on the *perception* of a risk, and the difference between yours, the management's and the customer's can be quite startling.

Analysing Risk

There are two types of risk:

- **External** (or Objective) Risk is that of an accident in the current situation if no changes are made to the flight path or the operation of systems.
- **Internal** (or Subjective) Risk. A risk that reflects the inability of the crew to implement a solution due to lack of knowledge or time to apply it. Internal risk increases linearly as the deadline for making and implementing a decision approaches.

The **Risk Factor** can be defined as anything that may increase the likelihood of an accident occurring.

The assessment of risk in a particular situation will be based on subjective perception and evaluation of situational factors. What this means in English is that the difference between perceived and actual risk depends on the amount of control you think you have, and familiarity. For example, it is a lot more risky to ride a bike through a busy city than it is to live near a nuclear power station, yet people still ride bikes along Main Street and don't want to live near nuclear power stations. The former situation allows you more control (you can always get off and walk) and is more familiar. Your perception of control is influenced by your fear of the unknown.

Risk is equal to *probability* multiplied by the *consequences* of what you propose to do, and your *exposure*. You essentially have four choices, based on the TEAM acronym:

- **Transfer** the risk (maybe with insurance)
- **Eliminate** the risk (don't do the job)
- **Accept** the risk (see *Risk Tolerability*, overleaf)
- **Mitigate** the effects of the risk. This means reducing a risk to bring it into a lower category. There may be three ways of doing this:
    - *Avoidance*. To be used when the risk exceeds the benefit gained.
    - *Reduction*. Don't take the risk so often, or reduce its consequences.
    - *Segregation*. Isolate the effects of the risk or build in some redundancy.

THE BODY

> 🛑 This section is meant to cover pilot examination requirements - it does not constitute medical advice.

The human body is wonderful, but only up to a point. It has limitations that affect your ability to fly efficiently, as your senses don't always tell you the truth, which is why you need extensive training to fly on instruments - you have to unlearn so much. The classic example is the "leans", where you think you're performing a particular manoeuvre, but your instruments tell you otherwise. However, although the sensors in the eyes and ears are actually quite sensitive, the brain isn't, and does not always notice their signals. Sometimes it even fills in bits by itself, according to various rules, including your expectations and past experience. Thus, at each stage in the perception process, there is the possibility of error, because we are not necessarily sensing reality. The reason why there is a *white balance* setting on a digital camera is because the brain interprets what is white in its own way and compensates all by itself - indoor bulbs actually glow quite red, and an overcast sky might have some blue in it, despite what you think you see. If the camera doesn't compensate, your pictures will be tinted the wrong way.

But why do you need to learn about the body? Well, parts of it are used to get the information you need to make decisions with, and, of course, if it isn't working properly, you can't process the information or implement any action based on it. For single pilots, it must be efficient because there is nobody else to take over if you get incapacitated. Also, presumably, you want to pass your next medical!

G Tolerance

Acceleration is the rate of change of speed or direction, or both. For example, getting to 60 mph in 6 seconds is an acceleration of 14 feet per second, per second.

If you pull back on the controls, your body (after Newton) wants to carry on in a straight line, but is forced upward by the seat, which feels the same as if you were being pushed into it. This extra pressure is called *g*, and it affects the whole body, including the blood, so the heart must change its action to keep the system running. The effects of g are compounded by hyperventilation, hypoxia, heat, hypoglycaemia (low blood sugar), smoking and alcohol, because they all affect the action of the heart.

The body can only cope with certain amounts of g-force, from the effects of acceleration that increase your weight artificially. With no acceleration, you are subject to 1g. However, we are often subject to forces beyond our limits, hence some illusions when the mind misinterprets the proper clues.

The types of acceleration include:

- **Linear** acceleration (Gx), which concerns itself with forward and backward movement in terms of speed only. During it, the **somatogravic illusion** can give you the impression of pitching up or climbing, making you want to push the nose down (governed by the **otoliths** in the ear). This is because, in level, unaccelerated flight, the only force that affects you is weight. If you accelerate, the fluid in the inner ear flows backwards and you end up with a resultant vector that gives you the feeling of pitching upwards. Pushing forward makes things worse because the weight vector is reduced, but you could also fly into the ground. The effect is more pronounced at night going into a black hole from a well-lit area, unfortunately confirmed by the artificial horizon, which suffers from the same effect. You get a pitch-down illusion from deceleration. The body can tolerate 45g horizontally, but if you don't wear shoulder straps, tolerance to forward deceleration reduces to below 25g, and you will jack-knife over your lapstrap with your head hitting whatever is in front of it at 12 times the speed of it coming the other way. This type of g causes breathing difficulties and affects the balance mechanism in the inner ear, but otherwise has slight physiological consequences.

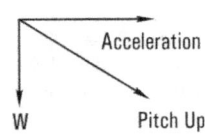

- **Radial** (centripetal) - about an external axis. It can lead to grey-out.
- **Angular** - about an internal axis, as when spinning.
- **Lateral** acceleration (Gy) has effects from left to right. It typically occurs when your direction changes, with an alteration in speed.
- **Vertical** acceleration (Gz) occurs while moving up or down. The body can tolerate 25g vertically. -Gz acts upwards and increases the blood flow to the head, leading to *red out*, facial pain and slowing down of the heart (your lower eyelids close at -3g). Blood vessels in the eyes and face may also burst. +Gz (otherwise known as *Positive g*) will *drain* the blood, with loss of vision, called *grey out*, at +3 Gz, so it will involve **tunnel vision** (loss of peripheral vision) above that (actually above +3.5 Gz). This could end up as *black out* (where you are fully conscious but cannot see) at +6g and unconsciousness between +7 and +8g. During substantial +g forces, the order of symptoms is: *grey-out, tunnel vision, black-out* and *unconsciousness*. Refer also to *Blood Circulation*, later. Increase long term +g tolerance by tightening your abdominal muscles (it helps veinous return), ducking your head (bending forward) and performing a kind of pressure breathing. A tilt-back seat is also useful, because it provides a supine body position that keeps the heart and brain at the same level so the heart works less.

Short-term acceleration lasts for **1 second or less**. *Long duration acceleration* lasts for **more than one second**.

Dem Bones

The skeleton does not keep the body upright - it works the other way round. Muscle tone dictates how you carry yourself, and the bones inside provide support. Lumbar support provides an even pressure for the spinal discs by allowing the lower spine to curve naturally.

Body Mass Index (BMI)

This is supposed to relate your weight to your height, and is calculated by dividing your weight by the square of your height.

The Central Nervous System

Whatever your body gets up to, the processes involved must be coordinated and integrated. This is done by the Central Nervous System, with a little help from the endocrine system. Although making an approach to land might seem to be automatic, the control responses that occur as a result of input from your eyes and ears, and experience, plus the feedback* required from your limbs so that you don't over-control, are all transmitted over complex nerve cells (*neurons*) for processing inside the CNS, which consists of the brain and spinal cord**, though it also includes the visual and aural systems (eyes and ears), proprioceptive system (the "seat-of-the-pants", which works off postural clues) and other senses.

*The **ideomotor phenomenon** relates to making motions unconsciously. The term is derived from *ideo* (idea, or mental representation) and *motor* (muscular action) and is most commonly used where a thought or mental image brings about a seemingly reflexive or automatic muscular reaction, often minuscule and outside of the awareness of the person concerned. Thus, as with reflexive responses to pain, the body sometimes reacts reflexively with an ideomotor effect to ideas alone without the person consciously deciding to take action. It is most important for the acquisition of complex perceptual motor skills

**Anything covered by bone.

Cells communicate with a combination of electrical and chemical signals, a process in which cholesterol plays a significant part. Chemical signals either diffuse between cells (*neurotransmitters*) or are disseminated in the blood (*hormones*) to act on more distant parts of the body.

The brain carries 25% of the body's cholesterol. Its availability can directly limit the ability to form synapses (points of passage of nerve impulses from one neuron to another). Not only that, cholesterol is synthesised into Vitamin D by the sun's rays. Low Vitamin D levels affect calcium absorption and serotonin production.

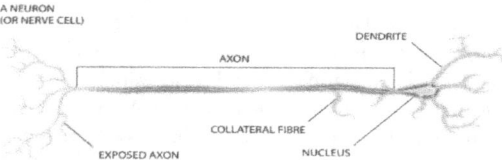

Neurons don't touch each other directly - if a message needs to be transmitted, a neurotransmitter (of which there are over 100 types, including serotonin) creates a connection called a *synapse* between them, having been triggered by an electrical signal. The chemical is destroyed after triggering a response in the next neuron. Modern drugs pretend to be neurotransmitters by providing a "key" to the receptor's "lock".

Neurites are extensions that connect with other neurons or muscles. Those that send impulses away are *axons*, and those that receive impulses are *dendrites*. Synapses are constantly being formed and broken where they meet.

Neurons are very thin and, as we shall see later, this makes it hard for electricity to move freely (there is a high resistance). To keep the signals going over relatively long distances, sodium (and potassium) ions outside a nerve act as booster stations (an ion is an atom with more or less electrons than it should have. Sodium has one less).

The first jolt of sodium creates holes further down that allows more sodium in. After the signal has passed, the nerve has lots of holes in it and is sloshing with sodium, which has to be repaired before it can fire again. This takes up around 80% of the energy going to the brain. Cold conditions will slow this activity down, which is why your fingers are more clumsy in the Arctic. Alcohol and anaesthetics have a similar effect. Adrenalin and caffeine speed things up!

Nervous system cells are capable of both efficient and rapid, or slow and generalised activity.

PERIPHERAL NERVOUS SYSTEM

This consists only of nerves, and connects the Central Nervous System with the sense organs, muscles and glands, and therefore with the outside world. The PNS is divided into:

- the **somatic** nervous system, which contains the peripheral pathways for communicating with the environment and control of skeletal muscles, and
- the **autonomic** nervous system, which regulates vital functions over which you have no conscious control, like heartbeat and breathing (unless you're a high grade Tibetan monk, of course), or anything that is not to do with skeletal muscle. The ANS in turn consists of the:
  - **sympathetic** nervous system, which prepares you for fight-or-flight (see *Stress*, later) and tends to act on several organs at once.
  - **parasympathetic** nervous system, which calms you down again, one organ at a time.
  - **enteric** system, which controls the gastro-intestinal process. As it contains more neurons than the spinal cord or peripheral nervous system, and has a degree of independence, it is often called the second brain, or the immune system.

Being under the influence of fight-or-flight is like being in a powerful car in permanent high gear, which you can't do all the time - you need rest & relaxation to allow time for the parasympathetic system to kick in, such as meditation, or a snooze in the back of the aircraft. Being in such a high state of readiness all the time produces steroids, and can lead to depression. It can actually be a problem during an emergency in a complex aircraft, where you have to force yourself to sit still and think your way through a problem.

The Brain

The brain is a switchboard that is constantly in touch with the 639 muscles inside the body. It can also store vast amounts of data - John van Neumann calculated that it stores around 2.8×10^{20} bits of information over the course of the average lifetime! Although the brain is only 2% of the body mass, it takes up to 20% of the volume of each heartbeat - its blood supply needs to be continuous, as it cannot store oxygen.

When their temporal lobes were stimulated (behind the temples), epileptic patients could recall past episodes in vivid detail. However, when rats had various parts of their brains removed, they could remember their way round a maze, which would suggest that, although memories are stored in the brain, they are distributed around the whole organ, rather than being allocated specific locations (people who have head injuries don't seem to forget halves of novels, or who their families are). Maybe each part of the brain contains enough information to reconstruct a memory, in the same way that a fragment of a hologram contains the complete image from the whole. Paul Pietsch flipped the brains of salamanders around (upside down, etc.) and found that they behaved perfectly normally whichever way round they were.

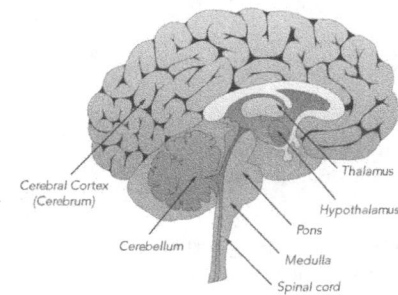

Many of the brain's departments merge into each other, and work closely together, but there are still three distinct areas. The "lower" level (central core) deals with basic survival, while the "higher" ones allow complex processes.

- The **Central Core** includes most of the brain stem, starting at the *medulla* where the spinal cord widens as it enters the skull. The medulla controls breathing and some reflexes that keep you upright. Also, the nerves coming from the spinal cord cross over here, so the right side of the brain connects to the left side of the body, and *vice versa*. Slightly above the medulla is the *cerebellum*, which concerns itself with (smooth) coordination of movement, and acts as a *reflex centre for the coordination of equilibrium*. The *thalamus* consists of two egg-shaped groups of nuclei. One acts as a relay station for messages, and the other regulates sleep and wakefulness. Just below that is the *hypothalamus*, which controls endocrine activity (through the pituitary gland) and maintains normal body functions, in terms of temperature, heart rate and blood pressure, which are disturbed under stress. For example, the body's core temperature should be between 35-38°C. It is maintained through mechanisms such as *vasorestriction* (narrowing of blood vessels), *sweating*, *shivering*, or *goose pimples*, when hot or cold. Below 32°C, with hypothermia, the demand for oxygen will initially increase, shivering will tend to cease, then apathy will set in. With hyperthermia (too hot), getting used to a hot country can take about 14 days. The hypothalamus is also called the *stress centre*.

- The **Limbic System** wraps itself round the Central Core and is closely connected to the hypothalamus. Part of it, the *hippocampus*, would appear to have something to do with short-term memory, in that, when it is missing, people can remember things that happened long ago,

but not recently. The Limbic System is often called the *interbrain*, as it has structures that communicate with both the higher and lower brain centres.

- The **Cerebral Cortex** is the surface of the Cerebrum, or the final layer that allows the development and storage of analytical skills, verbal and written communication, emotion, memory and analytical thought.

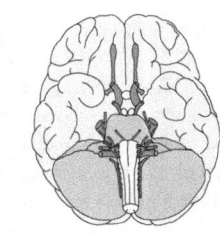

Cerebral Hemispheres are basically symmetrical, but the left and right halves are interconnected (through the corpus callosum), with women having more connections between them than men, which accounts for their ability to think of several things at once, often contradictory. Each hemisphere has four *lobes*. The hemispheres work in different ways, leading to two types of thinking:

- *Left Brain*, or logical - governs language, skilled in mathematics
- *Right Brain* - conceptual. The artist type

The left hemisphere therefore works with words, and the right hemisphere with pictures.

Although the two hemispheres work differently, they still work very much together.

The brain has different reservoirs of resources, depending on whether you are in the *information gathering*, *information processing* or *action* phase. Unlike muscles, which only react to stimulation, it has several constant electrical rhythms. The dominant one consists of alpha waves, and an increase in brain activity creates beta waves which are faster, but of less voltage. These are associated with the focussing of attention and problem-solving, so they make stress arousal more possible. There are also theta waves and delta waves, the latter being slow and usually only detectable during sleep. Concussion is unconsciousness resulting from a blow to the head.

The most important parts of the brain are the *brain stem*, *cerebellum* and *cerebrum*.

SENSORS

The body has two types of sensor:

- those that collect **precise data**, such as the eye's central vision, and hands and feet, and
- those that collect **general information** to confirm the precise data above, or to provide warnings.

Generally, information picked up by a sensor is only transmitted (and used by the brain) when it is needed.

Vision

LIGHT

In the electromagnetic spectrum, as radio waves get higher in frequency, they approach the lower reaches of visible light, which is what is detected by your eyes. Radio and light waves are of the same nature (just vibrating at different rates), so the eye can be viewed as a specialised radio receiver, or at least a frequency analyser. Sub-ranges within the range of visible light are detected as colour, with the lowest frequency being red and the highest violet, in this order: R O Y G B I V. Their combination creates white light, and black is the absence of any radiation, so black and white are not actually "colours".

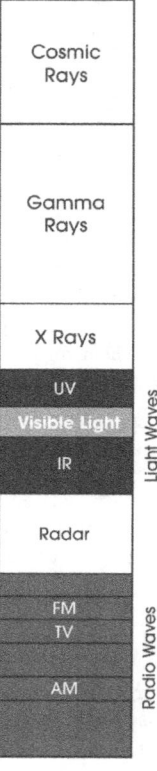

The diagram on the right shows how limited the range of visible light is against the spectrum of electromagnetic waves available. In fact, if the full spectrum were 2 yards long, visible light would occupy 1/32 of an inch.

The nature of the atom is discussed in *Electricity & Magnetism* but, essentially, when an electron is knocked away from its inner orbit round the atom's nucleus, one from a further orbit replaces it. In doing so, it has to adapt to a slower speed, giving up high frequency radiation in the process, and the more energy that is given up, the higher is that frequency. As well, the closer to the nucleus this happens, the more energy is surrendered.

All electromagnetic energy is produced by the movement of electrons into holes in the inner orbits of different atoms by a kick of energy coming from outside. In the case of light, this mostly comes from the Sun. For example, shifting the orbit of an electron in a sodium atom will create a yellowish light, while steely blue comes from a mercury atom. You see objects in daylight because you are able to detect radiations from the movement of their electrons. The use of heat, as obtained with fire, or applying electricity to a filament in a light bulb, has the same effect. However, no such artificial means can enable you to see the visible spectrum in its correct proportions. Red will only appear as red when the light shining on it contains the (slower) frequencies that can agitate the electrons in atoms that are able to give off red light. A London bus, therefore, reflects only the red frequencies and fails to reflect the rest. If the light striking the bus contained no red, you would not be able to see it.

Vision is your primary (and most dependable) source of information - **70% of data enters the visual channel**. It gets harder with age to distinguish moving objects; between 40 - 65, this ability diminishes by up to 50%, but this is only one limitation, and we need to examine the eye in detail to see how you overcome them all.

THE EYE

The eye is a dual sensor, for central and peripheral vision. The latter is imprecise, but it covers a large area, and is good for detecting movement. Central vision is more exact, and narrowly focussed. You can only read instruments with central vision.

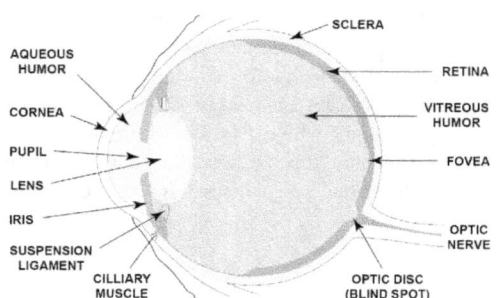

The eye is nearly round, and its rotation in its socket (and focussing) is controlled by external muscles. It has three coatings, or layers of membrane:

- the **sclerotic**, which has a transparent area at the front called the *cornea*, which bends light rays the most. Behind the cornea is the *lens*. Its purpose is to finish the job of bending light rays inwards and to focus them on the retina. The ciliary muscles surrounding the lens control its shape. This change of shape is *accommodation*, which can be affected by age or fatigue. When you are tired, accommodation is diminished, resulting in blurred images.

- the **choroid**, which lines the sclerotic and contains tiny blood vessels.

- the **retina**, at the back, which is the light sensitive part that detects electromagnetic waves at light frequencies, and converts them to electrical signals that are interpreted by the cerebral cortex in the brain. It is sensitive to hypoxia, as are the rods ((the parts of the retina sensitive to dim light).

 According to EASA, the optic system consists of the cornea, the lens and vitreous humour. The three coatings in the eye are the sclera, uvea and retina.

The fluid in the eye retains its shape and keeps the sensory ligaments tight. The ciliary muscles have to work to overcome this tension, which is why your eyes get tired after a lot of focussing on near objects.

The lens may be dislodged by careless rubbing of the eyes (for example when the humidity is low), an accidental knock or increased g forces.

As the cornea does not have its own blood supply, it gets its oxygen from the ambient air. Mild hypoxia and dehydration, from low humidity on the flight deck, may therefore increase the potential for cornea damage when using contact lenses. Bubbles may form under a contact lens if decompression is experienced.

 If you are cleared to use contact lenses, a pair of ordinary spectacles must be carried while exercising the privileges of your licence. Aircrew who wear spectacles must carry a spare pair during flight in any case.

HUMAN PERFORMANCE & LIMITATIONS
The Body

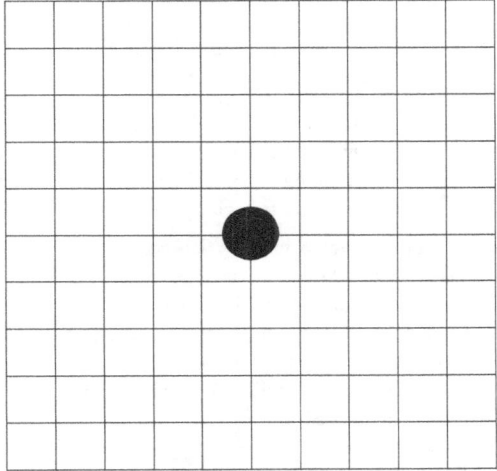

The lens, iris and cornea control the amount of light entering the eye through the *pupil*, which is the black bit inside the coloured iris. 70% of light is refracted by the cornea, and 30% by the lens. The more your iris is open, the less *depth of field** you have, so in darkness it is hard to see beyond or before the point of focus, and you may need glasses to help.

*The depth of field is an area either side of the focus point in which everything is sharp. The wider the iris, the shorter this distance is, and *vice versa*.

Generally, vision is better with more light, but too much produces glare (older people need twice as much light to see well). The iris appears black because any light that does not get absorbed by the retina is usually absorbed by a layer behind it called the *retinal pigment epithelium*. If it wasn't, your vision would be blurred by randomly scattered light. Redeye occurs when not all light can be absorbed and some is reflected back.

The retina is composed of ten very thin layers, with nerve endings that act as light sensors (actually, neurons) which are called *rods* and *cones*, in the ninth. Their names arise from the way they are shaped. Each is more efficient than the other in different kinds of light. Cones are sensitive to day or high-intensity light and rods (scotopic visual cells) are used at night or in low-intensity light. As the periphery of the retina consists mainly of rods, peripheral vision is less precise because they only see shades of grey and vague shapes (you see colours because the vibrations they give out are strong enough to wake the cones up, and the brain mixes the colours received by them). The cones need at least the light of a half moon to function at all.

The rods contain *visual purple*, also known as *rhodopsin*, which builds up over 30-45 minutes as light decreases until the approximate level of moonlight, which is when the rods take over from the cones. As rods are sensitive to shorter wavelengths of light, in very low light, blue objects are more likely to be seen than red (neither will be in colour), which is why cockpit lighting is sometimes red because it affects the rods (used for night vision) less than white light does.

Light waves from objects in the *right* visual field fall on the *left* half of each retina, for transmission to the *left* cerebral hemisphere, and *vice versa*. This is so that each side of the brain has input from both eyes at once, and that both of them work in concert. The size of the image on the retina decreases with distance, and is upside down and backwards. The *optic nerve* carries signals from the eye to the brain. The point where it spreads out to become the retina has no rods or cones, so there is a blind spot there. You don't normally notice it because the brain superimposes the images from each eye.

Once light falls on the retina, the visual pigment is bleached, which creates an electrical current. Once bleached, the pigment must be reactivated by a further chemical reaction called *nystagmus*, caused by the eye jerking to a new position, there to remain steady. The movement period (saccade) is edited out by the brain, and the multiple images are merged, so continuous vision is actually an illusion, as an *after image* is produced when light falls on the retina - that is, the image of what you are looking at remains there for a short period, as light has a momentum. As the eye does not need to be seeing constantly (and can therefore be regarded as a detector of *movement*), it can spend the spare time in repair and replacement of tissue. 30-40 images per second are taken in the average person, and an image takes about $1/50$ of a second to register. It has also been discovered that, when we blink, the visual cortex in the brain (where what the eye sees is interpreted) closes down for that period. As it happens, if 90% of a rat's visual cortex is removed, it can still perform quite complex tasks that require visual skills. Similarly, a cat can have up to 98% of its optic nerves severed without much effect.

All this means you also *see with the brain*, giving a difference between *seeing* and *perceiving*. It also means that problems with vision can arise from the brain's processing ability and not the eyes themselves. The eye's optical quality is actually very poor (you would get better results from a pinhole camera), hence the need for the brain, which can modify what you see, based on experience, and so is reliant on expectations. For example, if you were blind and could suddenly see an orange, you wouldn't recognise what it was until you were able to feel its shape and texture which, up till now, would have been your only experience of one (the ability to see in 3D is learned). If the brain fills in the gaps wrongly, you get visual illusions. **Less than 50% of what you see is actually based on information entering your eyes!** The remainder is pieced together out of your expectations of what you should be seeing.

Your mind can get so accustomed to seeing a given set of words that your unconscious can edit out what is really there and make you see what you expect to see, as experienced by writers who can miss a smelling pistake for ages. Pilots used to seeing a certain instrument picture can miss changes in the same way.

Close your left eye and stare at the dot in the middle of the grid in the picture at the top of the previous page with your right eye. As you move the page back and forth along your line of vision (about 10-15 inches away), the right one will vanish because it is falling inside your blind spot (so move your head as well as your eyes when scanning). Now close your right eye and stare at the dot on the right. The one on the left will vanish as well, *but all the lines on the grid will remain intact*. This is because your brain is filling in with what it thinks should be there. If we are only seeing about half of what is out there, what are we missing? How many readings on our instruments do we not see at all? The eye/brain combination is therefore not trustworthy, as it can tinker with its world view before you become conscious of it. In fact, visual information entering the brain is modified by the temporal lobes before being passed on to the visual cortices (*Pribram*).

The only part of the eye that sees perfectly clearly is in the centre of the retina, an area just larger than a pinhead, called the *fovea centralis*, where the first eight layers of the retina are missing, so the cones in it are directly exposed to light (that is, the light doesn't have to battle through the first layers) for clearer vision at that point. It is the area of best day vision, and no night vision at all, so you are subject to two blind spots at night (see below). The eye's ability to read alphanumeric information is limited to the foveal area. Inside it, the cones are connected singly to their own nerves. Elsewhere in the retina, one nerve may be connected to 100 receptors.

5° away from the foveal axis, sharp vision reduces by a quarter, and one-twentieth when 20° away. Outside of that, vision is quite blurred - if you look at the top part of this page, you will not see the rest clearly without shifting your vision. Our eyes also take in lines of text in little clumps (*fixations*) so the fovea can deal with them properly (the eye can only focus when it is not moving). The small jumps needed for this are called **saccades**, and the points where the eye stops to focus on fixations are *fixation points*. As your eyes jump between fixation points, nonfoveal vision is generating a preview of the next words so the brain can decide where the next point will be. The average saccade and rest period lasts for a third of a second. So, the illusion of seeing large areas clearly (that is, more than two words at a time) comes from the rapidity of shifting - attempting to do this otherwise means seeing without focussing, and gives you eyestrain. Sometimes your eye and brain can get out of the habit of looking at one point together. Vibrations can also cause blurred vision, from *tuned resonance oscillation of the eyeballs*.

NIGHT VISION

There are 3 types of vision. Night vision involves the latter 2:

- **Photopic**, which occurs by day or in high-intensity lighting, using **mostly cones**, as the rods bleach out and become less effective. Objects can be detected with peripheral vision, but central vision is mostly used anyway, because that's where the cones are

- **Mesopic**, for dawn, dusk and full moonlight, using both **rods and cones**. Colour perception reduces as the cones start to work less well, and off-centre scanning gets the best results

- **Scotopic**, for low light, and where vision becomes around 20/200 (see below), using **only the rods**. As the cones don't work at all, you also get a night blind spot, so you have to look to one side to see an object properly.

The eye is slow to adapt to darkness. It takes about 30 minutes, as opposed to about 10 seconds with high levels of illumination. This is because of the need to create visual purple (rhodopsin), a process requiring Vitamin A, of which the retina contains enormous amounts - having too little could result in night blindness. The pupil gets larger, to let more light in, which also reduces the depth of field, which will therefore increase focussing errors. Dark adaptation is an independent process for each eye. Night vision can be affected (through lack of oxygen) as low as 5 000 feet (1 600 m) under conditions of indifferent hypoxia (see later). In the compensatory stage, at 15 000 feet, it will degrade by as much as 25%. Otherwise, night vision is affected by age, cabin altitudes above 8,000 ft, smoking and alcohol.

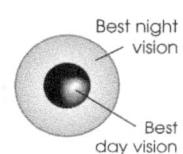

At night, with a low workload, cockpit lighting should be *increased to prevent low vigilance.*

Picture: Operation of the Eye

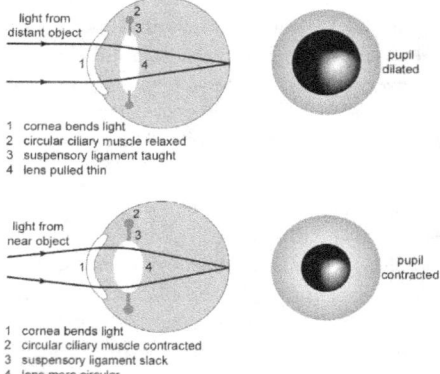

COLOUR BLINDNESS

Total colour-blindness (not colour deficiency) can be a bar to the issue of a flying licence, being subtle and only detectable with specialised tests. It results from a defect in the structure of the colour-sensitive cones in the retina - normally when a single group is missing, although it does not affect acuity. The most common form is red/green. Colour blindness is more common in men than it is with women, but women act as carriers.

FIELD OF VIEW

The field of view of each eye is about 120° left to right, and about 150° up and down. There is an overlap of 60° in the centre where binocular vision is possible.

HUMAN PERFORMANCE & LIMITATIONS
The Body

VISUAL ACUITY

This is the ability to perceive detail - while the eyes can receive light from a wide arc, they can only focus over an area of about 10 or 15°. In fact, the eye finds it hard to resolve anything that occupies an angle of less than 1 minute of arc, so the smallest object you can see from 3600 m away (2 nm) would have to be at least 1 metre wide (after the 1 in 60 rule). You would therefore only be able to see the fuselage of a light aircraft inside 2 nm. At typical closing speeds, you would have 30 seconds to see and avoid. Power lines are beyond the resolving power of the eye, which is why they are so hard to see.

An aircraft heading towards you can disappear from sight under the same circumstances.

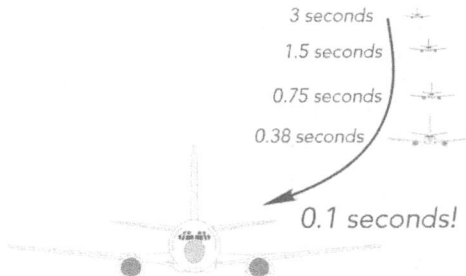

A high speed aircraft approaching head-on will grow the most in size very rapidly in the last moments, so it's possible for it to be hidden by a bug on the windscreen for a high proportion of its approach time. Lack of relative movement makes an object harder to detect.

You should be able to see another aircraft directly at 7 miles, or 2.5 miles if it was 45° off - at 60° it's down to half a mile! The reason why you must scan is because the eye needs to latch on to something. With an empty field of vision, your eyes will actually focus at relatively short distances, just under 1 metre ahead, and miss objects further away (*empty field myopia*). In other words, you effectively become short-sighted (myopic).

Normal vision is described as 20/20, meaning that you can see at 20 feet what a normal person can see at 20 feet. If the ratio, as a fraction, is greater than 1/1, visual acuity is better than normal, so 6/4 means you can see at 6 m what a normal person can only distinguish at 4 m. On the other hand, 6/9 is poor: Normal people can detect at 9 m what you cannot see above 6 m.

Clarity of vision is affected by:

- light available
- size and contours of objects
- distance of an object from the viewer
- contrast
- relative motion
- the clarity of the atmosphere

Visual acuity at high altitudes can be affected by anaemia, smoking, carbon monoxide and hypoxia.

DEPTH PERCEPTION

This is the process of forming 3D images from 2D information, in our case, 2 sets, from our eyes - and it's all done in the brain.

BINOCULAR NON-PICTORIAL CLUES

These rely on both eyes working together in two ways:

- **Retinal Disparity** - also known as *stereopsis*, this is the main cue to depth perception (up to 60m), and it depends on the difference in images received by each eye - the brain fuses the two images to get a 3D result and analyses the differences between them to deduce distance. This disparity gets greater when objects are close. If you hold one index finger close to your eyes, and the other one further away but behind, the closer one will seem to shift its position more when you look at them with one eye closed at a time. This is because the angle between the eyes is greater. Stereopsis helps you judge the *length* of runways (up to 200 feet).
- **Convergence** is another muscular clue where the eyes point more and more inward as an object gets closer and each eye sees an object from a different angle. By noticing the angle of convergence, the brain produces depth information over 6-20 feet. Speed is judged by the rate of change of the angle.

The effects of convergence and accommodation (below) are relatively negligible.

MONOCULAR NON-PICTORIAL CLUES

Accommodation is a (ciliary) muscular clue to distance, effective up to about 4 feet, from the change in curvature of the lens, which gets thicker when you focus on nearby objects.

MONOCULAR PICTORIAL CLUES

Vision is based on binocular vision at short distances, and rules of proportion and perspective (*monocular clues*) for objects further away (over 200 m). As the latter can be detected with one eye, they are not dependent on biological processes, except for focussing. They are most subject to illusion, including:

- *relative size* (larger objects appear to be closer)
- *overlap* (objects covered by others look further away)
- *relative height* (lower objects look closer)
- *texture gradient* (smooth surfaces look further away)
- *linear perspective* (more convergence, more distance)
- *shadowing*
- *relative brightness* (nearer objects are brighter)
- *motion parallax* (nearer objects seem to move more)

Differential size is the dominant cue at far distances, movement parallax at intermediate ones, and stereopsis up to 17 m (more if you fixate on the object). *Atmospheric perspective is where distant objects are less coloured and less distinct.*

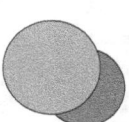 For example, the dark shape on the left is actually a half-moon, and it is level with the other one, even though it looks like as if it is further away.

Optical illusions, discussed overleaf, may occur when any of the above cues are missing.

DEFECTIVE VISION

A focussed image on the retina depends on the length of the eye against the focal length of the lens, which is adjusted by varying the thickness of the lens, as performed by the ciliary muscles.

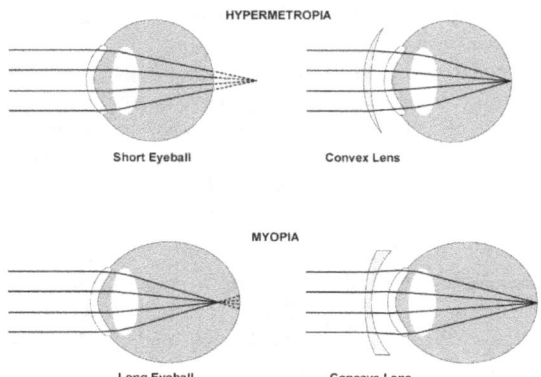

For best results, the image should come into focus directly on the retina - there is some evidence to suggest that muscular activity at the rear can adjust the body of the eye to help the lens.

Otherwise, the major causes of defective vision are:

- *Hypermetropia** - where the eyeball is too short, and images focus behind the retina (farsightedness). Requires a convex lens.
- *Myopia** - where the eyeball is too long, and images focus in front of the retina (short sight). Needs a concave lens.
- *Presbyopia* - the lens hardens, leading to *hypermetropia* and difficulty in focussing, lack of accommodation (comes with old age).
- *Cataracts* - the lens becomes opaque.
- *Glaucoma* - an increase in the pressure of liquid in the eyeball interferes with accommodation for a progressive narrowing of the visual field.
- *Astigmatism* - unequal curvature of cornea or lens. Corrected with a cylindrical lens.

*Both conditions cause blurred vision, which is correctable by glasses, that vary the refraction of the light waves until they focus in the proper place.

Night Myopia and Night Presbyopia

Night myopia (nearsightedness), also known as *twilight myopia*, causes some people who are slightly myopic in daylight to become more so after dark.

Also known as *red light presbyopia*, night presbyopia occurs in presbyopic individuals who are subjected to red light, which is found in some cockpits during night operations. Red light has the longest wavelength, so when you try to read instruments or charts in it, the demand for accommodation is more than if you were using white light, making it difficult to read small print. In effect, your depth of field is reduced.

Space Myopia

Also known as *Empty Field Myopia*, this describes the short-sightedness experienced when there is nothing to look at outside the cockpit. For example, when flying VFR on top, clouds prevent you from seeing the ground, and the light they reflect reduces your visual cues. Your eyes will tend to lock-in on the instruments (i.e. less than about 1 metre ahead) and remain fixated for that distance, so when you look outside, *the resulting myopia could stop you seeing other aircraft*. Look at the wingtips from time to time to allow relaxation of the *ciliary muscles* (the ones that control the shape of the lens for near and far vision).

OPTICAL ILLUSIONS

Flying is subject to illusions, especially when carrying out extreme manoeuvres and/or at night. The input from your senses is interpreted (rightly or wrongly) by your conscious and subconscious minds. The former handles the visual aspects, and the latter all the rest, through the peripheral nervous system, part of which, if you remember, runs your body automatically. When the subconscious becomes confused about your position in space (it assumes you are on the ground), the only link between you and reality is the visual system linked to the conscious mind, which is a lot slower and less capable in its processing ability. As the eyes are not affected by acceleration, centrifugal force or gravity, you must rely on your instruments when you get disorientated.

Much of what you "see" outside the central zone of attention (the fovea) is a reconstruction of what was there a few seconds ago, because the eyes simply do not have the bandwidth to stream video across their whole field of view. The visual cortex filters the data it gets from the rods and cones and uses it to identify objects that are inserted into a mental model of the world. Humans are prone to illusions when their mental models differ from the real world, in which case, protective measures would include comprehensive briefings and debriefings.

Illusions exist when what you sense does not match reality, but they are more than just mistaken perceptions.

They occur because our senses are limited, especially when it comes to the demands of flight - the missing bits tend to get filled in by the brain, sometimes wrongly. Even going to the cinema is an optical illusion: still frames are shown so quickly that it looks as if movement is taking place - the switching is done in the brain, using the eye's *persistence of vision*, which is the ability to retain an impression of the shape, colour and brightness of an image for a fraction of a second after light from the image stops being received. Without persistence of vision, this would not work.

Looking directly at an object underwater at any angle, other than the normal to the surface of the water, is difficult because the difference of densities of the air and the water cause the light rays to be refracted as they pass through the surface and the object appears to be in a position other than its actual position:

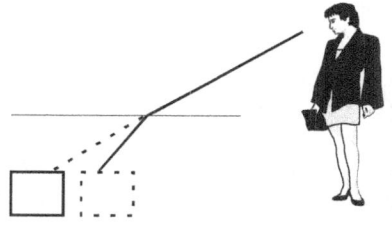

This has obvious parallels with looking at a runway through a wet windshield and *distortion* occurs, especially where water is thicker near the bottom (nearer to the windshield), causing a *prismatic effect* - like looking through a base-down prism, which tends to make objects look higher or closer. Raindrops on a windscreen can double the apparent size of lights outside and make you think you are closer to the runway than you really are. The reflections on the windshield can create a false horizon below the true one by as much as 5°, which means a difference of 200 feet at one mile.

This will be more apparent with high intensity runway lighting, which may also give you the same effect that actors have on stage, where they can't see the audience through the bright lighting. The lack of normal contrast will also upset your altitude perception, making you feel further away and higher than you are. As a result, on a final approach you could find yourself too low and fast.

Approaching an oil rig, particularly, the lighting will appear as a straight line above 1 nm away, an ellipse as you get closer, then a circle close to. As you have no depth perception, the closing speed is very hard to judge until you get very close, and pilots will either come to the hover just short or go steaming past and have to pitch nose-up to stop themselves overshooting.

In the image on the right (a Ponzo illusion), the two horizontal lines are the same length, but they look different because your perspective cues are not correct.

One classic illusion for pilots is *whiteout* (see *Meteorology*), defined by the American Meteorological Society as:

> "*An atmospheric optical phenomenon of the polar regions in which the observer appears to be engulfed in a uniformly white glow*".

That is, you can only see dark nearby objects - no shadows, horizon or clouds, and you lose depth perception. It can occur over unbroken snow cover beneath a uniformly overcast sky, when the light from both is about the same (you get brownout in dust clouds). Blowing snow doesn't help because you may also get a vectional illusion, and it's a particular problem if the ground is rising. *Flat light* is similar to whiteout, but it comes from different causes, where light is diffused through water droplets suspended in the air, particularly when clouds are low. *Objects seen through fog or haze will seem to be further away.* Approaching at night with no visual reference or landing aids can make you think you are higher than normal and there is a risk of landing short, or ducking under (see also the Kraft illusion, below).

A good fixed wing example of an optical illusion is a wider runway tending to make you think the ground is nearer than it actually is:

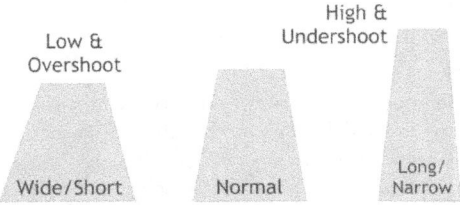

A narrow runway delays your reactions, possibly leading to an undershoot. In the diagram above, all three landing strips are the same distance and angle away from the aircraft, but the one on the left is wider and shorter (looks nearer, and low on the glideslope, so you might carry out a higher approach and flare too soon) and the one on the right is longer and thinner (looks further away and high on the glideslope, so you might go lower and flare too late, landing short while trying to keep the sight picture). So, if you are used to a runway 28 m wide, and land on one 40 m wide, there is a risk of performing a high approach, with an overshoot and a high roundout.

Similarly, being used to a runway 45 m wide and trying to land at one 28 m wide may make you think you are higher and produce a low (flatter) approach with an undershoot, with a late flare and a tendency to land short.

The best visual cues for height during the flare are your apparent speed and the texture of ground objects so, if there is no information, you should make an instrument approach and be aware of these illusions.

Illusions you might get with sloping ground include:

Problem	Illusion	Risk
Downslope	Too low	High approach/overshoot
Upslope	Too high	Low approach/undershoot
Rain	Closer	Low approach
Narrow	Too high	Low approach
Wide	Too low	High approach & flare
Bright lights	Too low	High approach

In short, if your approach angle is meant to be 3°, and the runway is already sloping up by 1°, you will think you are higher than you actually are and make you increase the rate of descent and land short, and *vice versa*. An approach to a downsloping runway will therefore tend to be started higher, with a steeper angle, because the perceived glide path angle is smaller than that of the actual glide path you think you are too low). However, the

slope away from the aircraft presents a smaller image to your eyes, and you see less of the runway, so you try to see more by flying too high to correct the apparent undershooting and land long. This is *hape constancy* (see the *Kraft Illusion*, below).

All are good reasons for using VASIS or a PAPI.

KRAFT ILLUSION

Normally, the aiming point on a runway on a constant approach remains stationary in the field of view, while the visual angle occupied by the runway is constantly changing. Boeing researchers found that if you are approaching on a dark night over unlighted terrain to a runway beyond which the horizon is indiscernible, when only runway lights are visible with city lights beyond, there may be a tendency to keep the visual angle of the whole runway constant. You may think you are too high and too far away, and make an initially steep approach that flattens out, ending up too low and landing short - often up to 3 miles away from the runway.

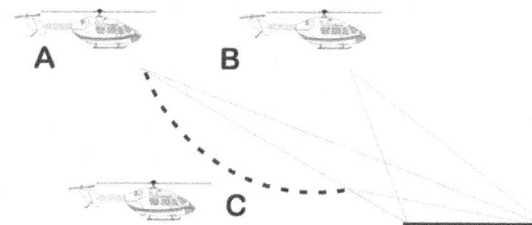

Upslope runways intensify the illusion. Long straight-in approaches over featureless terrain should be avoided.

VECTIONAL ILLUSIONS

These are caused by movement, as when sitting in a railway carriage and wondering whether it's the train next to you or the one you're in that is moving. It is *somatogyral* when you are moving and *oculogyral* when the object is moving (it's called the *illusion of relative movement* in the exam, but is actually *Motion Parallax*). It is dealt with under the *Vestibular System*, later.

Otherwise, helicopter pilots can get similar illusions when hovering close to moving water. The *waterfall effect* happens while hovering or in slow flight at low altitudes. The downwash causes the air to pick up water and displace it upward at the edge of the blades and downward directly under them, so you might see drops of water going down in your field of vision to give you a climbing sensation. Descending will put the helicopter in the water. Where there is a conflict between the two senses, the visual reference provides the more accurate picture. **The most important sense for spatial orientation is sight.**

AUTOKINESIS

This is one illusion you might come across at night, being the apparent motion of a stationary object, typically a star that can be mistaken for an aircraft. It is a particular threat when fixing your position by a single light source. When little or no light is on the surface and a prominent one comes into view, it may seem that the light is above the horizon, which could lead you to pitch into a steep attitude in keeping with the resulting false horizon. The light source may also appear to change colour. To help combat the phenomenon, look for other references, including with your peripheral vision.

HEIGHT

When mountain flying, it's often difficult to fly straight and level because the sloping ground around affects your judgment. Similarly, you can't judge your height when landing on a peak.

An aircraft that appears to be the same height as you will probably pass below you.

The solution to illusions is to use every piece of sensory information you can, including landing lights and instruments, plus *comprehensive briefing and debriefing*.

DESIGN EYE REFERENCE POINT

The DERP gives you the best visibility outside and inside while making as few head movements as possible. The pilot compartment should be designed for a clear, undistorted, and adequate external field of vision, so seats need to be adjustable to position your eyes as close to the DERP as possible for the best views while manipulating the controls (including the instruments). If you sit lower than the ideal position, you can lose a lot of vision downwards, so you might see fewer runway lights, and approach and flare judgment may suffer. On changing to an aircraft with a higher eye position, you may not be able to see the overshoot area, and initially taxi faster than you should.

SUNNIES

Pilots are exposed to higher light levels than most people, especially from below, as the eyes are recessed into the skull to protect them from light coming from above. Light may also be reflected from cloud, and there is less scattering of the rays by the atmosphere at altitude. In addition, at altitude, the horizon is lighter than the sky, which is the reverse of normality. High-energy blue light can cause cumulative damage to the retina over long periods. Ultra violet wavelengths can also cause damage, mainly to the lens, but most are filtered out by the cockpit windows. The above are good reasons to wear sunglasses, within certain limits.

Good sunglasses should be able to absorb enough visible light to eliminate glare without decreasing visual acuity, absorb UV and IR radiation and colours equally. A neutral-grey lens with 15% transmission (following British Standard 2724) would appear to be the most suitable, as it virtually eliminates invisible electromagnetic radiation. Sunglasses should also be made from scratch-resistant hard-coated polycarbonate with thin metal frames. Photochromic lenses are not advised because they take too long to change over (up to 30 minutes bleaching time), but even when fully bleached, they still absorb slightly more light than untinted lenses. Their operation also depends on UV light which is screened by the windscreen. Polaroids should be avoided in digital cockpits.

The Ears (Vestibular System)

The structure of the ears allows you to hear and maintain your balance (by sensing motion and gravity), but they are also important because an auditory stimulus most often the one to which most attention is paid. How many times do you answer the phone when you're busy, even though you've ignored everything else for hours?

13% of our knowledge is acquired through hearing.

The whole ear assembly is around 25 mm long, and the eardrum is the boundary between the outer and middle ears. Sound waves make it vibrate, and the vibrations are transmitted by a chain of linked bones in the **middle ear** (the smallest ones in the body) known as the *hammer, anvil* and *stirrup* (the *ossicles*) to the *cochlea* in the inner ear (via the *oval window*), which is full of fluid. The vestibule is the duct that contains the organs of balance.

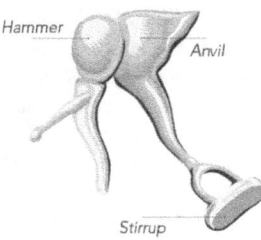

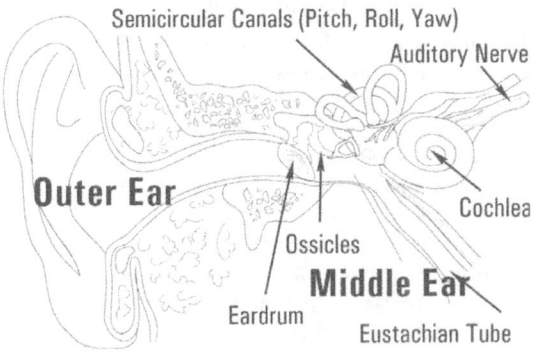

The cochlea is a tube which narrows progressively. It contains thousands of fibres (*cupula*) of different lengths that vibrate in sympathy with various frequencies. The fibres are linked to the brain and, as with sight, it is now, when the signal reaches the brain, that we "hear". The human audible range is 16-20 Hz to 20 KHz, with the most sensitive range between 500-4000 Hz.

As you climb and the outside air pressure reduces, the eardrum will bulge outwards, and *vice versa*. This difference in pressure is equalised by air leaking out through the *Eustachian Tube,* which is a canal that connects the middle ear to the back of the throat. The tube is normally collapsed as it can just about cope with walking uphill, but air expanding in the middle ear is enough to open it up (thus, pressures equalise more easily in the climb). When you descend, however, especially at low level, the pressure goes the other way and tends to keep the tube closed. Swallowing opens it up, allowing air to enter, which is why it helps to clear the ears when changing altitude. Blocked Eustachian tubes can be responsible for split eardrums, due to the inability to equalise pressure. As the eardrum takes around 6 weeks to heal, the best solution is not to go flying with a cold.

DEAFNESS

Hearing depends on the proper working of the *eighth cranial nerve*, which carries signals from the inner ear to the brain. If it gets damaged, deafness results. The nerve doesn't have to be severed - deterioration will occur if you don't get enough Vitamin B-Complex. Also, as the sensitive membrane in the cochlea gets damaged, the ability to hear some frequencies goes (see NIHL).

The frequency and intensity of sounds are important when it comes to deafness. Loudness is determined by how much the eardrum is bent by pressure waves, as measured in **decibels** (dB). Ear defenders reduce noise levels by up to 40 dB and ear plugs by only about 20. There are three types of hearing loss:

- **Sensori-neural**, where the ability to process sound is lost. In aviation, **high-tone deafness** is very common and the most dangerous. *Noise Induced Hearing Loss,* or **NIHL**, comes from prolonged exposure to loud noise, usually over 90 dB.

- **Conductive Hearing Loss** comes from interference with the transmission of sound waves from the outer to the inner ear. In other words, it is damage to the physical hearing mechanism (middle ear bones), which can include hardened ear wax!

- **Presbycusis**. Age-related hearing loss, causes loss of high tones.

DISORIENTATION

The three *semicircular canals* in the ear monitor **angular accelerations**. Two are vertical and one is horizontal (the vertical ones are at right angles to each other, so they can detect rotary motion in any plane). They use the fluid in the inner ear, which acts against sensory hairs (cupula) to send electrical signals to the brain so you can tell which way is up. The hairs enter the walls of the canals at a point called the *ampulla*. If your head is turned to the left, the fluid's inertia makes it stay where it is, but the canal's movement bends the hairs to the left. The signal is then sent to the brain for interpretation. **The danger lies when such movement is too slow to detect in the first place, and is gradually increased**, especially when you are affected by gravity and centrifugal force at the same time, as when in a steep turn, or holding.

While the semicircular canals sense *angular* acceleration, the **otolith organs** on the top of the cochlea in the inner ear pick up changes in *linear* movement. These consist of the **utricle**, for horizontal movement, and the **saccule**, for vertical. They both have sensory hairs at the bottom with calcium carbonate crystals at their ends. The crystals provide the inertia needed to bend the hairs, which send signals down sensory nerve fibres which are interpreted by the brain as motion.

Alcohol in the fleshy stalk of the otoliths may persist for days after all traces of it have vanished from the blood. It is not unusual for even small movements of the head to cause disorientation or motion sickness up to three days after alcohol was last consumed.

Additional sources of positional information include s*omatosensory receptors* inside the skin, joints and muscles. As they respond to pressure and stretching signals, they can be an important source of information about your equilibrium. They are called the "seat of the pants" sense because it was thought that you could tell which way was up by the seat of your pants sensing the most pressure. **The seat of the pants sense is completely unreliable as an attitude indicator when your body is moving in the aerial environment.**

On the ground we maintain balance with impressions from the eyes, the vestibular apparatus in the inner ear and various sensations from the muscles, joints, skin, etc. as coordinated by the nervous system, more or less in that order of importance. We grow used to being parallel to the trees and at right angles to the ground, and things feel strange when we are not. Disorientation is the state of confusion you get when the brain receives conflicting messages, such as a feeling of turning detected by the inner ear, but not confirmed by the eyes, which frequently produces nausea. It refers to a loss of your bearings in relation to position or movement, and is more likely to happen when you are subject to colds, in IMC, and changing between inside and outside visual references.

ILLUSIONS FROM OTOLITH ORGANS

Somatogravic illusions occur from movements of the head. If the otoliths are pulled backwards or forwards from inertial forces during acceleration or deceleration, you get the sensation of facing upwards or downwards (or climbing or descending) even though you have not moved your head.

The **oculogravic** illusion covers the visual aspects, making you think that the instrument panel is moving up or down during acceleration or deceleration.

ILLUSIONS FROM SEMICIRCULAR CANALS

The "leans" (**somatogyral** illusion) occur because your semicircular canals get used to a particular sustained motion in a very short time, especially if the roll rate is below the perceptible rate (sub-threshold bank). If you start a turn and keep it going until you reach a uniform velocity, your canals get used to the situation, because they lag, or are slow to respond. When you straighten up, they will try to tell you you're turning in the opposite direction, when you're actually flying straight and level (reducing bank then carrying out a long turn will do the same). It is the most common vestibular illusion.

Although your natural inclination is to obey your senses, your instruments are there as a cross-reference. In fact, the whole point of instrument training is to overcome the dependence. To combat the leans, close your eyes and shake your head vigorously from side to side for a couple of seconds, which will topple the semi-circular canals.

The **oculogyral illusion** is the visual element, where there is a false sensation of the motion of an object which might look as if it is rotating in the opposite direction even though it is actually stable in front of you.

The **graveyard spin** arises from the somatogyral illusion. During a prolonged spin, the fluid (endolymph) in the semi-circular canals settles, allowing the sensing hairs to erect. When a recovery is initiated (as with a prolonged turn), you get a strong sensation of entering in a spin in the *opposite* direction. If you react wrongly, you will re-enter the spin in the original direction.

The **Coriolis** illusion is an abnormal sensation that occurs when more than one set of semicircular canals are stimulated at the same time (cross coupling). It produces a sensation of tumbling in space. For example, in a roll to the right you may get a sensation of a yaw to the left if you move your head forward. In a steady turn, a sudden movement (greater than about 3° a second) of the head will be detected as a change in the turn rate.

The Coriolis illusion with relation to vertigo is easily demonstrated with a revolving chair - sit in one, and get someone to spin it while you have your chin on your breast. When you raise your head sharply, you will find yourself on the floor inside two seconds. This has obvious parallels with flying, so make all your head movements as gentle as possible, especially when making turns in IMC, or picking up a pen from the cockpit floor (mention of fluid, above, implies that, if you are dehydrated, you may also get spatial disorientation - if you feel thirsty, you are probably already 5% there).

Medications and alcohol can have similar effects, but alcohol will intensify the effects of medication. It's well known that lying down when drunk causes the ceiling to revolve, and this can lead to stationary objects appearing to move when standing upright. This is because the difference between the specific gravities of alcohol and inner fluid is enough to make the sensors move by themselves and be wrongly interpreted as a head movement. Since your head is not really moving, it looks as if the rest of the world is. This effect can be reproduced days after drinking only two pints of beer, long after alcohol is undetectable.

MOTION SICKNESS

This results from a continued stimulation of the inner ear.

Another illusion associated with the vestibular apparatus is *Vertigo*, or a loss of spatial awareness, resulting from *disease, accelerations, pressure changes* and *flashing lights*. It can be the result of *Coriolis Effect** from a mismatch between the information sent to the brain by the eyes and ears (as all semicircular canals are stimulated). *Pilot's Vertigo* is dizziness and a tumbling sensation from making head movements in a tight turn, or a sensation of rotation coming from multiple irritation of several semicircular canals. Aside from being *a sensory conflict within the vestibular system accompanied by nausea, vomiting and fear*, airsickness can also be caused by vibration, when the body (i.e. the skull), is vibrated at frequencies less than 0.5Hz, as found in turbulence.

In fact, vibrations within the frequency band of $1/10$ - 2 Hz are a contributory factor to air sickness because they upset the vestibular apparatus. Keep the head still and get someone to do the lookout, as closing eyes is not always an option!

*In a steady turn, a sudden movement (greater than about 3° a second) of the head will be detected as a change in the turn rate. This is a cross-coupled stimulation of the semi-circular canals, otherwise known as Coriolis Effect.

Make all your head movements as gently as possible, especially when making turns in IMC, or picking up a pen from the cockpit floor (mention of fluid, above, implies that if you are dehydrated, you may also get spatial disorientation - if you feel thirsty, you are probably already 5% there).

Medications and alcohol can have similar effects, but alcohol will intensify the effects of medication. It's well known that lying down when drunk causes the ceiling to revolve, and this can lead to stationary objects appearing to move when standing upright. This is because the brain detects the movement of fluid in the inner ear and tries to rationalise things through the eyes. In other words, eye movements are used to compensate for head movement - the difference between the specific gravities of alcohol and inner fluid is enough to cause the sensors to move by themselves and be wrongly interpreted as a head movement. Since your head is not really moving, it looks as if the rest of the world is. This effect can be reproduced days after drinking only two pints of beer, long after alcohol is undetectable.

You can get problems from colds, etc. as well, particularly a spinning sensation caused by a sudden difference in pressure between the inner portions of each ear.

The Respiratory System

Respiration is the process by which a living organism exchanges gases with its environment. Its main function (in humans) is to provide oxygen and remove excess carbon dioxide from body cells, but it also helps to maintain temperature and the acid base balance. Other functions include:

- acting as a blood filter or reservoir.
- acting as an air filter, warmer and humidifier.
- contributing to heat loss through ventilation.

It works at sea level because the **partial pressure** of oxygen in the atmosphere is higher than it is in the blood (this is reversed at high altitudes - see *Dalton's Law*, overleaf). The partial pressure of the respiratory gases within the pulmonary alveoli is 40 mmHg for CO_2, 47 mmHg for H_2O and 100 mmHg for oxygen.

External respiration concerns ventilation of the lungs and the transfer of gases through the pulmonary membrane into the blood. **Internal respiration** is about the transportation of gases to and from the tissues and exchanging gases in them. There are a number of conditions that interfere with them both and which could result in hypoxia of some description, discussed later.

Under normal conditions, respiration is a subconscious process that occurs at 12 - 20 breaths per minute, averaging 16, with a typical volume of air being exchanged of around 500 ml.

The respiratory system can be split into two regions.

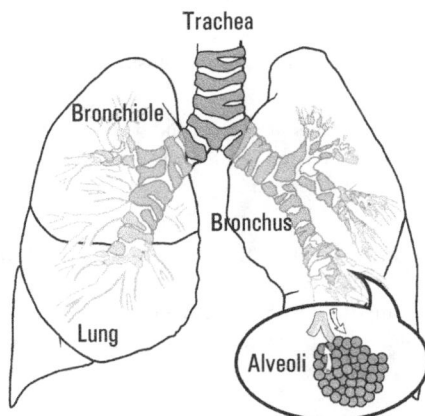

- The **conductive airways** contain the oral and nasal cavities, pharynx, larynx, trachea and the first several branches of bronchi, which distribute the gas to each lung. The **trachea** (windpipe) divides into two **bronchi** which divide again into **bronchioles**, which keep dividing until they end up as air sacs called **alveoli**.
- The **gas exchange region** contains bronchioles and alveolar ducts, which are lined with alveoli.

The two lungs are separated by the heart, airways and the major blood vessels in the centre of the chest, all of which are enclosed by the chest wall, which is a combination of ribs, cartilage and muscle. Each lung is covered by a thin, moist tissue called the *pleura*, which also lines the chest wall. The lungs and chest wall are elastic but, as you breathe in and out, the lungs recoil inward while the chest wall expands outward. These two opposing forces create a negative pressure in the pleural space between the rib cage and lung. If air enters that space, from in- or outside the lungs, the pressure can cause all or part of the affected lung to collapse. Medically, this condition is known as a *lung rupture*, or *pneumothorax*. Symptoms include breathlessness and chest pain on the affected side.

THE GENERAL GAS LAWS

A gas has three variables - *pressure (altitude)*, *density* and *temperature*, and a general gas law defines their relationship when there is no change of state or heat transfer. For example, if a gas were restrained in a rigid container (so the volume doesn't change), increasing the temperature makes the gas expand and increase the pressure inside, and *vice versa*. If the container were not rigid, the volume could change, and affect the gas's density (air density affects aircraft performance). Put another way, you can alter the volume of a gas by changing its pressure or temperature, or both.

PRESSURE

Static pressure (which plays a major part in breathing, lift, drag, and the operation of carburettors, amongst other things) is proportional to air temperature and density. It arises 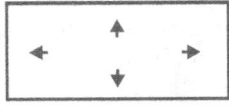 from the average continuous random motion of air molecules. As the random motion involves collisions between them, and they tend to repel each other, the end result is the formation of pressure in all directions. The motions average out at the speed of sound.

Air at rest is subject to *static* pressure, which results from the mass of air supported above the level concerned - it depends on the number and mass of air molecules (density), and how fast they are moving (temperature).

The shorthand notation for static pressure is p, and a 0 means at zero altitude, i.e. sea level (p_0). The shorthand notation for the ratio between the ambient and standard sea level static pressure (p/p_0), which is useful for performance purposes, is δ (delta).

Thus, at a given height, the only thing that stops the air above you falling to the ground is the pressure of the air below you acting upwards, so the total pressure acting on your aircraft is equal to the weight of the air above you.

We do not notice the pressure above us because there is an equal and opposite internal pressure inside the body which remains the same as we climb. As the pressure outside reduces, blood vessels can expand or even burst.

The weight of a column of air is commonly expressed in one of three ways:

- **Pounds per square inch** (psi). The force that air exerts in pounds over a square inch of a surface - about 14.7 lbs at sea level in the standard atmosphere (2116.2 lbs per square foot). This will be lower by 81% at 40,000 feet.

- **Inches of mercury** (Hg). If you fill a tube with mercury (because it is more dense than water and takes up less space), and tip it upside down into a bowl that is also full of mercury, the level in the tube will drop until the force exerted by atmospheric pressure on the mercury in the bowl equals the weight of the mercury in the tube. Atmospheric pressure under standard conditions will hold up a column of mercury that is 29.92 inches long.

- **Hectopascal**. Newtons/square metre is the SI unit for pressure. 1 N/m^2 is a *pascal*. The hPa, which has replaced the millibar, consists of 100 Pascals. 1 millibar is equal to 1 Hectopascal.

TEMPERATURE

The quantity of heat contained in a substance is a measure of the kinetic energy of the molecules it contains, depending on the temperature, mass and nature of the material concerned. A bucketful of warm water will melt more ice than a cupful of boiling water because it contains more heat. Thus, two bodies containing the same amounts of thermal energy may not have the same temperature, because temperature is a measure of the *quality* of heat (or the rate at which molecules are moving), which means it cannot strictly be measured, but only compared against some form of scale.

Officially, temperature is a measure of the average kinetic energy of air molecules measured in Kelvins (K), or absolute temperature (see later). Otherwise, two common ways of measuring temperature are *Fahrenheit* or *Celsius*, and it's a real pain to convert between the two.

The quick and easy way is to use a flight computer:

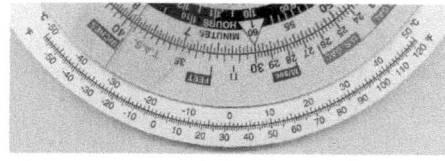

But here are the calculations if you want to show off:

```
F - C     Tc = (Tf - 32) x 5/9
C - F     Tf = Tc x 9/5 + 32
```

They work for any temperatures above freezing. The freezing level (in flight) is where the temperature is 0°C.

To find Fahrenheit from Celsius, you can also multiply °C by 1.8 and add 32. To find Celsius, subtract 32 from the Fahrenheit value and divide the remainder by 1.8.

Tip: 16°C is equal to 61°F, 15°C is 59°F and 30°C is 86°F, for gross error checks and quick conversions - however, given the standard of performance charts in the average flight manual, doubling the Celsius figures and adding 30 to get Fahrenheit, or subtracting 30 from Fahrenheit and dividing the remainder in half to get Celsius is probably good enough! The Fahrenheit scale assumes that water freezes at 32°, and boils at 212°. Celsius (which used to be called *Centigrade*, the Latin for one hundred degrees) starts at 0° and finishes at 100°, which is more logical, but the scale is coarser. The full range of each is 180 and 100 respectively, which is where the $9/5$ fraction comes from.

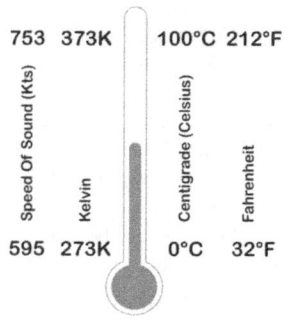

For each °C of cooling, a gas will reduce its volume by $1/273$, which brings us to scientific methods of temperature measurement, in the shape of Kelvins, which don't use a degree sign. -273.15°C is equal to 0K, or Absolute Zero, which is when all molecular motion is supposed to have stopped, and therefore has the least kinetic energy, although this is scientifically impossible. There should now be zero pressure because the air molecules are not moving, which is why absolute temperature is used in the gas equation.

You could also say that 0°C is equal to 273K, from which you can infer that the 1° steps in both scales are the same.

The shorthand for the ambient temperature is *T*, and that for the standard sea level air temperature of 288K is T_0. The ratio between the ambient and the standard sea level air temperatures (T/T_0) is θ (theta).

DENSITY

Density, or the mass of air occupying a given volume, depends on pressure, temperature and humidity, as measured in slugs per cubic foot. A slug is a unit of mass and is found by dividing the weight of an object by its acceleration due to gravity, so a person weighing 161 lbs would have a mass of 5 slugs (161 divided by 32.2). In standard ISA conditions, air has a density of around 1.225 kg/m^3. At 40,000 feet, the air density is around 25% of the sea level value.

The symbol for density is ρ (rho) and the density ratio (ρ/ρ_0) is called σ (sigma).

Density and pressure are directly related, and density and temperature are inversely related (the term *Density altitude* is used in relation to aerodynamic performance when the temperature is not standard).

Density and humidity (below) are also inversely related as water has less mass than air. When translated to altitude, the effects of changing pressure are offset by temperature changes, meaning that the expansion of a gas is much greater than any shrinking from temperature reductions.

HUMIDITY

To function properly, the human body requires a certain amount of humidity, which concerns the amount of invisible water (vapour) contained in a parcel of air. The *absolute humidity* is the actual mass, expressed in grams per cubic metre (i.e. as a volume). For a particular temperature, the *relative humidity* is a measure of how much moisture an air parcel *is* holding against the maximum it *could* hold at that temperature (and pressure) or, in other words, the *percentage saturation*, which will *decrease* if the air gets warmer. Thus, the amount of water vapour that air can hold is determined by the temperature.

Vertical Temperature Distribution

A parcel of air rising through the atmosphere meets air at lower pressure, so it expands and cools adiabatically (without heat transfer). The standard fall of temperature with height (the lapse rate) is 1.98°C per thousand feet.

In the lower levels of the stratosphere (see overleaf), the temperature is assumed to be mostly constant with height, but there is a gradual increase above 20 km (65 617 ft) due to the ozone (molecular oxygen). When you're up that high, the ozone is above toxic limits, so the air needs to be filtered (and monitored) before it comes into the cabin.

The Ideal Gas

An ideal (perfect) gas obeys the gas laws. Actually, no gas is really ideal, but they are considered to be so in low subsonic flow, which is about 30% of the speed of sound.

The *kinetic theory of gases* (from Maxwell, after Bernoulli) states that gases consist of molecules that are in constant motion, on which their properties depend. The *volume* of a gas is the space through which its molecules are free to move. From *Avogadro's Law*, which states that equal volumes of all gases at the same temperature and pressure contain the same number of molecules (assuming you could count them), you can deduce that the same number of molecules should have the same volume.

Contributions to the kinetic theory of gases include:

- **Charles'** Law, from a Frenchman, Jacques Charles, which states that, if the *pressure* remains constant, volume (and density) is very nearly proportional to the *absolute* temperature so, the hotter a gas gets, the more space it takes up, or the more you compress it into a smaller space, the hotter it gets, and *vice versa*. If you double the temperature of a gas, you double its volume. Put another way, equal volumes of different gases expand more or less equally for the same temperature if the pressure is kept constant, with the change in volume being $1/273$ of its initial volume at 0°C, for each degree change in temperature, up or down, so at -273°C the volume would be zero. This law (which is only approximately true anyway) helped Charles make the first meteorological flight in a balloon, taking a barometer with which to work out his height.

  Thus, if Spain and Iceland have the same pressure, the air in Iceland will be denser.

- **Boyle**, an Irish physicist, discovered that, for a perfect gas*, if *temperature* remains constant (i.e. it is **isothermal**), its volume and density vary inversely with its pressure so, if you double the pressure of a gas, you halve its volume. As you climb, and pressure reduces, the volume of the gases within various body cavities, such as the middle ear, sinuses, the gut, lungs and teeth, increases and may cause pain and/or discomfort. In practice, the temperature increases slightly as the pressure is raised, but it stabilises afterwards. Thus, a parcel of air taken from sea level to 34 000 feet would increase its size 4 times because the sea level pressure is reduced to a quarter at that height.

  *Only approximately with high pressures. Boyle's and Charles' laws are only accurate in small ranges.

  If it's 25°C all over Spain, the air density will be lower in the mountains than it is on the beach.

- **Dalton** says that the total pressure of a mixture of gases is the same as the sum of the *partial pressures* exerted by each of the gases in the mixture, assuming they don't react chemically with each other, which is relevant for oxygen. In other words, each gas's pressure contributes a part of the total according to its constituent proportion, or exerts the same pressure that it would do on its own, and the total pressure of the mixture is equal to their sum. This allows meteorologists to figure out how much water vapour there is in a given parcel of air - if they know the makeup of a gas on the ground, they can calculate the amounts for any altitude.

  So, after Dalton, if the pressure at a certain altitude were 986 hectopascals, the pressure from oxygen would be 21% of 986, or 207 hPa. An average set of lungs absorbs oxygen at a partial pressure of 3 psi, which is enough to saturate the blood. The overall and partial pressures of the gases in the atmosphere *decrease* with increasing altitude.

- **Gay-Lussac's Law** states that equal increases in temperature result in equal increases in pressure if the *volume* is kept constant.

When everything changes at once, you must use Boyle's and Charles' laws, in that order. By adding Gay-Lussac and Avogadro to the mix, you can get a single expression called the **General Gas Law**, which connects temperature, pressure and density:

$$p = RT\rho$$

ρ is the density, T the absolute temperature and p the pressure. R is a constant that depends on the gas (2.87 for dry air). The constant doesn't change, of course (unless you change the gas), and if temperature stays the same, pressure is proportional to density* - because you are increasing pressure by cramming more molecules into a smaller space, density automatically increases. If pressure stays the same, an increase in temperature reduces the density. So you can calculate density if you know the pressure and temperature.

*If density remains constant, pressure and temperature are directly proportional.

The **Combined Gas Equation**, which still involves Boyle's and Charles laws, is similar:

$$PV = WRT$$

Where P is pressure, V is Volume, W= Weight, T is Temperature and R is a constant, as above. Being constant, its value is not affected by variations in any of the others. The formula shows that, if you increase pressure without changing volume, the only ways you can balance the other side of the equation are to increase the temperature (T) or the mass (W) of the gas (although increasing the mass would involve a temperature rise anyway). On the other hand, you could increase the pressure by decreasing the volume, which will leave the right hand side of the equation unaffected, once the temperature has settled down.

DIFFUSION & FICK'S LAW

Diffusion is the process by which many substances get through membranes and into cells. It is the spreading of a gas or any substance in solution from a higher to a lower concentration (osmosis is a form of diffusion that concerns water). The greater the difference, the faster is the rate of diffusion. The alveoli, which are the final branchings of the respiratory tree, form an exchange surface that is specialised for diffusion and the exchange of oxygen and carbon dioxide (the villi do a similar job in the small intestine for the products of digestion).

The oxygen in the lung has to get across a thin membrane to reach the blood in the alveoli. The gas-blood barrier between the alveolar space and the pulmonary capillaries is extremely thin, to allow for a rapid exchange. To reach the blood, oxygen must diffuse through the *alveolar epithelium*, a thin interstitial space, and the *capillary endothelium*. The waste product, CO_2, is carried by the blood mainly as sodium bicarbonate, and broken down by enzymes. When CO_2 is released, it is diffused into the alveoli and breathed out.

The oxygen thus absorbed is carried to the tissues of the body, especially the brain, which is the most sensitive organ to its lack. **It is the carbon dioxide** (and acidity) **level in the blood that regulates respiration**, not the body's need for oxygen, so an increased level of CO_2 creates a shortness of breath - if you breathed in helium instead of oxygen, your rate of breathing would hardly change. The levels are monitored by several chemical receptors in the medulla that are very sensitive to CO_2. When the level is higher than normal, as it might be if you exercise hard, the rate of breathing is speeded up.

Tip: If you hyperventilate the lungs by breathing deeply and rapidly for a minute or so, you will remove enough carbon dioxide from the blood to remove the need to breathe for a while, not recommended under normal circumstances, as it is one of the dangers of high altitude flight, but it may help if you end up under water.

Graham's Law states that, under the same conditions, the rate of diffusion of a gas is inversely proportional to the square root of its density. Hydrogen will diffuse 4 times faster than oxygen does under the same conditions of temperature and pressure. **Fick's Law** states that the rate of diffusion is directly proportional to the membrane surface area and the concentration gradient, and is inversely proportional to the membrane thickness, so a large area subject to high pressures lets through more gas, but less if it is thick.

The diffusion of oxygen into the blood depends on *partial pressure gradients* (that is, in proportion to a gas's presence in the mix - it follows **Henry's Law*** and, presumably, Dalton's) so, as partial pressure falls, oxygen assimilation is impaired. Although the air gets thinner, the ratio of gases remains the same, so there is still 21% oxygen at 35,000 feet. However, even if you increase the proportion of oxygen to 100% as you climb, there is an altitude (around 33 700 feet**) where the pressure is so low that the partial pressure is less than that at sea level, so just having oxygen is not enough, because, as altitude increases, the partial pressure of water vapour and carbon dioxide in the lungs remains the same, reducing that of oxygen in the lungs still further (**the partial pressure of CO_2 in the alveoli is *lower* than it is in the blood**). Also, at altitude, other gases dissolved in the blood, such as nitrogen, may bubble out and cause the bends or similar effects. The term *aeroembolism* describes the liberation of gas bubbles when you climb up high.

*Henry's law states that the amount of gas dissolved in a liquid is proportional to the partial pressure of the gas above the liquid (assuming no chemical reaction) - when that pressure decreases, as it would in the climb, so does the gas (typically nitrogen) dissolved in the liquid.

STOP Fat can dissolve about 5 or 6 times more nitrogen than blood can, which can be a problem for an overweight person when it bubbles out.

Air in the alveoli contains water vapour and CO_2, so the relative pressures of oxygen and nitrogen are reduced against that of the atmosphere, at sea level. The partial pressure of oxygen thus becomes around 103 mmHg as opposed to 160 mmHg. It reduces to **55 mmHg past 10,000 feet, while the pressures of water vapour and CO_2 remain the same. The altitude where the atmospheric pressure equals that in the alveoli is 33 700 feet (109 mmHg), so breathing 100% oxygen at that height gives you the same oxygen tension in the alveoli as you would get at sea level. As the oxygen tension can reduce to 55 mmHg before any decrease in performance is noticed, the limiting altitude for 100% oxygen is 40 000 feet.

In summary, from 0-10 000 ft you can survive on normal air; above this, you need more oxygen, up to 33 700 feet, where you need pure oxygen to survive (breathing 100% oxygen at that height is the same as normal breathing at sea level. At 40 000' the equivalent is 10 000 feet). Above 40 000 feet, the oxygen needs pressure, meaning that you must exhale by force (exposure to O_3 is also significant). Having said all that, your learning ability can be compromised as low as 6 000 feet (*Source*: RAF).

Breathing	First Signs	Death
Air	10,000 ft	22,000 ft
100% Oxygen	38,000 ft	43,000 ft
Pressure Oxygen	45,000 ft	50,000 ft

You can expect symptoms of hypoxia (a deficiency in the amount of oxygen reaching the bodily tissues) between around 38 000 - 40 000 feet when breathing 100% oxygen without pressure.

RESPIRATION

Respiration begins when the chest cavity is expanded or contracted by the actions of the intercostal muscles and the diaphragm so that air rushes into the lungs to fill the empty space (or rushes out), due to the pressure gradients created between the mouth or nose (atmospheric) and the alveoli, from where oxygen is diffused (actually, pushed, under pressure) into the *haemoglobin* in the blood (haemoglobin is a protein molecule). This takes place 12-15 times a minute at rest (some say 16-18), exchanging about ½ ltr on average. This *tidal volume* (also known as V_T) is the volume of an individual breath (in and out). The rate of breathing is faster in small children and slower during sleep. It is controlled by the autonomic nervous system, but it can also change according to your activity.

The air inspired per minute is *respiratory minute volume*.

The maximum amount of gas you can hold in your lungs after breathing in is predictably called the *total lung capacity*, which is typically 6½ litres for a healthy adult. Normal breathing involves volumes of half that, or 3-3½ litres. It consists of four volumes:

- **Tidal Volume**
- **Inspiratory Reserve Volume** - a little extra in over the total volume (3100 ml).
- **Expiratory Reserve Volume** - a little extra out over the total volume (1200 ml). The gas left in the lungs after breathing out is the *functional residual capacity*, or the sum of ERV and *Residual Volume* (RV), below (about 3 litres).
- **Residual Volume**, always there, about 1.2 litres for a healthy young person.

The difference between total lung capacity and residual volume is the *vital capacity*, which is around 5 litres.

Lack of oxygen at altitude stimulates the rate of breathing, but this washes more carbon dioxide out of the blood, so the sensors in the brain slow it down again. Thus, the two factors that regulate breathing oppose each other at high altitudes. The net effect is a gradual increase.

AEROBIC RESPIRATION

This is the release of energy from the breakdown of glucose by combining it with oxygen inside living cells.

$$\text{Glucose} + O_2 \longrightarrow CO_2 + H_2O + \text{Energy}$$

Expired air contains 15% oxygen and 4% carbon dioxide.

Without enough oxygen, you get a bit of energy and a lot of lactic acid, and *anaerobic respiration*. The lactic acid must be converted to CO_2 + water to complete the process.

THE ATMOSPHERE

Life exists in the biosphere, of which the *atmosphere* is one of three components. The other two are the *lithosphere* (the solid part of the Earth) and the *hydrosphere* (the water, including water vapour). The biosphere is therefore within, and influenced by, the atmosphere, which is an ocean of gases around the Earth, and which moves with it, although it is in continuous motion from uneven heating, as discussed in *Meteorology*.

Various concentric(ish) layers have been identified over the years, which are not sharply defined because they are based on the way the temperature changes with altitude, latitude, and the type of terrain below. This means that their heights and locations can vary hourly.

Starting from the bottom, the layers include the *troposphere*, *stratosphere*, *mesosphere* and *thermosphere*, although the last two are not of much concern to the average pilot. In fact, many scientists say they are actually part of the *ionosphere*, which we will meet again in *Radio Navigation*. On the other hand, some say that the ionosphere is actually the bottom part of the thermosphere, while the upper part is the *exosphere*. Go figure.

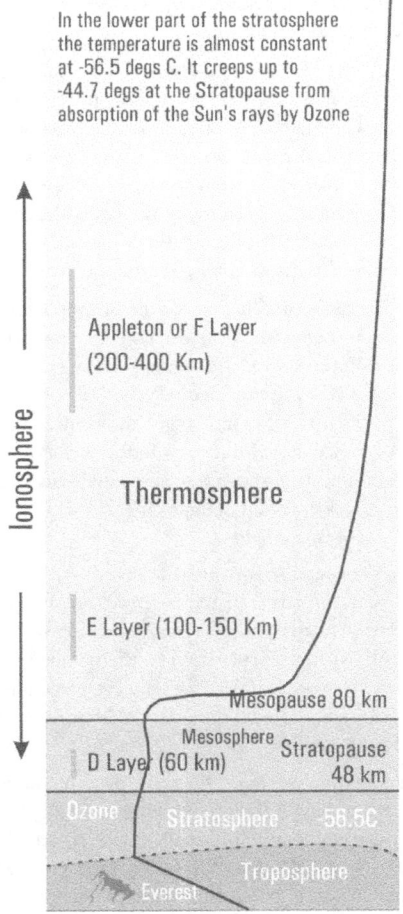

However, the first two layers do concern us, and we live at the bottom of the troposphere, which is at the shallowest and most dense area because it is compressed by the weight of the air above it. In fact, it contains around 85% of the total mass of the atmosphere. Almost all the remaining 15% of the atmosphere lies within the Stratosphere as, above about 25 km, less than 1% remains. The boundary (or transition zone) between them is the *tropopause*, where any clouds are made of ice crystals. It lies at an average height of 36 090 feet, or 11 km.

21% of the troposphere, luckily for us, is oxygen, but 78% is nitrogen (N_2), with 1% of odds and ends, like argon (0.9%) and CO_2 (0.03%), and others, that need not concern us here, plus bits of dust and the odd pollutant, and water in various forms in suspension (the nitrogen, as an inert gas, keeps the proportion of oxygen down, since it is actually quite corrosive). Normally, because of the constant mixing, these proportions remain constant (in dry air) up to about 80 km, but there are exceptions:

- **Water**. 2% of the Earth's total water supply can be found suspended in the atmosphere.
- **Ozone**. 0.001%. **This is toxic**, and the main gaseous constituent of airborne pollution. It can be removed from the cabin with ozone converters.

- **Carbon Dioxide** (CO_2). 0.05%. This absorbs infrared radiation and allegedly contributes to the greenhouse effect, described in *Meteorology*

If the air wasn't continually being stirred up, the heavier gases would simply sink to the lower levels.

Thus, the atmosphere provides oxygen for us to breathe, and filters out harmful cosmic rays, aside from helping to regulate the Earth's temperature. The main characteristic of the troposphere is that its temperature falls off with altitude (because gases cool as they expand), whilst that of the stratosphere is assumed to remain constant until it increases slightly in the latter stages as the Sun's energy has enough power to heat its molecules directly*. See *International Standard Atmosphere*, below.

*The **ozone layer** lies in the middle part of the Stratosphere, about 30 kilometres up (between 11-50 km, with the highest concentration at 80,000 feet), where the air absorbs ultraviolet radiation from sunlight (UVB better than UVA**), to break the bonds of the two atoms that make up oxygen molecules and allow the creation of molecules with three. On the surface, about 3% of the ozone found in the atmosphere is the main ingredient of *photochemical smog*, the sort found in large cities, in which chemical reactions occur in sunlight.

THE INTERNATIONAL STANDARD ATMOSPHERE (ISA)
Because the atmosphere (in terms of temperature, pressure and density) changes almost from minute to minute, we need some sort of model to work with, particularly when the volume of a gas varies so much with pressure. You can only get a true idea of the actual quantity of a gas if the volume it would have under some sort of standard is used.

To make sure that everyone works on the same page, a couple of typical scientists went to a typical place (at 40° N latitude) and took the average year round conditions, part of which turned out to be 1013.25 millibars (29.92" of mercury) and 15° Centigrade, which is 288K. This was adopted as the International Standard Atmosphere, and now everyone who makes altimeters, or whatever, does so according to its rules, so that everything is standard. In short, ISA is a standard that provides universal values of temperature, pressure, density and lapse rate, by which others can be compared. It not only covers conditions at sea level, but also variations with altitude, although viscosity has not been standardised (the chief difference between actual and standard air is the presence of water vapour, which is more to do with Meteorology).

In the standard atmosphere, ½ sea level pressure is at 18 000', one third at 27 500' and ¼ at 33 700'. Thus, pressure decreases with height, but not linearly, because air is compressible and therefore more dense in the lower layers - a layer 1 hectopascal deep is about equal to 27 feet at sea level - at 3 000 feet it's 30 feet, or around 90 feet at the heights jets fly at, i.e. 35 000 feet. The greatest rate of change is in the lowest 5000 feet.

The sea level pressure on which the standard atmosphere is based relates 1" of mercury to 1,000 feet of altitude, so you would expect to see an altimeter read 1 000 feet less if you set it to 28.92 instead of 29.92 inches. Other assumptions are that the air is a perfect dry gas and that the temperature reduces by 1.98°C per 1,000 feet up till around 36,090 feet (the tropopause) from which point (in the stratosphere) it is assumed to remain constant at -56.5°C.

OXYGEN
Pure oxygen is a colourless, tasteless, odourless and *non-combustible* gas that takes up about 21% of the air we breathe (it is corrosive because it belongs to the same chemical family as chlorine and fluorine, so too much is toxic). Although it doesn't burn itself, it does support combustion, which is why we need it, because the body turns food into heat, producing water and waste as by-products of burning fats. As we can't store oxygen, we survive from breath to breath, aside from the roughly one minutes' worth of "reserves" in the blood at any time.

How much you use depends on your physical activity and/or mental stress - for example, you need 4 times more for walking than sitting quietly. The proportion of oxygen to air (21%) actually remains constant up to about 9 km, but its *partial pressure decreases* because the barometric pressure does. However, water vapour and CO_2 have a constant partial pressure, so you can see that, at some point, they will restrict the partial pressure of oxygen. Above 15,000 feet, you just need extra oxygen. At 37,000 feet, you need 100%, and above 40,000 feet the oxygen must be supplied under pressure.

Put another way, the maximum altitude at which sea level conditions can be maintained by breathing 100% oxygen is 37 000 feet. The maximum allowable altitude without pressure breathing is 40 000 feet. The net result is you must use oxygen when the cabin altitude is over 10 000 feet. No extra is needed below 5 000 feet, as 95% of what you would find on the ground is there anyway. However, at over 8 000 feet, you may find measurable changes in blood pressure and respiration, although healthy people should perform OK. Lack of oxygen leads to.......

HYPOXIA
This is a condition where the oxygen concentration in the blood is below normal, or where oxygen cannot be used by the body, but anaemia can produce the same effect, as can alcohol. There are several types of hypoxia:

- **Hypoxic Hypoxia** arises from insufficient partial pressure to transfer oxygen to the cells, and is what people normally mean when they refer to the subject in general. It is otherwise known as *hypoventilation*, and is affected by altitude and poor health - the most dangerous sign is *impaired judgment* and *self criticism*. It has four stages:
    - **Indifferent Stage**. Slight effects on dark adaptation, as low as 6 000 feet.
    - **Compensatory Stage**. The body tries to increase its oxygen intake through faster breathing & heart rate, etc. Pulse rate, systolic blood pressure, circulation rate, and cardiac output all increase, and respiration increases in depth and rate. At 12 000 - 15 000 feet*, after 10-15 minutes, you may become drowsy and make frequent errors in judgment. You may also find it difficult to do simple tasks requiring alertness or muscular co-ordination. Hypoxia at this stage can be easily overlooked if you are preoccupied with your duties.

    *Night vision is significantly reduced (by more than 25%) at 15 000 feet with compensatory hypoxia.

- **Disturbance Stage**. The disturbance threshold is at 12 000 feet, where the body cannot compensate for the oxygen deficiency. You can become unconscious without symptoms, but you may get headaches, blue skin, etc.
- **Critical Stage**. Within 3-5 minutes, judgment and co-ordination usually deteriorate. You are close to incapacitation

- **Anaemic Hypoxia** (**Hypaemic**) is a reduction in the blood's carrying capacity, even if there is enough oxygen.
- **Stagnant** (Ischaemic) **Hypoxia** - poor blood circulation, possibly from excessive G forces.
- **Histotoxic Hypoxia**. The body cannot utilise oxygen, possibly due to toxins, like cyanide, or alcohol, which increases the physiological altitude.

So, there may really be too little oxygen, or you don't have enough blood (haemoglobin) to carry what oxygen you need around the body - you may have donated some, or have an ulcer. You might also be a smoker, with your haemoglobin affected by carbon monoxide (*hypaemic hypoxia*) so you are at an equivalent altitude of between 5000-7000 feet before getting airborne (short-term memory impairment starts at 12 000 feet). In fact, one pack of cigarettes a day reduces your capacity to transport oxygen via haemoglobin by between 5-8%. In short, hypoxia is a *reduced partial pressure* in the lungs.

The effects of hypoxia are like those of alcohol.

However, the most dangerous symptom for safe flight is the interference with reasoning and perception. When you give oxygen to someone with hypoxia, their symptoms temporarily get worse, so don't take the mask off!

As with carbon monoxide poisoning, the onset of hypoxia is insidious and can be recognised only by being very aware of the symptoms, which are aggravated by:

- *Altitude*. Less oxygen available, less pressure to keep it there
- *Time*. The more exposure, the greater the effect
- *Exercise*. Increases energy and oxygen usage
- *Cold*. Increases energy and oxygen usage
- *Illness*. Increases energy and oxygen usage
- *Fatigue*. Symptoms arise earlier
- *Drugs* or *alcohol*. Reduced tolerance
- *Smoking*. Haemoglobin has an affinity for CO (carbon monoxide) 210-250 times that of oxygen

Oxygen Requirements

The oxygen to be carried, and people who need masks, varies with *altitude, rate of descent* and *Minimum Safe Altitude*. The latter two depend on each other, in that it's no good having a good rate of descent if the MSA stops you. It may well be that, although you're at a level that requires fewer masks, the MSA may demand that you equip everybody. If you use a pressurised cabin*, oxygen equipment is not needed (except when it decompresses suddenly) because the partial pressure of oxygen will be correct. 8 000 feet is the maximum (cabin) altitude at which flying ability is not seriously affected by a lack of oxygen, and 10 000 feet is the level above which supplementary oxygen must be provided for rapid decompression and smoke and fumes (for the flight deck only).

*Air is pumped into a sealed cabin which has an exhaust valve to allow it to escape at a uniform rate, otherwise the cabin would get very hot from the compressed air. The pressure inside is kept between 6 000 - 8 000 feet.

The cabin pressurisation system reduces problems from gastrointestinal or trapped gases in the middle ear and sinuses, prevents hypoxia and allows the people inside the cabin to move about freely in a comfortable environment without oxygen masks or other life support equipment.

In a climb, in a non-pressurised aircraft with no supplemental oxygen, you will pass the critical threshold at around 22,000 feet. When using 100% oxygen without pressure, expect hypoxia at around 38,000-40,000 feet - this is the same as breathing ambient air at 10 000 feet.

Otherwise, non-pressurised aircraft (see CAT.IDE.H.240 and CAT.IDE.A.240) above 10,000 ft must have **supplemental oxygen equipment** that can store and dispense supplies. The amount is determined on the basis of cabin pressure altitude and flight duration, plus routes and emergency procedures in the company's operations manual. However, with prior approval, excursions of a short duration between 10,000 ft and 16,000 ft may be undertaken without supplemental oxygen, under procedures in the operations manual.

Usually, however, above 10 000 feet, you must have supplemental oxygen as follows:

- supply for the crew when above 10 000 feet PA.
- supply for cabin crew above 13 000 ft PA and for periods over 30 minutes between 10 000-13 000 ft.
- supply for all passengers above 13 000 feet PA.
- supply for 10% of passengers after 30 minutes between 10 000-13 000 feet.
- When cabin crew is needed, dedicated therapeutic oxygen for 1% of passengers, or one person, whichever is greater.

Between 10 000 - 25 000 feet, a continuous flow system is adequate (see *AGK*). Between 25 000 - 40 000 feet a demand system is used. Above 40 000 feet you need pressure demand.

PRESSURE CHANGES (BAROTRAUMA)

Aside from oxygen, the body contains many gases - some occur naturally, and some are created by the body's normal working processes, but they all expand and contract as the aircraft climbs and descends. Some need a way out, and some need a way back as well. Problems arising from such expansion are called **dysbarism**.

The direct effects of barotrauma are pains that arise from gases that expand and cannot escape, and the indirect effects include gases (typically nitrogen, because it tends to accumulate in the blood) that come out of solution in body tissues.

- Gas in the ears normally vents via the Eustachian tubes. If these are blocked, the pressure on either side of the eardrum is not balanced, which could lead to considerable pain, and/or a ruptured eardrum (**otic barotrauma**). It is also called **aerotitis**, and is **most likely** when flying with a respiratory infection **during a descent**, usually with a **reduction in hearing ability** and the feeling of increasing pressure. One countermeasure is to close your mouth, pinch the nose tight and blow out, to increase pressure in the mouth and throat, while swallowing or moving the lower jaw (*Valsalva manoeuvre*). When one ear clears and not the other, producing dizziness, you get **Pressure Vertigo**.

  If the middle ear becomes saturated with oxygen, as you might get when breathing pure oxygen in flight, you can get a delayed ear blockage which only clears several hours after landing. It is also called **oxygen ear**, and can be cleared with the Valsalva or Frenzel manoeuvres (not while climbing!).

- Although associated with the nose, the **sinuses** are hollow spaces or cavities inside the head surrounding the base of the nose and the eye sockets. Amongst other things, they act as sound boxes for the voice. Being hollow, the sinuses provide structural strength whilst keeping the head light; there are normally between 15-20 of them. Blockages arise from fluid that can't escape through the narrow passages and pain results from fluid pressure. As they are lined with a moist sensitive membrane that is continuous with that of the nose, they can get blocked when you have a cold and the membranes swell up. Sinus cavities are also vulnerable to imbalances of pressure, and are affected in the same way as eardrums are. **Barosinusitis** is caused by differences in pressure between the sinus cavity and the ambient air. Blocked sinuses can mean severe headaches.

- Gas in the gut can be vented from both ends. It can also expand the gut to more than twice its size, which leaves less room for the lungs to work in.

- **Barodontalgia**. Teeth may have small pockets of air in them, if filled, together with the gums. Although dentists nowadays are aware of people flying, and pack fillings a lot better, the public don't fly every day, as you do, so be sure. High altitude balloonists actually take their fillings out. **Barodontalgia arises especially when the sensitive tissues close to the root of a tooth are irritated**, and does not happen in the descent.

DECOMPRESSION SICKNESS (AEROEMBOLISM)

This results from the formation of nitrogen bubbles in body tissues and fluids after a cabin pressure loss at high altitude. Exposure to reduced pressure can lead to DCS because the body is normally saturated with nitrogen. When the ambient pressure is abruptly reduced, some of this nitrogen comes out of solution as bubbles (Henry's law).

Bubbles forming are especially painful in the joints, as you find with the *bends* (very similar to *Caisson disease*), so called because they tend to make you stoop with the pain. Other symptoms include the *creeps* (skin), *chokes* (lungs) and the *staggers* (brain). The bubbles do not redissolve on descent, so if you are affected you may need to go into a decompression chamber. At the very least, you should *descend as low as you can and land as soon as possible*.

The altitude where decompression sickness increases rapidly after ten minutes is 25 000 feet, assuming no scuba diving*. There is little risk below 18,000 feet and it is unlikely to occur below 14,000 ft.

*Diving before flight should be avoided, as extra nitrogen is absorbed while breathing pressurised gas, which will dissolve out as you surface again. A diver 30 feet under water is under twice the normal sea level pressure. When you go flying too soon, this is accentuated, and the symptoms can appear as low as 8,000 feet. Don't fly for 12 hours if the depth involved is less than 30 feet, or 24 hours when over that (there's no limit for plain snorkelling). Factors that *decrease* resistance to DCS include *scuba diving*, *obesity* and *old age*. If you get pains in the joints *within a few hours of landing*, see a doctor as soon as possible. DCS can be avoided by pre-oxygenation before exposure to high altitudes, which reduces the body store of nitrogen as much as possible.

Factors that *decrease* resistance to DCS include *scuba diving*, *obesity* and *old age*. If you get pains in the joints *within a few hours of landing*, see a doctor as soon as possible. DCS can be avoided by pre-oxygenation before exposure to high altitudes, which reduces the body store of nitrogen as much as possible.

TIME OF USEFUL CONSCIOUSNESS

It is dangerous to fly above 10,000 feet without using additional oxygen or being in a pressurised cabin.

When you climb, oxygen levels fall, but the CO_2 levels in your blood do not, and the brain does not know it has to compensate (high CO_2 levels are normally associated with an increase in physical activity, but the lack of oxygen at altitude is not due to hard work).

One definition states that TUC (see below) is the amount of time you can perform flying duties efficiently with inadequate oxygen, or the time from the interruption of the supply or exposure to an oxygen-poor environment, to when useful function is lost (it is *not* the time to total unconsciousness). However, this is more of a definition of *Effective Performance Time* (EPT). TUC is more to do with lack of oxygen. Officially, the TUC is: *The time during which you can act with physical and mental efficiency and alertness from when an adequate oxygen supply is no longer available*.

You won't pass out inside the times given below, but you will be pretty much useless in the cockpit unless you get your oxygen mask on and select 100% oxygen, preferably in a rapid and controlled descent to **below at least 10,000 ft cabin altitude, or the MSA, whichever is higher**.

If you don't, you will be in a state of *negative aspiration*, because the partial pressure of oxygen at that height is much lower than that in your blood, and the pressure gradient will force it back into your lungs, there to be sucked out even further due to Venturi effects (air is pulled out by the flow of air over a hole in the fuselage). The figures below will be *reduced* (by about half) in a *rapid decompression*, so check for the magic words (see the right hand column in the table below).

Height (ft)	Progressive Decompression		Rapid Decompression
	Seated	Active	
22 000	10 mins	5 mins	3 mins
30 000	1.25 mins	45 secs	30-45 secs
35 000	45 secs	30 secs	15-30 secs
40 000	30 secs	18 secs	12 secs

 The figures depend on cabin pressure altitude, vary individually, and are affected by physical activity, strength and time of decompression.

HYPERVENTILATION

The balance of O_2 against CO_2 in the body affects the alkaline/acidic properties of the blood, which in turn affects the rate of breathing. Hyperventilation is simply overbreathing, caused by exhaling more than you are inhaling, creating a drop in the partial pressure of oxygen, so there is a **lack** of CO_2 in the blood as the excess oxygen causes CO_2 to be washed out of the bloodstream. The plasma gets too alkaline (less acidic), and the arteries reduce in size, so less blood gets to the brain.

The usual cause is worry, fright or sudden shock, but hypoxia can be a factor - the symptoms are similar to hypoxia and include:

- **Dizziness**
- Pins and needles, **tingling**
- Blurred sight
- Hot/Cold feelings
- Anxiety
- Impaired performance
- Loss of consciousness

The last one is actually one of the best cures, since the body's automatic systems take over to restore normality. Whenever you are unsure of whether you are suffering from hyperventilation or hypoxia, treat for hypoxia, since this will almost always be the root cause - reach for the oxygen mask or a paper bag, which will increase the level of CO_2. You can treat hyperventilation by talking aloud through the procedure to calm the emotions and reduce the rate of breathing.

The Cardiovascular System

The body needs a constant supply of oxygenated blood for best performance.

The mechanics involve a double system which is joined at the heart. There is one circulation to the lungs and return (pulmonary), on the right side, and one to the rest of the body (systemic), on the left, so blood passes through the heart twice on each side. The system consists of the heart, arteries, arterioles, capillaries, veins and blood. It provides a transport system that links the external environment to the tissues and distributes essential substances, such as hormones, oxygen and nutrients around the body. It also removes carbon dioxide and other waste products from the tissues and delivers them to the lungs, kidneys and liver. The system can anticipate demands by increasing heart action before it is required.

Knowledge of the way blood circulates round the body is useful when trying to understand how blackout occurs. In the picture above, you can see that the largest blood vessels run parallel, so a downwards acceleration will pull blood away from the head and push it to the lower parts of the body. The heart is then working against the acceleration. In addition, the blood in the veins below the heart is prevented from returning in the normal way, so blood pressure and the supply to the brain are restricted, whilst it is increased in the abdomen and legs. This is why a tilt-back seat is useful, so that centrifugal force acts sideways rather than in a head-to-foot fashion (although it could stop you breathing!) An acceleration the other way will cause red-out.

THE HEART

This item is pear-shaped, and found lying slightly to the left inside the thoracic cavity. It is surrounded by a protective membrane containing a fluid filled cavity called the *pericardium*, which prevents friction between the heart and other tissues.

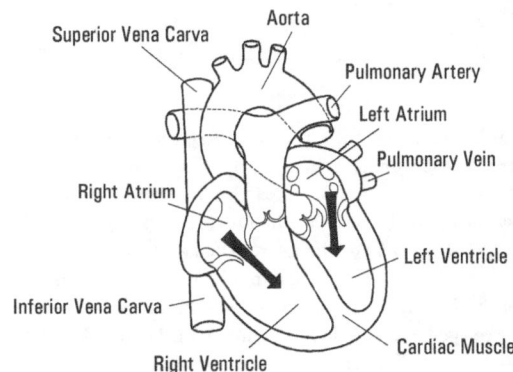

The rest comes up through a combination of non-return valves and muscular action. Chest movements also have a siphon effect. Heart muscles get their own blood from the *coronary arteries*.

Oxygen-rich haemoglobin in the red blood cells passes from the alveolar capillaries into the pulmonary vein and enters the left atrium at low pressure. It is pumped into the left ventricle and then at high pressure into the systemic circulation via the aorta, which is the body's main artery, so the left ventricle has the thickest muscle walls. The weight of blood above the height of the heart returns the deoxygenated blood through gravity to the right atrium, then the right ventricle to the lungs.

The rest comes up through a combination of non-return valves and muscular action. Chest movements also have a siphon effect. Heart muscles get their own blood from the *coronary arteries*.

Cardiac muscle can contract rhythmically without nervous input, in a *myogenic rhythm* (myo = muscle). Thus, the pumps do their work in phase, but deliver blood in series, throughout the body in one direction only. The heart does not rest in the same way as other muscles do - instead, it takes a mini-rest for a microsecond or two between beats.

Arteries carry oxygenated blood *from* the heart to the body (the *pulmonary artery* goes straight to the lungs) whilst veins return blood *to* the heart (again, the pulmonary vein has a direct connection from the lungs) at a lower pressure (veins are *drains*). The main vein in the body is the *cava*.

The blood pressure in the veins is very low, so they are often surrounded by muscle (e.g. in the legs) that acts like a secondary pump when you exercise. The elasticity of the artery walls helps to keep the blood pressure constant between heart contractions.

Arteries eventually turn into *arterioles* which eventually break up into minute vessels called *capillaries* that allow the diffusion of small molecular substances like oxygen, vitamins, minerals, water and amino acids to nourish cells. Carbon dioxide and water pass the other way in a process called *capillary exchange*. Arteries are less flexible than veins, so they are more prone to clogging.

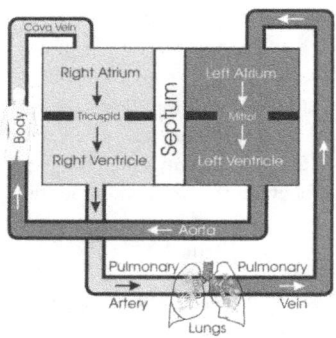

Note that, although blood from the heart is oxygenated, and that to the heart is de-oxygenated, the pulmonaries are reversed. In other words, pulmonary circulation carries deoxygenated blood from the right side of the heart to the lungs, and oxygenated blood back to the left side of the heart. The systemic circulation carries oxygenated blood from the left side of the heart to the head and body. The right side receives deoxygenated blood from the body, so oxygenated and deoxygenated blood is kept separate - the blood alternates between the two circulations.

As the blood pressure in the veins is very low, they are often surrounded by muscle (e.g. in the legs) that acts like a secondary pump when you exercise. The elasticity of the artery walls helps to keep the blood pressure constant between heart contractions.

The rate of contraction of the heart, or the *pulse rate*, is around 72 (70-80) beats a minute when at rest. It is influenced by *adrenalin*, *physical exercise* and the *treatment of glucose in the blood*. As the ventricle pumps about 70 ml of blood per beat, *cardiac output* is about 5 litres per minute (actually 4.9-5.3), or 7600 litres per day. Cardiac output is the volume of blood pumped per minute by each ventricle, and represents the total flow of blood through the pulmonary and systemic circuits. It comes from *stroke volume* and *heart rate* (the heart rate contributes most).

BLOOD

This is a liquid made up of:

- 55% straw coloured plasma, for transporting CO_2, nutrients and hormones, and
- 45% blood cells, which come in three varieties.
    - *Red cells* transport oxygen via *haemoglobin*.
    - *White cells* (*leukocytes*) fight infection.
    - *Platelets* are for clotting blood.

All are produced in *bone marrow*, which capacity diminishes as we grow older.

CO_2 in solution forms a weak carbonic acid which also helps to maintain the blood's acid balance. The amount of haemoglobin in the blood depends on the amount of oxygen in the lungs. Reductions in the amount of haemoglobin available reduces the blood's ability to transport oxygen (to cause anaemia, below). This could arise from either less red blood cells or the concentration of haemoglobin in them.

ANAEMIA

Anaemia means that there is not enough functional haemoglobin, there being too few red blood cells, and a limited capacity to transport oxygen (more iron often cures it). As a reminder, *Anaemic Hypoxia* is the lack of oxygen resulting from anaemia.

BLOOD PRESSURE

This is the amount of force that the blood exerts on the vessel walls, measured in **mmHg**. It is sensed by bundles of nerves in cavities called *sinuses*. There are two sets in the main arteries to the brain, and another on the aorta, the *carotid* and *aortic* 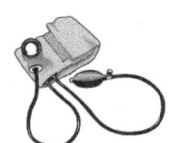 *sinus pressoreceptors*, respectively. When low blood pressure is detected, respiratory activity, heart rate and cardiac output all increase, and the brain varies secretions of two hormones to narrow the arteries. As the blood vessels can compensate for lack of blood by changing their size (otherwise you might get vapour locks when gases dissolve out into the new space), dehydration may produce symptoms of high blood pressure. As with electricity, the rate of blood flow through a vessel depends on the pressure gradient from one end to the other, plus the resistance. The resistance to blood flow depends on the *vessel dimensions* and *blood viscosity*.

The *systolic blood pressure* is the peak pressure as blood is pumped from the left ventricle into the aorta. The *diastolic* (relaxed) *pressure* is the lowest, produced when resting between beats - it is an indication of the resistance of the small arteries and capillaries to blood flow, or the load against which the heart has to work. The World Health Organisation says that "normal" blood pressure lies between 100-139 mmHg (systolic) and 60-89 mmHg (diastolic) - something like 120/80 (120 over 80). However, "standard" values are 100 and 60 mg, or 100/60, with the limits regarded as 160 and 100 mmHg, or 160/100. The higher the figures are, the harder the heart is working, and the greater is the risk of stroke* and coronary heart disease. As you get older, the systolic pressure should be roughly 100 plus your age in years, so for people aged over 50 it might be 160/100 as a maximum. The **arterial pressure in the upper arm** is equivalent to the pressure in the heart, which is why it is used to check your pressure in medicals.

*Where the blood supply to part of the brain is cut off.

HYPERTENSION & HYPOTENSION

Hypertension is known as a silent killer. As the blood pressure is persistently elevated with no external symptoms, vessel walls, heart and other organs may be severely damaged without you knowing. It is the culmination of many factors, including your weight, diet, bad habits and family history (most important). The symptoms are easily confused with hypoxia.

You have hypertension when your blood pressure exceeds:

Age	Pressures
<39	145/90
40-49	155/95
50+	160/100

Hypotension, on the other hand, is any blood pressure that is below the normal expected for given environment. It is a relative term because blood pressure normally varies greatly anyway with *activity*, *age*, *medications* and *underlying medical conditions*. Neurological conditions that can lead to low blood pressure include changing your position from lying down to the more vertical (*postural hypotension*), stroke, shock, lightheadedness after urinating or defecating, Parkinson's disease, neuropathy and simply fright. Non-neurologic conditions that can cause it include bleeding, infections, dehydration, heart disease, adrenal insufficiency, pregnancy, prolonged bed rest, poisoning, toxic shock syndrome and blood transfusion reactions.

DEEP VEIN THROMBOSIS (DVT)

This is a blood clot (thrombus) that develops *inside* a deep vein, usually in the lower leg, but also the arm, where it can cause pain. Blood clots in superficial veins under the skin are *superficial thrombophlebitis* and are much less serious. The clots are mostly small and do not cause symptoms, as the body can gradually break them down, but larger ones may partially or totally block the blood flow in a vein and cause symptoms such as:

- swelling of the calf, which is usually different from the mild ankle swelling you get from long haul flights.
- pain in the calf, or calf pain that is noticeable, or worse when standing or walking.

Although they are not always a sign of DVT, clots need medical advice. There is evidence that long haul flights (i.e. lasting four hours or more) may increase the risk of DVT as a result of prolonged immobility, which can happen during any form of long distance travel, whether by car, bus, train or air. Potential complications include:

- *Pulmonary embolism*, when a piece of the blood clot travels in the bloodstream to become lodged in the lungs and block the flow of blood, hours or even days afterwards. It may cause chest pain and shortness of breath.
- *Post thrombotic syndrome* happens if a DVT damages the valves in the vein so that, instead of flowing upwards, the blood pools in the lower leg. This can result in pain, swelling and ulcers on the leg.

Anticoagulant medicines are the most common treatment, which alter certain chemicals in the blood to stop clots forming so easily. Otherwise, you should:

- exercise your legs at least every 2-3 hours, starting with the muscles of your lower legs (which act as a pump for the blood in the veins) while sitting.
- wear loose-fitting clothing and compression stockings.
- keep hydrated (with water!)

HEART DISEASE

Heart disease can be grouped into 3 categories:

- *Hypertensive* - from high blood pressure, working the heart harder so it gets enlarged (anxiety, etc.)
- *Coronary*, or *Arteriosclerotic* - hardening of the (coronary) arteries through excessive calcium, or cholesterol, which again makes the heart work harder (bad diet). The coronary blood supply is blocked or restricted, and oxygen does not get to the affected cells, which die. Then you do, if enough are affected. This is a *myocardial infarction*, and such a heart attack is the commonest cause of death in men over 40.

  Arteriosclerosis exists where a build-up of fatty material in the linings of the coronary arteries makes them narrower. The fatty linings get harder as calcium deposits are added. The main result is *angina*, a symptom of which is a severe chest pain which radiates out to the left arm and up to the neck and jaws. *The origin of an angina pectoris* (chest pain) *and a cardiac infraction is a partial or total blockage of the coronary arteries*. Although angina pectoris (or stable angina) is a partial or total blockage (ischemia), the tissue does not die, there is just a reduction of O_2 to the tissues. The pain will go when you relax. When assessing an individual's risk in this area, you must consider *obesity*, *distress*, *smoking* and *family history*, amongst other things.

- *Valvular* or *rheumatic* - where valves cannot open or close properly, allowing back pressure to build up.

To reduce the risks of heart disease, *double your resting pulse for at least 20 minutes 3 times a week*. However, a recent US study has suggested that, although this will lengthen your life by around two years, that two years will be spent on the extra exercise! Otherwise, stop smoking, reduce stress and watch the diet........

The Digestive System

The gastro-intestinal system is there to digest nutrients and fluids so that they can be transformed into energy and be used for the rebuilding of tissues and other maintenance tasks (metabolism*). *Digestion* is the chemical process of breaking down the food you eat into substances that can be absorbed through the walls of the intestines, and transported to the rest of the body via the bloodstream, moving in a controlled fashion from the mouth to the other end. The stomach contains hydrochloric acid for this purpose, and the stomach lining is able to heal (from scratches, etc.) within 24 hours.

The metabolic workload is taken up by the liver, which makes glycogen (glucose in storage form), processes fats and proteins, removes waste products and takes part in the generation of body heat. It also changes the chemicals absorbed into useful products, such as vitamins, enzymes, bile (in the gall bladder) and cholesterol, as well as detoxifying drugs, medications and alcohol. The kidneys remove impurities and some waste products from the blood. They also maintain a fluid balance by adjusting the volume of blood through the retention or excretion of water - if there is not enough as serum in the blood, the urine is concentrated. If this is a prolonged condition, kidney stones may result.

*The body has no real reserves of water - it redistributes what it has with a system of priorities that is controlled by histamine over the neurotransmitter system. Histamine becomes more active when the body is dehydrated, and potassium levels may drop, causing heart palpitations.

The digestive system is controlled by the *enteric* nervous system (often called the second brain), as modulated by the brain via autonomic nerves and hormones. It is almost always active - not just when you eat!

The digestive process starts in the mouth, where food is chewed and mixed with saliva that starts to break down starches. After swallowing, it is propelled down the oesophagus which is around 8 inches long, to the stomach, using a rhythmic muscular movement called *peristalsis*, which is controlled by numerous automatic reflexes.

Once food reaches the stomach, it cannot normally pass back the way it came, because a muscular non-return valve stops it. After being churned in the stomach over 2-6 hours, the food is moved to the small intestine, which is a coiled tube about 20 feet long. More mixing takes place over 3-5 hours, as does absorption and digestion, then the mixture (called chyme) moves to the large intestine, or the colon, which is about 5 feet long.

The centres that control hunger and appetite are in the hypothalamus and are closely related to pleasure and pain. Since hunger and satiety are emotional states, the operation of the digestive system can be affected by other emotions, especially those that arise from stress - certainly, with anger, resentment and aggression, the stomach will increase its production of hydrochloric acid.

Stress arousal will also affect peristaltic rhythm. You get diarrhoea if the food is moved so fast through the intestines that water cannot be absorbed, and constipation if the food moves so slowly that too much is absorbed.

DIET

Regular exercise is beneficial to general health, but the most efficient way to lose weight is by eating less calories.

Dieting must be supervised, with no crash diets or supplements! The body's main fuel is glucose, which can either be converted from different types of food, or eaten directly. Levels of glucose are regulated by the *pancreas*, which secretes *insulin** to reduce blood sugar levels by getting it into cells or converting it into fat if there's no room.

*It also provides essential enzymes for digestion.

The body's three sources of nourishment include:

- **Carbohydrates**, which are long chains of identical sugar molecules converted into glucose to provide energy and which consist of:
    - Simple sugars
    - Complex sugars
    - Starch

Carbohydrates can provide immediate energy, and they come in different varieties, according to the *glycaemic index*, which measures how quickly they are absorbed. Wholewheat has a higher GI (72) than sugar (59)!

- **Fats** (and oils), which produce twice as much energy as carbohydrates for the same weight (i.e. they have more calories), but are harder to digest. However, they don't form triglycerides and add weight, which is what carbohydrates do. Fat molecules are three fatty acids attached to a molecule of glycerol.
- **Proteins**, which are constructed from long chains of amino acids, not all being carried in the body. Animal protein has to be broken down into peptides and amino acids before being reconstructed into what the body needs, which takes energy. Proteins are needed for growth, and repair and replacement of cells.

All are large insoluble molecules that must be broken down into smaller soluble ones before they can be absorbed, using enzymes. Trace elements should be got through a balanced diet. *Breakfast should bring in about 25% of the daily calorie intake.*

Although the body uses sugars, the processed stuff is one of the most harmful substances we can put into our bodies on a daily basis, and there is almost no processed food that does not contain it - even baked beans. Certainly, there is hardly a cereal product without it (did you ever wonder why cereals are fortified with vitamins? It's because they are all taken out first! Manufactured ones are never as good as the real thing because they are treated as invaders by the body). Sugar that is not needed to maintain adequate glucose levels and replenish stored glycogen in the liver and muscles is converted to fat, by insulin, which also tends to block the conversion of fat back to glucose, so a high insulin level makes it difficult to remove the fat it created in the first place. The problem is that our insulin levels are almost permanently high, which is something that our bodies are simply not built to cope with - the pancreas needs a rest! Thus, we should try to eat so that large spikes of insulin are not generated, which can be difficult in a normal pilot's lifestyle. That is, insulin should be injected into the bloodstream under more controlled conditions - processed foods are converted into glucose *very quickly*, which is the real problem. The type of carbohydrate you eat will determine how this happens (the Atkins diet works because it doesn't trigger insulin). As well, sugar has no vitamins, so it cannot process itself, and has to borrow what it needs from other sources, which creates a deficit of Vitamin B. After reading most of the diet books around, these conclusions can be drawn:

- It is not necessarily the fat you eat, but the fat created from sugar that is bad for your health.
- Don't eat anything processed - usually anything "white", or at least with white flour in it.
- Eat fruit by itself - although fruit contains sugars, it also contains enzymes and other beneficial substances, and does not stimulate so much insulin (around a third, in fact). However, once you combine fruit with other food, you get the full non-benefit. Also, fruit is digested mostly in the small intestine, and eating it after a large meal causes this to be delayed, with fermentation that causes indigestion.
- If you drink alcohol (in moderation!), dry (low sugar) red wine is best.

- Exercise, but not so much that you need to eat a lot to produce the glucose you need.
- Don't eat a heavy meal just before going to bed - calorie consumption is different in the evening.
- Drink lots of fluid (not with sugar or caffeine in! Caffeine can pull calcium out of your bones).
- Eat lots of fibre and water-based food, such as fruit, greens, tomatoes, etc. in their raw state - try for around 70% of your total diet.

And if you thought sugar was bad - think about monosodium glutamate, or MSG, labelled on food packets as *hydrolyzed vegetable protein*. MSG is injected into rats to make them morbidly obese so they can be experimented on. It triples the amount of insulin created by the pancreas, so if you ever needed proof that insulin can be bad for you, this is it. MSG is addictive.

HYPOGLYCAEMIA

The most common problems (in a normal pilot's lifestyle, anyway) are low blood sugar (*functional hypoglycaemia*), or eating too much (*reactive hypoglycaemia*), from missed meals and the like.

Although you may think it's better to have the wrong food than no food, be careful when it comes to eating chocolate bars instead of lunch, which will cause your blood sugar levels to rise so rapidly that too much insulin is released to compensate, which drives your blood sugar levels to a *lower* state than they were before - known as *rebound hypoglycaemia*. Here, the sugar is pushed into all cells of the body and not specifically reserved for the Central Nervous System. Apart from eating "real food", you will minimise the risks if you eat small snacks often instead of heavy meals after long periods with nothing. Complex (slow release) carbohydrates are best, like pasta, etc.

Hypoglycaemia is bad enough in the short term, but long-term can be regarded as a *disease*, aside from being responsible for alcohol cravings. Although not life threatening, it is a forerunner of many worse things and should be looked at. The important thing to watch appears to be the suddenness of any fall in blood sugar, and a big one can often trigger a heart attack. A high protein diet will tend to even things out, as protein helps the absorption of fat, which is inhibited if too much insulin is about. Warning signs include shakiness, sweatiness, irritability or anxiety, difficulty in speaking, headache, weakness, numbness or tingling around the lips, inability to think straight (or lack of concentration), palpitations and hunger. At its worst, hypoglycaemia could result in a coma, but you could also get seizure and fainting. Eat more if you exercise more.

HYPERGLYCAEMIA

This is the opposite of the above (and precedes it), an *excess* of blood sugar. Symptoms include tiredness, increased appetite and thirst, frequent urination, dry skin, flu-like aches, headaches, blurred vision and nausea. This condition causes dehydration, so have fluids around to help you. Also, decrease stress.

WATER & DEHYDRATION

The comfort range of the human body is 21-27°C with an associated relative humidity of 50%. *Too hot* is over 32°C, where blood vessels dilate to get rid of the heat and the heart cannot keep up, so you feel tired. Below about 10°C, you can lose heat quicker than it can be produced. You need water to:

- regulate body temperature.
- circulate nutrients & oxygen and remove waste from cells.
- prevent kidney stones, constipation and some urinary and colon cancers.

Pilots are exposed to a greater than average rate of dehydration, especially in a cockpit in hot weather which can be a more like a greenhouse. Even in Winter, and at altitude, the air can get very dry. So dry, in fact, that you don't need a towel after showering.

The body is composed of 60% water, so a person weighing 200 lbs should be carrying around 14 gallons. About half a gallon is usually lost per day, through perspiration, breathing or urination*. You can lose more if you are exercising, or are vomiting or have diarrhoea.

*Urine should normally have a slight yellowish tint from a pigment called urochrome. If it is dark yellow (and often smelly) you need more water.

STOP Hunger and thirst share the same signals to the brain, so try drinking water first!

When the brain senses an increase in body temperature, it secretes a saline solution to cool the surface of the skin through evaporation. At the same time, there is increased blood flow to the skin as the blood vessels expand (vasodilation). The temperature of the blood is lowered as it flows through the cooled skin, then it returns to the body core. There, it picks up excess heat, and the process continues until a satisfactory temperature is reached.

However, perspiration is only an option when the sweat can evaporate, so don't wear tight clothing or that which doesn't breathe. Also, there is no cooling benefit when perspiration drips off or is wiped away. Less evaporation occurs in high humidity, which is why we feel hotter on a sultry day.

Thirst appears after losing around 1.5 litres of water. When it gets to 3 litres, you get sluggish, tired, nauseated and irritable. You start getting clumsy by the time you lose about 4 litres. Headaches are likely, with an increase in core temperature, heart rate and breathing rate. Coping with the fluid loss becomes a top priority. Prolonged dehydration can result in kidney stones, which are small concentrated masses of mineral salts. They can be incredibly painful when they try to pass through the urinary tract. It's not something you need on finals!

DIABETES

Glucose in the blood provides energy, but sometimes the body cannot either produce the insulin in the first place that is required to get it into the cells (*Type 1* diabetes), or make use of it in the best way (*Type 2*). The former tends to appear in people under 40, and the latter in people over 40, although they can occur in either. Both can be treated by diet and/or insulin injections. Exercise is good, too, as it uses up blood sugar that would otherwise need insulin to remove it.

Since insulin is needed to get glucose into your cells, it follows that, if this is not done, blood sugar levels can be dangerously high. So important is this, that, if you were on a desert island with a bottle of blood pressure pills and a bottle of diabetes pills, you'd better take the blood pressure pills first! High blood pressure will tend to push proteins through the kidney walls, to be detected in urine.

ALCOHOL

There is only one rule - **flying and alcohol don't mix!**

Whilst nobody should object to you taking a drink or two the evening before a flight, you should remember that it can take over 3 days for alcohol to clear the system (it remains in the inner ear for longest). Within 8 hours of a planned departure, you should not drink alcohol at all.

The maximum blood level is officially 0.2 mg per ml*, a quarter of the driving limit in UK, but it's not only the alcohol that causes problems - the after-effects do as well, like the hangover, fatigue, dehydration, loss of blood sugar and toxins caused by metabolisation, etc. You are still under the influence with a hangover, and many non-alcoholic drinks have odd chemicals in them. The body even produces its own alcohol - around 0.04 mg per 100 ml. A further complication is that alcohol is absorbed (not digested!) with incredible speed and can go directly into the bloodstream through the walls of the intestine.

*40 mgm/100ml (half the legal driving limit) is associated with significant increases in pilot error.

Although it appears otherwise, alcohol is not a stimulant, but an *anaesthetic*, or a *depressant*, which puts to sleep those parts of the brain that deal with inhibitions - the problem is that these areas also cover judgment, comprehension and attention to detail. In fact, the effects of alcohol are the same as hypoxia, in that it prevents brain cells from using available oxygen. One significant effect of hypoxia in this context is the resulting inability to tell that something is wrong.

It takes the liver about 1 hour to break down 1 unit of alcohol into water and CO_2. Eating has no effect on the rate of absorption. Officially, alcohol leaves the body at 15 milligrams per 100 ml of blood per hour, but one figure is 0.01-0.015 mg% per hour. A blood alcohol level of 60 mg/100 ml will therefore take 4 hours to return to normal. 1 unit is, or used to be, considered to be the same as 1 measure of spirit, a glass of wine or half a pint of beer. The number of units per week beyond which physical damage is likely is 21 for men and 14 for women.

The WHO defines **alcoholism** as *when the excessive use of alcohol repeatedly damages a person's physical, mental or social life*. The primary outward symptom of alcoholism is drinking alone. The first step for curing alcoholism is the admission that you are an alcoholic, and willingness to accept treatment.

Although passengers get cabin service, persons under the influence of alcohol or drugs, of unsound mind or having the potential to cause trouble should not be allowed on board - certainly, no person should be drunk on any aircraft (people aren't generally aware that one drink at 6000 feet is the same as two at sea level). This is not being a spoilsport - drunks don't react properly in emergencies and could actually be dangerous to other people, so it's not just for their own good, but that of others as well.

CAT.GEN.MPA.100 (see *Operational Procedures*) states that crew members must not perform duties:

- when under the influence of psychoactive substances or alcohol or when unfit due to injury, fatigue, medication, sickness or similar causes.
- until a reasonable time has elapsed after deep water diving or following blood donation (**due to possible fainting** or **hypoxia** in the latter case).
- if applicable medical requirements are not fulfilled.
- if they are in any doubt of being able to accomplish their assigned duties.
- if they know or suspect that they are suffering from fatigue (see 7.f of Annex IV to Regulation (EC) No 216/2008)* or feel otherwise unfit, to the extent that the flight may be endangered.

No crew member must allow task achievement/ decision making to deteriorate to the extent that flight safety is endangered because of the effects of fatigue, taking into account, inter alia, fatigue accumulation, sleep deprivation, number of sectors flown, night duties or time zone changes. Rest periods must provide sufficient time to enable crew members to overcome the effects of the previous duties and to be well rested by the start of the following flight duty period.

Australian researchers found that being awake for 17 hours is as bad as a blood alcohol concentration of 0.05%, after which a slight lack of coordination is evident. The limit for driving in Canada, for example, is 0.08%.

Crew members must not:

- Consume alcohol less than 8 hours before the reporting time for flight duty or start of standby
- Start a flight duty period with a blood alcohol level over 0.2 promille (part per thousand).
- Consume alcohol during the flight duty period or while on standby.

 Most regulations are worded so that you can have a drink 8 hours before reporting time, but you must also not have alcohol in your system.

 In the UK, no specific limit is included in the Air Navigation Order, but the same limit described above is in the *Railways and Transport Safety Act*, 2003 (where the question of interpretation arises, reference is sometimes made to Road Transport in comparison, especially for production of licences).

MEDICATIONS

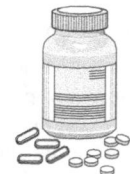

Although the symptoms of colds and sore throats, etc. are bad enough on the ground, they may actually become dangerous in flight by either distracting or harming you by getting more serious with height (such as bursting your eardrums, or worse). If you're under treatment for anything, including surgery, not only should you not fly, but you should also check that there will be no adverse effects on your physical or mental ability, as many preparations combine chemicals, and the mixture could make quite a cocktail. No drugs or alcohol should be taken within a few hours of each other, as even fairly widely accepted stuff such as aspirin can have unpredictable effects, especially in relation to hypoxia (it's as well to keep away from the office, too - nobody else will want what you've got).

 Too much aspirin can cause **gastric bleeding**. Codeine turns into a morphine-like substance inside the body - it is banned in some countries, such as the UAE because it is addictive and can cause constipation.

Particular ones to avoid are antibiotics (penicillin, tetracyclines), tranquilisers, antidepressants, sedatives, stimulants (caffeine, amphetamines), anti-histamines and anything for relieving high blood pressure, and, of course, anything not actually prescribed.

ANAESTHETICS

All procedures requiring local or regional anaesthetics disqualify you for flying for at least 12 hours.

DRUGS

Although altering your state of consciousness is one way of coping with stress, using drugs is not the way to do it. As with all short cuts, there are unwanted side effects. A study of airline pilots landing in a simulator found that performance was significantly impaired up to 24 hours after smoking one marijuana cigarette with 19 milligrams of THC, although the pilots thought they were doing OK.

BLOOD DONATIONS

Pilots are generally discouraged from giving blood (or plasma) when actively flying, because a donation may lead to a reduced tolerance of altitude. Some dental anaesthetics can cause problems for up to 24 hours or more, as can anything to do with immunisation. If you do give blood, try to leave a gap of 24 hours afterwards, including bone marrow donations, as the immediate effect is a reduction in blood pressure. Longer than 24 hours, it affects the composition of the blood, particularly the red corpuscles. Having donated blood, you should *rest supine for about 15-20 minutes, drink plenty of fluid and not fly for 24 hours*. After a general anaesthetic, see the doctor.

SMOKING

There are over 200 harmful chemicals in cigarette smoke, which are more concentrated in *sidestream smoke*, or that which has not been filtered through the cigarette, so passive smokers face the worst risks (cigarettes release 10 times more air pollution than a diesel engine - it is a Group A carcinogen). Here are some of the chemicals involved and common places they may be found:

- Carbon monoxide (car exhausts - see below)
- Arsenic (rat poison)
- Ammonia (window cleaner)
- Acetone (nail polish remover)
- Hydrogen cyanide (gas chambers)
- Naphthalene (mothballs)
- Sulphur compounds (matches)
- Formaldehyde (embalming fluid)

Otherwise, the addictive substance in tobacco is *nicotine*, and the substance that stops the alveoli doing their work is *tar*. Nicotine reduces the diameter of the arteries, which stimulates the release of adrenalin, to increase the heart rate and blood pressure. The risk of heart attack or strokes is increased in the order of 100%*, and gangrene by 500%.

*With high blood pressure or cholesterol, try 200%. If you are on the pill, 1000%!

FOOD POISONING

Food poisoning can also be a problem, and not just for passengers - the standard precaution is to select different items from the rest of the crew, even in the hotel, or at least eat at different times.

CAFFEINE

See under *Fatigue*, later.

CARBON MONOXIDE

Carbon monoxide (CO) is toxic gas that is created through the effects of incomplete combustion, when not enough oxygen has been available to create the proper waste product, namely carbon dioxide (CO_2). It typically gets into the cockpit from faulty engine exhausts, but other sources relevant to aviation can include cigarette smoke and cabin heaters. You can buy carbon monoxide detectors from most pilot shops that will act as an early warning, because it is colourless, tasteless, odourless and non-irritating, and extremely hard to detect. The precise way that the effects of carbon monoxide work on the body are complex and not fully understood, but when it is not ventilated it binds to haemoglobin better than oxygen does (by a factor of 210-250), and makes it retain up to four times more oxygen than it normally carries, so the blood oxygen content increases while the body does not get the supplies that it needs. Hence one of the symptoms being cherry red lips - if it simply blocked the intake of oxygen as is implied in the exams, your lips would be blue.

The symptoms of CO poisoning can resemble those of food poisoning and the flu, but without the associated high temperatures. A headache is the most common symptom. Others include:

- feeling sick (nausea) and dizziness
- feeling tired and confused
- vomiting with abdominal pain
- shortness of breath, difficulty breathing (dyspnoea)

The longer you breathe in CO gas, the worse the symptoms will get. You may lose your balance, vision and memory and, eventually, consciousness. This can happen within two hours if there is a lot of CO in the air, but the symptoms can occur over a number of days or months.

Later symptoms include:

- confusion
- memory loss
- co-ordination problems

To recover, turn off the cabin heat and open the air vents. Use 100% oxygen if you have it. It may take several days for a full recovery.

HUMAN PERFORMANCE & LIMITATIONS
The Body

COSMIC RADIATION

Records of such radiation are normally kept for any flights above 49 000 feet, as there is a possible link to cancer (it will certainly affect the Central Nervous System). There isn't much below 25 000 feet, but its effects are worst at high latitudes. The average annual amount of cosmic radiation received by crew members is about the same as the amount of background radiation.

Galactic radiation is a steady flow of particles from outside the solar system, which is reasonably predictable, should you get that high. Its effects increase with altitude. *Solar radiation* is of low energy and emanates from *solar flares* (see *Meteorology*) which are charged particles from the Sun.

MISCELLANEOUS

Don't forget to inform the authorities (in writing) of illnesses, personal injuries or presumed pregnancies that incapacitate you for more than 21 days. Pilots in accidents should be medically examined before flying again.

Incapacitation   040 02 03 03

There is always a danger that whoever is in the other front seat may become incapacitated; in the obvious case, they collapse and fall across the controls. Less noticeable is the sort that comes with boredom or lack of mental stimulation on longer trips, where you may physically be in the cockpit but mentally miles away. Even disorientation during instrument flight is included. There's not much you can do against the first type aside from levelling the aircraft and returning to a safe flight path, then ensuring that the unfit pilot cannot interfere. Call for a crew member or passenger to help, and tell ATC what's going on. Land as soon as you can *under the circumstances*, which is not as daft as it sounds - you might find it prudent to divert to a place with better aids or weather, which is further away, despite what the Company says about landing where they've got a base. *Do not* be rushed into an approach before you are ready, especially at an unfamiliar airfield. Your greatest responsibility is to the passengers.

Incapacitation can be *gradual* (insidious - the worst kind) or *sudden*, *subtle* or *overt*, *partial* or *complete* and may not be preceded by any warning. It is mostly caused by acute gastro-intestinal* disorders from suspect food and drink (try to allow 90 minutes between eating and flying).

Under the "Two Communications Rule", you are deemed to be incapacitated if you do not respond appropriately to a second verbal communication associated with a significant deviation from a standard operating procedure or flight profile. Do not be reluctant to take control if you have to - better safe than sorry.

*Gastro-enteritis is often caused by bacteria, and washing your hands is one of the most effective ways of preventing infection. The need for liquids will be greater than normal.

PARTIAL OR GRADUAL

Symptoms that might affect your handling ability, to the extent that you have to hand over control, could include severe pain (sudden severe headache or chest pain), dizziness, blurring or partial loss of vision, disorientation, vomiting or diarrhoea.

TWO PILOT

You must immediately inform the other pilot and hand over control, then inform the destination, base or whoever else and divert, bearing in mind the nature and severity of the symptoms and the availability of medical facilities. Naturally, as with any emergency, the company would prefer you to carry on (minimum inconvenience to the passengers) or return to base (minimum inconvenience to them), but appendicitis waits for no man! You should not take control again, and your harness must be locked to stop you falling over the controls if you get worse.

SINGLE PILOT

You should react before an illness becomes severe enough to affect your handling, so an immediate radio call is essential. The first consideration is for the safety of the passengers, so medical assistance for you must be a lesser priority, though the former may well depend on the latter.

SUDDEN OR COMPLETE

This may be subtle or overt, and give no warning; Murphy's Law dictates that fatal collapses occur during approach and landing, close to the ground. Detection of subtle incapacitation may be indirect, that is, only as a result of some expected action not being taken, so when you die maintaining your body position, the other pilot may not even notice until the expected order of events becomes interrupted.

TWO PILOT

Crew members should closely monitor the flight path, especially during takeoff, initial climb, final approach and landing, and immediately question any deviations. The fit pilot should assume control, if the controls are not interfered with, which is why you should wear full harness, which should be locked in place and the seat slid back as a matter of priority (use passengers or other crew if required). First aid should be delayed until the immediate problems are sorted out, then land as soon as practicable.

Disease

You often fly to places with very low standards of hygiene and/or disease-carrying insects (disinsecting procedures must be carried out at least 30 minutes before landing). Although not good for you in the long run, on such occasions, processed and packaged food can be a real lifesaver, as can bottled water. As with many things, prevention is better than cure - for malaria, certainly, a good tactic is to avoid being bitten (by the female Anopheles mosquito*) in the first place, by wearing appropriate clothing, even though it may be hot.

*Dengue is another fever spread by infected mosquitoes that are **active by day** – usually the Aedes Aegypti.

It is a misconception that illness starts when the symptoms first appear. There are often more subtle signs that are mostly ignored for some time, so you *are* sick well before you *get* sick. Changes in emotions are a good example, as are attitudes and personality traits - some personality types are more prone to illness than others. *Pathology* is the term used by medics to mean anything that is not normal, such as inflammation, which could occur through infection or injury (if the name of a body part ends in *itis*, you can be sure that inflammation has something to do with it). Otherwise, there are various types of disease:

ORGANIC DISEASE

Infectious diseases (colds & flu) are communicable, meaning that they can be transmitted from one host to another, and are regarded as acute, and short term. The microorganisms concerned (viruses, bacteria, fungi, parasites.) cause their damage by releasing poisons or toxins and reproducing in enough numbers to interfere with the normal operation of the body.

- **Typhoid** comes from infected milk.
- **Tetanus** comes from bacteria coming through the skin (typically a puncture) as spores. Vaccinations must be done every 10 years after the initial one.
- **Malaria** is one of the world's biggest killers.
- **TB** is an airborne contagion that is spread through coughing and sneezing.
- **Hepatitis**. Type A is most common, which can be vaccinated against, transmitted by contaminated food or water (as is cholera). B or C can be obtained through improperly sterilised needles or syringes.
- **Cholera** is caught through contaminated food or water, or faeces.
- **Yellow fever** is spread by infected mosquitoes.

Non-infectious diseases are typically caused by processes within the body, such as degeneration or heredity factors, but may include bad nutrition or a noxious environment. They are regarded as chronic.

PSYCHOSOMATIC DISEASE

These diseases stem from mind-body interaction (see *Stress*, below), although a *coping reaction*, which is often confused with a psychosomatic illness, is a closing down of a bodily system as a reaction to stress - typical cases are deafness and blindness, but physical disabilities count, too. Some lifestyles promote psychosomatic illness, and knowledge is the best prevention.

- The **psychogenic** variety refers to a physical disease due to emotional stress. There is organ damage, but no invasion or degeneration. These might include backaches, or migraines, or bronchial asthma, which often appear before stressful periods in peoples' lives.
- The **somatogenic** disorder works differently, in that an emotion such as anger or fear may bring down the body's immune system enough to allow a microorganism that may already be present to gain an influence, for which stress would be a catalyst.

STRESS

Flying requires considerable use of the brain, with observation and/or reaction to events, both inside and outside the aircraft. Psychology and aviation have been used to each other for some time; you may be familiar with selection tests and interviews. Part of why accidents happen is that some people are accidents waiting to happen! This depends on personality, but status, role and ability are also important, all discussed later.

Whatever influences the mind or emotions can alter the way we interpret the information on which we base decisions. For example, when under stress, because it's harder to concentrate, your judgment becomes impaired and you make rash decisions as you try to make the problem go away. In fact, during an emergency, people often go into denial - having been used to doing practice engine failures over wide open fields during training, it takes a while to get through the unfairness of it all as it happens for real over trees! By this time, the emergency will have rolled on. In psychology, this is the **normalcy bias**, which causes us to underestimate the possibility of disaster and its effects. As something has never happened before, it never will!

Modern technology (automation), allows us to achieve more in less time and has led to lifestyles of constant change, which is something that humans don't like in general. Just coping with change can be a major cause of stress, which can pull down your immune system and act as a catalyst for illnesses to take hold. It can all start with a mismatch between what you want and what you get.

Flying is stressful, but a little is good for you; it stops you slowing down and keeps you on your toes; this is the sort associated with success. However, the word is commonly used to mean both the source and an outcome of a problem. For example, we say we are *under* stress and that we are suffering *from* stress. In reality, stress is the outcome of being under pressure, which can either raise or lower your performance, depending on how it is perceived or reacted to, but eliminating pressure does not remove stress - the whole process, including the original pressure, must be managed. You do this by knowing when to use it to get things done.

Negative stress (or *dis*tress) occurs when we react to pressure in the wrong way. It can lead to fatigue, anxiety and an inability to cope, and is associated with frustration or failure. It can also make you ill - of the two systems that are designed to protect the body, only one can be active at any time. That is, when the adrenalin used for fight or flight kicks in, the immune system is suppressed, long term. Over your career, this can lead to failing medicals earlier. In fact, there is evidence to indicate that stress is behind many modern illnesses, certainly headaches, asthma, heart disease and hypertension. In short, stress disturbs the body's *homeostasis*, which is how it maintains its comfort and efficiency. The word comes from the Greek *homeos* and *stasis*, meaning *similar* and *condition*, respectively, and describes a state where the internal functions of the body are in stable equilibrium. Homeostasis preserves the body's internal sameness, particularly for temperature (but also water and blood glucose), by resisting and smoothing out changes. As it allows the body's internal environment to be independent of the external environment, it gives you a great amount of flexibility, especially with time, so you can interact more freely with the outside world without being tied down.

The reason why stress is a problem for the human body is evolutionary - the autonomic nervous system, if you remember, works as a whole unit, which may have been OK when coming across a T Rex, but not for the more everyday stuff we have to cope with today that is present in a more or less relentless stream. That is, a physical response to an emotional or physiological threat is inappropriate, because the effects take too long to dissipate with no physical action. In other words, fight or flight as a mechanism for improved performance is now redundant, as most threats are now not physical.

Fight or flight* stress (or pressure) is supposed to enable you to adapt to encountered situations - it is the body's response to a *stressor*, which is an internal or external stimulus that is *interpreted* as a threat to the body's equilibrium, and prepares it for action in various ways. Adrenalin starts to pump and many other changes take place as well, including a rise of sugar and fats in the blood (including cholesterol, from the liver), endorphins (from the hypothalamus), faster respiration, thicker blood (to carry more oxygen), tense muscles and the stopping of digestion (up to 70% of the immune system is in the gut), so more blood can be diverted to where it is needed. All this happens very quickly, but it cannot be maintained for long - if it is, the body can be adversely affected. Muscles can only contract or relax, and it takes a specific procedure to do the latter. The problem is that just thinking about a defensive action can make you adopt a posture without realising it. This is how hidden fears or anger can create muscle tension, especially in the cardiovascular or digestive systems. Thus, stress disorders are caused by chronic, long term overactivity.

*Most people recognise this physiological reaction as panic, which often triggers a number of other physical symptoms, but clinical psychologist, Dr Curtis Reisinger from Zucker Hillside Hospital in New York, has said the binary model of fight or flight is oversimplified. There would appear to be six possible responses to stress:

- Fighting a threat.
- Flight from a threat.
- Freezing and not reacting to a threat.
- Flooding: Being overcome with emotion.
- Fawn: Submitting and being compliant.
- Fatigue: Feeling very tired and needing sleep in response to a threat

The freeze response is similar to a rabbit caught in the headlights, whereas the fatigue response may create a powerful need to take a nap. Usually seen in children and babies, sleeping is one way for the body to restore energy by replenishing glucose in the brain which has been used up by undertaking low-level mental and physical tasks. However, it's not a very good reaction in situations of real danger, for obvious reasons.

Officially, the body's reaction to stress is the *non-specific response to the demands placed on a person*. If a threat continues to be perceived as such, the imbalances in body chemistry will eventually no longer be sustainable, and our performance will eventually suffer. The cortisol* and adrenalin (and other substances) combine to increase blood pressure, blood sugar and fats which, if continued over time, will result in the stress related illnesses above. In other words, chemicals and hormones that help us in the short term will kill us long term.

*Most animals produce up to 13 times the normal amount of ascorbic acid (Vitamin C) to counteract the inflammation caused by the cortisol. Humans (and monkeys and guinea pigs) cannot produce Vitamin C, so we have to get it from external sources.

Stress and preoccupation have their effects - a PA 31 pilot was doing a cargo flight with three scheduled stops, but he did not refuel or even shut down at any of them, so both engines stopped after the last delivery. He was anxious to get home as his wife was in hospital. This illustrates how stress can cause a *narrowing of the focus*, or a fixation on one problem to the exclusion of others. In a complex task, high levels of arousal can narrow the span of attention and make you fixate on smaller areas of attention. Although it produces faster responses, they can also be less accurate.

THE YERKES-DODSON LAW OF AROUSAL

This suggests that people can become complacent without much stress in their lives, and their performance increases when they become subject to a little but, when something unusual or unexpected happens and their responsibilities start to pile up, some sort of fuse blows when the stress becomes too much and they start to lose control - the harder they run around, the less they get done, and a vicious circle begins. We don't have time to rush! The model uses a graph of performance against arousal with an inverted U-shape which shows that, as arousal increases, performance increases to an optimum point, after which it falls off (the extreme left side represents sleep, and the extreme right, extreme panic). Below the breakpoint (mid point) is best.

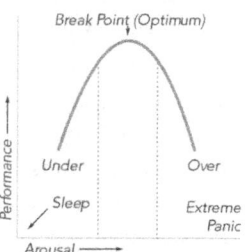

Peak performance is relative - it's not about being the best, but better!

The optimum arousal state is 115-145 heartbeats per minute. After 145, motor skills start to break down. After 175, the forebrain (which has something to do with decision making) is superseded by the mid-brain. Behaviour becomes more aggressive and blood is withdrawn into the body (from the brain and immune system) to restrict your bleeding if something happens. What happened to Rodney King in Los Angeles occurred *after* a high speed chase. This is why you rehearse emergencies, because, when under stress, you may well revert to former training - watch out for those levers in the wrong place on the new machine (i.e. *reversion*)! An overstressed pilot may show mental blocks, confusion, channelised attention, resignation, frustration, rage, deterioration in motor coordination, and fast speaking in a high-pitched voice.

THE GENERAL ADAPTATION SYNDROME

Stress is what you perceive it to be, so it is personal, and in the mind, but it can have a profound effect on the body. The *biological* reaction to stress is, after Selye, also called the *General Adaptation Syndrome*, associated with the autonomic nervous system, where adaptation means *the tendency of the body to fight to restore homeostasis against forces that upset the body's natural balance*. It's also known as the *Fight or Flight Response*, and it consists of three phases:

- **Alarm Phase** - where the stressor causes the body's resistance to fall as the sympathetic branch of the autonomic nervous system is activated. **Adrenalin** releases sugar into the blood, an acceleration of pulse and blood pressure, and an increase in the rate and depth of breathing, but no specific organ is affected. If the cause of stress is not removed, you move to.....

- **The Resistance Phase**, where the response is channelled into the specific organ system or the process most capable of dealing with or suppressing it. It is characterised by psychosomatic disorders over time, because the parasympathetic nervous system uses **cortisol** to prolong the mobilisation of energy in the body by converting fats to sugar.
- **Exhaustion Stage.** The body runs out of energy reserves and immunity, and there is a reduced metabolic rate and stress tolerance, which is why you feel tired and crave sugar (and gain weight).

As an example, the body can adapt to high blood pressure without constantly going into the alarm stage, but kidney and heart damage will eventually cause a problem as the resistance is forced into a stronger system. Unfortunately, the GAS assumes that everyone reacts to stress in the same way - it does not allow for the ability to perceive a situation as a threat or not, and to take action to change things. In other words, the threat itself is less important than the attitude of the person concerned. *Lazarus* (with *Cummings* & *Cooper*) suggests that the less you feel able to cope with a threat, the more stress you will experience.

WHAT IS EXCESSIVE STRESS?

Anything that has a strong enough influence to take your mind off the job in hand, or to make you concentrate less well on it. Not only are you not doing your job properly, but subconsciously feel guilty as well, which is enough to set up a little stress all of its own. We all like to feel we are doing the best we can, and it disturbs our self-image to feel that we're not. Consequently, we get angry at ourselves for being in such a position, which increases the stress, which further takes us away from the job, etc.

Common situations causing stress include grief, divorce, financial worries, working conditions, management pressure, pride, anger, get-home-itis*, motivation (or lack of), doubts (about abilities, etc.), timetable, passengers' expectations, etc. In fact, there are many life events in a long list, with each item weighted with *Life Change Units* (LCUs) according to its stress-producing capacity. They range from death of a spouse, partner or child at the top of the list (100 LCUs) to minor law violations (11 LCUs). A visit from the in-laws rates 29!

*Also known as the *end deterioration effect.*

The current list is the *Life Change Events Scale*, which can be grouped for convenience as follows:

- *physical* (environment, temperature)
- *physiological* (fatigue, illness)
- *emotional/psychological* (divorce, death, etc.)

All the above leads to anxiety, which is really based on fear, if you think about it (fear of people not liking you, of losing your job, etc.), but the common denominator is *change*, regardless of whether it is desirable or not. As anxiety itself can cause stress, you get a circulating problem. People have their own ways of dealing with stress, so what works for one does not necessarily work for another. This is due to the evaluation of the stress that particular person has, i.e. whether they feel they can cope and their perception of the problem. Symptoms of stress include:

- Anxiety, apprehension, depression, mood swings
- Fixation of attention
- Personality and voice pitch changes
- Reduced cognitive ability
- Poor emotional self-control
- Anger

STRESS MANAGEMENT

Prevention is better than cure - the worst time to deal with stress is when you are suffering from it. You will cope with stress better if you learn to cope with change first, then modify *your* position relative to the stressor. You can be affected in these areas:

- **Adaptation**. Life is full of change, but this is a problem with customers, and the lack of planning on their part. Many pilots visualise a task up to a week before they get going, but it commonly changes at the last minute!
- **Frustration** (too many people in the way, or thwarting of your goals). Pilots, in particular, have to reconcile the demands of two influential groups of people, namely customers and management.
- **Overload**, so much to do in so little time, particularly during a complex approach. A level of demand that exceeds your capacity to cope (delegation helps).
  - *Qualitative overload* occurs where the information is perceived to be beyond the capacity of our attention and the task becomes too difficult.
  - *Quantitative overload* just means too many responses in the time available.
- **Deprivation** (boredom or loneliness).
- **Biological/Personality** (anxiety, etc.)
- **Nutritional**. A stress prone diet includes sugar, caffeine and salt, and leads to vitamin depletion, especially B and C, because stress uses up the body's supplies that process sugar into energy. Salt regulates the body's water balance - too much leads to fluid retention, which leads to high blood pressure. Caffeine is just as bad as stress.
- **Noise and vibration**
- **Smoking**

Since most of the above occur simultaneously, it can be seen that stress has a wide scope, with no simple solution - it is actually a *lifestyle* problem, which means that one of the most effective means of stress management is to switch to one that eliminates or avoids such stressors. You could change your daily routine, eat more healthy food, change your job or partner, or even your personality (however, you can never really get rid of them all).

Good cockpit stress management begins with what causes stress - in a crisis in the cockpit, for example, you must first identify the source. Then, try to relax and think rationally, and use all available resources to help.

Having recognised the situation, eliminate or deal with the factors causing your stress. I like black humour myself, and some

HUMAN PERFORMANCE & LIMITATIONS
Stress

people favour eating, meditation or biofeedback machines that help them reduce their heart rate, etc., but most either adjust to the situation, or change it, or their thinking about it, or walk away. Since the primary fight or flight response is physical, which takes hours to undo, one of the quickest methods would be to get enough physical exercise to use up the chemicals that have been placed in your bloodstream. However, the willingness to recognise stress and to do something about it must be there; for example, if you don't admit there's a problem at home, there's not much you can do! It is not weakness to admit you have a problem - rather, it shows lack of judgment otherwise. As previously mentioned, it's your *attitude* towards stress that counts, not the situation itself, as other people may be able to cope with it very well. If you have the usual fight-or-flight symptoms over a relatively minor incident, you are stressed! This energy has nowhere to go and you end up in overdrive, with a very easily ignited short fuse to push you over the edge (see *Anger*).

COPING MECHANISMS

These are *psychological* reactions that involve dealing with the source of the stress.

- **Action Coping** means taking positive action in the **short term***, including removing yourself from the situation, addressing the problem or altering the situation enough to reduce the demands. In other words, *changing your behaviour*.

    *Long-term Stress Management involves a change of life-style or counselling.

- **Cognitive Coping** involves reducing the *Perceived Demand*, maybe by rationalisation or consulting with others. It concerns the modification of your perception or reaction to events (*changing your thinking*). Denial of the problem comes under this heading, where the conscious mind is prevented from being aware of the stressor.

- **Symptom-Directed Coping** involves treating the symptoms rather than the cause of stress, say by drinking (exercise is better), the use of drugs, coffee, tea, tobacco or meditation.

A major stressor for pilots is too much automation and not enough hands on flying. Experience helps you deal with stress.

Fatigue

Fatigue is a condition arising from mental and emotional strains that can reduce your efficiency. Although we do not use our muscles much, we do need to concentrate and use up mental resources. In fact, physical and mental fatigue work with each other to produce the effects.

The human system is not well suited to being continuously alert for events that are unlikely to happen, especially after staying awake for long periods so that, if the event does happen, you are less able to deal with it. A good example is Search and Rescue work where, near the end of a shift, you have mentally gone home, but you are still on duty and less keen to perform a task should it turn up. Prolonged exposure to fatigue (mental or physical) can reduce the capabilities of your immune system and make you quite ill. Like the frog in a saucepan of warm water that is getting hotter, you don't usually notice until you collapse in a heap at the end of the flying season. Helicopter pilots are especially prone to fatigue, due to the high workload and intense decision making, and vibration. The Canadian government compares four hours' worth to eight hours' hard labour and double that when longlining (not including the normal A-B stuff, of course and, naturally, fixed wing pilots on short sector work have similar strains, without the vibration).

Fatigue is typically caused by delayed sleep, sleep loss, desynchronisation of normal circadian rhythms and concentrated periods of physical or mental stress or exertion. Working long hours, during normal sleep hours or on rotating shifts, all produce fatigue to some extent.

A surprising amount (over 300) of bodily functions depend on the cycle of day and night - we have an internal (*circadian*) rhythm, which is modified by such things, which, oddly enough, is 25 hours*, although there are several body clocks that might run for slightly more or less than that. You naturally feel best when they're all in concert, but the slippery slope starts when they get out of line. For example, one reason why people feel bad on Monday mornings is because they have let their body clocks run free over the weekend, instead of using the usual timegivers (*zeitgebers*), like the cycle of night and day. So, when your alarm clock says it is 7 o'clock on Monday morning, your body thinks it is around 4 o'clock and wants to keep sleeping. With circadian rhythms, *sensorimotor performance is better in the evening and intellectual performance is better in the morning*.

*The study of bodily rhythms is called *chronobiology*.

The best known desynchronisation is jet lag (*circadian disrhythmia*), but it also happens when you work nights and sleep during the day. Bright light can fool your body into thinking it's day when it's not. One day for each time zone crossed is required before sleep and waking cycles get in tune with the new location*, and total internal synchronisation takes longer (kidneys may need up to 25 days). Even the type of time zone change can matter - 6 hours westward requires (for most people) about four days to adjust - try 7 for going the other way! This Eastward flying compresses the body's rhythm and does more damage than the expanded days going West. N-S travel appears to do no harm.

*You need 90 minutes per day in the new time zone. If the stay in the new location is less than 24 hours, you should try to remain on home time. If it is over 24 hours, get acclimatised to the new zone as soon as possible.

Symptoms of jet lag are tiredness, faulty judgment, decreased motivation and recent memory loss. They are aggravated by alcohol, smoking, high-altitude flight, overeating and depression, as found in a normal pilot's lifestyle. In view of all this, you have a maximum working day laid down by law, intended to ensure you are rested enough to fly properly (see *Flight Time & Duty Limitations* in *Operational Procedures*). The two types of fatigue are *acute* and *chronic*, the former being short-term, or more intense, and the latter arising from more long-term effects, like many episodes of acute fatigue, typically found after a long spell of fire suppression. Acute fatigue usually affects the body, and just needs a good nights' sleep to sort things out, whereas the chronic variety has a mental element, where you never want to see an aircraft again, even though things are physically the same from day to day. It typically happens after you've had no rest, food or recreation for some time, as seen in the example under *Error Management*. Symptoms are insomnia, loss of appetite, and even irrational behaviour. To control its effects, try rest, exercise and proper nutrition.

Foods low in carbohydrate or high in protein help fight fatigue, especially "healthy" ones, like fruit or yoghurt, or cereals, such as granola. Coffee, of course, contains caffeine, which keeps you awake (as does tea), but too much can lead to headaches and upset stomachs. People who drink unleaded coffee (decaffeinated) still report unpleasant side effects, as the process that removes caffeine is allegedly just as harmful, but in different ways. Caffeine has a half-life of about 3 hours, and although it might not stop you getting to sleep, it will affect its quality.

The effects of caffeine are measurable from **250 mg**, and your intake should be restricted to between 250-300 mg.

Trivia: ICAO Annex 1 excludes coffee and tobacco from the definition of *psychoactive substance*, but Coca Cola, Pepsi, Tea, and other substances containing caffeine, are there.

SLEEP

Nobody really knows what sleep is for, but the current working hypothesis is that it is necessary to restore and replenish the body and brain (it would seem that REM sleep refreshes the mind, and Slow Wave (NREM) sleep refreshes the body). However, if that were the only reason, you would sleep less after a slack day and more after a busy day, but the amount does not seem to vary, although people do need different amounts - Margaret Thatcher, when Prime Minister, only slept 5 hours each night. As for resting the body, you can do that in front of the TV, so it seems to be a mental thing.

Most people need about 8 hours' sleep, and you can do with less for a few days, creating a *sleep deficit*, but it's not only the amount of sleep you get, but *when* you get it that counts, so fatigue is just as likely to result from badly planned sequences of work and rest, or being too long away from base without a day off. One example comes from crop dusting, which happens real early in the morning or late in the evening, when the winds are lightest and don't spread whatever you are spraying where you don't want it. Most people would get a good nights' sleep in a tent on a warm summer's evening (especially when they camp for fun), but the authorities would rather you drove for two hours over bumpy roads, get 2-3 hours' sleep and drive back again. Go figure.

There is some evidence to suggest that several shorter periods of 3-4 hours during the 24 hours of a day are better for you than one 8 hour period of sleep.

Sleep is actually a state of altered consciousness, in which, although paralysed, you don't lose awareness of the external world, as any mother will tell you (it's actually where your brain focusses internally - consciousness seems to depend on certain regions of the brain stem for its function). It is part of a daily cycle that is 25 hours long - that is, the sleeping and waking rhythm is about an hour longer than the normal day of 24 hours, which itself is a mean figure anyway (*Moore-Ede, Sulzman & Fuller*, 1982). This is why flying West is easier on the system than flying East - the body's rhythm is extended the right way. Various factors, such as cycles of night or day, keep the natural 25-hour tendency in check. Normally, this *circadian rhythm* works with body temperature, so the body is coolest when it is hardest to stay awake, around 05:00 hours. The highest body temperature occurs at about 17:00 hours (it is important to be familiar with the circadian rhythm of body temperature because peak performance occurs at times of rising or high body temperature).

1 hour of quality sleep equals 2 hours of activity, so each sleeping hour gains 2 credit points (maximum 16) and each hour awake loses one. A *sleep debt* is the cumulative effect of not getting enough sleep. Its effects increase with workload and altitude.

8 hours' sleep overnight (the same as a minimum rest period) therefore means that you will be ready for sleep again 16 hours after waking. If your work pattern is disrupted, you can increase your "credit rating" with a short nap. Aside from interfering with the REM variety, alcohol interferes with sleep because of its diuretic action - repeated use disturbs sleep on a long term basis, to give you insomnia. The British Army thinks that a shave is about equal to 20 minutes' sleep, in terms of refreshing you, and washing your face or brushing your teeth are also good, as is moving around for 5-10 minutes. A person suffering sleep loss is unlikely to be aware of personal performance degradation, which may be present for up to 20 minutes after a nap.

Clinical Insomnia is being unable to sleep under normal conditions. *Situational insomnia* arises out of the circumstances, like sleeping in a strange bed or time zone (*circadian desynchronisation*). Although insomniacs may think they don't sleep at all, they actually spend their time in stages 1 and 2 (see below). *Sleep Apnea* stops people breathing for short periods up to a minute, and *Narcolepsy* (the inability to stop falling asleep when in sleep credit) makes them drop off at any time of the day.

Wilse Webb, a behaviourist, tried to persuade rats to stay awake when they would normally be asleep, but they would go back to their normal sleep routine once he stopped "reminding" them, which would suggest that the natural amount of sleep is regulated internally (he tried it with humans, too). The fact that how long you sleep depends on when you sleep also suggests that there are two components of the sleep system, and the former function is not an internal rhythm, but takes account of habits and routines - when these are taken away, people tend to sleep in shorter bursts. So, sleep can be resisted for a short time, but various parts of the brain will ensure that, sooner or later, sleep occurs. A Boeing 707 overshot LA International at 32,000 feet over the Pacific ocean after the whole crew had fallen asleep (one was only roused by ATC setting off alarms in the cockpit).

When we are asleep, the higher regions of the brain lose the ability to communicate - parts of the cerebral cortex which mediate perception, thought and action disconnect (*Science*, Sep 30 2005). It has been found that electronic signals do not pass beyond certain stimulated cells during sleep, so the brain "breaks down into little islands that cannot talk to one another." Conscious thought may therefore depend on the ability of the brain to integrate information, and REM sleep (see below), at least, may be a way of allowing the brain to defragment isolated pieces of information collected and processed during the day. Thus, the main role of deep sleep could be to allow for physical recovery and reconstitution of neural energy reserves.

Until 150 years ago, most people worked outdoors, and obtained enough natural sunlight. Sunlight increases the number of white blood cells, most of the lymphocytes, causing an upsurge in the defences against infectious diseases. It also stimulates the formation of Interferon, thereby preventing viruses from proliferating. Our bodies need clear information about day and night in order to regulate our waking and sleeping phases and the biorhythms associated with this.

Unfortunately, windows filter out many parts of the light spectrum. Professor Dr. Fritz Hollwich, of the University Eye Hospital in Munster, discovered that only around 25% of the light absorbed by our eyes is used directly for vision - the other 75% travels via the optic pathways to the brain and hypothalamus - the body's chief control system.

The pineal gland (which is not much bigger than a grain of rice) is extremely light sensitive. When it is dark, it synthesises and secretes a hormone called melatonin, which tells the body it is time for sleep. During this time the brain repairs cell damage and replaces the half a billion cells lost each day. Melatonin is an extremely powerful antioxidant that deals with free radicals (electrons left over in the repair process) that attack healthy cells. This why you should sleep in a dark room, bright full-spectrum light suppresses its production.

Even a night light inhibits melatonin production enough to increase the health risks of people who work nights and sleep during the day when it is hard to reproduce the darkness of night time. If parts of the light spectrum are missing, the body can enter a twilight state, comatose, neither fully awake nor asleep.

Types of Sleep

The sleep process is characterised by 5 stages (4 + REM) that take place over a typical cycle of about 90 minutes.

Stage 1 sleep is the light sleep you get into just after dozing off. It only lasts a few minutes before you go into Stage 2, which takes up around 50% of the total sleeping time (around 20 minutes). Stage 3 takes up 3-12%, while Stage 4 occupies 15-35%. Stages 3 and 4 are called *Orthodox Sleep*.

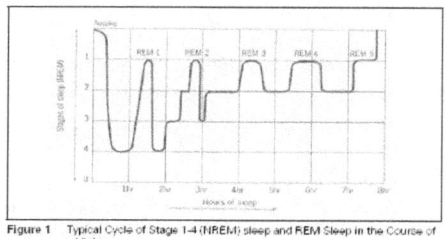

Figure 1 Typical Cycle of Stage 1-4 (NREM) sleep and REM Sleep in the Course of a Night

The duration of sleep periods is mainly governed by when in your circadian rhythm you try to sleep.

As you get deeper and deeper into sleep, it is progressively more difficult to be roused to wakefulness. It takes about 15-30 minutes to get into Stage 4, and you stay there for about 30-40 minutes before going back up through to Stage 1, the whole process lasting about 90 minutes. After this, you enter the first stage of REM sleep, so the sequence is 1 - 2 - 3 - 4 - 3 - 2 - REM - 2 - 3 - 4 - 3 - 2 - REM and so on.

In **Rapid Eye Movement** (or *paradoxical**) sleep, the body and brain become active, heart and metabolism increase and the eyes shift, hence the name. The brain is awake in a virtually paralysed body, so you are nearly awake anyway, and it is more difficult to get back to sleep for the next hour. Alcohol degrades REM sleep which, in adult humans typically occupies 20–25% of total sleep, about 90–120 minutes of a night's sleep (4-5 bouts).

*Nathaniel Kleitman (1895-1999), the Professor of Physiology at Chicago University, is credited with discovering rapid eye movement in sleep experiments.

He wanted to study the rolling movements of the eyes that only occur during sleep (and speeches by politicians). About an hour after the eye-rolling ended, they began to move very rapidly, about every 90 minutes, coinciding with changes in brainwave activity as the long, slow wavelengths of normal sleep were replaced by fast frequency patterns which were close to those obtained when awake. As it is most difficult to wake people up then, it is called paradoxical sleep. Signals from part of the brain stem (the reticular formation) paralyse the muscles.

The first REM period is between 5-10 minutes long, but the length of each one increases through the night, after the second cycle (you get up to four REM sessions per night, on average). Long term lack of REM sleep is not good for general health.

COMMUNICATION

This is the first cockpit tool to suffer from stress. Any relationship needs it to be successful. In fact, there is hardly any job in which it can be ignored. Lack of it can affect your physical health - in the 13th century, for example, Emperor Frederick experimented by cutting some babies off from all communication, instructing their nurses to stay silent. The babies all died. A study was once done on graduates of Stanford University, to find out what makes a great engineer. The responses indicated that technical expertise formed only 20% of the ingredients for success - the rest was due to people skills.

Communication in aviation is important because customers, for instance, should know exactly what your aircraft can and cannot do or, more particularly, what you will and will not do (especially with heliskiing!) For some reason, a fork lift driver who says that only 50 packages can be carried is believed, but pilots are assumed to be lying - most customers think that all you need to do is put in extra gas to lift the load.

The first requirement for communication is a common language, for which aviation uses English, or something more precise, namely "Aviation English", which uses standardised, abbreviated, precise and agreed terminology. However, we still have to make certain assumptions, otherwise everything would grind to a halt as we continually ask for clarification. Such assumptions would certainly include peoples' levels of knowledge and how they think about things. This is one reason for clear briefings - to ensure that we are not operating on assumptions in the cockpit! The aim is that people should understand what they need to do without the need for detailed explanations.

Thus, your ability to communicate will account for over 80% of your success in any walk of life. However, your current methods have more than likely been based on responses learned through childhood, and can almost certainly be improved. What happens is that you build a facade, either for emotional protection or because you have to behave in certain ways in order to get what you need (food, comfort, etc.), which does not necessarily have anything to do with the person that you really are. From that stems the playing of games and manipulation, hurting and punishment until you grow into a full-blown control freak. To be sure, personality plays some part, but most behaviour patterns are learnt. Luckily, communication skills can be learnt, too.

Communication is defined as the ability to put your ideas into someone's head and be sure of success, or to exchange information without it being changed. Or both. Unfortunately, even under ideal conditions, only about 30% is retained, due to inattention, misinterpretation, expectations and emotions. Your team needs to know what you want done, especially in an emergency, and requires feedback as to progress and satisfaction of your expectations. This could be through the spoken word* or body language (see overleaf). Officially, around 80% of all communication is achieved by factors other than words, otherwise known as *metacommunication*, which consists of those tools, other than the words, which complement them in order to communicate, such as body language, or "communicating around communication".

*In general, we listen at 900 words per minute and speak at 125 words per minute.

The ancient Greeks thought of communication between two people in three parts:

- **Ethos** - character (and credibility) of an individual.
- **Pathos** - emotional content.
- **Logos** - the logical content, and the least influential part of the process - it will only be listened to if the other two are clear. You can be as correct as you wish, but if character and emotion are missing, your message will not get across.

Implicit communication means that various interpretations may be placed on the information, so the sender can always claim afterwards to have been misunderstood. *Explicit communication* (as used in the Tenerife accident) has no ambiguity. Success in achieving the objectives of a message requires the matching of verbal, non-verbal and contextual meanings.

Verbal communication may be either *social* or *functional*. The former helps to build teamwork, and the latter is essential to flying, or operating, an aircraft. For a spoken or written message to be understood, the sender has to make sure that the receiver is using the same channel of communication, and language, and can make out the message's meaning. The *channel of communication* is the medium used to convey the message.

For the spoken word, this might be face-to-face, the radio or intercom, so communication is the exchange of thoughts, messages or information by many means, including speech, involving (according to Berlo):

- the **source** (sender)*
- the **message**
- the **channel**
- the **receiver***

Not forgetting *feedback*, which is the process of responding to a sender by confirming the reception of a message. It guarantees the understanding of a message without adding new information to it, and **should always relate to a specific situation**.

*The sender (on which communication heavily depends) and the receiver, as well as coding and decoding are prone to malfunctioning.

However, communication serves other functions than just exchanging information. It also helps the crew to share the same mental model of the flight and allows participation in the decision making process. Because it establishes the interpersonal climate in the cockpit, it sets the tone for management of the flight, and very much depends on the company culture.

Peoples' perceptions and background at either end may influence things - as in the movie *Life Of Brian*, a person at the back of a congregation might hear: "Blessed are the cheesemakers" instead of "Blessed are the peacemakers".

Effective Communication

From a CRM standpoint, effective communication plays a critical role in the alignment of mental models, but such skills require practice and reinforcement to be effective, particularly in the pressure of an emergency.

For effective communication, information should be sent according to the receiver's decoding abilities. If the sender finds the receiver competent, verbal redundancy content is reduced (i.e. cut out the crap). If the receiver is deemed incompetent, the message will be simplified.

Crew members must feel comfortable in providing input to a captain to assist his decision making. If a steep trans-cockpit authority gradient exists (see below), there is an increased risk that decisions will be made based on incomplete or inaccurate information. Modern CRM training encourages first officers to assert themselves, but this can be very difficult for certain people. Ideally, the process begins with non-threatening statements or questions. If they fail to address the concern, a more assertive approach must be taken. This escalation in communication strategies is difficult for new employees, who may be fearful of career implications.

On the other hand, a captain must ensure that crew members feel that their input is valued by actively seeking out and encouraging open communication. Inexperienced FOs will likely use subtle, non-aggressive communication strategies to voice concerns that they are afraid to raise. To ensure that a first officer's message has been received and understood, captains should provide timely and relevant feedback.

Effective communication demands certain skills, such as:

- *Seeking information* - good decisions are based on good information.
- *Problem solving*, especially with other people.
- *Listening* - active listening means not making assumptions about what the other person is saying, or what they really mean, so it *promotes a constructive solution of interpersonal conflicts*. You need to be patient, question and be supportive. Even low-time pilots have opinions! We can listen at up to 1200 words per minute (in general, 500 and speak at 125), so our inability to listen is not physical, but mental. It takes practice to listen properly (especially, don't interrupt!)
- *Stating your position* - or *assertiveness skills*, which does *not* mean being aggressive!

- *Resolving differences* - conflict resolution. Almost always, the best way to do this is ensure that the results are best for everyone concerned.
- *Communication skill selection*, or how to perform the communication you need.
- *Providing feedback*.

Efficiency in communication is sensitive to workload and interruptions (having interrupted the Captain, a copilot should remind him of his last previous action).

Body Language

The fact that somebody isn't talking does not mean they are not communicating (some female silences can be quite eloquent!) It is said that 7% of communication is accomplished verbally, 38% by unconscious signals, such as the tone of voice, and the remainder (55%) by non-verbal means, such as body language. In fact, before language was invented it was the only way to get your point across. It's certainly the most believed means of communication, since it will most likely reflect the true feelings of the person concerned.

Non-verbal communication can accompany the verbal kind, such as a smile during a face-to-face chat. It may be acknowledgment or feedback (a nod of the head). It can also be used when the verbal type is impossible, such as a thumbs-up when it's noisy. Body language can be very subtle, but powerful. For example, the word *No* with a smile will be interpreted quite differently from one accompanied by a smack in the mouth. Non-verbal communication may also include written information or notes, between pilots or the flight deck and cabin crew, but technology makes this even more important - it is the main way that systems speak to you - newer displays present data graphically. Unfortunately, the side-by side seating arrangements in the cockpit tend to lessen the effects of body language, so the choice of words (and their packaging) assumes a greater importance.

 Elements of body language should not be taken in isolation - folded arms may not mean hostility, but that the other person is merely cold. Always interpret body language over three or four indications. For example, posture is also an important part of an unspoken message. The way you sit or stand can show others a lot about how you are feeling, but it needs to be read with other clues, such as.....

GESTURES

These can be used in threatening or submissive ways, such as head movements, facial expressions and eye movements (or lack of eye movement if someone is ignoring you).

SOUNDS

You don't need words to convey a message - a deep sigh can say much, as can grunts and groans. In addition, the pitch and pace of a voice can be very expressive.

PROXIMITY & DISTANCE

Your personal space expands and contracts with the conditions you were raised in (the radius for Western cultures is roughly the same). It also varies in size according to the person being spoken to - for example, you might stand further away from your boss than from a colleague, which can be a way of finding out seniority. The same effect can happen by your positioning - somebody in charge is more likely to place themselves at the head of a table. Those who want to try and influence that person will naturally try to sit as close as possible, and those at the bottom of the pecking order will be furthest away.

"Those that think they are important will sit where they think they ought to sit. Those that are important will sit where they like."

QUESTIONS

Asking questions gives the impression that you are listening. Actually, the person who asks questions controls any conversation, because, once asked, the other person's mind flies to the answer, and you are in charge for as long as it takes to finish it. Open (implicit) questions require an extended answer, and are best for getting conversations going. Closed (explicit) questions require a specific answer, like *Yes*, or *No*, and can be used to bring a conversation to a conclusion (these are what we mostly use in aviation). However, they can be less than useful - a question such as "Have you got a pencil?" is no good when you want to borrow it!

Leading questions can be asked when situational awareness is lost, or where there is some doubt - for example: "Isn't that London down there?"

AURAL CLUES

These include the words themselves, how quickly they are spoken, and the sound or pitch of the voice, not forgetting the "ums" and "ahs" that people use when they are nervous. A good ploy is to stop listening to words and start listening to the tone. For example, you could emphasise each word in turn of this sentence and get a different meaning every time:

I never said your dog was ugly
I *never* said your dog was ugly
I never *said* your dog was ugly
I never said *your* dog was ugly
I never said your *dog* was ugly
I never said your dog *was* ugly
I never said your dog was *ugly*

Thus, it's not what you say that may cause a problem, but how you say it! In an emergency, you must use the proper language, so ATC can react properly, otherwise you won't get help but an increase in paperwork after you land!

LISTENING

We spend around 45% of our time in listening. ¾ of it is heard imprecisely, and ¾ of the remainder is forgotten within three weeks. It is also said that hearing is done with your ears, whereas listening is done with the mind. *Active Listening* means that whoever is speaking thinks you are understanding them, and that you appreciate the feelings behind the words. "Power" communicators have high levels of empathy. Key steps to proper listening include:

- *Listen* (with all the signals)
- Pause
- *Question* for clarification
- Paraphrase

Psychologists have a phrase, *Unconditional Positive Regard*, meaning that they always react in a positive and supportive non-judgmental way - they don't become angry or upset, but continue to smile and nod, which is probably why people go to them in the first place.

Barriers To Communication

Individual styles, body language and speech patterns all have their part to play in communication, and you need to be sensitive to and aware of their nuances. You also need to be aware of anything that might stop communication taking place. Barriers to communication include:

- Influence of authority, reluctance to ask questions.
- Difficulty in listening (noise, environment...)
- The door between the cabin and flight deck!
- Language (including use of jargon), culture.

not forgetting making assumptions, and anger, described below. You, therefore, have to put people at their ease and make them think they can talk to you or ask questions. In fact, there can be *lack* of communication and *poor* communication. The former might be a young first officer who is very computer-literate, but doesn't tell you what he's doing while continually texting. The latter, someone that tells you there is a problem, but not what it is, but an important component is speech - the words you say often have the opposite effect to what is intended, because they simply mean different things to different people.

As well, when people speak, the words become coded into some sort of indirect expression. This is because we grow up learning to be politically correct in order to get what we need from other people, thus hiding your real self behind some sort of language barrier and continual demands not to show emotion. For example, when a child asks questions at bedtime, the meaning behind the words is a request to stay a little longer. All too often, we take words at face value and confuse the real meanings for their presentation, if only because the real meat of any conversation tends to come at the end. Listeners have problems, too, because people have filters through which words have to struggle to be understood.

Responses that spoil communication include:

- **Judging**
- **Solution-giving**
- **Avoidance**

If one party is under stress, the more positive responses above will play their part in reducing communication.

CONFLICT

This is a confrontation between 2 or more people, with emotional overtones. The causes can include:

- Perception of injustice.
- Attacks on integrity.
- Difference in approach.
- A situation which opposes the participants, such as the introduction of new procedures.
- The exercise of power.

There are 5 stages of conflict:

- **Initiation**, which is where conflict is recognised, possibly by behaviour, but is often allowed to develop without knowing how to control it. It is also where there is the greatest chance to resolve a conflict before it gets more serious.
- **Escalation**. This is where conflict is visible, and it may get personal, and we start to lose any logical reasoning. It may involve projection onto others of motives that they may not have, and blame.
- **Polarisation**. Here, it gets ugly. Entrenched positions are taken and defended, emotions run high and behaviour can get childish.
- **Implosion/Explosion**. Conflict erupts. You may get withdrawal, yelling, aggression & violence.
- **Closure**. Things should be resolved by now, but there may be remaining underlying resentment.

The art of conflict resolution is *not to let it develop, especially in the cockpit! Conflict management involves the participation of all parties in finding an acceptable collective solution.*

ANGER

Anger held in becomes resentment - the trick is not to express it destructively. When you are angry your body pumps out adrenalin, and cortisol, which depresses your immune system, so being angry can have long-term health effects. Although losing it can make you feel better, it is only temporary and a huge exhaustive low follows as the hormones leave your system. Aggressive people are more susceptible to heart attacks, clogged arteries and higher cholesterol. However, anger is also a good means of blocking communication. This is because there are four types of angry person, each with their own language:

- those who are generally non-malicious, whose anger is quick to boil and just as quick to dissipate.
- those who are slow to anger, but keep a list of everything you did or said wrong since 1929.
- those who just like being angry.
- those who like after-effects rather than arguments.

If you learn more about your own makeup, you can avoid setting other people off. It will help you step back and *resolve* a conflict, if you can't avoid it in the first place. The body is not built to be in fight or flight mode as much as it is these days. You will therefore not be surprised to hear that it takes very little effort to trigger off an angry reaction after even the most trivial event. Such emotional triggers can easily make people explode but, at the very least, will affect the way you assess situations and react to them or, more importantly, make decisions. Emotions carry so much force and influence that they rule your actions before you calm down enough to think rationally.

As for health, one study at the Ochsner Clinic in New Orleans reports high levels of hostility in many heart attack victims, who also had higher levels of weight, cholesterol, anxiety and depression. Stress brought on by rage can also affect memory, creativity and sleep. Bacterial infections can increase during angry episodes, and you lay yourself wide open to upper respiratory problems, like flu.

People overcome anger in many ways:
- Eating
- Displacement (taking it out on the dog)
- Talking (a lot)
- Exercise (kill the tennis ball)
- Writing
- Yelling and screaming
- Swearing
- Sulking

Laughter or humour is a good defuser of anger, as is reminding yourself that it won't matter in a week anyway. Another good way to defuse it is to acknowledge the other person's reasons for being angry, because it is, at bottom, a frustrated demand for attention.

In fact, to be effective, a display of anger must:
- be directed at the target, with no retaliation.
- restore a sense of control or justice.
- result in changes of behaviour or outlook.
- use the same language (see above).

Otherwise, it will be non-productive. For the best results from any conflict, everyone needs to feel they are a winner (because the loser is still wound up). In our case, our customers need to feel they have come off best, and it's up to us to make them think they are, even if they're not.

 Anger also makes you blind to reason! This is because it puts you into the equivalent of a trance state.

Behavioural Styles

People trying to get their way may try to put you off-balance in many ways (this happens in interviews as well). Mothers, especially, use guilt, but, in the aviation world, you are most likely to come across bullying customers or management.

Bullies choose people who will go to great lengths to avoid conflict, typically a low-time pilot in a first job who doesn't want to lose it. The problem is that, somehow, these people seem to sense your vulnerability, probably because they are insecure and/or jealous themselves. Unfortunately, your behaviour can make it worse, and it is the only thing you have any control over. If you behave negatively, the other person has control of the situation, which is why they do it! Your negative reaction is their expected response, so if you do something different, by asking them why they are angry, for example, it puts *them* off balance! You can then try to direct the situation the way you want it.

Use the following steps in any altercation:
- STOP! Remain calm and don't react with gut feelings. Get all the facts!
- Defuse the situation.
- Ask questions that give the impression you really care - acknowledge their anger or concerns, and fix the problem if you can.

Here are some suggested behavioural styles:

- *Assertive.* These people have respect for themselves and others and are not afraid of sticking up (politely) for themselves. Being assertive is not the same thing as being aggressive.
- *Aggressive.* These people have no respect for other people, and have no problem expressing their anger, although they will blame others for it.
- *Passive.* These people have no respect for themselves and excessive respect for others. They very rarely stand up for themselves.
- *Passively Resistant.* These are passive people who actually try to stick up for themselves, but they use manipulative games to do it, because they still have to learn to deal with people up front (watch their body language).
- *Indirectly Aggressive.* These people use underhanded methods to get their way, such as by doing jobs improperly so they won't get asked to do them again, or by using backhanded sarcastic comments, the silent treatment or gossiping, etc.
- *Passive Aggressive.* These people feel one way, but act in another. They deny anger because they feel powerless.

PARENT-ADULT-CHILD

However, more common patterns are based on Eric Berne's *Transactional Analysis*, in which he postulates that people in any interaction take on one of three roles, *Parent*, *Adult* or *Child*, according to the circumstances. TA starts with the premise that people have multi-faceted personalities, which often conflict with each other. Eric Berne stated that, when two people meet, there is an interaction, in that one of them will speak through a *Transaction Stimulus* (the reaction from the other person is the *Transaction Response*). The person sending the Stimulus is the *Agent*, and the person responding is the *Respondent*. In other words, there is a *contractual* approach, with rights and responsibilities on each side, and *expectations*. Berne also said that people are made up of the three alter ego states above (which do not have the same usage as found in normal language):

- **Parent** conditioning that comes from authority figures, like our real parents, teachers, older people, next door neighbours, relatives, etc. Phrases like "you will never amount to anything!" remain in our consciousness to affect us for the rest of our lives. They can be removed, but not easily - later psychologists have suggested that the *exact phrase* must be used, hence the difficulty, as you can't remember what it was anyway! Absorbing mannerisms in this way is called *introjecting*. As mentioned before, we often have to behave in certain ways in order to survive, which have nothing to do with our real personalities. Parental behaviour includes scolding, finger pointing, always correcting and lecturing.
- **Adult**. This refers to our ability to think for ourselves. The adult starts to form when we are around ten months old, and is how we keep our Parent and Child under control. The Adult deals with the *here and now* and sees things how they *are*, not how they should be, or in terms of what we project onto others. In other words, there is no unhealthy baggage from the past.

- **Child**. The emotional body within each of us that usually is a series of replays from childhood. When anger or despair overcomes reason, the Child is in control. It is easier to change than the Parent.

Our feelings during an interaction determine which of the three states we will use. To communicate successfully with someone, you must be able to detect which state they are in, as successful communications must be complementary. For example, if the stimulus is Parent to Child, the response should be Child to Parent (the ideal is Adult-Adult, if you want a rational conversation!)

If a crossed transaction occurs, there is an ineffective communication, and either or both parties will be upset. For the relationship to continue smoothly, the agent or the respondent must rescue the situation with a complementary transaction.

Later, the original three Parent-Adult-Child components were sub-divided to form a new seven-element model, principally during the 1980's by Wagner, Joines and Mountain. This established *Controlling* and *Nurturing* aspects of the Parent mode, positive and negative, and the *Adapted* and *Free* aspects of the Child mode, again each with positive and negative aspects.

JUDGMENT

In short, judgment is the process of choosing between alternatives for the safest outcome. Factors that influence the exercise of good judgment include:

- *Lack of vigilance* - vigilance (consistent monitoring without lapses in attention) is the basis of situational awareness. You need to keep a constant watch on all that is going on around you, however tempting it may be to switch off for a while on a long navex. Monitor the fuel gauges, check for traffic and engine-off landing sites, all the time.
- *Distraction* - anything that stops you noticing a problem, like slowly backing into trees while releasing a cargo net. Keep pulling back to reaffirm your awareness of the big picture.
- *Peer Pressure* - we all like to be liked, by people in- or outside the company. Do they want you to fly overweight? Or in darkness, even though the passengers will be late back? Being too keen to please is part of a self-esteem problem. *Do not take on other peoples' problems!*
- *Insufficient Knowledge* - although you can look the regulations up in a book, this is not always the most convenient solution, so you need a working knowledge of what they contain, including checklists and limitations from the flight manual, etc. We don't all have an aircraft library, or have the time to refer to it even if there is one.
- *Unawareness of Consequences* - this is an aspect of insufficient knowledge, above. What are the consequences of what you propose to do? Have you thought things out thoroughly?
- *Forgetfulness of Consequences* - similar to the above

- *Ignoring the Consequences* - again, similar to the above, but more of a deliberate act (violation), since you are aware of the consequences of your proposed actions, but choose to ignore them.
- *Overconfidence* - this breeds carelessness, and a reluctance to pay attention to detail or be vigilant. Also, it inclines you to be hasty, and not consider all the options available to you. This is where a little self-knowledge and humility is a great help.

Fascination

This is where pilots fail to respond adequately to a clearly defined stimulus despite all the necessary cues being present and the proper response available.

A study in the 1950s (*Clark, Nicholson, and Graybiel*, 1953) classified experiences in 2 categories:

- **Type A**. This is fundamentally perceptual, where you concentrate on one aspect of the situation to such a degree that you reject other factors. Pilots become so intent on following a power line, for example, that they don't see the tower lines in the way.
- **Type B**. Here, you may perceive the significant aspects of the total situation, but still be unwilling or unable to make the proper response.

Habits

These are part of our lives; many are comforting and part of a routine that keeps us mentally the right way up. Others, however, are ones we could well do without, but they can be very difficult to break, because the person trying to break them is the very person trapped by them. Old habits are hard to break and new ones are hard to form because the behavioural patterns we repeat most often are etched into our neural pathways. Habit formation is how new behaviour becomes automatic (and changing your behaviour can form new habits), which is easier when the cues for existing habits are removed, as when moving to a new city. We learn habits as children, simply in order to survive, as mentioned previously and, in certain circumstances, habits can be dangerous - if you can't do anything about them, you at least need to be aware of them.

Habit can make you go for a familiar routine rather than trying for the best results - for example, *habit reversion* can occur after a pattern of behaviour has been established, mainly because you get so used to doing it - you may accidentally carry out a procedure you have used for years, even after recurrent training, which is quite possible under stress, but it can happen under normal circumstances - a Beaver pilot flew the turbine-engined variety after a long spell on the piston version, and ran the tanks dry before changing over, a normal practice in the bush, which caused quite a stir among the passengers.

Training is all very well, but don't let it limit your thinking. Also, don't confuse *stereotyping* with *probability*. You can always accept a probability that certain actions will solve a similar problem to one you've had before, but stereotyping implies that the same actions work every time. If you give an engineer a fuel load without planning for it, based on the fact that you always use that load, that is a *decision bias* based on habit (*frequency bias*).

Attitudes & Personality 040 03 05 01

Your *personality* is based on heredity, childhood, upbringing and experience. It could be defined as the *unique organisation of characteristics that determine the typical or standard behaviour of an individual toward the outside world*, although the word *attitude** also refers to the way in which you respond to other people or situations (the product of personal disposition and past experience). Both concern the way we look at life, or the sum total of the meaning and values we give to various events. Another definition of personality is *deep-seated characteristics that constitute the essence of a person*. Such characteristics are **stable** and **resistant to change**, because they have been developed by mid-adolescence.

*Attitude plus *behaviour* results in your *personality*.

Interactive Styles

When people work together to achieve common goals, the way they react together and the resulting harmony can have a significant effect on the outcome of their activities.

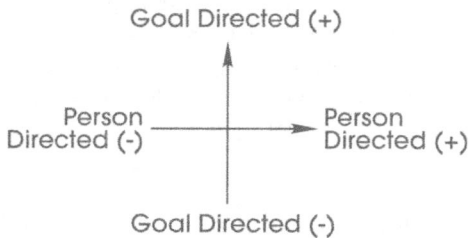

In this respect, people can be *person-oriented* (focussed on keeping the team happy) or *goal-oriented* (focussed on getting the job done, like most pilots, especially EMS ones), after *Blake & Manton's Grid Theory*.

With regard to interactive style:

- G+ will have a keen desire to complete the designated task.
- G- will tend to care little for the job and will not exert themselves unduly.
- P+ will have a concern for the other team members and will consult them as needed.
- P- couldn't care less about other team members.

A person too person-oriented (P+G-) is too democratic and likely to run a *laissez-faire* cockpit (see later), and one too goal-oriented (G+P-) may trample roughshod over peoples' feelings in trying to get the job done (1/9 - too autocratic). On the other hand, a person who scored as 9/1 would be more interested in the task or goal with little interest in people, and would be authoritarian, expecting obedience at all times. A 1/1 (P-G-) person is not interested in the task or the people involved. A 5/5 person would "go along to get along" but would not get the best out of any situation. At the top, a 9/9 person is a team manager who gets the task done by making the best use of individual team members. *The ideal professional pilot is person and goal oriented* (P+G+), being as concerned for the efficient operation of the flight as they are for morale and well being of other team members. However, many pilots are goal oriented*, which adds motivation and pressures (largely self-induced) to "get the job done" to impress customers and peers. Such pilots have an increased tendency to take risks, with a lower tendency to conform and a higher tendency to achieve (*Flight Safety Foundation*).

*EMS pilots typically tend to take too much note of their patient's welfare above fatigue or weather.

The term **power-distance** refers to the nature of the relationship between leaders and subordinates. Subordinates in high power-distance cultures tend to accept and expect autocratic leadership and are generally unwilling to question the acts or decisions of leaders.

Ability

People more readily accept deficiencies in personality and interactive style if they see that you are good at your job, although a perceived high ability has a negative side. It is possible for a P+ G- team member to allow a colleague, who is perceived as competent, to proceed much further on an inappropriate course of action because he feels that the colleague probably knows what he is doing.

Status

A dominant captain will question the actions of a junior first officer, but the opposite will not necessarily be so. The first officer will need to be absolutely sure that the Captain is getting it wrong before he says anything.

In some Middle and Far Eastern cultures, questioning a senior's course of action is unthinkable.

The least status-affected pilots would appear to be Australians, who place much greater emphasis on perceived ability than any other factor.

Role

Roles are partly defined by the expectations associated with a position. Pilots' roles can change, depending on whether they are the Pilot Flying or Pilot Non Flying, and according to their goals. It is very difficult for pilots to take control from others, because it shows a lack of faith in their ability. This reluctance to interfere is particularly noticeable when both pilots have the same status.

Having two Captains on board, with neither sure of who's in charge can be a problem! They may score points off each other, or be too gentlemanly, allowing an accident to happen while each says "After you, Nigel". How do you sort out the mess if you have someone in the left seat who is a First Officer pretending to be a Captain, and someone in the other seat who is a Captain pretending to be a First Officer? Senior commanders may not like taking orders (as co-pilot) from captains with less seniority.

HAZARDOUS ATTITUDES

Your attitudes are the product of *personal disposition* and *past experience*. *Behaviour* is the outward result of attitude and personality combined, and is adaptable. These attitudes have been identified as undesirable for the accident-prone person to possess:

- **Impulsivity**. Doing things without forethought - not stopping to think about what you're doing and ignoring the consequences. For example, a pilot and passengers who are anxious to get to their destination for a business presentation when thunderstorms are reported to be in a line across the route exhibit this attitude when they want to hurry and get going, before things get worse. Apply your training! *Slow down and think first!*

- **Anti-authority.** These people don't like being told what to do. They may either not respect the source of the authority, or are just plain ornery (with a deep source of bottled-up anger). Very often there's nothing wrong with this - if more people had questioned authority, we wouldn't have had half the wars, or we wouldn't get passengers pressurising pilots to do what they shouldn't. However, regulations have a purpose. They allow us to act with little information, since everything is supposed to be predictable, although that doesn't mean that rules should blindly be obeyed - sometimes breaking the rules saves lives. As mentioned, the DC 10 that had an engine fall off during takeoff could have kept flying if the nose had been lowered a little for speed, instead of being set at the "standard" angle of 6°, as per the simulator, which, in this case, stalled the aeroplane. The real anti-authority person is the one who keeps ignoring the Chief Pilot's instructions and feels constrained by rules & regulations. This attitude is demonstrated when the passengers arrive almost an hour late for a flight that requires a reservation and the pilot considers that those rules do not apply. The antidote is to *follow the rules* (mostly!)

- **Invulnerability**. People like this think that nothing untoward can happen to them, so they take more risks, or push the envelope - humility is the antidote, or the realisation that it *could* happen to you. One instructor I know cures people who insist on flying VFR helicopters in IMC conditions by taking them up into cloud (in a twin) and showing them how incapable they are of instrument flying, even though they can do the occasional turn with the foggles on. The point is taken! *Repetitive tasks must be done as if they were new every time, no matter how tedious they may be* - you can guarantee that the one time you don't check for water in fuel, it will be there! You display this trait if, during an operational check of the cabin pressurisation system, you discover that the rate control feature is inoperative and elect to disregard it and depart on the trip because you think you can handle the cabin pressure yourself.

- **Macho** people are afraid of looking small and are always subject to peer pressure, which means they care a lot about what other people think of them - thus, they have a very low opinion of themselves and take unnecessary chances for different reasons than aforementioned Invulnerable people, above. These are typically the high-powered intimidating company executives who have houses in the middle of nowhere with no navaids within miles. Such people may subconsciously put themselves in situations where they push the weather to test their own nerve. This is demonstrated if, while on an IFR flight, you emerge from a cloud to be within 300 feet of a helicopter and fly a little closer, just to show him. The antidote is *don't take chances*, or think you can fix things on the fly. You must stick up for yourself, with management and passengers.

- **Resignation**. The Lord only helps those who help themselves - you've got to do your bit! If you want help to win the lottery, buy the ticket first! The antidote is to realise you *can* make a difference, or to have more confidence in your abilities. *Complacency** would come under this heading.

*One definition of complacency is: "Self-satisfaction accompanied by a loss of awareness of danger." Another is "unjustified self-confidence". Once an activity is routine, you relax and reduce your mental effort, so the dangers are highest with the most skilled people. *Automatic behaviour* is most likely to result in complacency. High performers *remain vigilant, cross-check* their performance and *correct errors* before they are significant.

As you can see when you compare the opposites, each side of each coin above is as bad as the other - we should be somewhere in the middle, with a possible bias towards anti-authority and paranoia (you don't want management or customers putting you in awkward positions, and neither do you want them trying to kill you). The first step in neutralising a hazardous attitude is to recognise hazardous thoughts. Label the thoughts as such and correct them by stating the corresponding antidotes. Pilots must also learn to avoid classic behavioural traps:

- *Peer Pressure.*
- *Mind Set.* Allowing expectations to override reality, or the tendency to see or hear what we expect. Also known as a pre-determined opinion.
- *Get-There-Itis.* A fixation that clouds the vision and impairs judgment, plus disregard for other actions.
- *Duck-Under Syndrome.* Sneaking a peek by going below minima, like descending below MORA.
- *Scud Running.* Going VFR when you should be IFR.
- *Getting Behind the Aircraft.* Allowing events to control your actions, leading to..........
- *Loss of Situational Awareness.*
- *Getting Low On Fuel.*
- *Pushing the Envelope.* Exceeding design limitations in the belief that high performance will cover overestimated flying skills, or relying on manufacturer's fudge factors to go overweight.
- *Poor Planning.*

WHAT TYPE OF PERSON IS A PILOT?

Having decided what product we are selling (safe arrival), we can now talk about the best kind of person to produce it. We certainly have more intelligence than the average car driver. Or do we? Passing exams doesn't mean you're capable of doing a decent job or handling a crisis. There are stupid solicitors, professors, you name it. I have flown with 17,000-hour pilots who I wouldn't trust with a pram, and 1,000-hour types with whom I would trust anything.

I think it's fair to say that the public typically think of pilots (when they think of them at all) as outgoing types, often in the bar and having a lark, an image from all those World War II movies, and if you were cold, hungry, tired, frightened and inexperienced, you would probably behave that way, too, but life today is quite different.

A pilot should be a synthesis of the following headings:

- *Meticulous* - being prepared to do the same thing, the same way, every time, and not get bored, as that's the way you miss things.
- *Forward Thinking* - in the same way that an advanced driver is ready to deal with a corner before going into it, the advanced pilot positions the controls properly.
- *Responsible* - the "responsible position" that you hold as a commander is where you act with minimum direction but are personally responsible for the outcome of your activities. You are responsible for the machine without being directed by any other person in it.
- *Trustworthy* - people must be able to *trust* you - all of aviation runs on it. You trust the previous pilot not to have overstressed the machine, or to really have done 4.3 hours and not 6. Signatures count for a lot, and, by extension, your word.
- *Motivated*. Motivation is a drive to behave in a particular fashion, or an internal force which can affect the quality of performance, although excessive motivation together with high levels of stress will limit your attention-management capabilities. In short, you can get fixated.

WHAT IS COMMON BETWEEN COMPETENT PEOPLE?

Competency is based on the knowledge, skill and ability of an individual.

- *Intelligence*.
- *Personality*. "The sum total of physical, mental, emotional and social characteristics". To be accident prone, you are under- or overconfident. You might also be aggressive, independent, a risk taker, anxious, impersonal, competitive, and invulnerable, with a low stress tolerance, which, when you think about it, are all based on attention-seeking and fear. However, where personality really counts is during interactions with other people; behaviour breeds behaviour.
- *Leadership vs teamwork*. Leadership has been defined as facilitating the movement of a team toward the accomplishment of a task, in this case, the crew and the safe arrival of their passengers. This is a better definition than "Getting somebody to do what you want them to do" which implies a certain amount of manipulation, something more in the realm of management as a scientific process. A Leader, as opposed to a Manager, is a more positive force, inspirational, nurturing and many other words you could probably think of yourself.
- *Personal qualities* to passengers and colleagues.
- *Knowledge*, and the ability to apply it.

FLIGHT DECK MANAGEMENT

What sort of personality do you have? Do you leave everything to the last minute? Are you a placid type, or nervous and anxious? Do you have a low self-image or are you on the arrogant side? Do you succumb to pressure? Are you strong enough to stand up to the Chairman of the Board who insists he must get there NOW? It's better to ask for help and look stupid, than not to ask and risk looking worse. Unfortunately, the ability to laugh at yourself and not feel uncomfortable when you've cocked things up only comes with a certain degree of maturity. As you get older, you accept that mistakes are made; there's no shame in that, even the most experienced pilot couldn't fly at one time - the trick lies in not making the same mistake twice, or at least ensuring that the ones you make aren't the fatal ones. The team spirit of a crew depends on its members respecting each other and striving for the same goals.

The advantages of co-ordination are *redundancy*, *synergy* and *clarification of responsibility*. Co-ordinated co-operation allows for synergy (mutual reinforcement) between the captain and copilot, synchronised actions and the distribution of responsibilities. *Co-action* is a mode of co-operation which recommends working in parallel to achieve one objective.

Groups

Groups behave differently from individuals. That is, a person may carry out different actions in concert with others than they would have done solo - there is strong pressure just to conform when in a group, regardless of what the group gets up to, with a resulting high possibility of riskier decisions. Synergy arises from a group with a high degree of co-operation, where people in the group are motivated to support each other. Thus, groups are more likely than individuals to make decisions concerning risk, known as *risky shift*. In other words, if you put known risk takers together, the chances of them taking risks are amplified out of all proportion. *Conformity* concerns the likelihood of an individual to go along with a group decision, even if it is wrong, and it has been proved that the situations people are in, rather than their native personalities, make them behave as they do (vicious prison guards, etc.). The idea of being integrated into the team, to be recognised as a leader, or to avoid conflicts, may lead to a disposition to agree with decisions made by others. A request is more likely to be complied with if a greater one has previously been denied or a lesser one accepted (*compliance*). Crew decision making is most efficient if the crew members adapt their management styles to cope with the situation. *Cohesion* within a group is a major advantage in times of difficulty but, with too much, groupthink* can have negative results.

*More or less unconscious support from group members.

Military crews often fly together semi-permanently, which means that they become familiar with each others' habits as well as their strengths and weaknesses. However, this is not a practical option in civil aviation and, in a large airline, you will be flying and working with strangers almost all the time. Standard Operating Procedures enable each member of the crew to know what the others are likely to do. Efficient crew co-ordination will therefore depend on effective communications and co-operation.

To improve group decision making:

- Avoid personal judgments, and try to use logic.
- Avoid changing your mind only to reach agreement or avoid conflict. Only support solutions with which you can agree. If a decision has been made, accept it, unless you feel there is a hazard that has not been appreciated by the others.

- Avoid conflict-reducing techniques such as majority votes or middle course strategies.
- View differences of opinion as helpful rather than hindrances in decision making.

The role of CRM & LOFT (*Line Oriented Flight Training*) is to improve group performance!

LEADERS & FOLLOWERS

Leadership has been defined as *any behaviour that moves a group closer to attaining its goals* or, in the words of Henry Kissinger, *the art of taking people where they would not have gone themselves*. It can arise out of personality (as with a born leader), a situation, or group dynamics (interaction). Another definition is *the ability to get work done with and through others, while at the same time winning their confidence, respect, loyalty and willing co-operation*.

A leader's ideas and actions influence the thoughts and behaviour of others. Through example and persuasion, and understanding the goals and desires of the group, the leader is a means of change and influence. The quality of leaders depends on the success of their relationship with the team. A Leader, as opposed to a Manager, or Administrator, is a positive force. Leaders see the big picture, people, empowerment, and opportunity, and expect outperformance. They display emotional resolve, control their actions, think before they act, and accept responsibility for their actions before blaming others. Administrators, on the other hand, see detail, risk, budget and *control*, requiring just compliance with no mistakes.

Unfortunately, many seem to forget that most people know what their job is, and want to do it well, and that it's management's (in this case, the Captain's) function to create the proper environment in which to do it, then get out of the way and let people work things through, although they should not work unsupervised. If you keep checking on them (and therefore distracting them) they will eventually tell you anything just to get you off their backs and you will end up working with false information, and look even worse to your boss. A major part of this is setting a good example - if the Captain turns up neatly dressed and organised, it shows his attitude towards the work in hand, or demonstrates expectations.

An effective leader should perform certain functions, including *regulating information flow, directing activities, motivation* and *decision making*. *Synergy* allows the group to appear greater than the sum of its parts, or crew members, in our case. It's a new name for an old concept - for example, Montgomery wrote this years ago:

> "The real strength of an army is, and must be, far greater than the sum total of its parts; that extra strength is provided by morale, fighting spirit, mutual confidence between the leaders and the led and especially with the high command, the quality of comradeship, and many other intangible spiritual qualities."

You will get the best out of your staff if their goals align with those of your Company, and that happens when you give them the ability to make decisions, or assume responsibilities. Any problems are 99% down to bad leadership. Remember that you're not as concerned with what people get up to when you're there, but what they do when you're not there! It's all about giving people respect, which is reflected in your body language and tone of voice. Experienced doctors make mistakes, but only a very low proportion of them are actually sued. These are usually the ones that didn't treat their patients properly. The real measure of people lies in how they treat their subordinates - management's function is to serve! In short, if you want your staff to look after you, you have to look after them.

There is a difference between *leadership*, which is acquired, and *authority*, which is assigned - although, optimally, they should be combined - the authority of the Captain, or Chief Pilot, should be adequately balanced by assertiveness from the crew. *A follower's skills should be exercised in a supporting role that does not undermine the leader*. Of course, if special skills are held, sometimes the follower becomes the leader!

Monty also wrote this:

> "The acid test of an officer who aspires to high command is his ability to be able to grasp quickly the essentials of a military problem, to decide rapidly what he will do, and then to see that his subordinate commanders get on with the job. Above all, he has got to rid himself of all irrelevant detail: he must concentrate on the essentials, and on those details and only those details which are necessary to the proper carrying out of his plan - trusting his staff to effect all the necessary co-ordination."

Out of the military context, it applies equally to flight crews. Leadership has nothing to do with management!

AUTHORITY GRADIENTS

The term *Authority Gradient* defines situations where pilots and copilots may not communicate effectively in stressful situations if there is a significant difference in their experience, perceived expertise, or authority. There is some risk involved when, for example, a very senior captain is paired with a very junior first officer (check out the Tenerife incident in *Communications,* above).

- The **autocratic cockpit** exists when the Captain imposes decisions without consultation, ignoring the opinions of the other crew members. He rarely delegates, makes general comments which teach nothing, and becomes isolated from the rest of the crew, so can become **overloaded** in an emergency.

Forcefully made suggestions are regarded as either criticism or insubordination, so there is a tense and non-communicative atmosphere in the cockpit.

This scenario can occur when:

- An under-confident Captain uses authority to hide weaknesses. In fact, an under-confident and self-effacing co-pilot who is promoted to captain could be aggressive, if challenged.
- There is a large gap in the seniority and technical ability/knowledge between the Captain and the crew.

- The Captain has a very strong character and the co-pilot is weak and self-effacing.

 The Captain is still the Captain! In an emergency, and when pressed for time, the Captain must give the clear orders needed for immediate reaction.

- A **self-centred** cockpit is one where crew members tend to do their own thing without telling the others what is going on, assuming that they already know. This offers the least synergy and is the **most dangerous**. The most frequent result is that the co-pilot is ignored and may disengage, showing delayed responses and aggression.

- A **laissez-faire** cockpit exists when a passive approach by the captain allows decisions, choices and actions to be made by other crew members, with a major risk of an **inversion of authority.**

This situation tends to arise when the Captain is working with a competent crew. The leadership role may be filled by another crew member, or members may work on their own plans, without keeping the others informed.

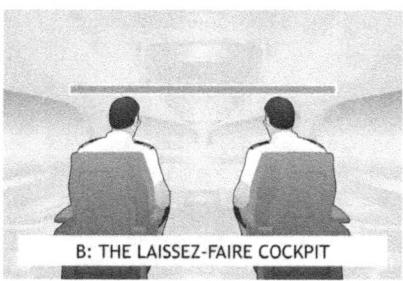
B: THE LAISSEZ-FAIRE COCKPIT

In a parenting context, it amounts to uninvolvement and borders on neglect.

- A **synergistic cockpit** (the ideal) exists when decisions are taken by the Captain with the help and participation of the other crew members (supports *team working*).

C: THE SYNERGYSTIC COCKPIT (THE IDEAL)

Here, a *democratic* and *co-operative* style is characterised by the leader, when conflicts arise, trying to clarify the causes and reasons of the conflict with all persons involved.

Multi-Crew

This term means that more than one person is flying the aircraft, and implies that they should be doing so as a team, which is defined as two or more people working together to perform a task as one. It is *not* the same as two superstars in the same cockpit working with each other!

Early multi-crew aircraft would need as many as five people on the flight deck, but modern ones can get by with two, both of whom can sometimes take on the tasks of the people who are not there now. For example, inertial navigation systems and GPS have reduced the need for a navigator, and FADECs and other automation have eliminated the flight engineer.

However, there are still so many tasks in a typical flight deck environment that they cannot be done effectively by one person, hence the need for *delegation*, which implies that someone must set the tasks to be performed and monitor them. That person is the Captain.

A Captain has full control and authority in the operation of the aircraft, without limitation, over other crew members and their duties during flight time, whether or not valid certificates are held for those functions. With that position comes responsibilities, not least of which is allowing others in the team a chance to develop (i.e. let the P2 get on with the emergency), and the need for humility, as when recognising that someone else may actually be better at doing what's required, and accepting that they may do it in a different way. Also, as mentioned, there is the need to be a leader, and motivate, rather than drive, people - in other words, set tasks and objectives, but not necessarily the way they are done.

Crews take their lead from the Captain.

Positive influences that F/Os have reported include:

- Good attitude towards the job and the company.
- Neat, professional uniform.
- Good briefing skills.
- Encouraging crews to speak up and/or express their opinions.

Negative ones are:

- Quiet demeanour.
- Negative attitude to job and Company.
- Failure to state expectations.
- Negative reaction to input.
- Inability to admit mistakes.

In return, the crew should provide positive support. If you're a First Officer, regardless of what your company says, it's your *job* to monitor the Captain and mention it if you think there's anything wrong, which is not to say you should be on the Captain's back - he is still the Boss and you could become a flight safety hazard.

With proper multi-crew operations, everyone should take the responsibility for the work of the team as a whole. Thus, any problems become *crew problems*.

The industry standard for multi-crew operations is to designate a *Pilot Flying* (PF), who controls the aircraft, and a Pilot Not Flying

(PNF), who handles other crew duties related to radio communications, checklist management, and FMS operation. Another function is monitoring, which is why some companies call him the *Pilot Monitoring* (PM). This division of duties is designed to optimize crew efficiency, prevent task saturation, and avoid confusion regarding in-flight responsibilities.

During an emergency, it is generally accepted that the captain should try to reduce information processing demands by delegating routine tasks to the first officer.

Thus, the multi-crew concept is meant to provide a higher level of safety by:

- reducing the workload by sharing tasks (a governor runaway on the Bell 212 requires the co-ordinated efforts of two people handling the throttles to be done properly).
- allowing better quality decisions, because actions should be discussed.
- allowing better error management by increasing situational awareness.

In order to do this properly, certain things need to be established, namely, are you a group of individuals working together or a fully functioning team? There is a subtle difference! These stages can turn one into the other:

- *Inclusion*, where individuals feel they are part of a team, and are motivated to do their best.
- *Control* - who is exerting it, and how?
- *Trust*, which must be achieved as quickly as possible. Crew members need good reason to justify their trust in the leader and each other.

All the above can be promoted with good crew briefings, during which you can show that you are comfortable in authority and can promote communication, and are prepared for the day's activities, establishing roles without making the boundaries too rigid. The first briefing during the assembly time before a trip is when the group decides in very short order how difficult each other will be to work with, particularly the Captain! For example, if the Captain decides to ignore certain procedures, or even cut them out altogether (doing it "his" way), the rest of the crew will be wondering what else will be ignored. A quick, curt briefing is likely to set up barriers, as is one that is at odds with subsequent actions.

Briefings should be short and precise (less than 10 items), and standard, so they can be *understood* and *reused* in similar situations. The usual ones include:

- **Crew Briefing**, before the flight, which is an opportunity for its members to knit together when they first meet. One trick I use when meeting lots of new students for the first time (I used to do seminars for computer technicians) is to catch them having their first coffee, give one of them a soft ball and get them to throw it amongst themselves for a short time. It's a great ice-breaker, and soon they are all chatting amongst themselves. It makes them less afraid of talking in the classroom and asking questions - plus, they are more likely to get involved, because the last thing you want is puddings sitting there. It applies to flight crews, too.

- **Departure**, during which routes are discussed
- **Pre-takeoff**, covering actions in emergencies
- **Approach**, routes and emergencies - for example, what to do if the glideslope goes out - do you carry on as a localiser only approach, or go around?

The latter three generally involve only the pilots.

Remember that briefings pull information out of long term memory and help to maintain situational awareness.

CHECKLISTS

These will have been written for normal and abnormal situations. The latter are specific events, with their own checklists, which means that sometimes you have to be creative and try to combine them if you have multiple emergencies. An abnormal situation should be positively identified before any action is taken, *after the aircraft is under control*. The crew member identifying it should call it out, then the PF should call for the appropriate checklist (not just "the checklist"!) Items should be called by the PM (or PNF), and the PF should respond if and when it is understood. To use them properly, *you need to be aware of what they are trying to achieve*. Long checklists should be subdivided, and there should be redundancies to cover critical points - the most important items should be at the beginning. Checklists should not be used with performing other actions.

Assertiveness

The feeling of being in control, with resultant self-esteem, has health implications - a study of civil servants found that the death rate of those in lower status jobs was three times higher.

Everybody has a personal space around them, one which includes thoughts and attitudes, and culture. In other words, maintaining an appropriate emotional distance is just as important as maintaining a physical one. You do this by not putting people down, or asking too many questions, offering unwanted advice, swamping them with affection, etc. In short, allowing somebody, including yourself, to be their own person. To see what I mean about personal space, sit down next to someone on a park bench. There will be a point beyond which you do not feel comfortable going past. Only when another person sits on the bench do you feel able to bunch up closer (there is also a respectful distance behind cars, hence people getting wound up when you get too close behind them).

Thus, there are many opportunities for others to invade your space, and you often have to defend it. This is known as being *assertive*, which should not be confused with being *aggressive* - assertion is a way of defending your space non-destructively - whether you do this aggressively is up to you! It is a positive and productive expression of yourself. People who allow others to invade their space, on the other hand, are *submissive*, or passive, which brings less responsibility and conflict, of course, and usually brings more approval, but many people use it as a form of control. Nevertheless, the most appropriate role for a Captain is often the submissive one, to get the job done. Being assertive lies between being aggressive or passive. If you assert yourself wrongly, you will generate a defensive response from the other person, and a request to reorganise two short words into a well-known phrase or saying. In other words, if you push, you will get pushed back, because the other person will not want to admit that they have affected your life, or are wrong. One pilot took off in a helicopter in bad weather, ignoring his wife who asked him not to take their son (he didn't wish to appear as if he was listening to what she said). The helicopter crashed into the side of a hill and killed them both.

This is where a sympathetic approach from you will help - certainly allowing enough time for the other person to reply, and to listen - then make your point again. It may take more than ten attempts to get your message across.

"The pilot who masters the simple engineering principles of his aircraft, who understands the why behind the reaction - immediately elevates himself to a new level of competence and safety"

Airframes

This section should be read in conjunction with *Principles Of Flight*, as some of the items required by the syllabus are covered there. Engineering limits for aircraft are lower than would normally be the case for, say, road or rail transport, due to weight and performance considerations, which is why you must keep within the limitations imposed by the flight manual or pilot's operating handbook.

The *airframe* is the complete structure of an aircraft, without the engines and instruments. It must be as light and as strong as possible to cope with the stresses found in flight, such as *compression, tension, torsion, shearing* and *bending*, all of which may be suffered at once during landings.

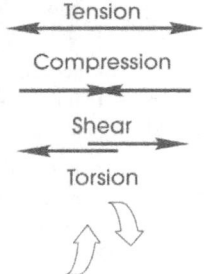

Modern airliners fly more hours in one year than some older aircraft did in their lifetimes. Their airframes have to take the strains of turbulence, pressurisation, take-off and landing, often several times a day, not to mention extremes of temperature - 30 minutes after taking off from Dubai, for example, an aircraft will be several degrees below freezing. Aluminium-copper alloys stand up to this kind of treatment best, while highly stressed parts such as the landing gear are made of forged steel.

FORCES INVOLVED

When it is stretched, a material is *in tension*, and its ability to withstand the tension is a measure of its *tensile strength*. When the material is squeezed, it is subject to *compression*, and it has a *compressive strength*. Torsion is a twisting force. If one face of a material is forced to slide against another, it is *in shear* - for example, in a stressed skin pressurised aircraft, the rivets holding the fuselage together are under shear loads.

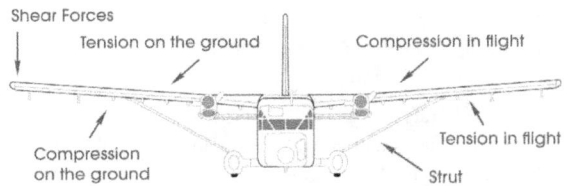

A structural member subjected to bending stresses is a *beam*, one subject to compression is a *strut* and one under tension is a *tie*. A beam supported at both ends, with a load at the centre, has its top in compression, its bottom in tension, with a shear at each end trying to slice it in half.

The maximum bending moments are underneath the load.

If the beam is supported at one end, as a wing may be when the aircraft is on the ground, the tension is at the top, the compression at the bottom, and only one end, the supported end, has a shear force. This is a *cantilever* - a cantilever wing containing fuel has its highest bending moments at the root, or the support, which is why they taper towards the tips. Bending loads from lift are carried by the upper and lower skin surfaces and the spar(s).

A fuselage is an example - when there is a download from the tail, which is needed to keep the nose up, it will act as a cantilever around the centre of gravity, which is one reason why correct loading is important. Sometimes fuel is kept in the stabiliser to stop this.

 Beams, struts and ties can change places, depending on the loads applied to them. For example, the (braced) wing strut in the aeroplane shown above is only a strut when it is on the ground. In flight, it becomes a tie, because the presence of lift reverses the loads.

Air loads are therefore opposite to those on the ground and the greatest stress will be during wing loading reversal on take-off and landing. These reversals can result in metal fatigue and structural failure from normal flight manoeuvres, plus turbulence and landing, etc., but threats to structural integrity also include overstressing, and operational hazards, such as bird strikes and corrosion. All are discussed later, under *Fatigue and Stress*, and in *Principles Of Flight* (the V-n diagram).

Struts are often hollow tubes, for lightness, because the centre part of one subject to compression is in what is called the **neutral plane,** being neither in tension nor compression, so the material there can be removed and made to serve a more useful purpose elsewhere. Unless struts are extremely short, they will tend to bend under load before failure occurs, so long struts are like cantilever beams when they have a load on them, with one side in compression and the other in tension.

Ties are often cables or wires, rather than solid tubes if they are only subject to tension, or tensile loads.

CLASSIFICATION OF STRUCTURES

The components inside an aircraft are *structural* or *non-structural*.

Structural components transfer loads and forces from one location to another, or absorb forces. Naturally, they must be strong enough to cope without failing or distortion (wings are prone to twisting, as is the fuselage when the control surfaces are moved, so they must be able to flex). They include wing spars, ribs, the fuselage, bulkheads etc. Non-structural components include doors, and some types of panel.

© Phil Croucher, 2018   EASA Professional Pilot Studies   2-1

- **Primary** structures are the most important. Failure here may cause structural collapse, loss of control or power, or serious injuries because stressed parts are not included in the definition.
- **Secondary** structures are parts of the airframe that could be primary but which have a reserve of strength to cope with stress.
- **Tertiary** structures are other parts that are lightly stressed or unstressed. Damage here does not normally affect safety.

FATIGUE & STRESS

Maintaining structural integrity is important for flight safety, aside from reducing maintenance and minimising costs. The statistical probability of losing an aircraft through structural failure should not exceed 0.001. The allowable average failure probability per flight hour for:

- **Minor failures** should be between 10^{-3} and 10^{-5} (probable). The worst effect would be a slight increase in crew workload and a slight reduction in functionality or safety margins (for the aeroplane), with physical discomfort for passengers.
- **Major failures** should be between 10^{-5} and 10^{-7} (remote probability), involving physical discomfort or a significant increase in workload for the crew, and a significant reduction in functionality or safety margins for the aircraft, plus physical distress, and maybe injuries for everyone else.
- **Hazardous failures** should be between 10^{-7} and 10^{-9} (extremely remote). These mean large reductions in functionality or safety margins, possibly serious or fatal injuries to a small number of passengers and crew, but mainly physical distress or excessive workload, with an impaired ability to perform any tasks.
- **Catastrophic failures** should be less than 10^{-9} (extremely improbable). These involve multiple passenger fatalities, and fatalities or incapacitation for the crew. The aircraft itself would be destroyed.

Design Philosophy

This will determine the life of an airframe, and a lot depends on what it is designed to do. An airliner, for example, will be used for relatively predictable flights but, even then, one designed for long distance travel cannot simply be used for short haul flights at higher frequencies because the lifetime of the components will be based on a predetermined spectrum of loading. The fatigue life of such a fuselage is based on pressurisation cycles, and repetitive cycles induce **hoop stresses** which can cause fatigue cracks. An executive aircraft, on the other hand, may have to deal with many situations. The HS 125 was designed to last for 20 years, based on 500 flights per year.

WEIGHTS & MASSES

The greater the mass of an aircraft, the greater the structural loads on it, especially for the wing roots and landing gear.

The loads on an airframe in steady flight are calculated and multiplied by a *load factor* (see *Principles of Flight*). How high the load factor must be mostly depends on how the aircraft is handled, or its task. A change of one unit in the load factor means a 1% change in the weight of the aircraft, so one designed for aerobatics will be more heavily built than one for normal duties, because it has to withstand higher stresses.

The relationship between the strength needed to carry a load (*Design Limit Load*) and ultimate strength (*Design Ultimate Load*) is the *factor of safety* or, put another way, the ratio of the ultimate load to the limit load, which is 1.5 for aircraft structures. Put yet another way, the DLL refers to the maximum load value of repeated stress during normal operations and the DUL is the DLL increased by a "safety factor" of 50% to ensure that there is enough strength for emergencies like heavy landings.

 Use of the term *safety factor* does not necessarily mean that it is safe to enter the area where structural damage may occur!

Thus, a part that should have a normal working load of 100 lbs must be strong enough to carry at least 150 lbs or, in other words, the structure must remain substantially intact after experiencing the DLL multiplied by 1.5.

- The **Maximum Zero Fuel Mass** is the weight of an aircraft, above which any increase in weight must consist entirely of fuel. It stops the wings from being stressed when there is too much weight in the cabin if the fuel tanks are in the wings. Unlike other weight limitations, the MZFW is not associated with handling or performance.
- The **Maximum Structural Take-off Mass** is the maximum permissible total mass at the start of the take-off run. The **Performance Limited Take-off Mass** takes into consideration any limitations for performance reasons (it might be a hot day). The **Regulated Take-off Mass** is the lowest of the two.
- Landing weights in transport aircraft are typically much smaller than take-off weights. The **Maximum Landing Mass** helps prevent the impact with the ground being transmitted through the undercarriage to the rest of the aircraft. This can only happen if the weight is within limits. This weight may very well be restricted performance-wise in a similar way to Take-off Mass, and could equally be a factor in further reducing your payload at the *start* of a flight. It's actually the Zero Fuel Mass, plus reserve and alternate fuel.

The weight of an aircraft also affects its performance, and the weight distribution affects its flying characteristics and stability, discussed later in the relevant sections.

SAFE LIFE

The reliability of a system is determined by the failure rate of the worst components of which it is made, and their service history. *Infant failures* are caused by weak components that are either badly made or not inspected properly. They require a long burn in period, after which they enter a *normal life period*, during which there should be relatively few failures, and random at that. The problem is that random errors cannot be avoided, even with the best maintenance, and neither can the time they occur be predicted, so routines (involving statistics) are adopted to minimise random failures.

- **Hard Time Maintenance** is used when the known deterioration of an item is limited to an acceptable level by maintenance at certain time periods.
- **On-condition Maintenance** is a preventive process in which an item is monitored continuously or at specified periods, without disassembly. Its performance is compared against a standard to see if it can stay in service. In other words, as long as the item meets the required standards (remains within limits), it will not need maintenance.

 The Mean Time To Failure (MTTF) does NOT indicate the maximum time a component can be used. A component with an MTTF of 3000 hours just means a 99.9% certainty of it surviving its normal life time without failure

Otherwise, the safe life principle is based on the replacement of parts after a given number of cycles or flight hours. Its length may depend on such items as:

- the **number of landings**.
- **hours flown** (components wear out).
- **calendar time**. Some engines have 3000 hours between overhauls, and a date limitation.
- **cycles**, which are usually more relevant with pressurised aircraft.

FAIL-SAFE

Fail-safe means that no one part of a system takes the complete load, as there are multiple paths to absorb it (and a weight penalty), meaning that there are parallel structural paths. The idea is that the limit load can be met even if an element fails. The concept came in with the DC-2 and DC-3, which suddenly started flying upwards of 40,000 hours per airframe, where a typical total was previously about 6,000. The Comet, which had fatigue round its windows, was also a factor in its introduction.

Flight controls and electrical systems use the same concept to provide a reliable service, especially autopilots, but one alternative is to use one system and have a backup switch in immediately in case of a failure.

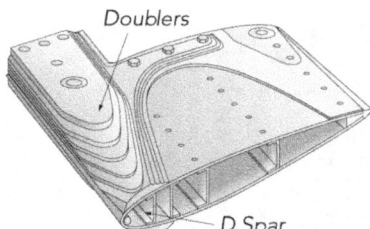

Because the remaining structure can withstand reasonable loads without failure, there is some sort of redundancy*, where nearby components can accept any loads placed on failed components. For example, a spar may have doublers (see picture above), so that cracks can be tolerated for a short while, say up to the next service inspection, or there could be four hydraulic systems (as with the 747).

*Any structural failure in a fail-safe system immediately removes the redundancy, which must be replaced with a regular inspections to maintain safety (inspect-safe) so that problems can be detected before they become critical.

DAMAGE TOLERANCE

Damage tolerance accepts that production flaws might exist, and they are detected and fixed before they become critical. It does not have the redundancy of fail-safe. Instead, loads are spread over a wider area. In theory, the strain is more bearable and cracks do not start in the first place. In addition, the structure will be lighter.

Strains & Stresses

Force is the product of mass multiplied by acceleration. As the mass of an aircraft in flight may be regarded as more or less constant (except for fuel usage, which will be relatively small), the forces encountered in flight may simply be expressed in terms of acceleration, with the largest changes taking place in the vertical axis. Accelerations can be measured with........

ACCELEROMETERS

An accelerometer is a device that measures acceleration forces, which may be static, like gravity, or dynamic, like those that move or vibrate the accelerometer. A basic one could consist of a mass attached to springs, restrained by a motor (*torquer*).

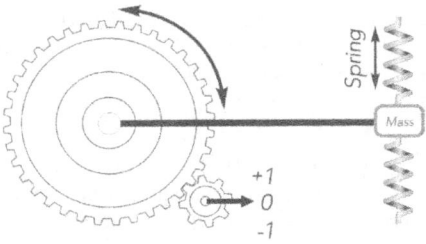

Movement of the mass stretches one spring and contracts the other, which moves the pointer over a scale calibrated in g units (it should read +1 in straight and level flight).

A positive acceleration will move the mass downwards, and a negative one will move it upwards. The displacement of the springs is directly proportional to the accelerating and decelerating forces, and the electrical current needed to return everything to rest after moving is a measure of the acceleration. Others involve E & I bars.

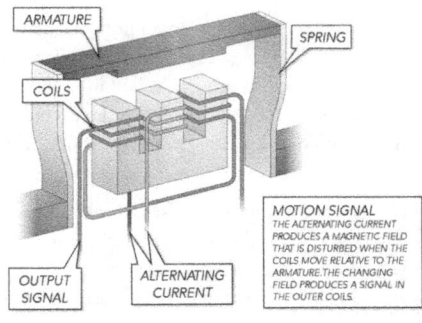

There are also electrical types that use the piezoelectric effect, where crystal structures that get stressed by accelerative forces can generate a voltage. You could also sense changes in capacitance - two capacitors next to each other would have a certain amount between them. If one is moved by an accelerative force, the value will change. Convert that to voltage, and you have an accelerometer.

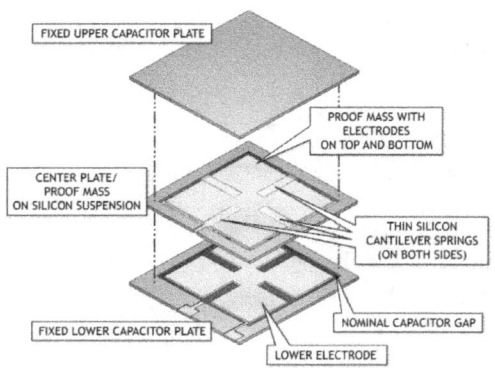

A typical modern use of this type would be to rotate the screen automatically in a mobile phone.

Such *Micro Electro-Mechanical Systems* (MEMS) are used in solid state accelerometers, rate sensor gyroscopes and magnetometers. Most use a tuning fork configuration, where two masses oscillate and move constantly in opposite directions.

STRENGTH

The strength of a material lies in its ability to resist the application of a force without breaking. The general term for the force of attraction between molecules (of the same kind) is *cohesion* (that between molecules of different kinds is *adhesion*). It is a short-range force, and if you break something, gas molecules attaching to the surfaces of broken parts stop them rejoining.

The tensile strength of a material depends on its cohesion. It is the maximum amount of tensile stress that a material can be subjected to before it fails, the definition of failure varying according to the material and design philosophy. The *Yield Strength* is stress that a material can withstand without permanent deformation. Where this is not clear (ductile* metals other than steel have no defined yield point) it is usually when permanent deformation of 0.2% of the original dimension results.

*If a metal rod can be drawn through a small hole and turned into a wire, it is *ductile* (one gram of platinum can stretch to nearly 600 km!) Metals that can be hammered or rolled into sheets, on the other hand, are *malleable*. In both processes, the metal's cohesion is strong enough to allow it to hold together during a shape change.

An object's ability to return to its original size or shape when stress forces are removed is called *elasticity*, typically encountered with operations within the normal flight envelope. For example, the extension of a spring is proportional to the force stretching it, up to a point. When a substance is on the verge of permanent change, it has reached its *elastic limit*. A rubber band usually returns to its original shape after being stretched but, if it is overstretched, will be unable to (the strain that remains is called *permanent set*). This can also happen to metals used in aircraft, and is to do with Hooke's Law, which concerns elastic behaviour. It can be demonstrated by the gradient of a straight line on a graph. If it is steep, the spring is stiff, and *vice versa*.

Once the elastic limit of a substance has been reached, it will be permanently deformed, as might happen outside the normal flight envelope. This is *plastic* behaviour, and will be shown on the straight line graph mentioned above by a smooth curve after the elastic limit is reached. During elastic behaviour, the particles in a material are pulled apart a little. In plastic behaviour, they slide past each other and change the structure of the material.

As the elastic limit of a material is reached at a lower load than its ultimate strength (the maximum stress a material can withstand), a member used in an aircraft must be stronger than the normal working load.

Two terms describe the elastic properties of a substance:

STRESS

When comparing materials, we are less concerned with the amount of force than the force per unit area, which is defined by the term *stress*, and expressed like this:

$$\text{Stress} = \frac{\text{Force}}{\text{Area}}$$

The units of stress are pascals, and 1 pascal is equal to 1 newton per square metre (1 N/m^2).

Stress (tensile, compressive or shear) arises from the internal forces in a body that resist external loads, as a tendency to recover the original shape. It is an internal force that opposes an external one. If too much stress is applied, the strength of the material may be exceeded and plasticity may take place before the item breaks (although the plastic region may be quite small). The stress needed to produce the first signs of plastic strain is the *yield stress*. *Direct* stress is at right angles to the line of action of the external forces, as with tension or compression. Shear stresses do not qualify because the forces concerned are applied in the same plane as the area being stressed.

STRAIN

Strain is the distortion caused in a body by the stress forces acting on it, from extension, contraction, and shear or slide. The change in dimensions is expressed as a percentage of the original dimensions:

$$\text{Strain} = \frac{\text{Change in length}}{\text{Original length}}$$

Hooke's Law says that, for an elastic material, stress is proportional to strain, or, *within the elastic limit of a material, any change in shape is directly proportional to the applied force producing it.* However, the rubber band's ability to resume its shape also depends on a relatively short time of stretching so, even if the amount of stretching is within limits, if it's done for a long time, deformation could still take place. This elongation is also called *creep*, which is relevant with turbine blades. It can be affected by the material used, the load applied, the duration of stress and the temperature, since warmth can make material more pliable. A sudden increase in strain is called *shock loading*.

Metal Fatigue

Applying a load to a metal produces a stress, measured from the load itself divided by the cross-sectional area. *Ultimate stress* is where the metal will fracture, after applying a single load, but repeated loads *well below* the level of ultimate stress will eventually have a similar effect, called *metal fatigue*. Because an aircraft has to be as light as possible, and the metal of which it is made has to work harder, it will be subject to *alternating loads* and *load reversals*. Essentially, if a material is continuously loaded and unloaded, it will eventually break.

Metal fatigue is the *initiation and propagation of microscopic cracks, due to the slippage of atomic planes within a metal component*. It occurs from the repeated application of stress and can be caused by flight and landing loads, and vibrations. However, an applied load only needs to be around 30% of the ultimate load or stress for a fatigue crack to occur, although it is true that a load this small must be applied many thousands of times to become significant.

 These fatigue cycles are cumulative and non-reversible throughout the life of a component! This is why the total number of hours in service, as opposed to time since new, is so important. The most significant factors include:

- the type of operation.
- the magnitude and frequency of loads.
- the quality of the material.

With metal, cracks almost always start on the surface of a structure that has anything out of the ordinary, such as sharp corners, fastener holes* or just discontinuity of shape. With composite materials, fatigue is not a consideration at stress cycles around 80% of ultimate stress, because the individual elements tend to fail rather than the structure itself. In this case, cracks will not appear, but the structure will weaken gradually, unlike metal, which is sudden.

*The points where fasteners are used to join parts together will be even more exposed. The local stress at any round hole in a sheet of metal under tension is 3 times the average. Fatigue cracks have three stages - *initiation*, *growth* and *final fracture*. Once started, corrosion helps a crack grow faster. A small hole is usually drilled at the end of a crack to stop it spreading (called *stop drilling*). Weak points such as holes and joins can be reduced by using adhesives instead of rivets and bolts and by casting wing skins in large panels.

GOLDEN RULES

Metal fatigue can now be controlled and predicted, and airworthiness can be extended if some rules are followed:

- Maintain accurate records.
- Keep within Flight Manual limitations.
- Do not use the wrong parts.
- Report all exceedances.

Corrosion

You can get corrosion when dissimilar metals are used together and one of them breaks down into various compounds, either by chemical or electrolytic action, or movement, such as fretting, stress or erosion.

When a steel bolt is used to hold an aluminium panel together, for example, you will get galvanic corrosion after moisture or some other electrically conductive substance acts as an electrolyte to form a "battery". When this occurs the aluminium, which is an anode, deteriorates because it receives metal ions from the steel bolt, or the cathode (see *Electricity & Magnetism*). In this case, you would see a white, powdery surface. This effect worsens with increased temperature and humidity, so the worst thing you can do with a wet aircraft in this respect is put it into a warm hangar (the same goes for your car, which is made up of panels dissimilar enough to cause a reaction when they get wet. Salt from the road conducts electricity better and only make things worse). This is one reason for electrical bonding between aircraft surfaces.

Engineers can prevent such corrosion with zinc-based paints, or by using a suitable jointing compound, or electrically isolating the panels. For example, if your battery is held against an aluminium firewall with a steel bracket, and the battery leaks, corrosion will start as soon as the battery's electrolyte meets the two metals, so a barrier between them will be cheap preventive medicine. Also, copper and cadmium are relatively close in terms of electrical potential, so steel terminals should be cadmium plated if you want to use them with copper cabling. On the other hand, aluminium and magnesium will corrode easily because they are far apart electrically.

Oxidation is the loss of at least one electron when two or more substances interact, which may or may not include oxygen. Oxygen is actually very caustic - with iron, for example, the oxygen creates a slow burning process, which results in rust. With copper, the same process results in a greenish layer of copper oxide. The metal itself is not weakened by oxidation, but the surface develops a patina after exposure to air and water. Outside paint on aircraft is constantly exposed to them. If it is not protected (say by a wax coating or polyurethane), the oxygen molecules in the air will eventually start interacting with the paint and the finish will get very dull.

Destructive oxidation cannot occur if the oxygen cannot penetrate a surface to reach the free radicals it craves.

STRESS CORROSION CRACKING (SCC)

This is the unexpected sudden failure of normally ductile metals subjected to tensile stress in a corrosive environment, especially metals at higher temperatures.

SCC is highly chemically specific, in that certain alloys will suffer from it only when exposed to a small number of chemical environments. The one that causes SCC for any alloy is often one which would normally have a mild corrosive effect. Hence, metal parts with severe SCC can look bright and shiny, yet have microscopic cracks. This makes it easy for SCC to go undetected before a failure.

SCC often progresses rapidly, and is more common among alloys than pure metals. The specific environment is of crucial importance, and only very small concentrations of certain highly active chemicals are needed to produce catastrophic cracking, often leading to devastating and unexpected failure.

Types Of Aeroplane

Aeroplanes are either low, or high wing. The idea behind low wings is to protect the crew in a crash, since they should hit the ground first. They also allow for shorter (and therefore lighter) retractable landing gear.

Aeroplanes can be single- or multi-engined, with fixed or retractable undercarriages, if they are landplanes, skis if they land on snow, and floats for water. *Monoplanes* have one pair of wings, and *biplanes* have two.

The Fuselage

The fuselage is where the pilot, passengers and cargo are placed, and to which any wings, tailplanes, and engines are attached. Its design is a compromise between the need to protect its occupants and to be aerodynamically shaped.

Older aircraft are made of a *truss construction**, or *frame and skin*, where aluminium or steel tubing is joined in a series of triangular shapes:

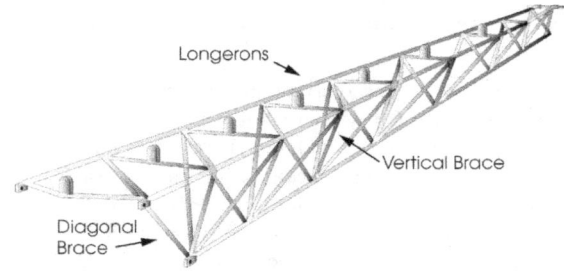

*Now mainly used for light training aircraft.

The idea is that the compression and tension stresses that arise from the bending loads that a fuselage is subjected to are alternately carried by the braces. When they are reversed, the loadings are reversed, so the stresses are spread evenly over the whole structure, avoiding their concentration at any one point.

The tubing might be covered with thin metal or fabric, which will act merely as a cover, making no contribution towards the strength of the assembly. Instead, each part is made strong enough to take a certain load (mostly tension or compression) by itself. Unfortunately, this makes them heavy - another disadvantage is that the crossbracing takes up space and leaves less room for seats, etc.

Having said that, some aircraft, such as Cessnas, use a steel truss construction for the forward part of the fuselage and semi-monocoque for the rear fuselage and tail cone.

An egg is a good example of a monocoque structure, which is handy, as *cocque* is French for *eggshell*. Monocoque therefore means *single shell*. Aside from saving weight, the big advantage of monocoque is that it leaves more space inside the aircraft, although it suits long, narrow fuselages best, because large diameter aircraft would require a thick skin, which would weigh too much - older flying boats, made of wood, were among the earliest examples. Not only that, to get passengers in, we have to punch holes in it, which weakens the structure.

To provide the strength needed, internal bracing is still needed to support the openings required.

Semi-monocoque is a compromise which uses longerons and (weaker) stringers to keep a light framework of vertical formers and bulkheads apart, and absorb the tensile and compression stresses from bending, while any torsional stress is taken up by the skin. In other words, most of the applied stresses are dissipated by the internal components, and a small percentage is absorbed by the skin. The internal structure of such components (like wings) can therefore be made weaker, and lighter.

The formers maintain the shape of the fuselage, and stringers stiffen the metal and stop it from buckling. Longerons take the main stresses. Thus, semi-monocoque construction is better able to sustain damage.

Bulkheads are similar to formers, but are placed at either end of a fuselage, or a compartment, or are designed to transmit concentrated loads. Frames are also vertical members, but are designed to maintain rigidity. A *firewall* can be a bulkhead, or a fireproof partition that separates an engine compartment from the cabin or from another engine. Engine compartment decking and firewalls are typically made of stainless steel or titanium sheeting.

This *stressed skin* approach (used with wings) uses high strength magnesium or aluminium alloys (i.e. Duralumin) to cope with normal bending and tangent stresses, and torsional moments.

Longerons and stringers are also attachment points for the skin. Methods of attachment include:

- **Riveting**, but the holes drilled for the rivets can produce stress points of their own (aluminium alloy rivets are light, small and strong *in shear*). The condition of the covering paint is a good indication of the state of the rivet underneath - black stuff is powder from *fretting* against the aircraft skin. Loose rivets can indicate excessive vibration. On modern aircraft, large parts are machined from single blocks of metal which are bonded together to produce a structure with even stress levels overall. Although this is expensive, large savings can be made.
- **Welding**
- **Bolting**
- **Pinning**
- **Adhesives** (bonding), as with composite materials

Pressurised aircraft need a more robust structure because the process creates hoop or circumferential stresses*. Holes must be sealed against leakage and arrangements must be made to get rid of various liquids, such as condensation. As doors and access panels may well be part of the aircraft structure, wide bodied aircraft also need a way of rapidly equalising pressures above and below the floor in case one comes off, otherwise the airframe could become distorted.

*The internal pressures will make the pressure vessel inside the fuselage expand and contract, which will create a tensile load at its circumference. There will also be stress longitudinally against the bulkheads at each end.

The fuselages of large transport aircraft are usually of semi-monocoque construction and use a number of sections joined end-to-end. The simplest format comprises a streamlined nose section that includes the flight deck, a parallel-sided cylindrical cabin section to which the wings are attached, and a tapered tail section carrying the empennage.

Longitudinal strength and rigidity may be supplemented by a **keel beam** that runs along the fuselage centreline through the wing centre section area, as with the L 1011.

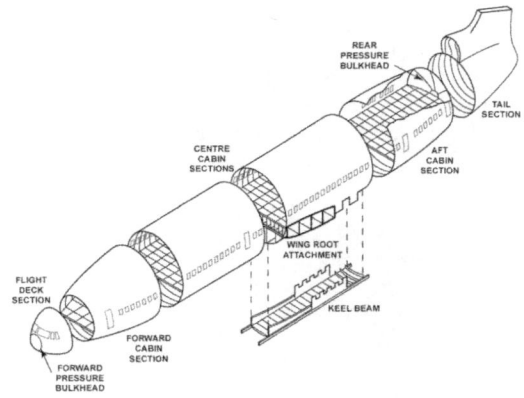

THE AREA RULE

This states that the area of a cross section (of a fuselage) should increase and decrease gradually either side of a maximum point. Adding wings to a fuselage increases the cross sectional area rather suddenly, so narrowing the fuselage where the wings and tail assembly attach to it to revert back to a gradual increase in cross section should reduce **wave drag**.

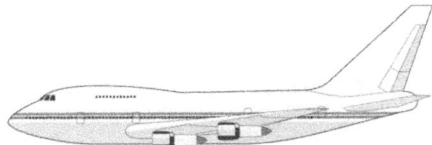

Boeing used the principle with the hump on the 747 which contains the cockpit and the upper passenger deck. It increases the cross-sectional area of the forward fuselage and smooths the volume distribution over the whole length of the aeroplane. By delaying the onset of wave drag, this allows a higher cruise speed than would normally be expected for such a large aircraft.

Materials Used

To be commercially viable, an aircraft must be light, yet strong enough to cope with the forces of flight. For this purpose, materials such as wood, fabric and carbon fibre are used, plus two types of metal - ferrous and non-ferrous. As you would expect, ferrous metals have something to do with iron, but many pure metals cannot be used by themselves. As iron is a weak metal, it must be mixed with carbon to turn it into steel, which still must be mixed with something else to get the characteristics needed. Most steels used in aircraft are alloy steels which have good fatigue properties, so they are used where strength is required, such as with landing gear supports. As a further example, aluminium is a third of the weight of steel, but it has only a third of the strength. Aluminium alloys are therefore light, easily machined and have good wear resistance. *Duralumin* (AL2024) is a brand name for a mix of aluminium, magnesium, manganese and copper (4%) which is hard to weld but has good thermal conductivity, hence its use with engine cylinders. As it loses strength in welding, a laminated form called AlClad may be used instead, which has thin layers of pure aluminium over a strong Duralumin core. Such copper based alloys are used instead of earlier zinc based ones because they are less likely to crack, if at all. In larger aircraft, steel and titanium alloys may be used for major load-bearing components.

Titanium alloys are light, corrosion and temperature resistant, with high structural strength, but are brittle and difficult to work as they need very sharp and special tools.

COMPOSITES

To meet the strength required for modern flight, modern construction materials are often designed at the molecule level. A filament of carbon (or graphite) can be spun out for more than a kilometre, finer than a human hair, and yet have 20 times the strength of metal. Secondary and non-load bearing components can be made from fibreglass reinforced plastic, Kevlar^{TM}, graphite-based compounds and other composite materials. Cabin floors, for example, are often made from an aluminium and fibreglass honeycomb sandwiched between aluminium sheeting, described below.

A "composite" is a material with two or more distinct constituents. Although concrete fits the description, in aviation, the word is taken to mean fibres embedded in some sort of resin (e.g. epoxy), and they are very strong in tension (Kevlar is one example, but so are carbon and glass - a carbon composite is much lighter and six times stiffer than aluminium). They can also be moulded into shapes consistent with the load, plus they are lighter, more flexible and resistant to corrosion and heat.

However, composites can be eroded easily by hail or sand, and may be difficult to repair. Not being electrically conductive, they also need arrangements for bonding, and for lightning conduction. The big difference from metal is that a composite has a more gradual deterioration profile.

There are two main classes of synthetic resin used:

- **Thermoplastics**, which soften when heated and *vice versa*.
- **Thermosetting resins**, which, with heat and a hardener, cure when heated, and stay that way (epoxy resin, etc.)

Laminated materials are produced from thermosetting resins and reinforcing materials, such as carbon fibres, which are laid out as a mat or in woven form (the direction depends on the loads to be transmitted), then impregnated with the basic resin. Several layers are stacked, then placed in a mould and cured.

When bulk is needed, a **honeycomb construction** helps keep things light. This is a framework made of a light core material (typically short hexagonal tubes) within metal or laminate sheeting. It is commonly used in cabin floors.

Laminated honeycombs have a core made of metal, glasscloth or Nomex, each face of which goes against one or more impregnated layers. The assembly is then oven cured. *Sandwich structural parts need additional provisions to carry concentrated loads.*

Otherwise, they are good for loads involving compression.

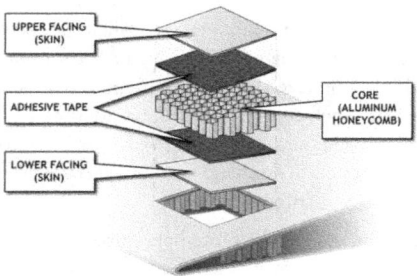

Wings, Etc

The forces involved in flight are trying to pull the wings off the fuselage, or at least deform them. The ailerons, for example, can apply a twisting force about the lateral centreline, similar to the feathering of a propeller. If a wing twists in one direction, and can offload the cause of the twist, it should return to its original position. This cycle (together with gusts) can result in **fluttering** (see *Flying Controls*) that produces high levels of stress inside.

Wings must therefore be as rigid (and as flexible) as possible, as any twisting can change their characteristics, so they are very rarely of monocoque construction (although struts and cables can help). The upward bending forces are mostly concentrated at the root, where they are fixed to the fuselage, which is why the strength of the wing roots limit the Maximum Zero Fuel Weight. The stress can be alleviated by mass balancing (see *Flight Controls*) or putting engines on pylons ahead of the wing.

You can reduce the bending stresses from flight with downward forces that oppose the upward force of lift, such as those from wing-mounted engines and the weight of fuel in wing tanks.

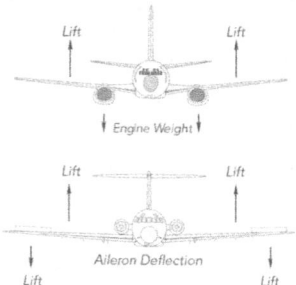

In aircraft with fuselage-mounted engines, or to compensate for usage of fuel from the outboard tanks, some aircraft have ailerons that are biased toward the up position to provide a stress-relieving downward force at the outer wings.

Wings (plus tailplanes and elevators) are designed and manufactured on the cantilever principle, where structural rigidity is provided entirely by their structural members. In other words, there is no external support, so all the strength is built within the wing. As less drag is involved, such wings are normally used for large and fast aircraft.

Their construction is similar to the fuselage, but **ribs** (in line with the airflow) are the equivalent of formers, which shape the wing. They are held in place with transverse beams called **spars***, that perform like longerons. In addition to shaping, the ribs absorb the torsional stresses that come from the movement of the Centre of Pressure discussed in *Principles Of Flight*.

*Spars are the main structural members, typically consisting of a web and girders. They run for the length of the wing, and support all distributed loads as well as concentrated weights such as those from the fuselage, landing gear and engines. The front spar may have engine mounts attached to it and landing gear can be fitted between them. The rear spar normally holds the ailerons and may be the support for high lift devices such as flaps. On a non-stressed skin type wing, the spars take up the vertical bending moments. Most larger aircraft have at least two front and rear main spars - a *multispar* construction with more is not common. Light aircraft have a *monospar* construction.

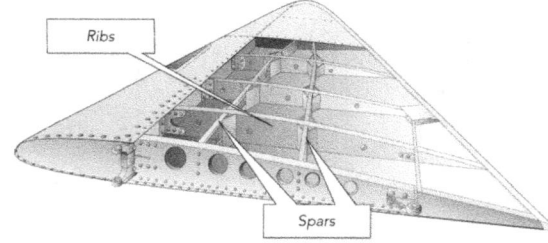

To keep the ribs light but strong, holes may be cut in them, but strength can be further added by curling the edges of the holes through 90° (stiffeners may be fitted vertically to a rib to increase the strength in this direction). The ribs are attached to the skin and the main spars (and any stringers between them) to produce a rigid structure.

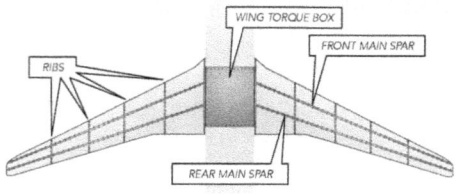

Wings can be bolted to a central structure called the **wing torque** (torsion) **box**, which is formed inside the front and rear spars and the upper and lower wing skins, and which carries all the lift and weight loads. As it is a cube, it can often be used as a fuel tank.

Stabilising Surfaces

The empennage contains the horizontal stabiliser and elevators (which may be combined), and the vertical fin.

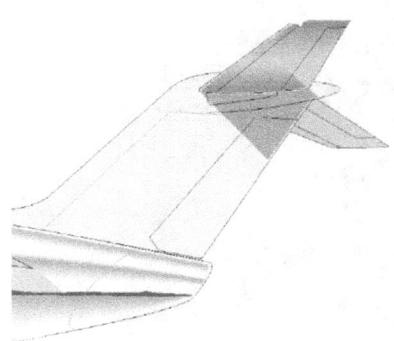

Otherwise, the construction of stabilising surfaces is more or less the same as that for the wings, but on a smaller scale, as lower lifting and twisting/bending stresses are involved (no forces are really involved until their associated control surfaces are deflected). Typically, horizontal and vertical stabilisers have a twin-spar construction, with the associated flying controls hinged to the rear one, which means that it is stronger than the front one, the other way round to how wings are made. The material used is mainly aluminium alloy.

During flight at high Mach numbers, the C of P moves rapidly fore and aft on the wings, which means large changes in the aerodynamic force generated by the horizontal stabiliser. In large aircraft, this could create major structural stresses. To compensate for this, aircraft operating at high Mach numbers have a Mach trimming device that automatically adjusts either the elevators or the tailplane to maintain longitudinal trim and prevent rapid load reversals.

Windows

Aside from allowing the flight crew to see outside clearly, windows must be able to withstand forces caused by the air flowing past the aircraft, precipitation, birds, insects and pressurisation. Their size is regulated, as are the amounts of vertical and horizontal slope.

Some aircraft have windscreen wipers, but they are best not used at all, unless the windscreen is made of glass. This is because, if the wipers are operated when the windscreen is dry, a perspex one will get scratched and marked and reduce visibility during normal weather. There are rain repellent products that work better, although these should still be used with caution - they are best only used when the rain is very heavy.

Window construction depends on where they are placed.

FLIGHT DECK

Windows on the flight deck are subject to differential pressures and temperatures, but the thermal load is particularly important, with the OAT, flight deck and heating mat temperatures to be considered (heating improves the strength of cockpit windows).

The first pilot needs a window that provides a sufficiently extensive, clear and undistorted view so that manoeuvres may be safely performed within the operating limitations, including taxying, take-off, approach and landing.

The windscreen panels in front must be arranged so that, if vision is lost through any of them, one or more remain available for use at a pilot station to permit continued safe flight and landing.

Light aircraft windows are usually made from perspex (acrylic), but they can use sandwiched laminated glass, with embedded heating elements, for preventing ice on small areas and protecting against birdstrikes, because the windscreen becomes flexible with the heat (it takes about 15 minutes to warm up). An electrically heated windscreen is made from glass and *polycarbonate laminate*, with inner surfaces made of soft polycarbonate. The principal directions of strength of each lamination will lie at 90° to each other.

Windscreen heating systems may have a green System On light and an amber System Failure light. They are kept on continuously to guard against thermal gradients and increase the life of the components, but cycle on and off to keep the temperature somewhere between 18-35°C. Power is usually from 3-phase AC. If the overheat warning light comes on, the heating elements will still work, but at a temperature 10-15°C higher than normal.

On more sophisticated aircraft, the front windscreens are usually triple paned with layers of transparent material between them. Put another way, strengthened glass with shock-absorbing clear vinyl interlayers and rubber pressure seals.

Side windows are also triple paned, but could be made of acrylic rather than glass. Heating in this case is for de-misting purposes and is permanently on during flight. If the windscreen heating fails, a reduced maximum pressure differential may be required with a slower maximum IAS limit below a specified height, due to the possibility of being hit by birds.

CABIN WINDOWS

These can also be subject to pressurisation differentials, and also require demisting. Cabin windows are therefore simpler, with generally only 2 or 3 layers, being vented to a silica gel capsule to keep them clear. They are also protected by a scratch screen.

Cabin window openings lie between fuselage frames and are strengthened by aluminium doublers, or reinforcing plates, around strong aluminium alloy frames. The frames are recessed so that the window can be fitted from inside the fuselage, to withstand pressurisation forces. After the Comet's problems, the corners were well-rounded to avoid any concentration of stresses, which could lead to stress cracking and fatigue failure due to the pressurisation cycles. For the same reason, the size of cabin window openings is limited in pressurised hulls.

Doors

In larger aircraft, the areas around doors and windows (and any access hatches) must be reinforced to help take the strain of pressurisation, where longerons and fuselage skins cannot be used. The reinforcement would be in the shape of a frame around the aperture.

A typical door assembly is shown below:

A plug-type door fits into its aperture from inside the fuselage and internal pressure holds it closed in flight.

To open, the door must be pulled inside the fuselage then turned and passed back through the aperture so that when fully open it is outside. Gates at the top and bottom of the door fold to reduce its height so it can pass through.

Aircraft doors must:

- Be openable from inside and outside
- Be lockable to prevent opening in flight
- Not jam during minor incidents
- Be fully open within 10 seconds (including after the failure of any power booster [usually pneumatic] system)
- Include a clear visual inspection panel (window) if not inward opening, and open clear of propellers
- Have an interlock to prevent pressurisation if the door is not locked

Any door that can be locked by a passenger (such as a toilet) must be able to be unlocked by a crew member. Doors used as emergency exits must have red exit signs.

However, there must be a manual inflation capability.

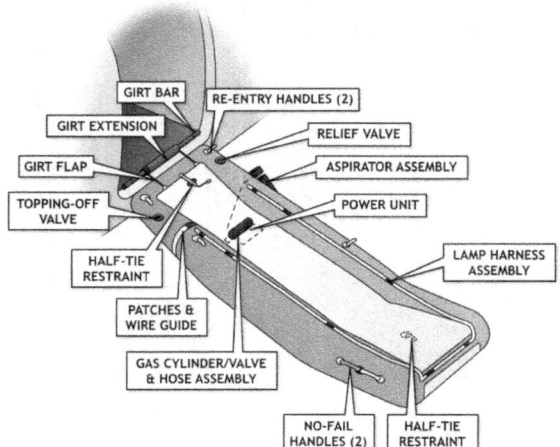

The slide is attached to the aircraft with a Girt bar.

EMERGENCY EXITS

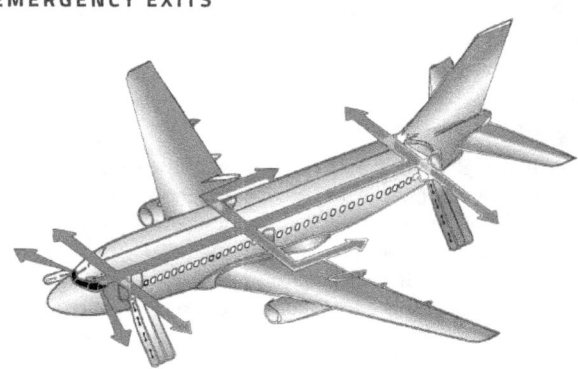

Emergency exits in transport aeroplanes (i.e. with a passenger capacity of 45 or more - typical example shown above) must be arranged to allow all passengers and crew members to leave within 90 seconds through 50% of the available emergency exits.

An exit is considered to be out of service when these elements are inoperative:

- external or internal door opening mechanism.
- door opening aid device.
- open door locking system.
- auxiliary means of evacuation.
- emergency lighting.

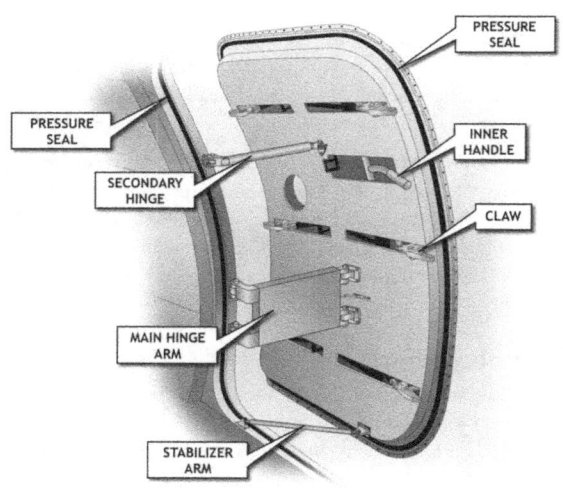

Any able bodied individual must be able to open an emergency exit from the instructions posted inside and outside. Emergency exits must be kept clear and gangways to them must be at least 20 inches wide. At least 2 emergency exits must be accessible from each seat. Overwing escape hatches must pull inwards and throw outwards, and may be fitted with an escape slide or a rope for assistance. If internal curtains are on the route to an emergency exit, there must be a way of securing them open, and they must be open for take-off and landing.

FLIGHT DECK

If the aircraft can carry more than 19 passengers, the flight deck must have a lockable door with a sign saying *Crew Only* on it. There must also be a means of escape from the flight deck, either to the side of each pilot or a roof escape hatch, with a means of lowering to the ground.

EMERGENCY SLIDES

Emergency exits with a sill height of 6 feet or more, with a landing leg collapsed, must have an escape slide that deploys within 10 seconds. The slide is activated automatically as the door opens and must be capable of being deployed in a 25kt wind from the worst direction (an automatic system stops the slide deploying when the door is opened from outside).

BREAK IN AREAS

Designated areas of the fuselage that are suitable for break-in by rescue crews in an emergency must have external markings with right angled corners, and be where there is no danger from normal systems such as hydraulics, electrics, oxygen, etc. The markings must be red or yellow and, if necessary, outlined in white to contrast with the background.

Landing Gear

The landing gear of an aircraft has a similar status to that of drains - unglamorous, but essential, especially as most airliners spend around 65% of their time on wheels - the proportion is much higher for privately owned machines.

Amongst other things, the gear assembly ensures that the shocks of taxying, take-off and landing are not transferred to the airframe. Take-off weights into the range of tons, and accelerations under load in the order of 200-odd knots all must be designed for, with a safety reserve of strength.

The gear is also supposed to absorb side loads in cross-winds - 25% of the vertical load combined with 75% of the maximum ground reaction and 40% drag load, all of which may be present anyway with STOL/VTOL aircraft.

The impact velocities to be absorbed include:

- 10ft/sec at the design landing weight.
- 6ft/sec at the design take-off weight.

combined with a maximum aft drag component of 25% of the vertical ground reaction. This is equivalent to landing at 115 knots from a 3° glide slope without a flare.

Wheels, brakes and hydraulics must also be able to cope with massive changes in pressure and temperature, from sub-zero at altitude (and very hot at supersonic speeds) to near boiling when braking. Such heat must be dissipated rapidly and safely.

The fatigue life of a gear assembly is expressed as mean times between overhaul or replacement, and is affected not just by the number of up or down cycles, but by vibration from wheels that are out of balance, vibration from the airframe, and corrosion.

PAVEMENT CLASSIFICATION

The landing gear supports the weight of the aircraft on the ground and helps you get around on it. Surfaces used for aircraft must be strong and drained, and the runway scored with grooves 2 inches apart to prevent aquaplaning.

Asphalt or concrete runways (or aprons*) have different load bearing abilities. To ensure that aircraft are not too heavy for them and, to prolong their life and prevent damage, there is a system involving an **Aircraft Classification Number** (the load exerted on a pavement by the landing gear) and a **Pavement Classification Number**, both of which are mutually dependent, in that the ACN must not exceed the PCN (subject to tyre pressures and All Up Mass).

*On landing, the aircraft is light on fuel and less than 5% of its weight affects the runway. On take-off, the aircraft is heavy but its weight moves from the wheels to the wings as it accelerates. It is during loading and taxying before departure that the apron can experience significant loads.

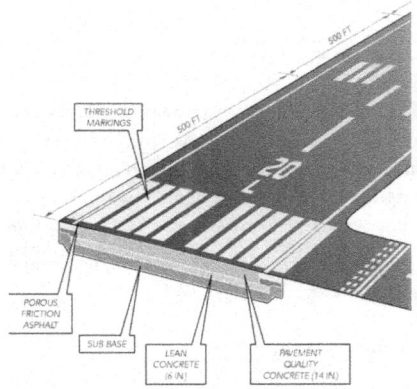

ACN

This is a unique number that expresses the relative effect of an aircraft (in terms of its weight and landing gear design) on a runway pavement for a specified standard subgrade category (ICAO), without specifying a particular thickness of pavement.

The ACN is twice the derived single-wheel load expressed in thousands of kilograms, with single-wheel tyre pressure standardised at 1.25 megapascals (=.09 ton/ft^2). The derived single-wheel load is a function of the sub-grade strength.

The ACN covers four subgrades for flexible or rigid pavements - *high*, *medium*, *low*, and *ultra low*.

PCN

The reported PCN indicates that an aircraft with an ACN equal to or less than that can operate on the pavement, subject to tyre pressures and all up mass.

For aircraft with a ramp mass equal to or less than 5 700 kg, the following information is reported:

- maximum allowable aircraft mass.
- maximum allowable tyre pressure.

The PCN is expressed as a five part code, separated by forward slashes. The first expresses the assessed strength of the pavement. The second is a letter (R or F), showing whether the pavement has a rigid (concrete) or flexible (asphalt) design. The third is a letter from A to D expressing the strength of what is underneath the pavement, called the *subgrade*, so a subgrade of A would be very strong (most likely reinforced concrete). D would be very weak, probably uncompacted soil.

The fourth part can be a letter, or a number with units expressing the maximum tyre pressure that the pavement can support, as follows:

Class	Max Tyre Pressure
W	No Limit
X	1.5 MPa (217 psi)
Y	1.0 MPa (145 psi)
Z	0.5 MPa (72 psi)

The fifth part describes how the first value was worked out. T means a technical evaluation, and U means usage, so a PCN of 80/R/B/W/T means that the underlying concrete has a bearing strength of 80, is rigid, on a medium subgrade, with no limit on tyre pressure, having been calculated via technical evaluation.

One reason why multiple gear systems are used on jet transports is weight distribution and lower ACNs.

TYPES OF UNDERCARRIAGE

A pair of wheels ahead of the centre of gravity with a swivelling tailwheel are known as *conventional landing gear*, because of the length of time it was in service.

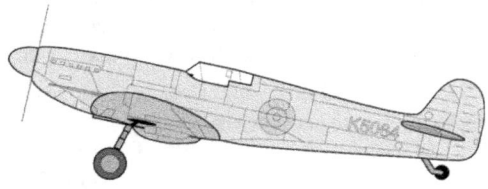

Although it can assist landing by producing large amounts of drag from the wings, it does make the coffee slide down the floor to the rear of the cockpit. At rest, the aeroplane sit tail-down with an angle of attack that is slightly less than the stalling angle with high lift devices extended, so you can do a nice three-point landing with the power off.

This arrangement has been replaced (since just before World War II) with the tricycle undercarriage, which has the main gear behind the centre of gravity and an auxiliary under the nose.

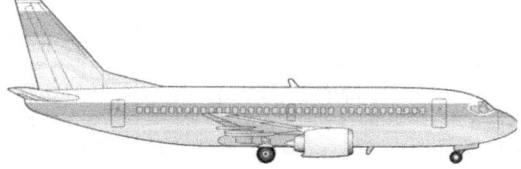

The tricycle is more stable on the ground, and you can see much more ahead, so there is also less chance of ground looping, especially in crosswinds. As nosing over is less of a problem, you can use higher speeds for landing and take-off, and the jet exhaust doesn't hit the ground.

Very slender aeroplanes with low aspect ratio wings use shorter nosewheel units to drop the nose below the main fuselage. This is because such wings cannot be stalled on landing, as the angles involved would be well beyond any possible aircraft attitudes - in effect, the aircraft continues flying. So, to prevent ballooning after touchdown, the low nose attitude is less than the angle of zero lift and the machine is held down on the ground aerodynamically. This makes rotation harder because the large download required from the tail section reduces the lift available, which is one reason why a canard might be used.

Slender aeroplanes with large pitching inertia take longer to respond to elevator inputs, so the undercarriage must be made stronger in case there is a late flare on landing and the associated heavy loads - the C of G is rotating about an instantaneous centre way ahead of it, so there is an additional downwards force involved. This gives you the feeling of being in a fairground ride as you flare while the gear and fuselage break up on the runway behind you.

For most light aircraft, the landing gear might be fixed in place (i.e. locked down and welded). Although this increases drag, they are simple to make and maintain, and cost less, and the drag can be minimised with a little streamlining. However, drag is a major problem with high performance aircraft, so retractable undercarriages were created, at the expense of weight, complexity and maintenance costs (landing gear needs frequent cleaning to get rid of dirt, grit, ice or snow).

The retractable undercarriage is supposed to improve performance, assuming you remember to raise it. The methods for moving the wheels up and down can be electrical, hydraulic, pneumatic, or even based on gravity, with an emergency manual system as a backup. Emergency extension is done with compressed nitrogen, a secondary hydraulic system, or freefall (gravity). Sequencing valves (see *Hydraulics*) ensure that the gear doors open before the gear moves up or down!

For example, when the gear lever is selected down in the picture below, the spool valve (A) is moved to allow fluid under pressure against various pistons (B).

Only when the gear door (C) has moved down to push against a spring (D) is the fluid allowed to flow along the pipe to the main gear piston at (E).

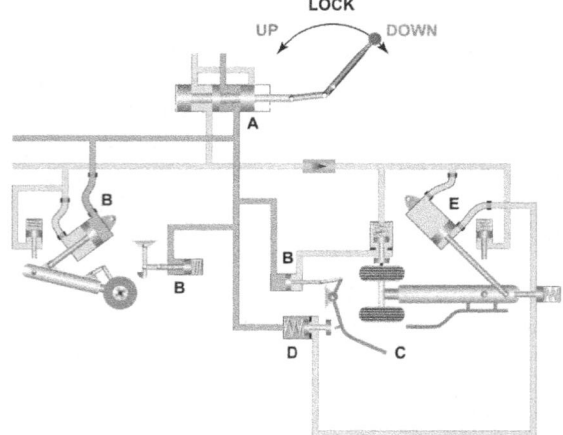

When the gear lever is selected up, the spool valve moves the other way to allow fluid under pressure to the opposite side of the pistons to reverse the process. Such systems are usually powered by engine driven pumps, but sometimes an independent power pack may be used.

AIRFRAMES
Fatigue & Stress

The gear selector on some aircraft may have an OFF setting which should be selected once the gear has been fully retracted to save wear and tear on components and prevent leaks due to the system being pressurised all the time (again, see *Hydraulics*).

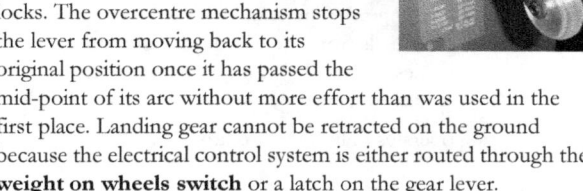

Main undercarriage units are locked down by *mechanical* and *overcentre geometric* locks. The overcentre mechanism stops the lever from moving back to its original position once it has passed the mid-point of its arc without more effort than was used in the first place. Landing gear cannot be retracted on the ground because the electrical control system is either routed through the **weight on wheels switch** or a latch on the gear lever.

Also known as *squat switches* or *undercarriage safety switches*, weight-on-wheels switches are normally micro or magnetic proximity switches mounted on the torsion link (see below) to make or break electrical circuits when the oleo extends or retracts. They are used to disable the undercarriage selector while on ground (normally by inserting a solenoid operated pin to physically prevent the gear lever from being moved), or lock out the gear up if the wheels don't self-centre properly. The squat switches on both main gear legs must break to allow gear retraction once airborne. A secondary method of stopping the gear being selected up when on the ground is with ground locking pins that physically stop the legs moving. They may also be used to:

- Prevent the use of reverse thrust in flight
- Control outflow valves on the ground (pressurisation)
- Stop airframe anti-icing being used on the ground
- Enable auto-spoilers to deploy, plus the auto-braking system
- Control electrical output to some anti-icing systems on the ground (e.g. galley outflow)
- Record landing times

A retractable landing gear unit will normally have an *oleo-pneumatic shock-absorber strut** supported in a *trunnion bearing* which is fixed to a *strengthened box section* in the fuselage (wheel bays are unpressurised).

*The oil supplies damping and the nitrogen supplies a springing effect by absorbing the initial shock of landing (the bounce, or release of landing inertia, is called *recoil*). The rate of extension is controlled by the oil. A motionless aircraft with weight on its wheels is in a static condition, where the weight is balanced by the gas pressure, so the piston ends up about halfway up its stroke. If the oleo leg is too short or too long, you have not enough or too much nitrogen, respectively.

There are considerable side and fore-and-aft loads during take-off, landing and taxying. To prevent damage or possible collapse, additional support is needed.

The assembly is braced longitudinally by drag struts and laterally by side struts. The side strut supports leg side loads and the drag strut supports the leg fore and aft.

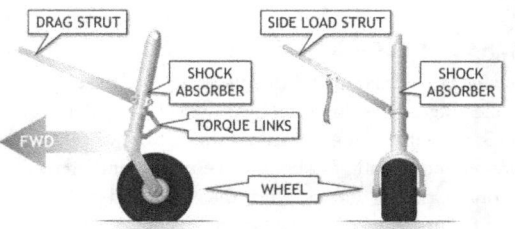

A scissor-link (or torsion link) stops the oleo in the shock absorber from rotating, so the wheels are kept aligned with the longitudinal axis. The highest loads on the torsion link occur when making tight turns during taxi manoeuvres. Crosswind landings don't help.

Types of wheel attachment include the following:

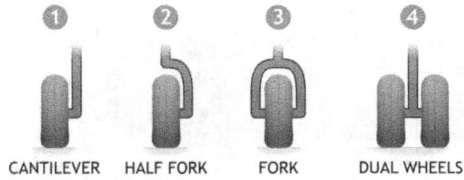

BOGIES

As mentioned above, heavy aircraft need to spread their weight over large areas to avoid damaging the hard standing. In addition, it's a lot easier to accelerate many small wheels rather than a few large ones, and a lot cheaper, as there will be less wear on the tyres (the greatest wear is on landing as the wheels spin up suddenly from zero speed).

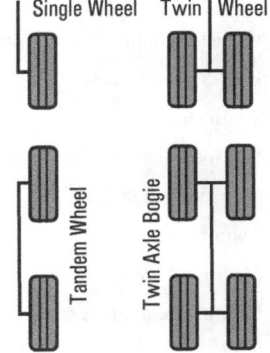

With the four wheel bogie, the reaction from braking can throw a bogie forward from its pivot point. Torque rods take the reaction to the main leg instead of the axle beams. Tyre scrubbing during ground handling and docking is minimised by allowing the rear pairs of wheels to castor, for which you need articulated hydraulic pipes.

BOGIE TILT

Some bogies tilt hydraulically (after lift off) as they move up and down, which allows them to fit into smaller wheel wells. If it doesn't happen, of course, there will be structural damage, aside from various services that depend on the tilting not getting the proper notification.

By using hop and damper linkages that make the rear pair of wheels touch the ground first, the ground contact with the runway and the wheel spin up can be made to absorb a lot of energy (approx 16%) before the main oleos begin to compress. This means that the oleo can be shorter, which saves both weight and space.

NOSE WHEEL STEERING

The nosewheel carries about 10% of the weight of the aircraft. On light ones, steering is done just by moving the rudder pedals. Nosewheels are self-centring to make sure that the wheels are in line before retraction and after being lowered for landing so that any input on the pedals does not turn the wheel and make life difficult. Self-centring uses a roller/spring system. Sometimes, hydraulic power is cut off as the nosewheel comes up.

On large aircraft, a steering wheel (or a tiller device) is used for steering, with help from the control surfaces as speed is increased (the tiller should be used for sharp taxi turns). Self-centring is done with a pair of cams in the upper and lower parts of the strut engaging with each other and turning the wheel as it comes up. The maximum castoring angles are about 55°.

Some nose wheels use a **chine** (a continuous annular fin) on each side of the upper sidewall of the tyre to deflect water from engines.

Shimmy

Nosewheels will also have an anti-shimmy facility. Shimmy is the rapid oscillation of a wheel during ground manoeuvres and take-off, or movement about its track, and is divergent in nature. It is caused by:

- Uneven tyre pressures or unevenly worn tyres.
- Unbalanced wheels.
- Worn shimmy damper or wheel bearings.
- Worn torque links (most probable).

Anti-shimmy designs include:

- Twin wheels.
- Marstrand tyres.
- Shimmy damper (friction for light aircraft, hydraulic for larger ones, or within steering apparatus - see below).
- Limiting the castoring ability of the nosewheel.

One type of damper consists of two actuating cylinders with an accumulator between them which forces fluid into both cylinders to hold a steady tension on the pistons. As the nosewheel is turned, one piston is pushed back to force the liquid ahead of it through a small hole, back to the accumulator, which slows down the piston's movement, and that of the nosewheel.

Turning Radius

Nosewheel steering can have an effect on turning radius, and wing tip clearance. The path followed by the outer wing tip will pass well ahead of the track of the nosewheel, and the pilot, who is also forward of the nosewheel. This needs clearance from ground obstructions. In the 757 for example, the outer wing and tailplane tip radius are greater than that of the nose. This is an important consideration when calculating performance, as some of the available runway length can be lost when lining up.

MAIN WHEEL STEERING

The purpose of main wheel body steering is to make turning easier and tighter around corners, to prevent side loads and scuffing of tyres, because the inner wheels can travel at different speeds to the outer ones and become locked. One technique is to taxi forward a short distance after making the final turn onto the parking bay. Another is not to make sharp turns.

Wide bodied aircraft have more than two sets of main gear, the ones on the wing being predictably called wing gears, and those on the fuselage called body gears. They can be turned separately in response to electrical signals from the nosegear. The main wheels (just the rear bogies in the A380) turn in the opposite direction to the nose wheel to reduce side loads.

Main wheel steering operates only when it is armed.

PUSHBACK

Because aircraft park nose-in to terminals, they are pushed back from them by a tractor attached to the nosewheel. If this is done too aggressively, the nose wheel system can be damaged, so it is locked out from the main system with a pin, which is removed after pushback is complete. Before carrying out normal towing operations involving sharp turns, the nosewheel steering can be disconnected at the nosegear torsion links with an APEX pin. This gives greater protection than just locking out the steering.

MONITORING

Aircraft with three sets of wheels typically have three green lights to tell you when the gear is down and locked, and one red one to tell you if there is a malfunction, and if any wheel is not locked. Earlier aircraft allowed the crew to look into the wheel well through an access panel to check witness marks on the wheels, but this is impractical.

Aircraft with more than three bogies will typically have only one green light, and you use the EICAS to find out the nature and location of any problem. Large transport aircraft may also have a warning system which operates:

- For landing, with flaps and slats down, and throttles set below a predetermined value.
- When part of the landing gear is not locked down.

A warning horn will sound continuously until either the gear becomes locked down (3 greens) or the throttles are advanced (as for a go-around).

HEAVY OR OVERWEIGHT LANDINGS

Heavy or overweight landings will primarily cause damage to the landing gear, support structures in the wings and fuselage, and wing and tailplane attachments. Additional structural damage may occur to the front pressure bulkhead, nose wheel drag and shock struts, with the possibility of the nose wheel collapsing.

Secondary damage will occur to the fuselage structure, its upper and lower skin, the wing structures and their upper and lower skins. If no damage is found in the primary area, the secondary area does not need to be inspected. There is more of a risk of a nose wheel landing with aeroplanes with no leading-edge lift augmentation devices, such as the HS 146.

AIRFRAMES
Fatigue & Stress

Wheels, Rims & Tyres

There are three main types of wheels:

- **Well-based** - similar to cars and fitted to light aircraft (with tubed tyres).
- **Detachable flange** - one side of the wheel can be removed by taking out a locking ring (tubeless).
- **Split hub** - can be separated down the centre and bolted together once the tyre has been fitted (tubeless tyres).

Wheels now tend to be made from aluminium alloys, because the earlier magnesium based ones had a tendency to catch fire, aside from being bulkier (using aluminium allows for more space between the rim and the brake for cooling purposes).

Excessive heating may cause a retracted tyre to burst within the wheel well. Fusible inserts are fitted on wheel rims (around 3 or 4, spaced equally) to reduce the risk.

They are hexagonal studs with a through-bored centre, closed with a eutectic alloy* and a rubber plug. The alloy melts at a pre-set temperature to blow out the rubber plug and allow a controlled deflation before a tyre explodes after, say, a maximum weight rejected take-off. Landing on a flat tyre is way more preferable than dealing with an in-flight tyre burst.

*One formed at the lowest possible solidification temperature for its constituents.

TYRES

Tyres represent a major part of maintenance costs, and their life depends on how they are used. Short or heavy landings, heavy braking and poor runway surfaces all contribute to making the average life of a tyre around 100 landings between remoulds and around 2-3 retreads.

When tyres touch the runway, and have to spin rapidly in a short time, they can creep round the wheel rim. However, the most likely time for creep is when the tyre is newly fitted. **Creep** is the circumferential movement of a tyre in relation to the wheel flange. Aside from the stress, creep can force the valve assembly to one side, so it is usual to monitor it by checking the alignment marks that are placed on the tyre when it is fitted (the white mark near the rim in the picture). If the movement reaches half the width of the paint marks, it's time to consult an engineer. A red spot is used to match up the tyre with the rim when balancing (a red band is a balance mark), and a grey/green one is an awl hole (vent position) that allows trapped gas between plies to escape.

- Up to 24 ins diameter - 1 inch of creep is allowed.
- 24 ins and above - 1½ ins of creep is acceptable.

A speed rating is present if a tyre is rated above 160 mph.

Tyres are normally inflated with the weight off the wheels, and 4% is added to compensate. Air can escape either through the valve or the carcass (not with tubeless). Cold tyres are rejected if they are over 10% below pressure. Between 5-10%, they can be re-inflated and checked the next day, then rejected if they are still more than 5% below. A tyre 5% below can be reinflated, but must be rejected if it reaches the same value by the next day. Hot tyres are rejected if they are more than 10% below the loaded pressure of other tyres on the same leg. Under-inflated tyres wear most on their shoulders and over-inflation leads to crown wear. Tyres should be inflated with nitrogen, because it has a reduced pressure change with altitude, but dry air can also be used. However, nitrogen must be used for aircraft over 5700 kg that have retractable landing gear. Typical inflation pressures are 30-50 psi for grass and 200 psi for paved surfaces. The permissible load decreases as inflation pressure decreases (see *aquaplaning*).

Pre-flight inspection should include:

- Creep within limits.
- No cuts or scores, swelling or bulges, especially in the side wall.
- No embedded objects.
- No signs of heat damage, particularly the bead.
- Correct inflation (5 - 10% above loaded inflation pressure is usually specified).

AIRCRAFT TYRE CONSTRUCTION

Tyres are classified by load, ply and speed rating. The ply rating identifies a tyre by its maximum recommended load and pressure - it is the index of tyre strength, not necessarily the number of cord piles used in its construction. The markings may be in full, as with 10 PLY RATING or abbreviated, such as 10PR. The speed rating is included for tyres used above 160 mph.

Most tyres are cross-ply, for an even load distribution, with multiple layers of nylon ply at alternating angles to the tread centreline (in radial tyres, the ply runs at 90°, which helps with cornering). High speed demands are covered by reinforcing the tread, described below. Radials are more flexible and can offer low weight, but tend to be less retreadable than a bias ply with weaker sidewalls.

TREAD

The tread is made from a specially compounded rubber that resists wear, cutting, chunking and heat build up. It is the abradable material in contact with the ground, which includes the crown and shoulder of the tyre.

Tread patterns need to provide the best compromise between maximum contact and the avoidance of aquaplaning by dispelling water. The most common pattern (if one is used) is the ribbed tread, where the ribs along the length of the circumference help with directional stability and the grooves between them allow water dispersal. Diamond treads are particularly suitable for unpaved airfields. You can go down to the depth of the pattern (on patterned tyres), or the marker tie bar or 2 mm above the bottom of the wear indicator on ribbed tyres, and they can be repaired several times.

A plain-treaded tyre is at its limits when cushion rubber is exposed. Tread separation and tyres bursting will involve:

- Smaller footprint (loading)
- lower braking efficiency
- FOD (hydraulic lines & engine ingestion)

AIRFRAMES
Fatigue & Stress

UNDERTREAD
A layer of rubber that is designed to improve the adhesion between tread/ ITF and the casing plies. During the retreading process, it acts as the interface for the application of fresh tread rubber.

THE CASING
The basic strength of the tyre is provided by the casing plies, which are layers of fabric cord coated with hi-modulus rubber on both sides. Casing plies are held in place by being wrapped around the beads to provide the casing ply turn up.

BEADS
The bead wire anchors the tyre to the rim to ensure an airtight seal. Beads consist of bundles of high-tensile steel wires, each strand of which is coated in rubber compound and wound into coils of the correct diameter for a given tyre size.

SIDEWALL
The area of the tyre between the shoulder and the bead, covered with a layer of specially formulated rubber treated with anti-oxidants. The sidewall protects the casing plies from the effects of weathering and offers resistance to cuts and flexing.

TUBED TYRES
The tyre is inflated with a rubber inner tube. The tyre casing (around the tube) is similar to that of a tubeless tyre, mentioned below, but the tubeless version has another inner lining of low leakage rubber. Tubed tyres are less subject to sudden blowouts, but the main problem is bending or breaking of the inflation valve after tyre creep.

TUBELESS TYRES
A tubeless tyre has no inner tube, so it is easier to balance, and lighter in weight (7½%). As well, the valve cannot be ripped out through movement inside, and there will be no rubbing during taxying, so there is less heat (they are 10ºC cooler when running and are vented to release air trapped in the casing during manufacture or normal permeation).

Other advantages are a lower risk of deflation through puncture (no bursting) and better adjustment to wheels. They also have a radial side casing (their mounting rim must be flawless), and require no rim protection between the rim flange and tyre removing device. Tubeless tyres have a layer of rubber bonded to the inside of the first casing ply from bead to bead to resist the permeation of nitrogen and moisture into the casing.

The Constant Speed Propeller
The first attempt to overcome the fact that the fixed pitch propeller is really only designed for one speed was the variable pitch propeller in the 1930s, which rotated the whole blade through a mechanism in the propeller hub. The degree of rotation was controlled by the pilot.

However, the constant speed propeller was a subsequent improvement, based on the idea that the power available depends not only on the efficiency of the propeller, but also the shaft power coming from the engine, which is directly proportional to engine RPM. For a given throttle setting, the engine RPM depends on the load on the crankshaft - going uphill in your car will slow the engine down if you keep in the same gear. In an aeroplane, the equivalent is the aerodynamic torque, which comes from the resistive component of aerodynamic force exerted on the propeller in the plane of rotation, acting through a moment arm to the shaft. This means that, every time the pitch was changed in a variable pitch propeller, the engine RPM changed as well, away from the optimum level.

The constant speed propeller changes the pitch automatically to keep the engine RPM constant. It performs pretty much the same function as the automatic gearbox does in a car, in that it "maintains engine RPM over varying conditions of road", or flight, in this case. The gearbox (or constant speed prop) is there because engines work best within a certain speed range - going too fast or slow is not good for them. In other words, a constant speed propeller can have its pitch adjusted for varying conditions. Most are hydraulically operated with a centrifugal governor operating a control valve that lets oil in to make the pitch coarser or releases it for fine pitch (best for take-off).

Once the RPM lever is set to a particular value, the engine RPM will stay constant regardless of the airspeed. Now, as forward speed increases on take-off, the pitch angle is increased by the governor to stop the propeller overspeeding, and the aircraft can progress to a higher velocity. For full speed in the cruise, coarse pitch is selected and the engine speed can be reduced to a more comfortable level, which reduces fuel consumption.

A double acting propeller uses oil pressure to move the blades towards both fine and coarse pitch angles. A single acting propeller uses oil pressure to move the blades towards the smaller pitch angle so that, if the engine fails, and the oil pressure, the blade feathers automatically to produce minimum drag (if feathering is not available, select fully coarse). Engine overload when changing power is avoided by increasing the propeller RPM before increasing the manifold pressure.

If engine oil pressure is lost, an electrical pump can be used to feather the propeller only. The feathering pump is an electrically driven oil pump that supplies the propeller with oil under pressure when the engine is shut down. Unfeathering is also done with pressurised oil from an accumulator or an electric pump - airflow will start the propeller spinning. You need a safe margin above V_{MC}* in case the engine does not start, as a windmilling propeller creates more drag.

*Minimum control speed in the air.

The pitch of the blades when fully fine and feathered is limited by mechanical stops, although the in-flight fine pitch stop can be varied to prevent a sudden massive selection of fully fine, and can be withdrawn to allow the prop to go to ground fine and reverse pitch. The superfine pitch setting establishes a zero blade angle to make its life easier. Superfine pitch requires less power for starting because early turboprop engines also had to drive a reduction gearbox, increasing its workload.

Most modern turboprops use a free turbine, which is not connected to the main spool of the engine. Superfine pitch can also be used to produce a great deal of extra drag in flight, called *discing**, similar to using spoilers on jets. It enables you to achieve steeper descent paths without gaining too much airspeed.

*Disking in the US.

AIRFRAMES
Fatigue & Stress

GEARING

The propeller's job is to convert the torque delivered from the rotation speed of the crankshaft into thrust. The problem is that the crankshaft or power turbine runs at so high a speed (typically 30,000 RPM for a turbine) that reduction gearing is needed to drive a transmission.

Epicyclic or planetary reduction gears (left, below) are used on radial engines:

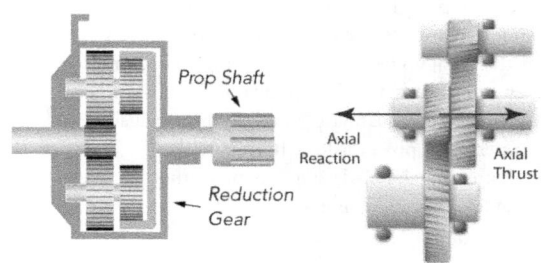

and spur reduction gearing (right above) is generally used with in-line engines.

Either may be used on horizontally opposed engines.

Roller bearings will normally support the propeller shaft, while a ball or roller thrust bearing transfers propeller thrust to the airframe, although plain bearings and a thrust washer may be used instead. Lubrication is normally from the engine oil system.

Measuring Torque

The torquemeter indicates the twisting force of the engine against the transmission, or the loads applied to the transmission shafts and gears. As propeller speed is more or less constant, it also shows the engine's power output.

Part of the reduction gearing can be used to measure the power output because axial thrust (movement) is generated when helically cut gears are used to transfer power from one shaft to another. That is, as the gears rotate they move slightly, the amount being proportional to the torque applied.

Turbine engines in turboprops have a smooth and uniform torque output due to their continuous combustion. Torque is the measure of power being used, being a force applied at a distance by a turning point. It is measured between the engine and the reduction gearbox, and can be expressed in newton-metres, brake or shaft horsepower and inch or foot pounds. It may be shown on a torque gauge (above) as a percentage.

```
Power = Torque x RPM
```

Having the torquemeter on the *output* shaft (as late as possible, as the measurement of torque absorbs power) allows engine torque to be closely monitored. Manifold pressure, on the other hand, is measured on the input side of the engine - MAP is at best a *predictor* of engine power output, whereas torque is its measurement. Changes in N_1 or TOT are the only way of determining whether the engine is meeting its specification, because the torque indication will always be the same.

An electronic torquemeter uses the same probe and phonic wheel system as an engine RPM indicator, on two concentric shafts. The torque shaft is connected to the engine and the reduction gear box. The reference shaft is only connected to the engine. There is a toothed wheel at the forward end of each shaft that rotates past the pickup to produce an AC voltage. As power changes, so does the phase relationship between the voltages from the toothed wheels, in proportion to the power used.

COUNTERWEIGHTS

These can be used to force the blades into increasing their angle of attack when power is lost. The blade angle is reduced by oil pressure so, when it is lost, the angle will increase, although there may be an automatic feathering system. Thus, with counterweights, loss of oil pressure feathers the blades. Otherwise, they go into full fine pitch. Now you have more choice - you can operate at high RPM and low manifold pressure, and *vice versa*. Using lower RPM in the cruise (with higher manifold pressure) helps fuel consumption, since the engine is going round fewer times per minute, and the losses from friction are less than at high RPM. However, using too much MAP against low RPM makes the engine work too hard and risk detonation.

PITCH STOPS

The constant speed range is not maintained at very low power settings. As the throttle setting is reduced, the CSU senses a reduction in RPM and fines off the propeller. Eventually the PCU piston will come into contact with a fine pitch stop in the cylinder, and the blade angle will remain constant. As the propeller has effectively become a fixed pitch unit, the low power setting means lower RPM. If the fine pitch stop prevents the blades from moving to such a fine pitch that reverse thrust would result in flight, it is known as a flight fine-pitch stop. It is withdrawn, either automatically or by the pilot, when the weight is on the wheels. There may also be a reverse pitch stop to perform a similar function.

The travel of the PCU piston in the coarse pitch direction is also limited, either to a maximum pitch to prevent overtorquing or to the feather blade angle, typically about 85°. It is withdrawn when feathering is selected.

FEATHERING

When the engine is not driving the propeller, the airflow creates a lifting force that causes it to rotate in the normal direction. This is referred to as windmilling. The finer the pitch of the propeller blades, the faster the rotation. Feathering allows the blades of a propeller to be moved through coarse pitch to a position where their leading edges face into the air stream so that no lift is created and they do not rotate. To do this, the propeller RPM lever is moved through the low (fully coarse) position. This physically lifts the piston valve, overriding the RPM spring and governor weights, and allows the booster pump to drive the PCU piston to the full extent of its travel in the coarse pitch direction. At the same time, the throttle is closed. As the RPM decreases, the output from the engine-driven booster pump falls, providing an alternative feathering supply to maintain oil pressure until the propeller is fully feathered. This may be from an electrically driven pump or an accumulator.

AIRFRAMES
Fatigue & Stress

At the same time, the throttle is closed. As the RPM decay the output from the engine-driven booster pump falls, so there is an alternative feathering supply to maintain oil pressure until the propeller is fully feathered. This may be from an electrically driven pump or an accumulator.

Without a feathering system, the blades will tend to move towards the smallest blade angle, using the centrifugal turning moment and/or spring forces. *Feathering stops* prevent the blades moving past the feathering position.

TURBOPROPS

Turboprops use oil-controlled systems - the power levers control the torque and the prop levers control pitch and RPM, very similar to a piston. Higher oil pressure creates flatter pitch and higher RPM so, if an engine fails and you lose oil pressure, the blades will feather, which is what you want anyway. Springs or compressed nitrogen may assist the process. The turboprop uses three propeller governors - the primary, the overspeed and fuel-topping governors.

The Fuel Control Unit (FCU) and a turbine governor work together to keep the propeller RPM constant over a range of power settings. As you push the levers forward, the FCU sends more fuel to the combustion chambers which eventually makes the turbines spin faster. This is sensed by the governor which makes the blades coarsen their pitch to absorb the extra energy and provide more thrust.

- The **primary governor** works just like the constant-speed version on a piston aircraft. It uses a valve controlled by the prop levers that makes flyweights control the oil going to the hub (see right). If RPM decreases, the flyweights slow down and are drawn inwards. They are usually held out by centrifugal force against springs. This allows more oil in to reduce the pitch.

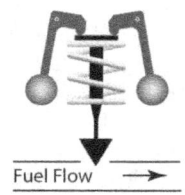

- The **overspeed governor** is a relief valve that increases the blade angle automatically if the primary governor fails, to control RPM within the maximum limits.

- The **fuel-topping governor** also prevents overspeeding, but only within a small margin over the selected lever setting. It adjusts fuel flow instead.

On some systems, like the Garret, the engine and propeller RPM are linked so that both increase or decrease by the same amount. Free turbine engines, like the PT6, allow the engine RPM to vary slightly without affecting the propellers much because the power turbine is independent of the main engine.

Changes in power output are not directly related to engine speed but to the turbine inlet temperature, which is determined by the fuel flow. Increased fuel flow increases the turbine inlet temperature to make more energy available at the turbine. The absorbed energy is transmitted to the propeller as torque, and it increases its blade angle to keep the engine RPM the same.

Negative torque occurs when the propeller spins faster than the reduction gear and drives the engine instead of the other way round. It may happen when:

- the fuel flow is interrupted.
- with gust loads on the propeller.
- during the descent, with high compressor bleeds at low power.
- during shutdown.

Should the negative torque exceed the maximum limit of the Negative Torque Signal (NTS), a safety coupling disengages the reduction gear from the engine.

There is a safety coupling that disengages the reduction gear from the engine if it goes above a preset negative torque value that is higher than that covered by the NTS (it is a backup feature). Re-engagement is also automatic during feathering or engine shutdown. An autofeather system is a thrust sensitive signal which operates if power is lost. It operates by automatically increasing the blade angle to the feather position. It is armed during take-off and landing.

GROUND OPERATIONS

Below the flight idle position, the system is not sensitive enough to allow the fine movements needed for ground operations. The *Beta range* (or *ground range*) is the aft range of the **power lever** that is accessed through a gate (the prop lever remains forward as set for landing). Here, the propeller blade angle is not controlled by the RPM lever through the governor, but by the power lever through an oil pressure control system. It puts the props nearer to flat pitch (or superfine) for ground manoeuvres.

This is because a lot of thrust is generated even at idle, unlike piston-engined machines, which produce little.

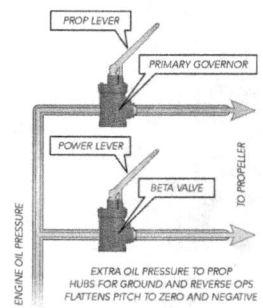

The *beta valve* bypasses the primary governor to send more oil to the hub, and allows the power lever to control only propeller pitch in the beta range, as opposed to its normal torque. *Low pitch stops* or hydromechanical locking devices stop the propeller entering the Beta range or even reverse pitch in the cruise. In reverse range, the power lever controls pitch and torque.

The *Alpha range* (in the forward part, between flight idle and maximum power) has the opposite function.

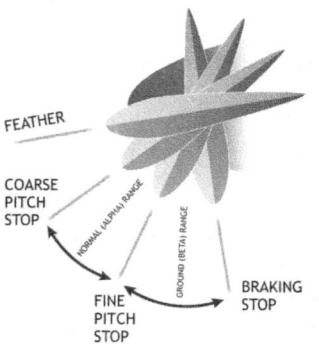

Thus, power output and propeller RPM are controlled at the same time with one lever. There is a lever for residual control, called the *condition lever*, which sets the propeller for normal flight, that is, handing over control to the power lever, and for starting and feathering. When the power lever is moved aft of ground idle, the pitch reduces to zero (i.e. flat pitch), then is reversed for reverse thrust.

REVERSE THRUST

This is feature that involves using negative pitch, past the fine pitch angle (sometimes called braking propellers). Special locks linked to the landing gear stop this being used in flight. Bearings in the propeller shaft take the load in the opposite direction, and arrangements are made to ensure that the airflow into the engine is not interrupted.

Using reverse thrust makes a lot of noise, but this doesn't mean that the process is efficient - around 80% of the loss in kinetic energy is still through the brakes.

Turboprop power levers are lifted back past an idle gate on the quadrant. This puts the propellers into negative pitch after initially increasing drag by flattening it (engine power will increase as negative pitch is applied).

Tip: When selecting reverse thrust on a multi-engined aircraft, pause for a second or two at 20% reverse power to ensure that you do not have an asymmetric situation.

SYNCHRONISATION

On take-off, the throttles are pushed fully forward. If left to themselves, the engine speeds will typically not be the same, and the difference between them will be enough to produce an uncomfortable beat, or vibration. In most light aircraft, matching engine speeds to remove the beating is done manually - all it needs is a light movement of one of the RPM levers - if you fly one machine regularly, you will soon get used to which one it is.

However, Constant Speed Units (CSUs) can be matched to the exact speeds automatically with a synchroniser or synchrosope. A tachogenerator (or frequency generator) on each engine generates a signal that is proportional to within 100 RPM of the engine speed. A synchroscope measures the difference in alternator output frequencies - the rotor is fed by the alternator on the master engine and the stator by the alternator on the slave so it can match its RPM to the master, usually the left engine on a twin-engined machine, or any engine when you have four.

A typical system comprises a phonic wheel, a magnetic pickup, and a control box that compares the two signals. The engine with the higher voltage or frequency determines which way the actuator will rotate.

Synchronisation will not take place on take-off or landing just in case the master engine fails, in which case the slaves will follow and "fail" as well!

Synchrophasing allows you to set relative positions of the propeller blades as well. Pulse generators on each No 1 propeller blade ensure that all blades start off at the same relative position at the same time.

FLIGHT CONTROLS

The effectiveness of a control depends on:

- its distance from the centre of gravity (large moments).
- the control surface area.
- the degree of deflection.
- dynamic pressure (IAS).

Aeroelasticity

Unfortunately, the flexibility an aircraft needs can cause problems at high speeds. The aerodynamic forces at such speeds can distort the structure and produce elastic forces and aerodynamic loading (*Divergence*, below). For example, when an aileron at the end of a long, flexible wing is moved downwards, the line of action of the lift is moved clockwise to the rear and actually twists the wing the opposite way* until it is halted by the structural rigidity. If the aerodynamic twisting is sufficient, the lift will decrease and the aircraft will roll in the opposite direction to that expected. Upward aileron is worse because a stall will occur. The unloaded wing will spring back until the airflow restores itself. This kind of twisting moment will continue until either a state of equilibrium is reached, or structural failure.

*Around the torsional (feathering) axis.

Aeroelasticity, or aero-elastic coupling, is the interaction between aerodynamic loads and elastic strain on the airframe, or whether a component bends or twists under the loads imposed by flight (control reversal and flutter).

In brief, a material is said to be wholly elastic if the strain cause by a stress goes away when the stress is removed. If the strain does not go away we have a plastic situation, and the material will acquire a permanent set.

At low airspeeds, the aerodynamic forces are relatively small, and the effects are negligible, but this is not so at higher speeds - although the aerodynamic force is proportional to V^2, torsional stiffness remains constant. At some high speed the aerodynamic force buildup may overcome the resisting torsional stiffness to create a divergence. The speed at which this occurs will be higher than the design dive speeds V_D/M_D. All aeroelastic distortion is generally destabilising, with swept wings and surfaces with high aspect ratios suffering the most. Well worked machines with looses joints can display similar effects.

DYNAMIC AEROELASTICITY

Flutter is the dynamic instability of an elastic structure in a flow of fluid, resulting from feedback between the body's deflection and the force exerted by the flow. Put another way, flutter is a *divergent oscillatory motion of a control surface from the interaction of aerodynamic and inertia forces, and the stiffness of the structure*. Just changing the mass distribution or the stiffness of one component can induce flutter in another. This could be just a buzz in the structure, or it could develop with great speed and cause serious damage to or lead to destruction of the aeroplane, as with Braniff Flight 542.

- **Flexural flutter** is caused by the C of G of a control surface being offset from the control hinge line, with flexing as lift changes. It is prevented or reduced by introducing a mass balance in front of the torsion axis so the C of G of the control surface is better placed (see *Balance*).

- Also known as *Cyclic Deformation*, **Torsional Flutter** occurs when increased lift on a control surface causes a turning moment about a torsional axis such as the leading edge radius of an aerofoil. In short, the wing is made to twist. If the twisting becomes excessive, control reversal is possible. If the cycle is repeated and divergent (see below), it could lead to fatigue failure.
- **Buffeting** is high-frequency instability caused by airflow separation or shock wave oscillations from one object striking another. It is a random vibration that usually affects the tail unit caused by the airflow downstream of the wing.

DIVERGENCE

This is a phenomenon in which elastic twist suddenly becomes theoretically infinite, typically causing a spectacular failure. It occurs when a lifting surface deflects under an aerodynamic load and adds to the applied load, or moves it so that the twisting effect is increased (see above). The increased load deflects the structure further.

CONTROL REVERSAL

This is the loss (or reversal) of an expected response from a control surface, because the main lifting surface becomes deformed. It only occurs in wings that have ailerons or other surfaces that can reverse their usual functions in circumstances such as high speed flight.

When an aileron is deflected downwards, it increases the C_L of the wing at that point, well behind the flexural centre, and there is a tendency for the wing to twist. This is especially so with outboard ailerons, at the point of least torsional stiffness. This gets worse with speed, so much so that the twisting will create a negative angle of attack. Having said that, it is only likely on aircraft that are not designed for high subsonic or transonic flight when a limiting airspeed is exceeded. High speed aileron reversal can be delayed with inboard and outboard ailerons and/or roll control spoilers*. The inboard ailerons are placed where the wing structure is naturally stiffer, and work at all speeds. The outboard ailerons work only at low speed, being deactivated when the flaps are retracted and vice versa.

*On most high speed jet transport aircraft, roll control spoilers are used as well. Because they are further forward and on a stiffer part of the wing, they do not distort the wing structure to the same degree as do ailerons.

TRANSONIC AEROELASTICITY

Flow is highly non-linear in the transonic regime, dominated by moving shock waves. It is mission-critical for aircraft that fly through transonic Mach numbers.

FLY BY WIRE

Manual flight control systems typically use various mechanical parts such as rods, cables, pulleys, counterweights, and even chains to transmit the forces from the cockpit controls directly to the control surfaces. *Fly By Wire* systems, on the other hand, use electrical signals over electrical cables that connect to hydraulic actuators at the control surfaces. The flight controls operate transducers in the shape of *Rotary Variable Differential Transformers* (RVDTs), which produce command signals based on voltages that are proportional to the movement of the control. The computer compares the demand with the stored flying characteristics, and the algebraic output is transmitted to the control surface. The computer will ensure that the demand is met without imposing out-of-limit manoeuvres and that the flight envelope is not exceeded. Most systems are *active control*.

There is some controversy as to whether the programmers actually talk to pilots but, if nothing else, FBW systems **save weight** and reduce maintenance requirements. Its use can also create more space in various locations, particularly the cockpit, at the expense of software quality and control (there is also improvement in piloting quality over the flight envelope). Sometimes, sidesticks replace conventional control columns. Redundancy is achieved by having multiple pathways for signals, or multiple computers for the same task, and the computers are continually self-checking.

The software used for flight controls is certified at the highest level of safety (Level A). Since the use of software is uncertain (hard to test properly, etc.), some attention is given to the design of systems as well. Software levels are defined according to the effects of a software failure:

Level	Contribution
A	Catastrophic
B	Hazardous
C	Major
D	Minor
E	No Effect

Long Range Operations are categorised according to the severity of the expected conditions, i.e. *benign*, *demanding* and *severe*.

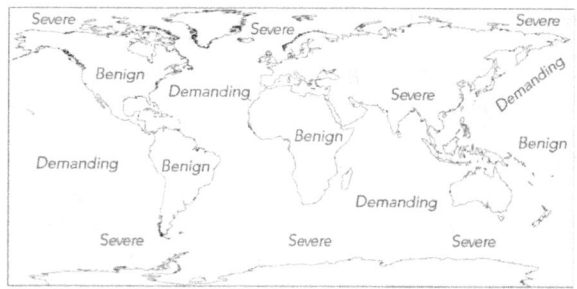

The Himalayan region is classified as severe because of the height of the terrain - it is above 10 000 feet, so a pressurisation or engine failure would cause problems.

Under ETOPS rules, twin-engined aircraft can only fly for up to 180 minutes over benign or demanding climatic regions. See *Operational Procedures*.

CONTROL LOCKS

Control surfaces are normally locked when the machine is on the ground to prevent them being damaged by the wind. For light aircraft, locks can be fitted externally on the flying surfaces or internally on the cockpit controls. However, for larger aircraft with electro-hydraulic systems, the controls lock automatically when power is removed. Other locks on larger aircraft include mechanical, lever and cable operated bolts or pins that are engaged within the aircraft. Reversible flight controls must have gust locks which are essential for manual controls (on a cable operated system, they will stop the control column from moving if the controls do not have servo tabs). Most gust locks will also prevent take-off.

CONTROL JAMMING

Most transport aircraft have protection against this, with provisions for disconnecting any part of the system that becomes blocked.

CONTROL STOPS

Manually operated controls are fitted with stops to limit their range of movement.

- Primary stops are fitted to the control surfaces.
- Secondary stops are fitted to the cockpit controls.

TOCWS

The *Take-off Configuration Warning System* provides a warning on the ground before take-off if the aircraft is incorrectly configured as the throttles are advanced. It takes note of:

- Control locks removed
- All powered flying controls operative
- Feel simulators operative
- Flap settings correct
- Slat settings correct
- Trim within limits
- Aileron up-set* armed but not applied
- Speedbrakes and/or spoilers in
- Doors locked

*Aileron upset is a system that biases the ailerons up to move the wing's centre of pressure inwards to reduce wing bending stresses. In addition to TOCWS, control surface position indicators may be provided.

Primary Flight Controls

Control surfaces in large aircraft are usually fitted in pairs, such as inboard and outboard ailerons on each wing, inboard and outboard elevators and even upper and lower rudders (on the DC 10, which also splits each part into forward and aft sections*). This ensures that the controls are effective at high and low speeds, particularly with lateral control, and to allow for failures, as each one has an independent system. For example, at low speeds only the outboard ailerons are used - at high speeds, they are locked out and the inboard ailerons take over. In this way, the forces involved act closer to the longitudinal axis to reduce twisting of the wings.

*The forward parts are operated by the rudder pedals, while the aft sections are hinged to the forward sections and linked with pushrods to the vertical stabiliser. This provides a finer control and improves efficiency.

As a control surface is moved, the aerofoil concerned moves the opposite way because the deflection increases the local angle of attack, reducing from the change in relative airflow, which gradually reduces the increase in lift and dampens the movement. If there is an opposite control, the local angle of attack would also change and provide a damping moment.

The greater the rate of movement, the greater the damping. Because the camber changes, the centre of pressure moves towards the trailing edge. As speed increases, the deflection angle required to achieve a given change in attitude reduces - if you double the speed, you only need a quarter of the control deflection. Put another way, if you double the speed, the control becomes four times more effective. At slow speeds, therefore, you need large deflections because the controls are sloppy, which is a point to remember when flying low and slow. Powered controls must be reliable, especially when operating them is beyond the strength of humans. Such reliability would involve duplication and separation of sources. There are 4 ways of actuating flying controls, including manual, electric*, pneumatic* and hydraulic*.

*Can be *power operated* or power *assisted*. With the latter, moving the cockpit control moves the flying control and a pilot valve (see *Hydraulics*). With the former, the control only affects the pilot valve. Controls are *reversible* if aerodynamic loads provide feedback (feel) to the pilot (power assisted). They do not need artificial feel.

Controls are *irreversible* (power operated) if there is no feedback, and artificial feel (Q-feel) is needed. If you activate the rudder trim on the ground, for example, the rudder will move, and the pedals will move correctly. In fact, trimming of the rudder (and aileron) is achieved by adjusting the zero force point.

Q-Feel uses static and pitot inputs to prevent overstressing powered controls.

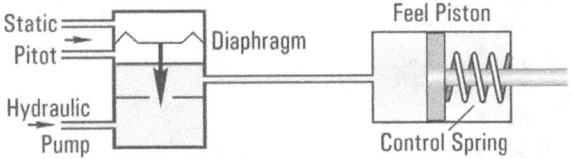

It is normally duplicated and fitted **in parallel** with control runs, and is supposed to increase control column or rudder pedal force when increases in airspeed and control deflection occur. A **q feel pot**(entiometer) controls hydraulic pressure to a feel piston that is connected to a control run. As airspeed rises, dynamic (pitot) pressure increases and moves the diaphragm upwards. This allows greater hydraulic flow and pressure behind the piston, and a greater resistance to control movement is sensed by the pilot. Different feel values are provided for each axis. The most used hydraulic fluid is mineral based and stored in a reservoir. The controls and indicators for the feel system include an On-Off switch to energise the feel unit motors and a pressure failure indication for each system.

Note that controls do not move in isolation - an adjustment in one causes a secondary effect in another and must be allowed for, as discussed below. For example, an uncontrolled yaw results in a roll, because one wing is moving faster and generates more lift on that side.

AIRFRAMES
Flight Controls

PITCH (ELEVATOR)

The elevator controls *pitching* (where the nose goes up and down) by increasing the angle of attack above or below the tailplane, according to whether it is raised up or forced down by moving the control column in the cockpit. If it is pushed forward, the elevator is forced down into the airflow underneath the stabiliser, the angle of attack is increased, the tail rises because more lift is created and the nose goes down. The opposite happens if it is pulled back. The tail is involved with:

- **Control**. Obtained by having part or all of the tail hinged and connected to the cockpit controls.
- **Balance**. The forces on a wing change with the angle of attack, but weight does not, or it does so only slowly as fuel is used. As lift usually moves aft as speed increases, the greater the spread between it and the C of G, the more downward force is required from the tail.
- **Stability**. An increased angle of attack should create forces that reduce it. Ignoring downwash, if part of the tail is fixed, an increased alpha on the wing produces an increased upward force on the tail which tends to push the nose down.

Naturally, the tail should do the above with *minimum drag*.

Sometimes, there is no elevator, but the whole stabiliser is moved, in which case it is a *stabilator*. A *variable incidence* tailplane (as opposed to a fixed incidence one, with an elevator and trim tab) allows for more powerful trim. The best C of G position for a stuck stabiliser depends on what you were doing at the time. In the cruise, the aircraft would be set for a low pitch attitude and angle of attack, with gear and flaps up. To land, you would need to put the gear and flaps down, which would produce a nose down pitching moment that would be increased by a stabiliser stuck in the cruise position. A forward C of G would make things worse, so you need an aft C of G in this case, with little flap, and a higher than usual landing speed, as deceleration would make the nose go down further.

A *Canard* has its horizontal stabiliser on the front of an aircraft - it has the advantage of a longer moment arm, so the stabilising surfaces can be smaller. Both sets of surfaces provide positive lift, The stabiliser is at a slightly greater angle of incidence than the wing so, when the aircraft pitches up there is a restoring nose-down pitching moment. Because the foreplane reaches the stalling angle of attack before the mainplane does, the canard is (in theory) unstallable, since the nose drops to initiate a stall recovery. Unfortunately, there is a problem when both planes stall!

YAW (RUDDER)

The rudder does much the same thing, but sideways, to make the nose *yaw*, or move left and right. It is controlled by the foot pedals - whichever one goes forward moves the rudder to that side, where more lift is created and the fin is forced sideways in the appropriate direction, to produce a flat turn with a skid (you don't use the rudder to turn, but to fine tune one initiated by the ailerons, or stop it going the wrong way - see *Low and Slow*).

If the rudder deflection makes the fin exceed its critical angle of attack the fin will stall, as would any aerofoil. At high speeds or high altitudes, the rudder deflection must therefore be limited to avoid over-stressing the system.

Yawing causes the wing on the outside of the turn to speed up, which increases the lift on that side to make the aircraft roll into the yaw. Some aircraft can change the ratio between pedal and rudder movement*. When they are banked, the rudder deflects to yaw the aircraft into the turn and reduce the adverse yaw effect. Thus, if you roll to the right, you get less yaw to the left. The fin and rudder can stall if there is enough camber when the rudder is deflected. A dorsal extension to the fin can increase the stalling angle, as can a low aspect ratio fin.

*A **rudder ratio changing system** reduces the deflection for a given pedal movement as the speed increases. The 747, for example, uses a dynamic pressure (q) sensing gear change unit. The pressure/speed signals are fed to ratio changers in hydraulic power actuators which reduce control surface displacement as airspeed increases.

There is a variable stop system for rudder and pedals.

ROLL (AILERONS)

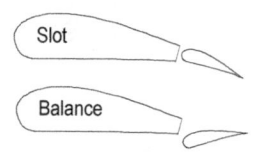

Conventional ailerons are on and hinged from, the wing trailing edge as far out as possible for maximum leverage. They may be operated directly by cables from the control column hand wheel or by moving the stick sideways.

The cables of a mechanically operated system are tensioned to a pre-determined load to compensate for thermal expansion. The cable run terminates at a pulley wheel and/or lever attached to the control surface.

The ailerons make the aircraft roll around the longitudinal axis (they act like horizontal rudders). If you move the control column to the left, the right aileron goes down, increasing the angle of attack on that side, and the left one goes up, decreasing it, causing a roll in the same direction.

Frise or *differential* ailerons are used to counteract aileron drag caused by the downgoing aileron. Frise ailerons have an asymmetric leading edge, so that the downgoing one creates more drag because its hinge is offset. It also produces a slot (i.e. a gap between its upper surface and the rear of the wing) to smooth out the airflow over it.

Differential ailerons move the down aileron through a smaller angle so, in a level turn to the right, the right aileron moves up more than the left aileron moves down.

AILERON REVERSAL

The ailerons are at the end of the wings simply because the flaps are already near the roots. If the wings twist, as they may do when the ailerons are used at high speeds, the effects of the ailerons may reverse and reduce the available rate of roll. Such aero-elastic distortion may also affect stability in pitch and yaw. In essence, when the aileron goes down, the wings will go down instead of up. Aileron reversal speed is normally outside the flight envelope, but you may still get these effects at any high forward speed.

Large (transport) aircraft may have multiple ailerons, with one set disabled at certain speeds - the 767's (outboard) second set on each wing is locked at 240 kts, as only smaller ailerons (with a short moment arm) are needed at high speeds, otherwise aileron deflection would cause a wing to twist around its torsional axis, enough to reduce the angle of attack and make it ineffective. In addition, beyond a certain *aileron reversal speed*, you would get a negative value and the roll will be the opposite of what you expect (see below). At low speeds, the inboard ailerons can supplement the outer ones to increase the rolling rate. Such mixed use is automatic.

Aileron snatch results from the centre of pressure moving rapidly back and forth over the aileron at high angles of attack. It is prevented by placing a rubber seal between the aileron and the wing. Roll spoilers (see below) can either assist or replace ailerons. When the flaps are lowered, their outer parts, or even the whole flap, can also be used as ailerons. Ailerons that droop when the flaps are deployed are called **flaperons**. These can produce a considerable increase in $C_{L_{max}}$.

AILERON DROOP
Ailerons are usually rigged to be slightly down when the roll control is in the neutral position. This is to correct for any upfloat during flight where the pressure differential over the wing makes the ailerons move upwards to increase the drag. If they are made to droop, in flight, drooped ailerons assume a normal position.

COMBINED CONTROLS

ELEVONS
These are combined elevators and ailerons. If you are trying to control pitch, they move in the same direction simultaneously. If you are trying to roll, they do so in opposite directions. However, there is no space at the trailing edge for flaps, resulting in a very high nose up attitude when landing and poor visibility - to improve it, Concorde had to lower its nose.

FLAPERONS
Combined flaps and ailerons – aileron deflection is limited so roll control can be a problem.

RUDDERVATORS
The control surfaces on the angled stabilisers are called **ruddervators**, as they work as both rudder and elevators, so you will be using the control column in one axis together with the rudder pedals.

TAILERONS
Combined elevators and ailerons.

Secondary Flight Controls
Tabs, slats and flaps, which vary the lift by changing the airflow pattern, wing area, or both, are secondary flight controls that modify the effects of the primary controls.

High lift devices reduce the take-off and landing distances required by allowing the aircraft to get the lift it needs at lower airspeeds. Put another way, they increase the coefficient of lift so you can reduce the V (speed) in the Lift formula, which is handy in aircraft that are designed for high speed flight. As they are part of the wing, increasing the sweep angle reduces their effectiveness.

Whereas flaps increase lift by changing the camber and/or area of the wings, spoilers and speed brakes do the opposite by changing the airflow over the wing to *reduce* lift. This is of great importance, especially when the engines have to be kept at high RPM while you are trying to descend. Speed brakes work together simultaneously, but spoilers work individually to assist in roll control.

TRIM
Depending on how power is used and how the controls are positioned, it may take some force to keep the aircraft in a particular attitude. That is, for any combination of power and control position, they will move freely with a certain range, but take a lot of force to go outside of it - an increase of speed from the trimmed position at low speed has more effect on stick force than it does at high speed.

These extra forces can be trimmed out with a wheel or similar device in the cockpit which operates a small control surface in the elevator (for example), so you have a secondary surface attached to a primary surface that applies a continuous force to relieve pilot workload.

If there is a double switch on the elevator trim, it is there to reduce the chances of a trim runaway.

Most large aeroplanes do not have aileron or rudder trim - instead, the artificial feel mechanism is adjusted.

Some aircraft use fuel for longitudinal trim. For example, Concorde used to pump fuel to and from its centre tanks to the fin tanks for supersonic flight, and the tailplanes of the 747-400 and A300 series are used as fuel tanks and pitch trim. The trim sheet will show the tail trim setting needed for take-off, and the needle of the trim indicator will show in a take-off segment coloured white or green.

A trim tab is hinged at the rear of the starboard elevator and is usually controlled by two handwheels through a chain, cable, rod and gear system in the *opposite* direction to the elevator (when the autopilot is engaged, pitch adjustments are made by a *servo motor* connected to the tab). The wheel moves the surface up or down in the airflow, which moves the elevator the opposite way and does the work you would otherwise have to do to keep it there. If the trim wheel is moved forward, it forces the trim surface upwards, which creates more lift between it and the elevator, which therefore is forced down, creating more lift underneath the tail which lifts and forces the nose down. The thing to remember for exams is that the control column, when moved forward, moves the elevator *down*, whereas the trim wheel moves its attached surface *up*. If the elevator gets jammed, the controls reverse. As they are independently controlled, *trim tabs remain fixed* for all positions of the controls they serve. They are also the only forms of balance that are used after the controls are moved - all the others are automatic. Power not only alters the effectiveness of the primary controls but also that of the trim tabs. Reducing power makes the nose pitch down because the trim tab has become less effective and cannot hold the nose in position. Compared with the elevator trim system, a stabiliser trim system has certain advantages:

- it is **less sensitive to flutter**
- when jammed, it is easier to control the aeroplane
- it has a larger range of speeds and C of G positions
- the neutral position of the control column does not alter after trimming for a speed change. After trimming for a speed decrease, the neutral position of the control column moves aft with an elevator trim system.

Jet transport aeroplanes with power assisted controls are normally fitted with adjustable stabilisers instead of elevators with trim tabs because they are able to generate the higher forces required by such aeroplanes. The main advantages are:

- No trim drag from the normal elevator.
- Full travel for the elevator.
- Smaller elevators are required.

Trimmable stabilisers are usually hydraulically powered and controlled by trim switches on the control yoke, or by trim wheels, or even the autopilot. The current settings are shown by indicators near the throttle levers. The green band shows the take-off range.

An out of trim stabiliser can produce such a powerful pitching moment that even full elevator deflection may be unable to overcome it. Rotation will be difficult if the machine is nose heavy. If the THS is at the maximum nose up position, the nose wheel will lift off early. So important is this that an alarm will sound if the aircraft is incorrectly configured.

If you take off in a jet transport aeroplane with its C of G on the aft limit, and the trimmable horizontal stabiliser set to the maximum nose down position (a higher leading edge) for take-off, the rotation will be normal, using normal rotation technique. An aeroplane with a forward C of G has the stabilator leading edge lower than if the C of G was in the trimmed position. If the stabilator is jammed in the cruise position, you need a higher landing speed or a lower flap setting to land.

Balance tabs provide aerodynamic balance and make it easier to move the controls by automatically moving the trim tab - it is easy to overcontrol when using them.

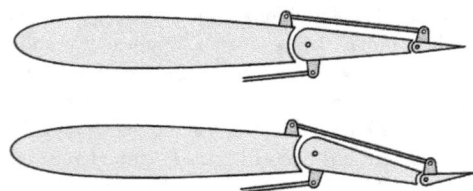

An *anti-balance* or *anti-servo* tab moves automatically *in the same sense as the main control*, and is provided to increase the force required to move it, so the further it is deflected, the greater the force (the angle of attack increases at a greater rate on the tab). This both aids the control's return to neutral and (more importantly) stops it moving to full deflection due to aerodynamic forces, thus resisting over-controlling and overstress, especially when controls have low aerodynamic loading. It also makes hydraulically boosted controls more effective.

It is outboard of the spring tab on the port elevator.

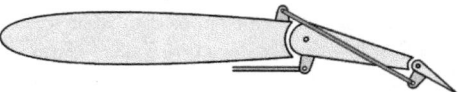

The purpose of a **servo tab** is simply to reduce stick forces, as opposed to a trim tab, which is supposed to reduce them to zero. Servo tabs are situated on the right of the port elevator, and work in a similar way to anti-servo tabs, except that only the tab is moved by the controls, and the force of the airflow over it makes the primary surface move - servo tabs are less effective at slow speeds as their function is to assist in moving large control surfaces, rather than holding them in one position.

Servo tabs move in the *opposite* direction to the surfaces to which they are attached, through a mechanism on the port elevator torque tube.

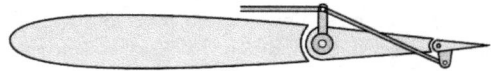

Normally, when control forces are light, the tab is part of the elevator, but when they exceed 25 lbs, a spring compresses to deflect the tab and produce an aerodynamic force to aid movement of the elevator. If the surface to which they relate jams, you get *control reversal*. At high airspeeds a spring tab will behave like a servo tab - spring tabs use springs with a preset strength to allow the tab to be effective above a certain stick load. External locks fitted to the main control surfaces will not prevent movement of a servo tab or its control.

A *servomechanism* is a *closed loop control system in which a small power input controls a much larger power output in a strictly proportionate manner.*

A *control tab* does a similar job, but is manually controlled - it is only there for when the hydraulics fail and you need help with control movements.

Trim surfaces may also be found on rudders, depending on the complexity of the machine, which helps when you have to fly with one engine out. You may occasionally see a *fixed trim tab*, which is there to provide a fixed amount of trim to make the machine fly true (it may be one wing low, for example, from the factory). It must only be altered by an engineer.

Interesting Aside: One of the Dambusters' Lancasters had to get home using only trim controls, after an aileron cable snapped, with flat turns from the rudders (Shannon said afterwards that it was a better landing than usual).

BALANCE

A flight control that is hinged at its leading edge is quite hard to move, especially on heavy or fast aeroplanes (at high speeds, control surfaces may flutter due to buffeting, especially if the wings are flexible with a high aspect ratio). Placing the hinge away from the leading edge (an inset hinge line) can reduce your workload, which is how aerodynamic balancing comes in, where a surface in front of the hinge line will produce an opposing force that will reduce the moment, aside from reducing the gap between the lifting force and the hinge.

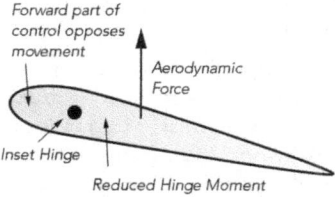

However, if the hinge is too far back, the C of P of the control surface may move ahead of the hinge and cause an overbalance.

An alternative method is to fit a streamlined balancing weight (usually lead) forward of the hinge. It may be inside the control surface itself, or fitted externally (*Mass Balance*). A graduated horn balance will prevent an over balance at high speeds.

FLAPS

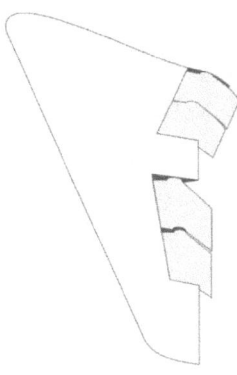

The more camber a wing has, the more of the upper surface is exposed to accelerate the airflow and the more lift is created. However, at some point you will get more drag than lift, which you can only really tolerate when landing, particularly over obstacles in short spaces. Normally, you want more lift than drag. It would be handy, therefore, to be able to change the camber to suit the conditions. The Wright Brothers bent the wing, but modern aerofoils don't allow this. Instead, only part of the wing is "bent".

Flaps (as designed for deck landings) are hinged devices on the trailing edges of wings*, inboard of the ailerons, that temporarily increase the camber for certain modes of flight, like landing, and sometimes take-off (not in the PA 31, or aircraft without enough power to overcome the extra drag that reduces acceleration), where you might be going very much slower than normal and need a boost - in fact, *flaps produce the required lift at lower speed by increasing the upper camber and the negative pressure underneath* because the chord line moves further down at the rear and changes the angle of attack against the relative airflow (pushing the nose down restores the original angle).

*Ailerons, elevators and rudders fall within this definition.

Thus, the reason for using flaps (or any other low speed lift-producing device) is to change the shape of the wing required for high speed flight into one suitable for low speed flight. Without it you would need several miles of runway to get airborne. Or land, in which case you need sturdier (and heavier) undercarriages.

Flaps increase the lift coefficient to beyond the normal maximum in the clean condition. They increase the lift *available* but not the lift *delivered*. Induced drag hardly changes but parasite drag increases. As a result, V_{MD} decreases, which reduces the range of unstable speeds.

Certain high flap angles can produce more drag than lift, so your acceleration and climb gradient may be reduced unacceptably (you need to accelerate before you can pull the flaps in). In 1971, an RAF Andover, which is a STOL aircraft, crashed at the Rome airshow when the co-pilot selected landing flap (30°) instead of take-off flap (25°). Unfortunately, the Captain didn't notice.

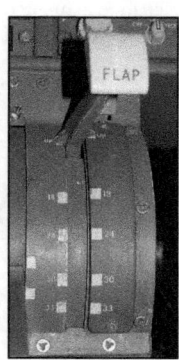

In this case, the L/D ratio reduces. Too much flap on take-off reduces acceleration - many aircraft, such as the PA31, do not use it. The flap setting that gives the shortest take-off run is called the *optimum flap setting*, typically about 15-20°. It is used when the Take Off Run Available is the limiting factor in performance (especially when you are hot and high), and is what your Maximum Take Off Mass (MTOM) should be based on (if the climb gradient is limiting use maximum flap).

If the MTOM is limited by the climb gradient, the minimum flap setting (for the least drag) will maximise the take-off weight, so if the climb gradient is the most limiting factor, the best one to use is 0°. If the Take-off Run Available (runway) is reduced, or other factors which increase the ground roll are most limiting, the *optimum* permissible flap setting for take-off should be used to maximise the take-off weight.

For a prop-driven aeroplane, the minimum drag speed gets below approach speed anyway, providing speed stability. However, there is a point beyond which the extra surface structure in the airflow produces more drag than lift, which is made use of when trying to bring the speed down, as with a short-field landing, or increase the angle of approach without much sacrifice in speed. Sometimes, the ailerons are made to move in sympathy with flaps.

When flaps are extended in a straight and level flight at constant IAS, the lift coefficient will eventually decrease. To remain in level flight the lift force must stay the same, and to have that with constant IAS, the coefficient of lift (C_L) must be constant. Therefore, as the flaps go down, the pitch angle must be reduced to keep C_L the same.

There is a **maximum flap extension speed**, as they are not designed for high speed flight. A flap load relief system will typically prevent full extension at a greater speed than V_{FE} (maximum flap extension speed).

Once lowered, flaps should not normally be raised until you are actually on the ground. On a missed approach, they should be raised after power is applied, in easy stages. The aircraft becomes less stable when flaps are extended, because the lateral CP moves inboard, so it becomes more manoeuvrable in roll. Longitudinal stability is decreased.

 Because the flaps do not extend all the way to the wingtips, the lift force must move toward the wing roots. This means that the pressure differences above and below the area of wing close to the tips must reduce, as will the strength of tip vortices.

All trailing edge flaps produce a nose-down pitching moment, from the change in pressure distribution as the centre of pressure move backwards, but sometimes they affect the airflow over the tailplane enough to go nose-up.

The increased pressure differential between the upper and lower surfaces also augments the upwash and downwash, which may affect the airflow over the tailplane and its longitudinal stabilising effect. Generally, when flaps are lowered, they produce a negative change in angle of attack of the tailplane, and a download is required to balance the aircraft in pitch.

Types Of Flap

Various designs create different effects, but the **Fowler flap** is considered to be the most efficient, despite their complexity - they do not just drop down from the wing, but slide out from the back first. The Fairey-Youngman flap achieves the same result, but drop first and then slide back. These are the only ones that increase the wing area and the camber at the same time. These are the only ones that increase the wing area and the camber at the same time. As such, they affect the critical angle of attack (stalling angle) and the Coefficient of Lift (C_L), providing around 90% of an increase. Fowler flaps are also almost always slotted flaps (below), which allow air to escape from the lower to the upper surface, accelerating as it does so, to re-energise the boundary layer and delay the stall.

Ailerons, rudders and elevators are **plain flaps**, which only increase the camber with no change in surface area. They produce a nose-down pitching moment because the C of P moves aft. Plain flaps typically produce a 50% increase in lift at a given IAS (although it can nearly double), but there is a maximum because the increased camber encourages boundary layer separation over the upper surface of the wing, which reduces the critical angle to about 12°. During the landing, as less pitch up is required, visibility ahead is better.

The plain flap increases drag considerably, which is fine for approach and landing, but not during take-off and climb, so plain flaps are best suited to low speed aircraft.

If you need flaps during take-off, it is usually limited to small amounts only for normal aeroplanes but STOL aircraft use considerably more.

The (older) **split flap** (as invented by Orville Wright) leaves the upper surface unbroken while the bottom part moves downwards (but not rearwards), which changes the mean chord. Past the mid position, they increase drag without increasing lift, which is why they are only used for landing. Split flaps can produce up to a 60% increase in lift, with a large increase in drag, so they are mainly used for approach and landing. As with plain flaps, they create a nose-down pitching moment, but it is less, and the stalling angle of attack is only marginally reduced, to around 14°, due to the same boundary layer separation.

A **slotted flap** has a gap between the trailing edge of the wing and its leading edge, which acts like a venturi to let air flow from the high pressure area beneath the wing to the low-pressure area above it.

The additional kinetic energy makes the air flow further back along the upper surface of the flap before separating to stabilise the boundary layer. In fact, a new boundary layer is formed over the flap which remains attached over very high flap deflections. This increases C_{Lmax} by about 65% and increases the stalling angle of attack by 1 or 2°. The drag produced is much less than with plain or split flaps, so it can be used in a limited way during take-off as well as landing.

In summary, a slotted flap increases C_{Lmax} by increasing the camber of the aerofoil and re-energising the airflow by preventing it from breaking away.

Double or triple slotted flaps allow slow, steep approaches at reasonable aircraft attitudes, although there is a marked nose-down pitching moment because the C of P moves way back. Leading edge devices (below) usually fix this. There is a 70% increase in C_{LMAX} with an associated stalling angle of about 18°.

This is what happens with the angle of attack against C_L:

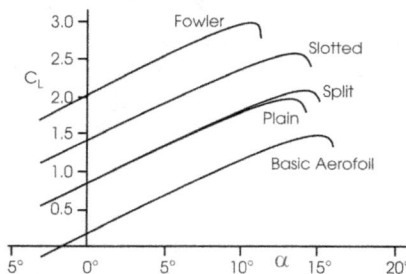

The increase in C_L when flaps are deployed looks like this:

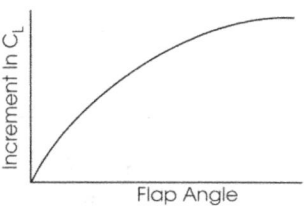

It is linear initially, but reduces markedly as the maximum flap angle is approached.

The increase in C_D looks like this:

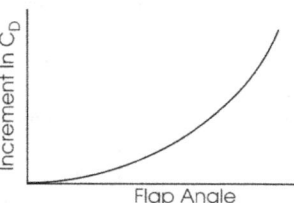

At lower flap angles, the increase is small, but it is markedly greater as the flap angle is increased.

Finally, this is how different types of flap affect the relationship between C_L and C_D:

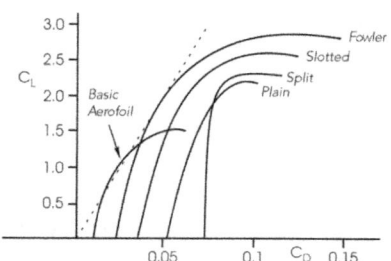

The tangent from the origin to each of the curves shows the efficiency and the L/D ratio for each of them. That with the steepest gradient is the most efficient and has the best L/D ratio. As shown, it is the Fowler flap.

ASYMMETRIC FLAPS

Should flaps operate *asymmetrically* (that is, one side works, but the other doesn't), the aircraft will **roll** to the retracted side*, though less so with leading edge flaps. If it happens, immediately select flaps up and apply the appropriate aileron and rudder, but this is a good reason for only selecting flap in small quantities in the first place - the influence of ailerons will not be enough to counteract that of full asymmetric flaps.

*Asymmetric slats create a yawing moment.

LEADING EDGE DEVICES

With a high-speed aerofoil (that has a small leading edge radius) the boundary layer can separate when trailing edge flaps are lowered. Leading edge flaps modify the leading edge radius and the slots associated with them re-energise the boundary layer.

Leading edge devices, especially slots, only incur a relatively small drag penalty, so the lift/drag ratio is improved rather than reduced. In fact, extending the slats 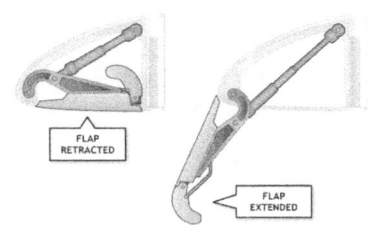 provides the most positive contribution to C_{Lmax} regardless of the flap position - they produce about 60% extra lift.

Leading edge devices can be deployed with any flap setting and go to the full-out position. They increase the camber of the wing, and hence the acceleration, and assist with the boundary layer. They affect the critical angle of attack (α_{CRIT}). Trailing edge devices, on the other hand, can be selected to varying degrees because they affect the coefficient of lift (C_L). Both take the aircraft away from the stall.

The *Krueger flap* (as found on a 747, ten on each wing) extends *forward* from the inboard leading edge of swept wing aircraft.

The nose folds to vary the effective camber, and does *not* form a slot (see below). An alternative is the *drooped leading edge flap*.

Krueger flaps increase the lift by around 50% but they actually produce poorer aerodynamic efficiency, so the wing stalls earlier. However, they do allow steeper climbing and gliding angles and better control at low speeds (you need slots and flaps to get slow landing speeds and adequate lateral control). With swept wings, Krueger flaps are fitted inboard and slots outboard to ensure that the wing root stalls before the wing tip.

SLATS

It is more common to use devices such as slats, which are small aerofoils that open forward of the main one to create a slot and smooth out the airflow, or guide it over the top of the wing at an optimum angle. The "downwash" from an extended slat makes the high velocity air rushing through the slot stick to the upper surface of the wing for longer. The idea is to modify the pressure distribution over the top surface of the aerofoil. The slat is highly cambered and has a lower pressure over its top surface, but the flow interaction results in a higher pressure over the main aerofoil, which offsets the adverse pressure gradient and delays flow separation. Thus, slats increase boundary layer energy and prolong the stall to allow a higher critical angle of attack - they can increase C_{LMAX} by more than 70% (about the same as a plain flap) and the stalling angle of attack from 15% to 20%. At high angles of attack, the slat increases the upper curvature of the wing and the pressure distribution above it.

The angle of attack of the slat is 12-15% less than that of the main wing, in any position, with reference to the relative airflow. With automatic slats, it is the location of the stagnation point that determines their open or closed position. When it is established on the slat, the positive pressure stops it opening. However, at high angles of attack, the stagnation point migrates downward along the lower surface of the wing. This creates an upwash under the slats and reduces the pressure on their leading edge. This allows them to open (the ones on the ME-109 would pop out at about 120 mph in a tight turn).

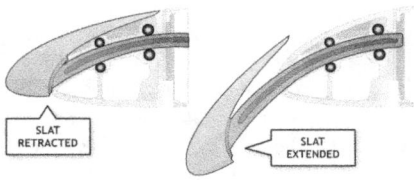

After take-off, slats are retracted after flaps because they allow large decreases in stall speed with relatively less drag. Slats can be manually operated (unpopular with pilots), or automatic (unpopular with designers).

SLOTS

(fixed ones, at least) are openings between a slat and the leading edge of a wing that create a venturi effect as air flows from the lower to the upper surface at high angles of attack, to produce around 50% extra lift.

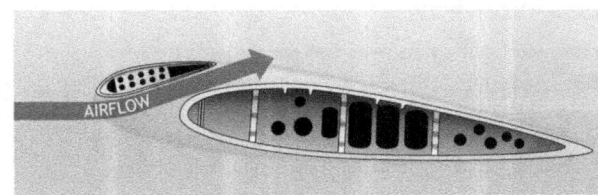

Because the air directed through the slot has lots of energy, it re-energises the boundary layer and extends the laminar flow, moving the transition point to the rear, reducing the area of turbulent flow over the wing. This reduces the loss of lift and drag, and increases the stalling angle of attack. Slots can give improved lateral control at and above the critical angle, sometimes by as much as 10°, across the length of the wing, or just as far as the ailerons. Leading edge slots are more effective than slotted flaps.

SPOILERS

Slow landing requires the highest possible C_{Lmax} - if both wings are already working hard at their maximum limits, you can only control the aircraft laterally by reducing the C_{Lmax} on the

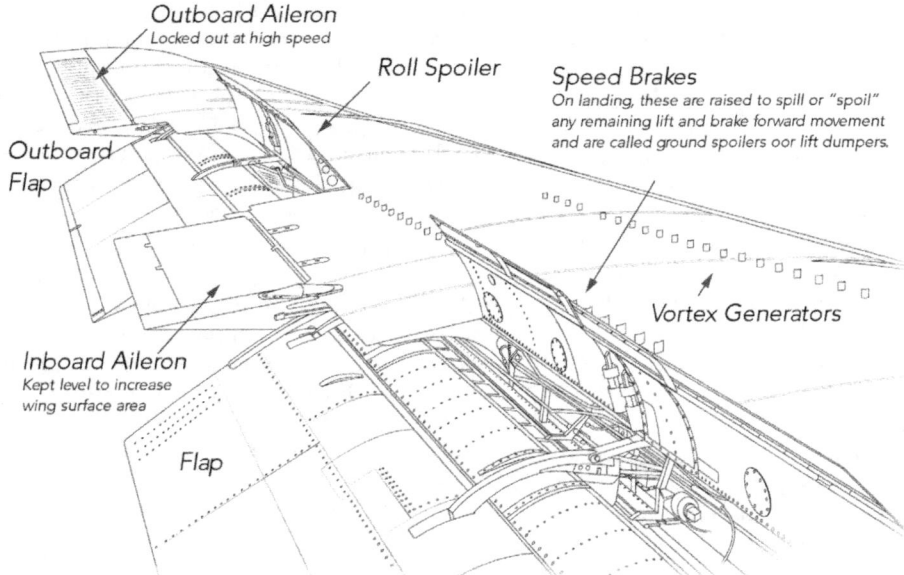

relevant side. Whereas ailerons change the effective camber of the outer part of the wing, spoilers create a turbulent flow over it to destroy the lift and stall the wing to produce the same effect, but on the other side. They extend into the boundary layer and force it to separate. Speed brakes thus allow you to keep the engine speed high with low airspeed. Spoiling the lift is a much more effective method because jet engines operate with a time lag, and modern aircraft are very slick, so drag is created without altering the shape of the wing, essentially producing the same effect as introducing a barn door into the airflow, though not as big, of course (they are flat panels on the upper wing). If they go up on one wing, the wing drops, since it is producing less lift than the other. Thus, the aircraft rolls in the direction of the *upgoing* spoilers. The downgoing wing puts the aileron up to counteract adverse aileron yaw, so: "Roll spoilers up, aileron up - DOWNGOING WING".

When they work with the ailerons (in which case they are being used as a flying control, the combination often works better than either*) or during the landing ground run they may be linked with the brakes to increase the weight on the wheels, helping with the braking action and making sure the machine doesn't bounce back up in the air again (ground spoilers are effectively speed brakes that kill lift once on the ground, which activate when the main wheels spin up). Reverse thrust automatically deploys them on an abandoned take-off. When you extend a spoiler, C_D is *increased*, and C_L is *decreased*.

*On some aircraft, like the MU-2, spoilers are used instead of ailerons, as they are less complicated and more effective anyway (you need new crosswind landing skills!) If you have ailerons, spoilers allow them to be made smaller and make more room for flaps. Ailerons and spoilers usually have separate control columns.

Spoilers are locked down in the cruise, for obvious reasons, especially as the low pressure above a wing can suck them out of their sockets (spoiler float).

The benefits of using spoilers include:

- No adverse yaw.
- Wing twisting is reduced as they act forward of the ailerons.
- No flutter.
- They are clear of the trailing edge so room can be made for flaps.

The use of spoilers can be asymmetrical or symmetrical.

SPEED BRAKES

Speed brakes are designed to make descent easier without decreasing power enough to cool the engine and are especially useful in aeroplanes with high service ceilings. They are also good for setting up the right approach speed and descent pattern in the landing configuration. The brakes, when extended, create drag without altering the curvature of the wing and are usually fitted far enough back along the chord so they do not disrupt too much lift and are located laterally where they will not disturb the airflow over the tailplane. They are usually small metal blades housed in a fitting concealed in the wing that, when activated from the cockpit, pivot up to form a plate. On some types of aircraft, speed brakes are incorporated into the rear fuselage and consist of two hinged doors that open into the slipstream.

Principles of Flight

Many of the definitions given below do not just apply to Principles of Flight, but originate from mechanics (the science of how objects interact with forces) and can be used with many other aspects of aviation. For example, vectors can not only be used to describe the forces acting on an aerofoil, but can also show the relationships between heading and track when affected by the wind, which is useful in Navigation.

DEFINITIONS

- Axes

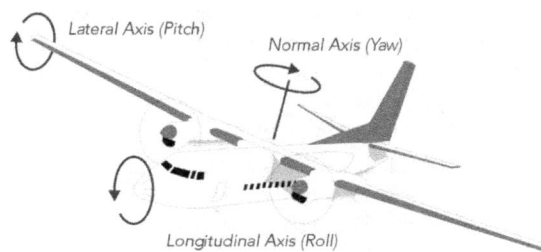

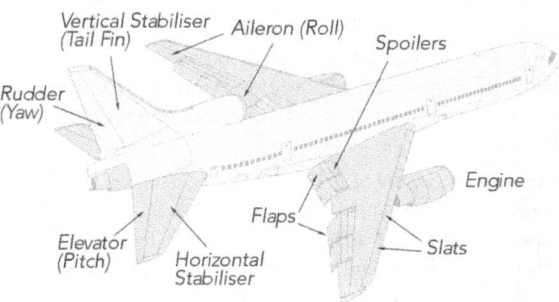

- The **longitudinal axis** of an aeroplane extends fore and aft, through the fuselage. Movement about it is **roll**, controlled by the ailerons, and supplemented by spoilers on larger aircraft, which use two sets of ailerons anyway, one being locked out at high speed. This is the only axis with airflow parallel to it, which is relevant for stability. The **angle of bank** (used for rolling) is between the *lateral* axis and the horizon.
- The **lateral axis** runs from wing tip to wing tip (it parallels the span at 90° to the normal axis). Movement around this axis is **pitch** (the angle between the longitudinal axis and the plane of the horizon) and it is controlled by the elevators.
- The **vertical** or **normal** axis is perpendicular to the longitudinal and lateral axes. Movement around it is **yaw,** primarily controlled by the rudder, having been moved by the pedals.

All axes run through the Centre of Gravity. **Translation** occurs *along* an axis, **rotation** occurs *about* an axis.

- **Velocity**. The rate of change of position *in a given direction*. Unfortunately, this word is often used instead of *speed*, as the units used are the same, but speed is only concerned with the time taken over a distance travelled, not which way you are going. For example, velocity can be a combination of airspeed and heading, expressing how fast an aircraft is travelling and in which direction.

With respect to velocity:

- **Straight** means flight on a constant heading.
- **Level** means flight at a constant altitude, where the vertical speed is zero.
- **Climbing** means flight at a constant airspeed and constant positive vertical speed (if your airspeed is decreasing you are zooming).
- **Descending** means flight at a constant airspeed and negative vertical speed (if your airspeed is increasing you are diving).
- **Turning** means that your heading is changing. The **heading** is the angle between the longitudinal axis and a reference line in the plane of the horizon (usually some variety of North).
- **Vector**. A quantity with size and direction, such as force or velocity. Non-directional *scalar* quantities like speed or mass have size only, and can be combined by simple addition or subtraction, whereas the length of a vector is

proportional to the quantity involved. For example, a speed of 60 knots might involve a line 6 inches long, with each inch standing for 10 knots (all other lines in the drawing must have the same scale).

Now you can work out problems with diagrams, because vectors can be combined to produce a *resultant* such as Total Reaction shown on the right (the single force which is exactly equivalent to two, or more, forces is called their 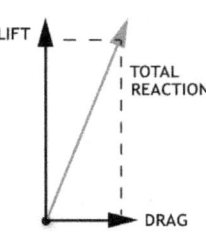 resultant. When two forces are applied to or from a point, their resultant is the diagonal of a parallelogram based on that point). The *resolution* of a vector is the process of finding its effect in two mutually perpendicular directions. A **vector diagram** is a picture of a vector with an arrow showing the direction the force is acting in.

- **Mass**. The quantity of matter in a body, which is constant if the number of subatomic particles in it remains unaltered. It is functionally identical to weight when gravity is present, as described below. The Centre of Mass of an object is where the sum total of its mass is said to act. The **mass centroid** is a line joining the Centres of Mass of thin slices of a body. It is important when designing propellers and balancing things that rotate. Newton also defined mass in terms of inertia in that, the greater the mass of a body, the greater the force needed to move it.

  The basis of flight is the *conservation of mass* (from Lavoisier) applied to a fluid. The principles include:

  - **Continuity**, where mass can neither be created nor destroyed, but it may change form into something else, like heat with an engine, or chemical energy (from the engine) into kinetic energy (movement). In a steady flow process (where flow rates don't change over time) the inflow should equal the outflow, or what goes in must come out, whatever might happen in the middle. This is like Kirchhoff's electrical law, and Bernoulli's *Venturi Effect*.
  - The **Conservation Of Momentum** is Newton's second law applied to a continuum, but that's not important right now ☺.
  - The **Conservation Of Energy** is similar to the First Law of Thermodynamics (see *Engines* for the second), and to *Continuity*, in that the energy of a closed system (other things being equal) remains constant during a process.

- **Density** is the mass of a specific volume of air, divided by its volume.
- **Gravity**. The force of attraction between masses, which is greater with mass and closeness together.

  The **Centre Of Gravity** is the point around which all moments arising from gravity are equal to zero, where an object's weight (or gravitational attraction) passes through, or where its mass is concentrated. When stationary on the ground, the total weight of an aircraft acts vertically through its Centre of Gravity, parallel to the gravity vector (autopilots rotate aircraft around their Centres of Gravity). The C of G could also be described as the average location of a body's weight force, or its point of balance. The forward limits are primarily determined by control response and the rear one by decreasing stability.

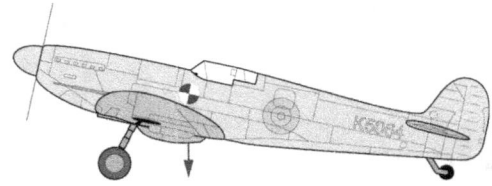

- **Weight**. This is the effect of the local gravity vector (g) on a mass that provides a force acting down, toward the centre of the Earth. This may not be constant, as gravity varies around the world but, as the atmosphere occupies only $1/600$ of the space taken up by the Earth, its influence can at least be considered as constant.

   Although pounds and kilograms are commonly used as weight values, they are actually to do with mass - as weight is a force it should, strictly speaking, be expressed in newtons, which arise from multiplying kg by m/s^2. **G** is shorthand for any force or acceleration that is equivalent to weight, so 2G is twice the weight involved. *G* shares the same units as acceleration which, under gravity (g) is 32.2 feet per second, per second, but SI (below) uses metres (9.81 m/s^2). Acceleration as G forces can affect the body in flight (see *Human Factors*).

- **The SI System**. The *International System of Units* now recommended for scientific purposes instead of CGS (*centimetre*, *gram*, and *second*) and Imperial.

  Unfortunately, nobody told the manufacturers, so the SI system is the politically correct one. You will also need a working knowledge of the traditional systems, also shown in the tables below.

Primary units are:

Item	SI	Anglo-American
Mass	kilogram (kg)	0.0685 slug
Weight (Force)	newton (N) (kgm/s^2)	0.2248 lb
Length	metre (m)	3.281 feet 39.4 inches
Time	second (s)	second
Temperature	kelvin (K)	celsius (C)

These are derived units:

Item	SI	Anglo-American
Weight	kg (9.807 N)	2.2046 lbs
Density	kg/m^3	lbs/ft^3
Pressure	pascal (N/m^2)	millibar
Velocity	m/sec	3.281 ft/sec
Acceleration	m/s^2	3.281 ft/sec^2
g	9.807m/s^2	32.2 ft/sec^2
Power	watt (Nm/s)	.7376 ft.lb/sec hp
Metric hp	75 kgm/s	.9863 hp
English HP	76.04 kgm/s	550 ft.lb/sec
Energy	joule	

N/m^2 is used for wing loading and dynamic pressure.

- **Work**. A resultant force is said to do work when it moves a body in the direction in which it is acting, so it is equivalent to *force x distance*, or *force x velocity*, if you bring time into it, and start thinking in terms of power (below). If an object doesn't move even if a force is applied, no work is done, although it obviously has in the casual sense.
- **Power**. Power (the rate of doing work, or force x velocity) is measured in *horsepower*, which has a standard value of 33,000 ft/lbs per minute, or 550 per second, based on the idea that a standard horse (in a British mine) could lift 100 pounds out of a vertical shaft while walking away at about 4 mph (330 fpm). When you lift a weight, you work against gravity and the power you need depends on the weight of the item concerned and how high you raise it. So, if you lift 10 lbs over 55 feet, or 55 lbs over 10 feet, you require 550 ft-lbs, the product of weight multiplied by distance, but that 550 ft-lbs must be used within 1 second to be a horsepower. The SI unit is the watt, which is 1 joule/second. 1 horsepower equates to 0.746 kilowatts, or 746 watts (to convert kW to hp, multiply by 1.34).
- **Pressure**. The force per unit area on a surface arising from the time rate of change of momentum of the gas molecules impacting on it, usually defined at a point normal to the surface.
- **Energy**. A measure of the ability of a body (or unit of mass) to do work, in joules (the unit of work) or newton-metres (weight multiplied by distance). An aircraft can have three types of energy:
  - **Potential energy**, which comes from its position in a gravity field (usually height). 50 lbs at 100 feet has a potential energy of 500 ft-lbs. Similarly, 50 newtons at 100 metres has a potential energy of 5 000 joules. When an object is dropped, its potential energy progressively converts to.....
  - **Kinetic energy**, which comes from movement (the energy of motion), and is actually a measure of the ability of a body that has velocity to do work when it is brought to rest (mostly a sudden stop!) and can change to **pressure energy**. If you integrate the rate of change of momentum with differential calculus, the formula *mass* x *velocity* (mv) becomes ½mv^2, meaning kinetic energy, which will be significant when we look at *Lift*.
  - **Chemical energy**, from the engines.

An aircraft in straight and level flight has heaps of all three. A reduction in chemical energy (losing an engine) will cause a descent if all other factors remain constant.

- **Viscosity**. As air has a certain thickness, some of it will stick to an airframe as it tries to push its way through the atmosphere, which takes energy to overcome. This is expressed by viscosity, which is also relevant for the internal friction between the layers of oil when it comes to lubrication. The higher the viscosity, and the thicker the fluid, the slower the flow.
- **Compressibility**. As you start to move, air is compressed against the frontal surfaces, and may change density. This is ignored below about 300 kts because the molecules repel each other, and the error is only around 5%. Above it, the effects can be significant (see the table below), so any instruments or aerofoils relying on air pressure won't work so well without adjustment. For any speed above 300 kts, compressibility must be accounted for. The Machmeter automatically corrects for this error. 300 kts is easily achieved at higher altitudes where TAS increases markedly.

Speed (kts)	Error
175	Less than 2%
260	4%
347	7%
436	11%
522	16%

To predict the effects of compressibility, you need to be able to determine the ....

- **Mach Number**. Compressibility effects depend on the relationship of airspeed to the speed of sound (see *High Speed Flight*, later). They can be delayed with aerofoil shaping, or streamlining.
- **Angle Of Attack.** The angle between the chord line of an aerofoil and the Relative Airflow.

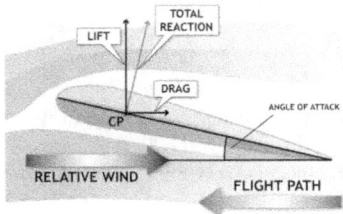

The most efficient angle of attack at which to fly is where you get the best lift/drag ratio.

NEWTON'S LAWS

Aside from inventing the catflap (true!), Sir Isaac Newton formulated three laws of motion that govern material bodies, which are also relevant to flight:

The First Law

In the absence of an unbalanced force, *an object at rest (or in motion) will remain at rest (or in motion at that velocity) until acted upon by an external force,* otherwise known as *Inertia*. In other words, an object in a steady state is neither accelerating nor decelerating (although it might be moving) and you must apply a force to make it move or change direction (or if you observe an acceleration, there must be a force behind it). As air has mass, it is capable of applying force, which becomes a problem at the speed of sound because the air compresses so much that it behaves like a brick wall, which is a force in anyone's language.

Related to the first Law are:

- **Inertia**. A force resisting change that gives a body the tendency to remain at rest, or carry on with what it's doing - in other words, not to change its present state, or to maintain a constant velocity, and be hard to get moving (but see *Momentum*, below, about stopping). To do its work, air must possess the property of inertia. Inertia should not be confused with Momentum, as even bodies at rest have inertia. Both can add stress to the materials used in aircraft, as found with wings that flex on takeoff or landing.

- **Momentum**. The quantity of motion in a body, or its resistance to being brought to rest.

    As it is a vector quantity, momentum concerns the *velocity* of a body as well as its mass, so the formula *mass x velocity* denotes how much is moving and how fast (only bodies with velocity can have momentum). If either mass or velocity increase, the momentum increases and you need a bigger force to change the body's state of motion. Any change in momentum is proportional to the size of the forces involved - a bullet and a steamroller may have similar momenta, but they have different masses and speeds. For example, a heavy aircraft taxying at a high rate of knots requires more power to stop than if it were going at walking pace. You could also use a relatively small force for a longer time. The letter *p* signifies momentum.

The Second Law

The rate of change of motion (of a body) [acceleration] *is directly proportional to the force acting on it, along its line of action, inversely proportional to the body's mass.* Put more precisely, when a body is made to change its state, its acceleration is proportional to, and in the direction of, the applied force.

Acceleration is the rate of change of motion in speed and/or direction (velocity), divided by time. If you change one or the other, or both, an object is accelerating, as with a turning aircraft affected by centripetal force.

 Although the word *acceleration* refers to any change in velocity, *deceleration* also indicates a decrease.

Force and mass are related, in that doubling both produces the same value of acceleration. Doubling the force doubles the acceleration if mass stays the same, and doubling mass for the same force halves the acceleration, which therefore depends on force divided by mass (and force is proportional to mass multiplied by acceleration). As force is measured in *newtons* (Kgm/s^2), represented by the letter F, if 30 newtons is applied to a mass of 10 kg, the acceleration is 30 divided by 10, or 3 m/s^2. 1 kg is equivalent to 9.81 newtons, usually rounded to 10.

 A *slug* is a unit of mass that accelerates at 1 ft/sec when acted on by a force of 1 pound.

The Third Law

If one body exerts a force on another body, the second body will exert an equal and opposite force on the first body, popularised as: *For every action, there is an equal and opposite reaction.* This law is made use of by propellers and jet engines to drive aeroplanes (and autogyros) forward.

Force is a dynamic influence that changes a body's state of rest to one of motion, or changes its rate of motion. In simple terms, a push (the only forces that truly pull are gravity, magnetism and electrical attraction, and even gravity is suspect these days). Force is equal to *mass x acceleration* (f=m.a). In studying the principles of flight, we are looking at how accelerating a mass (of air) produces a force called Lift that overcomes gravity, or Weight. In this respect, we are interested in its speed and density. The speed concerns kinetic energy, or the additional (dynamic) pressure that is there because the air is moving. However, it is the differences in static pressure that give us lift (and drag), as we shall see later.

In fact, four forces act on an aircraft in flight, called *Lift*, *Weight*, *Thrust* and *Drag*.

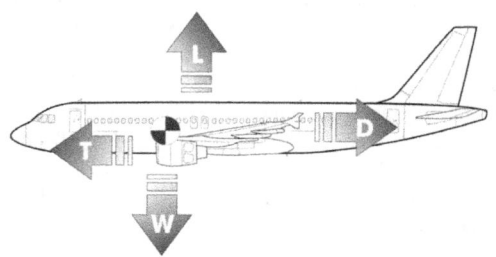

For now, lift makes a flying machine go up, weight makes it go down, thrust makes it go forward, and drag tries to stop it. Creating an imbalance between them is what makes an aircraft go in one direction or another.

- **Centrifugal Force**. Under Newton's first law, a moving body will travel along a straight path (with constant velocity) unless a force acts on it from the outside. With circular motion, the constant force pushing a body to the centre is *centripetal force*, inwards along the radius of a curve. It is an accelerating force, as it affects velocity in terms of its line of direction, and is proportional to the body's mass.

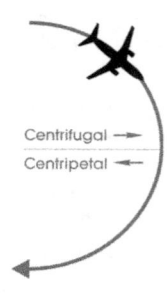

PRINCIPLES OF FLIGHT
Airflow

However, under Newton's third law the opposite reaction is *centrifugal force*, which is a fictitious one acting *outwards* (it is called a reaction force as it is only there because centripetal force is). It increases with *mass*, the *square of rotational speed*, and the *distance from the axis*, as shown here.

$$\frac{m \times V^2}{r}$$

Centrifugal force is inversely proportional to the radius of the curve, so the smaller a curve is, the more influence centrifugal force has.

 Being fictitious, centrifugal force does not act on the body in motion - the only one actually involved is centripetal force. It is the *removal* of centripetal force that allows a blade to fly from a propeller hub when it is released, not the application of centrifugal force.

- A **couple** is a combination of two equal, parallel and opposite forces that produces a rotation. In the picture below, the combination of Lift and Weight produces a couple that creates a nose down attitude. The *moment* of a couple is one of its forces multiplied by the distance between them both.

- A **moment** is the turning effect of a force about a point, in foot-pounds or newton-metres. **Torque** is similar, but is a continuous force in one direction.

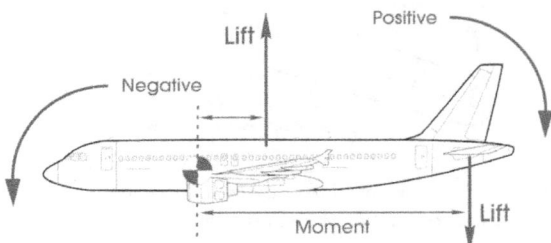

The size of a moment arises from the force involved multiplied by the distance from the point concerned to the line of action of the force. In the picture above, the two lift values are different, yet they balance because of their relative distances from the Centre of Gravity. Clockwise movement is positive, because it involves a nose-up pitching moment, and anticlockwise is negative.

- **Equilibrium** is state of balance between forces, where the sum of the clockwise moments is equal to that of anticlockwise moments (zero acceleration), as with straight and level flight.

 Sometimes forces may be in balance, but not in equilibrium, as in a turn with a constant bank angle (where you are accelerating).

AIRFLOW

Air is a fluid. Under the Archimedes Principle, an aircraft surrounded by it will be supported (or experience an apparent loss of weight) by a force equal to the weight of the air it displaces (buoyancy). Weight acts downwards and buoyancy acts upwards, so the two cancel each other out when the 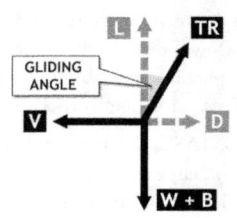 aircraft is in a steady, or unaccelerated, state, where the net force is zero. In the diagram, an aircraft is moving at constant velocity (V) in air otherwise at rest. Put another way, it could be at rest, with the air streaming past it, at -V. In theory, the situation is the same in both cases so, even if you tie an aeroplane down, a strong wind will make it want to fly up, but air at rest has less turbulence than moving air, so there are limits. In other words, it is the *relative* speed that matters.

The speed at which an object moves through the air is called *airspeed*, and the various types are described briefly below. The path an object takes through the air is the *flight path*, and the air going the other way is variously called the *relative airflow, undisturbed airflow* or *relative wind*. As it is the resultant of two vectors, it may also be called the resultant wind.

Here are the relevant airspeeds: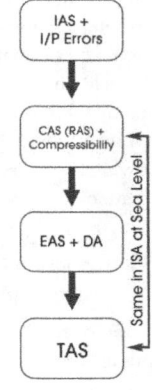

- **Indicated airspeed** (IAS) is read directly and corrected for instrument error, to become...

- **Calibrated airspeed** (CAS) is IAS corrected for position errors, which are highest at extreme speeds. They are about the same in the cruise.

- **Equivalent Airspeed** (EAS) is CAS corrected for compressibility (relative density), or factors arising from high speeds above around 300 kts (where the static pressure inside the pitot tube is higher than that outside the aircraft, and the two do not cancel out). It provides the same dynamic pressure that you would get from TAS at sea level (in ISA).

- **True Air Speed** (TAS) is the CAS corrected for altitude and temperature, or density. In ISA conditions at sea level, CAS will be equal to TAS. *It is the only speed* and the only one used for navigation - the others are pressures and deal with aircraft behaviour! TAS is also the only speed affected by density - on average, it increases by 2% over IAS for every 1,000 feet you climb, which can be significant when you land halfway up a mountain, especially on a warm day subject to low pressures.

To find out what happens to various speeds in the climb or descent, remember this picture: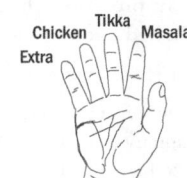

The initial letters stand for *Equivalent, Calibrated* and *True* airspeeds, and *Mach number*. In the climb, select which one remains constant, and the speeds to the right will be increasing, with the ones to the left decreasing. The reverse for the descent.

Above the tropopause (i.e. when isothermal) the Mach number and TAS will react in the same way at the same time (they will remain parallel), but remember that pressure changes and they will increase relative to IAS.

Whereas IAS is displayed in light aircraft, CAS tends to be shown on large aircraft (rather than IAS) because the corrections are made by computer. When air density is high, as it would be on a cold day, IAS can exceed TAS.

 Also, on light aircraft, the speeds for takeoff, flaps down, etc. tend to be fixed. In transport aircraft, they vary according to the weight, although they do have limits. Accurate flight planning is important, because the Flight Management System needs the weight to set the controls correctly.

The *Total Reaction* (TR) shown above, which acts at around 90° to the chord line, is the resultant of two components, one **at right angles** to V, called *Lift*, and one **opposite** (parallel) to V, called *Drag*. The angle between TR and L (the gliding, or lean-back) angle should be as small as possible to keep the drag vector short (the real trick) and the lift vector long and nearly vertical. It is governed by the ratio between Lift and Drag (or the Lift/Drag ratio), which is governed by the shape of an aerofoil and the angle at which it meets the airflow. It is broadly equivalent to the angle of attack.

 Lift does not necessarily act upwards, or in opposition to weight, and drag does not necessarily act in a horizontal direction.

The motion of fluids is still not fully understood, so one or two assumptions are made, for low speeds, at least:

- Fluids are **non-viscous**, so internal friction can be ignored outside the boundary layer, below.
- Their **flow is steady**, so velocity is constant.
- **Flow is irrotational** (it doesn't spin), with no angular momentum about any point, although this can be a factor for the Momentum Theory of propeller operation, discussed later.
- At slow speeds (below about 30% of the speed of sound), air is **incompressible** because its internal friction (as molecules bump against each other) is so low that it can be ignored. *Incompressibility* in this context simply means that there is no change in density when the pressure changes - at slow speeds, air is considered to behave like a liquid.

As it has mass, air can exert force, do work and transfer energy. As a quantity, it's normally measured in cubic feet. The ability for air to do work is affected by its density, which reduces as you go higher or the air gets warmer. Aerodynamic effects depend on:

- **air pressure**, which acts perpendicular to the surface of a body, and
- **friction**, which acts parallel to it (in shear).

As the friction is confined to only a small area near the surface (the boundary layer, overleaf), the pressure distribution around the aerofoil is what does the work.

Airflow is usually three-dimensional because it can move in any direction in space, where tip vortices (at the end of a wing) may be involved. One- or two-dimensional flows are simplifications for modelling purposes - for example, one-dimensional flow (as with propeller wash) ignores any properties at 90° (normal) to its flow. In two-dimensional flow, the motion of fluid particles is identical in the direction of flow, so airflow is two-dimensional when it concerns a cross section of an aerofoil of infinite span (having no end point), and it is three-dimensional when it starts moving sideways on its way to the trailing edge. Turbulent air is three-dimensional.

The two primary 3-dimensional factors that affect the performance of a wing are aspect ratio (tip losses) and wing sweep (transonic flow), all discussed later.

Streamlines & Streamtubes

The passage of air over an aerofoil in a steady path is called a streamline flow*, because a line drawn in a fluid so that its tangent at each point lies in the direction of the fluid's velocity (at that point) is a **streamline**.

*When a fluid's velocity at each point is the same for each particle in terms of time, the motion is described as steady, or a streamline flow. Turbulent flows are unsteady.

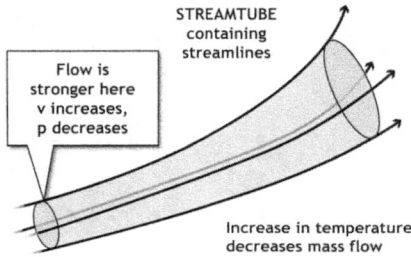

Streamlines are therefore imaginary curves along which individual particles of fluid flow. Their density is proportional to their size (or strength) in that, the closer they are together, the stronger is the flow (and the **negative** or **suction pressure**), so they can be used to illustrate increases and decreases in pressure and velocity by being drawn as converging or diverging.

Assuming the air is incompressible, we can say that:

$$A_1 V_1 = A_2 V_2$$

or that the area and velocity on one side of the equation or at one end of the streamtube is the equivalent of those on the other side or at the other end. In other words, if you mess with the area, the velocity changes, and vice versa.

Therefore, if you reduce the cross-sectional area of a tube (or a pipe) and force the streamlines closer together, their velocity will increase (water flows faster if you squeeze the end of a garden hose). Put another way, air flowing into a smaller space must either accelerate or change its density because the law of conservation says that matter cannot be destroyed. Below about a third of the speed of sound, the air density doesn't change much, because the natural repulsion between air molecules keeps it more or less constant, but it will do so at more than about 300 kts, which reduces density, so we are now talking about:

$$\rho_1 A_1 V_1 = \rho_2 A_2 V_2$$

PRINCIPLES OF FLIGHT
Airflow

A streamline drawn through each point of a closed curve creates a **stream tube**, which is a tubular region of fluid surrounded by streamlines. As streamlines do not intersect*, the same streamlines must pass through a streamtube at all points along its length. There is therefore no flow across the surface of a streamtube, so the mass entering it per second is the same as that leaving it per second, as expressed by the continuity equation.

*Pathlines in turbulent flow can cross each other.

If the temperature is increased (assuming velocity is constant), the mass flow will reduce. If density is halved, drag will reduce by a factor of 2.

Propeller wash is a good example of a streamtube:

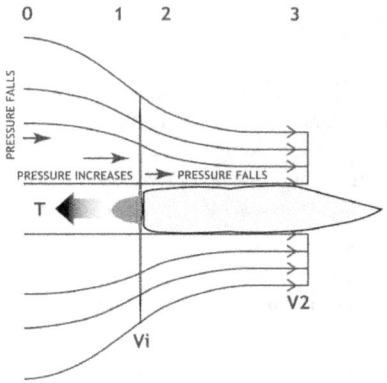

Vortex flow (e.g. at the wingtips) is partly streamline and partly turbulent. As vortices rotate, they lose energy and get larger.

The Boundary Layer

Having said that air is assumed to be non-viscous, certain aerodynamic effects cannot be explained without regard to viscosity, which makes air tend to stick to a surface moving through it and produce a resistance (skin friction). In fact, you won't get lift without it. Ludwig Prandtl discovered that, up to a certain critical airspeed, *close to the surface*, air flowing over or around a body will hug its shape and be quite well-behaved, flowing in a *laminar* fashion, after which it breaks up to form vortices that may interfere with any lifting action.

Airflow is laminar if it follows a smooth path *while it is accelerating* and its parallel layers do not interfere with each other. That is, it is non-turbulent, and its layers have different velocities. This is because air can flow freely and conform to the outline of any containers involved (as with Coanda, below).

Such a fluid can be a liquid or a gas.

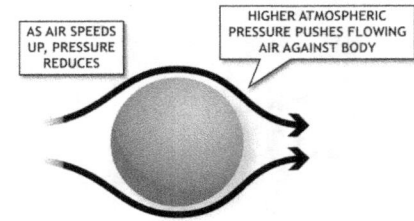

The drag coefficient of a sphere is around 0.25.

Ignoring viscosity*, airflow tends to follow the outline of a body because its pressure reduces when it speeds up on its way round. It wants to follow a straight line (after Newton's First Law), but it cannot, so the same pressure cannot be exerted on the surface it is travelling over. A lower static pressure is therefore created, relative to the air at atmospheric pressure further out from the body, and the air flow is pushed against the surface.

*If you don't ignore viscosity, friction between the air and the surface of the body creates turbulence and a lower pressure behind the sphere (see *The Flat Plate*, below).

 The force from atmospheric pressure acts against *all* surfaces. It is instrumental in concentrating the airflow over the upper surface of an aerofoil.

The net force around the sphere is zero, as the flow of air above and below is the same so, if we want it to do something we need an imbalance. In reality, viscosity will create one at the trailing edge (discussed later), but this can be done simply by cutting off its bottom half, at which point there will be a tendency for it to move upwards due to the reduced pressure on top.

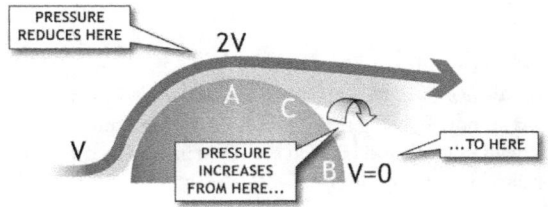

If the velocity of the airflow as it meets the new body at rest is given a value of V, it will be more as it goes over the top (at A, above). The static pressure at A will therefore be lower, but the pressure is still high at B, so the air cannot force its way there due to the adverse pressure gradient. This reverses the flow around point C, where it is about to break away. Beyond C it forms into an eddying wake, which increases the resistance.

 The flow over the half cylinder represented above is an ideal flow - in real life, friction between the surface and the air reduces its energy, which may create an area of low pressure behind - again, as happens in mountains.

The shape of an aerofoil behind its thickest point tapers away to minimise this effect and ensure that the air breaks away as much as possible near the trailing edge, so the turbulent wake remains as small as possible. If you go through a car wash, and your car remains wet, you will notice drops of water staying still on the bodywork, no matter how fast you drive. The layer in which this happens is called the *boundary layer*. Friction makes the air in its lower areas slow progressively until, at the surface (within a distance of one molecule), its relative speed could be zero, hence the water mentioned above being unaffected.

The boundary layer exists where the speed of the air flowing within it is less than 99% of the free stream (air not affected by the aircraft). This is the customary edge to the boundary layer, because one is needed, but there is no precise cutoff point, just a fading of influence. Just as the surface slows down the relative motion of the air, the air will try to drag the surface along with its flow. This is *viscous friction*, and is part of how **surface friction** (drag) is produced.

Looked at another way, an object moving through air pulls a few air molecules along with it (due to viscosity), at around the same speed as the object. The layer of air from the surface to where nothing is dragged along at all is the *laminar (i.e. layered) boundary layer*, which is typically about 1 mm thick at the leading edge and 1.8 mm at the *transition point*, near the thickest part of the aerofoil, where it becomes the *turbulent boundary layer*, and which has the strongest change in velocity close to the surface. The maximum depth is around 18 mm.

The transition point occurs where the airflow over the surface begins to slow down at, or slightly behind, the point of maximum suction.

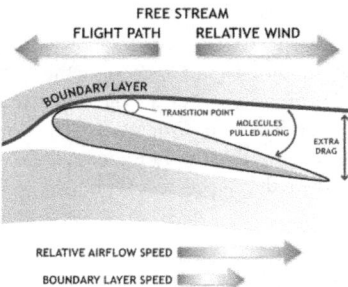

The laminar boundary layer has no velocity components (turbulence) normal to the surface (although, being picky, around 1% of the turbulent layer is actually smooth and is called the laminar sub-layer, which has a depth of around 18 mm).

The turbulent boundary layer has more kinetic energy and is less likely to separate, and may even be deliberately designed in to go round corners, especially on high speed wings. The position of the transition point between the two layers depends on:

- the condition of the surface (any obstruction will create a turbulent layer).
- the speed and size of the aerofoil (a rapidly slowing boundary layer will become turbulent).
- the adverse pressure gradient.

to create a wedge of air that resists the aerofoil's movement as *drag*, which is covered later. The transition point moves *forward* with increased speed (or increased angle of attack), which is something to do with the Reynolds number*, and more of the aerofoil becomes affected by the turbulent area, which increases the amount of skin friction. The point where turbulent airflow leaves the surface to create wake turbulence is the *separation point* (the boundary layer is considered to be turbulent between the transition and separation points). The air *accelerates* to the transition point.

*The Reynolds number expresses the ratio of pressure against viscosity forces in the flow of a fluid, or the relationship between dimensions and profile drag (it depends which book you read). It is dimensionless, meaning that it has no units, and was developed to relate scale models in wind tunnels to their real-life counterparts. Fluid flow is turbulent when the RN is greater than 2000. It is laminar below that. The Reynolds number and the surface conditions determine the characteristics of the boundary layer, which becomes thinner as the Reynolds number increases, but there is always a bit of friction drag which can never be entirely eliminated. This has some relevance to stalling, later.

SUMMARY

- The forces around aerofoils include forces from pressure *against* or *from* the surfaces at right angles, and friction *along* them, so the air is slowed down (due to viscosity) according to their smoothness.

- The layer of air immediately in contact with the surface is slowed down the most and subsequent ones less until it reaches the *free stream flow rate*. This layer is *laminar* (streamlined) and *turbulent*.

- The point where it goes from laminar to turbulent is the *transition point*. The layer thickens to create extra drag that tries to stop the aerofoil moving through the air.

Bernoulli's Theorem

In the special case where density is constant (and we assume it to be so below about 30% of the speed of sound*), the relationship between static and dynamic pressure can be defined by Bernoulli's equation which, building on the principle of conservation of energy, states that *in the streamline flow of an ideal fluid* (i.e. non-turbulent), *the quantity of energy remains constant..*

*In theory, the effects of compressibility must be considered at Mach numbers below around 0.3 but, in practice, the equations concerned can be used without significant error up to between M 0.6 and 0.7.

Total pressure is the sum of potential, kinetic (dynamic) and pressure (static) energy.

If air is at rest, it is subject to *static* pressure, and when moving, *dynamic* pressure as well. When a fluid speeds up, static pressure converts to dynamic pressure, and its value reduces because their sum must stay the same.

As dynamic pressure depends on velocity, we can say that the pressure inside a fluid decreases where its speed increases, or that an incompressible fluid speeds up through a restriction in direct inverse proportion to the reduction in area, which is balanced by a decrease in pressure. In a moving stream of fluid:

```
density x area x velocity = constant
```

but, at low speeds, you can disregard the density.

The end result is that, if you take a tube with a smaller diameter at its centre than at either end, and blow air through it, the pressure in the centre becomes less because the speed increases. It does this because the mass flow must remain the same. The correct number of air molecules will get through the hole if they go faster

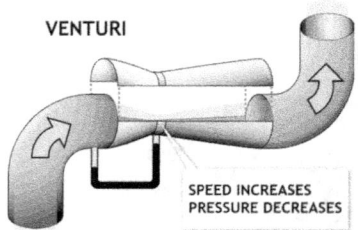

Newton's laws state that there must be an imbalance of force to provide the change in velocity (acceleration), which comes from a difference in static pressure between

the start of the tube and the constriction. This is the potential energy mentioned above.

Regard it as a streamtube with rigid walls. If you take the top half away, the phenomenon still works on the remaining (lower) half, which looks like the top surface of an aerofoil because a layer of undisturbed air (at the higher atmospheric pressure) replaces the missing bit. The imbalance creates an upward force we call lift.

You can see this yourself by taking a large piece of paper and folding it back over the top of your hand, keeping hold of it with your fingers. If you blow across the top, you will see the paper rise. Similarly, a high wind will lift the roof from a house rather than blow it off. Used sideways, this is how yachts use the wind to get along. Note, however, that this is a closed system, and assumed to be frictionless. Mainly, though, the theorem only applies **if no energy is imparted to the system** - a propeller is an actuator, so Bernoulli assumes less importance, except maybe to start things off.

The molecules of air taking the longer route may be up to 30% of the distance away from their original fellows, depending on the angle of attack, which means that the faster flow over the top has the effect of bending the airflow downwards, especially at the trailing edge of a wing. However, since the speed of the flowing air (on top of the aerofoil) is increased, its pressure is reduced, which allows atmospheric pressure to push the machine up from underneath. This is because, when the airstream meets the curved upper surface, its tendency to stick to the aerofoil is interrupted when it is diverted upwards. In terms of laminar flow, the air molecule under the wing goes with the flow and is held against it by air pressure. The one that goes over the top gets pulled away by the lower pressure, and has a harder time keeping next to the surface. The inertia that stops it creates a lower pressure. This is not helped by the dents and scratches on the average aerofoil, which help to give it a bumpier ride.

To reinforce the point - as air flows around an obstruction and does not pile up against it (like sand would), the same mass must flow away as flows towards it. As the obstruction makes the distance longer (over the top), the flow must accelerate. The net result is a cocoon of lower pressure (created by the aerofoil) surrounded by atmospheric pressure, with a bias to the upper end. The aerofoil has no choice but to go up.

Note the *stagnation point* at the point of impact just under the leading edge:

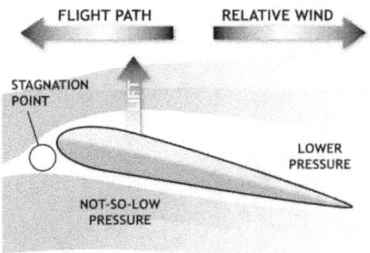

That is where the velocity of the relative airflow is zero and the surface pressure is higher than atmospheric. The air molecules are brought to rest for an instant before being given the choice of going over or under an aerofoil so, between the top and bottom edges, there is only a difference of one molecule. The essential point to note is that the flow does not divide precisely at the tip of the aerofoil, but at a stagnation point somewhere under the leading edge, which effectively increases the upper surface area, and will carry on so doing as the angle of attack increases, up to the stall. That is, as the angle of attack increases, the stagnation point moves down on the profile, to increase the size of the upper area (and, incidentally, increase the adverse pressure gradient). The pressure differential imparts acceleration to produce an upwash.

The stagnation point can also be used as a trigger for stall warning devices such as the flapper switch.

 The pressure at the stagnation point is *total pressure*. As the aircraft is accelerated, the dynamic pressure increases with the square of the TAS until you get to a speed where the dynamic pressure is equal to the ambient pressure, but this does not mean that pressure becomes zero. The increased dynamic pressure comes from the extra energy needed for the acceleration (i.e. thrust). The dynamic pressure becomes greater, so the total pressure will end up greater than its initial value. Put another way, at the stagnation point the total static pressure is the sum of static pressure plus the converted dynamic pressure. When air flows through a shock wave, however (see *High Speed Flight*), it is abruptly compressed, which converts some of the pressure energy into heat, to reduce the total pressure.

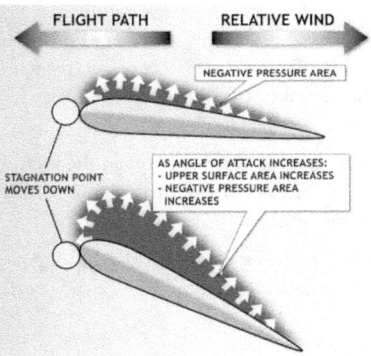

There is also a stagnation point at the trailing edge, where the airflows from the upper and lower surfaces meet.

Of course, all this can be proven mathematically. In physics, the formula for kinetic energy (that arising from movement, and measured in joules) is:

$$\tfrac{1}{2} \text{Mass} \times V^2$$

Where V stands for *Velocity*. In other words, the faster an object of a given mass moves, the more kinetic energy it possesses. We know that air has mass (density is mass per cubic foot), because it contains molecules that can exert pressure (against your hand in a wind, for example), so we can replace *Mass* in the formula above with *air density*, which uses the Greek symbol *rho*:

$$\tfrac{1}{2} \rho V^2$$

The more dense the air is, the more molecules that are available to push against an object. Combine that with speed, and you get *dynamic pressure* (q), which is represented by the above formula. Given that the total pressure is constant, if you increase speed, the dynamic pressure will automatically increase, if density remains constant. Therefore, static pressure will decrease. The difference between total and static pressure is how airspeed is measured. Bernoulli's equation can therefore be written as below, where pt = total pressure, ps = static and q = dynamic pressure:

$$pt = ps + q$$

q is measured in N/m^2.

THE AEROFOIL

An aerofoil is a device that can create a lift reaction from the air. To understand how it does this, we must remind ourselves of how static pressure works, but first....

The Flat Plate

A flat plate held at right angles to a flow of air is impacted by kinetic energy.

As the airflow decelerates to zero, the kinetic energy is converted completely to pressure energy and, if you take the area of the flat plate (S) into account, you can work out the force involved as $\frac{1}{2}\rho v^2 S$. To find the amount of the resistance to movement of the plate, you need some sort of coefficient (or correction factor) which, in the case of the flat plate, is about 1.2 (more about such coefficients under *Lift* or *Drag*, later).

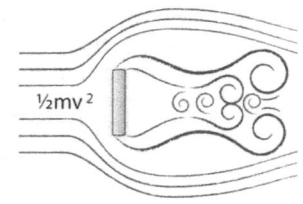

In other words, the formula for kinetic energy in the picture needs to be modified by 1.2 to get the correct figure for the amount of resistance encountered.

If you streamline the flat plate, by creating a smoother profile, but keeping the same frontal area, you can reduce the coefficient to something like 0.06.

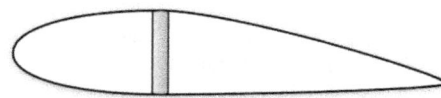

A resistance is felt in the first place because the pressure behind the plate decreases by more than the increase in front due to the increased velocity that creates turbulence and an artificial low pressure (form drag).

The difference is enough to suck the plate backwards.

This resistance can be diverted upwards by holding the plate at an angle to the airflow. Although the drag is reduced, the relative pressures are still the same (i.e. less above) for the same reasons, but the action of diverting the air downwards will also make the plate try to rise into the air.

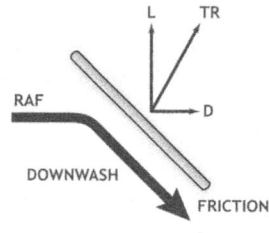

We now have two reasons behind the production of Lift.

The Total Reaction should be roughly at right angles to the flat plate, but friction from the air's viscosity at the trailing edge actually causes it to tilt slightly. Note that the TR is a net effect of distributed loads, and the TR vector is an equivalent value that works through one point. The centroid of the distributed forces on the wing is called the *Centre Of Pressure*, discussed later. This is similar to carrying a large piece of plywood in a strong wind. That the air flows downwards from an aerofoil can easily be proven by flying low over some ground fog or a field full of wavy crops, where you will see a disturbance that can only have come from downflowing air (*Stick & Rudder*).

However, the plank of plywood is a brute force solution, so the aerofoil will be shaped to reduce the turbulence and create a better reduction of pressure (it is more efficient to *accelerate* air downwards than to hit an inclined plane, as the air passing over the top cannot change direction quickly enough. This is what the curvature, or camber, on the upper surface, mentioned overleaf, is for). The process takes advantage of Bernoulli's *venturi effect*.

A third reason behind lift is that downward flowing air also comes from wingtip vortices, which curl inwards from the tips as the higher pressure from underneath an aerofoil interacts with the lower pressure air above, to produce a downward flow that is stronger at the tips than at the root (*source*: NASA).

Picture: DARK BLUE WORLD (2001) by Jan Sverak

Static Pressure

The weight of the air in a column that is 1 foot square at sea level is 2116.16 lbs (on a standard day). This pressure surrounds an aircraft from above, below and all around.

 Pressure is the ratio between an applied force that is perpendicular to a surface and the area of the surface concerned. As it is measured in terms of the force it will produce on an area, it should really be expressed in newtons (sea level pressure is around 101 kN/m^2) but, for convenience, we use the (incorrect) values for weight, i.e. kilograms or pounds.

That is, the aircraft is being squeezed from all directions at a static pressure of around 2000 lbs per square foot at sea level. If you can reduce the pressure above its aerofoils by more than the weight of the aircraft, it will fly, which is what we do mechanically, by moving forward to concentrate the airflow over the top of the wing and bring its streamlines closer together. The resulting difference in pressure between the upper and lower surfaces is the equivalent of the **wing loading** (when unaccelerated), which is the weight of an aeroplane divided by the gross wing area. It is equivalent because L = W in level unaccelerated flight.

As an example, an aircraft weighing 6 000 lbs with a wing area of 300 square feet will have a wing loading of 20 lbs per square foot, which is typical for a light aircraft, so all you have to do is decrease the static pressure above the wing by at least that amount to make it fly. Thus, it is static pressure that is directly involved with flight, but we cannot affect static pressure directly. Instead, we change the dynamic pressure over the upper surface of the wings, especially in the first quarter, where pressure is decreased the most relative to the lower surface to create the change we need - this is discussed under *Bernoulli's Theorem*.

 The aircraft is not sucked up into the air, despite the use of the word *suction*, as forces generally do not pull. Atmospheric pressure **from underneath** pushes it up because there is less static pressure above (this is the same reaction force that you would get from the surface of the Earth when the aircraft is on the ground).

There is enough upwards pressure on a 10 ft^2 ceiling to support a 737. In fact, a difference in pressure of only 1% between the upper and lower surfaces of a wing is 1000 N/m^2, where the normal loading is between 500 to 5000*. No movement (of the aircraft) would be necessary were it not for the need to reduce the static pressure on the upper surface by changing the dynamic pressure.

*This pressure difference would be halved at 18 000 feet. If you add the effects of heat (friction) if you fly too fast, the flyable part of the atmosphere becomes quite small.

Q: How much of a difference in pressure around the wings is needed to create a force equal to 1000 N/m^2?

The units used for the force per unit of wing area and pressure are the same, i.e. newtons per square metre, so the answer is simply 1000 N/m^2. However, 1 Newton per square metre is equal to the pascal - so the answer could also be 1000 pascals. It could also be 10 hectopascals (*hecto* = hundreds), or 10 millibars, as 1 hPa is equal to 1 millibar. It depends on the choices available in the question.

Profile

The side view of an aerofoil is its *profile*.

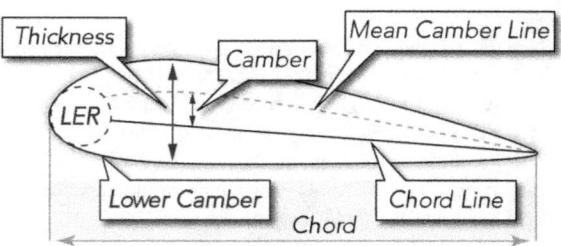

It can be changed in many ways. For example, collecting ice will alter its shape and therefore its lift producing characteristics, and make it heavier. In other words, if ice or snow, or any other contamination collects on an aerofoil, there is a reduction of lift (or C_{Lmax} reduces - see later), and the extra weight makes things worse. The largest ice build-up will be on the frontal areas of the aircraft, typically where the stagnation point is located.

Ice with a rough surface can cause high surface friction and a marked reduction in the energy in the boundary layer, meaning more drag and less lift. If you factor in the extra weight from the ice, you will need more power, plus you will get a lower stalling angle of attack and a higher stalling speed.

 Be very careful when landing - the distance required may increase by 40-50%! Better still, don't take off with any ice on the machine in the first place, although it is possible to collect it before descending. Leading edge roughness (within about 20% of chord) can have a major effect on the maximum lift produced. During takeoff, the aerodynamic effect of ice on the wing leading edge can be very critical in the latter stages of the rotation, because it will crack off as the fuselage flexes. Frost on the upper surface of a wing has the same effect, although not so much, but it could still cause problems on takeoff, particularly as the angle of attack indicator or alpha sensor (see later) will work normally, so the wing will stall before it activates. Heavy rain may wear the leading edge, and increase profile drag.

A large leading edge radius makes it easier for the air to follow the upper surface at high angles of attack. A small one can cause separation at the leading edge (rather than further back) and create a vicious stall. Extending the flaps with ice on the stabiliser may stall it and initiate a vertical dive.

THE CHORD LINE

The chord line is a *straight line* which joins the leading and trailing edges of an aerofoil (actually, the ends of the mean camber line, or the centres of curvature at each end), and it is the size of the angle that the chord line makes with the relative airflow that is so

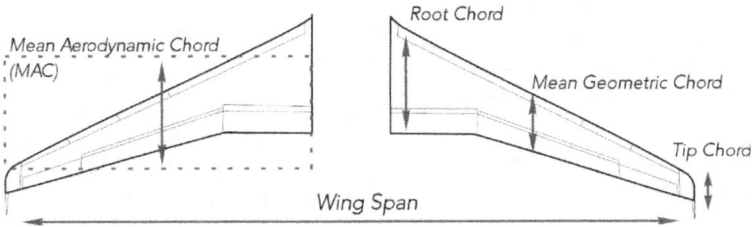

important in the creation of lift. The *chord* is the length of the chord line. The *mean chord** (C_{AV}) is determined by dividing the **gross wing area** by the wing span (the gross wing area includes the fuselage in between the wings. The **net wing area** doesn't).

*The mathematical average of the chord lengths. Not always the same as the *Mean Aerodynamic Chord* (MAC), which is an equivalent chord drawn through the centroid of a wing that is easier to use when working with swept wings and is discussed further in *Mass & Balance*. For now, the MAC is the chord of a section of an imaginary aerofoil on a wing which would have the same force vectors over the flight range as the actual wing.

THICKNESS

Thickness describes the greatest distance between the upper and lower surfaces of an aerofoil. Somewhere near the point of maximum thickness, you get *maximum velocity* and *minimum pressure*. The ratio of thickness to chord of an aerofoil section is an important factor and is expressed in *percentage of chord* (so you can change size without changing shape). It seems that a TCR of around 1:7 (15%), typical of subsonic wings, produces very little form drag. Reducing the effective thickness/chord ratio is how we get extra speed out of an aerofoil before it gets into the transonic range (see also *High Speed Flight*).

CAMBER

The word *camber* is popularly used to mean the curvature of an aerofoil but, technically, it refers to the distance of the *mean camber* line from the chord line, although EASA says that an aerofoil is cambered when the line connecting the centres of all inscribed circles is curved. The mean camber also joins the leading and trailing edges, but at an equal distance from the upper and lower surfaces. For a symmetrical aerofoil, the mean camber line is identical to the chord line. Otherwise, it will be a curve biased towards the thickest side.

A positively cambered aerofoil has the greatest curvature on its upper surface, and a negatively cambered one has it on the lower surface (like a regular aerofoil upside down). A symmetrical aerofoil has no camber in the true sense.

The maximum camber is just referred to as "the camber", because it is the only dimension worth bothering about. It is there to smooth out and accelerate the airflow over the upper surface of the aerofoil. Had the aerofoil been a flat plate, there would have been severe turbulence over the upper surface.

Increasing the camber also *concentrates* the airflow and makes it speed up to assist the reduction of pressure on the upper surface.

 If the mean camber line crosses the chord line, the aerofoil is *reflexed*. Reflexed aerofoils can compensate for nose down pitching moments with nose up ones.

Planform

This is the shape of an aerofoil as viewed from above. It could be *rectangular*, *tapered* (from root to tip), *elliptical*, *delta* or *swept* (back or forward). Large, wide aerofoils, for example, are good for large transport aircraft, and short, stubby ones will be found on fast sports aircraft.

To get the most efficient structural weight and stiffness, you need a highly tapered planform, but a compromise is usually made between a taper with washout and section variation to obtain as near as possible the elliptical lift distribution, later.

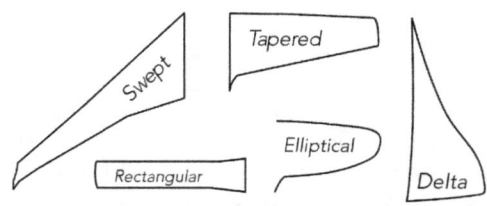

The **taper ratio** is the ratio of the tip chord (Ct) to the root chord (Cr). The best is around 2.5:1.

ASPECT RATIO

The *aspect ratio* of a wing is the relationship between its length and width, or *span* and *mean geometric chord* (the ratio between the square of the wing span and the wing area). Aerofoils can have equal surface areas (and hence roughly the same lift production) but different aspect ratios, depending on what they were designed for. The higher the ratio of length to width, the less induced drag you get (later), because a lower ratio of the surface is exposed to the tip losses from wake vortices, but such wings are not stiff and are best used at low speeds because they can flutter, which is a divergent oscillation due to the interaction of inertia and aerodynamic forces, and the stiffness of the structure (see *AGK*).

Glider wings have high aspect ratios. High speed aircraft, on the other hand, have low aspect ratio wings with a high loading, which makes takeoff and landing interesting. Concorde's aspect ratio is less than 1.

More under *High Speed Flight*, later.

Angle Of Incidence

A wing is fitted at a fixed angle to the longitudinal axis (based on the wing root chord line) so it can start altering the velocity of the air coming the other way, although the intention is to make the fuselage fly level in the cruise.

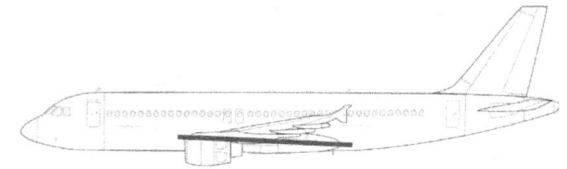

This means that you can improve visibility and reduce drag. In practice, the wing is set at the best *lift/drag ratio*, or the point when you get the most lift for the least drag at the optimum angle of around 4°.

WASHOUT (GEOMETRIC TWIST)

The angle of incidence may be varied throughout the length of a wing. Washout is the reduction in the angle of incidence of an aerofoil from root to tip.(or *washin* if you go the other way). It is also known as geometric twist.

Washout is used because the outer edges of the wing (or propeller, which acts on the same principle) may be moving faster than the rest in some manoeuvres (a turn, for example), creating more lift and stress. In addition, it allows the outer parts of a wing to still be creating lift at slower speeds when the inner edges are stalled, as they might be when landing.

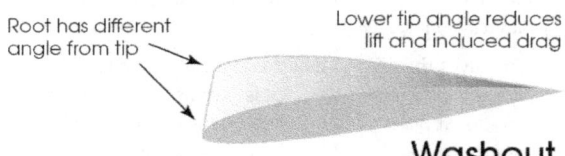

Washout

Wing twist (geometric and aerodynamic*) is used to:

- improve stall characteristics, so the wing tips can reach their stall angle of attack later and keep the machine flying at low speeds.
- reduce induced drag (later).

***Aerodynamic washout** changes the *shape* of the wing from root to tip by tapering or with flaps or slots. Too much washout may lead to zero or negative lift at small angles of attack, as found when in the cruise.

Angle Of Attack

The *angle of attack* is an *aerodynamic* angle between the chord line and the relative wind*.

*To be picky, the angle between the chord line and the free stream is the *geometric* angle of attack. That between the zero lift line and the free stream is the *aerodynamic* angle of attack. They are both the same in a symmetrical aerofoil.

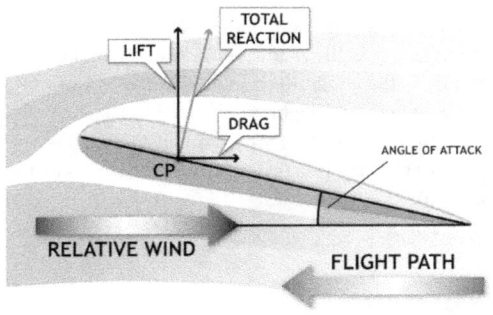

To be even more picky, the above definition is only valid for 2-dimensional flow - EASA uses the longitudinal axis as a reference for 3-dimensional flow.

And, as if we didn't have enough to deal with, the air impacting on the leading edge has an increased pressure (maximum at the stagnation point), which creates a gradient between the leading edge and the upper surface, along which the airflow is attracted (this is less vigorous with swept wings).

The new angle created by the resulting upwash produces a lower true angle of attack, called the *effective* angle of attack, because the relative airflow moves upwards (see *Induced Drag*, later) to become the effective relative airflow, being the vector sum of all the airflows that are affecting the aerofoil. The *induced* angle of attack is the angle between the effective and relative airflows. It is larger at low speeds or with greater tip vortices (and downwash*), so it is in our interest to keep them small.

The "angle of attack" consists of the effective and induced angles of attack.

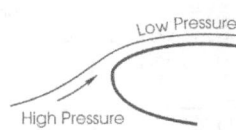

*Downwash at the trailing edge occurs because the flow over the upper surface is faster.

When we change the angle of attack from the zero lift position, we are creating an unbalanced shape against the airflow in order to create an unbalanced force. A positively cambered (asymmetric) aerofoil produces some lift at zero angle of attack because of the excess upper surface exposed to the airflow (that is, the bulk of its mass is above the chord line). To get zero lift, it must be slightly nose down. However, although the pressure values are the same on both surfaces, the relative pressure *distributions* are not. The Centre of Pressure of the upper surface is further aft than that of the lower surface, which produces a nose down pitching moment. Therefore, when the lift coefficient of a *negatively* cambered aerofoil section is zero, the pitching moment must be nose up, or positive.

A **symmetrical** aerofoil needs a small angle of attack to produce lift because the upper and lower surfaces are of equal size, which is why they are less efficient at producing lift than asymmetric ones, although they are easier and cheaper to make. *A symmetrical aerofoil at 0° produces no lift and some drag.* Symmetrical aerofoils also do not produce pitching moments.

You can fly at a high speed with a small angle of attack, or a slow speed with a high one. The generally accepted optimum is between 3-4°, and the maximum around 16°. Each speed in unaccelerated flight has its own angle of attack (for a particular weight or wing loading), whether you are climbing, descending or straight and level. Thus, not only must you change the angle of attack when you change airspeed, but the airspeed will also change when you alter the angle of attack. This has some relevance when gliding for range, where you fly at a higher speed, but have a lower angle of attack as a result, and less drag.

The angle of attack on a jet increases in this order:

- Long Range Cruise
- Maximum Range Cruise
- Max L/D ratio (L/D_{max})
- Minimum Rate of Descent
- C_{Lmax}

All are discussed in more detail later.

Centre Of Pressure

Some parts of a wing may produce more lift than others, due to the variations in static pressure. The pressures created by an aerofoil at any point may be represented by a vector at right angles to its surface, whose length is proportional to the difference between absolute pressure and the free stream static pressure. The length of the vector concerned represents the pressure involved. There is a marked decrease over the upper surface, followed by a gentle increase.

The greatest decrease is forward of the thickest part, from *leading edge suction*.

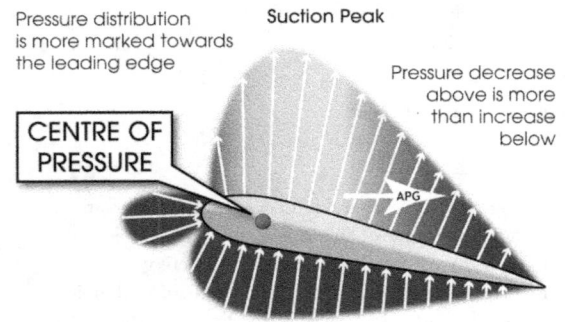

All the vectors can be represented by a single resultant acting at a particular point, called the Centre of Pressure, which is a theoretical point on the chord line through which the resultant of all forces (i.e. the total reaction) is said to act, so the sum of all moments there is zero.

The C of P is where the pressure distribution produces no moments, found around 25% of the way from the leading edge, simply because more lift is generated there but, on **asymmetrical aerofoils**, it moves steadily forward along the chord line as the angle of attack is increased, until **just before** the stalling angle, where it moves rapidly backwards as the suction peak collapses, usually behind the C of G of the aircraft so the nose will drop (its most forward point is just before the stalling angle).

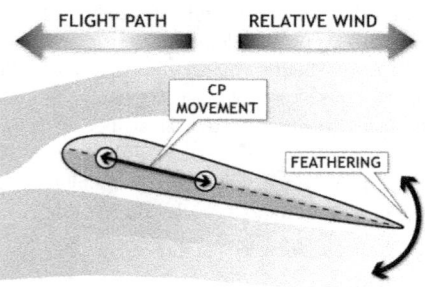

The upper surface lift reaction can act through a different point than that of the lower surface, as there will be a C of P for both surfaces (with a positive camber, the lower one tends to be forward of the upper one), so there will be a couple. Forward movement of the C of P is classed as unstable, because it ends up forward of the aerofoil's C of G and makes things worse.

On **symmetrical aerofoils**, the position of the C of P is (more or less) fixed because the lift on the upper and lower surfaces acts through points opposite each other, so its position is independent of the angle of attack for its usual values (i.e. below the stall).

In level flight, the velocity of the airflow is maximum at the Centre of Pressure. When trailing edge flaps are lowered, the C of P moves aft to create a nose down pitching moment and a reduced stalling angle. As the Mach number increases from subsonic to supersonic (see *High Speed Flight*), the Centre of Pressure will move to the mid-chord position.

Aerodynamic Centre

One problem with changing the angle of attack is that the angle of incidence of the wing can change as well. If the wing is pivoted at its trailing edge, forward movement of the C of P makes it pitch up more than it should (at a decreasing rate), when the angle of attack is increased.

Similarly, if you pivot the wing at its leading edge, as the C of P moves forward when the angle of attack is increased, the rate of change of nose-down pitch would increase. This is because, on top of the lift acting through the C of P, there is a twisting couple from the chordwise pressure distribution because lift acts through different points on each surface. Even with no lift, the wing would be twisted nose down. Somewhere along the chord line, there is a point where the angle of incidence does not change, or where the rate of pitch change would be constant, typically found at 25% of chord (50% when supersonic). The twisting moment is not zero, however, as the unequal pressure distribution is still there.

The aerodynamic centre is the *fixed* point* on the chord line about which moments are constant when the angle of attack changes. Put more simply, it is where the moment from the pressure distribution does not change with angle of attack, or where changes in lift coefficient from changing the angle of attack are offset by changes in distance between the Centre of Pressure and Centre of Gravity (of the wing). The equivalent for the whole aircraft is the *neutral point*, discussed below.

*It moves when you go supersonic, from roughly 25% of chord to around 50%. The C of P can move, but it never quite reaches the aerodynamic centre, which is co-located with the C of P on symmetrical aerofoils.

The AC is relevant to gusts and longitudinal stability - if the C of G is ahead of it, changes in lift create a nose down moment that returns the aircraft to the equilibrium angle of attack. If an aeroplane in straight and level flight is subjected to a strong vertical gust, the point on the wing where the instantaneous variation in wing lift effectively acts is known as the aerodynamic centre (of the wing).

STALLING

The stall is a condition in which an aerofoil cannot support an aircraft in flight because either not enough air is flowing over it, or the air is turbulent, or without energy. It exists when an increase in angle of attack decreases lift.

When its upper surface is mainly covered in separated airflow, and the air cannot accelerate fast enough to follow it, an aerofoil is stalled. An aerofoil starts to be less efficient at producing lift when it is inclined sharply upwards with low speed so, instead of cutting its way smoothly through the air, as it would normally do at a higher airspeed and a lower angle, it leaves a turbulent area of lower pressure behind, as with the flat plate.

There are three types of stall:
- A **trailing edge stall** from separation at the trailing edge, which moves towards the leading edge as the angle

of attack is increased. This is a gentle decrease in lift from its maximum value.

- A **leading edge stall** that forms as a short bubble is formed near the leading edge. When it bursts, there is a rapid change of flow over the upper surface, producing a sudden drop in lift and in increase in profile drag.
- A **thin aerofoil stall** starts with a long stable bubble which gradually gets longer before it bursts.

The type of stall is strongly influenced by the geometry of the front part of the aerofoil, the most important factors being the shape of the mean camber line in the first 15% and the leading edge radius, which should be large enough to ease the flow from the stagnation point to the upper surface without high centrifugal forces that would create separation. The tangent to the mean line at the trailing edge should make the smallest possible angle with the streamline of the incoming flow.

 In the stall, the first control to be lost is the aileron, but longitudinal and directional control is also reduced, because of the low speed of the airflow over the elevator and rudder, hence the danger of spinning.

The stalling angle (also called the critical angle, or α_{CRIT}) is that *above which* the aerofoil stalls (not the point of stall), or where lift is maximum. Although lift is still being produced after that angle, the aerofoil has a hard time producing it. The EAS just below this point is the Basic Stalling Speed (V_S), which is the lowest possible steady speed in level flight for a given weight, or the minimum steady flight speed at which a clean aircraft with its engines throttled back is controllable (Class A aircraft use V_{SR}*). Both are found by reducing speed by 1 knot per second until the stall is identified.

*Light aircraft base their stall speed on V_{S0} (gear & flaps set for landing, power off) and V_{S1}** (unaccelerated and clean, i.e. power off, gear and flaps up). Heavier ones use a reference stall speed, V_{SR}, which may not be less than a 1g stall speed (i.e. unaccelerated) and is usually around 6% higher than V_S.

**The stall speed (minimum steady flight speed) in a specific configuration.

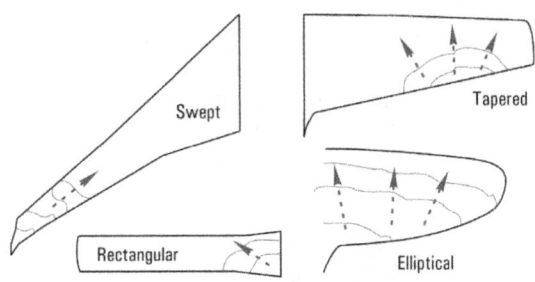

Because the angle of attack can vary across the wingspan, some parts of a wing can stall before others. On a rectangular wing (say on the Cherokee), the stall will start at the root, which is most desirable because the tips will stall last. You get warning of the stall by buffeting over the tail surfaces as the disturbed airflow hits them. As the ailerons remain effective in this case, a wing drop at the stall is avoided. Having said that, it is a structurally and aerodynamically inefficient wing. It is used only on low speed, light aircraft.

 Frost, ice or snow all decrease the critical angle of attack.

An elliptical wing (or one with elliptical loading), on the other hand, as used on the Spitfire*, has its lift dropping off exponentially towards the tips, meaning that the lift distribution matches the shape of the wing and that lift and induced drag are evenly distributed, so that the whole wing stalls at the same time. It doesn't necessarily have less induced drag than other wings, it distributes it more evenly.

*The elliptical shape was chosen to fit the wheels and guns into what needed to be a thin wing. Although they are nearly ideal, the major disadvantages with elliptical wings revolve around mechanical layout and construction.

To get the most efficient structural weight and stiffness, you need a highly tapered planform, but these can produce poor stall characteristics, as mentioned below.

The **taper ratio** is the ratio of the tip chord (Ct) to the root chord (Cr). The best is around 2.5:1.

It is rare to find aircraft with a tip chord that is less than one third of the root chord.

You can see that a tapered planform can get very close to the characteristics of an elliptical wing (and is cheaper to make), although it does give rise to aileron buffet, wing drop* and a reduced nose down pitching moment at the stall. This could mean that the aircraft rolls, especially when landing. This is because you are deliberately bringing the wing near to the stall, which starts close to the wingtip where the aileron is situated. The fix is *washout*, mentioned previously, or reducing the camber. A compromise is usually made between a taper with washout and section variation to obtain as near as possible the elliptical lift distribution. The Dash-8 uses an untapered centre section for its wings with tapered outer sections.

*With a tapered wing, most of the lift is produced at the root, so the downwash there is significantly greater than it is at the tip. This means that the effective angle of attack is greater at the tip than it is at the root, so the tip stalls first. As well, the local wing loading (lift per unit area) tends to be greater toward the tip.

Ways of stopping wing tips stalling too early include having the outboard sections of leading edge devices extend automatically within certain alpha* values (angles of attack), to re-energise the flow over the top surface of the wing immediately aft of them, which delays the breakup of the streamline flow until more inboard areas have stalled (it also improves the effectiveness of the outboard ailerons near the stall).

*Because speeds are often an imprecise measure of attitude, the Alpha (α) angle is used instead by military and jet transport aircraft (and the Wright Brothers). It is also used by flight control computers and aircraft data recorders.

Wing fences, or **stall fences**, are small vertical fins a couple of inches high running with the chord (but not necessarily for the whole length) on the upper surface of a wing.

Its purpose is to stop air moving towards the tips at high angles of attack (swept wing*) or controls the airflow around the flaps (straight).

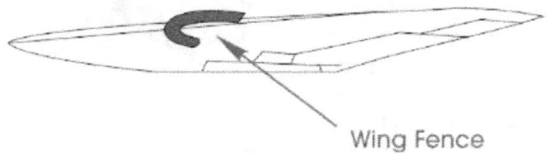

Wing Fence

*The tendency of a swept wing to stall at the tips is due to the spanwise movement of the boundary layer that creates a pool of slow moving air in that area after it meets the adverse pressure gradient and is forced sideways.

The outward drift can cause a low speed pitch up, so the wing fence can improve low speed handling.

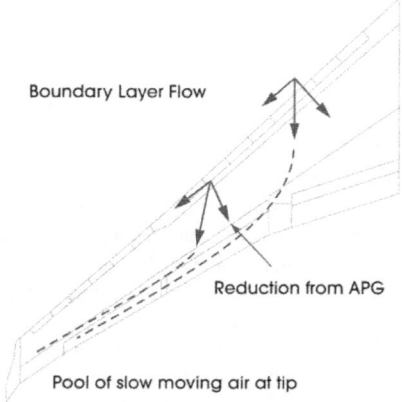

 Pitching up is a form of longitudinal instability. Aircraft with a large inertia in pitch may overshoot a demanded increase in angle of attack, so anticipation is required, especially at high angles of attack, otherwise the aircraft may pitch up beyond the stall. On some T-tail aircraft, pitching up can lead to a deep stall attitude.

In addition, the C of P moves differently. As there is less lift coming from the tips, it moves inwards, towards the root, as well as moving forwards.

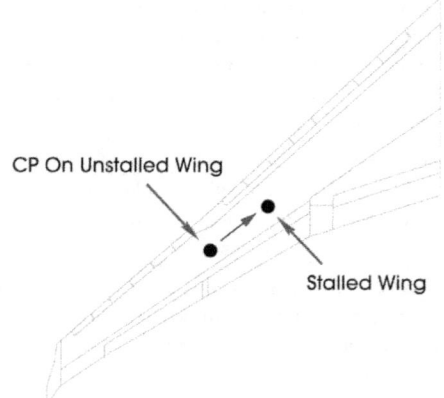

When a swept wing is loaded, as it would be in a turn, the end of the wing bends and twists, because that is where the wing loading is highest. This is because most of the wing is behind the main structural member, so the angle of attack is reduced at the tip (similar to washout).

Wing fences help to prevent such movement. Otherwise, they effectively split the wing into two sections at the boundary between the flaps and ailerons, isolating their effects from each other to stop the spanwise movement that creates induced drag - a trailing vortex, as the wing tip vortex is sometimes called, that rotates in the opposite direction to the usual one from the wing tip scours away the local boundary layer. This improves stability and control near the stall. Handling is also improved at slow speeds and help is given with the stall.

The **Saw Tooth** (or *Dog Tooth*) does the same by producing a sudden change in chord length as a notch at the leading edge (that is, the end of swept wing suddenly juts forward), as used on military jets such as the F4 Phantom. It tends to anchor the ram's horn vortex at that point 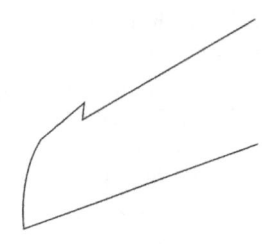 and stops it moving further inboard. By acting as a vortex generator, it also reduces the outflow of the boundary layer.

Because tip stall is reduced, the pitch up tendency at the stall will be reduced but, as the thickness/chord ratio of the tip area is reduced, the critical Mach number* can be increased. Also, the C of P of the extended wing is further forward than it would otherwise be, so the mean C of P of the whole wing is further forward. When the tip eventually stalls, the forward movement of the C of P is less marked, giving a less pronounced pitch up moment.

*The speed at which local airflow becomes sonic on any part of the airframe.

Shark teeth are near the root, on inner leading edges within the stagnation region at normal pitch attitudes. They also stick out into the upper airflow, causing turbulence, and stall the inner wing before the tips.

A **leading edge notch** (as fitted to the Lightning) works in a similar way to the saw tooth, except that the thickness/chord ratio is not affected (although it is sometimes combined with a wing section outboard of the notch that has an increased t/c ratio).

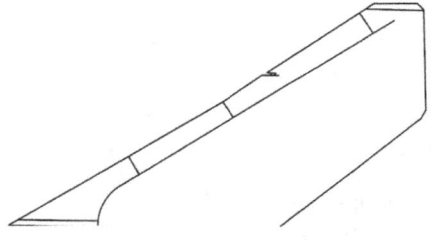

By creating a vortex over the wing behind the leading edge, the size of the vortex over the tip area is reduced, and with it the magnitude of the tip stall.

The notched leading edge is often used with the saw tooth to intensify the inboard vortex behind the devices and create a stronger restraining effect upon the outflow of the boundary layer (as used on the Avro Arrow).

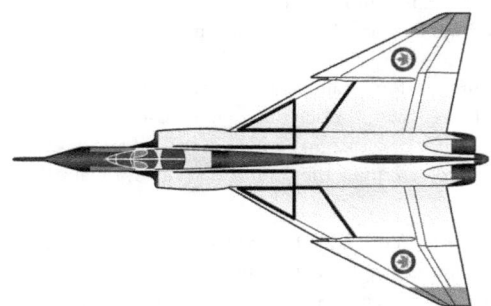

Mach 2.4 in the 1950s. Marvellous.

Vortilons are small fences *under* the leading edge of a wing that extend forward of it - fences, but underneath. They shed vortices over the upper surface at very high angles of attack that behave like aerodynamic wing fences when the boundary layer needs the most help. Engine pylons can do a similar job.

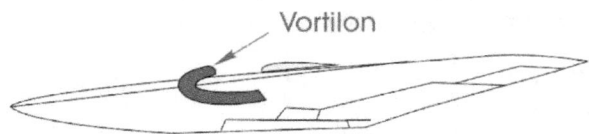

The boundary layer becomes sluggish over the rear part of a wing section as it flows against the adverse pressure gradient. **Vortex Generators** are small vertical plates that rise above the wing surface (normally towards the leading edge) into the free stream to re-energise the boundary layer and inhibit its outward flow.

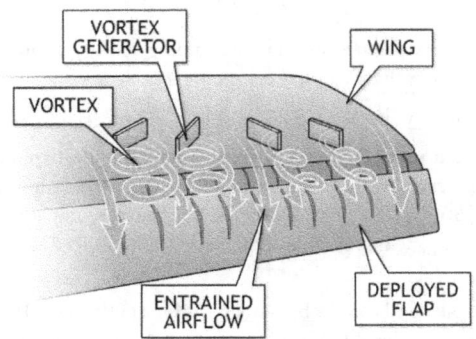

They reduce the drag from supersonic flow by creating vortices that bring high velocity, high energy air nearer to the surface to reduce or delay separation. The small amount of drag they create is more than compensated for by the energy regained from the earlier separation.

However, they are only a temporary protection because they are positioned more or less where the first shock waves form when approaching the speed of sound, and just buy you time to slow down again - they are not intended for permanent use at high speeds. They are also sometimes used on the outer section of the main wings to re-energise the boundary layer over the ailerons.

The stall happens in the first place because the air under heavier pressure below the wing finds it easier to creep *forwards* over the upper surface from the trailing edge as the angle of attack increases.

In other words, it goes the wrong way because the upper air has started to slow down and is less able to stop it. This is because it has longer to travel and more surface friction to cope with, so it doesn't have the energy to keep flowing and create the same pressure differential, and the lift is reduced (the pressure at the trailing edge is atmospheric anyway). Thus, boundary layer separation originates from the adverse pressure gradient, when air starts flowing in the *reverse* direction to the free stream, forcing itself under the normal airflow which has started to slow down, making it detach. If you were to attach some wool to the trailing edge, you would see it point *forwards*, well before the stall. As a non-swept aerofoil stalls, it starts to pitch down as the airflow starts to react about the midpoint of the lower surface instead of at 25% of chord, and the Centre of Pressure (below) moves behind the C of G.

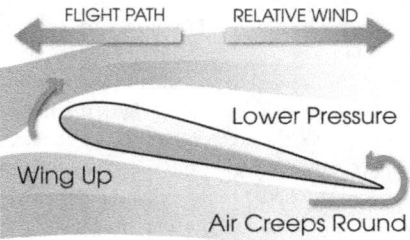

 The stall happens because the angle of attack is too high, not because the airspeed is too low. You can stall at a very high speed in a turn.

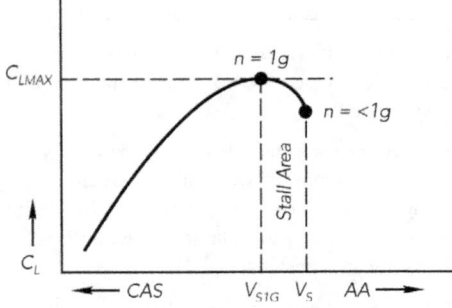

Stall Speeds

The stalling speed is the lowest speed at which an aeroplane is controllable in straight and level flight with the engine throttled back and the C of G at the forward limit. The stall always happens at the same angle of attack (α or alpha) for a particular shape of aerofoil and aeroplane configuration, but the speed at which it occurs can vary according to:

- **Aircraft weight**. Stalling speed is directly proportional to the weight of the aeroplane because of the increased wing loading*. If you pull out of a dive, or start a turn, you artificially make the aeroplane heavier with an increased load factor, so you will stall quicker, at a higher speed (stall speed increases). Jet transports (as opposed to piston engined machines) can have wide variations in stall speed in this respect, as fuel is used up.

- **Wing area**. This, with weight, above, is simply wing loading. Aircraft with higher wing loadings have higher stall speeds.
- C_{Lmax}. The maximum lift coefficient (below) is affected by camber and high lift devices, because the wings need help at low speeds. This, again, produces large variations in stall speeds for jet transport aircraft.
- **Air density**. The stalling speed TAS increases with altitude, whereas EAS doesn't (and neither do IAS and CAS if you ignore compressibility).

*The wing loading is the dominant factor. As V_S (the basic stalling speed) is proportional to the square root of the load factor, doubling the wing loading (for example) will affect the stall speed by the square root of 2, or 1.41. Halving it reduces the stall speed to about 70% (1/1.41).

These factors also need to be considered:

- **C of G position**. Other things being equal, the stall speed increases when the C of G moves forward, and vice versa. This is because a greater down force is needed from the tail and which adds to the weight supported by the wings. Ignoring weight, the further forward the C of G, the greater the angle of attack at any given airspeed, and the higher the speed at which the stalling angle is reached. On the other hand, recovery is easier because the weight of the aircraft is helping to lower the nose. A typical change in EAS between the forward and aft positions is around 5 knots.
- **Speed**. This has a similar effect to the C of G position, in that high speeds need a down force from the elevator. Both are helped by using variable incidence tailplanes.
- **Turbulence**. The stalling speed may increase.

Aircraft certification regulations ensure that there is a safe margin above the basic stalling speeds by establishing minimum takeoff and landing speeds.

Light aircraft that are certified under FAR/**CS 23** use V_{S0} and V_{S1}, both of which are established with the throttle closed and the engine(s) idling, and the C of G in a place that provides the highest stall speed (i.e. at the forward limit) and with the maximum mass for the circumstances.

V_{S0} is the stall speed or the minimum steady flight speed in the landing configuration (that's what the 0 means). It is 10% below the minimum speed for flap extension to provide a safety margin, so the lower end of the white arc (for flap extension) on the ASI is 1.1 V_{S0}. V_R (the rotate speed) must be at least V_{S1} for single engined aircraft and 1.1 V_{S1} for multi-engined aircraft. Both types must reach at least 1.2V_{S1} by 50 feet. The target V_{REF}** for Class B aircraft (under CS 23) is at least 1.3 V_{S0}.

**V_{REF} is the term used by airlines for the airspeed you need to achieve on short final (i.e. at screen height), used in the sense of V_{REF} + 5, and so on. As it is factored on stalling speed, it is affected by weight. L equals W only in straight, level, unaccelerated flight, when W can otherwise be replaced by L so, if an aircraft is creating more lift than weight (as in a turn), its stalling speed will increase. In fact, it becomes equal to V_S multiplied by the square root of the load factor, later. Because swept wing aircraft don't stall the same way as other aircraft do (it is very hard to detect, for one thing), they base their takeoff and landing speeds on a margin above the stall reference speed, V_{SR}. It is used to determine the landing distance for manual landings.

Change 15 of JAR 25 (Oct 2000) introduced the idea of the reference stall speed V_{SR} being the same as V_{S1G}, which is the minimum speed at which an aeroplane can develop a lift force normal to the flight path equal to its weight. It corresponds to C_{Lmax}, just before the lift starts to decrease*, when n still = 1.

*The lift collapses at V_S, which used to be 0.94 of V_{1SG}.

All Airbus documentation uses the new convention, even though FAR 25 makes no reference to a 1G stalling speed.

Thus, V_{SR} is established by the manufacturer (25.103) and must be at least the 1G stall speed. The speed at 35 feet after takeoff must be at least 1.13 V_{SR1} for most transport aircraft.

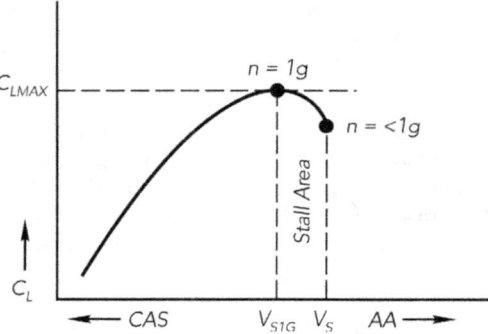

V_{SR0} is the stall reference speed in the landing configuration. It is around 6% faster than V_{S0} and cannot be less than V_{S1G}.

V_{REF} for Class A aircraft (CS 25) is at least 1.23 V_{SR0}.

Any apparent increase in weight increases the stall speed, as does any reduction in the value of C_{Lmax}, the maximum amount of lift that can be produced. When flaps are deployed, the value of C_{Lmax} increases and the basic stalling speed will decrease.

Flight manuals tend to be a bit shy on stating stall speeds. If you know the value in level flight (for a particular weight), you can find the approximate stalling speed for any other weight with this formula:

$$V_2 = V_1 \times \sqrt{\frac{W2}{W1}}$$

In the formula, V_2 is the new stalling speed, V_1 the old one, W_2 the new weight and W_1 the old weight (W_1 and V_1 could also be the values in the flight manual). Given a stalling speed of 130 kts for an aircraft weighing 160,000 kg, the approximate stalling speed at 190,000 kg is 154 kts. A rule of thumb is that the % increase in stalling speed is half the % increase in all-up weight.

 Lift is not equal to Weight in manoeuvres, so the Weight must be divided by the cosine of the angle of bank (see *Load Factor*, below).

Having said that, in straight & level flight, L does equal W, so you can find V_S like this:

$$V_S = \sqrt{\frac{W}{S} \times C_{LMAX} \times \tfrac{1}{2}\rho}$$

You can simplify it still further if you remember that W divided by S is the wing loading......

$$V_S = \sqrt{\frac{WL}{C_{LMAX} \times \tfrac{1}{2}\rho}}$$

This will be the unaccelerated (true) stall speed.

EFFECTS OF POWER

Stall speeds are usually given for power off, or at least with the engines at idle. Leaving the power on will provide a lower stalling speed (assuming no change in weight and configuration), but there may also be a more violent wing drop at the stall, especially with single-engined propeller driven aircraft.

The decrease in stalling speed with power on is due to the vertical component of thrust, which can be significant if the angle of attack is high.

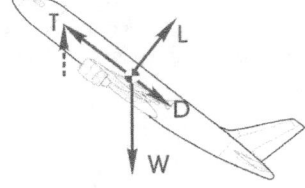

The effects of propeller wash can also delay the stall by producing a much higher dynamic pressure than the free stream to create greater lift at zero thrust. However, because only the areas of the wing inside the prop wash are affected, the tip may stall first. The induced flow has a similar effect to boundary layer control and increases the angle of attack for maximum lift (although this may cause the aeroplane to drop suddenly when reducing power on landing). In a jet, as there is little induced flow, the stall speed is more or less the same whether power is applied or not.

Recovery from a power-on stall should involve less height loss, as the response from the engines is fast.

RECOVERY FROM DIVES

All the considerations about turning apply to recovering from dives, which are simply turns in the looping plane.

At twice the speed, you need four times the room to accomplish a turn. This goes for diving as well!

EFFECTS OF ALTITUDE

Ignoring the very small differences between EAS and IAS, and assuming constant weight and aircraft configuration in straight and level flight, as C_{Lmax} and S are constant at the stalling angle, an aircraft will stall at a constant IAS, regardless of altitude.

The Stall Inducer

A stall inducer, stall strip or root spoiler, may be fitted at the inboard end of a wing.

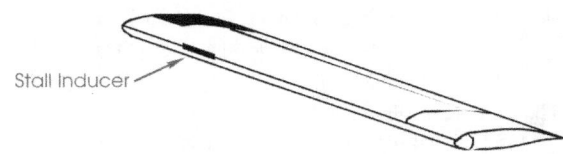

The strip has very little effect at normal angles of attack but, at high angles, it spoils the airflow over the wing behind it, causing a buffet on the tailplane and ensuring that the section of the wing where it is fitted stalls first.

Stall Warning

Adequate advance warning of the stall must be available - the greater of at least 2 knots or 2% above the speed that any device that pushes the nose down operates. A stall warning should come on 6 knots before the stall, where there will be an increased nose-down tendency.

Under CS 25 (large aeroplanes) there must be enough of a warning to prevent inadvertent stalling with the flaps and landing gear in any normal position. However, systems are inhibited when the aircraft is on the ground. When the speed is reduced, the warning must start at a speed exceeding the stall speed by at least 5 kts or 5% CAS.

The inputs to the stall warning computer would include the angle of attack and the deflection of flaps and slats.

You usually know the stall is coming in a light aircraft because it starts bouncing around (buffeting). Heavy aircraft with powered controls must use stick shakers or pushers to simulate the pre-stall buffeting that would otherwise be masked by powered controls (a detector senses the **angle of attack** and its **rate of change**), meaning that it operates before the stall.

A pre-stall pusher is used when the basic aerodynamic stall characteristics are not certifiable, typically used when leading edge stall occurs (no slats). A post-stall pusher is normally used when the basic aerodynamic stall characteristics are acceptable, but when other characteristics are uncertifiable, as with the possibility of deep stall or if identification of the stall is deficient.

If the shaker is ignored, the pusher starts the recovery procedure at a higher angle of attack, which is to reduce the incidence to below the warning activation value while applying the maximum power to minimise any height loss (dangerous situations that require stick pushers include *excessive wing drop* and *deep stall**). If it is too late, the recovery action is the same, but lateral correction is not applied until after the wings are unstalled, to prevent a wing dropping.

*Also known as super stall - it is a stable stall with an almost constant pitch attitude.

ANGLE OF ATTACK (ALPHA) SENSORS

Angle of attack sensors activate stall warning devices. The simplest is the flapper switch, which is a vane fitted to the leading edge of the wing at, or just below, the stagnation point at normal angles of attack. A small vane that protrudes forward is connected to an electrical switch. As the angle of attack increases, the stagnation point moves lower on the leading edge to move the flapper.

- **Vane Sensors** are free to line up with relative airflow, clear of wash from wings or engine pods, usually one on each side of the nose. The vane is attached to the rotor of a synchro, which rotates.

  The vane is initially aligned against reference marks on the fuselage that represent a clean pitch attitude with the wings at the most efficient angle. The output from the synchro (see *Instruments*) as it is moved by the vane is transmitted to the stall warning system. The circuit is de-energised on the ground. In short, the position of the vanes relative to zero alpha is measured by a transducer and sent to the flight systems.

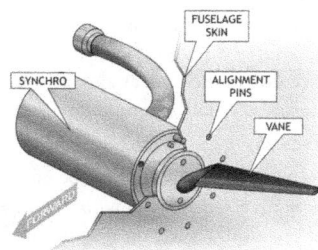

The vane also detects the *rate* of change, which information is sent to the stick pusher, if fitted.

- **Pressure Sensors** are aerofoil sections with pressure measuring holes placed symmetrically above and below the leading edge. The chord line is at zero alpha, so the difference in pressure between the upper and lower sets of holes is the angle of arrival of the airflow. A pressure transducer changes this to electronic data and calculates alpha (you could also use the pressure differential to move a paddle in a box, with paddle position converted to alpha electronically).

Pitching Moments

If the C of G is too far forward, the couple between it and the C of P is long enough to produce a large nose down pitch from the lift/weight vectors. The moment is counterbalanced by a down force from the tailplane.

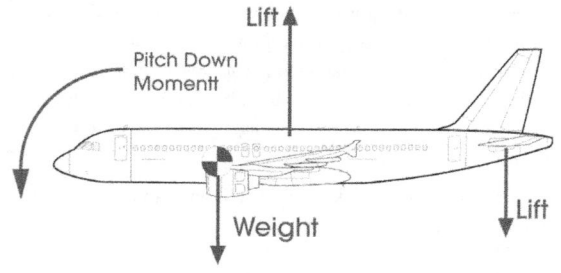

The change in downwash angle behind the wing also affects the tailplane's pitching moments.

The picture below shows the moments about the C of G before the stall, when the nose down pitch from the lift (behind the C of G) is balanced by the nose up pitch from the tail.

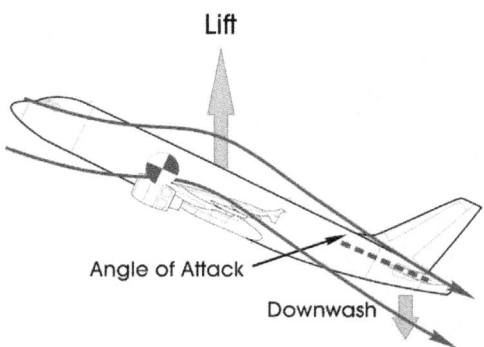

If you reduce the speed, the elevator must be deflected upwards to maintain altitude, and the downward load on the tail is increased. Static stability, where the aircraft tries to recover, means that further elevator movement is needed to stop the nose dropping. The low tail becomes affected by the turbulent, low energy air from the wake off the wings, which reduces its efficiency. Put simply, the tail becomes less effective as the aircraft begins to stall, but this is offset slightly by the angle of attack above it.

Here is the stall, where the normal nose-down pitching moment kicks in as the C of P moves back. The wake from the wings (turbulence) now goes above the tail, reducing its inefficiency, but the angle of attack has moved to the other side of the elevator and the lift moment increases the nose down pitch.

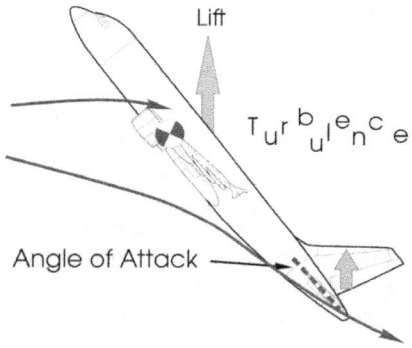

Essentially, if you increase airspeed, you need a smaller angle of attack and the C of P moves backwards. If it gets behind the C of G, the tailplane must supply a downwards force in high speed flight. On the other hand, at low speeds, it will have to supply an upwards force if the C of P manages to get ahead of the C of G.

Either way, a longer distance between the C of G and the elevator will tend to make the aeroplane longitudinally overstable (see *Stability*, below), meaning that you will need more control input to pull the column back on landing, and you may run out of range. For optimum fuel efficiency, though, it should be somewhere near the aft limit, because less tail-down force is then required, and a lower angle of attack, and less drag.

PRINCIPLES OF FLIGHT
Stalling

Deep (Super) Stall

With swept wings, the nose *pitches up* in the stall (the wing tips are behind the C of G). This increases the angle of attack, taking the wings deeper into the stall, hence the name. The loss of lift causes a descent, so you are going down or, rather, wallowing down, and the change in relative airflow increases the angle of attack even further - a stable stall with an almost constant pitch attitude. In June 1966, a Trident I deep-stalled during testing, eventually flopping onto the ground, which is when stick pushers and shakers were created, some with automatic full throttle select, to stop the entry into the stall in the first place. However, they didn't stop Air France 447 (from Rio de Janeiro to Paris) from crashing on the 1st of June 2009, having entered a deep stall at altitude.

How easy it is to recover partly depends on the tailplane (although the sweep of the wing is the most important factor). A T-tail is in turbulent air from the stalled wings (as are the engines), so it will be of less use (if at all) in getting the nose down than a conventional low-wing one.

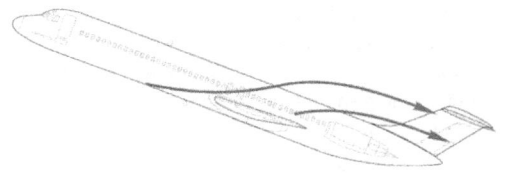

There is also a significant reduction in the effectiveness of the rudder, which is why such input is not recommended when stalling an airliner - using one at high subsonic speeds can result in opposite yaw, because the faster wing gets a substantial increase in drag to produce the effect. A yaw damper can monitor directional control requirements and input very small amounts at the earliest opportunity.

 The main factor in stall recovery in a typical training aircraft is minimum loss of altitude. With a swept wing aircraft the priority is to **get out of the stall fast** - if you've got altitude, use it! That is, dive if you must (up to -15° pitch) to reduce the angle of attack. Once clearly out of the stall, smoothly recover. The loss of height is rarely more than 3000 feet anyway (if you are *that* close to the ground, you may get a runway assisted go-around ☺).

Tail Stall

Tail stall occurs at relatively low angles of attack, but above V_S, often with flaps extended. When it occurs, a buffet is felt through the control column. This is similar to a stall of the main wing and may be incorrectly diagnosed.

Leading Edge Separation

On thin wings that have sharp leading edges, as used in high-speed aircraft, a form of laminar flow separation may occur above the leading edge. A stationary vortex, called a bubble, forms between the separated layer and the wing surface, modifying the airflow pattern:

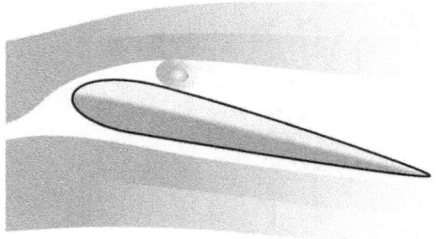

As the angle of attack is increased, the vortex will collapse and the wing will stall abruptly. If the bubble is able to extend over the chord length, it will be more gradual.

Stalling in the Turn

During a turn, an aircraft is not in a state of equilibrium, as you need an imbalance of forces to make it turn in the first place and deflect it continually from a straight line. This imbalance would be centripetal force, which is created from the horizontal component of the deflected Lift vector, which also has to keep the machine up in the air.

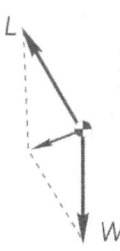 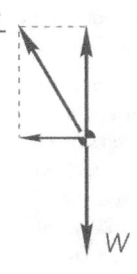 Initially, as you bank, the Lift vector is tilted, and the resultant between it and the Weight vector will make the aircraft move down and sideways. To make the sideways force more horizontal, you will have to make the Lift vector longer, which is done by increasing the angle of attack. More power will then be required to overcome the increased drag. It follows that, if you don't have much power, your angle of bank will be limited.

This has the effect of providing an equivalent force to balance Weight and maintain a level turn.

The size of the centripetal force ultimately depends on the all-up weight of the aircraft, the TAS and the turn radius.

PRINCIPLES OF FLIGHT
Stalling

Put another way, to turn at a constant altitude, an aircraft must be banked in the direction of the turn, which tilts the lift vector to the lower wing, making part of it act towards the centre of the turn and accelerate the aircraft that way.

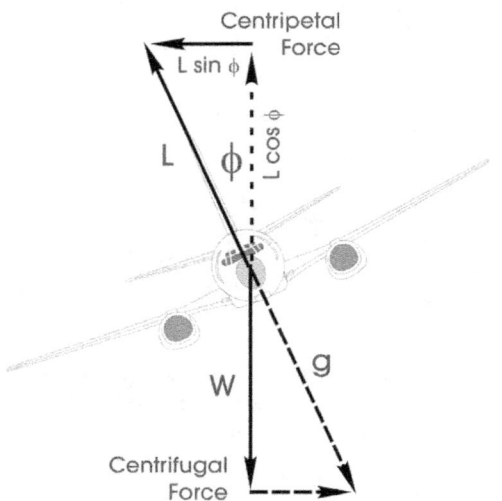

This also reduces the vertical component, so lift no longer equals the weight of the aircraft or stays in line with it. The horizontal component is centripetal force, which must be compensated for by extra lift from the wings. Lift must be increased enough to make $L \cos \phi = W$ (Lift as modified by the cosine of the angle of bank). If this is done by increasing the angle of attack, there will be extra drag, so power must be increased. If there is a power restriction, then the angle of bank will be limited.

The bank angle achieved will depend on the radius of the turn and the TAS - you won't be able to turn if you are already at the stall speed in straight and level flight, but if you are faster, the angle of attack will be lower, so you can get a higher bank angle before you stall. The angle of bank is independent of Weight. That is to say, for a given TAS and radius, centripetal force will increase in proportion to the weight, but so will Lift, so its inclination will be the same whatever the weight, and is obtained at the same angle of bank.

In a level turn at a constant angle of bank, and in climbing and descending turns, the outer wing travels fastest. As a result, the inner wing will have a greater alpha and, subject to the ailerons*, will stall first, but the increased lift on the descending wing produces roll damping.

*Be careful near the stall on takeoff! If you turn right, for example, the *left* wing will drop because using the aileron takes it past the stall. In Canada, this is called the farmer's takeoff, and it catches many people out.

In a steady balanced turn, the only acceleration is along the normal axis. In an uncoordinated turn, however, there is a lateral acceleration acting towards the centre of the turn (slip, with too much bank), or away from the centre of the turn (skid, with not enough bank).

A slip can be corrected by increasing the speed or reducing the angle of bank whilst applying more rudder. For a skid, reduce speed or increase the bank angle while applying less rudder.

LOAD (INERTIA) FACTOR

The strength of an aeroplane essentially revolves around how much its wings can carry without being damaged, and the wing loading depends on what you are doing with it. If you are doing anything that involves centrifugal force, its weight will artificially increase.

In other words, Lift and Weight (for example) are not equal in other than steady level flight, so the relationship between them is important when calculating G forces (Lift is greater than Weight in turns). The increase in lift required to maintain height in a turn is an increase in the load factor (n). It can be calculated by dividing the weight of the aircraft by the cosine of the angle of bank, and indicates by how many times Lift is bigger (or smaller) than Weight. When L exceeds W, the load factor is said to be positive, and vice versa. As they are both forces, they can be expressed as mass (m) multiplied by acceleration (a) which, for Weight, is due to gravity (g). During a manoeuvre, the apparent weight of everything in the aircraft is increased by a factor (n) of the weight due to gravity (g). *Weight appears to increase in the opposite direction to the force directing the acceleration.*

However, in basic terms, the load factor is the ratio of lift produced (or the actual load supported by the wings) to the normal weight of an aircraft, expressed in multiples of g (as the load factor is a ratio, there should be no units, but g is a convenient standard to use).

```
Actual Weight (Lift)
Normal Weight
```

The Load Factor is small below 30° of bank (around 20%) but increases rapidly beyond this bank angle. The greater the angle of bank, the greater the load factor will be, compared to weight.

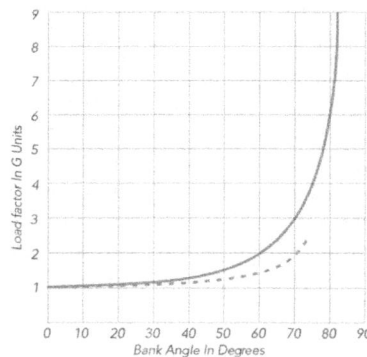

In a 60° bank turn, *the effective weight of your aircraft doubles.*

Bank	Load Factor	Stall Speed
30°	1.2 (20% more)	1.07 (7% more)
45°	1.41 (41% more)	1.19 (19% more)
60°	2 (100% more)	1.41 (41% more)

The stall speed also increases, as the *square root* of the load factor (the dotted line in the picture above). To calculate the stalling speed in a manoeuvre, multiply it like so:

PRINCIPLES OF FLIGHT
Stalling

$$V_{SO} \text{ in turn} = V_{SO} \times \sqrt{V_{LF}}$$

or:

$$V_{NEW} = V_{OLD} \times \sqrt{n}$$

For example, in a 60° turn, the load factor is 2, the square root of which is 1.41 (41%). The manoeuvre stalling speed is 41% higher than the basic stalling speed. An aircraft that normally stalls at 60 knots at a given weight will do so at 85 knots in a 60° bank turn (65 x 1.414).

To find the increase in stalling speed in a 45° banked turn:

$$\frac{1}{\cos 45 \ (0.71)}$$

which produces 1.41, as shown in the table above. The square root of that is 1.19, an increase of 19%.

To find the g involved, divide the new speed by the stall speed and square the result:

$$\frac{150}{60} = 2.5 \times 2.5 = 6.25G$$

 This also applies to pull-ups or, in reverse, the effects of gusts, below. If you pull 4g while pulling out of a dive, your stall speed will double. In level flight, you will stall before you reach the 4g value (check out *Limit Load Factor*, below).

If you push the controls the other way, you will get negative g, so keep hold of loose items in the cockpit, and that lunch you had earlier! Aircraft take less negative g because humans do.

SPEED INCREASE
Given a load factor of 1.95 and 1.9VS, what will be the load factor at $2V_S$?

The new V_S divided by the old V_S is 2 divided by 1.9, which is 1.05. Squaring that gives 1.1 which needs to be multiplied by the original load factor. of 1.95, giving 2.1.

TURNING
To find the load factor in a turn, given the TAS (200 kts) and radius of the turn (2000m):

$$\tan \varphi = \frac{TAS^2}{g \times Radius}$$

Note that the above formula is rearranged!

Convert the TAS to metres per second:

$$200 \times 0.515 = 103 \text{ m/s}$$

The tan of φ is:

$$\frac{103^2}{10 \times 2000}$$

The inverse tan of 0.53 is 27.94, the cosine of which is 0.88, the reciprocal of which is 1.13.

To **find the lift** in a turn, we still need:

$$\frac{1}{\cos \varphi}$$

then apply mass x acceleration on the result (2). Thus, with a 60° bank angle and a mass of 2000 kg, we get:

$$2000 \times 9.81 = 19,620 \times 2 = 39,240$$

CLIMBING
The basic formula is:

$$\text{Sin climb angle} = \frac{Gradient}{100}$$

A gradient of, say, 20% would end up as 0.2 if you divide 20 by 100. The inverse sine of that is 11.53 (climb angle), the cosine of which is 0.97.

LIMIT LOAD FACTOR (MANOEUVRE ENVELOPE)
In general, the excess load that can be applied to the wings depends on how fast you are flying. At slow speeds, there is not much leeway left on top of what the aircraft is already using to stay airborne, so the load cannot become excessive whatever you do with the controls. At high speeds, however, the lifting capacity of the wing is so much (due to the V^2 part of the lift formula) that a sudden movement of the controls or a strong gust may increase the load beyond safe limits. All aircraft have speed restrictions for flying in turbulence.

When you run into it on a VFR flight, you can change your speed, attitude and/or direction with little trouble. However, when IFR, you need to check with ATC when you slow down to turbulence speed, change levels or turn back the other way, so you could be in turbulence for a while before it gets sorted out.

It would be impossible to design an aeroplane to cope with every situation. For example, fighters and training aircraft are typically built to withstand forces from +7 down to -3g (being based on human limits), while transport aircraft have much lower boundaries, between +2.5 and -0.5g. As *g* is equal to lift divided by weight, the g limits must be reduced if the weight is increased in order to keep the same safety margins.

As the load factor increases with the angle of bank, at some bank angle, you will reach a limiting load factor.

The Limit Load Factor is a boundary associated with **permanent structural deformation** of one or more parts of an aeroplane Up to that limit, deformations will be elastic in nature so that, when things return to normal, the aircraft will resume its natural shape. However, within a boundary of 1.5 times the limit load factor (the safety factor, described below), deformations will be permanent, with structural *change* but not *failure* as obtained beyond the safety factor. This would be the *Ultimate Load Factor*.

The problem lies not just with the wings - there are fixed weight components such as the engines to consider as well. The load factor described above is an overall value for a particular weight so, if the aircraft gets lighter, those components are thrown about more and have a disproportionate effect. In other words, the manoeuvring speed must decrease if the weight does. For example, the baggage compartment has a placarded weight to ensure that baggage in it does not increase the load factor in that area. 200 lbs at 3.8 becomes 760 lbs, which is designed in, but twice that isn't!

The **flight regime** of any aircraft includes all combinations of speeds, altitudes, weights, centres of gravity and configurations, as determined by aerodynamics, propulsion, structure and dynamics.

PRINCIPLES OF FLIGHT
Stalling

- The **Limit Load** is the maximum load that can be anticipated in service.
- The **Ultimate Load** (see *Fatigue & Stress*) is the load at which the structure fails.
- The **Safety Factor** is the ratio of the ultimate load to the limit load, 1.5* in the case of aircraft structures. It is lower than would normally be the case for other situations due to weight considerations, which is why you must keep within the weight limitations.

*If its structure is set to fail at 12,500 lbs, an aircraft can weigh up to 8,333 lbs.

The borders of the flight regime are referred to as the **manoeuvring envelope**, or the operating limits in terms speeds and normal accelerations shown as a graph, assuming no sideslipping, rolling or yawing (i.e. no failed engines), at maximum all up weight (except aircraft designed for aerobatics). The manoeuvring envelope begins with a zero load factor.

From the envelope, you can find:

- Basic stalling speed.
- Available load factor at any height and speed.
- Maximum EAS at any height.
- Stalling speed at any height and load factor.

The **gust envelope**, discussed later, shows the range of g loadings generated by gusts at various speeds, beginning at +1g. Combining them produces the **flight envelope**, for which a protection system may prevent the exceedance of certain limits, namely angle of attack, speed and pitch.

One of the first limits involved is the stalling speed. At V_S (the basic stalling speed), Weight is equal to the maximum Lift available, or L_{max}. You can plot manoeuvring stall speeds against the load factor on the manoeuvring load, or V–n*, diagram.

*Airspeed (V) versus Load factor (n). Also called the V-g diagram. Amongst other things, it is the basis of the colour coding on the ASI:

It starts off like this:

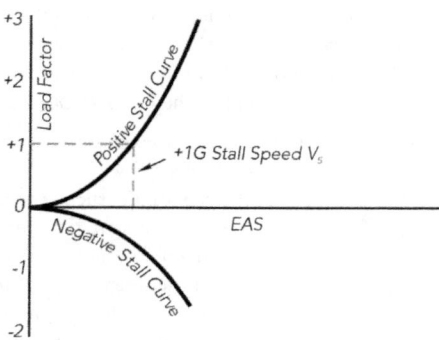

It shows that, as the speed increases, so does the stall speed in relation to the load factor. Left of the stall curve, there is not enough lift available. It also shows that you can fly below V_S if the load factor is less than one. As most aerofoils have a positive camber, the positive stall angles will be higher than the negative ones, as is shown by the longer lines.

The load factors (or the amount of stress with which your aircraft can safely cope) depend on its role, or the category it is certified in.

- **Large aeroplanes**, due to structural limitations, have lower limits than smaller ones. Under FAR/CS 25 (CAR 525 in Canada), the positive limit manoeuvring load factor (n) for any speed up to V_D* must be at least:

$$2.1 + \frac{24000}{W + 10000}$$

except that *n* must be at least 2.5 and need not be greater than 3.8 where W is the MTOM in lbs.

*Design dive speed, which may be limited by Mach number at altitude.

The negative limit manoeuvring load factor must be at least -1.0 at speeds up to V_C (design cruise speed), and must vary linearly with speed from the V_C value to zero at V_D, the dive speed, which is factorised downward to give V_{NE}.

You can use lower load factors if design features make it impossible to exceed them in flight.

- For **light aircraft** (under FAR/CS 23) the positive limit manoeuvring load factor must be at least:
  - **Normal & Commuter**, use the formula above, but *n* **need not** be more than 3.8 (**at least** 2.5). Thus, you can pull up to 3.8g with no danger of permanent deformation or structural damage.
  - **Utility**, 4.4 x gross weight.
  - **Acrobatic**, 6 x gross weight.

This graph is for a Normal Category aeroplane:

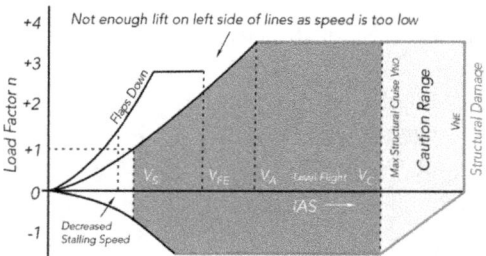

It shows that the aeroplane will stall at +1g, which is the speed at the lower end of the green arc on the ASI. The Maximum Structural Cruise speed (V_{NO}) should not be exceeded in rough air, at the top end of the green arc. That is, the Caution range (yellow arc) should only be used in smooth air.

The negative limit manoeuvring load factor must be at least 0.4 the positive load factor for normal and commuter machines (-1 to -1.52), utility machines (-1.76), or acrobatic aeroplanes (-3). Again, use lower load factors if they cannot be exceeded in flight.

The **Ultimate Load Factor** includes a **safety factor** of 1.5 (discussed further below), which gives you between +5.7 and -2.28 for Normal and Commuter aircraft.

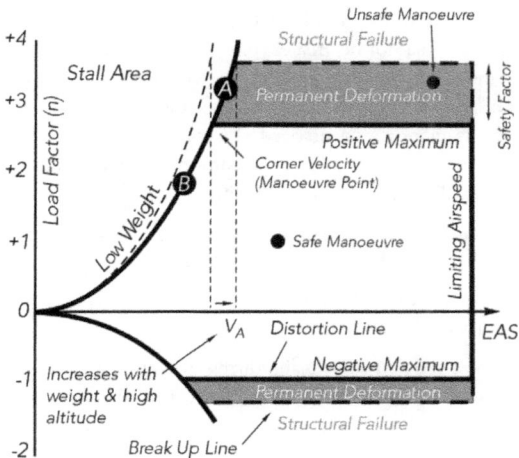

When this limit is reached, the primary structure will start to fall off, to follow the secondary structure which will have already gone. In other words, how much damage you do will depend on how far past the Limit Load Factor you go. Since you don't necessarily know who flew it before, it would be a good idea not to go past it at all. Thus, a light aircraft weighing less than 4,118 lbs must have a load factor between +3.8 and -1.52. The range for a commuter aircraft weighing 30,000 lbs would only need to be between +2.7 and -1.08. The flight manual should state the range for a particular aircraft.

V_A is the design manoeuvring speed*, or the highest speed at which an aeroplane will stall before exceeding the maximum load factor (or the highest speed at which **sudden, nose up full elevator deflection can be made without exceeding the design limits** or overstressing the aircraft). Its maximum value can be found by multiplying V_{S1} by the square root of the maximum load factor. As mass reduces, V_A will reduce as V_{S1} reduces. At the positive limit load factor (usually 3.8g) the aircraft will stall at V_A, the design manoeuvring speed. V_g is the stall speed at the negative limit load factor (usually -1.5g).

*Design speeds are EAS. Performance speeds are CAS.

The curve between 0 and the corner velocity (V_A) in the diagram above represents the aerodynamic limit on the load factor imposed by C_{Lmax}. The stall region is above it.

Thus, manoeuvring speed (V_A) (with flaps retracted) is the stall speed at the design load factor or, put another way, V_A must be at least the stalling speed at the design load factor (see *Radius Of Turn*, below). An aeroplane in the Normal category will stall at 3.8g so, if you fly below V_A, you cannot exceed the limits because the machine will stall first, and you can use full control deflection. If you stall at manoeuvring speed, you must be on a curved flight path involving a high g force.

 As weight is reduced, V_A reduces (as does V_S) because, although there is less stress on the wings with a lighter aircraft, it remains the same for other components, and full control deflection will still cause problems. Also, the maximum limit with flaps extended need only be 2g, so V_A only applies with flaps retracted. This is why using flaps in turbulence should be avoided.

Airliners normally operate within +2.5 to -1g (+2g with flaps extended) (distortion lines) which keep a 50% safety margin inside +3.75 and -1.5g (break up lines) so, if any maximum load factor is exceeded by more than 50%, structural failure will occur, giving us another two limits, the design ultimate positive and negative load factors.

The significance of V_A (for jet transports) is reduced at high cruising altitudes because of buffet onset limits. If you then add the maximum speed, you get something like the graph above.

 Use of the term *safety factor* does not mean that it is safe to enter the area where structural damage may occur!

As the stresses involved are a function of the dynamic pressure acting on the aircraft, the envelopes based on equivalent airspeeds - TAS is not relevant.

In other words, V_A is the dividing line between exceeding the limit load factor and stalling before you get any problems. Put yet another way, below V_A, if you pull too much g, you will stall first. Above it, you can exceed g limits before stalling. Manoeuvrability decreases above this speed, so the manoeuvre point gives you the fastest and tightest turns, where you can move the controls instantaneously without damage. The right hand vertical line is the high speed limit and is usually chosen to be the dive speed as the dynamic pressure otherwise would be too high and cause aileron reversal, flutter, etc.

At Point A, you cannot fly at C_{Lmax}, otherwise you would exceed the positive limit load factor. Point B is the highest load factor that can be obtained at that velocity.

 The boundaries of the basic envelope assume that C_{Lmax} remains constant but, against Mach numbers, it can vary with compressibility*, Reynolds number and adverse pressure gradient.

*Increasing the angle of attack increases the local acceleration over the wing so that the critical Mach number (M_{CRIT}) is reached at a progressively lower free stream Mach number (M_{FS}). The subsequent shockwaves are nearer the leading edge and, as the flow behind the shock breaks away and is turbulent, an increased part of the wing is subject to separated flow and the loss of lift is greater. With moderately thick wings, this loss could occur at an extremely low M_{FS}.

The reduction in C_{Lmax} means that the wing produces less lift than was expected at any particular speed, so the available load factor is reduced and a new curve must be produced. As each EAS corresponds to a higher Mach number at altitude, C_{Lmax} will decline further and new curves must be drawn for each altitude, although the Mach number at which the maximum load factor occurs will remain the same. Lift boundaries also exist for negative load factors.

PRINCIPLES OF FLIGHT
Stalling

The chart below includes the stall buffet boundary (C_{Nmax}) with flaps down, and significant speeds.

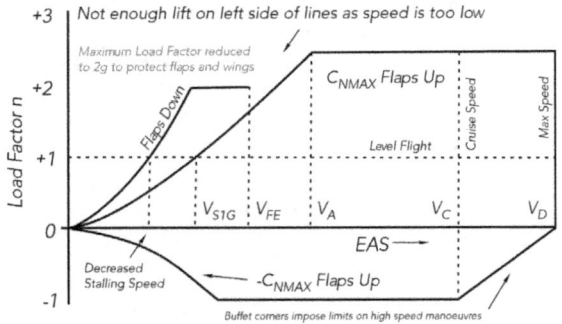

A lower **rolling g limit** can be imposed because the wing structure must provide the strength to withstand the twisting forces on top of the normal g.

Buffet Corners (on the bottom right of the diagram above, and often on the top right) are imposed because, if high air loads are combined with high loadings, the weakest part of the structure is more likely to fail, even more if the tailplane is buffeted by the turbulent wake of the wings. A typical example is aileron reversal, which actually governs the V_{NE} in the Challenger 350.

 Although extending the flaps for turbulence in the cruise reduces the stall speed and increases the margin to the stall, the margin to structural limitations reduces by a greater amount.

 The designer uses EAS but, at altitude, TAS is more relevant. As the common factor between them is relative air density, at altitude, any given TAS relates to a much lower EAS. The design EAS values of V_A, V_C and V_D are therefore reduced above 20,000 feet, usually in steps. As altitude is increased, the TAS/EAS at which M_{CRIT} is encountered decreases to less than V_D, modifying the envelope. For high sub- or transonic aircraft, a complete envelope will show Mach number limits for each altitude.

 V_C and V_D, being design speeds, will not be in the flight manual, but the speeds in the flight manual are based on them.

The designer needs V_C to be as low as possible to reduce the strain on the airframe, but pilots want it to be high so they can throw the machine around. In fact, for the Normal and Utility categories, V_C should be 38 times the square root of the wing loading (W/S) so, for an aeroplane with one of 16 lbs per square foot, that would be 152 mph (38 x 4), or 132 knots. V_D must be 1.4 times V_C for the Normal category. Note the restriction above V_C for negative G in the picture above. There should be a large enough margin between V_C and V_D to ensure that you don't get near to V_{NE} during normal manoeuvring.

- As weight increases, so does the stall speed - the curved stall lines move to the right. As V_{NE} is not affected by weight, the speed range stays the same.

- Below about 25,000 feet, stall speed (as EAS) is near constant - the stall lines are unaffected. At high altitudes, compressibility increases the stall speeds, so the curved stall lines move to the right. Also, V_{NE} reduces as the Mach number limits are reached - the envelope reduces as the speed limit moves left.

V_{MO} is the highest speed at which a large aircraft (over 5,700 kg MCTOM) can fly (CS 25). It is the equivalent of V_{NE} for light aircraft (below) and also may not be deliberately exceeded in any flight regime, and must not be greater than V_C, being sufficiently below V_D to make it highly unlikely that V_D will be inadvertently exceeded in normal operations (it is actually set at around 0.8 V_D). Because it is an indicated airspeed, the corresponding Mach number will increase with altitude (the maximum operating Mach number (M_{MO}) will kick in between 24,000 - 29,000 feet).

- When climbing at a constant IAS, you can exceed M_{MO} (at constant Mach number, TAS decreases).

- When descending at a constant Mach number, you can exceed V_{MO}.

A Climb Speed Schedule means using different combinations of speeds during defined portions of a flight, say, from the initial climb to TOC.

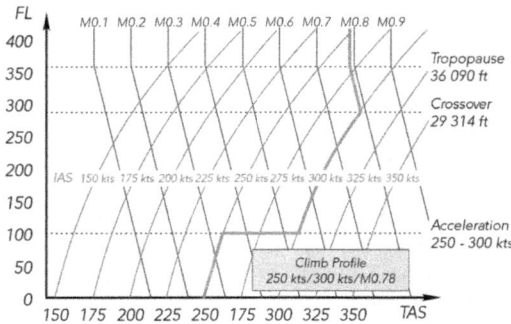

V_{NE} is the highest speed at which any aircraft under CS 23 (other than turbine aircraft) can fly. It is set at 0.9 V_D so that speed upsets can be recovered. It is shown by a radial red line on the airspeed indicator at the high speed end of the yellow arc.

V_{NE} is the highest speed at which any aircraft under CS 23 (other than turbine aircraft) can fly. It is set at 0.9 V_D so that speed upsets can be recovered. It is shown by a radial red line on the airspeed indicator at the high speed end of the yellow arc.

V_{NO} is the maximum structural cruise speed or normal operating limit for small aircraft. It must be not greater than the lesser of V_C or 0·89 V_{NE}. On the airspeed indicator, it occupies the upper limit of the green arc. From V_{NO} - V_{NE} there is a yellow arc, which is the caution range, within which you may fly only in smooth air, and even then only with caution.

V_{FE} is the highest speed for flaps fully extended.

V_{FO} is the maximum speed at which the flaps may be operated, either extended or retracted.

V_{LO} is the highest speed at which the landing gear can be safely extended or retracted.

V_{LE} is the highest speed for flight with the gear fully extended, slightly higher than V_{LO}.

PRINCIPLES OF FLIGHT
Stalling

GUST LOAD FACTOR

You might not intend to throw the machine around, but air currents, or gusts, have an accelerating effect in the same way as ordinary manoeuvres do, operating in any direction and getting worse with high speeds. The recommended speed for flight in rough air must be high enough to prevent a stall and low enough to prevent damage to the airframe. Both are catered for by calculating the stall speed for the gust then making sure that the aircraft is strong enough to cope with it.

Aircraft are designed to cope with gusts up to 56 feet per second at V_B, which is the design speed for maximum gust intensity. In fact, the stall would occur before exceeding the limit load factor so, in turbulence, there would be maximum protection at that speed. However, V_B is quite low, and it would take a while to slow down to it from V_C, so there must also be the ability to cope with vertical gusts of 56 feet per second at MSL* (EAS) at V_C. The maximum vertical gust limitations of V_B also apply to V_C. Those for V_D are exactly half the limitations at V_B and V_C.

*44 feet per second at 15 000 feet and 26 feet per second at 50 000 feet.

In practice, a slightly higher speed than V_B is used for turbulence penetration, namely V_{RA}/M_{RA} (rough-air speeds). Both will provide adequate protection from over-stressing the aircraft, together with maximum protection from an inadvertent stall.

A vertical gust can be otherwise known as an updraught or a downdraught, i.e. a rising or descending column of air (it might also be referred to as *sharp edged*, meaning that the transition from smooth air is instantaneous). The vertical component of a gust can significantly change the angle of attack (**with no elevator deflection**), when the relative airflow comes more from below.

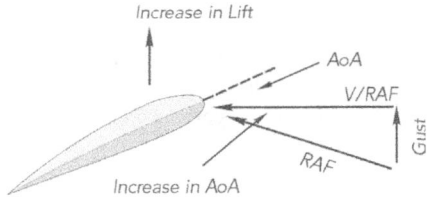

You can calculate the approximate load factor, as the C_L curve* is mostly linear (see the C_{Lmax} graph below). From an initial load factor of 1, a percentage increase in angle of attack will provide the same percentage increase in load factor. Put another way, a 1° change in angle of attack will change the C_L by 0·1.

*Coefficient of Lift, which indicates how good an aerofoil is at producing Lift, explained more fully later.

If you want a formula, divide the gust speed by the TAS to get the tangent of the angle of attack:

```
Tan AoA = Gust
          TAS
```

So, if an aircraft flying straight and level has a C_L of 0·35 and experiences a vertical gust which increases the angle of attack by 3°, what will the load factor be?

In straight and level flight, *n* will be 1, or 0.35. A 3° increase in angle of attack will produce 3 x 0.1 = 0.3. The C_L will increase to 0.35 + 0.3 = 0.65.

$$n = \frac{0.65}{0.35} = 1.86$$

A gust that increases the angle of attack by 3° will increase the load factor to 1.86. Although Lift is proportional to V^2, because the angle of attack is proportional to V, so is the impact of the gust. Put more in English, the gust speeds are to do with EAS, but the angle of attack is a function of the TAS and the speed of the gust. Gust speeds are taken to be 66 feet per second but, as the mathematical probability of exceeding the design limits at higher speeds is lower, gust speeds can be lower in these situations as well. The assumed gust velocity at V_B is 66 fps from MSL to 20,000 feet, decreasing to 38 fps at 50,000 feet. At V_C* it is 56 fps at MSL, 44 fps at 15,000 feet and 21 fps at 60,000 feet. The values are halved at VD**.

*As per the requirements of CS 25.335 and 23.335. It must be far enough away from V_B and V_D to allow for speed upsets. For example, under CS 25, V_C should be at least 43 kts above V_B and up to 0.8 V_D (CS 23 is similar). V_C does not have to exceed the maximum speed in level flight at maximum continuous power (V_H) or, in CS 23, 0.9 V_H at sea level.

**Based on an upset at V_C that creates a shallow dive. If that speed cannot be used, a demonstrated speed may be used called V_{DF}, which is the flight demonstrated design dive speed.

Our V–n diagram is now a gust load diagram, in which the gust lines originate from zero speed and a load factor of 1.

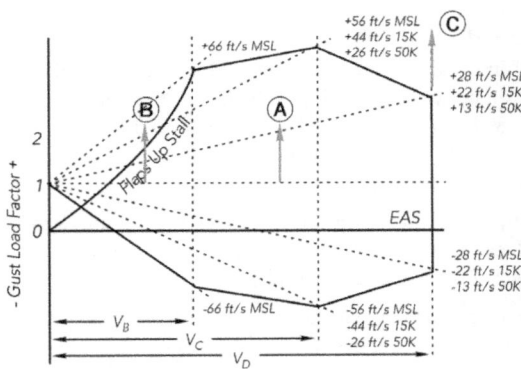

These values were originally established for military requirements in the 1940s, but are still valid today, due to the capabilities of the design engineers back then.

The figures used in the diagram above come from amendment 16 to JAR 25 - ICAO uses 66, 50 and 25 ft/sec up to FL 200, then 38, 25 and 12.5 at FL 500.

If the machine gets lighter, the gust lines will get further apart and more dangerous.

Notice that, for speeds above V_B, the diagram is symmetrical around the *n=1* line. You can see that, if an aircraft at 1g (Point A) is subject to a 28 fps gust, it will suddenly find itself subjected to 2g. At Point B, at a much slower speed, you will stall first. Point C is off the scale.

A GA aircraft should be able to withstand gusts with a velocity of 56 feet per second from sea level up to 20,000 feet. Between there and 50,000 feet, the gust velocity decreases to 38 fps. It must be able to safely fly at V_A when gusts of 66 feet per second are encountered, and carry gust loads of up to 28 feet per second at dive speed, as can be seen from the vertical gust velocities (dotted lines) plotted from the 1 value on the vertical axis, which represents straight and level flight in smooth air.

The equation that creates the lines is like this:

```
LF_G = 1 + k(V x G)
```

The number 1 means that, if there is no gust, the load factor will be 1 (which is why they start at 1 in the graph). The values in the brackets show that the gust load depends on the TAS (V) and the strength of the gust. The effect of wing design is small because the *k* value refers to the slope of the C_L vs alpha curve below according to the wing loading and wing design - a high wing loading means a lower k value, and less of an influence from turbulence.

Thus, because the C_L changes less for a given change in angle of attack for swept wing aircraft (their curve is shallower), turbulence affects them less, as the gust load factor decreases.

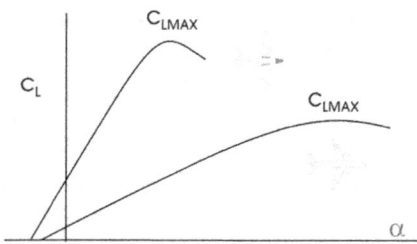

You can see from the graph that:

- If Lift equals Weight, the stall speed will be least at the maximum value of the lift coefficient (C_{Lmax}), and that the higher its value, the lower the stall speed will be. Thus, an aircraft with a straight wing has a lower V_S for the same weight and wing area.
- Swept wing aircraft must use a higher angle of attack to achieve maximum lift (or their C_{Lmax} is slightly lower). Their stall angle of attack is higher.
- There is a sudden reduction of C_L for straight wing aircraft at the stall, but not for swept wings.
- The straight wing aircraft will reach its maximum lift at an earlier angle of attack, but the lift produced decreases rapidly with further increases.

Anyhow, the load limits in the gust load diagram are established where the dotted lines cross selected reference speeds. Joining them together sets out the **Gust Envelope** within which the aircraft must operate.

 The gradient of the positive stall curve is shallower than that in the manoeuvring envelope, because a vertical gust, by increasing the effective angle of attack, increases the airspeed at which the stalling angle is reached.

The recommended speed for flight in turbulence, or rough air (V_{RA}) also comes from the above graph. V_{RA} must lie within the range of speeds for which the requirements associated with V_S are met, and must be sufficiently less than V_{MO} to ensure that likely speed variations in rough air will not cause the overspeed warning to operate too frequently.

As with the manoeuvring envelope, the effects of gross weight, altitude and Mach number must be accounted for. The gust load diagram is drawn up for particular values of each and the complete envelope will show the effects of flight at various altitudes and gross weights. Because an aerofoil with a high aspect ratio is less resistant to bending loads, the aspect ratio and the sweepback must be considered as well.

When wing loading increases (i.e. the aircraft gets heavier), the gust load factor decreases, as it does with lower speeds. What this means in real life is that, if you are flying an aeroplane with a quarter of the wing loading of another type, the turbulence would be four times worse for you. If your aircraft has straight wings (as opposed to swept wings) it will be even worse. Reducing the speed will reduce the effects.

RATE OF TURN

The rate of turn is the angle through which an aircraft turns divided by the time taken, quantified in degrees per minute. Assuming the turn is balanced, the rate of turn is dependent on the speed of the aeroplane and its angle of bank. The slower the aeroplane and the greater its angle of bank, the greater will be the rate of turn. At a constant rate of turn, the angle of bank depends on the TAS. If you increase speed, to maintain a rate one turn (see below) the bank angle and the radius must be increased.

To avoid exceeding the limiting load factor, transport aircraft are usually limited to 3° per second, otherwise known as a Rate 1 Turn, being the ratio of TAS to the radius involved. The proper calculation is to divide the circumference by the speed. You will end up with:

```
Rate =  TAS (fps) x 57.296
           Radius (ft)
```

 The rate of turn is inversely proportional to V, not V^2. An aeroplane with double the speed of another will take twice as long to turn and 4 times the radius so to do (the radius is proportional to V^2).

RADIUS OF TURN

Only the angle of bank and speed will modify the radius of a turn. Put another way, for a given angle of bank, the radius of turn is proportional to the velocity squared (V^2). Weight has no bearing, either - a large aeroplane will use the same radius as a small one, at the same TAS.

To calculate the radius of a Rate 1 turn:

$$R = \frac{V}{60\pi}$$

or:

$$R = \frac{V}{\cancel{188.5}\ 200}$$

(call it 200 for government work).

 ICAO requires all turns in the hold to be made at a 25° angle of bank or at 3° per second, whichever requires the lesser bank. A rate 1 turn at more than 180 knots TAS would need more than 25°, so just use that for turns in faster aircraft.

So, given a speed and an angle of bank:

$$R = \frac{V^2}{g \times \tan \varphi}$$

where φ is the angle of bank, and ignoring any slip.

As 1 knot is 0.515 metres per second (call it 0.5), for 500 knots with a bank angle of 30°, and rounding g up to 10, we have a radius of around 10 824 m or nearly 11 km:

$$R = \frac{250^2}{g \times \tan \varphi}$$

$$R = \frac{62500}{10 \times 0.5774}$$

The accurate calculation is:

$$R = \frac{66306.25}{9.81 \times 0.5774}$$

11 034 m. Close enough!

👍 **Rule Of Thumb**: For those dark rainy nights just use 1% of the groundspeed - 11 km is around 6 nm.

For a metric example, at 70 kts with a bank angle of 45°:

$$70 \times 0.515 = 36.05$$

which, squared, is 1299.6. The tangent of 45° is 1, and multiplying by g produces 9.81. Dividing that into 1294 gives 132 m.

Your altitude will affect the relationship between the various factors involved for a given IAS.

- The angle of bank for a given radius at a constant IAS will increase with altitude.
- The radius of turn for a given angle of bank and IAS will increase with altitude.
- The rate of turn for a given angle of bank and IAS will decrease with altitude.

The graph below plots various turn radii against a series of bank angles. It may seem obvious, but it shows that the greater the angle of bank for a given velocity, the less is the radius involved.

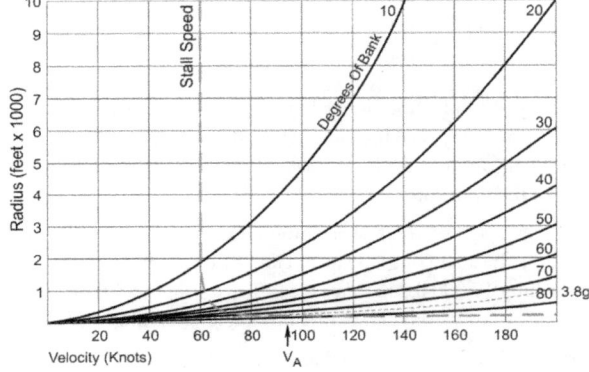

Not so obvious is that there are only very slight differences between anything above 45°*. As you are well below the 3.8g limit shown at that point, it means you can use the flaps, as the g involved will only have a value of 1.41 (41%), as described in *Load Factor*, above (with flaps extended, most aeroplanes are limited to 2g). As the stall speed is then only 1.19 V_S, using 1.3 V_S allows a safety margin. You may well get a tighter turn anyway if you use flaps, because the stall speed will reduce.

*You need a lot more power after this point as the weight of the aircraft will have increased due to the load factor.

The minimum radius occurs where the 3.8g line crosses the stalling speed line, which increases dramatically after about 30° of bank. This is V_A, the manoeuvring speed for the tightest turn.

BANK OF ANGLE

To find the angle of bank for a standard rate balanced turn:

$$\tan \varphi = \frac{2\pi V}{gt}$$

👍 **Rule Of Thumb**: Divide the TAS by 10, then add half of the answer - at 120 knots, it would therefore be 18°. For interest, this table shows you how accurate it is:

TAS (kts)	Correct	RoT
50	8°	12°
100	15°	17°
150	22°	22°
200	29°	27°
250	34°	32°

It's close enough between 100-250 knots.

Q. What angle of bank can an aircraft flying at 1.3 V_S use without stalling? **A.** Load factor is equal to 1/cos bank angle, so we end up with 0.769, or 39.7°.

Q. To **find the bank angle** given the TAS and radius of turn:

$$\tan \varphi = \frac{(0.515 \times V)^2}{\text{radius} \times 10}$$

As a reminder, 0.515 turns the TAS in knots into m/s, which you must use if you want metres for the radius (plus m/s² for g). Assuming 170 knots, and a radius of 1000m:

$$170 \times 0.515 = 87.55$$

which, squared, produces 7665 in round figures.

1000 x 9.81 = 9810 which, divided into 7665 produces 0.78 which turns out to be 37.95°.

Q. To find out how long it takes to do a **complete circle**, given the bank angle (45°) and TAS (200 kts) we start with the radius, which is found with:

$$R = \frac{V^2}{g \times \tan \varphi}$$

$$1060.9 = \frac{10,609}{10}$$

200 x 0.515 gives us 103 - square that to get 10,609. The tan of 45° is 1.

$$\frac{2\pi \times 1060.9}{10,609} = \frac{6662.45}{10,609} = 0.63$$

Multiply 0.63 by 100 to obtain 63 seconds.

The Spin

In a spin, the angle of attack of the dropping wing is increased well beyond the stall, due to the change in relative velocity, as the upgoing wing reduces its angle of attack. Any attempt to raise the dropping wing with the ailerons will just make things worse. At the same time, the increased drag on the downgoing wing creates a yaw, leading you into autorotation, often called the incipient spin. Once the rolling and yawing motions become self-sustaining, the aircraft is spinning.

Recovery comes from reducing the rolling moment and/or trying to yaw the other way. Of the two, the yawing moment is the more important, but the rudder (the normal yaw control) is not the only game in town. First, set idle power, then full opposite rudder, push the control column forward until the spin stops, keeping the ailerons in the neutral position. You may need to use the ailerons, depending on the type.

FORCES IN FLIGHT

The forces acting on an aerofoil are Lift, Weight, Thrust and Drag, all of which must be balanced for straight and level flight. Having said that, given that static pressure is responsible for Drag and Lift, because it both supports the aircraft against gravity and impedes its movement, we are really dealing with only one force, but we split it up for convenience. In an aeroplane, they would all resolve into something like this:

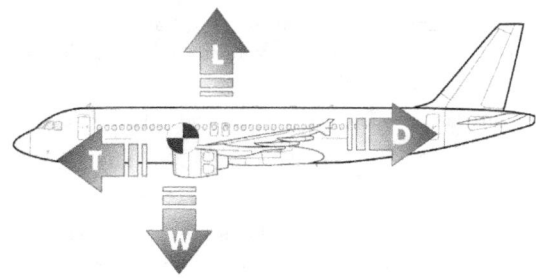

They are not in line with each other, because the idea is to balance the couples - the nose down tendency of the L/W couple is balanced by the nose up tendency of T/D, which is relatively weak, so the ideal position would be to have T & D as wide apart as possible. As this cannot always be done, the tailplane is placed at an angle of attack that produces a down force in level flight.

The other point to note is that each vector is a resultant of the forces associated with it. That is, Lift is the sum of *all* the forces acting perpendicular to the flight path (or undisturbed airflow) - it doesn't just act through the point shown (the neutral point) but also comes from the elevator and the fuselage. Certainly, not all parts of the wing produce the same amount of lift.

Weight always acts through the Centre of Gravity towards the centre of the Earth, but it is not always opposed by Lift (this only happens in straight and level flight). Ignoring the use of fuel and load factors, Weight is the only vector that does not vary. Also, Thrust (technically) acts where the engines are pointed but, for our purposes, it is assumed to be parallel and opposite to the drag vector, along the longitudinal axis, when the thrust line is parallel to the line of flight - thrust is greater than drag at slow speeds near the stall in level flight, and in the climb.

This is how the vectors might look as a parallelogram of forces when added together for straight and level flight*, where T = D and L = W:

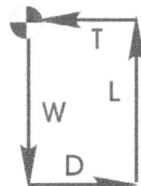

*When forces acting at a point are in equilibrium, the resulting polygon will be a closed figure.

The Climb

This is how they would look in a climb:

Climbing is done by converting excess propulsive energy (above that needed for straight and level flight) into potential energy, which is based on height.

Thrust is now greater than Drag, which is still at right angles to Lift, which is less than Weight because it doesn't oppose it. This is how it would look in most textbooks:

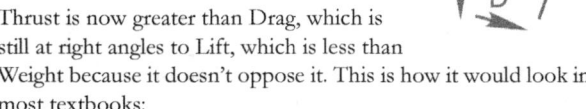

In a steady climb, weight acquires a rearward component* which is below, parallel to and in the same direction as drag, and must be compensated for by extra thrust (in fact, in a vertical climb, weight is opposed by engine thrust). There is also a component opposing Lift.

*The sine of γ can be found by dividing the difference between Thrust and Drag by Weight:

$$\text{Sin (Climb angle)} = \frac{T - D}{W}$$

Which, when you think about it, really means excess thrust over weight. In the first stages of the climb, Thrust is significantly larger than Drag, and it must be at least 1.3 times the Drag in a twin to make the gradient.

You get the best *angle* of climb at maximum excess thrust, so thrust controls the angle or gradient of climb. For example, if an aircraft weighing 10 000 lbs has an excess thrust value of 5 000 lbs, the equation works out at 0.5, or a 30° angle of climb.

Having said all that, Lift is accepted as equal to Weight up to about 15° angle of climb, as the cosine used to calculate it is still close to 1 at 0.9659. This means that, although induced drag is less in the climb (less lift) the difference is negligible at less than 2%. For example, an aircraft with a mass of 75 000 kg, with a weight of 735 750 N would have a Lift force of 724 572 for a climb angle of 10°. The difference between Lift and Weight is quite small. To maintain a constant IAS, power must be increased because the IAS decreases with altitude (relative to TAS), which is significant for aircraft with a high rate of climb (if the angle is less than γ, the climb will be accelerative).

Put another way, to get the maximum *angle* of climb, you should fly at the speed that produces the maximum difference between thrust and drag, or the greatest distance between the thrust available and thrust required curves. With a piston engined aircraft, whose thrust reduces as the speed is increased beyond lift off speed, this will be as low as is safe above it (around V_{IMP}).

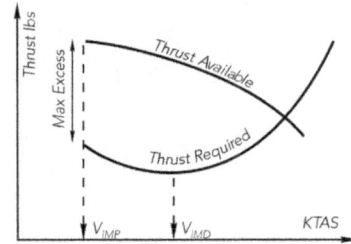

However, this is very close to the stall speed so a margin of 10 knots may be added for controllability purposes.

For jets, where thrust doesn't change much with speed, this will be at minimum drag speed (V_{IMD}).

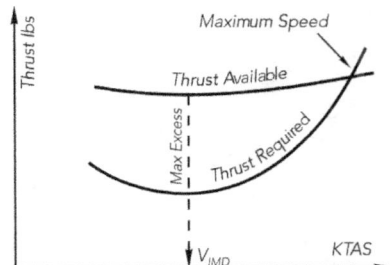

You could call the drag involved the *Thrust Required* (for straight & level flight), and the thrust actually produced the *Thrust Available*. The former has almost everything to do with the airframe, and nothing to do with the powerplant, while the latter is the opposite. Thus, if we know the variations of thrust with velocity and altitude, the Thrust curve can be added to the Drag curve, as shown above.

The points where the thrust and drag curves intersect represent the minimum and maximum speeds in straight and level flight. Above the maximum speed or below the minimum speed, there is not enough thrust to overcome the drag. In fact, the true lower speed limitation would be the stall.

Here is an alternative view:

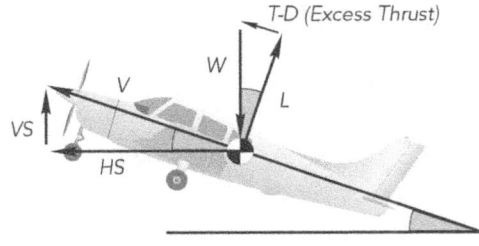

VS = Vertical Speed, or Rate Of Climb which, in this case, is the vertical component of Velocity (V), or TAS (two aeroplanes climbing at the same angle will only have the same vertical speed if they have the same TAS).

The point of the similar triangles is to emphasise that they are all affected when the vectors change. For example, increasing Thrust will increase the angle of climb.

The horizontal speed (HS) is TAS multiplied by the cosine of the climb angle, as affected by the wind (with zero wind it is groundspeed).

If Thrust exceeds Drag (in straight & level flight, at a given speed), the aircraft can accelerate, climb, or turn, or perform other manoeuvres.

CLIMB GRADIENT

The climb gradient is the ratio of the change of height in feet for every 100 feet of horizontal distance travelled in that time (*Rise over Run*). It depends on the excess thrust available (and weight). As thrust available is constant for a turbojet as its speed increases, if it flies faster, the excess thrust available increases until L/D_{max} and the climb gradient will also increase. At L/D_{max} there is maximum excess thrust available, or the maximum climb gradient.

The gradient can be positive (climbing) or negative (descending). To get it, divide the height gained (H) by the ground distance travelled (D), allowing for wind (without the wind, you get the *Still Air Gradient*).

The climb gradient decreases with increasing flap angle and increasing temperature.

$$\text{Gradient} = \frac{H}{D} \times 100$$

Which is the same as VS divided by HS (above), or:

$$\text{Tan (Climb angle)} = \frac{T - D}{L} \times \frac{100}{g}$$

(the triangles are similar).

However, remembering that if the climb angle is less than 15°, you can assume L = W:

$$\text{Climb Gradient} = \frac{T - D}{W}$$

To express the gradient as a percentage:

$$\frac{\text{height gain(ft)}}{\text{distance (ft)}} \times 100 = \text{gradient\%}$$

If an aircraft has a rate of climb of 500 fpm at 100 kts, first convert the speed to feet per minute:

$$\frac{100 \times 6080}{60} = 10,133 \text{ fpm}$$

In one minute you will have flown 10,133 feet through the air* and gained 500 feet in height so the gradient is:

$$\frac{500}{10133} \times 100 = 4.9344\%$$

or 5% for government work.

*This is TAS, not groundspeed, but the angle is small so there is not much difference. As a rule of thumb, ignoring units, divide the ROC in fpm by the TAS in knots.

With 20 knots of headwind, the groundspeed above would be 80 kts.

$$\frac{80 \times 6080}{60} = 8106 \text{ fpm}$$

For a 6% gradient, or thereabouts.

So, just to complicate matters, what climb gradient would you get from a four engined aeroplane that loses an engine (this might be indicated by the words "second segment")? It weighs 55 000 kg, with a L/D ratio of 11:1 and the thrust from each engine is 23 000 N. It is performing a straight, steady climb on the remaining 3 engines.

Remembering that the weight value in the formula above is actually mass x gravity, we can use:

$$\text{Climb Gradient} = \frac{T - D}{M \times G}$$

or:

$$\text{Gradient} = \frac{69\ 000 - 50\ 000}{550\ 000}$$

69 000 is the output from 3 engines (23 000 x 3). The drag value comes from dividing the weight (55 000 x 9.8, or 10) by 11. Multiplying by 100, the answer is 3.5%.

EXAMPLES

1. Given a thrust value of 60 newtons, and a drag value of 50 newtons, if an aircraft weighs 200 newtons, what is the climb gradient?

$$5\% = \frac{60 - 50}{200} \times 100$$

2. If a twin engined aeroplane with a mass of 40 tonnes is in a straight, steady, wings-level climb, what is its climb gradient, given a thrust value of 40 000N per engine, an L/D ratio of 11:1 and a g value of 10 m/s²?

$$\text{Climb Gradient} = \frac{80\ 000 - 36364}{400\ 000}$$

The thrust is quite easy to figure out (40 000 x 2 engines), and the weight is simply the mass multiplied by g (40 000 x 10). Divide that by 11, the L/D ratio, to get the drag value of 36 364 (assuming L = W). Number-crunch that lot and multiply by 100 to get 11% in round figures.

3. What should the mass of a twin-engined aircraft be to achieve a gradient of at least 4% in the second segment, given a drag value of 40 000 N and a thrust per engine of 50 000 N?

$$W = \frac{50\ 000 - 40\ 000}{4} \times 100$$

Divide the weight in newtons by the acceleration from gravity (assume 10) to get a mass of 25 000 kg.

4. If a twin-engined aircraft with an L/D ratio of 11:1 and a mass of 60 000 kg has a thrust per engine of 75 000 N, what is its climb gradient?

The weight in newtons is 600 000, and so, approximately, is the Lift. The drag is 54 545 N. Total thrust is 150 000 N, so the gradient is 16% in round figures.

5. If an aircraft with a mass of 10 000 lbs requires 700 HP to fly straight and level at a constant speed, assuming its mass doesn't change, what rate of climb would you get if there was an excess of 300 hp available? 1 HP = 33 000 ft/lbs (see *Definitions*).

$$990 \text{ fpm} = \frac{300 \times 33\ 000}{10\ 000}$$

Tip: To convert an angle of climb to a gradient, simply place the speed index of the flight computer against 3°, and the approximate gradient (5%) is against the 10 index (the exact gradient is against 10.5 on the inner scale).

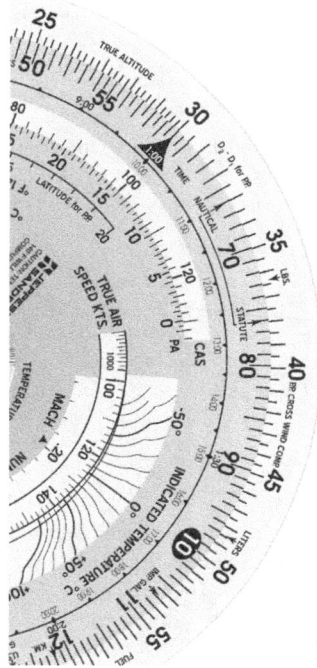

EFFECTS OF WEIGHT & ALTITUDE

As thrust and excess power both reduce in the climb, the angle and rate of climb will reduce, as they would if an engine fails or the flaps are deployed, or there is an increase in weight (same as loss of thrust).

RATE OF CLIMB

For the *rate* of climb, we are talking about excess *power*** over weight. Power is the rate of doing work, and is thrust multiplied by TAS, so power available is thrust available x TAS, and power required is drag x TAS.

$$\text{Sin (Vertical Speed)} = \frac{TAS(T - D)}{W}$$

**Power available minus power required. The maximum excess power produces the best rate of climb.

This formula:

$$\frac{\text{Power avail} - \text{Power reqd}}{\text{TAS}}$$

is the same thing, but 1 kt = 101.3 ft/min (around 1/0.987).

For small angles, if the TAS and the angle of climb double, so will the rate of climb, which therefore depends on them both:

$$\text{ROC} = \text{Angle of Climb} \times \text{TAS}$$

You could also say that the ROC is approximately the % gradient x the TAS, so you could use:

$$\text{FPM} = \frac{(\text{TAS} \times \%)}{0.987}$$

The rate of climb is not affected by wind.

Tip: As the Rate Of Climb (ROC) is the height gained in 1 minute, you can find it if you know the gradient and can work out the ground distance covered in that time.

$$\frac{\text{TAS} \times \% \times 6080}{60} = \text{fpm}$$

If a twin-engined aircraft climbing at 180 kts has a climb gradient of 2.4%, what is the rate of climb?

$$\frac{180 \times 2.4 \times 6080}{6000} = 437 \text{ fpm}$$

6000 comes from 60 multiplied by the 100 part of the gradient figure.

Tip: The 6000 and 6080 figures virtually cancel each other out, so just multiply the TAS by the gradient to get a close enough figure (432 in this case).

POWER AVAILABLE

Power *available* = Thrust x TAS. If Thrust = Drag, speed will remain constant. If Thrust < drag, speed will reduce, and if thrust > drag, speed will increase.

In the graph below, you can see that the power available curve for a jet is different from that of a piston-engined aircraft. This is because the thrust it produces is more or less constant at any speed, so you get a straight line when you multiply the thrust by the appropriate airspeed.

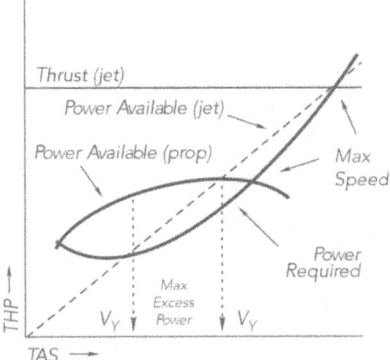

Thus, if you have no speed, you have no power, although you might have plenty of thrust. On the other hand, an aircraft always needs power when it is moving, even when no thrust is being used, as found when gliding. All this proves that thrust and power are not the same thing.

The jet has a wide range of speeds that provide the maximum power - its power required curve* is quite shallow, so the highest speed is used, for maximum efficiency. When climbing at a fixed IAS, the angle of attack stays the same.

*Drag can be expressed in terms of power required (for level flight) to overcome it. As power is force x velocity, the power required can be found by multiplying drag by velocity. Note that the power required curve shown below has nothing to do with engine power - it is simply the drag curve replotted in terms of power, and the speed at which minimum power is required is not the same as the speed for minimum drag. With the piston, under the same conditions and for a given BHP, the power available varies at both ends of the speed range because the propeller shows inefficiencies at low and high airspeeds, due to angle of attack and compressibility effects, respectively.

The engine output of all propeller aircraft is expressed in terms of power, which is really energy per unit time, or thrust multiplied by velocity. Shaft horsepower is what comes out of the engine to the propeller.

It's worth noting that the type of powerplant involved is irrelevant when it comes to the power required curve because only drag and speed come into the equation.

Remember that, when you reduce power, the power available curve will move down, while the power required curve stays where it is. In the situation below, the aircraft can no longer climb, but only fly level at one airspeed.

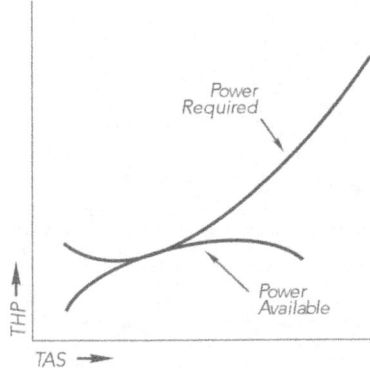

The power available must be more than that required to maintain a steady climb. The speed at which excess power (that available minus that required) and rate of climb are maximum is V_Y. The maximum climb gradient is attained at V_X, which is derived from the thrust curves.

It is proportional to the excess thrust (that available minus drag) divided by the weight. The maximum climb angle at any given

PRINCIPLES OF FLIGHT
Forces In Flight

weight depends upon the airspeed. At the absolute ceiling* V_X is equal to V_Y and the best angle and rate of climb are zero.

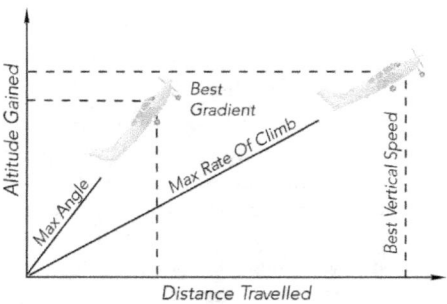

During a climb at maximum power, if you reduce the IAS progressively from the maximum rate of climb speed (V_Y) to the stalling speed (V_S), the angle of climb will increase, then decrease as you pass through V_X (best angle of climb speed) to V_S.

*The **service** (gross) **ceiling** in ISA conditions is the altitude where the best rate of climb decreases to a specified minimum, usually 100 ft/min for propeller aircraft and 500 ft/min for jets, or the maximum practical pressure altitude. Above it, the power available, excess power and best rate of climb all continue to decrease. The **absolute ceiling*** is reached when power available is just equal to power required, and excess power and rate of climb are zero, as are excess thrust and best angle of climb. As it takes a long time to get there, it can normally be ignored. The **net ceiling** is where the best rate of climb decreases to 150 ft/min for prop aircraft and 750 ft/min for jets.

It is the maximum altitude for the cruise.

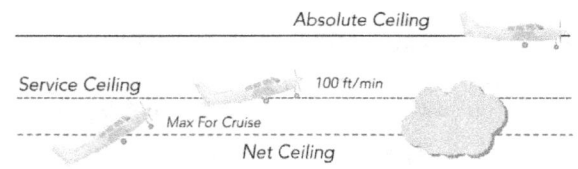

*The absolute ceiling in the Challenger 350 is FL 450 - it is governed by the 4 minutes it takes to get back down to sea level in a hurry.

The chart below is the climb graph for a typical light twin. To determine its single-engine service ceiling, enter the graph on the right hand side at 100 fpm, then go up to the aircraft weight (at altitude).

Go left to the ISA reference line and the result would be approximately 15 200 feet.

POWER REQUIRED

The performance of your machine is essentially the difference between power available and power required.

Because power required depends on drag x TAS, it does not matter what engines you are using.

In the climb, the power required increases because you must increase TAS to maintain a constant IAS. This comes from the formula:

```
Power Required = Drag x TAS
```

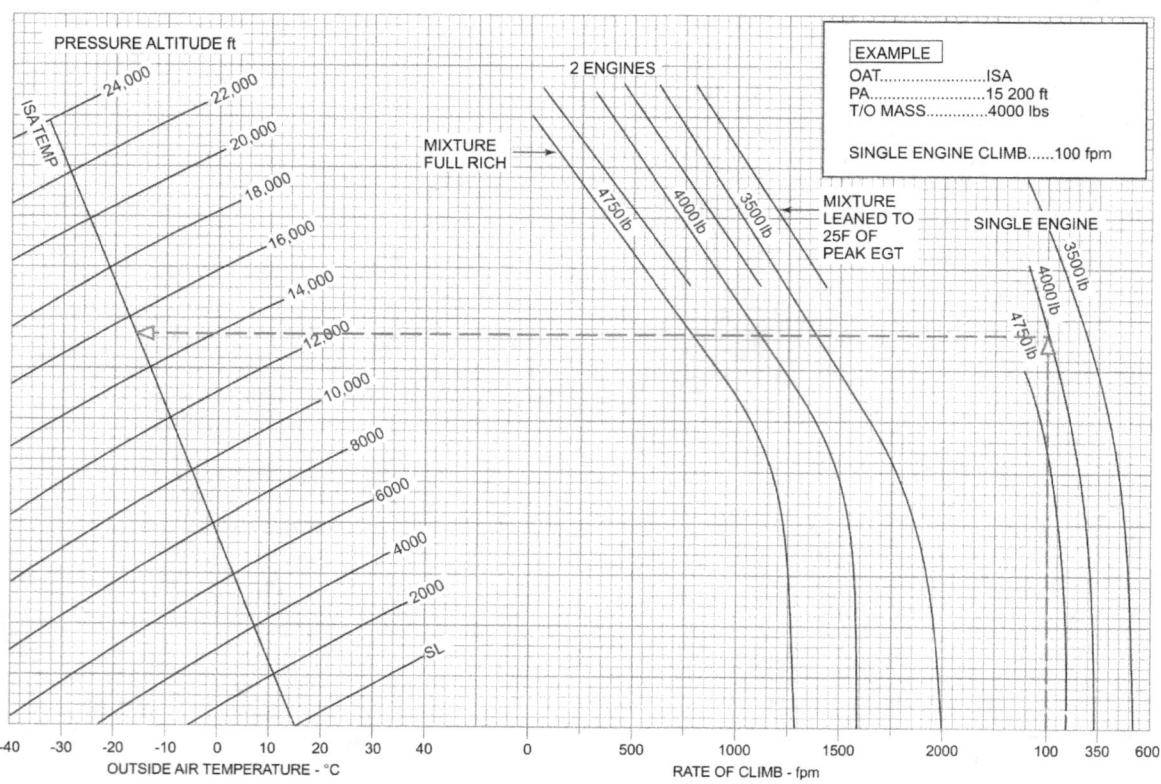

PRINCIPLES OF FLIGHT
Forces In Flight

It derives from the fact that *Power* (the rate of doing work) is equal to *Force* x *Distance* (i.e. work) divided by *Time*. The power required curve (see picture below) really represents the power needed to overcome the various types of drag (determined for each speed by multiplying the drag found at that speed by the TAS), so it's similar in shape to the drag curve, but skewed a bit because extra velocity is involved. TAS is used because it is the only speed that gives a measure of the actual distance covered (there is a disproportionate requirement for power at low speeds in order to overcome the high induced drag).

POWER REQUIRED & DRAG CURVES
In the picture, the dashed line is the total drag curve.

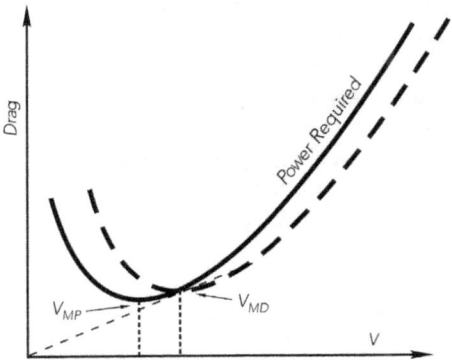

The solid line is power required curve.

Notice that V_{MP} is 0.76 x V_{MD}, and the tangent to the power curve (best range) is at minimum drag speed.

The tangent business works as follows:

```
Work = Force x Distance
```

therefore:

$$\text{Distance} = \frac{\text{Work}}{\text{Force}}$$

If work remains constant, to obtain maximum distance, the force used must be minimal. The speed to achieve this is obtained from the power required curve:

Because:

$$\text{Tan } \theta = \frac{\text{power}}{\text{velocity}}$$

and:

```
power = force x velocity
```

You can end up with (substituting):

$$\text{Tan } \theta = \frac{\text{force x velocity}}{\text{velocity}}$$

or:

```
Tan θ = force
```

So, when the angle of the tangent to the curve is minimum, you get the best speed for the most range.

Similarly for endurance, where the work available must be spread over the longest possible time. If:

$$\text{Power} = \frac{\text{Work}}{\text{Time}}$$

$$\text{Time} = \frac{\text{Work}}{\text{Power}}$$

Again, if work remains constant, the power must be minimal to ensure maximum time.

DESCENT
If the result of the equations above is negative, you are descending:

Here, Thrust is less than Drag.

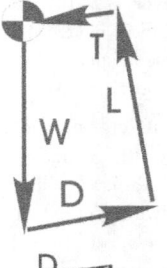

If you take the thrust away, you are gliding (discussed later):

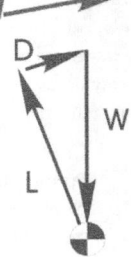

In steady descending flight (i.e. unaccelerated), the equilibrium of forces acting on an aeroplane is given by the formula:

```
D = T + W sin gamma (γ)
```

Theta (θ) is the pitch angle and gamma (γ) is the flight path angle. Alpha (the angle of attack) is the difference between them.

 In the EASA learning objectives, Gamma is defined as the flight path angle with climb being positive. However, it can be used as a descent angle, so the sign would be reversed.

In a powered descent, Thrust is greater than Drag:

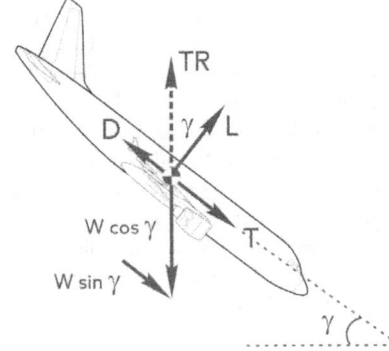

If the Thrust is removed, it is replaced by W sin γ, which should equal Drag for equilibrium. By changing the dive angle, the aircraft will glide at different speeds, depending on the values of Drag, Weight and the glide angle.

© Phil Croucher, 2018

The range can be found by dividing the height by the tangent of the glide angle so, for maximum range, the glide angle must be as small as possible (the glide angle is degraded when you use trailing edge flaps).

Tip: Range can also be found by multiplying the height by lift over drag.

 Flaps increase drag more than they provide lift, so you need to put the nose down to maintain airspeed. This increases the descent angle, which reduces the range.

Increasing Weight needs more Lift, so you get more Drag. However, L and D will increase in the same proportion, so the L/D ratio will stay the same. The overall effect will be an increase in speed. If there is no change in glide angle or range, you simply end up with a higher rate of descent.

Wind affects only the horizontal component of velocity, which changes the groundspeed The rate of descent determines how long the aircraft will stay up so, if you keep the same gliding time, a headwind will reduce the range by decreasing the groundspeed, and vice versa. If you keep the glide angle constant, increasing velocity increases groundspeed and rate of descent, so you cannot stay up as long. Increasing speed while keeping the glide angle constant means increasing weight.

 Controlling the rate of descent properly is an important factors in instrument flying. Whereas a climb results from excess power, a descent is the result of a horsepower deficit.

By controlling the deficit, you can control the rate of descent at a given airspeed, which is important when trying to maintain the ILS glidepath. Some approach charts have a small chart that shows rates of descent against airspeed in nil wind conditions, which means that the wind will effectively turn them into groundspeeds. With a headwind, you will fall below the glideslope if you try to maintain the airspeed shown and vice versa. As you don't really know the groundspeed, all you can do is set the speed and use power to maintain the required rate of descent. This must be reduced as you descend. If you just adjust the attitude (nose down) you will arrive too fast at the threshold and float.

Gliding

The three forces acting on a gliding aircraft are Lift, Weight and Drag (no Thrust* - see picture below). H represents horizontal speed, and V represents vertical speed (rate of descent). The ratio of H to V (or height to distance) is the glide ratio, or the distance flown forward for altitude lost. This is equal to the ratio of L to D as the triangles are similar. As the angle between the Lift vector and its resultant (W) is the same as the one between the flight path and the horizontal (the gliding angle), for maximum distance (and minimum sink rate), the gliding angle should be as small as possible. This depends on an angle of attack that provides the best L/D ratio.

*Even with no Thrust, you still need power to stay airborne. This comes from Drag multiplied by TAS.

With angles of glide less than 15°, the cosine concerned is around 1 anyway, so the speed can be very close to the cruise speed in level flight - at greater angles, it must be reduced. The rate of descent will become less at lower altitudes as the TAS decreases.

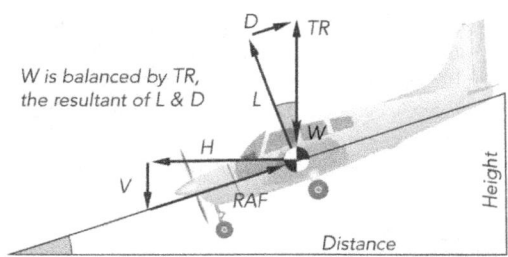

You can calculate the glide range in still air by multiplying the L/D ratio by your altitude. The answer will be in feet, so divide it by 6080 to get nautical miles. So, from 35 000 feet with a L/D ratio of 6:1, you will glide for 210 000 feet, or around 35 nm.

The glide range is not affected by weight*, and neither is the glide angle (at the best L/D ratio) - only the speed. As drag depends on IAS, the best glide speed at a given weight is constant, regardless of altitude, but the rate of descent will decrease at lower altitudes as TAS decreases.

*The increased weight makes the aircraft move faster down the descent path (so glide speed is affected), which increases the lift without the need to change the angle of attack (the proportions are the same, as an increase in the Weight vector is balanced by increases in the Lift and Drag vectors). However, as a heavier aircraft has a higher gliding speed, it will cover the same distance as a lighter aircraft but in a shorter time. Furthermore, the heavy aeroplane will have a reduced glide endurance.

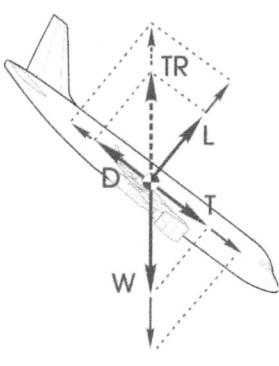

The picture below is a typical comparison of the rate of sink against velocity at sea level and at altitude.

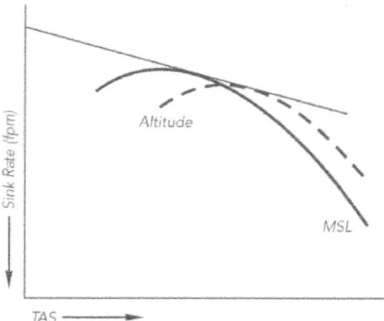

It looks like an upside down power curve because it is! The minimum rate of descent is found at the top of each curve. The tangent line indicates the speed for maximum range. As it hits both curves at the same point, the glide ratio for maximum distance is the same for all altitudes, although the aeroplane will be sinking faster at altitude, and travelling at a faster speed.

The wind has no effect on gliding for endurance, but it has a marked effect on gliding for range when you want to arrive at a specific point. Naturally, an aeroplane will glide less over the ground when flying into wind, and further with a tail wind. Speed should be increased in a headwind because you can then use a lower angle of attack, and your exposure to the headwind is less (lowering the nose when going for range is not intuitive, but it works).

Similarly, if you want a steeper approach, increase the drag.

The speed for range is not a specific speed, but a range of speeds covered by the tangent's broad intersection point with the curve in the picture below. This is also the best ratio of C_L to C_D (Lift/Drag).

The origin itself can be moved forwards or backwards to take into account the effects of headwind or tailwind.

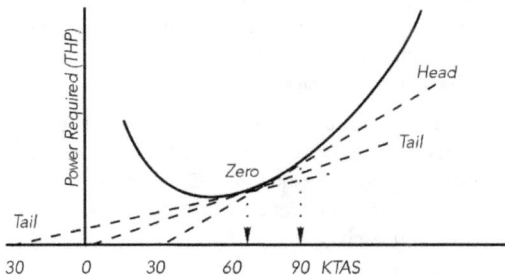

Like endurance speed, the range speed is usually increased slightly for handling reasons at low altitudes and reduced at high altitudes.

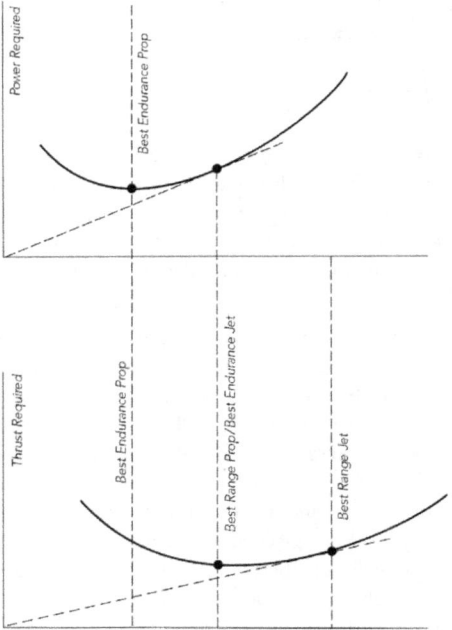

Tip: In general, other things being equal, the best glide speed in zero wind for a propeller driven aeroplane is the same as that required for best range in level flight, if parasite drag remains unaltered (i.e. the gear and flaps stay up) and, for a jet, it is the same as best endurance speed. When it comes to propellers, the most lift for the least drag translates to the most thrust for the least power lost. Gliding for maximum endurance, on the other hand, involves slower speeds and higher angles of attack.

For a given weight, as long as you use the correct IAS, range is unaffected at altitude, but the rate of descent will increase because of the increased TAS.

In any descent, you are converting potential energy into kinetic energy. Gliding at the minimum rate of descent means that this energy conversion is at the least possible rate. As the rate of doing work is defined as power, you must use the minimum power speed (V_{MP}).

Lift

There are many theories about how lift is generated, but none of them really explain the facts. First there is the flat plate at an angle that deflects air downwards, assisted by its tip vortices, then the aerofoil shape that smooths out turbulence and helps the pressure differential.

Even the formula used to calculate Lift (described below) has been constructed to explain certain observed effects. The Wright brothers certainly didn't know it!

Lift is said to act through the centre of pressure at 90° to drag and the relative airflow. It does not always oppose Weight! You can increase it in 4 ways, in this order:

- Increase speed for more reaction over the top surface of the aerofoil.
- Increase the angle of attack (up to the stall).
- Increase the lift producing areas.
- Fly in denser air (lower, or in a colder air mass).

Remember that the wings are not the only source of Lift - the Space Shuttle also uses the fuselage, which is why it has short stubby wings.

One method of lift generation (used by Concorde and some helicopter rotor blades) is to use the separated flow above sharply swept back wings, which rolls into stable, cone-shaped vortices. As the airspeed in them is high, the pressure is low.

THE LIFT FORMULA

The formula for calculating lift is:

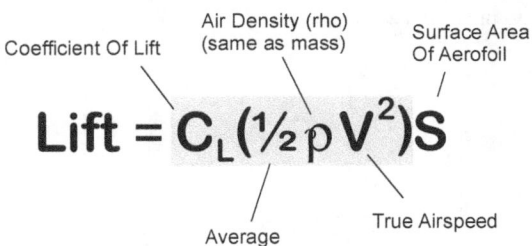

$$\text{Lift} = C_L(\tfrac{1}{2}\rho V^2)S$$

The figures in brackets represent kinetic energy* (or Indicated Air Speed) measured in joules, and the figures before the S represent the average pressure difference between the upper and lower surfaces in lbs/sq ft. The result is multiplied by the surface area to get the total lift.

*As density is mass per cubic foot.

Put more in plain English, lift is equal to the coefficient of lift multiplied by the wing area and dynamic pressure.

- The **Coefficient of Lift** is a dimensionless number that is the product of **design** (thickness and camber) and **angle of attack**, or the relative pressure distribution above and below an aerofoil. It is dimensionless because it expresses how much dynamic pressure is harnessed by it to create lift. If it is all converted, the C_L is 1. If it is not, the Coefficient of Lift provides a correction factor.

We need just the right amount of lift, or components would be stressed. For example, the dynamic pressure in the free stream flowing past the average Cessna in the cruise is around 29 lbs per sq ft. The wing loading of the Cessna 172 is 14 lbs per sq ft, so its wing only needs to capture around half of that free stream to do its work, a C_L of 0.48. In contrast, a Learjet would require a C_L of 0.39, and Concorde 0.22. The higher the speed*, the more dynamic pressure increases and the less needs to be captured, hence the lower C_L. The value of C_L therefore acts like a factor, as in 0.48 x dynamic pressure.

*The value of C_L will be maximum at, or just before, the stall, which you can see from the formula - if C_L increases on one side of the formula, the other side (L) will also increase, until lift can no longer be produced. Similarly, reducing speed (V) decreases lift so, to keep the same value, you must change the aerofoil shape and/or angle of attack if you change the speed, and *vice versa*. If speed is doubled, C_L must be reduced to a quarter of its previous value. Put another way, if you half the speed, C_L must be quadrupled.

Although ice adds weight, it also changes the shape of the aerofoil and will therefore affect C_L and C_D. C_L can also be affected by washout.

If you know how much lift is being produced, you can work out C_L by playing with the lift formula:

$$C_L = \frac{Lift}{\frac{1}{2}\rho V^2 S}$$

You could then plot a lift curve (see picture below), then work out how much lift is available for different sizes of aerofoil at different speeds just by plugging the figures into the formula.

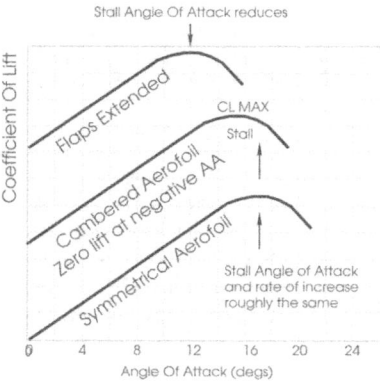

The shape of the curve at the peak shows how abrupt the stall would be (based on the aerofoil's leading edge radius - a small one separates the flow earlier). The linear (straight) part shows that C_L is proportional to the angle of attack, meaning that, if you double the angle of attack, you double the lift. The middle curve is for a cambered aerofoil because it is producing some lift at zero angle of attack. The top one is for flaps extended, or with even more camber. A symmetrical aerofoil (no camber), when its chord is in line with the RAF, will provide no lift, or, when the angle of attack is zero, the C_L will be zero.

As the three curves are parallel to each other, it can be seen that a change in angle of attack produces the same change in C_L for all three. It can also be seen that C_{Lmax} increases with camber, and the zero lift angle of attack decreases, plus the angle of attack for a given C_L becomes less, which is why you have to lower the nose when you lower the flaps (you also stall at a lesser angle of attack with flaps extended). Slats increase C_{Lmax} and the stalling angle of attack.

Although C_{Lmax} is slightly lower for a swept wing because not all the surface area is used, the stalling angle of attack is significantly increased. This means that a transport aircraft with swept wings and slats has its nose higher on approach.

If you wanted to find the speed for a particular angle of attack (or lift coefficient):

$$V^2 = \frac{Lift}{C_L \frac{1}{2} \rho S}$$

The TAS can be worked out by deriving the square root of the values on the right:

$$V = \sqrt{\frac{Lift}{C_L \frac{1}{2} \rho S}}$$

Tip: If you substitute C_L for C_{Lmax}, you will have the stalling speed. As the only variables are speed and lift, the stalling speed is proportional to the square root of Lift. Also, remember that Lift is equal to Weight in level, unaccelerated flight., so you can substitute them in the formula.

 To an aerospace engineer, the stall occurs at C_{Lmax}, which represents the highest lifting capability of an aircraft but, to the rest of the world, it occurs when all lift is lost! The key to this paradox is to recognise the difference between lift and the lift coefficient. As mentioned, the former is the product of the wing area and dynamic pressure, as modified by C_L. For a given altitude and wing area, lift depends on the lift coefficient and velocity, so you can have a very high C_L with a low value of lift if you are flying slowly.

- ½. This creates the average.
- ρ (rho) = air density. If this doubles, so will Lift.
- V = **TAS**. True Airspeed depends on Indicated Airspeed (IAS) and air density, which decreases with altitude, so you need a higher TAS to get the same lift as you go up.

PRINCIPLES OF FLIGHT
Forces In Flight

At height, the aircraft encounters less resistance, or drag. In a descent, the air gets more dense, so you get more drag, more friction, and the machine decelerates. Thus, TAS could be seen as a function of the resistance found when flying in the air. In level flight, if lift remains constant and the IAS changes, the value of C_L must change to maintain the balance of the formula. If the speed doubles, because it is squared, C_L must be divided by 4. Similarly, if the speed is halved, C_L must be multiplied by 4.

- **S** = the surface area of the lift producing surfaces, i.e. the planform, not the total wetted area of the aeroplane.

In level flight, the weight of the aircraft is balanced by the lift produced and, according to the formula, lift will decrease when any of the terms on the other side of the equation decreases. If speed is reduced, C_L must be increased, usually by increasing the angle of attack, to restore the lift to its former value. As a rule of thumb, the percentage change to the stalling speed is equal to half the percentage change to the all-up weight.

Weight

A force acting through the Centre of Gravity, not always in opposition to lift.

Thrust

The force that makes the aircraft move through the air, assumed to be parallel to and in the opposite direction to Drag*. However, this is a simplification because, when the angle of attack is increased, thrust acts in the same direction as lift.

*Thrust is equal to drag multiplied by the cosine of α, which is seldom more than 10°, so thrust along the direction of flight is nearly 99% of the total anyway.

Although the output of any aircraft engine is referred to in terms of thrust, it is the convention to say that thrust comes from jet engines and power comes from piston engines because, technically, it goes to the shaft. The propeller, of course, produces thrust.

Drag

 The definitions below are the older ones that haven't really gone away, despite attempts in 1958 to change them.

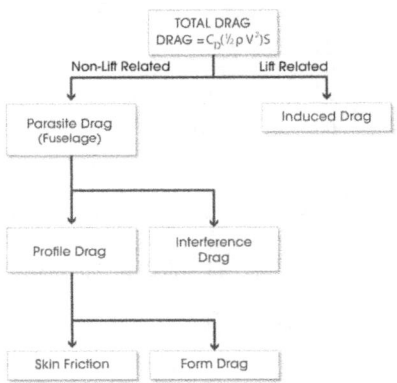

Drag is the difference in static pressure across a plane perpendicular to the flight path, which is how it is measured in a wind tunnel, where the speed of the airflow is measured just in front of and just behind the model. If the speed is the same, then so is the dynamic pressure, and the static pressure, and there is no drag, but this would only happen if there is no air motion behind an aircraft once it passes. As it is always faster (and static pressure is lower), this would never be the case.

Drag acts in the opposite direction to thrust, parallel to the relative airflow. As it retards motion and increases fuel consumption, it also affects range, endurance and maximum speed.

- **Induced Drag**. Sometimes called *Vortex Drag* or *Lift Dependent Drag* (LDD), this type of drag only exists when lift is created, as air at different pressures mixes behind the trailing edge.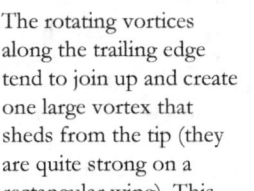

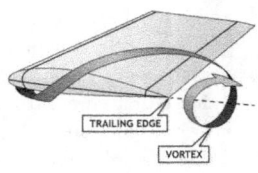 The rotating vortices along the trailing edge tend to join up and create one large vortex that sheds from the tip (they are quite strong on a rectangular wing). This reduces the difference in static pressure above and below the wing in that area, because the vortices descend **inside the wingspan**, so less lift is produced at the tips, resulting in tip losses over about 6% of the wing surface.

It also makes the air trailing behind the tips flow lower than that from the root. The starting vortex creates a counter flow that reduces the speed of the flow underneath the wing to increase the pressure underneath, while the flow above the wing is increased, to reduce the pressure further.

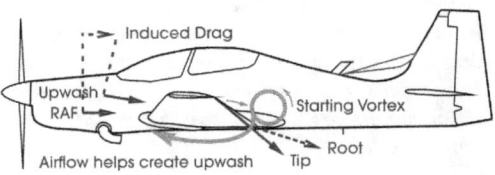

The resulting pressure field helps to create the upwash at the front of the wing, through a process called *circulation*. The air doesn't rotate about the wing, but we get an equivalent effect if you imagine that the airflow over the upper surface is the same as the average speed plus a bit, and that through the lower surface is similar to the average speed minus a bit - rather like the difference between a headwind or a tailwind when it comes to groundspeed. The virtual vortex around the wing is called the *bound vortex*.

The *Magnus Effect* works on the principle that any object that is rotated so as to produce a vortex or circulation will generate lift when placed in a stream of air.

When an aerofoil is rapidly accelerated from rest, as it might be when taking off, the airflows above and below will initially merge smoothly at the trailing edge in a process called the *Kutta condition*. However, as the speed of the flow increases, the boundary layer will start to separate (due to the adverse pressure gradient) and form the starting vortex which will eventually leave the surface and proceed downstream to become part of the wake turbulence mentioned at the end of this chapter. As this helps to create the differences in speed and pressure required, the viscosity involved plays a significant part in the creation of lift. This is because, without its influence, the streamlines would close up behind all parts of the aircraft and provide no turbulent wake. As there is a loss of energy in the boundary layer, Bernoulli does not apply because the amount of energy is supposed to remain constant.

As the lift vector is tilted, it is decreased, the drag is increased, and the extra, being the difference between that from the upwash and that from the relative airflow is induced drag. This creates an induced angle of attack, which means a lesser, *effective* angle of attack than the geometrical version. The stronger the vortices, the greater is the reduction in effective angle of attack, so it must be increased to regain the lost lift - this is where induced drag comes from. A benefit is that the wing will now not stall (especially at the tips) until this angle is reached, a little later. As there is more circulation at large angles of attack, and thus more upwash, this explains why induced drag is greatest at large angles of attack.

 Induced drag does not come directly from the lift producing surfaces. They produce profile drag, below. Induced drag depends on the downwash velocity induced by the tip vortices, so it doesn't exist in 2-dimensional flow. Because of this, the more modern term *Trailing Vortex Drag* is now preferred.

If no lift is induced, there is no induced drag. Similarly, the more lift there is, the more induced drag there is. It is inversely proportional to the square of the velocity, so halving air velocity increases induced drag four times. The coefficient of induced drag (C_{Di}) is the ratio of C_L^2 and aspect ratio. *It is reduced by increasing airspeed, using long, narrow wings (with high aspect ratios), or by reducing the lift coefficient, which itself can be done with washout or design.*

As well as distributing lift more evenly, washout reduces the angle of attack at the tips, reducing induced drag.

Induced Drag increases when air density decreases, so it can be a problem for high flying aeroplanes. **Winglets** are vertical aerofoils on the wingtip that are best used at altitude on aircraft using high angles of attack. They **cut down induced drag** by reducing the area of the wing tip that is affected by vortices (winglets are often a compromise between gaining extra lift and making sure the wings don't hit the hangar doors). The spill of high pressure air beneath the wing to the lower pressure above is reduced, and two smaller vortices (at the base and the tip) are created, instead of one big one, for less drag and wake turbulence, and the inboard flow can be used to create thrust, hence the reduction in induced drag. Put another way, winglets produce their own horseshoe vortex systems that partially cancel the main wing trailing vortices where the wing curves up to form the winglet. The inwash effect (towards the fuselage) produces a force on the winglet that has a forward thrust (or negative drag) component.

Winglets improve the range of long-range aircraft (like the 747-400) more than short-range commuter jets, but the 777 doesn't appear to need them. The reduction in induced drag is more than the increase in profile drag.

Note that any method of stopping vortices from being generated by air spilling over wing tips improves efficiency - these may include wing tip tanks, wing tip plates, or droop tips (a tip tank raises and drops the wingtip at the same time). That is, to reduce induced drag, the *effective* span must be greater than the *actual* span. In summary, induced drag varies with taper, sweepback, altitude, aspect ratio, angle of attack, and speed. It arises from making air accelerate to cause a differential pressure above and below the wing as well as wing tip spillage, so it all starts with Camber.

C_{Di} is proportional to C_L^2. It is the ratio of C_L^2 and aspect ratio.

- **Parasite Drag** (or *zero lift drag*) comes from anything that is not actually creating lift, like the fuselage or undercarriage. Unlike induced drag, it *increases* with speed and consists of:

  - **Interference Drag** is the result of the interaction of airflow around adjoining aerofoil surfaces. In other words, if you added the various types of drag together, the result would be less than the total - interference drag is the difference.

  - **Profile Drag** is caused by the action of the aerofoil passing through the air, and depends on its cross-section (i.e. its profile - it's like parasite drag for wings). It consists of:

    - **Form Drag**, or *Pressure Drag*, from the difference between the high pressure in the front and the low pressure to the rear (i.e. sucking back by the decreased pressure in the wake - nothing to do with high pressure at the stagnation point). Eddies form when the streamline flow is disturbed, as when a flat plate is held at 90° to the airflow, where you would get 100% form drag. It is minimised by *streamlining* - the best shape is round at the front and sharp behind, so the airflow separates slowly. Form drag is directly proportional to the airspeed.

PRINCIPLES OF FLIGHT
Forces In Flight

- **Skin Friction** (also known as *surface friction drag* or *viscous drag*) is tangential to the surface, from inside the boundary layer. It arises from the surface area, the viscosity of the air, and rate of change of velocity. As viscosity increases with temperature, you get more skin friction on a hot day, although the type of surface doesn't matter. Skin friction and form drag are about equal at a 0.25 thickness ratio.

Profile Drag is therefore due to the smoothness (or otherwise) and shape of the lift producing surfaces. It is directly proportional to the square of the speed and is only relevant for 2D flow.

Parasite Drag* only varies with speed and is directly proportional to V^2 so, if the speed is doubled, the drag is quadrupled. For a 10% increase in speed, multiply by 1.1, the square of which is 1.21.the increase in parasite drag is 21%.

*The Wright brothers called it *head resistance*.

OTHERS

Aileron Drag, from downgoing ailerons, causes a yaw in the opposite direction to a turn. *Wave drag* comes from shock waves in high speed flight, from energy drag and boundary layer separation (the energy for a temperature rise across a shockwave is a drag on the aircraft). It is alleviated by sweepback and vortex generators on the upper side of the wing.

Cooling Drag comes from air flowing through the engine compartment, where a continuous flow of air over the cylinders is required. More momentum is lost through the engine compartment than can be added by heat, hence the drag force. This is alleviated by the use of cowl flaps.

In summary, drag can be reduced to two general types:
- **Pressure drag**, from an imbalance of surface pressure acting in the direction of the drag.
- **Friction drag**, from the effects of shear stress acting in the direction of the drag.

DRAG FORMULA

The formula for Drag is similar to that for Lift:

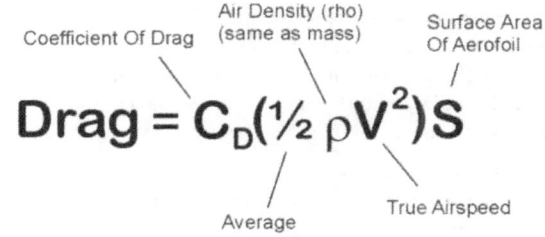

The V^2 factor takes it out of all proportion once you get out of the low speed regime - an aircraft at 150 kts encounters 100 times the drag at 15 kts. This square law means that small increases in speed need larger amounts of thrust.

C_D, the drag coefficient, represents the potential of a body to interfere with smooth airflow over it, or how much of the force produced by dynamic pressure gets converted to drag. As with lift, shape is important, not size, and the angle of attack must be considered. The remainder of the formula works as it does for lift, except that the force is measured parallel to the airflow.

LIFT/DRAG RATIO

For a given weight and altitude*, you can maintain level flight any speed (between the minimum and maximum limits) by varying the angle of attack so that the lift developed is always equal to the weight, and the lift formula remains balanced.

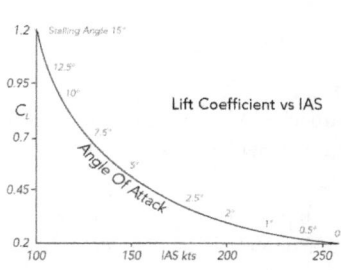

*More correctly, weight and air density. When maintaining the same lift, the other factors in the lift formula have a fixed relationship (they are otherwise variable by themselves). This is shown above.

Each angle of attack has a corresponding IAS, C_L and C_D, although compressibility will reduce the effectiveness of C_L, meaning that the angle of attack will need to be adjusted slightly. If the IAS decreases, the others will have to increase, and vice versa. However, as the angle of attack increases, so does induced drag, and hence the total, so you will need more thrust, and fuel. Thus, for a given amount of lift, you need the least value of drag, or the most lift for the least drag.

Typically, the greatest lifting effort comes at an angle of attack of about 16° and least drag occurs at around –2°, but the ratio of lift to drag at these extreme ranges is low. What we need is the maximum lift against the drag obtained at the same angle of attack, or the best L/D ratio. The optimum angle of attack for this is around 4°.

 The maximum L/D ratio occurs in the same conditions as minimum drag or, put another way, minimum drag occurs when L/D is maximum.

If the lift equation is divided by the drag equation, their similarity means that most of their elements cancel out - only C_L and C_D remain. It follows that C_L/C_D is the same as L/D, so it is also true to say that minimum drag occurs (at a single value of angle of attack) when C_L/C_D is maximum. **Minimum drag does not mean minimum drag coefficient!** Neither does it mean C_{Lmax}, which occurs at the stall where drag is very high.

As minimum drag is only a function of the ratio of C_L/C_D and not of altitude (i.e. density), its actual value and the ISS at which it occurs for a given aircraft at a given weight will not vary with altitude. However, the TAS at which it occurs will generally increase as altitude increases.

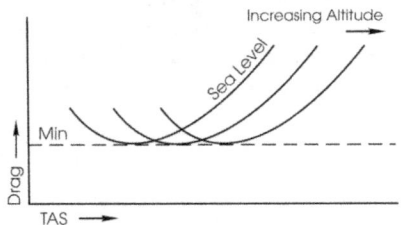

For a particular IAS/EAS, the dynamic pressure is the same at all altitudes, so a graph of drag versus IAS/EAS is the same for all altitudes.

Typically, the best C_L/C_D ratio occurs at 4°, the accepted optimum (so the L/D ratio increases from 0-4°, and decreases above 4°).

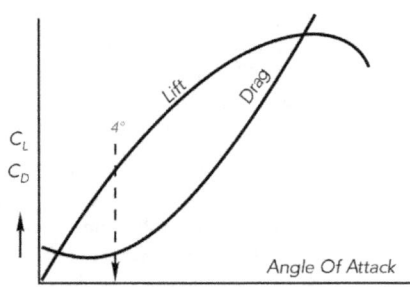

This is the angle of attack at which you get the greatest surplus between the two, which is not necessarily the lowest point on the drag curve, which simply represents the point where you get the least drag. Neither does a high L/D ratio mean that the wing is producing maximum lift.

For a given angle of attack, the L/D ratio is unaffected by density changes.

One way to find C_L and C_D at minimum drag is to plot one against the other as shown in the polar diagram below. The maximum value of the ratio between them is found where a line from the origin lies tangent to the curve - this will also be at minimum drag.

The normal relationship of C_L to C_D for a clean aircraft is shown in the drag polar diagram below, on the left.

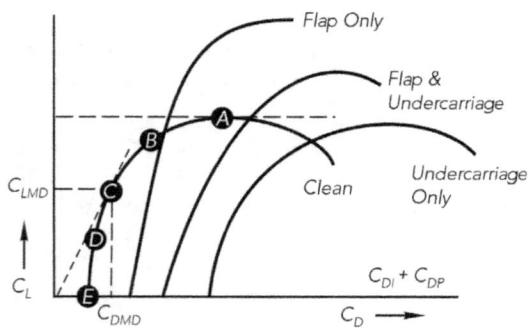

Virtually all the aerodynamic information about an aeroplane with regard to performance is contained within the drag polar,

which can be expressed as an equation or a plot of one as a graph, as shown above (the label was coined by the same guy who designed the Eiffel Tower).

Each point on the curve corresponds to a different angle of attack, at which the TR makes an angle with respect to the relative wind, which can be plotted on a graph. If you change the angle of attack, you can locate another point, and so on, and show the aerodynamic coefficients as polar coordinates, hence the name.

You can deduce a lot of information from it. For example:

- **Point A** is C_{Lmax}. As it occurs at the critical angle of attack, it exists just before the stall.
- **Point B** is V_{MP}, or the speed for minimum power, for the minimum sink rate. It is 0.76 V_{MD}.
- **Point C** is C_L/C_{Dmax}, or V_{MD}. The best L/D ratio allows you to figure out the minimum glide angle and, if you know your speed, your rate of descent.
- **Point D** is 1.32 V_{IMD}, for maximum range in a jet.
- **Point E** is the zero lift angle of attack ($C_L = 0$), so there is no lift and no induced drag (the lower part of the curve represents fast speed as the angle of attack is small). Any drag is therefore parasite drag.

The slope of the graph at any point is given by:

$$\frac{C_L}{C_D}$$

which is just another expression for the Lift/Drag ratio, the maximum value of which is found where a line drawn from the origin is tangential to the curve (V_{IMD}). The slope is less either side of that point. The angle of attack associated with the point of tangency corresponds to the angle of attack for L/D_{max}. This is sometimes called the *design point* for the aircraft, and the associated C_L value is sometimes called the *design lift coefficient*.

The angle between the vertical line for C_L and where it meets the angle of attack plot is also that between the Lift & TR vectors.

The only other points of interest with reference to Lift is C_{Lmax} at the peak of the curve, for the lowest speed in unaccelerated horizontal flight, and that the maximum Lift/Drag ratio does *not* correspond to the point of minimum drag. In reality, when an aeroplane is at its zero lift angle of attack, parasite drag may be slightly higher than its minimum value but, for wings with a moderate camber, this is usually ignored. In addition, as C_L and C_D are functions of the Mach number, changing it will create a different drag polar although, at low subsonic Mach numbers, this is ignored. The largest differences arise near the critical Mach number and above (see *High Speed Flight*).

Flap deflection also affects C_D, and a similar graph can be drawn for the various types to show their efficiencies, as covered in *Airframes & Systems*.

If the flaps are lowered, the C_D increases, so the graph moves to the right, and gets higher as C_L increases substantially (however, the ratio of C_L/C_D decreases*). If the undercarriage is lowered as well, the C_D will increase even more, but C_L will decrease again (if you only put the gear down, there is no extra lift to offset the drag, so the figure simply moves to the right).

*There is more drag per unit of lift, so climb performance will reduce.

The start for the clean polar does not start at the origin, but is offset, as parasite drag does not change with C_L. Otherwise the shape of the curve is due to induced drag changing with C_L^2. The optimum area for the design wing loading is dictated by the C_L obtained at the peak of the L/D curve.

The airspeed where drag is minimum can be seen from a graph that compares the total to the values of parasite and induced drag (below). You can see that, as airspeed increases, parasite drag increases, but as airspeed reduces, induced drag increases (i.e. both ways increase total drag). Thus, accelerating from V_S to V_{NE} makes the total drag decrease until V_{IMD}, then increase.

There are also two speeds at which drag is the same, one slow and one fast, but they have different components.

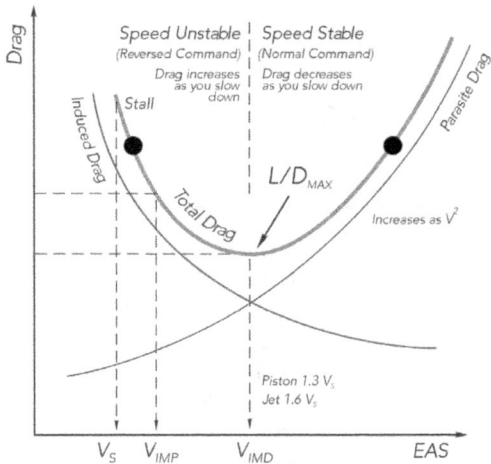

 There is no induced drag in two dimensional flow! A total drag curve is valid for a particular aircraft at one weight in level flight - the above is a generic example.

The picture below is more realistic, where the point of minimum drag is 1.3 V_S for the piston, but is higher at around 1.6 for a jet, or more.

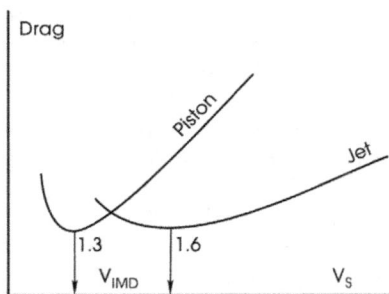

You can see that flight below V_{IMD}* on a piston-engined aeroplane suffers from a steep drag curve, but that for the jet is shallower (although the induced drag part is steeper), so there are fewer noticeable changes in flying qualities. Be careful not to drop below V_{IMD}.

*The IAS for minimum drag. It represents the optimum angle of attack of about 4° and is also the speed for the best lift/drag ratio (in level flight), typically used for holding. As minimum thrust is needed at that point, and thrust is equal to fuel flow, V_{IMD} is also the best endurance speed for jets. In climbs or descents, though, V_{IMD} does not produce the best L/D ratio, as lift is less in those manoeuvres.

 V_{IMD} produces the lowest drag, not the lowest *power required* (V_{MP}), where best glide endurance occurs (for the minimum sink rate). It is speed unstable because it lies to the left of V_{MD}.

Also, for a particular EAS, the dynamic pressure will be the same at all altitudes, so a plot of drag against EAS will apply at all of them. However, if TAS is used, the curve will move to the right with altitude.

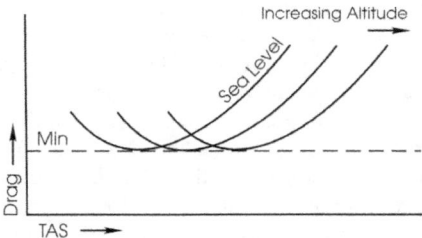

An increase in weight means an increase in the lift required, so the curve will then move up and to the right due to the rise in induced drag (minimum drag and V_{IMD} will both increase, and speed stability will reduce).

On the other hand, lowering the undercarriage (or flaps) increases the cross-sectional area, making the total drag curve move up and to the left. Induced drag is not affected, but the parasite drag curve is steepened, so their point of intersection (and V_{MD}) reduces, although total drag increases. The range of speed stability will be greater.

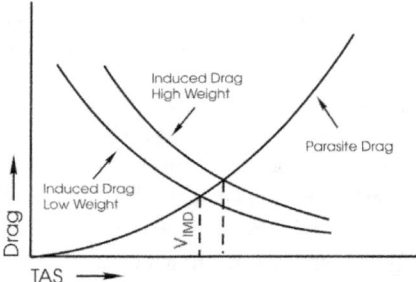

The same happens if an engine fails, where induced drag increases only slightly.

STABLE SPEEDS
The speed range below L/D_{max} (the left half, or the back side of the power curve) is the *speed unstable regime*, which means that drag increases when you slow down and power must be *added* to maintain *slower* speeds, otherwise you would get a further speed decrease. This is why the back side is also called the *area of reverse command*, where airspeed must be controlled with alpha or nose position, and rate of descent with thrust. As acceleration continues at an increasing rate, you must keep using the throttle to maintain a set speed, so maintaining flight at speeds below V_{IMD} is associated with a higher workload. It is also associated with high angles of attack.

On the other hand, the area above L/D_{max} (on the right) is the *speed stable regime*, where the aircraft recovers speed by itself after a disturbance (when an aircraft maintains a preset speed without any other outside influence, we have speed stability). You don't therefore need to use the throttles that much, as speed increases are met with a drag increase, which slows things down again. Similarly, a speed decrease is met with a drag decrease so the aircraft speeds up. You get low angles of attack on this side. Jets, unfortunately, make their approaches in the speed unstable regime, because they have a higher V_{IMD} (minimum drag speed), but this is eased with flap, which reduces V_{IMD} by moving the total drag curve to the left. The area around V_{IMD} where the curve is quite shallow either side is known as speed neutral.

The difference in speed stability between jet and propeller driven aircraft is due to propeller wash, which varies the lift value of the parts of the wing exposed to it, and the downward force from the horizontal stabiliser. This means that adding power can pitch the nose up, while decreasing power pitches it down. For jets with engines on or in the fuselage, power changes mainly affect airspeed with little pitch change, but on low winged aircraft with under-wing mounted engines, the low thrust line (below the C of G) creates pitching moments that are very similar to prop aircraft. Pushers and canards* are different - by design, a canard will stall before the mainplane, which will make the aircraft pitch nose down, moving the mainplane further away from the stall (actually, it may not be possible to stall the mainplane of some modern swept wing and delta aircraft that have canards).

*Canards have the foreplane in front of the mainplane.

If the gradient of the drag curve is very steep, a small change in speed produces a large change in drag, which increases the effects of stability or otherwise. Swept wing aircraft tend to have low drag coefficients, which gives them shallower drag curves. The range of speed instability is reduced below V_{IMD}, but it is more difficult to maintain a given speed at or above V_{IMD}.

Tip: At V_{IMD}, parasite drag equals induced drag. You can use this to work out fuel flow if you remember that induced drag is proportional to the square of the weight, so if you increase W by 10%, V_{IMD} increases by 5%*. For example, if aircraft weight is decreased by (say) 0.9, you would square that and reduce induced drag by the answer (parasite drag does not change with mass), which is 0.81. Thus total drag becomes 99.19% of its original value, and is the same factor to apply to original fuel flow.

*Minimum drag is directly proportional to W.

EFFECTS OF SPEED

The ram effect at the compressor air intake increases with forward speed, by forcing air into the engine at a greater velocity. The design of the intake converts that velocity into pressure, increasing the density, and engine thrust (see curve B, below).

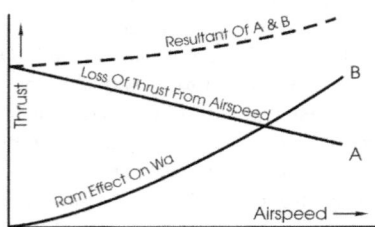

The increased air density must be matched by an increased fuel flow to keep the mixture correct.

At subsonic airspeeds, net thrust decreases slightly with increased airspeed and fuel consumption increases as shown in the graphs on the right.

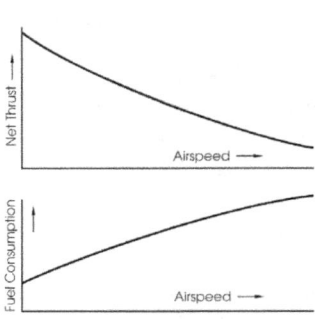

The specific fuel consumption (SFC) of a turbojet increases with airspeed. SFC is defined as the fuel flow per unit of time per unit of thrust, which is usually pounds of fuel burned per hour per pound of thrust developed (lb/hr/lb.thrust). This is shown here:

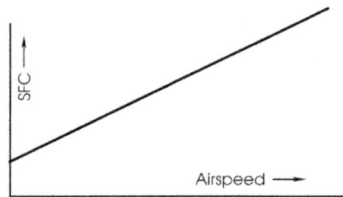

In turboprops, SFC is defined as lb.fuel/hr/SHP. Because the shaft horsepower increases with airspeed, SFC shows an increase up to the maximum prop efficiency airspeed (about 350 knots).

The highest speed that can be achieved is where the power available equals the power required (i.e. where their curves intersect). Minimum speed is not usually defined by power or thrust but by stability or stall requirements.

For a prop-driven aircraft, the lowest point of the curve is the TAS at which the least power is needed (as opposed to producing the least drag) and is therefore the best for endurance in level flight.

The bottom point also represents the maximum rate of climb speed because the gap between power required and power available is greatest there. You need more power when you fly above or below minimum power speed.

As mentioned, maximum endurance is obtained at the speed where the rate of fuel consumption is lowest. As thrust is equal to drag on a jet, the lowest fuel consumption and maximum endurance is obtained at the bottom of the thrust required (total drag) curve. This speed generally remains constant with altitude, but it is usually increased slightly for handling reasons and to keep away from the back side of the drag curve at a speed of V_{IMD}, into which it is very easy to slip with a jet. The IAS/EAS is reduced at high altitudes to reduce the drag you would get at high Mach numbers.

For maximum range, though (for a given fuel flow), we need the greatest TAS for the fuel used, as fuel flow is proportional to thrust which, in steady flight, is equal to drag. That is, for minimum fuel consumption (and maximum range) we need the most speed for the least drag. This point on the thrust required (total drag) curve is to the right of the bottom point and is found by drawing a tangent to the curve from the origin.

As speed increases beyond V_{IMD} (on the drag curve) the rate of increase in drag is initially quite small, less than the rate of increase in TAS. Thus, increasing the TAS within this speed range increases the drag slightly, but the payoff is better speed. Where a tangent that is drawn from the origin touches the drag curve, you will find Velocity Maximum Cruise Range (V_{MRC} or $V_{I/Dmax}$).

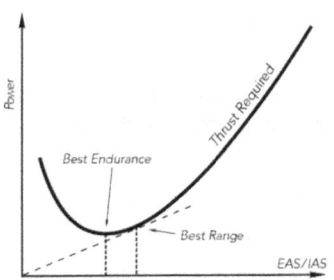

It gives the minimum fuel consumption, which in turn means the maximum attainable range for any given fuel load. Flying faster than V_{MRC} increases some costs and decreases others, so the lowest overall cost is achieved at the speed which gives the best compromise between them. This is usually slightly faster than V_{MRC}, which itself is faster than M_{CRIT}.

Not many aeroplanes are flown at V_{IMD} or M_{MD}, nor necessarily below the critical Mach number (discussed later), because the idea is to get where you're going with the least fuel, which should be done at best range speed, which is higher (1.32 V_{IMD}).

The best cruise speed would be higher even than that, as the cost of fuel is a minor part of the whole process.

 Fuel costs are not minimised at the speed of the lowest fuel flow. More important is that burnt for each nautical mile, covered in *Flight Planning*.

V_{MR} is at the bottom of the drag curve for a piston/prop. V_{ME} is at the bottom of the power curve.

EFFECTS OF WEIGHT

If the speed stays the same, the excess lift produced over the weight will make the aeroplane gradually increase its altitude (a cruise climb). If you try to stay in level flight by reducing the angle of attack, the speed will (gradually) increase. Now, the thrust must be reduced.

Put another way, as the fuel is used, the excess power available increases and the power required decreases. If the weight is increased, the power available decreases and the power required would increase.

The changes to the power curves are similar to those resulting form a change of altitude.

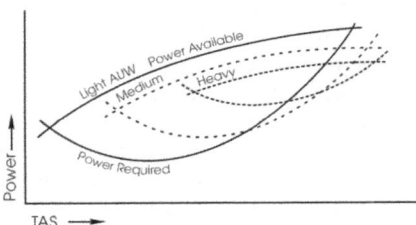

EFFECTS OF TEMPERATURE

At lower levels, outside air temperature has a marked effect upon engine performance for a given altitude. This is of particular importance to take-off performance of gas turbine engines. When the air temperature is lower than standard, the increased density will increase the mass of air entering the compressor so, for a given engine RPM, the thrust is greater, but the compressor will need more power to maintain the same speed in the denser air, so more fuel is needed. Alternatively, if the fuel supply is not increased, engine speed will decrease.

When the air temperature is higher than standard, the reduced density produces a decrease in thrust for a given RPM. The engine cannot be safely operated much beyond 100% so, if you want the mass flow for takeoff thrust, the air density must be restored, so some form of thrust augmentation must be used, such as water or water-methanol injection, as discussed elsewhere.

EFFECTS OF ENGINE RPM

The mass flow of air from turbine engine compressors depends on their speed of rotation. Also, the change of thrust (mass flow) is most marked at high engine speeds. For this reason, cruising RPM is usually 85% - 90% of maximum RPM. This is why high engine RPM is a good idea during the approach, especially as turbine engines are slow to spool up.

FLAT RATED THRUST

The thrust from a turbine engine is directly related to the density of the air in which it is operating. For example, in the climb, the thrust will decrease with altitude due to the decreasing air density. Sometimes, however, you can get the same value of thrust over a range of altitudes, regardless of the temperature. In other words, if the engine RPM limit is reached before the TOT limit, within the range of temperatures affected by the RPM, the thrust available will not be affected.

FADECs overcome this by automatic compensation that adjusts the engine speed to maintain thrust at a value demanded by the throttle lever angle.

Engine thrust is displayed as Engine Pressure Ratio on an EPR gauge or EICAS:

To select the required thrust (EPR), the throttle lever angle is adjusted until the command EPR needle is aligned with the reference bug set by the thrust management system. The system will automatically adjust the fuel flow, and thus engine speed, to maintain the required thrust with varying altitude, airspeed and inlet air temperature. In other words, thrust is maintained at a constant (flat) value regardless of changes in air density.

Such a system is known as a flat rated system and the engines using it are flat rated engines.

EFFECTS OF ALTITUDE

A decrease in air density has the following effects:

- At a constant weight, the relationship between EAS and the angle of attack will not be affected higher up, but less lift is developed because there is less air density (at a high cruising TAS, more lift is lost from compressibility). To remain level, the angle of attack or the speed must be increased.
- Although the reduced density at altitude reduces drag, to maintain level flight, an increased angle of attack would increase drag, which would cancel out the benefits of the decreased density. The overall change is very little.
- There is also less power available at altitude. Because drag is virtually the same at all altitudes, the power required to maintain level flight increases with altitude, so the power available and power required curves get closer together, resulting in a decrease of the maximum possible speed and an increase in minimum speed. In other words, the range of speeds available in level flight decreases with an increase of altitude.

If the relevant curves are plotted against EAS they move up the graph, but when plotted against TAS they also move to the right.

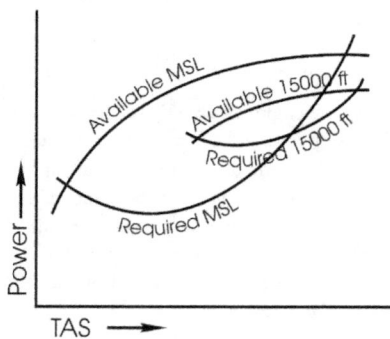

GROUND EFFECT

This is an effect that is measurable within about half a wingspan of the ground, where about 10% of the wingtip vortices cannot develop fully (to block 75%, you need to be within 1/20 of a wingspan). You get a little more lift because of the increased effective angle of attack, but the main factor is lower induced drag due to reduced vortices, and reduced upwash and downwash. This explains why you need a higher angle of attack as you fly out of ground effect on takeoff (a higher rotate speed can provide more momentum to compensate). There is a change to longitudinal stability and trim, in that you get generally increased stability, a greater elevator deflection is required, and a change in position error at the static vents (there is usually an increase in local pressure at the static source for a lower IAS & altitude).

As the closer to the ground you are, the greater the effect is, a low wing aircraft is affected more than a high wing aircraft would be. It is a useful tool for bush operations, but could mean you get airborne sooner than expected, and excess speed in the flare may cause floating, so the landing distance will be greater.

FORMULAE

Power (force x velocity) is normally expressed in terms of *horsepower*, where one horsepower is equal to 33,000 ft/lbs/min (550 ft/lbs/sec). Using that information, you can calculate the rate of climb for an aeroplane that is able to produce 60 hp more than the power required to maintain level flight, and weighing 6 000 lbs:

$$330 \text{ fpm} = \frac{60 \times 33000}{6000}$$

Work is done when a force moves *against a resistance*. Put another way, you must apply a force to overcome the resistance set up by an object being moved.

You need force to overcome drag, so you can say that:

$$\text{Force} = \text{Drag}$$

Because work is equal to:

$$\text{Force} \times \text{Distance}$$

It is also equal to:

$$\text{Drag} \times \text{Distance}$$

Power is the rate of doing work, so:

$$\text{Power} = \frac{\text{Work}}{\text{Time}}$$

or:

$$\text{Power} = \frac{\text{Drag} \times \text{Distance}}{\text{Time}}$$

But distance divided by time is velocity, so:

$$\text{Power} = \text{Drag} \times \text{Velocity}$$

But the formula for drag is:

$$D = C_D \tfrac{1}{2} \rho V^2 S$$

Now we get:

$$\text{Power} = C_D \tfrac{1}{2} \rho V^2 S \times V$$

or:

$$\text{Power} = C_D \tfrac{1}{2} \rho V^3 S$$

This means that, while drag might increase as the *square* of the speed, the power to overcome it varies as the *cube* of the speed. If you double your speed, you will quadruple the drag and require 8 times more power, hence the steep rise in the power needed to overcome parasite drag.

The power required refers to that required for level flight. The power curve above shows that you need 200 hp to fly at 300 knots. If your engine was rated at only 200 hp, you would not be able to make that speed because you have to multiply the BHP rating of the engine by the propeller efficiency to get the power available for thrust (THP). As prop efficiency is only around 75-80%, you really need an engine rated at around 250 bhp, bearing in mind that you don't normally cruise at full power, but typically at 75%, so now we're talking about nearly 350 bhp.

Referring again to the same diagram, because the power available is the thrust horsepower available, the power available curve is the same shape as the propeller efficiency curve. Where it crosses with the power required curve is the maximum speed in level flight. You could reduce speed to use less power (and fuel), but only down to the minimum point. Beyond that, you are on the back side of the power curve, where induced drag begins to have a disproportionate influence.

As with the drag curve, there will be two speeds for each power setting - at 65% power, you can typically fly at around 65 or 140 knots, down to the minimum power point, the one speed at which it will take the least horsepower to maintain altitude, although it would be prudent to add a small increase.

STABILITY & EQUILIBRIUM

A cambered aerofoil cannot create lift and remain in equilibrium, because the centres of pressure of the upper and lower surfaces are misaligned and create a nose-down pitching moment. A horizontal tail surface some distance from the C of G is needed as a countermeasure.

An aircraft is in a state of equilibrium (or trimmed) when the vector sum of all the forces involved equals zero, with no acceleration or pitching moment. If this equilibrium should be disturbed, in an ideal world, a stable aircraft would go back to what it was doing before, with no input from the controls*. The significance lies with turbulence, or wind gusts, which have the most to do with your machine being knocked off its flight path.

*Stability is actually to do with what the aircraft wants to do without your interference by preventing pitching moments, sideslips, slips and skids. Keeping the same heading is your job.

Unfortunately, stability problems don't become apparent until you are airborne, which is why cargo operations have so many accidents in this area. Understanding longitudinal stability is particularly important - when whatever you have loaded places the C of G close to the aft limit (behind the centre of pressure), there will be less effort needed to pull back on the control column to make the horizontal stabiliser do its work. Having said that, an aft C of G may be preferred for performance reasons.

Remember that the purpose of the horizontal stabiliser is to pull the tail down. It does this inside the downwash from the wings which both pushes the tail down and creates an angle of attack on the upper surface.

The pitching, rolling and yawing planes translate to *longitudinal*, *lateral* and *directional* stability, respectively.

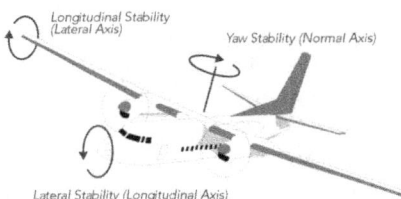

An aircraft is *inherently stable* if its stability is enhanced by design features. An aircraft may be stable in one flight condition, but not in others.

Static Stability

This is the *initial* (or primary) ability to return to a desired attitude or its short term reaction:

- An aircraft that uses a restoring moment to return to its original position after a disturbance is **statically stable**, or has positive static stability (the only condition that leads to dynamic stability).

- An aircraft that moves further away from its original position is **statically unstable,** or has negative static stability. This is usually only possible if energy is added, such as mishandling the controls, so it is rare. Statically unstable aeroplanes are never dynamically stable.

- An aircraft that takes up a new position away from the first position without needing a force to maintain it is **neutrally stable**.

Dynamic Stability

Dynamic stability reflects the long term (secondary) ability of a **statically stable** aircraft to settle down after a series of oscillations (the aircraft must be statically stable before it can oscillate at all). That is, a statically stable aircraft will *start* on its way back to where it came from, but overshooting brings it into dynamic stability, which is governed by mass or inertia.

Adding a damper*, such as a hydraulic or an aerodynamic one, adds another force, proportional to velocity in the opposite sense to the direction of moment. Fighting this force reduces the amplitude of the oscillation with time.

*You get damping whenever a force is produced on a body that is proportional to its velocity.

If the force opposes the motion, it is positive, like that exerted by a spring, and it contributes to static stability, but a spring will not return to the equilibrium point - it will oscillate back and forth around it.

- If oscillations damp themselves out, the aircraft is **dynamically stable**, as measured by the time taken to settle down at half amplitude (i.e. half the original deviation).

  All statically stable conventional aeroplanes are dynamically stable at high speeds, although they may be dynamically unstable at low speeds.

- If the amplitude of the oscillations increases, the aircraft is **dynamically unstable**. Thus, it is not a desirable condition unless positive static stability is within limits.

- If oscillations continue at a constant amplitude, the aircraft is (dynamically) **neutrally stable**.

However, with any aircraft, a movement in one plane induces a movement in another (for example, you hardly ever get a pure yaw, as it produces a sideslip and a roll).

In practice, static & dynamic stability are of academic interest, because you will hardly ever want to fly hands off, and you are more interested in how heavy the controls are and the feedback they give to you.

Directional Stability

Directional stability makes sure that the machine keeps pointing into the relative wind, which is what the feathers on arrows do (keeping it on the same heading is your job). An aeroplane is directionally stable (around the *normal* axis) if an increased angle of yaw results in a change of yawing moment that decreases it, avoiding a slip or skid. All it needs is the C of P of the correcting force to be aft of the C of G. The size of the vertical fin needed for such stability depends on the side areas presented by the aircraft. Flying boats, for example, typically require a large fin as the bulk of the bodywork is forward.

Directional static stability reduces with an aft C of G, reducing the correcting yawing moment in a sideslip. There is a greater need for active rudder input to ensure zero sideslip in turns, but it is easier to fly deliberate sideslip if you want to. The wing drop at the stall also tends to be greater.

A swept back wing also affects directional stability, when one wing presents a longer leading edge to the airflow if the aircraft is yawed, producing more drag on the opposite side and slowing it down, yawing it back.

With more lift being generated by the left wing in the picture below, there is a tendency to roll during a yaw.

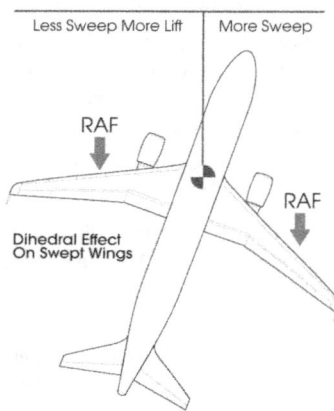

In the diagram below, the relative air flow impacts the vertical fin at an angle of attack that creates enough lift to move the fuselage back to its original position:

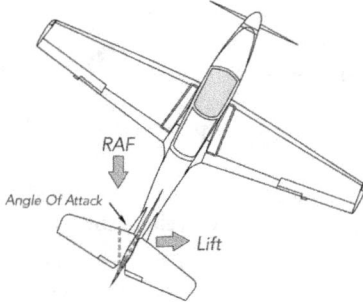

Tip: Directional stability is often greater if the rudder pedals are held central.

THE FUSELAGE

The fuselage has a generally destabilising effect upon static directional stability because, in subsonic flight, the C of G is well aft of the C of P of the fuselage so, in a sideslip, the relative airflow exerts a greater yawing moment forward of the C of G than aft of it. This is why an aircraft needs a vertical stabiliser (fin) to overcome the destabilising influence of the fuselage. The effect is often noticeable at high angles of attack, when the fin is stalled by the disturbed airflow from the fuselage and the aircraft becomes directionally unstable.

To combat this, strakes or ventral fins are sometimes fitted. These are flat plates or strips underneath the rear fuselage, running parallel to the centreline, forming a keel surface aft of the C of G. They increase directional stability in normal flight and help maintain it even if the fin begins to stall. Such devices are usually found on short-bodied training and military aircraft, rather than large jet transports. You could also use multiple vertical tails, such as twin fins small additional fins on the tailplane.

Dorsal Fin

The dorsal fin is an extension of the fin, running forwards along the top of the fuselage:

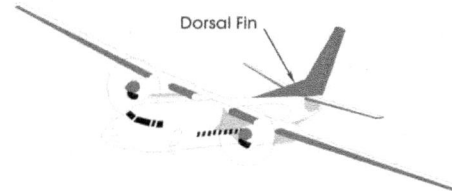

The fin significantly increases the side surface area aft of the C of G, and increases static directional stability by increasing the yawing moment and the weathercocking effect. Secondly, by reducing the effective aspect ratio of the vertical fin it increases its stalling angle of attack, so the fin remains effective at greater sideslip angles.

Longitudinal Stability

Longitudinal stability revolves around the *lateral* axis, and concerns stability in pitch It is identical to directional stability, if the impact point of the lift is behind the Centre of Gravity*, which is designed to be ahead of the Centre of Pressure anyway.

*In which case elevators are not required. Their deflection to achieve a changed angle of attack does not usually affect longitudinal stability - this is the job of the fixed part of the horizontal stabiliser, which also concerns itself with control and balance.

Control is obtained by having part or all of the horizontal stabiliser hinged and connected to the control column (on the Piper Super Cub, the whole unit is hinged, as it is with many transport aircraft). Balancing is required because the forces on a wing move when the angle of attack changes, but gravitational forces do not.

An aeroplane is longitudinally stable when an increased angle of attack creates forces that reduce it, although all the machine is trying to do is maintain its speed through the angle of attack. If the initial change is nose-up (positive) the resultant pitching moment must be nose-down (negative), and vice versa. Wing downwash has a negative effect. If the C of P of the wing is behind the C of G, when the nose pitches up, the increased angle of attack increases the lift vector, which reacts around the lateral axis through the C of G to put the nose down again.

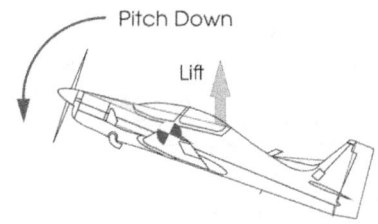

 There is a limit to the C of G's forward position, based on the availability of control movement. The more forward it is, the more the elevators must be moved to get the nose up during takeoff or landing. The elevator trim tab has little effect due to the low airspeed in these phases of flight. In addition, if the C of G is forward of the C of P, you need more of a down force from the horizontal stabiliser, which acts in the same direction as weight and therefore needs to be counteracted with more lift. This means more (induced) drag and lower fuel consumption because greater thrust is needed to maintain a constant airspeed. The extra is drag caused by the position of the stabiliser, or *trim drag*.

The aft C of G limit can be determined by the minimum acceptable static longitudinal stability.

An aircraft with its C of P in front of the C of G is statically (and dynamically) unstable, in that any nose up pitching will be *increased* by the destabilising moment from the forward movement of the C of P and the increased lift.

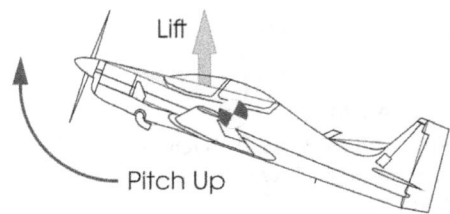

Longitudinal stability is not affected by the degree of positive camber because camber produces a constant pitch down moment that is independent of the angle of attack. A cambered aerofoil has the resultant force acting further back along the chord than the bottom resultant one so it will pitch nose down. With a symmetrical aerofoil, the top and bottom lift forces act through the same position, so there is no pitching moment.

MODES

The types of motion in a dynamic system are called modes. There are two involved with longitudinal stability:

- The **long** (low frequency) **period**, or phugoid, is the only one really noticeable in light aeroplanes.

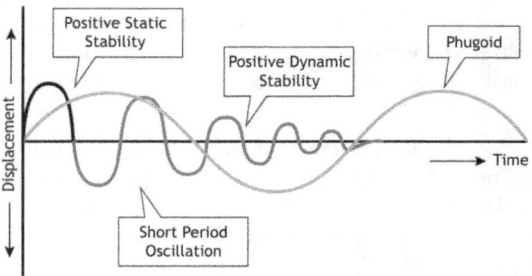

A phugoid (sometimes called *hunting*) is the path a particle takes when it is subject to gravity vertically, but is acted upon by a force at right angles and proportional to V^2. Put another way, it refers to the size of the oscillation for dynamic stability (you could loosely call it porpoising). There is a large-amplitude variation of airspeed, pitch angle, and altitude, with almost no variation in angle of attack. It is really a slow interchange of kinetic energy (velocity) and potential energy (height) about some equilibrium energy level as the aircraft attempts to re-establish the steady flight condition from which it was disturbed. The motion is so slow that the effects of inertia and damping are low. Although **the damping is very weak**, the period is so long that you normally correct for it without realising. Typically it lasts for between 20–60 seconds.

- The **short** (high frequency) **period mode** is an oscillation about the **lateral axis** that might get to half amplitude in rather less than a second, **with almost no effect on airspeed**. In small aircraft, a disturbance will normally be damped within around two oscillations - this damping **must be heavy** as corrections from the pilot could get out of phase and cause Pilot Induced Oscillations (PIOs). Large aircraft, especially those at high altitudes, need help from the autopilot.

Stability in pitch is therefore a function of the tailplane, which is the part of an aeroplane that provides the greatest positive contribution to *static* longitudinal stability. Although it produces relatively little lift, its C of P is some distance from the C of G of the aircraft, so its moment arm (and its influence) is large. It is the primary source of pitch stability and is dependent on the location of the C of G for its effectiveness*.

In the picture below, the tailplane's angle of attack has increased, which allows it to produce more lift and lower the nose.

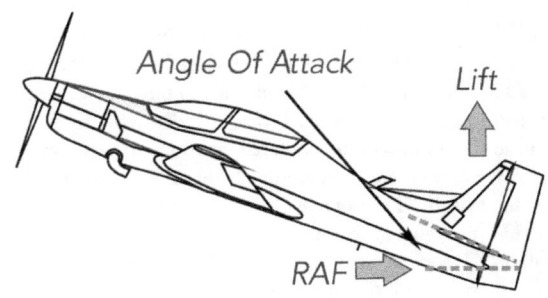

*In some aircraft, such as the 747, you can alter the position of the C of G by moving fuel between the tanks.

On the other hand, if there is an increased downwash angle from the wings (as the angle of attack increases), its effective angle of attack will be reduced, as will be its restoring moment and longitudinal stability of the aircraft (the neutral point would be further forward).

Other factors that will affect the downwash at the tail include extending the trailing-edge flaps and increasing the camber of the wing. However, this also moves the C of P to the rear to provide a stabilising nose-down moment. Usually, using high lift devices is de-stabilising.

THE NEUTRAL (TRIM) POINT

There is a point along the longitudinal axis at which the destabilising effect will exactly offset the work of the tailplane, or the location of the C of G at which the aircraft is neutrally stable, and where the tail moment is the same as the wing moment (where the aircraft is said to be in trim*). The angle of attack at which it occurs depends on the longitudinal dihedral.

*Straight and level flight requires a zero pitching moment about the C of G, with Lift equal to Weight. Static stability also requires that the total pitching moment coefficient (C_m) changes with the angle of attack.

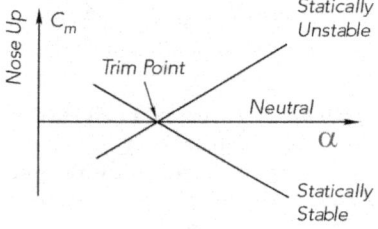

The negative slope in the picture above represents positive static longitudinal stability. The greater the slope, the greater its value. The horizontal line represents zero static longitudinal stability. The trim point is the value of the angle of attack at which C_m is zero, corresponding to the aerodynamic centre for the aircraft. For angles of attack less than this, Cm is positive (i.e. nose up) and vice versa.

The distance between the Datum and the Neutral Point in straight and level flight is the *Static* or *C of G Margin*. It is defined as the distance of the C of G from the Neutral Point divided by the mean aerodynamic chord, or *c*. It will have a minimum value when the C of G is at the Neutral Point, and a positive value when the C of G is forward of it. The greater the margin, the greater is an aircraft's longitudinal stability.

If the C of G is in front of the neutral point, the aircraft will be positively stable, or will have static longitudinal stability. As the C of G moves aft, it becomes less stable in roll and pitch, and the required control deflection is reduced (that is, it gets a bit twitchy). If the C of G moves beyond the maximum aft position, the aircraft officially becomes longitudinally unstable, which is why the aft limit of the C of G envelope is always forward of it (the NP defines the most aft position of the C of G without static instability). Keeping the C of G within limits keeps the stability (and therefore controllability) within limits.

The maximum aft position is (amongst others) limited by the minimum value of the stick force per g (see below) so, as the C of G moves forward, stick force per g increases (the stick force per g has limits to ensure controllability). An increase in speed from the trimmed position at low speed has more of an effect than it does at high speeds.

If the nose is pitched up, the opposing nose down moment from the horizontal tailplane can temporarily increase longitudinal stability, so the C of G could be slightly further aft than the neutral point without resulting in neutral stability. This is the *Manoeuvre Point*.

EXAMPLES

1. If the maximum pull force of an aircraft is 60 lbs, and the design load limit is 6g, the stick force per g required to manoeuvre the aircraft to its design load limit is 10 lbs/g.

An increase of 5 is required from 1G, so divide 50 by 5.

2. The manoeuvre stability of a large jet transport aeroplane is 280 N/g. What stick force is required to pull it to the limit manoeuvring load factor from a trimmed horizontal straight and steady flight?

In straight and level (balanced) flight the aircraft is at 1g and the trimmed stick force is zero. If it is subjected to a positive g manoeuvre, stability* resists the movement and stick force increases. You must subtract 1g from the given g value, so 2.5 - 1 = 1.5 x 150 = 225N.

*Stability increases in a manoeuvre due to changes in angle of attack, called aerodynamic damping. Increased stability increases stick forces.

The limit load factor is 2.5g, so 1.5 x 280 = 420N.

3. If a stick force of 20 lbs is needed to pull 4g from the trimmed position, the stick force gradient is:

$$\frac{20 \text{lbs}}{3g} = 6.6 \text{ lbs/g}$$

STICK FORCE STABILITY

Where stability concerns the tendency to return to equilibrium when displaced, *controllability* relates to how easy it is to displace it from that equilibrium.

Static longitudinal stability is normally indicated in terms of stick force against airspeed measured about a trimmed point of equilibrium.

Certification procedures start in trim at low speed in level flight, and specify a minimum stick force/speed gradient.

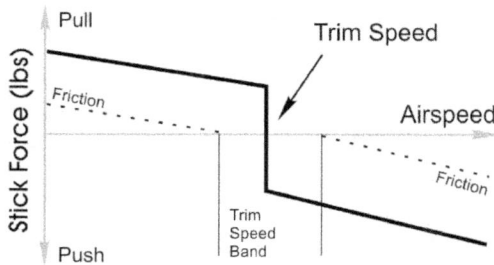

PRINCIPLES OF FLIGHT
Stability & Equilibrium

The picture shows that, to slow down, you would increase the pull force, and to increase speed you would push more. The level of stability is indicated by the steepness of the slope - a very stable aircraft would need significantly more pull force, and vice versa. If you need to pull to maintain straight and level flight as the airspeed is increased, you have an unstable condition, as would be found if the C of G is too far aft. You can recognise stick force stability during flight if you have to pull to maintain a speed below the trim speed and vice versa.

The dashed lines show the effects of the friction in the control runs that must be overcome before the control surface will move in the first place. The *trim speed band* is a range of airspeeds in which no stick force or retrimming is needed. For a given amount of friction, the lower the slope of the curve (less positively stable) the wider the trim speed band.

- Stick *position* stability relates to the direction in which the controls are moved to achieve an effect - pulling back to fly slowly and forward to fly faster (i.e. normal) is positive. This does not change if the C of G moves within its range, or after trimming.

- Stick *force* stability concerns how hard it is to change airspeed from a trimmed condition - it is easier to measure the force needed to keep the stick in position than by how much it must be moved. The forces involved can be useful cues for judging airspeed. The more stable the aircraft is, the more push force is needed - at least 1 lb per 6 knots change in speed is typical. This effect increases with a forward C of G and vice versa. This also depends on the trim tab setting and varies as the square of the EAS. Upward deflection of a trim tab causes a nose down pitch for an increase in speed, but needs less of a push force to lower the elevator. This is a decrease in stick force that still requires a forward push, so stick position stability is constant.

A high limit load factor enables the manufacturer to design for a lower stick force per g. As stick force limits are specified in **CS 23/25**, you cannot exceed the maximum value, so increasing the limit load factor provides a greater range and difference.

An increase of 10 kts from the trimmed position at low speed has more effect on stick force than the same increase at high speeds.

As stick force and stick position stability are alternative ways of measuring or displaying values for longitudinal stability (stick position less so), they don't exist unless the aircraft is longitudinally stable in the first place.

In the Cm diagram below, in which the slope is a measure of longitudinal stability, changing a trim tab setting moves the line up or down without altering the degree of slope.

In Part 1, the aircraft wants to pitch up but, as alpha increases, that force reduces, so it is self correcting and positively stable. Where the trace crosses the horizontal line, Cm is zero, and the aircraft is in trim. At Point 2, the aircraft has zero static longitudinal stability for a brief period. In Part 3, any increase in alpha will increase the nose up moment. The aircraft is negatively stable (i.e. it has **static longitudinal instability**), typical of entering an unrecoverable deep stall (deep stalling is an example of negative pitch stability, with the highest angle of attack).

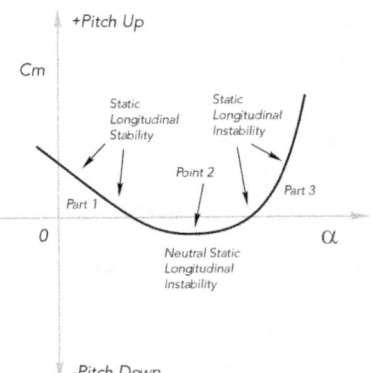

The following diagram is good for all angles of attack.

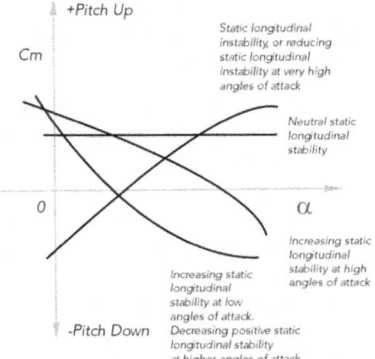

These are worth a look as well:

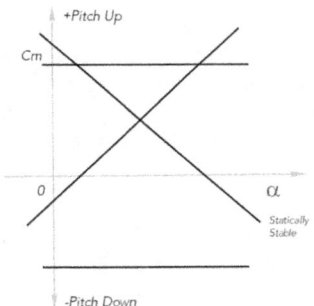

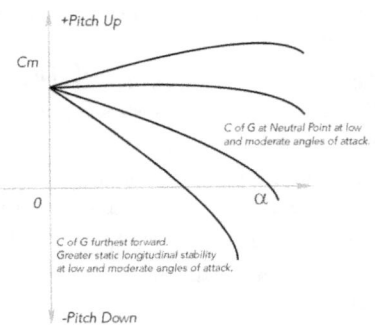

Remember that, when a control surface is moved directly, an adjustable trim tab remains fixed for all positions. If there is not enough stick force per g, a bobweight can be used to pull the control column forwards.

The **stick force gradient** is the force needed to change the load factor by a given amount.

STICK FIXED & STICK FREE STABILITY

Although moving the elevator (or stabiliser) does not affect stability, it does change the pitching moment, and the lift coefficient at which equilibrium (trim) will occur. When these changes occur at fixed elevator positions, we have stick-fixed stability (stick position stability is when the C of G is forward of the stick-fixed neutral point).

If the elevators are allowed to float, as they might if your hands are not on the controls (or stick-free), they will tend to align with the free stream when the angle of attack of the tailplane is changed. If its angle of attack is increased the elevators will tend to float up and reduce the restoring moment of the horizontal tail surfaces. As a result, the stick-free stability of the aircraft is usually less than the stick-fixed stability.

Put another way, the position of the neutral point will be different for each condition, which will alter the static margin (which will be greater in stick-fixed conditions).

THE FUSELAGE

The effect of the fuselage (and the engine nacelles), is usually destabilising. If the aerodynamic centre of the fuselage is ahead of that of the wing, their combination is further forward, so the C of G of the aircraft is relatively further aft and its longitudinal stability is reduced. The induced upwash ahead of the wing increases the destabilising influence in front of the wing, at the same time as the downwash behind the wing reduces it.

If the thrust line does not pass through the C of G, extending the landing gear lowers the position of the drag line, so any variation in thrust with changes of the angle of attack cause changes in the pitching moment. Relative to the C of G, a high thrust line has a stabilising influence and a low thrust line a destabilising one.

Lateral Stability

An aeroplane is laterally stable (around the *longitudinal* axis) if an increased angle of roll is decreased by a change of rolling moment - only in level flight is keeping the wings level of any importance - lateral stability is actually to do with avoiding sideslips*. As the airflow is parallel to the longitudinal axis, there is no aerodynamic force to correct or maintain a roll once the ailerons have stopped moving.

*A strong static lateral stability is needed to prevent the tendency to enter a spiral dive. However, if it is too strong, you would need to use too much aileron to combat any crosswind on landing.

Aeroplanes are, in theory, neutrally stable in roll*, but most are laterally unstable because, in a turn, the outer wing flies faster and produces more lift, making them roll further into the turn.

*If an aircraft has neutral static lateral stability, after a wing drop, the wing would remain in the new position.

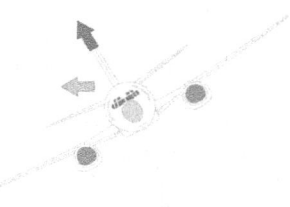

This is one reason why entering a roll from using the rudder on its own is called the dihedral effect, otherwise known as the *secondary effect of rudder*, if you remember your instructor's lessons, or *rolling moment due to sideslip,* which is the basic reason why an aircraft turns when you bank it. As you bank, lift is inclined, which creates a sideways vector that ultimately creates a slip.

There are three ways to correct this tendency.

DIHEDRAL

A dihedral is the angle between two intersecting planes. On an aeroplane, it is **the angle between the 0.25 chord line and the lateral axis**. Looked at from the front, the wing tips will be higher than the roots (the term *dihedral* is commonly used instead of *lateral dihedral*).

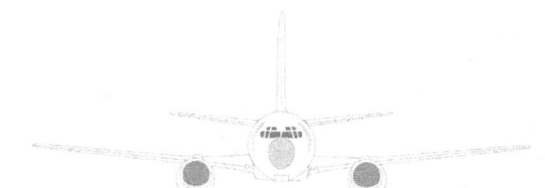

Longitudinal dihedral refers to the relationship between the angles of incidence of the wing and tailplane (or *canard*), which actually contributes to longitudinal stability.

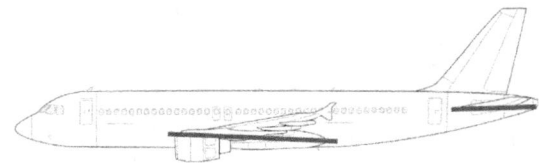

If the flight path is disturbed, the resultant between weight and lift creates a sideslip in which the lower wing will produce more lift to restore level flight.

This is because the increased angle of attack from the change in relative airflow now comes from below.

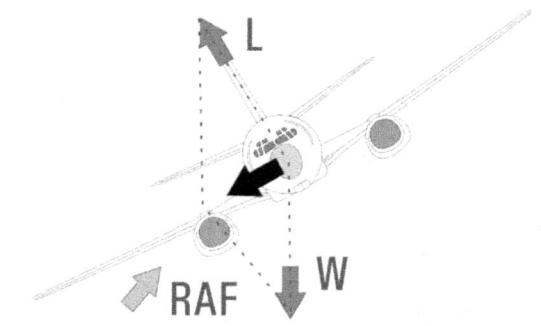

This creates an opposite roll to the slip. If you had your hands on the controls all the time, of course, like the Wright Brothers did, you wouldn't need a dihedral. The side force against the fin (if it is above the C of G) will assist recovery. A swept back wing makes the aircraft behave as if it had a greater degree of dihedral (it is called the dihedral effect*) when one wing becomes more swept in a slip than the other, so it becomes more perpendicular to the airflow and creates more lift on that side.

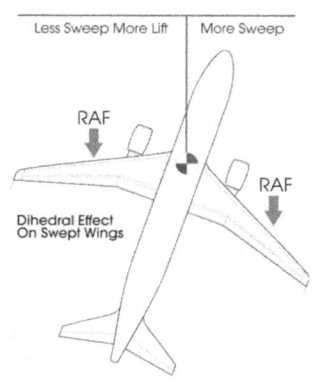

Dihedral Effect On Swept Wings

*Because dihedral is so important, lateral stability is often called the dihedral effect. It is *decreased* when the flaps are extended.

If an aircraft has a lot of weight away from the centre, say with tip tanks, it will take longer to start a turn and will slip for longer - the dihedral effect works better on such aircraft. This leads to aircraft being spirally divergent or liable to suffer from Dutch Roll, overleaf.

If you sideslip at a constant speed and angle, a higher dihedral angle will require more lateral control force.

Anhedral is the opposite, where the tips of the wings are lower in the horizontal plane than the roots are.

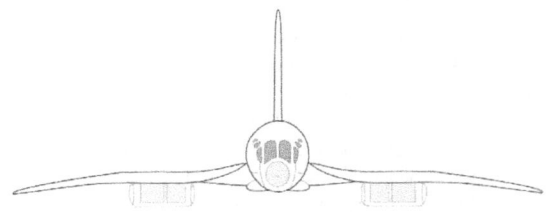

Anhedral *reduces* lateral stability, and is often used to reduce the excessive lateral stability. This can be so strong that your feet are best left off the pedals. This is especially so with high wing aircraft like the BAe 146. The tailplane of the Falcon has anhedral to improve low speed flying qualities - it reduces the effect of wing downwash.

Trim
There is no real difference between trimming swept or a straight wing aircraft - trim in yaw*, then in roll. However, other things being equal, because a swept wing has greater lateral stability (dihedral effect) than a straight wing, any sideslip due to directional mistrimming will generate a greater rolling moment, which will appear as a greater out of trim condition in roll.

*Typically, the ball is trimmed to neutral because that is the primary indication but, in wings level flight, this may not be zero sideslip, especially at high power settings with a single propeller, or with twin props when both rotate in the same direction. This is due to a lateral aerodynamic force from an asymmetry in the airflow over each side of the fuselage and fin which, for equilibrium, must be countered by an opposing force generated by sideslip.

Excessive lateral static stability is undesirable for transport aeroplanes because there would be excessive demands on roll control during a sideslip.

WING & FUSELAGE INTERFERENCE
The flow of air round the fuselage can be likened to the flow of air round a cylinder. If the upper wing is blanked by the fuselage it loses lift, so you can get a dihedral effect even if there isn't any.

High Wing
High-winged aircraft, or those with their wings above the C of G and the longitudinal axis, are more laterally stable than mid-wing or low winged aircraft. Such a feature is useful for maintaining ground clearance below engines or propellers. If there is too much lateral stability as a result, a little anhedral can be introduced to counteract it.

Sideslip produces the restoring force. The lower wing is influenced by upwash and the upper wing by downwash, to increase and decrease the respective angles of attack. The air also flows over the top of the wings to create a **positive dihedral effect**, even if there is not much of one in the first place.

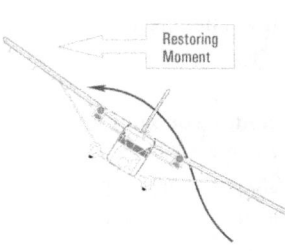

Low Wing
With a low wing aircraft, the air flows underneath the wing and tends to destabilise the machine.

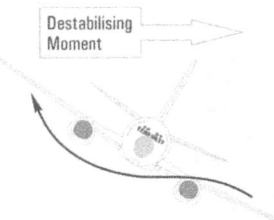

This provides negative lateral stability.

Coupling
Roll and yaw do not occur independently - each one involves the other at some stage. The interaction between rotations between planes is called coupling.

With airflow from the left, the initial tendency of a directionally and laterally stable aircraft is to move its nose to the left and its right wing downwards.

ADVERSE YAW
In a roll, the down-going wing has an increased angle of attack and a forward lift vector because the relative airflow is coming from below the horizontal.

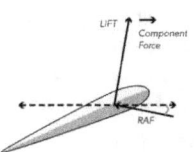

The lift vector for the upgoing wing is less forward, because the relative airflow is coming from above the horizontal.

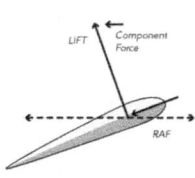

If you use the ailerons by themselves, the down aileron on the outside of the turn creates more drag as it increases the camber of the wing. It also reduces its induced drag while the up-going wing increases its induced drag. The difference is enough to create a yaw in the opposite direction to the turn, which is the main reason why we have a rudder. This can be overcome with:

- **differential ailerons**, where the up-going aileron is made to move through a larger angle than the down-going aileron.
- **frise ailerons**, which have an asymmetric leading edge. The up-going aileron sticks out below the lower surface of the wing to increase the drag.
- **control coupling**, where the aileron and rudder controls are interconnected.
- **spoilers**, where a flat plate is raised into airflow to increase the drag on the down-going wing.

SPIRAL DIVERGENCE

Almost all light aeroplanes have plenty of directional stability with limited dihedral capability. If one is trimmed to fly straight and level and then left to fend for itself, random turbulence will cause a slight bank angle and a slight turn as the fin tends to make the aircraft yaw in the direction of the roll. Because the outer wing is travelling faster, the bank angle and rolling moment will slowly increase. Although the rate of divergence is usually gradual and easily controlled, the process can carry on until the end result is an extremely steep (spiral) dive at a high airspeed, bank angle, and load factor. If a high performance aircraft is subject to a prolonged yaw involving the rudder or asymmetric power, it will dive spirally quite quickly. The problem is that the aeroplane will respond to disturbances in two ways, laterally and directionally - *at the same time!* As it yaws, its refusal to sideslip will make it lift one wing and drop the other.

An aircraft is more sensitive to spiral dives when it has static directional stability and weak static lateral stability, so spiral stability can be increased by reducing the size of the fin, or increasing its aspect ratio (with straight wings).

To recover, remove the power, roll level, then raise the nose slowly without overstressing the aeroplane. **Spirally divergent aeroplanes cannot recover on their own.**

DUTCH ROLL

Jet transport aeroplanes with swept wings, on the other hand, have a very strong dihedral effect (as described above), so the machine will not spiral, but wallow around in a combination of roll and yaw, in that order*. This is technically known as oscillatory stability. Dihedral and sweep dictate the lateral qualities. The fin and rudder size dictate the directional ones.

*If it were the other way round, it would be **snaking**, which happens on aeroplanes with more mass outboard from the centre, and lots of inertia around the normal axis. Once they start yawing, they start skidding, then rolling, and so on. For machines with low lateral stability (straight wing)s, the heading may swing back and forth a few degrees at a time. Otherwise, a yaw damper will be required. Snaking is more pronounced at low true airspeeds and high altitudes (as is Dutch roll).

Anyhow, Dutch roll is "a second order composite stability characteristic that results from the lateral-directional cross-axis coupling of two separate responses to sideslip". Of course it is. It occurs when lateral stability is stronger than directional stability, particularly below the critical Mach number, i.e. at slower speeds, so the machine will not turn quickly enough when it rolls. This is similar to, but not quite the same as, the short period mode in pitch. It is commonly found in aircraft with swept wings that have a high loading, at low airspeeds and high altitudes. If a swept wing aircraft is yawed to starboard, the port wing will produce more lift and start a roll to the right (see *Dihedral Effect*). However, the port wing also develops more drag because more of it is exposed to the airflow, which starts a yaw to port. which helps the starboard wing create more lift, and so on.

Essentially, the machine rolls in one direction and yaws in another, but the roll happens before the yaw in a sideslip. As each cause (and effect) is usually less energetic than the previous one, the motion will eventually die away. If random turbulence causes a slight bank, the aeroplane will slip towards the bank, but the dihedral effect* quickly starts a recovery, at which point a turn (yaw) will start, but **lagging behind the roll**, so the machine now rolls the other way. Inertia causes an overshoot, for a slip in the opposite direction and a repeat of the whole process. Each oscillation is usually larger than the one before.

*In a sideslip, the effective span of the wings is changed and the forward one creates more lift for a short time, because it presents more of a span to the airflow than the other. This makes it rise, hence the roll. However, the increased lift also creates more drag to pull the wing back, starting an oscillation. A dorsal or ventral fin will reduce Dutch roll by increasing directional stability and lateral *dynamic* stability while decreasing lateral *static* stability (Learjets 31, 31A and 55C have *Delta Fins* which improve directional stability, enough not to need yaw dampers).

A *Yaw Damper* (often essential equipment) uses gyros to sense and correct changes in yaw, but the tendency to Dutch roll may be used by increasing the anhedral. As the initial cause is a slip, many machines use slip sensors connected to a yaw damper that applies rudder in the relevant direction to correct things.

Dutch roll is more of a problem at high altitude where the thinner air provides less of a damping effect. It is also more likely at slow speeds because directional stability is reduced. The generic recovery procedure is to leave the rudder pedals alone and make one large movement with the ailerons in the opposite direction to the roll on each cycle until control is regained.

PROPELLERS

When stationary on the ground, the power from a jet engine is zero, but the thrust can be considerable, which is why it is used to measure turbine engine performance. The thrust from a propeller, on the other hand, is variable (and so is the efficiency), but the power can be considerable, even when stationary.

PRINCIPLES OF FLIGHT
Propellers

Officially, a propeller's function is to *convert crankshaft rotary movement into thrust*, by moving a large column of air backwards, to propel the aircraft forward (it pushes against the air behind). As a propeller is an aerofoil, the thrust it creates is equivalent to the lift produced by a wing - it's just used differently. A *tractor* (at the nose) will propel fast, turbulent air over the lifting surfaces, whereas a *pusher* (somewhere behind the fuselage) provides better high speed performance because it doesn't produce so much drag. On the other hand, the tractor bites into clean air, while a pusher spins in air that is already disturbed.

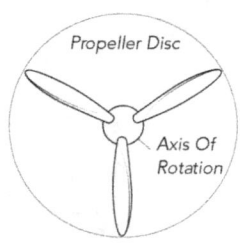

Thus, propellers are just aerofoils with a twist in them (*washout*) to spread the "lift" (thrust) evenly over their whole length, as the tips run faster than the centre and need less of an angle of attack (the word *pitch* is sometimes used loosely to describe this). In fact, as far as the exams are concerned, the blade is twisted to *keep the local angle of attack constant along the blade*, although the real purpose is to balance the amount of lift as much as possible. The basic fixed pitch propeller is averaged to cope with many flight conditions, so is not perfect for them all, particularly taking off, where its angle of attack will be highest or, more accurately, its blade pitch would be too coarse*. The problem is that you have to make the engine run faster to get more performance from such a propeller, and engines work best within a certain speed range. Not only that, once the airflow becomes more than that with which the propeller can cope.

*Aside from improving takeoff performance, a constant speed propeller reduces fuel consumption over a range of cruise speeds.

 With propellers, the concern is not so much with forces perpendicular and parallel to the airflow (e.g. Lift & Drag), but those along the axis of the aeroplane (Thrust) and at right angles to the Plane Of Rotation (Torque).

Two blades are usually used, for maximum lightness and efficiency, but 3 or 4 might be used if two blades would be too long, as they might be near a fuselage. This also produces less vibration if there is an asymmetrical airflow, due to the more even spread. To produce their peak thrust, propellers must be at an extremely fine pitch angle. When the propeller is moving forward the most slowly is the time when the engine must be run fastest to get maximum thrust. However, after only a relatively small speed the engine would overspeed, at which point a coarser pitch is needed. The first action for an overspeed would be to close the throttle.

Propellers with two pitch angles were developed around 1930, and still used in 1939 on the Hurricane and Spitfire, but propellers with infinitely variable pitch angles were not long in coming, as discussed below. Changing the speed of the aircraft changes the airflow into the propeller disc, and the angle of attack of the blades. If you increase speed, the angle of attack reduces, and if you slow down, it increases, affecting the L/D ratio, meaning that a fixed pitch propeller gets less efficient away from its optimum speed, which is usually the cruise, but some propellers are designed for climbing. Also, propeller thrust is not the same as propeller efficiency - when the brakes are released*, the thrust will be high because the angle of attack is high, but efficiency will be zero.

*Thrust is greatest before brake release and reduces with speed as the angle of attack decreases, so you get the maximum when stationary on the ground and minimum (with maximum drag) at maximum forward speed. Thrust also bends blades forward, while torque bends them against the direction of rotation.

What you need is a way of varying the pitch of the propeller to suit different conditions of flight, such as a fine pitch for takeoff and climb and a relatively coarse pitch for the cruise, where the blades move a longer distance per rotation due to the higher angle of attack. That is, the blade angle increases with increasing TAS. Constant speed propellers can do this automatically.

To determine the relationship between the THP delivered by a propeller and the BHP from the engine that drives it, the propeller blade can be split into infinitely small parts. This allows the integrated thrust and drag forces of a propeller blade to represent those of the whole blade*. The rotational velocity around its axis is an angular velocity usually expressed in RPM.

*As based on a section at 75% of the radius.

On the ground, with the engine running, the only airflow over the propeller blades is that arising from their rotation. So everything starts from this diagram:

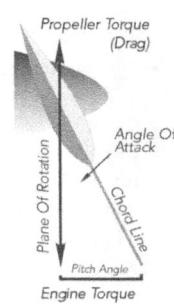

The angle between the chord line of the blade and the relative airflow, which (in this case only) coincides with the plane of rotation, is the angle of attack, which (here) is the same as the pitch angle.

The pitch angle is the angle between the chord line and a reference line based on the propeller hub.

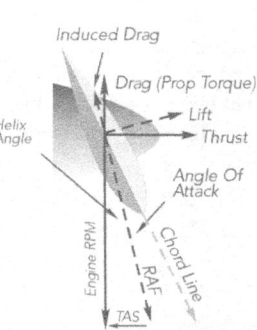

As the throttle is moved forward, the RPM vector gets longer. Once you start moving forward, air flowing through the propeller disc (TAS) has to fit into the pitch angle, so the angle of attack must reduce to accommodate it. The angle between the resultant airflow (helical path) and the plane of rotation is called the *helix angle*, or the angle of advance. The relative airflow is now not parallel to the plane of rotation, but between it and the chord line. As the RAF vector moves, so does the lift vector, because it must remain at right angles to the RAF. Thus, not all of the lift vector is contributing to thrust, and the difference (induced drag) is added to profile drag. In other words, the forward component Lift is now Thrust and the remainder, as drag, is working against the blade.

As full power is applied, the TAS increases, and the angle of attack reduces, and so does the thrust as you go down the runway, much more than the drag reduction. In the climb, the air becomes less dense, reducing it further, and the TAS will increase with altitude, reducing the thrust even more (in a turboprop, the ram effect in the engine intakes helps offset this).

If you slow down, the angle of attack will increase, which will increase the drag markedly.

 Maximum *thrust* comes with the maximum angle of attack. Maximum *efficiency* is to do with the power *from* the propeller compared to the power going *to* it.

Efficiency with a turboprop is expressed in terms of Thrust Horsepower (THP) divided by Shaft Horsepower (SHP), and for a piston prop as Thrust Horsepower (THP) divided by Brake Horsepower (BHP). The propeller's purpose is to create THP from SHP or BHP.

1 HP is equal to 325.66 lbs x knots, so if you fly at that speed, 1 lb of thrust equates to 1 THP. A 1000 HP engine will therefore produce 1000 lbs of thrust. Above that speed, 1 THP will produce less than 1 lb of thrust and vice versa. For example, at 10 knots, the same engine will produce 32,566 lbs (assuming the same efficiency), because the amount of thrust falls off with velocity. This is why jets have an advantage in terms of maximum speed.

The formula concerned is:

$$T = \frac{325.66 \times THP}{V}$$

It is flawed, in that thrust approaches infinity as V gets to zero, so it cannot be solved for the beginning of the takeoff roll. In the real world, the propeller has a maximum speed anyway. If the blade were not twisted, the lift at the tip would be enough to bend it. The washout isn't perfect, and there is a residual force (*Thrust Bending Force*), which tries to bend the blades forward, especially at the tips, which are thinner. Centrifugal force tries to stretch the blades and throw off their pitch* and there is also a **torque bending force** that bends the blade in the opposite direction to its rotation, in the plane of rotation, or perpendicular to the thrust bending force.

*See *Centrifugal Turning Moment* in *Airframes & Systems*. The *Aerodynamic Turning Moment* tends to increase the pitch of a blade when its Centre Of Pressure lies forward of the torsional (feathering) axis.

This graph shows the variations in efficiency of a fixed pitch propeller with TAS at a constant RPM:

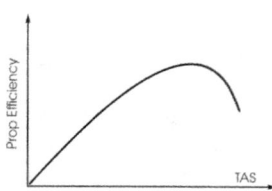

Increasing blade camber improves the power absorption capability.

In medium horizontal turbulence, the pitch angle of a constant speed propeller would alter slightly. If you run an engine with a fixed pitch propeller attached to it at full RPM when stationary and facing into a strong wind, you would get higher RPM than you would in still air.

Geometric pitch is how far a propeller should move forward in one rotation when the helix angle is equal to the blade angle (i.e. zero angle of attack). The *nominal* or *standard geometrical pitch* of a complete propeller is that of a section at two thirds of the radius.

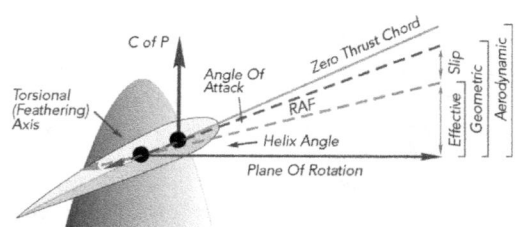

The *effective pitch* is how far it actually moves. The difference between the two is *propeller slip*, and is a measure of the efficiency or otherwise of the process (it is directly related to the angle of attack. Effective pitch is governed by the helix angle). As with wings, the angle of attack is best at around 3-4°, the normal value for a fixed pitch propeller in the cruise.

The surface with the greatest pressure is the *thrust face* (at the rear when producing forward thrust). The *pressure face* is therefore at the front. Because certain parts of a propeller have to give priority to strength and not aerodynamics, such as the root, only that area between 60-90% of the tip radius is actually effective at producing thrust (there are tip losses as well, as there are with wings). The greatest amount is found at around 75%, hence the reference to blade angles at the 75% station.

WINDMILLING

A propeller that is driven by airflow only is said to be windmilling. This is how the forces involved look:

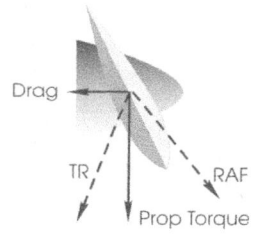

In a twin-engined aircraft, a windmilling propeller can produce asymmetric forces that can make the aeroplane uncontrollable. To keep above the stall, power on the good engine must be increased, and the increased thrust on top of the drag from the windmilling propeller can produce a yawing moment that is too great for the rudder to cope with, especially at low airspeeds (see *Multi-Engined Operations*, below).

The TR produces a twisting moment about the pitch change axis which involves centrifugal and aerodynamic turning moments, discussed later.

SOLIDITY

Solidity (or the **area ratio**) describes how much propeller you can see against air, from the front. The more blades there are, or the higher their chord, the more "solid" the disk formed by the blades is. So, if you put in a larger engine, you would have to increase solidity to compensate, or absorb power from the engine. You could fit another prop (counter-rotating), or make the present blades bigger, but it's more efficient to use more blades, up to where they get too close to previous blades.

Solidity is therefore the ratio between how much of the propeller disk area is taken up by the blades, or the total blade area divided by the disc area - more blades means more solidity, up to a maximum of 1, which represents a solid disk and no propeller wash, so adding more blades beyond a certain maximum decreases propeller efficiency.

Solidity can be calculated as follows:

```
Solidity = No of Blades x Chord
           Circumference
```

The solidity at any point on the radius of the propeller disc is the ratio of total blade chord at that radius (usually 70%) to the total circumference at that radius.

THE P FACTOR (ASYMMETRIC THRUST)

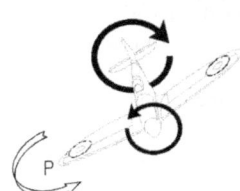

A rotating propeller creates various forces that may be allowed for in the design stages, including *gyroscopic precession* (see *Instruments*), where lifting the tail tends to make the nose yaw to the left.

Torque results from the airframe going the opposite way to the direction of rotation (see picture), although this was more of a problem with rotary engines than modern ones on machines with better design. In any event, as torque acts on a short lever arm and stability on a long one (the wings), under normal circumstances, the torque effect (in terms of producing a yaw) is quite small, given the relative lengths of the propeller and the wings (the reaction from a fixed pitch propeller would be greatest at low speeds with maximum engine power). The worst scenario occurs as you accelerate the engine, especially at, or near the stall on machines with short wings and powerful engines.

Anyhow, the effect is to produce a *roll*, which is countered by washout on the upgoing wing. This is a factor that is often forgotten about when instrument flying, especially in the climb.

In the climb, or at least with a positive angle of attack, the propeller blade that is going down has an increased angle of attack (and more of the blade exposed to the airflow) while the one going up has a reduced angle of attack, so thrust is offset to the right, with clockwise rotating propellers (the downgoing blade also travels further in relation to the aircraft than the upgoing one. As it does so in the same time, its relative speed and aerodynamic force are higher).

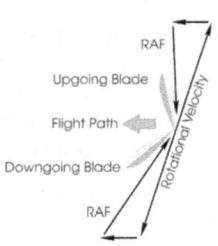

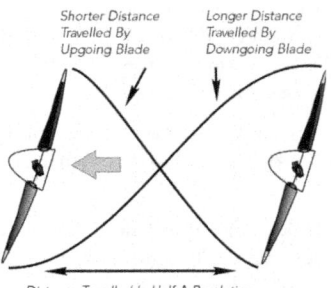

Thus, you can expect a little left yaw and to use a little right rudder to stop the machine slipping, including when you are flying at less than cruise speed, even in level flight, but it is most noticeable with tail wheel aircraft on takeoff and landing*, or with high angles of attack.

*You get gyroscopic precession as the tail is lifted - the force applied to the top of the prop disk is felt 90° away in the direction of rotation, to cause a yaw. The combined precessions may cause a ground loop if you raise the tail too early. With a clockwise rotating propeller on a single-engined aeroplane, a pitch up (or inclined blade) will produce a yaw to the right.

Counter rotating propellers cancel out torque and gyroscopic effects, and aircraft with tricycle undercarriages suffer less from precession effects on take off because of their attitude. On twin-engined machines with a single rudder that is bypassed by both propeller slipstreams, rudder control in the early stages of a takeoff will be weak.

This asymmetric loading is the *P factor*, and is one aspect of the problems caused by the *critical engine*, discussed in *Multi-Engined Operations*, below., but the main element involving yaw is the rotational velocity imparted to the slipstream by the propeller (see next column).

The propeller torque reaction will also force a wheel into the ground on takeoff and make the aircraft steer wrongly - for example, with a clockwise rotating propeller (seen from behind), the airframe will want to go the other way and put pressure on the port wheel (this will also create a **yaw to the left**). It is actually in the same direction as the slipstream effect, below.

SLIPSTREAM

Slipstream results from rotating air going round and round the fuselage until it eventually hits the tail fin, forcing it one way or the other (thus causing yaw), depending on which way round the propeller is going. This adds to the P factor, but it is not so marked on multi-engined machines. It is actually the main reason why the nose moves to the left. Or right.

It is most prominent at low airspeeds with high power settings, and can be reduced by offsetting the fin, as most flight is spent in the cruise, or placing the fin as far as possible from the propeller (or even having a fin and rudder on the opposite side of the fuselage, i.e. underneath, as well). In addition, the engine (and the thrust line) may be offset by a few degrees. Of course, there is always the rudder trim to help.

Thus, most single engined propeller aeroplanes yaw to the right, needing left rudder whenever power is **reduced** below the cruise setting, so *left rudder is needed in a descent with low power*.

The term also refers to the effects of propwash over the wing, where a local increase in dynamic pressure that produces more lift behind the propellers, relative to the power off situation so, with the wing at the stall, you need a lower IAS to support the weight. Having said that, the reduction is small, so the major effect is an increase in the attitude at which the aircraft will stall. The wings will stall progressively from the tips which are at a higher angle of attack than the sections behind the props, so there is an increased chance of dropping the wing at the stall.

PROPELLER TIP SPEED

There are few problems until the speed of sound is reached, when compressibility effects mean that more power is needed for no appreciable increase in thrust. Propeller tip speeds are normally established at less than 0.8 times the speed of sound.

Tip speed can be calculated by multiplying the RPM by $2\pi r$ (the circumference) to get feet per minute. Divide by 60 to get that in feet per second. Dividing by 101.3, which is the feet per minute equivalent of 1 knot, gives you the speed in knots. Remembering that:

$$\text{Speed} = \frac{\text{Distance}}{\text{Time}}$$

To find the speed of a section of a blade that is 8 feet out from the root and rotating at 394 RPM:

$$\frac{394 \times 2\pi 8}{101.3}$$

The answer is 195 knots.

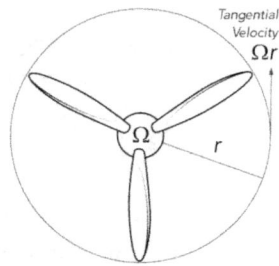

Alternatively (as RPM is an engineering quantity), the angular velocity (Ω) in rads (from physics), or the blade frequency (Hz), multiplied by the radius will give you the answer in feet per second. To get the frequency, multiply the RPM by 2π then divide by 60.

PROBLEMS

Whenever a propeller is producing thrust it is subject to mechanical forces that can damage it, so preflight checking for dents and scratches is important. There are also vibrations from a piston engine which can set up a series of standing waves along the propeller span.

The waves cause local stress points which change their position with engine RPM - there may be a red line on the RPM gauge that indicates critical areas to be avoided.

Multi-Engined Operations

Although the loss of power in a light twin is 50%, the climb performance will be reduced by at least 80%. You can also expect a yaw due to the asymmetric thrust which must be balanced with the rudder, and a roll from the reduced prop wash over one wing (also affected by yaw towards the dead engine). The roll forces are balanced by banking towards the working engine. Having said that, ailerons should be used with care, because the secondary effect of roll is yaw.

When an engine fails, thrust is drastically reduced while drag is increased, and the thrust and drag lines move away from the centreline of the aircraft to increase the yawing moment when the centre of lift moves from the dead engine to the live one.

For most light twins there is an airspeed:

- below which directional control cannot be maintained on the ground (V_{MCG}). This, and its equivalent for landing (V_{MCL}, for overshoots) are based on the yawing moments at maximum thrust values, **with the C of G on the aft limit**, at least for V_{MCG}, and with no nose wheel steering (or deviations from the straight line path by more than 30 feet), but the two main variables are the airfield elevation and temperature. If there is too much thrust, as there could be from a jet at low levels, you could really have a bad day, so observe those EPR values! Conversely, the yawing moment from an engine failure at high temperatures or altitudes will be lower, so V_{MCG} can be lower. V_{MCL} can be limited by roll rate.

- below which directional control cannot be maintained, when airborne at sea level (V_{MCA}). It is denoted by a red radial line on the ASI, and depends on the density altitude and the location of the engine. The equilibrium of moments about the normal axis comes from deflection of the rudder, and the equilibrium of forces along the lateral axis requires either bank angle or a side slip, or a combination.

  V_{MCA} cannot be greater than 1.13 V_{SR}. The aircraft must be outside ground effect and the heading must be maintained within 20°.

- below which you should not intentionally shut an engine down (V_{SSE}).

- that will provide the best single engine rate of climb or, put another way, the slowest loss of altitude (V_{YSE}). This is usually lower than V_Y, and is represented by a blue radial on the ASI.

- that will give the steepest angle of climb with one engine inoperative (V_{XSE}). It is used only to clear obstacles during the initial climb after takeoff, as it also provides less cooling airflow for the engine and requires more rudder control than V_{YSE}.

All are described more fully in context below, and in the *Performance* chapter.

Takeoff should be made using at least V_{MCA} +5 kts, AEO, followed by an acceleration to V_Y (or V_X if there are obstacles), which should be maintained with takeoff power until you get to a safe height. For a cruise climb, maybe use V_Y plus 10 - 15 knots - this will cool the engines better and provide more visibility, as well as improving fuel consumption. However, if an engine fails, establish V_{YSE} or V_{XSE}, as appropriate.

 There is no guarantee you can maintain altitude, let alone climb - you can only expect to maintain heading.

In the picture below, the left engine has failed, so the aircraft is yawing to the left. The moment will be greater if the engines are outboard, which would usually be the case with propellers because of the clearance required from the fuselage. Jets can have their engines closer.

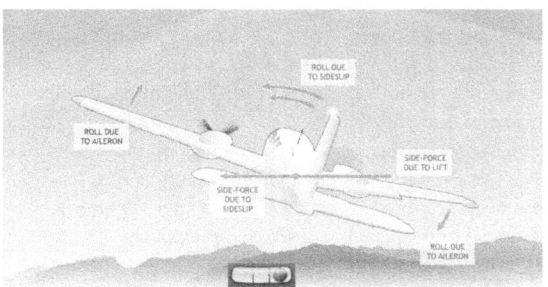

BANK TOWARDS LIVE ENGINE - FORCES AND MOMENTS BALANCED

Aside from the yaw, the machine will also roll towards the dead engine because the propeller slipstream increases the lift from the operating side. The force from the right rudder input that is needed to keep the machine straight creates a sideslip and parasite drag increases because the streamlining of the fuselage is distorted.

If you slow down at this point, you must use more rudder until the full travel is reached (which is why this situation is worse during takeoff). This occurs at a limiting speed called V_{MC}, or V_{MCA} (Minimum Control in the Air).

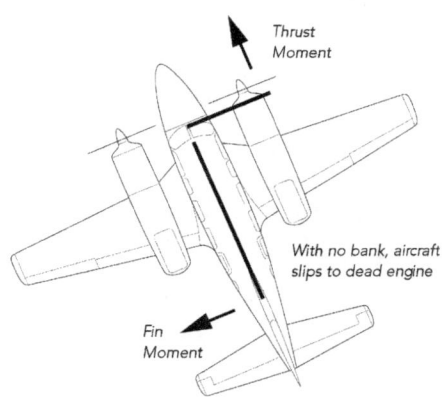

The manufacturer establishes V_{MC} as the minimum airspeed at which you can recover directional control within 20° of the original heading, using no more than 5° of bank if one engine fails. The following are assumed:

- takeoff power set on both engines
- the C of G at its furthest aft position
- flaps in set for takeoff
- the landing gear retracted
- the propeller windmilling at takeoff pitch (or feathered if the procedure is automatic)

The bank is 5° because too much would stall the fin.

However, sudden engine failures are not common, so the V_{MCA} as established may be different if all of the above conditions are not satisfied. If you fly slower than V_{MCA}, there will be insufficient force from the fin (assuming it doesn't stall first) to maintain directional control and the aeroplane will begin to yaw out of control. **DO NOT** fly below V_{MCA} on one engine!

Especially, do not fly at speeds approaching it, except when training or during flight tests*.

*V_{SSE} is there to reduce the potential for accidents due to loss of control after an engine is shut down at or near minimum control speed. Training should only be made at a safe altitude at a speed above V_{SSE}, with power on the good engine set for maximum continuous operation. Airspeed should then be reduced slowly until directional control can no longer be maintained, or the first sign of a stall is obtained.

As V_{MC} assumes that maximum power is used on the operating engine, the easiest way to regain control at or below that speed is simply to reduce power. Then drop the nose, accelerate past V_{MCA}, return power to the operating engine and accelerate to V_{YSE} (the blue line on the ASI).

Because maximum power is mostly available at sea level, V_{MC} decreases with altitude until it becomes lower than the stall speed and of no concern, so you can maintain directional control at lower airspeeds than at sea level. Nevertheless, do not practice stalls with one engine out, or you might lose control. To get rid of the slip, bank (about 5°) towards the good engine, which inclines the lift vector and create a sideways force to cover it.

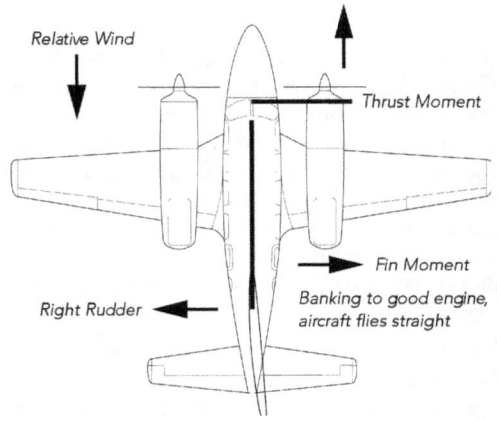

This is because, with full power on the working engine, the machine will tend to roll as well as yaw into the inoperative one as airspeed drops below V_{MC}, and gets worse as speed is reduced. Aileron drag will increase the yaw, leading to a violent roll if a stall occurs. Banking at least 5° into the good engine ensures controllability above V_{MC} and minimum drag for best climb performance, because the lift is inclined in the same direction to provide a small turning force that allows less rudder, reducing drag and giving you some leeway for later problems should they arise. Stall characteristics will not be degraded, either. The ball should not be in the centre - in fact, it should be displaced slightly towards the lower wing.

A forward C of G will give you a smaller V_{MCA} and an aft one will give you a greater V_{MCA} - the one in the flight manual (and displayed on the ASI) is based on the C of G being at the aft limit as the distance between the C of G and the vertical stabiliser will be smaller.

As thrust is greatest at slow speeds when using propellers, the vertical fin must therefore produce more force at lower speeds. With a jet, as thrust remains constant, the fin must produce the same force at all speeds.

THE CRITICAL ENGINE

When the propellers rotate the same way on a light twin (such as the PA 23), the failure of one engine in the climb may cause more problems than the other would - in the case of the Aztec, the downgoing blades are on the right side of each engine, as the propellers rotate clockwise when viewed from the rear, so there is more of a turning moment if the left engine fails, as the thrust line from the downgoing blade of the right propeller is further away from the longitudinal axis.

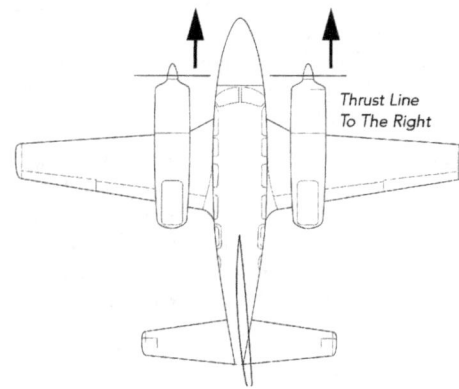

Thrust Line To The Right

The left engine in this case is called the critical engine, because its loss has the worst effect. Later aircraft (such as some PA 31s or the PA 34) have counter-rotating propellers (that is, the right engine rotates the other way). Although you will still need to use the rudder if an engine fails, you won't need it in the climb under normal circumstances as there is no critical engine. The slipstream going back over the flight controls will also be asymmetric, and some parts will be more responsive (there will also be no propeller wash on the dead side and there is a rolling action towards it).

In a propeller-driven twin, somewhere between 60-80% of the lift comes from the prop wash over a wing (hence the difference between power-on and power-off stall speeds). If an engine stops at a slow speed, the affected wing will stall (power-off stall speed is *higher*), so you not only get asymmetric thrust, but also asymmetric lift, giving a yaw *and roll* to the dead engine.

This is why you must bank into the good engine to regain the lift that was lost.

Increasing thrust on the operating engine will increase the yaw, as will displacing it further from the centreline. Drag from a windmilling propeller will have the same effect, but the propeller will also be turning the dead engine against all those cylinders - one very good reason for feathering it. Reduced lift from the reduced slipstream adds to the yawing tendency. Because the wing with the good engine goes faster it develops more lift and could lead to a sideslip and a spiral dive if the situation is not corrected immediately with rudder, the dead prop feathered and full power applied to the live engine.

JETS

The exhaust stream from jet engines does not usually flow over the wings, so there is no significant change in lift when one engine fails. Despite that, the critical engines are the outboard and/or upwind ones. With a crosswind from the right, No 4 engine (on the far right) would therefore be the critical one, and *vice versa* (with a crosswind on takeoff, the wheels act as a pivot while the tail weathercocks the nose into wind).

The Trident I and the Boeing 727 (1963) were an attempt to remove asymmetric handling problems and make takeoffs in low visibility more of a possibility. They had three engines at the rear with the horizontal stabiliser high on the tail fin. However, engine failure increases the possibility of damage to the others because they are all close together, and the fuel pipes run through the fuselage from the wings to the engines. There was also the potential to deep stall, as discussed previously.

*Rear mounted engines affect longitudinal trim less when thrust values change. Some Tridents had three and a half engines - the extra boost engine was used only for takeoff and the takeoff climb.

HIGH SPEED FLIGHT

Planes driven by jet engines are very slick, in that there is no automatic drag effect from reducing power as you would get with a propeller, so there is a tendency to overspeed when you couple that with powerful engines. This means that **constant attention is required**. As mentioned elsewhere, it's like driving a powerful car in permanent high gear, so autopilots are routinely used to keep such aircraft under control and within performance and structural limits.

Large aircraft also have high inertia, because they have more momentum (control forces are a lot higher, so brute force in the shape of hydraulics is often needed). Any force applied to change that momentum will have a lesser effect, and the machine will carry on doing something wrong while you make a correction, so you cannot now afford to wait until a situation has developed before doing something about it. Good jet pilots correct problems before they happen! Such anticipation is why you must know the power settings against flap settings, plus associated trim changes. For example, to increase power, you must give the engine time to spool up, with a little delay between applying power and seeing the result, which again means you need more anticipation. As well, if you reduce power, then increase it again, the engine will spin down to a low RPM then wind all the way up again. This is why, on approach, that relatively high thrust is maintained against all those lift-and-therefore-drag-producing devices, so the power is there when you need it.

You need to know your weight, because it affects the operational characteristics. For example, an extra 10 000 lbs could mean around 4 kts less speed and some embarrassment when the takeoff speed figures have been wrongly computed (you need to be accurate within 5,000 lbs for takeoff, for a possible error margin of 2 knots).

As fuel is used in a swept wing jet aeroplane, the C of G moves forward, so big jets need a wider range within which to work and a greater range of travel for the elevator. The elevator, of course, is subject to stalling, so the variable incidence tailplane (where the elevator remains in the streamlined position) was developed to keep things within the proper range. These are very powerful, because the surface area involved is extremely large, so you don't need to move it very much. This is why any movements should be controlled, using short bursts, and the elevator (which is smaller than normal) is used for normal manoeuvres. Because you can move the whole tailplane, the elevator remains available over its full range.

Variable incidence tailplanes are actually used for a number of reasons, especially when you combine them:

- The C of G envelope is larger, which is useful when the fuel is used from tanks in swept wings.
- You get a larger speed range and a higher V_{NE}.
- The system can cope with large changes in trim when the flaps and slats are extended.
- Less trim drag is caused by the system, which increases the maximum range and endurance.

The strength of the tail structure is often a limiting factor because a high download is required from the elevators to keep the wings at an angle of attack that will produce a large amount of lift when manoeuvring. In addition, the loads on the airframe may be large enough to cause aeroelastic distortion, which will affect stability and make the behaviour of the aircraft (and its controls) unpredictable. A Mach number limitation is usually imposed when buffeting may lead to structural failure or when loss of control due to compressibility characteristics may cause the aircraft to exceed the structural limitation before control can be regained.

Turbine engines run best at high speed (90% of the maximum RPM). To obtain maximum power, the aeroplane should be flown at high altitudes. Put another way, at lower levels, you will not be able to make best use of the engine, because there will be a lot of power that cannot be used before you reach the limits of the airframe. As it happens, the best conditions for the airframe are also found at high altitude because drag varies only with EAS. At a constant EAS the drag decrease with increased altitude due to the decreased air density. However, the TAS increases, so the distance travelled for the fuel used to overcome drag is increased. It is most economical to fly jet aeroplanes at high altitudes.

If you fly slower than the optimum speed, you will get controllability and stability problems, and if you fly faster, you will get more drag.

High speed aircraft have low aspect ratio wings with a high wing loading. If you add sweepback, at high angles of attack, the rate of change in C_L is very slow, almost flat, in fact, while changes in C_D are very large (with high aspect ratio wings, large changes in drag occur only at the stall). This means that climb performance will be marginal at low speeds.

There is no particular stall point, but you get lots of drag so, if you over-rotate, you will likely not get out of ground effect. On the other hand, you need higher power settings for the approach - DO NOT just ease the nose up!

As the angle of attack is high, you can expect less directional stability as the fin will be less effective due to interference from the fuselage.

 The correct climbing speeds must be observed - if they fall too low, especially at higher altitudes, the rate of climb can be seriously reduced and the only way of regaining speed quickly is to dive but, because of the reduced excess thrust needed to climb, a lot of height may be lost in the dive before climbing speed is regained.

On landing, a steep flight path will require a flare, but you simply won't have the manoeuvrability (no-flare landings are preferred) - as the lift curve is shallow, a large rotation is required to get the lift you need and you will just sink. The best gliding speed will be above that for the best L/D ratio for the most flare options.

A long wheel base can be a problem with taxying, and you can often lose sight of the taxiway.

The factors to be considered include:

- **Compressibility**. The effects may occur at lower Mach numbers as the aircraft ages and the external finish deteriorates.
- **Buffeting**.
- **Aircraft Behaviour**.
- **Change of trim**, longitudinal (porpoising) or lateral (wing dropping). This can vary with the rate of change of speed.
- **Control Effectiveness**. This deteriorates at the high Mach numbers and low IAS* found at high altitudes. Due to positioning, only part of the lifting surface is affected by movement of the control surface behind it, so changes of forces are smaller. The control surface may also be operating in turbulent airflow.

   *The force exerted by the deflection of a control surface is proportional to the IAS, whereas the kinetic energy of the aircraft depends on the TAS. The time taken to recover from a spin, for example, is greater at high altitudes.

   The air loads from a high IAS (usually at lower levels, where the air is denser) may distort the airframe enough to cause control reversal (see *Flight Controls* in *AGK*) or changes in lift, if the structural limits are not exceeded. Hydraulic jacks may stall and limit the range of movement.

The Mach number shows how close you are to the speed of sound, which is called Mach 1.0. Mach numbers (designated with the letter M) have no units, but simply show a ratio between two speeds, TAS and the local speed of sound, as seen with this formula:

$$M = \frac{TAS}{S}$$

where S is the local speed of sound, which changes only with temperature (pressure and density cancel each other out, although a gas with a lower density than air will have a higher speed of sound), so if your TAS is 250 kts and the local speed of sound is 600, your Mach number is 0.42. The local speed of sound, on the other hand, is found with this formula:

```
S = 38.94 X √kelvin
```

For mental arithmetic, you can also use:

```
S = 644 + 1.2 TATc
```

The result is in knots, and to get kelvin, add 273 to the Celsius temperature. As the result is proportional to the square root of the absolute temperature, height is not a factor (the speed of sound changes with altitude only because the temperature does). For example, at MSL in ISA conditions, it will be 661.7 kts, and it will be the same at FL100 if the OAT is 15°C. Put another way, if the speed of sound at sea level is 662 kts and 574 (ish) at 36 000 feet where the temperature is -56.5°C, a Machmeter (see *Instruments*) will still read 1.0.

As we have seen, below around 200-300 knots, air is assumed to be incompressible. What that really means is that the effects are not worth bothering about below that speed. Air is actually compressible at any speed, otherwise any disturbance in it would be felt instantly miles away. Small disturbances (or pressure waves) travel through a given material at a fixed speed called the speed of sound, which is mostly based on the (absolute) temperature of the medium and, to a lesser degree, the frequency of the sound. People trying to break speed records use the warmest air they can find.

 Although we are talking about air, the speed of sound for water is several times greater, and higher still for metals.

A wave will start off as a very small rise in pressure followed by an equal and opposite fall, so the air molecules will go back to where they were after the disturbance has died down. The limit to how quickly they can move is the speed of sound. In the picture below, an aeroplane is flying through successive points from left to right, each point being 1 second later that the last, and centred on its respective circle. The situation shows the time for the final point, on the right, from which the sound wave has not yet departed.

The speed of sound is given the letter a, and the airspeed is given the letter u.

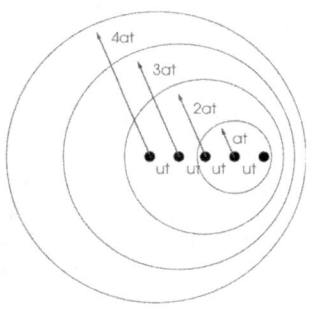

The wave from the centre of the first (smallest) circle has a radius of at, or the speed of sound over 1 second, in this case. The remaining circles are correspondingly larger.

You can see the potential cruising Mach number, which must be ut divided by at or, in this case, $4ut$ over at, roughly 0.7. You reach Mach 1 when u is equal to a, at which point the atmosphere is aware of the coming aircraft which is actually already there! The wave that now travels along with the nose of the aircraft is called a shock wave, but a weak one, as you would get with a very pointed or thin body is simply called a Mach wave.

Thus, small disturbances simply create Mach waves, which are associated with small bodies. However, aircraft are large enough to create **shock waves**, through which changes are much more severe (see below). Air passing through either of them experiences an increase in temperature, density and pressure* and a decrease in velocity. The only difference is in magnitude.

*Decreasing pressure is associated with expansion waves, which are generally found between shock waves. The density, pressure and temperature in front of an expansion wave are higher than they are behind. When air is passing through one, the local speed of sound decreases, the Mach number increases and static temperature decreases.

When the source moves ahead of the waves, they bunch up to form a *Mach Line* in 2-dimensional flow that divides areas where the source can be "heard" and where it cannot. It is at right angles to the direction of movement (or the Mach angle* is 90°) at Mach 1, so it is a normal shock wave, perpendicular to the local airflow. The Mach angle would be 30° at Mach 2. When supersonic, a Mach cone is formed in 3-dimensional flow, yet another boundary over which a wave cannot pass (see picture above). At speeds above Mach 1, pressure disturbances from the aircraft will affect only the flow within the Mach cone. Where the cone touches the surface of the Earth, the sudden change in pressure creates a sonic boom (so the sonic boom moves over the Earth at the ground speed of the aircraft).

*The sine of the Mach angle is equal to $1/M$.

In two-dimensional flow, the Mach cone is replaced by a wedge, which is cut by Mach Lines.

If the wing leading edge is inside the Mach cone from the nose, the velocity of the component of airflow that is perpendicular to the leading edge is subsonic (a *subsonic leading edge*), which produces much less wave drag.

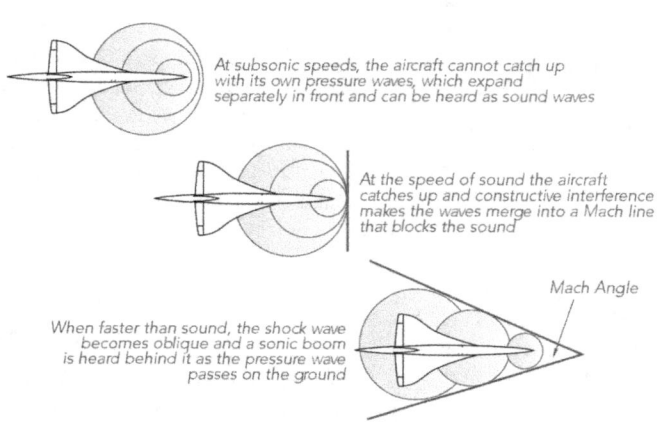

At subsonic speeds, the aircraft cannot catch up with its own pressure waves, which expand separately in front and can be heard as sound waves

At the speed of sound the aircraft catches up and constructive interference makes the waves merge into a Mach line that blocks the sound

When faster than sound, the shock wave becomes oblique and a sonic boom is heard behind it as the pressure wave passes on the ground

Mach Angle

PRINCIPLES OF FLIGHT
High Speed Flight

In this respect we must consider 3 speed ranges:

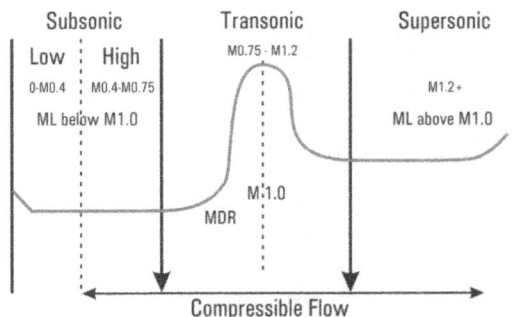

- **Subsonic flight**, up to about 0.75 Mach, or the critical Mach number (M_{CRIT}), which is the maximum airspeed at which all airflow is below the speed of sound and the air has time to get out of the way (it can also be defined as the Free Stream Mach number at which a local Mach number* reaches unity, or where compressibility effects first become apparent). M_{CRIT} actually marks the lower end of the band of Mach numbers where a local one (M_L) may be supersonic. It therefore marks the boundary between subsonic and transonic speeds. It follows that, the less the air is accelerated over the wing, the higher M_{CRIT} can be, which is done either with a lower camber or a higher sweep. M_{CRIT} for the Spitfire is around 0.9M. At M_{CRIT}, there are few, if any, shock waves, in a very small region, so there is no significant increase in drag, or changes in performance or handling, so M_{CRIT} is really of academic interest to pilots.

*The air will be accelerated at different rates over the aircraft. There will also be local temperature changes. Both effects combine to produce local Mach numbers (M_L) which will be higher or lower than, or even the same as, the Free Stream Mach number (M_{FS}).

M_{CRIT} can be increased by using thin, sweptback aerofoils and area ruling, or reducing weight.

- **Transonic flight** lies between M_{CRIT} - 1.2M, where some airflow is subsonic and some is supersonic. This is not a good place to be as things are unpredictable - ailerons are less effective here simply because their overall effect is small anyway.
- **Supersonic** is between 1.2-5M, where all airflow around the aircraft is above the speed of sound.
- **Hypersonic** speed is greater than Mach 5. Friction ionises the air molecules so they interfere with radio traffic, which is why contact is lost with spacecraft when they re-enter the atmosphere.

The *Critical Drag Rise Mach Number* is the speed at which there is a significant rise in drag from the formation of shockwaves, that are in turn due to flow separation, a type of form drag. It is also called the *Drag Divergence Mach Number*. For most aerofoils, its value is higher than M_{CRIT} by 5 - 10%, so it is a transonic effect, and it is also increased by sweepback. The drag coefficient can rise to more than 10 times its low speed value, generally peaking at Mach 1.

The Aerofoil

Small disturbances simply create Mach waves, which are associated with small bodies. However, aircraft are large enough to create shock waves, through which changes are much more severe. Air passing through either of them experiences an increase in temperature and pressure* and a decrease in velocity. The only difference is in magnitude.

*Decreasing pressure is associated with expansion waves, which are generally found between shock waves.

The density, pressure and temperature in front of an expansion wave are higher than they are behind. When air is passing through an expansion wave, the local speed of sound decreases, the Mach number increases and static temperature decreases.

SHOCK WAVES

In supersonic flow, unlike subsonic flow, the upper and lower surfaces of an aerofoil are essentially isolated from each other and make their own contributions to the total lift created (with subsonic aerofoils, the two surfaces combine as a whole). When an aerofoil finally reaches the speed of sound, a **shock wave** forms where the flow decelerates to subsonic speed due to the pressure waves that are moving forward from the trailing edge.

Shock waves therefore form where the two airflows meet.

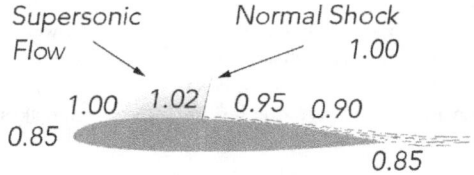

Flight At M 0.85

A shock wave is a sudden discontinuity in airflow at which there is a considerable (and instantaneous) increase in density, pressure and temperature that causes an equally sudden decrease in velocity that makes the boundary layer separate and become turbulent, creating a large reduction in lift directly behind the wave. In other words, the airflow gets warmer and denser at the same time - passing air through a shockwave makes it behave as if it were inside a container that suddenly shrinks in volume. Where the supersonic flow is forced to decelerate to subsonic speed, the air is compressed instantaneously until its pressure is equal to that immediately behind the shockwave. As its volume decreases, its density must increase, along with its temperature, due to the sudden compression.

The turbulence also causes buffeting, and the increased temperature causes the local speed of sound to increase. This, plus the reduced velocity, can cause the Mach number to decrease. Because the compression is very sudden, some pressure energy is converted into heat, so total pressure also decreases. A *shock stall* comes from separation of the boundary layer behind the shock wave, during which the angle of attack may have the lowest value of any type of stall. Shock stall occurs when the lift coefficient, as a function of Mach number, reaches its maximum value.

Because the compression is very sudden, some pressure energy is converted into heat, so total pressure decreases.

As the energy required for all this comes from the forward movement of the aircraft, it is a (wave) drag penalty.

It's like deploying air brakes - there is a marked increase in (wave) drag because the size of the disturbed wake has increased. This is similar to a low speed stall, except that the angle of attack is small and the speed is high, instead of the other way round. This is called a Mach stall, or Mach Tuck (see below).

It is called a normal shock wave because it is normal to the aerofoil surface, namely at 90° (perpendicular to the local airflow), and it first appears at the point of maximum velocity. Separation occurs close behind it.

As the Mach number gets higher, it will move further downstream, to the trailing edge.

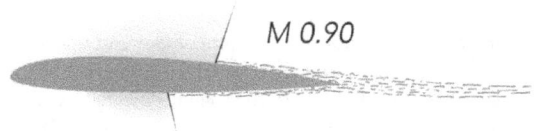

The least energy loss through a normal shock wave is just above Mach 1. The pressure and velocity distribution over the wing behind the wave creates significant variations in local values of lift and drag, which alter the pitching moment on the wing and the trim of the aircraft. The controls may also be affected.

The lower surface shock wave forms later because the lower camber is less, but this means that it is more forward than the upper one. The centre of pressure moves aft, and the resulting pitching moment only increases the aerofoil's speed and makes things worse.

On a typical transonic aerofoil, the rearward shift occurs at around M0.89 - M0.98.

The drag from the normal shockwaves goes away when you go supersonic, but you also get two shock waves. One is a bow wave ahead of the wing (which appears at Mach 1), so form drag now involves high pressure in front rather than low pressure behind, as with subsonic flight.

The other wave is a trailing oblique shock wave at the rear. This would be from the normal shock waves that formed in transonic flight moving back to the trailing edge to create some wave drag* but, as it does not affect the boundary layer, there is no form drag. That comes from the bow wave** in front, which is the main drag problem in supersonic flight.

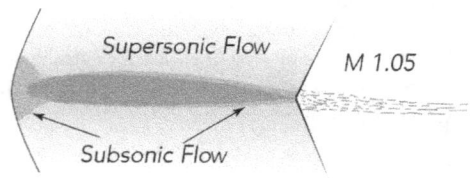

*Subsonic speeds produce minimum wave drag, which is reduced with vortex generators.

*If there is a radius at the leading edge of a wing, the shock wave at the front will detach, leaving a small area of subsonic flow between the wave and the leading edge. The speed of sound is locally higher from the increase in compressibility and temperature. M_{DET} is the M_{FS} at which there is only a small movement of the bow wave with increasing speed. The separation occurs because a portion of the boundary layer remains subsonic and gets thicker. It is the upper limit of the transonic speed range.

The changes through oblique shock waves are much less, because the air passes through at an angle.

 Oblique shockwaves slow down the air passing through them, but not down to subsonic speed, as through a normal shockwave. The airflow behind an oblique shockwave is supersonic (the airflow at right angles to it, however, is subsonic).

The front of a shock wave moves across the Earth's surface at the ground speed of the aeroplane.

In summary:

- A shock wave on the upper surface moves the centre of pressure aft.
- A shock wave at the root of the wing means a loss of lift at the front of a swept wing.
- A shock wave reduces downwash at the tail.

All three effects will make the nose pitch down, so the machine get more unstable as the Mach number increases.

CONTROLS

When deflected, the conventional hinged flap type of control surface should create an aerodynamic force ahead of the control that is usually greater than that produced by the control surface itself. When a shock wave is established on the lifting surface ahead of the control surface, the pressure variations cannot be transmitted forward through the shock wave. As a result, the effect of control surface is reduced, as only the flow over it is modified. The effectiveness of the control is even further reduced when the shock wave is established at the trailing edge.

This has led to the replacement of the tailplane and elevator configuration with the all-moving horizontal stabiliser in high-speed aircraft. When the shock wave is actually on the control surface, its deflection will cause the wave to move, with consequent large alterations of the position and magnitude of the aerodynamic forces acting on the control. This may result in high frequency vibration of the control surfaces, which is known as *control buzz*.

MACH TUCK

At transonic speeds (above the critical Mach number) Mach Tuck (or *tuck under*, or *jet upset*) occurs when the C of P moves so far back as speed is increased that the nose pitches down, to increase speed and move it further back, and so on, until you end up in a steep dive that you can't get out of (the reduced download from the tail due to flow separation doesn't help).

In fact, the C of P moves rapidly fore and aft on the wings, which means large changes in the aerodynamic force generated by the horizontal stabiliser. In large aircraft, this could create major structural stresses.

The Mach trim system is designed to minimise the adverse effects of changes in the position of the centre of pressure. It prevents tuck under by continually deflecting the horizontal stabiliser slightly more than is needed to maintain longitudinal stability and allow M_{MO} to increase, to take advantage of favourable drag figures. It also helps with confusing control problems as the speed gets really high, when the nose-down tendency means not pushing the control column forward, but pulling it back. There is enough of an input in the other direction to still give a progressive increase in push force as Mach number is increased. In other words, the Mach trimmer corrects the change in stick force stability of a swept wing aeroplane above a certain Mach number, or for insufficient stick force velocity at high Mach numbers.

If the Mach trimmer fails, the Mach number must be limited.

SUPERCRITICAL WING

The purpose of the supercritical wing is to delay the formation of the shockwave and to achieve higher *subsonic* speeds by using a relatively thick wing, with a **larger nose radius**. As it happens, supercritical wings will develop no noticeable shock waves even when just above M_{CRIT}.

The idea is not to increase the value of M_{CRIT}, but to increase the *increment* between M_{CRIT} and M_{DD}, so M_{DD} is increased with a top surface that is **relatively flat** (less acceleration). The underside is bulged and the trailing edge is often downturned (i.e. an extreme positive camber for the rear 30%), to recover some of the lost lift from the upper surface (it also stabilises the flow and reduces drag from separation at the trailing edge). There is therefore a more gentle lift over a wider band than standard wings.

Maintaining the thickness/chord ratio while changing to a supercritical wing section will increase the range.

Although the design of a supercritical wing means that is can be made deeper, there are practical limits to how thin a wing can be - you have to get the fuel and landing gear in, and there are structural problems, too, so........

SWEEPBACK

If the leading edge of the wing is very sharp, the bow wave can attach to it and get rid of the subsonic high pressure area in front. This happens at the *Detachment Mach Number* (M_{DET}), above which there is only a small movement with an increase in speed (and above which all local Mach numbers are supersonic). The shock wave sitting on the trailing edge may also affect the flying controls - the ailerons can freeze, as found by Spitfire pilots who put their machines into high speed dives.

Anyhow, in the case of a thin wing (like the double wedge shape below), lift is created from the higher pressure underneath the first part of the wing and the lower pressure over the upper surface of the rear half.

The pressure distribution is rectangular. The leading edge is more pointed, its profile is nearly symmetrical and its point of maximum camber is further back, often up to 50% of chord, over which the airflow is speeded up relatively gradually. The pressure distribution is also more even, but nothing comes for free. Any irregularity in the surface (dust, etc.) will move the transition point to that part, so manufacturing and maintenance tolerances must be that much greater. If you can suck the boundary layer into the wing near the trailing edge, you can use a thicker aerofoil. You could also use part of the (jet) engine exhaust to blow it away.

The air has enough momentum to flow past the bend in the middle safely. If an aeroplane accelerates to supersonic speeds, the centre of pressure and aerodynamic centre move to the mid chord position, making the distance from the C of G longer. This increases longitudinal stability and explains why the controls get heavier. The Mach trim function is installed to minimise the adverse effects of such changes. Unfortunately, in subsonic flight, this creates a very high stalling speed for which you will need very long runways.

Unless, of course, you don't need to land again, so such wings are found on missiles, not transport aircraft. Another option is to sweep the wing.

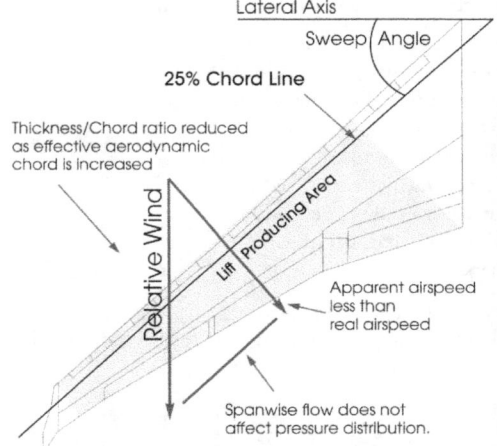

A swept wing is angled forward or aft from a right angle to the fuselage (usually aft, as shown below). There are two components to the airflow, one parallel to the wingspan (which is ignored as it has no chordwise velocity), and the other at right angles across the chord with a velocity slower than the free stream, whose size depends on the sweep angle*. For example, a 37° sweep produces a chordwise flow that is 80% of the free stream speed. 45° produces 71%, so the wing thinks it is flying slower. A 30° sweep will increase M_{CRIT} up to about M 0.75.

*Due to various effects, such as those in the boundary layer, the actual reduction of the chordwiise component is 50% of the theoretical value.

The amount of sweep depends on how fast you want to go. Subsonic aircraft at speeds less than 0.9 M need a sweep angle of between 25° - 30° along the quarter chord line. At twice the speed of sound, it should be more than 60°, but very thin, as found with the Lightning.

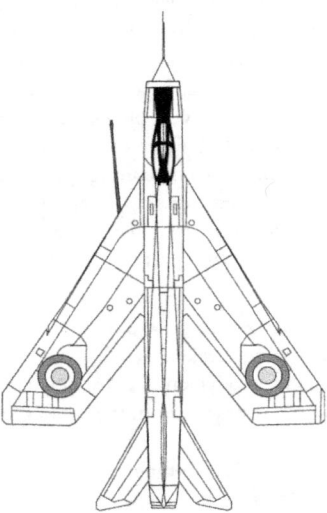

However, although they suffer from less drag and are less susceptible to turbulence, sweptback wings produce less lift (because not all of the surface is used), which means flying faster to compensate (or using Delta wings* to increase the area), which can be a problem when taking off and landing, hence the use of high lift devices, such as slats and slotted flaps.

*Delta wings, as used with Concorde, can use relatively short and straight spars, and tend to be thicker at the root. They were developed by German engineers during WWII, and come in two variations, according to their flow patterns. The older broad type was used by the Vulcan bomber, and is essentially a swept wing with a lot of taper.

Although they are designed to operate with attached flow for most flight conditions, separated conical-vortex flow will occur at high angles of attack.

Concorde has slender delta wings with very sharp leading edges that provoke separation even at the low angles of attack that are used in the cruise. There is also a warp that ensures that the vortices grow evenly along the leading edge*. In this way, tip stall does not occur, as the flow is already separated and stable.

*The curved leading edges create a shape called an *ogive*, rather than a true Delta. The shape of the ogive moves the C of P to the rear and reduces its variations in position with angle of attack and speed.

The flow over a delta wing with a low aspect ratio at low speeds consists of two vortices along the highly swept leading edges that trail downstream over the top of the wing. If the leading edge is sharp, the flow will separate along the whole length and curl into a primary vortex above the wing just inboard of the leading edge. There is a secondary vortex underneath. Both are strong and generally stable, creating a lower pressure above the wing than normal (the difference is called *vortex lift*). This allows lift to increase over a wider range of angles of attack, up to around 35°, hence the large nose high attitude on landing.

 As they are needed to allow subsonic aircraft to cruise at higher Mach numbers, swept wings are only an advantage in the transonic range (they are the least sensitive to turbulence). There is little advantage at sustained supersonic speeds (not quick dashes as you might get with a fighter) because you need the lowest possible thickness/chord ratios.

Lift is proportional to the component of velocity that is at right angles to the leading edge - i.e. TAS multiplied by the cosine of the sweep angle. The reduction in lift can also be compensated for with tapering, as shown above (although you could increase the speed as far as the wing is concerned, other parts of the aircraft might slow you down). There is also a tendency towards Dutch roll, discussed previously.

Swept wings can also reduce the effects of drag caused by the bow wave in supersonic flight, if the sweep is parallel to the shock wave (i.e. swept by at least the Mach angle, or 30° at Mach 2). In this way, you can use a subsonic aerofoil without a sharp leading edge at supersonic speeds, at the expense of Dutch roll effects and a large nose-high attitude for landing, due to a large stalling angle of attack.

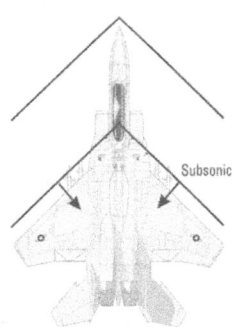

Speed Control

Turbine engines need careful handling to get the best results. Operating procedures must be memorised and the programming of the management systems must be exact so that everyone sees what they expect to see on the instruments, and the difference between normal and abnormal indications. While taxying, you must take care that nothing is sucked into them, obstacles are avoided and that you don't blow anything over.

PRINCIPLES OF FLIGHT
High Speed Flight

TAKEOFF

Takeoff power will set for either full or reduced power, which will improve engine life and reduces noise levels. For reduced power, you use an assumed temperature of the day and read off the power figures required when setting the parameters for the engine. You will be using the maximum TORA, TODA and EDA (see *Performance*) but there will still be enough room to stop if an engine fails before V_1*. A twin-spool engine in very cold conditions will be governed by the EPR and, in hot and high conditions, the exhaust temperature or HP RPM will be the limiting factor. Take off power is limited to 5 minutes, unless in an emergency.

*The speed at or beyond which takeoff can no longer be aborted.

THE CLIMB

After takeoff the undercarriage is raised and the aircraft climbs away under takeoff power, making due allowance for noise abatement. On some aircraft, the climb procedures are carried out with the vertical navigation facility from the FMS.

 If you use maximum continuous power (you may be hot and high), it is a much higher setting than climb power, with a lower time limit.

In the early stages of a climb, your flight path and speed are governed by performance regulations, so the fuel you use cannot be altered. With an engine out, commercial transport aeroplanes must climb initially at a minimum speed of V_2 until at least 400 feet above the aerodrome, which is the minimum flap retraction height. In this situation, with a problem, you would normally land back at the departure aerodrome or its alternate, after dumping fuel to get the landing weight down. Otherwise, with all engines operating, you would progress through V_2, V_3 and V_4 to flap retraction height, then reduce pitch for acceleration and climb. As flaps and slats are retracted, you would typically aim for V_{ZF} + 10 kts (Zero Flap speed) until 3,000 feet, then go for enroute climb speed.

Around M0.7 - M0.8, you change from a fixed IAS to a fixed Mach number, whereupon TAS and IAS start to reduce (this altitude may be selected by the company, and will be in the ops manual). For a fixed Mach number in level flight, IAS stays the same when moving into colder air, but TAS will decrease by around 1 kt per °C, and *vice versa*. As a fixed Mach number is a percentage value of the speed of sound, the TAS will follow the same rules - that is, it will increase and decrease in line with temperature, other things being equal. However, long range cruise uses a variable Mach number according to aircraft weight, so light weights mean a lower Mach number, and vice versa. If the temperature and flight level remain unchanged, Mach number (and TAS) will decrease as fuel burns off.

 Remember to keep a check on the engine instruments, especially with older aircraft. For example, the temperature normally drops in the climb and, with a twin spool, at least, the LP RPM will increase relative to the HP, to where it reaches its limits for the height and temperature concerned and the engine should be throttled back. This is because the LP governor is set for takeoff power and the LP RPM will be much higher than that expected in the climb.

At high subsonic speeds, the shock wave starts to change the shape of the power curve, at M_{CDR}. There is no effect on the climb as long as this is above V_Y but, with altitude, M_{CDR} decreases with EAS until it coincides with V_Y. You can continue the climb (if power is available) until EAS falls below V_X towards some sort of minimum control speed (and hold it until M_{MO}), but this is your absolute ceiling, or *coffin corner*, where stall speed and M_{CRIT} merge, and you cannot vary speed or altitude. V_Y is accepted as being equal to or greater than V_X.

THE CRUISE
MAXIMUM RANGE SPEED

This gives you the most lift for the least drag, for the most economy, and the most miles per gallon. The biggest factor concerning your range will be the wind, which will reduce your groundspeed when on the nose, causing you to use more fuel. However, a slight increase in airspeed, say 5-10%, will get you there sooner with only a slight effect on fuel consumption. A common rule of thumb is to increase your airspeed by half the headwind value.

MAXIMUM ENDURANCE SPEED

This gives you the most time in the air for least amount of fuel, which is useful when waiting for the weather to clear, or when asked to hold clear of a control zone but, in practice, it gives you little or no controllability, so there will be a recommended endurance speed in the flight manual, which is a few knots above the theoretical value. The endurance for a piston/propeller aeroplane is longer the lower you can fly (allowing for safety, of course) but, for a jet aeroplane, fly as high as is practicable. Turbulence and flaps will affect the speed considerably. There is more drag with endurance speed than there is with range speed, which is higher. Wind has no effect on endurance speeds.

LONG RANGE CRUISE

LRC is higher than maximum range speed, and is used as the standard speed for the cruise. Boeing and Airbus say that it is 4% faster than best range speed for 99% of the range. There are advantages (mainly commercial) for using it, the main one being money because, as well as fuel, you save time by flying the route faster (although this gives a slightly higher fuel burn, the cost of the airframe time is way higher). LRC is also a better speed in a headwind.

THE BUFFET ONSET BOUNDARY (BOB) CHART

As the idea is to get the fastest possible speed for the least possible drag, and fuel burn, jets are flown at high altitudes. Although this means thin air and less drag, the cruising speed will be much closer to stalling speed, sometimes as little as 10% away, as discussed below.

Buffet is vibration which, if excessive and prolonged, could cause structural damage and interfere with the control surfaces.

- The *low speed buffet*, which can be violent, means you are near the stall - the pre-stall buffet occurs at around 1.2 V_S, *increasing* with altitude.

- The *high speed buffet*, on the other hand (which may involve a complete loss of elevator control), occurs near the maximum speed from shock-induced separation.

Except for the low speed variety, there should be no perceptible buffet at any speed up to V_{MO}/M_{MO} (CS 25).

PRINCIPLES OF FLIGHT
High Speed Flight

At low altitudes, the low speed, high alpha stall speed remains constant but compressibility becomes significant higher up and C_{Lmax} reduces at speeds above about 0.4M. In fact, at sea level, the airframe will normally limit the airspeed before the high speed buffet is reached.

As altitude increases the following effects occur:

- With reducing temperature and LSS, a given Mach number leads to a reduced TAS and lower EAS.
- The EAS corresponding to the Mach number of onset of the high speed buffet/shock stall reduces with increasing altitude.
- As the EAS falls, the required C_L, and therefore angle of attack, increases. The airflow over the top wing surface speeds up to reduce the Mach number for buffet onset.

M_{MO} is the *Maximum Mach Operating Speed*. It is displayed by a self-adjusting red-and-white needle called a *barber pole*.

Put another way, V_{MO} and M_{MO} are the maximum IAS and Mach number that can be flown intentionally (V_{MO} should not be greater than V_C). They provide for normal strength and handling qualities. In some jets, you can exceed them in the climb without exceeding maximum continuous power. The speed range for the cruise is, therefore, between 1.2 V_S and V_{MO}/M_{MO}, which will decrease as altitude is increased, because the high speed buffet occurs at *lower* speeds with altitude.

When the buffets merge, or the speed range reduces to zero*, the aircraft is at its *aerodynamic ceiling*, which should not be confused with the service ceiling, as per power available. The high speed buffet is the more likely one to be experienced, as exceeding V_{MO}/M_{MO} is not uncommon (gusts, or emergency descents). Warnings will sound at around 10kts above V_{MO} or 0.01M above M_{MO}.

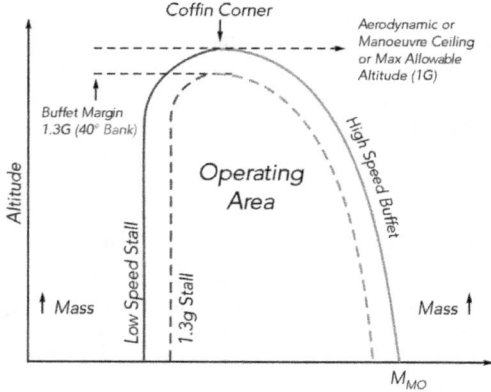

At the maximum cruising altitude, based on the 1.3g margin, a manoeuvre with a load factor of 1.3 will cause buffet onset. To increase the buffet margin, you would have to fly lower with the same Mach number.

*The margin between the speeds is called *coffin corner*, or the point at which, if you reduce speed, you stall and, if you increase speed, you get a *shock stall*, which comes from separation of the boundary layer behind the shock wave, during which type the angle of attack may have its smallest value. Shock stall occurs when the lift coefficient, as a function of Mach number, reaches its maximum value.

The margin is further reduced by g forces from turning and turbulence, and extra weight (the dotted lines in the picture below) and you will want to choose a level that gives you enough breathing space, typically within 5 knots of stalling or reaching M_{CRIT}. Reducing weight or altitude will help.

Coffin corner is an occupational hazard with high speed subsonic flight, although the Challenger 350 can do steep turns at FL 450 because it doesn't have one. The TAS increases with altitude and could be in the region of 350 kts at 40 000 feet (as opposed to around 150 kts at sea level). At the same time, the critical Mach number might be 0.9, or 500 kts, give or take. The aircraft must be flown between these two speeds because turbulence or harsh manoeuvres will increase the stall speed and reduce M_{CRIT}. As dynamic stability is reduced and damping is diminished, the aeroplane is less stable and any control movements used for recovery must be made **slowly and smoothly**. This means *gentle* turns (within 25° of bank) to maintain safety margins. This is not so bad in good weather (except for CAT) but, in bad weather, turbulence will require correction which is more difficult as altitude increases. Limiting the wing loading is the only practical way to reduce the stall speed (although the maximum limit is fixed for all weights, the lower limit increases as weight is increased, so the range of speeds available for normal operations increases as the weight reduces with fuel burn). If you were to pull up suddenly in between a set of Mach number boundaries, the lower one will increase and the upper one will decrease.

The margin between the speeds is called the speed margin, and for each speed along this scale, there is a Manoeuvre Margin expressed in Load Factor and Bank Angle.

ATC often ask you to reduce to minimum speed, so you need to know the minimum load factor and bank angle that can be accepted. A load factor of 1.4g is one suggestion for good weather and 1.5g for bad weather.

Knowing the minimum load factor (bank angle), you can enter any manoeuvre capability curve to find out the corresponding speed.

The Buffet Onset Boundary (BOB) chart provides yet another envelope within which it is safe to operate in the cruise. It indicates the Mach numbers for the onset of the low speed and high speed (Mach) buffets for various altitudes and weights (masses), but C of G position, bank angles and load factors may also be considered.

For any given weight, C of G position and airspeed, the maximum operating altitude is that at which you can achieve a positive normal acceleration increment of 0.3g without exceeding the buffet onset boundary. The chart overleaf is drawn for 1.3g.

The general rule is, the bigger the load factor, the better the manoeuvre margin. At any given weight and speed (Mach number), the higher the altitude, the lower is the load factor and the narrower is the manoeuvre margin.

Examples

1. Using the chart overleaf, and given:

   Airspeed: M0.72
   Altitude: 35,000 ft
   Gross weight: 50,000 kg
   C of G:10% MAC

   To find the 1g low and high speed buffets, and manoeuvre margin to initial buffet (load factor & bank angle):

   - Enter the graph with the Mach number (A).
   - Move up to the altitude line (B).
   - Move across to the reference line (C).
   - Follow the %MAC line to 10% (D).
   - Move across to the weight line (E).
   - Move vertically down to find the load factor and bank angle for initial buffet, 1.47g and 47° of bank.
   - From E move down the weight line to point F.
   - Move to the altitude line (G) via the %MAC line.
   - Move down to speed scale to find 1g high speed buffet boundary of M0.814.
   - Move left to intercept the altitude line again (H) to find the 1g low speed buffet boundary of M0.54 (178 knots).

2. Using the chart, and given:

   1.3 g
   38 000 kg
   CG 25% MAC
   FL350

   Find the Low and high speed margins.

   - Enter the chart on the right hand side at 1.3g.
   - Go up to the mass line.
   - Go across to the MAC reference.
   - Go across to the FL slope and the two speeds will be found underneath each one:
     - Low Speed: M0.53
     - High Speed: M0.83

THE DESCENT

When descending above the tropopause, with a constant mass and Mach number, the coefficient of lift will decrease. As the temperature above the tropopause is assumed to be constant, so the Mach number, the speed of sound and the TAS will not change. However, the pressure is increasing, so the angle of attack must be reduced to maintain the same Mach number.

As the lift coefficient is a function of the angle of attack, it must reduce as well.

THE APPROACH

The range of acceleration for a gas turbine is in two sections, with a borderline at about 80%. Below this figure, acceleration is slow; above it, acceleration rates improve as you set the throttle higher. This is due to the relative inefficiency of the engine at low power settings, the inertia of the rotating assemblies, the FCU trying to stop the turbine inlet temperatures from exceeding their limitations, and the almost exponential increase in fuel flow at higher RPM settings. However, rapid acceleration will be required during a go-around - it is usual to set an approach RPM from which engine acceleration can be achieved quickly; especially if bleed air is being used for, say, anti-icing. Acceleration times are longer on a single spool engine as compared to those with a twin or triple spool.

A lower RPM is set when the landing is assured.

LANDING

Good landings result from being set up properly on the approach, which comes in turn from proper planning, as mentioned elsewhere - do not put yourself in the way of having to make abrupt control inputs on finals. For this reason, high descent rates (and speeds) should also be avoided. In any case, approaches are started way earlier than with piston-engined aircraft, because holding takes such a hit on the fuel consumption.

Normal procedure is to set things up so you cross an imaginary 15 m screen before the threshold at V_{REF}, then reduce to 1.15 V_{SO} on the roundout (not too late, Hoskins!) Hold the glideslope down to the flare, planning to touchdown at the ILS reference point at 1000 feet in. You need to keep the power on to prevent sink, and enough stabiliser trim to keep the elevator effective.

When over the threshold, flare, cut to idle, allow for drift and land firmly if the runway is wet (that is, drive it onto the ground to reduce the chance of hydroplaning). When down, relax the back pressure and allow the nosewheel to touch the runway smoothly. You should not need any more forward movement than that - according to the 757 Training Manual, large nose-down control column movements before the nosewheel touches the runway can mean pitch rates that cause structural damage, because the elevator still has enough strength to be dangerous (it's needed for go-arounds).

Anyhow, keep the ailerons level, and apply reverse thrust immediately on landing, where it is most effective (that is, at higher speeds). It also keeps the brakes cool for later. Shortly after touchdown, extend the spoilers, to reduce lift and increase drag, then use the brakes which are more effective anyway when the weight is being taken by the gear and the wheels have more contact with the runway.

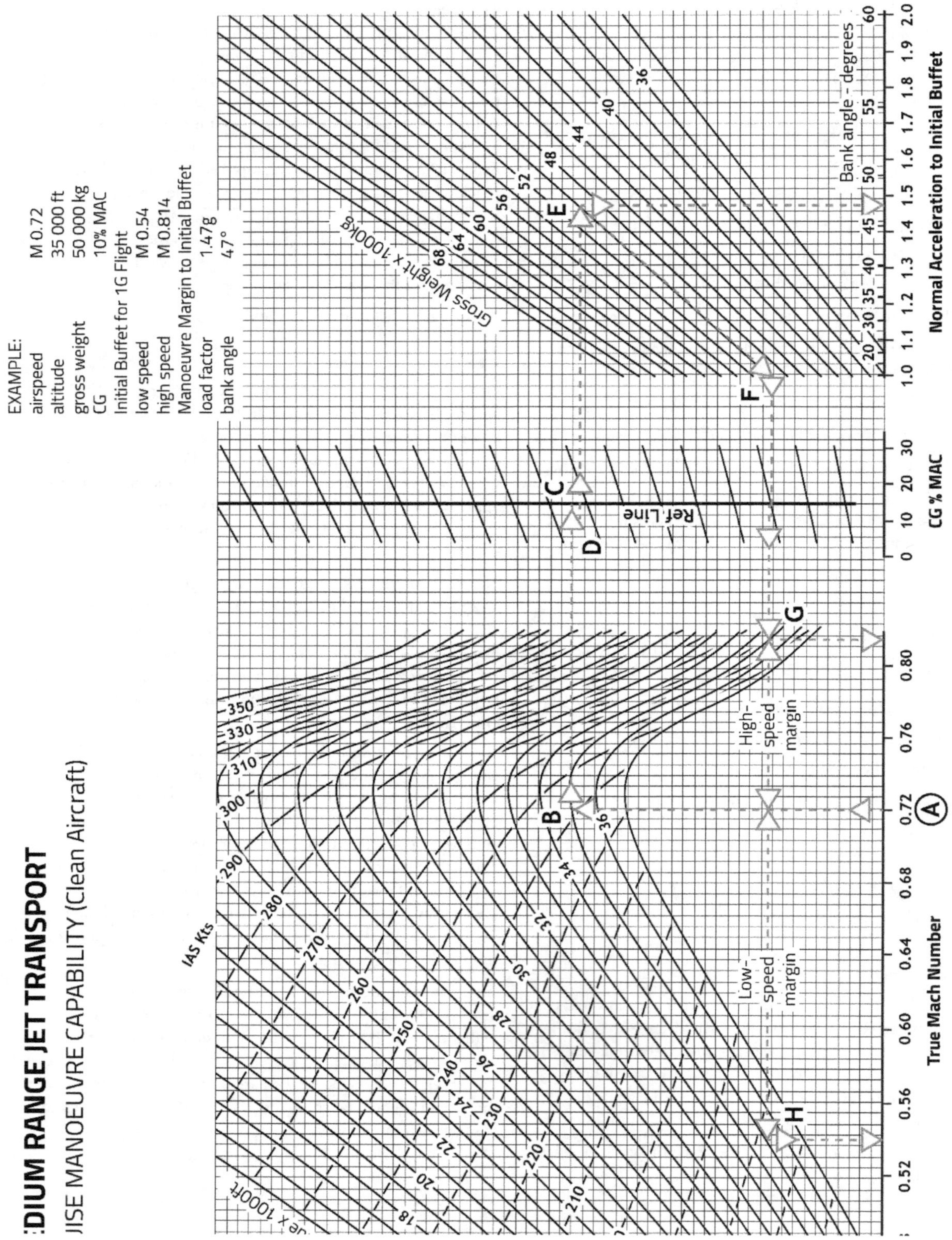

EDIUM RANGE JET TRANSPORT
UISE MANOEUVRE CAPABILITY (Clean Aircraft)
EXAMPLE:
airspeed M 0.72
altitude 35 000 ft
gross weight 50 000 kg
CG 10% MAC
Initial Buffet for 1G Flight
low speed M 0.54
high speed M 0.814
Manoeuvre Margin to Initial Buffet
load factor 1.47g
bank angle 47°
IAS Kts
Gross Weight x 1000kg
Ref Line
Low-speed margin
High-speed margin
Bank angle - degrees
True Mach Number
CG % MAC
Normal Acceleration to Initial Buffet

WAKE TURBULENCE

This is a by-product of lift behind every aircraft, (including helicopters) in forward flight, originating from induced drag. Wake turbulence is particularly severe from heavy machines, and worst at slow speeds, as found on takeoff or landing.

Combined with the wing-bound vortex (i.e. the virtual circulation), the trailing vortices create a horseshoe system, which is closed when the circuit is completed with the starting vortex that is formed and left behind just above the runway when the aircraft rotates on takeoff (you get more of these whenever there is an increase in wing circulation, such as with violent manoeuvres). You get *stopping vorticity* in the opposite sense whenever the "circulation" is reduced. Although these vortices eventually dampen down, they can persist for several minutes and create dangers for following aircraft. As mentioned previously, they are a significant factor in creating what most people call induced drag.

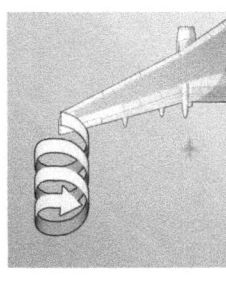

Wake vortices are horizontally concentrated whirlwinds streaming off the wingtips, from the separation point between high pressure below and low pressure above the wing. Air flowing over the top of the wing tends to flow inward due to the reduced pressure sucking it in, while that under the wing tends to flow outwards because it is of higher pressure and pushes outwards.

Where the lower air curls over the wingtip, it combines with the upper air to form a clockwise flow (on the left wing - on the right it is counter clockwise).

Wake generation begins when the nosewheel lifts off (i.e. as lift is generated) on takeoff and continues until it touches down again after landing. Vortices (one from each wing) drift downwind, at about 400-500 fpm for larger aircraft, levelling out at about 900 feet below the altitude at which they were generated. Eventually they expand to occupy an oval area about 1 wingspan high and 2 wide, one on each side of the aircraft. The distance between them will be about ¾ of the wingspan or rotor disc:

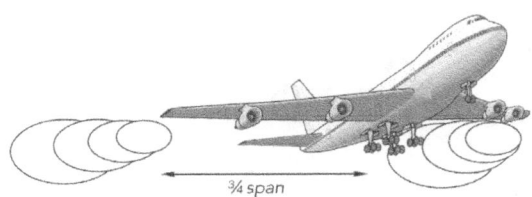

Heavy, slow aeroplanes produce the most severe vortices. Flaps, etc. have little effect in breaking them up, so even clean aircraft are dangerous*. Inside a vortex core, you could get roll rates as much as 80° per second and downdraughts of over 1500 feet per minute, so avoid them. The effects become undetectable after a time, varying from a few seconds to a few minutes after their production, although they have been detected 20 minutes later. Vortices are most hazardous to other aircraft during takeoff, initial climb, final approach and landing, but you should be careful within 1,000 feet below and behind a heavy aircraft.

*The worst combination is *heavy*, *clean* and *slow*.

Those from large aircraft tend to move away from one another so, on a calm day, the runway itself will remain free, depending on how near the runway edge the offending wings were. They will also drift with wind, so your landings and takeoffs will be upwind of moving heavy aircraft, before the point of takeoff and after that of landing. A crosswind will increase the movement of the downwind vortex and decrease that of the upwind one. A light wind of 3-7 knots could mean the upwind one actually stays in the touchdown zone and the downwind one moves to another runway. As a tailwind can also move the vortices of previous aircraft into the touchdown zone, a light quartering tailwind is the most dangerous hazard.

Although there is a danger of shockloading, the biggest problem is loss of control near the ground. It is safest above the approach and takeoff path of the other aircraft, or when landing beyond its touchdown point (or lifting off before its takeoff point) but, for general purposes, allow **at least 3 minutes** behind any greater than the Light category (especially widebodies) for the effects to disappear (but see the table below).

Aircraft are grouped as follows:

Category	ICAO & Flt Plan (kg)	UK
Heavy (H)*	136,000 or more	136,000 or more
Medium (M)	7,000-136,000	40,000-136,000
Small (S)	Not ICAO	17,000-40,000
Light (L)	7,000 or less	17,000 or less

Windshear

Windshear is caused by variations in the direction and/or speed of the local wind over height and/or horizontal distance. In abnormal circumstances it can be very dangerous by displacing an aeroplane abruptly from its intended flight path enough that substantial control input is required (see also *Meteorology*).

An aircraft encountering windshear can maintain its speed over the ground because of its momentum (the larger the aircraft, the easier this is), although a change in the wind component will, in the short term, change the airspeed, rather than the groundspeed.

If the windshear comes from a reduction in headwind component (or an increase in the tailwind component) this is an energy loss and will result in a reduction in IAS. Lift is therefor reduced and the aircraft will, if not corrected, lose height or increase its rate of descent or decrease its rate of climb. It is a common phenomenon in mountainous areas, or near thunderstorms. In these circumstances, engine reaction time is a critical factor.

On the other hand, an increase in headwind component (or a decrease in tailwind component) is an energy gain and provides an increase in IAS.

Such variations are more serious when close to the ground during an approach or shortly after takeoff.

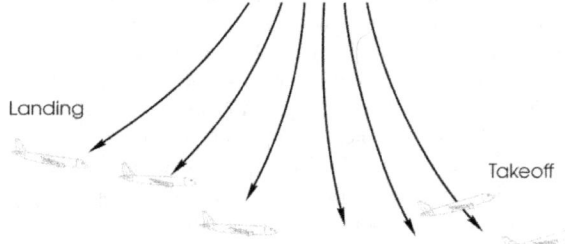

Good indications of potential windshear are windsocks or plumes of smoke pointing in opposite directions, or reports of differing wind velocities around an airfield.

Virga (precipitation that evaporates before it reaches the ground) is also a good visual sign for......

DOWNDRAUGHT

When landing near a thunderstorm, and flying through a gust front into the cold air coming out of the base of the storm (the left side of the picture above), the airspeed increases, but the groundspeed remains constant, because of inertia. This will result in a **short-term** performance increase and a gain in altitude (the second aircraft from the left). If you reduce power to cope with it, you will end up like the third aircraft.

When taking off near a thunderstorm, and the headwind component decreases sharply and/or becomes a tailwind component (an energy loss), the groundspeed remains constant (inertia again) but the airspeed decreases sharply, with an equally sharp loss of lift.

ACTIONS TO BE TAKEN

One tactic is to increase airspeed on the approach (if the runway is long enough to cope). If the loss of airspeed is unexpected, the recommended actions are:

- Increase power rapidly (full go-around if needed).
- Raise the nose to check the descent.
- Coordinate power and pitch.
- Be prepared to carry out a missed approach.

For downbursts near thunderstorms:

- Use maximum power as soon as possible.
- Adopt a pitch angle of about 15° and hold it. Do not chase airspeed.

Refer to the stick shaker when holding or increasing pitch attitude, easing the back pressure as required to obtain and hold a slightly lower attitude.

"The pilot who masters the simple engineering principles of his aircraft, who understands the why behind the reaction - immediately elevates himself to a new level of competence and safety"

SYSTEMS

The motive power for the systems used to operate an aircraft comes mostly from the engine (with independent backup), and they may work singly, or in combination, frequently with one type of system controlling another (electric switches controlling hydraulic rams, for example). It is important to know which way any system goes when it fails - that is, does it fail open or fail closed?

A basic system of whatever type (which needs to be a closed loop) will consist of a *reservoir* (such as a fuel tank or a battery) to contain whatever flows around it and ensure that the delivery is constant and consistent, with no highs, lows, or shocks.

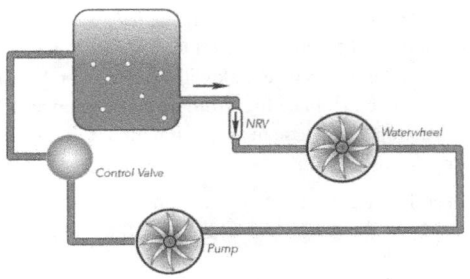

In the very basic system shown above, the fluid leaves the reservoir under the power of potential energy (the height of the fluid), to power the water wheel and whatever might be attached to it. Meanwhile, the pump takes the used fluid and pumps it back to the reservoir. A strong enough pump could run the whole system.

To keep things clean there may be a filter, and some sort of bypass in case things get clogged. There are two variables in any system - the amount of stuff in it and its pressure. You can use a small amount at high pressure or a larger amount at a lower one.

Whatever system is involved, as pilots, we are more interested in how power flows through the system rather than the details.

Picture Below: Typical Fuel Tank Arrangement

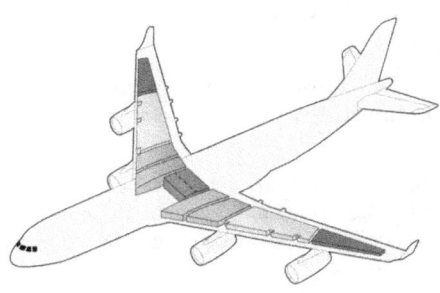

FUEL SUPPLY

The purpose of the fuel system is to deliver clean fuel to the engine. The simplest way is to use gravity feed, which needs the fuel cells to be above the engine to work properly, thus providing potential energy.

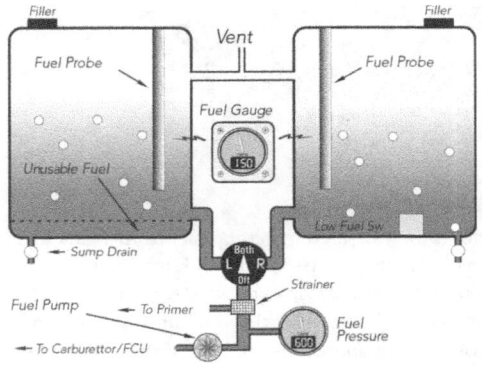

Modern requirements, however, mean that fuel cells are in all manner of strange places, and come in many different shapes and sizes (together with a C of G system all of their own). Typically, they are in the wing, and are not always a tank - instead, the wing can be sealed so it can contain fuel, with the ribs and spars inside also acting as baffles (this is known as a *wet wing* system). **Integral** fuel tanks are part of the aircraft structure which are sealed during manufacture to provide a tank, typically used in the wing centre section of smaller aircraft. This saves weight and space. In large aircraft, the wing torque box is sealed and compartmented to contain fuel. A fuel-tight seal is achieved with a sealant between mating surfaces and a fuel proof coating over the interior. In light aircraft often only the wing centre section is used as an integral fuel tank, many do not incorporate them at all.

Provision is made for draining off fuel and/or water from the lowest point in the tank, in the form of a sump drain.

Fuel tanks are generally not heated on transport aircraft.

SYSTEMS
Fuel Supply

Flexible tanks are tailored to fit into an available space in a wing or fuselage. They are made from reinforced rubber or plastic sheeting and are attached by cords or buttons to the structure around the tank bay. Wing fuel tanks in light aircraft are often flexible types.

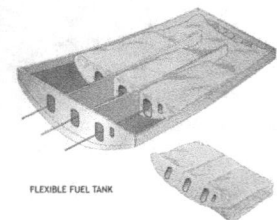

Rigid tanks can be used for extra storage in the fuselage or, in military aircraft, carried externally. They are generally made of aluminium alloy.

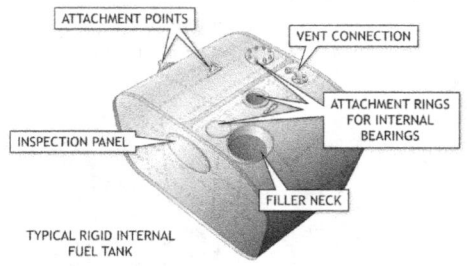

Fuel Transfer

Various methods may be used to get the fuel from a tank to an engine, all involving fuel pumps and filters. Each engine will have its own pump, but there may also be a *boost pump*, in the tank, to pressurise the fuel slightly and prevent vapour locks, as some lines may pass through unpressurised parts of the aircraft. Boost pumps are lubricated by the fuel they work on, so don't run them dry or you will burn them out. Those in transport aircraft are supplied with 115V AC and typically operate at pressures between 20-50 psi.

Fuel tanks are vented to atmosphere, to prevent a vacuum forming inside the tanks as the fuel level is reduced (and to stop the tank from collapsing). They also prevent excess pressure forming inside the tanks.

The vents might be in the fuel cap, or be an overflow pipe in the tank or, on large aircraft, through air intakes underneath the wing. If the gauge reads more than it should, there's too much venting - you've likely left the fuel cap off! Under CS 23 & 25, 2% of the total space in each tank is required for venting.

Fuel systems are typically designed as left and right halves so that contamination on one side does not spread to the other, although you are still able to transfer (crossfeed) to opposite engines in an emergency, or for trim purposes.

At high all-up weights in a swept wing aircraft, for example, there is structural benefit in concentrating the weight in the outer wings to reduce the bending moment from high wing loads. As fuel is used, however, the C of G will shift.

If all the usable fuel in the wing tanks is burned off, the landing weight distribution will be wrong.

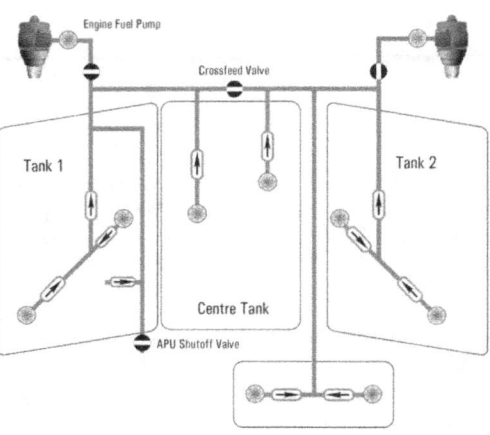

Fuel management systems are usually automatic*, with the option of a crossfeed if an engine fails. Due to Zero Fuel Mass considerations, fuel in the centre tank will be used first. Swept wing aircraft, however, can use fuel from all tanks at once to prevent the aircraft getting nose heavy, as it would if the tip tanks were used first.

*Special procedures are used for fuel consumption in flight to minimise g loads on the wings and to preserve the fuel in the main tanks for landing.

Direct feed from a tank to its own engine is normally used for takeoff. When established in the climb, the centre tank is usually selected, backed up by booster pumps in the inboard wing tanks, with the outboard booster pumps off.

The centre pumps have a higher output pressure than those in the wing tanks, so the flow from the centre tank will have priority. With the inter-engine valves open, all engines will be fed from it. When the centre tank is empty, the inboard pumps will continue to supply all engines, and the centre pumps can be turned off. A tank pump low pressure warning light illuminates for each pump when the tank is empty.

When the amount of fuel in the inboard tanks is the same as that in the outboard tanks, the outboard booster pumps are turned on and the inter-engine valves closed. The system is now configured for tank-to-engine feed for the remainder of the flight, unless uneven fuel burn or an engine failure results in a fuel load imbalance.

The crossfeed is used to transfer fuel if this occurs, or to feed an engine from other than its own tank. The crossfeed would be open with an engine out.

The booster pumps are at the low point of the fuel tanks, one forward, one aft. During takeoff and climb, the aft pumps are used. During a descent with a low fuel quantity, the rear pump inlets may be uncovered, so the forward pumps should be used. However, for a go-around with low fuel, the aft pumps should be used, as acceleration and climb may uncover the forward pump inlets.

The pressure of a low pressure fuel pump is measured with an aneroid capsule.

Picture Below: Twin fuel control panel set for crossfeed

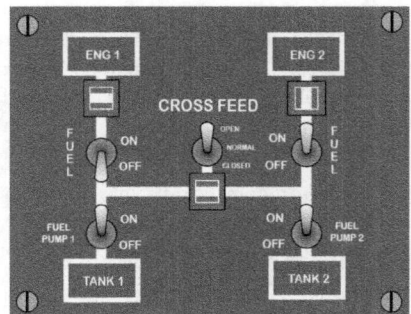

Fuel flow is measured out after the high pressure valve.

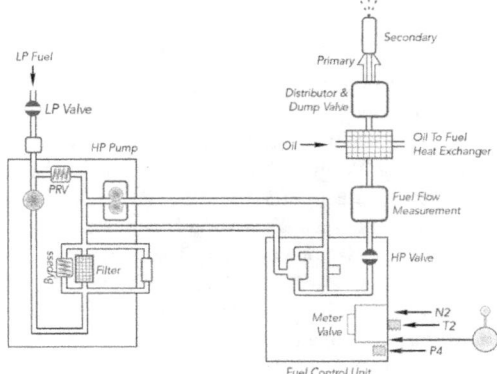

Picture Below: 737 Fuel System

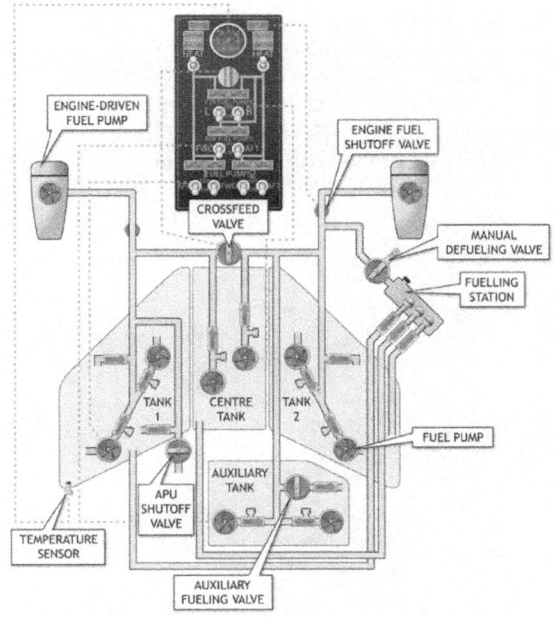

Jet engines typically burn up to five times more fuel at takeoff power than in the cruise at high altitude. To cope with peak demands, a **collector bay** (or a **header tank**, same thing) collects the input from several wing tanks to ensure an uninterrupted supply as the aircraft moves around in flight or when changing tanks - it acts like a relay tank.

Surge tanks near wingtips also control fuel movement. They are made in the same way as integral tanks are, and form part of the venting system. They are normally empty and are designed to collect fuel from the vent lines and return it to the tanks, especially during refuelling to full tank loads. Some vent surge tanks include a pump.

A **feed box** in a fuel tank increases the fuel level at the location of the boost pumps. **Clack valves** live in the baffles in fuel tanks - they work like a cat flap to allow fuel to drain to the centre tanks. **Flapper valves** are spring-loaded doors that stop reverse movement of fuel back to the main tanks from the collector bay. Baffle check valves stop fuel flowing to the wingtip.

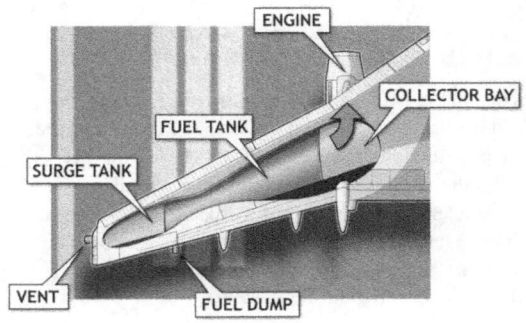

Fuel Heating

Fuel should be heated before it passes through the low pressure filters, to ensure that any droplets of water in suspension fuel do not enter the filters as ice and cause a blockage. Solid, wax-like particles begin to form in kerosene (Jet A) at temperatures below -40°C. They can also clog fuel filters, and heating the fuel prevents this.

Fuel can be heated as it passes through heat exchangers that transfer heat from engine oil to the fuel, but compressor bleed air from the engine can also be used. Both are usually thermostatically controlled, maintaining the fuel temperature within pre-set limits above 0°C, although manual control is possible.

Manually controlled systems include a warning lamp, activated by a pressure differential switch in the fuel filter. If the flow through the filter is restricted by ice or wax, the differential pressure across it increases until it is enough to operate the icing warning lamp. The heat exchanger valve is then opened to admit hot compressor bleed air until the fuel temperature gauge reaches a limiting value.

Refuelling

Refuelling is carried out with the overwing method or pressure refuelling. The former involves placing the fuel nozzle into the opening in the top of the tank. The fuel is then transferred under low pressure from the bowser to the tank. However, pressure refuelling is used on most jet transport aircraft. With it, fuel under pressure and at a high flow rate is transferred from the bowser or dispenser via a coupling at a refuelling centre under one wing. The panel may contain valve selection switches and tank gauges so that you can control the process from one place. When a tank becomes full, a float operated shut off valve is closed by the rising fuel level.

Pressure refuelling takes place at around 50 psi. It is used so that fuel caps can remain closed when it's raining, and the fuel pumps can remain idle when auxiliary tanks are filled. An automatic shut off valve can also be used to prevent overfilling, but the equipment does add an extra 100 lbs or so to the weight of a typical small jet.

A volumetric topoff valve is a fuel level switch that switches off the refuel valve at the right moment, using float switches.

FUEL ZONES

These should be established before fuelling starts. They should extend at least 6 m (20 feet) radially from the filling and venting points on the aircraft and fuelling equipment. Within this zone, smoking, use of naked lights and operation of non-approved switches should be forbidden.

Unless fuelling takes place in a designated area, No Smoking signs should be displayed at least 15 metres (50 feet) from the fuelling equipment and tank vents. APUs with an exhaust discharge into the zone should, if needed during fuelling, be started before filler caps are removed. If fuelling stops, the APU should not be restarted until it has stopped. GPUs should be located as far as practical from the aircraft and should not be connected or disconnected during fuelling.

Fire extinguishers should be readily accessible and preferably be CO_2 and/or BCF.

 Fuelling with passengers embarking or disembarking (or even on board) is not allowed when fuelling with AVGAS, or with wide-cut fuel with no static dissipator, or in any aircraft with less than 20 seats, especially with engines running.

Precautions

The aircraft should be connected to an effective earthing point and the fuelling equipment. After fuelling, bonding wires should not be removed until the filler caps have been refitted or the pressure fuelling hose disconnected.

When overwing fuelling, the hose nozzle should be bonded to the aircraft structure before removing the tank filler cap. When pressure fuelling, the fuel tank pressure relief valves should, if possible, be checked for correct operation and the bonding lead on the nozzle should be connected to the receptacle next to the fuelling point, *before* connecting the nozzle.

SPECIAL PRECAUTIONS

Aircraft should not be fuelled within 30 m (100 feet) of radar equipment, under test or in use, in aircraft or ground installations. When any part of a landing gear appears to be overheated, the fire service should be called and fuelling should not take place until the heat has dissipated. Extreme caution should be exercised during electrical storms. Fuelling should be suspended during severe electrical disturbances near aerodromes.

Photographic flash bulbs and electronic flash equipment should not be used.

When a loading bridge is used for an aircraft fitted with automatic inflatable chutes, those at the rear doors should be manned and prepared for use as an emergency escape route by a cabin attendant. Where slide actuation requires the manual fitting of an attachment to the aircraft e.g. a girt bar, the slide should be engaged throughout the fuelling process. When a loading bridge is not available, one set of steps should be at the (opened) main passenger door normally used for passengers.

If your aircraft does not have automatic inflatable chutes, and when a loading bridge is in use, one set of steps should be at another opened main passenger door and preferably at the other end of the aircraft. When a loading bridge is not available, passenger steps should be at two of the main passenger doors (preferably one forward and one aft) which must be open (integral stairways may be used).

Fuel Jettison

These systems allow you to dump fuel when the aircraft is heavier than its permissible landing weight, as may happen after takeoff. They are required for all transport category aircraft where the Maximum Takeoff Weight is significantly higher than the Maximum Landing Weight, unless it has been shown that they can meet a climb gradient of 3.2% at MTOW less the fuel for a 15-minute circuit between takeoff and landing again, or where the landing weight is not a problem. That is, the system must be able to bring you down to landing weight within 15 minutes (from MTOM to MLM at a typical rate of 3-4 tonnes/minute). Fuel jettisoning is permitted to an extent consistent with reaching the aerodrome with the required fuel reserves, if a safe procedure is used. Typically, however, the pump that draws fuel from a standpipe in the tank is used for jettisoning. This ensures that a specified quantity of fuel remains in the tanks. It is not a good idea to dump fuel near thunderstorms, however, or in turbulence (aircraft with underwing engines do it with flaps up). The *No Smoking* light should be on and passengers briefed and radio silence observed as much as possible, especially with HF. Dumping should be done either over the sea or above 10,000 feet agl, but it is an emergency procedure, so these should not be too rigidly observed - exceptionally, you can do it over 7,000 feet agl in Winter and 4,000 in Summer.

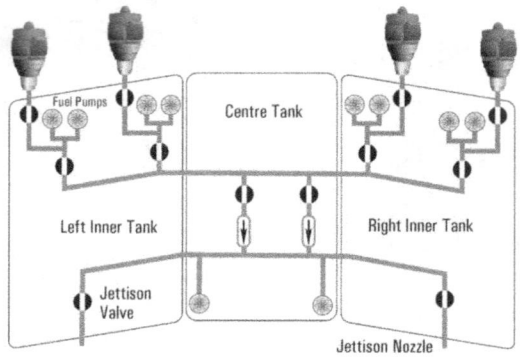

After jettisoning fuel, you must be able to climb to 10 000 feet and fly at maximum range speed for 45 minutes.

If time permits:
- Inform ATC.
- Avoid areas of static/cloud.
- Do not fly in circles or turn down wind.
- Be at a safe altitude and speed.
- Clean aircraft configuration.
- No smoking.
- Non-essential electrical equipment - off.
- No HF radios on.
- Use a designated dumping area.
- Ensure positive fuel feed to the engines.

Fuel System Monitoring

The fuel system must be properly managed in order to maintain a proper supply of fuel to the engines, whilst avoiding excessive movement of the C of G or undue stresses on the wings.

Fuel quantity is measured by the level in the tank, but may be shown as volume or weight. The measurement can be done by *float type* (resistance) or *capacitive* contents gauges.

 Although many fuel gauges are accurate, they should never be relied upon as the final guide to what you have in the tanks, especially if they are calibrated with lbs or kg - fuel weight (per gallon) varies with specific gravity and temperature, so instrument readings will vary as well. Reading the book *Free Fall*, about the Gimli Glider is very instructive about this - a 767 had to make a dead stick landing at Gimli (in Manitoba, Canada) after running out of fuel in the cruise, from a combination of circumstances, including misleading fuel gauges and confusing lbs for kg (the whole episode is very instructive about CRM).

Fuel system indications available to the pilot normally consist of contents, fuel low, pressure, flow, transfer status and filter condition.

Fuel Measurement Sticks

These must be used when the fuel quantity cannot be determined by the gauges.

The **dipstick** is a calibrated stick that is inserted into the top of a tank. When it is removed, the level of wetness on the stick indicates the level of fuel in the tank.

The **dripstick** is a calibrated tube in the bottom of a tank. You pull it down enough to allow fuel to drip through the centre when the top of the stick reaches the fuel level.

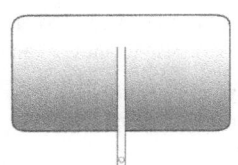

On the 737, there are 5 for each wing tank and none for the centre tank. All 5 must be read and the measurements recorded. The quantity is then calculated from data tables.

MAGNETIC FUEL LEVEL INDICATOR
The MFLI is a variation on the dripstick.

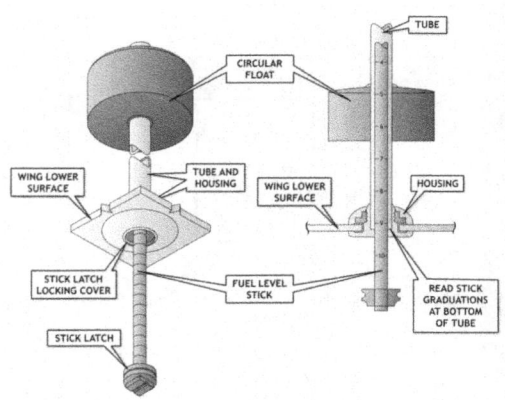

It eliminates fuel leakage by using a float on a sealed tube that contains a calibrated inner tube. There is a magnet in the float and inner tube. When the calibrated tube falls to the point where its magnet links with the one in the float, you can read the tank contents off the bit that sticks out.

HYDRAULICS

 Although the word *hydraulics* technically refers to water (i.e. hydro), it is commonly used to refer to any system operated by a fluid, particularly oil.

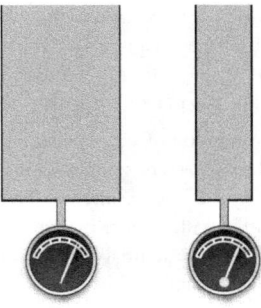

Moving the controls directly on some aircraft is physically impossible, so hydraulic components called *Power Control Units* (PCUs) may be used instead. Movement of the controls operates control valves that allow a metered amount of hydraulic fluid through to move the surfaces a specific distance. As there is no feedback, artificial feel units may be built in to provide this in proportion to the control movement.

Liquids have minimal compressibility so, when pressure is applied, it is taken up throughout the whole system. It is the *height*, or head, of the fluid that matters, not the shape of the container or the weight of the fluid. This why we speak of inches of mercury rather than Newtons/m^2.

In fact, *Pascal's Principle* states that the static pressure exerted by a fluid is the same on all surfaces touched by it or, when pressure is applied to an enclosed fluid, it is transmitted uniformly in all directions, assuming the fluid concerned is confined and doesn't compress.

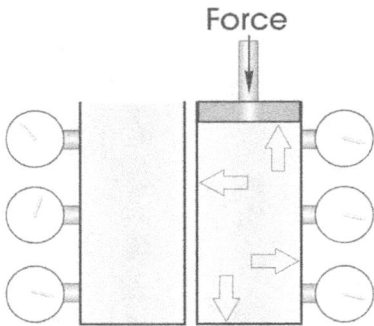

The pressure would be at 90° to the internal walls of the vessel, as you would see if you bored a hole in it - the liquid spray would be perpendicular to the surface (but the pressure would be lower outside). This makes hydraulics a useful way of transferring movement round corners and into strange places, as the forces produced can be very powerful, hence their use in aircraft to reduce the forces that would otherwise be required to move the flying controls. As well, cables stretch and linkages wear. If you add friction to the mix, much of your control input, with traditional methods, will not even get to the control surfaces concerned. Hydraulics can therefore provide an alternative, lighter weight solution to moving large or difficult to move control surfaces.

If a tube is placed into the middle of the piston in the diagram above, water will fill the tube until the weight of water in the tube equals the weight placed on the piston, equal to the sectional area of the tube, in pounds per square inch.

If the weight is atmospheric pressure and the tube is long enough with a vacuum inside, and one square inch in cross-section, eventually the weight of the water in the tube would equal the pressure outside, in pounds per square inch (14.7).

Hydraulic power is a function of *system pressure* and *volume flow*. In fact, *high pressure* and *small flow* are symptomatic of a hydraulic system - 3,000 psi is typical in large aircraft. This allows more energy to be transmitted with smaller piston areas, so it saves weight. The trade-off is the potential for leaks and the need to protect against lines bursting.

3 quantities must be considered with hydraulics:

- Force (F)
- Cross-section (A)
- Pressure (P)

They are related as follows:

    F = P x A

In the picture below, a force of P lbs is applied to the small piston (A), which produces a system pressure of P ÷ a lbs per square inch (1000 ÷ 25 = **40 psi**). The system pressure is constant throughout the system, and produces a force on the larger piston (B) equal to P ÷ a x A, in this case 2 000 lbs. This would be the case if Piston B could not move. As the output area is twice the input area, the output force is double the input. However, if you wanted to *move* piston B, piston A would have to move twice the distance that Piston B moves to keep the numbers the same Put another way, the effort travels farther than the load, but in proportion to piston area - if piston B is ten times larger than piston A, it would only move a tenth of the distance of piston A. Thus, a gain in force is obtained at the expense of distance and speed, as the rate of movement is affected as well. The work done would be the same in either case - 10 lbs over ten inches is 100 ft-lbs. So is 100 lbs over 1 inch.

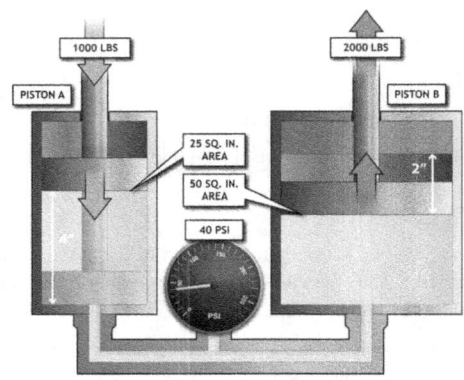

The component that transforms force into pressure is called a **master cylinder,** in the above case, piston A. Piston B would be an actuating cylinder. To find the pressure exerted by a force of 2 000 lbs over a piston 25 square inches wide, divide the applied force by the area to get 80 psi. Conversely, 800 psi applied to a piston of 12 sq ins means a total output force of 9600 lbs.

You can change a hydraulic force by altering the input ratio against the output ratio, which is a similar effect to moving the position of a fulcrum under a lever to get a different leverage. When a small force overcomes a larger resisting force, you gain a **mechanical advantage**.

System Components

Let's try to build a system with some of the components described later, using a Bramah's Press.

If you move the force of 20 Newtons downward by 4 cm, the other piston will be moved upwards by 1 cm.

When you let the force go, however, both pistons will move back to their original locations, so you need something to stop that happening.

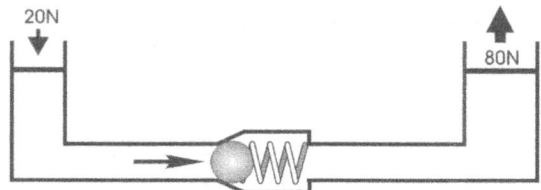

A non-return valve is a spring loaded device that allows fluid to flow in one direction only. It will be marked with an arrow to show which direction that is.

Now, when the piston on the right has been pushed up, it will stay up, due to the pressure trapped between it and the NRV. However, you can only do this once, because pulling the left hand piston back up will leave a lower pressure between it and the NRV unless you can let more fluid through, which you must do to repeat the process.

Enter the reservoir, with another NRV between it and the other side of the piston. There will be a hole in the piston to allow the fluid through, with yet another NRV to keep it in the system. When you push the piston down, the NRV in it closes, and the one in the pipe allows fluid through to push up the second piston. At the same time, the depression above the first piston allows fluid to flow in from the reservoir.

On the upstroke, the delivery NRV closes, trapping fluid above the first piston until pressure increases enough to open the NRV in the piston and allow fluid through again.

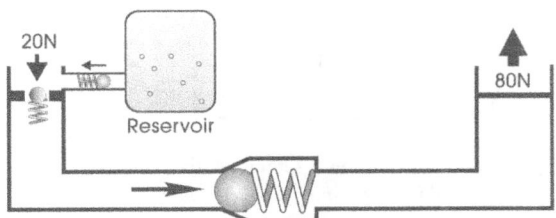

To reset the system, by allowing fluid from underneath the second piston back to the reservoir, add a pipe between them, with a release valve to act as the switch.

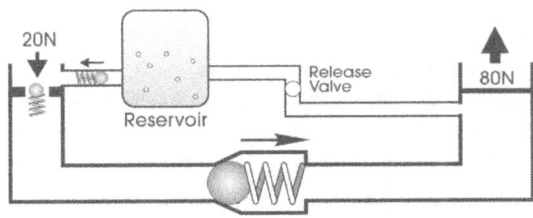

Now replace the first piston with an engine driven pump, attach the second piston to a component that is required to do some work, and you have the workings of a rudimentary hydraulic system.

A couple of extra components now need to be mentioned.

The engine driven pump is running all the time, and when the jack is fully extended the pressure may be too high for the system to cope with. The pressure relief valve is there to dump fluid back to the reservoir in this case.

In between the pump and the system itself there is a filter to keep any foreign bodies out of the fluid.

Lastly, the jack cannot return to its original position by itself, so you need a selector valve to deliver fluid under pressure to the other side of the piston so it can move the other way.

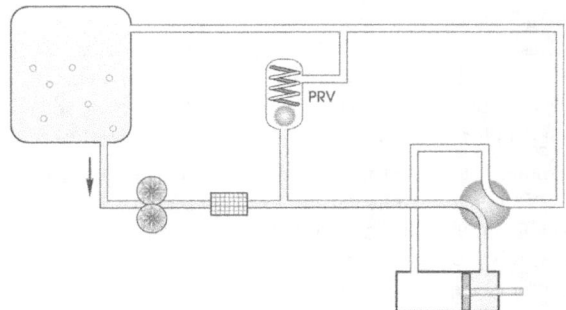

Power for a hydraulic system can be mechanical or electrical, being driven by an engine or gearbox. Standby systems are usually driven by electric motors or a gearbox.

Flight deck indications include *temperature*, *pressure* and *contents*. If only the temperature changes, for example, and the contents and pressure stay the same, you have an internal leak. Other indications would mean external leaks.

THE RESERVOIR

The reservoir stores the fluid at the highest point in the system. It may be pressurised* (by bleed air from the engine), but typically not for light aircraft, as they do not fly high enough to need it.

Pressurisation, when used, provides a positive supply of foam free fluid at the pump inlet.

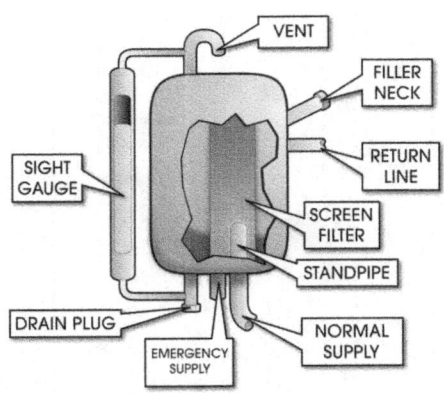

*Modern hydraulic equipment operates at high speeds and requires constant lubrication. Pressurising the reservoir ensures a positive pressure of fluid in the pipes, preventing cavitation, especially during the induction strokes of the pistons concerned. Pressurised reservoirs also prevent foaming at high altitudes.

The reservoir must contain enough fluid for the system and a bit more for emergencies. It must also provide room for expansion as the oil will acquire air bubbles as it flows round the system. A de-aerator will remove them, and the airspace above the normal fluid level will allow any trapped air to escape. If the system starts to leak, the reservoir will help to ensure that there is a ready supply to replace the lost fluid.

Thus, the fluid level in a reservoir will fluctuate according to system demands, accumulator pressure and jack displacement - when they contract, there must be somewhere for the displaced fluid to go. In this way, the pressure surges that you would otherwise get if there were no space are minimised. If there is only one reservoir, and there is an emergency hand-powered hydraulic facility, the fluid from the reservoir for less important services will be taken from a standpipe *at the bottom*, so there will always be fluid for emergencies.

A reservoir may also have baffles to stop the fluid from sloshing around or foaming, and a sight gauge to allow you to check the fluid level before flight (using a dipstick could introduce impurities, even if there is a filter in the system). The vent is there to allow air in to stop a vacuum forming as the level falls. Fluid temperature will typically be measured in the reservoir. Overheat detectors will be found at the pumps.

 There is a shutoff valve between the reservoir and the engine pump, which is normally open. It closes when the engine fire switch is pulled. If it is closed for a long period, it must not be reopened because there has been no cooling and lubrication for the time it has been closed. Sometimes a tech log entry is required to indicate that the valve has been closed.

JACKS

The purpose of the jack is to transform hydraulic pressure into linear motion.

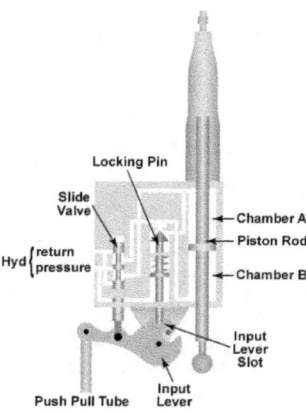

- *Single-acting* jacks move in one direction only, and are pulled back to their original positions non-hydraulically, maybe with a spring. They are usually used as locking devices, where the fluid pressure overcomes the spring tension. A typical use is to keep undercarriages locked in the up position.

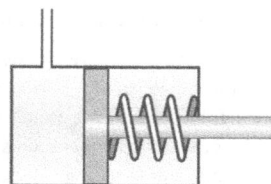

- *Double-acting* jacks can move either way according to where hydraulic fluid is injected - the spool/slide valve diverts system pressure to the side of an actuator where it is needed. However, because the piston is only connected on one side, you can exert more pressure on the other side, because the shaft isn't there.

This could be used to raise an undercarriage against gravity, which would assist it the other way.

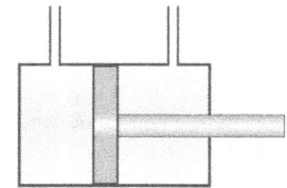

- *Balanced jacks* have a connecting rod either side of the piston, so you get an equal force whichever way the piston is moved, useful for steering and flying controls.

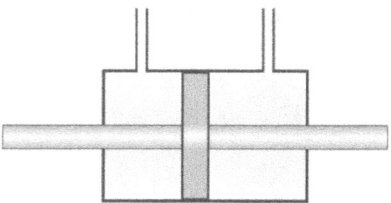

In a *fully powered* system (i.e. power operated), the controls only activate the spool/slide valve, and the fluid pressure will move the actuator concerned. When the servo moves, a feedback linkage closes the spool valve pistons over the two actuator ports to trap hydraulic fluid inside the working cylinder. With such an **irreversible** flight control system, the trapped fluid causes a hydraulic lock that freezes the controls so they cannot be moved by the control surface. In this case, there is no feedback to the controls, so artificial feel systems need to be introduced.

For a *boosted* system (i.e. power assisted, or reversible), the input and output are connected to the control linkage, as shown below, so the pilot's efforts will be assisted by a set percentage, such as 4:1, which will apply 4 units of servo power for every one from the cockpit.

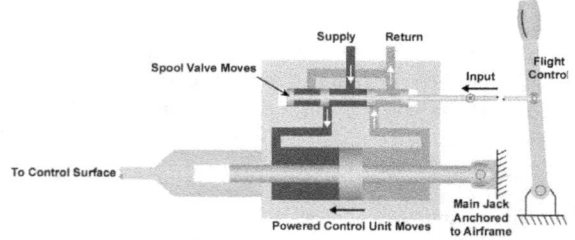

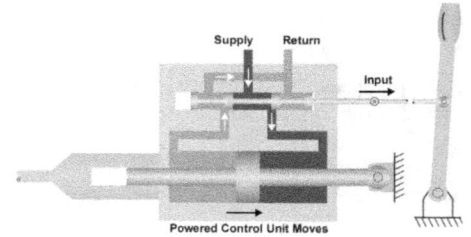

SELECTOR VALVES

Otherwise known as Directional Control Valves in the real world, these send system pressure to either side of an actuator, or jack, and provide for a return path for the unused fluid. In some systems, selector valves are operated electrically (by a solenoid) and are fail safe, so the hydraulic switch in the cockpit, when switched off, turns on the solenoid, so that, if the electrics fail, the solenoid reverts to the position where fluid can flow again.

A rotary selector valve spins to direct fluid into channels:

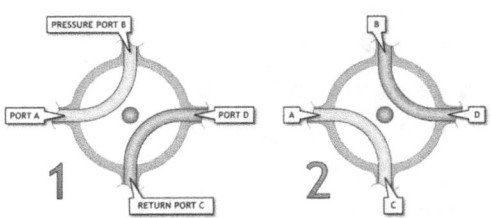

The above picture shows a closed centre valve. When it is in the Off position, the flow of fluid is blocked, and the system stays at its operating pressure at all times. The four-way, closed-centre selector valve is the most commonly used valve in aircraft hydraulics. There are two types, rotary (as shown above) or spool valve.

A spool valve uses a sliding piston:

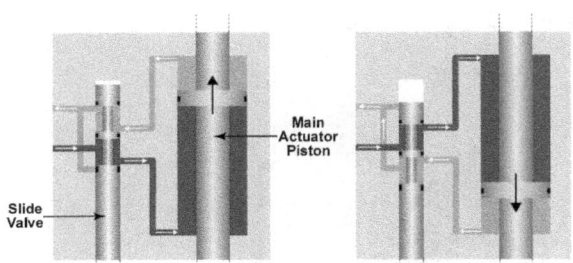

A *mechanical null* is the half stroke displacement of the control valve spool between stops. A *hydraulic null* exists when the spool is positioned equally over the ports feeding fluid to extend and retract the actuator, so it takes the same displacement of the spool to initiate a motion to extend or retract.

Hydraulic systems are classified according to the selector valves they use. In an **open centre** system using more than 1 selector valve, the valves are arranged one behind the other, in series. The open centre is needed so that fluid can reach all jacks when only one is being operated.

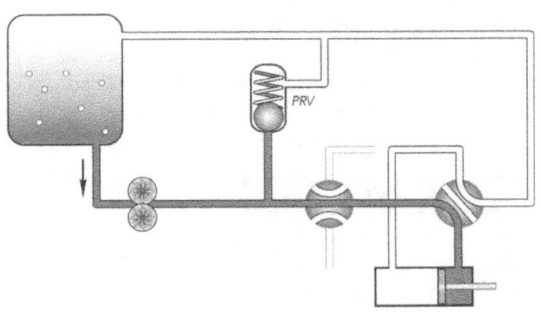

In other words, the term *open centre* refers to the open central path of the control valve when it is in the neutral position, and the fluid goes back to the reservoir.

An open centre system therefore has fluid flow but no pressure when the selector valve is off, so pressure is only present when an actuator is operated. Put more technically, it is pressurised to a specific demand.

When the jack has finished moving, the pump pressure builds up to return the selector valve to its neutral (open centre) position.

A **closed centre** system allows you to run several items at once - that is, in parallel, with varying fluid flows (the quantity of fluid to each device can be controlled by line or valve size, with less heat build up as compared to the flow dividers needed in a comparable open centre system). The components that generate the pressure form a complete loop called the closed centre in which pressure is almost constant, so fluid is under pressure all the time the pump is operating, and pressure varies in direct proportion to system demands. A non-return (check) valve traps the pressured oil in the circuit.

As the control valve has no central pathway (it is closed), the flow of fluid from the pump is stopped and it can take a rest when it is not needed.

When the accumulator is charged to full pressure, an automatic cutout (unloading) valve diverts the pump flow back to the reservoir. When a selector valve is operated, fluid from the accumulator actuates the relevant jack. As the pressure drops, the ACOV allows recharging of the accumulator to take place.

This system is effective when fluid is needed only for a short time. When more is needed for longer periods, the accumulator needs to be very large.

Otherwise, a closed centre system does not need relief valves because the pump simply shuts off by itself when standby pressure is reached. The prevents heat building up in systems where relief pressure is frequently reached.

The size of the lines, valves, and cylinders can also be tailored to the flow requirements of each function, and it is more efficient with functions such as brakes, which need a lot of force with very little movement of the piston. By holding the valve open, standby pressure is constantly applied to the brake piston with no efficiency loss because the pump has returned to standby.

A **servo** is a combination of a selector valve and an actuator in one unit. Servos are used when precise control is needed over the distance a component moves.

When the pilot valve of a servo is opened, it is automatically closed by the servo's movement because the pilot valve housing moves as well (the two are attached). The pilot valve itself is held stationary by the operator, and the ports again become blocked by the pilot valve stopping the piston when it has moved the required distance.

A **Sloppy Link** is the connection point between the control linkage, pilot valve, and servo piston rod. It allows the servo piston to be moved either by fluid pressure or manually by providing a limited amount of slack between connecting linkage and pilot valve. Now the pilot valve can be moved to an On position by the linkage without moving the piston rod.

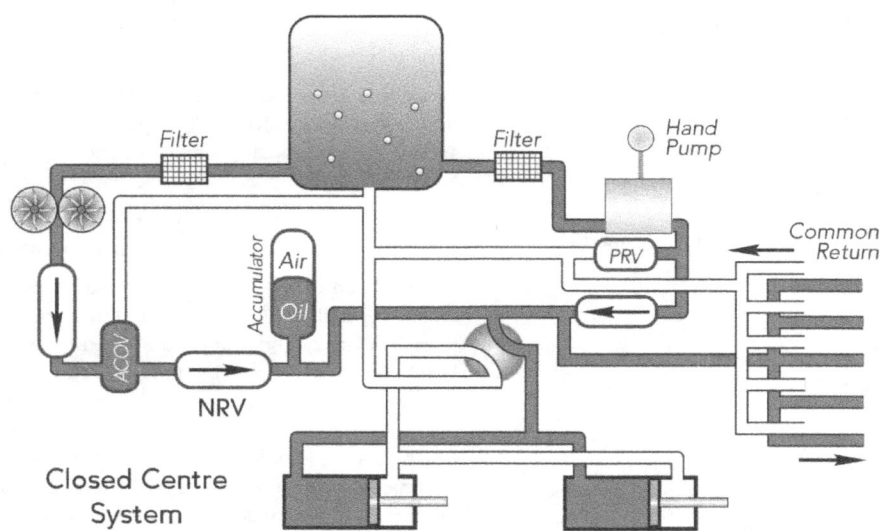

Closed Centre System

SECURITY COMPONENTS

These would include the filters, pressure relief valves, bypasses, fire shutoff valves and, in some cases........

THE ACCUMULATOR

An accumulator is a container in which a piston or a diaphragm separates hydraulic fluid under normal system pressure from an inert gas (usually nitrogen) which is also under pressure, having been charged up on the ground (any gauge will show the system pressure*). An inert gas is used because oxygen and oil can become explosive if you combine them under high pressure.

*If an accumulator is precharged to, say, 1000 psi (as is usually found on large transport aircraft), and the system is pressurised to 3000, the pressure on the gas side should read 3000 psi, i.e. system pressure.

Tip: Accumulator pressure can be checked by exercising the system with the pumps inoperative and observing the indications just before they drop to zero.

Part of an accumulator's job is to store energy in the form of hydraulic fluid under pressure that can be used for a short time if the main system fails or needs help at peak times - that is, in a failure, you can still move the controls for a few seconds, at least enough to bring the speed back to where the forces are controllable. The stored pressure also allows an initial impetus to be given when a selection is made (i.e it reduces lag). You can also think of an accumulator as a shock absorber, since a valve opening in a highly pressurised system makes quite an impact on the hydraulic lines. Yet another function is to use the stored pressure to reduce the number of times the hydraulic pump has to switch on and off when there is low demand, which saves wear and tear. As the output from an accumulator can be more (temporarily) than that from the system anyway, you can then save weight and expense by using pumps of lesser capacity, and size. An accumulator on a brake system allows you to move the aircraft without having to run the engines.

The bladder (diaphragm) is thinner and larger in diameter at the top (near the air valve) tapering to a smaller diameter. The accumulator's operation is based on Barlow's formula for hoop stress, which states that the stress in a circle is directly proportional to its diameter and wall thickness. Thus, for a certain thickness, a larger diameter circle will stretch faster than one with a small diameter or, for a certain diameter, a thin wall hoop will stretch faster. The bladder will therefore stretch at its largest diameter and thinnest wall (that is, at the top), pushing itself outward against the walls.

Picture Below: Types Of Accumulators

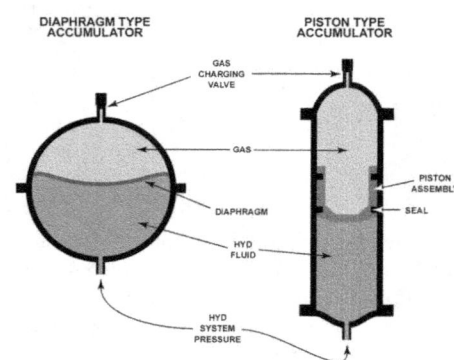

As pressure builds up in the system, the gas in the accumulator is compressed until the fluid and gas pressures equalise inside it at normal system pressure, at which point the pump runs down to idle speed and pressure is maintained by the accumulator. As soon as the system pressure drops, the nitrogen expands against the bladder to force out the fluid on the other side, which keeps the system pressurised for a short while, until the pump kicks in again. Depending on how much and how harshly you use the controls, the accumulators will usually bleed off their stored pressure inside about 20-30 seconds. The capacity of an accumulator is what it can supply during discharge.

If gas pressure is too high, there will be less fluid in the system, and more on/off cycles as the pump kicks in and out. If gas pressure is too low, you can expect rapid fluctuations in fluid pressure as surges are not absorbed. A piston would also hit against the stops and cause *hammering*, which should be investigated immediately, or at least as soon as possible if you are flying. A *cutout valve* sits between the pump and the accumulator.

While the pump is keeping system pressure up, the valve will be closed. When the accumulator is doing the work, it will open, so fluid can be dumped back to the reservoir. A low pressure switch will set off an alarm if the pump output pressure is not enough. There will be a non-return valve upstream of the accumulator to stop fluid going back to the reservoir.

HYDRAULIC FLUID

Speaking of shocks to the system, hydraulic fluids are specially made to withstand high pressures and temperatures without vaporising, so make sure you use the proper stuff. The ideal hydraulic fluid should be:

- incompressible
- have a low viscosity (to minimise power consumption and resistance to flow)
- have good lubrication properties
- **be non-flammable** (or at least have a wide temperature range) and non-toxic
- have a low freezing point and a high boiling point, with no foaming
- thermally stable
- anti-corrosive
- have a high flash point
- have low emulsifying characteristics

It should also be compatible with the seals and materials used, that is, it should not cause corrosion. Being coloured helps as well, so that leaks show up better. Did I mention stability? I thought not.

The three main types of fluid are:

- **Vegetable** (Castor). May be yellow or almost colourless (i.e. straw) and must be used with pure rubber seals and hoses. It is found in some braking systems, but not often in power systems.
- **Mineral**. Normally **red**, for **synthetic rubber** seals and hoses in braking systems, power systems and shock absorbers. As it is based on petroleum, mineral-based fluid can be flammable, so if it leaks out, it can catch fire, especially if the leak is in the form of a spray. Used on older aircraft.
- **Synthetic**. Phosphate Ester based, may be green, purple or blue (Skydrol*) and must only be used with Teflon, Ethylene Propylene or Butyl Rubber seals and hoses, as it is hostile to rubber. It is **fire and cavitation resistant** with a wide temperature range (between around -55°C to over +105°C), but it becomes acidic if overheated, and will attack electrical insulations. It will also be harmful to the skin and eyes. It is **the most common fluid used** in modern hydraulic systems.

They cannot be mixed, because using incorrect fluid could damage the seals. You must use the fluid specified in the Flight Manual.

*DTD 585 and MIL-H-5606 are red. Skydrol 500B is light purple. Other grades are green or blue.

NON-RETURN (CHECK*) VALVES

These allow fluid to move in one direction only. In the USA, they are known as hydraulic fuses.

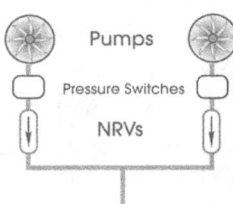

In the picture above, the NRV stops any back flow of fluid through its respective pump which could happen if it fails.

*It is a check valve if there is a specific force on the inlet.

HYDRAULIC FUSE

See above. Otherwise known as a lockout valve, the hydraulic fuse is designed to limit or stop the flow of fluid from a leak, so that the main circuit is not affected. For example, you don't want a leak in one brake line to be responsible for losing the fluid from the whole circuit. A leak has the effect of decreasing fluid pressure.

Fuses are fitted upstream of non-essential services, and allow either a specific amount of fluid through or a specific maximum rate before closing off. One type of valve shuts off the flow when pressure drops enough across it.

PUMPS

Having a powered pump means that hydraulic fluid is always available when it is required. Hydraulic systems are *passive* when they don't use a pump (or, rather, they use a hand pump and the system isn't pressurised until it is used), and *active* when they do. Hand pumps are normally connected to the bottom of the reservoir.

Systems will typically have at least 2 pumps in parallel. After the pump will be a pressure switch that operates a light if the pump output pressure falls below a given value.

With 2 pumps running, normal pressure will be the same as if 1 was running, but the flow rate will be doubled. Should a pump fail, the pressure remains the same but the flow rate will be halved. This will not affect smaller components, but larger ones may operate at a slower rate giving longer operating times.

Modern aircraft may have many hydraulic systems that are colour coded for ease of identification.

In the picture below, each system has at least 2 pumps that are driven from different sources, so that an engine failure does not mean a system failure.

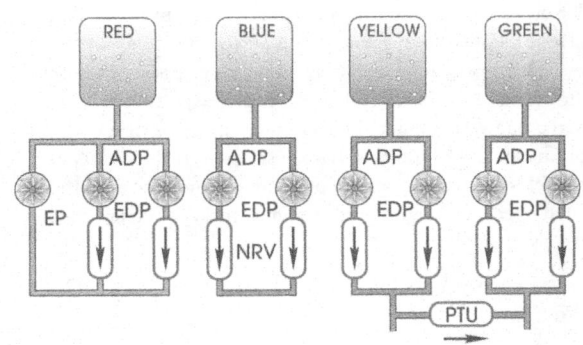

- EP - Electrical Pump
- EDP - Engine Driven Pump
- ADP - Air (Turbine) Driven Pump
- NRV - Non Return Valve
- PTU - Power Transfer Unit

Major services will be supplied by at least 2 systems to protect against their loss. For example, a hydraulic motor in one system may be used to drive a hydraulic pump in another, also known as a *Power Transfer Unit*.

In the 757, for example, there are three independent hydraulic systems, left, centre and right. The left and right systems have one engine driven pump (EDP) and an electric one. The centre system uses two electric pumps with possibly Ram Air Turbine (RAT) powered pump as a back-up. Once deployed in flight, the RAT is normally stowed on the ground by maintenance.

Normally, each system powers all primary flying controls and some spoiler surfaces. In the left engine fails on takeoff, a Power Transfer Unit (PTU) supplies power from the right system to retract the landing gear and flaps, etc. (the power transfer unit transfers *energy* from one system to another - there is no transfer of fluid).

Support pumps may back up engine driven pumps - these may be electric or air driven. Support pumps usually start up automatically when they are needed, for example just after takeoff when there is a lot of hydraulic activity going on and the engine driven pumps need a boost. In this case, they might also be called demand pumps. The outputs from main and support pumps will be fed through check valves to stop them from interacting.

A hydraulic pump's mechanical action first creates a vacuum at the pump inlet, which allows atmospheric pressure to force in liquid from the reservoir. Then it delivers the liquid to the outlet, forcing it into the hydraulic system. The fluid may be slightly pressurised as it enters the pumps to prevent vapour lock. *Pressure gauges show the outlet pressure from the pump.*

There are many types of pump - constant or variable *volume*, or constant or variable *pressure*. They can also be piston or gear based. Hand pumps allow for ground servicing and emergencies, and are usually double acting. Variable displacement pumps adjust the amount of fluid pumped to the amount of fluid required, so that fluid only moves when necessary. **Constant Volume** (or constant delivery) pumps deliver a fixed amount of fluid, which means that you need to dump excess fluid back to the reservoir when it is not required (the combination of pump and valve creates a constant pressure source). An Automatic Cut Out Valve (or a pressure regulator, with an accumulator) provides an idling circuit when no hydraulic service is selected or when the accumulator is full. When the pressure gets high enough, the pump cuts out and system pressure is maintained by the accumulator until another service is selected. If the ACOV fails in the closed position, system pressure will increase until the relief valve opens. Constant volume pumps mean less engine wear.

Piston type constant volume pumps have multiple pistons driven at an angle by a drive shaft through a universal joint, which makes the rotary motion of the shaft turn into linear motion of the pistons that pumps the fluid.

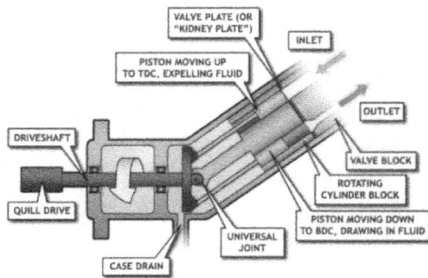

There is always a residual flow for lubrication and cooling.

For low pressure systems, up to about 200 psi, a gear-type pump with two meshed gears that revolve in a housing is the simplest solution.

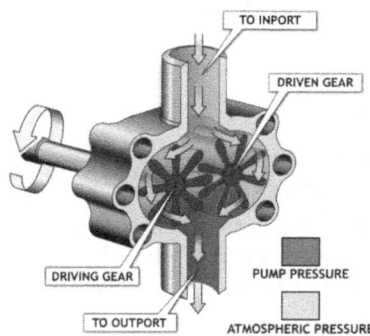

The gears are turned by a shaft which has a shear pin or section that will break under excessive loads (something might get jammed. If a hydraulic pump seizes, the **quill drive** will shear to offload and protect the gearbox). The inlet port to the pump is fed straight from the reservoir, and the outlet is connected to the pressure line. As the teeth pass the inlet port, fluid is trapped between them and the housing, and carried round to where the teeth mesh again to displace the fluid into the outlet port. This produces a positive flow under pressure into the line. The meshing in the centre prevents any back flow, although some fluid may be allowed to leak past for cooling and lubrication purposes.

One rotation of the shaft displaces a fixed quantity of fluid that is determined by the geometry of the motor (i.e. the rate of flow determines it speed), and the output is proportional to the RPM. The pressure drop across it is determined by the torque it is applying. A constant delivery type pump requires a pressure regulator.

With **Variable Volume** (Constant Pressure or Delivery) pumps, fluid output varies with the demands of the system (it is open centred), and sorts out its own pressure. In simple terms, the pump only works when it is needed. Although it doesn't need an accumulator, it does need a bypass to prevent over-pressurisation.

Axial piston pumps can produce high pressure and can be offloaded to reduce power consumption.

Hydraulic pumps used on large commercial aeroplanes (i.e. using high pressure over around 3000 psi, so that flying controls can be hydraulically assisted while running multiple systems) use pumps with a tilting swashplate to vary the stroke of the pistons. They resemble the constant volume pump, but the cylinder block and pistons are co-axial, rather than being at an angle. It is the tilted swashplate, and not the drive, that creates the eccentric movement (the swash plate angle is adjusted by the control piston).

When the system pressure is low, spring pressure on the control piston tilts the swashplate (or yoke) to its maximum angle to make the pistons use the full length of their strokes for maximum output (this is how they are at start up). In the minimum stroke position, a small flow through the pump is maintained to keep the parts lubricated and cooled, and to overcome internal leakage.

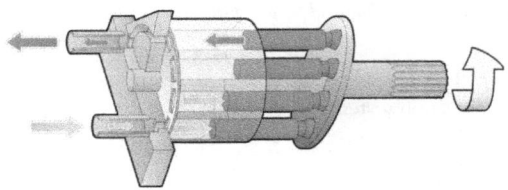

RAM AIR TURBINE

There are normally at least 2 main supplies to each unit. If both fail, a Ram Air Turbine (RAT) can keep things going. It consists of a propeller driven generator and/or hydraulic pump which, when dropped into the airflow, provides the appropriate power supply to certain systems, such as the flying controls, which includes flaps and spoilers, but not the landing gear. The RAT is stowed in a bay under the fuselage and is kept there by an uplock. To deploy the unit, the uplock is released mechanically or by the firing of a small explosive charge (squib).

On some aircraft with more than one set of control surfaces, if one fails, control is maintained by the remaining surfaces at a reduced rate.

WARNINGS

Warning systems are designed to throw an electrical switch when the pressure at the point being tested is too low or high (in other words, a pressure switch will operate a warning light). Fluid from the pressure line holds a piston up against a return spring, which forces the piston down if the pressure drops, to contact the switch button. For high pressure systems, the return spring holds the piston away from the switch button.

Where two hydraulic systems are fitted, loss of one will normally be indicated in the cockpit by a Master Caution, and amber light and loss of pressure indications.

Internal leakages will cause a higher fluid temperature. Overheat detectors are usually installed at the pumps.

Sluggish operation indicates that there is air in the system, which requires bleeding.

SEALS

Without seals to stop fluid from leaking or going where it shouldn't, no hydraulic system would work properly.

Static seals, gaskets and packing are squeezed between two surfaces. *Dynamic* seals come between sliding surfaces and vary in shape according to the fluid pressure and location. U and V (chevron) rings*, for example, only work in one direction, while O rings and square seals work both ways.

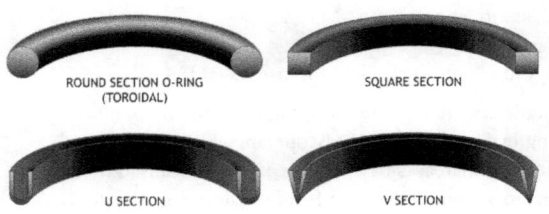

*Oil and pressure to the inverse side, air to the pointed side. If internal, must be in pairs or back-to-back

Dynamic seals need lubrication, so a little seepage is acceptable in their case. An O ring in a high pressure system will also have backing rings to retain its shape and keep it in place, to stop it being squeezed.

Seals can be made from natural or synthetic rubber, or other materials, depending on the fluid used. Using the wrong type will degrade the seals which are easily damaged by dirt and grit.

FILTRATION

The fluid in the system must be as clean as possible to stop any seals, or the working surfaces of the components being damaged. Gauze strainers are normally found in reservoir filler necks, filtering new fluid down to 100 microns (1 micron is a millionth of a metre).

Micronic filters are fitted in suction or pressure lines, or pressure and return lines. They have valves to let the fluid in and out (inlet and outlet) and the filter (through which the fluid is forced) is inside a sump, or housing.

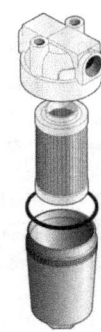

When impurities build up on the element inside the filter housing, the flow rate through the filter will reduce and there will be an increase in the input pressure and a reduction in the output pressure. The difference will increase in proportion to the clogging.

When a filter gets clogged, it is bypassed, and the system will be working with unfiltered fluid.

When the element (which can be paper or metal) has to be changed, the valves close automatically when the housing is removed, so no air or dirt gets in, and no fluid gets out. You can clean and re-use metal filters.

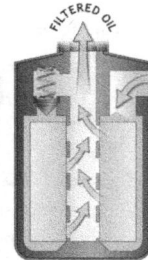 

CLEAN FILTER — CLOGGED FILTER (BYPASS VALVE OPEN)

Popout indicators (checked before flight) warn you of an impending bypass situation. They operate when the pressure inside the filter increases beyond a certain limit, caused by the contaminants stopping the fluid from flowing. Some systems also have an electrical warning, using a light in the cockpit.

False indications on those cold mornings, when the fluid is sluggish anyway, are prevented with a bi-metal spring.

PRIORITY VALVE

This is an American term for a **Pressure Maintaining Valve**. It maintains the pressure in a primary service, such as flying controls, regardless of what a secondary service may require. Put more simply, it gives priority to one system over another, ensuring that available pressure is directed to essential services after the system pressure drops. When the main system pressure exceeds a certain value, tension in a spring is overcome and the secondary system gets a service.

RESTRICTOR VALVE

A restrictor is designed to allow limited flow in one direction and full flow in the other, so that the speed of a service can be controlled. For example, it can restrict flow in a landing gear up line and create a restriction during gear down selection. It can also restrict flow in the flap down line and create a restriction during flap up selection.

Because it restricts the speed of operation of an actuator, the restrictor valve also prevents cavitation. The direction of flow is marked by a dotted arrow on the valve body.

THE SHUTTLE VALVE

Sometimes, fluid must come from more than one source to meet the demands of a complex system. At other times, an emergency system might be needed to provide pressure if the normal system fails (the emergency system will usually only actuate essential components). The shuttle valve can isolate the normal system

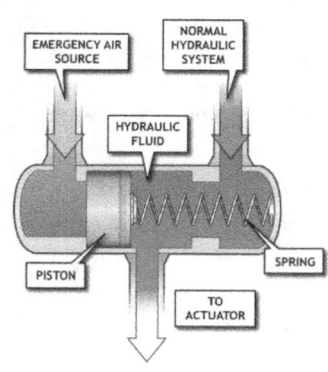

from an alternate or emergency one, or provide **best pressure** to a service. A typical shuttle valve contains three ports— normal system inlet, alternate or emergency system inlet, and an outlet. Inside, there is a sliding part predictably called the shuttle, whose purpose is to seal off an inlet port, which itself will contain a *shuttle seat*.

When a shuttle valve is in its normal position, fluid can flow freely from the normal system inlet port, through the valve, and out through the outlet port to the actuating unit. The shuttle is seated against the alternate system inlet port and held there by normal system pressure and the *shuttle valve spring*, where it remains until the alternate system is activated (if the shuttle is stuck in the normal position, emergency use cannot be undertaken). Fluid under pressure is then directed from the alternate system to the shuttle valve, forcing the shuttle to seal off the normal inlet port. Fluid from the alternate system then has a free flow to the outlet port. The shuttle may be one of four types: *sliding plunger*, *spring-loaded piston*, *spring-loaded ball*, or *spring-loaded poppet*.

Aside from hydraulic systems, the shuttle valve can be found in engine fire protection systems.

SEQUENCE VALVE

Sequence valves confirm that one action has been completed before anther takes place. They are used in undercarriage systems to make sure that everything operates in the correct order. For example, because gravity can help the gear come down, there could be an artificial reduction of pressure in the downlines, as compared to the up lines, which means that the doors might not open all the way. A sequence valve can block the return fluid until the pressure in the down lines is enough.

PRESSURE REDUCING VALVE

Used when you want two pressure values in a system.

RESTRICTOR VALVE

Controls the rate of movement of a service, or slows down a service in one direction.

FLOW CONTROL VALVE

Smooths the flow to a system and/or dampens out surges in system pressure. A **modulator** is a flow control valve specific to brake systems that speeds up the operation of an anti-skid system (see *ABS*, below).

PRESSURE RELAY

These are used in older systems with a long distance from the hydraulic bay to the pressure gauge in the cockpit. Their purpose is to cut off the supply to the gauge if there is a leak from the pipe to the gauge. There is normally no flow through the relay because it merely transmits pressure. If there is a leak, the flow cuts off the supply to preserve pressure for the services (i.e. the gauge reading is lost but they still operate).

BRAKE CONTROL VALVE

These are complex - their importance lies in what capabilities are required, such as progressive or differential braking (the latter for nose-wheel steering).

THERMAL RELIEF

A thermal relief valve prevents damage to components in the closed part of a hydraulic system due to heat expansion. It senses the ambient fluid temperature, and when it exceeds a predetermined value, the valve depressurises the system. It is set higher than the Automatic Cut Out Valve (ACOV) pressure.

PRESSURE RELIEF VALVES

These are pressure limiting or safety devices that prevent pressure from building up to where it might blow a seal or burst or damage the container in which it is installed. They are there to relieve excessive pressures from thermal expansion, surges and other failures. For example, when a jack reaches its full travel, a pressure relief valve may allow fluid to bypass it and unload the pump. The *cracking pressure* is that at which the PRV opens.

Main system relief valves operate within certain specific pressure limits to relieve complete pump output when in the open position, from where excess fluid is directed to the reservoir return line. In systems designed to operate normally at 3,000 psi, the relief valve might be set to be completely open at 3,650 psi and reseat at 3,190 psi.

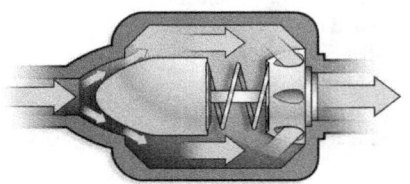

A coil spring at one end of a piston retains it against a stop on the valve housing, and the poppet valve, just inside the pressure port, is spring seated over a passage through the valve. When fluid pressure reaches 3,650 psi (for example), the piston is forced to depress the coil spring and move clear of the poppet valve, so the fluid can flow through the valve into the return line. When pressure is reduced to 3,190 psi, the coil spring reseats the piston against the poppet valve, and fluid flow ceases.

Pressure relief valves may be separate components in their own right, or be found within others, such as filters. The simplest form is a ball or piston held in place with a spring, whose tension can be adjusted to change the cracking pressure. If the fluid pressure gets too high, the ball is moved against the spring to allow fluid past. A valve not seating correctly would result in low oil pressure.

Wheel Brakes

Brakes serve four primary functions:

- To slow down and stop an aircraft during a normal landing with a reasonable rate of deceleration and minimal wear.
- To stop an aircraft after an aborted takeoff under the worst conditions of weight, altitude, temperature and critical speed.
- To allow the engines to be run up to full power without the wheels rotating.
- To allow ground manoeuvring without excessive pedal loads or snatching.

Except for the aborted takeoff, braking must be effective, smooth, and within the same temperature range.

Wheel brakes therefore apply friction to the main wheels to slow them down and stop them rotating, converting kinetic energy into thermal energy in the process (in other words, they get hot). The speed of this energy conversion controls the rate of deceleration. The energy rating of the brakes must match or exceed the kinetic energy generated at maximum landing weight and speed due to the heat generated. In fact, the brake energy level can easily restrict your takeoff or landing weight. So serious is this problem that firewires are fitted inside wheel wells - one checklist action on getting a fire warning is to lower the gear so the brakes can cool in the slipstream. Tyres used on transport aircraft have fusible plugs which will melt at high temperatures to prevent an explosion.

The type of brake unit used primarily depends on the weight of the aircraft:

- **Drum brakes**. Not used on modern aircraft.
- **Single disc brakes** used on light aircraft.
- **Multi-disc brakes** used on heavier aircraft (a parking brake will have its own components)

Inside the cockpit, a brake pressure indicator will indicate the accumulator or system pressure - not the pressure at the brakes. There may also be a temperature indicator.

BRAKE PEDALS

For light aircraft, there will be a master cylinder for each brake pedal, a reservoir, the brakes and connecting pipes.

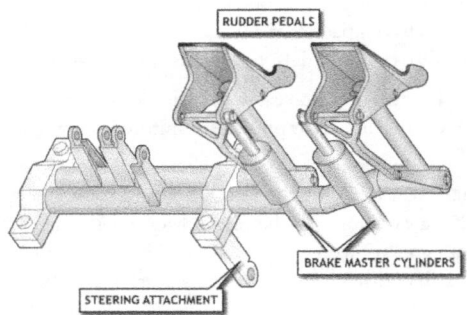

The toe pedal activates the master cylinder directly, and a piston inside forces fluid along the lines to activate the brakes. The amount of braking force depends on how hard you push the pedals. When you release the pressure on the pedals, a spring in the master cylinder returns the piston to its original position. A brake accumulator may provide a reserve of power if the main system fails.

Large aircraft use the main hydraulic system because of the power requirements. The amount of braking is varied with the pressure put on the pedals.

SYSTEMS
Hydraulics

DRUM BRAKES

Drum brakes use pneumatically inflated air sacs or hydraulically operated pistons inside a wheel assembly to push asbestos lined shoes against a rotating drum when the brake pedals are pushed. When they are released, a spring moves the shoes away.

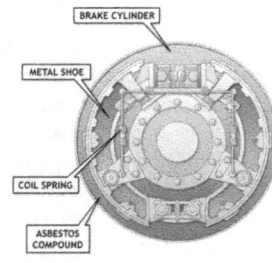

Drum brakes are not very efficient and suffer from **brake fade** when they overheat, caused by the gas given off by the vaporisation, at high temperatures, of the binding material in the brake linings which gets trapped between the brake pad and drum.

This makes the pad float on a blanket of vapour, so they are less effective. The pads can also glaze from the heat, reducing the friction effect.

DISK BRAKES

These were designed to overcome the brake fade problem, although the material used for the brake linings is largely responsible for the improvements (carbon/steel). Older aircraft use steel discs and pressures of around 1800 psi. Newer ones use carbon fibre and 3000 psi. Carbon disk packs not only act as a heat sink, but they are much lighter, so they save weight. The disc is exposed to the open air and sandwiched between pads that are pushed into the disc by the pedals, to slow its rotation down.

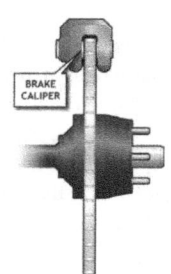

Small aircraft use single disk brakes, which can be checked visually for wear, while indicator pins are monitored on bigger machines.

Multi disk brakes consist of interleaved stators and rotors. Applying the brakes compresses the stator discs together and brings them into contact with the rotors. An adjuster assembly maintains the correct distance between the stators and rotors as they wear through use.

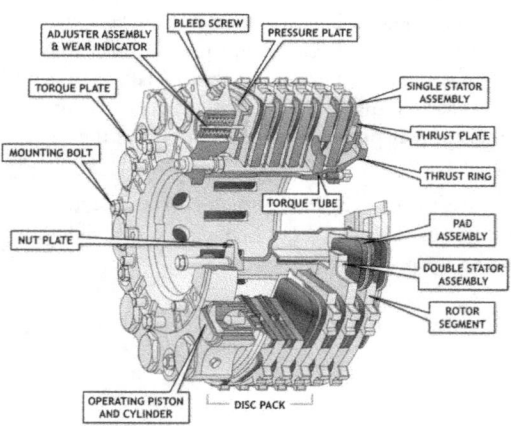

They are checked in the On position. As long as there is some part of the wear indicator pin sticking out, the brakes are assumed to be serviceable.

A spring pulls the brakes off when released and sets the running distance between the discs and linings.

ANTI SKID

The brakes are supposed to convert the kinetic energy of the aircraft into heat energy, through the friction from the brakes. If the wheel stops rotating (that is, it locks) and the tyre ends up skidding on the runway, the energy transfer moves between the tyre and the runway. If the runway is wet, directional control may be lost.

Anti-skid systems are supposed to stop the wheels locking when the brakes are applied. Locked wheels not only extend the landing run, but you could also get burst tyres, especially with bogie type landing gear, where some weight transference to the wheels usually locks them. With these systems, the brake pressure is released when the wheels are about to stop rotating. This allows for maximum braking, especially on slippery runways where hydroplaning may be a problem. Each wheel has a speed measurement device, and a control unit compares its rotation speed with what it should be on a dry runway. If the speed is less than 85% (meaning that heavy braking is making the wheels slow down too quickly), valves are opened at intervals (many times a second) to relieve the hydraulic pressure enough to stop the wheels locking. The brakes are reapplied when the wheel speeds up again.

The system can only work if the wheels are spinning in the first place. If the brakes were applied before touching down, there would be no way of sensing as to whether the wheels were locked. A protection circuit called *touch down protection* or *control* stops the brakes being applied during the approach to landing.

 If your system requires you to use them (some don't), do not release the pressure on the brake pedals during the landing roll - you should hold constant pedal pressure and let ABS do the work.

There are two types of ABS:

- **Electronic**. The wheel rotation speed is checked electronically against a reference (the nose wheel speed in the Airbus), using a small DC generator whose output is proportional to the speed of the wheel. Any discrepancy results in a reduction in brake pressure on that wheel only, based on the discharge rate of a capacitor. When the wheel speeds up, pressure is reapplied.

- **Mechanical**. A flywheel in a **Maxaret unit** (inside the wheel rim) rotates at the same speed as the tyre. When the wheel slows rapidly (because of a skid) the Maxaret unit tends to over-run against spring pressure, generating an error signal and reducing the brake pressure on that wheel only. When the wheel speeds up, pressure is reapplied.

AUTOMATIC BRAKING

On multi-bogeyed systems, there is no feedback to tell you if you are braking too hard, so it can be done for you - the system applies the brakes on touchdown and during the landing roll without anyone touching the pedals, although you can use the brakes manually at any time (this disengages the automatic service). Once a spinup of the main wheels has been detected, the brakes will be applied to maintain a certain deceleration rate so, if you use reverse thrust, the brake pressure will reduce, but it will increase again as reverse thrust is terminated.

The system can be armed at 5 settings - 1, 2, 3, 4 or maximum. 1 or 2 would be used for a normal dry runway with enough length to cope with the landing roll. 3 or 4 would be used for slippery, wet or icy runways. Maximum is used for emergencies - as it is still less than the maximum you would get with manual braking, if you need more, just press the toe pedals. The rate of deceleration is detected by the INS, and the braking effort is adjusted by the autobrake computer. Autobrakes are cancelled during landing by **pilot action**, such as touching the brake pedals, advancing the throttles or pushing the TOGA button.

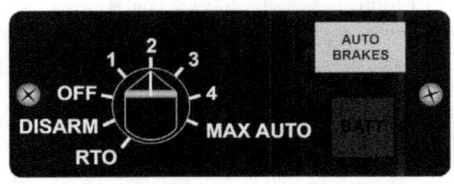

On some widebodied aircraft, auto brakes will even work through a rejected takeoff - if yours can, there will be an RTO ARM switch on the control panel. Certain indications of an aborted takeoff must exist, however. In the 767, moving the thrust levers below 85% during the takeoff roll will do it. RTO brake pressure is the same as you get with full manual braking.

When the system is working, normal brake pressure is isolated with a shuttle valve.

RETRACTION BRAKING

Although, on light aircraft, dabbing the brakes is a typical after takeoff action, doing that on a large aircraft can cause damage to the struts and wheel wells from gyroscopic forces. Automatic retraction braking applies a light pressure to slow the wheels down properly. It is activated when the gear selector is moved to the UP position.

Aquaplaning/Hydroplaning

A contaminated runway has significant amounts of standing water, ice, slush, snow or even heavy frost along its surface. The most important factors are loss of friction when decelerating, and displacement of (and impingement drag when accelerating through) whatever is on it, so it may be difficult to steer, and takeoff and accelerate-stop distances may be increased due to the slower acceleration, as will landing distance because of poor braking action and aquaplaning, which is a condition where the built-up pressure of liquid under the tyres at a certain speed will equal the weight of the aircraft and the liquid on the runway creeps under the tyres, with the consequent loss of traction, so there may be a period during which, if one of your engines stops on takeoff, you will be unable to either continue or stop within the remaining runway, and go water-skiing off the end (actually, you're more likely to go off the side, so choosing a longer runway won't necessarily help). The duration of this risk period is variable, but will vary according to weight, water depth, tyre pressure and speed. It only needs a tenth of an inch of contaminant to do this.

The three types of hydroplaning are:

- **Dynamic hydroplaning**, which is the basic sort, arising from standing water (*lift off speed* is the important consideration here). It comes with as two subtypes, *partial* and *full*, both more likely when water depth is over 6 mm.
- **Viscous hydroplaning** involves a thin layer of liquid on a slippery surface, such as the traces of rubber left on the landing area of a runway which fill in the small holes (one reason why it's dangerous to drive after a rain shower in Summer). In other words, it is caused by a *smooth* and *dirty* runway surface, at a lower speed than dynamic hydroplaning, and you should particularly watch out for the white markings - it can almost be like landing on ice.
- **Reverted rubber hydroplaning** happens when a locked tyre generates enough heat from friction to boil the film of water on the surface and cause the steam to stop the tyre touching the runway. The heat causes the rubber to revert to its basic chemical properties, i.e. black and runny.

Although there are many factors, the most important is tyre pressure. A rough speed at which aquaplaning can occur is about 9 times the square root of your tyre pressures (see the formula below), 100 pounds per square inch therefore giving you about 90 kts (7.7 times if the tyre isn't rotating) - if this is higher than your expected take-off speed you're naturally safer than otherwise. The point to note is that if you start aquaplaning above the critical speed, you can expect the process to continue below it, that is, you will slide around to well below the speed you would have expected it to start if you were taking off.

Most factors that will assist you under these circumstances are directly under your control, and it's even more important to arrive for a "positive" landing at the required 50 feet above the threshold at the recommended speed on the recommended glideslope than for normal situations (the positive landing helps the wheels break through the water). Under-inflating tyres doesn't help - each 2 or 3 lbs below proper pressure will lower the aquaplaning speed by 1 knot, so be careful if you've descended rapidly from a colder altitude. Naturally, you should try not to use the brakes, but as much aerodynamic braking as you can, after lowering the nose as quickly as possible to reduce the angle of attack and place weight on the wheels.

The (rotating wheel) formula is:

$$Vp = 34.5 \ \sqrt{(p)}$$

Vp is the ground speed in knots and p is the tyre pressure when using bars (for PSI, use 9 instead of 34.5. The stationary wheel formula uses 7.7, so you might get partial hydroplaning while the wheels spin up).

ELECTRICITY & MAGNETISM

The term *electricity* comes from the Greek word for amber, *elektron*. As far as pilots (and engineers) are concerned, it is not a source of energy in and of itself, but a way of transmitting energy (or data) from one point to another. For this, it has to be produced, transmitted, applied and controlled, with switches and/or computers.

As you cannot see electricity, some imagination* must be used in order to understand it, but the whole process is very like the movement of water (current) in a hose. The difference is that you have to put the water into the hose, whereas the charge is already present in an electrical cable - all you have to do is set it in motion.

*Nobody knows whether an electron is a negative charge with no mass, or a particle that has a negative charge.

Some airmanship points first:

- Take care not to overheat electrical equipment when it is switched on (for checking) during a preflight check (there is no airflow to cool it).
- Do not start or stop engines with unnecessary electrical equipment switched on.
- Avoid using the starter motor for too long - there is usually a limit of one or two attempts for around 30 secs each, after which you must let it cool down before trying again. Also, starters don't have fuses - make sure the warning light is out after starting!
- Check that the generator or alternator is working properly after starting, and often during flight.
- Do not switch all electrical services on at once!
- Make sure the Battery Master Switch is off before you leave the aircraft after flight (many pilots leave the anti-collision light on to remind them).

Atomic Theory

Matter is anything that has mass and volume. For our purposes, it exists as a solid, liquid or gas, but it can be a plasma as well. An **element** is a substance that cannot be reduced to a simpler form by chemical means because it contains only one type of atom - what distinguishes one element from another is the number of protons, neutrons and electrons in the atoms it contains. A **compound** contains 2 or more elements (many atoms) - one example is water, which has 2 hydrogen atoms and one of oxygen.

However, for most purposes, the atom is the most basic building block of matter. The word derives from the Greek *a tomos* which means "not cut", or that you can't reduce (or cut) an atom into anything smaller. A molecule is a collection of atoms in a chemical compound, the smallest part of an object that retains its identity (meaning that, if you split a molecule, the substance changes its character). By the time Einstein came along, it had been discovered that atoms are both a lot smaller and a lot bigger than was originally thought. If you enlarged an apple until it became the size of the Earth, for example, the atoms inside would be the size of cherries (and the atmosphere would have the thickness of clingfilm). Gold leaf has the thickness of about 5 atoms - if this book were printed on gold leaf, and you multiplied it by 4, the thickness would be that of a single sheet of paper.

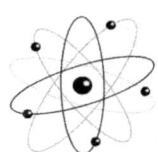

The diagram on the left is a loose depiction of the inside of an atom (the Bohr model). The large ball in the middle is the *nucleus* and the smaller ones spinning rapidly round it are a cloud of *electrons*, which are **negatively charged particles** and around 2,000 times smaller in size. The nucleus contains positive- and neutrally charged particles, called *protons* and *neutrons* (which both contain quarks and other strange things). The neutrons are there to bind the protons together, as particles of a like charge are repelled. As an example of how large atoms can be, if the nucleus were the size of the apple above, the first electron would be found anywhere between 1-10 miles away, and be hardly visible at that.

In an atom, there are an equal number of electrons to protons, to make it electrically neutral, or uncharged. An atom with one extra electron is *negatively* charged, and an atom with one missing is *positively* charged, or "carrying a positive charge", which is a bit strange, as all it has done is lost an electron. This is called *ionisation*, because an unbalanced (charged) atom is an *ion*, which we will come across in *Radio Navigation* when we discuss the ionosphere that surrounds the Earth. Some components, like transistors, depend on the movement of electrons or holes (missing electrons) one way or the other.

None of the components of an atom are physical in nature - they are actually electromagnetic charges, or tiny whirlwinds of electromagnetic force. The negative electrons are held in place by the positive protons with *electrostatic attraction*, as particles with opposite charges attract each other. Once an electron leaves an atom, lines of force exist between them, to create a kind of electrical "tension" which is made use of in radio transmissions. Electrons spin round the nucleus at around 600 miles/second so, bearing in mind the relative distances above, you can see that they work quite hard! In fact, they move so quickly round a nucleus that they give the *illusion* of a more solid construction because our senses don't work fast enough to detect the difference.

So, an atom is not solid and is mostly full of nothing.

Of course, Einstein proved that energy is really matter in another form with his formula:

$$e=mc^2$$

In other words, energy is equal to the mass of a body multiplied by the speed of light, squared. Matter converts into energy and back again depending on what you do with its velocity.

Electrons possess kinetic energy from their movement, and potential energy from their position. Those spinning round an atom occupy *energy levels*, or *shells*, like the orbits of the planets around the Sun, except that the planets have unique orbits - electrons can share theirs! The first shell can hold up to 2 electrons, and the second up to 8, but it's the outer one that is important. Unbalanced electrons in the last shell of an atom determine its valency, and are therefore called valence electrons. Valency is the property of atoms to combine with or displace others, or the number of chemical bonds that an atom can form.

Insulators & Conductors

Some atoms don't have much of a hold on their free electrons, and allow them to move around easily because their valence shells overlap. The materials made from these atoms (such as copper) are called **conductors**, and they have a low resistance to the flow of current, meaning that it flows easily. Silver is best, and copper is next by 6%, but gold is commonly used because it doesn't corrode and cause bad connections. Carbon is a non-metal that can conduct slightly, and some non-conducting liquids can do it if they are ionised - they are called *electrolytes*, and the process is *electrolysis*. Ionised gases can also conduct electricity, as with fluorescent lighting, or the ionosphere. Contrary to popular belief, electricity can flow across a vacuum.

If a conductor is positioned perpendicular to a magnetic field, a force will be exerted on the conductor.

Insulators, by contrast, may have their outer shells full, and they may not overlap, so no movement of electrons will take place. This makes them useful for keeping conductors from touching each other, otherwise electricity would flow where you don't want it and create a short circuit. Examples of insulators are glass, or the plastic coating around a cable, or non-ionised liquids or gases.

SEMICONDUCTORS

A substance that is normally an insulator but which can become a conductor depending on which way the current flows is a semiconductor.

As semiconductors can produce changes in circuit conditions, they are known as *active* components, as opposed to the more passive capacitors and resistors, which is why they are also called **solid state devices**, meaning no moving parts. As they have more to do with digital electronics, they are discussed later, under *Computers, Etc*.

Electricity

This involves the movement of electrons (or a statistical average of electron drift). In theory, if you line up a series of atoms in an electrical cable, and remove an electron from one end, the resulting hole is filled by a free electron from the previous atom, because the others are trying to repel each other, and so on.

That is, you have created a (very) slight **difference** in pressure, or potential, between each end of the cable. This causes the movement of free electrons, or an electric current, to the area with less electrons (from high to low pressure). Put another way, electrons are pulled towards the holes at the positive end, but this won't happen without a complete circuit, described later.

Although the electrical force moves at a speed close to that of light, individual electrons move relatively slowly (actually about 0.3 mph!), because they collide at random as they push each other along.

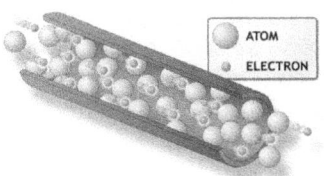

You can separate electrons from their atoms and make them move in 6 different ways:

- **Heat**. The usual way of using heat is to apply it to the junction of two dissimilar metals, such as iron and copper. How much electricity you get depends on the temperature difference between the ends of the wires (the cold junction should stay constant). A component built like this is the thermocouple that detects the heat coming from the back of a turbine engine. The electricity it produces drives a temperature gauge in the cockpit. As you don't need batteries for this, you have at least one gauge that works when the electrics fail.

- **Friction**. When rubbing two materials together, such as glass and silk (two insulators), electrons may be forced out of their orbits in the glass by friction and transferred to the silk, which acquires a negative charge of **static electricity**, later. The glass acquires a positive charge.

- **Chemical Action**. Used in batteries, later.

- **Light**. Photo-electric or solar cells create reactions between two substances when exposed to light.

- **Pressure**. Certain materials, such as quartz, can produce an electric charge when pressure is applied to them. This principle is also used in carbon pile voltage regulators (described later) to control the amount of electricity fed into a battery by a generator. Applying electricity to such a substance can also make it expand or contract.

- **Magnetism**. This is the most common method, using relative motion between a coil of wire and a magnet. It is described later on in this section.

THE ELECTRONIC TIDE

Transferring electrons to a place and leaving them there sets up a stress (field) between them (the electrostatic or dielectric attraction mentioned before) and the original location. This is relieved only when the electrons flow back to where they came from. The electrostatic field is represented by lines extending in all directions from a charged body and terminating where there is an equal and opposite charge (the field flows away from a positive charge and towards a negative charge. Lines going in the same direction repel each other, as per *Magnetism*, later).

- **emf** (electromotive force) is the *open circuit* pressure, or the total voltage a battery or generator is *capable* of generating (open circuit means that it is not connected to anything). It is that which maintains a flow to create a difference in potential across each component, and occurs when some other form of energy is converted to electrical energy. When the circuit is open (no current flow), the p.d. at the terminals is equal to the e.m.f. It is the *electrical energy per unit of charge from the source*.

- **p.d.** is the "pressure" difference (or energy transfer) between two points such as across a component such as a lamp, because some of the charge gets used up (it arises when there are more electrons at one end of a cable than the other). Thus, the voltage measured in a circuit when current is flowing is smaller than the maximum, because of internal resistance and the work required to overcome it. Put another way, p.d. involves

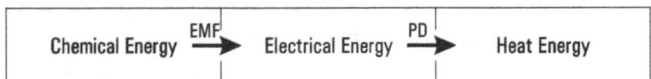

the conversion of electrical energy into another form, such as heat, having first been converted from, say, chemical energy to get emf. Electrons coming from a battery contain a potential charge that is used up as it goes through a component and work is done. The reason behind bonding the parts of a fuselage together is to produce a zero potential over the airframe - if the bonding breaks down, there will be a series of varying differences in potential all over the place.

Essentially, **the voltage coming out of a component is not the same as that going in**, as some of it gets used up. Kirchoff's second law (later) states that all the voltage drops* in a closed circuit equal the total voltage applied to the circuit.

For example, in the picture below of a series circuit, the emf from the battery divides between two lamps.

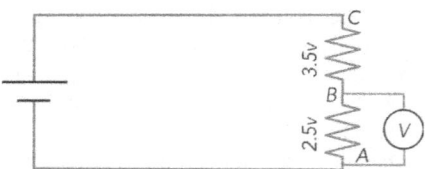

*The difference between a supply voltage and a load voltage, or the loss in electrical pressure used to force electrons through the various resistances. A 10 volt battery connected to a 2 volt device would have a p.d. between them of 8 volts.

A voltmeter connected across the bottom lamp (in parallel) reads 2.5 volts, and one across the top one reads 3.5 volts. If point A has zero potential* (Earth), the p.d. at B is 2.5 volts, and at C, 6 volts. The battery is therefore a 6 volt one (2.5 + 3.5).

*Similar to mean sea level. With the term *potential difference*, from mechanics, the emphasis should be on the word *potential*, since it refers to potential energy, or the energy available due to position (a better expression is *difference in potential*).

To make this clearer, the work involved in pushing together electrons that repel each other is like pushing a large snowball ball up a hill that is getting steeper.

The closer you get to the top, the more work you have to do to move it.

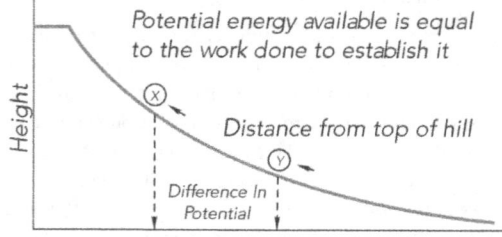

There is a greater potential at X than there is at Y, which is what creates the pressure for a current, assuming the electron at X is allowed to flow to Y.

So, although the number of electrons (current) flowing at each point of the circuit is the same, the pressure or energy behind them (voltage) can vary.

STOP The current does not flow because of the p.d. - the p.d. exists because current is flowing.

If you take a positively charged body (one with more holes than electrons in its atoms) and bring it close to a neutrally charged one, there will be a migration of negative electrons towards the new body (the blue is the negative quality). This is an *electronic tide*.

If you move the positively charged sphere back and forth, the tide will do likewise. These are called *induced charges*, brought about by a process of *induction*, in this case electrostatic. As electrons are moving, one way or another, you now have a drift of electrons, or an electric current.

The electrons do not all rush completely to one side - the centre of the neutral body remains neutral, in that the negative charge gradually increases from the centre to the end. As the electrons have all moved over, there are holes in the atoms on the other side of the body, and there is a similar gradient from the centre to the positive end.

If you replaced the positively charged sphere with a negatively charged one, the result would be the opposite - namely, the negative electrons would be repelled and flow to the other side of the neutral body. If you replaced the air between the two bodies with glass or mica, you could do this at a much smaller distance because you are condensing the field. See *Capacitors*.

Coulomb's Law states that the attractive or repellent force between charged bodies is directly proportional to the product of their individual charges, and inversely proportional to the square of the distance between them.

TYPES OF ELECTRICITY

There are three:

- That which stays right where it is, or **static electricity**, although it can jump across small gaps (this can be a problem with underslung loads on helicopters, especially in dry snow). As this force does not generally move, it is called *static*, meaning electricity that goes nowhere in particular, but which can build up to create a charge that can be attractive or repellent (no conductor is needed).

SYSTEMS
Electricity & Magnetism

You discharge static electricity by providing a path for the electrons to move. *Static discharge wicks* are used on aircraft for this purpose, because the airframe can develop its own static potential. They  allow the charge to concentrate, then discharge to air to avoid radio interference - the visible discharge of static electricity to the air is called *St. Elmo's fire*. A conducting bead in the tyres will do the same job on the ground. Static (and sparks) are why you bond an aircraft and a refuelling vehicle together, and aircraft surfaces to each other.

- That which goes in one direction, usually at one speed and value, called **Direct Current.**
- That which flip-flops back and forth, called **Alternating Current.**

It is AC which concerns us when it comes to radio.

Circuits

There must be an unbroken connection between any components for electricity to flow. A complete circuit is any combination of a conductor and a source of emf that allows electrons to travel round it in a continuous stream. If a circuit is broken (usually with a switch), it is an *open* circuit (as opposed to *closed*), and no current flows. **With open circuits, the loss of continuity stops everything in the circuit from working.**

A cable going to a component must have one returning to its origin as an earth return, to create a *dipole circuit*. However, you can use the fuselage as a return path, which means that you only need one length of cable - the battery will be connected to the fuselage by its *negative* pole. This saves weight and space, but you do need bonding through the fuselage. Further weight savings can be made with busbars, and alternating current, both described later.

SERIES CIRCUITS

A series circuit exists when its elements are connected end to end, creating *one path* for the current to flow in, so if one fails, everything stops (as with Christmas tree lights).

Referring again to the picture of a series circuit above, although both lamps would have the same brightness, they would be dim, because the battery has to push the same charge through the first bulb, then the second. Less charge is flowing per second, so energy is transferred slowly from the battery. The flow of current is the same throughout the circuit.

PARALLEL CIRCUITS

In a parallel circuit, components occupy separate paths, *across* the voltage source (another term for this is a *shunt* connection). In a parallel circuit, the loss of one component does not result in a circuit failure.

In the picture below, both lights would again have equal brightness, but this time they would be bright, as the battery can push the charge along two alternative paths.

More charge can flow around the circuit per second so energy is transferred quickly from the battery.

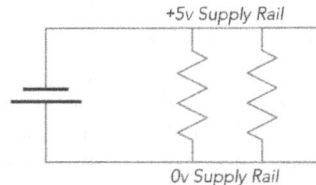

There is more energy in the 5v supply rail, so the current will naturally follow the gradient and flow towards 0.

COMPLEX CIRCUITS

Simply a circuit where the components are connected in combinations of series-parallel.

Voltage

Voltage is a measure of how much energy a charge has. It is like the head of pressure behind the movement of water in a hose. The volt is the p.d. that must exist between two points if the energy transformed is 1 joule when 1 coulomb of electricity (1 amp) passes for one second.

 There is never voltage "at" a place - only a potential difference relative to somewhere else, measured in volts.

Current

The flow of charge (electrons) in a conductor is called the *current*. The rate of current flow is the number of electrons passing any section of the conductor in one second, expressed in terms of *amperes*, or *amps* (an ampere is the movement of 1 coulomb per second). Small currents may be measured in *milliamperes* or *microamperes*. However, one electron has such a small charge that it is hardly detectable. You need a larger unit to work with, such as the *coulomb*, which consists of 6.28×10^{18} electrons (think of a coulomb of electrons in the same way as you would a pint of beer). The symbol for a coulomb is *C*.

Remember: The rate of current flow is measured in amps, and the charge is measured in coulombs.

The more electrons that move along a wire in a given time, the higher the current that is measured, so if you increase the voltage, current will increase automatically, other things being equal. Put more technically, *current will increase with voltage if the resistance, or opposition to flow, remains constant*. It follows that, to control the current, you can vary either the voltage or the resistance, discussed below.

In a series circuit, the current is the same throughout. In a parallel circuit it changes with individual values of resistance (although the voltage will stay the same).

Resistance

A waterwheel produces work when it is turned, but it also slows down the flow of water. Electricity is affected in the same way, in that the amount of current applied to a component is not the same as that coming out the other end. The electrical energy supplied to a circuit is changed into other forms of energy by any appliances connected to it that impede its flow, or have resistance. For best economy, you need to move the most current with the least waste, in a circuit with as little resistance as possible.

A conductor has a low resistance to current, and an insulator has a high one, but even a good conductor slows electrons down, because a new electron joining an atom is repelled by those already there, and some energy is lost. This increases the temperature. The more work you make electricity do, the hotter things get, which is how electric fires work. If you make it work harder, you get light as well, hence light bulbs. Each material has a specific resistance (2.82 for aluminium) against a standard, but its actual resistance depends on its cross section and length. If your conductor is thick and short, you won't meet much resistance. If it is long and thin, on the other hand, you have to force the current along, which takes more work. Electrical energy is proportional to the difference in potential across the component (volts) multiplied by the rate of flow of the moving current, which is affected by the type of material and its cross-sectional area (resistance). In other words:

```
pd across component
current that gets through
```

The more current that gets through a component with a given p.d., the less resistance it has. It is *directly proportional* to *temperature* and *conductor length*, and *inversely proportional* to *cross-sectional area*, so the warmer, longer and thinner a cable is, the more resistance it has. So, if resistance is such a drag, why use it? The answer is that resistance can limit current, or control voltage*, for which the heat is a penalty. It is associated with the *dissipation* of energy, and power is used up (as heat) when it is present. Such power cannot be recovered. For example, you have a starter motor which draws 50 amps at 28.5 volts when it is working hard (see *Ohm's Law*, below). If even a tiny resistance of 0.1 Ohm (which cannot be measured with an multimeter) appears in the circuit, you will lose 5 volts, and the motor will only be working with 23.5 volts Because there is a square law involved, that's over 30% of your cranking power gone.

*A switch is a very crude way of controlling current. Resistors used properly can allow much finer adjustments. For example, a volume control is a variable resistor, and combinations of switches and resistors are the basis of logic gates, described in *Computers, Etc*. A connection taken from the junction between two resistors connected in series can obtain a portion of the voltage, so you can create a specific voltage drop for a particular purpose. Indeed, this is the main use of resistors in any circuit. LEDs, for example, typically operate at around 2 volts. In a 5 volt circuit, they would need some sort of step down.

*Potential dividers*** are used in sensor circuits, where a voltage can be changed if the environment changes.

Resistors in **series act as *voltage* dividers. Resistors in **parallel** are *current* dividers.

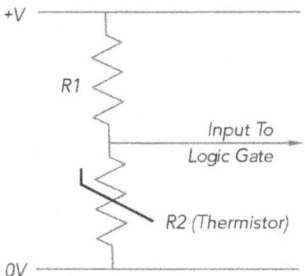

In the picture, the lower resistor is a thermistor, which is heat sensitive, in that, when it is cold, it has a high resistance and *vice versa*. Because the thermistor is on the bottom, such a high resistance allows more current to flow from R1 to the logic gate. Later on, we will see how this can be combined in a circuit to do work. It has to be that way round because having the thermistor on top would block the current and the logic gate would get a low value.

The symbol for resistance is Ω (omega), but in diagrams the zigzag symbol given below is used. In formulae, resistance is signified by the letter R.

 The symbol can mean either a specific component or the amount of resistance present. A resistor slows down electrons in the *entire circuit*, not just at the resistor. In circuit diagrams, however, connecting lines are assumed to have no resistance.

For resistors in **series**, total (or *equivalent*) resistance is simply the sum of them all:

$$R_{TOTAL} = R_1 + R_2 \text{ etc}$$

This is because the same *current* flows through them, and the total is higher than any individual resistance, as the "conductor" is effectively longer. Thus, the current flow will decrease.

Resistors connected in **parallel** present a lower combined resistance because they have an increased cross-sectional area. In other words, if they all have the same value, the current divides equally between them all. As the voltage (p.d.) remains the same, and therefore so does the current through each resistor, the total current increases - it is doubled with two resistors in parallel.

Put another way, the effective resistance is reduced - by half with two resistors.

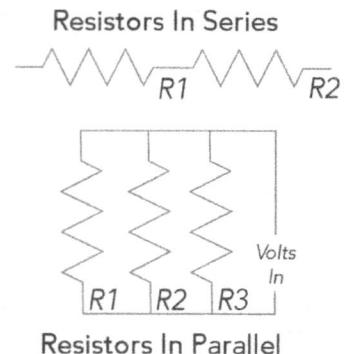

If they do not all have the same value, those with *lower* resistance will draw *more* current (components are protected against excessive current with fuses and circuit breakers, described later).

Tip: Two identical resistors in parallel have half the resistance of one! To calculate the ohmic value of a pair of resistors in parallel, divide their product by their sum.

Essentially, *the resultant is smaller than the smallest resistance*, and you can often answer an exam question just by knowing that. That is, if the resistances were 3 ohms each in the diagram, they would collectively behave like a 1 ohm resistor. Individual resistors do not then have to cope with maximum current, which is useful when adding loads in a sharing situation.

Now you find total resistance by adding the reciprocals:

$$\frac{1}{R_{TOTAL}} = \frac{1}{R1} + \frac{1}{R2} \text{ etc}$$

Instead of resistance, think of its opposite, conductance, which is simply the reciprocal. Find the sum of the conductances, then reverse it to find the resistance, as the reciprocal of the total resistance is the sum of the reciprocals of the individual resistors, which sounds a lot worse than it is. For example, with 4 resistances in parallel, of 1, 3, 8 and 15 ohms, find the unknown total R.

Turned into reciprocals, the formula would look like this:

$$\frac{1}{R} = \frac{1}{1} + \frac{1}{3} + \frac{1}{8} + \frac{1}{15}$$

The lowest common denominator is 120, so....

$$\frac{1}{R} = \frac{120 + 40 + 15 + 8}{120}$$

which becomes:

$$\frac{1}{R} = \frac{183}{120}$$

The non-reciprocal of which is:

$$\frac{R}{1} = \frac{120}{183}$$

As the denominator is greater than the numerator, the answer is less than 1. This makes sense as, if you imagined the same situation with water pipes, more liquid will flow through several of them connected in parallel than through one, which is the same as having less resistance. If one conductor is split into two, resistance doubles in each half (because the cross sectional area is reduced), so total resistance is half that of one.

Ohm's Law

The ratio of the voltage across, and the current flowing through, a conductor is constant, and equal to the value of the resistance. If you increase the voltage (pressure) in a circuit, you increase the current (number of electrons) automatically. On the other hand, given a constant voltage, current flow decreases if you increase the resistance. Current flow is therefore *directly proportional* to voltage and *inversely proportional* to resistance.

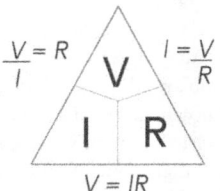

Ohm's Law describes the fixed relationship between voltage, current and resistance, and is useful for finding the unknown factor in a circuit if you know the values of the other two and have forgotten the relevant measuring instrument (actually, it's very hard to measure current, and it's mostly calculated anyway). Ohm's law does not apply to all conductors, but it is valid for most metals if their temperature remains constant.

The symbols for the elements in the formula are *I* for current (amps), *R* for resistance (ohms), *V* for voltage, and they come together in this formula:

```
V (or PD) = I x R
```

or (rearranged slightly):

```
I = V
    R
```

So, if you have a 24 volt battery, and a load has 12 ohms of resistance, there are 2 amps of current:

```
24 = I(2) x 12
```

Aircraft systems typically use 24-volts because of the weight savings you get when a higher voltage is used - lower current means lighter cabling.

This formula can be useful in many ways - given that the resistance of an aluminium cable is about 60% greater than a copper one of the same length and cross section, you could use the formula to calculate how much larger the replacement would have to be.

 If you connect a heavy load to a battery, the battery's voltage will drop as it tries to satisfy Ohm's Law. If the required current cannot be produced, it pushes out as much as it can and the voltage will reduce to whatever Ohm's Law says it should be.

Ohm's law often has to be combined with something like:

KIRCHOFF'S LAWS

These are generalisations that make it easier to calculate the currents involved with complex resistances.

- **First:** At any junction of resistances, the total current flowing in is equal to the current flowing out. In other words, electricity does not accumulate at any point in a circuit.

- **Second:** This is a generalisation of Ohm's Law. In any closed circuit, the sum of the products of current and resistance (drops in potential) equals the voltage applied to the circuit (emf) - the law of conservation of energy for electrical circuits. In other words, voltage drops and sources are equal.

Both are very useful (in combination with Ohm's Law) to find unknown values in a circuit. For example, in a circuit with two resistors that have voltage drops across them of 14 and 10 volts, the source voltage must be 24v.

SYSTEMS
Electricity & Magnetism

Bridge Circuits

Kirchoff's laws are the basis of the **Wheatstone Bridge**, which was invented by Samuel Hunter Christie in 1833 and improved and popularised by Sir Charles Wheatstone in 1843. It measures an unknown electrical resistance by balancing two legs of a bridge circuit, one of which includes the unknown component. They are commonly used in Air Data Computers that use solid state capsules.

In the diagram below, a DC current flows through R1 and R2, and R3 and R4, so the potential difference across both pairs is the same. If R1 and R2 are of equal value, the p.d. across each is half the supply value.

Equally for R3 and R4, so everything is in balance.

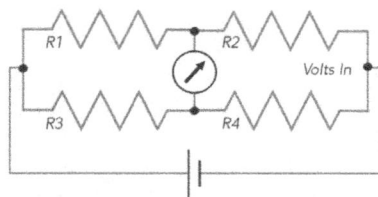

If you have a resistance you don't know, say R4, you can simply vary R3 until the bridge is balanced again. It is the ratio between R1 and R2 that is significant rather than their values. This is why they are called the ratio arms.

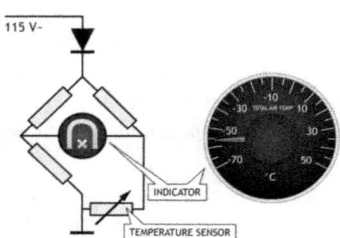

As the bridge becomes unbalanced, the varying voltage across the middle can be measured with a voltmeter. For temperature measurement purposes, for example, you can replace the voltmeter with a wiper arm that is positioned by a servo loop, and how far the arm moves is a measure of the temperature change. It will be centred at 15°C.

The same principle can be used with fuel measurement, using a resistive circuit that has floats connected to a Wheatstone Bridge, typically powered by DC.

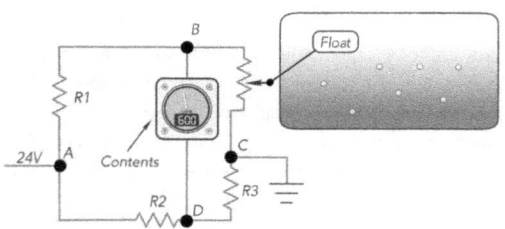

The float may be made of specially treated cork, or a sealed (lightweight) metal cylinder attached to an arm that is pivoted to allow angular movement to be transmitted to an electrical element consisting of a wiper arm and a potentiometer (variable resistance), so, as the fuel level changes, the float arm's movement alters the resistance.

The three fixed resistances (R1, R2 and R3) have the same value. If the variable resistance (RV) is also the same, Ohm's law says that the current through each side of the bridge (ABC and ADC) will be the same. As there is no current through the indicator, it will read zero (i.e. an empty tank). As the level of fuel in the tank rises and lifts the float, the variable resistance increases, the current flow through ABC (which contains the variable resistance) will be less than that through ADC, creating a higher voltage at B than D. Current will flow from B to D, through the indicator, which would show a quantity in the tank.

Float type indicators provide information on *volume*, whose indication varies with temperature. One advantage is their easy construction. Neither are they affected by voltage variations (if a galvanometer is used), but they are influenced by *attitude**, *acceleration*, and *temperature variations* (if calibrated for weight rather than volume).

*Resistive systems are calibrated for level attitudes so the indications will otherwise be inaccurate.

Power (watts)

The *rate* at which electrons are moved about is called *electrical power*, represented by the letter P, which is measured in *watts*, after James Watt (the watt is the SI derived unit of power, equal to the transfer of one joule per second. 746 watts equal 1 horsepower). However, as watts are very small units, we tend to use kilowatts (kW) instead, and count them in thousands (0.01kv is 10 volts!) With DC, power consumed (wattage) is determined by multiplying the voltage across a circuit by the current going through it (in amps):

$$P = V \times I$$

The amount of power changes when voltage and/or current changes but, in practice, we can only change voltage and resistance. Put another way, if the current changes, it is because either V or R has changed. If the resistance is held constant, the power varies directly with the square of the voltage - starting with 1 volt and 0.5 amps (0.5 watts), you will progress through 2 volts and 2 watts, and 3 volts and 9 watts (it also varies with the square of the current).

Power lost as heat is often called the *IR loss*, as the heat depends on current and resistance. The above formula (*Joule's Law*) best represents heat energy lost by a circuit.

But V is also equal to I x R under Ohm's Law. If you substitute one for the other, you only need to use current and resistance to find power:

$$P = IR \times I$$
$$P = I^2 R$$

But you can also use just voltage and resistance:

$$I = \frac{V}{R}$$

To give:

$$P = \frac{V}{R} \times V$$

$$P = \frac{V^2}{R}$$

Thus, there are three formulae for calculating power, depending on the information you have to hand.

If a 240v light bulb is rated at 60W, what is its resistance?

$$R = \frac{V^2}{P}$$

$$R = \frac{57600}{60} = 960 \text{ ohms}$$

This is only correct for DC.

The total power equals the sum of the power consumed by each component. In general, for maximum power transmission, E and I (voltage and current) must be as large as possible, but the current is limited by the size of the wire, and the voltage by the insulation.

It is easier and cheaper to make a line with good insulation, so you can transmit a higher voltage, than to make one able to carry high current, as power loss is proportional to the square of the current, which should be as low as possible. This is one reason for using alternating current, as high voltages are easier to achieve with it. Sending signals down long cables is more effective when they are based on voltage rather than current.

POWER RATINGS

The power rating, expressed in watts, represents the rate at which a device converts electrical energy into another form of energy, as is done with speakers. A 60 watt bulb is capable of converting more electrical energy into light than a 40 watt bulb. In some devices, the wattage rating indicates the maximum design power at a specific voltage, such as the bulbs mentioned above. Others, such as resistors, can use any combination of voltage and current up to the maximum specified (there will be a 50% safety factor built in).

The *efficiency* of an electrical device is the ratio between the power converted to useful energy divided by the power it consumes. This will always be less than 1 due to various losses (especially with AC generators).

Circuit Protection

A **short circuit** exists when the full current comes into contact with the grounded part of the circuit. This can be more than the circuit is built to handle, so electrical equipment may be protected in many ways.

 The **Battery Master Switch** controls the power to all circuits, and others will control smaller groups of equipment, such as the **Avionics Master Switch** for the radios and navigation aids. The battery switch may be in two parts, one for the battery, and the other for the alternator, which needs DC for its electromagnet.

Circuits will be otherwise protected by **fuses** or **circuit breakers**, which are designed to interrupt the flow of current where specific conditions that generate a lot of heat exist. One difference between the two is that a fuse will blow *before* the full fault current is reached, and the circuit breaker will trip afterwards, in which case both it and the item protected must be able to take the full fault current for a short time. Neither are designed to protect equipment as such - rather, they are there to protect the cabling and connectors which are not easy to replace and may be old and/or inaccessible if a fire starts.

Circuit protection devices should only be reset or replaced once if the item is needed for flight safety, after allowing them to cool, and you know why it blew in the first place.

Generally, circuit breakers are resettable, fuses are not.

FUSES

A fuse is a deliberately weak part of a circuit so, in theory, instead of replacing wiring in odd places, all you do is change the fuse. Technically, a fuse is a *thermal device wired in series with the load protected*, meaning that all the current passes through it, and it *melts* because it *overheats* from *excess current*. Fuses are placed as close to a power distribution point as possible to minimise runs of unprotected cable.

To put this in perspective, and to show how potentially useless they can be, **fuses protect your wiring**. Not components. Put more simply, the fuse is there to isolate the upstream system from faulty downstream equipment that is drawing too much current. If a component is meant to draw 5A and is working properly, it will only draw 5A. You cannot force, say, 8A into it. **If too much current is flowing through a device it is because something is already wrong with it.** This can be a potential fire hazard, as current flowing in a conductor creates heat.

The amount of current needed to melt a fuse is way more than would destroy any equipment connected to it. Taking a 240v domestic example, which is around double of what is floating around the average airliner, a BS 3036 30A (wire) fuse will only melt at 45 amps – and even then, it'll take nearly 3 hours! If you want it to melt within a second, you'll need to put around 105 amps through it.

 As the current is large, there is no fuse protection for starter motors, which is why there is a warning light that must be checked after you start a piston engine.

You must carry spare fuses - EASA require the higher of 10% of the number for each rating, with at least 3.

Fuses must be replaced with those of the *correct* value. They are rated according to the number of amperes they carry, which must be a lower figure than the lowest rated equipment. As well, fuse capacity should be double the amperage requirement. So, in a 100-watt circuit using 25 volts (i.e. 4 amps), you need an 8-amp fuse. Generally, the lowest rated fuse is selected for reliable operation, but for emergency equipment (anything that will affect safety), the highest rating is used consistent with cable protection.

A *high rupturing fuse* is also known as a *heavy duty* fuse.

CIRCUIT BREAKERS

A circuit breaker is a combination of a relay and a solenoid, both described later. It is relatively slow acting (a magnetic circuit breaker has a quicker response), and can be used in AC and DC circuits, being a button that pops out when a fuse would otherwise break, so it is a *resettable mechanical trip device,* activated by the heating of a bimetallic strip element, where one metal expanding more than another pops it open.

Thermal trip circuit breakers show black when closed and white when they are open.

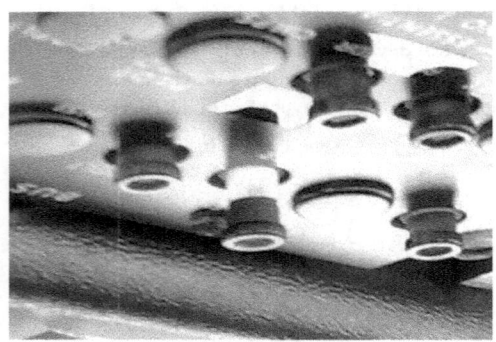

A *trip-free* circuit breaker will trip even if it is held in, and therefore does not remake a circuit, so pilots don't make the situation worse! A magnetic one is a *quick tripping response protection system.* A *flush fit* circuit breaker cannot be manually tripped or pulled.

 Although they are the most commonly used method of circuit protection, try not to use a circuit breaker as a switch. This cannot always be avoided, but it is still not good practice.

CURRENT LIMITERS

These are like fuses, but with a much higher melting point so that a higher (short term) overload current can be carried. They will limit the current to a predetermined value and are used typically to sectionalise heavy duty supply circuits.

LIMITING RESISTORS

These are used in DC circuits where initial current surges may be very high, as with starter motors or inverters.

Capacitance

Where two separate, nearby, conductors have a current flowing through them, there is an electric field flowing through the insulation (dielectric) between them. Even two wires close together can have this property. A circuit has capacitance if it can store energy as an electric field. Whereas resistors can control the amount of current in a circuit, capacitors can control how quickly the p.d. across a component changes, so they allow you to design circuits that involve timing (see *Storage*, below). Potential energy is also associated with *elasticity*, which can be represented by a stretched spring, or a hydraulic accumulator, including smoothing fluctuations and absorbing surges. Electrically, you can do the same thing with a capacitor.

Normally, electrons cannot enter a conductor unless there is a path for an equal amount of them to leave, which is why you need a circuit. However, a conductor can hold a greater charge if it is near another one and there is an electric field in the space between them (see below).

You are concentrating the region over which the field extends, which is why capacitors were originally called condensers. The number of extra free electrons added to the conductor (or free electrons taken away) is directly proportional to the field flux between them.

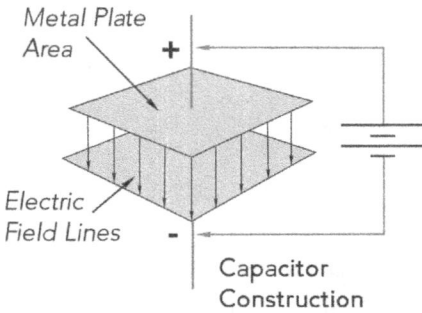

STORAGE

In an electronic circuit, you often need to store small quantities of electricity for short periods of time. Because they can store electricity* (or energy), capacitors can make a circuit dynamic. If you had two circuits, each with a battery, a switch and a light bulb, but one with a capacitor, the capacitor can introduce a time delay before the bulb goes on or off (as can a coil, or a solenoid, for different reasons). This is because capacitors tend to resist changes in voltage drop.

*A capacitor's storage ability is not actually used much in radio - they are more useful for their ability to pass AC and block DC, as described overleaf.

Capacitance is the ratio of the stored charge to the applied voltage. The larger the capacitance, the larger the charge you can store from a given voltage. It depends on:

- the **dielectric** used. Glass, for example, has 5.1 times the capacity of dry air and fuel has double (water has 80). The reason that solids are more effective than air is that, when the charge starts or stops, a momentary flow of electrons begins or ends. This wouldn't happen if there was nothing there at all. This increase is called *permittivity* (see below). *It is the dielectric that holds the charge.*

- **distance** between the plates (they cannot touch or there would be a short circuit).

- the **parallel surface area.**

Thus, capacitance is more when the conductors are nearer to each other, or larger. If they are relatively far apart, you will get more leakage from the field, which is the basis of radio transmission, discussed in *Radio Navigation*. If you had 100 volts between two plates and introduced a third one between them, you would get two capacitors in series, with a p.d. of 50 volts each, so they have the same charge but half the voltage. To get back to 100 volts you would have to double the charge. That is to say, halving the spacing doubles the capacitance, which is inversely proportional to the spacing between the plates (it is directly proportional to the cross-sectional area). For capacitors in parallel, the total capacitance is the sum of them (the opposite of how resistance works):

$$C_{TOTAL} = C1 + C2 \text{ etc}$$

They add up because you are increasing the plate area whilst the spacing stays the same.

Treat capacitors in series as for resistors in parallel:

$$\frac{1}{C_{TOTAL}} = \frac{1}{C1} + \frac{1}{C2} \text{ etc}$$

or:

$$C_{TOTAL} = \frac{C1 \times C2}{C1 + C2}$$

Total capacitance will be less than that of the smallest capacitor, because connecting them in series increases the space between all the plates and reducing the p.d. across each capacitor.

The unit of capacitance is the *farad* (F), named after Faraday. It represents 1 amp for 1 second with a change of 1 volt stored as 1 joule of energy. As it happens, this is too large to be used in most circuits (the capacitor concerned wouldn't even fit into a room), so *microfarads* (μf), representing millionths, are used instead.

CURRENT FLOW

When voltage is applied across the capacitor in the diagram below, one plate becomes negatively charged with electrons leaving the battery. At the same time, electrons leave the other plate to resupply the battery, leaving that plate positively charged.

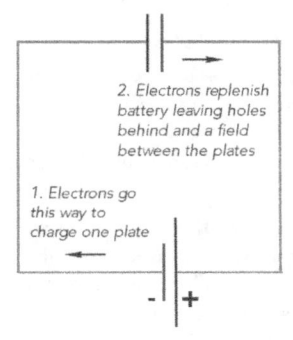

1. Electrons go this way to charge one plate
2. Electrons replenish battery leaving holes behind and a field between the plates

This effect is called *polarisation*. The current flows until the charge across the capacitor is equal to the battery emf, at which point everything stops. However, you now have more electrons and holes than you would normally have on the respective plates, which carry equal and opposite charges, attracting each other, and an electric field of force (charge) between them. There is a "strain" on the dielectric (hence the word "tension", as in *High Tension*). DC will not normally pass across the gap, unless the voltage is very high and the gap very small, in which case there may be a spark. Thus, a fully charged capacitor acts as an open circuit to DC because, as it reaches the maximum charge and therefore matches the supply voltage, the current becomes zero. **No current will flow if you simply charge the capacitor** (with DC).

If the source of voltage is taken away, the voltage across the capacitor stays where it is, but will leak in the reverse direction over time so, until this happens, capacitors behave like batteries, since they preserve a difference of potential between the plates for a short time. This is how you can change the batteries in your mobile phone without backup power. Capacitors are also used in computer memory cells to store information, and as suppressors on electric motors, or in magnetos.

If a capacitor discharges through a high resistance, the current will be relatively large at first, but will gradually die away, so you get a lot of current in one shot but, through a small resistance, the current alternates rapidly in relatively weak cycles.

Alternating current appears to pass through capacitors because the plates change between positive and negative on each cycle as the charge on them builds up and decays. The rapid change of p.d. looks like current "flowing".

If the frequency of the alternating current is high enough, the capacitor will behave as if it were a low value resistor, because it will never become charged in either direction. At lower frequencies, this "resistance" will be higher because charging can take place, and be maximum at zero frequency if you ignore leakage. This quality of resistance varying with frequency is actually called *reactance*, which is useful for filtering frequencies, especially with radio.

If the frequency of the supply in a series capacitive circuit is decreased, the current flowing in it will decrease. When the AC voltage across a capacitor is kept constant and the frequency is increased, the current through the capacitor will increase.

PERMITTIVITY

The factor by which capacitance is increased when an insulator (dielectric) fills the space between the plates is called the *dielectric constant*, or permittivity of the material, which is the quality that allows it to store an electrical charge, or a measure of its ability to allow an electric flux to be established. It is the relationship between flux density and electric field strength.

A material with high permittivity can store more charge than one with lower permittivity. It is a physical quantity that describes how an electric field affects and is affected by a dielectric, or *a constant of proportionality that relates the electric field in a material to the electric displacement in that material.*

The *absolute permittivity* of a substance (or the constant for a given material) is given relative to that of a vacuum, or the *permittivity of free space*. The *relative permittivity* of a particular dielectric (the dielectric constant) is the ratio of its absolute permittivity to that of free space, or of using an insulator rather than a vacuum. The relative permittivity of air is usually 1, since the difference between that and a vacuum is negligible for our purposes.

Thus, permittivity relates to a material's ability to isolate (or "permit") an electric field - as mentioned above, solids are better at being a dielectric than air, and the increased permittivity allows the same charge to be stored with a smaller electric field (and a smaller voltage), leading to increased capacitance. This is how capacitive fuel measurement takes place, using the difference between fuel and air when they are used as a dielectric.

APPLICATIONS FOR CAPACITORS

- Short term storage of DC charges.
- Coupling AC circuits where no DC is wanted.
- Filtering out AC where DC is wanted.
- Timing circuits - with potential dividers, they can create time delays in logic circuits as they charge.
- With an inductor (later), creating tuned circuits that resonate at a particular frequency.

FUEL MEASUREMENT

Capacitance fuel systems are fitted to larger aircraft because they measure fuel mass rather than volume (Specific Fuel Consumption is the weight of fuel used in one hour to develop 1 pound of thrust).

The capacity of a capacitor depends on the nature of its dielectric (see *Electricity*). Fuel has twice the capacitance of air so a full tank has twice the capacitive reactance as an empty one. A simple system will have a variable capacitor in the fuel tank, an amplifier, and an indicator, plus a compensator to correct for fuel temperature and a densitometer to adjust for specific gravity or fuel type (Jet A-1 or Jet B). The complete circuit forms an electrical bridge that is constantly being rebalanced around the differences between the tank and reference capacitors. The calculation is *Permittivity* (E) multiplied by the *area of the plates* (A), divided by *distance* (D) between them. The signal is amplified and used to drive a motor inside the indicator.

A *capacitance probe* that runs the full height of the tank consists of two tubes, one inside the other, with fuel between them. The two tubes are fed with AC so the "capacitor" formed by the tubes (fuel is the dielectric) charges and discharges alternately. The amount of discharge varies according to whether the dielectric is fuel or air, so the electrical signal produced is proportional to the tank's contents.

On their own, the detectors can only measure the height of fuel (volume), so a datum or *reference capacitor* compensates for *density* to ensure that weight is indicated correctly (if not told otherwise, assume you have a compensated system, as most aircraft use them). Any increase in density from the contraction of fuel as it cools will increase the capacitance.

In a compensated system, the indicated fuel weight remains the same if the temperature changes.

Compensation works on the basis that variations in fuel capacitance follow permittivity, which describes how an electric field affects and is affected by a dielectric. Thus, permittivity relates to a material's ability to transmit (or "permit") an electric field. For example, in a capacitor, an increased permittivity allows the same charge to be stored with a smaller electric field (and a smaller voltage), leading to increased capacitance.

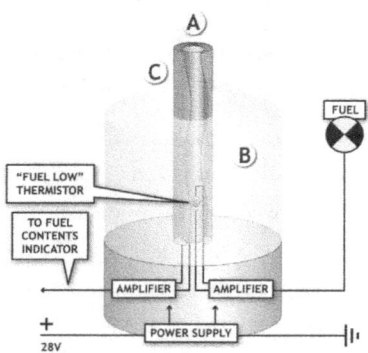

To ensure that only permittivity is measured, the compensator unit is placed in the bottom of the tank so it is always covered with fuel, which means that capacitance is not measured by fuel quantity. When temperature increases, permittivity will increase and so will capacitance, and the bridge circuit becomes unbalanced. The voltage so produced drives a motor that drives a potentiometer that decreases the resistance. As this is biased towards a full tank condition, an increase in fuel quantity is indicated. Indication errors will still be there because density also varies with temperature, but these are minor in comparison, so errors are minimised.

There are many sensors connected in parallel, because fuel has a habit of sloshing around - this ensures that a more accurate average reading is taken.

There is always a continuous zero signal (i.e. empty) in a parallel system that is normally suppressed by the signal from the probes. If it fails, your gauge will suddenly read empty, or whatever the manufacturer chooses. A test routine simulates the empty signal.

If a fuel tank with a capacitive contents system has water in it, but no fuel, the gauge will be inaccurate because water has a very high dielectric constant of about 80, as opposed to 2 (fuel) or 1 (air). The reading, however will be greater than zero - possibly full, because the gauge could over-read by as much as 8000%.

Measuring Instruments

THE AMMETER

Current is measured in series using *ammeters*, or *loadmeters*, both presenting the information in different ways. They need a low resistance so they don't affect the current they are measuring. Ammeters measure coulombs per second, and there is one per generator.

A **centre-reading** ammeter's needle (right) is typically associated with DC generators and light aircraft and should always be in the + side of the gauge (not too much!), to show a positive charge going into the battery. It is connected to the battery's positive lead. In other words,  it is a two-way device that shows you what is going on between the battery and the generator. With the battery on and the engine off, the needle will show a negative reading in the minus range, or a discharge. If a discharge is shown with the engine running, the generator is not up to the job and the difference has to be made up by the battery. Switch things off until you get a positive reading.

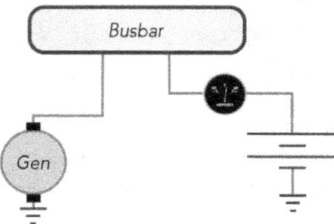

The other type is also called a **loadmeter**. It is often associated with DC generators and/or turbine engines, and measures electrical loads rather than battery charging, so it is a one-way device connected only to the generator.

The display starts at zero, and shows positive numbers, sometimes as a percentage. With the battery on and the engine off, it will read zero.

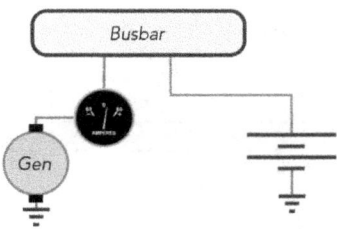

The *peak startup draw* (when the load is first applied) is always heavier than that used by a device when it is running. That is, components draw more current in the initial stages, until the flow settles down*. Typically, when you switch on the generator after starting an engine, the loadmeter will read high at first, then decrease as the battery becomes topped up. Only after reaching a certain figure on its way down (say 0.7) should you switch the electrical services on.

*A high rate of charge after starting an engine is only allowed for a short period.

THE VOLTMETER

A voltmeter is an ammeter that includes a multiplier resistor in parallel with the circuit, so the drop in voltage across the resistance is a measure of the voltage in the circuit - a high voltage is indicated if the current flow is large, and *vice versa*. A *Voltmeter is connected in parallel*, so the current does not pass through the meter instead of the circuit and affect the readings.

A good voltmeter therefore has a very high resistance.

Power Distribution (Busbars)

The lighter an aircraft is, the better, so it's impractical (if only for weight saving) to run a wire from the battery (and back) to every component it supplies. A better solution is to run a single (big) wire to a distribution point and then (via fuses or circuit breakers) to any electrical appliances, to serve all of them from the end of that line, and use the fuselage as an Earth return, which is what a busbar system is all about.

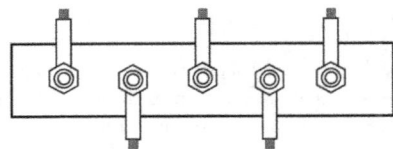

Physically, an electrical bus is a metal bar with provisions to make electrical contact with a number of devices that use electricity. Electrically, it's a conduit between components, like the memory bus in a computer.

There's nothing to stop you having main buses supplying secondary ones, but the system must ensure that problems on or near it do not endanger any components connected to it, so services supplied by a busbar are normally in parallel, to enable isolation and keep voltages equal.

REQUIREMENTS

There are certain requirements for busbars:

- If a power source fails, equipment must not be deprived of power unless the total demand exceeds the supply.
- Earthing faults should produce the least possible fire risk and the minimum effect on systems.
- Equipment faults must not endanger the supply to other equipment.

The above can be met by:

- paralleling generators
- adequate circuit protection devices
- isolating faulty generators

For isolation purposes, components are graded in order of importance in an emergency: *vital*, *essential* and *non-essential*.

- **Vital** services include items that are wired directly to the battery, so they will carry on working when the generators fail (emergency lighting, etc.) The term *hot bus* or *direct bus* means that the bus is always live (i.e. it has no switches), so you must switch devices attached to it off when you close down, as with the fuel boost pumps in some aircraft. There may be a secondary battery switch for this purpose. The hot bus not only allows items to be powered if alternators or generators fail, but also allows the engine(s) to be started when they are not working anyway. All aircraft need standby electrical power systems, in case the normal one goes down. For small ones, this is usually the main battery, which is oversized for this reason. The problem is, it's time-limited to 30 minutes. Larger aircraft use an *Auxiliary Power Unit* (APU).
- **Essential** services are those needed for safe flight that can still be run by a generator or the battery.
- **Non-essential** services are things like galleys which can be isolated for load-shedding purposes.

Most multi-engined aircraft have left and right main buses, and a battery master bus for a few essential items, but there the similarity ends. There are so many variations that it's difficult to keep track, and getting acquainted with a new type of aircraft can be quite difficult, especially when the Flight Manual is less than perfect. Essential things to know about buses are what they power, how to reroute power to them and how to isolate them, a bit like fuel systems (the bus tie does the same job as a crossfeed). It can be closed if power is lost on one side to route electricity to the other.

There are three types of busbar system:

SPLIT

Busbars can be split to protect delicate equipment from large variations in electrical power, as is found when starting. In other words, there are two separate systems that are not operated in parallel. In many aircraft, the Avionics Master Switch serves as a link between busbars.

 The Avionics Master Switch would also be a circuit breaker, and useful for reducing wear and tear on the switches of the radios and navaids.

Split busbars are normally found in twin engined aircraft, where each generator feeds its own busbar. However, they are not necessarily paralleled because this can be problematic, especially with AC, so they don't need advanced circuitry, and each generator can run with a slightly different frequency. If a generator fails, its circuit breaker (GCB) will close (as instructed by a Generator Control Unit), and a bus tie breaker (BTB, or changeover relay) will connect the busbars automatically so the loads can be taken care of by the other generator. The APU is brought on line by the transfer relay, at which point the BTB will reopen. When the BTB is closed on the ground, both busbars can be served by external power or the generator on the APU.

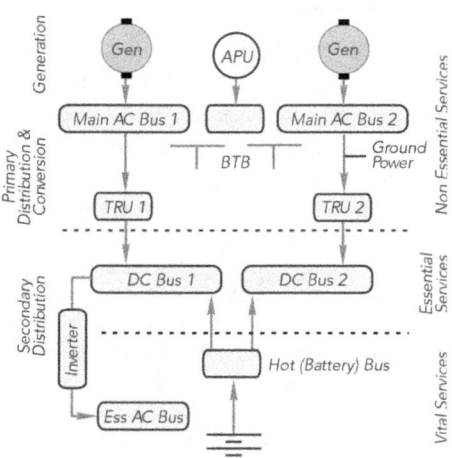

Above is a theoretical example of a split busbar system. It shows the possible location of typical components. Each generator has its own bus with non-essential services connected to it (passengers' coffee), or those that don't matter if it fails. Both are ultimately connected in parallel to a combining busbar which carries the essential services (pilots' coffee), so they will always have at least one source of power. Notice that the essential AC bus comes off the essential DC bus via an inverter. The battery is connected to the DC buses, so it can be charged, yet still supply essential components if both generators fail.

PARALLEL

Normally found on 3-engined aircraft such as the L-1011, MD-11, DC-10 and B-727*, in which all the generators are paralleled onto one bus once the engines are working. Loads can be supplied and controlled independently, so voltage must be independent of the load, but current must be proportional to them. It used to be the Flight Engineer's job to look after them, because they need careful matching before the bus tie is closed to synchronise the frequency and voltage.

*The 727 has a parallel system with a synchronising bus. This is one where several buses are connected together with bus ties (I know the 727 only has 3 engines, but the picture below shows the principle):

The Generator Circuit Breaker (GCB) is controlled by the generator switch in the cockpit. Bus tie breakers are normally closed, being controlled by a bus tie switch.

The split system breaker simply splits the system in half so that 1 & 2 and 3 & 4 can be separate buses in their own right. It therefore provides a measure of control and protection and system isolation. It is designed to open automatically if you try to parallel external power sources on to the bus (they cannot be synchronised). On some aircraft, you have to close it manually (with a switch) when you connect external power.

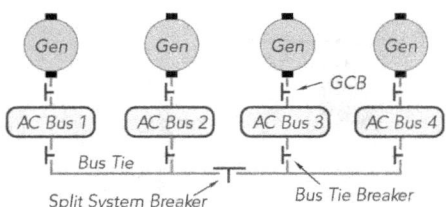

 On some aircraft, you cannot do this if the system is already using its own generators, or if it has the wrong voltage, frequency and phase.

SPLIT PARALLEL

Found in the B747-400, but may also be in the A-380, this system allows generators to be isolated or paralleled, so you have more options.

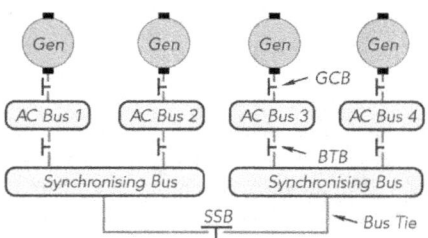

Again, each generator has its own bus bar. Pairs of them may be paralleled with a synchronising, or combining, bus bar. On a four-engined aeroplane closing the split system breaker (SSB) will parallel all four generators. As each generator phase is connected to its own busbar, there are three for each generator from which single phase supplies can be taken. The supplies for larger induction motors are therefore taken by connecting all three (for simplicity, only one is shown). Non-essential AC is taken from the busbar. Essential AC is taken from one that has an automatic alternate source of power, the synchronising busbar. As the generators run on part loads, their life expectancy is increased, and the system absorbs large transient loads.

STANDBY BUSES

Some aircraft have their essential services covered through extensions that are connected to main buses through relays that are normally closed. This allows you to power those circuits from standby power sources if required, which would normally be inverters from the main battery.

MONITORING

Because the larger load is in kilowatts, the maximum load is expressed in kW in the limitations section of the flight manual. You would normally check the kW readings to ensure equal load sharing*. The kVAR reading gives you an idea of what the voltage regulator is up to.

*Frequency matching shares the real load (kW) and voltage matching shares the reactive load (kVAR).

SYSTEMS
Electricity & Magnetism

FAULT PROTECTION

When generators are paralleled or isolated, there is some automatic control to ensure that frequency and voltage remain within limits. Typical faults that might trip an associated circuit breaker include:

- Synchronising bus faults, which will trip a bus tie breaker.
- CSDU (see later) disconnections, or over- and undervoltages, which come from voltage regulators and will trip the GCB.
- Excitation or voltage problems, which will trip the relevant GCBs if their generators are paralleled.
- If the generator is isolated, the field breaker will trip and disconnect the voltage regulator (used to keep the battery charging voltage constant). When the generator field breaker (control relay) trips, the voltage regulator disconnects from the excitation field and the GCB will also trip.
- A frequency problem or operation of an engine fire switch will trip the field breaker.

Batteries

Certain chemicals, when they are combined with some metals, can make electrons flow as direct current, until all the electrons disappear from the metal, causing it to eventually get eaten away - as the atoms comprising the metal lose electrons, they cease to be the same atoms and therefore cease to exist in their former state - if you could put the electrons back, you would regain your metal plate, and recharge the battery (they don't have to be the same electrons). A primary (dry) cell is enclosed in a metal case which gets eaten away as the battery discharges. This process is not reversible. Primary cells are typically used in flashlights as a throwaway item.

A secondary cell can be recharged, and usually has a liquid involved in its construction.

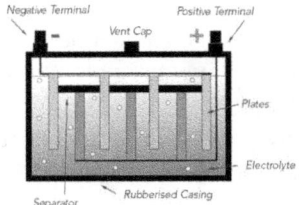

A "battery" is a *collection* of secondary cells, which have a charge of about 2.2 volts each (lead-acid), or 1.2 (Ni-Cad), hence the need to combine them to do anything useful. Lead-Acid batteries will have 12 cells, and Ni-Cads 19 or 20 to produce the 24 volts needed for aircraft. To be the equivalent of a 12v lead-acid battery, a NiCad needs between 10-11 cells.

If one cell is dead, the battery is unserviceable.

A cell consists of alternating positive and negative *plates* surrounded by a liquid called an *electrolyte*. Different materials are better or worse at this job, so you might get more or less voltage out of one type of battery compared to another. The two types used in aircraft are *lead acid*, as found in cars (shown above), and *NiCad*, as found in older portable computers, now replaced by Lithium Ion. People who use both will already understand the difference but, in simple terms, the lead acid's output tends to fall off steadily with discharge, whereas a NiCad can pump out a constant power until it can do no more, meaning that its *closed-circuit voltage* remains nearly constant until it is rapidly discharged.

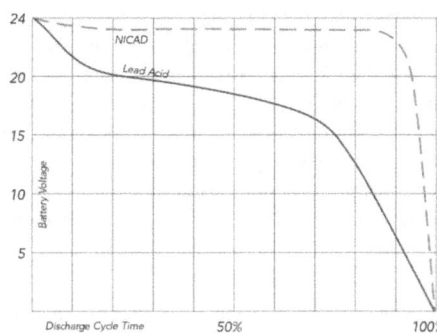

As well, a NiCad is more compact, has a longer shelf life, reduced charging time, recovers more quickly, and has a low internal resistance, so it's good for starting turbines.

In the early days, say, up till the 1950s, *vented* lead-acid batteries were used almost exclusively, until vented NiCads came along, with their superior performance at low temperatures, and in low voltage full discharge high-cycle applications. *Sealed* lead-acid batteries were subsequently invented, for better reliability, and are now more common, as NiCads do not perform so well in extended standby applications, such as with battery backups for IRS, etc.

An aircraft battery's purpose is to:

- maintain a supply under transient conditions.
- help with short term heavy loads.
- supply total power for a short time in emergencies.
- start the engines, where it also has to excite the alternators.

However, it needs the right conditions - at -30°C, a battery has less than half its power to start an engine that needs 350% more effort to get going! This is because, when it is cold, a battery's internal resistance increases (in the Arctic, you take them out at night to keep them warm).

A flat battery has maximum internal resistance, which will generate lots of heat when an attempt is made to charge it (on a bench, only a very small current is used). It is therefore not a good idea to continue a flight if your battery gets discharged. In any case, it should be replaced before the next flight. One problem is, for it to work, an alternator needs current from a battery, and your machine's electrics won't work if it isn't there.

BATTERY CAPACITY

The capacity or holding power of a battery is a measure of its ability to produce current over a specified period of time. The number of cells will determine the voltage it produces, but the area of the plates inside, the amount of active material in the plates and how much electrolyte there is determines the *ampere-hour* capacity, or amps multiplied by hours. A typical rating is 12-18 amp/hours (which rate will go down the faster you use it).

The definition of electrical current is the amount of charge flowing down a wire per second, expressed as:

Current = $\dfrac{\text{Charge}}{\text{Time}}$

So current is a time-derived value. A battery delivering 45 Amps for 2.5 hours could deliver 90 Amps for 1.25 hours (double the current, but for half the time) or 22.5 Amps for 5 hours (half the current, but for twice as long). Or any combination in between. The battery's rating is therefore 112.5 ampere-hours (45 x 2.5). The minimum capacity is 80%, so a 20 amp/hour battery actually pumping out 20 amps should last at least 48 minutes, or 0.8 hours. A battery is supposed to provide enough power for 30 minutes when fully charged, although it is never wise to rely on any battery for more than about 20 minutes. This is particularly relevant if your aircraft has an EFIS display, or a FADEC! A flat battery doesn't do warning lights much good, either.

To get an idea of your aircraft's capabilities, add up the current requirements of essential services and divide them into the amp/hour rating. So, if your devices collectively use 45 amps, and your battery supplies 45 amp-hours, you should be able to get an hours' use out of it. When faced with such an emergency, it is usual to use the navaids, for example, to get a position fix, then turn them off until you start feeling a little lost, then turn them on again until you are once more certain of your position. The same with radios. This will get a little extra time out of your battery.

POLARITY

The polarities of a battery are positive and negative, marked plus (+) or minus (-), or coloured red and black, respectively, and electrons flow from the negative (-) electrode, through the circuit the battery is connected to, back to the positive (+), because the negative end has the most electrons (the terms are indeed misleading, and the words *positively charged* even more so, but they were coined a long time ago and it's a hard thing to change).

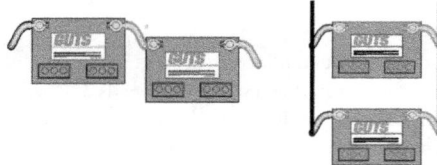

If you join batteries in *series*, that is, one after the other, with the positive of one connected to the negative of the next (left, below), you will get a voltage which is the *sum* of them both, but with the same *current capacity as one*.

If you join them in *parallel*, with the positive and negative connected to each other (right, above) you would get the *voltage of one* battery, but the *current capacity* of *all* of them, so you can use them for longer. This is because anything connected in series keeps the same current, and anything in parallel keeps the voltage. Since a typical aircraft runs on a 24-volt system, you would therefore connect two (12v) car batteries in series (better yet, two sets in parallel). Be aware, though, that terminals are different sizes to stop them being confused, so you need an adapter to connect them up in the middle (jumper cables may open up and spark when a load is applied).

 Ensure that batteries have an electrical load on them before completing a circuit. A battery condition check is best done with a load on.

In an earth return circuit, the negative pole of the battery is connected to the fuselage (negative earth). This is for weight saving, easier fault detection and reduction of risks associated with short circuits.

CHARGING

When charging, the **constant voltage** method uses a reducing current as the battery's state of charge improves. This requires less time and supervision than the constant current method, which takes longer and includes a risk of overcharging. Because of the battery's internal resistance, which causes a voltage drop, the external charging voltage must be greater than that of the battery.

During engine operation, the battery is recharged with a *DC or AC generator (alternator)*, using the constant voltage method via a voltage regulator. Charging a battery from an AC system requires a *Transformer Rectifier Unit* (TRU).

An AC generator alternator will charge at low RPM (a DC generator doesn't much), but some aircraft use a *starter/generator* to save space, despite this advantage. The same unit spins the engine on startup, and switched over when it's running to become a generator because their construction is the same, as we shall see later.

A Battery Control Unit isolates the battery from the bus when it is charged, and when the battery overheats or has an internal short circuit.

LEAD ACID

The lead-acid battery is made of alternating lead peroxide (+) and lead (-) plates, with separators in between, and an electrolyte made of sulphuric acid (37%) and water (63%), which can be neutralised with sodium bicarbonate (bicarbonate of soda).

The oxygen in the lead peroxide has an affinity for the H_2 in the sulphuric acid and the other plate likes the SO_4, so there is a tension between the plates which would create lead sulphate on one plate and water on the other, if the battery were part of a circuit. The formation of water dilutes the electrolyte and reduces its relative density, which is why the state of charge of a lead-acid battery is measured with a hydrometer (see below). Another test is to compare the on- and off-load voltages.

One plate turning into lead sulphate as electrons are lost is allegedly what the term *sulphated* means, which describes a fully discharged battery (it results from mistreatment).

NICKEL-CADMIUM

When uncharged, the positive electrode of a NiCad cell is *nickelous hydroxide*, and the negative is *cadmium hydroxide*. In the charged condition, the positive electrode is *nickelic hydroxide*, and the negative metallic is cadmium, meaning that the chemical reaction is in the plates. The electrolyte is *potassium hydroxide*, which is only there as a path for the current flow - it plays no part in the chemical reaction, so it will show little change over charge/recharge process. If you spill any electrolyte from a NiCad, you can neutralise it with a weak acid solution such as *dilute boric acid*.

During the latter part of a charge cycle, and during overcharge, nickel-cadmium batteries generate oxygen at the positive (nickel) electrode and hydrogen at the negative (cadmium) one (at full charge), which must normally be vented. To allow the system to be overchargeable while sealed, the battery is built with excess negative capacity so that the positive electrode reaches its full charge first. Since the negative electrode will not have reached full charge, it will not give off any hydrogen.

However, NiCads have short memories, in that if you charge them when they have only discharged a little way, they will think they have a lesser power rating which is only noticeable when you try to use all the charge, which won't be there in an emergency. To stop them causing hot starts they need regular *deep cycling* to keep them awake. Thus, although it's good practice to start an aircraft, for example, from a battery cart, to preserve the ship's battery for better reliability in remote places, occasionally a battery start is good for the system as it will help to eliminate the memory effect. The actual term is *voltage depression*, where there is a slight dip in the voltage near the end of a discharge. The dip goes below the normal output voltage, which makes you think the cell has actually discharged - a common occurrence with home movie cameras! As the battery is charged, the voltage depression point moves toward the beginning of the discharge period.

Another problem with NiCads is that they can catch fire when too much current is drawn and then replaced, a process called *Thermal Runaway*, which happens when an increase in temperature leads to a further increase because the battery's internal resistance decreases as its temperature rises. This is why some aircraft have a *Battery Temp* caution light on the warning panel which means you must land *immediately*, before the battery catches fire and takes other stuff with it, if it doesn't burn its way through the airframe and fall out. Yet another problem is that a NiCad cell will lose about 1% of its charge per day.

 Lithium Ion batteries, as found in most modern laptops and Portable Electronic Devices, can also overheat and burst into flame, so be wary about putting such devices in a remote baggage compartment.

CAPACITY CHECKS

Battery capacity checks should be made every 3 months. The minimum acceptable is 80%. Because the electrolyte remains unchanged, there is no way to tell the real state of a Ni-Cad's charge by checking its relative density. Checking the voltage is no good, either, because a NiCad can produce a constant voltage for some time, even when discharged, and closed-circuit voltage changes very little.

On the other hand, a *hydrometer* (see right) can be used to check the relative density and hence the state of charge of a lead-acid battery, but not when it is installed in the machine, in case the (acidic) electrolyte gets spilled (aside from corrosion, it can also create grounding paths). The relative density of electrolyte is 1.25 fully charged, and 1.3 when cold.

If you have to measure capacity whilst the battery is in the aircraft, the open and closed circuit voltages can be compared (e.g. on-load and off-load). The voltage will fall significantly as charge diminishes. Otherwise, you can use a *voltmeter* while a load is applied.

Magnetism

Magnetism is important because, without it, we would not have electricity. It is an invisible force which is defined as the property of an object to attract certain metallic substances, mostly ferric (iron based).

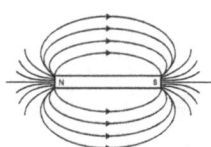 A magnet is therefore a ferrous substance, typically a soft iron bar, that has lines of magnetic force running through and around it in the shape of a *magnetic field* (the Earth is a magnet as well). The lines are called the *magnetic flux*, expressed by the Greek letter φ (phi). The *flux density* is the number of lines within a magnetic field, and the flux is stronger when the lines are closer together (at the ends), similar to streamtubes. The picture above left is often used to show what iron filings do in a magnetic field, but the lines of force do not actually flow as shown).

Attraction or repulsion between two magnets varies inversely as the square of the distance between them.

Magnets can be permanent or temporary, whose magnetism is lost after the magnetising force is removed. However, there is (almost) always a small amount left, called *residual magnetism*, which is useful for getting generators and motors to work in the initial stages. Even when a material is permanently magnetised, it can only be driven back to zero by a field in the opposite direction. This is called *hysteresis*, and is used widely in the recording of information on disks or tape.

Lines of magnetic flux always form closed loops and behave like stretched elastic bands, in that they are always trying to shorten themselves. This property is made use of in electric motors to turn the moving parts. As an example, the lines of flux between the North- and South-seeking poles in the bottom magnet below are as short as possible. On the top one, however, where the two poles are the same, the flux lines are pushed out towards the sides and do not shorten.

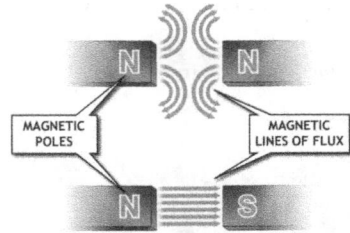

All magnets have a N seeking and a S seeking pole, and like poles will repel each other - unlike poles attract (parallel lines of flux moving in the same direction repel each other). If you had a bar magnet, its North seeking Pole would point towards the Earth's (magnetic) North Pole. This is what a compass is all about, under *Instruments*. The thing to remember is that the South Pole is marked as North, because that's the end that seeks North.

Iron and steel (and nickel and cobalt, slightly) are the only elements to be attracted by a magnet, and which can be magnetised. In their non-magnetic states, the theory is that the molecules in such metals are arranged at random, and their poles cancel each other out. When stroked with another magnet, the molecules align with each other and their magnetic fields combine to create the magnet as a whole. Heat or rough treatment can destroy this effect.

Through *magnetic induction*, an unmagnetised iron bar held close to a permanent magnet will attract iron filings in its own right, without being permanently magnetised (the magnetic flux temporarily aligns the crystals in the bar).

ELECTROMAGNETISM

When a current flows through a cable, there is a magnetic field associated with it, with a clockwise* action if you look at it from the rear.

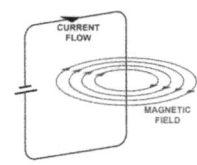

*The movement of electrons creates the field - it is nothing to do with the conductor. The flux lines do not actually rotate.

The magnetic field will become stronger if the wire is made into a coil and even stronger if the coil is placed around some easily magnetised material, such as iron, which becomes a magnet for as long as a current flows. As an iron bar has a greater permeability than air (or a lower reluctance*), it can concentrate the flux better into a smaller area.

*Reluctance with magnetism is equivalent to resistance.

In a coil, the magnetic field around the cable cuts the next loop in line. The fields merge to produce a large one through and around the whole coil, resembling that of a bar magnet (it can take up a N-S position if suspended).

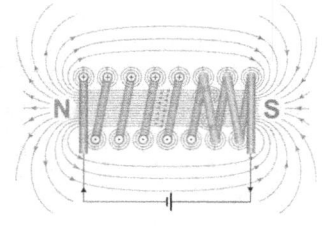

If a conductor, particularly soft iron, is moved within a magnetic field, or if a magnetic field is moved around a conductor, so that the conductor cuts flux lines, current can be made to flow in the conductor.

This is called *electromagnetic induction* (from Faraday).

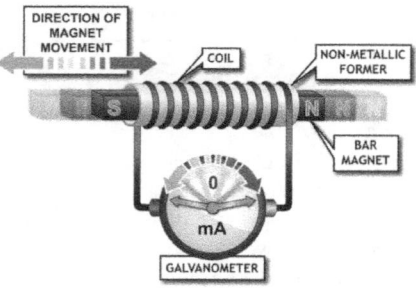

In the picture above, as the magnet moves, a current is induced in the coil and the needle moves in the relevant direction. The strength of the induced emf depends on the size of the magnetic field, the number of turns in the coil or the speed the bar's movement. Induced magnetism is usually proportional to the current that creates it, but no more can be created when saturation occurs. A changing magnetic field (as produced by an alternating current) around a stationary conductor also produces an electric current in the conductor, with the size of the voltage proportional to the rate of change of the field.

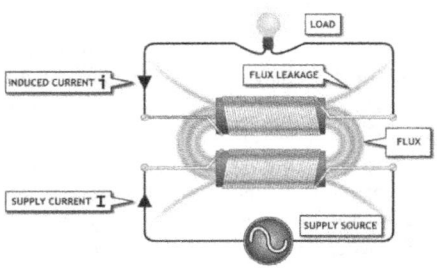

Mutual induction occurs between two coils close enough to each other to have currents induced in them. In the picture above, because there is AC flowing through the bottom coil, there must be a changing magnetic field around it, which interacts with the other coil into which it induces a current.

Mutual inductance is greatest when one coil is wound round the other, as found inside a magneto, and least when they are at right angles to each other.

INDUCTANCE

An inductor is a coil (solenoid) of insulated wire, possibly wound over a ferrous metal former. A changing flow of current can turn the coil into an electromagnet that will induce its own current in the opposite direction (sometimes called *back emf*). Inductance is the degree of self-induction, and it can also happen between complete circuits that are near to each other (see *Transformers*, below). There is no induction if the current is steady so, with DC, there will only be an effect as the switch is closed and opened, and the current rises and falls, hence the use of contact points in magnetos. In this case, the coil acts merely as a resistance but, with AC, the constant changes set up a reverse current. Inductance can therefore oppose a change in current flow or induce a voltage when there is a change. All conductors have this property, but for best results you need a coil.

Ordinary resistance to DC does not therefore change when a wire is coiled, but its "resistance" to AC (inductance) can be, to provide, for example, small opposition to low frequency AC and a high opposition high frequency AC, which is useful when filtering out unwanted radio signals.

To produce back emf, the magnetic fields around the cable induce a current the other way, stopping the main current from rising too quickly. The effect is that, when you first apply current, the inductor appears to have a high resistance (that does not generate heat), which drops once flow becomes constant, leaving you with the normal resistance you would find in any wire. In this respect, the inductor has the opposite effect of a capacitor. Practically, an inductor slows down the rise and fall of current, and behaves like the flywheel in an engine, or a large mass, such as a locomotive - the more inductance there is, the larger is the locomotive and the effort needed to get it moving, or slow down. In an AC circuit, this acts to resist current flow., more with a higher frequency.

This ability to "store" energy magnetically is due to inertia, because the current is moving as it does its work (it is like kinetic energy). Thus, the circuit discharges quicker if you apply the brakes, or add resistance. A capacitor, on the other hand, stores electrostatically, as nothing is moving, so the discharge rate increases when you *release* the brakes, or remove resistance. This is proportional to the speed with which the current changes, so when it collapses to zero very quickly, as when you use the contact breakers in a magneto, the back emf will be very large, and enough to jump across a gap. In conjunction with capacitors, inductors can produce electrical resonance at particular frequencies, which is useful when tuning radios.

The unit of inductance is the *henry*, and its symbol is *L*. To find totals, treat inductance as resistance. For example, the total inductance of several inductors in series is the sum of the individual inductances. For example, 0.03 plus 0.03 results in a total inductance of 0.06 henrys.

Transformers

In low power circuits, you can limit current with resistors, but where large currents get involved, the heat generated could well melt the equipment. It can also be wasteful. For example, stepping 240 volts down to 24 would involve wasting around 216 volts. In an AC circuit, coils can also restrict voltage by using their impedance (resistance, sort of). If you can vary the inductance of a coil, you can control the voltage with little waste.

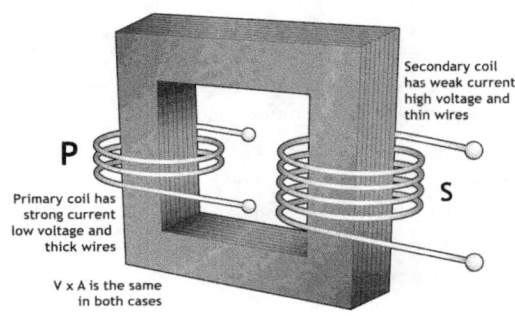

Transformers are a special application of inductance, commonly used in magnetos to boost voltage from 24-28v to whatever is needed to jump across the gap of a spark plug, but they have other uses, such as electrical isolation, because they are able to create electricity without any wires, as mentioned in *mutual induction*, above.

Transformers consist of electrically separate coils on a common laminated* iron core which are *magnetically coupled* when an induced emf is created in one (the *secondary*) by a change of current in the other (the *primary*).

*The laminations must be insulated from each other, otherwise the core itself will behave like a one-turn coil, and will have very large eddy currents induced in it, which will cause overheating. Armatures of motors or generators are laminated for the same reason. There are always power losses with transformers, usually as heat.

That is, an alternating current (or fluctuating DC) in the primary coil sets up an alternating magnetic flux. Self-induction in the primary creates an opposite voltage in the secondary that is nearly the same as the original (there are some losses). The difference between the two is just enough to set up an alternating magnetic flux in the core. Mutual induction then allows a voltage to be established in the secondary. In this way, we can get an electrical current without moving conductors and magnetic fields around each other, as you would have to with a generator. The voltage induced depends on the relative number of turns between the windings, or the *turns ratio* - a transformer with 1000 turns on the primary coil and 500 on the secondary has a turns ratio of 2:1 and an output voltage that is half of the input, but Ohm's law states that there will be more current (the power must remain constant), so the secondary windings must be thicker.

The voltage induced depends on the relative number of turns between the windings, or the *turns ratio*. For example, a transformer with 1000 turns on the primary coil and 500 on the secondary has a turns ratio of 2:1 and an output voltage that is half of the input, but Ohm's Law says that there will be more current (the power must remain constant), so the secondary windings must be thicker.

If the voltage is below the design limits, the current will increase and the transformer could overheat. Having said that, the efficiency of modern transformers is over 90%.

An **autotransformer** has part of the primary or secondary winding in common with the other, commonly used in 3-phase circuits, or radio. Autotransformers can be smaller, lighter and cheaper than standard transformers, but they do not provide electrical isolation between the primary and secondary coils.

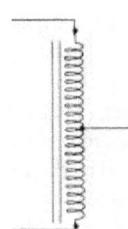

THE SOLENOID

The word *solenoid* actually refers to a coil of insulated wire, but as they are often wrapped around a movable metal core, thus creating an electromagnet, its common usage means a *solenoid switch*, or *solenoid valve*, such as those used to operate starter motors. A speaker uses a solenoid. Some aircraft use switches in the cockpit to operate a solenoid that controls the hydraulic system. They are held on by the solenoid as long as current flows. When it stops, the switches revert to the off position. When electricity is passed through the coil, a magnetic field is created, and the core is drawn in to the centre. If the core is pulled back against a spring, when power is switched off and the magnetic field collapses, it returns to its original position.

Thus, a solenoid could be defined as a device that turns electrical energy into linear motion. One is used with a starter motor, for example, because starters draw so much current that a normal switch would burn out (a large one can draw over 200 amps). The job of a solenoid (and the relay, to a lesser extent) is to keep heavy duty currents out of the cockpit, so you only need cables to be thick enough to operate the solenoid, thus saving weight. The cockpit starter switch therefore operates a relay which triggers a solenoid (which can handle the current) and which operates the machinery concerned. In this way, a small switch can start a large reaction in a remote location.

The strength of a solenoid can be increased by adding more turns or current, or using a soft iron core.

THE RELAY

A relay is a magnetic switch that does a similar job to a solenoid, but the only bit that moves is a contact, as a relay consists of a **non-movable** soft iron core surrounded by a coil. The force produced by the resulting electromagnet moves switching contacts back and forth.

Your microphone switch operates a relay that turns the aircraft radio from a receiver into a transmitter.

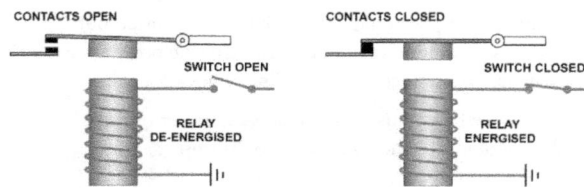

Relays are used for low-current switching or interruption of electrical current, typically used with a voltage regulator, or in conjunction with a logic gate, whose output will not be enough to drive the component concerned (the gate will, however, be able to drive a relay, which can do the work. In such cases, a protective diode will stop the logic gate being damaged when the relay demagnetises).

When a relay opens or closes, there is arcing between the movable and stationary silver alloy contacts, which causes pitting on their surfaces, and extra resistance between them. This means extra heat, plus a lower voltage under load that will need extra amperage to complete the same task. If the component controlled by the relay is also faulty, there may be more of a current draw than the relay is rated for.

The arcing occurs because there is a back emf - the coil in a relay has inductance like any other. A relay using a 6v supply can produce a spike of 100v or more when it disconnects, as the current drops rapidly to zero.

A normally open relay has its contacts open when it is de-energised. A normally closed one is the opposite. If a turbine engine starter relay fails in the open position, the starter/generator will not turn the engine. If it fails closed, the starter/generator will turn as soon as the battery is switched on, and will not switch off.

In the example shown, the relays connect various power sources to a distribution busbar. When the relevant relay is closed, that source can supply the bus.

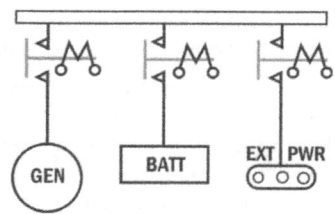

Differential Relays
In multi-engined aircraft, these ensure that generator voltages are almost equal before they are paralleled. They allow a generator to feed the busbar when no other supplies are involved. They are controlled by the difference in voltage between them, and close when the generator voltage is above that of the busbar. They open with reverse current.

Reverse Current Relays
As the name suggests, these are designed to operate whenever current flows in the reverse direction, to protect components from backfeeds caused by internal faults. For example, there is often one to stop a battery discharging back through a generator or, more typically, when paralleling DC generators, preventing a weak one from being driven by the others (you could also isolate it). RCRs are found in DC generating circuits and consist of two coils wound on a core, plus a spring-controlled armature and contact assembly. When the generator voltage builds up to a value that exceeds the battery's, the shunt winding of the relay produces enough magnetism to attract the core and close the contacts. However, when the generator voltage falls below the battery voltage, the battery starts to discharge through the generator (i.e. the current reverses), so the current in the series-field winding, and thus the voltage across it also reverses, reversing the magnetic field. The relay armature is pulled up by its spring tension and the contacts open, to disconnect the generator from the battery.

When the reverse current cut out fails to operate, the reverse current circuit breaker should trip.

Direct Current
As mentioned, this is current that flows in one direction only. It can be produced in many ways, but aviators are concerned with electromagnetism and chemical action (see *Batteries*).

THE GENERATOR
The electrical equipment on an aircraft may only be run by the battery for a short while, otherwise you would have to keep stopping to recharge it. Long term, the power must come from the aircraft itself, using a self-contained generating device. For DC systems, this is a generator, or dynamo - for AC, an alternator, although the term *AC generator* is often used instead. The battery's function is really for short-term storage and to act as a buffer when the generator's output fluctuates.

Generators use magnetism to create DC. A simple one exists when a coil of wire (a conductor) is spun between the poles of a magnet to induce a current in the loop.

The magnet can be permanent*, or an electromagnet formed from battery current or the generator's own (the electromagnet produces better results and is more efficient, in that more control is available). The current so generated is actually AC, because each arm of the rotary coil cuts the flux one way, then the other. It can be converted to DC electronically with a *rectifier* (described later) or mechanically at source, in which case the slip rings are replaced with a *commutator*. To produce a current in the first place, the generator does not need help from the battery (like the alternator does) because there is residual magnetism in the field winding poles.

*Any small generator using a permanent magnet is commonly called a magneto.

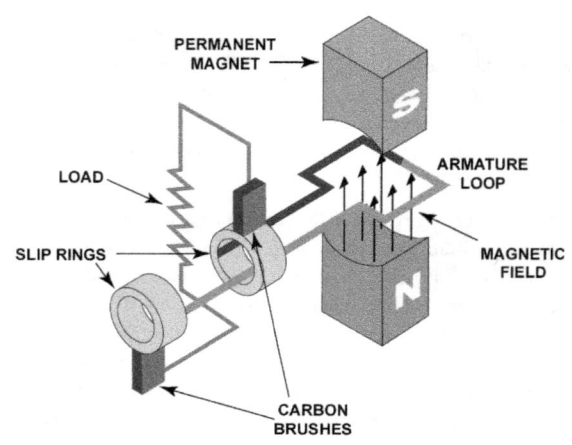

SYSTEMS
Electricity & Magnetism

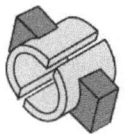

The commutator is really an adapted pair of the slip rings used in an alternator, combined and split into two halves which are placed opposite and insulated from each other, and attached to one end of the rotating loop through *brushes*, so called because the original designs used copper ones as contacts, but which have now been replaced by spring-loaded carbon blocks which simply wear out and are replaced from time to time (they need moisture for lubrication, which is a problem at high altitudes). Thus, a commutator is a *mechanical means of periodically reversing current*, or an automatic reversing switch, which is ideal for converting the AC from the loop into DC in the circuit, otherwise the current would keep reversing. As the rotor spins, the brushes contact each segment in turn, just as the current flow stops and is about to go in the other direction (actually twice per cycle). In this way, the polarity of the brushes remains constant, as does that of the commutator, and DC voltage is produced.

However, the supply in the simple generator is a series of positive pulses, which can be jerky *commutator ripple*), which can be minimised with more loops and connections, or more poles through which the coil(s) can rotate.

Complex generators have several commutators to ensure a smooth output and a constant supply.

In the pictures below, the armature loop is rotating clockwise.

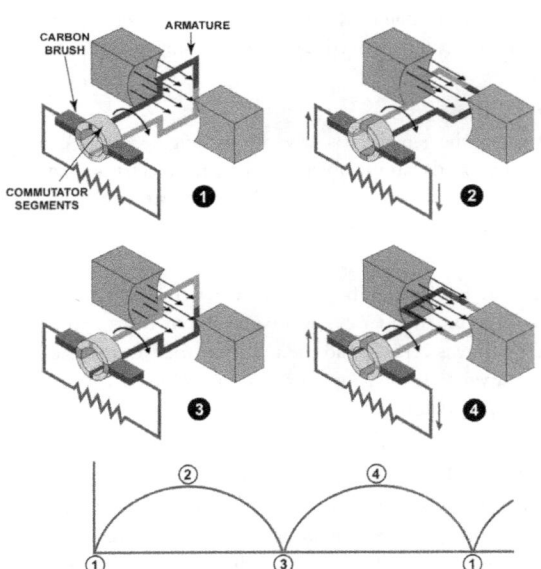

In position 1, the loop is perpendicular to the magnetic field, at 0°, so the conductors are moving parallel to it, and not cutting any lines of magnetic force, so there is no emf being generated in the loop. In moving to position 2, the conductors move progressively through more lines of force until they reach 90°, where maximum current is generated. The black conductor has moved down, while the grey one has moved up. Since they are in series, the voltage across the brushes is the sum of the two emfs. Positions 3 and 4 produces the same result, but the current flows in the reverse direction.

In summary, the output of a generator depends on the:

- number of turns in the armature
- **strength of the field current**
- rotation speed of the armature, and
- supplied load

Generators are rated in Kilowatts.

CONSTRUCTION

This is how a generator is constructed:

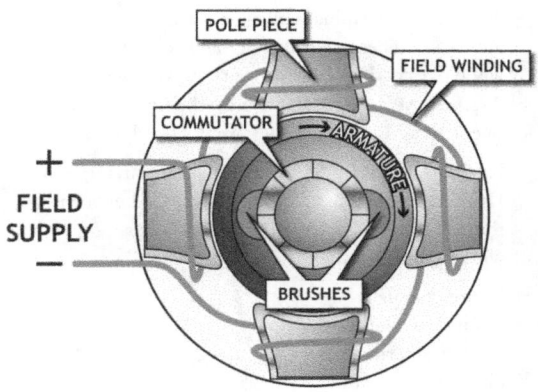

The major parts are a field frame (or yoke), a rotating armature (which includes the commutator, described below) and a brush assembly. The field frame completes the magnetic circuit between the poles and supports the rest of the device. The above is a four pole generator frame. The poles are of alternating polarity and are usually laminated to reduce losses from eddy currents. Their function is to concentrate the lines of force from the field coils, as with any other iron core in an electromagnet (permanent magnets would work, but would make the generator too large). Because the pole pieces project out from the frame to reduce the air gap between them and the armature, they are called *salient poles*.

The armature (usually drum-type) has many coils wound on an iron core, called *windings*. The distance between each winding is the same, coinciding with the number of segments on the commutator. As the armature will rotate in the (electro)magnetic field created by the poles, it is also laminated to prevent eddy currents.

EXCITATION

When the field current is taken from the generator itself, it is *self-excited*. The types available are:

- **Permanent magnet**. Only used by small machines (i.e. magnetos).
- **Separately excited**. By DC from another source (practically all AC generators).
- **Self-excited**. Excited by current from the machine itself (e.g. with DC generators).

- **Series wound** - the armature, field coils and external circuit (the load) are all connected, so the resistance of the load governs the field current (you need *few* turns of *large wire* in the field windings as the current can be large). That is, the voltage produced depends on the external load, so regulation is difficult (the terminal voltage rises as the current increases). These are not suitable for paralleling - when overloaded, they have a rising voltage profile. As, if the voltage regulator fails, the field coil will overload and overheat, they are not used in aviation.

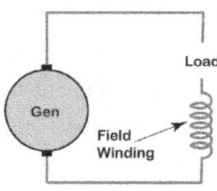

Having said that, a **feeder fault** (short circuit) in a DC circuit arises from a flux imbalance between the voltage coil (electromagnet) and the series winding turn.

- **Shunt** (parallel) **wound**, where the armature current is divided between the field winding and the load. In this type, emf will fall as the load increases and the flow through the field coils becomes smaller relative to the armature. As the field winding has a high resistance, the maximum current flows through the external circuit. This is the most common type used in aircraft, as it is stable (self righting) when load sharing. A rheostat can be used to adjust the field current to prevent the tendency of the terminal voltage to droop.

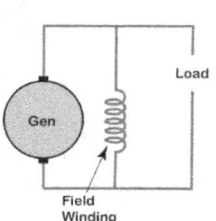

There must be *residual magnetism* in the core, enough to get the whole process started, but if it is lost or reversed, say through excessive heat or shockloading, it can be restored by briefly passing a current through it, a process known as *flashing the field*. There must also be a minimum rotation speed.

- **Compound wound** - one field coil in series (for the load) and one parallel with the armature (for the field). The coils carry currents in the same direction. With a light load, the machine behaves like a shunt, but as the load increases the series coil adjusts the voltage to be constant. The rising characteristics of the series and the falling characteristics of the shunt windings mean that it is hard to get a steady voltage that is independent of the load. Compound generators overcome the drop in voltage that occurs with shunt windings when the load is increased, as the series field reinforces it. Ultimately, the voltage rises slightly as the load is increased, so it is less stable for sharing.

They are used in larger aircraft, typically for hydraulic pumps that have heavy periods of use and lower periods in steady flight, plus others that use starter/generators.

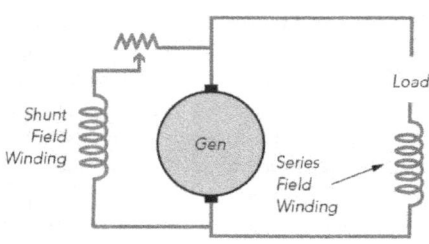

As soon as the induced current starts to flow, a generator will start behaving like a motor. This is because their construction is the same, but the motor tries to work in the opposite sense, after Lenz's law*. This is so powerful that 600-ton trains can be slowed down from 40 to 3 mph on a down gradient of 1 in 37.

*A moving magnet induces a current flow that opposes the movement of the magnet.

Speaking of motors, a **starter-generator** (as fitted to many turbine engines) has at least two sets of field windings and an armature winding, to save weight and space. A series field is used for starting, as a high torque is required. Once the engine has started, and you no longer need the starter, the other (shunt) windings are used. The back emf becomes the supply voltage on switchover. Smaller aircraft can get their DC by using rectified output from a frequency wild AC generator, in which silicon diodes are used as a bridge rectifier (see later), but these have no residual magnetism, so they need DC from the ship's battery to self-excite.

VOLTAGE REGULATION

Problem 1 is that the generator is driven by an engine, which can run at different speeds, and Problem 2 is that the electrical loads may change, so the next step is to **vary the field current** of a generator in sympathy with the engine and/or load to keep the voltage constant.

The field current is regulated because you can't change the generator's speed independently, or the number of wires in the coil. Its output line is sensed, and the regulator tries to maintain it at a constant value. If the generator's output is low, it will increase the field strength.

Alternatively, if an overvoltage occurs, the regulator changes the resistance of the field circuit to lower the output voltage. In this case, the voltage regulator acts as a variable resistor between the external field connection and the ground. A reverse current relay between the generator and the bus stops the battery discharging through the generator, putting the generator online again as soon as its voltage rises above the battery's. It is open when everything is switched off.

Older generators that need a lot of field current use a **carbon pile** regulator. The carbon pile is a stack of carbon discs in a ceramic tube which vary their resistance when compressed. The larger the compression, the lower the resistance and *vice versa*. As resistance decreases, current through the field coils increases. The stack is biased towards full compression (least resistance) by a spring, so you can get a current straight away, and an electrical connection is made to each end of the stack so that the generator output flows through it.

Picture: Carbon Pile Voltage Regulator

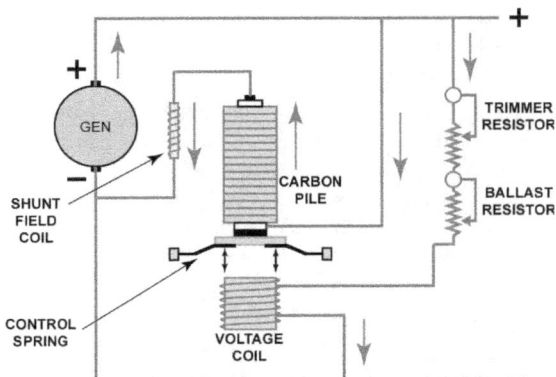

An electromagnet is placed under the stack (i.e. voltage control coil) which influences the tension of the spring against the discs, and is in parallel with the generator output, so the current flow will be proportional to the generator voltage. As the current varies in the coil, it will increase or decrease the strength of the magnetic field, to vary the compression effect of the spring. This affects the current flow and the strength of the field coil until the required output voltage of the generator is achieved.

With the **vibrating contact** version, used on lower-output systems, voltage is controlled by rapidly switching a fixed resistance in and out with an electromagnet (voltage coil) opening a pair of normally spring loaded closed contacts.

When generator output voltage is low, the current through the voltage coil is not enough to open the contact points. They open at a predetermined current through the voltage coil - when they do, field current flows through the fixed resistance causing its value to fall and produce an output voltage of the required level.

This is repeated rapidly, between 50-200 times a second, effectively maintaining a steady voltage while causing a lot of wear and tear.

Picture: Vibrating Coil Voltage Regulator

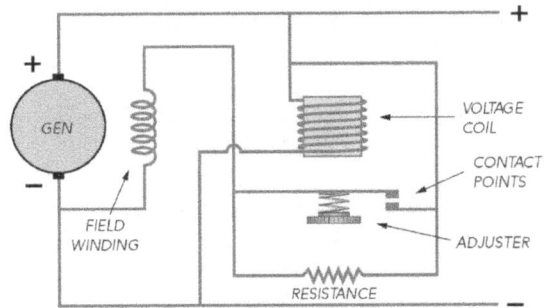

Below is a layout for a typical battery-generator system.

The battery stores electrical energy, which is replenished by the generator, as directed by the voltage regulator, which acts like the automatic cutout valve found in a hydraulic system.

The dotted lines indicate the equipment required for a twin-engined aircraft. The paralleling relay ensures that each generator takes its share of the load (this is not required with alternators, as discussed later).

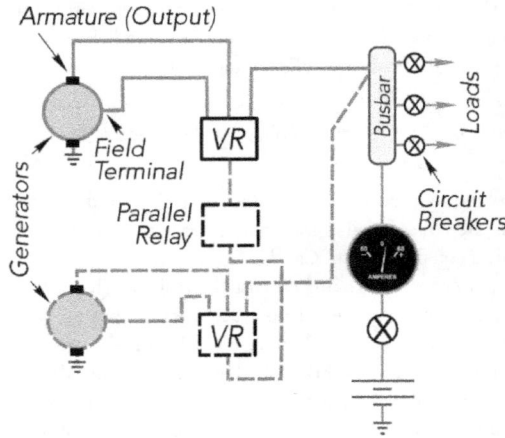

The limit for DC systems is around 400 A, due to the limitations of high current protection devices, amongst other things (known as contactors). A 28 V DC system delivering 400 A would only produce 12 kW, which is OK for light aircraft and business jets, but even they sometimes need the higher amounts demanded by modern transport aircraft which need something between 20-90 kVA per channel, or even higher.

Load Sharing

Multiple (DC) generators are run in parallel (for maximum power) because, if the associated engine fails, there should not be an interruption in the primary power supply. In addition, the system will be able to handle the switching of high transient loads and the generators will last longer. The downside is that you need more circuitry, mainly for protection, as a fault can affect the whole system. You also need ammeters so the crew can check that the load sharing is being carried out properly.

AC generators in parallel need matching for **voltage** and **phase**, which makes the process problematical, especially with **real** and **reactive** loads. This is why bus tie breakers are used to switch busbars in and out as required instead.

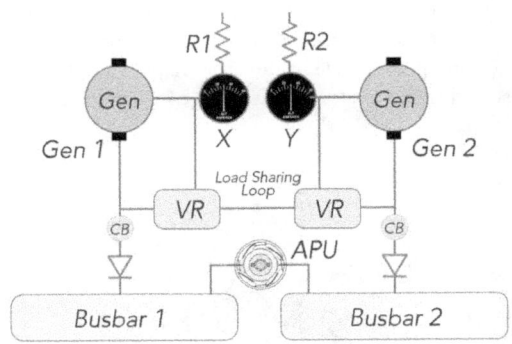

DC generators are paralleled through their field circuits, and each has a voltage regulator connected **in series with the shunt field coil**. Ensuring that output voltages are as **near equal as possible** (within about 2%) is done with paralleling coils between the voltage regulators, through which difference voltage flows, so the voltage regulators control the generator output, but are themselves controlled by an equalising circuit. When the first engine is started, a current flows in the generator's field coil via its voltage regulator. The warning light goes out and the ammeter (or loadmeter) shows the current taken (the warning light indicates that the generator is undervolting or no longer feeding the busbar).

If a generator fails (in a pair), the voltage will stay the same, but the power available reduces.

The load sharing loop consists of equalising coils wound on the same core as the voltage coil in the voltage regulator). If the load is being shared equally, points X and Y will be at the same potential because the voltage drop across the resistors (R1 & R2) will be the same. As the voltage drops vary when one or the other generators takes more load, X or Y will become more negative and more current will flow to that point through the equalising circuit. The resultant magnetic fields will change the magnetic pulls on the voltage regulators to change their outputs and rebalance the system. The relevant circuit breakers are reverse current types because a normal one will not trip if there is a short on its outgoing side. The diodes (see *Semiconductors*) protect the generators from each other.

Protection is required in DC circuits for:

- **Reverse current**. Current should normally flow from the generator to the system. Reverse current relays sense current flowing the wrong way and switch the generator out of the circuit.
- **Overvoltage**, from over-excitation. Line contactors (circuit beakers) will switch the generator out.
- **Undervoltage**. Similar to reverse current when one generator is involved, otherwise the equalising circuit will try to make the lagging generator work harder, which could damage it.

DC MOTORS

A motor converts electrical energy into mechanical energy. It is a current carrying conductor inside a magnetic field that experiences a Lorenz/emf force.

Motors are essentially the reverse of generators. As before, the field winding is carried around the inside of the casing, around pole pieces. The armature, which is magnetised and revolves inside, has a commutator, to which brushes are pressed. If many coils are used, the commutator is split into a corresponding number of pieces.

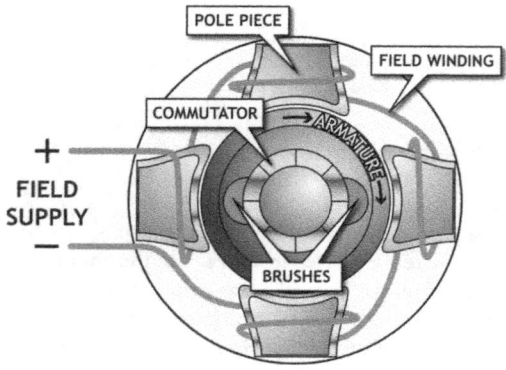

The commutator plays a very important part in the operation of a DC motor because it causes the current going through the loop to reverse just when unlike poles are facing each other, which causes a reversal in the polarity of the field, so that repulsion exists instead of attraction and the loop carries on rotating.

Since every current has an associated magnetic field, the one produced in the field winding as it is energised is repelled by the field already on the armature and the motor starts to spin. As mentioned previously, lines of magnetic flux behave like elastic bands, in that, when they are displaced, the tendency is to push back and create a force which starts the movement.

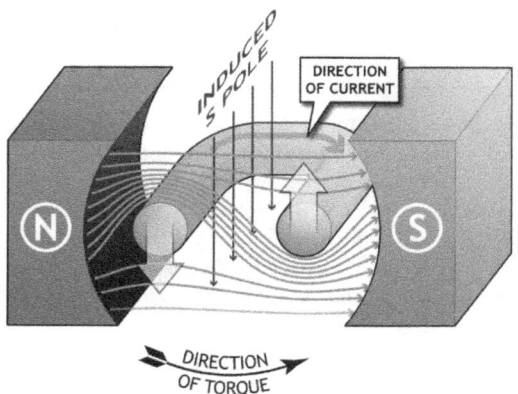

Just as the generator has a reverse motor effect, the DC motor can behave like a generator. This leads to a self-adjusting characteristic, in that, as the load is increased, the motor slows down its rate of increase.

Where you use a particular type of motor can depend on its *speed* or *torque* characteristics. The turning force (or torque) that a DC motor produces arises from the interaction of the magnetic field with the armature current, so torque is the product of the main and armature currents. However, when they are first started, large DC motors have no back emf to slow things down, so a resistor may be connected in series with the armature to limit the current to a safe value, otherwise the heat generated would break down the insulation on the cables. The resistance is gradually reduced as speed builds up.

Types Of Motor

As with DC generators, DC motors are classified by the ways in which their field excitation circuits are arranged.

- **Series wound** motors have their field and armature windings in series, so the same current flows through both, adding them together. As the output depends on their product, these motors have a high starting torque because, in the initial stages, there is little back emf, so all the current provided is used. As the magnetic flux is strong, the windings must take a large current, so they need heavy wire (for low resistance) and a load, because the back emf will not be enough to stop the motor accelerating to destruction. Thus, series wound motors run slower with heavy loads and dangerously fast with light ones. They are commonly used as starter motors.
- As a **shunt wound** motor is wired in parallel, the back emf in the armature coil does not affect the field coil, so the only large current in the early stages is in the

armature. The field winding uses relatively thin wires to keep its resistance high and the field's value to a minimum. There is a low starting torque, and the motor settles mostly at a constant speed. As well, the motor is more stable. Shunt wound motors are considered to be constant voltage, so they will run at practically constant speeds under normal conditions, whatever the load (within about 5%). As such machines have a low starting torque, they are usually started with the load disconnected. To reverse the direction of rotation, reverse the polarity of the stator or the rotor.

- A **compound wound** motor can have a high starting torque, and will not overspeed. The series winding opposes the shunt winding and weakens the field as the load increases, to provide an almost constant speed (the motor runs quicker if the field weakens, as the back emf that caps the speed becomes less). If the fluxes act in opposition, the machine is known as a *short shunt*, and will behave like a series motor. If the flux is strengthened, it is a long shunt machine, with the constant speed characteristics of a shunt motor.

A *split field* motor can rotate forwards and backwards, which is useful when you want to operate something in two directions. It has two field windings in opposite directions controlled by a double throw switch to reverse the polarity as required (intended for brief operation).

To keep the weight down, DC motors often have to work hard, so they require cooling periods. For example, you may only be allowed 3 attempts at starting, with a 30-second gap between them. Then you have to wait 30 minutes before trying again.

Starter/Generators

These units combine two functions, those of a generator and a DC motor, which saves both weight and space. The DC motor function is used to start the engine, then the unit is switched over to be a generator at a predetermined speed, after a short wait (say 1 minute), to allow the system to stabilise and the battery to recover before it receives a charge. A *changeover relay* is used for the process. Because generators don't work well at low speeds, they are usually used in turbine engines that run at high RPM.

Alternating Current

Alternating Current is electricity that continually reverses its polarity (and direction), and magnitude. That is, the electrons flow in one direction, then back to where they came from, accelerating and decelerating all the time. The quicker this is done, that is, the higher the frequency, the less distance is involved. As a result, the free electrons don't actually move very far, and the conductor length can therefore be shortened. With AC, moving half a coulomb back and forth produces the same current (1 amp) as moving 1 coulomb in one direction for the same distance. The essential point is *movement*, and many devices, such as light bulbs, only care that electrons move, and not which way they move, in order to work. Changing the connections to a battery quickly from one terminal to the other would achieve the same effect, but the results would be jerky, and the waves virtually square, because there would be a near 90° rise when on, and a 90° drop when off. In contrast, transitions from an alternator are smooth and like *sine waves*, as shown below (AC is assumed to be as a sine wave unless otherwise stated).

Most modern aircraft (large ones, at least) use AC as a primary power source, using a *Transformer-Rectifier Unit* (TRU) to get any DC they require (there are no AC batteries, so you still need DC for backup systems!) AC is typically used for flight instruments and fuel quantity systems, and its advantages include:

- **Better performance** from AC generators (more amps per unit weight), which may also be brushless, so there is less wear and fire risk. An AC generator can be even smaller (and lighter)
- **Ease of converting** voltage and current, either to different values (with transformers) or rectification between AC & DC.
- **Lighter cabling**. There is a point beyond which the size and weight of DC components become a disadvantage, as well as the power loss you get when transmitting electricity over longer cable runs. For example, with DC, you would have to have a high starting voltage to get only a relatively small one at the other end, even between the nose of an aircraft and the engine starter motor.

As an example, if you transmitted 250 volts of DC over a cable with a resistance of 1 ohm, the current would be 80 amps, if the generator had a capacity of 20 kW. This gives a voltage drop over the cable of 80 volts, so the receiving end only gets 170. The power loss would be in the order of 6400 watts (20 000 - (170 x 80)). If you raise the voltage to 10,000, as you could with AC, the generator would only need to produce 2 amps of current. Ohm's Law now gives a voltage drop of 2 volts and a power loss of only 4 watts.

Aside from the lack of batteries, and the fact that excitation must be supplied from the battery, about the only disadvantage is that AC requires frequency control*.

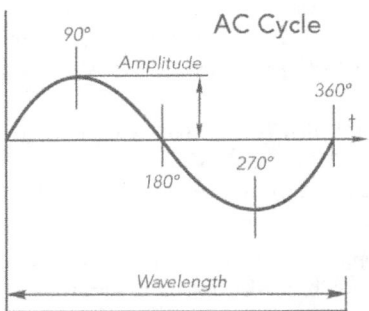

*A *cycle* is a complete set of varying conditions, in this case a transition from zero through a peak, down to a trough and back up to zero, so the more cycles you can fit into a particular time scale (the higher the frequency), the shorter the length of the wave is. One cycle per second is called 1 hertz (Hz), and constant frequency systems on aircraft use 400 Hz as the standard. The steeper parts of the wave represent periods when the conductor cuts the most lines of magnetic flux.

Alternating currents below 20 kHz are audio frequencies (AF), and those above that are radio frequencies (RF). The value of the frequency is often as important as the supply voltage - most AC motors have their speed determined by frequency. The rate at which the frequency varies is, when it comes to radio, in millions of cycles.

After Ohm's law, you divide the voltage by the resistance to find the current at any moment. The catch is that, as the voltage is changing, so is the current, as resistance remains constant, and current is proportional to voltage.

PHASES

The difference between the peak (or crest) and the base line of a wave is the *amplitude* (or, loosely, volume, but also power). When the *frequencies* (and hence wavelengths) of two waves coincide, that is, they pass through zero

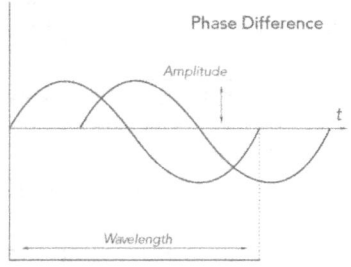

and attain their peak values in the same direction at the same time, they are *in phase* (the same amplitude is not required). When the points do not coincide, they are *out of phase* by the angle created when the second wave starts its cycle.

This is the basis of operation of the VOR and many other navigation aids.

 The word *phase* can mean the number of alternating currents being produced and/or carried by the same circuit (as in *single phase* or *three phase*), or the relationship between voltage and current in an AC circuit. There are times, when using radio, when you want them to be out of phase, and a coil or capacitor is introduced into the circuit to make current *lag* behind voltage, or *lead*.

The simplest forms of AC are good enough for light bulbs, etc., because the human eye is not quick enough to catch the flickering effect, and the bulb will stay warm anyway while the power drops and rises again, but electric motors need a more constant source of power. Aside from that, a single phase generator is uneconomical because a lot of winding space would be wasted.

Constant Frequency AC systems run at 400 Hz (the most used frequency in aircraft). This is partly because of the effects of inductive and capacitive reactance, which both depend on frequency, and paralleling, discussed below.

Using 400 Hz (as opposed to 50 or 60) means that smaller and lighter components can be used, albeit with some induction loss, but weight savings are more important with aircraft. You need 4 sets of wiring for a 3-phase system (3 live plus a neutral), but they are smaller, so you still save weight.

To produce 400 Hz with the 2- pole generator shown previously (i.e. with one North and one South Pole), the armature would need to rotate at 400 RPM. It follows that, the more pairs of poles you have, the slower can be the running speed.

The formula for calculating the frequency of an AC generator is:

$$Hz = \frac{RPM \times pairs\ of\ poles}{60}$$

So, to produce AC at 400 Hz, you need 4 pairs of poles in an AC generator running at 6000 RPM, or 3 pairs at 8000 RPM (8 poles for 6000, 6 for 8000). A generator with a 4 pole rotor (i.e. two pairs) must turn at 12 000 RPM.

Three-phase AC is essentially 3 AC lines in parallel, with their peaks a third of a cycle behind each other to reduce the changeover effect. You can therefore have 3 separate alternating currents running down the same cable. In such *polyphase systems*, loads can draw power at a uniform rate, so a machine can run steadily under a uniform torque because the power peaks and zero values do not coincide. In addition, you can use conductors with less of a cross section, which saves weight. Using multi-phase AC also means you can create a rotating magnetic field, which is handy when it comes to AC motors.

Although you can use any number of phases, most of the advantages are available with three, which is why three-phase is in general use (it was designed by the US military over 50 years ago). With it, three coils are at 120° (electrical degrees) to each other, so the voltages differ in phase by the same amount. Electrical degrees are used because there is often more than one coil per phase, and more than one electrical cycle for each geometrical cycle.

The advantages of polyphase systems include:

- Additional phases increase total AC power as a function of the square root of the number of phases, so 115 volts multiplied by the square root of three (1.732) will give you over 199 volts from a 3-phase system, hence the 115/200 designation.
- Heating loss and the line voltage drop are less.
- Loads can draw power at a uniform rate.
- AC Generators can work in parallel.
- Phases can be connected to different loads.
- Fewer copper coils are needed to generate the necessary current, which allows for a smaller and lighter alternator.

OPPOSITION TO FLOW

Resistance, or electrical friction, affects AC in much the same way as it does DC - some of the electrical energy is converted to heat and there is a voltage drop across the component, due to the power required for the current to pass through it. In addition, as the frequency of the current increases (say up to VHF level), it concentrates more and more into the outside surfaces of the conductor (the *skin effect*), meaning that no current flows in the centre. The effect of increasing the frequency of the current is therefore to increase the resistance as the current is concentrated into a smaller area. This is why stranded cable is used on the RF (i.e. high frequency) side of a radio receiver. Otherwise, current flow is affected by *real* and *reactive* loads (capacitive or inductive).

If an alternator runs below its normal frequency, inductive devices will overheat, as the current will increase as inductive reactance reduces.

REACTANCE

Reactance is the property of resisting or impeding the flow of alternating current or voltage. It occurs when the voltage and current in a circuit are out of phase with each other due to the action of an inductor (coil) or a capacitor.

It is part of the total opposition to the flow of AC, also expressed in ohms, being an extra to resistance (the two together are called *impedance*, and very relevant when it comes to radio antennae). 400 Hz appears to cope with it best. It is overcome with reactive power from the generator, similar to drag being overcome with engine power - in both cases, the power is non-productive.

 Resistors are static components, with which the current flow will be the same after the initial application of power. However, when you apply a fixed DC voltage to a capacitor, it will draw a high current as it charges up, and appear to be a short circuit. Once the capacitor is charged, however, the current flow stops and it will look like an open circuit. With AC, the capacitor would always be "passing" a current as it charges and discharges in each direction. What current you get depends on the time it takes to charge (its capacity) and how often the AC changes (its frequency). In other words, the reactive nature of a capacitor (or an inductor) alters the relative timing of voltage and current.

As current flows through a resistor, the voltage across its end terminals will be in phase with the current.

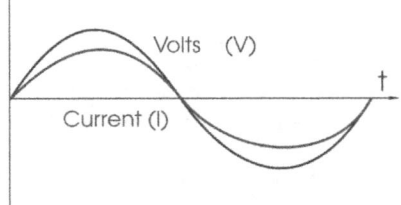

As capacitors take time to charge up, the voltage flowing through one will peak late and lag behind the current.

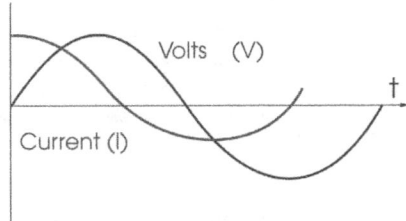

Changing the values of voltage and current has no effect on their phase relationship.

As inductors oppose the flow of current, it cannot change instantly, so the voltage will peak early, or lead:

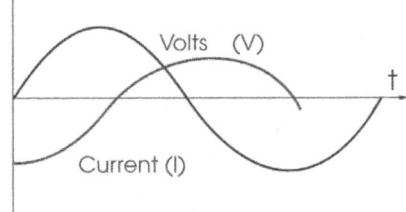

If you had an inductor and a capacitor in the same circuit, the voltages across them would cancel out to some extent, as they are out of phase by 180°. In practice, there will be a little resistance left. In a circuit with resistance and inductance, the current has two components, one flowing against the resistance and one against the inductance, so there are two emfs (see *Resonance*, overleaf).

*emf is the reference, so current leads or lags on it.

The "resistance" coming from inductors or capacitors is called reactance, also measured in Ohms. Both change with AC frequency, as described below:

- **Inductive reactance** is the opposition in an inductive circuit (as with a coil). When you apply a voltage to an inductor a magnetic field slows the current down while the voltage is allowed to build up freely. The amount of back emf depends on the rate of change of the current, in that, the larger its frequency, the larger will be the reverse current, so the effect decreases with lower frequencies. Any device relying on magnetic fields is a form of inductor, like motors, generators, transformers, and coils. Using an inductor in a circuit causes it to become inefficient because it makes the current lag behind the voltage or applied emf*. Resistance tempers this somewhat, because it acts in series with the coil, so the resulting phase shift will be between 0-90°. If there were no resistance (which would never happen) the phase shift would be 90°. This effect is increased by the inductance of the coil and the frequency of the current, in that the more of each, the greater the opposition.

- **Capacitive reactance** exists in a capacitive circuit, and it decreases with an increase in frequency. Unlike inductive reactance, changes to the current occur *before* any changes to the voltage because, when you first apply a voltage at its lowest value, the current will be at its highest. A capacitor in an AC circuit builds up a charge as supply voltage rises, which opposes and reduces the current flow so that, when the maximum supply voltage is applied, the current is zero. As the supply voltage falls, the capacitor starts to discharge, hitting a maximum rate when the supply voltage is zero, so the current is maximum when voltage is zero and *vice versa*, or current leads voltage by 90°.

    Capacitive reactance is also measured in ohms, and is inversely proportional to AC frequency, meaning that when frequency is high reactance is low, and when it is low reactance is high. Capacitors therefore act as low resistances to high frequencies and high resistances to low frequencies.

 The term *reactance* is only used when voltage and current are out of phase with each other. When they are in phase, the term *resistance* applies.

In summary, the effect of reactance varies with the frequency of the current, in that an increase in frequency causes an increase in inductive reactance and a decrease in capacitive reactance. Coils therefore oppose high frequencies, while capacitors oppose low frequencies. Adding a resistance reduces the lead or lag angle.

IMPEDANCE
Impedance is the total opposition to the flow of AC, so any voltage drop is proportional to the product of current and impedance, which consists of resistance and reactance of whatever type (capacitive or inductive). Its symbol is Z, and its

value is always greater than resistance, except at resonance (see below), when Z = R. *Impedance is the vector sum of resistance and reactance* - the total equivalent resistance at any given frequency, and the square root of the squares of reactance and resistance added together. Put more simply, it is the result of RMS Volts divided by RMS amps (overleaf).

Total impedance is not simply the algebraic sum of resistance and reactance. Capacitive and inductive reactance can cancel each other out and the total (effective) reactance is then the *difference* between the two. The phase shift characteristics (i.e. whether voltage or current is leading) will be determined by the largest value. For example, in a circuit with 20 ohms of inductive reactance and 36 of capacitive, the total will be 16 ohms of capacitive reactance. Therefore current will lead voltage.

As the inductive and capacitive reactance are 90° out of phase with the resistance, and their maximum values occur at different times, vector addition must be used for calculations. Impedance matching (as used in avionics) means that a device works best when a circuit to which an input or an output is connected has the same impedance as the input or output. A low impedance circuit should not be connected to a high impedance one without allowing for power losses, hence the use of transformers (the connection between a 75 ohm coaxial TV cable and a flat TV twin lead, which has an impedance of 300 ohms has a transformer in it).

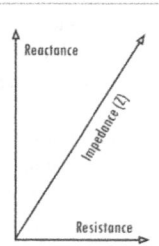

RESONANCE

We know that the frequency of an AC voltage applied to a series circuit determines its reactance or, put another way, the quicker the changes in current, the more opposition is experienced.

The current has three components:

- One flowing against the resistance, in phase with the applied emf
- One flowing against inductance which is lagging behind the emf
- One from capacitance which is leading the emf, in opposition to that flowing against inductance

If the inductive reactance is larger than the capacitive (usual for higher frequencies), the circuit is inductive and the voltage leads the current. If the capacitive is the larger reactance (for lower frequencies), the circuit is capacitive, and the voltage lags behind the current. Somewhere in the middle, the reactances will be equal and that of the circuit will be zero, meaning that impedance will be minimum, and equal to the "normal" circuit resistance (R). The voltage across the circuit and the current in it will be in phase. This condition is *series resonance* which occurs at the circuit's *resonant frequency*.

Put another way, in an AC circuit, current and emf are only in phase when either:

- the circuit contains only resistance.
- the leading effect on the current from capacitance is balanced by the lagging effect from inductance.

The second condition refers to a state of resonance.

A resonant, or *tuned*, circuit is one where the inductive and capacitive reactances (that is, concerning voltage and current) are equal, and cancel each other out because they have opposite polarity. The reactive elements (L and C) have values that cause the circuit to vibrate electrically in sympathy with the electrical supply, which can reinforce the voltage or current in the circuit. The principle is used when selecting a radio frequency, where the tuning knob is connected to a variable capacitor. This means that an alternating current is required - an inductor in a DC circuit would have no effect, aside from the normal resistance in the wire wrapped round the coil.

Circuits not containing components with resistance, capacitance, and inductance can still exhibit their effects. For example, a coaxial cable has some capacitance and some inductance whose values are very small, but not negligible in sensitive circuits. As such a circuit presents a low opposition to a voltage at the resonant frequency, the current is large, so the circuit can differentiate between voltages at different frequencies. In other words, it is *selective*. This is OK in an electronic circuit with a high resistance, but in a power circuit with low resistance it can cause damage.

RMS VALUES

As alternating current is constantly changing, how do you compare it to DC without measuring both in a circuit? Using a measuring instrument on an AC circuit is problematic because the average value is nothing, and the needle would be waving about anyway. In practice, such peak values are calculated from the Root Mean Square value and multiplied by the square root of 2 (for a pure sine wave). If AC is passed through a wire that is wound around a thermojunction, a millivoltmeter would respond in proportion the square of the AC.

The heating effect is proportional to the square of the current (I^2), so here we are concerned with the average squared value*, or *mean square*, since the normal average is zero, and you need something to work on. As you don't refer to square amperes, you then need find the square root of that (the *root mean square*) to get a suitable figure.

*Taking a current that is fluctuating between 5 and 8 volts as an example, the average would be 6.5 volts, but the square of that (42.25) does not give a true measure of the heating effect. The average of the squares (25 + 64), which is the correct figure, would actually be 44.5.

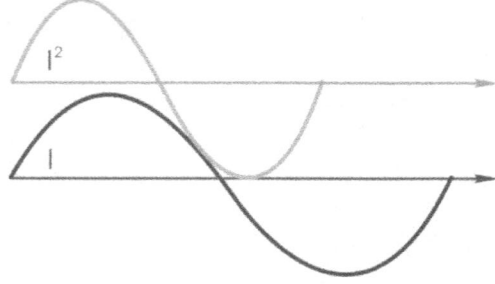

The power used in an AC circuit is the average of all the instantaneous values of power (or heating) in a complete cycle. If the circuit is in phase, the power curve is entirely above the zero axis, because two positives or two negatives make a plus (the square of a negative quantity is positive).

In the diagram above, the grey sine wave is the *square* of the black one. Now its average value is not zero, but half of the maximum of the squared current.

If you take a cycle and sample it 90 times (once per degree), square the values, then find the mean and its square root, you get 0.7071 times the peak value (often called the *virtual value*).

```
RMS =  peak value
         √2
```

The peak is found by multiplying the RMS* by 1.414, which is the square root of 2. If the peak to peak voltage is 400 volts, RMS is 141 volts. To convert from RMS to amplitude, divide RMS by 0.707. In summary, as an AC waveform is not square, its peak voltage is 1.414 times that of DC to have the same energy (RMS is effective current).

*Whenever an alternating current or voltage is specified, it is always the RMS value that is referred to.

The insulation of any component must be capable of standing the peak value of an AC.

In the diagram, the shaded area inside the curve over the square DC wave has the same energy as the shaded parts outside the curve. the horizontal straight line represents a DC voltage.

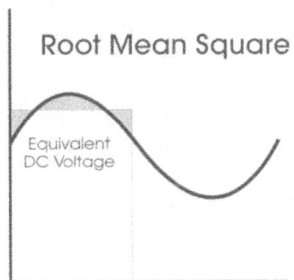

POWER

A current that is always dying away and building up again is less effective than a steady one. For best efficiency, AC must be synchronised with the voltage and be undistorted. Electrostatic and electromagnetic forces can affect the phase relationship between voltage and current in AC circuits, which affects the power gained.

For DC, where voltage and current are always in phase, power consumed is derived simply from their product - 1 volt (E) and 1 ampere (I) *flowing in the same direction* form the watt. However, with AC, the volt-ampere product (VA) does not necessarily give the power consumed, as a current flowing in the opposite direction puts power back into the supply. In other words, power is derived from the product of current and *that part of the voltage that is in phase with it*, so you can have current and emf without power! Having said that, for non-inductive loads, such as light bulbs and electric heaters, volts multiplied by amps can equal watts consumed. For example, when the VA product is positive, as it would be when they are in phase, all the power goes to the load (two minuses are positive so, when voltage and current are both negative, there will still be a positive power value).

However, when the VA product is negative, as it might be when voltage and current get out of phase, the load returns power to the supply and can turn a motor into a generator. If the phase angle between voltage and current is 90°, the load will return as much power to the supply as it consumes, and the average power will be zero. Thus, to find out how much power you will get from an AC circuit, you must multiply amps by volts as usual, and the cosine (power factor) of the phase angle between them.

This is **True Power, Real Power,** or **Effective Power**, being that needed to drive the current loads and measured in kW. Its symbol is *P*. Put another way, components such as heaters and lights do real work and use real power, expressed in watts and indicated on a voltmeter. Other components (i.e. transformers) use up power without apparently doing anything. This is called reactive power, mentioned below. The real load from an AC generator is proportional to its RPM and the torque supplied by its drive, both of which must be matched.

Apparent Power is simply the total of what is produced, or the RMS volt-ampere product (VAR/ kVAR). Its symbol is *S*, and it has more to do with voltage regulation and field strengths. In fact, RMS values of current and emf are also called *virtual* current and emf, with their product of *virtual watts*. So, to find the true power in an AC circuit, you find the component of emf that is in phase with the current, and multiply it by the virtual current (see *Power Factor*, below).

Reactive (Imaginary) Power (Q) is what is used when overcoming reactance (current flowing in the opposite direction), and is measured in *Volt-Amps Reactive* (VAR). It is a small value compared to the kw from real power, being the vector sum of the inductive and capacitive currents, and voltage, representing the energy alternately stored and returned to the system by capacitors and/or inductors. Although reactive power does not produce useful work, it still needs to be generated and distributed so that enough true power is available for electrical processes to run. Because of this quality, it is also called *wattless Power*. The more voltage and current are out of phase, the more this will be - any phase angle between 0° and 90° means that it will take more power to deliver a fixed amount of current because of the reactive losses. Thus, you will never get full power from an AC generator, except when everything is in phase, as with just resistance (light bulbs, etc.) or with equal values of inductive and capacitive reactance, as found in a tuned circuit.

```
kVA = kW + kVAR
```

In a loadsharing situation, the kVA and kVAR loads must be carefully synchronised.

THE POWER FACTOR

This expresses the relationship between true and apparent power, or by how much current and voltage are out of phase with each other. With reactance and resistance present, there is always a phase difference between current and voltage. The ratio between the actual power consumed (True Power, in watts) to the Apparent Power (VA) that could have been transmitted if the current were in phase and undistorted is the Power Factor:

```
Power factor = kw (Real Power)
               kVA (Apparent Power)
```

Put another way, the power factor is the amount by which apparent power must be multiplied to get true power. It is the cosine of the phase angle of the circuit. Thus, the traditional **volts** x **amps** formula becomes:

```
watts = volts x amps x power factor
```

As an example, imagine towing an aeroplane:

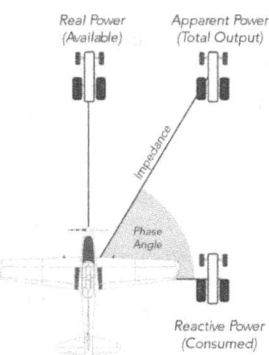

If the tug is directly in front of the aeroplane, all the power will be used for the job, and the power factor will be 1. As the tug moves away from the direct line, the amount of work needed for towing would steadily increase until, eventually, the tug would be at the side and the aeroplane would not move at all. The power factor now would be zero. If the tug were to take up any position between directly ahead and to the side, some power would be available for towing, and some would be wasted. In our case, real power would be measured in watts, and apparent power (along the rope) as volt-amperes, or VA (it is higher than real power). The reactive power is the wasted energy.

The formula for apparent power is:

    P = EI

EI is RMS volts x amps.

True power is calculated from another trigonometric function, namely the cosine of the phase angle (cos q):

    P = EI cos q

The cosine of zero is 1, so in a purely resistive circuit it is ignored, which is why it is not in the first formula.

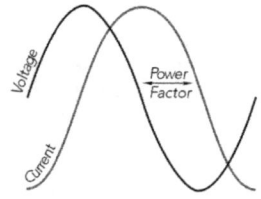

The picture above is a *phasor diagram* which shows the relationship between Reactive, Real and Apparent Power. The Real Power equals the Apparent Power multiplied by the cosine of the phase angle between voltage and current.

In a circuit where reactance and resistance are equal, voltage and current are displaced by 45°, the cosine of which is 0.7071, so the power factor is 0.7071. This means the circuit has used around 70% of the energy supplied by the source and returned around 30%. This is important when you are trying to decide what size of cable to use in a circuit.

A 1.84 kW load supplied with a power factor of 0.4 would require a 20A cable, while the same load supplied at unity would only need an 8A cable.

So, the power factor determines what percentage of power is used up in watts, and what percentage returns to the source as wattless power.

Power loss is proportional to the square of the current:

    P = I²R

The power factor is *leading* if there is more capacitive than inductive reactance, or *lagging* if they are the other way round. Electric motors result in a lagging power factor because they are more inductive than capacitive.

Inductive reactance decreases when the frequency decreases with frequency. Capacitive reactance decreases with an increase in frequency. We need a constant frequency to keep them equal.

The type of capacitance can be found by dividing a circuit's resistance by its impedance, so, if there is 50 ohms of resistance, 50 ohms of inductive reactance and 80 of capacitive reactance, the power factor will be 0.857, or that just under 86% of the current is in phase with voltage.

A poor power factor can arise from either a significant phase difference between voltage and current, or harmonic distortion. Poor phase angles are usually the result of an inductive load such as an induction motor or a power transformer, because some current is used to create the magnetic field. This can be improved by placing capacitors in parallel with the circuits, which should actually be kept to a minimum to avoid resonance. The energy now moves between the capacitors and the inductive load, reducing the current flow from the line. That is, the capacitor catches the current and reflects it back, instead of having it flow all the way back to the generator. Capacitors reduce the lagging of the inductive component and the losses in the supply.

Typical output would be between 30-90 kVA for the largest aircraft, so, if a 90 kVA AC generator has a power factor of 0.75, what is the useful output? 67.5 kW. Talking of big jets, they often have kW- kVAR meters that show the true power in kilowatts that the system is using. Pressing a button nearby changes the circuitry so that it will read the reactive power in kilo-volt-amps, showing how hard the alternator is working.

THE AC GENERATOR

An inverter creates AC (from DC), but so does an AC generator, which is similar in construction to a DC generator, but using *slip rings* instead of commutators, so current reversals are not modified. Each end of the loop connects to a separate ring.

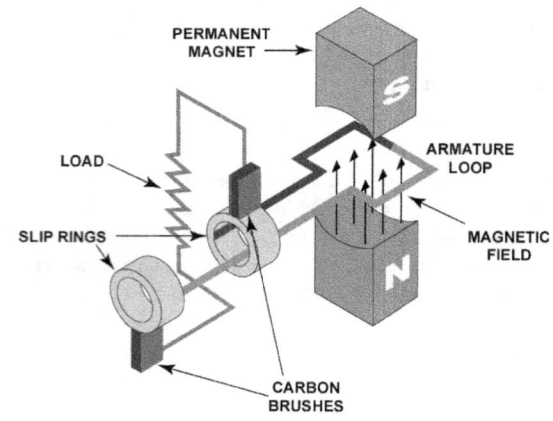

Slip rings are not used in the brushless generators used at high altitude, discussed later.

There are two types of alternator, one with a *revolving armature* (shown above) and one with a *revolving field* which is more common in aviation (to save confusion, the term *rotor* means rotating parts, and *stator* means fixed parts).

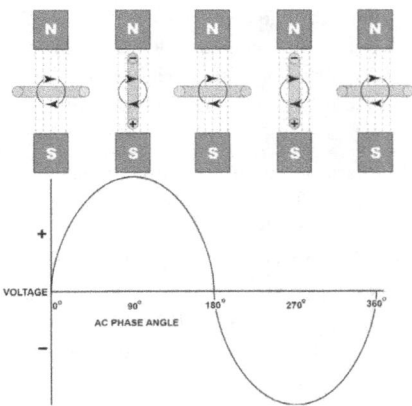

The revolving armature type resembles the DC generator insofar as the armature rotates inside a stationary magnetic field. The other has the opposite - the field comes from an electromagnet rotating within a stationary armature winding (in the case) so that the output can be connected directly to the load, as opposed to going through slip rings (insulation is easier).

Instead, the slip rings only need to convey the excitation current.

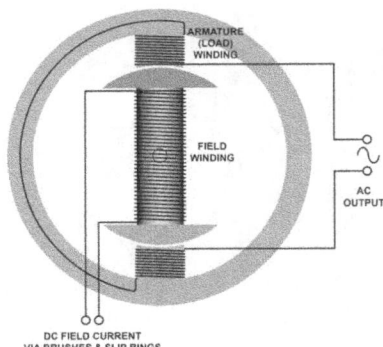

In this case, the excitation comes from an external DC source, namely the battery, hence the use of a dual switch.

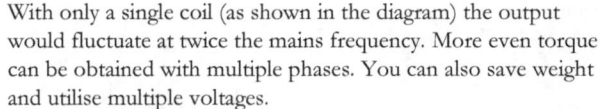

A revolving field AC generator has two main elements:

- An engine driven rotor which has the field coils wound on it. Power for the coils (to turn them into an electromagnet) comes through the slip rings and brushes from a DC source, typically the battery (hence the alternator switch next to the battery switch). This is why flying with a dud battery can be problematic. The on-off switch can isolate the alternator from the electrical system and should be turned off if the alternator fails.

- Stator windings carry three sets (or pairs) of coils (i.e. phase windings), in which the current is generated by the rotating field windings.

With only a single coil (as shown in the diagram) the output would fluctuate at twice the mains frequency. More even torque can be obtained with multiple phases. You can also save weight and utilise multiple voltages.

The picture below shows a typical battery-alternator system for a light aircraft - the dotted lines are the equipment required for twin engines.

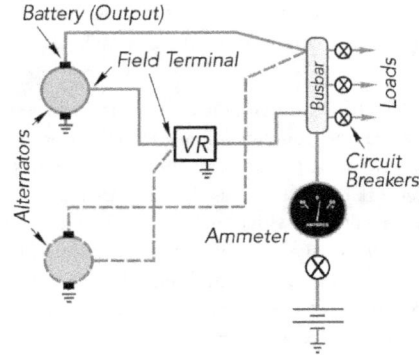

A 3-phase system can use the same frame, field and armature core, so you can save material and weight (in fact, you get three generators in one). In addition, transmitting a load over 3 sets of wires rather than one means less of a heating effect and less of a power drop, if only because power is drawn at a uniform rate.

With 3-phase, the windings are 120° apart and may be wired as a *mesh* (*delta*) or *star*. The star (on the left, below) is the most commonly found in aviation, with one end of each coil joined to a common neutral point, **with which you can get two voltages** - a *line voltage* between any two phases, and a *phase voltage* between line and neutral, as the current flows away from the centre.

Line voltage is 1.73 x phase voltage, and line current is equal to phase current (1.732 is the square root of 3).

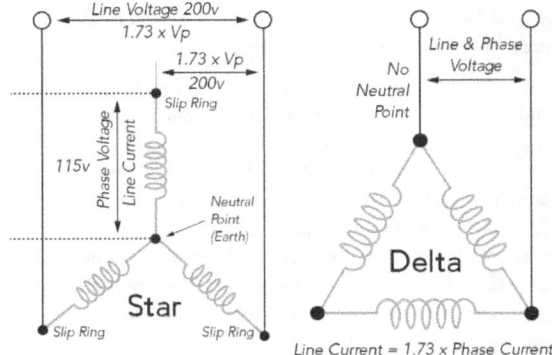

When one coil is vertical, and therefore not crossing any flux lines, and not producing any current, the others are producing equal current in opposite directions, so the algebraic sum of all three voltages is zero. Thus, you only need three slip rings, because you can interconnect the other

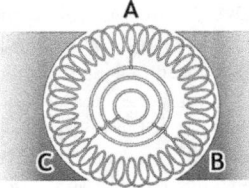

three cables. In practice, a neutral wire is taken from the interconnected ends on the outside, with the slip rings in the middle.

The neutral wire allows you to treat the unit as three single phase systems, so you get three generators in one. The star winding can cope with unbalanced loads on different busbars, meaning that you can switch things on and off quite easily, unlike the delta, which will overheat from the extra current. If one phase becomes earthed, its voltage drops to zero. Although the other phases will still work, a protection circuit will switch the generator off.

With a mesh or delta (right, above), the three coils are in series as a closed circuit, so a short circuit will make all phases drop to zero (one terminal is earthed to the airframe). This design is only used for small motors because, unless the emfs are equal, circulating currents will exist which makes them less useful for generators. Here, line voltage is equal to phase voltage and line current is 1.73 x phase current. The difference between the two is that a star generates a high voltage at a low current (thinner cables required) and can produce a greater output for a given size. A delta generates a low voltage at a high current. You can switch between both to maximise efficiency if both are present.

The frequency of the current provided by an alternator depends on the number of **pairs of poles** and **rotation speed**, which is linked to engine RPM. In fact, many aircraft sample the alternator output to provide the engine tachometer indication. Refer to *Induction Motors,* below.

FREQUENCY WILD SYSTEMS
Alternators are *frequency wild* if their speed is not controlled, meaning that their frequencies can vary with speed, so they cannot be paralleled. Such items would only be used on systems that are not affected by frequency, like heating or lighting (which are resistive), on simple aircraft where the primary supply is DC (light aircraft usually have frequency wild bridge rectified alternators). The alternator is driven off the engine by a fan belt, so its output varies with engine RPM. Having said all that, frequency wild can be stabilised with a TRU or inverter - that is, you can parallel the TRUs if you cannot parallel the generators.

When you switch the battery on, the busbar receives a minimum voltage, and the ammeter will show a negative value, or a discharge. There will also be a low voltage light flashing somewhere, indicating that the busbar is below its minimum level, because the alternator is not working. The alternator switch must be selected ON to provide the initial excitation from the battery, but this will be overridden from the alternator's own output once the engine has started. When the alternator output exceeds the minimum voltage, the undervoltage light will go out and the ammeter will show a positive reading.

Fault protection includes:
- **Over/under voltage**. If the voltage goes over around 15.5 volts, the voltage regulator will break the field and lock it out, making the undervoltage light come on. You can switch the alternator off for a few seconds to reset the system, but only once. If voltage reduces, or the alternator is switched off, the warning lamp will come on, and go off when the voltage is restored.
- **Overheating**. The generator should be switched off and allowed to cool once the warning light comes on.
- **Over/under frequency.**
- **Over/under excitation**.

For larger aircraft, alternator output is typically 200 volts, 3-phase, varying in frequency between 280-540 Hz to cover the whole range of engine RPM. The initial excitation again comes from the battery (or ground power), switched in by resetting the alternator switch.

After the engine has started, and the generator warning light goes out, moving the control switch to ON allows some current to be fed back to the generator from the *Bridge Rectifier Pack*, which sits after the voltage regulator, to allow self-excitation.

CONSTANT SPEED DRIVE UNIT/IDG
To keep inductive and capacitive reactance under control, aircraft systems should be supplied with AC at a constant frequency, as almost exclusively used on large jet aircraft. The 747, for example, parallels its generators to make sure that all the systems have the power they require. If one fails, you loadshed.

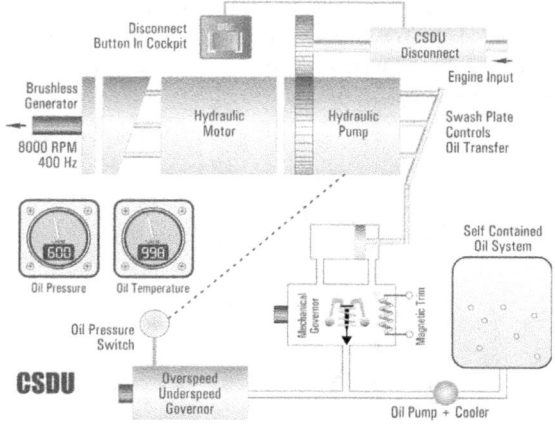

The 737, on the other hand, has each generator supplying around half the load. If one fails, the other can power the whole system, with or without loadshedding, without the APU generator being brought on line. Here, the generators do not supply common busbars - they are not paralleled, so there is no need to synchronise their frequencies, although they are kept within certain limits.

As the engines cannot be relied upon to maintain a constant speed (on which the aircraft's constant AC frequency depends), there needs to be some sort of interim arrangement between the engine and its alternator.

The hydraulically operated Constant Speed Drive Unit* keeps the AC generator's rotational speed constant (usually about 8,000 RPM), for a nominal frequency of 400 Hz, ranging between 380-420. 400 Hz is low enough not to interfere with radios and high enough to allow better component designs, although there are (or have been) reliability issues.

*Modern technology allows systems without a CSDU. Variable output is fed to a full wave rectifier, where it is converted to DC and filtered, then chopped into square wave outputs, separated and summed for 400 Hz AC. If used in modern aircraft, the

CSDU and (brushless) alternator can be combined in one unit, the **Integrated Drive Generator** (IDG). It is cooled by oil, which involves a heat exchanger.

Note that a voltage regulator is still required in order to maintain constant voltages under load.

Otherwise, the CSDU may be cooled with ram air or its own oil supply. It is connected to the engine by a clutch (the CSD disconnect) which can be used at any RPM, but preferably at idle, to reduce loads. An electromechanical disconnect mechanism is used for emergencies, provided the engine is running.

Once a CSDU has been disconnected, it is not available for the rest of the flight. It can only be reinstated on the ground, with the engine shut down.

The system uses differential oil pressure between a hydraulic pump and a hydraulic motor. The oil temperature is a function of the work being done, in that, if it rises, the load has increased. Instruments in the cockpit will show the temperature rise, which is the important value - there may be two or just one showing the IN and RISE figures. However, you can also expect an oil pressure indication in the cockpit.

Low oil pressure and high oil temperature are good reasons for disconnection in flight.

The oil transfer is controlled by an eccentric swashplate whose angle of inclination is controlled by movement of a piston inside a centrifugal governor (see picture below). This may be further refined by a magnetic trim device that adjusts the flyweights in the governor. The pressure exerted on the motor piston by the pump determines the rotational speed of a centre plate, in that, the higher the pressure, the faster it will rotate. When the engine and generator speeds are equal, the system is known as *on speed*. There is no oil transfer and the governors are in the neutral position. If the throttle setting is reduced, the engine will slow down and the output of the hydraulic pump will reduce. As the generator is now faster than the engine, an overdrive condition exists, which will be sensed by the governor, and the angle of the swashplate will be increased, as will the stroke of its pistons. For an under-drive condition, the reverse happens.

Fault protection includes:

- **Quill Drive**. A drive shaft with a weak point that prevents engine stoppage if the IDG seizes.
- **Over/Under-excitation**. For parallel faults, a protection device trips in when the excitation to the field of one generator varies one way or the other, sensed when it takes more or less than its share of the reactive load. The fault signal has an inverse time function that trips the Bus Tie Breaker (BTB) of the over-excited generator. A voltage regulator or reactive load-sharing circuit could cause this fault. An under-excitation fault opens the:
  - **Exciter Control Relay**, which will open with the GCB (below) if there is an AC generator fault on a twin-engined aircraft.
  - **Generator Breaker** (GCB). This closes when the generator's voltage is greater than the battery's, and opens when the opposite is true.
- **Bus Tie Breaker** (BTB). Used when there is a phase imbalance between an AC generator on the main busbars and other AC generators.

When under excitation occurs, the exciter relay doesn't always trip, but the generator does. This is sensed when the under-excited generator takes less than its share of reactive load, and a fault signal makes the BTB trip in a fixed time (3-5 sec). This could be from a fault in a reactive sharing circuit, a generator, or voltage regulator.

- **Over/Under voltage**. Protection is given when the line voltage goes over around 225v, or when high currents occur (i.e. undervoltage and overheating, where burning out is a possibility). This device operates on an inverse time function, which means that the voltage determines the time in which the offending generator is de-energised by tripping the GCR (Generator Control Relay) and GCB. The GCR de-energises the field, and the GCB trips the generator off the busbar. A detector, set to operate within 3 volts of 100 or 130 v, sends a signal via a time delay to two solid state switches (the delay allows the CSDU to react in time). On detecting a persistent overvoltage fault on an AC generator, the **exciter and generator breakers** are opened. If voltage reduces, or the alternator is switched off, the warning lamp comes on, and goes off when the voltage is restored. For undervoltage, the GCR and GCB are tripped in a fixed time (3-5 seconds), resulting in the generator shutting down.
- **Overheating**. The generator should be switched off and cooled once the warning light comes on.
- **Differential Protection**. Differences between the generator and busbar are sensed by transformers and the field automatically de-excited.
- **Over/Under Frequency** (Over/Under speed). If this is left unchecked, the inductive loads can be damaged. Older systems use a pressure switch in the CSDU, but modern ones detect changes in frequency. Overspeeding causes the GCB to trip and the CSDU goes into underdrive. The GCB still trips for an underspeed, but the generator is removed from the busbar. As the heaviest loads are inductive, under frequency is most hazardous. When an underspeed fault is detected, the generator breaker is opened.
- **IDG (CSDU) Disconnect**. Oil pressure and temperature are monitored in the cockpit and you can disconnect if there is a problem, but the system can only be reset with engines stopped.
- **Bearing Failure**. If there is too much clearance in generator bearings, a warning light will come on.
- **Negative Sequence Voltage Protection**. This detects line-to-line or line-to-earth faults after the protected zone and makes the BTBs trip.

Modern AC Generator Control Units have permanent indications to record failures, and all the commands from the control panel are applied through them, except for the dog clutch release.

A **feeder** is the wire or bus bar connecting the load with the AC generator. It may short out or have some sort of leakage with Earth or another phase or open circuit that means the disconnected wire is known as a **feeder fault**. **Feeder fault protection** is associated with paralleling generators and the term *balancing circuit* is the same as *equalising circuit*. On removing a faulty generator from the bus, the equalising circuit is also taken out of the system and the remaining generator will retain its standard voltage control. Load shedding may be required.

The results may include:

- Automatic disconnection of the generator from the AC busbar.
- Opening of the generator field current relay.
- Opening of the main relay of the generator breaker
- Opening of the balancing circuit connecting two generators.
- Lighting of an indicator lamp.

Time delays allow any protection devices to trip before equipment is removed from busbars. Warning lights include excessive temperature and low oil pressure.

The phrase *generator with another generator* refers to a parallel busbar and the tie breaker needs to be tripped, plus something else for the generator (usually exciter and generator relays). *Modern twin jet/ twin engine* means a split busbar and the tie breaker should not be closed. A single generator is on its own, so no tie breaker.

BRUSHLESS GENERATOR

A brushless generator minimises the normal losses from slip rings and brushes. The assembly is in three parts, starting with a pilot exciter that uses a permanent magnet (PMG) to generate single phase AC that is fed into a voltage regulator, from where it comes out as DC (having been rectified) into a stator coil in the Main Exciter.

A current is induced into each of three coils in the main exciter field producing a three-phase current, which is again full-wave rectified to DC which ends up in the Main Generator's rotating field rotor. The six diodes are kept cool with ram air directed down the shaft.

The exciter field resistance is temperature compensated by a thermistor which keeps a nearly constant resistance at the regulator output terminals. As the field coil rotates it induces current in the stator output windings. Some of the output is fed back to the voltage regulator to help control the field excitation. On starting, in a brushless AC generator with no commutator rings, the generator is activated by a set of permanent magnets.

The flow of power is shown by the red dashed line.

VOLTAGE REGULATION

The output is regulated by varying the current to the field windings. A voltage regulator senses the output and adjusts the field current when the voltage rises above a set value (typically 28.5 V). The current is cut off around 2000 times a second.

LOAD SHARING

Sharing AC generators is problematical because, if two, or more, become out of balance, a current will flow between them, and those with lower voltages are driven, causing a stress on their drive shafts, which may break, as they have a deliberate *weak link*, the mechanical equivalent of a fuse.

As frequency wild systems cannot be paralleled, *their phase relationship is unimportant*. Constant frequency systems, on the other hand, are designed to be paralleled, typically using a *split* or *parallel busbar* system, described previously.

A split busbar ensures that the supplies never actually meet. Each generator has its own busbar and, if one fails (as detected by a voltage controller), the load is transferred to the other with the help of a changeover relay (bus tie).

An alternator working with others must have its excitation (for reactive loads), speed (voltage, frequency) and phases adjusted (i.e. real and reactive load vectors must be synchronised). The process uses a *synchroniser*, which is simply a couple of small transformers. One has its primary across the busbars and the other is across the terminals of the alternator. The secondaries are connected in series with each other. When the emf of the alternator is in phase opposition to the p.d. on the busbar, the emfs of the secondaries are added together to drive a voltmeter to its highest reading.

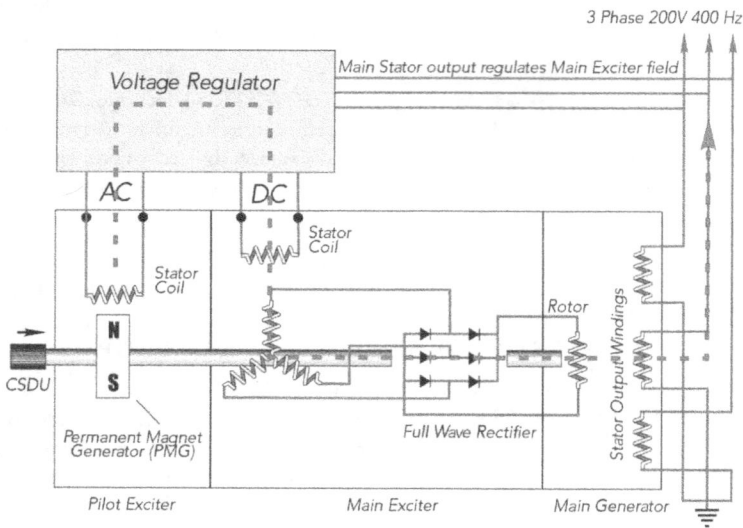

In a paralleled 3-phase AC system, with varying loads, the most efficient generator would be compound wound.

 Parallel systems have the same advantages (and disadvantages) as paralleled DC systems, but they are not suitable when independence is required, as with ETOPS. The Boeing 737, for example, uses a *non-parallel* 115/200 volt, 3 phase AC from two 40 kVA generators. A third generator is driven by an APU. In a *parallel busbar* system, all AC generators can be connected to one distribution busbar, so voltages, frequencies and phases (as well as real and reactive loads, mentioned below) must be kept within very strict limits by *phase discriminators*.

Real Load Sharing (Speed)

The real load (in kW) is the useful power available, and reactive power (in kVAR) is the resultant of the inductive and capacitive currents and voltage in the system.

Real load sharing is determined by the rotational speeds of the generators and hence the voltage phase relationships. Generators are synchronous, so they lock together with respect to frequency when they work in parallel. The system frequency ends up as that of the generator with the highest output, which means it is carrying more of the load. The imbalance is overcome with an error detector which senses current change in a load sharing loop. The signals are sent to the electromagnetic coil in the governor of each CSDU to restore the balanced condition.

Real loadsharing control is effected by automatic adjustment of the torque on each generator at the output drive shaft, via the CSDU. The field from the coil interacts with permanent magnet flyweights to produce a torque which, together with centrifugal force, allows fine adjustment of the governor control valve and CSD speed.

Picture Below: Brushless Generator

Reactive Load Sharing (Voltage)

This depends on the relative sizes of the output voltages, which depend on the settings of the relevant *voltage regulators* and **field excitation current**. The circuitry is similar to that for real load sharing, but the current transformers are connected to the primary windings of mutual reactors, which only deliver signals proportional to the generator's reactive load.

In a paralleled AC system, the reactive load is borne by the voltage regulators.

POWER CONVERSION

DC from AC (Rectifiers)

AC is used when it comes to generating large amounts of power, but most radio and computer equipment uses DC, and 12v at that. That part of the problem is easy - a transformer can be used to step the voltage down (or up) as required. Then a *rectifier* is used to convert the AC into DC by extracting the peaks from the AC waveform. That is, the alternating current is only allowed to flow through a series of diodes in one direction and every second half is turned upside down.

The diode can be a *half-wave* rectifier*, in which current will flow only on alternative half-cycles (left, below):

Half Wave   Full Wave

*A halfwave rectifier for a single phase requires one diode, but the lost half cycles are used in trying to drive the current in the reverse direction, and are wasted as heat. To use those cycles, four diodes (*anti-phase*) allow full wave rectification. You need 3 diodes for a half wave rectifier on 3 phase, and 6 for a full wave.

In the diagram below, when A is positive against C, current will flow from A to B, through R (the load), then D to C. When it is negative, current will flow from C to B, through R, D to A. However, the current is still not steady, even though it is now flowing in one direction (you can detect it with a suitable instrument). A capacitor smooths the final result, inside a *filter circuit*. There might be a *bleeder resistor* of a very high value across the capacitor's terminals to ensure it discharges when the power is switched off.

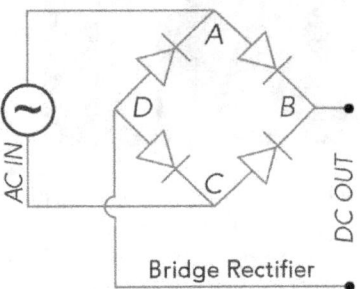
Bridge Rectifier

AC from DC

Inverters produce AC from DC. This might be because an older aircraft using DC has new equipment that requires AC. For example, you may not get any fuel indications until you switch the inverters on, because the capacitive fuel indication system requires AC with which to work. A **rotary inverter** is a DC motor driving an AC generator.

A **static inverter** is electrical, with no moving parts (and therefore much more reliable), that contains a signal generator and amplifier producing a square or sine wave, which is reshaped into a sine wave. They generate very little heat, so you don't need cooling air. Also, as they do not suffer from arcing at low air pressures, as rotary inverters do, there is no need for them to be within the pressure hull.

AUXILIARY POWER UNIT

Before the engines are started, power can be supplied from a Ground Power Unit (GPU), but more typically from an Auxiliary Power Unit, which is more able to meet large power demands. The APU is usually a small axial flow gas turbine that usually sits in the tail* (behind a firewall) and which drives the same type of AC generator that is fitted to the main engines (supplying 115v, 400 Hz power after the engines have been started). The generator will be driven through an accessory gearbox.

*It will be high to stop it ingesting anything nasty. It is usually covered by a door which naturally must be opened (electrically) before you operate the APU. This is mostly automatic.

The APU also has a compressor that can supply bleed air to the pneumatic system (used for starting the main engines) and the air conditioning. The APU can still be used when the main engines are operating, especially to replace a failed generator. As the APU runs at a constant speed, it does not need any sort of speed regulation.

In emergencies, a Ram Air Turbine can drop down from the fuselage, to spin in the airflow. There may even be a generator driven by the hydraulic system.

In large aircraft, the ship's battery will only be used to start the APU, and to provide limited DC power in real emergencies. The APU otherwise has its own battery.

The fuel for the APU will come from the main tanks, and will normally be delivered under pressure from an AC driven pump, but there is a DC one if AC is not available. The DC pump will run off the ship's battery, as will the fuel valve, which will open when the APU is started and close automatically on shutdown.

Below is a typical control panel for an APU:

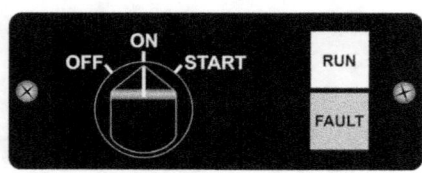

The RUN light is white, and will be illuminated when the APU is at its proper running speed. The FAULT light is amber, and it will tell you when the APU has shut down due to a fault, or when the fuel shutoff valve is not in its commanded position.

Picture: Typical Power Sources

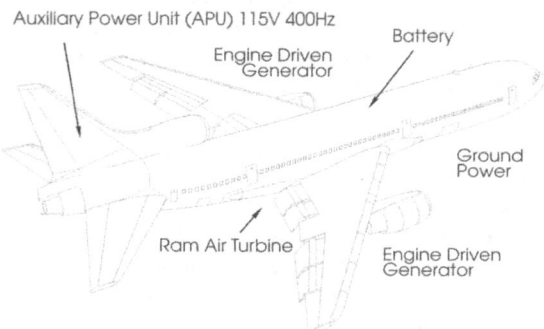

The OFF selection closes the APU bleed valve and initiates the shutdown cooling cycle after it has closed. The ON position is for normal operations. It opens the bleed valve and the door, arms the bleed valve and energises a fuel pump. The start sequence will commence when the door is fully open. The START position is spring loaded and is used to initiate the automatic start sequence, before returning to the ON position.

The instruments that tell you what an earlier type of APU is up to might include RPM, EGT and oil indicators. Modern ones use the EICAS/EICAM displays.

AC MOTORS

There are three main types of AC motor - the *synchronous*, the *induction* (asynchronous), and the *series*, or *commutator* motor, which is more commonly found in domestic appliances. We are only concerned about synchronous and induction motors.

There are also three sizes of motor:

- **Large**, with an output of at least 3 kW, which are normally 3-phase
- **Medium-Small**. The output starts at 50W, mostly based on single-phase operation. Those below 750W are also called *Fractional Horsepower*
- **Miniature**. Below 50W, in instruments and servos

AC motors use a rotating magnetic field. 3-phase currents set up magnetic fields that can be resolved into a single field revolving in the air gap between the rotor and stator. At 400 Hz, this will be 24 000 RPM. By using a stationary winding with a rotating field, you only need two slip rings, which makes construction easier and reduces losses.

INDUCTION MOTORS

Induction motors are often called *squirrel cage motors*, because the rotor that spins in the middle is based on those things that hamsters run around in (their proper name is just the *cage*, or *short-circuited rotor*).

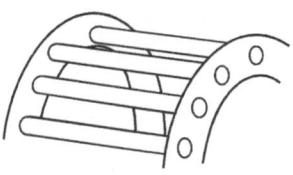

The bars are copper or aluminium, shorted together by rings at each end (apparently you can get better starting and quieter running if the bars are slightly skewed). There are no connections to or from the rotor, or moving parts, aside from the rotor itself when it is made to spin. As a brush or commutator is not required, or slip rings, there are less parts to wear out and less interference with radios.

The rotating magnetic field induces large currents in the spokes of the squirrel cage (because of the short-circuiting), which produces a magnetic field that interacts with the outer rotating field, in the opposite direction, after Lenz's law, making it spin.

As the field rotates through one revolution over each AC cycle, at 50 Hz, you will get 3000 RPM.

However, the rotor will never turn at the synchronous speed of the rotating field, or there would be no induced current. The difference between the speed of the rotor and the rotating field is *slip*. At full loads, it is around 4%.

As mentioned, you can obtain the speed from the number of pole pairs and the frequency of the AC supply:

```
RPM = Hz x 60
      pole pairs
```

The speed of a 4 pole motor at 400 Hertz is 12 000 RPM.

If a phase is lost while it is running, the motor will still run, at about half speed, but it cannot be restarted (if it is not running, it will refuse to spin and probably blow the fuses in the other phases). When the load on an induction motor becomes so great that it cannot be carried by it, the motor will stop. This is the *pullout point*. To change the direction of rotation, you just swap two cables round.

The squirrel cage is simple and cheap, so it is used in smaller motors, but it takes a large starting current and has a relatively low starting torque (unless it has a high resistance, but that is inefficient). It therefore doesn't like starting against heavy loads and often must be run up to speed first. In fact, it has similar characteristics to a DC shunt wound motor. As a result, the greatest torque on an induction motor is at start up. Gyroscopes based on them should not be used in the speeding up phase.

Although the most common winding (in the rotating element) is the squirrel cage (i.e. short circuited), another type has coils in the rotor slots, to produce a *wound rotor*, in three sections, out to three slip rings, so that starting resistances can be included in the rotor circuit. They are gradually cut out as the rotor speeds up until the slip rings are short-circuited.

A two-phase motor has two windings 90° apart, but their voltages come from different sources. One is the *reference* phase, and the other a *control* phase. By varying the phasing and amplitude of the currents in the control phase, you can control the direction of rotation and the speed. Such motors are not as smooth or powerful as 3-phase motors, so they are used in lesser roles, such as servo motors.

Split-phase motors also have two windings 90° apart, but one is capacitive and the other is resistive, connected in parallel across a single phase AC supply. The current in the capacitive winding leads that in the resistive winding by around 90° (called *phase splitting*). These motors are also used in lesser roles, as they operate like 2-phase motors.

Synchronous

Synchronous motors are particularly suited for constant speed operation, since their rotors only run at the same speed as the rotating magnetic field, which is determined by the *frequency* of the AC supplied.

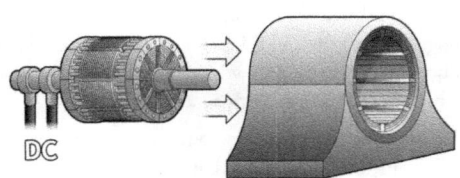

In a synchronous motor, the squirrel cage is replaced with a magnet, either permanent, for low power requirements, or an electromagnet for higher outputs. There, the rotor is supplied with a DC current (from a generator or a rectifier) that creates an electromagnet with North and South Poles to line up with the opposite poles in the rotating field.

As long as the pull between the magnets is large enough, the rotor will run at the same speed as the rotating field. If the load exceeds the maximum torque, the rotor will stall and stop.

Synchronous motors cannot start without being driven, or having their rotor connected as a self-starting circuit. That is, since the field is already rotating at the eventual speed, it rushes past the rotor poles so quickly that the rotor does not have a chance to get started, so the rotor is repelled first in one direction and then the other (in other words, inertia plays a part). Thus, the motor must be accelerated before it can synchronise, so it may need a separate starting mechanism. This is done mostly with a small induction motor, often called a *pony motor*.

Once the rotor is near to synchronous speed, the rotor's DC field is energized by a mechanical switch that operates on centrifugal force. This makes it lock the rotor in step with the rotating field. Full torque is developed, and the load is driven.

COMPUTERS, ETC

You can represent and store information electrically in many ways - a capacitor, for example, can store an electrical charge which can be measured and related to a value that can be used for calculations in an analogue computer. However, capacitors leak over time - as the mathematical values would therefore change by themselves, and measurements would become less accurate (assuming the mechanism was adequate in the first place), a better way of using those charges is to detect the presence (or not) of a signal, regardless of its strength, which is how digital circuits work (see *Bits & Bytes*, below).

As with all computerised equipment, an aircraft with digital equipment must be grounded when not flying to guard against static damage!

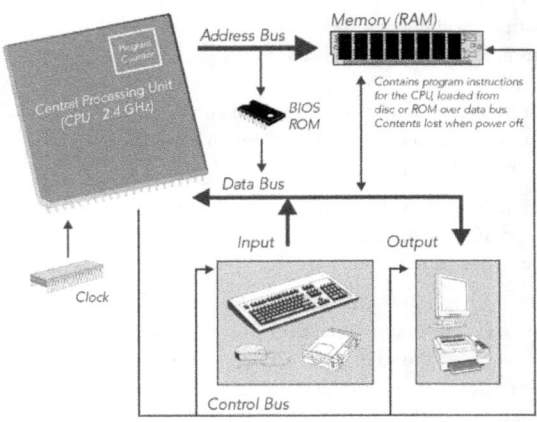

There are many computers in modern aircraft, and they all work in pretty much the same way, although they won't all have a keyboard and screen. Essentially, a Central Processor (CPU), which is the brains and does all the work, is connected to memory and other peripheral chips (that may control instruments, screens, keyboards, etc.) over various buses that control memory or data. The CPU itself consists of an Arithmetic and Logic Unit (ALU), a control and timing unit*, and registers.

*The control unit is supposed to sequence and coordinate operations.

You can see that the memory is linked to the CPU and the Arithmetic & Logic Unit (ALU) inside it.

Multiprocessing involves several CPUs inside one computer (it is not the same as multitasking, which can be done with just one CPU, and is less powerful because it is a software solution). In fact, modern technology allows several CPUs inside one chip (multithreading), which only works if the software is aware of the facility (it must be said, however, that much of the computer equipment used in aircraft is nothing like modern).

Some systems use multiprocessors that can run several tasks in parallel.

If any part of the computer needs attention, it *interrupts* the CPU, which is more efficient than having the CPU poll each device in turn, and wasting cycles when the device(s) are quite happy to be left alone, thank you very much.

Hardware

The term *hardware* covers the physical aspects of a computer, such as keyboards, screens, hard drives, etc. Keyboards and mice are *input* devices, and screens and printers do *output*.

INTEGRATED CIRCUITS

These are now found in a wide variety of equipment - not just computers. An integrated circuit is essentially a complete piece of electrical equipment inside one chip, including resistors, transistors, wiring, etc., which are therefore very small indeed.

The picture on the right is of an EEPROM, or *Electrically Erasable Programmable Read Only Memory*, which is simply a chip that can be cleared with a small voltage and reprogrammed. Such chips are used in Flight Management Systems, for

example, to contain navigation or performance databases. You cannot normally change the contents, but an engineer can with special equipment when it's time for an update.

The integrated circuit inside is very small, and it has to interface with the rest of the world, which is why it is in a bigger chip so that we humans can manipulate it.

The transistor (later) prompted the development of integrated circuits. As it is able to move electrons through solid material instead of requiring the vacuum in a valve, the transistor has a much lower internal resistance and uses a lot less power. Cost is therefore reduced and, most important for aviation, weight, while increasing reliability.

The most useful application of integrated circuits is within computers, which use large numbers of identical logic circuits to make yes/no decisions. In other words, switching. If you operated five switches in their various binary combinations, you could obtain any number between 1 and 31. Adding one more switch (for 32) allows any number between 1 and 63. With only 46 switches, you can get any number between 1 and 100 trillion! The ability to check this number of switches at once is one reason why computers are fast, aside from the fact that they are run at high clock speeds anyway.

MEMORY

Memory contains the instructions that tell the Central Processor what to do, as well as the data created by its activities. As a computer works with bits that are either on or off, memory chips work by keeping electronic switches in one state or the other for as long as they are required (since they are capacitors, which leak their charges, memory cells are refreshed every other cycle). Where these states can be changed at will or, more properly, the operating system is able to reach every part of memory, it is called *Random Access Memory*, or RAM, which comes from when magnetic tapes were used for storage, and information could only be accessed sequentially; that is, not at random. A ROM, on the other hand, has its electronic switches permanently on or off, so they can't be changed (by pilots anyway), hence *Read Only Memory*. ROMs are *non-volatile*, meaning that data inside isn't lost when the power is off. System memory, on the other hand, is volatile, so it is vulnerable to power loss.

Memory is counted in K, which is actually 1024 bits, as opposed to 1000, because of the binary counting used by computers, so you get 4096 instead of 4000.

More permanent storage is provided by magnetic materials (such as the coating on floppy or hard disks), or optical means, such as DVD-ROMs, or flash memory.

Virtual memory is space used on a permanent medium (typically a hard drive) to store data that is too much for system memory to hold. The process of moving data from one to the other is called *paging*, because memory is dealt with in pages.

BUSES

A bus is a shared connection between devices, of which a computer has several; for example, the *processor bus* connects the CPU to its support chips, the *memory bus* connects it to memory.

So, buses are electronic pathways between the various parts of a computer, which could be 8-bit, 16-bit, 32-bit, depending on how much data is transferred around at once. The problem with the average desktop PC is that the rest of the machine, in terms of bus width and speed, won't necessarily have the same capability as the CPU, so you might get data bottlenecks. For example, the CPU may be running at 2000 mph (2 GHz), but the screen and hard drive, the busiest components, are sitting in the PCI bus, running at 330 mph (33 MHz). The memory bus will be somewhere in between. A fast CPU won't mean a thing if the rest of the machine is crippled, as with a Celeron.

Some computerised devices in aircraft are better designed than this, but many use purpose built chips that contain the same CPU and support chips as a PC in one package. The FADEC in a Bell 407 uses a single-board computer which transmits data to the engine with the RS 232 protocol, which is quite old. Some components, such as an EGPWS or a GPS, will use a PCMCIA bus to get data in and out, which is just as old.

THE BIOS

The instructions that turn a computer into a useful machine come in three stages, starting with application programs, which are loaded by an operating system, which in turn is loaded by a bootstrap loader in the BIOS (the *Basic Input/Output System*). There may be several BIOSes, a good example being the one on the video card that controls the interface between it and the computer. However, more important to the machine as a whole is the *System BIOS* which is a collection of assembly language routines that allow programs and the components of a computer to communicate with each other at the hardware level. It therefore works in two directions at once and is active all the time your computer is switched on. In this way, software doesn't have to talk to a device directly, but can call a BIOS routine instead.

Software

The term *software* refers to programming instructions that make the hardware work together. More technically, the software controls the switching of electrons in transistors (using quantum rules) so you don't have to keep changing the wiring. The software used in computers on aircraft must follow RTCA/DO-178B. There are two types of software:

OPERATING SYSTEMS

A computer is only a machine, so it needs instructions to run itself. For example, it can only put letters on the screen after you press a key if it's told to. However, it's a waste of time including those instructions in every application program, which is why computers have operating systems. These are *collections* of programs that perform standard housekeeping tasks, such as translating keypushes into screen displays, changing colours on the screen, or simply moving data from one part of the computer to another. Other (application) software is then written up to the operating system level, without worrying about what sort of hardware it's dealing with. This saves programmers producing the same code that everyone uses over and over again.

Every computer has an operating system, and they ultimately all do the same job. Some are more user-friendly, though (on the Macintosh), and some are downright user-hostile (like Unix). That used on IBM-compatibles is commonly called Windows, and mostly lies somewhere in between.

A multitasking operating system switches rapidly between several running tasks.

APPLICATIONS

This is software that turns the computer into something useful, such as wordprocessors, or spreadsheets, or in the case of aviation, that runs the FADEC, or even the complete aircraft (there can be 150 computers in the average jet transport). It is so important these days, that checking the software version is part of the checklist.

Firmware

This is a cross between hardware and software, when programs are contained within Read Only Memory, or a chip, as opposed to being kept on a hard drive, so such software loads quicker and cannot be erased.

Electronic Systems

"Normal" electronic equipment consists of components such as capacitors, resistors, transistors, etc., which can be assembled into just a few basic circuits, like amplifiers. Electronic *systems* are composed of such circuits, which are used as building blocks, so you can deal with larger systems in concept form rather than getting involved with detail, especially since the introduction of integrated circuits, where the distinction between circuits and systems is much less clear cut. Now, you only need to know what a "black box" does, rather than how it works.

Two main types of circuits are used - linear (analogue) or digital. Linear circuits handle signals that change smoothly over a range of values. That is, the output will be an exact copy of the input, but larger, so there is a linear connection between them - doubling the input would double the output, for example.

An analogue signal is *analogous* to whatever it represents, and relatively smooth; the voltage over a telephone line, for instance, rises and falls in sympathy with the loudness of your voice - the fluctuating size of the signal is what's actually measured. Compare this with a digital signal, which is jerky, and like tapping on a pipe to get a message through rather than using the flow of material through it (the word *analogue*, is often taken to mean *non-digital*).

Digital electronics involves electronic manipulation of, or by, numbers, to obtain economy, reliability and speed. For convenience, only two numbers are used, and a state of On or Off is called a *Binary Digit*, or *Bit* for short.

ANALOGUE VS DIGITAL

The digital on-off signals that a computer generates as bits arise from switches (that is, transistors) making and breaking contact several million times a second, forming electrical pulses in the shape of square waves, with a very sharp rise as the connection is made, a plateau as the switch is held on and a sharp fall as the contact breaks. An *On* condition is recognised once the pulse reaches a certain threshold, and Off when it drops below. As further protection against spurious signals, the computer will only react to signals of a certain duration.

Digital systems are *discrete state* systems, in which only a fixed number of states are allowed, in our case, two.

Imagine the difference by comparing a normal light switch with a dimmer. You might get more choice with analogue, but it is more expensive to create and maintain.

An analogue system is therefore a *continuous state* or *continuously variable* system, which is able to cope with any value within certain limits. With all the variables involved, the accuracy of transmission can be as low as 0.1%. Digital signals can get quite distorted before you lose the ability to detect what they mean, since you are only dealing with the presence or absence of a signal rather than its value.

An *Analogue-Digital converter* (or *Digital-Analogue*) is simply a device that converts between digital and analogue signals, since there may be occasions when you want to take advantage of the benefits of either system.

NUMBERS

The decimal system is useless for counting numbers in this case, since you need to be able to discriminate between 10 levels of voltage. For example, say you had the answer to Life, The Universe and Everything*, which is 42. To calculate it, you must multiply 6 by 7, so you start with 7 volts. Now you have to feed it into an amplifier with a gain of 6 to get 42 volts. Easy enough, but if you start multiplying by thousands, you will soon have problems!

*from *The Hitchhiker's Guide To The Galaxy*.

Using only 2 numbers is a lot better, hence the use of the binary system, mentioned below. Now, all you need to do is find out whether a voltage exists or not, rather than how large it is, and use more wires for the bigger numbers, or put them in memory and use them in a sequence.

A bit is represented on paper by a 1 for On or 0 for Off (the same as on power switches for electrical appliances). To place one character on the screen takes eight bits (a byte), so when a machine is spoken of as being eight- or sixteen-bit, it's effectively dealing with one or two letters of the alphabet at the same time - a 32-bit computer can therefore cope with 4 characters in one go. 2 bytes are called a *word*, 4 bytes (32-bits) are a *double word* and 16 bytes are a *paragraph*. 4 bits are a *nybble*.

Because it uses multiples of 8, a computer will also count to a base of 16, or hexadecimal, which uses letters as well as numbers, and the order is 0 1 2 3 4 5 6 7 8 9 A B C D E F, as numbers run out after 9. However, older systems, including transponders, use an octal system, from 0-7.

BINARY MATHEMATICS

With the decimal system, the numbers run from 0 to 9, and when you go past 9 you return to zero but place a 1 to the left of it (a *carry*, in the next column) to indicate that you have gone through the sequence once. Once you go past 19, the 1 is changed to 2, for twice round, and so on. With binary, you do the same, by starting with 0, progressing to 1, then returning to 0 but with a 1 to the left of it. However, this is not ten, but rather one-zero, meaning 2 in the decimal system. 11 (one-one) is 3, and so on. You naturally end up with long sequences, but computers can handle this with ease.

As a bit has only two possible values, 0 or 1, there are only four possible combinations of inputs, which are:

```
0 + 0 = 0
0 + 1 = 1
1 + 0 = 1
1 + 1 = 10
```

The fourth line shows that you need to account for two output bits when two input bits are added: the sum and a possible carry. Put another way, if you need a quantity larger than 1, the symbols will just repeat themselves. As with decimals, the least significant digit is on the right.

The first figure represents 2^0, which actually means 1, and the second (from the right) is 2^1, the third 2^2, and so on:

Digit	5th	4th	3rd	2nd	1st
Power	2^4	2^3	2^2	2^1	2^0
Decimal	16	8	4	2	1

The binary system doubles every time, so a binary number of 11001 really means 1 + 0 + 0 + 8 + 16, which equals 25 (all you do is add the powers). To convert decimal to binary, divide each successive number by 2 and take note of the remainders.

SEMICONDUCTORS REVISITED

The main reason as to whether a substance is an insulator, a conductor or a semiconductor is the spacing of its energy bands. With semiconductors, the size of the gap between the top of the highest full energy band (the *valence* band) and the bottom of the next empty one (the *conduction* band) is quite small, so some electrons, given some heat energy, can jump more easily to the conduction band (with metals, resistance increases with temperature, but it *decreases* with semiconductors because the number of charge carriers increases). Electricity can flow one way and not another (i.e. resistance is higher in one direction), depending on how you apply the current. The most common semiconductor material is either germanium (Ge) or silicon (Si), whose atoms will link up to share their valence electrons.

In those materials, each atom shares one electron with another in a *covalent bond* which is so strong that it takes a lot of energy to break. As all the outer electrons form covalent bonds, and cannot move, the resulting crystal is a good insulator. However, you can add an impurity by doping the main material with another that may have more or less electrons in its outer shell, which degrades it and adds electrons or holes. For example, as silicon has four valence electrons, you can add phosphorous (which has 5) to create N-type material (N=negative). Adding Boron, with 3 valence electrons, makes a P-type (positive).

THE DIODE

The "orbit" of an electron is not the same as any other at the same level, because it might not have the same energy. This means that an energy shell will not necessarily be a precise line, but a slightly fuzzy band consisting of several orbiting electrons. The fuzziness is increased because you only know the position of any electron within a certain probability range. The degree of fuzziness depends on the temperature - normally, absolute zero is used.

Another name for a shell would therefore be an energy band, so the outside one is the valence band, which is the only one that may not be completely full. The gap between bands is called the *forbidden gap*. When an electron jumps, it leaves a hole in the valence band. Although holes can give the illusion of movement, this happens only in the valence band. Electrons move in the conduction band, which is an empty band beyond the valence band, where electrons that manage to escape are assumed to go. In an insulator, there is no forbidden gap between them. In a conductor, there is quite a large one* (in electronic terms). Any increase in energy will move an electron into the gap, where it can't exist, so it hops back into the valence band. In a conductor, the electron can hop easily to the conduction band where it is free to roam.

*In germanium, the gap between the valence and conduction bands is quite small, so you only need a little heat to close it enough to allow an electron to jump over. As it is nearly a semiconductor in its own right, it is known as an *intrinsic semiconductor*.

An *extrinsic semiconductor* is a substance like silicon that is doped with phosphorous or boron to produce a material that has one more electron or one more hole, respectively. These would be known as *n-type* or *p-type*. N and P refer to the type of chemical used to dope pure silicon.

The surface where one type changes to the other is a *junction*, and it is the key to modern solid-state electronics.

In the top picture below, of a junction diode, holes and electrons are repelled from the battery and interact as normal, allowing electrons to pass to the positive side of the battery and holes to pass to the negative side, so the *n* side loses energy and the *p* side gains it. There are no holes or free electrons in the junction because they diffuse into each other (and cancel each other out) at the atomic level over the junction (the depletion region). Essentially, when electrons hit the junction, they become valence electrons, so they can move through the holes in the P type material.

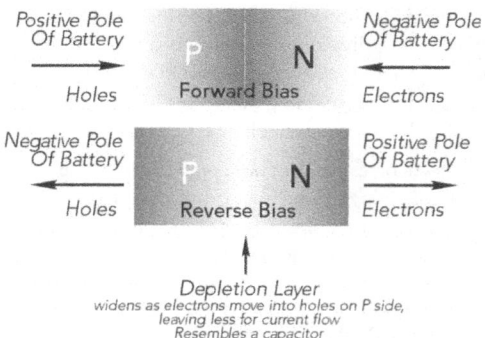

Depletion Layer widens as electrons move into holes on P side, leaving less for current flow Resembles a capacitor

The electrons and holes are forced away from the power supply *toward* the junction, and the depletion region is compressed until it disappears. The barrier is broken and current can flow through the device. This is known as being *forward biased*, and the *forward voltage drop* is almost constant (0.7v for silicon, 0.3v for germanium), regardless of the current, assuming normal temperatures. Resistance is low in the forward direction.

In the lower example, a positive voltage is applied to the n-type material and electrons start filling the p-type material. Holes and electrons are pulled *away* from the junction, so the depletion region expands to take up the entire structure, which allows very little current flow (the *reverse leakage current*). This is *reverse biasing*, where the junction behaves like a capacitor. If the voltage gets too much, a reverse breakdown occurs, which fries the diode. You now have the electrical equivalent of a non-return valve.

THE ZENER DIODE

The maximum safe reverse voltage for diodes is low. In fact, they usually fry if any attempt is made to push current through them in the wrong direction.

A Zener diode allows current to flow in the reverse direction if the voltage is larger than a *breakdown voltage*. As the voltage dropped is known and fixed, the Zener diode can maintain an output voltage within a fraction of a volt, while the input voltage can vary over a range of several, so it is typically used to maintain a fixed voltage, if there is a resistor to limit the current. If the output voltage rises due to a reduction in load current, the Zener takes current from the supply to keep the output constant. It is therefore useful for *voltage stabilisation*.

Below is an example of a lighting circuit:

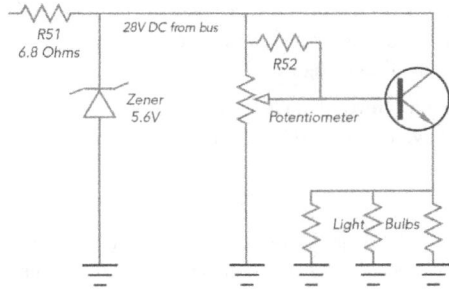

It is a simplified version of that used in the Bell 206. Between them, the Zener diode, transistor and resistor R51 regulate the amount of voltage to the instrument lights. R51 protects the circuit from excess current in conjunction with the Zener diode, which is set to pass current when the voltage across it exceeds 5.6 volts.

Using Ohm's law, when the current through R51 exceeds around 3.3 amps, its rating of 6.8 ohms means that the voltage drop across it will be about 22.4 volts. If you subtract that from the 28v on the bus, you are left with the 5.6 volts setting of the Zener diode, which therefore acts like a pressure relief valve - any current more than 3.3 amps is fed to Earth through it.

As the potentiometer is rotated (on the overhead console), the voltage applied to the base of the transistor varies, and so does the voltage applied to the light bulbs.

Zener diodes are always reverse biased.

THE TRANSISTOR

The transistor is essentially two diodes back-to-back, one forward biased and the other reverse biased. Transistor action is the turning on (and controlling) of a large current through the high resistance (reverse biased) collector-base junction by a small current through the low resistance (forward biased) base-emitter junction. This is how the name arises, as *transistor* is a contraction of *transfer-resistor*, as in transferring resistance. Essentially, the emitter injects charge carriers at one end and the collector absorbs them at the other. The base controls how fast they go.

Thus, you can have more electrons (or holes) flow one way or the other for a given input, depending on the transistor's construction, either P-N-P or N-P-N. On the right is the symbol for an NPN bipolar transistor, which is the easiest one to understand because it works just like the triode valve - the base is equivalent to the grid, the emitter is the cathode and the collector is the anode. The arrow indicates conventional current flow, which is opposite to the electron flow. As the *n* material is more heavily doped* than the *p* material, it has more free electrons.

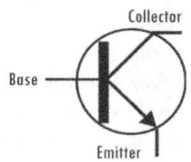

*The Collector is moderately doped, the Emitter is heavily doped and the Base is significantly less doped, so there are relatively few free holes in the picture above of an NPN transistor. When the base is made positive with respect to the emitter (i.e it gains more holes), current will flow in the base. If the collector is more positive, some of it is attracted into the collector-emitter circuit, so there is a gain in current due to the difference in resistance between the input and output (low when forward biased, high the other way). As power derives from the square of the current multiplied by the resistance, the current varies only slightly, but there is a large transfer of power.

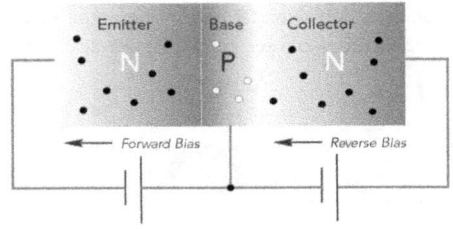

In other words, as a weak signal (perhaps a voice wave) increases or decreases the emitter-base voltage, the emitter-collector voltage varies in sympathy, and the transistor can be thought of as a controlling device, or a switch at the atomic level, especially when the forward biasing of the base current is done with a variable resistor, such as a volume control or a dimmer switch, as we have seen already.

So, a small amount of voltage from the base can regulate a large amount across the emitter-collector, in the order of 20 - 1 000, depending on the device, which is why transistors are also used for amplification.

Whereas the NPN depends on the movement of electrons, the PNP depends on the movement of positively charged holes, so the polarities of the applied voltages must be reversed to get the same effects. The base will therefore be made negative with respect to the emitter, and the collector made negative with respect to the base and emitter.

TRANSDUCERS

Transducers (as used in Air Data Computers) change energy from one form to another so that electronic components can communicate with the outside world. Examples include microphones, LEDs, speakers, CRTs.

THE THYRISTOR

This is a semiconductor that is mainly used for rectification and switching, particularly as a relay with no moving parts. It has four layers to the transistor's three (NPNP or PNPN), but the third layer is always the controlling one. It is known as the *gate*. When reverse biased, it behaves like a normal diode and allows no current through. When forward biased, the current does not flow until the bias voltage reaches a *breakover value*. The voltage at which breakover occurs is varied by changing the size of the current at the gate, known as *firing*.

A thyristor could be used for detecting momentary over-temperatures when starting a jet engine, because once current flow is initiated, it will continue until the forward bias voltage is reduced to a very low value. Instead of coming on momentarily, and risking not being seen, now the overtemperature light will stay on until it is reset.

LOGIC GATES

Two-state components are often called *logic elements*, which ultimately form complete *logic systems* or *circuits*. When the voltage to be detected is above a certain level, it is called a **Logic 1**, and when below, a **Logic 0** (this could also be *High* or *Low* or *True* or *False*). A logic gate could be seen as a simple two-position switch.

For mathematical operations with only two states to work with (i.e. yes or no), you need elements which have two binary inputs and one binary output - the three from which all binary logic may be constructed are the AND, OR, and NOT gates, which combine logical input signals in various ways to produce the desired outputs, and which may be found in various chips all over a computer (there are also three combinations, discussed below):

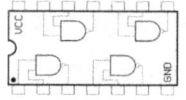 

All arise from the requirements of *Boolean logic*, originally developed by George Boole in 1854 in an effort to express complex ideas in a simple fashion. With Boolean mathematics, there is no such thing as subtraction, because that implies negative numbers (since division is compounded subtraction, that is not allowed either). However, multiplication is valid, and is the same as in real algebra: anything multiplied by 0 is 0, and anything multiplied by 1 remains unchanged.

The reason you need logic gates can be shown by an example. To a computer, it is not enough to say that if you operate the On switch of a radio, it will come on. It needs more information, because it is intrinsically stupid and needs to be told precisely what to do.

For example, you or I would know what to do if instructed to leave a room, but a computer would need to be told:

- Stand up
- Walk forward two paces
- Stop
- Put out hand
- Grasp door handle
- Turn door handle
- Pull door
- Check to see if door hits foot
- If yes, move foot
- If not, pull door further open

You get the picture.

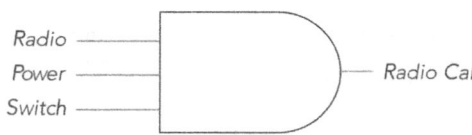

In the above case, *if* the On switch is operated, *and* the radio is serviceable, *and* there is power, it will turn on.

Now, after Boole, you can say:

```
Radio Call = Switch x Radio x Power
```

or, to be pedantic:

```
Radio Call = Switch.Radio.Power
```

Programmers, incidentally, have to anticipate every stupid thing that a computer (or user) might do, and create error messages for each one. Note that, in logic terms, the period (.) means + and the + sign means OR. Go figure.

Boolean algebra has three main logical operations: NOT, AND and OR, which were extended later in time:

THE AND GATE

With an AND gate, the inputs must all have logic 1 signals applied to them for the output to be a logic 1 (i.e. *True*, as opposed to *False*). If any of the inputs are logic 0 (*False*), the output will be logic 0 as well, so it acts as if all its switches were in series. Most AND gates have 2, 3 or 4 inputs, but you can actually have as many as you want - on an EGPWS, for example, you may need to test for many conditions. AND gates are certainly used in fire detection systems, where two systems in parallel must trigger for the fire to be reported, in case of false alarms. In other words, the switch must be on *and* the fuse must be unbroken for our radio to work.

This might also be useful with an autopilot, for example, which will not engage unless a certain series of conditions is met.

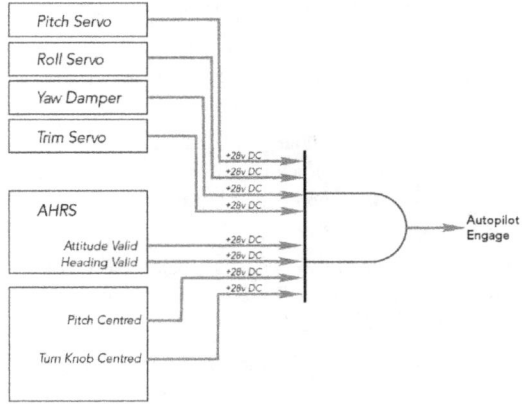

Also, if one input is held open, a stream of pulses could pass through the other inputs.

If you incorporate a potential divider, you can create an alarm circuit - as we used a thermistor previously, a suitable one could warn you when part of the aircraft (say a cargo hold) is getting too cold.

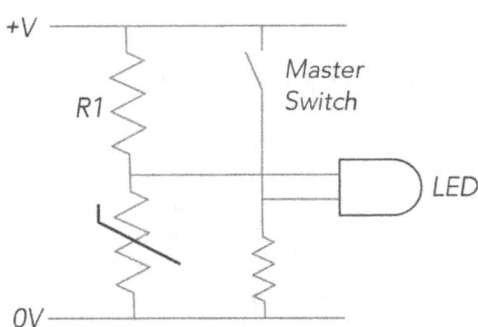

The signal from the divider to the logic gate will be high when the temperature is low, and the Master Switch will provide the other high signal required by the AND gate to issue a logic 1 to the warning LED.

Because an AND gate can only produce an output when all the inputs are at logic 1 (i.e. at the same time), it could also be known as an "all or nothing" gate.

The symbols used in this book (and by the examiners) are older ones rather than the "correct" ones used by the IEC: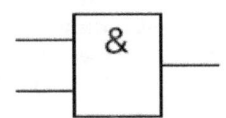

THE OR GATE

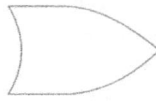 This allows the output to be true (1) if any one (or more) of its inputs are true (if the switch is off *or* the fuse is broken, the radio will not work). Put another way, the output is always 1, unless both inputs are 0. It may also be referred to as an "any or all" gate, as if its switches were in parallel.

This could be used with two baggage doors - if one is not secure it can activate a warning light.

Several of them can be used in the matrix of a computer keyboard:

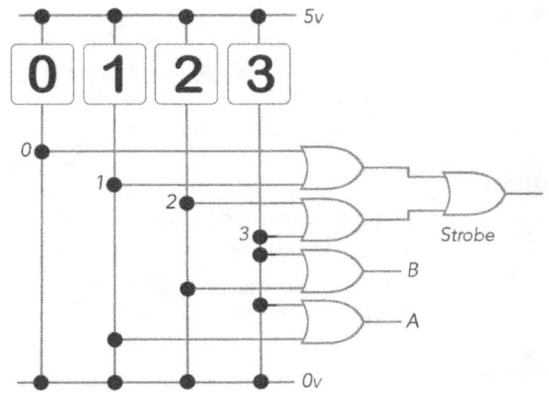

THE NOT GATE

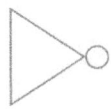 Otherwise known as an *Inverter*, the NOT gate has one input and one output. Whatever state is applied to the input, the opposite will appear at the output, or a signal can be produced without an input, and *vice versa*. Instead the equivalent of a relay might be energised by the 1 (On) signal to pull the other switch in the opposite direction. For a better explanation of why you might want to invert a signal, see *NAND Gate*, below.

When the small circle is on the input, it means that the signal must be low (0) for it to be an activating signal - this would be useful, for example, if you wanted to detect a current on the line that would represent a fault - a logic 0 would mean no faults. A NOT gate can be used in a generator circuit breaker control to ensure that output from the generator cannot be connected to a bus if the aircraft is receiving ground power.

THE NAND GATE

 The NAND function is an AND followed by a NOT, so the result is the opposite of what comes out of an AND gate. It is called a NAND because the Boolean convention is to state the NOT first, or NOT-AND contracted to NAND.

Both inputs must have 1 signals for the output to be 0, and *vice versa* - with either input at 0, the output will be logic 1. In other words, two switches in series operate a relay to reverse the output. Essentially, with a NAND gate, the output is always 1, except when both inputs are 1.

The NAND gate is quite useful, because you can use it as a basis for making any other gate, even though it could be the long way round (in practice, the various gates can be made in easier ways). For example, with both inputs from the same source, the NAND gate becomes an inverter, or a NOT gate. Two of those feeding into another NAND gate creates an OR gate. Connecting another inverter to the output of the NAND gate creates an AND gate. This way, you could make an entire processor out of NAND gates, which themselves can be built out of two transistors and three resistors.

 Logic gates are hard-wired, meaning that, if you want to change a function you have to add or remove or otherwise modify a component. You can change the function of a microprocessor, on the other hand, simply by changing its software.

THE NOR GATE

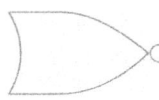 This is an OR followed by a NOT, or an OR with an inverted output. It forces the output to 0 when an input is true. Two switches in parallel operate the relay.

THE XOR GATE

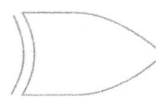 This produces a Logic 1 signal if only one input is 1, but not both.

However, it is not in the Learning Objectives.

TRUTH TABLES

A truth table expresses all possible combinations of the inputs and outputs of a logic gate in terms of binary digits (i.e. 0 and 1). This is a truth table for an AND gate:

A (2^1)	B (2^0)	C
0	0	0
0	1	0
1	0	0
1	1	1

This is on for a NOR gate:

A (2^1)	B (2^0)	C
0	0	1
0	1	0
1	0	0
1	1	0

The number of inputs is represented by 2^n, where n is the number of inputs, so the table above has 2 input columns for the basic gate on the left. 2^2 equals 4, which is why there are 4 rows (you always work from right to left).

FIRE DETECTION

If you applied for a licence to run a night club in a confined space on top of several hundred tons of a liquid with a relatively low flash point that was placed not ten feet away from a flames of several hundred degrees, you would be laughed out of court, yet that is what we do with large jets daily.

Fire is a chemical reaction involving rapid oxidation or burning of a fuel. It has three elements - fuel, oxygen and heat. Take one away and it stops, although it's fair to say that cold does more to put out a fire than anything else. With dangerous goods, you can get fire from the reaction of flammable materials with an oxidising agent - you don't need a source of ignition.

Although the atmosphere's oxygen content is 21%, fire only needs 18% to burn.

- A **Class A** fire is an ordinary one, that is, of normal combustible material on which water is usually effective (e.g. solids, like wood and paper, but not metal - see Class D). Symbol: *Triangle*

- A **Class B** fire is in a flammable liquid, such as oil or grease, or anything that melts to create a flammable liquid or vapour. Symbol: *Square*

- A **Class C** fire is electrical, or *anything near an electrical supply*, for which you need a non-conducting extinguisher (e.g. don't use foam or water). Thus, in any building, you should always consider C. Symbol: *Circle*

- A **Class D** fire covers other materials, like metals, that *may* burn, such as magnesium, titanium, potassium or sodium, as used in fireworks or aircraft (also brakes). Use Dry Powder, which will absorb the heat from the material, or sand. Halon should not be used on burning metals because, at the high temperatures involved, it could form phosgene, which is a poison gas.

 Fire Categories are not in the UK question bank because of the variations between countries - they are included here for information.

For B and C, you could use either CO_2 or Dry Powder (which ruins the avionics), but the fumes may be toxic, so you will need plenty of ventilation afterwards. The extinguisher colour codes are black and blue, respectively (foam is cream). You can use Halon (BCF) on anything, especially in the cockpit, if you're allowed to use it. *In the cockpit of a transport aeroplane, at least one manual fire-extinguisher must be conveniently located containing Halon.*

To help you identify the source, smoke associated with electrical fires is usually grey or tan and very irritating to the nose or eyes (it doesn't smell too good, either). Anything else (say from the heater) tends to be white, but you may get some black from upholstery. If you think you have an electrical fire, it's no good just using the extinguisher, because you may be treating the symptom and not the cause, although there is a school of thought that advocates not using an extinguisher at all if you can possibly help it, due to the fumes and stuff you have to breathe in until you land, particularly with Halon/BCF which has been banned from everywhere else except aviation for this very reason (unfortunately, it's darn good at putting out fires!) Whatever you do, transmit a Mayday before it's too late - you can always downgrade it afterwards. Bear in mind also that your first strike with your extinguisher is the best, because the contents and pressure decrease from then on.

Some points not related to the exams, but still useful:

- Fire doubles in size every two minutes.
- Never tackle a blaze that is bigger than you.
- Fire extinguishers are only meant for small fires, and even then they should be used to help give you an escape route.
- Always have an escape route behind you.
- Only hold the handle on a CO_2 extinguisher, or you will get frostbite.

A **Fire Zone** is an area designated by the manufacturer where there is a perceived risk of fire and may have both fire detection and protection. Typical examples are:

- **Engine bays/APUs***
- **Main gear wheel wells**
- Electrical bays
- Hydraulic bays
- Baggage holds
- Toilets and galley areas

*A fixed extinguisher would be aimed at the low pressure end of the outside of the engine compressor.

Detectors cover large areas and must give rapid warnings within 5 seconds of a large temperature rise. They will reset within 30 seconds once the temperature reduces.

Warning systems have a warning light for each engine and an aural alert that is common to all engines.

Engines

The main type of detection system for engines uses a Firewire, of which there are two types - one uses a continuous wire loop with a negative coefficient of resistance, the other (the most common) uses a positive coefficient of capacitance. Both systems use AC power, but their test circuits use DC. As the materials in the firewire are affected by the heat, a current will flow and, at a predetermined level, will operate the bell and the appropriate engine light.

Systems usually have 2 independent loops with both being needed to initiate a warning. A break in a loop will not affect operation of the system, but fault protection circuits inhibit the detector when the detection line is grounded.

Jet engine systems are divided into three zones:

- **Zone 1** surrounds the hydraulic pumps, ancillary gearbox, engine lubrication oil reservoir, fuel control unit, etc. It is the most likely place for a fire to start and is the only one with fire detection and remotely operated fire extinguishers. To reduce the chance of fire spreading, the zone is kept at a lower pressure than other bays by a ventilation system.
- **Zone 2** is where compressor blades could touch the engine case and create a metal fire, indicated via the engine vibration monitoring system. This zone is hotter than Zone 1.
- **Zone 3** is the hottest Zone, as it surrounds the engine and jet pipe behind the combustion chamber. A bulkhead separates it from Zone 1.

If a combustible fluid or gas has to pass through a hot zone, it must go through a double-skinned pipe.

Systems

Fire detection systems are on the essential bus, meaning that they get priority for electrical current.

Unit type detectors use either thermocouples or switches operated by differential expansion of metals. Unit detectors monitor specific points, while continuous detectors are routed around a potential fire zone for maximum coverage.

GASEOUS SYSTEMS

Gaseous fie loops are tested by heating the sensor.

FIREWIRE

The principle of operation of a firewire is *positive coefficient of capacitance, negative coefficient of resistance*. On resistance and capacitance variation type fire detection loops (described below), a fire alarm is initiated by an increase in temperature detected at any isolated point of the loops or generally on all of them.

When testing a fire detection system, the lights and loops (warnings and wiring) are tested.

A **Resistive** fire detection system has two independent loops of wire around the area to be protected, which both have to be activated to guard against false alarms - an AND logic gate helps with the process. A central electrode surrounded by crystal filler sits inside a capillary tube, and the two ends are brought together at a junction linked to a Wheatstone Bridge (no current flows because it is an endless loop).

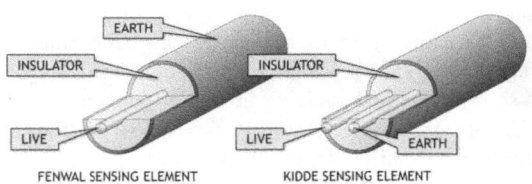

The capillary tube is earthed to the aircraft. As temperature increases, the resistance of the filler material decreases, allowing the electricity to run to Earth via the capillary tube. The resulting flow unbalances the bridge and sends a signal to the warning panel. Sometimes, however, these can short out, particularly on misty or humid days, or if the capillary tube gets crushed, and create false alarms (escaping compressor bleed air from a turbine engine can do this, too). Another system uses the resistance drop to allow the current to increase enough to energise the system.

The wires in a **capacitance** system look identical to those in a resistive one, but the central electrode is connected to an amplifier unit which charges the central electrode for a set time then discharges it into the measuring unit, where its capacitance is compared to a reference value. In a fire, the capacitance will *increase* with temperature. The measuring unit senses this and sends a signal to the warning panel. If the fire wire earths out, the loss of capacitance will prevent a fire warning from being given (this is a *no-fault* system, or Fault Free Fire Detector).

A fire detector that operates on the *rate of temperature rise* is a **thermocouple** system, described elsewhere. In an aircraft, the potentially hot area could be the engine compartment, and the cooler area the cockpit. When a fire starts, current increases in the hot end, with the rise compared to a reference.

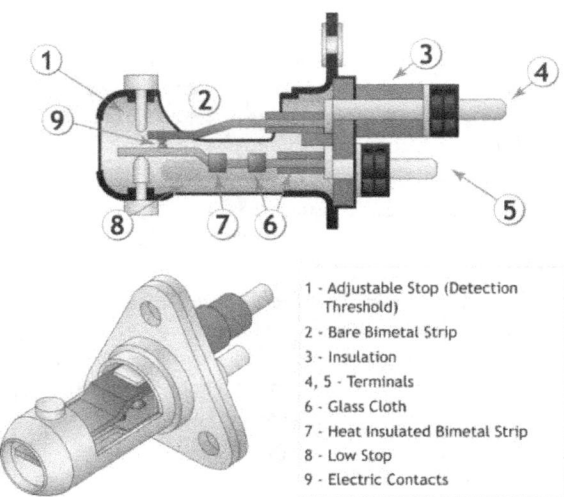

1 - Adjustable Stop (Detection Threshold)
2 - Bare Bimetal Strip
3 - Insulation
4, 5 - Terminals
6 - Glass Cloth
7 - Heat Insulated Bimetal Strip
8 - Low Stop
9 - Electric Contacts

Some detectors use **bimetallic strips**, consisting of low- and high-temperature coefficient metals welded together.

As the temperature rises, one will expand more than the other and bend the assembly enough to make contact with a switch. One bimetallic strip may be partially heat insulated with glass-cloth and the other may be bare. Bimetal strip detectors are arranged in *parallel*, and they *close* during a fire (under normal circumstances, the electrical contact is open). Only when the temperature increases enough to bend one strip and make the contact does the alarm trigger. In the picture, if the temperature rises quickly, the bare strip bends the most and breaks the contact as soon as the threshold is reached. If the temperature rises slowly, both strips will bend at the same rate, but the lower one is longer and runs up against a stop while the bare strip keeps bending, which also breaks the contact.

Fire detection systems have test circuits for continuity checks.

Cargo Compartments

If there is a fire in a compartment in the lower half of the fuselage, turn off the ventilation. Similarly, in an air-conditioned hold, turn off the air conditioning. You should not use oxygen masks when the cabin is affected by smoke, because it allows the smoke to mix with the oxygen. Compartments must have provisions for safeguarding against fires after these classifications:

CLASS A

A fire is easily discernible to crew at their stations, and all parts of must be easily accessible in flight (e.g. a passenger compartment, or cockpit). There must be a hand fire extinguisher for each compartment.

CLASS B

Typically an avionics bay or similar, where enough access must be provided in flight to enable the crew to effectively reach the whole compartment and its contents with a hand extinguisher, and the compartment must be able to contain hazardous amounts of smoke, flames, or extinguishing agent. There must be a separate smoke or fire detector system to give warning at the pilot or flight engineer station, a hand fire extinguisher, and it must be lined with fire-resistant material.

CLASS C

These compartments do not conform with the other categories. There must be a separate smoke or fire detector system to give warning at the pilot or flight engineer station, with a built-in extinguishing system controlled from them, because they are remote. Hazardous quantities of smoke, flames, or extinguishing agents must be contained. Ventilation and draft must allow extinguishing agents to control any fire. The compartment must be lined with fire-resistant material.

CLASS D

A fire here is completely confined without endangering the safety of the aeroplane or occupants. These must be able to contain hazardous quantities of smoke, flames, or noxious gases, control ventilation and draughts so fires do not go beyond safe limits, and be completely lined with fire-resistant material Consideration must be given to the effects of heat on critical parts nearby.

CLASS E

On cargo aeroplanes, cabin areas classed as E must be completely lined with fire-resistant material, have separate smoke or fire detection systems to give warning at flight stations, have a means to shut off ventilating airflow to or within, and the controls for it must be accessible to the flight crew in the crew compartment, and be able to contain hazardous quantities of smoke, flames, or gases.

Crew emergency exits must be accessible in all conditions.

SMOKE DETECTION

Smoke detectors in the home are very useful for telling you when the toast is done. In aircraft, however, the detection of smoke is one way in which fire is detected, and is particularly important. Detectors are required in unmanned compartments and toilets and are installed in the upper cargo compartments (Class E). Remote ones are fitted in underfloor bays where there is a chance of fire.

 Remote smoke detectors in toilets give a visual or aural warning in the cabin or a visual one in the cockpit.

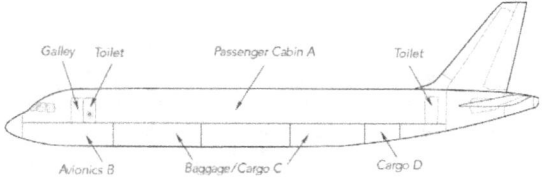

SYSTEMS
Fire Protection

Tip: Speaking of remote compartments, be aware that talcum powder, if it escapes from a passenger's baggage, can set off a smoke alarm, as can dust.

Smoke detectors come in several forms:

- CO detectors in cabins.
- Yellow silica gel that turns green in the presence of CO (more CO, more green).
- Visual smoke detectors in which a sample of air is drawn through a tube with a backing light and visually checked by the crew.

Smoke detectors work in two ways (both normally give an aural and/or visual warning):

- *Ion detection systems* use a bit of radioactive material that bombards oxygen particles in the surrounding air with alpha particles. Ions are thus created which allow a small current to pass through the air across the chamber (somewhat like a fluorescent light tube). Smoke will block the passage of current because they absorb the alpha particles. This blockage is detected and used to trigger an alarm.

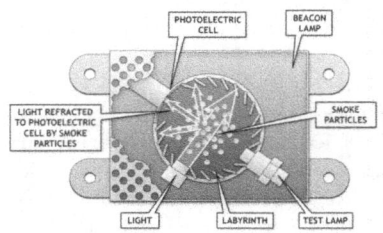

- *Optical detection systems* use a current of air drawn through a labyrinth with a lamp at one end and a photoelectric cell at the other. The labyrinth ensures that the one cannot be seen by the other directly. Smoke and fumes, however, allow light to refract and reflect and be seen by the photoelectric cell, to create an electrical current which can be used to trigger an alarm. The system is tested with a relay switch that lights a bulb next to the photoelectric cell.

FIRE PROTECTION

The standard fire drill (for a turbine engine) is:

- Cancel the Fire Bell
- Close the throttle
- Shut the HP Cock
- Pull the fire handle. This prepares the engine for the extinguishant, typically closing the LP fuel valve, arming the extinguishing system, closing isolation and de-icing valves, isolating associated generators*, etc. - it does NOT fire the extinguisher bottle! That is a separate process performed after the throttle has been closed for the engine.

*Opening the exciter control relay and generator breaker.

- Discharge the fire extinguisher

The engine fire warning system on a multi-engined aircraft has an individual warning light and possibly a bell or a similar loud noise (with EICAS or ECAM, there might be a warning message on the screen, such as **FIRE ENG 1**).

The fire handle warning light is there to help make sure you've got the right engine - it goes out when the detected fire is out.

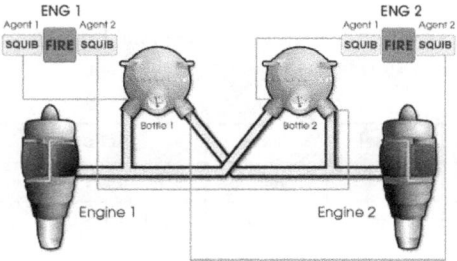

There is one squib per engine, but the contents (usually freon, but older systems used halon) can be switched to either as appropriate, using a shuttle valve. Squibs must discharge within 0.5 - 2 seconds. There will be a warning light in the cockpit to tell you when the extinguishing agent has been discharged.

A fault protection circuit in a fire detection system will inhibit fire detection when the detection line is connected to ground, so if a system with no fault protection has single-loop continuous components, the alarm will be triggered if the line is accidentally grounded.

APU

The APU will cut off its own fuel supply, shut the ventilation doors and shut down (actually, the extinguishing agent is discharged automatically, but will be withheld until the fuel is off and doors are closed, so that any air that might promote the fire is isolated). There is an aural warning horn in the front wheel well to warn ground personnel that the APU extinguisher has been discharged.

ENGINE STARTING

Modern turbines are spun over until they are self-sustaining, with compressed air (or a starter/generator), commonly bled from the APU, to start the No 1, or Master, engine, which is then used to start any others through a crossfeed system of pipes and valves. Any electric motor used for this purpose would be too heavy! Early jets would use the exhaust from another machine to spin an engine over for starting.

On The Ground

Engine fire drills may vary considerably between different types, and these will have to be memorised, but there are some general points that can be made. One is, before evacuating the aircraft, make sure the parking brake is off, so it can be moved somewhere safer if things get out of hand, always being aware that it could run off by itself, as well! If the fire has been caused by spilt fuel, has spread to the ground under the wing and the other engine has been started, taxi clear of the area (or more specifically, the fuel on the ground) before evacuation, keeping the fire on the downwind side. If the other engine has not been started, evacuate first, carrying out what drills you can. Always approach hot landing gear from the front or rear (the safest extinguisher for wheel fires is dry powder).

Component parts of wheels are ejected laterally in an explosion, so it is best to approach hot ones from the front or the rear. Water and CO_2 extinguishers are not used because they cool things down too quickly.

Fire Extinguishers

Hand-held fire extinguishers are coloured red and have different coloured labels as shown below:

Type	Label	Fire	Action
Water	Red	Material	Removes Heat
Powder	Blue	Fluid/Brakes	Isolates O_2
Halon	Green	All Classes	Stops reaction between O_2 & Fuel
CO_2	Black	Electrics/Engine	Removes Heat

These are the appropriate extinguishers for their fires:

Fire	Extinguisher	Remarks
Ordinary Combustibles	Water Dry Chemical Chemical Foam	Risk of flare up after using Dry Chemical*
Flammable or combustible liquids	Halon Dry Chemical Foam/CO_2	Halon is toxic and needs ventilation
Energised Electrical Equipment	Halon Dry Chemical CO_2	
Combustible Metals	Dry powder	Sand can be used for a magnesium fire

*Dry Chemical is multi-purpose and can be used on the first 3 types but it is corrosive and a respiratory irritant.

If CO_2, BCF or Halon are used on an engine fire, the engine should be turned over afterwards. If you use foam or dry powder the engine must be stripped and rebuilt.

ICAO Doc 9137-AN/898, Part 1 - Rescue and Fire Fighting, 12.2.4 states that: too rapid cooling of a **hot wheel**, especially if localised, may cause explosive failure of the wheel. Solid streams of water may be used as a last resort. Water fog or indirect solid stream can be used to cool hot brakes. Dry chemical is an effective extinguishing agent but is not recommended.

Here are the fire extinguishers needed for the cabin:

MOPSC	Number
7 - 30	1 of any type
31 - 60	2 (1 Halon)
61 - 200	3 (2 Halon)
201 - 300	4 (2 Halon)
301 - 400	5 (2 Halon)
401 - 500	6 (2 Halon)
501 - 600	7 (2 Halon)
601 or more	8 (2 Halon)

On top of those, you need at least 1 Halon on the flight deck and at least one in any galley not in the passenger compartment. At least 1 must be available for use in each cargo compartment.

OXYGEN SYSTEMS

To recap from *Human Factors*, air at sea level contains about 21% of oxygen at a pressure of around 14.7 psi. Air above sea level contains the same percentage of oxygen but at a reduced pressure, so it has less oxygen by mass. Thus, less oxygen is available and the lower pressure reduces the rate of absorption into the blood. 8 000 feet is the maximum (cabin) altitude at which flying ability is considered to be not seriously affected by a lack of oxygen, and 10 000 feet is the level above which **supplementary oxygen** must be provided for **accidental decompression**, and smoke and fumes (flight deck only).

Oxygen for commercial air transport is obtained from:

- **Gas bottles** (used for the flight deck, but may be used for the cabin). Replenishment of onboard oxygen bottles (i.e. not portable) must be done with the engines off.

- **Chemical generators**, used for the cabin, toilets and smoke hoods. Sodium Chlorate reacts with iron filings to give off a smelly type of oxygen after being triggered electrically or mechanically, and the passenger breathes a mixture of oxygen and cabin air. As a lot of heat is generated, *there must be no smoking, or grease nearby**, and there will be a heat shield involved. It is a one-shot solution that only lasts for 12-15 minutes (but at least 10). Each installation supplies between 1-5 seats. There must be enough for at least 110% of passenger seats fitted (for infants, cabin staff moving about cabin when problem occurs, at least 2 per toilet for mother and baby). Chemical generators have a life of around 10 years if they are not operated. One disadvantage is that the flow cannot be modulated - another is that less capacity is involved. Advantages are easier maintenance and reduced risks of explosion.

*Oil or grease traces may not be near or on parts of an oxygen installation as there is a risk of explosion when it is used with oxygen under pressure. The heat discolours a stripe on the outside of the generator to show its use.

If there is smoke in the cockpit, the crew oxygen regulator should be set to 100%. *Diluted mode* means that the crew will breathe a mixture of oxygen and cabin air.

Smoke hoods, if used, are available for the crew only and must last for 15 minutes. They cover the whole head and have a continuous flow. **Smoke masks** cover the whole face and provide a flow of oxygen on request.

Gaseous Systems

The main oxygen system is there for pressurisation failures, but you might also need oxygen in a fire or with other hazardous fumes in the cabin, or even with a medical emergency. Oxygen is normally carried as a pressurised gas in cylinders up to **1800 psi**, which is reduced by various regulators before reaching the mask where the supply can be adjusted according to requirements. The access to the system is pneumatic.

A gaseous system provides greater autonomy, has reversible functioning, and its flow can be regulated. If its maximum operating pressure is exceeded, the oxygen will be discharged overboard through a safety plug.

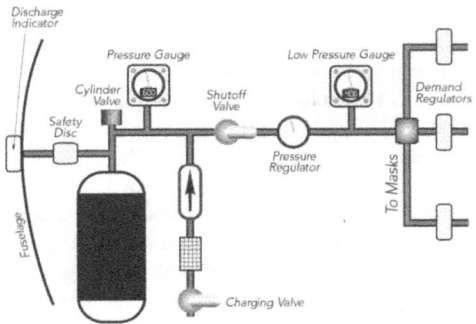

Oxygen cylinders are black with white necks (all green in the USA). There are three types of gaseous system, discussed below.

CONTINUOUS FLOW

This type is intended for passengers. High pressure oxygen gets to the mask through a pressure reducing valve (if it fails, there is a pressure relief valve to relieve the overpressure). The line and shutoff valves are in the On position during flight, which allows for immediate flow in an emergency. The masks normally plug in, but on larger aircraft they can be permanently attached. They have a flow indicator. As the system is constantly pressurised, all you need to do is give a sharp tug to start the flow.

A continuous flow mask *cannot* be used when smoke is in the cabin because they will mix. It has a face piece and a plastic bag that can expand. The bag is a *rebreather*, because it allows air to be reused to a certain extent. Flow must be adjusted for different altitudes. If it is not enough, the flow indicator will show a red line. Otherwise, when the oxygen mask is pulled downwards, the passenger breathes a mixture of oxygen and cabin air (100% oxygen is supplied to the mask then mixed with cabin air through holes in the mask). An overpressure disc in line with the bottle allows the contents to escape to atmosphere if an overpressure occurs (a red indicator shows at the discharge port on the outside of the aircraft). The bottles have a shut off valve which is only operated for maintenance purposes.

DILUTER DEMAND

Oxygen is delivered for mixing with air *when inhaling* (in *Normal* mode). That is, proportions of cabin air and oxygen are mixed according to the altitude*. This type is used for crews because they have individual regulators.

*If the cabin altitude rises to 33 000 feet (i.e. above 32 000), the system will supply 100% oxygen, which equates to 21% oxygen at sea level. The maximum allowable cabin altitude is around 40 000 feet when 100% oxygen is used, which is similar to the conditions at 8000 feet.

The oxygen received at the inlet to the regulator is reduced to an intermediate pressure of 400 psi. If the supply lever is On, and *Normal* is selected, the inhalation creates a depression that causes a diaphragm to move and open the demand valve through which oxygen flows into the mask. On exhalation, a valve in the mask closes and a back pressure builds up in the supply tube and the regulator. This closes the diaphragm and the oxygen supply. An aneroid capsule controls the amount of air that mixes with the oxygen by moving a metering valve, up till 32 000 feet.

A doll's eye indicator or blinker indicates when oxygen is flowing. There is a relief valve to protect the lungs from over-pressurisation. The system is tested by pressing *Test Mask*, so oxygen flows at more than emergency pressure to detect leaks.

PORTABLE

A portable walk-around kit is also needed on commercial pressurised aircraft and larger commercial unpressurised aircraft. They protect the eyes, nose and mouth while allowing verbal communication and must give protection for at least 15 minutes. A 120 litre bottle should have a flow rate of:

- 2 ltrs/min for 60 minutes at the **Normal** setting, which mixes cabin air with the oxygen, reducing its consumption according to the cabin altitude - the oxygen/air ratio increases when the altitude does. When it is selected, oxygen will only be supplied when the user breathes in (oxygen on demand).

- 4 ltrs/min for 30 minutes at the **High** setting.

- 10 ltrs/min for 12 mins at the **Emergency** setting, which supplies 100% oxygen at a slight over-pressure, on demand or as a continuous flow, depending on the system. This ensures that leaks from the mask seal will be outwards and stops fumes entering the mask. When selected to 100%, the regulator air valve is closed and 100% oxygen is supplied on demand regardless of cabin altitude.

The times will vary according to the cabin altitude and rate of breathing. The dial reads green when the cylinder is full, amber when it is ¾ full and red when ½ full.

CHEMICAL GENERATORS

The personal panel drops down (released electrically) before the cabin altitude reaches 15 000 feet, or if selected by the pilots. The panel itself is actuated by an electrical solenoid for a chemical system or by a pneumatic solenoid in the gaseous system.

When the panel drops, the masks fall to the *half hung* position. Oxygen does not flow to the mask until the user pulls the mask down to its full length. Oxygen then flows continuously at a low pressure to the mask. This is not enough for the average person so cabin air is also drawn into the mask. Most masks have some form of filter system for the induced cabin air. It is not possible to receive 100% oxygen from cabin masks.

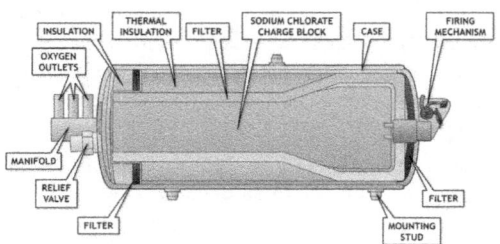

PROTECTIVE BREATHING EQUIPMENT

Modern transport aircraft flight deck positions have Protective Breathing Equipment (PBE) in the shape of quick donning masks, which must be donnable within 5 seconds with one hand, without disturbing spectacles or interfering with emergency drills. After being put on, immediate communication with other crew members must be possible, with uninterrupted radio communications.

 At a cabin altitude of 25 000 feet the crew have around 2 minutes of useful consciousness, which rapidly reduces to 10 seconds at 41 000 feet.

It is therefore a good idea to have one pilot on oxygen at or above FL 410 in case of a rapid decompression.

FIRST AID SYSTEMS

These are provided from a gaseous source, sometimes the main aircraft system, but a separate bottle is often supplied. They are purely for therapeutic use where a passenger is suffering from the lack of oxygen and the cabin may be greater than 8 000 feet due to a system failure and the supplementary system has expired. When cabin crews are needed, there must be enough therapeutic oxygen for 2% of the passengers carried, but at least 2, for the time the cabin could be above 8 000 feet for that route.

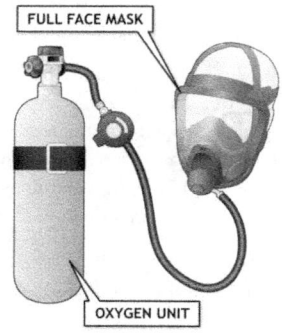

Non-Pressurised Aircraft

Above 10 000 feet, you need supplemental oxygen:

- for the crew when above 10 000 feet PA
- for cabin crew above 13 000 ft PA and for periods over 30 minutes between 10 000-13 000 ft
- for all passengers above 13 000 feet PA
- for 10% of passengers after 30 minutes between 10 000-13 000 feet.

Pressurised Aircraft

FLIGHT DECK

For cabin altitudes between 10 000 - 13 000 feet, oxygen is required after 30 minutes, or full time above 13 000 feet. There must always be a supply of at least:

- 30 minutes for aircraft certified up to 25 000 feet
- 2 hours for aircraft certified above 25 000 feet

CABIN CREW

For cabin altitudes between 10 000 - 13 000 feet, oxygen is required after 30 minutes, or full time above 13 000 feet. There must always be a supply of at least 30 minutes.

PASSENGERS

Oxygen is required for:

- 10% of passengers at cabin altitudes between 10 000 - 14 000 feet, and full time after 30 minutes.
- 30% of passengers whenever the cabin altitude is above 14 000 feet
- 100% of passengers whenever the cabin altitude is above 15 000 feet

The minimum passenger supply is always 10 minutes (which allows for descent to 15 000 feet). Preflight stuff includes ensuring that oxygen masks are accessible for the crew, and passengers are aware of where their masks are. Check the security of the circular dilution valve filter (a foam disc) on all of them, together with the pressure. Beards will naturally reduce their efficiency. Briefings should include the importance of not smoking and monitoring the flow indicator. All *No Smoking* signs should be on when using it. If you know you will need oxygen at night, it's best to start using it from takeoff.

PNEUMATICS

Compressed air can be used for many purposes that are now done with hydraulics, but it is still useful in other ways. Although it is more compressible than hydraulic fluid, and the response times are slower (and less precise), a good reason for using it instead is that you already fly through it, so you don't necessarily need to carry it in storage tanks, or need return pipes and systems, as it can be exhausted to the atmosphere. This can save a great deal of weight. For all that, however, pneumatics tend to be used on slower aircraft (e.g. the F 27) as primary systems.

In general, force is calculated in the same way as it is for hydraulics, but the difference is volume - halving it will double the pressure inside a cylinder. Similarly for temperature. When heat is applied to a cylinder, the gas inside will expand and provide a force to move a piston or, if it is restrained, increase the pressure inside.

Disadvantages are that the system is not self-lubricating, and any water content can freeze at altitude.

Piston Engine

An air supply is required for instruments (pitot-static), heating and de-icing. The usual supply is ram air, but fans can also be used, as can compressors driven by the engine with many other components. A compressor uses a piston inside a cylinder, like a reciprocating engine. There are even cooling fins, as air heats up when it is subject to pressure (compressors are also positioned to get maximum benefit from air cooling). When the piston descends, air is sucked in through an inlet valve at the top of the cylinder. There is a *delivery valve* about halfway down the chamber, through which air from the previous upstroke is forced as the piston descends - it will have got there through a transfer valve in the top of the piston, which allows air through when it gets compressed as the piston goes up. Continuous delivery happens because the space underneath the piston is small, and the excess goes out through the delivery valve. Valves are spring-loaded.

A *high pressure relief valve* is fitted near the compressor to keep it warm, so it doesn't freeze up. Its purpose is to protect the system by allowing excess air to escape if a component fails and blocks things up. Although it is adjustable, it is *not* the way to control the pressure! That's done with the *pressure regulating valve*, which is between the manifold and the low pressure bleed valve. Also near the compressor is an *anti-freezer* full of methanol, which stops ice forming from the moisture in the air being compressed. An alternative solution is a *dehydrator* with silica crystals in, that absorb any moisture. An air bottle can act as a temporary supply of pressure when the system is overloaded or switched off - it gets charged up during normal operations, although the system is filled before flight through a *ground charging valve*. The pipes going into the bottle actually extend inside by about 4 inches (forming *stack pipes*), so that oil or water that escapes the relevant traps doesn't get out. Where such a system powers wheel brakes, a typical gauge in the cockpit shows the pressure in the main system along the top, and wheel pressure on each side underneath.

Turbine Engine

Compressed air can be supplied by bleeds from the engines, the APU or a high pressure ground source, which would be used before starting the engines. The HP compressor is normally used at low power settings, but as the engine speed is increased, the IP or LP compressor takes over. The automatic changeover is done with a regulating valve. The bleed air system can consist of:

- pneumatic ducts
- isolation valve
- pressure regulating valve
- engine bleed valve
- fan air pre-cooler
- temperature and pressure sensors

Malfunctions of a bleed air system could include:

- Overtemperature
- Overpressure
- Low pressure
- Overheating and duct leaks

Cabin Pressurisation

The ambient pressure at sea level is 14.7psi, and 10.9 psi at 8 000 feet, At 30 000 feet, it is 4.4psi. Although an aeroplane can operate up there, the people inside it cannot without special procedures and equipment. It is much more practical to maintain the cabin at a lowish altitude than to give everyone on board an individual oxygen set (it interferes with the coffee).

The equipment required includes a pressure vessel inside the aircraft that is kept at 8 000 feet (or 15 000 feet if anything fails), regardless of the altitude outside. The pressure vessel does not occupy the whole space inside the fuselage, but uses pressure bulkheads and the outer skin to contain the passenger compartment and some or all of the cargo areas. Control cables, plus assorted wiring and piping have to pass through it, and doors and windows have to be accommodated, so it is by no means airtight*. Bleed air from the engines is used to pressurise the cabin, and the *outflow* or *variable discharge* valves (operated by the pilots) control the air's orderly rate of escape, assisted by pressure controllers. In the cruise, therefore, the outflow valves will be partially open. If they close fully, with air conditioning on, the pressure differential would go to the maximum value.

*A bullethole is likely to be accepted as just one more leak. A much larger hole, however, appearing rapidly, will cause a rupture in the cabin wall.

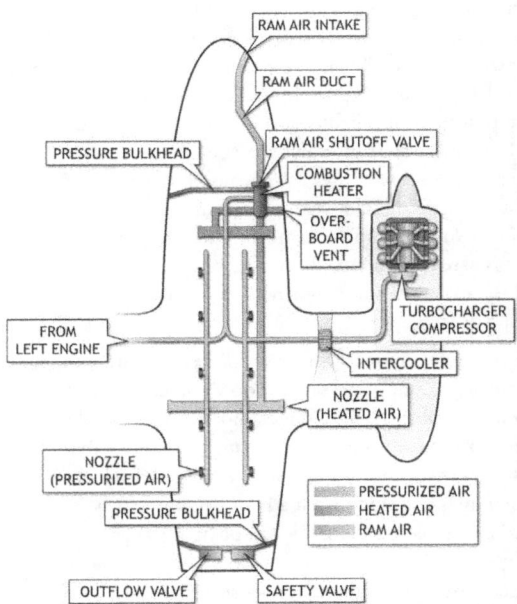

The *pressurisation cycle* concerns the rise and fall of differential pressure, which is the ratio between the pressure inside the cabin and atmospheric pressure outside. The *max diff*, or *maximum differential* for short, is the maximum ratio that the system can maintain. One is set for every type as there can be large variations between them. For turbo-props it is around 5 - 6 psi, whereas transport aircraft use between 7 and 9 psi. Modern pressure hulls are normally designed for a maximum pressure differential of 8.6 - 8.9 lbs/in^2.

If you maintain mean sea level pressure inside the cabin at 40,000 feet, the pressure differential across the skin of the hull would be 12 lbs psi. With a cabin altitude of 8,000 feet, it would reduce to

8.3 lbs psi. At 30 000 feet, is 10.9 psi (cabin) minus 4.4 psi (aircraft altitude) leaving 6.5 psi. The maximum altitude for pressurisation with a cabin altitude of 8000 feet will therefore be around 43 000 feet.

The positive cabin differential pressure at the maximum cabin altitude can limit the maximum operating altitude. *The maximum operating altitude comes from the maximum positive cabin differential pressure at the maximum cabin altitude.*

The maximum negative* differential pressure is ½ psi.

*The pressure hull is designed to deal with relatively high pressure acting outwards on the pressure hull (positive differential pressure). If, during a descent to sea level, the cabin altitude remains at 8,000 feet (when the copilot forgets to set the system for landing), the pressure outside the aircraft would be greater than that inside (negative differential pressure), so the pressure loading would be the reverse of that for which the pressure hull is designed. On the ground, opening inward-opening doors is dangerous and outward opening ones impossible. Inward relief valves open automatically at a differential pressure of, typically 0.5 psi whenever the outside air pressure exceeds that in the cabin.

If you maintain altitude when the differential pressure has got to the required value in normal flight conditions, there will be a constant air mass flow through the cabin.

The pressure limiting safety valve ensures that the absolute maximum pressure differential is never exceeded. It is usually combined with the inward relief valve and spring-loaded to open at a differential pressure slightly higher than the controlled maximum. Normally, it is lightly spring-loaded in the shut position. In many aircraft the valve may be opened on the ground to ensure that pressures are equalised. It is closed before takeoff. To maintain the same cabin pressure during a climb, the system must be used in **isobaric mode** (the other mode is **constant pressure differential**). In a manual system, the rate of change of the cabin altitude is normally controlled by a rate of change selector.

The desired cabin altitude is usually set before takeoff, although there is a small amount of pressurisation while taxying to keep engine fumes out of the cabin. In fact, modern aircraft cabins are slightly pressurised for takeoff and landing to reduce cabin pressure swings (the cabin and the aircraft should reach zero feet at the same time - you don't want a hard landing with a pressurised cabin. Not only that, it can be hard to open the doors). If you run along the runway with the conditioning system off (to reduce the load on the engines), some air is drawn from the outflow valves and will show a slight cabin climb. On rotation, this is reversed as ram air passes into the cabin. Such pressure swings can cause distress to passengers (and crews), making it a better idea to pressurise the aircraft early on. Modern aircraft use the APU anyway.

Then the system will "climb" automatically at an assigned rate, more slowly than atmospheric pressure. Automatic systems only require you to enter an initial cruising flight level and the landing airfield elevation. Typically, there will be two gauges in the cockpit, one to show the cabin's rate of climb (looks like a VSI), and the other with two needles, one to show the cabin altitude and a smaller one to show the ratio of the cabin pressure to the outside.

On the dial mentioned below, the max diff will be marked with a line, and the VSI will show a descent as cabin pressure is increased. Normal rates of change are 500 feet per minute in the climb, and 300 in descent. A warning system must be fitted over 25,000 feet. The EASA max rate of climb or descent is 1500 fpm. If, during the cruise with air-conditioning packs ON, the outflow valve(s) close, what would be the result? The pressure differential would go to the maximum value.

CABIN ALTITUDE DIFFERENTIAL PRESSURE INDICATOR   RATE OF CLIMB INDICATOR

The altitude warning system operates at 10 000 feet.

Components

There are two of each component listed below to ensure that the system continues to work if one fails, with the exception of the pressure controller which has varying modes of operation* instead (including manual). For aircraft flying over water there may be a ditching switch, which closes the outflow valves to stop water getting in.

*The system will automatically revert to a standby mode or manual control if any of the following take place:

- Power supply failure to the pressure controller
- The cabin rate of climb exceeds 1800 ft/min
- The cabin altitude exceeds 14 000 ft

A pressurisation system contains:

- Two outflow valves
- Two safety (positive pressure relief) valves
- Two reverse pressure (inward relief) valves
- Pressure Controller
- Flight Deck indications:
    - Differential Pressure
    - Cabin pressure altitude
    - Cabin altitude rate of change
- Warning system, including sensors

Air from the conditioning system provides the higher pressure inside the cabin. The rate at which it discharges to atmosphere dictates whether the cabin climbs, descends or remains "straight and level". **Outflow valves** (or discharge valves) limit the rate at which the air escapes and change their positions as demanded by the controller. If the cabin needs to climb the valves motor further open to allow more air to escape, or close a little if the cabin needs to descend. For a steady cabin altitude the valves remain partially open, allowing the same amount of air to escape as that coming in from the conditioning system.

Outflow valves are now driven electrically. Previously, pneumatic pressure has been used.

Positive pressure **relief valves** dump excess pressure overboard when max diff is exceeded (they work at 1 or ½ psi above max diff). *Negative pressure relief valves* stop the outside air pressure getting above that of the cabin (½ psi) - they keep cabin pressure to a minimum level for when the cabin can't catch up, which is something the aircraft is not designed to take, as with a fast descent. They may sometimes be called *pressurisation safety valves*, or *inward relief valves*, respectively, all mechanically operated.

Dump valves allow you to manually dump the pressure in an emergency, which could be from a system failure or smoke in the cabin. **Squat switches** on the landing gear make sure the cabin is depressurised before takeoff and after landing (they activate the dump valve).

The **pressure controller** measures the various pressures in- and outside the pressure hull and their rate of change. The air pressures are used as a pneumatic power source within it. Depending on your selections of cabin altitude and rate of change, the controller signals the outflow valves to adjust their positions as required. A feedback system enables the controller to sense the effects and whether further movement of the valve is needed. The controller also has a max diff capsule to give an automatic overriding Open signal to the outflow valve if maximum differential pressure is reached until the system is back within limits. If the controller itself has a problem, the system can be controlled semi-automatically or manually. For example, if the cabin VSI indicates a rate of descent when it fails, the differential pressure will rise to its maximum value, which will open the safety relief valves.

Secondary systems are dependent on aircraft type, but at some failure stage the pilot will be operating the outflow valves towards open or closed directly from a switch.

SYSTEM OPERATION

The required settings for the maximum expected aircraft altitude will be on a pressurisation control panel. Once the flight and land altitudes are set, modern cabins in automatic mode will climb and descend as required. If the system fails, a standby mode allows the altitude to be set and the rate of climb or descent to be adjusted. If these options are unavailable, you can operate the outflow valves directly with a 3-position switch (using AC or DC). A band of lights above the panel shows which mode is being used. A yellow light indicates system failure, while green shows the working system in use.

The instruments will continue to indicate if a power failure occurs. They are inter-related, in that, as well as an indication of a higher cabin altitude, a cabin rate of climb and reduction in differential pressure will be indicated.

Older aircraft should not take off or land when pressurised. Maximum limits will be placarded on the flight deck as a reminder that limits must not be exceeded or damage to the aircraft structure could result.

CALCULATIONS

In case the system fails, you will need to know how to revert to doing it manually, so a few calculations are in order. To find out the cabin rate of climb, find the change in altitude, then the time taken to get to the one you want. Then divide the change by the climb time. So, if you start at 2,000 feet and want a cabin altitude of 8,000 feet, you divide the resulting 6,000-foot difference by the time taken to get to the real altitude of, say, FL 250.

Remember: The cabin can descend (or ascend) at a different rate than the airframe!

When descending, cabin altitude must decrease proportionally with the real altitude so that both reach sea level (or airfield elevation) at the same time, so apply whatever you calculate as the time for descent to the cabin altitude as well (this is important, because a pressurised airframe can be stressed during a landing, although some aircraft are always slightly pressurised. Not only that, it can be hard to open the doors). Modern systems need to know the destination elevation at TOD so it can be worked out automatically.

For max diff, you can use a table or a graph.

Altitude (ft)	Ambient (psi)
0	14.7
4 000	12.7
8 000	10.9
12 000	9.3
16 000	8
20 000	6.75
24 000	5.7
28 000	4.8
32 000	4

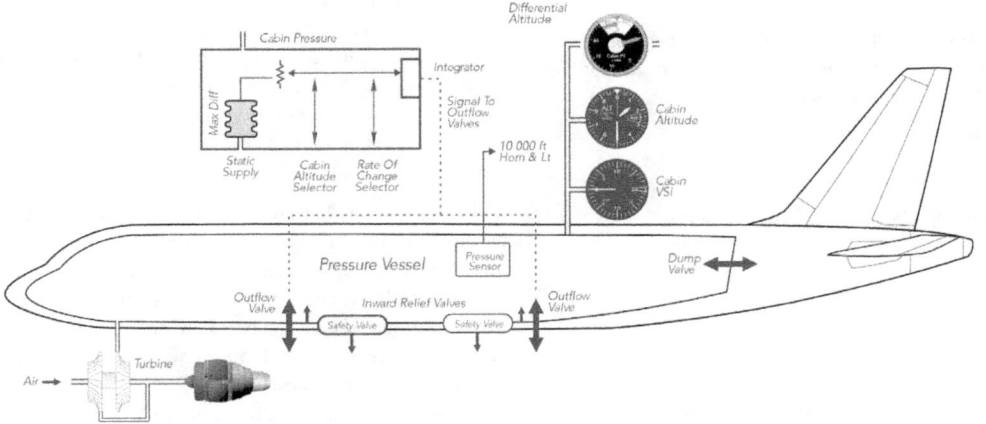

At FL 320 with a cabin altitude of 4 000 feet, the differential pressure will be 8.7 psi. This is derived from the difference aircraft altitude (4 psi ambient) and the cabin altitude (12.7 psi ambient).

Using a graph, at 16 000 feet with a pressure differential of 3 psi, the cabin altitude will be 8 000 feet.

Interpolate between the 4 and 2 psi lines to make a 3 psi line, then match it with a straight line across from 16 000 feet. Where the lines cross. move down to see 8 000 ft.

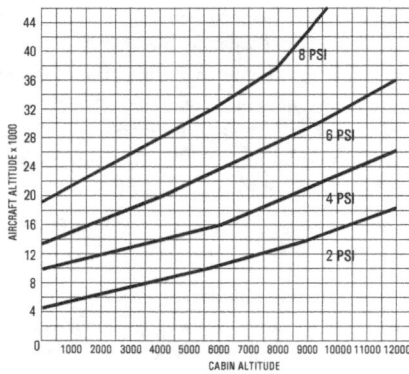

TESTING

All this inflating and deflating of cabins places a stress on the airframe, of course, as a result of which the life of an airframe can be limited by cycles, to save embarrassing incidents when the rivets fail. Pressurisation systems are ground tested by submarining the cabin to below sea level. Pressure inside is raised to about 24 psi to give a pressure differential of about 9 psi. This procedure needs at least 2 people around (or even 3). Climbing the cabin back to sea level too rapidly can lead to condensation in the cabin.

Blow out panels, which open automatically to equalise the pressure across the floor structure, may prevent distortion of the floor during a rapid decompression.

EMERGENCIES

If the cabin altitude increases past 10 000 feet, an intermittent horn sounds and a warning light illuminates. The horn may be cancelled (too noisy!) but the light will stay on until the cabin altitude is below 10 000 feet. Many items may cause a slow depressurisation, including leaking components within the pressure shell. Also, the pressure controller may develop a fault that makes the outflow valves open. In manual mode, the outflow valves can be operated directly. The instruments must be monitored to ensure that the cabin reacts as expected. For loss of pressurisation these drills must be carried out:

- Oxygen masks on
- Establish communications
- Commence emergency descent - monitor terrain

Then:

- Check for structural integrity
- Close all vents
- Air supplies all on
- Attempt to re-establish control of the system

AIR CONDITIONING

Hot bleed air from the engines is cooled by the air conditioning system before being used for pressurisation.

An environmental control system should provide a favourable atmosphere for instruments and equipment, in terms of temperature and humidity*, aside from allowing the crew to work in comfort. Conditioned air is controlled in respect of *temperature* and *pressure*, particularly below ambient temperature, and cabin air should be changed continuously at 1.5 kg/min to prevent the buildup of CO_2, water, dust, fumes and smells. Each passenger and crew compartment must be ventilated and each crew compartment must have enough fresh air (at least 10 cubic feet per minute per crew member) to enable crew members to perform their duties without undue discomfort or fatigue.

*Typically not for short haul.

Crew and passenger compartment air must be free from harmful or hazardous concentrations of gases or vapours*. In meeting this requirement, the following apply (allowing for reasonably probable failures or malfunctioning of the ventilation, heating, pressurisation or other systems and equipment):

- Carbon monoxide concentrations over one part in 20 000 parts of air are considered hazardous. In any case they should not exceed 50 parts per million by volume (under CS 25.831(b)(1)).
- Carbon dioxide concentrations must not exceed 3% by volume (sea level equivalent) for any period greater than 5 minutes.

*If this is reasonably probable, smoke evacuation must be readily accomplished, starting with full pressurisation and without de-pressurising beyond safe limits.

Means must be provided to enable the occupants of the flight deck* and crew compartments (unless ventilated by air interchange with other compartments or areas under all operating conditions) to independently control the temperature and quantity of ventilation air supplied to their compartment.

*CS 25.831(f). Not required if the total volume of the flight crew and passenger compartments is 800 cubic feet or less, and the air inlets and passages that allow air to flow between them are arranged to provide compartment temperatures within 2.8°C (5°F) of each other with adequate ventilation to occupants in both compartments. The temperature and ventilation controls must be accessible to the flight crew. The normal flow rate in a large cabin should be 1 lb per seat per minute, but at least 0.5 lbs if any part of the (duplicated) system fails. In emergency, this can drop to 0.4 for any period over 5 minutes. Any duplication ensures that the minimum rate is maintained. In any case, each person should get at least 10 cubic feet of conditioned air per minute.

EASA recommends that the cabin temperature should be kept between 15-30°C, as there is no specific provision, but **18-24°C** seems to be the industry standard, with relative humidity between 30-60% (again, no specific recommendations). If the cabin temperature is kept close to **18°C** the ideal humidity would be **60%**. It comes from the domestic water supply (i.e. the galley). If it is difficult to carry water for this purpose, one compromise is to reduce the humidity to 30%, which does not significantly reduce comfort. Humidity is controlled by spraying water into the air conditioning ducting.

Passenger and crew compartments must allow adequate air distribution to all parts. The velocity of air from the system should not cause discomfort, and should not normally exceed 120 ft/min with individual air supplies closed but with normal air cooling equipment operating. The distribution of air to compartments should ensure that there are no areas where air movement velocities are less than 10 ft/min. Air intakes essential to the operation of the air supply shall be suitably protected against blockage by ice, dirt etc.

There are several parts to the average air conditioning system, including the *air supply*, *flow control*, *cooling* and *heating systems*, *temperature control* and *distribution*. They all work in the same way, by compressing a liquid, and taking some of the heat created away by running cool air past it. When that air is expanded again, it absorbs heat from the environment and makes it cooler, with the amount of cooling being proportional to the change in volume.

Heat always flows from the hot to the cold substance.

Air Supply & Ventilation

At the basic level, air is drawn into the cabin and mixed with a supply of warm air for the right temperature. How air is sucked in depends on the system being used:

RAM AIR SYSTEMS

Ram air can cool a cabin directly, being allowed in through valves which regulate airflow typically coming in through the nose. If ram air is not available, for example, when on the ground, a blower could circulate the air instead. Ram air is used on small, unpressurised machines not needing much throughput, with any heating either coming from the engine exhaust (by using a muff) or a unit that is self-contained - fuel burnt in it provides the heat, which is mixed with ram air through simple control valves.

The air itself is scooped in through an inlet in the nose or on the fuselage. Ram air ventilation may be provided throughout the cockpit and cabin through a series of ducts in windows and doors.

RAM AIR AND COMPRESSORS (OR BLOWERS)

These are used in conjunction with ram air, or instead of it when on the ground. They can be driven by the engine, to pump ram air from the wing leading edge or engine fairing into a system similar to the Bleed Air system, below. However, there will also be filters and silencers.

ENGINE BLEED AIR

Here, a supply from the high pressure (i.e. hot) end of the compressor of an engine (or the APU, on a large pressurised aircraft) is tapped. This ensures that an adequate supply is available at reduced thrust settings, such as during the descent.

Being hot (200-400°C), it needs to be cooled, so the air passes through a shutoff valve (used for isolation purposes), then to a pressure-reducing valve to calm things down before proceeding to the cold air unit. One benefit of using compressor air is that it is relatively uncontaminated, from either dirt or fumes, although the air is unfiltered.

Heating

Heating can come from a compressor bleed, be electrical, or come from a separate source, such as the Janitrol heater. The simplest system, mostly used in single-engined aircraft, uses a muff round the exhaust that makes air flowing through it warmer, on its way to the cabin. Ram air flow is guided around the outside of the engine exhaust where a heat transfer takes place. The hot air is passed to a temperature control valve and then to a mixing chamber, also called a plenum chamber.

Some ram air bypasses the muff and is used as a cold supply to the plenum chamber via a cold air control valve. Depending on temperature selection the final temperature entering the aircraft will be a mix of the hot and cold air.

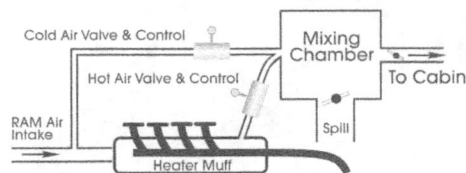

There may also be a progressive On/Off control that selects the quantity of air to enter the cabin, part of which may flow over the inside of the windscreen as a demister. A separate fresh air supply can be ducted into the cabin and distributed to individual outlets (through punkah louvres) next to each seat.

A disadvantage is a danger of carbon monoxide poisoning if the exhaust is leaking. The muff around the exhaust is double skinned to protect against this, and frequent maintenance checks are needed. Slightly more complicated is what can best be described as a flame in a tube, under some control, of course, around which air is forced (the *Janitrol*). These need a rundown period which should be observed, otherwise carbon will form on the igniter and stop it from firing up again. As mentioned above, a compressor heats air up through pressure, and a butterfly valve can restrict airflow for the same result (*choke valve*). However, because of the availability of cold air, it is easier to cool down hot air than the other way round. A turbine powered machine can use bleed air from an engine, which can be mixed with outside air to regulate the temperature.

Temperature regulation of an air conditioning system is automatically controlled by sensing the output temperature from the control valve in relation to the temperature set on the control panel. Associated warning devices include a green System On light and an amber bleed air failure light.

A humidifier is sometimes used at high altitudes, so short haul flights are not often adjusted for humidity.

Systems

Systems can be based on air or vapour cycles. Air cycle systems* use the air surrounding the aircraft for cooling the heat exchangers, which at altitude is cold anyway and, since you're already flying through the stuff, you don't have to use up fuel by carrying lots of refrigerant.

*The term *air cycle unit* is also used to refer to the bootstrap, or cold air, unit mentioned below. The term *bootstrap* means a self-sustaining process that proceeds without external help, as when a compressor and turbine share a common shaft and one drives the other. Cabin air is usually taken from the low pressure stage of the HP compressor, and the high pressures stage if needed.

AIR CYCLE

This system is fed with low pressure engine bleed air because, although light and less expensive, air cycle systems do not provide the mass flow needed for machines with high cooling needs (if low pressure is not available, high pressure bleeds can be used instead).

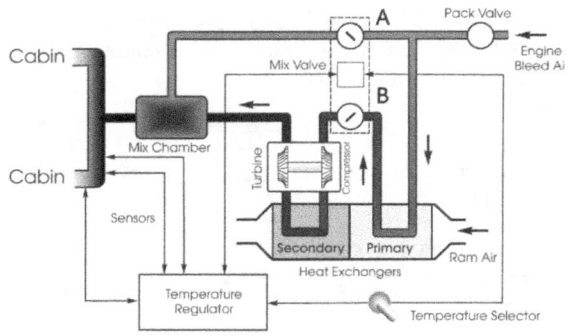

There are three main types of air cycle systems:

- **Bootstrap**. The bootstrap (or turbo-compressor) above is heavier and more complex than the brake turbine mentioned below, but it uses less power. It is used where high pressure bleed air is not a good idea, in small turbo-prop and high by-pass engines.

  It first uses a **P**rimary heat exchanger to pre-cool the air before it is fed to a **C**ompressor, where its pressure and temperature are boosted enough to provide a significant contrast in both against the turbine. The air then goes to a **S**econdary heat exchanger to remove any unwanted temperature rise in the compressor. *The main temperature reduction comes from the heat exchangers, and the maximum temperature drop is in the second exchanger.* An expansion **T**urbine then extracts work from the air by driving the compressor. The resulting expansion cools the air because, if the pressure is reduced, so is the temperature. After the air has cooled, any water vapour in it will naturally condense out, to form fog or high humidity, so the air leaving the expansion turbine is also passed through a water separator. This uses centrifugal force to throw the water particles into a coalescer bag that absorbs the moisture, which can be injected into the outside air entering the secondary heat exchanger to improve its performance (it also helps with humidity control). The air can now be combined in a mixing chamber with some uncooled engine bleed air to warm the air to any desired temperature.

  The so-called **three wheel system** uses *Pack Cooling Fans* (driven electrically or by the turbine) to provide airflow in slow flight or on the ground.

- A **pack inlet flow valve** (pack valve) is there to maintain a constant and sufficient mass flow of air to ventilate the cabin.

VAPOUR CYCLE

A vapour cycle system, which uses its own refrigerant, can supplement an air cycle system, as it can be used without the engines running (being essentially a refrigerator, it also has its own compressor). It is self-contained, and mainly used on small aircraft. Vapour cycle systems use less power, and can place cool air accurately, but they can also reduce humidity, which is why they might be chosen over other systems. With them, a gas refrigerant (usually Freon) is converted between a liquid and a gas as it is pumped round, collecting heat (as a gas) at one end of the system, which is removed when the vapour is compressed into a liquid at the other end (outside). This is why another name for the heat exchanger is a *condenser*. It therefore "moves" heat from one place to another, being compressed, cooled, expanded and heated, in that order. The power required to do this depends on the difference in temperatures and the amount of air to be treated, and the temperature change depends on the rate of compression or expansion.

The liquid used in the system (the *refrigerant*) will have special properties, such as a low boiling point and the ability to change state readily from liquid to vapour, and *vice versa*. You control the temperature around the system by varying the pressure of the refrigerant at any point.

Freon normally boils at 4°C. Although water is actually the lightest refrigerant, with the highest latent heat value, its boiling point is too high for best use. You need a lot of latent heat to make a liquid change its state to a gas. If you can accompany this with expansion, you can suck a lot of heat from the atmosphere. This expansion takes place inside an *evaporator*. As air flows over it, heat will be extracted from the air.

In a more complex system, a *compressor*, which is driven by the engine, can compress the refrigerant vapour to increase its pressure and temperature, and its boiling point. The compressor keeps a difference going between the low and high pressure sides of the system by increasing the pressure of the refrigerant going into the condenser, and reducing the pressure in the evaporator, to aid expansion. The vapour is transferred to a *condenser*, which is a heat exchanger (like a radiator in a car) that uses external airflow to cool the refrigerant enough to turn it into a liquid (i.e. condensing it), so that it gives up its latent heat into the ram air. Water is removed now to stop the system corroding. A liquid moves through an expansion valve to reduce its pressure and boiling point before it goes into an *evaporator*, where the process happens again. The *expansion valve* is a metering device that responds to temperature to increase or decrease the refrigerant flow. In other words, the evaporator is another heat exchanger that sucks heat from the air going into the cabin as it passes over the expanding (and therefore cooling) refrigerant. It is a long, thin tube, coiled to save space. The air now gets so cool that you need water traps to stop the system freezing from the moisture. The water extractor and humidifier are downstream of the cold air unit.

In an *open circuit* vapour cycle system, evaporated refrigerant is lost to atmosphere, and wasted. In a *closed circuit* system, as found in those square units in motels, it is recycled by evaporation and condensation.

Temperature Control

Temperature regulation is automatically controlled by sensing the output temperature from the control valve in relation to temperature set on the control panel. If colder cabin temperature is selected, the cold air unit runs faster.

If automatic control of an air conditioning system fails, you can revert to manual control and 'beep' the control valve to the required setting. Warnings include a green System On light with amber bleed air failure lights.

AUTOMATIC FLIGHT CONTROL

The basic role of an autopilot (or any automatic flight control system) is to *decrease pilot workload* with *attitude retention*. In addition, AFCS systems can:

- Overcome stability and control deficiencies
- Improve handling or ride qualities
- Perform manoeuvres that are difficult for pilots, maybe because of the length of time involved, the lack of visual cues or the accuracy required

Stabilisation and control is achieved by a closed loop control system (servomechanism), where small power inputs control much larger power outputs, in proportion.

Systems must be capable of continuous operation, be able to detect errors and amplify error signals for correction, monitor the reaction and control the closing of the servo loop by providing feedback signals.

 Always, always, monitor the output from the autopilot. That is, do not assume that the autopilot is doing what you need, especially on landing. There have been many cases of the throttles being closed by the autopilot on the approach, too late to do anything about it. For this reason, the flying pilot's hands are required to be on the throttle levers on the way in to land.

Control Loops

The *inner loop* of a system concerns itself with events internal to the aircraft, such as movement of the controls, and their disturbances in pitch, roll and yaw, etc. about a single axis, so it is only concerned with stability.

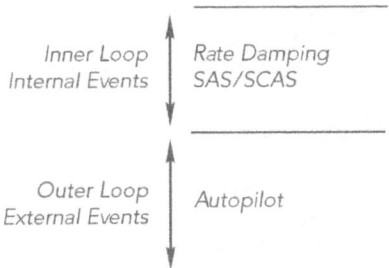

On its own, the inner loop would be a stability augmentation (or auto stabilisation) system that is able to hold an attitude by detecting and correcting deviations for a limited time - typically around 20 seconds. For example, yaw stability augmentation is required in most jet aircraft to suppress Dutch roll (or keep a military fast jet steady while you fire a missile). This can range from a single-channel, limited authority system which can be easily over-ridden, to a full authority system with full redundancy (the term *triplex* means three complete systems working in parallel). Such yaw dampers can be engaged separately.

The runway alignment feature of the 767 is part of the autoland system. It lines up the longitudinal axis with the runway just before landing so there is no crab angle at touchdown in a crosswind, using a combination of rudder and aileron to produce a wind down effect. It can also counteract the asymmetric effect if an engine fails on the approach.

The SAS can be controlled by an outer loop system that makes higher level decisions, such as which way to fly, and anything else to do with the outside world. Command modes, coupled to the appropriate autopilot channel, are selected on the Mode Control Panel, or MCP.

Only one autopilot should be engaged at any time (A or B), except for automatic landings, where a second one with a monitoring function can be engaged below 1 500 feet AGL.

A closed loop system can measure the output from your control system and feed it back to the input side, determine the difference between what you want (input) and what you are getting (output), then tell the system to reduce or cancel the error so you end up with the output you wanted in the first place.

The average AFCS has many such loops working inside each other. The small inner loops deal with elevator angles, etc,. then more complicated ones encircle them, working up through holding specific aircraft attitudes to delivering rates of climb, speeds etc.

System Contents

An Automatic Flight Control System includes:

- **Autopilot(s).** Large passenger transport aircraft have more than one, and possibly three. One of which will be responding to inner and/or outer loop commands. During automatic landings all autopilot channels are engaged, for redundancy.

- **Flight Director.** This senses any deviations from the planned flight path and presents the information as correction command information on the ADI and HSI. In automatic flight, these commands may be fed to the autopilot(s).

- **Flight Management System** (FMS). A complex digital system which is capable of controlling the flight path and thrust management to achieve a least-time or least-cost operation. It usually receives data from a flight control computer, an air data computer, a thrust management computer, EICAS, the flight controls and various airframe, engine and navigational sensors. Its outputs are the outer loop signals to the autopilots and autothrottle. It may also be called the *Autopilot Flight Director System* (AFDS).

- **Central Air Data Computer**. The CADC receives manometric data (don't ask) from the pitot and static sources, together with a transducer generated signal representing the true air temperature. The computer can produce airspeed data, Mach number and pressure altitude. The CADC outputs are used for automatic speed, rate of climb/descent, altitude and Mach trim control.
- **Autothrottle**. An automatic system that adjusts engine thrust to suit the flight conditions through takeoff, climb, cruise, descent, approach and landing or even a go-around.

All the above are supplemented by equipment on the ground, such as the ILS, runway guidance, etc.

The outer loop data inputs, which are relevant to the desired flight path, are coupled to the autopilot in terms of hold, lock or capture. For example, a system maintaining a pre-selected altitude is using height (or altitude) hold.

The term *capture* refers to intercepting radio beams from ground-based aids such as ILS or VOR, so the machine can capture a glideslope and subsequently hold it.

In large aeroplanes, the autopilot is used for almost every manoeuvre except for taxying and takeoff, and landings if you don't have autoland. This is because the tolerances for navigation and aircraft separation are very tight, whether you're in a departure or arrival procedure or simply flying long distance in RVSM airspace. Probably the only time you will fly the machine completely in manual is on your initial interview! An automatic pilot ensures piloting and guidance in the horizontal and vertical planes, stabilising and monitoring movement around the C of G. The inputs must be proportional to the rate and degree of any deviations, as you don't want them to get too large.

Autopilots that control attitudes in pitch, roll and yaw are **3-axis**. A **2-axis** autopilot controls pitch and roll, and a single-axis controls roll only (the **wing-leveller**, which is the most basic function, along with speed along track). Some will even handle an engine failure. An **operational autopilot** is one that allows you to perform complete tasks, like make an approach to a predetermined point.

Either way, you should be able to maintain an altitude or heading, intercept and follow a radial* and keep to a climb or descent pattern, by controlling vertical speed.

*When following a radial, the results can be unsettling to passengers, as the system doesn't anticipate the needle's movement, but keeps going past the radial and recorrecting. A better way is to use the heading bug and chase the needles yourself so you don't spill the coffee.

Having said that, more modern systems are better at it.

Near the VOR cone of confusion, the roll channel temporarily switches to heading mode.

Your flight can be broken down into several phases:
- Takeoff**
- Climb to cruise altitude (including the SID)
- Cruise (including step climbs and descents)
- Descent (including STAR)
- Approach**
- Landing**

**Extreme vigilance is required! The above are explained in excruciating detail later.

In a transport aeroplane, to cover the above phases, an autopilot comprises display devices, sensors, comparators, computers, amplifiers and servo-actuators, plus navigation equipment, flight instruments, the Air Data Computer, and the Flight Management System. All this is supplemented by equipment on the ground, such as the ILS, runway guidance, etc.

System Protection

For automatic landings, a concept of *system redundancy* means that multiple systems are used in such a way that a single failure has a minimal effect on aircraft performance.

When one autopilot is used in the cruise, the system is considered to be fail safe, in that a pitch trim disconnect will give you back a correctly trimmed aircraft within the manoeuvre envelope (automatic synchronisation gives the autopilot a smooth takeover, in the climb, cruise and descent). The only time more than one autopilot can be engaged is for an autoland with APP selected, which brings in the redundancy factor.

- With three autopilots, the system is **Fail Active** because the other two can be used if one fails. That is, one failure leaves the overall system still working, and you can still land automatically. On the EFIS, the message **LAND 3** means that all autopilots are working. Other names include **Fail Operational** or **Fail Survival**.
- A system with only two autopilots is **Fail Passive** because you cannot autoland with only one - it would automatically disconnect at a pre-determined height and **manual intervention** is involved, so some sort of warning is required. Such a system can fail without excessive deviation from the flight path or out of trim condition that would degrade safety, as with a single autopilot in the cruise (with only one autopilot for climbing, cruising and approach, the system is also fail-passive). Another name is **Fail Soft**. You get the disconnection without the effects of a failure.

Thus, an automatic landing system that keeps operating after a failure below alert height is *Fail Operational*, although it will then operate as *Fail-Passive*, meaning that the landing must be continued manually if something else fails. If there is a secondary independent guidance system to help with the manual landing, you have a *fail-operational hybrid* system. To stop events such as system runaways, you can either limit the authority of an actuator, or the rate at which it can travel.

- **Comparators** check if an attitude change is in the same sense as actuator movement, such as the nose pitching down when such a command has been given. If it is, the system is disconnected.
- **Rate Trigger**. If a rate of change exceeds a certain value (based on system runaway parameters), the system will be disconnected.
- **Multi-channel**. A *duplex system* has two lanes, each with a sensor, a computer, an actuator, and switching circuits. Outputs from the two actuators are averaged before any commands are passed to the control surfaces, so if one gets a runaway, it will be (in theory) counteracted by the other. If using comparator monitoring, this can produce *fail operational* capability. *Triplex* and *quadruplex* speak for themselves - the difference is that, if one system fails, it can be outvoted by the others and automatically disengaged. If the others have a problem, they will all disconnect and return the aircraft to the pilot in a safe, trimmed condition.

Interlocks stop the autopilot being used if the system isn't ready, and cause it to disengage on failures. They are switches and relays that ensure satisfactory engagement.

Control Laws

These are rules that the autopilot computer has to follow, or how control demands are translated into movement of the control surfaces, but they also determine the fundamental response of the aircraft and set safety limits for automatic flight (that is, a control law will protect the aircraft from overstress or overspeed). Put more simply, control laws allow a fly-by-wire system to position the flight controls for the most efficient response. They are electrical algorithms that figure out the proper signals to be sent to the electrohydraulic actuators. For example, the control law of a transport aeroplane autopilot control channel may be defined as *the relationship between the computer input deviation data and the output control deflection signals* (don't blame me, I didn't write it). Try this:

For each control channel (pitch, roll and yaw) the piloting law is the relationship between the deflection of the control surface commanded by the computer (BETA c) and the offset epsilon at the computer input. Yuk.

The laws apply to the whole flight envelope, with regard to pitch and bank attitudes, depending on speed. On the longitudinal axis, they may combine the load factor and changes in pitch as data sources. Trimming is automatic and ensures neutral stability.

On Airbuses*, at least, for safety and redundancy, there are 3 flight control laws:

- **Normal Law** provides envelope protection and autotrim.
- **Alternate Law** provides reduced protection and speed stability if a computer fails, but pitch trim is automatic, as with Normal Law. Degradation from Normal is automatic, depending on the failure.
- **Direct Law** has no envelope protection and the sidestick moves the control surfaces in proportion to the input. The stabiliser trim is moved manually as there is no electric trim. *The Airbus always lands in direct law* - in some failures, the only way the system knows you are going to land is by extending the gear, so the system will change from Alternate to Direct law automatically.

*FBW Boeings use *Normal, Secondary* and *Direct*. The Direct mode on the 777 and 787 is essentially an analogue mode, similar to normal flying controls.

On an Airbus, mechanical backup control of the Trimmable Horizontal Stabiliser and rudder is always available. It is the only way to maintain control if all the flight control computers fail or there is a total loss of electrical power. The aircraft is controlled with trim wheels, rudder pedals, and engine thrust until a higher law can be restored.

Normal Law

This is the normal operating configuration, which is not affected by the failure of any single computer. Put another way, it is used when all, or nearly all, of the aircraft systems are available. It covers 3-axis control and flight envelope protection.

- **Manoeuvre protection** prevents damage from overstress. The flight control computers prevent control surface movement that would exceed preset G limits. Pitch protection may range from between 30° nose up to 15° nose down (Airbus).
- **High speed protection** activates just above V_{MO}/M_{MO}. A gentle pitch up is produced by the flight control computers to limit further acceleration, which is limited even if full forward stick is applied. If high speed protection activates, automatic pitch trim in the nose down direction is deactivated and the autopilot, if engaged, disengages. *It is always possible to overspeed the aircraft* - the flight control computers merely limit the maximum attainable speed to within safe limits.
- **Angle of attack protection** (on the A320 at least) includes:
    - **Alpha Protection.**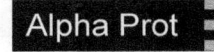
      The angle of attack where the flight control computers intervene to prevent alpha from reaching a stall value, represented by the amber and black band on the PFD. If the speed falls into it, the pitch command logic changes from load factor demand to commanding an angle of attack while additional nose up trim is inhibited, although nose down trim is still available. The autopilot, if engaged, disengages and the pitch attitude is lowered. If the stick is pulled further aft, the angle of attack will reach........
    - **Alpha Maximum**. Above 100 ft AGL, this speed corresponds to the maximum angle of attack that the ELACs (**EL**evator **A**ileron **C**omputers) will allow. As it is a lower value than Alpha stall, it is nearly impossible to stall in normal law. Note that, although the Flight Augmentation Computers (FACs) continuously compute airspeeds corresponding to the alpha protection values and display them on the

airspeed tape, these speeds are for reference only. The actual angles of attack for Alpha Prot and Alpha Max are computed by the ELACs based on angle of attack, not airspeed. If autothrust is available, the airspeed is unlikely to reach Alpha Max anyway because Alpha Floor will probably activate beforehand.

- **Alpha Floor**. This operates automatically between Alpha Protection and Alpha Max. It is a predictive function of the autothrust system which activates based on the current trend if it thinks that thrust will be required. It is normally available from just after takeoff down to 100 ft radio altitude in configuration 1 or greater. It is only available in normal law. Applying a large pitch up control input while Alpha Protection is active will trigger it. As Alpha Floor is predictive (and independent), it can be triggered at any airspeed (including those significantly higher than Alpha Prot), so it won't be seen on the airspeed tape. If Alpha Floor activates, TOGA thrust is automatically applied, regardless of the position of the thrust lever. Alpha Floor activation does not require autothrust to be engaged, but it must be available (i.e. working).

PITCH CONTROL

A specific pitch input results in the same G change regardless of the current airspeed.

- **Neutral Stick** – Requests no change in G, and the flight control computers maintain approximately 1G. Pitch attitude remains relatively constant.
- **Aft Stick** – Requests a positive G change. The flight control computers order the elevators to move by the required amount to provide the requested G change, resulting in the nose pitching up.
- **Forward Stick** - Requests a negative G change. The flight control computers order the elevators to move by the required amount to provide the requested G change, resulting in the nose pitching down.

The Trimmable Horizontal Stabilizer (THS) is trimmed up or down for pitch trimming. It is a much more active part of pitch control on the Airbus than on many other aircraft. When a G (pitch) change is commanded, the elevators move initially to provide the commanded change. If they need to stay there, THS movement is commanded until the elevators are centred.

On the Airbus, manual pitch trim inputs are not required.

- **Ground Mode** is a direct stick to flight control relationship that enables a pilot to check the flight controls and rotate the aircraft on takeoff.
- **Flight Mode** provides load factor demand in pitch, and all protections are available.
- **Landing Mode** gives the flare and touchdown a conventional feel. At 50 feet AGL (measured by the RAs), the ELACs (**EL**evator **A**ileron **C**omputers) memorise the pitch attitude. At 30 feet AGL, they add a gentle nose down command, which the pilot counters with an aft stick input.

ROLL CONTROL

For the roll rate:

- **Neutral Stick** – A zero roll rate is requested. The aircraft essentially maintains the current bank angle.
- **Full Stick Deflection** – Requests a 15°/sec roll rate.
- **Stick Slightly Left/Right of Centre**. Requests between 0 and 15°/sec roll rate.

Automatic pitch trim is available up to 33° of bank in order to maintain altitude during turns. If the bank angle exceeds 33° and the stick is released, the bank angle returns to 33°. This is positive spiral stability.

In normal flight, the FCCs (on an Airbus) will not allow bank angles greater than 67°.

YAW CONTROL

Yaw orders associated with bank are processed by the ELACs then passed on to the Flight Augmentation Computers (FACs) which then direct hydraulic servos to move the rudder.

Alternate Law

At least two or more failures must occur for the flight controls to degrade from Normal to Alternate Law.

Direct Law

This produces a direct stick to flight control surface relationship, although stick inputs are still processed by the FCCs and transferred to the flight control surfaces. The computers, however, carry out pilot orders exactly as they are signalled. Unlike Normal or Alternate laws, the computers have no authority to modify or override stick inputs, so there are no protections or stabilities. In other words, this is the basic mechanical connection between input and output - a nose-up pitch demand applied and held will initiate a nose up pitch rate. As natural stability opposes the increase in angle of attack, the pitch rate will slow to zero and the aircraft will hold a new attitude. It will obey direct control inputs and behave normally.

Pitch Rate Demand/Attitude Hold Law

In this system, a nose-up pitch input applied and held will react as above, but the computer will continuously increase deflection of the elevators to maintain a constant pitch rate. With zero pitch input there will be zero change, so zero pitch input is an attitude hold condition. This means that, in a positive alpha vertical gust, attitude will not change, but the extra lift will balloon the machine above the intended flight path. The disadvantage is that the flight path is not maintained under zero input and continual autopilot control inputs are needed.

G Demand/Flightpath Hold Law

This depends on level flight being a constant 1G flight path. Increased G makes the aircraft go up, and reduced G makes it go down. In response to a nose-up pitch input, the computer initiates a demand for more G and calculates the necessary elevator angle, so a pitch input calls for a flight path change and zero pitch input is a flight path hold demand. This is inherently good for maintaining a defined flight path, but there is an inherent lag in response from gusts, which leads to sharp and rapid computed corrections, particularly at low speed.

C* Law

This is a common control law which blends g and pitch-rate feedback, being basically a flight path hold law with some pitch rate demand at low speed to improve response on the approach. At low speed in a C* airplane, pitch rate applies whereas, at higher speeds, g applies. The changeover is transparent and occurs, for example, at about 210 kts in an A320. Boeing use a modified version called C*U where U* represents forward speed and which provides apparent speed stability.

Automatic Trim

The function of automatic trim is to:

- Reduce to zero the hinge moment of the entire (elevator) control surface to relieve the load on the servo-actuator
- Maintain the stability & manoeuvrability trade-off in the flight envelope
- Transfer a stabilised aeroplane to the pilot during autopilot disengagement (i.e. ensure it is properly trimmed when the autopilot is disengaged)
- For pitch, cancel the hinge moment of the elevator

Automatic trimming is normally effected only about the pitch axis so the aircraft is trimmed if the pilot has to take over on disengagement.

MACH TRIM

For aircraft with a tendency to tuck under, the *Mach trim* compensates for backing up of the aerodynamic centre at high Mach numbers by moving the elevator nose-up, but only above a predetermined Mach number. The Mach number is read from the ADC, and a signal is generated that drives a screw jack which operates the elevator.

YAW DAMPER

A yawing motion (whether pilot-induced or otherwise) can lead to Dutch Roll. The vertical stabiliser and the rudder can be used to develop forces that can overcome it.

TA yawing motion (whether pilot-induced or otherwise) can lead to Dutch Roll. The vertical stabiliser and the rudder can be used to develop forces that can overcome it. Their effectiveness depends on their size and the speed of the aircraft, in that the yaw damper is more effective at higher speeds. A rate gyroscope (on the vertical axis) provides the signals needed to start off the yaw damper actuator, which in turn activates the main actuator to the rudder. The commands sent out are added to or subtracted from the commands from the pilot or autopilot, but the rudder pedals do not move.

This can be done in manual or automatic flight.

Yaw dampers are not designed to provide balanced turns.

STICK SHAKER/PUSHER

This is a device fitted to the yoke as an aid to prevent stalling - when the angle of attack, or alpha, approaches a critical value, the stick is made to shake as a warning. If it is ignored, the stick pusher applies down elevator.

SIDESTICKS

Each sidestick has a takeover button. In normal flight, simultaneous inputs from both pilots will be summed algebraically, but priority will be given to the pilot who depresses, and holds depressed, the takeover button on his stick. A green light on the glareshield tells the pilot he has priority, while a red light tells the non-priority pilot that his stick is dead. He can then retake control by depressing his takeover button. If he elects instead to release his stick, the green light in front of the priority pilot will go out. The priority pilot can then release the takeover button, extinguishing the red light and returning the aircraft to normal flight control. If the non-priority pilot does not release his stick, however, because he is incapacitated, the priority pilot keeps his takeover button depressed for 30 seconds and then the dead stick is electronically latched. As soon as the obstruction is removed and the dead stick centred, it is automatically delatched.

That has proved to be one of the problems with the Airbus if you read the incident reports. There is an indicator in the panel showing the control input but it is hard to look at when you are taken by surprise. Another recurring problem has been the failure to punch the priority button when the PNF jumps on the controls in an attempt to put things right and salvage a situation.

Autothrottle

This is a system that controls engine thrust to maintain some other value (PM, EPR or airspeed) within the design limits. It is designed to operate with an AFCS and FMS to maintain speed and a vertical flight path. Its actual purpose is to maintain constant engine power or airspeed.

Speed control is achieved by simply controlling thrust (during takeoff it holds N_1). When the vertical flight path is the parameter, speed is controlled with pitch while full (for climb) or idle (for descent) power is set so, in a steady climb, N_1 will be automatically adjusted. When flying an ILS approach manually, it can be used to hold the IAS in SPEED mode.

When it comes to flexible takeoff modes (as you might use with a low takeoff mass, a low temperature or a high pressure to save engine wear when you don't need to use full power), you select a higher temperature than the ambient temperature to achieve a reduced power setting.

Autoland

An autoland approach is a precision approach to touchdown and possibly the landing run (the procedure is complete at the beginning of the ground roll). It is performed by the autopilot, which gets its position information and/or steering commands from onboard navigation equipment.

Autoland is intended for conditions of low visibility, meaning fog, with little wind. It is *not* designed for crosswinds over 15 kts, hand flying, or turbulence!

Semi-automatic mode with respect to landings means that the autopilot maintains the ILS and the autothrottle maintains a constant speed until DH, to disengage automatically at around 100'. *Automatic Mode* maintains the ILS until the flare, the autothrottle decreases thrust at around 30 ft, and the flare and ground roll are performed automatically.

Coupled Approach

A coupled approach is one performed by an autopilot that gets its position information and/or steering commands from onboard navigation equipment. Coupled non-precision approaches should be discontinued and flown manually when 50 feet below the MDA, and coupled precision approaches should be flown manually below 50 feet AGL. During a Cat II automatic approach, height data is supplied by a radio altimeter.

On an autopilot coupled approach, Go Around mode is engaged by pushing a button on the throttles. When an automatic landing is interrupted by a go-around, the autothrottle reacts immediately upon pilot action on the TO/GA (Take-off/Go-around) switch to recover the maximum thrust, the autopilot monitors the climb and the rotation of the aeroplane, ad the pilot retracts the landing gear and reduces the flap to reduce the drag.

USING AN AUTOPILOT

The most basic function of an autopilot is maintaining speed along the track and keeping the wings horizontal.

The Flight Mode Annunciator (FMA) is at the top of the Primary Flight Display (PFD).

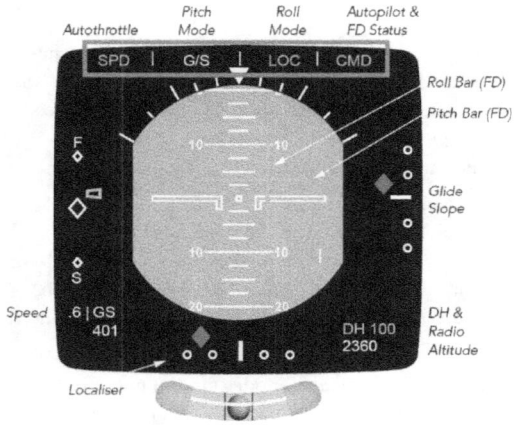

It indicates the current autoflight system status and displays any modes currently in use.

There are 3 columns in later versions (the above is a very old example):

- The left one is for speed control modes.
- The centre one is for lateral control modes (LNAV), where the ailerons are used to control the heading.
- The right one is for vertical control modes (VNAV).
    - In **speed mode**, the autopilot will climb or descend to a selected height at a speed selected by the pilot (usually economy speed). The pitch attitude is adjusted with the elevators.
    - In **path mode**, the elevators are used to hold a vertical flight path, such as a constant attitude in the cruise. Once the FMC has calculated the optimum descent profile, the elevators will be used to adjust the pitch attitude. Speed will be controlled by engine thrust, using autothrottle.

Typically, before takeoff, you would engage the Pitch, Roll and Yaw channels, plus the Flight Director so you can see what inputs are required (the full autopilot is not normally switched on for takeoff or landing).

In fact, engagement of an autopilot is not possible when:

- The electrical supply is faulty
- The turn control knob is not set to centre off
- There is a synchronisation fault
- There is a fault in the attitude reference unit

If you ever want to fly the machine yourself, you must use the *Disengage* button on the cyclic to release the system's grip of death on the controls, but most systems allow you to manoeuvre in pitch and roll without disengaging the autopilot, either by using the panel described above, or by *control wheel steering*, which allows the controls to be moved without the autopilot dropping off line. The new attitude is held once the control wheel is released. *Touch control steering* uses a thumb switch on the control yoke, which disengages the autopilot while the controls are moved, and re-engages it once the switch is released.

The power switch for the autopilot may have 3 selections:

- **OFF**, which speaks for itself
- **FDIR**. The Flight Director's job is to reduce your workload by indicating the manoeuvres required to execute, achieve or maintain a flight condition. It does this by presenting data as control commands to show you the *optimal way to achieve your flight path*. In other words, the flight director gives you directions about *how to position the controls* rather than the attitude of the aircraft. This means you get no information about the flight path, for which you need a separate navigation display. When the FD bars centralise, you have only made the proper control inputs, not reached the optimum flight path! The flight director can be used without the autopilot, although the autopilot can use the FD to tell you what it's doing.

    Remember: The FD doesn't tell the aircraft what to do - *command bars* show you the control inputs. All you need to do is align them as they move.

    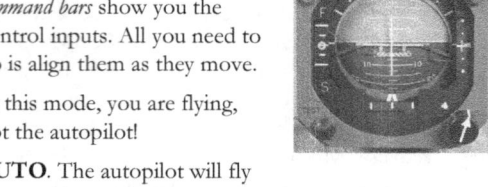

    In this mode, you are flying, not the autopilot!

- **AUTO**. The autopilot will fly the machine according to your selections below

Here is a list of potentially available functions (some will not be present on simpler autopilots, or they may be labelled differently!)

- **WLV**. The Wing Leveller simply holds the wings level while you figure out what to do next. It's a handy button to punch in an overload situation and will hold the wings at the current level of bank, or level them for you if you engage it with less than a certain figure, typically 7°.

Engaging an autopilot and selecting no modes will provide attitude hold with auto trim.

- **HDG HOLD**. Heading Hold follows the heading bug on the HSI or DG. To turn, simply move the heading bug to the desired direction and the machine will follow. The bank attitude input is proportional to the deviation between the selected and current headings, but not exceeding a given value. **Tip:** Ensure the heading bug is in place before engaging the HDG button, or the machine will seek the heading straight away!

- **LOC**. The Localizer will fly an ILS localiser, which is more sensitive than a VOR radial, as is used with the NAV button. Pushing this button just arms the system - *your current HDG mode will remain in force until the localiser needle starts to move into the centre.* At that point, the LOC will go from ARMED to ACTIVE, and start flying for you, dis-engaging any previous modes.

- **G/S**. Flies the glideslope portion of the ILS, in the same way as LOC handles the localiser.

- **ALT**. Holds the current or pre-selected altitude. If you hit this button, the system should maintain the altitude you are currently sitting at, i.e. whatever pressure is outside the aircraft. Adjusting the altimeter afterwards should make no difference unless it is linked in with the autopilot.

- **V/S**. Holds a constant vertical speed. To climb or descend, push VS (*Vertical Speed*) and select the rate of climb or descent with a knob on the VSI. This will disable ALT, if selected. At the required altitude, reselect the ALT button to maintain. You can operate the autothrottle in SPEED mode.

- **SPD**. Holds a pre-selected airspeed.

- **FLCH**. Flight Level Change is commonly used to change altitude by allowing you to add or take away power while holding an airspeed. This is like SPD, but, if you have auto-throttle, FLCH will automatically add or take away power.

- **PTCH**. Use Pitch-Sync to hold the nose at a constant pitch attitude, like the Wing-Leveller.

- **LNAV**. Allows you to follow a programmed route from the FMC database, based on great circle tracks, tracking waypoints on the flight plan.

- **VNAV**. The pitch channel is controlled by the FMC to achieve the vertical profiles required by the flight plan, also controlling autothrottle inputs to maintain the thrust required for the profile.

- **BC**. The Back Course is a second localiser that works in the opposite sense to the proper ILS to fly along the extended centreline once you have missed the runway and have to carry out a Missed Approach. However, some airfields save money by making you use the Back Course as a proper ILS, although you won't have a glideslope. When coming back in the other way, it is back to front. Pushing this button reverses the commands to make it look right. It does not work with an HSI.

- **NAV** (or **VOR**). This keeps you coupled to a selected radial on the HSI, which must naturally be slaved to whatever navaid you are using. The problem is that it can chase the heading too much, and will overshoot and come back rather than make small adjustments to creep up on the selected heading. It is often more practical and comfortable for passengers to use HDG mode and move the heading bug yourself if time permits. In addition, you have better roll rates and maximum bank angles. In the cone of confusion, the last good heading is held until you get through it.

In the picture below, the light behind the ALT button is lit, indicating that the height-keeping function has been selected. This and the HDG button are the most used functions, so much so, that they are usually the automatic selections when the thing is switched on in the first place, to maintain pitch and roll.

VS, FLCH and HDG all do their thing the moment they are engaged. Others, like ALT, G/S and LOC, on the other hand, sit there on standby (armed) until they intercept the altitude, glideslope or localiser required.

That is, *they will not do anything until then.*

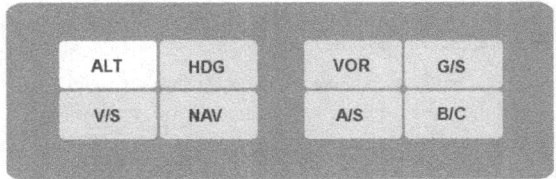

Example

You set the machine up straight and level at 3,000 feet and push the ALT and HDG buttons. Now you can take your hands off and read the instructions, as the autopilot will maintain that level and whatever heading you set with the heading bug until you tell it otherwise. Now you want to climb to 6,000 feet, so you need to dial this figure into the altitude window (you would also set your cleared altitude before you take off). How you want to get there determines what button you push next. You could hit the vertical speed (V/S) button, then select a rate of climb on the VSI until you get to the selected altitude.

FLCH or SPD, on the other hand, will pitch the nose up and maintain the currently indicated speed, leaving you to add power as needed. Again, this mode should disengage automatically when you get to the selected altitude.

PHASES OF FLIGHT

For a large jet, before you get airborne, the AFCS should be serviceable and the FMS programmed with the lateral and vertical flight path profiles for the route and flight levels (don't forget to press the EXECUTE button!)

Takeoff

Line up on the runway (check the compass with the runway direction), with the Flight Director on, the autothrottle armed and set to N_1 (RPM), and with the takeoff speeds and power bugged on the instruments.

Press the TOGA (Take Off/Go-Around) switch on the throttle lever(s), which will then advance automatically while you keep straight on the runway.

At some preset speed, which is typically about 60 kts, the throttle hold will automatically be engaged and the pitch command bars will indicate a nose-up requirement. You do this at VR (rotate speed), at a rate of about 3° per second. Once you lift off, merge the flight director bars, to reach and maintain V_2 (Takeoff Safety Speed). At around 400 ft AGL (i.e. a safe height), assuming an engine hasn't failed, you can engage the autopilot, followed by L NAV and V NAV on the MCP.

The Climb

With the gear and flaps retracted, V NAV engaged and the altitude alert system set to one above your present altitude, the autothrottle will provide maximum climb power (it knows this from the FMC). Pitch will be adjusted for the correct climb speed, also from the FMC.

When you approach the preset altitude (and assuming altitude alert is set for this level) the AFCS tells the autopilot to adjust the pitch attitude for the cruise.

The Cruise

The FMC generates a signal that is proportional to the required cruise speed (usually maximum economy*), leaving the autothrottle to adjust the power.

*This speed will change as you use fuel and the aircraft weight reduces, and the temperature varies. The power and pitch will be adjusted automatically.

The autopilot will use the FMC and INS to keep to the pre-programmed route, using the roll channel - L NAV must be selected for this.

Descent

The FMC knows the best point at which to start descending. Assuming the altitude alert is set to a *lower* altitude than your present one, the autothrottle will reduce engine power to flight idle. It then re-arms so that, if you suddenly level off, it can increase power.

The pitch angles are changed to achieve the most economical flight speed. The required radio aids are tuned and identified.

Approach, Flare & Landing

To use autoland, both pilots must be qualified, the aircraft certified and serviceable for the process and the airfield operational down to the required minima. 2 independent radio altimeters are also required. Automatic landing is a dual channel approach, with at least two autopilots capable of following ILS signals* engaged, so any others need to be armed (in the cruise and the initial stages of the approach, only one channel is used. In fact, only one autopilot may be engaged in all modes of flight, except when performing an autoland, where you can use others at/below 1500 feet AGL). Engagement is done by pressing the **APPR** switch on the flight control panel at a specified stage of the approach.

*The glideslope must be captured by 1500 feet AGL.

The localiser and glideslope modes are also armed. Altitude information comes from the radio altimeter once you get within range (usually 2500 feet). The picture above shows the profile of an automatic landing for a fail operational (and subsequently fail passive) system with triple redundancy.

For autoland certification, 2 autopilots are needed to monitor each other. A fail soft (fail passive) system has two autopilots and, upon failure of either, no autoland can be completed. The annunciation will be **Land 2**. A fail operational (fail active) system has 3 autopilots so, after a single autopilot failure, you can still land automatically because there are 2 operational autopilots as per the requirement. The annunciation will be **Land 3**.

At 1500 ft (radio altitude) the localiser and glideslope are captured, and the armed off-line channels automatically engage to provide triple channel operation. The FMA will show **LOC** and **GS**. Flare mode is armed in pitch (ROLLOUT in roll), and an autoland status annunciator shows **LAND 3**, or **LAND 2**, depending on which channels are voted into operation. The pitch and roll axes are adjusted according to the requirements of the localiser and glideslope. At 330 feet, the aircraft is trimmed by the horizontal stabiliser into a nose-up attitude for the flare.

Flare mode is automatically engaged when the gear is 45 feet above the ground, and the glideslope is disconnected. This is based on the pitch attitude, radio altitude and the known distance between the gear, the fuselage and radalt antenna. Flare mode now controls the pitch for a 2 fps descent path. The autothrottle also retards and the thrust reduces so the engines are at idle on touchdown. Flare mode disengages at about 5 feet, and the system transitions to touchdown and ROLL OUT mode. At 2 feet, the pitch reduces to 2° and, on touchdown, the elevators are commanded to lower the nose so that the wheels touch the runway (and stay there). The autopilot will use the ILS signals and the rudder and nosewheel to stay on the runway centreline.

After the weight on wheel switches are energised, the autothrottle disengages after 2 seconds or when reverse thrust is applied, but the AFCS is still in charge until you deselect it, which you must do before turning off the runway or the localiser will try to keep you on it.

If a go-around is initiated from a single autopilot coupled ILS approach, the autothrottle will sect GA power as soon as the TOGA switch (on the throttle) is pressed, but the pilot must carry out the procedure and clean up the aircraft. Normally, it would be flown by the autopilot.

Picture Below: 737 Flight Control System

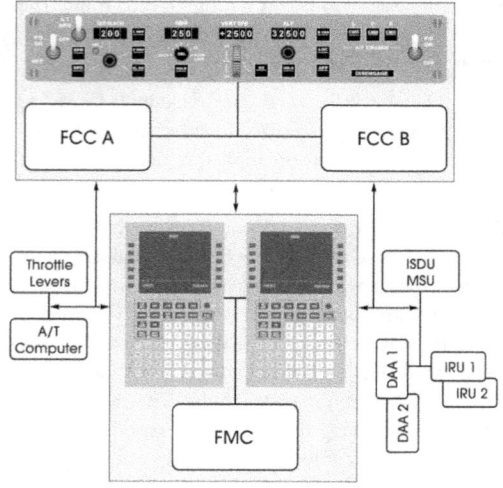

SYSTEMS
Automatic Flight Control

You tell the aircraft what to do through the Mode Control Panel (MCP) along the top centre of the instrument panel

The inputs from the MCP are sent to the Flight Control Computers (FCCs). These compare the demands from the MCP to what the aircraft is actually doing, using information from the Air Data Computer (ADC). Suitable signals are then sent to the flight control actuators.

The Boeing 737

The AFCS (see above) consists of:

- an **Autopilot Flight Director System** (AFDS), with:
  - two independent **Flight Control Computers** (FCCs), A and B, controlled from the AFDS panel, which send commands to their respective autopilot roll and pitch loops, and which operate the controls through their own hydraulic servos. Each FCC positions its own FD command bars which move to show the pitch and roll attitudes needed to follow the lateral and vertical profile.
- an **Autothrottle** (A/T).
- a **Flight Management Computer** (FMC), which provides command information to the autothrottle to keep the speed of the N_1 (fan) within the limits at high engine speeds and that target values are met, plus command airspeeds for the A/T and AFDS. The status of the AFCS is displayed on each pilot's ADI display.

  The FMC has 3 independent computing units, one for navigation calculations, one for performance and one to manage the throughput of data (I/O).

  The FMC will be certified to navigate accurately within a VOR/DME and GPS environment. In other words, your position is established with radio inputs and/or the IRU (see below). Put another way, the IRU's purpose (usually the left one) is to integrate the information from the sensors into a solution that is better than what you would get from individual ones, and provide a Best Position every 5 seconds. As the FMC assumes that radio positions are best, the BP is heavily biased towards them. The updated Best Position is used to correct the System Position, which is what is used for LNAV.
- an **Inertial Reference System** (IRS - see *Instruments*).
- Other **navigation equipment**.

Crews communicate with the FMS through the panel above and the FMS Control Display Units (CDUs), described in *Instruments*.

DATALINK

The basic system contains:

- a Communication Management Unit (CMU), which can be connected to:
  - Multipurpose Control & Display Unit (MCDU).
  - Communication Unit (VHF, HF, Satcom).

Departure and Oceanic clearances can be received over Datalink.
ACARS allows AOC and ATC messages to be sent via datalink

STORAGE

The FMS needs storage to contain the databases for Navigation and Performance. The Navigation database is essentially the Airway Manual (from whichever supplier you choose) on a chip, and the Performance database contains an average model of the aircraft and engines, being the flight manual on a chip. However, this can be tweaked to suit particular aircraft. There is a main Navigation database that is valid to a specified date, and a supplementary that contains revisions for the next period, in case you pass the specified date on a trip.

The storage involves three types of memory:

- **EEPROM**, or its older version EPROM. *Electrically Erasable Programmable Read Only Memory* keeps its data permanently, but cannot be written to, meaning it cannot be changed by pilots!
- **NVRAM**, or *Non-Volatile Random Access Memory*. This also keeps its data, as it is battery backed (but normally powered from the computer), but can also be written to, so minor changes can be made in flight, or saved data can be loaded from a tape of flash drive for particular flights. This is where the Navigation and Performance databases are.
- **RAM**. This is working memory, which is volatile, meaning that its data is lost when the power is lost.

FLIGHT DIRECTOR

If the autopilot is not engaged, you must use the controls to follow the bars. If it is engaged, the FD simply tells you what the autopilot is up to (autocoupling).

Flight Director operation is selected by the Flight Director switch (one at each side of the panel below, for Captain and F/O), and is available in manual and automatic flight. The command bar position depends on what command modes are selected, as shown by an illuminated switch, which can be pressed to deselect the mode (if engagement of a mode would conflict with the current operation, pressing the switch has no effect). All modes can be disengaged by selecting another command mode or disengaging the autopilot and switching off the FDs.

The autopilot may be engaged in Control Wheel Steering (CWS) or Command (CMD) modes. During single channel operation (i.e. all modes other than **APP**roach) only one autopilot can be engaged, so engaging a second autopilot disengages the first.

- For **CWS** operation, the autopilot follows the control column (the forces required are similar to those in manual operation). That is, you can make inputs to the autopilot by moving the normal control wheel. When the column is released, the autopilot holds the attitude unless the aileron pressure is released with 6° or less of bank angle, in which case the wings are held level on the existing heading. This mode allows for the current pitch and roll angles when it becomes active.
- In **CMD**, the roll and pitch modes can be manually overridden by applying more force to the control column than is applied by CWS mode. This will place the autopilot into CWS operation. Having said that, manual pitch override is inhibited when the FD system

is in APP mode with two autopilots engaged. Whether the autopilot remains in CWS or returns to CMD depends on the modes selected and the extent of deviations during the override.

IAS/MACH HOLD MODE

This is provided by the autopilot pitch channel in the climb at a constant IAS or Mach number, or the autothrottle in the altitude or glide path holding mode.

ALTITUDE ACQUIRE MODE

This is a transition manoeuvre that is entered automatically from a Vertical Speed (V/S), Level Change (LVL CHG) or VNAV climb or descent to a selected altitude, set by the Altitude Selector on the MCP. It is displayed digitally in the Altitude Display window.

ALTITUDE HOLD (ALT HOLD) MODE

The altitude hold mode will, by using pitch commands, either maintain the selected altitude or achieve the selected altitude. When not at the selected altitude, this mode is initiated by either pressing the ALT HOLD switch or selecting a new altitude whilst in ALT HOLD at the current altitude. While changing altitudes, with ALT HOLD depressed, the selector switch will be illuminated until you reach the selected altitude. When in ALT HOLD at the selected altitude LVL CHG, V/S and VNAV climb and descent modes are inhibited.

VERTICAL SPEED (V/S) MODE

The V/S mode uses pitch commands to hold the selected vertical speed (ROC/ROD) and to the autothrottle to hold the selected IAS. The V/S mode has an armed and an engaged state. Pressing V/S engages V/S mode (unless already engaged in ALT HOLD or after glideslope capture). This is annunciated and the vertical speed display changes to show the present V/S. The desired V/S can now be selected with the V/S thumbwheel. V/S mode becomes armed if, while in ALT HOLD at the selected altitude, a new altitude is selected which differs by more than 100 ft. V/S Armed is annunciated and V/S mode is engaged by moving the thumbwheel.

LEVEL CHANGE (LVL CHG) MODE

The LVL CHG mode co-ordinates pitch and thrust to make automatic climbs and descents to pre-selected altitudes and airspeeds. A LVL CHG climb or descent is initiated by selecting a new altitude and pressing the LVL CHG mode selector.

VERTICAL NAVIGATION (VNAV) MODE

Pressing the VNAV mode selector engages VNAV mode and the FMC commands AFDS pitch and autothrottle to fly the pre-selected vertical flight profile in the FMC. This profile includes pre-programmed climbs, cruise altitudes, speeds, descents and height constraints at specified waypoints. The vertical profile usually ends with an ILS approach to the destination. The ADI displays with VNAV engaged are VNAV PTH or VNAV SPD for the pitch engaged mode and SPD, N_1, RETARD or ARM for the autothrottle engaged mode.

LATERAL NAVIGATION (LNAV) MODE

With LNAV engaged the FMC applies roll commands to the AFDS to intercept and track the pre-programmed active route, including as and ILS approaches. For LNAV to engage there must be an active route in the FMC. LNAV mode will automatically disengage if the active route is not captured within certain criteria or if it is overridden by selecting HDG SEL. During automatic flight along a pre-programmed vertical and lateral flight path, VNAV and LNAV are the usual pitch and roll engaged modes of AFDS operation.

HEADING SELECT (HDG SEL) MODE

Pressing the HDG SEL switch sends roll commands to the AFDS to turn the aircraft onto, and maintain, the heading in the display. The bank angle during the turn is limited by the Bank Angle Selector, and is proportional the amount of deviation from the selected heading, and TAS, but not above a specified minimum.

VOR/LOC MODE

Pressing the VOR/LOC switch sends roll commands to the AFDS to turn the aircraft onto, and maintain, a selected VOR course if a VOR frequency is tuned, or the localiser inbound course if such a frequency is tuned.

APPROACH (APP) MODE (DUAL AUTOPILOT)

When APP is selected the AFDS is armed to capture and hold the ILS localiser and glideslope. For an automatic landing, both autopilots must be engaged for dual operation. This provides fail passive control throughout the flare and touchdown, or an automatic go-around. During fail passive operation, the flight controls respond to the autopilot demanding the lesser movement, which protects against servomotor runaway. The approach and landing sequence is similar to that described above.

AUTOMATIC GO-AROUND

This requires dual autopilot operation. It arms automatically when FLARE ARMED is annunciated. Go-around mode is engaged by pressing a TO/GA (take-off/go-around) switch. Upon engagement the autothrottle advances the thrust levers for go- around N_1 RPM.

The autopilot initially commands a 15° nose-up pitch attitude, to climb at a programmed rate and to maintain the existing track. At 400 feet radio altitude, other pitch and roll modes may be selected. Below 400 ft, the autopilots must be disengaged to change them.

The two Flight Directors operate in the same command modes as the autopilot, but drive the command bars on the Captain's and First Officer's ADIs.

Exceptions are:

- **Takeoff**, a Flight Director only mode. The FD initially commands 10° nose-down pitch and wings level. At 60 kts on the takeoff roll, this changes to 15° nose-up, wings level until enough of a rate of climb is acquired. Thereafter it commands pitch to maintain the selected IAS + 20 kts. Above 400 ft RA, an autopilot can be engaged in CMD.

- **Flare**. There is no flare capability during a normal (not automatic) approach. At around 50 ft RA on an ILS approach the command bars retract.

AUTOTHROTTLE

This provides automatic thrust control for values based on FMC and MCP inputs (within engine operating limits).

It is armed by pressing **A/T ARM** on the MCP, at which point a green light will illuminate:

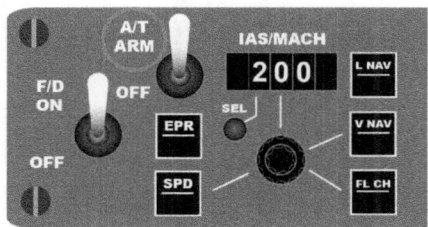

It is engaged by TOGA switches and disengaged on thrust levers. It can also be disengaged by positioning the A/T ARM switch to OFF (where a flashing red disengage warning will activate).

Each thrust lever has its own servomotor. The autothrottle can be operated in many modes, as follows.

- **Takeoff Mode**. This is engaged by pressing either TO/GA switch with the aircraft on the ground, the autothrottle armed and desired take-off N_1 RPM selected on the FMC panel. The autothrottle then advances the thrust levers to takeoff thrust. At 64 kts IAS, thrust hold engages to stop the autothrottle changing the lever positions until 400 ft RA, and around 18 seconds after lift off. Reduction to climb thrust can then be made by pressing the N_1 selector.
- **N_1 Mode**. The autothrottle positions the thrust levers to maintain the limiting N_1 set on the FMC.
- **MCP Speed Mode**. This is available throughout the flight, after the takeoff phase. The autothrottle positions the thrust levers to maintain the target speed in the MCP window (200 in the above example), but not above the N_1 limit. The autothrottle tries to equalise N_1 on both engines, but with no greater than 8° between the levers.
- **FMC Speed**. Maintains the flight profile of the VNAV path (no indication in MCP speed window).
- **Retard Mode**. During a LVL CHG or VNAV descent the autothrottle retards the thrust levers, if necessary until they reach the aft stop. During landing retard mode engages 22 seconds after FLARE is engaged, or at approximately 27 ft RA, whichever occurs first.
- **Go-Around Mode**. The autothrottle GA mode arms when descending below 2000 ft RA and may be engaged at any time until 2 seconds after touchdown, by pressing either TO/GA switch. Once engaged, the autothrottle advances the thrust levers to the reduced GA setting for a 1000 to 2000 ft per minute climb rate.

ICING & PROTECTION

Ice adversely affects performance, not only by adding weight, but also by altering the shape of lift producing surfaces, which increases your stalling speed. If you attempt to maintain the altitude by increasing the angle of attack, the ice will form below and behind the leading edge of the wing, which is why there is a minimum speed for aircraft that are certified for icing conditions - the angle of attack will then have a maximum value.

On top of all that, fuel could freeze in wing tanks, as could control surfaces, and slush collected on takeoff could stop the gear from operating, as well as instruments.

However, icing does not typically occur above about 25,000 feet, and there is no airframe icing above 40,000 ft.

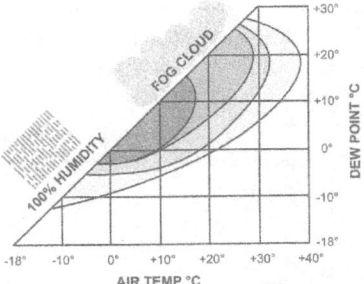

If icing conditions are reported or forecast, your aircraft must be adequately equipped, unless current weather or pilot reports indicate that icing conditions no longer exist.

The ability of an object to accumulate ice is known as its *catch* or *collection efficiency*, which is inversely proportional to the shape of the surface. In other words, a sharp-edged object is better at catching ice than a blunt-edged one is, because it deflects air less (but speed is also a factor). If the rate of catch is low and the droplets are small, you can expect to see rime ice rather than clear ice (in cumulus cloud, you are most likely to see clear ice if you have a high catch rate). It's the *rate of accretion* that's important, not the type of icing, although clear ice is definitely worse than rime ice, since the latter contains air bubbles and is much lighter and slower to build. It also goes forward from the leading edge as opposed to spreading backwards. Variations on clear ice are *freezing rain* and *freezing drizzle*, both of which have larger droplets and are caused by rain falling through colder air, becoming supercooled and turning into ice pellets as they come across freezing temperatures (if you get wet snow, it's colder upstairs or, rather, it's above freezing where you are). In layer cloud, the amount of liquid water will increase with height and become at its maximum near the cloud tops when temperatures are not far below freezing.

In **piston engines**, impact icing restricts the flow of air into the engine by blocking the intakes. Carburettor icing occurs inside the venturi from evaporation and expansion of the fuel, **between -10°C and +30°C**, with a relative humidity of 30% or more and a reduced power setting. It is most severe between -5°C and +18°C in cloud, fog or precipitation at any power setting (60% RH), but most engine failures happen during the cruise.

SYSTEMS
Icing & Protection

 Because it is more volatile, MOGAS can produce carburettor icing - the chart below is not valid for MOGAS. Expect icing at up to 20°C higher than the figures for AVGAS.

Fuel injected engines have few problems with induction icing, but otherwise they are subject to all the others.

In **turbine engines**, ice can form across and near the intakes, and can break off and cause damage to the blades inside. High airspeeds increase the mass flow of air entering into the engine, and hence the number of water droplets. The pressure reduction inside the intake can also cause an adiabatic temperature decrease. Icing can occur at temperatures up to around +5°C.

Icing equipment is not certified if you are carrying deposits from ground operations or storage, so ensure that *all* frost, ice and snow is removed *before* you get airborne, if only because the aircraft systems don't get really under way till then. The idea is a "clean aircraft concept" which means that nothing should be on the outside of an aircraft that should not be there, except, perhaps, for deicing fluid, but even that is suspect.

Ice should be removed from at least all critical areas in the 5 minutes before takeoff, including hoar frost on the fuselage, because even a bad paint job will increase drag, which is relevant if you're heavy, and it will have a similar effect (*hoar frost* is a light frosty deposit that typically appears on a parked aircraft after a clear cold night, and both temperature and dewpoint of the collecting surface are below freezing. It can usually be seen through). These areas include control surfaces, propellers, stabilisers, control linkages, etc. Hoar frost comes about through *deposition*, where water vapour changes directly into ice crystals. A heavy coat of frost will increase stall speed by 5-10%. If it comes to that, ice, snow or frost about as rough as medium sandpaper on the leading edge or top of a wing reduces lift by 30% and increases drag by 40%. Fine particles the size of a grain of salt even sparsely distributed (say, 1 per square centimetre) can destroy lift enough to prevent takeoff. Normally, the Captain must check that no ice accretion is present on the airframe before takeoff, except as mentioned in the Flight Manual.

Strictly speaking, de-icing systems are turned on after a bit of ice has built up (rubber boots on leading edges), whereas *anti-icing* systems try to stop it forming in the first place. Anti-icing systems include those round engine intakes, which are fed with a bleed from the compressor, and pitot heating.

*Pitot tubes are always heated, static ports may be heated. If a thermal deicing system gets too hot, there should be warning lights. Fuel tanks are not heated, as the freezing point of Jet A1 is around -50°C, but fuel on its way to the engines is heated with a fuel/oil heat exchanger, which also cools engine and hydraulic oil. Larger jets use hot N_2 bleed air (i.e. from the HP compressor) for engines and wings, and electrical systems for other components.

When using bleed air in the descent, the engine speed is often not fast enough to cope, so sometimes you have to increase the idle speed.

Thermal anti-icing is commonly used on wings. A second inner skin provides a small gap between it and the leading edge of a wing, through which **heated air** is ducted to warm everything up. The hot air itself can come from compressor bleeds, or heating ram air through a heat exchanger in an engine exhaust, as found on many turbo-props. Air can also be blown past a cylinder in which a fuel/air mixture is burned. The air is cycled round the surfaces to reduce the maximum demand at any moment. As with other uses of bleed air, anti-icing take up engine power, so are used only in flight.

Fluid de-icing is more common on small, propeller-driven aircraft, but can be used on older turbo-props. The *weeping wing* allows deicing fluid (glycol) to creep out of tiny holes in the leading edge of the affected surface but, if the aircraft is too small, the supplies you need can easily make you overweight. Put another way, a major limitation is the amount of fluid you can carry (at least 30 minutes).

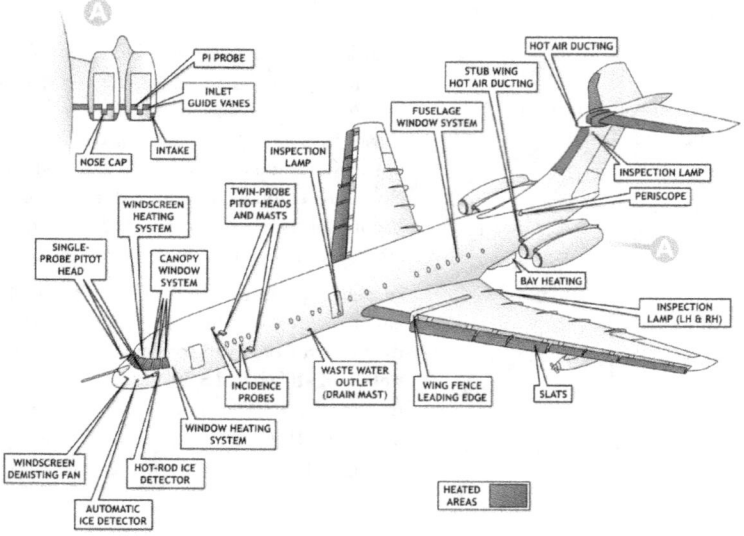

SYSTEMS
Icing & Protection

Inflatable boots are used in certain of piston-engine and most turbo-prop aircraft. The system consists of:

- Air supply
- Air distribution system
- Pneumatic de-icer boots (made of rubber)
- Controls and indications

When switched on, pressure is allowed cyclically* into the pneumatic sections to inflate the tubes. Ice breaks up and is carried away by the air flow, then air is dumped to atmosphere. The tubes are then fully deflated by a vacuum supply, which holds the boots flat against the wing when the system is off.

*The system uses a timed cycle, with each section on for about 20 seconds, then off for about 80 seconds.

The system can be damaged by refuelling and bright sunlight. **Do not operate it until after around 1.5 cm ice has formed on the leading edges.**

Electrically powered thermal devices are typically used on small surfaces, such as pitot tubes and windscreens and, occasionally, propellers.

Windshields

A layer of transparent conductive material (also known as Gold Film) in the windscreen is supplied from the aircraft AC system, although the control unit may be DC.

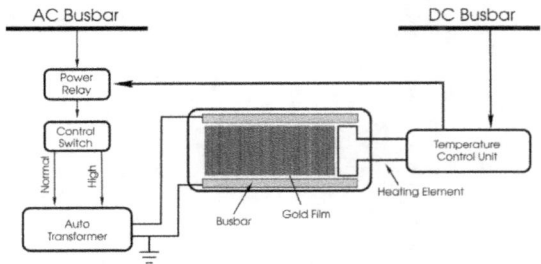

The heating process will keep the screen flexible and the flight crew will have normal and failure indications. The (inner) glass panel is the load-bearing agent. The vinyl interlayer is the fail-safe load carrying member and stops the window shattering if the inner panel fails. The outer glass panel provides rigidity and a scratch resistant surface.

There is a conductive film on the inner surface of the outer glass panel that allows electrical heating for anti-icing and de-fogging, but damage from arcing* can lead to visibility problems (if the electrical supply fails, you can use the warm air demister). A conductive coating on the outer panel also assists with dissipating static electricity from the windscreen.

*Indicated by a breakdown in the conductive coating resulting in local overheating that causes further damage to the panel.

Other problems include delamination, or separation of the vinyl windscreen plies which, if neglected, can cause visibility or electrical problems. The limits to what is allowed should be in the flight manual.

Propellers

These systems tend to be electrical, but they only need to cover the leading edges, and over the first third of the blade radius (because the outer two thirds flex enough to shed any ice). As well, not all the blades are heated at the same time. The picture shows a side view of a typical electrical deicing system. Some send pulses down the leading edge of a propeller blade every 5 seconds or so. De-icing of a propeller with fluid is done with slinger rings.

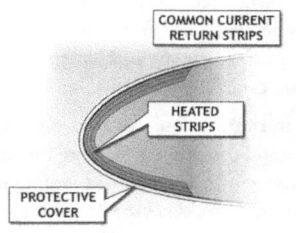

Be very careful when using flaps while landing with lots of ice on board - it could stall the horizontal stabiliser. Adding a few knots is also a good idea, assuming the runway is long enough.

Power Plant & Air Intakes

The engine air intake nacelle and spinner of a gas turbine or turbo fan engine are anti-iced from the aircraft pneumatic supply, but mechanical pneumatic devices can only be used for de-icing. Some systems may also include the LP compressor stator vanes. Engines that use a probe to sense intake pressure (a P_1 probe) will use the engine ant-ice air to prevent build up on the probe. Turbo Prop aircraft tend to use electrical systems that employ a cyclic system to anti-ice their intakes.

Switching the system on activates engine cowl anti-ice valves that are electrically controlled and pressure operated. Correction to maximum EPR indication and limits is automatic. As a protection against flame-out, the engine ignition is selected On manually or automatically. Sometimes, the engine RPM must be maintained within certain parameters, dependent upon altitude.

Ice Detectors

The **hot rod** is placed in a spot that is visible to the pilot, typically sticking out from the fuselage just below the window. The detector represents the wing - if there is no ice on the detector, there is none on the wing. It may be heated to allow you to remove ice and allow further icing assessments to be made, and there will be a built-in floodlight to let you see what's going on at night.

With the **dynamic pressure detector**, holes in the leading edge of the detector sense pitot pressure. Those in the trailing edge just detect static pressure. When the holes in the leading edge get iced up, **a decrease in dynamic pressure is detected**. As the capsule expands, an electrical contact puts on a light (usually blue) and maybe a case heater. The light only goes out when manually cancelled or an anti-icing system is switched on.

The **rotary detector** uses a rubber-mounted motor to drive a rotor against a knife-edge cutter that are separated by a small (.05mm) gap. As ice building up blocks the gap, the cutting action of the rotor produces a torque reaction that rotates the motor on its mounts. This operates a micro-switch that puts on a light in the cockpit, which stays on until pilot manually cancels it. In another version, the ice build up can affect the resistance between the rotor and cutter, which can also provide a basis for detection.

The **vibrating detector** oscillates ultrasonically at 40 kHz, which reduces when ice forms on the probe. The circuit detects the change in frequency and puts on a warning light, plus a timed heater to clear the ice and return to detection mode. The light must be cancelled manually.

The **inferential detector** uses two sensors. One is open to the airflow and the other is sheltered from it. When ice forms on the open detector, the change in temperature is monitored and, at a pre-set level, the detector illuminates a light in the cockpit. As with other systems, the light must be cancelled manually.

Propeller anti-icing systems are mainly electrical (there are some fluid based systems), but the power requirement is reduced by using a cyclic timer, as the blades are heated in turn. The spinner system is on all the time to stop ice forming and entering the engine. The Propeller system breaks the adhesion of the ice and centrifugal force throws it off. The whole system should be switched on before entering icing conditions.

Windscreen anti-icing is also electrical (being AC powered and DC controlled). It uses either gold film or very fine heating elements between the layers and is permanently on whilst the aircraft is airborne (it is switched on during taxi). The high setting is only used with severe icing). A yellow warning light (which is put on by an overheat sensor) shows only that power has been removed by Temperature Control Unit (when up to about 40°C) and not that the system has failed.

If the Cb trips, resetting it in cold temperatures may shatter the windscreen when heat is reapplied.

There is usually also a blown, hot-air, windscreen demisting system.

Pitot heads, angle of attack indicators and domestic drains are all anti-iced with electrical heaters that are permanently on when airborne and may be set to reduced levels by wheels-on micro-switches. There may also be ice inspection lights on various parts of the aircraft to enable them to be inspected at night in icing conditions. This would include engine intakes and wing leading edges.

"The pilot who masters the simple engineering principles of his aircraft, who understands the why behind the reaction - immediately elevates himself to a new level of competence and safety"

ENGINES

An engine is a device for converting the stored energy of fuel into useful work. In a steam engine, for example, the fuel is burnt in a separate furnace, which boils water and produces steam to drive the pistons. It is therefore an external combustion engine. In an *internal* combustion engine, the fuel is burnt in a confined space, and the increase in temperature produces an increase in pressure which is used to operate the engine. Chemical energy is converted into heat energy, and then into mechanical energy, which may also drive electrical, hydraulic and pneumatic systems, so engines are also called *powerplants*.

In doing this, air is sucked in, mixed with fuel, compressed, set on fire and slung out (*suck, push, bang, blow* for short or, more technically, *induction, compression, power* and *exhaust*). Piston and jet engines use more or less the same sequence of events, but the difference is that the power comes from the ignition stage in the piston, and the exhaust stage in the turbine, which is always ignited. The piston engine only ignites when the spark plugs operate (the turbine is also lighter, and spins a lot faster).

Aside from the engine itself, there are a few subsystems:

- Cooling
- Lubrication
- Ignition
- Fuel supply and carburation, which mixes the fuel with the air, ready to be burnt

The amount of thrust provided by an engine and/or propeller combination is related to the amount of air moved back, and the speed at which it is thrown out. If m kg of air is given a velocity of v m/second, the momentum given to it is mv, so Thrust = mv (per second). A propeller engine uses a large m with a small v, and a gas turbine uses a small m with a large v.

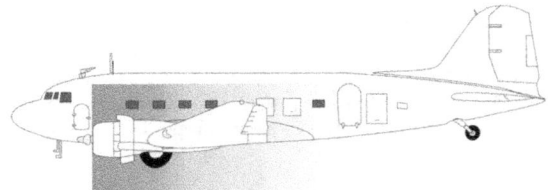

10 kg of air with a velocity of 1 m/s should therefore provide the same thrust as 1 kg of air with a velocity of 10 m/s. However, the rate at which kinetic energy is given to the air (the work done) is $\frac{1}{2}mv^2$ watts. The first case uses 5 watts and the second 50 watts, so a piston engine (with a propeller) looks to be more efficient because less kinetic energy is imparted to the air, but propellers are only efficient up to certain speeds, below which jets use too much fuel relative to the work done.

Although a propeller-driven aircraft has a maximum efficiency of about 82% at around 380 mph, this falls off rapidly after 450. At 600 mph, which is the maximum a prop-driven aircraft can fly anyway, propeller efficiency is only around 30%. Officially, piston engines are best below about 217 kts (250 mph), turboprops between 217-390 kts (250-450 mph) and jets above that. On top of that, at sea level, turbojets are operating on very thick air. The vast amounts of thrust, while good for taking off, are too much for level flight, because you would have to exceed the maximum speed to make use of it. As you increase altitude, however, the excess thrust reduces and you have a high TAS at a low IAS, for lower drag. The cold temperature also keeps the turbine temperatures down, so all the benefits of a jet are obtained at high altitudes.

In summary, the airstream from a propeller has a large diameter and moves around the same speed as the aircraft. The output from a jet engine is hot and thin, and very much faster, which is fuel-inefficient and noisy (the noise comes from hot air meeting the cold air outside too quickly). However, at higher speeds, jets are only used because propellers don't work at all.

ENGINE POWER

When you lift a weight, you work against gravity, and the power you need depends on the weight of the item concerned and how high you raise it so, if you lift 10 lbs over 55 feet, or 55 lbs over 10 feet, you require 550 ft-lbs, the product of weight multiplied by distance. However, the horsepower is a measure of *the rate of doing work*, so time is a factor - that 550 ft-lbs must be used within 1 second to qualify as a horsepower.

- The raw power developed inside the cylinders is **indicated horsepower**, so called because an indicator is used to measure the pressure.
- **Friction horsepower** means accumulated losses that increase with RPM.
- **Brake horsepower** is indicated power minus friction horsepower, where a prony brake places a known resistance against the engine's motion. It is used when the method of determining the power is important.
- **Shaft horsepower** is the equivalent to the thrust from a turboprop engine - it is not normally used for piston engines, and is measured after a certain amount of gearing down has taken place. It is usually synonymous

with BHP, and is used to emphasise the power at the output shaft.

- **Thrust horsepower** is the equivalent of the thrust from a jet engine. Piston engines use *brake* horsepower and turboprops use *shaft* horsepower, which are converted into thrust by the propeller, so you need an equivalent by which you can compare them, namely *thrust horsepower* (THP), which is expressed as:

```
Thrust (lbs) x Velocity
     550 (ft/lbs)
```

As a propeller is involved, it will be less than BHP and could be expressed as the product of SHP and propeller efficiency. The power developed depends on how much the throttle is opened.

- **Equivalent shaft horsepower** (see *Turbines*) refers to turboprop engines that develop a small amount of residual jet thrust added to shaft horsepower (thrust HP + shaft HP). The propeller of a typical turboprop accounts for around 90% of total thrust. Around 7% comes from the exhaust jet.

Shaft or brake horsepower are most familiar to pilots, and the most useful, as BHP is considered to be constant for all speed ranges, being simply a combination of engine RPM and manifold pressure, and relatively easy to measure with instruments in the cockpit. THP is more theoretical and more of interest to engineers, as pilots have no direct way of measuring it.

A propeller is only 85% efficient in converting BHP to THP (propeller efficiency is THP divided by BHP). As engine output is often too great for the transmission, the manufacturer may *derate* it to match them properly. Derating provides a power reserve in emergency, but its actual purpose is to better match engines and transmissions at altitude, or to provide a wider range of altitudes where they can work together.

In a reciprocating engine, to measure the power exerted on the pistons (indicated horsepower), you need to know the pressure acting on them, the cylinder dimensions, and the RPM of the crankshaft (the time element).

If:

- P = MEP in psi*
- L = the stroke in feet
- A = the area of the piston in sq ins
- N = the number of cylinders
- E = the working strokes per minute (RPM/2)

You can find the work done on all cylinders per minute:

```
IHP = PLANE
      33 000
```

*The pressure generated at the point of ignition will be high, but will reduce as the piston moves, so you need an average value. This we could call the *Mean Effective Pressure* at, say, 130 psi, if the original pressure is 500.

The formula for multi-cylinder engine displacement (capacity) is:

```
piston area x stroke x no cylinders
```

Efficiency

Efficiency concerns the ratio between the work put in and the work got out from an engine. As there will always be losses through conduction, friction and waste from the exhaust, no engine is even close to 100% efficiency.

THERMAL EFFICIENCY

This measures how much heat energy is converted to kinetic energy in the form of increased gas velocity (in a gas turbine engine), expressed as a percentage.

The First Law of Thermodynamics states that energy may be changed from one form to another, but not created or destroyed. As far as engines are concerned, it means that heat and mechanical work are mutually convertible, and that the rate of exchange is constant and measurable. However, the second law says (more or less) that: *Heat flows from a hot substance to a cold one unaided, but energy from an external source is needed for it to flow the other way.* That is, you might be able to convert most of your work into heat, but turning heat into work will incur serious losses, which is another way of saying that engines are grossly inefficient - if it were otherwise, exhausts would be cold!

In fact, engines waste as much energy in heat as the power they produce - the approximate thermal efficiency (global output) of a 4-stroke aircraft engine is 30%, although 25% is more typical of a multi-valve racing engine. About 40% is lost through the exhaust gases, and another large chunk through the cooling mechanism. Although allowing the engine to run hotter will stop some of this loss, the lubricating oil and other parts need to be kept within specified temperature limits to do their work properly. In addition, not all the fuel is burnt properly in the first place, especially if a carburettor is used.

A piston engine keeps its efficiency at almost any power setting because each combustion cycle produces more or less the same amount of heat. As power is altered with a piston engine by changing RPM or manifold pressure, they can run reasonably well at partial power. Turbine engine efficiency, on the other hand, is directly related to the percentage of power being produced, in that specific fuel consumption (see below), in terms of lbs per hour per horsepower*, is better at high power settings because the engine is running hotter. In other words, its thermodynamic efficiency improves because the gradient between the hot gas and the cold environment is very high. This is the *delta temperature*. A rough guide to thermal efficiency is the Engine Pressure Ratio (EPR), or the difference between what goes in and what comes out.

*Turbine fuel contains 17 500 BTUs per pound. 1 horsepower is 550 foot-pounds per second. At 778 foot-pounds per BTU, 1 HP is around 2 545 BTUs per hour.

A turbine engine is less efficient at partial power because of the lower temperature gradient.

SPECIFIC HEAT

This is the heat needed to raise the unit weight of a substance through 1°. If you heat a gas in a constant *volume*, the gas does not expand and therefore does no work. At constant *pressure*, on the other hand, the gas expands, so you get a higher value of specific heat. A gas's internal energy comes from the heat stored in it (which is relevant for Meteorology as well). If you apply more, the gas may increase its temperature or volume, or both, depending on the conditions. If the temperature rises, the gas has increased its internal energy. Any remainder is used up in external work as it expands.

An *isothermal process* is carried out at constant temperature so, although its internal energy may not change, work can still be done by or on the gas as it expands or contracts. During such expansion, the work done (in heat units) is equal to the heat supplied to the gas. In an *adiabatic process* (also relevant for Meteorology), no heat is added to or lost from the gas. Any work done through expansion must come at the expense of the heat energy stored in it and hence its internal energy, so its temperature falls. Any work done in compressing the gas, however, increases its internal energy and raises its temperature.

PROPULSIVE EFFICIENCY

This measures how much kinetic energy is converted to propulsion in terms of forward speed. As you might expect, some sort of formula is involved.....

$$PE = \frac{TAS \times 2}{TAS + V_{je}}$$

Where V_{je} represents the velocity of the outflow of gases from a turbine engine (jet efflux).

The function of a propulsive device is to produce thrust, which is the net result of the distribution of pressure and shear stresses on the device. There is zero propulsive efficiency when TAS is zero with a high outflow and maximum PE when TAS equals the speed of the outflow.

For a turbojet, V_{je} is designed to meet cruise TAS at cruise altitude. For turboprops, at low altitudes and speeds, V_{je} is reduced and the mass flow is increased.

PE can also be expressed as....

MECHANICAL EFFICIENCY

This is the ratio of brake to indicated horsepower, or power output to input. You can expect about 80% ME from a piston engine due to friction and pumping losses.

SPECIFIC FUEL CONSUMPTION

SFC is directly related to thermal and propulsive efficiency, measuring overall efficiency. It is the weight of fuel used in one hour to develop 1 pound of thrust, or the mass required to produce unit power for unit time.

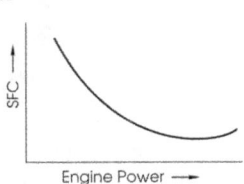

The picture represents specific fuel consumption against engine power of a turbine engine. Notice that the curve turns up as power is increased past a certain point, meaning that too much power can choke the engine and reduce its efficiency. This leads to an anomaly, in that a more powerful machine might carry less of a payload.

As the measurable primary output of a jet engine is thrust, SFC for a jet is often called *Thrust* Specific Fuel Consumption to distinguish it from a piston engine, which uses power.

VOLUMETRIC EFFICIENCY

To do with reciprocating engines and covered below.....

RECIPROCATING ENGINES 021 10

A typical piston engine consists of a series of identical cylinders which can be arranged in many ways, according to what the engine is going to be used for. The difference between engines designed for cars and those designed for aircraft is mainly the power to weight ratio, or the power delivered relative to their size. Aircraft engines undergo much more in terms of development to ensure that the materials are just strong enough for the job, having due regard for safety and reliability.

Aircraft engines also have more cylinders, which reduces vibration and allows for smooth operation, an important factor if the aircraft itself is lightly built. Having more than four cylinders means you don't need a flywheel*, which saves further weight, but this also means that if the engine stops you need something like a propeller to keep it going.

*The flywheel is a large heavy disc designed to keep the crankshaft turning through those cycles where energy is not produced, as only one stroke out of four per cylinder produces any. Using 6 cylinders provides an overlap because the power stroke is not active all the way down.

Another difference is that aircraft engines are built to run continuously at 60-75% power, or more when taking off. A car engine typically uses only 15% of its maximum power even on the motorway, and very rarely tops more than 80%. In addition, car engines produce their maximum power at high RPM. Aircraft engines are designed to run slower (to reduce internal stresses) and are made of sturdier construction, so the chances of mechanical failure are minimised.

On top of all that, an aircraft engine is expected to work at high altitudes (in low temperatures), which will require some form of adjustable mixture control.

A **radial engine** has its cylinders in a circle, with the pistons attached to the crankshaft in the centre.

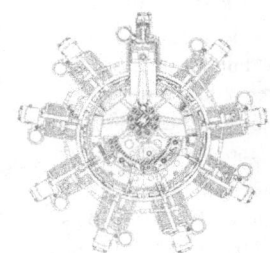

On a stationary engine, the cylinders stay still, and the crankshaft moves, but rotary engines kept the crankshaft still while the cylinders moved. Maintenance was interesting!

Aside from this, although the radial has a good power-to-weight ratio, and excellent cooling characteristics from the airflow, the large frontal area produces a lot of drag.

The most common piston engine used in modern aircraft is the four-stroke petrol, with an even number of horizontally opposed cylinders (typically 4 or 6) arranged opposite each other, to cancel some opposing forces out:

The *cylinder* in which the piston slides up and down is just that, being a large hole drilled in the engine casing and lined with steel for increased wear resistance, but it is closed at the top end by the valves (one each for the *inlet* and *exhaust*), to provide an airtight seal. Cylinder barrels are made of high tensile steel, but the cylinder head and jackets will be of a light alloy, usually Duralumin.

Screwed into the top of the cylinder are two spark plugs, and inside the cylinder is a *piston*, which acts like a pump, since it pulls air and fuel in, and pushes the burnt exhaust gases out.

Photo: Lycoming Horizontally Opposed Engine

As the piston is meant to be gastight, and no fit is perfect, there are two or three metal rings round it (the *scraper* ring at the bottom is for cleaning) to press against the cylinder wall and stop the escape of anything from one sealed portion of the cylinder to the other because, on the one hand, the engine will not produce full power if the burnt gases leak out and, on the other, oil will seep through to the head from the lubrication system, mix with the fuel and air and cause a lot of bluish grey smoke (if you are getting mysterious oil leaks from your car, and everything seems to be done up underneath, check your piston rings, as they may be allowing pressurised gases through to the sump to force the oil out). This means that hydraulicing* may be a problem the next time you start.

This means that hydraulicing* may be a problem the next time you start.

*Where oil gets past the rings and fills the combustion chamber.

Piston crowns are generally concave, but they may be convex to reduce the size of the combustion chamber and produce more power.

The piston is very slightly tapered towards the top, so its sides will be parallel with the cylinder walls when it gets hot. In this respect, the piston's crown and skirt do not have the benefit of the cooling that the cylinder wall gets from the system in use, so heat can only escape from the piston to the cylinder wall through the intervening film of oil, or the air inside the crankcase.

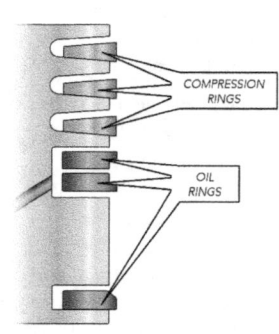

The piston is attached to the *crankpin* on the *crankshaft*, via the *connecting rod* (or conrod, for short). The small end goes to the piston (held in place with a gudgeon pin) and the big end to the crankshaft (if either end fractures, the engine will start clattering loudly). The conrod turns the back and forth (reciprocating) motion of the piston into rotary motion at the crankshaft, which is not straight, but offset for each piston connected to it, one after the other.

The crankshaft must be tough enough to stand constant hammering and alternating stresses as it spins. There will be one throw for each piston (each throw has two webs and a crank pin to which the big end of the piston is connected). Throws are separated by journals, which are placed into *main bearings*, in which they rotate.

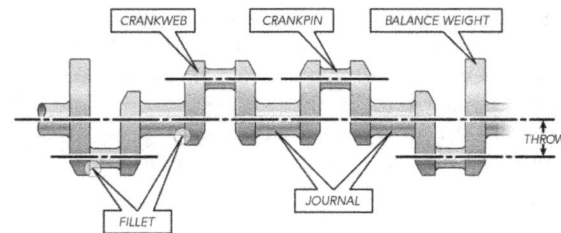

The crankshaft will rotate clockwise (from the front) as the piston is pushed downwards to the lowest point of its travel, where the centres of the gudgeon pin, crank pin and crankshaft will all be in a straight line (the crank pin will be directly under the centre of the crankshaft). As any pressure from the piston will have no turning effect on the crankshaft, this position is called a *dead centre*, in this case the Bottom Dead Centre, or BDC. The Top Dead Centre (TDC) exists at the other extreme of the piston's travel. The TDC is an important factor in the timing of the spark that ignites the fuel/air mixture, mentioned later. Movement of the piston from one dead centre to another is known as the *stroke*, and there are two strokes of the piston to every revolution of the crankshaft. The stroke of a piston engine is equal to twice the crank throw.

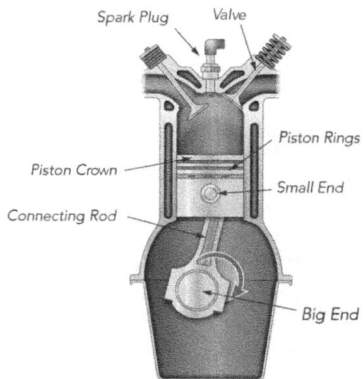

The diameter of the cylinder is the *bore*, and a *square engine* is one where the stroke equals the bore. A *short stroke* engine (i.e. most aircraft engines) permits lighter construction and reduces vibration.

The 4-Stroke (Otto) Cycle

The four stroke engine is attributed to Nikolaus Otto because he was the first person to build a car with one in 1876. It was actually patented by Alphonse Beau de Rochas in 1861. In simple terms, pressure is introduced onto the upper surface of the piston by burning a mixture of fuel and air in the confined space at the top of the cylinder. One complete stroke of the piston is used for each of the operations involved, namely *induction*, *compression*, *power* and *exhaust*. The problem is that, if you have only one cylinder, the power stroke is the only one that does any

ENGINES
Reciprocating Engines

useful work - the other three simply wear the engine out. It makes sense, therefore to have more than one cylinder, at least four, so that you get a power stroke somewhere in the engine for each cycle.

It all starts with the piston at *Top Dead Centre* (TDC), ready to start moving down to decrease the pressure in the cylinder, and suck in a fuel/air mixture from the carburettor, through the inlet valve, which has just opened (left, below). Atmospheric pressure also helps to force the fuel and air in.

The valve closes as the piston reaches Bottom Dead Centre (BDC), so the chamber is filled to maximum. With both valves closed, the piston starts moving up again (right, above), compressing and therefore heating the mix, as well as increasing its density, which helps the flame ignite quicker because the particles are closer together (heating helps to increase pressure).

 The weight of charge remains the same. For a very short period the volume remains relatively constant while the spark plug fires and makes the pressure and temperature increase rapidly as the fuel ignites.

The spark plug actually fires just before TDC (in the modified Otto cycle), with a spark from the magneto, which is rotating with the engine. This gives the fuel time to catch fire, and produce the optimum expansion at 10° *after* TDC, which is when it is actually needed. Under power (at high speeds) the spark can occur 30° beforehand (when idling, it is more like 10°).

The ignited gases expand adiabatically, and the temperature drops because their volume increases as the piston is forced downwards, in a smooth movement, making the crankshaft rotate, plus whatever is attached to it (left, above). Then the crankshaft's rotation, assisted by a flywheel, if there is one, forces the piston up again with the exhaust valve open to let the burnt gases escape. You get the maximum pressure in the cylinder when combustion is complete.

 Although there were four cycles, the crankshaft only went round twice (and the camshaft once). Valves open and close once each for every two revolutions of the crankshaft. At 2400 RPM, that's 20 times a second.

INDICATOR DIAGRAM

In the diagram on the right, of pressure against volume, the useful work area is enclosed by two adiabatic and two isochoric gas state change lines.

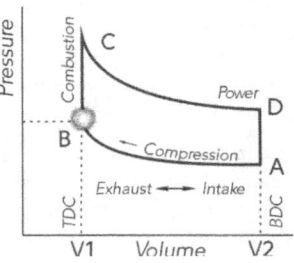

V_1 (TDC) represents the space above the piston at the top of its stroke (the clearance volume).

V_2 (BDC) is the volume enclosed when the piston is at the bottom of the cylinder. V_2 minus V_1 is the *swept volume*, or *the area of the top of the piston multiplied by the distance of movement of the piston*. The ratio of V_2 over V_1 is the *compression ratio*, which is an expression of the number of times the volume above the piston *before* compression is greater than that *after* compression, or the big space divided by the small space - the *total volume* above the piston at V_2 is the clearance volume plus the swept volume, so divide that by the clearance volume.

In the theoretical Otto cycle, the induction stroke ends at A. The pressure should be the same as atmospheric, but it's lower, because the piston creates a vacuum as it descends. The compression stroke occurs from A to B, where both valves are closed. The compression is adiabatic, and no heat enters or leaves the cylinder.

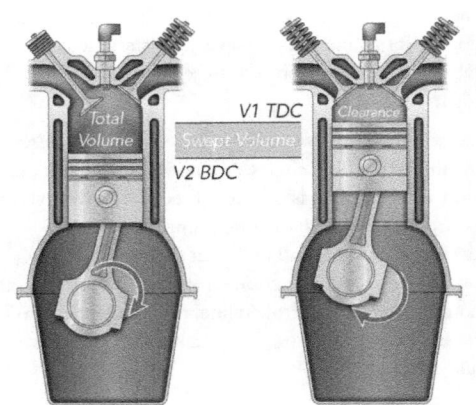

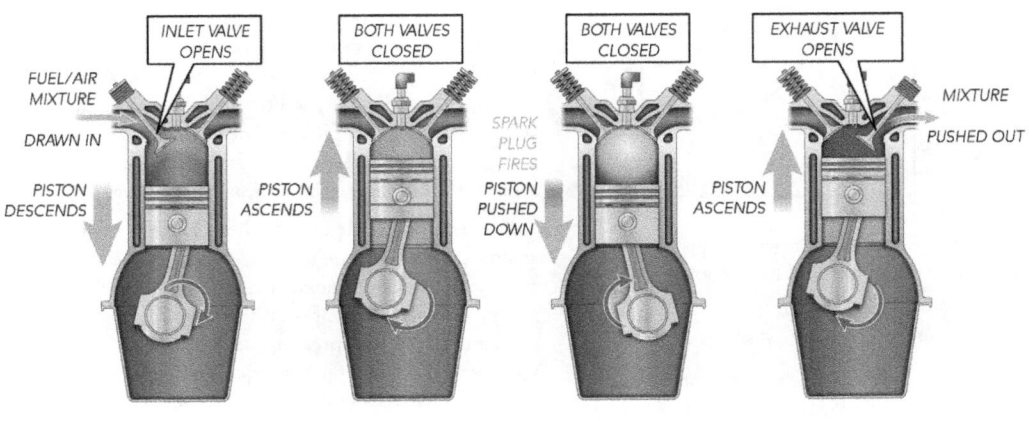

Ignition occurs at B, where the gases resulting from the ignition expand adiabatically in a constant volume, increasing the pressure and leading to the power stroke and the expansion between C to D. At D, the initial rejection of the exhaust occurs and the gases are eventually removed to the atmosphere in the opposite direction to the intake.

The area enclosed by the solid lines is an indication of the *net* work performed. The intake pressure is less than the exhaust pressure and the negative differential represents a pumping loss. Because of the initial rejection of the exhaust gases along the line D-A, the gases take a bit of a short cut (the curved lines actually extend to the right). The unused gases can be used to run other devices, such as a turbocharger.

The Otto cycle takes place very quickly, so the gases swirl. There are also large temperature gradients, so the gas cannot be treated as if it had constant temperature. As well, ignition takes a finite time to propagate through the fuel-air mixture, so pressures will vary within the gas.

Diesel Engines

Why not compress the charge more in a four stroke, and get even better efficiency? Because as the charge is compressed it heats up, until at higher compressions it heats enough to explode at the wrong time (see *Abnormal Combustion*, below) which may create enough pressure to exceed the strength of the engine components. This creates holes in pistons or cylinder heads, which is not considered to be a Good Thing.

However, diesel engines can take advantage of this effect and use "compression ignition" instead of a spark plug, so they can achieve double the compression of Otto engines and are consequently more efficient.

Formerly known as *compression ignition* engines (Rudolf Diesel patented one in 1892), these engines do not require spark plugs or carburation - instead, fuel is injected directly into the cylinder at high pressure (so you need a strong pump) just as the temperature increases to around 800°C at the end of the compression stroke, so the induction stroke only pulls in air, and only air is compressed (in a petrol engine, fuel is injected into the air before it reaches the cylinder). This makes the indicator diagram quite different.

Again, the compression stroke takes place from A to B. The air is compressed adiabatically to about 1/20 of its original volume, and it gets hot. From B to C, fuel is injected in an atomised form. It burns steadily to make the pressure on the piston constant. From C to D, the power stroke moves the piston down as adiabatic expansion takes place. From D to A, cooling and exhaust occurs.

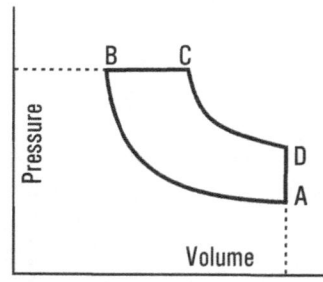

*Detonation (abnormal combustion) is not an issue.

The original idea was to operate the engine at constant pressure, but this is difficult, so part of the fuel is burnt at constant volume, as with the Otto cycle, and the rest at constant pressure. Because it receives a full charge of air, the mixture ratio is extremely variable, ranging from 100:1 at idle to 15:1 (stoichiometric) at full power.

The diesel engine has a higher thermal efficiency than the petrol engine because the compression ratio is much higher, but it is noisier, heavier, and bigger for a given power. Incomplete combustion also makes for considerable pollution (soot) as there is no mixture control. The power also depends on fuel flow.

A glow plug is used to help start it. This is a small heating element in the cylinder that is energised when the Master switch is turned on (there might be a GLOW ON caption on the PFD to show that power is getting to it. It should go off after a few seconds to show that the engine is now hot enough to start).

Compression Ratio

A heat engine is one that converts heat in a gas (added by a fuel) to do work. All combustion engines, like the Otto cycle (four stroke), Diesel and Brayton Cycle (gas turbine) are heat engines. Their efficiency of a piston engine is largely governed by the compression ratio. The space between the crown (top) of the piston and the cylinder head, into which the fuel/air mixture is pulled and later compressed, is the *combustion chamber*, which gets larger and smaller as the piston goes up and down. Piston crowns are generally concave, but they may be convex to reduce the size of the combustion chamber and produce more power.

More power is obtained with a higher compression ratio because the compression pressure is higher - as the mixture ignites, the pressure rises to about four times its previous value, which naturally, up to a point*, increases the Mean Effective Pressure. At higher compression ratios, temperature increases at a slower rate than pressure does, so at pressure ratios of, say, 16:1, the small temperature gain is lost in the inefficiencies introduced by the rise in pressure. Between 14:1 and 25:1 is good for diesel engines - petrol engines must have a typical ratio of 8:1 or 12:1 (with 100 octane fuel) because the heat from compression would cause abnormal combustion, described later.

*The compression ratio has a maximum limit because of the possible early ignition of the fuel/air mixture. This is called detonation.

Volumetric Efficiency

Whatever power you get from an engine ultimately depends on how much fuel (and air) mixture you can cram into the cylinders. Volumetric efficiency is the measure of how much mass charge *is* pulled in against what *could* be taken in, or fill the swept volume, in standard conditions*, or how well the engine can breathe (if you restrict its air supply it will not work so well). It is therefore an indication of the efficiency with which compression can be achieved, and a high cylinder head temperature decreases it.

*More technically, the ratio of the volume of the induced charge at atmospheric pressure to the volume displaced by the piston. In a normally aspirated engine, the induced charge pressure is always less than ambient so, if the reduced-pressure gas is at ambient atmospheric pressure, its volume would be less than that volume displaced by the piston, so an unsupercharged piston engine always has a volumetric efficiency of less than 100%.

The value is about 75% for a normally aspirated engine, due to various leakages and losses, or even the nature of the passages through which the mixture has to pass**, hence the need for supercharging, but it will improve with increased atmospheric pressure (i.e. flying in denser air) or compression ratio.

**The bigger the valve openings and the smoother the passages, the less lag there will be from the gases (this inertia is the reason why valves are made to open and close early, as explained below). In addition, if the mixture is too hot at the inlet valve, or the scavenging is poor, you will not get a full charge.

Valves & Timing

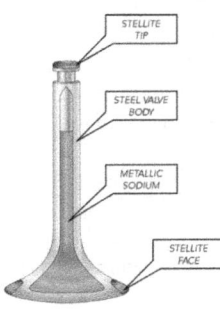

The cylinder head (which is bolted to the top of the engine casing) contains valves which must open and close at precise times to allow the fuel/air mixture in and exhaust gases out (*fuel* or *inlet* valves, and *exhaust valves*). *Poppet valves* (see left) are often hollow, or partly filled with sodium pellets to encourage heat transfer, especially the exhaust valve, which helps considerably with minimising abnormal combustion. They are made of steel, and are tough enough to take the hammering as they open and close, and the extreme temperatures. Valves have two springs around the shaft to return them to their original positions - the second reduces *valve bounce* due to its different size and resonance, and provides for some sort of redundancy.

As it turns, the crankshaft will turn a smaller version of itself, called a *camshaft*, which rotates at *half the crankshaft speed* (i.e. once per cycle), and is linked directly to the valve rocker at the top of the cylinder by a long metal rod, the bottom end of which is enclosed in a *tappet* (to save wear). The top end of the rod hits the valve rocker directly, pushing the valve open. As the engine gets hotter, these rods expand, so there is a little clearance to allow for this, called the *valve rocker clearance* (valve rockers are *not* tappets). If the valve rocker clearance is too large, the valve will not open so much, which will reduce volumetric efficiency. If the gap is too small, there will be loss of compression because the valves won't close properly. Hydraulic tappets take up the slack automatically so you don't have to keep adjusting the valve rocker clearance.

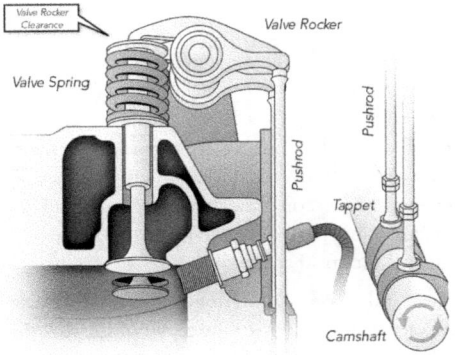

Valve design is actually very important for efficiency. If the inlet valve is too small, or it doesn't open enough, volumetric efficiency is reduced. Its position is also important, because you need some turbulence inside the cylinder to spread the flame more rapidly. For this reason, there should be no obstructions to the flow of gases after they have passed through the inlet valve. Too small an exhaust valve stops the burnt gases escaping quickly and creates a back pressure that heats the engine up.

 A *hydraulic lock* (hydraulicing) occurs when there is some liquid in the cylinder when you start up that is equal to, or greater than the swept volume, and which stops the piston moving during the compression stroke, when both valves are closed. Damage (usually a broken connecting rod) occurs once the preceding cylinders have fired since the piston is forced against the liquid, which is incompressible. In a radial engine, the fluid is likely to be oil, in the bottom cylinder. In a horizontally opposed engine, however, the liquid is more likely to be accumulated fuel, in one of the forward cylinders. Be careful when operating the fuel boost pump during a failed start, and do not over-prime on sloping ground.

In theory, the fuel/air mixture should enter the cylinder during the piston's travel from TDC to BDC (top to bottom), with the exhaust gases leaving it between BDC to TDC, but things are not quite as simple as that! In practice, a small part of the piston's up and down movement is immaterial relative to the work done - this is called *ineffective crank angle*. In other words, the piston hardly moves up and down relative to the rotary motion of the crankshaft, and the valves may as well be open as not. Thus, the theoretical valve and ignition timing can be adjusted to improve overall efficiency.

As an engine is complicated, with a lot happening in a short time, some anticipation here and there doesn't go amiss. Opening valves early (in the *modified* Otto Cycle) is called *valve lead*, and being late is called *valve lag*. When they are both open at the same time, you get *valve overlap*, where the exhaust gases on their way out reduce the pressure in the manifold, which helps to pull in the incoming fuel/air mix (this is more effective at altitude, where the atmospheric pressure is lower). Valve overlap also promotes easier valve timing, only occurring between the exhaust and induction strokes.

Opening the inlet valve early means that it is fully open as the induction stroke starts, which overcomes the fuel/air mix's inertia, so there is no time lag between the piston moving down and the mix actually moving. Its momentum when the piston finally stops at BDC means that as much of the mix as possible is crammed in and the valve closes *after* BDC to make sure. At the end of the power stroke, as its force weakens, you may as well open the exhaust valve early so that the remaining internal pressure can force the gases out early. It closes late to take advantage of the gas's momentum.

Ignition   021 10 07

Near the end of the compression stroke, you need a spark with enough energy to ignite the fuel/air mixture in the cylinder **just before** Top Dead Centre (where the piston gets to the top of its stroke), because the burning fuel needs to build up to its maximum pressure. In early engines, any timing adjustments (advancing or retarding) were done by the pilot, but now they are done automatically. Magnetos have fixed timing, meaning that any settings must be a compromise, which is not the best for low or high RPM.

The whole mechanism that provides the spark at the critical moment consists of spark plugs, leads and magnetos, etc., in duplicate (one magneto will serve one plug per cylinder, and the second the other).

The duplication is actually for efficiency, as the magneto doesn't work that well at low RPM, but a side benefit is, obviously, safety. Two sparks provide two flame fronts within the cylinder, which decreases the time needed for the complete fuel charge to start burning, so most of the fuel can be already burning at a lower temperature and pressure. In a cylinder with only one spark plug, lower octane portions of the fuel mixture far from the original flame front can explode, lighting off another flame front in a different part of the cylinder at a different time, leading to engine knock. Thus, two flame fronts can help to decrease the octane requirement for any given engine.

The magneto, which is actually a small generator based around a permanent magnet, contains a transformer and all the circuitry needed to boost the low primary voltage (24-28 volts) to one large enough to jump across a small preset gap at the plug electrodes (up to 20,000 v - this depends on the amount of turns in the secondary coil). A car has a similar system, but not all in one unit.

The magneto is a precision instrument. It needs to generate several hundred sparks per second, timed to occur at a precise instant on the compression stroke.

When doing power checks before takeoff, they are checked against each other for power and whether they actually are independent - there should be a slight, but discernible drop in RPM (around 100) when one magneto is switched off during the power check. If they stay the same, they are interconnected somehow. When running up, set the magnetos to *Both* between testing each one singly to allow the engine to stabilise at the proper RPM and to burn off oil and fuel that may have accumulated on the plugs that have been switched off. Any rough running at this point usually indicates fouled plugs which are typically cleared by leaning the mixture for a while.

The ignition switches in the cockpit, when selected OFF, ground the magnetos to Earth through the *primary circuit**, although you can open the secondary as well. As any connection can fail, magnetos should always be regarded as being live as far as safety is concerned. Normally, **magnetos will always work when the rotor inside is being spun.** They do not need any external influence or power.

*This means that, if one magneto fails, you will get a dead cut if you switch the other one off.

The magneto works by magnetic induction, which requires that a conductor (or a wire) moves in a magnetic flux, or a magnetic flux moves past a conductor, whichever is convenient. In this way, current flow is induced in the conductor, if it is part of a complete circuit. It does not matter whether the flux field is developing or collapsing; the induction effect is the same. If the conductor is part of a coil, the induced current can also be used to step up the voltage, as would be done with a transformer.

A distributor rotor contacts a spark lead, which completes the secondary coil's circuit. At the right moment, a contact breaker opens, to break the primary circuit, so the flux field of the primary coil collapses and induces a current in the secondary coil windings. The primary coils are thicker because they carry more current. As the secondary carries more voltage, its current must be reduced to compensate, so it can be made of thinner wire. The number of windings in the secondary coil, or the ratio of its windings to the primary, determines the voltage at this point, but it is in the order of 20 000 volts, so that a spark can jump across the plug gap and ignite the fuel/air mixture.

Magnetos in high altitude aircraft are pressurised to prevent arcing or flashover within the distributor. They are usually painted grey or dark blue (as opposed to black).

ROTATING ARMATURE

In a *rotating armature* magneto, a rotor (armature) rotates in the gap between two ends of a horseshoe permanent magnet. The rotor is actually an engine-driven shaft, which is surrounded by two sets of coils, a *primary* then a *secondary* winding. As the rotor spins, the conductor, which is the primary coil, moves within the flux field of the permanent magnet. This induces an alternating current into the coil and its associated circuit. The coil produces its own flux field which starts to build up.

ROTATING MAGNET

For engines needing more powerful magnetos (maybe they have more than 4 or 6 cylinders), a rotating magnet is used. Here, the primary and secondary windings are around the horseshoe-shaped former, or core (in other words, they are stationary). The rotating shaft spins a permanent magnet, which has as many lobes as there are cylinders, so the core and primary windings (because they are nearby) have currents induced in them.

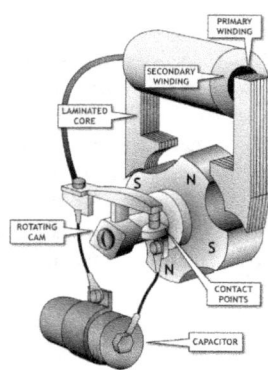

The core is subjected to an increasing and decreasing magnetic field and a change in polarity every time the magnet travels through 90°. The alternating pulses create an alternating flux in the primary coil. The core is laminated to keep eddy currents that will cause the device to overheat to a minimum, and to help collapse the magnetic field more quickly when required. The ends of the core are concave to keep the magnets as near perpendicular to the flux field as possible.

The most efficient induction of current into the conductor is when the conductor moves at 90° to the plane of the flux field, where the conductor cuts more lines of flux per unit of distance travelled (left, below).

The rotating magnet induces a current of up to 200 volts in the primary circuit, which has a magnetic field that opposes any decrease in the field in the core (back emf).

In this way, the core flux is held to a high value for as long as possible, at least until the rotating magnet gets a few degrees past the neutral position (right, below). In this position, the magnetic flux is short-circuited and the flow in the primary circuit is effectively cut off, to generate the required current in the secondary coil, although the timing will not be accurate, as the flux lines are not all broken at once. However, if the breakers open when the flux is changing most rapidly, you will get a sharp cutoff and a high rate of change, and maximum energy will be transferred (by inductive coupling) from the primary to the secondary when the rotor is quickly reversing the magnetism in the core across the secondary.

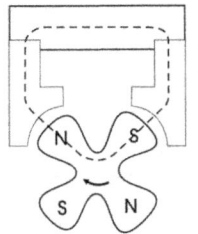 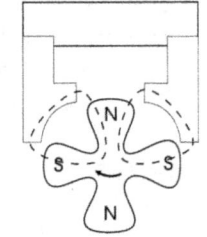

Essentially, as the contact breakers open, the primary current and its associated magnetic field collapses across the secondary, inducing a current in it, but the field collapses across the primary as well and generates enough current to produce a long-lasting spark across the points, which will eventually wear them out. As this stops the magnetic field from collapsing until the points are far apart, the capacitor (below) absorbs that extra current.

The end result is that the AC is converted into a series of precise pulses due to the action of the contact breakers.

CONTACT BREAKER

A voltage is only generated in the secondary coil when the current through the primary is changing. Such changes only occur with DC when the circuit opens and closes.

Inside the primary circuit of both types of magneto is a set of contact points that do just that, making the flux reversals more abrupt when they open and close at critical moments. When the points are closed, current flows in the primary coil and a flux field builds up around it, affecting the core. When a spark is needed, the points open, and the field collapses across the secondary, inducing a current which is fed to the spark plugs through the distributor.

The points are opened by a *rocker arm*, which is moved by a cam as many times per revolution as there are lobes on the cam. A spring returns the rocker arm to its normal position.

CAPACITOR (CONDENSER)

The more sudden the breaking of the primary circuit, the greater will be the voltage swing and the more current will be induced in the secondary coil. The capacitor across the contact points helps to create a good strong spark at the plug, and it does this by absorbing the charge that would otherwise go across the points and slow down the collapse of the field. This is a *spark quench*.

This prevents damage to the points from arcing and pitting. Without the capacitor the spark only ceases when either the voltage drops or the points open enough to stop an arc forming, about ten times as long as it would otherwise take to stop. When the capacitor discharges back into the primary coil, its collapsing field is more rapidly suppressed and a higher secondary output is produced. The capacitor and coil, when the points open, form a tuned circuit, which makes the current in the primary oscillate rapidly back and forth with a peak-to-peak voltage swing of about 400v, sustaining the spark for about 2 thousandths of a second (2mS), or several degrees of crankshaft revolution.

DISTRIBUTION

The high voltage generated is fed (from the secondary coil) to the plugs by a *distributor*, which is essentially a rotor spinning inside a cap at the end of the magneto holding heavy screened cables going to the plugs.

The rotor contacts each cable in turn, but they are not matched to the plugs in order, as one cylinder would receive the spark at the wrong time. Instead, the cables are out of order, on a four-cylinder engine as 1342 or 1243). On a 6 cylinder engine, the firing order is determined by the manufacturer.

The leads to the spark plugs together form an *ignition harness*. They are shielded with braided wire to minimise radio interference (one reason for checking them on a preflight inspection).

ADVANCING & RETARDING

Ignition is automatically *advanced* as RPM increases, and *retarded* when starting up (the spark is intensified as well). It must be advanced at high engine RPM because the flame rate and time for combustion remain constant.

The engine is spinning slowly in the initial stages, at around 120 RPM, so the magneto is spinning at 60 RPM, as it is driven by the camshaft, at half the speed of the crankshaft. It needs around 200 RPM to produce a proper spark, so a coiled spring is used to temporarily increase the magneto's speed of rotation. In addition, the spark would occur too early, since, at normal RPM, it typically occurs about 25° before TDC. If the piston is pushed down too early, it might try to turn the crankshaft in the wrong direction, resulting in a kick-back. We therefore need something to temporarily make the spark occur later in the cycle. An *impulse coupling* attached to the left magneto provides a high energy *retarded* spark (on TDC) during startup, as the engine is rotating very slowly at that point, and the strength of the spark depends on the speed of rotation of the magneto. The spark must also occur *later* than usual to ensure that the piston is beyond TDC as the gases start to burn and exert pressure.

In the coupling, flyweights react against two stop-pins in the magneto housing as the engine (and magneto shaft) is turned over. The locked flyweights hold the magneto still whilst a spring is wound up until a certain amount of rotation has occurred, when projections on the housing release the flyweights. The spring unwinds and spins the magneto to produce the spark. Once the engine fires, a centrifugal clutch disconnects the mechanism and spring. The spark is produced normally with the engine rotation.

ENGINES
Reciprocating Engines

Abnormal Combustion

 Popping back is most likely in a running piston engine at low RPM with a weak mixture, meaning that the manifold pressure is high, as is the CHT.

DETONATION

During combustion, the hydrogen and carbon in the gasoline, and oxygen from the air, combine to form carbon dioxide and water vapour, and the nitrogen (from the air), which is inert, acts as a buffer to create controlled combustion rather than an explosion. The result should be a rapid and steady burning of the mixture that produces a uniform pressure rise on the piston, with a flame rate of around 60 - 80 feet per second. The flame front actually moves across the cylinder through a series of chain reactions, with their rate of progress limited by the remaining, cooler, unburned charge. It is not an explosion, but a very rapid, orderly burning of the fuel-air charge—normally from two different ignition sources.

Ignition normally happens just before Top Dead Centre, to allow the flame to build up. In other words, burning of the fuel/air mixture starts in the latter part of the compression stroke and carries through to the early part of the power stroke. The flame front is accelerated by using two spark plugs so that heat is released more rapidly and the pressure rise is quicker. Where the last portion of the mixture burns almost instantaneously (i.e. too fast, at 1000 feet per second), you get detonation. It is a product of the characteristics of the fuel and engine design, which will ultimately limit the compression ratio. The primary cause is excessive pressure in the cylinder head, but using low grade fuel doesn't help.

Detonation is the explosive auto-ignition *after* the planned spark, at high pressure and temperature in the unburnt part of the mixture ahead of the flame front, where small, localised pockets of the fuel-air charge, frequently occur very close to the cylinder wall, auto ignite ahead of the flame front and create a shock wave in the combustion chamber, where many isolated areas of ignition may exist at the same time. This shock wave travels at the speed of sound in that medium (at near 4000°C, very much faster than on a standard day!), and bounces back and forth at the specific frequency for that speed (this is the pinging* you can hear in a car engine that is detonating). Although it is similar to pre-ignition, below, the timing is different.

*Detonation is otherwise known as *pinking*. You will hear it in your car if you make it work too hard (try going uphill in high gear). It can cause the temperatures inside the cylinder head to rise to the melting point of the components, with the piston usually going first. The hot gases leak past the piston rings, pressurise the crankcase and blow the oil out. Net result: seized engine and holes in pistons.

Detonation can be caused by:

- using low grade fuel
- too lean a mixture
- too high a manifold pressure
- an overheated engine

When detonation is recognised (through rough running, high cylinder head temperatures, or loss of power), you should *reduce manifold pressure* and *richen the mixture*, or cool the engine (or even increase engine RPM). The long-term cure is to use fuel with a higher octane rating.

PRE-IGNITION

Ignition of the charge by hotspots in the combustion chamber is called *surface ignition*. It is also called *pre-ignition* when it happens *before* the charge is supposed to be ignited by the spark plug. Put another way, the piston receives a "hammer blow" on its way up the compression stroke, i.e. early, rather than on its way down on the power stroke.

Gases may leave the combustion chamber while still burning, producing local hotspots and detonation. Thus, pre-ignition is a product of overheating, especially where the mixture has been leaned too much (meaning that the engine is not being cooled adequately), and deposits inside the combustion chamber that are glowing bright red (more from misuse of the throttle than the mixture control, as when increasing power without adjusting the mixture). Cure it by enriching the mixture.

As opposed to detonation, where EGTs don't change much while CHTs rise, pre-ignition produces rapidly falling EGTs and rapidly rising CHTs.

 If an engine does not shut down (dieselling), there is either excessive carbon formation in the cylinder head or the ground wire between the magneto and the ignition switch is disconnected.

Pre-ignition tends to affect only one or two cylinders.

OCTANE RATINGS

Because of the above problems, piston engines use fuel with an *anti-knock additive*, which used to be lead, to ensure that fuel ignites smoothly, and doesn't explode, and to stop it igniting before it's meant to. The octane rating of a fuel refers to its anti-knock value. In the days before carburettors, fuel was much more volatile, and could be ignited from ten feet away. Lead, of course, is no longer politically correct so, in cars, at least, the timing of engines is adjusted to produce the same effect with unleaded fuel.

The aviation industry still uses it, though. The "LL" in 100LL stands for *low lead*, but there is still about four times more than is needed. As well as the lead (as TEL - *Tetra-Ethyl Lead*), a scavenging agent (*Ethylene DiBromide*, or EDB) is added to ensure that the lead is vaporised as far as possible, ready to be expelled from the cylinder with other gases, otherwise the lead deposits would stick to the insides. This is not 100% successful, but the results are best at high temperatures and worst at low ones. The unwanted extras result in fouling of spark plugs, heavy deposits in the combustion chamber, erosion of valve seats and stems, sticking valves and piston rings and general accumulation of sludge and restriction of flow through fine oil passages, so it makes you wonder which is worse (in fact, petrol is not the only fuel you can use - Japanese Zeros used to outfly American aeroplanes because they used ethyl alcohol). The *octane rating* reflects the ability of fuel to *expand evenly*.

Higher octane fuels allow higher compression ratios than are possible with "normal" fuels without detonation. If fuel of a lower octane rating than is recommended in the Flight Manual is used, you should never use full throttle.

Cooling

The gases burning in the engine can produce temperatures as high as 2500°C. This will be absorbed by the various engine parts according to the temperature itself, the surface area exposed and the duration of the exposure. If left unchecked, this heat could cause those parts to distort and malfunction, or even cause pre-ignition or detonation. The function of the cooling system is therefore to remove heat from the engine at a high enough rate to keep its temperatures within safe working limits (overcooling can produce as many problems as undercooling - you need heat to vaporise the fuel, for example, and you don't want water vapour condensing on the insides). Liquid contaminants, such as water, must be boiled off.

Two of the main divisions of reciprocating engines is how they are cooled. Air cooled cylinders must necessarily be in the airstream so that they are cooled equally. The position of liquid cooled engines is not so limited.

AIR COOLING

Air cooling is simple, as heat radiates directly into the air from the warm parts. Fins on a cylinder head, for instance, increase the surface area through which this can happen*. The best engines for this tend to be those that allow the same amount of airflow over each cylinder, such as radials, but others, such as in-lines or those with a V formation may need fans and shrouds to help, or their cylinders would have to be very far apart to let air through. In any case, the first cylinders would be the coolest.

*Fins are usually found on the cylinder head, round the barrel and inside the piston head. Cooling air can be directed around the cylinder with suitably shaped baffles.

Air cooled engines can be run hotter because their limits are measured by the temperature of the oil.

LIQUID COOLING

You need around 2000 times more air to remove a given amount of heat from an engine than you would if you used water or a suitable liquid. There is a metal jacket around the warm parts (particularly the cylinders), and the space between them is filled with a liquid such as water (70%), with ethylene glycol (30%) added to solve certain limitations (boiling at low temperatures at high altitudes). This makes the construction of the cylinders more complex as they also have to be watertight.

The liquid is pumped through a radiator which sticks out into the airflow to cool it down before it recirculates. Because all this fluid has to be heated, the engine takes a little longer to warm up, and there is also the extra weight to consider, not to mention leaks, extra maintenance and the possibility of freezing in cold weather, which is why water is not generally used*. The boiling problem can also be solved by operating the system under pressure, for which you also need a *thermostat*, which is a bypass valve that regulates the movement of fluid.

*Plain water is not used because it freezes on cold nights and expands, which can crack the engine. It also has a corrosive effect. Instead, it is mixed with glycol to increase its boiling point and lower its freezing point.

The Carburettor   082 10 04

It is not the fuel, but its vapour that burns, so you need a way of ensuring that fuel is vaporised and mixed with air in the right proportions rapidly enough to feed an engine. The carburettor does just this and delivers the mixture to the inlet manifold* for its onward journey to the cylinders. It does this with a small bore jet in its choke tube that allows fuel to spray in a fine mist.

*A channel that serves manifold, or multiple, cylinders.

Carburettors in aircraft engines typically contain more than one complete carburation unit (i.e. float chamber, jets, butterfly, etc.) In fact, one carburettor will usually serve three or four cylinders to ensure that each one gets its fair share of the fuel/air mixture.

Float type carburettors depend on the pressure difference between the venturi throat and atmospheric pressure for their operation, using the Venturi principle. As the speed of the air increases through the choke, the pressure reduces., enough for atmospheric pressure to push fuel into it via the main nozzle, which is connected directly to the fuel system through a series of pumps and jets. As the main nozzle is inside the low pressure area, the fuel is forced to expand, which cools everything, so be careful with carburettor icing, which can form well in advance of any other type. In fact, if you could make one small enough, there's no reason why an air conditioning unit could not achieve the same effect. It would certainly work better than a carburettor.

There is a fuel strainer **upstream of the needle valve** (not shown). The **diffuser** (or compensating jet) is a perforated tube within the main fuel passage. It keeps the mixture ratio constant at high and low power settings by ensuring that the fuel flow is proportional to the volume of air through the choke. This stops the main jet from supplying too much fuel as the speed of the engine is increased.

It emulsifies the fuel, improves vaporisation and delivers the vapour to the fuel nozzle.

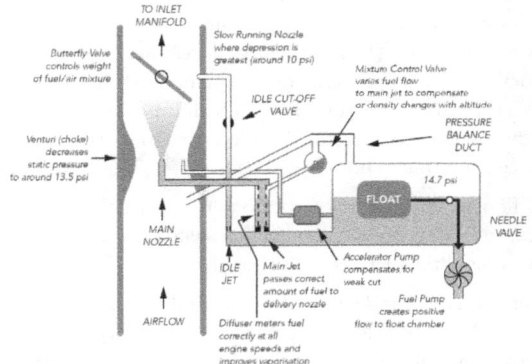

The diffuser is a perforated tube within the main fuel passage.

The perforations are normally below the static fuel level, so they are completely covered at low RPM. As they increase, the fuel level in the diffuser drops, uncovering the upper perforations to allow a bleed of air at intake pressure into the tube and to raise the pressure slightly above that in the venturi. Thus, the pressure differential across the main jet is decreased slightly, reducing the fuel flow through the jet slightly.

The higher the engine RPM, the more the float chamber level falls, uncovering more perforations to allow more air at intake pressure into the tube. The increase in pressure differential across the main jet is thus limited with increasing speed.

The perforations are carefully graduated to ensure that the pressure drop across the main jet, and the fuel flow through it, is matched to the airflow through the venturi at a constant ratio over the whole speed range of the engine. The diffuser also helps with atomisation because it introduces air into the fuel, which will break up into tiny droplets to form an emulsion. Since this is less dense than liquid fuel, it can be drawn to the lip of the discharge nozzle more readily. Also, the emulsion will have a larger surface area, so it will evaporate more quickly.

In carburettors where a diffuser tube is not used, an air bleed into the fuel feed from the main jet to the nozzle is introduced to create such an emulsion.

Just before the carburettor ends and the inlet manifold begins is a *butterfly valve*, which is best compared to a coin in a tube - when the throttle is closed, the butterfly valve is closed, and *vice versa*. One problem is that fuel splashes against it and condenses, which doesn't help with vaporisation or atomization much.

Even when the butterfly is fully open, there is still resistance to the flow of fuel from its sideways presentation. New car engines have eliminated it altogether by making the throttle increase the inlet valve opening time to get the same effect.

All the above is fine, but a small complication arises, in that we pilots keep wanting to change the speed of the engine. For example, when the butterfly is closed, the engine still needs fuel, but the pressure differential between the venturi and the float chamber is very small, so there is an *idle jet* that bypasses the butterfly to keep the engine ticking over (the jet is actually a hole next to the butterfly, and it's sometimes called the *slow running jet*).

Also, when you need power in a hurry, there is a small lag from inertia between the time you open the throttle and the time the engine starts to speed up, because the air supply responds more quickly than the fuel does, which gives you a *weak cut* (a momentarily weak mixture), so a small squirt of fuel is delivered separately to compensate, by an *accelerator pump*. When starting an engine from cold, therefore, resist the temptation to pump the throttle, because all you will do is flood it with large drops of fuel. A better tactic is to open the throttle v e r y s l o w l y, so that the accelerator pump doesn't kick in.

To start a flooded engine that has a carburettor, place the mixture control in cutoff, with the ignition switch off, and the throttle open until the fuel has been cleared.

Because aircraft go up, and air gets less plentiful at height, there is a danger of the fuel/air mixture getting out of balance as you climb - the engine will not work at all if the ratio of fuel to air is not correct. A mixture that has too much fuel against air is *rich*, while one the other way round is *weak*. The *mixture control* is provided to adjust for this as you increase altitude - for example, you would set it fully rich for takeoff and landing (this is also for cooling). The "normal" mixture is about 15:1 of air to fuel by *weight*, but this is not critical over a wide range. However, 18:1 would be considered weak. The *mixture ratio* is that between the *masses* of *fuel* and *air* entering the *cylinder* (air to fuel).

So, the mixture control's main purpose is to adjust the fuel flow to get the right fuel:air ratio, to correct for variations resulting from reduced air density at altitude. Leaning makes the engine run hotter and give you more power for less fuel; a 112 hp aircraft cruising at 4000 feet and 85 knots might burn 5 gallons an hour when rich, but only 4.5 when leaned, giving a range of 116 miles as opposed to 100 - a saving, or an increase, of 16%. The mixture control's secondary function is to cut off the fuel supply to the engine on the ground when you want to stop it (you don't just switch the magnetos off).

 Most normally aspirated engines can be leaned at any altitude when the power is set *below* about 75% (cruise power for Lycomings is normally between 55-75%). Thus, leaning off at more than cruise power (i.e. in the climb) should *not* be carried out, as many engines rely on a rich mixture for cooling. It may save fuel, but petrol has a high latent heat content, and the excess fuel reduces the temperature when it evaporates.

FUEL PRIMING

A *fuel primer* is a small hand pump that puts neat fuel directly into either the induction manifold (near the combustion chamber) or the inlet valve port. It should be used before starting a cold engine to promote the presence of fuel vapour (you rarely need to prime a warm engine). Injection systems do not need primers.

Tip: As the primer injects fuel into the manifold, you can put fuel into your engine if it quits because of carb icing.

Aside from the fire hazard, excessive priming should be avoided because it washes lubricant off the cylinder walls.

CARBURETTOR ICING

This is actually one aspect of *induction system icing*. The other two are *fuel icing*, arising from water suspended in fuel, and *impact ice*, which builds up on the airframe around the various intakes that serve the engine, usually found with fuel injected engines (discussed below).

The venturi's purpose is to accelerate airflow by restricting the size of the passageway, which reduces the pressure* and allows the fuel to be pulled in. Unfortunately, this also reduces the temperature*, as does the fuel vaporisation, hence the problem.

*With a closed butterfly valve, there is a very large acceleration of the air, leading to large drops in pressure and temperature.

The lower temperature means greater relative humidity - as the vaporisation takes its latent heat from the surroundings (i.e. the body of the carburettor), the situation gets worse. In fact, the vaporisation (and cooling) can carry on most of the way to the cylinders, causing the problem to persist, especially when the butterfly is semi-closed, which produces another restriction and more of the same. Any water vapour present under those conditions will turn directly to ice. Note also that warm air produces *more ice* because it holds more moisture.

Thus, even on a warm day, if it's humid, carburettor icing is a danger, especially with small throttle openings where there's less area for the ice to block off in the first place (such as when descending, or at low power settings). Also, the temperature drop (between the OAT and that in the venturi) can be anywhere between 20-30°C, so icing can happen even when the OAT is as high as 21°C (70°F), or more. Tests have produced icing at descent power at temperatures above 30°C, with a relative humidity below 30%, in clear air. Because it is more volatile, and likely to contain more water, you can expect more fuel and carb icing with MOGAS than with AVGAS.

 These values are above 0°C OAT - *airframe* icing only occurs at sub-zero temperatures (with the possible exception of hoar frost).

Carb icing usually arises from the action of the venturi in the throat, just before the butterfly, so it is most likely in the *venturi* and the *throttle valve*, at low power settings. The first indication of such icing during the cruise in an aircraft with a constant speed propeller is most likely to be a decrease in manifold pressure.

Fuel freezing may be prevented with additives.

Note that carb ice is not only a function of the engine and atmospheric conditions, it can also be due to intake design. A PA 28 is less inclined to get carb icing than a DR400, even though both have the same engine and carb.

Impact Icing

In piston engines, impact icing restricts the flow of air into the engine by blocking the intakes.

In turbine engines, icing can occur at high revolutions, with water droplets in cloud or fog (or clear air if the relative humidity is high enough) at temperatures up to around +5°C. It can form across and near the intakes, and can break off and cause damage to the blades inside. High airspeeds increase the mass flow of air entering into the engine, and the number of water droplets. The pressure reduction inside the intake can also cause an adiabatic temperature decrease.

Carburettor Heat

 If you pass the air going into the carburettor across the hot air coming from the exhaust manifold, you can warm it up and prevent ice from occurring. This is controlled by a carburettor heat control in the cockpit. Usually, a temperature gauge is used with an arc on it, showing the danger range. Use carb heat to keep the needle in the right place.

 Carb heat reduces air *density*, so the mixture gets *richer*, to decrease engine performance. Try not to use it on the ground as it bypasses the air filter into the carburettor.

Tip: If you decide that you need carb heat, you will need it quickly, as things are getting worse! To improve the effect, use the leanest setting you can manage without making the engine stumble. You're not developing full power with carb ice anyway, so you're not going to damage it by overleaning (carb ice will have made the mixture richer anyway, but leaning it to normal and thereafter to peak lean will result in more heat from the exhaust, which increases the carb heat that you need.

As the carb heat begins to have an effect, consider flying at a reduced power setting (and leaning more if need be), as less volume of air going through the carb at the lower power setting needs less total heat to warm it and melt ice.

Apply carb heat just before the power is reduced to approach a runway, because the heat exchanger will have the most heat in it. Otherwise, if the carb should ice up during a glide approach, you won't know it has done so until you try to go around and it's awfully quiet when you open the throttle. Only turn it off within gliding range of the threshold because it is using unfiltered air.

Also, do not use carburettor heat for long periods, and do not take off with it on unless the flight manual says you can. With smaller engines, use full settings for every application - that is, carb heat either on or off, with no in-betweens - the greatest risk is at reduced power.

Rough running may increase as melted ice goes through the engine. Also, be careful you don't get an overboost or too high an RPM when you reselect cold. Of course, piston-engined aeroplanes have an advantage if the engine stops from carb icing, as the propeller keeps the engine turning, giving you a chance to do something about it.

Fuel Injection   021 10 04 02

Most of the above problems with the carburettor are avoided with fuel injection, where fuel is metered directly to the cylinders according to power requirements, automatically taking air density into account. Ice is not formed because there is no carburettor and hence a venturi to create drops in temperature (the float chamber is replaced with an engine driven pump).

The fuel is also atomised more thoroughly as it is forced in a continuous stream through a small nozzle at high pressure. The process is thus more precise than a carburettor, which uses a more scattergun approach, where cylinders get excess fuel. As a result of fuel injection, engine response is quicker and smoother, fuel efficiency is improved (you need less fuel for the same power output) and exhaust emissions are cleaner. The process of delivering the fuel is known as **fuel metering**.

Most systems are mechanical, but injection timing may be controlled electrically (backed up mechanically). One benefit is being able to use it without the engine running, which is useful for priming.

There are three methods of delivery:

- Direct
- Indirect
- Injection carburettor

The injectors* are spring loaded valves which open and close at specific pressures to pump fuel into the cylinder head. The pump will include a rotating disc valve that rotates at half engine speed to distribute fuel to each cylinder in turn.

*The pressure injector delivers fuel to the jets constantly.

Engine RPM is controlled by another disc which is operated by the throttle lever. This controls the length of time that the injector is open.

Most systems also have a speed limiting governor in which more fuel than is required is forced into a **governed fuel chamber** that is separated by a diaphragm from the **metered fuel chamber**. Thus, the pressure in the governed chamber is always constant (any excess goes through a relief valve).

As the governor rotates, its bobweights fly out to open a **needle valve** that allows the fuel to proceed into the **metered fuel chamber**, where the difference in pressure between the governed and metered chambers acting on the diaphragm is used to try and close the needle valve and balance its movements. The pressure across the diaphragm is proportional to the square of the RPM, so the fuel flow through the jets varies directly with engine speed. The fuel flow through the **main jet** is governed by **boost pressure** and **exhaust back pressure**. Increasing the boost (with the throttle) compresses a series of evacuated **MAP** (Manifold Absolute Pressure) **capsules**. This makes the main metering needle withdraw from the main jet to increase the fuel flow through it because the hole gets bigger (the needle is tapered to automatically control the mixture strength).

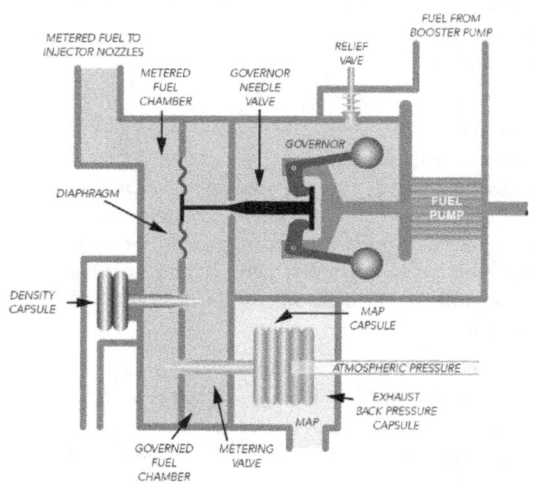

Normally, as atmospheric pressure falls with altitude, the exhaust gases find it easier to escape, as the pressure differential between the inside and the outside of the engine is larger. This improves volumetric efficiency because more of the fuel/air mixture can be pulled in. With a carburettor, the extra depression automatically pulls more fuel into the throat to keep the mixture correct but, in an injected system, some compensation is needed, or the mixture would be weak (the improved volumetric efficiency makes more air in the manifold available to be drawn into the cylinders). This is provided by **back pressure capsules**, which are connected internally to atmospheric pressure, and externally to the MAP capsules. As altitude increases, the back pressure capsules are compressed by the greater difference between MAP and atmospheric pressure, opening the main needle valve. To compensate for the reduction in density of the inlet charge when the temperature increases, a thermometer bulb in the inlet manifold controls the position of a second capsule-controlled needle valve. The capsule chamber is connected to the thermometer bulb by a liquid-filled capillary tube. When the manifold air temperature increases, the liquid expands and compresses the capsule. This closes the needle valve, reducing the fuel flow to match the air density.

A common problem with fuel injected engines is blocked jets, from dirt in fuel, which is why there has to be an efficient filtering system.

Superchargers

When the piston descends during the induction stroke, the pressure in the cylinder is lowered from the suction effect, which allows the fuel/air mixture to be pushed in by atmospheric pressure. This also means that the density (and mass) of the charge is less than it could be. The power output from a piston engine is directly proportional to the pressure of the charge, or that in the induction system (inlet manifold) during the induction stroke (this would be the *Manifold Absolute Pressure,* or MAP, as it indicates the pressure above absolute zero. It is measured between the throttle and inlet valves). When using a fixed pitch propeller, monitoring the MAP is essential to ensure that not too much torque is being applied to the propeller.

In other words, as the supply of air (and therefore oxygen) reduces with height, less air (or, rather, oxygen) gets in to the carburettor and not all the fuel will be burnt, so your power available will be less than the maximum possible. If air is forced into the cylinders under a pressure that is higher than atmospheric, you can artificially increase its density, and the volumetric efficiency of the engine is improved because the horsepower developed depends on engine RPM and the fuel/air mixture (manifold pressure) going into the engine.

The more air you pack into a smaller space, the more oxygen will be included, so you have to add more fuel to keep the mixture correct. The power output increases slightly anyway in the climb, because the exhaust back pressure and inlet temperature reduce, to increase volumetric efficiency.

The supercharger's function is to *increase the service ceiling* of an aircraft,* by compressing the fuel/air mixture to *maintain sea level power at altitude,* although it is more accurate to say that a supercharged engine, at whatever height, will produce as much power as an unsupercharged engine of similar capacity and RPM would at ground level. If you allowed it to, the supercharged engine would give out too much power at ground level, so you either have to restrict what it can do or make it very strong, which will make it heavier.

*The pressure altitude where the ROC reduces to a specific low value at full climb thrust, such as 100 fpm. The **absolute ceiling** is when you can only (just) maintain level flight.

The **rated height** is that at which ground level power can be maintained.

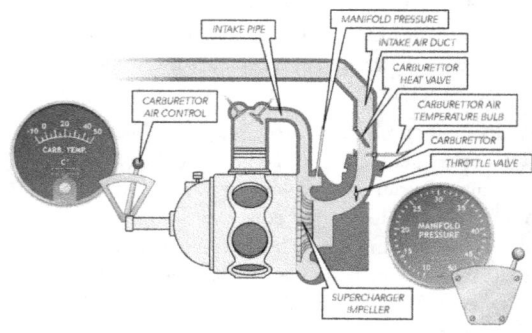

The supercharger maintains a mass flow rate with a constant inlet pressure and a reducing outlet pressure, as the exhaust gases can escape more easily, so power increases to full throttle altitude, then decreases. Its RPM cannot be changed because it is directly linked to the engine, so the air supply is controlled by the throttle, which is why the supercharger is downstream of it, aside from allowing the fuel vapour to help cool the compressed air. In this case, the output pressure is equal to the MAP. The lowest pressure is downstream of the throttle.

The supercharger gives the fuel/air mix a high velocity which is gradually reduced as it passes through diffuser vanes, to increase the pressure in the induction manifold. That is, kinetic energy is changed into pressure energy. Pressure is greatest at the supercharger outlet, as indicated on the MAP gauge, the reading of which should be constant from sea level to the *critical altitude*, which is the highest that can be attained for a given MAP, or the pressure altitude at which the waste gate of a turbocharger is fully closed (see below).

Although some work is wasted and the efficiency of the cycle is reduced because of the increased weight of the aircraft and the engine has to drive the supercharger. The overall result is an improvement in power of around 40% for the same fuel consumption. Compressing the air by up to three or more times the ambient pressure increases its temperature, so you can use a smaller compression ratio because the engine doesn't have to work so hard. However, if it gets too high, detonation could occur, so the compressed air is fed into the manifold *beyond* the carburettor so that the fuel, as it vaporises, will cool it.

Having said that, a high performance supercharger may use an **intercooler** instead, which will widen the detonation margin (intercoolers offer so much detonation protection that they are a high priority with turbochargers, described below). As supercharging is similar to increasing the compression ratio, you need high octane fuel. Also, at high altitudes, when throttled back to avoid overboosting, the temperature in the carburettor may drop low enough to cause ice to form at the butterfly, even at full rated power*. This is why many supercharged aircraft have a carburettor air temperature gauge. With a rated altitude of 12,000 feet, the temperature rise across a supercharger would be in the order of 150°C.

*The maximum horsepower that can be obtained from an engine safely operated at continuous power.

The most common type of supercharger is centrifugal (with a *radial compressor*) run directly from the engine, (typically 9 times the crankshaft speed) between the carburettor and the inlet manifold. A two-stage supercharger has two rotating impellers, with the output from the first connected as the input to the second.

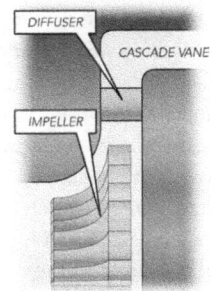

Automatic Boost Control

The crude method of restricting the power output is simply to place a gate on the throttle, which can be over-ridden in an emergency. A more elegant way is to place an evacuated capsule between the throttle and the butterfly valve which opens the butterfly automatically until it is fully open at the rated altitude. In other words, the length of the throttle linkage changes as the capsule contracts or expands, which ultimately controls the weight of charge entering the cylinder. The capsule is exposed to the inlet pressure while being linked to the throttle via an oil operated servo piston. The oil comes from the engine lubrication system.

When the capsule is compressed, the throttle is partly closed, and *vice versa*. When the engine starts, the induction manifold pressure falls to a low value which is sensed by the capsule, which expands, to make oil flow below the servo piston, which is forced to the top of its stroke. If the throttle is opened any more, the capsules compress and the oil supply is eventually cut off and re-directed above the piston, to make it go down and close the throttle. The boost cannot rise above the *rated boost*, which is the maximum continuous value that can be selected (it can be exceeded with an override for take-offs and emergencies).

 Rated boost is less than takeoff boost.

When things are in equilibrium, any tendency for pressure to fall in the inlet is counteracted by a progressive opening of the throttle because more oil is introduced underneath the servo piston until you reach the altitude where the throttle is fully open. This *rated altitude* is that, above which, the induction manifold pressure *falls*, just like it does with a normally aspirated engine. The *full throttle height* is the altitude up to which a given boost setting can be maintained at a given engine RPM, so the lower the boost pressure you select, the higher it can be maintained by the automatic system. The rated altitude is also full throttle height at rated boost and normal RPM for that boost.

HANDLING

With superchargers, engine speed should be kept as low as possible to minimise losses from friction and adiabatic heating, which will cause the charge's density to reduce, followed by the engine power. You get maximum efficiency with the throttle fully open and the engine RPM as low as it can be without causing detonation. Two-speed superchargers, which use variable gearing, are an attempt to overcome the problems of operating the engine at high speeds at high altitudes.

 Superchargers (and turbochargers) need special attention, especially when they are older, as under- or overboosting (with full power or descending rapidly) can cause significant damage.

Turbochargers

Because they are internal devices, and driven by the engine, superchargers can use up a lot of power (150 HP in a Merlin) and therefore fuel, increasing costs and reducing the range of the aircraft. They must also be controlled and continually adjusted by the pilot. Turbochargers use the engine's spent exhaust gases to operate an automatic *wastegate* in parallel with the turbocharger so they are external exhaust-driven superchargers. In fact, the word *turbocharger* is a contraction of *turbosupercharger*.

A turbocharger is an external device that operates *before* the carburettor or fuel metering device. It is *ground boosted* when it maintains a manifold pressure above sea level. The control system tries to maintain a constant boost pressure, but a pressure ratio controller senses the altitude and limits the manifold pressure in the climb. The amount of power in the exhaust gas depends on the difference between the exhaust pressure and the outside air pressure, which increases with altitude.

This allows a turbocharger to compensate for changing altitude without using up any extra power by driving all that machinery. In other words, the manifold pressure is controlled within preset parameters, and as long as the system is working properly and the pilot is smooth on the controls, a turbocharger will not overboost the engine and damage it.

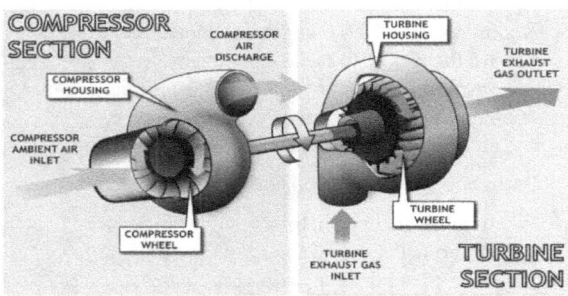

 As the exhaust is involved, preflight checks should include security of the exhaust pipes, so that carbon monoxide doesn't get into the cabin.

Turbochargers provide a constant *air pressure* to the engine, but the air temperature is increased from the compression so, at higher temperatures, the density of air supplied to the engine is less anyway, which is why you will never obtain the full theoretical capability of the turbocharger. The reduced density reduces volumetric efficiency, which can be partly restored with an aftercooler. *Turbocharger intercoolers* (between the compressor and throttle) prevent detonation at high altitudes, using ambient air to cool the intake air. The lowest pressure is downstream of the air filter. The output pressure is always higher than MAP, as the manifold is downstream of the butterfly, which lowers the pressure even when it is fully open.

The power output of a turbocharger decreases until the critical altitude, then decreases at a faster rate because the exhaust back pressure increases and the gases cannot escape so easily.

BOOTSTRAPPING

This is a condition that occurs at high altitude and low engine RPM, which can be made to disappear by increasing RPM or descending. It is an over-reaction to rapid throttle movement, caused by inertia of the rotating assemblies, leading to large pressure fluctuations and overboosting. A pressure relief valve in the induction manifold also cures it. Cessna defines it as "The unstable manifold pressure condition that occurs when the wastegate closes at high altitude under low RPM operation." In other words, it occurs when the manifold pressure begins to fall off as the RPM is reduced. The wastegate has fully closed and the turbo is not spinning fast enough to produce the desired manifold pressure. Controls should be moved smoothly and not too rapidly, and in the correct sequence.

Tip: To preserve the life of the turbocharger, let the engine run for a little while before shutting it down (check the flight manual for minimum times - usually 2 minutes), to stabilise the temperature and reduce the chances of distortion or having the engine oil which lubricates it coking (caking) on hotspots.

THE WASTEGATE

Without a wastegate, the amount of boost created by a turbocharger varies with the pressure of the engine's exhaust, which varies with engine speed. At higher RPM, therefore, more boost will be created. However, most engines can only take about 10 PSI, if not less. With a wastegate, once the engine produces more exhaust pressure than the system will allow, a flap opens to redirect excess exhaust away from the turbine blades. That is, when the waste gate is open, the exhaust gases are being dumped overboard before reaching the turbine blades. The wastegate is opened by a spring, and closed with oil pressure, so it is a fail-safe system. As exhaust back pressure increases when the wastegate is closed, engine power reduces slightly. As the temperature reduces, this means that engine power remains much the same up to full throttle height for that power.

If the waste gate seizes in the climb before reaching the critical altitude, the manifold pressure decreases.

There are two types of wastegate:

- An **internal** wastegate lives on the turbo unit itself. The gate is opened via an actuator which driven by a diaphragm. Excess exhaust gas is then fed directly into the exhaust system.

- An **external** wastegate is separate from the turbo unit and does not require an actuator. Excess exhaust gas can either be fed into the exhaust system or it can be vented straight out and into the atmosphere. External wastegates generally use a valve like the poppet valve in the cylinder head. However, they are controlled by pneumatics rather than a camshaft and open in the opposite direction

Most modern turbocharged aircraft use a hydraulic wastegate control with engine oil as the fluid. A wastegate is closed by oil pressure and opened by spring pressure.

On the oil output side of the wastegate actuator (i.e. *downstream*) sits the density controller, an air-controlled oil valve which senses upper deck pressure and controls how fast oil can bleed from the wastegate actuator back to the engine at full throttle. As you climb and air density drops, the density controller slowly closes the valve and traps more oil in the actuator, closing the wastegate to increase the speed of the turbocharger and maintain rated power. If the waste gate seizes with the throttle open in a descent, you will get an increase in power that may cause you to exceed the maximum Manifold Air Pressure, as well as cylinder head temperature limits.

ENGINES
Turbines

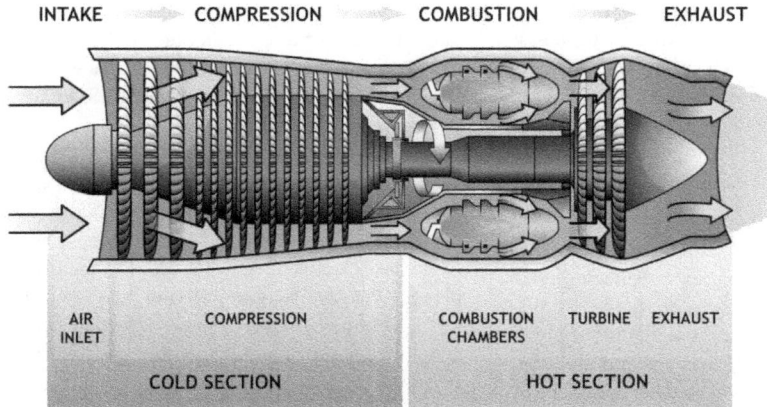

TURBINES

The same principles apply to jet engines as reciprocating ones, only they're applied in a different way. For example, in the piston engine, part or all of the functions of induction, compression, power and exhaust happen in the combustion chamber, which is not necessarily the best place for them all. A turbine engine's components can be designed specially for their tasks. Turbines are lighter and produce more power than piston engines do, although they are precision instruments because they spin faster, and must be handled more gently.

Turbines also use cheaper fuel, because compression is not a factor in producing their power, although avgas can sometimes be mixed with jet fuel (see the flight manual), at the expense of reduced maintenance periods, because it doesn't lubricate the fuel pumps so well (there is also a lot of crud* left on the turbine blades from the anti-knock additives and, being a thin fuel, will "bubble out" quicker at lower altitudes. It extracts heat and allows vapour bubbles to form in fuel lines, to create air locks).

Whereas a piston engine relies on a precisely timed sequence of individual events, with all the bits flying back and forth violently, jet engines just spin round, although their "simplicity" depends hugely on their quality of design and manufacture. Also, jet engines run on a continuous cycle (the *Brayton Cycle*), with everything happening at the same time, at *constant pressure* (piston engines are *constant volume*). A typical air-fuel ratio is 60:1.

During the cycle, there are changes in temperature, pressure and volume. Combining Boyle's and Charles' laws means that the product of pressure and volume of a gas is proportional to its absolute temperature, so heat changes are directly proportional to the work added to or taken from the gas flow. The changes occur at 3 places:

- Air enters the engine at A, and is compressed adiabatically up till B. Pressure and temperature increase, and volume decreases.
- During combustion (B to C), fuel is added and burnt, so the temperature and volume increase while pressure remains more or less constant (there is a small drop from the velocity increase).
- From C to D the gases expand adiabatically through the turbine and jet pipe, back to atmosphere. Some of the energy is converted into mechanical power by the turbine, reducing the pressure, temperature and velocity, and the rest provides the propulsion.

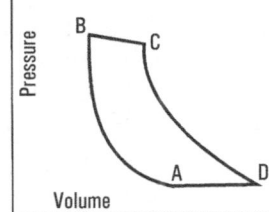

A turbine is lighter and produces more power than a piston engine, although it is much more of a precision instrument because it spins faster, and needs to be handled more gently.

In a jet aeroplane, thrust is used to propel the machine forward directly. In a turboprop, the stream of hot gases is intercepted by a turbine, which drives a propeller gearbox. Unfortunately, about two thirds of the energy thus produced is simply used to keep the engine running. Most of the rest is used by the power turbine to drive the gearbox and blades, leaving just enough energy to ensure the hot gases fall out of the engine by themselves, so you don't need extra components to drain more energy. As hot air is used in this way, the engine is called a *gas producer*, and the output is measured in shaft horsepower. In other words, the engine's function is to produce enough hot air to spin the turbines that drive the propellers.

 The first point for the transitioning pilot to grasp is that the payback for mistreating a piston engine is immediate, and likely to affect you directly, whereas that with a turbine may affect a pilot further down, as damage is cumulative.

Due to thermal wear and shock, starting up puts more wear and tear on a turbine engine than any other operation, within certain limits. Consequently, *start cycles* on the engine are counted, meaning that you count the number of starts you do during the day and put them in the Tech Log when you finish flying. Cycles can be more important than total hours, especially when you fly short missions. If you divide the cost of an engine by the start cycles you are allowed, it will give you an idea of how much it costs just to start the machine up.

Tip: One of the biggest things to unlearn when moving from piston to turbine is to keep your finger on the starter button once things start happening (with a piston, you tend to take your finger off straight away when the engine starts) - now you *don't* take your finger off *until the engine becomes self-sustaining*. Before then, it relies heavily on the battery to keep it turning. It follows that, if the battery is weak, the engine won't spin as fast, the cooling airflow is reduced, the whole process becomes hotter and you could melt the back end with a hot start, aside from losing the instruments if you have an EFIS display, so you won't see what's going on to stop it anyway. *Always check the voltage from the battery before starting a turbine engine!*

Learn to recognize a weak battery by how rapidly the igniter snaps and how quickly the engine pitch increases as it spins up. Another good ploy is to watch by how much the fuel pressure drops as you hit the starter. If it drops to near zero, the battery is weak. When in doubt, *use external power*. If the aircraft doesn't fly much, a NiCad battery will get worse between deep cycles, and even sitting for a day will make it lose its charge.

Hot starts are mainly due to:
- finger trouble
- a weak battery
- suspect fuel control

You can help avoid the finger trouble by making sure the throttle is fully closed *before* you press the starter button.

A *hung start* exists (at very low RPM, or below ground idle) when the fuel has been introduced before the engine has been accelerated enough by the starter. It just sits there, weakening the battery, and the throughput of fuel is not enough to accelerate the engine, so the temperature increases. You get a *wet start* when the engine doesn't light off at all (e.g. it's flooded), in which case you should wait a while and vent the engine before starting again. It is even more important to have airflow for cooling at this point, so an external start is also recommended.

If you believe a hot start is imminent, the procedure is to roll the throttle closed, past the idle stop *while continuing to motor the starter!* **Read that again**. Release the starter in such a case and the Turbine Outlet Temperature (TOT) will skyrocket, and there's nothing you can do to stop it - remember, *the starter motors the compressor stages*, which channel cool air through the engine. Unless cool air keeps moving the exhaust gases on their way out, the turbine will suffer damage. If you have time, pull the igniter circuit breaker as well, but if the throttle is closed, there should not be any fuel getting through anyway.

Tip: When you reduce power in normal flight, the engine RPM will slow down as less fuel is pumped through it, and if you want to increase power, there will be a slight delay as the engine spools up to the speed required. In fact, as you make the demand for power, the engine will continue spooling *down*, then start spooling up. It is therefore important to learn to anticipate power demands to reduce the chances of the engine surging (see *The Compressor*, below).

Thrust Distribution

Whereas a piston engine is controlled by varying the *airflow*, power (or thrust) in a jet is varied by changing the *fuel flow*, to create more heat and expansion and keep the internal pressure constant. Newton's third law (the one about opposite reactions) applies to jets and propeller driven aircraft.

Turbine engines create continuously expanding gases, the energy from which is used for propulsion. Thrust is equal to the change in momentum of the air entering and leaving, which is the reaction to the force required to accelerate a mass of air through the system, varying with changes in TAS. In fact, one formula is:

$$\text{Thrust} = \text{Mass Flow} \times V_{ex} - S$$

Where V_{ex} is the exhaust velocity and S is the speed of the aircraft (see below for variations). In other words, thrust is the product of mass airflow and acceleration, as assisted by the temperature gradient from the front to the back of the engine, plus the density of the air entering the engine. The colder it is, the more thrust you get because of the larger mass of air contained in a smaller volume (thrust depends on mass flow).

You get the highest thrust values at low airspeeds, with the maximum at zero, as limited by the maximum turbine temperature, which depends on how well the components cope with heat. You get zero thrust when the exhaust velocity equals the TAS (i.e. in the cruise).

To find the **static thrust** (at full power with the wheels chocked), use this formula:

$$\text{Thrust} = \frac{WV}{g}$$

To find **dynamic thrust** (at full power when airborne):

$$\text{Thrust} = \frac{W \times (V2 - V1)}{g}$$

Where *W* is the total weight of air passing through the engine over a given period of time (i.e. lbs per second), *V1* is the initial velocity of the air in feet per second at the intake (i.e. the speed of the aircraft), V2 is the final velocity of the air at the jet pipe (V_{ex}). *g* is gravity.

 Both equations are essentially the same but, with static thrust, V1 would be zero, so there is no need to bother with it.

To find the thrust developed in terms of horsepower:

$$\text{THP} = \frac{T \times V}{550}$$

Where *T* is in lbs, *V* is in feet per second and the horsepower is 550 ft/lbs per second.

In some parts of the engine, particularly the combustion chamber, the forces act forward and, in others, they act rearward, due to the changes in pressure and momentum as the gas stream reacts to the rotating components and the engine structure. When work is being done on the gas, as in the forward half of the engine, positive thrust is produced, but when the gas is doing work, as when expanding through the turbine at the rear, the thrust is negative. The amount by which the forward forces exceed the rearward ones is the *rated thrust*, but you can get a little extra with a choked nozzle in the same way as water runs faster through a garden hose by restricting the end.

Certified ratings include *Maximum Takeoff Thrust*, *Maximum Continuous Thrust* and *Go-Around Thrust*.

This picture compares the static pressure and temperature, flow velocity and thrust values averaged over a local cross section of a turbine engine (the air flows from left to right, starting with the diffuser at the free stream velocity).

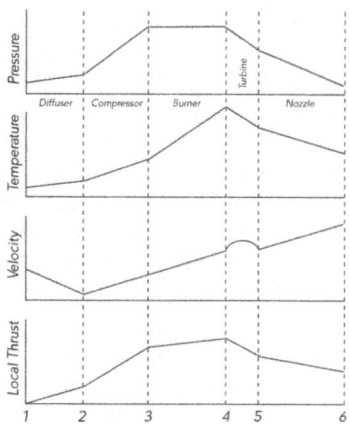

The air is slowed down in the diffuser, so pressure and temperature will increase. The compressor blades then increase them more, then the fuel/air mixture is burnt at constant pressure, but with increasing temperature and velocity until leaving the nozzle.

Note how the thrust increases until the rear of the burner, then it decreases through the turbine and nozzle because it increases the rearward load against the rear face of the burner, reducing the forward load from the impact of the gases against the front faces.

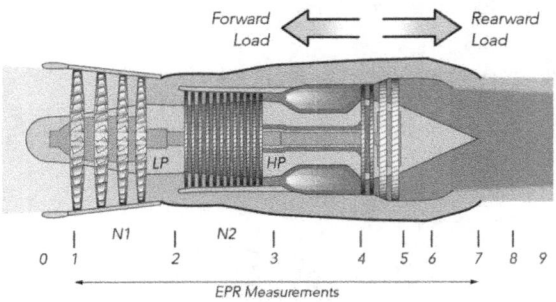

However, the net thrust produced by the engine still has a positive value.

STATION NUMBERS

Locations on engines are given station numbers for ease of reference. For example, the term T4 means the temperature at Station 4.

Free stream conditions are labelled 0 and the entrance to the inlet is Station 1. The exit of the inlet, or the beginning of the compressor, is Station 2. The compressor exit and burner entrance is Station 3 while the burner exit and turbine entrance is Station 4. The exit of the turbine is Station 5 and the flow conditions upstream of the afterburner occur at Station 6. Station 7 is at the entrance to the nozzle and station 8 is at the nozzle throat. Some nozzles have an additional section downstream of the throat which would be Station 9.

CONVERSION OF ENERGY

Energy (or the capacity to do work) comes in two forms, *potential* and *kinetic*. There is a constant interchange between the two in that fuel (before it is burnt) contains potential energy, and the kinetic energy is from motion of the air. With gas turbines, the energy from *pressure*, *heat* and *velocity* is constantly being changed from one form to another although, in the combustion chamber, heat energy is added from burning fuel. The conversions (on subsonic airflows) are done with convergent and divergent ducts, after Bernoulli.

- In a **convergent** duct, velocity increases, and (static) pressure and temperature decrease.
- In a **divergent** duct, velocity decreases, and (static) pressure and temperature increase.

For example, the nozzle forms a convergent duct which increases the velocity of the gas stream, in high thrust conditions reaching the speed of sound. Unless you increase the temperature, and hence the speed of sound, this is the maximum (this produces *nozzle thrust* on top of *momentum thrust*. The two combined produce *net thrust*). At constant RPM, the pressure ratio of the compressor and the temperature rise across it remain constant above the theoretical tropopause. As you climb, and density decreases, however, the mass flow into the engine reduces and the fuel supply must be reduced to stop the turbine getting too hot. This effect is offset a little, because the ambient air temperature will also have reduced, which lowers the temperature of the air after compression.

As the lower temperature also increases the air density slightly, the greater mass of air entering the engine plus the lower temperature after compression allows a little more fuel to be burnt without exceeding temperature limits. However, because the air temperature starts to remain constant at 36,090 feet, this effect reduces, so that the optimum cruising level for a jet is 36,000 feet.

The higher expansion ratio (from the higher temperature inside the engine) gives the gas more momentum on its way out, which is why gas turbine engines are more efficient at higher altitudes - you get more thrust per pound of air. The engine's power output reduces at a lower rate than the air density does.

Humidity reduces air density, but the moisture content has a cooling effect on the air before it starts to burn. To keep the temperature at the entry to the turbine the same, the fuel flow should be increased.

On a cold day, the mass of air entering the engine is greater, and so is the thrust, but more power is required to drive the compressor, so more fuel is needed to keep the speed up (on a hot day, this is reversed). If the fuel control system does not pump more fuel through, the engine will slow down. In some aircraft, the fuel flow remains constant at low temperatures and, although RPM may fall, the mass flow is greater and thrust will stay the same.

Thrust is the force developed by the engines to move the aeroplane forward. In a jet, the loads from the changes in momentum and pressure of the gases on the engine structure (the forward load) are the thrust forces, which often exceed whatever's coming out of the back. The excess forward force from the rearward flow of gases is called the rated thrust of the engine. It is measured by comparing the discharge pressure with that of the intake, or the Engine Pressure Ratio (EPR). At constant RPM, the thrust is directly proportional to the airspeed.

THROTTLE POSITION

Thrust with a piston/propeller combination is proportional to the engine RPM, MAP and propeller blade angle. At constant RPM, therefore, thrust is proportional to the throttle position, meaning that one or two inches of throttle movement at any part of the throttle quadrant produces the same change in thrust.

On a jet, however, thrust is proportional to RPM (mass flow) and temperature (the fuel/air ratio), so you get more thrust per inch at higher engine speeds, where the throttle is in the higher parts of the quadrant. At lower engine speeds, you need to open the levers a lot more. For example, if you increase the N_1 (LP compressor speed) of a CFM56-3 engine (737) from 80-90%, you will add about 5000 lbs of thrust. From 30-40%, you will add only about 1000 lbs, so the Thrust/N_1 curve of a jet engine is logarithmic. Engine thrust is proportional to the ratio of the engine speed to the TAS, around 3.5:2 for a propeller driven aeroplane. This means a considerable delay in producing thrust, especially at low RPM. If you are too heavy on the levers you could overfuel the engine and make the compressor surge, which is described later.

A closed throttle with a piston/propeller aeroplane produces a lot of drag. In fact, at reverse idle, the prop is already producing 60% of its maximum value, even before you engage reverse.

In a jet, there will always be residual thrust, which is why you need thrust reversers and good brakes. Or a long runway. On approach, with no propeller wash, to get more lift you have to accelerate the whole aeroplane.

Engine Construction

Gas turbine engines consist of a series of casings that contain the rotating parts, and a combustion chamber into which the fuel is injected and burnt.

These are essential requirements for any turbine engine:

- A means of compressing the air after entering the intake. This is both to be able to use the engine at low speeds (see *Ramjet*, below), and to increase its temperature and pressure.
- A combustion chamber in which to burn the fuel and make it expand.
- Turbine wheels to extract energy from the hot gases to drive the compressor and maybe (on a turboprop) a transmission.
- A fuel system that supplies the correct quantity of fuel to the combustion chamber at the correct pressure for the amount of air passing through.
- A means of igniting the fuel.
- An exhaust duct.
- A lubrication system.
- A starting system.

In any case, the five basic parts of a jet engine are the *inlet*, the *compressor*, *combustor*, *turbine* and *nozzle* (the bit joining the compressor to the combustor is the *diffuser*, which decreases the velocity of the air flow and increase the temperature). To save space, they could be combined or doubled back on themselves in some engines.

Types Of Engine

Turbine engines come in all shapes and sizes.....

THE RAMJET

The ram jet has no moving parts. It works by passing air entering the intake through a divergent duct, so part of the flow is converted to static pressure energy. Adding heat from combustion increases the total energy, and the expanding hot gas passes through a convergent duct (the propelling nozzle) where some of its heat and static pressure energy are converted to dynamic energy.

The problem is that the ram jet must be moving through the air as the heat energy is added, and aircraft engines need to be working on the ground and at low speeds. This is why a compressor is used, as described below.

However, the ram effect (in a normal gas turbine) is useful in restoring the thrust that is lost as speed is gained. In the graph below, at 400 knots, the thrust from forward movement jumps from around 4,000 lbs to 6,500.

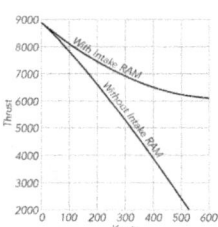

TURBOPROPS

Below about 400 knots, propellers are more efficient than pure jet engines.

In direct drive turboprop engines, the propeller is driven directly from the compressor shaft though a reduction gear assembly, which is not shown in this twin spool axial flow (in line with the engine axis) version:

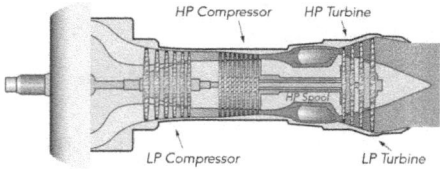

The (hot) expanding gases from the combustion chambers power a high pressure turbine, which is on the same shaft as the high pressure compressor, forming the **HP spool**. Exhaust gas from the HP turbine powers a second turbine that is on the same shaft as the low pressure compressor, forming the **LP spool**. Thus, with a twin spool engine, you get two engines in one. The HP spool is hollow and concentric with the LP spool, but they are mechanically independent, although the HP spool rotates much faster (and is smaller to avoid compressibility problems). This rotating assembly also drives the propeller through reduction gearing.

This one uses a centrifugal compressor as well:

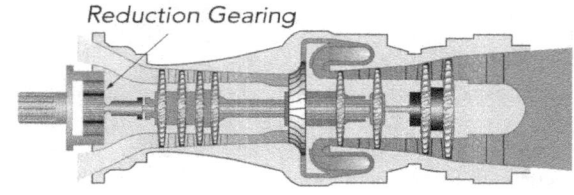

Early examples used one turbine to drive the compressor and the propeller, but more modern engines use a free power turbine that is independent of the compressor.

Free turbine engines are easier to turn by hand when they are stopped because the propeller is only connected to the second stage turbine. This also means that parts can be removed more easily for maintenance.

Direct drive engines are designed to operate at a more or less fixed RPM, so adding power by adding more fuel does not result in a significant change. This means that the internal aerodynamics can be set close to the optimum. Thus, they are more responsive and fuel efficient, but the ground idle speed is high, and can be noisy as a result.

Props at low blade angles after shutdown indicate a direct drive system (due to centrifugal start locks that place them there to lower the resistance to starting). Feathered blades mean a free turbine, because start locks are not required - the starter does not need to drive the whole assembly.

TURBOJET

This is the most basic form of workable gas turbine, with a compressor, combustion chamber and turbine, which extracts just enough energy from the flow of hot air to drive the compressor. The rest escapes through a nozzle, which is convergent for a subsonic aircraft, to provide the high speed acceleration the propels the aircraft forward.

BYPASS

The word *bypass* involves the mixing of hot and cold flows of air - otherwise there is no difference between a bypass or a front fan engine, mentioned below.

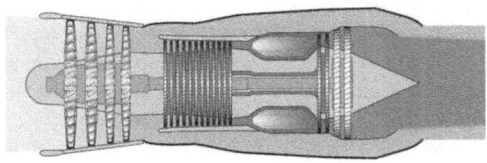

The above is also a twin-spool*, with a 4-stage LP compressor and a 12-stage HP compressor, and high temperatures at the back for greater thrust. Because the air mass flow is way more than that required for combustion, some of the output from the LP compressor is made to bypass the HP compressor, the combustion chambers, and the turbines to mix with the hot gas stream in the exhaust, just upstream of the propelling nozzle.

*The rise in temperature as air flows through a compressor increases the speed of sound, so the high pressure stages of the engine can run at higher speeds without increasing the mass flow through the engine.

Trivia: As a point of interest, bypass and ducted fans (and afterburners) were conceived by Sir Frank Whittle in 1936 before he came up with the turbojet. He was concerned that its propulsive efficiency would be lower (50% at 500 mph) than a propeller would be at moderate speeds. His solution was to gear the jet down by using an extra turbine to drive a low pressure fan that could cope with more air than the engine could and force it back as a cold jet, for a propulsive efficiency of 75% or more. This also resupplied oxygen to the air affected by the afterburner.

Although Whittle's 1932 patent included axial and centrifugal compressors, he chose the centrifugal for his first engine in 1937 because it provided a lower compression ratio and he needed to have it work right from the start because he only had £2,000 to hand rather than the £30,000 he needed. It fired up and worked first time, but it wouldn't shut down due to the fuel pooling in the combustion chamber.

For reasons best known to themselves, the Air Ministry at the time decided that no useful results would be gained from Whittle's work, and people would not want to fly faster than 250 mph anyway*, so the bypass was never exploited. With a more progressive attitude, something like the Meteor would have been ready in 1939.

*The Under Secretary of State for Air said in 1934:

> "Scientific investigation into the possibilities of jet propulsion has given no indication that this method can be a serious competitor to the airscrew engine combination....."

It was a similar story with radar. Go figure.

The lower gas velocity is offset by the much greater mass flow, to create significantly more thrust than the single-spool pure jet. As well, the lower exit velocity of the gas means that there is less noise. The ratio of unheated (cold) air to the hot air heated by combustion, is known as the *bypass ratio*. In this case, the ratio is less than 2:1, so it is a low bypass engine (supersonic aircraft are unlikely to need more than 1.5, often around 0.2. or 0.3).

The bypass ratio is found by dividing the external mass flow by the internal mass flow (or the difference between the amount of air accelerated only by the fan against that passing through the engine). The higher the figure, the more efficient the engine, at the expense of maximum thrust capability because the turbine drives larger fans (its rotation speed is also limited by tip speed, or shock stall). Thus, a turbofan engine with a bypass mass flow of 300 kg/s and 50 kg/s through the HP compressor has a bypass ratio of 6.

This not only gives better thrust (actually, more than double), but also provides cooling, and less noise, because the temperature differential between the gases and the air is not so great. It's also quite good at keeping ice crystals away from the engine core. The result is a large, relatively slow-moving column of cold air enclosing a thin, hot and fast exhaust, so the basic turbofan imparts a moderate change in velocity to a moderate mass of air. The back of the engine runs a lot hotter, though, even white-hot in the early days. Low bypass (or turbojet) engines are noisiest from behind, and high bypass is noisiest from the front.

The fan blades, for interest, are built to bend and recover if they get struck by anything up to a 4 lb goose (in fact, an RB 211-535 engine on a 757 once sucked in and spat out four Canada geese without a burp). Their spinners are designed to deflect rain and/or hail into the bypass duct. If the LP shaft in a twin spool gas turbine engine ruptures, the LP turbine may overspeed.

TURBOFAN

As you can get more thrust from a larger stream of slow moving air, the *fanjet*, or *turbofan*, is a low speed propeller (with lots of blades) enclosed in a duct, driven by the low pressure (LP) part of the compressor (and the rearmost turbine), so you don't waste power from air that spills centrifugally out of the sides, and you don't get the compressibility effects that you would get with propellers.

This is a triple spool ducted fan engine.

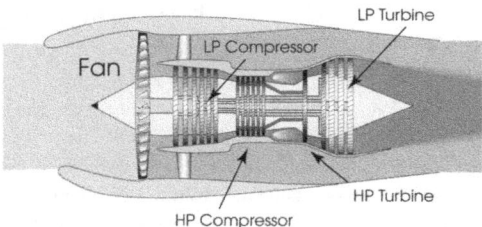

One advantage with three spools is that you don't need so many variable guide vanes to prevent compressor stall at low speeds. They all run inside each other, with the HP turbine driving the HP compressor, the LP turbine driving the LP compressor, and a final turbine driving the ducted fan (in a twin spool, the LP compressor drives the fan and runs at the same speed).

The mass of air accelerated by the fan is at least 5 times greater than that passing through the engine. With virtually no tip losses, and acceleration of the fan air through a propelling nozzle, the thrust produced is much greater than you would get from a propeller driven with the same shaft horsepower. Thus, the propulsive efficiency is better than that of the low bypass engine and is maintained to higher airspeed than the turboprop. Varying the thrust should not be done too frequently, because low cycle fatigue for the HP turbine blades is more severe. Another problem (during starting) is that you may get no N_1 rotation, even though the N_2 is accelerating normally.

After successfully starting a high bypass turbofan engine, the air starter is centrifugally disengaged by the coupling between the N_2 spool and the starter.

The ducted fan at the front acts as a first stage compressor and accelerates air around the outside of the engine so that the airflows mix downstream of the turbine. As this air is not burned, it does not accelerate so much, less kinetic energy is imparted to it and the process is more efficient. Around 70% of the thrust can be produced by the fan.

For best economy and low noise, subsonic turbofans have a bypass ratio of between 5:1 to 8:1, or more, so the LP compressor (fan) is very large.

The Inlet

This is where air enters the system. Although the inlet is normally considered to be part of the airframe, it can contribute a lot to engine efficiency. Its function is to convert ram-air pressure (from forward movement) into static pressure, ready for the compressor, for which inlet ducts should be as straight and smooth as possible, producing a minimal boundary layer, and delivering the air to the compressor with an even pressure distribution. In fact, the air enters the nozzle at less than the flight speed* and is further slowed before the compressor (below) causes a substantial rise in pressure and temperature.

*The inlet velocity is actually at flight speed, but in the opposite direction. The jet pipe velocity goes the other way, much faster - it is this difference that produces thrust.

In fact, the air intake should do three things:

- Let in the maximum amount of air from the free stream to the engine.
- Diffuse the airflow with minimum losses, so the air is delivered to the compressor at the maximum pressure with minimum turbulence (as close as possible to total free stream pressure).
- Create as little drag as possible.

The shape of a duct is used to change the velocity and pressure of the air as it flows through the engine.

- In a **convergent** duct, velocity increases, and (static) pressure and temperature decrease.
- In a **divergent** duct, velocity decreases, and (static) pressure and temperature increase.

As momentum is the product of *mass x velocity*, any increase in either will increase thrust in proportion so, other things being equal, an increase in airspeed leads to more air being compressed at the intake and a greater mass of air entering the engine. *Total head pressure* is the air pressure when it is brought to rest in front of anything moving through it, and it increases with aircraft speed. However, some of it is lost through skin friction, the formation of shock waves and the increased temperature (through compression). To get the maximum effect, you need as great a *pressure recovery factor* as possible. The smoothest flow through the compressor is at around 0.4M at the compressor inlet, where the air pressure should also be evenly distributed.

In subsonic aircraft, the inlet ducts are divergent and therefore act as diffusers. Supersonic aircraft use convergent ducts, but when subsonic, they need the opposite, so supersonic aircraft use variable geometry.

For subsonic to low supersonic speeds, the ideal shape for an intake is the short, circular*, pitot type. Pressure recovery is possible because it is divergent - its diameter is less at the front. This means that the air is slowed down and compressed before it gets to the compressor. At higher speeds, shock waves at the lip impair the airflow and the pressure recovery. Having said that, shock waves can be used to slow air down on purpose, as used in the *External/Internal Compression Intake*.

*This may have to be modified for the fuselage or wings.

At high Mach numbers, you must change the throat area and use spill valves to keep the airflow under control (a problem with Concord). Spill valves prevent turbulence over the face of the compressor at low speeds by dumping air overboard. A wedge decreases or increases the throat area as it moves in or out.

Because the air is slowed down before being accelerated again, the resulting *intake momentum drag* reduces the potential thrust. Low bypass engines suffer from this initially, but thrust will increase slightly but steadily above M0.5 as mass flow increases. High bypass engines, on the other hand, reduce thrust as Mach number increases. Blow-in doors at the inlet provide the engine with additional air at high power settings and low air speeds.

Jet thrust decreases generally with increased altitude and temperature, which is shown by the limiting TGT (*Total Gas Temperature*). If this stops you applying more power, a lower OAT allows a little more RPM, and throughput of air, and thrust. Of course, if it's very cold outside, you will hit compressor RPM limits before the TGT. Either way, thrust has a finite limit.

Above an ambient temperature of ISA +15°C, thrust varies with temperature. It is constant below that because it is independent of the air temperature (the engine is *flat rated*). The 737 uses N_1 (LP compressor RPM) as an indication of power, but others use EPR, explained in the *Compressor* section, below. Note that *power* is a measure of *thrust* x *speed*, so it is not the same as thrust.

Speaking of 737s, if you increase N_1 of a CFM56-3 engine from 80-90%, you will add about 5000 lbs of thrust. From 30-40%, you will add only about 1000 lbs of thrust, so the Thrust/N_1 curve of a jet engine is logarithmic. Engine thrust is approximately proportional to engine speed$^{3.5}$, against speed^2 for a prop aircraft.

PARTICLE SEPARATORS

The air travelling through the inlet may well include other odds and ends, like sand (in the desert), dust, leaves, etc. Various methods are used to combat this, but they do restrict the airflow and have an effect on performance, as filters and separators at the inlet reduce the efficiency of the air intake.

A particle separator uses centrifugal force from inlet air to create small swirls that pick up small particles and drop them into a *sediment trap*.

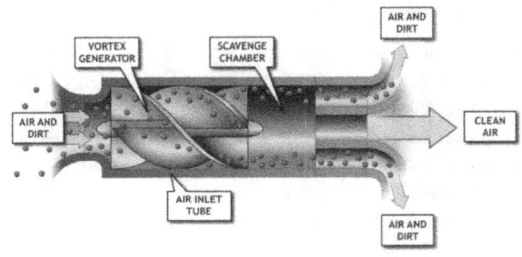

They work with snow as well. The crude method is simply to stick a piece of gauze over the inlet.

The Compressor

After entering the intake, the air is compressed, adding pressure and heat energy which must come from another part of the engine, as energy is not created (or destroyed). Adding heat energy means that less fuel is required. The compressor is a rotating mass of impellers or blades, designed to take vast quantities of air, compress it (and heat it) for onward movement to the combustor (below), so it's an air pump, sometimes with the weight of air that is delivered determined by the engine RPM. That is, for any specified RPM, the volume of air will be a definite amount. The compressor allows you to start moving from zero velocity without a launching device, as is needed for a ramjet. As with a supercharger, compressing air means that you can add more fuel to a given volume of air, plus it increases the velocity of the gases out of the back end.

For maximum efficiency, a compressor must have the least possible pressure loss, to save the turbine from having to drive it so hard. This requires aerodynamic stability, so the tip speeds of the compressor blades should not be close to the speed of sound - 0.9M is about right. A high compression ratio allows a higher pressure in the combustion chamber, which allows a greater pressure differential to the atmosphere, so you get a higher nozzle velocity and more thrust for the same amount of fuel (and frontal area). The compression ratio could be nearly 10:1 for a centrifugal compressor, and 25:1 for an axial, and the temperature rise be up to 750°C. Such high temperatures may restrict the maximum output because less fuel is burnt before the maximum temperature limits at the turbine inlet are reached.

 The air being so hot has some significance if the fire detection system in your machine is set to trigger off at a similar temperature, as a compressor leak could give you a false fire indication.

The compressor is an ideal place from which to tap small amounts of bleed air for other purposes, such as anti-ice, cooling or sealing, where back pressure is used to stop other gases going the wrong way. However, using bleed air reduces that available for cooling so the back end temperature will rise slightly. For anti-ice systems, the bleed is taken from the rear of the compressor (discharge air) because it has already been heated from compression. It will typically flow through the compressor shell and hollow struts, and the inlet guide vanes.

The two types of compressor (axial or centrifugal) both give high kinetic energy to a quantity of air with a high speed rotating element, then convert the energy into pressure through a diffusing stage. Some engines use both types, so they can be made shorter without greatly affecting the cross-sectional area.

CENTRIFUGAL COMPRESSORS

 The centrifugal compressor uses impellers to fling air *outwards* into channels leading to the combustion chamber, via a diffuser, being a development of those used in superchargers. It has a *high compression ratio by stage* and a *large diameter*, so it makes an engine shorter, but wider. However, the large frontal area makes it hard to create multiple stages.

You can place impellers one after the other, or back to back, as in the picture below but, in the latter case, the rear face is less efficient because the air is pre-heated, although there is a greater mass flow without an increase in diameter, producing less drag.

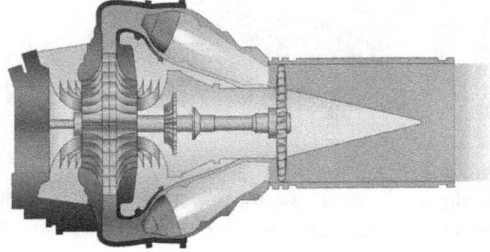

The centrifugal compressor must turn at high speeds to get even a typical pressure ratio of only 3.5:1 (i.e. 3.5 atmospheres), as opposed to the near 40:1 that can be obtained with an axial compressor, below.

As air is accelerated across the face of the impeller, a low pressure is created at the eye, to pull more air in. The rotating guide vanes on the impeller form divergent air passages that increase the velocity of the air and introduce a slight pressure rise across the impeller. They are curved in the direction of rotation to ease the pick up as the air comes in from the front and has to change direction.

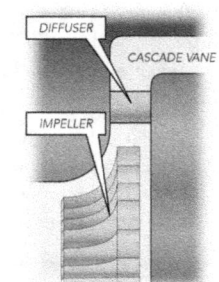

Before it gets here, the air will have passed through a *plenum chamber** which reduces the air's velocity with *swirl vanes*, which also direct the air to the rotating guide vanes at a suitable angle.

*A space around the engine from where the compressor can draw air that is free from foreign bodies.

After the compressor, the air is forced into a diffuser, which surrounds the impeller, and whose vanes form **divergent passages** that slow the air down and increase its pressure **and temperature**, turning kinetic energy into pressure energy to produce the highest value in the engine. The pressure rise between the impeller and diffuser is about 50:50.

The tip clearance between the impeller and the diffuser is critical - too large a gap will cause leakage and one too small will make them rub together (the clearance is about an inch). This scrubbing effect will lead to aerodynamic buffeting which causes unsteady airflow and vibration. The passages are arranged to form the most suitable angle under *running conditions*, so there could be some turbulence outside these.

AXIAL COMPRESSORS

Because the air in a centrifugal compressor has to be bent at high speeds (supersonic in places), there are losses that become more apparent as higher pressures are required.

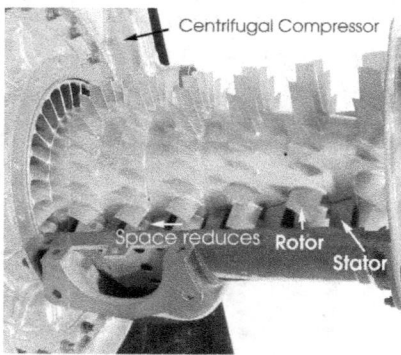

The axial compressor consists of a drum to which are attached rings of rotating blades called *rotors* followed by rings of stationary ones called *stators*, or *stator vanes*, whose purpose is to take out the twist and bend and shape the airflow into the right position for the next rotor wheel: In other words, the air passes alternately through rotors and stators.

Rotors and stators have aerofoil sections and are designed to form divergent passages. They are also twisted, so the stagger angle measured between the blade chord and the axis of rotation increases from root to tip (washout). This should both even out the angle of attack along the blade and create a spanwise pressure gradient (along the length) to counteract the tendency of the air to flow towards the tips as everything rotates.

Rotor blades are strong enough to withstand centrifugal forces. In the lower pressure stages of the compressor, the temperature is not so high, so the blades can be made of aluminium alloy, but stainless steel or titanium are used in the latter stages.

The stator blades in the front row are also known as **Inlet Guide Vanes**, and their job is to present the flow of air to the first rotors at the best angle of attack, which is a product of the (divergent) angle induced by the IGVs and the speed of rotation so, as the rotors spin faster, the angle of attack will change. To keep this as close as possible to the optimum, the first three rows of stators can often vary their position with the rotational speed of the engine, predictably being called Variable Guide Vanes (adjustable ones are closed at idle and fully open at about 70% engine RPM). If this cannot be done, there will be a **bleed valve** (or a **variable bypass valve**) between the LP and HP compressors that will dump excess airflow out of the casing at low compressor RPM.

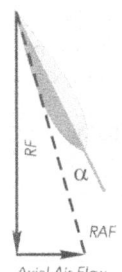

After passing the rotor blades, the airflow passes into the stator stage where more divergent passages convert velocity energy into pressure energy. The stator blades guide the air onto the next rotor blades at the correct angle, and so the process is repeated. It should be noted that, depending on the number of stages, a particle of air moving from stage to stage may only move through 180° from front to back.

Each rotating wheel with its set of stators is one stage of compression, so several together (on a shaft) constitute a *multistage compressor*, used because the temperature and pressure increases (between 1.1-1.2 for the latter) across each stage are relatively small and need boosting. This keeps the rate of diffusion and deflection angles of the blades small, and keep any turbulence within limits.

Axial compressors usually have more stages than their driving turbines because the turbine throws out much more power than the compressor uses up.

As the air pressure increases, the volume required will decrease, so the cross-sectional area of the air annulus gets smaller towards the rear of the compressor, which helps to maintain a constant axial speed in the cruise. In other words, the blades get shorter towards the discharge end to form a convergent duct from the casing as a whole, in an effort to sustain axial velocity. This is to maintain the air velocity as the pressure *increases,* and to better suit the air density. The final stator blades straighten the airflow to remove any turbulence and ensure that it reaches the combustion chamber at a uniform axial velocity.

During the compression process, there will be a steady rise in temperature, so the air will have pressure and temperature energy when it enters the combustion chamber, although its velocity will be slightly lower than when it entered the intake.

This is reflected in the diagram below:

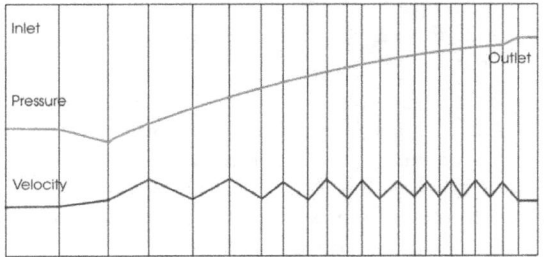

A dual compressor has stages in tandem, but on different shafts at different speeds, for higher compression ratios.

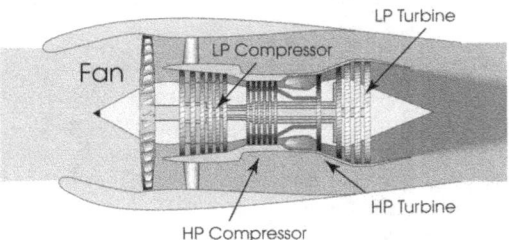

The first in line would be the low pressure compressor (N_1), driven by the low pressure turbine, (which would also be the slowest), via the low pressure shaft, which rotates inside the high pressure shaft, and which performs the same function for the high pressure compressor (N_2) and turbine. The N_2 shaft runs the opposite way to N_1, so the torques cancel each other out, relieving stress on the engine mounts (in some engines, N_2 is the intermediate shaft and N_3 the high power). The combination of shafts and compressor is a *spool*.

Splitting the compressor in two, with each part driven by its own turbine, allows them to be run at different speeds - at low RPM, the LP compressor runs slower, and the HP compressor runs faster than it would if there were only one. In fact, at idling speed, the LP compressor runs at half the speed of the HP compressor. This increases to 75% at maximum power, especially at altitude where its speed would rise from reduced air density. As well, a split compressor means less inertia, so responses to power demands are quicker - sometimes 10% of the time required for a single spool. When starting, only the HP (or N3) compressor is used, being the smallest, so you can use a lighter starter motor. A rotor shaft will be supported by ball and roller bearings (see *Lubrication*), and be coupled to the turbine shaft in such a way that small variations in alignment are allowed.

Because the clearance between the casing and the blade is so critical, blades are often made with a *knife edge tip*. As the blade heats up, it rubs against the casing and the knife edge beds in to provide a minimal clearance.

The **Compressor Pressure Ratio** (CPR) is the difference between the air pressure going in and coming out of the compressor - it should always be higher than the back pressure from the turbine, or the airflow could go the wrong way - that for a centrifugal compressor is 4:1.

The **Engine Pressure Ratio** (EPR), on the other hand, is how you measure power output on a turbojet or turbofan (turboprops use torque). It is the difference between air pressure at both ends of the whole engine, or an indication of thrust obtained by sensing pressure at various stages in it (depending on the aircraft). It is normally the ratio of the turbine discharge pressure and the compressor inlet pressure, and the normal measure of power output for turbojets or turbofans, except for the 737, which uses N_1, or the low pressure spool - if it is three times the size out of the back, EPR is 3. EPR is affected by CPR.

However, EPR gauges should not be used by themselves, but cross-referenced with other instruments, especially when the probes might ice up. The relevance of this becomes apparent with an engine failure after V_1, where some aircraft (with automatic controls) allow full throttle without exceeding performance limits. Others need the levers to be set more accurately, and a likely idea of what the limits will be before takeoff.

EPR settings vary with altitude and temperature. When using the tables, enter with the temperature and pressure altitude, remembering to make adjustments if you use bleed air (check the notes on the chart, which will be set up for a default). As there are so many variables, you might find it easier to create a table:

	Eng 1	Eng 2
Table	2.17	2.18
A/C off	+0.6	
Other		-0.5
T/O EPR	2.23	2.13

If you have an EPR for each temperature and PA (like the 737), use the lower. If an EPR is set at a constant pressure, with increasing OAT, thrust remains constant.

You need the minimum inlet pressure at the compressor for maximum CPR, EPR and thermal efficiency.

The effect of a blocked EPR intake varies with airspeed. At the start of the takeoff run, the pressure in the inlet is very low, due to the vacuum cleaner effect (the air is being sucked through the engine), hence the potential for foreign object damage (FOD). On the other hand, downstream of the turbines, the pressure is very high from the high engine RPM. The combination gives a very high initial EPR which gradually reduces during takeoff as the air is compressed more. Maximum EPR for any stage of flight is calculated by computer, and it is easy to go over the indicated value. If performance allows, a reduced EPR may be used to save engine wear. A typical value is 35:1.

COMPRESSOR STALL & SURGE

For maximum efficiency, and because engines have to react quickly, you need to operate the compressor blades as close to the stall as possible, but the stalling involved is not quite the same as that on an aerofoil, as compressor blades cannot change their position relative to the airflow they meet. They are affected by an *effective* angle of attack, which depends on the velocity of the airflow and the speed at which the blades are moving. In a centrifugal compressor, for example, there are normally more impeller vanes than diffuser vanes, so not all the diffuser passages will have smooth airflow. Pressure will therefore be less in the more turbulent ones, and air may turn back on itself and flow from the smooth channels into turbulent ones, and back.

In an axial compressor, the various stages have dissimilar airflow stages, especially at lower speeds, where the air has more of a tendency to break away from the blade contours and cause a stall because its volume reduces so little - it is therefore too fast and chokes the compressor. If the throttle is closed too quickly, the mass airflow reduces quicker than the RPM does, so the angle of attack of the blades in the early stage increases beyond the stall.

If the throttle is opened too quickly, the extra fuel increases the velocity of the gas too fast through the turbine, which chokes, so pressure in the combustion chamber becomes greater than that leaving the compressor and everything backs up. The graphs below show the surge envelope in situations where the throttle is opened rapidly at high and low RPM. The **surge line** indicates the pressure ratio above which surge will occur. The working line is where the engine will lie in a normal steady state combination of RPM, air mass flow, and compression ratio. The distance between the two is a measure of the engine's resistance to surge.

Because the pressure rise in the combustion chamber occurs before the increase in RPM and mass flow, the engine initially moves closer to the surge line before returning to the working line at a higher RPM as indicated by points A, B and C in the top diagram, which shows the effects of acceleration at high RPM (A - B shows the initial rise in pressure ratio and B-C indicates the recovery to the working line in the new conditions).

If the throttle is opened too quickly, the surge line will be crossed, initiating a compressor surge. If it is severe enough or prolonged, rising temperatures and loss of RPM and mass flow will stop the engine returning to the working line without pilot intervention. In extreme cases, the engine will move deeper into the surge area rather than recovering as indicated by points D, E, F and G in the lower graph, for low RPM (the dotted line between F and G indicates the actual path taken).

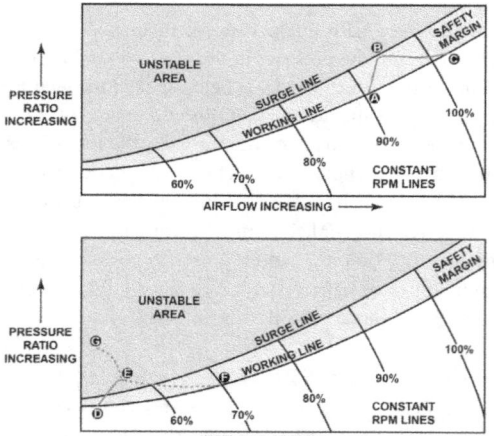

Because the margin between the working and the surge lines increases with RPM, surge is particularly likely when starting or accelerating from low speed. To overcome this, there are many stall and surge prevention devices, such as variable inlet guide vanes (or stators) in front of the first stage of the compressor.

Some engines have a small valve (a *compressor bleed*) in the late stages of the compressor (or between the axial and centrifugal compressors) that opens at low RPM (when the engine cannot shift as much air) to dump the extra volume overboard and correct the airflow.

A bleed air system makes the compressor see less restrictions by staying open until a certain pressure ratio is obtained. In other words, it aids acceleration without stalling, because the engine is made to use a higher pressure and the excess is bled out. The valve closes when acceleration is required so that the additional pressure better matches the increased fuel flow.

Bleed valves can be operated hydraulically (using fuel pressure) or pneumatically. In the pneumatic system, the valve is spring loaded in the open position. At low RPM, the airflow through a venturi creates a depression that operates a linkage to close the valve when required.

A **compressor stall** reduces engine efficiency. A *cold stall* only affects a few blades, whereas a *hot stall* involves them all, and may mean severe damage from the hot gases coming out of the combustor when the airflow becomes reversed inside the engine (as the air is being compressed, it will try to spring back the way it came, as might happen if the intake gets blocked). In a *transient stall*, you will just hear the odd bang (and a bigger one when a blade flies through the side), but in a more steady stall, there will be a roaring sound and severe vibration with a sound like a machine gun but, mostly, you should just hear a coughing sound from the engine. In the extreme, compressor surge is accompanied by loud banging noises and severe engine vibration. The only things you can do are to reduce the fuel flow and angle of attack on the compressor blades, or increase speed. Energy wasted in simply churning air in this way is called *compressor surge*, which can also be experienced in supercharged piston engines, although centrifugal compressors suffer less because they have lower compression ratios. In mild cases, the engine will keep running, but if it gets starved of air it will stop.

The causes of compressor stall are not necessarily internal - there could be ingestion of debris or otherwise dirty air (smoke, etc.), distorted flow through the intake during abrupt manoeuvres, re-ingestion of exhaust gases - even erosion can cause blades to stall. An axial-centrifugal engine increases an engine's resistance to this by a factor of 10 as the centrifugal compressor is essentially not affected by sand and dust erosion.

 You may have to report surging to maintenance, especially with a fixed turbine engine as compressor surge can feed through a transmission system.

A stall usually starts when the airflow stagnates in the front stages of the compressor. It is most likely in compressors designed for high pressure ratios running at high RPM. Severe compressor stall can be indicated by a rise in TOT and changes in the vibration level.

SUMMARY

Although the two terms are used synonymously, stall can occur in a compressor whenever the smooth airflow over the blade profile is disturbed. Stalling can be caused by damaged or deformed compressor blades (see picture above) or malfunctioning IGV controls or a sticking bleed valve. Icing can be another cause.

If the stall spreads to all stages, the airflow will break down completely and the compressor will surge. A localised stall will only involve a slight vibration and poor acceleration (or deceleration).

Otherwise, surging is essentially due to an incorrect fuel/air ratio in the combustion chamber. If overfuelling occurs, either from too much fuel or too little air, there will be too great an expansion of the gas stream. This will set up a pressure wave which is felt back along the compressor and causing successive stages to stall.

A surge will be accompanied by a loud bang, a rapid winding down of the engine and a rapid rise in gas temperature.

Common causes of surging are:

- Rapid increase in fuel flow when RPM increases
- Low engine RPM
- Air going into the engine from the wrong direction, in a crosswind, or restricted (from icing)
- Contaminated or damaged compressor blades

Symptoms of surging include:

- Loss of thrust
- Odd noises & vibrations
- RPM fluctuations
- Increased TOT
- Burning gases out of various orifices

To reduce the chances of surge, operate the power lever or throttle smoothly. To get out of it, slowly reduce power, but keep an eye on the temperature!

The Combustion Chamber

The combustion system's purpose is to provide a smooth stream of uniformly heated gas, with the least loss of pressure and the maximum release of heat, which accelerates the gases back towards the turbine. It does this because there is a wall of highly compressed air at the front end. If there is a drain valve, it is there for the removal of unburnt fuel.

The combustion chamber is made from two tubes that are highly temperature-resistant (made from something like titanium) - one is an inner liner, or flame tube, which is pierced with calibrated holes, and the other is an outer casing. Space is made for a fuel burner which sprays fuel as a constant atomised stream into the inner liner, and an igniter plug that provides the high energy spark needed to start the process off. Between the two is an air gap, through which any air that does not go into the combustion chamber passes (secondary air).

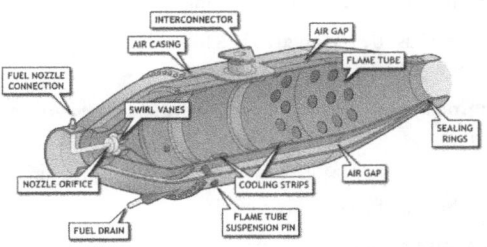

Fuel nozzles are shrouded to prevent carbon build up. They also have swirl vanes to reduce the average axial flow speed to stabilise the flame front, and swirl the incoming air to enhance the mixing of fuel with air.

As combustion occurs at constant pressure* (the gases expand to compensate), the combustion chamber can be relatively lightly constructed.

*In practice about 5% is lost through the turbulence that is needed to mix the air and fuel properly when keeping the flame stable.

The air is heated by burning the fuel after it has been injected into the airstream as a continuous stream. As the combustion chamber has a fixed size, the hot gases must increase their speed to escape, and they are delivered to the turbine below the limiting speed of its blades.

Once the flame is lit by the spark igniter during the start, it stays that way till the engine is shut down (you could say that the engine is on fire all the time, and it's only when it becomes uncontained that it becomes an emergency).

Fuel enters the combustion chamber at high pressure (1000 psi or more) through fuel nozzles that are designed to atomise it into a spray of vapour and fine liquid droplets, typically a millionth of an inch across (small droplets burn quicker and only need a small combustion chamber to achieve a given power). Meanwhile, the air is made to flow as slowly as possible* - every additional fraction of a second means an inch or so on the length of the combustion chamber, which introduces a weakness.

*Kerosene burns relatively slowly at 60 - 80 feet per second.

AIRFLOW

Air enters the combustion chamber at around the same velocity at which it entered the intake, which is enough to blow the flame out if it wasn't modified in some way.

The diffuser section reduces the air velocity from the compressor, and further diffusion on entering the combustion chamber as a divergent duct reduces it more, to about 60-80 feet per second. This is still too high for stable burning, so the air is given a swirl to slow it down even more - primary air (see below) must have a near-zero velocity on entering the flame tube to create a region of low pressure round the flame to keep it alight.

The ratio of air to fuel may vary from 45:1 to as much as 130:1, which is way too high for the optimum combustion ratio of 15:1, so the combustion chamber introduces a small proportion of the airflow (up to about 20-30%) into the primary, or combustion zone of the chamber.

Primary air comes directly in through the snout of the combustion chamber. About 12% of it passes through the swirl vanes, which creates a toroidal vortex that resembles a ring doughnut or a smoke ring - low static pressure in the centre encourages the air to reverse back into the incoming flow so that, once ignition starts, the flame is fed back to the burner head, shortening and concentrating it into an area of low velocity recirculation.

The centre of the vortex is also where the conical spray of fuel intersects the airflow, so the fuel is broken up and mixed with the air. *The highest temperature in a running turbine engine is in the primary zone of the combustion chamber,* with a flame temperature between 1800-2000°C.

The remainder of the primary air passes through the colander, or flare, where it meets the fuel spray at right angles to the spray cone. This shapes the flame and keeps it from touching the flame tube.

Downstream of the **primary zone** is the **dilution zone**, where the remaining 80% mixes with the products of combustion to bring the temperature into a range that the turbine blades can cope with.

Secondary air gets into the air gap between the two casings and comes back into the combustion chamber through holes a little way downstream. This cools the hot gas and provides more oxygen for the burning process.

The airflow and flame stabilisation in a typical combustion chamber is shown below:

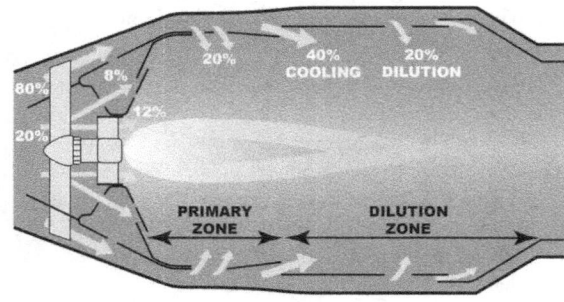

Tertiary air, also from the air gap, cools the flame tube before it is mixed into the gases downstream of the secondary air. Aside from *diluting* the high temperatures, it helps to distribute the heat uniformly through the gas so that it reaches the entry to the turbine at a more acceptable level, as local hot spots could damage it.

Some cooling air enters the flame tube through windows or corrugations which are shaped to form a skin of cooling air over its inner face.

The final section of the combustion chamber forms a convergent duct in which pressure energy is converted to velocity energy before it enters the turbines.

In summary, air entering the combustion chamber has high pressure and heat energy, low volume, and relatively low velocity. Heat energy is added to it by burning fuel, so the rising T (see the formula for the Combined Gas Law, above) should cause a rise in pressure. However, the same mass of gas is now occupying a larger volume (V), which offsets the temperature rise, meaning that the pressure remains virtually constant.

This pressure energy remains more or less constant over the whole length of the combustion chamber (as does the heat energy), while the velocity energy is decreased by the turbulence from the burning gases. When the stream of gases reaches the convergent section of the chamber, pressure energy will be lost and velocity energy gained while heat energy will remain fairly constant.

TYPES OF CHAMBER

Multiple combustion chambers were used on early engines, particularly those with centrifugal compressors.

The separate tubes were interconnected so that the pressures within the various chambers were equalised, but 2 igniters were needed to ensure that as much fuel as possible was ignited at the same time. Although they have a high resistance to distortion, a lot of material is needed for their construction and they use up a lot of space, aside from being prone to hotspots.

Turbo-annular, cannular or can-annular are all names given to systems where the individual flame tubes are mounted inside a common annular air casing, which simplifies construction, and eases maintenance and inspection. The diameter of the casing can be significantly reduced for the same mass airflow and there is a considerable saving in materials and weight.

Axial flow engines now tend to have **annular** combustion chambers, with a continuous circular casing (an *annulus,* or sleeve) around the compressor drive housing, open to the compressor at one end and the turbine at the other.

Fuel spray nozzles are disposed around the annulus near the front end. As the whole of the area around the engine is used for combustion, the combustion chamber can be shorter for the same overall diameter. Construction is lighter and simpler, and flame propagation is more efficient, so local hot spots are less likely, as is a flameout. As the total surface area is reduced, less cooling air is needed, giving greater combustion efficiency. Thus, the annular combustion chamber virtually eliminates unburned fuel, reducing air pollution and increasing thermal efficiency, and reducing the thermal load distribution on the HP turbine.

BURNERS (ATOMISERS)

The purpose of the fuel injectors is to supply a continuous spray of finely atomised fuel that will mix readily with air to form an easily combustible mixture (it's the vapour that burns, not the fuel itself). To achieve this, the fuel must be supplied at enough pressure to produce a cone-shaped spray into the centre of the toroidal vortex. If the pressure is too low, the fuel will come out as a film and, if it is too high, a solid jet.

A less common type is the vaporising burner, in which air is mixed with fuel and passes through tubes which are placed in hot air. The vaporised fuel/air mixture is ejected from the tubes in the opposite direction to the airflow, where it is burnt. The flame will extract the weight of air it needs for combustion from the airflow. If it is too much, then less is available for cooling. The rate of expansion will be too great and a pressure wave will be felt back along the compressor, causing successive stages to stall (from rear to front) until a surge condition exists. A fairly common reason for underfuelling is blocked burners, which can make the engine fail to reach self-sustaining speed.

The fuel system must be sensitive to the following variables, and react accordingly:

- **Engine speed**. The faster the engine spins, the greater the mass of airflow, so more fuel is needed.
- **Altitude**. Higher levels mean less dense air, a smaller mass flow and less fuel required.
- **Air temperature**. Cooler air is more dense, so a greater mass flow means more fuel is needed.

- **Acceleration**. The faster the rate of acceleration (or deceleration), the more rapid should be the response.
- **Intake pressure**. The higher this is, the higher will be the air density and the more fuel is required.
- **Specific gravity**. The higher this is, the higher the weight of fuel is available for a given volume. Compensation is automatic in modern systems.

Early gas turbine engines used a simple spray nozzle with a single discharge orifice called a **simplex burner** in which fuel is supplied through tangential holes to a chamber before being discharged. The swirling motion imparted to the fuel assists with atomisation, and varying its supply pressure varies the quantity of fuel discharged.

Because the flow of a liquid through an orifice is proportional to the square root of the pressure drop across it, the range of pressures needed to create the range of fuel flows required were between about 30 - 3000 psi. Fuel pumps of the time could not cope with that and maintenance of the required spray pattern proved to be impossible over such a wide range.

The **duplex** (or duple) **burner** has two orifices. At low supply pressures (small throttle openings), fuel only flows to the primary one. As the throttle is opened, and fuel supply pressure to the burner increases, a spring-loaded pressurising valve progressively opens to admit fuel to the main orifices. Thus, for a relatively narrow supply pressure range, fuel flow can be varied over a wide range, and pressure remains adequate for efficient atomisation.

A **spill burner** is similar to the simplex, but there is a passage from the swirl chamber through which fuel can be spilled back to the fuel pump supply at a controlled rate. At high demand rates (maximum engine RPM) the spill valve is closed and all the fuel is sprayed from the nozzle. At low demand rates (minimum engine RPM at high altitude), the valve is opened so that most of the fuel supplied to the swirl chamber is spilled away. Because the supply pressure is high there is enough of a swirl to ensure that the small quantity discharged is efficiently atomised. A complex fuel system is needed to control both supply and spill pressures to meet the fuel flow requirements over the full operating range of the engine.

Many modern gas turbine engines use **air spray nozzles**, where some of the primary air (for combustion) mixes with the fuel supply. This aeration achieves more efficient combustion of the fuel and requires lower fuel pressures.

The pressurising and dump valve admits fuel to the burners only if the fuel pressure is high enough for atomisation.

The Turbine

The turbine's purpose is to extract energy from the hot gases and expand them to a lower pressure and temperature, to drive the compressor and maybe some accessories (the turbine stages absorb around 75% of the energy from combustion to drive the compressors). As the gases are hot and fast, the turbine has to withstand a lot of stress, particularly when starting, where the temperature rise is very quick. Over the blades, this can be anywhere between 850-1700°C, and the pressure against them can be in the order of 50 tons per square inch, so the operating temperature is limited by the materials used. The highest temperatures occur on the first stators after the combustion chamber. Those further downstream are typically not measured but predicted from a known rise.

The gases leave the combustion chamber through nozzle guide vanes (one for each turbine stage), which both direct the flow onto the turbine blades at the correct angle and form convergent ducts that increase the velocity of the gas at the expense of heat and pressure energy. They are cooled by compressor delivery air.

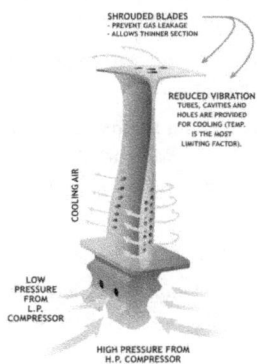

For an **impulse turbine**, the high velocity is obtained through *convergent* nozzle guide vanes *before* the gases go across the blades, where velocity is lost, with negligible changes in pressure or temperature. *In an impulse blade section, pressure drops across the nozzle guide vanes but remains constant across the blades.* This is because the space between the blades is constant.

The blades are shaped to produce a large deflection of the gas, being given they are given a swirl in the direction of rotation. The effect is to push the blades round, like a waterwheel, so Newton's second law applies. However, only the blade root can take the best advantage of the gas velocity. In a **reaction turbine***, the gases expand across the blades as well as the stators.

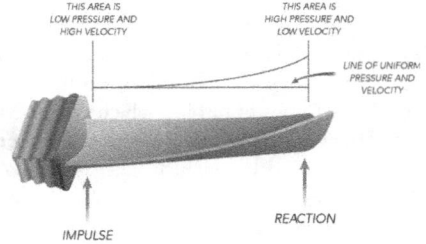

Reaction types use a narrowing (convergent) gap to provide a reaction approximately opposite to the direction of blade rotation, so Newton's third law applies. Here, the pressure drop takes place between the rotor blades - the NGVs just alter or guide the flow of air without changing pressure. A velocity increase provides the reaction.

*They actually start off as impulse blades, but are called reaction blades to distinguish them from the pure impulse variety. Modern blades are split roughly 50-50 - as the reaction turbine obtains maximum torque at the blade tip, the impulse-reaction blade has impulse characteristics at the root, a combination in the middle and reaction characteristics at the tip. Turbine blades wash in to get the best of both.

In summary:

- Impulse Turbine
    - Over the NGVs, pressure and temperature decrease, velocity increases.
    - Over the blades, pressure and temperature remain constant while velocity decreases.
- Reaction Turbine
    - Over the NGVs, pressure and temperature remain constant, but the direction changes.
    - Over the blades, pressure and temperature decrease while velocity increases.

The overall effect is for pressure and thermal energy to reduce through each section while velocity rises and falls much as it does through the compressor, including a lower velocity at the end rather than the beginning.

Tip shrouds increase turbine efficiency.

Put another way, the gas flow will enter the exhaust duct (at the end of the turbine section) at a P_4 and V_4 sort of equal to P_1 and V_1, but T_4 will be less than T_3 (but much higher than T_1).

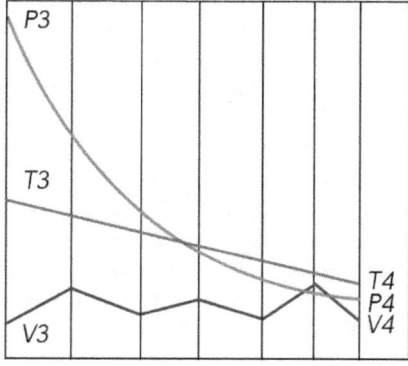

In a **free turbine** engine, the exhaust gases go through two turbine stages, a compressor turbine, which drives the compressor directly, and a power turbine, which is connected to the transmission. **There is no direct connection between the engine and the gearbox it drives**, which is helpful when starting, as one less turbine needs to be driven. In other words, a free turbine does not drive a compressor.

The energy delivered to the free turbine stages depends on how fast the gas generator is rotating.

In the picture, the drive shaft comes out of the hot end of the engine, but it could be made to run inside the compressor shaft to come out of the cool end at the front.

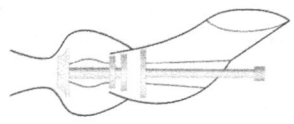

The compressor is allowed to run at different speeds to make sure that the power turbine maintains a constant RPM for any value of collective pitch. This means that the power delivered to the rotors depends only on engine torque, and that the free turbine is better for multi-engine systems because only the compressor speed needs to be adjusted to maintain rotor RPM.

With a **fixed turbine**, all parts of the engine run at the same speed, and fuel flow is changed to alter the temperature and velocity of the air. This makes the engine a little less responsive, and the compressor might not run at its optimum speed.

TURBINE BLADES

Turbine blades are mostly held in place with *fir tree fittings*. Centrifugal force ensures a tight fit, and such loose fits limit vibration damage (this technique is used on axial compressor blades as well).

This is so that the whole turbine wheel does not need replacing if a blade gets damaged. Because they are not rigidly fixed to it, a ticking sound when the wheel is turned by hand is normal.

Turbine *blade creep* is a change in blade length from a combination of heat and centrifugal force when spinning. The blades stretch when the engine is running, and cool and shrink after shutdown, but not to their original sizes.

If you overtemp the engine, the change will be permanent but, because it is not spinning so fast when you start, you are allowed a higher temperature, as there is less risk.

There are three stages of creep:

- **Primary**, with rapid expansion, occurring over a relatively short period when the blade is new.
- **Secondary**, which is more or less constant after the initial elongation, through the life of the engine.
- **Tertiary**, where rapid and fundamental changes occur, until the blade fractures.

The greatest risk created by a free turbine overspeed is the bursting of the free turbine disk.

Turbine Active Clearance Control (TACC) is a method of changing blade length by using bleed air to change the temperature of the casing. This is to provide enhanced clearances between the blade tips and the casing.

SEALING

The turbine engine does not have as many closed areas as a piston engine, so how are different regions sealed off? One method is to use (HP) air pressure, and another is to use a labyrinth seal, which is a mechanical seal that fits around a shaft to prevent leakage between the fixed and rotating parts of a turbine. In this case, HP air uses the labyrinth to prevent high temperature gases from reaching the front face of the turbine disc. The rear face is protected by the exhaust cone.

The seal consists of solid wheels on the rotating part with machined grooves that interlock with stationary gates, so that whatever fluid is being blocked has to pass through a long and difficult path to escape. Thus, there is a non-contact sealing action - at higher speeds, centrifugal motion forces the liquid towards the outside and away from any passages.

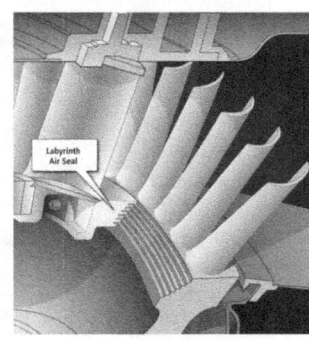

Similarly, any liquid that escapes the main chamber becomes entrapped in a labyrinth chamber, where it is forced into a vortex-like motion to prevent its escape and repel any other fluid. Because labyrinth seals are non-contact, they do not wear out, and can cope with the high speeds associated with turbines.

The Exhaust

The exhaust system conducts the gases as they come out of the turbine (between 750 -1200 feet per second) to the atmosphere at a suitable velocity to provide the thrust. It must be able to obtain the correct balance of pressure and velocity to prevent flow separation.

It consists of:

- **The Exhaust Cone**. This reduces the velocity of the gases by diffusion to prevent friction losses (down to about 950 fps, or Mach 0.5 at the temperatures involved, relative to the casing), and ensures that the gas flow is axial at the tip, to remove any whirl component from the turbine. It also stops hot gases flowing across the rear face of the turbine disc to prevent overheating.
- **The Jet Pipe**. This is insulated to stop heat reaching the fuselage. Its length and diameter are important - a short, small pipe means high gas velocities and minimum loss of thrust.
- **The Nozzle**. This restricts is a convergent duct, which accelerates the exhaust gases before they flow out of the engine to atmosphere. The reaction to this is a major contribution to the overall thrust produced. For maximise effect, its velocity must be as high as possible. As long as it is lower than the local speed of sound, the rate of acceleration is proportional to the pressure drop across the nozzle, meaning that the acceleration is proportional to the difference between jet pipe and ambient pressure. If the jet pipe pressure is increased, the velocity at the throat of the nozzle will increase until it equals the local speed of sound, after which further increases will not produce an acceleration. Instead, the gas will be discharged to atmosphere above ambient pressure, expanding wastefully and reducing the overall efficiency of the engine. The propelling nozzle at this stage is said to be choked.

To get more velocity, the local speed of sound can be increased with a convergent inlet attached to a divergent outlet, rather like a venturi. As the jet pipe pressure is increased beyond the choked condition, the increasing temperature and pressure downstream of the throat increases the local speed of sound, to restore the relationship between pressure drop and acceleration, causing the gas to continue its acceleration in the divergent section. That is, the gas in the convergent section remains choked in the narrowest part. Downstream of the throat, however, its velocity increases as the local speed of sound increases in that area. The overall effect is an increase in gas velocity and thrust.

The area of the nozzle is quite critical and is specified and calibrated during manufacture. Any changes will naturally have a significant effect on engine performance.

In the bypass engine, two gas streams must be dealt with, the cold (bypass) air and the hot exhaust gas. In low bypass engines, they are combined in a mixer unit before passing through the propelling nozzle.

In high bypass ratio engines, they are exhausted separately through hot and cold coaxial propelling nozzles. However, you can get more thrust if both streams are ejected through a common, or integrated, exhaust nozzle.

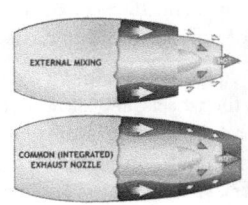

REVERSE THRUST

Modern aircraft have high wing loadings and therefore have to keep the speed up to keep the wings from stalling, which makes life difficult when the runway is short. Brakes create their own problems, so some help is needed*, especially when jets have low drag values once the nosewheel is on the ground, and there is always residual thrust when the throttles are back to idle.

*Having said that, thrust reversal is not allowed for certification, as it may not be available anyway in an emergency, so brakes are the main way of stopping. However, using reversers for routine landings saves a lot in brake wear and tear (and money) - and using them early keeps the brakes cool and reduces brake fade. Because wheel braking is reduced, the possibility of losing directional control is much less. They can also be used for pushing back from the terminal.

A thrust reverser redirects the exhaust gases outside the engine in the opposite direction to its normal flow to help the brakes, using up to just less than 50% of the engine's rated power, because it is not possible to deflect gases efficiently through 180°. A more typical angle is 45°.

Because aircraft must stop in a specified distance with one engine out (when reverse thrust is not available anyway), flight planning calculations do not take it into account. Taking off on icy or contaminated runways is not allowed when reverse thrust is unserviceable. The normal landing distance graphs in the flight manual assume that it is available and will be used, so the reduction in length is accounted for, which is not the case with OEI graphs. Having said that, the reduction in distance with it working is not that large.

Reversers should not be used until the nosewheel touches down, as their use shifts the weight on to it. As their main function is to relieve the strain on the brakes, performance calculations are based on maximum braking (which is not used routinely).

The process is most effective at high speeds, and pulls all sorts of crud into the engines at low speeds, so it should be engaged early (you could also get surging from the re-ingestion of hot air). Only a few (older) aircraft will allow reverse thrust to be deployed in flight - you would typically use 75% of N_1 as a throttle setting, and 100% in an emergency. At low speeds, re-ingestion of the jet efflux may cause overheating.

Normally, squat switches in the main undercarriage sense any weight on the wheels, and allow an isolation valve controlling bleed air from the compressor to open once the throttles are at idle. The reverser controls will be piggy-backed onto the normal thrust levers, so they are to hand when required. As they are interlocked, reverse thrust cannot be selected until the thrust levers are at the rear of the idle setting. Thrust cannot be increased to a high setting unless the reversers are in full reverse.

The reversers are designed for fail-safe operation. If the hydraulic pressure fails, a mechanical lock holds them in the forward thrust position. There are cockpit indications as to when the reversers are unlocked, moving to and in the reverse position.

In pure jet and low bypass engines the gas stream from the propelling nozzle is redirected to produce a forward component of velocity, so that reaction thrust is reversed from the normal, to oppose the forward motion of the aircraft. There are two basic types of **hot gas stream** system, the clamshell door and the bucket-target. Both types have to withstand a lot of heat.

Typically, on jet aircraft without bypass, **clamshells** forming part of the jetpipe block the escape of exhaust gases to direct them forward:

They are pneumatically operated doors which, in their normal (forward thrust) position, allow the normal gas stream to flow through the exhaust nozzle. When reverse thrust is selected, the doors rotate to block off the normal gas stream and divert it through ducts to cascade vanes, which direct the hot gas forward, creating thrust in the opposite direction. The pneumatic rams that operate the doors exert their maximum force when the doors are in the normal (forward thrust) position. This holds them against the reverse duct seals, preventing gas leakage and loss of forward thrust.

Buckets can also be introduced directly into the exhaust stream (they are hydraulically operated). In the forward thrust position, the bucket-shaped doors form a concentric tube around the propelling nozzle. When reverse thrust is selected, hydraulic actuators move the doors, using push rods, to deflect the stream from the propelling nozzle forwards, to create the reversal.

Cascade types are used with high bypass engines, because there is usually little ground clearance. In this case, the equivalent of clamshells operate *inside* the engine to redirect **cool bypass air** out of the sides (cheaper). **Petal Door Reversers** do much the same.

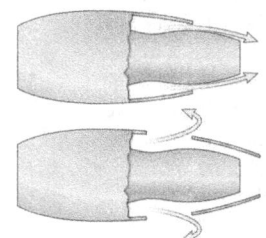

Cold stream reverser systems are usually operated by air motors using screwjacks, or hydraulic rams and push rods.

A reverse thrust alert will occur on the flight deck when the reverser doors are unlocked with the reverse lever in the stowed position, and when the doors are stowed with the lever in the deployed position.

THRUST AUGMENTATION

Instead of fitting larger ones, it is more economical to arrange for the engines to produce more power for short periods at critical times, like during takeoff and climb, as used by Concorde.

Afterburning means introducing more fuel into the hot gas stream between the turbine and the nozzle - there is always some residual oxygen to support its burning. This provides more heat, more expansion and more thrust, at the expense of (much) more fuel consumption. However, when you are not using the afterburner, the normal thrust is slightly less, because the jet pipe is different and the engine is heavier.

You also need a variable jet pipe to allow the gases more movement to prevent choking.

At very high speeds, you can bypass the engine to create a ramjet, where the air is directly burnt in the jetpipe (you only need a compressor when the engine is not moving).

WATER INJECTION

The power you get from a turbine engine depends largely on the density of the gases flowing through it so, if you increase the density altitude, you lose thrust.

You can boost power, or restore it when the air is less dense, by cooling the hot gases with water, or a mixture of water and methanol. The methanol has the properties of anti-freeze and can also be burnt, so it can restore the turbine inlet temperature without you having to adjust the fuel flow. (the Harrier can use its 227 litres of water in 90 seconds at full power in the hover).

Water can be injected into the compressor inlet, but axial flow engines like it better in the combustion chamber, because the mass flow in the turbine is increased, relative to the compressor, so there is less of a pressure and temperature drop across it. Another benefit is that you can burn more fuel before reaching the limiting temperatures.

ENGINES
Turbines

NOISE SUPPRESSION

The main sources of engine noise are the fan, compressor, turbine and exhaust velocity. Noise increases with airflow, but mostly in the exhaust, where the differences in temperature of the airflows creates turbulence. Mixing of the exhaust gas stream and atmospheric air (with corrugated nozzles) reduces noise, but you can absorb noise as well with honeycomb materials. The pure jet (i.e. no bypass) engine has the highest exhaust gas velocity and various methods have been created (when retro-fitted, these are often known as hush kits.

One method of encouraging mixing is to pass the exhaust gas through many radially mounted nozzles rather than just one. As the size of the individual gas streams is reduced, the frequency of the sound is increased. Since high frequency sound is attenuated more rapidly with distance in air, the sound at a given distance from the aircraft is less intense.

A similar effect to the multiple-tube nozzle can be obtained with a corrugated perimeter that resembles a "ring" of nozzles with the same total outlet area as that necessary for a single one.

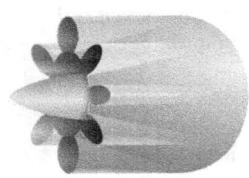

Starting & Ignition

You need two simultaneously operated systems here - one to spin the engine fast enough to create a reasonable airflow and the other to ignite the fuel/air mixture. Both systems must also be usable separately - for example, you often need to turn the engine over without ignition, or use the ignition system without the starter (for relight - an *auto relight* system is designed to restart the engine should it flame out, providing a continuous spark from the igniter all the time it is switched on).

Spinning the engine can be done electrically, with gas (air), or hydraulically. Whatever you use, it must be reliable, because losing momentum during a start will simply burn out the back end if the ignition process isn't stopped quickly enough. Smaller aircraft may use an electric starter/generator, but most modern civil aircraft use air starting because it is simple and economical to operate the pressure required being taken from another engine, such as the APU.

Power output is transmitted from a turbine through a reduction gear and a clutch to the starter output shaft which is connected to the engine.

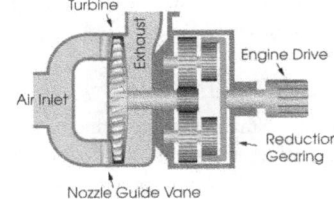

IGNITION

In the gas turbine engine, a flame exists as long as fuel is flowing, so ignition is only needed when starting up and to stabilise combustion, and when auto-relight is required. As starting takes place under many conditions, a high-energy (often dual) system is used.

A high energy ignition unit is connected to its own igniter plug (this is **not** a spark plug) and the two plugs in a dual system occupy different positions in the combustion section. The igniters are normally energised when the start lever (or HP cock) is set to start delivering fuel. Once the engine has reached self-sustaining speed (above which it will accelerate to normal running speed by itself), the igniters are de-energised.

A high-energy, twelve-joule DC ignition unit electrical system is shown below.

A trembler mechanism (vibrator) provides DC to operate an induction coil, the output of which is rectified to put a high voltage charge on a reservoir capacitor. When the voltage in the capacitor equals the breakdown value of a sealed discharge gap, it discharges to an igniter plug to produce a sequence of flashovers across the face of the plug. The function of the choke is to extend the period of discharge at the plug.

High-energy ignition systems are particularly necessary where ignition is likely to be difficult, such as when re-lighting after a flameout at high altitude.

For continuous operation, a low-energy, 3 Joule system is adequate and will result in longer life for the igniter plugs (continuous operation is necessary where flame extinction might occur, such as heavy rain, snow or icing).

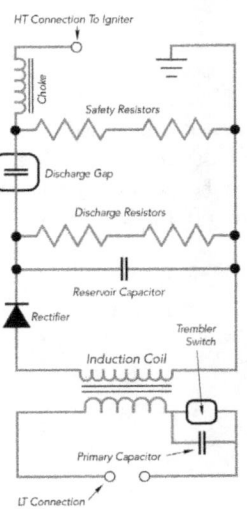

In them, AC is passed through a step-up transformer to charge a capacitor with high voltage. Otherwise, it works in pretty much the same way as the HT system above.

Ignition systems normally have a duty cycle specified, typically 10 minutes of continuous operation at a time. This prevents damage and possible malfunctions. In bad weather with the ignition on, it is just a matter of switching from one system to the other every ten minutes, or as otherwise specified.

Some systems can be automatically energised when the angle of attack indicator senses an incipient stall condition, as compressor stall and surging are would not be welcome.

Igniter plugs are usually of the surface discharge type which, when energised, produce a high energy flashover of 60-100 discharges per minute, as opposed to a gap-jumping spark.

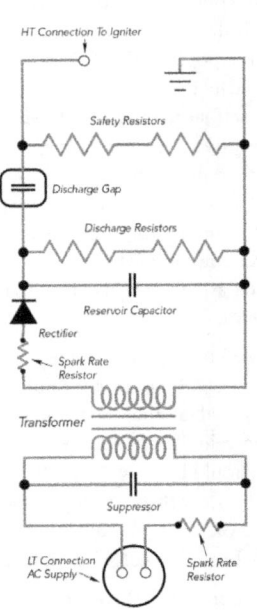

STARTING SEQUENCE

The starter rotates the compressor when the start control switch is activated.

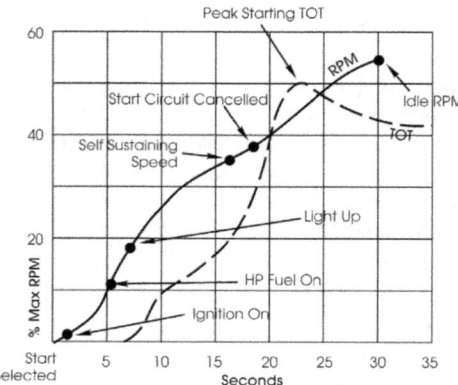

As soon as the starter has accelerated the compressor enough to establish the airflow through the engine, the ignition is turned on, then the fuel. Both are achieved by moving the start lever from cut-off to Idle.

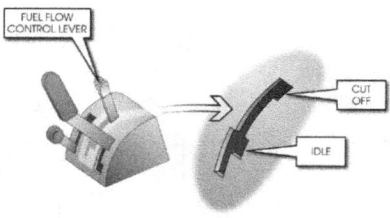

After light up, helped by the starter motor, the engine accelerates. The fuel flow is not enough to keep the engine accelerating on its own - if the starter is disengaged now, the engine may not accelerate, or may do so, but too slowly. It may even decelerate. This is why the starter is needed after light up, and until just above self-sustaining speed. After that, the engine can look after itself. Above self-sustaining speed, the starter and ignition are cut off, either automatically or by releasing the starter switch. The engine now accelerates to, and stabilises at, idle RPM. The higher the RPM before the starter is cut off, the shorter will be the time required until idle RPM is reached. The entire cycle takes between 20-90 seconds, depending upon the type of engine and the conditions.

You need to be aware of the maximum time for the start cycle, and be prepared to discontinue it when either the cycle time will be exceeded (a hung start), or the EGT will exceed the maximum starting value (a hot start*). In the latter case, the start lever (HP cock) should be closed and the sequence cancelled. The engine can subsequently be motored with start lever closed and the ignition off, to cool the hot section down. If the starter has already been de-energised, follow the recommended procedures.

*The automatic fuel control systems on modern engines are designed to prevent hung and hot starts.

If the engine is slow to accelerate, the ignition circuit may be cancelled by a time switch before self-sustaining speed has been exceeded. In this case, the engine may well continue to turn, but will not accelerate beyond self-sustaining speed. If this condition is allowed to persist, the TOT may become excessive, since fuel flow will be excessive for the airflow at such a low RPM.

If light up does not occur, the engine will not accelerate and TOT will stay very low. With the fuel flow started, the combustion chamber(s) will flood and the excess fuel must be allowed to drain off (a wet start), in which case the procedure is to turn the ignition off and motor the engine on the starter to blow out the excess fuel, and only attempt light up (with the ignition on) when it has gone - this may require allowing the engine to stop and allow the combustion chamber drain valves to open. Otherwise, there will be a firework display known as torching, when the residual fuel ignites at the next start attempt and is ejected from the jet pipe as a stream of flaming fuel.

FLIGHT START OR RE-LIGHT

When an engine has been shut down in flight, you may need to descend and/or reduce speed to obtain a positive re-light (this is called the re-light envelope). If the engine is windmilling fast enough, you might not need the starter and just need ignition and fuel. For a re-light in flight, the start switch is selected to something like *Flight Start*, which will start the ignition. Fuel flow is initiated with the start lever to open the HP cock, and a rising EGT and RPM will confirm a satisfactory re-light. The engine will stabilise at idle RPM which, at altitude, will be higher than what you would expect at ground idle. The ignition can now be switched off and the thrust lever gradually advanced to increase power. You need speed for this - attempting a windmilling re-light with too little airspeed will cause problems - in this case, you need the starter.

Rear mounted engines are very prone to disturbed airflow, as if you didn't have enough to cope with in a deep stall. An auto-relight system may be programmed to switch on when the stick shaker is activated.

Engine Position

On a modern jet, the engines are slung in pods underneath the wings, which not only provides a cleaner wing shape, but also helps to pull the wing down in flight, so the wing itself can be made of lighter construction. However, trying to roll near the ground can damage them! Engines at the rear minimise asymmetric problems, but wings need to be made stronger, and are therefore heavier. Engines are also closer together (a failure of one could damage the others) and the fuel pipes have to run through the fuselage.

Auxiliary Power Unit

The APU is a small turbine engine that provides power or compressed air, and is not intended for direct propulsion. In other words, it's a spare engine that runs the air conditioning and electrical systems when the aircraft is on the ground, or in an emergency when in flight, through a gearbox or suitable transmission. It also saves you relying on ground power units when starting. Sometimes, you can use the APU to power various systems so that the main engines can give a little extra if you are heavy.

The APU generator may only be used if no other power source is feeding the busbar.

ENGINES
Turbines

Automatic controls on APUs provide correct sequencing of the starting cycle as well as protection against high turbine gas temperature (TGT), overspeed, loss of oil pressure and high oil temperature. A load compressor mounted on the gearbox containing the generator and ancillary drives (just after the centrifugal compressor, but sometimes the same one as the APU power section, sharing the same air supply), provides air to the aircraft pneumatic system.

In essence, the APU drives a generator through a gearbox, which also drives the usual accessories, like fuel pumps, oil pumps, etc. You will find it in a remote (unpressurised) part of the aircraft, behind a firewall.

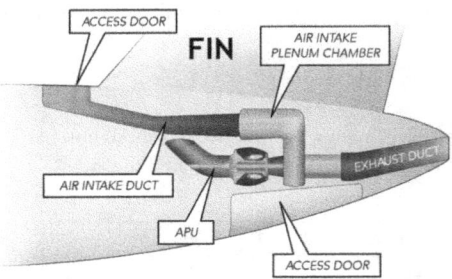

The air supply comes through inlets that open and close automatically on startup and shutdown. Their position will be indicated somewhere near the control panel in the cockpit. APUs must be stopped and started outside refuelling operations (GPUs must be outside the zone).

Air for combustion is supplied from the plenum chamber to the combustion chamber. In some units, a regulated supply of bleed air is ducted from the plenum chamber for the air conditioning and main engine air-starting systems.

FUEL SYSTEM

Starting will be done from the ship's batteries, or one for the APU. It is ready for loading 1 minute after the blue (AVAIL) light comes on. It can be shut down 2 minutes after working without a load on. Being a turbine, an APU qualifies as one of the most powerful vacuum cleaners around, so loose articles, etc. should be put away. Also, they are noisy, so wear ear defenders.

STARTING

Starting and operating in flight are subject to altitude and speed limitations. If the starter motor is isolated in flight (through a weight on wheels (squat) switch), in flight starts are windmilled and have different limitations, such as a lower altitude and higher speed, so the in-flight start envelope will be narrower. Windmilling means that the only battery power used is to operate the doors, speaking of which, the inlet duct door needs to be more complex. As these are the only items that use electrical power, if you are unlucky to get a double generator failure (on a twin-engined aircraft) the aircraft batteries are not depleted by unsuccessful attempts to start the APU.

 APUs are notoriously difficult to start after being at high altitude for a long time, because the lubricating oil will have become cold soaked.

The main APU control and indication panel is on the flight deck. The starting sequence is initiated by closing the master control switch (toggle or push type). This opens the air intake doors, then the starter motor winds up the APU. The fuel supply and ignition controls are activated as and when the appropriate speeds are achieved. Such automatic controls protect against high TOT, overspeed, loss of pressure and high oil temperature.

Picture: Typical APU Cockpit Panels

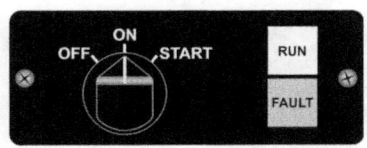

After light up has taken place, the engine accelerates, with the continued help of the starter motor, typically to between 35% and 50% of governed RPM. At this point, the starter motor circuit is de-energised and the engine accelerates to governed speed under its own power. At about 95% of the governed speed the ignition circuit is cancelled by the centrifugal switch and combustion becomes self-sustaining.

The unit should be rune with no load for a minute or so, to allow all of its parts to reach normal working temperatures before selecting any loads. There is an overspeed sensing system that will automatically shut down the APU if the governed speed is exceeded, typically at around 110%.

FIRE PROTECTION & COOLING

The APU compartment has its own continuous-wire fire detection system and its own single-shot fire extinguisher. In addition to activating visual and aural warnings, the detection circuit will automatically activate the shut down procedure. The fire extinguisher is activated by manually operated switches on the APU control panel. In some, it is discharged automatically when the circuit is activated.

A fan, driven from the accessories gearbox, provides cooling and ventilation of the APU compartment and cooling air for the generator and lubricating oil   cooler.

Ram Air Turbine

This is an air-driven turbine that drives an emergency alternator, for use if the engine-driven alternators fail.

A typical unit comprises a single stage turbine with a direct drive to the alternator, which has a lower output than the engine driven alternators, but it will be able to meet essential electrical requirements. The unit is normally stowed in a compartment closed by a hinged door.

When activated, the door opens and the device is deployed into the air stream, where it is rotated by the airflow passing through its blades. Variable incidence inlet guide vanes control the airflow using a flyweight type governor.

A variable pitch two-bladed propeller may be used as the driving unit and certain aircraft have a ram air turbine driving an emergency hydraulic pump.

Typically, the unit is in the underside of the wing root fairing and is deployed mechanically by spring action when a release catch is activated from the flight deck.

FUEL

To make fuel, crude oil is boiled up in what is effectively a giant still. The heavy stuff drops to the bottom, whilst the lighter parts (gasoline and kerosene) are distilled off the top. This is repeated at higher temperatures.

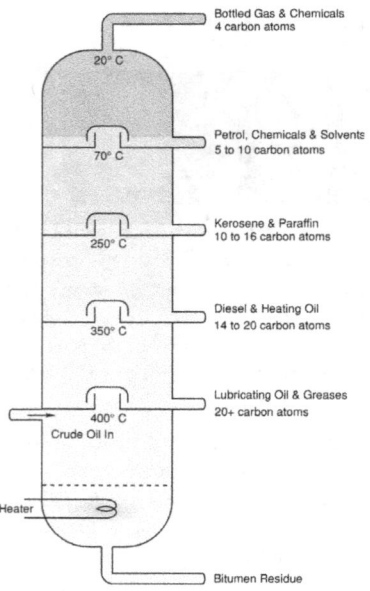

Jet and piston fuels mix differently with contaminants (particularly water), which is due to variations in their specific gravities and temperature. The specific gravity of water, for example, is so close to Avtur that it can take up to 4 hours for it to settle out, whereas the same process may take as little as half an hour with Avgas. As a result, there is always water suspended in jet fuel, which must be kept within strict limits, hence two filtration stages, for solids and water. The latter doesn't burn, of course, and it can freeze, but it's the fungi that gather round the interface between water and fuel that is the real problem - it turns into a dark-coloured slime which clings to tank walls and supporting structures, which not only alters the fuel chemically, but will block filters as well. Not much water is required for this - trace elements are enough, although, in reduced temperatures, dissolved water will escape as free water, and look like fog. Water in jet fuel is the reason for *icing inhibitors*, which will combine with the water and lower its freezing point, so that ice crystals do not form and block the lines, although this is really more relevant for aeroplanes at high altitude. However, machines operating in the Arctic can be affected too, and fuel heaters or filters are more popular these days anyway (on jet aircraft, they are fitted to each engine).

Each day before flying, or after a long turnaround time, and when the fuel is settled, carry out a water check in aircraft and containers. Collect samples in a transparent container and check for sediment, free water or cloudiness - if there is only one liquid, ensure it is not all water. Aviation fuel is "clean" if a one-quart sample is clear of sediment when viewed through a clean, dry, clear glass container, and looks clear and bright. Cloudiness indicates the presence of water, which is heavier than fuel, so it should sink to the bottom eventually. Aircraft parked overnight should ideally have their tanks completely filled to stop condensation, although the amount of water found under these circumstances in a small aircraft is unlikely to be more than a tablespoonful.

Fuel's volatility increases with altitude and temperature, so it will evaporate away quicker. This can cause *vapour locking*, where a bubble may form in the pipes and stop the fuel flowing. Increasing the pressure in the pipes helps with this, which is why boost pumps are installed.

The *flash point* is the *lowest* temperature at which fuel can produce a flammable mixture when vapour forms, so a volatile mixture has a low flash point. The *Reid vapour pressure* is that required to keep a liquid as a liquid, or the pressure measured where only a small fraction of the fuel vaporises, so a volatile fluid has a high vapour pressure.

Avgas

Aviation gasoline is made of lighter hydrocarbons and has a specific gravity of around 0.72. It is coloured this way:

Colour	Fuel
Red	80/87
Blue	100LL
Green	100/130

AVGAS fuelling points on aircraft are painted red with white lettering. If you cannot use the recommended fuel (in the flight manual) you must use a higher grade. Too low a grade causes detonation and increases cylinder head and oil temperature indications.

MOGAS

Motor Gasoline, for road vehicles, is colourless, and should not be used in temperatures above 20°C or at altitudes greater than 6000 feet. An aircraft using MOGAS is likely to be affected more by vapour locking and carburettor icing. You should be using fungicide in temperatures greater than 25°C.

Jet Fuel

This is less volatile than AVGAS, but will still catch fire, given the chance - technically, it has a higher flash point, but a lower freezing point, and it gets more viscous as it cools, so it gets harder to pump. At the freezing point, the hydrocarbons turn into waxy crystals. The specific gravity of jet fuel is between 0.75 to 0.84, but most flight manuals peg it down to 0.79.

Jet A, standard for commercial and general aviation (in the USA, at least), is narrow-cut kerosene, usually with no additives. **Jet A1** has a lower freezing point than Jet A, and possibly (but rarely) something for dissipating static, and inhibiting fungus. It is used for long haul flights where the temperature gets very low. **Jet B** is a naphtha-type fuel made by blending straight-run kerosene with lower-boiling distillate, so it's wide-cut, lighter (i.e. less dense) and has a very low flash point (it's actually 2/3 kerosene and 1/3 naphtha, but in an emergency you can swap the naphtha for avgas to get pretty much the same thing). It contains static dissipators, and is mainly used by military aircraft - **the FCU may need to be adjusted** if you want to use it, although it is being phased out, at least by Esso. The only significant demand for it these days is in really cold places.

Try not to mix Jet A and Jet B - the mixture in the right proportions can ignite through static, as Air Canada found when they lost a DC-8 on the ramp in the 70s. The static can come simply from movement of fuel through the lines (it has to cross many materials). Jet A weighs about 5% more per litre than Jet B, but it gives you a longer range, as turbines work on the weight of the fuel they burn, not the quantity (hence the use of kg/hr for fuel flow, for example). So, if you load the same amount of fuel, your machine will weigh more with Jet A, but if you fill the tanks, you will use fewer litres and less money (this is one reason, aside from its lubrication qualities, for not using AVGAS - its specific gravity is lower. However, AVTUR has more water in suspension and residual wax that must be heated to stop it blocking pipes.

 The only fuel allowed in a hangar (other than in a tank) is AVTUR, for checking and calibrating purposes.

Fuel Control

Regulating the fuel injected into the combustion chamber is how the power, or thrust, of a gas turbine is controlled. When more is required, the throttle is opened and the fuel pressure* to the burners increases from the greater fuel flow. This increases the temperature in the combustion chamber, which increases the gas flow through the turbine to give a higher engine speed and greater airflow.

*This is measured in the line between the booster pump and the engine or at the outlet of the high pressure filter. Fuel flow is measured in the line between the FCU and the engine burners.

Having set the throttle, fuel flow, and therefore mass air flow, is controlled automatically for changes in air density, altitude, air temperature and speed. This is done with a **Fuel Control Unit**, or FCU, discussed below.

Turboprops use free turbine engines, where the power turbine drives the transmission system that turns the blades. As they must be run at a more or less constant speed, so must the power turbine. This means that the energy from the gas producer (compressor) must be variable, so there is no common relationship between the speeds of the gas generator and the power turbine. This is why there are two RPM gauges. This table shows the various abbreviations used:

Type Of RPM	Symbol
Gas Generator	N_G or N_1
Free Power Turbine	N_F or N_2

The purpose of any fuel system is (aside from delivering clean fuel) to maintain the correct fuel/air ratio for efficient combustion under all operating conditions. This is typically 15:1 by weight for kerosene but, in a gas turbine engine, you need another 45 parts or so of air for cooling. If the fuel system cannot keep up, you could lose the flame from underfuelling or cause a surge from overfuelling - this can easily happen since the fuel can be sent to the combustion chamber before the compressor has had time to spool up and pump the air through.

Overfuelling is therefore necessary, but any acceleration should be controlled. The fuel system must also allow for:

- **Altitude**, **Temperature** and **Pressure**, and therefore density and mass flow.
- **Propeller Speed**, where N_G must change to cope with variations in N_R.
- **Specific Gravity**, and therefore the weight of the fuel per unit volume.

Consideration must also be given to fuel cleanliness and pressure, and the possibilities of overspeeding.

SYSTEMS

There are two main types of system:

- With **pressure control**, pressure upstream (before) the throttle varies as the throttle is opened or closed. This can be used to vary the output from the engine driven pump by varying its input. As this relies on a varying output, it can only be used with a variable displacement pump, below.
- With **flow control**, the pressure differential across the metering valve is maintained at a constant value. The control system senses any variations and varies the pump output until the differential is restored to its original value. This system can use any of the pumps described below, and can be either mechanical or pneumatic.

PUMPS

In most gas turbine fuel control systems, altering the output from the HP (engine driven) pump, which has enough pressure to atomise the fuel, varies the supply to the burners. There are two main categories of engine-driven pump, as also used with hydraulic systems.

The **variable delivery** type, driven by the gas generator, contains a number of pistons that are spring-loaded against a variable-angled swashplate.

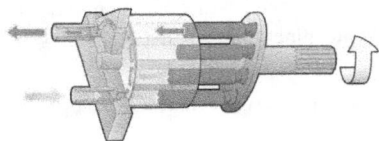

The angle of the swashplate is controlled by a servo mechanism that is spring loaded to the maximum angle position, because that's the way it shuts down (so if the drive fails, you always get a fuel supply).

The servo mechanism has a piston connected to a lug on the swashplate. One side of the piston is sensitive to the output pressure of the pump, while the other side is spring loaded and sensitive to reduced fuel (servo) pressure. If more fuel is demanded, the servo pressure is reduced, the output pressure overcomes the servo pressure and the spring force, moving the piston to reduce the swashplate angle and the length of the piston stroke, and consequently the output.

If the amount of fuel being bled off decreases, the servo pressure will increase and, helped by the spring, will move the piston to increase the swashplate angle, and the length of the piston stroke, and pump output. In this way, the output of the pump can be made to suit the requirements of the engine, as the pump is driven by the gas generator, and will run at a speed proportional to N_G. Even at a constant speed, the piston can still be moved with an altitude compensator.

Constant delivery pumps use two gears meshing together, as used on small American engines, because the output is not as high as piston types.

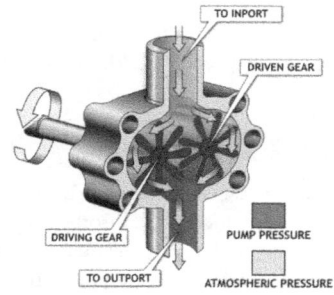

Again, the gears are driven by the gas generator and the pressurised fuel is carried around the outside of the gears. The meshing in the middle prevents any blowback.

Although the pump's speed is again proportional to N_G, being constant delivery, there needs to be a way of spilling any excess back into the inlet side. If the spill valve shown below opens to increase the fuel being bypassed, the output pressure from the pump decreases, and vice versa.

This is how it fits into the system:

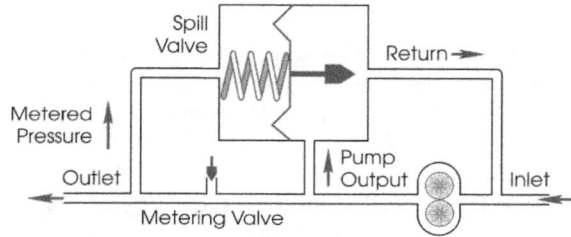

Otherwise, fuel flows from the tanks to the HP pump through a low pressure (LP) system. The LP fuel pump ensures a constant supply at a suitable pressure to prevent vapour locking and cavitation.

The LP system usually includes a fuel heater to stop ice crystals forming.

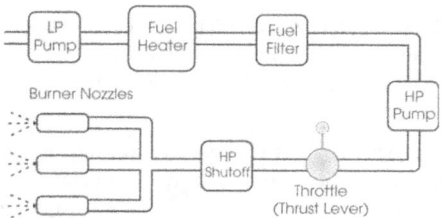

The HP cock shuts off the fuel downstream of the HP pump to ensure that it is not damaged, because it relies on the fuel for lubrication. Closing the LP cock (which is upstream) would therefore damage the HP pump by starving it of fuel.

Ignition is activated before the fuel is delivered by the HP Shutoff Valve (HPSOV) to the fuel nozzles.

FCU

The *Fuel Control Unit* does more or less the same job as a carburettor on a piston engine, except that it uses springs and centrifugal bobweights to meter fuel according to demand.

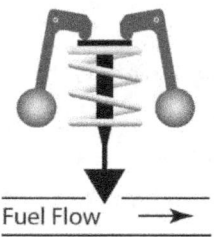

The methods of delivery can be fixed (with a return loop) or variable. The inputs to a variable delivery FCU are pressure, RPM, temperature & throttle position.

The FCU is protected from debris damage by a fine filter between HP fuel pump and the governor unit. Control of acceleration/deceleration is usually within the throttle valve mechanism. A dashpot limits the rate at which the throttle valve opens or closes, regardless of how rapidly the lever is moved.

HP Pump pressure is kept constant by the control piston. If the pump discharge pressure rises, it moves up, reducing the pump swashplate angle and the output. If the discharge pressure falls, the piston moves down, under the influence of the pressure control spring, increasing the pump's output. HP pump pressure is supplied to the throttle valve while supplying the servo system with a constant supply through a fixed orifice.

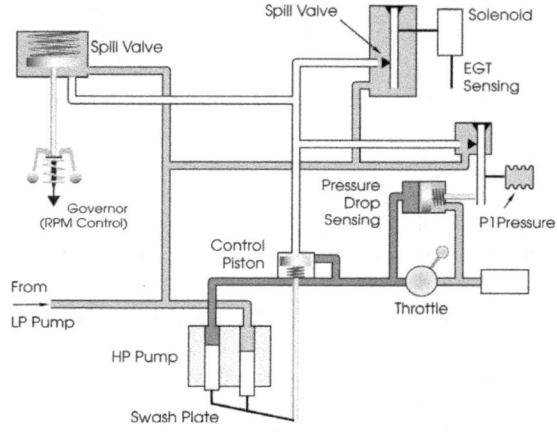

Servo pressure is controlled by spill valves, which control the rate at which fuel is spilled back to the LP system. If the flow through the spill valves exactly equals the supply through the control piston's fixed orifice, servo pressure will remain constant. If spill exceeds supply, it will fall. If the spill is less than the supply, servo pressure will rise.

How much the throttle valve is opened determines the pressure drop across it. As the control piston ensures a constant supply pressure, the more the valve is opened, the less the pressure drop across it will be. Opening the throttle increases the pressure to the burner nozzles (throttle outlet pressure), and inlet pressure is maintained constant by the servo-operated control piston. The pressure drop across the throttle valve is sensed by a spring-loaded diaphragm, which controls a spill valve.

If the throttle is opened for more power, the pressure drop across the diaphragm decreases and the spring force moves the diaphragm to close the spill valve. Pump servo pressure increases, which acts upon the control piston to increase HP pump output, increasing fuel flow to the burner nozzles. Closing the throttle increases the pressure drop across the diaphragm, opening the spill valve to decrease the pump servo pressure, which decreases the output from the HP pump.

Engine RPM is sensed by an engine-driven governor, which positions a spill valve. If RPM increases, the governor flyweights move out to open the spill valve and reduce pump servo pressure. This makes the control piston decrease the output from the HP pump and engine RPM will fall back to the pre-set value. If the RPM drops below this value, the governor spring overcomes the force of the flyweights to close the spill valve, increasing servo pressure and HP pump output.

P_1 pressure (compressor air) is sensed by a capsule attached to a spill valve. An increase in intake pressure (due to decreased altitude, air temperature/density or increased airspeed) requires a higher fuel flow. Increased pressure will expand the pressure-sensing capsule, closing the spill valve to increase pump servo pressure and HP pump output. A fall in air intake pressure will have the reverse effect.

The exhaust gas temperature should be limited to avoid damage to the turbine blades and inlet guide vanes. EGT is sensed by thermocouples **between the gas generator and power turbines**, and the electrical output, which is proportional to temperature, activates a solenoid that opens a spill valve as temperature increases, reducing pump servo pressure and therefore the HP pump output.

Pressure governed fuel control systems are quite commonly used for turbojets and turbo- prop engines. Alternative hydro-mechanical fuel control systems are the flow, combined acceleration and speed and pressure ratio systems. The type chosen will depend upon engine operating parameters and type.

FLOW CONTROL

Flow control systems differ from pressure control in that fuel pump delivery pressure is proportional to engine speed, as opposed to being kept constant. The output (fuel flow) is controlled to maintain a constant pressure drop across the throttle valve at constant air intake conditions. The system is better suited to engines requiring large fuel flows. The control system components, except the HP fuel pump, within a combined fuel control unit are.

These components are:

- The **engine speed governor** is a hydro-mechanical device that senses engine speed and produces a proportional hydraulic servo pressure to control fuel pump stroke (and output). Primary inputs would include the N_2, compressor discharge pressure and inlet temperature, fuel shutoff and the angle of the thrust lever (the Throttle Lever Angle information is sent to the FADEC over a direct connection).
- The **altitude sensing unit** is a barometric pressure control, which senses air intake (P_1) pressure and operates a spill valve to control servo pressure (and fuel flow) in conditions below governing speed.
- The **acceleration control unit** senses compressor delivery pressure and adjusts a spill valve to control servo pressure to match fuel flow to airflow.
- **Gas Temperature Control.** If the gas temperature exceeds a maximum limit a solenoid-operated proportioning valve is progressively energised to open a spill valve and reduce servo pressure, reducing fuel flow.

COMBINED ACCELERATION & SPEED CONTROL

This is a mechanical system that does not use spill valves. The controlling unit is a fuel flow regulator, which is engine driven and controls engine speed by adjusting the fuel flow. It contains two governors, a speed control governor and a pressure-drop control governor. The speed control governor is set by the throttle lever and controls fuel flow to the burners with a sleeve valve.

The pressure-drop governor senses any pressure drop from an increased fuel flow and maintains it by adjusting a second sleeve valve, at a set value relative to engine RPM. A capsule unit compares compressor inlet and outlet pressures and adjusts the fuel flow to match the airflow. Engine gas temperature is sensed electrically and a rotary actuator automatically adjusts the throttle mechanism if the maximum temperature is reached.

PRESSURE RATIO CONTROL SYSTEM

This is a mechanical system, similar to speed and acceleration control, which uses the ratio of HP compressor delivery pressure (P_4) to air intake pressure (P_1), to control fuel flow. However, this system is particularly responsive to surging or flame out. Either condition will cause the P_4/P_1 pressure ratio to be abnormally low and the system will substantially reduce, or even shut off, fuel flow to the burners.

ELECTRONIC CONTROL (FADEC)

The initials stand for *Full Authority Digital Electronic Control*. It's a computer that controls the fuel system, based on information from various sensors, such as exhaust temperature, engine RPM, control movement, etc. Data is always flowing from the engine sensors to the computer, and is typically stored in temporary memory. When anomalies are detected, on some machines, the previous 10 seconds' worth is captured, and the next 50 seconds' worth is recorded. This data is tagged by time and date.

Input and output data is checked, but the engine will continue to operate normally with a single input data failure, so a FADEC is single fault tolerant. Power for the FADEC comes from a source on the engine.

The end result is a more precise control of engine and propeller speeds under varying flight conditions, particularly with reference to overspeeding. Other benefits include automatic starting, optimal fuel metering, faster response to power demands, better care of the engine (so more time between overhauls) and reduction of pilot workload through automation. It is also better at limiting. Being a computer, it is software-based, and one preflight check is to ensure that the right software is loaded! Also, as it's a computer, it can monitor many parameters, which is why you might see more caution lights. It will typically have two main items, the *Engine Control Unit* (ECU), on the airframe, with a processor inside, such as a 486. There is also the *Hydro Mechanical Unit* (HMU) on the engine, which works rather like the old-style FCU when the FADEC is disabled. There will also be sensors and relays for the transmission of information around the system. Many signals will be repeated to the relevant instruments.

A FADEC has the following functions:
- Flow regulation
- Automatic starting sequence
- Transmission of engine data to pilot's instruments
- Thrust management and protection of limits
- Prevent overtemperature or overspeed

A slightly less sophisticated system is the Full Authority Fuel Control (FAFC). It is electronically controlled, but does not have the same control of transient conditions in the compressor airflow system.

Engine Handling

Pulling full power just because it's there is not always a good idea. Limitations may be there for other reasons - for example, the transmission might not be able to take that much, so excessive use of power will ruin your gearbox well before the engine (and will show up as metal particles in the oil). Many turbine failures are the result of pulling too many cycles from minimum to maximum N_G (gas producer RPM), so if you don't need 100% torque, it's best not to use it. With some turbine engines, you must keep a track of the number of times you fluctuate between a range of power settings because of the heat stress. It's also best not to reduce power to the bottom stop when descending, either, and to make power changes gently, avoiding over- and undershoots.

Maximum Continuous Power is the setting that may be used indefinitely, but any between that and maximum power (usually shown as a yellow arc on the instruments - see left) will only be available for a set time limit, typically 30 minutes.

While I'm not suggesting that you should, piston engines will accept their limits being slightly exceeded from time to time with no great harm being done. Having said that, the speed at which the average Lycoming engine disintegrates is about 3450 RPM, which doesn't leave you an awful lot of room when it runs normally at 3300! Turbines, however, are less forgiving than pistons and give fewer warnings of trouble because of the closer tolerances to which they are made. This is why regular power checks should be carried out on them to keep an eye on their health. The other difference is that damage to a piston engine caused by mishandling tends to affect you, straight away, whereas that in a turbine tends to affect others down the line.

Apart from sympathetic handling, the greatest factor in preserving engine life is temperature and its rate of change. Over- and under-leaning are detrimental to engine life, and sudden cooling is as bad as overheating - chopping the throttle at height causes the cylinder head to shrink and crack with the obvious results - the thermal shock and extra lead is worth about $100 in terms of lost engine life. In other words, don't let the propeller drive the engine, but rather cut power to the point where it's doing a little work. This is because the reduced power lowers the pressure that keeps piston rings against the wall of the cylinder, so oil leaks past and glazes on the hot surfaces, degrading any sealing from compression. The only way to get rid of the glaze is by *honing*, which means a top-end overhaul. For the same reasons, a new (or rebuilt) engine should be run in hard, at least at 65% power, but preferably 70-75%, according to Textron Lycoming, so the rings are forced to seat in properly. This means not flying above 8000 feet density altitude for non-turbocharged engines. Richer mixtures are important as well. Also, open the engine compartment after shutting down on a hot day, as many external components will have suddenly lost their cooling.

After flight, many engines have a rundown period which must be strictly observed if you want to keep it for any length of time. As engines get smaller relative to power output, they have to work harder. Also, in turbines, there are no heavy areas to act as heat sinks, like the fins on a piston engine, which results in localised hotspots which may deform, but are safe if cooled properly, with the help of circulating oil inside the engine. If you shut down too quickly, the cooling air is not blown over the turbine blades and the oil no longer circulates, which means that it carbonises on the still-hot surfaces, and can build up enough to stop the parts from turning (i.e. the rotor blades may seize in their seals). This coking up could seize the engine in 50 hours or less.

Because starter systems on piston engines don't have fuses (too much current), if the starter light remains on after you release the starter button (on a piston engine), it means that the starter is still engaged. There is a small gear on the starter motor and a very large one on the engine, so the starter motor will be driven at a very high RPM. You must shut down *immediately* to avoid serious damage.

GENERAL RULES

- Without exception, observe the red-line temperature limits during takeoff, climb and high performance cruise power operation. This includes the cylinder head and oil temperatures, and exhaust temperature if you have one.
- Mixtures should be adjusted slowly. Always return the mixture control (slowly!) to full rich before increasing the power setting.
- Do not shock cool the cylinders. The maximum recommended temperature change should not exceed 10°C per minute.
- Use full rich mixture during takeoff or climb but, for fixed pitch propellers, lean to maximum RPM at full throttle before takeoff at 5000 feet density altitude or higher. Keep full throttle operations on the ground to a minimum. For direct-drive, normally aspirated engines with a prop governor, but without fuel flow or EGT, set the throttle to full power and lean mixture at max RPM.

TURBINES

The performance of a gas turbine engine depends on the mass of air passing through the engine and the acceleration imparted to it the engine. In turbojet and turbofan engines, the performance is measured in terms of thrust at the propelling nozzle. In the turboprop, it is measured as shaft horsepower (SHP).

Static thrust, or gross thrust, is that produced when the aircraft is stationary or when the engine is on a test bench, the product of the mass of air and its speed out of the back. Net thrust is that produced in flight so, to calculate it, you therefore need to take into account the speed of the aircraft. The mass of air (and the thrust developed) depends on the air density, which varies with temperature and pressure. Forward speed also helps, as there is a ram effect at the air intake when the aircraft is moving.

The thrust from a gas turbine engine is usually set by a single lever, called the throttle, or power lever. Engine RPM is then governed within certain limits.

The gas temperature should always be monitored, particularly when starting the engine, since the turbine nozzle guide vanes and first stage blades can easily be damaged from overheating. The compressor is only really efficient at high RPM, typically above 85% of the maximum. When the engines are being run at low RPM in flight, the acceleration will be much slower, so demands for power need to be though about in advance - especially as the fuel system will almost certainly be slugged to limit the fuel flow, to avoid compressor stall and surge.

The operating parameter indications in the cockpit are.

- **Thrust**. Generally shown as Engine Pressure Ratio (EPR), usually the ratio between jet pipe pressure and LP compressor inlet pressure, although on large fan engines it is often an integration of fan discharge/turbine outlet pressure to LP compressor inlet pressure.

- **Torque**. The power output of a turboprop engine is usually indicated by a torquemeter, as measured in the transmission. Comparisons are made between torque readings and reference values.

- **RPM**. Usually measured as a percentage of maximum RPM. On multi-spool engines, HP spool RPM (N_2) is always measured. LP spool or fan speed (N_1) can be indicated as well.

- **TGT**. Turbine Gas Temperature, also referred to as Jet Pipe Temperature (JPT), Exhaust Gas Temperature (EGT), Turbine Outlet Temperature (TOT), or even T4, is the most critical of engine temperatures. It is measured with thermocouples.

- **Lubricating Oil Temperature and Pressure**. Gas turbines have high rotational speeds so the oil has to work harder. One reason for high temperatures at a constant power setting is a failed heat exchanger.

- **Fuel Temperature & Pressure**. Indication of the LP fuel supply is provided.

- **Fuel Flow**. An indication of the fuel flow is given for each engine, as it provides a valuable indication of unit performance. A fuel-used indicator can also be used.

- **Vibration Monitoring**. Gas turbine engines normally don't vibrate much, so vibration is a good indication of incipient failure. Typical causes of vibration can be a damaged fan, compressor or turbine blade. Vibration monitors transmit a signal of relative amplitude of vibration within relevant critical frequency ranges.

TAKEOFF
Using reduced power helps the engines to last longer, and reduces noise levels, although the runway length will be used more or less to its full extent, as the take-off ground run and take-off distance will both be increased. For a twin-spool engine in very cold conditions, the pressure ratio will be the limiting factor. When hot and high, it will be the exhaust temperature or HP RPM. Takeoff power is limited to 5 minutes, unless there is an emergency.

INITIAL CLIMB
After takeoff the undercarriage is raised and the aircraft climbs away under takeoff power, which is reduced at some stage, usually to noise abatement settings.

Once such procedures are out of the way, climb power is set, relevant speeds are achieved and the flaps/slats are raised. The aircraft will climb away at climb speed and eventually level off at cruise height. During an initial climb from a hot and high airfield, maximum continuous power may be specified, but be aware that this is a much higher value and its over-use will shorten the life of the engines.

CLIMB
Using the appropriate climb power for the weight, the climb will eventually change to one based on Mach number as opposed to IAS. The engine power indications must be checked - do not assume that the machine knows everything! For example, as the temperature drops (usually) in the climb, on a twin spool and older engines, the LP RPM will increase relative to the HP RPM, eventually reaching the limits for the height and temperature, because the LP governor is set for takeoff power. The engine must be throttled back to keep within limits. As with any automation, on modern aircraft, the instruments still need to be monitored so you can check that they are producing what it says on the tin.

CRUISE
Engine power is reduced progressively as you level off. As fuel is burnt, the weight of the aircraft reduces, the speed increases and the power is reduced to maintain the selected speed. Settings are in terms of RPM or EPR, which will vary with the ambient conditions.

If an engine fails, drift down may well be a factor, and until you get to a stabilising height, maximum continuous or climb power may be required on the remaining engines.

DESCENT
The power is usually set to idle and the aircraft descended at the recommended IAS/Mach Number. The RPM achieved at this point are significantly higher than those you would get lower down and is to do with minimum flow settings in the FCU. If bleed air is required for anti-icing purposes a higher RPM may be specified anyway.

 Gas turbines do not accelerate very well from low RPM, due to their relative inefficiency, the inertia of the rotating bits, the FCU trying to keep the TITs in line and the exponential increase in fuel flow at the higher settings. The range is in two sections with the borderline at around 80%.

Rapid acceleration will be required during a go-around, so the approach RPM are set to a value from which engine acceleration can be achieved quickly, especially if bleed air is being used for, say, for anti-icing (on older aircraft, full or maximum continuous power is used. Otherwise, it is handled by the FMS through EPR). Acceleration times are longer anyway on a single spool engine as compared to those of a twin or triple spool engine. A lower RPM is properly set when the landing is assured.

Landing

At the touch down point, idle is selected and, when the wheels are on the ground, the spoilers are extended, followed by reverse thrust, which is most effective at a higher IAS. This is usually cancelled at about 60 knots to avoid ingestion of foreign objects, unless the aircraft will not come to a stop. Spoilers and brakes are applied automatically on some, with the help of weight-on-wheel switches. The aircraft is taxied in using minimum power.

Gas turbine engines are shut down by closing the HP fuel cock first, then the LP cock. When starting one at altitude, the ground idle RPM will be greater than at sea level.

ENGINE INSTRUMENTS

A turbine engine has to operate within certain limits - it must not be run too fast, or too hot, or have too much strain imposed on it. The greatest stress is in the hot section, or the first stage of the high pressure turbine. When jet engines are cold, they are internally pressure limited*. As the temperature rises, they become LPRPM limited, then HPRPM limited, and finally EGT limited. The more you stay away from turbine temperature limits, the more life expectancy the engine will get (on takeoff, these limits are only approached for a very short time). However, they are normally capped by a **flat rating**. A flat rated engine can maintain its power up to a certain temperature, even if the density reduces - it will therefore be temperature limited if the OAT is higher than the flat rated temperature. If you are using maximum takeoff thrust with an OAT that is below that temperature, the thrust lever will not be at its maximum stop.

*If the inlet temperature decreases, the full rated thrust and pressure inside the engine increase. The maximum thrust value at a temperature that is limited by the pressure inside the engine is flat rated power. Once the temperature goes above that limit, an EGT limiter governs the flow of fuel to the engine and the thrust will reduce.

The Tachometer

Engine RPM are a direct indication of power, so the tachometer is a primary engine instrument. Turbines rotate so fast that the numbers are too large to make sense of, so percentages are used instead (that is, 100% means full power), so that engines can be compared easily.

MECHANICAL TACHOMETERS

These are found on older piston-engined aircraft, where the feed is taken from the crankshaft.

There is a long, flexible drive shaft from the engine to the indicator, which runs at a quarter of the engine speed to reduce wear and tear. This is the reason for the 4:1 step-up gear in the base of the instrument. The longest practical length for such a

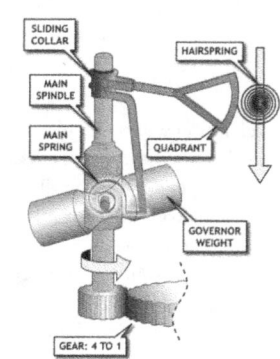

cable is 30 feet. A governor weight assumes a more horizontal position as the speed of the engine increases, which makes a sliding collar move up and down the shaft, driving a linkage to the indicator. The governor moves against a spring that moves it back to its home position when the engine speed is reduced.

Another type uses the flexible shaft to turn a magnet inside an aluminium drag cup to set up eddy currents that make the cup turn at the same speed as the magnet. The cup is supported on a shaft to which is attached a pointer and a controlling spring which opposes the turning force so that, for any one speed, the eddy current drag and spring tension are in equilibrium, and the pointer is steady.

ELECTRICAL TACHOMETERS

On more modern aircraft, tachogenerators driven by the engine can put out DC, or single- or three-phase AC, which can drive a voltmeter calibrated in RPM over electrical cabling. The lack of moving parts allows engines to be further away from the cockpit, and you don't need separate power supplies. With the DC version, output voltage varies with RPM, and drives a moving coil indicator which needs a commutator and carbon brushes, so there is wear and sparking which can cause radio interference (or fires). Also, voltage loss in transmission leads to indication errors. A single-phase brushless AC generator, on the other hand, has its output rectified to DC, so the mechanical problems are not there, but indication errors are. One disadvantage of a single phase AC generator tachometer is the possibility of the values transmitted being affected by line resistance, but spurious signals from a DC generator's commutator are avoided and the information is independent.

A Three-Phase AC Tachogenerator has its AC frequency varying with RPM, to drive a squirrel cage motor at the instrument. Frequency is proportional to transmitter drive speed. These normally rotate slightly slower than the generator, with the slip depending on the torque required. Because frequency is sensed rather than voltage, voltage losses are not a problem, but extra wiring is needed to carry three phases.

ELECTRONIC TACHOMETERS

It is not always possible to drive a tacho generator from some points in a turbine engine. In these cases, a system with fewer moving parts is used (alternating current is required for the system to work).

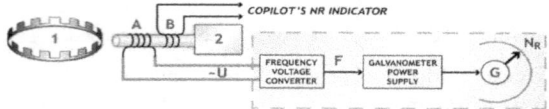

The picture above shows a suitable system for measuring propeller RPM, but the principles are the same for engines. RPM is sensed by a magnetic probe by a toothed wheel, called a phonic wheel.

The probe counts the passage of teeth on the wheel as it rotates by changes induced in its magnetic field, which creates an electrical current whose frequency changes in proportion to the RPM. This is calculated by a PFM box* and the results fed to an indicator in the cockpit.

*Pure Magic.

Manifold Pressure Gauge

These are only found on certain reciprocating engines where engine power needs to be accurately set, such as those with superchargers and constant speed propellers.

The power output from a piston engine depends on its speed and the absolute pressure in the inlet manifold. As the pressure in the induction system is below the ambient air pressure at idle or low power settings, using absolute pressure saves you dealing with positive or negative numbers.

The faster the engine runs, the more working cycles there are per minute, which is how fixed pitch propellers are operated. In this case, the MAP is adjusted automatically - the only power reference is the RPM gauge.

The Manifold Absolute Pressure (MAP) gauge shows the absolute pressure of the fuel/air mixture in inches at a point in the induction system, and is required equipment for a variable pitch propeller, which therefore has two controls that regulate the power and performance of the engine. Engine and propeller RPM are set by the RPM lever in the middle. The lever to the left (not always in a Beech) sets the MAP and engine power.

The pressure is measured downstream of the carburettor or FCU, and downstream of any supercharger. The measuring port in the induction system is connected by tubing to a bellows or diaphragm in the instrument. As the MAP gauge is an aneroid barometer, it will read ambient pressure when the engine is stopped (around 30 inches).

The higher the pressure is, the higher the density of the fuel/air mix* is, and more is potentially available for heat release, so you can get some idea of the engine's power output - that extracted from the charge is proportional to the manifold pressure, as discussed previously. Turbine machines use a torquemeter. The maximum horsepower output you can get from an engine when it is operated at safe continuous RPM & MAP is the *rated power*, or rated boost, marked as a red line on the MAP gauge.

*Richness is real ratio relative to the theoretical ratio.

The point beyond which it will be impossible to obtain rated boost is called the *critical altitude*. This doesn't mean that the aircraft stops climbing, however - the manifold pressure available at full throttle will simply be less than the rated boost. As every value of manifold pressure will have its own full throttle height, the critical altitude is simply full throttle height for rated boost.

 Boost pressure is generally considered to be any manifold pressure above 30 ins Hg*. The boost gauge has one side connected to the induction system and the other to a sealed chamber which is kept at sea level pressure.

*Ambient pressure is *static boost*. If there is a break in the line between the MAP gauge and the induction system, the gauge will show atmospheric pressure.

The *service ceiling* is the altitude at which you can achieve 100 fpm rate of climb. The *absolute ceiling* is when you can only (just) maintain level flight. You can extend the service ceiling by *supercharging* or *turbocharging*, discussed above.

Remember, the throttle controls the horsepower, and engine RPM is concerned with the load (if you kept the throttle setting constant, and increased the load, you will find that the engine RPM will drop). High MAP and low RPM makes an engine work too hard, and means severe wear and damage, and detonation, so observe the limits.

The reading on the gauge increases as the throttle is opened but, in an unsupercharged engine, it will drop with height for a given throttle setting, because there is less atmospheric pressure to push the useful charge into the cylinder, and you must keep opening the throttle.

When the engine is stopped, the MAP gauge will read atmospheric pressure, just below 30 inches (1013 hPa). When the engine is running, MAP is below atmospheric because of the pressure drop across the butterfly valve (the engine is sucking air in). For a non-turbocharged engine at maximum power, the manifold pressure is very close to atmospheric, so you get maximum power by letting the engine breathe freely. The manifold pressure can be higher than atmospheric if you use a turbocharger.

Humidity has an effect, too, although it is less with turbines. The more water there is in the air, the less air gets into the engine, therefore the mixture is richer and burns slower. The point is that performance graphs do not show this, so factor them by around 10% if the air is wet, say after a shower. You will get the most engine power when it's cold and dry, in high pressure conditions.

The Torquemeter

This has been covered under *Airframes & Systems*.

Temperature

Operating at higher than intended temperatures will cause *loss of power, excessive oil consumption and damage to the engine*.

PISTON ENGINES

In a piston aeroplane, the **Cylinder Head Temperature** (CHT) gauge (which uses a thermocouple) shows the temperature of one selected cylinder, usually a rearmost in a horizontally opposed engine, which is not necessarily the one that reaches peak temperature first, even though it may end up as the hottest, so a margin of 25° rich off peak may still not be enough to stop another cylinder from getting too close to peak for comfort, or even lean.

Knowledge of the **Exhaust Gas Temperature** (EGT), on the other hand, is needed for leaning the mixture efficiently. The probe is in the exhaust manifold of a fuel injected engine. Leaning the mixture reduces the excess fuel and makes the reading increase until there is none and the needle reaches its peak, where there is complete combustion (you get around 15% more range at this best SFC point). If you lean slightly rich, you will obtain maximum cruise power.

The reason the temperature cools either side of the peak reading is that on the one hand (rich), there is too much fuel and, on the other (lean), there is too much air (having said that, the hottest CHT is between 25-50° *rich* off peak EGT, because that's where the peak cylinder pressure occurs, with a high rate of heat transfer to the cylinder head, so you need to lean past it).

However, although being lean of peak works, there is much more potential for causing damage to the engine if it is mismanaged - it needs more monitoring to be used effectively, as the temperature at the exhaust will still be high, which is not good for the valves, and particularly acute with high performance turbocharged engines - the Australians found that leaning causes lead oxybromide deposits to cling to parts inside the combustion chamber, which could become hotspots and cause detonation (the lead appears as a result of chemical changes in avgas as it burns). At richer settings, the lead either doesn't form or is swept out of the cylinder.

Tip: Don't forget to enrich the mixture before increasing power when at peak EGT, or when increasing to more than 75% power. Move the engine controls slowly and smoothly, particularly with a turbocharger. Harsh movements (on older engines) will result in a cough and splutter and having no power can be embarrassing.

Tip: An EGT gauge is a fast-reading instrument that responds almost instantly to changes in power and the fuel/air mixture. The CHT gauge, on the other hand, measures the core temperature near one of the combustion chambers, so it reacts more slowly and may not represent the whole picture, especially when there is only one carburettor supplying several cylinders and one may be hotter than the others. The *oil temperature gauge* (which reacts very slowly to changes) is the best measure of how heat is balanced around the engine, which means that having the correct amount of oil in it is essential, if only for cooling purposes. However, having too much oil can be just as much a problem as having too little, as it can creep up the pushrod tubes and pick up heat directly from the cylinders.

One consideration with low power when it's very cold is that the engine may not warm up properly and water that forms from combustion may not evaporate, so oil won't lubricate properly.

Although many flight manuals state that, as soon as an engine is running without stuttering, it's safe to use it to its fullest extent, try warming up for a few minutes before applying any load, at least until you get a positive indication on the oil temperature (and pressure) gauges. This ensures a film of oil over all parts, and no excessive wear. In addition, when the oil is cold, its pressure will be higher, and too much throttle will only ensure that the pressure valves will let unfiltered oil into the system (high oil pressure spikes are also bad for the oil cooler).

Even better, warm the engine before you start it, because the insides contract at different rates - in really cold weather the cylinders may have the grip of death on the pistons and cause some strain when you turn the starter (manufacturers tend to suggest preheating around -10°C, but many pilots do it around 0°C. Don't forget the oil cooler, as warm oil from the engine meeting cold oil inside might also cause a burst). Equally important is not letting an engine idle when it's cold, as it must be fast enough to create a splash of oil inside (about 1,000 RPM is fine).

TURBINE OUTLET TEMPERATURE

One of the most important instruments in your cockpit is the *Turbine Outlet Temperature* (TOT) gauge, which shows the heat coming out of the back end.

It is particularly important during starting because, if the battery is too weak to spin the engine properly, there will be less airflow through it, and not as much cooling available, leading to a hot start and an expensive repair as the back end melts. During flight, on hot days, this temperature may well be the limiting factor in the payload you can take, even if you have lots of torque left.

A red triangle, or dot, or diamond on an engine instrument face or glass indicates the maximum limits for high transients, as found when starting

High temperatures in the 700-1000°C range are measured with *thermocouples*, which are based on the idea that dissimilar metals welded together can create an electrical potential at their junction, proportional to the temperature (the very small voltages are detected by a *galvanometer*). In other words, the voltage output is determined by the difference in heat between the two ends, if the cold end is kept at a constant temperature (intermediate metals in the circuit will not modify the emf either if their contact points are kept at equal temperatures). Thermocouples are wired in parallel so the failure of one does not stop the whole system. As external power is not needed, when you shut down on some aircraft, you can check that the TOT is not moving rapidly out of limits.

For higher temperatures, a *radiation pyrometer* measures the frequency of emitted radiation, and can deduce the actual turbine blade temperature. Its advantage is that it can perform measurements independent of the supply voltage.

The reason why the Turbine Outlet Temperature is measured after the turbine wheels is because it is simply too hot for a thermocouple to survive anywhere else. Instead, a more severe limit is imposed on the TOT to protect the turbine(s) at the other end. The heat is kept within limits with cooling air extracted from the compressor, which is driven by the turbine.

An instrument may contain *overspeed detectors* in the form of pointers or warning lights. These may only be reset by engineering, for obvious reasons.

Fuel Flowmeters

The Flight Management Computer needs to know the aircraft weight, which will include the fuel on board, in order to calculate the relevant speeds and ensure they are within limits (the 757 uses this information to calculate flap settings on the run). To do this, we need to know how much fuel has been used over a flight. Such information may be displayed on a cockpit gauge and passed to the autopilot and navigation systems.

The fuel flow may be measured by volume (litres or gallons) or mass (lbs or kg) over time, usually between the FCU and engine burners (an instrument that shows how much fuel has been used as well as the rate of flow is an *integrated flowmeter*). The display in the cockpit can be analogue or digital, and the information can also be passed to autopilot or navigation systems

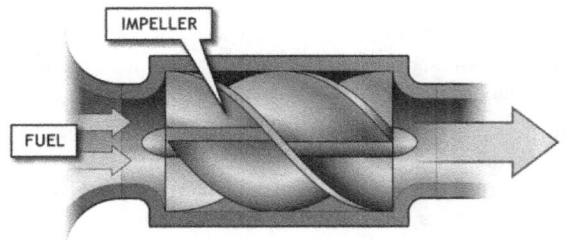

The flow is proportional to the square root of the pressure drop across an orifice. Many light aircraft simply use an adapted pressure gauge - in piston engines with fuel injection systems the fuel pressure is directly proportional to engine power and therefore to fuel consumption. Fuel pressure gauges often also have fuel flow or engine power indications. The coloured arcs on the face of the instrument will be similar to those of the MAP gauge, namely a blue arc for cruise power and lean mixtures and a green one for higher power and richer mixtures. More modern systems use an electrical sensor that reacts to the change in torque or speed of an impeller that has a magnet in one blade. Pick off coils have a sinusoidal signal induced in them, proportional to the speed of the impeller, which is proportional to the fuel flow. The signal can be corrected for temperature. A still more modern method is to measure a phase shift between impulses. In a turbine, the flow meter is fitted after the HP cock and before the spray nozzle.

LUBRICATION

Friction can be quite handy, but not inside an engine! Without a way of making all the surfaces rub smoothly against each other, they would get hot, and suffer from scoring damage. Oil does many things, including:

- **Cooling**. Oil is hot when it comes out of an engine, and to preserve its lubricating qualities it must be cooled. This is why monitoring oil temperature is so important. Hot oil is cooled in an oil cooler, which is exposed to the airflow.
- **Cushioning.** A film of oil has three distinct layers, the outside two of which cling to each surface, and the middle one moves between them, providing some sort of buffer.
- **Flushing & Cleaning**. Oil carries contaminants to the oil filter where they are blocked.
- **Lubrication**. Reduces friction in two ways:
  - *Film Lubrication*, where a thin film of oil between two surfaces stops them touching. The thinner the oil (i.e. the less viscous), the easier the movement is.
  - *Boundary Lubrication* is a state of near breakdown where the film above is reduced to next to nothing.
- **Sealing**
- **Prevention Of Corrosion**

Types Of Lubrication System

In aircraft, oil reaches bearing under pressure through holes in the crankshaft and bearings, rather than with splash and mist. The oil passes through as each set of holes line up per revolution.

WET SUMP

This is very simple, because the engine oil is kept in a sump which is under (and part of) the engine, where the crankshaft and other moving parts rotate, splashing it all around (*splash and mist lubrication*). When you start the engine, the oil is sucked from the sump through a filter to the galleries around the engine casing.

It is generally thought that wet sump systems do not use a pump, but they can, as with the Piper Cherokee. Wet sump systems tend not to be used on modern aero engines, as the bearings are starved of oil when the aircraft is inverted.

DRY SUMP

A dry sump system keeps the oil in a tank *outside* the engine (sometimes above it for gravity feed), and the oil is force fed under pressure to where it is needed - the sump in this case is used merely as a collector for stray oil dripping off the components inside. Because the engine parts aren't having to make their way through oil in the sump, they have less work to do and more power is therefore available. Less oil is also needed.

The "oil pump" is actually two pumps running on the same shaft - the scavenge pump and the engine oil pump.

The scavenge pump (which pulls oil *from* the engine) has the greater capacity in order to keep the sump dry, or to stop oil accumulating in the engine, especially after an unusual attitude, where oil might not necessarily be in the collection area until the machine is righted again, and the pump must cope with the surge (also, overnight, the crankcase drains into the sump and there will be oil remaining when the machine is started if the pumps were the same size). In practice, the scavenge pump is 25-30% larger than the pressure pump.

Pumps are usually mesh gear types, where one gear is driven, which drives the other, to force oil round the outside of the gears within their housing.

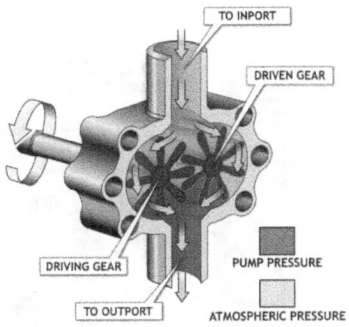

Engine oil reservoirs are sometimes at the front of the engine because the hot oil can heat the air intake.

Pressure is regulated by the *oil pressure relief valve*, which compensates for oil pump speed and viscosity variations with engine speed changes through the tension on its spring - in fact, engine oil pressure is adjusted by changing the spring pressure*. If oil pressure gets too high here, the pressure relief valve dumps it back to the reservoir. One symptom of problems with the relief valve is *lower than normal oil pressure*, with *steady oil temperature*.

*The reading on the oil pressure gauge is the pressure of the oil on the *outlet* side of the pressure pump. In other words, the oil pressure in a piston engine is measured immediately downstream of the oil pump.

An oil cooler in the return line to the oil tank cools things down after the oil has passed through the scavenge pump (that is, the oil cooler is *downstream* of the scavenge pump), if it is above a certain temperature. If not, it is fed directly to the engine.

CHIP DETECTORS

Modern engines work at the edge of technology in terms of speed and temperature. They have to deliver maximum performance, reliably and safely, while being as lightly constructed as possible.

For example, the main engine bearings need to cope with internal engine speeds and pressures on top of any loads generated by what we do with the aircraft. The contact areas between the balls or rollers and the bearing races they run against are only microns thick, and repeated stress can lead to flakes of metal breaking off the bearing surfaces (this is known as *spalling*). The resulting rough contact surfaces will result in the bearing breaking up and the engine seizing.

Inside engines (and transmissions) are magnetic chip detectors, which are designed to pick up stray bits of metal floating in the oil. They provide **warning of impending failure** without having to inspect filters.

Chip detectors should be as close as possible to the element being monitored, but always upstream of filters and coolers. When enough metal has built up, an electrical contact is bridged, with the aim of illuminating a light in your cockpit to warn you of the situation. Metal particles not picked up should be trapped by an oil filter. Naturally, if all this is detected early enough, costly repairs or even the loss of the engine should be avoided.

Fine particles occur during normal engine operation, and more frequently during running in (in the first 50 hours or so) but larger ones that occur more frequently can indicate some sort of failure. The problem is that multiple particles can give the same continuity as a single large particle, so you still don't really know what's going on round there.

The magnetic detectors are there to *warn of impending failure*, and are designed to be removable for frequent checking, but can often not be put back. There may or may not be a connection to warning systems in the flight deck.

TURBINE ENGINES

In a turboprop engine, the oil system also supports the propeller reduction gearing and provides oil for the propeller pitch control mechanism.

The oil must protect against corrosion, and its viscosity must be low enough to flow at low starting temperatures, but high enough to absorb mechanical loads which, luckily, are lower than in a piston engine, so gas turbine oil is thinner. This makes starting in low temperatures easier, and you can start (without pre-heating the oil), down to -40°C. Mineral oils are not generally consistent enough in terms of viscosity over the wide temperature ranges of a gas turbine, so synthetic low viscosity oils are used.

Self-contained recirculatory systems are the norm. Oil is contained in a tank and distributed around the engine by oil pumps, with enough of a reserve in the tank to cope with normal, minor losses in flight. Some short duration engines use a total loss system, in which oil is expended overboard after circulation, through the engine.

Picture Below: Dry Sump Lubrication System

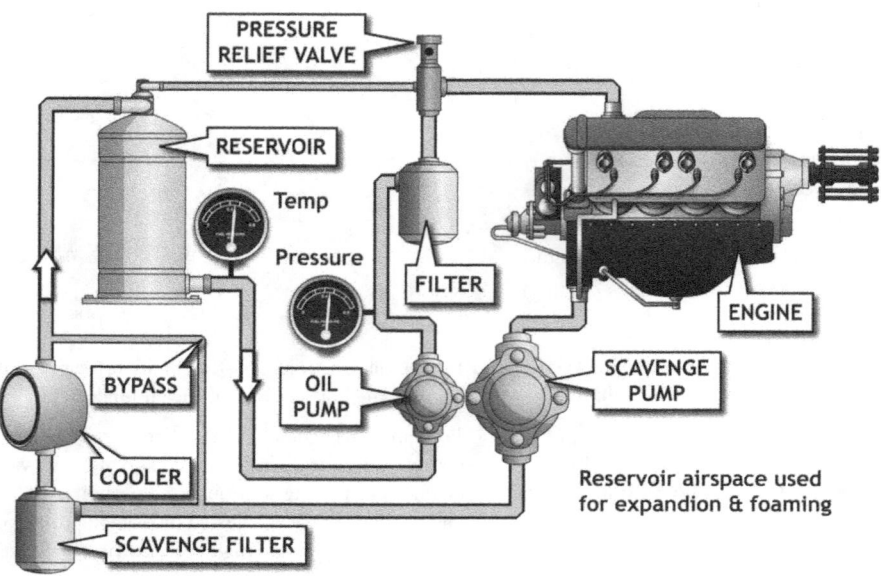

There are two basic types of recirculatory system - the pressure relief valve and full flow systems, both dry sump. In both, the factors crucial to safe operation are oil temperature and pressure, as indicated on the flight deck.

Pressure Relief Valve System

The flow to the bearing chambers is controlled with a constant pressure in the supply line. A spring-loaded pressure relief valve on the outlet side of the pressure pump opens to return oil to the suction side of the pump (as shown), or the tank. The valve starts to open at a pressure corresponding to engine idling speed. The faster the engine (and, therefore, the pump), the more the relief valve opens to maintain the pressure.

One problem system is the tendency of bearing chamber pressure to increase with engine speed. This creates a back pressure that reduces the oil flow to the bearing chambers, so this system is unsuitable for engines where high bearing chamber pressures are necessary because of high bearing loads. The problem can be reduced to some extent by helping the spring force with bearing chamber pressure, but where the chamber pressure is necessarily high, the full flow system, is used.

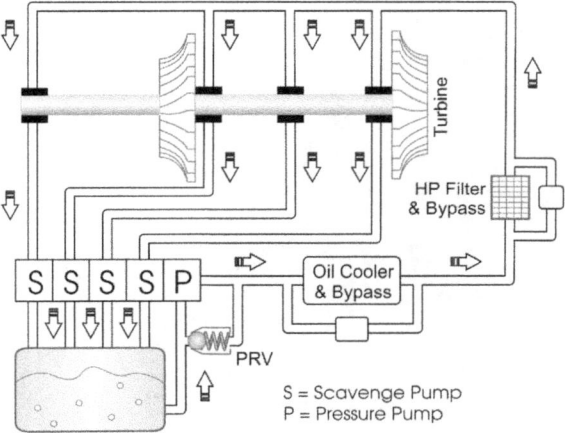

Full Flow System

This system does not use a pressure relief valve, but feeds the output of the oil pressure pump direct to the oil supply line to the bearing chambers. Thus, the higher the engine (and pump) speed the greater the quantity of oil supplied to the bearings. Because all the oil pumped is supplied to the bearings, with none being spilled back by a pressure relief valve, pump sizes can be smaller.

Because of the higher pressures, pressure-limiting bypass valves are fitted with components such as coolers and filters, which could otherwise be damaged.

System Components

The oil tank is mounted externally on the engine. Its content can be checked with a sight glass or dipstick. Replenishment may be by pressure or gravity filling. There will be a de-aeration device in the return line to remove air from the oil returning from the bearing chambers.

The scavenge pumps and pressure pumps are usually spur gear types, although vane or gerotor (Roots type) pumps can be used. The scavenge and pressure pumps are contained in a common casing with a single drive from the accessory gearbox.

Oil distribution is usually a spray from a jet orifice.

The oil cooler is a heat exchanger connected to the low pressure area that uses a matrix of tubes through which the cooling medium (fuel or air) flows. Engine oil is directed over the outside of the tubes and heat is transferred by conduction.

A pressure maintaining valve ensures that the oil pressure is higher than the fuel pressure to ensure that fuel does not get into the oil system and then the hot regions of the engine, which would be a potential fire hazard. In other words, if a tube fails, you will get oil in the fuel rather than fuel in the oil. Having said that, some engine manufacturers have the pressures the other way round, as with the Boeing 777.

When downstream of the HP fuel pump, internal leakage of the exchanger will make the oil level rise.

A bypass valve protects the cooler and the engine if the cooler gets blocked.

Small particles of metallic debris from the bearing chambers and gearboxes are collected by magnetic chip detectors in the scavenge side of the system.

Bearings

Gas turbine engine bearings can be ball or roller types. Roller bearings are shown in the picture:

To reduce the transmission of vibration from the rotating assembly to the bearing housing, oil is fed to a narrow clearance between the outer race (cage) of the bearing and the housing. The film of oil filling the clearance absorbs the radial shock loads of vibration. Air, which tends to accumulate in the oil at the bearings, is separated and exhausted to atmosphere, before the oil returns to the tank, by a centrifugal breather.

The lubricating oil is filtered at various points to stop debris floating around, with coarse strainers at the tank outlet and/or scavenger pump inlet.

If the oil filter becomes clogged, the oil supply to the bearings in gas turbine engines is maintained with differential pressure that opens the filter bypass valve.

Engine Oils

An engine that is not used enough develops corrosion very quickly on the inside, and rust flakes, which are very abrasive, will circulate when the engine is started, which is why you have to change the oil even when you don't fly a lot. Another reason is an increased water content, which will have an acidic effect once it mixes with the by-products of combustion. The most wear takes place in the first seconds of a cold start, after the oil has been allowed to settle. Priming will wash whatever oil is left off the cylinder walls, so don't do too much, and maintain minimum RPM to let the oil circulate. The pressure will be high just after starting, but will reduce to normal once the engine warms up. Excessive oil pressure is acceptable *for a few seconds* on a cold day.

In fact, after starting a cold engine, particularly in winter, you can allow the oil pressure not to rise for about 30 seconds, because it may be too thick to get through the passages until it gets warm. Otherwise, you should shut the engine down immediately.

 If you use high power before the engine is warmed up, bearings and other parts will suffer from oil starvation.

When flying, the oil temperature and pressure gauges work with each other. If the pressure is low, expect the temperature to rise because it is working harder, unless there is none going past the temperature detector.

VISCOSITY

Oils come in various thicknesses, or *viscosities*, which indicate their resistance to flow. The lower the viscosity number, the thinner the oil is, so you would use 120 oil in Summer, 100 in Fall or Spring, 80 in Winter and 65 in the Arctic. To keep the oil thin, in the cold, one trick is to pour a few litres of petrol into the oil just after closing down at night, so it is very thin in the morning and you can start the engine. By the time the oil has warmed up, the petrol has evaporated and you can carry on (but check the flight manual to see if such *Oil Dilution* is acceptable).

MINERAL OIL (RED BAND)

Mineral oil (castor oil) has no additives and is now only used in new or overhauled engines, to help them bed in. This is because it can oxidise when exposed to high temperatures or when it gets frothy, and form a sludge in low temperatures, and there are better modern oils for long term use. Look for a label on the oil filler to make sure that you only use this type of oil.

DETERGENT OIL

This has chemicals that help with cleaning, etc., including keeping particles suspended, but it is no longer available.

ASHLESS DISPERSANT (AD) OIL

This does not form carbon like mineral oil does, although it does get dark soon after an oil change. It has an additive that causes the components of sludge to repel each other and remain in suspension until they reach the oil filter, where they are screened out. It is the most used oil.

SYNTHETIC OILS

Synthetic oils have been developed to cover wide temperature ranges, for jets at high altitudes and reciprocating engines operating at high temperatures. However, synthetic oil is expensive, and another drawback is that it holds contaminants longer.

MIXING OILS

The official stance is that you should not mix oils, period, especially mineral oil. However, within their basic groups, there is an element of compatibility, but you should never use motor vehicle oil, because it is designed for liquid cooled engines that operate at lower temperatures.

AD oil is compatible with mineral oil, at the expense of some of its advantages. However, not enough data is available to confirm that the same situation exists with synthetic oil, so it would not be a good idea to mix it.

INSTRUMENTS

ircraft instruments base their readings on the measurement and comparison of the different temperatures and pressures found inside and outside the aircraft. They will cover four areas of aircraft operation - *Control, Performance, Navigation,* and *Miscellaneous,* which includes voltmeters, gear position indicators, etc.

Instruments must be able to be read easily, in terms of position, lighting and clarity. They can have up to four sub-systems, not all of which will be in the same case:

- Detection (e.g. temperature probe).
- Measurement (aneroid capsule).
- Coupling (suitable linkage between measurement and indication).
- Indication (pointer, or digital display).

At the point of measurement, a measuring body absorbs some energy and converts it to a quantity that has a functional relationship with the quantity measured. As some energy is absorbed, that quantity will never be the same as the true value. Corrections are usually included with amplification signals because the sample is small.

Displays can be *circular*, as shown on the right, or *straight* (like a tape) or *digital*, or even a combination, as with this display from an AW 139):

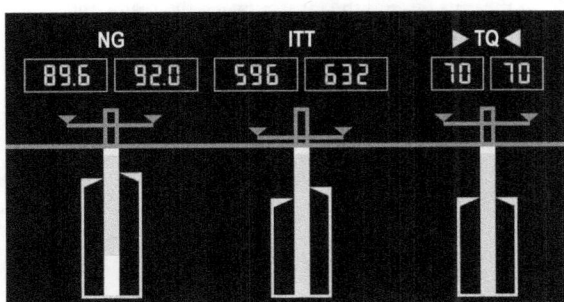

Instruments can also be classified into four groups, after the variations in properties of certain materials against variations in temperature:

- **Expansion**
- **Vapour-pressure**
- **Electrical**, based on:
    - *Resistance*, or
    - *Increase in electromotive force*
- **Radiation**

Most will be electrical.

Right: Circular Instrument

Lighting

White lighting is usually combined with grey cockpit interiors because:

- you have unrestricted use of colour
- warning indicators become more prominent
- black instrument cases against a grey background will emphasize their size and shape

Individual instruments may be lit by:

- integral lighting, which is built into the instrument
- ring, eyebrow, or post lighting, all of which are fitted to the outside of the instrument case
- floodlighting

PRESSURE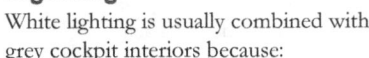

In many systems, the pressure of a liquid or gas must be measured and indicated, either directly, where the source of pressure is connected to the instrument (mostly Bourdon tubes), or remotely, where it can be some distance away, with electrical signals being sent instead. Such systems would have a transmitter at the pressure source and an indicator on a panel. This means you won't have yucky fluids in the cockpit, and you don't have to carry a lot of plumbing. Indicators can be based on *synchronous receivers, DC* or *AC ratiometers* or *servos*.

Pressure is the *force per unit area*, or the force exerted on an area divided by the size of that area:

$$P = \frac{F}{A}$$

where F is Force (N) and A is the Area in m^2. The result:

$$\frac{N}{m^2}$$

is equal to 1 *pascal* (Pa), which is the standard unit of pressure under the SI system (see *Principles of Flight*).

There are several types of pressure, including:

- **Absolute pressure**, or the difference between the pressure of a fluid and absolute zero (a vacuum). It is usually measured in inches of mercury, as on a Manifold

Air Pressure gauge. It would be the sum of gauge pressure (next) and atmospheric pressure, and is what forces the fuel and air charge into the cylinders of a piston engine.

- **Gauge pressure**, on the other hand, is measured against ambient air pressure, so it is absolute pressure minus atmospheric pressure. In other words, any variance from atmospheric pressure is called gauge pressure. For example, fuel and oil pressure instruments indicate the amount that the pump has raised the pressure of the fluid above that of the atmosphere Note that it can be positive or negative. If the absolute pressure stays constant, gauge pressure varies with atmospheric pressure.
- **Differential pressure** is just the difference in pressure between two points, as represented by the airspeed indicator. Two inlet ports may be used, with each connected to one of the sealed volumes whose pressure is to be monitored.

Pressure Sensing

Pressure is measured against a reference, such as a column of mercury, or by acting over a known area and measuring the force produced. Aneroid gauges use metallic pressure sensing elements that flex under pressure.

Aneroid means *without fluid*, or *not wet* (depends on which book you read), to distinguish between aneroid and hydrostatic gauges, which do use fluid, although aneroid gauges can be used to measure liquid pressure. The pressure sensing element may be a Bourdon tube, a diaphragm, a capsule, or bellows, all of which will change their shape in response to the pressure. The deflection is transmitted by a suitable linkage that will rotate a pointer around a graduated dial, or activate a secondary transducer that might control a digital display, the most common of which measure changes in capacitance that follow the mechanical deflection.

In order of sensitivity, you have:

DIAPHRAGMS

Diaphragms are circular metal discs that are corrugated for strength, to provide larger deflections. They detect low pressures. One side of the disc is exposed to the pressure to be measured, and the other is linked to the indicating mechanism.

ANEROID CAPSULES

In gauges used for small measurements, or for absolute pressure, the gear train and needle may be driven by an enclosed and sealed chamber, called an *aneroid*, as used in aneroid barometers, altimeters, altitude recording barographs, and the altitude telemetry instruments in weather balloon radiosondes. The sealed chamber is used as a reference pressure and the needles are driven by the external pressure.

A capsule consists of two diaphragms placed face to face and joined at their edges to form a chamber that may be completely sealed or left open to a source of (absolute) pressure. They are also used for low(ish) pressures, but are more sensitive than diaphragms.

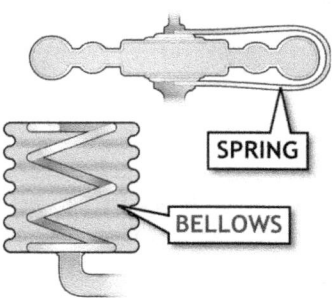

BELLOWS

Bellows are an extension of the capsule (think of them as several unsealed capsules joined together), but operate like a helical compression spring - indeed, there may even be a spring inside to increase the *spring rate* and to help the bellows return to its normal length once the source of pressure is removed. They are used for higher pressures.

THE BOURDON TUBE

The most common pressure sensor was invented by French watchmaker Eugene Bourdon in 1849, in which a C-shaped elliptical hollow spring tube is sealed at one end, with the other end connected to a source of pressure. The pressure differential from the inside to the outside causes the tube to change from an elliptical to a more circular shape, and to straighten out, rather like an uncoiling hose. Which way it moves is determined by the curvature of the tubing, as the inside radius is slightly shorter than that on the outside, and the ratio between the major and minor axes depends on what sensitivity you need - the larger the ratio, the greater it is.

The pressure range is governed by the *tubing wall thickness* and the *radius of the curvature*.

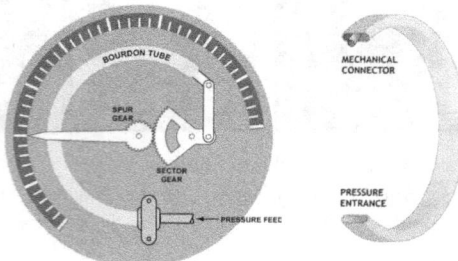

A specific pressure causes movement for a specific distance. When the pressure is removed, the tube returns to its original shape. To do this, the material used requires a form of heat treatment (*spring tempering*) to make it retain its original shape closely while allowing some elasticity under a load. Beryllium copper, phosphor bronze, and various alloys of steel and stainless steel are good for this purpose, but steel has a limited service life due to corrosion. Most gauges use phosphor bronze.

In summary, a Bourdon-based gauge uses a coiled tube which causes the rotation of an indicator arm connected to it, as it expands due to pressure increase.

INSTRUMENTS
Temperature

MANOMETER

The term *manometer* is often used to refer specifically to liquid column hydrostatic instruments. These consist of a vertical column of liquid in a tube whose ends are exposed to different pressures, with the difference in fluid height being proportional to the pressure difference.

The simplest design is a closed-end U-shape, with one side connected to the region of interest. A force equal to the applied pressure multiplied by the area of the bore will force the liquid downwards until, eventually, the two levels will stand the same distance above and below the original level. If you take into account the area of the tube bore and the density of the liquid, you can calculate pressure from the difference in the levels. Any fluid can be used, but mercury is preferred for its high density and low vapour pressure, so the tube can be shorter.

Manometers are used for calibration purposes.

TEMPERATURE

Knowledge of the air temperature is needed for performance calculations, anti-ice control and calculation of true airspeed (TAS), amongst other things.

The white arc on a temperature gauge represents a special operating range. A yellow arc is an exceptional range.

Total Air Temperature (TAT)

In the same way that we must deal with two types of pressure (static and dynamic), there are two types of temperature (static and total). On large jets, TAT is used to determine maximum N_1 or EPR. It is displayed with a calculated OAT in the cockpit.

Whatever detects the temperature must necessarily be in the airstream. At higher speeds, the boundary layer can be slowed down or stopped (relatively speaking) and be affected by adiabatic compression (and friction) that raises the temperature, so whatever temperature is indicated will be higher than the Static (Outside) Air Temperature (SAT) by an amount that is proportional to TAS, so the errors get larger as speed increases (although RAM rise is negligible up to about Mach 0.3).

TAT is the temperature that would be recorded if you could stop dead during flight (i.e. with nothing frictionally induced - on the ground, TAT/RAT = SAT). It is technically the maximum rise possible (SAT + 100% of RAM Rise), and can be thought of as the *indicated* air temperature, or what the aircraft feels, which is the same as the OAT plus adiabatic heating. In modern aircraft, TAT & SAT come from the ADC, because the information is needed for the Flight Management System. If your system cannot measure TAT correctly, you must use a Recovery Factor (see below).

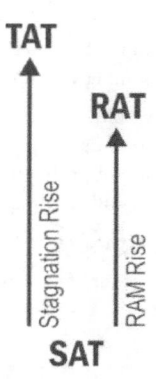

TAT is higher than or equal to SAT, depending on the Mach number and the SAT.

Static Air Temperature (SAT)

Where the air has only partially been brought to rest (as it would be if you used a more basic thermometer than the Rosemount, mentioned overleaf), you don't get so much of a temperature rise. The difference is called *RAM rise*, and the indicated temperature is *RAM Air Temperature*, which is equal to SAT + a percentage of RAM Rise.

As SAT is calculated, it may also be called the *Corrected* or *True Outside Air Temperature* (COAT).

The formula used is:

$$SAT = \frac{TAT}{(1 + 0.2\ KM^2)}$$

Where K = recovery factor (below) and M = Mach no.

The ADC does this as a function of Mach number. If you don't have one, you can obtain TAS as a function of Calibrated Airspeed and local air density (or static air temperature and pressure altitude which determine density) on the flight computer.

Recovery Factor

The difference between TAT and SAT is the *stagnation rise*, and the proportion of stagnation temperature that can actually be sensed by the aircraft instruments is the *recovery factor* or *K value*, which is governed by the thermometer. Thus, the recovery factor expresses the sensitivity of a temperature sensor as a percentage. It is determined by flight testing and will be found in the flight manual.

With a recovery factor of 1, a thermometer is measuring TAT, which is SAT + 100% of stagnation rise. If a more basic thermometer has a recovery factor of 0.8, it is only measuring SAT + 80% of the RAM rise, or the temperature of air that has been brought only partially to rest, so the measured temperature is called the Ram Air Temperature (RAT), and the difference between it and the Static Air Temperature is called the ram rise. If the recovery factor is zero, only SAT is measured. For example, what is the Ram Air Temperature if the SAT is -20°C, the stagnation rise is 10°C and recovery factor 80%?

$$-20 + 8 = -12°C$$

If a temperature sensor with a recovery factor of 0.75 indicates 30° and the SAT is 25°, what is the RAM rise? 6.7°. The trick is to remember that the 5° is 0.75.

RAT would only equal TAT when the ram rise is equal to the full stagnation rise (using a thermometer with a K factor of 1). The Rosemount probe (below) is assumed to have a K factor of 1.0, hence its other name of *Total Air Temperature Probe*.

Recovery is factored in for Mach number compressibility.

The recovery factor of a flush bulb temperature sensor varies between 0.75 - 0.9.

Thermometers

REMOTE BULB THERMOMETER

This consists of a bulb and a Bourdon tube filled with liquid or vapour, so the Bourdon tube could also loosely be regarded as measuring temperature (as expressed by one exam question), but it is still really measuring pressure. Expansion of the liquid causes the tube to lengthen, which moves the indicator, using the usual suitable linkage, as described above. With the vapour system, only the bulb has liquid in, which alters the pressure in the tube as it expands, with the same results, but you will get indicator errors with changes in atmospheric pressure.

RESISTIVE COIL THERMOMETER

The small, but stable, resistance of a nickel or platinum coil changes with absolute temperature. The coil is in a circuit with a fixed voltage, changes in which (from resistance) are measured with a meter calibrated in °C.

BIMETALLIC STRIP THERMOMETER

Below about 150 kts, a thermometer like that shown below is good enough for getting the OAT.

The probe sticks out into the airstream, and the dial is inside the cockpit. The works consist of a helical (coil-shaped) bimetallic strip that twists as the temperature changes, and moves the pointer.

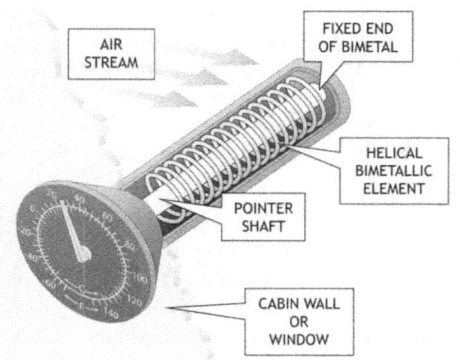

The probe cannot be shrouded from the Sun, and it is necessarily next to the fuselage skin, so its readings can be affected by kinetic heating, even at low speeds - at 150 kts, the rise can be around 3°. Being crude instruments, they are also subject to other errors, so a professional rule of thumb is to assume an error of about 2-3°.

THERMISTOR

The change in resistance with these is greater than with a resistive coil, and therefore easier to detect, but you don't get the same results from one instrument to another, thus consistency is a disadvantage. The information, however, is extracted in the same way as the coil, above.

RATIOMETER

This device measures an unknown electrical resistance by balancing two legs of a (Wheatstone) bridge circuit, one of which includes the unknown component. They are commonly used in Air Data Computers that use solid state capsules. As the bridge becomes unbalanced, the varying voltage across the middle can be measured.

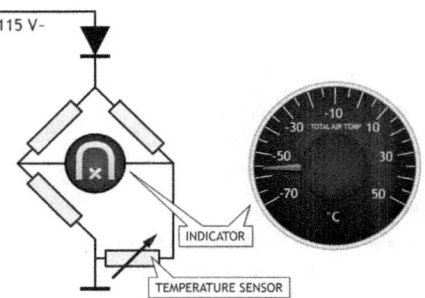

For temperature measurement purposes, you can replace the voltmeter with a wiper arm that is positioned by a servo loop, and how far the arm moves is a measure of the temperature change. It will centre at 15°C.

The main advantage of this device is that it works independently of the supply voltage.

THE ROSEMOUNT PROBE

Otherwise known as the *Total Air Temperature Probe*, this has a small (i.e. quick reacting) platinum* based resistance coil inside concentric cylinders, mounted on a streamlined strut around 50 mm or so from the fuselage skin, which therefore has little influence on it (skin temperature can be increased by kinetic energy).

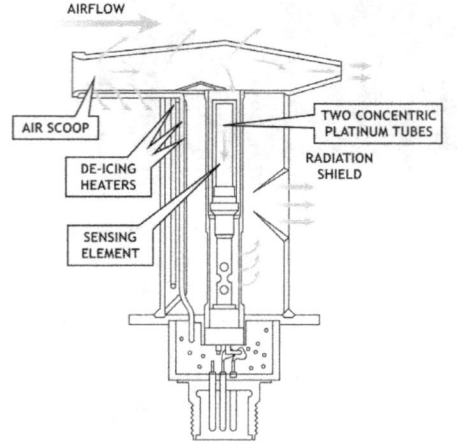

The probe is open at the front with a smaller hole at the back to allow air to flow through, but it is forced through 90° to encourage water and dust particles to separate as it speeds up, so the aircraft must be moving for the probe to work (although the airflow through the probe is quite slow because of the restrictions within it).

A heating element prevents icing (the detector works on vibration), and is self-compensating, in that, as temperature rises, so does resistance in the element, which reduces the heater current. Although the heater affects the temperature sensed, the error is small, around 1°C at Mach 0.1 and 0.15°C at Mach 1.0, so light aircraft that use the probe aren't affected anyway.

Aside from skin temperature, direct sunlight will give an artificially high reading and, when flying from cloud to clear air, readings will be low for however long it takes for moisture to evaporate from the element in the probe.

*An uncompensated instrument has one platinum sensor. A fully compensated one has 2.

Errors

Instrument error comes from the usual imperfections in manufacturing and can be sorted out by fine calibration. *Environmental error* is caused by solar heating or icing, for which the Rosemount probe has a heater. Probes are usually mounted to keep them in shadow, but the residual effects of environmental error can only be minimised, and not corrected for. Some heating is caused by compression as air is brought to rest, which is the difference between SAT and TAT, so it is only a problem when you need to find SAT. There is also frictional heating in the boundary layer, but both heating errors can be fully compensated for, either automatically or by calculation. Flat plate sensors, with their sensing element flush with the aircraft skin, are susceptible to environmental errors because of their relative lack of shielding. They are affected by frictional heating in the boundary layer (not compressibility), and instrument error.

TEMPERATURE COMPENSATION

Various methods can be used to make an instrument over- or under-read according to which way the temperature is going. For example, a thermal junction can get hot by itself, which will vary the emf it produces and give you false readings. In mechanical terms, a bimetal strip made of invar and brass or steel can be attached to a capsule to make it expand or contract slightly, or you could arrange to vary the resistance of an electrical current.

FLIGHT INSTRUMENTS

The artificial horizon or attitude indicator (AI*) is in the centre, because it is a primary instrument (it tells you which way is up), the heading indicator is below, No 1 altimeter at the top right, the vertical speed indicator below that, and the airspeed indicator at the top left with turn coordinator underneath.

The idea is to have the most important instruments as close together as possible to reduce the scanning distance.

*An ADI is an *Attitude Director Indicator*. It contains Flight Director bars.

The idea is to have the most important instruments as close together as possible to reduce the scanning distance.

As mentioned, instruments cover four areas of aircraft operation:

- **Control**, such as the artificial horizon and engine instruments
- **Performance**, that show you what the aircraft is doing (ASI, VSI, altimeter, compass)
- **Navigation** (VOR, ADF, DME)
- **Miscellaneous** (Warning flags, gear position indicators, pressure and temperature, etc)

A *primary instrument* is one which gives instant and constant readouts (also called *direct*), and is the one whose indications you want to keep steady. A *secondary instrument* is one that you have to deduce things from, such as the altimeter increasing, telling you that the pitch must have changed* (you might also say that the altimeter gives you an indirect indication of pitch attitude). The ASI and VSI also give indirect indications of pitch, and the HI and TC indicate bank. A primary instrument will tell you at what rate things are changing, but a secondary one will only indicate that change is taking place.

*The needle, ball and airspeed method of instrument flying refers to the Sperry turn indicator - as long as the needle and ball were centred, you were flying in a straight line. In a turn, keeping the ball centred meant you were not slipping or skidding, and holding the correct airspeed meant you were either flying straight and level or climbing or descending at a constant rate. In this case, the primary instruments were the ASI, turn and bank indicator and the VSI. However, using such slow, indirect indications is mentally tiring, as attitudes have to be continually deduced, which led to the development of the artificial horizon and DGI, that gave more instantaneous readings (once gyros became more reliable!)

Instruments are further grouped under the headings of *pitch*, *bank* and *power*.

Pitch

- **Artificial Horizon** (Attitude Indicator). The most important pitch instrument, because it gives direct, instantaneous readings.
- **Altimeter**. Although it indicates pitch indirectly, it is a primary pitch instrument.
- **Airspeed Indicator.** Secondary pitch instrument, although its value becomes less at higher airspeeds, as changes are more pronounced and the range indicated by the needle is less and more difficult to read. Any given power setting has only one pitch attitude where altitude and airspeed are constant.
- **Vertical Speed Indicator** (VSI). A secondary pitch instrument, to be used with the altimeter. Don't forget that it will give a brief reverse indication if you jerk the controls.

Bank

- **Artificial Horizon** (Attitude Indicator). Also the most important bank instrument, for similar reasons under *Pitch*, above.
- **Heading Indicator.** An indirect instrument, because if you change heading, bank must be involved somewhere.
- **Turn Coordinator**. Shows a rate of turn (3°/sec for rate 1), so it is an indirect indication of bank.

Power   022 01 03

Power instruments are not strictly in the traditional T, but you have to check them anyway. In this respect, **the ASI is a primary power instrument**, as it changes in relation to power application.

Engine and temperature instruments have already been covered elsewhere.

PITOT-STATIC SYSTEM   022 02 01

This consists of a series of pipes around the cockpit through which air flows to feed three common instruments: the altimeter, the ASI and the VSI.

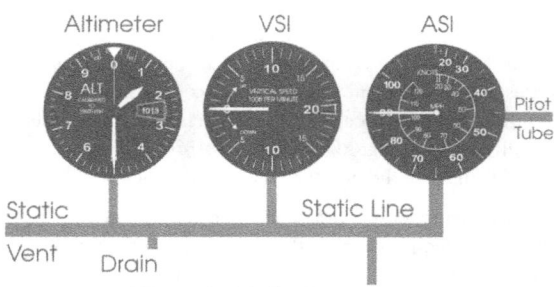

An aircraft is acted on from all directions by *static pressure*, which is fed into the system through static lines that are connected to static ports or static vents on *both sides* of the machine, to ensure that they balance out when it yaws, or performs strange manoeuvres (static balancing). They may or may not be heated (generally not on smaller machines). Warning lights associated with pitot/static heating systems usually come on when the heating element or the power relay has failed, so one light can have two meanings.

The static pressure is so called because it stays pretty much the same, except when there is disturbed airflow around the static ports. It's the normal barometric pressure that decreases with height, so any changes are relatively slow. Information from the static ports may also be fed to non-flight systems, such as autopilots or flight directors.

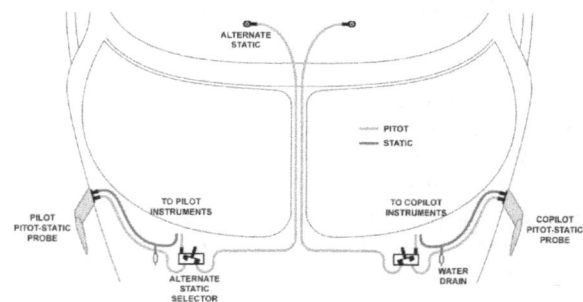

An *alternate static source* takes its feed from inside the aircraft in case the main one starts leaking or gets blocked, either through ice, a bird strike, or whatever. When it is used, some error will be introduced into the instrument readings because the cabin air pressure is affected by the airflow over the cabin (there are also different pressure errors), so indicated airspeeds and altitudes will read slightly *higher* than normal (that is, the altimeter and ASI will over-read). The VSI will show a momentary reverse as the alternate source is selected, then it will stabilise and produce normal readings. If the alternate gets blocked, or you don't have one, smashing the VSI glass (preferably not the ASI or altimeter) will have the same effect.

INSTRUMENTS
Pitot-Static System

Otherwise known as the *Total Pressure Probe*, the *pitot tube* (pronounced pee-toe) is used to detect *total pressure* (as mentioned by Bernoulli). It is connected to the ASI and sticks out beyond the boundary layer. Total pressure (sometimes called *stagnation pressure*) is the pressure obtained when a moving gas is brought to a stop through an adiabatic process - in this case, it includes the static pressure that affects the aircraft from all sides, and an extra element that comes from forward movement, since the pitot tube is pointed towards the direction of flight (within 5°). If the fluid (air) is an ideal one (meaning not viscous), total pressure is equal to the sum of potential energy, kinetic energy and pressure energy, but the first is ignored in a pitot tube, and the kinetic energy is converted to pressure energy anyway.

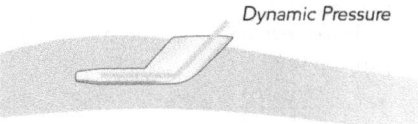

Dynamic Pressure

This creates an equal volume above the level of the flow, which is *dynamic pressure*, and a measure of airspeed. In simple terms, dynamic pressure of the air against the front surfaces of an aircraft (as detected by the pitot tube) is greater than the pressure of the undisturbed air sensed through the static ports. The difference is proportional to the square of the speed, so instruments can be calibrated in units of speed, such as knots.

The formula for *dynamic pressure* is:

```
Dynamic Pressure = ½ρV²
```

Where ρ (the Greek letter "rho") is air density and V the true velocity. As you can see, its strength depends on the speed of the relative airflow, and its density.

You cannot measure dynamic pressure in isolation, as static pressure is always present, so you should really write:

```
q = (q + ps) - ps
```

The pitot tube may be heated to stop it icing up, so watch your hands (tell the passengers). If the pitot is not at the front, it will be in another relatively undisturbed place, parallel to the relative airflow for best effect. Sometimes, a static source will be incorporated in a pitot head, as a small hole or series of holes around the side of the base.

A pitot tube failure will affect the ASI. A static system failure affects the ASI, VSI and altimeter.

If the static system fails:

- The ASI will over-read in the descent and under-read in the climb
- The altimeter will read the same in the climb or descent
- The VSI will read zero

If the pitot system fails:

- The ASI will under-read in the descent and over-read in the climb

Pitot-static systems are checked during regular maintenance, usually something like every 2 years for IFR machines. Preflight checks will be simpler, usually just making sure that nothing is blocking the holes (take the red covers off!) and that the heating works. Do not blow into the holes, at least, not with instruments connected (or with the pitot heat on!)

Errors

Errors in measurement will affect displayed speed, height and vertical speed. Accuracy depends on the shape of the probe and where it is placed. The total *pressure error* comes in two categories, *position* or *configuration error* (inherent from the design), and *manoeuvre error*, from the way you handle the machine, which mostly affects the VSI. Position error is defined as the *amount by which the local static pressure differs from that in the free stream airflow*, so it will vary substantially with the Mach number. The ASI and altimeter can develop positive or negative position errors. Configuration errors will have been established during flight testing, and can be displayed on calibration cards or programmed out by electronics, if you have them. Standby instruments, however, will have uncorrected errors given on a calibration card.

Configuration errors will have been established during flight testing, and can be displayed on calibration cards or programmed out by electronics, if you have them. Standby instruments, however, will not have the luxury, and will have uncorrected errors given on a calibration card.

The greatest errors occur when manoeuvring. If the left port gets blocked, for example, the altimeter over-reads when sideslipping to the left but is otherwise OK in symmetric flight although, in theory, with static ports in pairs on opposite sides of the fuselage (at right angles to the relative wind so they are not affected by speed), any errors due to sideslip should be eliminated.

Parallax error is due to the angle from which you read the instrument.

Here is a summary of the errors involved:

Situation	ASI	Altimeter	VSI
Blocked Pitot	Zero	Works.	Works.
Blocked pitot & drain + open static.	High in climb, low in descent.	Works.	Works.
Blocked static + open pitot.	Low in climb, high in descent.	Frozen.	Frozen.
Alternate static.	Reads high.	Reads high.	Momentary climb.
Broken VSI glass.	Reads high.	Reads high.	Reverses.

Air Data Computer

Aircraft operating at high speeds and altitudes can get significant instrument errors if they use the probes found on smaller aircraft. As well, the traditional pitot-static system uses a lot of pipes from the air data instruments (altimeter, ASI and VSI). The ADC was developed in an attempt to reduce the plumbing and improve reliability and accuracy, by allowing the instruments to be operated electrically from remote places.

The ADC is a "black box" that sits between the usual sensors (static and dynamic pressures, but also TAT) and the instruments, translating them into electrical equivalents for transmission to the relevant indicators, which have no pressure sensing elements, so they can be simpler (and cheaper) to make.

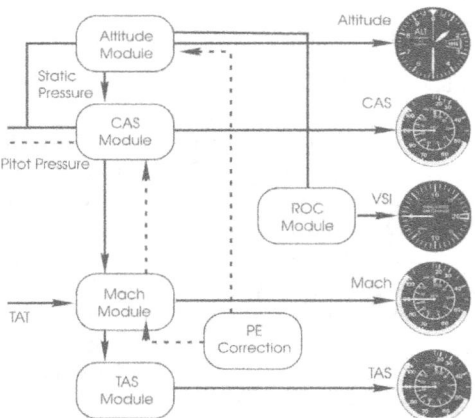

The TAT value is needed to correct for the compressibility errors found at high speeds, and the TAT probe uses a standard formula to calculate SAT, which value is also needed to correct for non-standard temperatures.

Each module is a *servomechanism* (described later) whose output signals are fed through a *transducer* (such as the E & I bar used in a servo altimeter) before being transmitted to their associated indicators.

The data can also be fed to the autopilot and Flight Director, Flight Management System, GPWS, area navigation aids, instrument comparison systems, and the EFIS symbol generators to be converted for electronic display. Standby instruments use the pitot-static plumbing. There are two ADCs in most modern air transport aircraft to provide redundancy.

The most significant advantages of an air data computer (ADC) are position error correction, so the ADC puts out CAS, not IAS, and remote data transmission capability. It works on TAT, and static and total pressures.

THE ALTIMETER

Static pressure is inversely proportional to altitude, so if you know the static pressure, you can figure out how high you are (in the standard atmosphere).

The altimeter is a barometer with the scale marked in feet rather than millibars. It does not measure the true height, but the weight of the air above the aircraft, which compresses the capsule

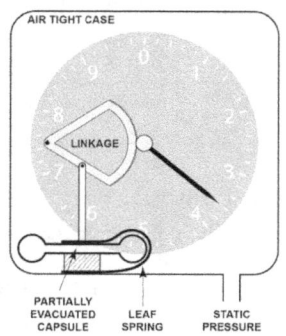

inside. As you go up, pressure is less, so the altimeter translates air pressure into an *estimate* of altitude, although it will be better sealed than a barometer, so air pressure in the cockpit doesn't affect it - the only pressure that should be there is static pressure from the pitot-static system. The readings could be inaccurate due to temperature and pressure variations from standard.

Inside a *sensitive* altimeter are *two* aneroid capsules (vacuums), which are corrugated for strength and kept open with a large leaf spring (a *simple* altimeter is a little more basic, with only one capsule - they are commonly used as cabin altimeters on pressurised aeroplanes since, at high altitudes, the capsule's movements are difficult to detect). The capsules' movements as you go up and down are magnified through the spring by a "suitable linkage" that connects directly to the pointer, using jewelled bearings. If the capsules expand, as they would when you go up, the pointer increases the reading. There is also a temperature compensation system to correct any spring and linkage tensions. Outside, there is a small knob, linked to a subscale which is visible through a small window. Rotating the knob causes the subscale to move and adjust the instrument to an *altimeter setting* (see *Meteorology*).

Caution: The three-needle display (on the right, below) can be easily misread:

The dials work like a clock. The long, thin pointer indicates hundreds of feet and the short, wide one, thousands. A very thin one, maybe with an inverted triangle at the end, as above, shows feet in ten thousands.

Only in standard ISA conditions will the true altitude be indicated directly. When it is extremely cold (below about -16°C), it will be a lot lower than shown, so corrections must be applied (altitudes given with radar vectors from ATC are corrected already). If this is something you need to take note of, you could perhaps mark the corrections directly on to the approach chart, next to the heights they refer to (you must recalculate *every* significant height).

Servo Altimeter

The servo-assisted altimeter typically uses a digital readout and is connected to the ADC. In this instrument, the aneroid capsules are connected to one end of a pivoting magnet (an I-bar) which influences an E-bar that has windings on each of its arms. At sea level, it has a tolerance of ±30 feet.

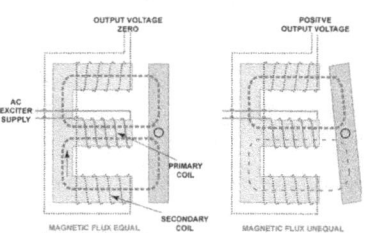

An AC current is fed to the primary winding on the centre arm, and as long as the gaps between the E and the I bars are equidistant, no voltage is induced in the coils on the other arms. The E-bars are wired in opposite directions and are connected in series to an amplifier unit - one example of the use of transformers.

Once the capsules increase or decrease in size, however, the gaps vary in size to create different magnetic fluxes and an output voltage that will be in or out of phase with the voltage in the primary coil, according to the direction of the displacement. Its magnitude will vary with the amount of the deflection.

The signal goes to the amplifier, then the servomotor control winding so the pointer and height counters are driven in the relevant directions (more about servos *later*). At the same time, the servomotor gear train spins a worm gear that rotates the cam and cam follower to try and balance the magnetic fluxes at the I-bars, reaching the null point when the aircraft is levelled off and no more voltages are produced.

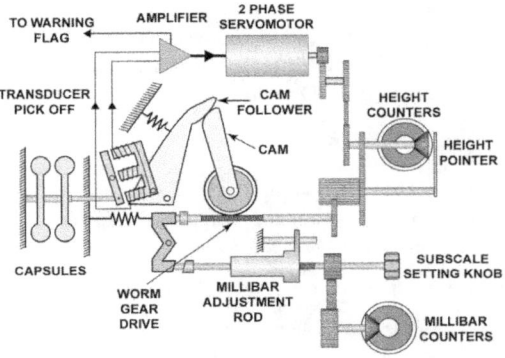

Turning the altimeter setting knob on the front drives the worm gear directly. All this complexity allows increased sensitivity at higher altitudes, as the aneroid capsules only have to drive the I-bar and not the whole instrument. The rest is done by the servo motor, which removes lag and pressure errors, and can drive more robust displays.

If servo altimeters are used, a standby pneumatic one must be in close proximity and easily visible.

Encoding Altimeter

An *encoding altimeter* is used with a transponder in Mode C so that your altitude can be shown on an ATC ground radar display.

The encoding assembly is mechanically activated by the aneroid capsule. Older versions consist of a light source, various lenses and an encoder disc with a special pattern on it (in eleven concentric circles) that works like a bar code when the light is reflected from it to produce binary inputs that correspond to 100-ft increments in altitude. One turn of the disc covers the complete range of the altimeter. Naturally, there are now digital versions of the same thing that can also be fitted externally.

 The adjustment knob does not affect what ATC see on their radar screens! All encoding systems transmit your altitude corrected to 29.92 inches, or 1013.25 hPa which is the pressure altitude. The ground equipment makes any regional corrections directly.

Errors

Altimeters suffer from:

- **Mechanical errors**, which include:
  - *Scale error.* The difference between the indicated altitude and the basic altitude at which the measurement is taken.
  - *Friction error.* Causes irregular or jerky movement of the needle when the inner workings are sticking together. It is fixed by gentle tapping or vibration.
  - *Position error* can arise from unusual attitudes or the behaviour of the airflow due to the shape of the surrounding fuselage as opposed to the smooth free stream. It is sometimes confused with "installation error", and is generally greater at low airspeeds as the angle of attack is abnormal, but manoeuvring doesn't help. On an aircraft with 2 altimeters, and only one compensated for position error, in straight symmetrical flight, the higher the speed, the greater the error will be between them, but an ADC should compensate (a non-compensated altimeter, however, will indicate a higher altitude). If the static source on the right gets blocked, in a sideslip to the right, the altimeter will over-read.

- **Temperature error**, caused by linkages in the instrument shrinking or expanding, but this includes the temperature of the atmosphere, particularly when cold (see the *Meteorology* section). If the temperature is lower than ISA, *you* are lower! A correction is required whenever temperatures are significantly below standard. For temperatures down to -15°C, the calculation is 4% for every 10°C of deviation from ISA, and the same deviation is assumed to apply for all heights. At a constant indicated altitude over a warm air mass, the altimeter reading will be less than true altitude. Going into a colder air mass, it will over-read. This error is zero at sea level and increases with altitude.

- **Elastic error**, which includes:
  - *Hysteresis,* an irregular response to pressure changes (technically where changes lag behind the force that produces them) because a capsule under stress provides an imperfect response. This varies a lot with time passed at an altitude and is measured by the difference in two readings, when increasing and decreasing. Essentially, the altimeter gets used to a certain position and takes time to catch up if you move from it. The effects are negligible in slow climbs or descents, but a rapid descent will cause a delay, which is fixed with a vibrator, whose purpose is also to make the linkages work more smoothly. Indicated readings will lag behind true altitude, and the aircraft will be lower than indicated.
  - *Drift.* A slow increase in readings without an increase in altitude after levelling off from a climb - after descending the readings should return to normal. Drift should not be more than around

0.2% for every 15,000 ft change in altitude for flights over an hour long.

- *Secular error.* The slow change over time of the entire scale error curve, mainly from internal stresses in the metal. Fixed by resetting zero.
- **Time lag** from the distance a pressure change has to travel in the pipes, at its worst during rapid altitude changes. Due to lag, the altimeter will under-read in a climb, and over-read in a descent.
- **Reversal error**, a momentary display in the wrong direction after an abrupt attitude change.

Between areas with different pressures, you could be at a different height than expected.

For example, flying from high to low pressure, your altimeter would over-read (from HIGH to LOW, your instrument is HIGH), so you would be lower than planned and liable for a nasty surprise, especially in the lee of a mountain wave. Conversely, going from low into high pressure, without the altimeter setting being adjusted, the altimeter will indicate lower than the actual altitude above sea level. The same goes when you move between areas with different temperatures.

Surface Temp (ISA)	Correction
-16°C to -30°C	+10%
-31°C to -50°C	+20%
-51°C or below	+25%

Another factor is the creation of wind from a temperature difference. A cooler column of air has a lower pressure at a given altitude, and the warmer one has a higher pressure, causing air to move from left to right in this case so, after Buys Ballot, low temperature is to the left in the Northern hemisphere with your back to the wind. The vertical distance between two pressure levels is less in cold air. Pressure in upper levels depends on the mean temperature of the column of air beneath the point.

You can refuse IFR assigned altitudes if temperature error reduces obstacle clearance limits to an unacceptable level, but once the assigned altitude has been accepted, you cannot adjust it for altimeter temperature error. When the aerodrome temperature is -30°C or colder, add 1,000 feet to the MSA to ensure obstacle clearance. The difference between True and Indicated altitude is called the D value.

Altimetry

Altimetry is the science of measuring vertical distances in the atmosphere. The decrease of pressure with altitude depends on gravity and air density (the *hydrostatic balance*).

```
pressure = g x density x height diff
```

As vertical pressure variation follows the general gas laws, if you know the pressure on the ground and that at your height, you can work out your distance from the surface. For meteorology, 1 hPa is taken to be 27 feet in the lower atmosphere - for all other purposes, it is 30 ft.

 The word *height* refers to the vertical distance from a particular datum, usually the surface of an airfield (QFE, as used in Europe, is the airfield datum pressure, which makes the altimeter read your height above the airfield).

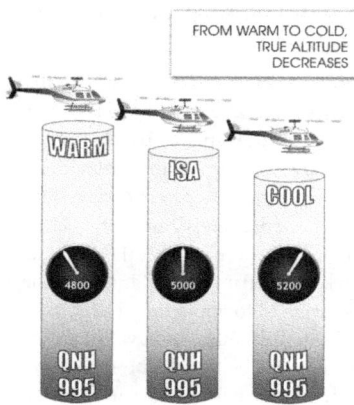

The standard atmosphere has a temperature element that also affects the altimeter. Remembering that air density decreases as it gets warmer, a point in your imaginary column of air above a station would be higher on a warm day than otherwise. If, therefore, as is typical near the Rockies in Winter, the air is *very much* colder than standard (actually below about -16°C), you will be lower than you should be (actually, the phrase above is still valid, in that going from HIGH *temperature* to LOW, your instruments will be HIGH). A *cold low* will lower True Altitude to a point where it is dangerous to fly in mountains.

This is serious because, in low temperatures, combined with other effects from the movement of wind over ridges, you could be *as much as 3,000 feet below your projected altitude* (although, with some navaids, you rely more on a radio signal than the altimeter). You could have a 150-foot difference on a published minimum of 500 feet and be too close to the ground. Normally, down to -15°C, you would apply a 4% increase for every 10°C below standard. In simple terms, when the surface temperature is well *below* ISA, correct your altitudes by:

Altitude means vertical distance above *sea level*, so the aircraft in the picture below has a height of 1,000 feet (above the aerodrome, or QFE) and an altitude of 1,500 feet (above the sea, or QNH). The difference is the *elevation* of the aerodrome.

Elevation is the vertical distance of a point on the Earth's surface from mean sea level. *Indicated altitude* is what is shown on the dial at the current altimeter setting. *Calibrated altitude* is the indicated altitude corrected for instrument and position error. *True Altitude* is the actual one above mean sea level, and is discussed later.

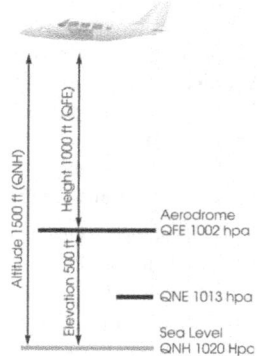

CRUISING LEVELS

Cruising levels are expressed in terms of:

- **Flight Levels** - the altimeter reading with two digits knocked off the end. FL 30 means 3,000 feet when set to 1013.25 hPa. Usually, the *lowest usable FL* corresponds to, or is immediately above, the minimum flight altitude. Flight levels must be used above the transition altitude (below).
- **Altitudes**, below the lowest usable flight level, or at or below the transition altitude, based on QNH.
- **Heights** - used within the traffic pattern and based on QFE, if used, taken from the airfield elevation, but the threshold elevation is used for instrument runways if there is more than a 2 m difference, and precision approach runways.

TRANSITION ALTITUDE

A transition altitude is normally specified for an aerodrome **by the State in which it is located**. It is as low as possible, but normally at least 3,000 feet in Europe, rounded up to the nearest 1,000. In the USA and Canada, and other countries, it is 17,999 ft. Below the Transition Altitude, vertical position is controlled by reference to altitude. Above it, Flight Levels are used, for which the altimeter must be set to 1013.

The *Transition Level* is the lowest available flight level (see below) above the Transition Altitude when the altimeter is set to 1013.2 hPa, so it would normally be FL 30 in UK, including when the QNH is more than standard. However, if the QNH is less than standard, the transition level will be higher than that. The Transition Level is determined **by the ATS unit concerned**, since it varies with pressure from day to day, and it is always *higher* than the Transition Altitude. The difference between transition altitude and transition level is the *Transition Layer*, which will be *more than zero and less than 500 feet*.

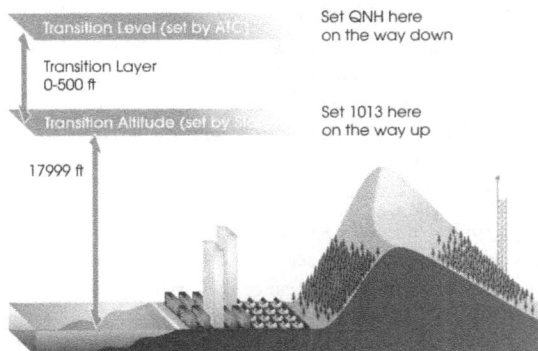

The change in reference between flight levels and altitudes is made, when climbing, at the Transition Altitude, and, when descending, at the Transition Level. In other words, when passing through the transition layer, report flight levels when going up and altitudes when going down. When descending to go below Transition Level, if you are cleared to a Flight Level, you must keep 1013 set on your altimeter. If you are cleared to an altitude, and no more FL reports are needed, set the QNH as soon as you start descending and report altitudes. Flight level zero is at the atmospheric pressure level of 1013.25 hPa. Consecutive Flight Levels are separated by intervals of at least 500 feet.

EXAMPLE

If the QNH is 985 hPa and the transition altitude is 3,000 ft, how deep is the transition layer (1 hPa=30ft)?

For this, you need to work out the pressure altitude at 3,000 ft.

```
1013 - 985 = 28 hPa difference
28 x 30 = 840
3000 + 840 = 3840 ft PA
```

The next flight level is FL 40 which is at 4,000 ft PA. The transition layer is:

```
4000 - 3840 = 260 ft thick
```

ALTIMETER SETTINGS

Three altimeter settings are used throughout a flight:

- **QFE** (Field Elevation) is used near an airfield, particularly in the circuit, showing the approximate height above the aerodrome reference point. At the field elevation (FE), the altimeter will therefore read zero feet, and the QFE will be shown in the subscale. *Airfield QFE* is measured at the highest point of the airfield surface, and *Touchdown QFE* at the touchdown point.
- **QNH** (*Nautical Height*) is used for general transit elsewhere, below the transition altitude, showing the approximate altitude above sea level (at the aerodrome reference point, it shows the field elevation). It is forecast for 1 or 2 (or even 3 in Australia) hours ahead over large areas, so don't expect accuracy. It is QFE reduced to MSL **under ISA conditions** and should not differ from Local QNH by more than about 5 hPa although, in places like New Guinea, there could be a 10 hPa difference between the highlands in the centre and the coast.
- **QNE** (*Nautical Elevation*) is the altimeter reading at the runway threshold with 1013.25 on the subscale, used when the subscale does not go low enough to set QFE. It is a height, not a setting or a flight level.

QFF is similar to QNH, but is the QFE reduced to MSL using long term mean conditions at the surface, including temperature and water vapour content (the temperature between there and sea level is assumed to be constant). QFF allows accurate surface charts to be drawn, as it is the basis of isobars. When above MSL and warmer than ISA, it will be less than QNH, and more when the temperature is colder than ISA (the opposite below MSL). For meteorologists only!

The barometric pressure is constantly changing and varies from one place to another. What would happen if you departed the spot in the diagram above and returned several hours later to find the 1020 QNH above had reduced to 995 hPa? The altimeter would be over-reading by 675 feet and you would only be 325 feet off the ground (1020 - 995 x 27 = 675, 1500 - 675 = 825 AMSL = 325 AGL). The altimeter needs constant updating as you fly.

Although altimeters are calibrated to ISA, the actual sea level pressure varies from hour to hour, and place to place. You would be very lucky to hit the standard atmosphere more than, say, 25% of the time, so you need a means of adjusting any instruments based on it to cope with the differences. To allow you to set the zero reference correctly, an altimeter has a *setting window* (also called the Kollsman window) in which you can adjust the figures of a *subscale* for the correct pressure on the ground by turning a knob on the front.

This is actually part of an important preflight check, where you make sure that if you turn the knob to the right, the height readings increase, and *vice versa*. If the subscale is set wrongly, the zero reference will be displaced by an amount proportional to 1 inch per 1,000 feet, so your relative height to obstacles, like mountains, will not be maintained.

For example, if the proper altimeter setting is 29.92 inches, but you have 30.92 inches set in the subscale, the altimeter will be over-reading by 1,000 feet. When flying from high to low pressure, your altimeter will also over-read (from HIGH to LOW, it is HIGH), so you would be lower than planned and liable for a nasty surprise. It's therefore much safer to be going the other way (that is, from LOW to HIGH, where your instrument is LOW).

To convert from inches to hectopascals, start at 29.92 and find the difference between it and the current pressure. Divide the difference by 0.03 inches and apply the result to 1013. In other words, 1 hPa is about equal to 0.03". For example, if the current pressure is 30.02, that is, 0.1" above 29.92" (or 3 x 0.03), add 3 hPa and set 1016.

A more formal way is to use this formula:

$$\frac{\text{hectopascals}}{1013.25} = \frac{\text{ins}}{29.92}$$

TRUE ALTITUDE

This is your (geometric) elevation above mean sea level, being the distance you could normally find with a tape measure, but it is impractical to throw one out of the window, so we use instruments such as the altimeter instead, to show an indicated altitude.

The only time an altimeter will indicate true altitude is in ISA conditions. As such conditions are rare, indications are almost always in error due to temperature.

The difference between true and standard (ISA) altitude is 4 feet per thousand feet per degree of deviation from ISA. That is, true altitude changes by 4% for every 10°C deviation from ISA conditions, or 2% for every 5.5°C*.

*4% is correct for the stratosphere, but it's more like 3.5% for lower altitudes. 4% for every 11°C is more accurate.

One source of error can occur when the temperature at a level might be close to ISA, when the lapse rate is not.

 All calculations should be rounded to the nearest lower hPa. The barometric lapse rate near mean sea level is 27 ft (8m) per hPa. Also, the airport elevation must be taken into account - that is, *only use the layer between the ground and the position of the aircraft*. In practice, true altitude is obtained from knowing the OAT at the level you are flying at, and using a flight computer. This will be reasonably accurate when the actual lapse rate is, or is near, that of ISA, i.e., 2°C per 1,000 feet, but if it's very hot, or very cold, you need further adjustments.

INDICATED ALTITUDE

Indicated and Pressure Altitudes are the same in ISA conditions.

CALIBRATED ALTITUDE

The Indicated Altitude corrected for airspeed, altitude, imperfect pressure lines, etc.becomes Calibrated Altitude.

ABSOLUTE ALTITUDE

The geometric height above terrain - what would be measured by a radar altimeter.

PRESSURE ALTITUDE

Pressure altitude is the height in the standard atmosphere that you may find a given pressure, usually 29.92" or 1013 Mb, but actually whatever you set on the altimeter - if you set 1013 on the subscale and the needles read 6,000 feet, the PA *for that setting* is 6,000 feet. So what is indicated is the height of the pressure selected. PA is a starting point for any calculations for performance, TAS, etc., and is the altimeter setting used above the transition altitude, where all altimeters must be set to 1013 hPa so that everybody is using the same standard (every country has a different transition altitude). Below the transition altitude, local altimeter settings are used.

If an altimeter is set to 1013, it is measuring Pressure Altitude with respect to Mean Sea Level. In ISA conditions, Pressure Altitude is the same as True Altitude.

If the sea level pressure is different from 1013, obstacle clearance heights and airfield elevations, etc. must be converted before using them. To do this, get the local altimeter setting, find the difference between it and 29.92 (or 1013), convert it to feet (1"=1,000 or 1 hPa=27 feet at sea level), then apply it the *opposite* side of 29.92. You could also get PA from the altimeter, by placing 29.92 or 1013 in the setting window, and reading the figures directly. The significance of this concerns performance - if the pressure on the surface is less than standard, you are effectively at a higher altitude, and your machine will not fly so well. You often need to calculate the pressure altitude of a location so you know your performance.

For example, for a strip on the side of a mountain at 400 feet above sea level, with an altimeter setting of 29.72, your PA at that location would actually be 600 feet, since the difference between 29.92 and 29.72 is 0.2, or 200 feet *added*, and where you would enter your performance charts, since they are set for the standard atmosphere (the altimeter setting is *below* the standard pressure, so your answer should be *above*). Again, you are *adding* because the sea is *lower*, and the figures ought to be higher (see the examples below).

Pressure levels with altitude are:

Height	Pressure Level
Surface	1013
10,000	700
18,000	500
24,000	400
30,000	300
34,000	250
38,000	200

Calculations

Tip: *Always* draw a diagram and place the numbers in order, with the large ones at the bottom. When on a local QNH for an airport, errors from variations in ISA only apply to height above the airfield elevation - local QNH (which is calculated under ISA) applies up till then.

Q: What minimum flight level will clear high ground rising to 1800 m AMSL by at least 1500 ft on a track of 225°(M), if the Regional QNH is 990 hPa? How much is the clearance at that level? (1 hPa=27 feet).

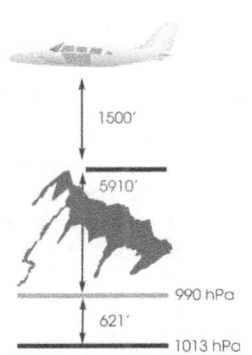

A: 1800 m is equal to 5910 ft. The difference between the QNH and QNE (1013 - 990) is 23 hPa, or 621 feet. Your minimum height is 621 + 5910 + 1500, or 8031 feet. The next applicable even flight level is FL 100, and the high ground is cleared by 3469 feet (10000 - 621 - 5910).

Q: An aeroplane is flying at 2500 feet AGL near an airfield which is 350 ft AMSL. The QFE is 982 hPa. If another aircraft flies over at FL 40, what is the approximate vertical separation between them? (1 hPa = 27 feet)

A: 664 feet. 350 feet divided by 27 is 13 hPa, so the QNH is 995 (982 + 13). The difference between the QNH and QNE is 18 hPa, so sea level is 485 above the standard pressure level. Add 2500 feet to 485 and 350 to get 3336 and subtract that from 4,000.

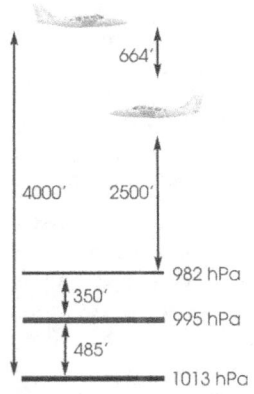

Q. A westbound aircraft is VFR at 8,500 feet. The OAT is -18°C and the altimeter is set to the nearest airport (30.22 - field elevation 2,000 ft). By how much will the aircraft clear a 7,500 ft ridge in the flight path?

A. This involves a temperature correction, with the complication that the QNH is measured at 2,000 ft AMSL. ISA at 8 230 ft (the pressure altitude at 8,500 ft AMSL on the QNH of 30.22" Hg) is -1° to the nearest degree, so the deviation is -17°C. Correction is made for the difference between the elevation and aircraft altitude, i.e:

    8,500 - 2000 = 6500

Adjust by 4 ft per 1000 ft per °10C:

    4 x 6.5 x 17 = 44.2

The conditions are below ISA, so the true altitude is less than indicated. The aircraft is at 8 456 feet, which will be 956 feet above the ridge.

DENSITY ALTITUDE

This is the altitude in the Standard Atmosphere at which the prevailing density occurs, meaning your real altitude from the effects of height, temperature and humidity, and is used to establish performance, as it is a figure that expresses where your machine thinks it is, as opposed to where it actually is - see *Performance*. For now, it is *pressure altitude corrected for non-standard temperature* (ignoring humidity), or the true air temperature at a given level. Thus, density altitude has the same value as pressure altitude at standard temperature.

To find DA on the flight computer, set the aerodrome elevation or Pressure Altitude against the temperature in the *airspeed* window.

In the picture, the temperature is -21°C at 10 100 feet. The indicated airspeed is 350 kts, and the TAS is 396. The Density Altitude is 8100 feet - quite a difference!

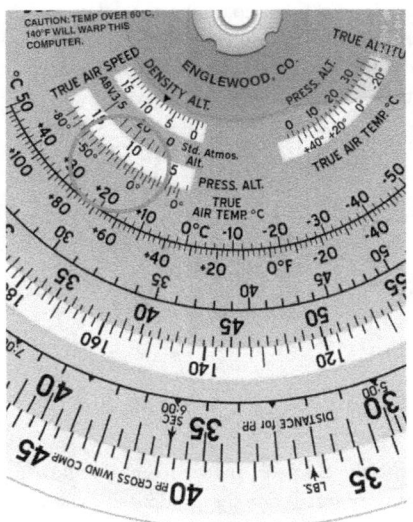

If you want a formula:

    PA ± (118.8 x ISA Dev)

(Multiplying the ISA Dev by 120 is usually good enough, and should be used in the exams).

Altimeter Checks

Rotating the knob through ±10 hPa must produce a corresponding height difference of about ±300 ft in the relevant directions. At a known elevation on the aerodrome, vibrate the instrument by tapping, unless mechanical vibration is available:

- Set the scale to the current QNH. The altimeter should indicate the elevation, plus the height of the altimeter above it, within ± 20 m or 60 ft for altimeters with a test range of 0-9,000 m (0-30,000 ft) and ± 25 m or 80 ft for altimeters with a test range of 0-15,000 m (0-50,000 ft)
- Set the current QFE. The altimeter should indicate the height of the altimeter in relation to the QFE reference point, with the same tolerances
- Both should be set to the aerodrome QFE and should indicate within ±80' of zero, within 60 or 80' of each other. Thus, they can misread by up to 120 or 160 feet and still be "serviceable"
- With No 1 on QFE and No 2 on aerodrome QNH, the difference should equal the aerodrome elevation AMSL, to within 80 feet
- With both on aerodrome QNH, indications should be within ±80 feet of aerodrome elevation, and 80 feet of each other

No 1 is the handling pilot's primary instrument and No 2 the secondary.

According to CS 25 the tolerance for an altimeter at MSL is ±30' per 100 kts CAS.

AIRSPEED INDICATOR   022 02 06

To find airspeed, you need to compare the general pressure outside the aircraft (the static pressure) with the pressure created from its movement through the air, so this instrument is connected to both the static and pitot pressure systems.

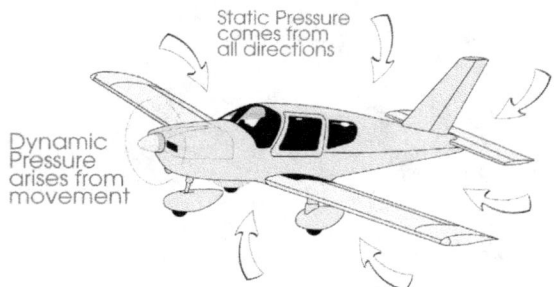

The ASI is similar to the altimeter inside, except that the capsule is fed directly with pitot (total) pressure, and its size will vary as a function of the dynamic pressure. The static port's job is to cancel out the effects of the air surrounding the aircraft. As the capsule expands under the pressure of the ram air, static air in the case can escape through the static port. If it were otherwise, the capsule would not be able to expand.

The ASI is a pressure gauge with its dial marked in knots or mph instead of PSI. It captures **total pressure** then subtracts static pressure to get dynamic pressure, which is proportional to forward speed. The needle is connected to the capsule through the usual suitable linkage.

Dynamic pressure varies with the square of the airspeed.

The combination of static and dynamic pressure is the *stagnation pressure*, because airflow is being brought to rest inside the pitot tube, or stagnating.

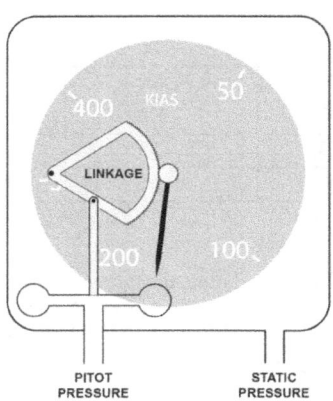

Because the atmosphere gets less dense as you climb, the IAS must be corrected. The rate is 1.75% per 1,000 feet.

There are several variations on the airspeed theme:

- **Indicated airspeed** (IAS) is the direct reading, corrected only for instrument error - turbulent flow around the pressure head accounts for 95%. Modern instruments have little error, so the direct reading is effectively IAS. A given IAS can result from flying through high density air at a low speed, or low density at a greater TAS (below), as you might get at high altitudes. The ASI cannot compensate for changes in density, but can only indicate the combination of density and velocity of the air.

- **Calibrated airspeed** (CAS) is the IAS corrected for pressure (system) errors, which are highest at low speeds and high angles of attack (IAS and CAS are about the same at speeds above the cruise). It was once known as the *Rectified Air Speed* (RAS), and is a measure of the dynamic pressure at *low speeds*. Instrument and position errors can be corrected out by the Air Data Computer in modern aircraft. *An aircraft at the same weight always takes off at the same CAS.*

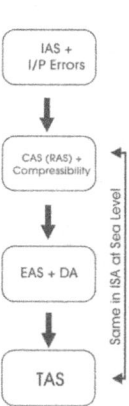

- **Equivalent Airspeed** (EAS) is CAS compensated for compressibility, or factors arising from high speeds. It is the speed that gives the same dynamic pressure that would come from TAS at sea level. It does not consider density error, and is effectively IAS/CAS where such errors are small (below 200 kts and 20,000 feet it will be around 1-2 kts). EAS is lower than or equal to CAS, because, as the air is compressed inside the pitot tube, the dynamic pressure is greater than it should be, and the correction is a **negative** value, so it could be regarded as a form of error. The bridge between EAS and TAS is Density Altitude. It's hardly worth working out because at the speeds and altitudes where it is significant, a constant Mach number is used anyway (see below).

- **True Air Speed** (TAS) is the CAS corrected for altitude and temperature, or density (its original calibration is based on the standard atmosphere). *It is the only speed* and the only figure used for navigation - the others are pressures and are to do with aircraft behaviour! On average, the TAS increases by 2% over the IAS for every 1,000 feet.

If air density remains constant, the relationship between IAS and TAS will remain constant so, if we double the IAS (in conditions of constant density) we will double the TAS. Dynamic pressure is proportional to the square of the TAS so, if we multiply the TAS by 2 the dynamic pressure increases by 4. With 4 times as much dynamic pressure and the same wing area, we need ¼ of the initial C_L to generate the same amount of lift.

You can find TAS from the CAS and Air Density, which can be derived from Pressure Altitude and temperature which may involve a conversion from Fahrenheit to Centigrade (and from miles per hour to knots). Thus, in ISA conditions at sea level, CAS = TAS. However, as an example, given an altimeter setting of 30.40", an indicated altitude of 3450', an OAT of 41°F and an IAS of 138 mph, let's find the TAS in knots. For the moment, take CAS as 118 kts, having converted 138 mph to 120 kts and looked it up on an imaginary graph (if there isn't one, the question will contain the information required). 41°F also converts to 5°C. The PA is found in the usual way, remembering that 1" equals 1,000'. The difference between 29.92" and 30.40" is 0.48, or 480 feet, which gives 2970' when subtracted from 3450' (29.92 is the "higher" figure in terms of distance above ground).

The TAS is 122 kts, and the Density Altitude (out of interest) is 2500'. If the TAS were over 300 kts, you have to apply a compressibility correction, which will bring TAS and CAS closer together.

If you maintain a constant CAS in level unaccelerated flight, from warm to cold air, TAS will *decrease* as air density *increases*, and *vice versa*. Thus, in ISA conditions, when descending at constant CAS, TAS decreases.

If you climb at constant IAS, you will be climbing at a constant dynamic pressure, but air density decreases, so you need more V^2 to produce the same dynamic pressure.

At 40,000 ft for example, ρ is about ¼ of its sea level value, so V^2 must be 4 times its own sea level value to keep dynamic pressure constant. In fact, TAS is twice the IAS, a point to be remembered when landing on high runways as the ground run will be longer.

To find out what happens to various speeds in the climb or descent, remember this picture:

The initial letters stand for *Equivalent, Calibrated* and *True* airspeeds, and *Mach number*. In the climb, select which one remains constant, and the speeds to the

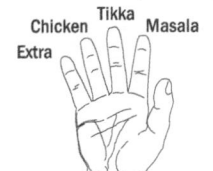
Chicken Tikka Masala Extra

right will be increasing, with the ones to the left decreasing. The reverse for the descent.

Above the tropopause (in an isothermal atmosphere) the Mach number and TAS will react in the same way at the same time.

Colour Coding   022 02 05

Various colours are specified for ASIs.

The limits are:

- **Green scale**: The normal operating range. Starting at the flaps up, gear up, power-off stall speed, or V_{S1}, and ending at the maximum structural cruising speed, V_{NO}/V_{MO}, where no damage will occur in moderate vertical gusts.

- **White scale**: The flap operating range. The lower limit is the power-off stall speed with the recommended landing flaps at gross weight with the gear extended and the cowl flaps closed (V_{S0}). The upper limit is the maximum (full) flap operating speed, or V_{FE}.

- **Yellow scale**: Starting at the maximum structural cruising speed, i.e. V_{NO}/V_{MO}, and ending at the never-exceed speed, or V_{NE} (the red line). Strong vertical gusts could cause structural damage if you fly in this range.

Modern jets have a red and white striped barber pole indicator for M_{MO} (the maximum safe Mach number against altitude), which is a limit speed pointer that moves according to conditions, unlike the red V_{NE} line described above, which is fixed (Mach numbers depend on temperature).

Such an instrument is often called a CSI, or *Combined Speed Pointer* or even a MASI, if it is combined with an ASI (but see also *The Machmeter*, later), because it also contains an altitude capsule that is connected to the limit speed pointer with the usual suitable linkage. The capsule expands or contracts

according to altitude. In the picture, the Mach number is 0.814, and the TAS is 264 knots.

INSTRUMENTS
Airspeed Indicator

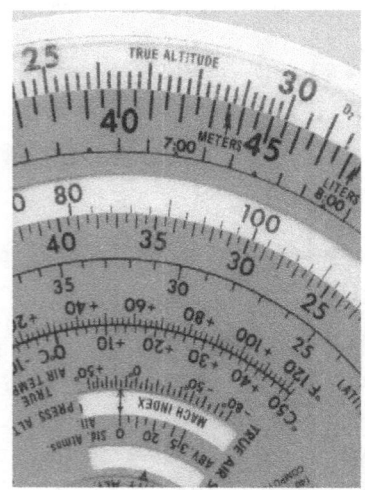

On the flight computer, if you set the *Mach Index* opposite the temperature, you can read the speed of sound directly against the inner scale 1.0. In the picture below, the Index (a double-headed arrow) is in a window at the bottom. TAS 280 corresponds to a Mach No of 0.424.

At low levels, limiting speeds will be expressed as IAS, which is used for the takeoff and initial climb, during which the TAS increases while the speed of sound decreases with the temperature. At higher levels, a Mach number is used, with the changeover point somewhere around 25,000 feet. A speed of M 0.9 at low level could be 550 kts, as opposed to 350 kts at 35,000 feet, which may be too high for the airframe. For example, an aircraft with a V_{MO} (maximum safe IAS, based on EAS) of 350 kts and an M_{MO} of 0.84 is climbing to FL 360 in standard conditions at 330 kts IAS until M 0.83 is reached.

As it passes 10,000 ft, the IAS pointer will show 330 kts with a Mach number of 0.59 (see picture below). As it passes 20,000 ft, the IAS pointer will still show 330 kts, but the Mach value will be 0.71. At 28,000 ft the Mach number will be 0.83, at which point the aircraft is flown at a constant Mach number so, on passing 30,000 ft the IAS pointer will show 316 kts. At 36,000 ft it will show 277 kts.

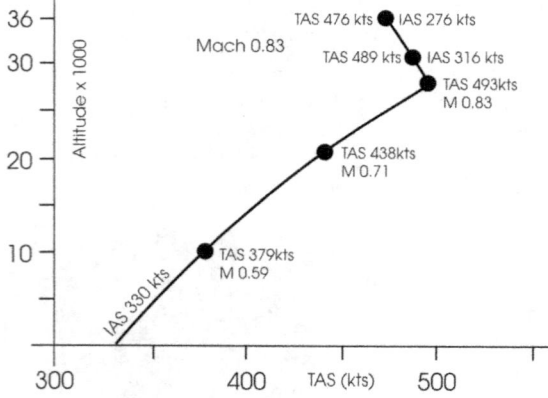

A constant CAS and flight level produces a Mach number that is independent of temperature - i.e. it will not change.

A command bug is normally set to indicate the target speed or used as a datum for the autothrottle in automatic flight. Other bugs may be on the bezel (outside the glass), which can be used to define, for example, V speeds, mentioned below.

Errors

The ASI suffers from position and attitude errors*, plus those from the instrument itself, and lag. It is very susceptible to position error, which can be up to 10 or 20 kts at low speeds (check the flight manual), because the instrument will be calibrated for greatest accuracy in a particular flight condition (i.e. straight & level), otherwise the stagnation point will move to a different position.

*It will indicate wrongly in a sideslip.

If dynamic pressure is captured by the static port, the ASI will under-read, but the static pressure is lower along the fuselage anyway in flight, and the ASI will then over-read. calibration error will be greatest at the extremes of the operating envelope, that is, at very high and very low IAS, especially in larger aircraft.

However, density error is also important, since changes in air density affect the dynamic pressure, and make the ASI under-read at altitude (the ASI only reads TAS when density is standard, so to find it you have to apply a correction to CAS). The effect of temperature extending and contracting the linkages is fixed by a bimetallic strip that distorts to correct the expansion.

At high speeds (over 300 kts TAS, or 200 kts IAS) a further correction is made for air being compressed as it is brought to rest in the pitot tube. In the capsule, it will end up more dense than usual, and will vary the capsule's proportionality of expansion with dynamic pressure. At high altitudes with thinner air, the air flowing into the capsule is more easily compressed and will make the instrument over-read.

If the pitot tube and its drain get blocked, the ASI will behave like an altimeter because it has only static information - its readings (i.e. your airspeed) will increase (read high) as you climb, read low in the descent and not change at all when airspeed varies. This is a typical icing situation so, as you get higher, there is a danger that you will try to bring the speed back until you stall (without knowing why) which is what happened when the crew of one large jet missed the checklist item for the pitot heat. As static pressure *increases*, the ASI reading will *decrease*, and *vice versa*. If the drain hole remains open, however, IAS will read zero, as there is no differential between static and dynamic pressures, due to the drain hole allowing pressure in the lines to drop to atmospheric. A leak in the pitot total pressure line of a non-pressurised aircraft would cause an ASI to under-read.

If the static port gets blocked, the pressure inside the instrument (but outside the capsule) remains the same. The ASI will still read correctly in the cruise as long as the OAT doesn't change but, in the descent, it will over-read because the static element of pitot pressure increases inside the capsule - you will be closer to the stall than you think. In the climb, the static element of pitot pressure decreases, which causes a partial collapse of the capsule, so the instrument will under-read.

SQUARE LAW COMPENSATION

In addition being calibrated according to the St Venant formula (for compressibility), ASIs work on a differential pressure that varies with the square of the airspeed, and if you plotted the results linearly, the graph would look something like this:

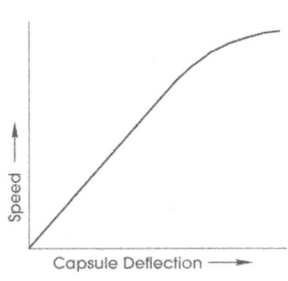

If you translated that to the instrument, you would end up with a logarithmic scale that would be difficult to read at low speed, and the whole speed range would be too big to fit in the display. To create a linear display, either the capsule or the linkage must be adjusted to produce the correct results or, rather, the indication moves at the same rate as the airspeed. Usually, the length or the point of leverage of a lever is adjusted to produce increased pointer movements for small deflections and decreased ones for large deflections. It is the *principle of variable magnification*.

V-Speeds

More in *Performance*!

Speed	Explanation
V_{LE}	Max gear extended
V_{LO}	Max gear operating
V_{NE}	Never Exceed speed.
V_{NO}	Normal Operations. 10% less than V_{NE}.
V_{MCG}	Minimum control speed on the ground
V_{MCA}	Minimum control speed in the air Now just referred to as V_{MC}
V_1	Decision speed - must be greater than V_{MCG} because you need to control the aircraft
V_R	Rotation speed - must be greater than V_{MCA} because you need to control the aircraft
V_{LOF}	Lift off speed

Increasing the flap angle has no effect on V_{MCG} or V_{MCA}, but it lowers the minimum value of V_1 because it decreases V_{LOF}. However, the maximum value of V_1 is increased because drag is increased.

THE MACHMETER

Here, we are interested in the *Free-Stream Mach Number*, which is assumed to be far enough away to be unaffected by the aircraft. In the Type A Machmeter, shown here, dynamic pressure is measured by an airspeed capsule, while the static pressure is measured by an aneroid capsule at right angles to it. A complex linkage detects their movement ratios. In other words, an ASI and an altimeter (in the same casing) feed their movements to a *main shaft*, which is connected to a *ratio arm*, then a *ranging arm*, to the *indicator* (rat ran in). When altitude decreases, the ratio arm slides to the end of the ranging arm, which reduces the ASI's involvement in the whole affair. As you go higher, it slides to the root, giving it more influence. Thus, the Mach number is found by dividing the dynamic pressure by the static pressure - *there are no temperature sensors*.

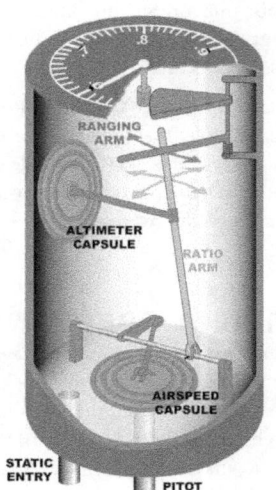

Type B Machmeters use the Air Data Computer, which does have a temperature sensor and is therefore able to correct properly for temperature rise and can display more accurate figures, usually to three decimal places.

Errors

Since the instrument contains an ASI and an altimeter, it suffers from both sets of errors, with those from the ASI being numerically predominant. However, these are very small, so the indicated Mach number is taken as the true Mach number.

The Machmeter does not suffer from compressibility error, though, as compressibility is a function of D-S* divided by S*, and it is this ratio which is use to calculate the Mach number.

*The static element of pitot pressure.

The Machmeter does not suffer from density error either, because it cancels out on both sides of the equation.

Machmeter readings are subject to *position pressure error, due to* incorrect pressure sensing from disturbed airflow around the pitot tube and/or static ports. If the pitot becomes blocked, the Machmeter shows the same errors as an ASI. The Mach number will stay unchanged until static pressure changes in a climb or a descent.

Blocked static sources mean that excess static pressure is trapped in the *case* and will cause the instrument to under-read below the altitude at which the blockage occurred (in a descent it will over-read above that altitude). If the static line fractures inside the pressure hull, static pressure will be too high and it will under-read. Likewise, if the pitot line leaks, the instrument will under read. At high speeds, temperature become artificially increased at speeds above about 300 kts, because of compressibility (this is already accounted for in the CR flight computer, so don't add any figures again from charts or tables).

The static pressure (S) on the top line of the equation above is the static element of pitot pressure. It should be cancelled out by the static pressure surrounding the capsule (S) on the bottom line, but this is artificially low due to the blockage. The airspeed capsule is expanded.

The static pressure (S) on the bottom line is also affecting the altitude capsule. It should increase during the descent, but the blockage stops this, so the altitude capsule remains in its expanded state. Because both capsules are expanded, the instrument is will over-read.

VERTICAL SPEED INDICATOR

There is a capsule inside this, too, but it is connected only to the static system. However, there is a *restrictor*, or *calibrated leak* between the inside and outside of the capsule that makes the pressure outside it lag behind, so the VSI measures the *rate of change* of *static pressure* with height, based on pressure difference between the inside of the capsule and the inside of the casing.

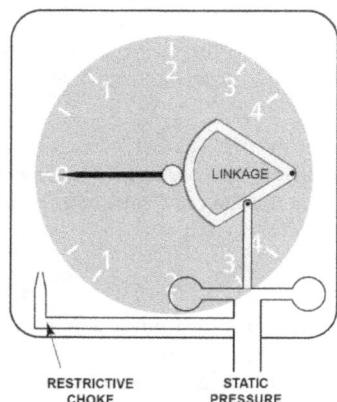

In other words, the difference between the instantaneous static pressure and that shortly beforehand is measured, with one chamber (the capsule) being inside the other (the case). Static pressure is fed in directly to the capsule so that any changes are due to movement of the aircraft. The flow through the restrictive choke, however, is constant, so the pressure in the case is always lagging behind that in the capsule, and we are dealing with the rate of change in static pressure, as determined by vertical speed.

During level flight there is no pressure differential across the metering unit, but in a descent (for example), static pressure increases and flows into the capsule and case. The capsule will expand as normal, but the restrictor will keep the pressure inside relatively low and create a differential that distorts the capsule. A suitable linkage transfers the capsule's movements to the dial.

The VSI is a trend *and* a rate instrument, showing the direction of movement (up or down), and how fast you're going, in hundreds of feet per minute on a logarithmic scale*, with zero at the 9 o'clock position, so it is horizontal when straight and level. Any movement up or down is shown in the relevant direction.

*The advantage is that, at low rates of climb or descent, the pointer movement is much larger and easier to read.

About 10% of the indicated vertical speed should be used to determine the number of feet to lead by when levelling off from a climb or descent.

Between +50°C and -20°C, the VSI is accurate within limits of ±200 feet per minute.

Errors

A complex choke system self-compensates for temperature, density and air viscosity, using two capillary tubes to give a laminar flow and two sharp-edged orifices for a turbulent flow. Errors that result from the two types are of opposite sign and cancel each other out.

Aside from the usual position error, the VSI suffers from lag, which may last up to 6-8 seconds before the air inside and outside the capsule stabilizes. This means that, for example, once you level off and the altimeter is stable, the VSI will take a few more seconds to settle to neutral. There is also *reversal error*, which occurs when abrupt changes cause movement briefly in the opposite direction.

If the static source becomes blocked, pressure differentials disappear and the instrument reads zero. If the restrictor gets blocked, there is a greater difference in the rate of pressure change so the VSI will over-read. A leak in the case will make the instrument over-indicate in the climb and under-indicate in the descent.

Diaphragm overload stops prevent damage if the rate of climb or descent exceeds the maximum design values of the instrument, so an aircraft descending at 6,000 ft per minute might only indicate 4,000 ft per minute.

 When breaking the glass of the VSI if the static source gets blocked, remember that the flow of air will be through the capillary tube, which is designed to create a lag. This means that the ASI and altimeter will lag as well! The rate of climb will indicate in reverse. Breaking the glass of the other two would have a similar effect to using alternate static.

IVSI

An *instantaneous (or Inertial Lead) VSI* uses two accelerometers in the static line, or a static input to an acceleration pump, to reduce lag errors, which introduces turning errors.

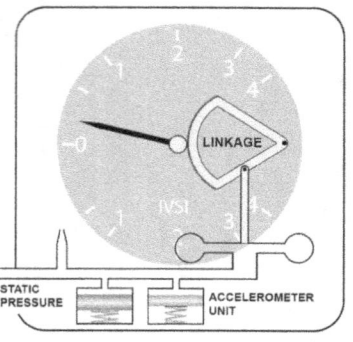

The accelerometers are small cylinders with weights inside (they act like pistons), held in balance by springs and their own mass. The weights are centralised when stabilised in the climb or descent, but, when levelling, they act in opposing directions to sharply reduce instrument indications by puffing air into the appropriate places (inertia causes an immediate differential pressure). When returning to level flight from large angles of bank, the IVSI will initially show a climb. If the turn is maintained it will stabilise to zero, then indicate a descent on rollout. Thus, IVSIs should not be relied upon while initiating or ending turns at bank angles of more than about 40°.

THE COMPASS   022 03/061 02

The Earth has its own magnetic field, with lines of force that are more or less parallel with the curvature of the Earth, but increasing their angle towards the Poles until they move vertically downwards in a circle surrounding the true pole.

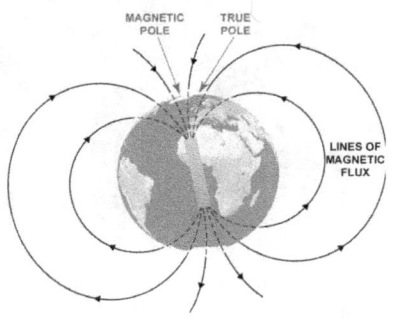

Although the origin of the Earth's magnetic field is not known, the Earth has its blue pole near the North pole and the direction of the magnetic force pointing straight down to the Earth's surface. In fact, the geographic North Pole is magnetically a South Pole, and *vice versa*, which is why the North end of a compass needle points to it.

A Direct Reading Magnetic Compass (DRMC) has a pivoted magnet that is free to align itself with the horizontal component of the Earth's magnetic field.

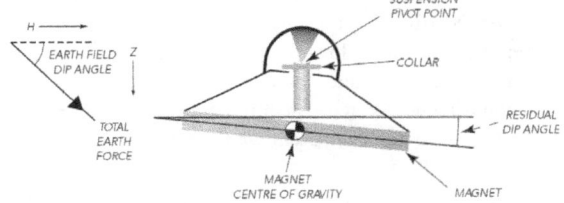

It must have certain properties to do this, namely:

- **Horizontality**. The needle must dip as little as possible, so the centre of gravity is made to lie below the pivot point, with pendulous magnets, that oppose the vertical component of the Earth's magnetic force (Z). Although there is still some dip, if it is less than 3° at mid-latitudes, it is OK.
- **Sensitivity**. This can be improved by increasing the length and/or the pole strength of the magnet. However, multiple magnets will do just as well, and they can also be employed as the weights under the pivot point mentioned above. Pole strength can be increased by using special alloys. In addition, you could use a jewelled pivot to reduce friction, and a suspension fluid which both lubricates it and reduces the effective weight

of the whole assembly. Modern compasses are sensitive, down to 0.01 gauss, but even that gives excessive hunting (in fact, you need gyro assistance when the magnetic field is below about 0.06 gauss).

- **Aperiodicity**. The ability to settle quickly after a disturbance, without overshooting or oscillating, which is helped by the (transparent) suspension liquid and a wire spider assembly. The two magnets above are also useful here, as they keep the mass of the assembly near the pivot, reducing inertia. Light alloys reduce inertia even more.

Being magnetic, the compass will be affected by all the fields generated by the aircraft itself, causing a phenomenon called *Deviation*, which is discussed under *The Compass Swing*, below. To try and eliminate errors, particularly magnetic dip, a remote indicating gyrocompass may be used, which is slaved to a DGI (discussed later). The master unit is mounted near the rear of the aircraft, so it is removed from as much influence as possible (hence the term *remote*). It contains a gyroscope under the influence of a magnetic element.

The usage limits lie between 73°N and 60°S.

E2B

A typical E2B direct indicating *standby* compass, as used in most aircraft today, consists of a floating inverted bowl suspended on a pedestal in kerosene, for damping (the transparent liquid also increases sensitivity and aperiodicity). The bearings are marked on the outside of the bowl, and there are two parallel magnetised needles inside, suspended under the pivot point, as mentioned.

Here is what the insides look like:

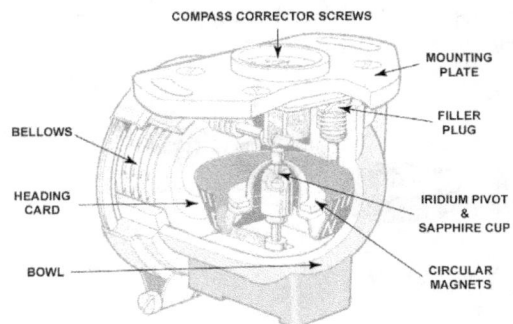

Dip

As the compass needle tries to follow the Earth's lines of force, it dips near the Poles, to where it is vertical (and unreadable), due to the vertical component of the Earth's magnetic force, which is called Z (in UK, the dip angle is around 67°). The bit we are interested in is H, the directive component, which is zero at the poles. At the Equator, there is no dip, so H is maximum, but as soon as you move away, the compass's Centre of Gravity becomes misaligned with its pivot point, and will move towards the Equator, or away from the nearer Pole.

H is about the same at magnetic latitudes 50°N and S, but the formula used to calculate the dip angle is:

$$\text{Dip} = \text{Cos}^{-1} \frac{H}{T}$$

Dip should obviously be minimised as much as possible, and is the reason why true tracks and headings are flown in Polar areas - the North and South magnetic Poles are the only places on the Earth where a freely suspended magnetic compass will stand vertical. On Northern routes, the dip effect causes a compass to turn much slower than you are used to in lower latitudes.

Magnetic dip is the angle between the horizontal and vertical forces acting on a compass needle toward the nearer pole. Its existence is why the limits of a magnetic compass lie between 73°N and 60°S (it is most effective about midway between the magnetic Poles). An *aclinic line* is a line representing points of zero magnetic dip. An *isoclinal line* connects points of equal dip. As the magnetic pole and lines of force do not coincide with either the true poles or lines of longitude, there is a way of accounting for any magnetic variation, discussed below. Unfortunately, although the C of G's position below the suspension point assists with minimising Z (and dip), it also gives rise to errors. Before you start relying on the compass (either to navigate or align your DGI), make sure you are in steady, level flight. Also, make turns gently, because the swirling fluid will keep the compass moving afterwards.

ACCELERATION ERRORS

These are caused by inertia on East-West headings. Because the C of G of the compass is under the pivot point, accelerating displaces the C of G behind the pivot point and makes the bulk of the compass lag behind the machine. If you were just going N-S, all you would get is extra dip, but because you are going East or West, the displaced C of G, not being vertically in line with the pivot point, creates a couple that makes the compass turn in the direction of the acceleration (clockwise when heading East) to read less than 90° during the turn. A deceleration has the opposite effect.

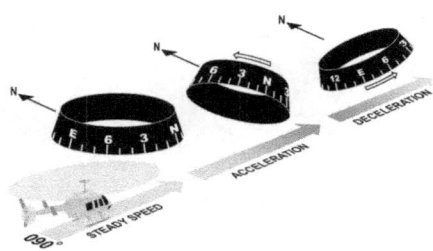

Acceleration errors are maximum on East/West headings and near the magnetic Poles, and nil on North/South headings, and at the Equator. The term here is ANDS - *Accelerate North, Decelerate South*, or SAND in the Southern Hemisphere. In the Northern Hemisphere flying East, if you accelerate, the needle deflects to the nearest Pole (North, for an easterly deviation) and South when you decelerate so, if you take off on runway 45 in the Northern hemisphere, the compass will read below 045°.

- During deceleration after landing on runway 18 (a Southerly direction), a compass in the Northern hemisphere would indicate no apparent turn.

- During deceleration after a landing in an Easterly direction, a magnetic compass in the Northern hemisphere indicates an apparent turn South.

- During deceleration after a landing in a Westerly direction, a magnetic compass in the Southern hemisphere indicates an apparent turn North.

TURNING ERRORS

These are the main cause of error in a DRMC.

A Mr Keith Lucas discovered that a simple compass underestimates turns on Northerly headings, and over-estimates them on Southerly ones in the Northern hemisphere (UNOS, and ONUS in the South). This happens because you are banking and the compass tries to follow the lines of dip, with a little help from liquid swirl. To put it another way, to eliminate the hemispheres from the equation, during turns through the *nearest* Pole (within 35°), the compass is sluggish, so you need to roll out early. During turns through the *furthest* Pole, it will be lively, so roll out late. The errors are maximum (30°) at the Poles and decrease by 10° towards East and West, where they are nil, so the lead/lag required is approximately equal to the latitude. Turning errors can have two elements, both of which work in the same sense:

- **Magnetic**, which depends on the angle of bank. In a turn from North to East, for example, the North-seeking end will move down towards Earth, so its readings will decrease and a turn in the opposite direction will be indicated. The more the bank, the more the error, so it is more apparent with a fast aircraft for the same rate of turn.

    Turning error actually depends on the tangent of the angle of dip multiplied by the cosine of the heading and the angle of bank. It is nil on E-W headings because the cosine is nil. For a 5° angle of bank, the error will be in the order of 30°.

    As an example, when flying South, you decide to make a right turn and fly due North. As soon as you start the turn, the compass will indicate a turn of around 30°, even though the nose has hardly moved - an extra fast turn is shown in the direction of the bank. It will then slow down so that the reading is approximately correct on passing through West, then it will lag as you approach North, so you roll out early, anticipating by the number of degrees of your latitude, plus an allowance for rollout.

- **Dynamic**, which depends on speed and the rate of turn. In a flat turn, the dip makes the C of G of the compass move toward the Equator and it moves to the outside of the turn, producing a clockwise movement as above.

A rough calculation as to how much to overshoot or anticipate by when turning to the North or South comes from this formula:

$$\frac{\text{Bank Angle} + \text{Latitude}}{2}$$

So, to turn right on to a southerly heading with 20° bank at 20°N, you stop on an approximate heading of 200°.

In practice, just overshoot or undershoot by an amount equal to the latitude, regardless of the bank angle.

 In real life, you would simply do a timed turn at 3° per second - such calculations would have a low priority on a dark rainy night.

Direction

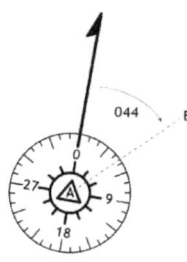

Direction (for us) is the position of one point relative to another, regardless of distance between them, measured in an angular fashion from the observer's meridian with reference to True, Magnetic or Grid North, using up to 360 numerical degrees*.

*The complete circle of direction (or *compass rose*) is split into 360 *degrees*, which are split into 60 *minutes* and 60 *seconds*, so the complete expression of an angle is in degrees, minutes and seconds - 30° 45' 53". North is 0°, so, going round the clock, East is 90°, South is 180° and West is 270° (the *cardinal* directions. NE, SE, SW & NW are intercardinal).

A *bearing* is a direction obtained by observation. It is the horizontal clockwise angle from a North baseline, or the angle between whichever North you use and any line between two points, such as that between A and B in the diagram above. The bearing is 044°, and the opposite is the *reciprocal*, found by adding or subtracting 180°, or 224°. Because you go clockwise, and the largest number is 360°, 355° is less than 010°.

This is not the same as the *relative bearing* from your aircraft, as measured from the longitudinal axis!

- **True North** is a line from any point on the Earth's surface to the North Pole, along the local meridian. Modern navigation systems such as INS/IRS output True North and their readings are changed to magnetic according to a lookup table.

- **Magnetic North** is the direction to the North *magnetic* pole, as shown by the North-seeking needle of a magnetic compass. Its usual symbol is a line ending with half an arrowhead. It was discovered by Soviet explorers to be the rim of a magnetic circle 1,000 miles in circumference, around 600 miles from the True Pole, around Northern Canada. It moves by 1° every 5 years.

- **Grid North** is a line established with vertical grid lines drawn on a map, explained later. It may be symbolised with the letters *GN* or *y*

All meridians run North to South.

MAGNETIC BEARINGS

The North *Magnetic* Pole was discovered by Soviet explorers to be the rim of a magnetic circle 1,000 miles in circumference, around 600 miles from the True Pole. Both magnetic Poles move slowly around their respective True Poles, over a period of around 960 years. The North magnetic pole and various lines of force described below change their positions to the West.

That there is a True and a Magnetic North indicates that a compass will not point towards True North, since it relies on magnetism for its operation, and the two Norths (or Souths) do not coincide at their respective Poles. This is because the Earth generates its own magnetism, which may be varied by local deposits of metals under the ground, for example, which bend the magnetic flux lines. The way to Magnetic North will therefore vary across the ground from place to place, and a freely suspended compass will turn to the direction of the *local* magnetic field (the *Horizontal Component* is toward Magnetic North). As well, the lines of force will be vertical near the poles.

Variation

To find the direction of the geographical Pole, or True North, you have to apply a correction called variation, which is the angle between the magnetic and true meridians (that is, variation is the correction that must be applied to magnetic headings or courses (at the same place) to make them true. It is technically called *declination*. If the magnetic meridian is to the right of the true one, variation is Easterly and has a plus (+) sign (think of what it makes the compass rose do). If it is left, it is Westerly and has a minus (-) sign So, -8 is really 8W. The **Magnetic Track Angle** (MTA) is the direction of the path of an aircraft across the Earth's surface against *Magnetic North*. The phrase to remember is *Variation East, Magnetic Least, Variation West, Magnetic Best so*, if the variation on your map is, say, 21° West, the final result should be 21° *more* than the true track found when you drew your line.

- If you travel over many variations, use an average about every 200 miles.

- Variation on a VOR bearing is applied *at the station*, and on an ADF *at the aircraft*.

 Magnetic information in a Flight Management System is stored in *each IRS memory* - it is applied to the true calculated heading.

Variation can change temporarily from sunspot activity or magnetic storms. This is more of a problem in the Arctic or Antarctic areas, where the change can be ±5° for an hour or more. On a map, or chart, which would be drawn initially for True North, there is a dotted line called an *isogonal* that represents the local magnetic variation to be applied to any direction you wish to plan a flight on.

The charted values of magnetic variation normally change annually due to magnetic pole movement, causing values at all locations to increase or decrease. When plotted, isogonals are accurate worldwide to ±2°. They converge on both poles, geographic and magnetic.

An *agonic line* exists where magnetic variation is zero, or where the True and Magnetic meridians are parallel. There's one near Frankfurt, running North/South.

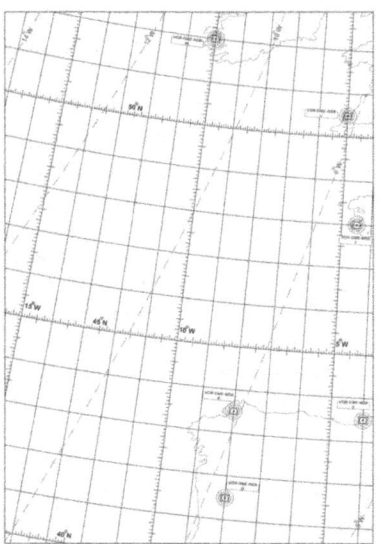

The compass cannot be corrected for variation.

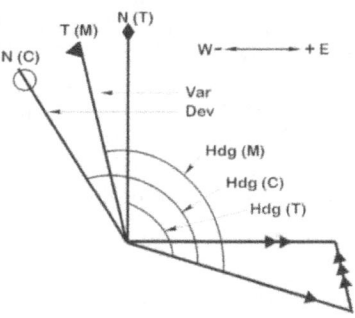

DEVIATION

Errors in the compass, plus an aircraft's own magnetism, from metal, and electrical currents, and residual magnetism from hammering, etc. during manufacture, make the compass deflect from Magnetic North. This is deviation, which is unique to an aircraft, or even a compass position. It is applied to the compass heading to get the magnetic heading, and *vice versa*.

The net result of an aircraft's magnetic forces is represented by a dot somewhere behind the wings or rotor head. On Northerly headings, the dot lies behind the South part of the needle and merely concentrates the magnetic force. On Easterly headings, however, the dot is West of the South part of the needle and causes an Easterly deviation, and *vice versa*. It is proportional to Z and inversely proportional to H.

Deviation is the difference between a heading measured from the magnetic meridian and the same heading measured by a compass, at the same place. It is defined by the number of degrees which must be added (algebraically) to the observed reading to get the magnetic reading. Two aircraft flying in formation would have slightly different headings due to their deviations.

When deviation is West, compass North is to the West of magnetic North. When deviation is East, compass North is to the East of magnetic North. The phrase here is *Deviation West, Compass Best, Deviation East, Compass Least*, similar to Variation. This means that if the compass is reading 005° when it should be reading 360°, the deviation is 5° West, or -5°, as it must be "added" to the observed reading to get the proper one. If it is reading 346°, the deviation is 14° East, or +14°.

Thus, positive deviations deflect the compass needle to the right, and will have a plus sign even though the heading reads less. Negative deviations deflect the needle to the left and have a minus sign, although the heading increases. The key is to realise that they are based on what the deviation does to the heading on the compass rose.

Deviation varies with the heading and its values are displayed on a correction card next to the compass (they should not exceed 1° after correction). The values are obtained after a *compass swing*, a complex procedure normally done by an engineer, described soon.

For	Steer
000	001
045	043
090	089
135	133
180	184
225	223
270	269
315	316

Allowing for deviation is called *compensation*. So:

```
HDG(T) ± VAR ± DEV = HDG (C)
```

EXAMPLES

1. With a compass heading of 030°, deviation of 3°W and variation of 8°E, what is the true heading?

C	D	M	V	T
030	3W	027	8E	035

The Compass Swing

The magnetic compass is incompatible with aircraft, if only because it needs to be placed where it can be seen, which is typically in the middle of any stray magnetism.

The magnetic compass is incompatible with aircraft, if only because it needs to be placed where it can be seen, which is typically in the middle of any stray magnetism.

A compass swing allows you to find out by how much a compass reads differently from the proper figures on any heading, then make corrections that cancel out as many deviations as possible. In other words, the idea is to measure the angle between Magnetic and Compass North.

Airfields have clear areas in which this can be done. The aircraft is taxied there and everything electrical that would be used in flight turned on. Then the aircraft compass is compared against a landing compass on several headings by an engineer standing out in the rain (you need to find the errors on the cardinal and quadrantal points, so the aircraft is placed on each in turn). The deviations are reduced by adjusting magnets inside the compass and a calibration swing is done to see what deviations or residuals are left. Those figures are written on the deviation card.

INSTRUMENTS
The Compass

A compass swing should be done:

- on installation of the compass in the first place.
- as per maintenance schedules.
- whenever there is any doubt about accuracy.
- after a shock to the airframe or a lightning strike.
- if the aircraft has been left standing on the same heading for some time or has been moved to a significantly different latitude.
- when major components or electrical installations change.

Aircraft have built-in magnetism, whose influence on a compass can be classified broadly into 3 components, *hard iron*, *soft iron* and *electrical*. You can sum the individual effects and replace them with a single equivalent source.

HARD IRON

This is a more or less permanent effect that arises because the aircraft will have been on a particular heading* at a particular latitude for some time (more then three weeks or so) when it was being made, and will have absorbed some of the Earth's magnetism at that point. As such, it is the controlling factor in deviation. The effect is increased by hammering, and it will weaken when the machine starts flying, but some permanent magnetism will always remain. It is therefore unlikely to change.

There are vertical and horizontal effects, which are corrected with magnets. The field caused by such permanent magnetism is visualised as three components at the compass position:

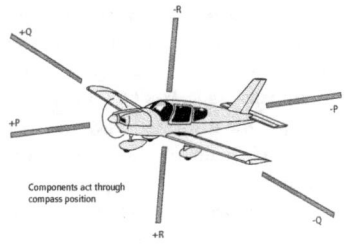

- **P** - fore and aft.
  It is minus if it pulls the red end of the compass needle to the rear (blue at the back), and plus if it pulls it to the front (blue at the front).
- **Q** - left to right (athwartships). Plus if it pulls the red end to starboard (blue starboard), minus if it pulls to port (blue to port).
- **R** - Up and down. Plus if it pulls the red end down (blue to the bottom), and minus if it pulls upwards (blue to the top). In level flight, it has no effect on the compass. Once it comes out of the vertical, however, the horizontal vector affects P and Q. When nose-up, for example, R will be acting forward, acting like P, so its maxima will be E-W (like Q when banking). The amount of the deviation depends on the value of R, and the angle between the longitudinal and horizontal axes. In practice, it is small enough to be ignored.

*P and Q only. If you built an aircraft at the magnetic Equator, where the Earth's lines of force are horizontal, you would get a fair amount of P and Q, and no R. If you built it facing SE in the Northern Hemisphere, you would get +PQR. R is always positive if the machine is built in the Northern Hemisphere, and negative otherwise.

The capital letters represent hard iron effects. Small letters are used for soft iron effects, described below.

P is zero when facing North, but will remain attracted to North as a 360° turn is started and cause a deviation that depends on the component's polarity. It will be maximum when facing East, zero again at South, maximum again at West (in the opposite direction) and zero at North, so it is a sine relationship with the aircraft's heading. The maximum deviation from P is called *Coefficient B*, which is expressed as an angle. Coefficients are discussed overleaf. Component Q's maxima are on North and South, and vary as the cosine of the aircraft heading. The maximum deviation is resolved with Coefficient C.

In summary, hard iron magnetism is permanent, and does not change with latitude, but the deviation caused by it increases with latitude because the H force is weaker, and the compass magnets are more easily deflected.

SOFT IRON

This is a temporary influence that only appears when the metal in the aircraft is affected by the Earth's magnetic field and, to a lesser extent, electrical systems (i.e. induced magnetism). That is, induced magnetism is from ferrous metals that are not permanently magnetised. The effect of soft iron depends on the heading and attitude of the aircraft, and its geographical position. As your heading changes, so does the soft iron magnetism.

As your heading changes, so does the soft iron magnetism.

Soft iron has a vertical element that is stronger in high latitudes because H is reduced. The horizontal element is also split further into X and Y to match the longitudinal and lateral axes of the aircraft. Soft iron magnetism is visualised as coming from 9 soft iron rods near the compass that are affected by the Earth's magnetic field. The rods have length, but no thickness, and are *imaginary* - that is, they are simply a mathematical device that explains certain effects. You cannot use "bar magnets" as with hard iron magnetism, because of confusion as to which way the fields go in turns.

The rods are labelled with small letters (a - k) and are related to the XYZ components mentioned above like this: aX, bY, cZ, dX, eY, fZ, gX, hY and kZ.

The important ones are:

- cZ - fore and aft
- fZ - athwartships
- kZ - Vertical axes

cZ and fZ act like P and Q because they do not change polarity with heading. As Z acts vertically, it does not affect directional properties, and its sign will only change if the aircraft moved to the other magnetic hemisphere.

ELECTRICAL

Current flowing through a conductor produces a magnetic field that can deflect a compass needle. There can also be effects from lightning strikes.

COEFFICIENTS

Deviations from the components of hard and soft iron can be resolved into:

- **Coefficient A**, which is constant on all headings, and is found by dividing the sum of the deviations on the cardinal and intercardinal points by 8, so it is an average. It is caused by asymmetric soft iron around the compass, and is similar to a deviation caused by the lubber line being out of alignment. As the two are hard to tell apart, it is simplest just to move the compass.

  Apparent A (as opposed to Real A from soft iron) may be caused by an error in the magnetic bearing of an object used for swinging. Both are allowed for by rotating the compass by the result.

Aircraft	L/C	Result
000	352	+8
045	040	+5
090	094	-4
135	130	+5
180	172	+8
225	226	-1
270	273	-3
315	316	-1

For example, the sum of the numbers in the right hand column is 17. Divided by 8, this gives a correction of 2° to be applied to all headings (if the aircraft is headed North and the compass reads 5°, the error deviation is classed as -5°, meaning that the aircraft compass is under-reading and 5° must be subtracted to make it correct).

- **Coefficient B** is like a **fore-and-aft** magnet and is used to resolve deviations from P + cZ. It produces maximum values on East and West (zero on N-S), varying as the **sine** of the heading. It is the result of dividing E - W by 2.

- **Coefficient C** is like an **athwartships** magnet, with maximum values on North and South, varying as the **cosine** of the heading. It is used to resolve deviations from Q + cZ and is the result of dividing N - S by 2.

- **Coefficient D** is for soft iron on quadrantals*.
- **Coefficient E** is for soft iron on cardinal points*.

*D & E are not particularly important. Put another way, dealing with A, B and C is enough trouble so we leave them alone. D is not compensated for anyway as it is in the vertical plane.

- Residuals should not exceed 1° for a gyromagnetic compass and 3° for a direct reader.
- Combined changes (say from multiple electrical items) should not exceed 2°
- Deviations in level flight should not exceed 10°
- The maximum limits are ±3° for a gyromagnetic compass and ±15° for a direct reader.

Errors from B and C are corrected before those from Coefficient A (in fact, C is done first), and are minimised by equal and opposite effects to those from the aircraft.

The E2B uses *scissor magnets*, and electromagnets are used in gyro compasses.

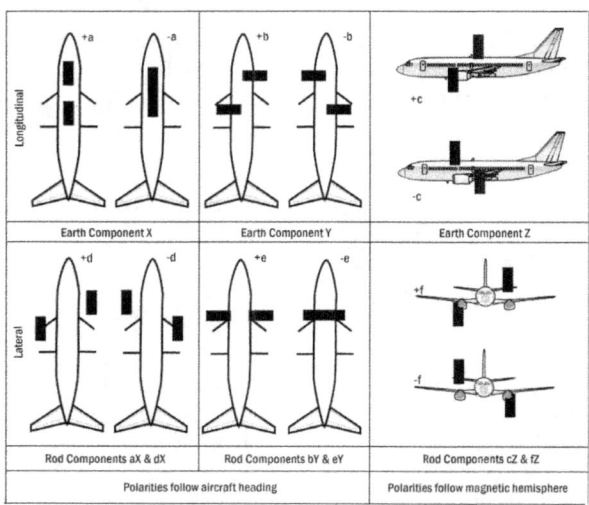

GYROSCOPES

Gyros are used in aircraft to establish three reference planes, namely Pitch, Roll and Yaw but, as they only have two reference rings (or gimbals - see *Types Of Gyroscope*, below), we need more than one to get the information we need. In fact, three instruments are usually run by gyroscopes, the *Attitude Indicator* (artificial horizon), *Directional Gyroscopic Indicator* (DGI) and *Turn Indicator or Coordinator*. The first two are typically suction-powered and the last by electricity, but many are now all electric.

Gyros (and accelerometers) are also called *inertial sensors* because they use resistance to changes in momentum to sense angular (gyro) and linear motion (accelerometer).

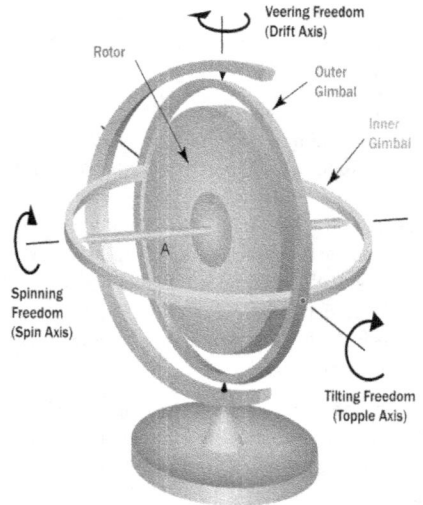

INSTRUMENTS
Gyroscopes

The Earth itself is a gyroscope. Around the Equator it spins at around 1,000 knots, as opposed to the more typical 250 knots for man-made gyroscopes. As such, it is able to maintain its present position in space to within 1° of the North Star. The problem for us is that we need the gyros to maintain a position with reference to the Earth, hence the various correction mechanisms, described later.

A gyroscope is a heavy rotating mass on a vertical or horizontal axis*, suspended in inner and outer *gimbals* which are in *frames*. Its operation depends on the resistance to deflection of a spinning wheel or disc, and only its Centre of Gravity remains fixed in space. The gyro is free to turn in any direction around it.

*A gyroscope's axis of rotation defines its orientation. A vertical gyro has its axis in *Earth Vertical* (as opposed to aircraft vertical) and a horizontal gyro is in *Earth Horizontal*, but more properly aligned with North.

You need a gimbal for each axis to be measured, so an artificial horizon has 2, because it measures pitch and roll.

Rigidity

The spinning allows the gyro to maintain its own position in space, regardless of whatever it is attached to is doing. In other words, it resists attempts to displace it from its position. If you attached one to a camera in a helicopter, the helicopter could be bumping around all over the place due to wind or pilot input, and the camera would not move from where the operator put it. The same applies with the instruments mentioned above, as we shall see shortly. In fact, the gyro does not move, but the Earth moving around the gyro gives you that impression. The magnitude of this apparent movement depends on your latitude or, rather, the sine (drift) or cosine (topple) of your latitude.

Rigidity can be increased with:

- faster spin speeds
- increasing the gyro's peripheral mass
- increasing the gyro's radius

The greater the rigidity, the more force will be required to move the spinning gyro, which is an example of the *Law of Conservation of Angular Momentum*.

Precession & Wander

Any movement of the gyro's spin axis from its initial alignment is called *precession*. A force applied to a gyroscope's spinning mass is felt 90° away from where it is applied, in the direction of rotation. Put another way, pressure applied to the vertical axis is felt around the horizontal axis, and vice versa.

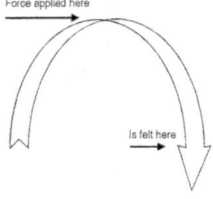

A mundane example comes from riding a bicycle - when you apply a force to turn one way or another, it is done at the top of the wheels, but the turning movement appears 90° later, hence the turn. More technically, precession is the *angular change in the plane of rotation under the influence of an applied force*. It is not wanted in some instruments, such as directional gyros.

The rate of precession depends on:

- the strength and direction of the applied force
- the rotor's moment of inertia (degree of rigidity)
- the rotor's angular velocity

WANDER

When a gyro moves from a preset position because of precession, it is said to wander.

The gyro is *drifting* when the axis wanders *horizontally*, and *toppling* when it wanders *vertically* (the term *topple* also refers to the tumbling that occurs when a gyro reaches a limit stop and a rapid precession occurs around a misaligned axis). Thus, a gyro with only a vertical axis cannot drift. Both are affected by real and apparent wander.

This is covered under *DGI*, where it is most relevant.

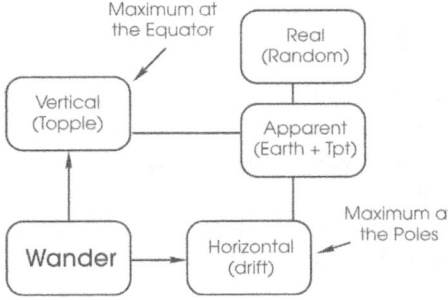

Drift occurs at 15° per hour multiplied by the sine of the latitude. Topple occurs at 15° per hour multiplied by the cosine of the latitude.

Types Of Gyroscope

The conventional gyro uses the principle of stored mechanical energy (inertia).

3 PLANES OF FREEDOM

Gyros with 3 planes of freedom have 2 gimbals and total freedom of movement around 3 axes. There are 3 types:

- **Space Gyro**. Free to move in all directions with reference to space. Theoretical.
- **Tied Gyro**. As above, with the spin axis tied down in one local plane. 2 *degrees* of freedom (see below). An example is the DGI, where the spin axis is tied to the yawing plane.
- **Earth Gyro**. As above, but the spin axis is tied *Earth vertically* by gravity, e.g. the artificial horizon.

2 PLANES OF FREEDOM

These show a rate of movement rather than a position:

- **Rate Gyro**. One gimbal, free to move around 2 axes (including the spin axis). Designed to show the rate of movement about the axis at right angles to the two free axes, as used in the turn and slip indicator, or the turn coordinator.

- **Rate Integrating Gyro.** These are used in Inertial Navigation Systems, and their gimbals are restrained by the viscosity of a fluid, as opposed to the springs that are used by rate gyros. The fluid's viscosity is affected by temperature, so a warm-up period is required. It is so dense that the weight of the rotor and can is effectively zero. As the aircraft turns about the sensitive axis, the precession is used to generate an error signal, the magnitude of which signifies the rate at which the aircraft is turning about the axis.

DEGREES OF FREEDOM (GIMBALS)

A French method of classifying gyroscopes uses the numbers of axes *not* including the spin axis, so a gyro with 3 *planes* of freedom has 2 *degrees* of freedom. A degree of freedom is the ability to move around an axis, so we count the number of gimbals. The spin axis cannot precess, but each gimbal allows it to do so in one other direction.

An airborne instrument, with a gyro that has 2 degrees of freedom and a horizontal spin axis could be a DGI.

- *Spinning* freedom is about an axis perpendicular through the centre
- *Tilting* freedom is about a horizontal axis at right angles to the spin axis
- *Veering* freedom is about a vertical axis perpendicular to the spin and tilt axes

Degs	Gyro	Purpose
1º	Rate	Turn Indicator
	Rate Integrating	Inertial Navigation
2º	Earth	A/H
	Tied	DGI
3º	Space	Theoretical

Attitude gyros use rigidity in space for their operation, while rate gyros use precession.

GIMBAL LOCK

In a 3-gimbal system, two gimbals can end up in line, effectively removing one from the equation. A fourth gimbal (used with Inertial Navigation Systems) can keep the 2nd and 3rd gimbals at right angles to each other to prevent gimbal lock.

Power

As mentioned, air-driven gyroscopic instruments are made to spin through suction or pressure (heading and attitude indicator) or electricity (turn instruments) although many are now all electric (even then, there should be separate and independent power supplies. If there is only one, you need suction, too).

SUCTION

With suction, air is usually *sucked out* of the casing, to create a vacuum that will be indicated on a gauge in the cockpit. It is part of the checklist before flight to ensure you have enough for the instruments to work properly, typically 4-5 inches of mercury.

If it is reading low, the filters are blocked or equipment is worn, and the gyros will run too slowly. If the reading is too high, the gyros will run too fast (the rotation speed of an air driven gyro is usually between 9,000 - 12,000 RPM).

Vanes (small bucket-shapes) on the gyro mass catch the air movement and force it to go round at several thousand RPM. The rest of the vacuum system has a pump driven by the engine, a relief valve, an air filter, and enough tubing for the connections. Older aircraft may have a venturi tube on the side to create the initial vacuum.

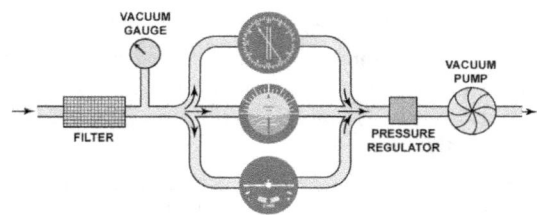

The relief valve is kept closed with a spring, which is pre-adjusted for the required vacuum so that air pressure acting on the outside of the valve is balanced against spring tension. If the adjusted value sis exceeded, the outside air pressure overcomes the spring, opening the valve to allow outside air to flow into the system until balance is restored.

A pressure-operated system is similar, but the inlet and outlet connections are reversed on each instrument

ELECTRICITY

At high altitudes, suction-driven gyros can lose rigidity because they cannot produce so much vacuum. They also require large amounts of plumbing. These can be resolved with electrical gyros, whose advantages include:

- Faster spin speed, therefore greater rigidity
- Spin speed is easier to initiate and maintain, as aircraft power is regulated, and you don't need other systems running first
- The container can be sealed to keep dirt out - suction driven instruments necessarily have a hole in them to let air in
- More stable operating temperature
- The ability to work at higher altitudes
- Acceleration errors are minimised because there is no heavy mass underneath the gyro. Any there will be due to the mercury sloshing around.

The motor is usually a squirrel cage, using a power supply of 115v 400 Hz 3-phase AC in large aircraft, while smaller ones can have an inverter built in to produce 26 V (AC motors tend to be used in artificial horizons, while DC is used in turn and bank indicators). There must be some form of failure indication to show loss of power.

Fast erection involves giving the motors a higher error signal, which can be done in unaccelerated flight.

Ring Laser Gyros

These are used in inertial reference systems and use a partially silvered mirror (prismatic sensor) and 2 contra-rotating laser beams that go the opposite direction to each other in a precisely drilled tunnel round a triangular block of a vitro ceramic material* that does not expand or contract with temperature (it is very hard) - any change in length would produce the equivalent to real wander in a mechanical gyro (the mirror position or the discharge current can be altered to compensate). Noise from imperfections in mirrors is the same as random wander.

*The material used does not distort with age, which can degrade the accuracy and destroy the gas tight seal necessary to contain the helium and neon gases used in creating the laser. Two anodes and a common cathode create electrical discharges within the gases which cause the channels to act as gain tubes, producing the beams. Put more precisely, the gas or plasma is ionised by the voltage, causing helium atoms to collide with, and transfer energy to, the neon atoms.

The servo mirror can move. The collecting mirror allows a small amount of light through so one beam can be flipped around by the prism and meet with the other one that is aimed directly at the detector, which determines any fringe pattern generated by interference when the beams are out of phase. They are in phase (coherent) when there is no acceleration. The counter-propagating waves normally beat together to set up a standing wave pattern inside the cavity. The optical path must be kept th a length that is a multiple of the lasing wavelength, that is, an exact number of wavelengths at the frequency for peak power.

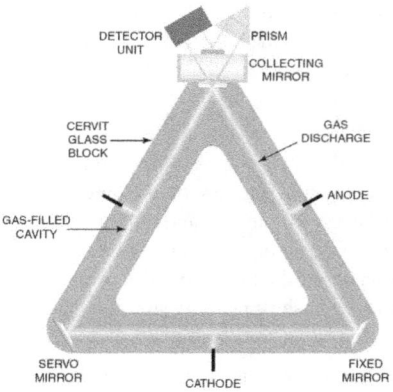

The resonant structure (the triangular block), is designed such that each beam will only resonate at one spot frequency. If the ring is stationary, the resonant frequency for both directions will be identical, as the path lengths are identical. When the beams combine at the detector they interfere with each other to form a fringe pattern of light bars at the photoelectric cells of the detector.

If the path length of the waves is altered artificially by movement, their frequencies change and so do their transit times. The light beam travelling in the same direction as the rotation must travel a slightly longer path while the opposite beam will travel over a shorter one.

There will be a change in the interference pattern, causing the light bars to move in a direction that depends on the direction of rotation of the RLG and the distance moved will depend on the rate of rotation. This output is converted to pulse signals that are representative of the rate and direction of rotation of the RLG.

Compared to conventional gyros, laser gyros are more accurate, and have a longer life cycle, as there are no moving parts (apart from the *dither motor* below) and therefore no friction. They are also very quick to align, smaller, use less power and do not suffer from precession.

LOCK IN

Picture: Ring laser gyros as used in an Inertial Unit:

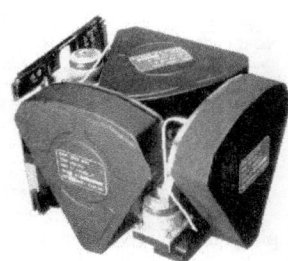

At low input rates, the frequency differences become very near zero due to back scatter from one beam affecting the other. This makes them both synchronise.

Dithering is the name of the technique, using a piezo-electric motor, that is used to counteract it. The entire apparatus is rotated clockwise and anti-clockwise about its axis at a rate convenient to the mechanical resonance of the system, ensuring that the angular velocity of the system is usually far from the lock-in threshold. Typical rates are 400 Hz, with a peak dither velocity of 1 arc-second per second.

ARTIFICIAL HORIZON

Otherwise known as the *attitude indicator*, or an *attitude and director indicator* (ADI) if it incorporates a flight director, this instrument represents the natural horizon and indicates the pitch and bank attitudes, that is, whether the nose is up or down, or the wings are level or not. It does not necessarily show climb, descent, or turns.

Given that a gyro tries to keep its position in space, as you move around, it needs to be kept level with the Earth's surface, so there is an erection mechanism, described below. The spin axis is *vertically mounted* (in line with Earth Vertical) so the instrument suffers from topple, in a cosine relationship. The housing (and aircraft) can rotate around it. The assembly is inside an *outer gimbal*, which is Earth Horizontal, with 2 degrees of freedom.

The instrument's C of G is below the suspension point, so it is nearly vertical when it is switched on, which reduces the erection time. In the suction-driven version, four *pendulous vanes* cover holes through which air tries to pass, but is blocked by the vanes as long as the instrument is vertical. When it is not vertical, the vanes, which are suspended from a pivot and kept vertical by gravity, open the hole by differing amounts to let more or less air through as required, to provide the correcting force.

In other words, the pendulous vane stays vertical*, but more of the hole is exposed as the instrument moves.

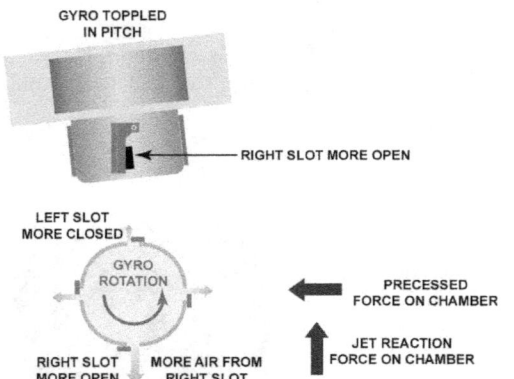

*To be picky, it is affected by centrifugal force, and will not be properly effective (see *Errors* below). This can be minimised with an offset for the vanes for a particular rate of bank (compensation tilt).

As it has a slow erection speed, and is relatively slow to operate, this system is not perfect in accelerated flight. Electrical systems are more responsive.

The aircraft symbol is attached to the casing and therefore the aircraft. The *horizon bar* (which stays in line with the Earth) is connected to the rear of the frame and to the housing with a *guide pin*, so when the nose pitches up, the outer gimbal comes off the horizontal. The movement is amplified by the beam bar and the guide pin is driven down - in a descent it goes up. Rolling rotates the instrument case.

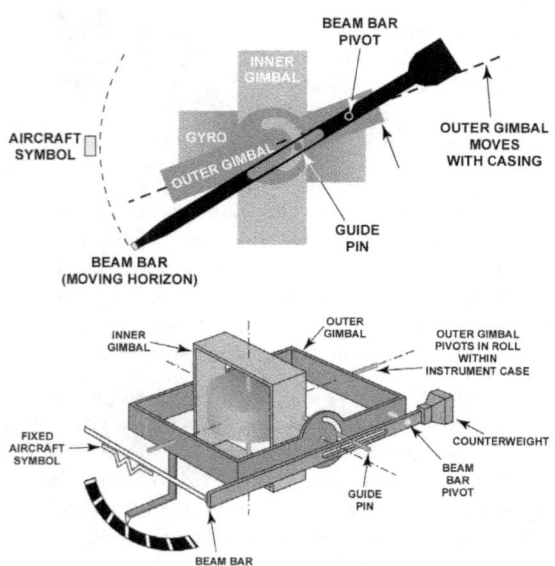

A standby artificial horizon must have its own power supply and its own gyro.

Errors

With all the rotating parts, there is bound to be friction, which will cause some errors in the readings. Others include *acceleration error*, during forward movement (as in a takeoff) which gives a false climb to the *right** - this is because of the pendulous mounting - the heavy bottom of the (suction) gyro suffers from inertia and creates an imbalance between misplaced centres of gravity (roll error) and closing one of the suction ports (pitch error) - the effect is similar to the compass. The resulting forces precess 90° away for false readings. Deceleration shows a false descent and roll to port.

When an aircraft has turned through 360° with a constant attitude and bank, both will be correct on a classic instrument. Having turned only 90°, you will observe too much nose-up and too little bank. At 180°, the nose will still be too high, but with a correct amount of bank. At 270°, too nose high, but with the bank too high. Centrifugal force created during a turn will also displace the mass of the instrument's heavy bottom, but modern designs minimise turning errors at low rates of turn.

*Electrical artificial horizons will show a climbing turn to the *left*, because they normally spin the opposite way.

Thus, an instrument showing a climb to either direction indicates *pitch* and *roll* errors. The pitch error is due to acceleration on the pendulous vanes, and the roll error comes from the inertia of the bottom-heavy housing.

Electrical Version

In an electrical artificial horizon, two *torque motors* are used, one parallel to the lateral axis, and one to the longitudinal axis. The laterally mounted one detects movement in roll, and a correction from the torque motor is applied to the pitch axis. Displacement in pitch is detected by the longitudinal switch which corrects around the roll axis.

The mercury switches that sense topple of the spin axis in the fore and aft plane and athwartships are on the inner gimbal. The torque motor associated with the fore and aft one is attached to the outer gimbal. It applies a torque about the roll axis, which is then precessed to act about the pitch axis. The torque motor associated with the athwartships mercury switch applies a force about the pitch axis, which is precessed to act about the roll axis.

The torque motors are squirrel-cage type laminated iron rotors mounted concentrically round a stator, with two windings - one for a constant field, called the *reference winding*, and the other is in two parts so it can be reversible, called the *control winding*.

Levelling switches are sealed glass tubes containing 3 electrodes (one at each end and one in the middle) and a small blob of mercury. An inert gas is also present to stop any arcing as the mercury comes into contact with the electrodes. The glass tubes are set at right angles to each other on a switch block behind the gyro housing.

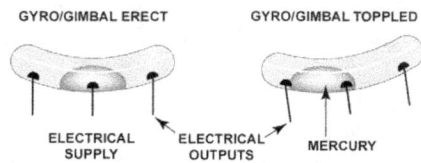

In the normal operating position, the mercury is in contact with the centre electrode, which is connected to the reference winding. If a displacement happens, the mercury makes contact with one of the side electrodes which completes a circuit to the relevant part of the control winding to apply the necessary torque correction. In fact, the voltage to the reference winding is fed via a capacitor and, as we know, this will cause the current to lead the voltage by 90°. As there is no capacitance in the control winding, it lags the reference winding by 90°. The resulting magnetic field rotates the stator in the required direction, at the same time cutting the conductor in the squirrel-cage winding and inducing a further magnetic field that makes the rotor follow the stator field. This is immediately opposed because the rotor is fixed to the case, so a reactive torque is set up to cause the required amount of precession to correct the instrument.

HEADING INDICATOR (DGI)

This is used to give a stable heading reference free from compass errors. It works in a similar way to the artificial horizon, except that the spin axis is *aircraft horizontal* in the *yawing plane*. That is, the spin axis is parallel to the surface of the Earth, so it can only turn in the horizontal plane and it will only be affected by drift.

The casing turns round a **horizontally tied gyro**, which has a compass card mounted on it, so the aircraft rotates around the compass card:

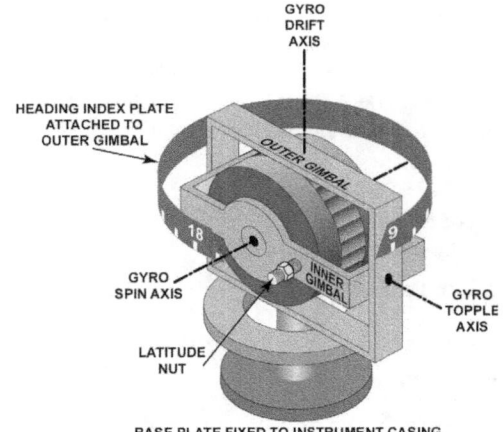

The instrument has **two degrees of freedom** with typical limits of 55° in pitch and roll. To help with re-erection after toppling, the mass of the gyro is spun at 10,000-12,000 RPM, with air jets from twin sources, very close to each other. When the gyro does not lie in the yawing plane, one jet (the drive component) will be pushing the gyro round, but the other (erection component) will strike the rim and cause a precession force at the top.

This is correcting for fine topple. The caging knob deals with gross topple.

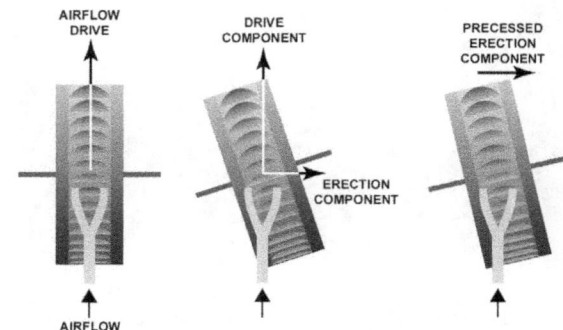

DGI indications are only valid for limited periods due to:

- rotation of the Earth.
- aircraft movement over the surface of the Earth.
- mechanical imperfections, plus low rotor speeds.
- gimbal system geometry (i.e. gimballing errors, which are small and transient inaccuracies that occur whenever the inner and outer gimbals are not at right angles to each other. This is particularly relevant when the spin axis is primarily horizontal, as with the DGI. Taking a descending turn as an example, the outer gimbal will be forced to rotate by a small amount about its own axis in order to maintain the spin axis horizontal. The amount of this rotation will be translated into a heading error for the duration of the manoeuvre.

These are the reasons why the DGI is aligned with the compass every 15 minutes or so remembering, of course, to do it in level, unaccelerated flight, to avoid errors.

Wander

If you just sat in your aircraft (at the North Pole) and watched the DGI, you would see it change from its original setting at a rate of 15° per hour, all by itself, if you applied no compensation. This is because the gyro is trying to maintain its own position in space, and the Earth is moving. There are two main types of wander:

- **Real**, or mechanical (the main cause), which comes from friction in the bearings, power fluctuations and other imperfections, although this is less than 1° per hour in modern systems and may be considered negligible. However, it is unpredictable and can be measured only by checking your heading. This is sometimes called random wander as the effect is supposed to be unintentional. A perfect gyro (in a question) has no imperfections, and no random wander, so you need not account for it.

- **Apparent**, where the spin axis remains aligned to a point in space as the plane of reference changes, making the gyro *appear* to precess. It consists of:
    - **Earth Rate** (N-S), from the Earth's rotation. Although there is a vertical component, the horizontal component is meant when talking about this (assuming you are stationary). So, at the Poles,

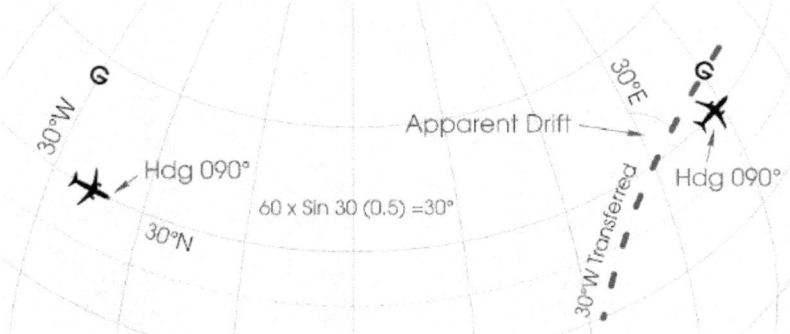

the gyro will appear to move at 15.04° per hour (in the horizontal plane) because that is the rate at which the Earth is spinning and orbiting round the Sun. The only time this won't happen is at the Equator (if the gyro's axis is aligned with a meridian and is parallel to the Earth's axis). Thus, it varies with the sine of the latitude, to the right in the Northern hemisphere and the left in the Southern hemisphere. The sign is negative in the Northern Hemisphere because the gyro under-reads as the Earth rotates. In the picture above, an aircraft that has its DGI aligned to True North at 30°W heads off in an Easterly direction. By the time it reaches 30°E, the spin axis of the DGI is to the right of True North, making it under-read. The reverse is true in the Southern hemisphere. You can see from the formula in the middle of the picture that the amount of drift can be calculated.

At 60°N, the apparent drift rate of a free gyro is 13° per hour to the right, or anticlockwise (the sine of 15° is 0.87). At 45°N, it would be 10.5° and, at 15°N, 4° per hour.

Apparent drift is corrected with a latitude nut (below).

- **Transport Wander** (E-W). Here, the spin axis appears to move because you are crossing meridians and convergency is added to the mix, similar to the above. Here, flight to the West causes over-reading, and Eastward flight causes under-reading* (in the Northern hemisphere) so, if you held a steady heading of 090°, because the gyro is under-reading, you will be turning away to the *right* of Earth track and your *true heading* is *increasing*. This is not normally corrected for in light aircraft, but is minimised by resetting the gyro every 15 minutes or so.

*Eastward flight increases apparent drift because the gyro is rotating faster than the speed of the Earth, and Westward flight reduces it, so errors will be more than 15° per hour, and less, respectively. N/S travel will only be a problem as far as the latitude in the formula changes, so mean latitudes are used. A minor variation (**grid transport**) occurs when the great circle track curves away from a straight line track, and is proportional to the difference between convergence of the meridians as shown on the chart against how they should be on the Earth, and the rate at which you cross them.

LATITUDE NUT

The latitude nut (on the inner gimbal) introduces an equal and opposite precession force to counteract apparent drift - this is usually for 45° of latitude when the device comes out of the box. In other words, a real wander is introduced to correct for fine drift. When wound outwards, the latitude nut exerts a greater force against the balance weight on the other side of the inner gimbal, where it is mounted. Assuming no other influence, going North of the preset latitude causes the DGI to under-read. Going South makes it over-read.

Watch out for aircraft flying in one hemisphere with their latitude nuts set for the *other* hemisphere. Use mean latitude for ER and TW where there is a North or South track component (**Note:** do not take mean latitude for a latitude nut - it only has one set value). Use the E or W component of groundspeed for TW calculations, taken from TAS and W/V.

TOTAL GYRO DRIFT

This is the sum of the Earth Rate + Transport Wander + Latitude Nut + Random (Real) Wander.

- The **Earth Rate** is:

    ```
    15° x sine latitude/hr
    ```

- **Transport Wander** is:

    ```
    ch long x sine latitude/hr
    ```

    or:

    $$\frac{GS \times \tan lat}{60}$$

- The **Latitude Nut** is:

    ```
    15° x sine of latitude setting
    ```

The resulting *drift budget* is the drift rate, in degrees per hour. Multiply it by the time period. The signs for the Northern hemisphere are:

- *Earth Rate* (-)
- *Latitude Nut* (+)
- *Transport Wander* East (-) West (+)

Reverse them for the Southern Hemisphere. So, for a DI with a Latitude Nut set for 40°N at 240 kts groundspeed on a Westerly heading at 50°N, you would add +9.64, -11.49 and +4.77 together to get +2.92° per hour.

R	E(A)	L	T
0	-11.49	9.64	4.77

If you move to 30°S with a latitude nut set for 45°N, the rate would be 18.1° per hour, from:

```
+15 x 0.5 = 7.5/hr
+15 x 0.7 = 10.6
```

You may be given Real Drift (perfect gyros have no random wander). On the DGI, *gross topple* is corrected with the *caging knob*, which grabs the gimbals and holds the gyro in one position. You can also turn the knob to move the gyro about the yaw axis, which turns the compass card so you can realign the instrument with the compass.

 Drift (at 15° per hour) is multiplied by the sine of the latitude, and topple by the cosine of the latitude.

EXAMPLE

1. What is the hourly wander rate at 49°N?

```
-15 x 0.7547 = 11.32/hr
```

The minus sign before the 15 indicates the Northern hemisphere. If this were corrected by a latitude nut, the observed drift would be zero.

2. Flying from 60°N 010°E to 60°N 020°E over 1.5 hours in nil wind conditions, a perfect gyro compass with no latitude nut is aligned with the true North. What constant gyro heading should be followed on departure?

(a) 66
(b) 80
(c) 76
(d) 85

Only Apparent and Transport Wander need be calculated here. The former is -19.54 (NH) and the latter -8.66 (heading East). The total is -28.2 which, halved (as you are maintaining a constant gyro heading), is - 14 which, subtracted from 90 gives the answer 76.

The Gyromagnetic Compass

A direct-reading compass's indications get weaker near the Poles, are subject to short term inaccuracies in the shape of turning and acceleration errors, and can only be read in one position in the aircraft. Neither can it drive or send information to other instruments. The gyromagnetic compass tries to resolve these problems by stabilising (gyroscopically) a magnetic compass and providing electrical outputs to the instruments that need to be read by the crew, or systems like IRS or INS. It is continually sampled for errors and short- and long term corrections are sent to the compass and gyro. So a gyrocompass is a DGI that aligns itself. In an area with a weak magnetic flux, like the Poles, you have to disable the automatic slaving and use the instrument as a DGI. The main components are:

- The **Gyroscope**, which provides short-term stability for azimuth reference. It will have 2 degrees of freedom and the input axis will be vertical (so the spin axis is horizontal).
- An **erection mechanism** to keep the axis horizontal.
- The **flux valve**, which is the detecting element for the Earth's magnetic field. It will be as far away from external magnetic influences as possible, say, in a tailboom or the rear of the fuselage and, if it ceases to provide reliable information, may generate a red HDG message on the HSI. It will provide a torque on the sensitive axis.
- The **Transmission and Display System** is simply the mechanism by which information is sent to the crew stations and instruments that need it. There is a feedback system to keep everything synchronised.
- A **torque motor** to make the gyro precess in azimuth at about 2° per minute. A dot shows in a small window on the display when the gyro is being precessed in one direction and a cross shows when it is being precessed in the other. In normal operations, they should alternate quickly. There is a manual rapid precession system.

The most significant errors are:

- *Apparent & Real Wander*
- *Gimballing*
- *Mechanical Defects*
- *Low Rotor Speed*

THE FLUX VALVE

You cannot directly measure the Earth's magnetic flux, because its H component is steady, but you can produce your own flux that changes with H, then measure and interpret the resulting voltage. This is done with a device that has three transformers at 120° to each other, with a curved horn at their ends to maximise reception.

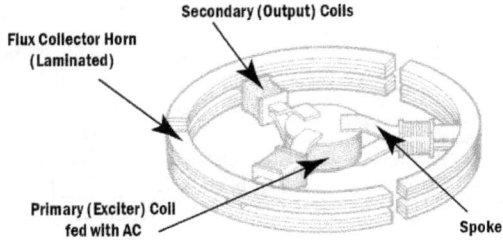

Using three spokes ensures that we know which way is North (or South). They are made of two identical parallel permalloy* strips on top of each other, with insulation between them and the transformer windings around them in series, in opposite directions.

*Permalloy loses its magnetic influence once the power is gone or, rather, it has a low hysteresis factor. It also magnetises very quickly.

The two poles of the resulting electromagnet cancel each other out and, without other magnetic sources (i.e. from the Earth), the total flux in another winding that is wound round the whole assembly is zero, as would be found when that spoke is at 90° to the Earth's magnetic field and both strips are detecting the same constant component of H. The maximum influence is obtained when the spoke is in line with the Earth's magnetic field, and any in between vary as the cosine of the magnetic heading.

In the picture below, a different value of H is present in each spoke, due to the angle between it and Magnetic North. The size of the field in each spoke now needs to be measured and transmitted to the rest of the equipment.

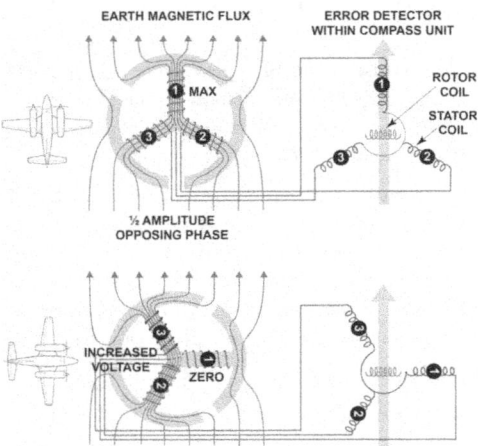

An exciter coil is placed in the centre, and fed with 400 Hz single phase AC so that a reversing magnetic field is created through the primary coil round each spoke. When the AC reaches its peak, so much magnetism is produced that the spokes cannot deal with any from the Earth. In other words, ignoring any external magnetic influences, the cores would just saturate at the 90° and 270° phase points of the primary winding alternating current flow.

However, as the current reverses, the spokes become demagnetised, so current can be induced as the Earth's flux lines cut across them. As long as the aircraft is on a fixed heading, the field remains constant. When it turns, the field changes and a current is induced in the secondary coil. This varies the induction in each leg and the secondary pickoff coils produce a complex phased signal, part of which is more prone to saturation because the H element is working in the same sense. Where it is in the opposite sense, the magnetic peaks are simply reduced and can be measured.

More technically, adding magnetism from the Earth saturates a spoke before one of its AC peaks, and it won't die away for a similar period afterwards. The two fields no longer cancel each other out, and there is a blip of AC in the pickoff coil that varies with the Earth's magnetism. That is, when AC is pumped through a flux valve it produces a ripple at twice the frequency of the original current, so a sinusoidal voltage with a frequency of 800 Hz is obtained, with its amplitude directly in proportion with the Earth's magnetic field and the cosine of the magnetic heading. Thus, induction from the H component is greater in one permalloy strip than the other, over an extended AC angle, the fields will no longer cancel out, and H will attain twice its original value.

The secondary coil has converted pulses of saturated magnetism to voltage.

Comparing the graphs below should provide some idea of what is happening.

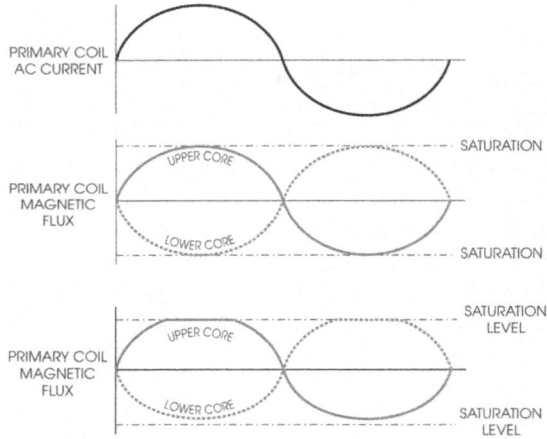

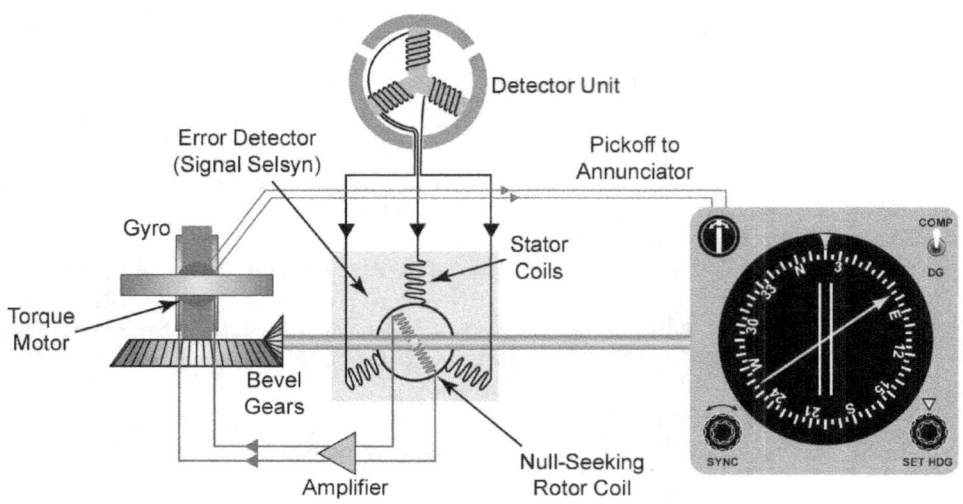

In the centre picture, no external magnetic influence is evident at the flux valve, so both cores only just achieve saturation twice during each 360° cycle of the AC fed to the primary coil.

In the bottom picture, the Earth's own magnetic field applies a magnetic bias to the system, so one core will become totally saturated at 90° and the other at 270°. The different magnetic field strengths produce a current in the secondary winding.

The flux valve assembly rotates with the aircraft. It also dangles from a *Hooke's Joint* (the technical term is *pendulous*) so it will swing within limits of around ±25°, to allow the aircraft to bank a little before it becomes inaccurate (it can switch itself off in a steep turn to avoid turning errors). The chamber that encloses the Hooke's joint also contains a viscous fluid to dampen any unwanted movement. This is to capture as much of the Earth's H force as possible, rather than the Z force which will produce turning and acceleration errors (as the DGI part uses slow acting torquers, acceleration errors are barely noticeable).

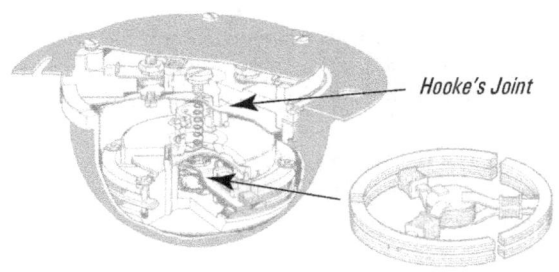

Hooke's Joint

As the system *senses* rather than *seeks*, it is more sensitive.

Heading information from the flux valve is compared to whatever the display is indicating and the results sent to an *error detector* or *selsyn unit* (self-synchroniser).

The signals then go through an amplifier to the torque motor, which precesses the directional gyro in the horizontal plane at 2° per minute. On its way, the current also flows through the *annunciator*, which is a small dial with a dot or a cross, depending on the current direction, whose purpose is to tell you that synchronisation is taking place correctly. The *synchronisation knob* is there for manual correction of gross topple in level flight. That is, it has the same function as the caging knob.

ERRORS

Gimballing errors arise from banking, and will disappear once a turn is complete.

Horizontal accelerations (Coriolis, turning) that make the flux valve tilt can cause heading errors. They will not be seen immediately and the rate of any heading error introduction depends on the limiting precession rate and the response time of the system (time constant).

- **Turning Error**. Although a high rate of turn in a fast aircraft would show the greatest heading error, the time spent in the turn is minimal - slow prolonged turns at high speeds generate the greatest errors. They decay after level flight is resumed. Errors from tilting can be limited by switching to an unslaved directional gyro mode whenever turns are sensed by suitable devices.

- **Coriolis Error**. An aircraft flies a curved path in space, so there will be a central force acting to displace the valve. The error is calculable, depending on groundspeed, latitude, dip and track, and can be compensated for automatically.

- **Vehicle Movement Error**. Whenever flying a true or magnetic rhumb line the aircraft must turn to maintain a constant track with reference to converging meridians. As with Coriolis error, the acceleration displaces the detector from the local horizontal plane. A correction can be applied in a similar manner to the Coriolis error.

- **Vibration**. This results in a heading oscillation, whose mean is not the actual mean heading. As the gyro slaving loop tends to average flux valve headings over time, the gyro would eventually precess to the erroneous flux valve mean heading. This can be limited to small values by careful design of the pendulous detector damping mechanism and through the detector's location in the aircraft.

As deviation is corrected electromagnetically, deviation cards are not needed.

TURN COORDINATOR

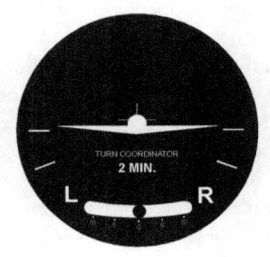

This is actually a combination of two instruments, one power driven, and the other not. The idea is to measure the *yaw* rate for low *bank* rates, and since yaw and bank have to be measured, the instrument is made sensitive to both by having its axis (i.e. the gimbal ring) *tilted upwards* by about 30-35°, though it is less sensitive to roll.

The roll is sensed first, and the rate increases when the correct angle of bank is set. This is what the instrument is sensing. Displacement remains constant for a given bank, regardless of airspeed. A small aircraft tilts to indicate whether you are banking, so it is a useful backup to the artificial horizon, especially as the gyro is electrically operated and not affected if the suction system fails (although it gives you a rudimentary indication of bank, turns without the other instruments are done with timing). It becomes very useful when you are not able to use the full panel, as the amount that the wings of the aircraft move also indicates the rate of turn.

When the wings in the little aircraft hit one of the lower marks you are in a Rate 1 turn, which takes two minutes to go through 360°, making 3° per second.

Underneath the indicator is a steel ball (or similar) in a clear tube containing fluid, for damping purposes, called an *inclinometer*, which indicates the quality of the turn (it doesn't affect the rate of turn). When a turn is balanced*, centrifugal force offsets the pull of gravity and keeps the ball in the centre of the tube. In a slip (below, left), where the rate of turn is not enough for the angle of bank, the centrifugal force will be weak and the ball will fall to the inside of the turn.

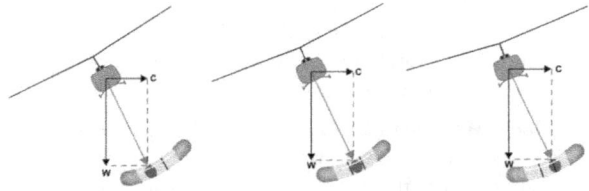

In a *skid*, the turn is too fast, so the extra centrifugal force causes the ball to be displaced more, to the outside of the turn (right, above).

*A turn is balanced if more than one half of the ball is inside the indicator marks.

Turn And Bank (Slip) Indicator

This instrument has a vertical needle instead of the horizontal small aircraft in the artificial horizon. As such it will only give you the *rate* of turn, since it is only sensitive to yaw, which is what is measured for **low bank angles**. It has the spin axis across the aircraft, so it spins up and away from you, with one end of the spindle held in place with a spring, so it has **one degree of freedom**. The spin rate is 10,000 RPM, and there are mechanical stops to keep it from going more than 45° either side of the centre.

The gyro is aircraft horizontal with 2 **planes of freedom**. During normal operation, the spring keeps the spin axis horizontal so the turn pointer is at zero, and the gyro's rigidity will tend to keep it there. The yaw induced when you turn is precessed to the top and bottom of the gyro. As the springs stretch to cope with gyro movement around the longitudinal axis, they apply a force that produces a *secondary precession* equal to and in the same direction as the rate of turn. In other words, a turn makes the gyro move, to create a primary precession that stretches a spring that creates another in the same direction as the original force.

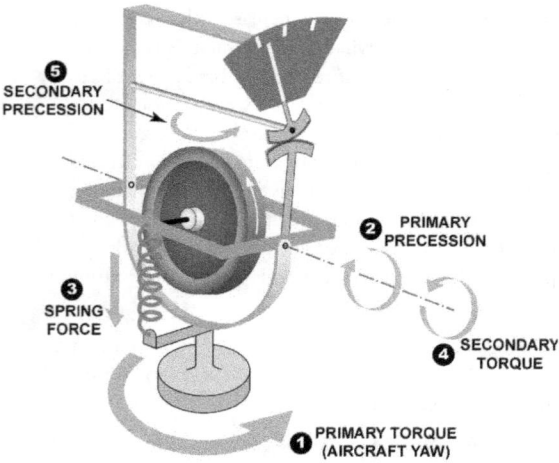

Without the spring, you would still see a turn indication, but would have no idea of its magnitude, so the spring controls the angular deflection of the gimbal ring and introduces its own

precessing force. As the precession is equal to the rate of turn multiplied by the angular momentum, the force is a measure of the rate of turn.

In the picture above the aircraft is turning left and the yawing moment is the primary applied force **1**. This is precessed through 90°, producing the primary precessed force **2**, which makes the gyro topple. The amount of tilt determines the rate of turn indicated on the instrument.

As the gyro topples the spring stretches, giving the secondary applied force **3**. This is again precessed through 90°, providing the secondary precessed force **5**.

When the secondary precessed force is equal to the primary applied force, the secondary precession caused by the spring is proportional to the actual rate of turn. The gyro ceases to topple, and the angle between the spin axis and the yawing plane is proportional to the rate of turn.

ERRORS

All errors cause the instrument to under-read, except when the rate of turn is less than rate 1, when rotor speed is faster than normal, and the springs are slack. The ball is sensitive to gravity and centrifugal force.

If the TAS is within 100 knots of the calibrated TAS, the error in the indicated rate of turn should not be more than ±5% of the actual rate of turn.

During low rate turns there is little or no change of pitch required to maintain level flight. During steeper turns, however, the nose must be raised to maintain height. Any pitching moment while the spin axis is displaced from the yawing plane create additional precession, causing the instrument to over-indicate the rate of turn. As it is not normally used to monitor steep turns, this error does not seriously restrict its effectiveness.

If the rotor speed is low, the instrument will under-read the actual rate of turn because the gyro is less rigid and will precess more quickly. The amount of secondary torque required to produce the secondary precession that matches the aircraft's rate of turn is therefore less than it should be, is achieved with less spring stretch and less tilt of the spin axis. Less tilt means that a lower rate of turn is indicated. Conversely, with the gyro overspeeding, the balance of forces is only achieved when the spring is stretched by more than the correct amount, because the gyro is too rigid, so the indicated rate of turn is greater than it should be.

A weak spring (due to age) needs to be stretched further. This will result in a greater tilt of the spin axis, causing the instrument to over- indicate the rate of turn.

 This instrument gets less accurate as the bank increases. In a level turn with a 90° bank angle, the needle would centre itself, because you would be performing a loop in the horizontal plane.

INSTRUMENTS
Flight Management Systems

FLIGHT MANAGEMENT SYSTEMS

Understanding the FMS for your aircraft is vital for modern operations*. Luckily, they are similar between types, so that, if you understand the inner workings of the one on the Boeing 777, you can bluff your way through on the 737, 747, 757 and 767 (but not the 787). The FMS chosen for the EASA exams is based on the 737**. As the idea is to reduce pilot workload (and to make sure they don't make mistakes!), the autopilot should usually be left alone to do the job.

*Air France 447 is one of the best known examples of why. On June 1st 2009, it was flying from Rio de Janeiro to Paris when it disappeared from radar over the middle of the Atlantic Ocean. It had flown through a thunderstorm, and there was no distress signal. The pitot tubes had frozen over in the storm, which made the autopilot disengage, and the pilots could not maintain enough airspeed to stay in the air due to the incorrect airspeed readings in the cockpit.

**This would be the Smith version. Larger Boeings tend to use the Honeywell, as used in the Airbus and others, which comes in two flavours, one biased to Europe and one to the US.

The software used for the FMS is certified at a level equal to or lower than that for Fly By Wire. It can provide guidance for RNAV and non-precision approaches.

The procedures given here are generic and geared towards the exams. Your company's procedures will likely be very different.

Basic procedures include passing everything you enter through a logic check, with independent verification of entries when inputting the initial position through lat & long on the keyboard (from separate source documents). This is to avoid elementary mistakes such as transposing N and S or E and W. It is safer to use the database!

Although the idea is to enter your route before you start, you can get airborne with just the first waypoints and put the rest in later when you have the time (although including the destination ICAO code at least gives it a start for calculating the fuel). Whichever way you work, *one person should always fly the aeroplane*.

You should always understand the difference between where the FMS thinks you are and where you actually are. One tip is to use machine messages as a trigger to check your position, even if it is only a quick check.

A Flight Management System is a **mode-selectable colour flight display** that can be defined as a *Global 3D Flight Management System*, whose function is to provide automatic navigation along planned routes (LNAV) and optimum flight profiles (VNAV), plus performance management for *managed guidance** by the crew. The system can manage altitude, speed, direction, multiple navigation sources and power, and estimate waypoint ETAs and fuel remaining, amongst other things.

*Managed guidance exists when the FMS controls the autopilot. *Selected guidance* is when it controls the pilot!

If the autopilot is not available, the FMS can at least drive the Flight Director so you can fly manually. It first arrived with the Airbus A320, to manage flight paths.

A true FMS normally consists of 2 Flight Management Computers (FMCs) and 2 (M)CDUs, one each for the Captain and First Officer.

A dual configuration means that the system can be used as a sole means of navigation, although backup traditional systems are usually present. With 2 systems, you have *redundancy* and *integrity*, as they can check each other.

You can also use P/RNAV airways, down to 2 nm wide, and perform FMS approaches in non-radar environments.

The data must be presented on different displays, so there is a 3-position switch that can be set to NORMAL, BOTH ON L or BOTH ON R (from that, you will deduce that there are Left and Right systems).

With the switch on L or R, the system behaves like one FMC. The primary (Master) provides the guidance commands and maps the display, and the secondary (Slave) is synchronised with it. In NORMAL mode, the tasks are shared, each system effectively handling its own side of the aircraft, with separate inputs (and information synchronised through a common bus), except that your position and velocity (and guidance) come from a weighted average. The *composite navigation solution* is a second aircraft state calculated in each FMC from both error estimates. When the FMC switch is set to the ALTN position, the related CDU and EFIS displays will be connected to the other computer.

Single mode exists where only one FMS is operational. *Backup mode* exists when the FMC has failed in certain areas but still works a bit. You might have to *downmode* to Single FMC if there is a miscompare between databases on the start-up check, for example. An FMC can be *brickwalled* if there is too much of a discrepancy.

Data is combined from many sources, such as navigation systems, the Air Data Computer (airspeed, etc.), route information and operating requirements, to provide a centralised source of information and control for navigation and performance, if only to help manage fuel costs by calculating optimum levels, etc.

Aside from the Mode Control Panel:

the main interface between the crew and the FMS is the Control Display Unit, or CDU:

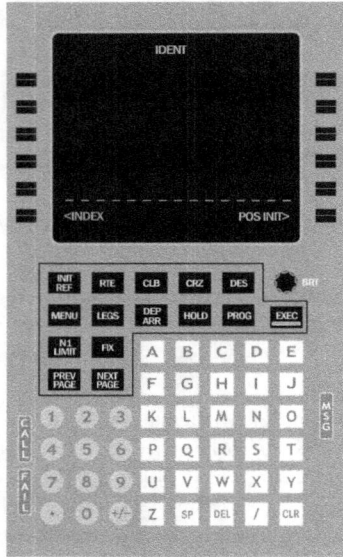

It is used before flight to manually input dispatch information to the IRSs and the FMC.

The alphanumeric keys represent the same characters as they would on any keyboard, except that the **SP** button is the space bar. The delete key clears a selected line, while the clear key deletes single characters.

The 15 function keys are short cuts that provide access to major functions, including:

- **MENU**. Provides access to the FMC and other subsystems.
- **INIT REF**. Provides access to these pages:
    - IDENT. Aircraft ID and navigation database verification.
    - POS. Position initialisation (on the ground) and position reference in flight.
    - PERF. Performance initialisation (gross weight, cost index).
    - THRUST LIM
    - TAKEOFF. Parameter reference and initialisation.
    - APPROACH. Parameter reference and initialisation.
    - NAVDATA. Information and saved flight plans.

The most relevant page for the phase of flight will automatically be displayed. IDENT or POS, for example will show during the preflight phase.

- **RTE**. The ROUTE page displays the waypoint fixes and how the system proposes to get to them.
- **CLB**. Climb thrust and altitude control.
- **CRZ**. For managing the cruise in terms of altitude, fuel and speed.
- **DES**. Descent speed, fuel and planning.
- **LEGS**. Similar to the ROUTE page, but showing every fix to be overflown, as opposed to only the major ones. It is used often to manage altitude and speed, and to enter waypoints into the flight plan.
- **DEP/ARR**. Used to select published SIDs and STARs.
- **HOLD**. Allows you to add holding procedures to the active flight plan (which can be changed any time before takeoff and throughout the flight.
- **PROG**. Monitors the progress of the flight in terms of time, distance and fuel consumption.
- **EXEC**. This only works when the light bar on it is showing. It is used to confirm changes to the plan. When it is active, you will see an <ERASE prompt so you can erase a proposed action quickly.
- **N1 LIM**. Selects and controls engine performance limits during takeoff, climb, cruise and descent.
- **FIX**. Allows you to place waypoints on to the display in relation to known points within the navigation database. They do not have to be part of the active flight plan and are shown as green.
- **NEXT PAGE/PREV PAGE**. If the display has more than one page, these cycle round them.

Amongst other things, the Flight Management Computers (FMCs) can perform the following functions:

- **Flight Planning**. The basis of the flight profile is the route (or the *lateral flight profile*) you will fly from the departure point to the destination. The items making up the route are known as the *flight plan* (not to be confused with the ATC form).

    The information will come initially from the navigation database, and might consist of a departure airport (and runway) a SID, enroute waypoints (see overleaf) and airways, a STAR, and an approach procedure to a specific runway, although the latter two are often not selected until ATC at the destination is contacted. Once you're happy with all that, the details are assembled into a buffer where they are used for computing the lateral and vertical profiles. The information can also be transmitted from the ground via DataLink.

- **Navigation Computation** and Display, automatically tuning navigation aids and interfacing with the IRS to provide a great circle track to any point. The FMC knows where it is from data supplied by the usual sources, plus IRS. The Best Position is generated every 5 seconds, based on the IRS, as adjusted for the Radio

INSTRUMENTS
Flight Management Systems

Position, as the FMS assumes that radio is more accurate. The new Best Position updates the System Position, which is used for LNAV (Lateral Navigation).

Operation of the FMC is based around the track to a fix and the groundspeed to get there. However, LNAV can also factor in the TAS to work out the angle of bank to fly a holding pattern (for example) and construct the dimensions of the hold each time it passes over the fix. LNAV (see *Radio Navigation*) can fly the pattern drawn on the approach charts, based on the information entered into the Hold page and the TAS (this is a lot better than the guesstimates you fly with steam driven instruments). Normal deviation from the flight path should not exceed 0.1 nm, but if it is working DME/DME only, this would be 0.3 nm.

- **Issue commands** in pitch, roll and thrust. Vertical Navigation, for example, is controlled by speed or rates of climb or descent. With speed control, the autothrottle is given a target thrust setting and the elevator will be used to control the speed and provide a variable rate of climb. When vertical speed is controlled, the elevator is controlled directly and the autothrottle will be adjusted to provide a fixed ROC/ROD and a variable speed.
- Manage fuel
- Compute weight and balance
- Manage performance. For this, the gross weight, cost index target altitude and the route need to be fed into the system - you won't get a vertical navigation profile until the performance initialisation page has been completed. A least cost performance model is used, and the default setting is for ECON.

Output can be sent to the EFIS displays, flight director, mode control panel, autothrottle and engine controls.

An **Air Data Inertial Reference Unit** (ADIRU) supplies the following information to the EFIS displays as well as other systems, such as the engines, autopilot, etc.:

- **Air Data Reference** (airspeed, angle of attack and altitude). The ADR is a small computer that corrects pitot-static information (airspeed, altitude, vertical speed) for high altitude operations.
- **Inertial Reference** (position & attitude). The IRU senses and computes linear accelerations and angular rates about each axis. This is used for pitch and roll displays and navigation calculations.

The ADIRU acts as a single, fault tolerant source of navigational data for both pilots. The term has come to mean any integrated ADC/IRS unit, and may be complemented by a *Secondary Attitude Air Reference Unit* (SAARU), as with the Boeing 777 (see *Inertial Navigation*). The ADIRU shows air data from the left pitot/static on the captain's side and the SAARU shows that from the right pitot/static on the FO's side. The ADR is a small computer that corrects pitot-static information (airspeed, altitude, vertical speed) for high altitude operations. AD and IR functions are combined because some of their functions overlap - for example, the IRU knows how fast you are moving, and in what direction, and the ADR knows the TAS.

The ADIRU can operate with 115 v AC or 28 v DC. The power supply feeds the ADR, the IR, the ISDU and the Air Data Modules (ADMs).

An **ADIRS** contains up to three fault tolerant ADIRUs, an associated control and display unit (CDU) in the cockpit and remotely mounted air data modules (ADMs). No 3 is a redundant unit that can supply data to the P1 or P2 display if the

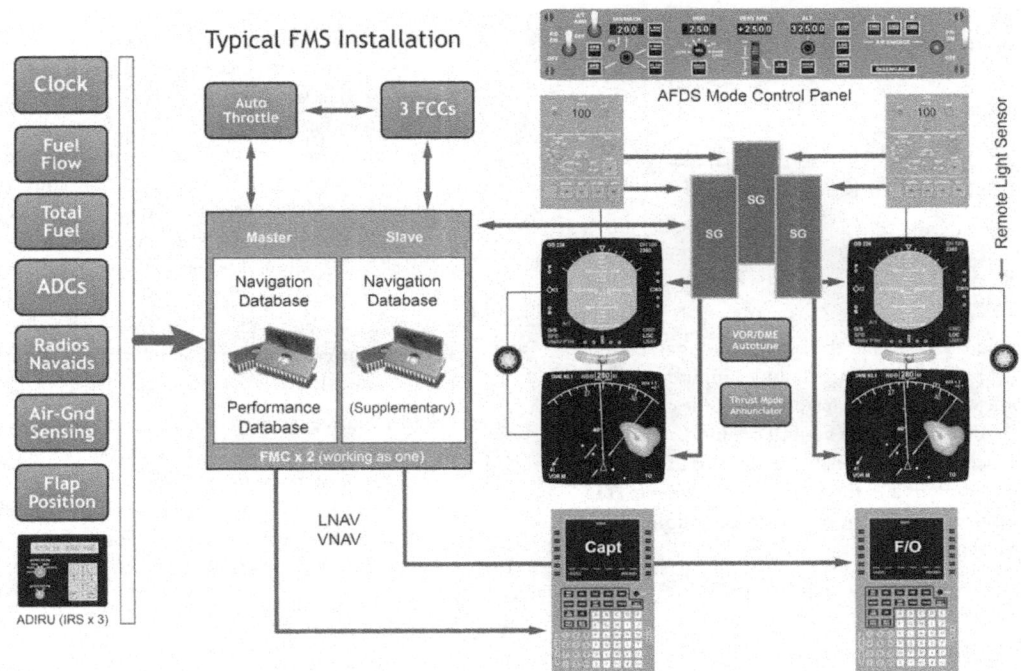

other two fail. As No 3 is the only alternate source of air and inertial reference data, there is no cross-channel redundancy between 1 and 2.

An inertial reference fault in 1 or 2 will cause a loss of attitude and navigation information on their associated PFD and ND screens. An ADR fault will cause the loss of airspeed and altitude information on the affected display. Either way, the information can only be restored by selecting No. 3.

To do its job properly, the system needs information, such as clock time, aircraft weights, fuel loaded, winds, ISA deviations, etc., particularly *databases* of waypoints, navaids, airways, procedures, airports, and other data. Most of the information for a flight is in the FMC. Items such as navigation facilities, reporting points and airway designators can be input using up to 5 alphanumerics.

Whilst searching for it, ensure that someone is flying the aircraft!

LNAV/VNAV

Lateral Navigation, and VNAV (*Vertical Navigation*) are used with custom routes in the navigation database, and were first fully integrated on the 757/767. Because the original use of the FMS was simply to take over routine tasks and improve fuel efficiency, not all installations can perform LNAV/VNAV. Luckily, most modern ones do, and the FMS is now the primary tool for Performance Based Navigation, discussed in *Radio Navigation*.

LNAV

LNAV provides guidance (steering) along the lateral path of the flight plan.

VNAV

VNAV is a function in the FMS that allows the vertical path of an aircraft to be better controlled and managed, so optimal profiles can be used. It also allows more sophisticated guidance along a SID or a STAR, directing the autopilot along a three-dimensional tube in space to not only fly over the relevant waypoints, but also to arrive at each one at the desired altitude, as per any clearances or restrictions. On charts:

- An **AT** altitude is double lined: $\overline{\underline{4600}}$
- An **AT or Above** altitude is underlined: $\underline{4600}$
- An **AT or Below** altitude is overlined: $\overline{4600}$
- A Window is mixed:

$$\overline{6000}$$
$$\underline{5000}$$

VNAV should provide steering and thrust commands along the vertical path, usually based on the baro altitude* input from the ADC, although some systems do not have autothrottle capability. In other words, VNAV provides the vertical component of the flight plan along the chosen vertical path, taking into account altitude and speed restrictions and the limits of the airframe. **It is not intended to be used when not on the lateral flight path or purposely deviating from it.**

*There is a temperature compensation facility for ISA differences along the vertical profile.

- **Takeoff** uses a speed based climb (i.e. safety speed until acceleration height or flap retraction).
- **Climb** is speed based, using the most economical (ECON) or pilot selected speed (SEL SPD).
- **Cruise** is a 3D path based level segments determined by economics or pilot selection, including cruise-climb or cruise-descent.
- **Descent** is path-based, using an idle or near idle profile in terms of performance. A geometric path is shallower, and typically non-idle, used where restrictions have a higher priority. Although it is constructed upstream, i.e. from the lowest waypoint, the descent starts at the TOD, proceeding through the approach to the beginning of the missed approach. Put another way, the end of descent waypoint is the anchor position. The path can be made shallower by the system) as a protection for potential overspeeds to cope with adverse or unforecast winds and temperatures.
- **Approach** is a path-based descent determined by the approach procedure's vertical angle. It is a separate phase within the descent phase. LNAV minima indicate non-precision approaches, using the usual minimum step-down altitude below which you may not descend. That is, without vertical guidance, you must remain **at or above** the MDA without the required visual reference, or you need to conduct a missed approach at the missed approach waypoint (MAWP). LNAV/VNAV and LPV minima refer to APV approaches (RNAV approaches with vertical guidance).
- **Missed Approach** is similar to the climb phase - speed-based to a pre-determined altitude and waypoint.

Databases

There are two loadable databases that support the core flight management functions. These are:

- a **Navigation** database, for data relating to airports, navaids, airways, terminal procedures, etc., with RNP values for the associated airspace. In short, an airway manual in a chip. It does two jobs, relating to *navigation* and *flight planning*. It must be updated every 28 days (the RAC cycle) - the information, which may come from many commercial sources, is valid to the next expiry date, plus the next revisions. There is a permanent database and a supplementary one, which can be switched over at the right time. The data is checked at each phase of the process, from reception to loading. Pilots can insert extra (temporary) navigation data between updates (they cannot modify the original data).
- a **Performance** database, which is only updated when performance parameters change. It contains an average model of the aircraft and its engines, flight envelopes and operating limits, to correct for various conditions of flight. You can fine tune it and load defaults through the CDU, with alterations kept in NVRAM.

The system uses EPROMS for permanent storage, which cannot be changed in flight (but they can by engineers on the ground). Such NVRAM (*Non-Volatile RAM*) is Random Access Memory that keeps its contents when the power is switched off because it either uses a backup battery or flash memory ("normal" RAM, which does lose information when the power is off is called *volatile*). This allows you to update navigation data between updates. Navigation and Performance also have their own processors, and there is a third to handle I/O (Input and Output) and the Built In Test (BIT). The information needed by them all is kept in (volatile) main memory.

In Use

Central control means that you will select radio and navaid frequencies through the FMS control panel, or CDU - you should not see separate boxes in the cockpit. That is, the CDU is the principal pilot interface to the FMS and any other systems that interact with it. You enter data with the *alphanumeric keyboard* and *line select* keys, and you *must* get used to the menu system!

The display screen shows 14 lines which can display 24 characters across in large or small fonts. There are three basic areas - the top line carries the title of the page you are on, plus its status, whether ACTive, or MODified, etc.

Text, or data lines (1-6) are in the middle area, aligned left and right and are adjusted by the Line Select Keys on either side of the display.

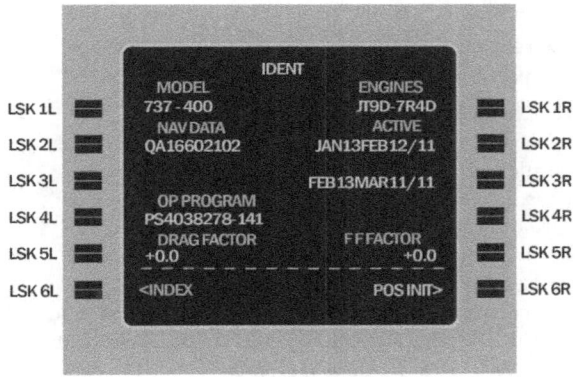

The first three pages of the FMC/CDU that normally appear on initial start-up of the B737-400 Electronic Flight Instrument System are IDENT - POS INIT - RTE.

Each data line has an information line above it describing what the text line is for (predictably called the title line). Data lines may also include prompts for input from the crew. When you see boxes, typically with gross weight figures, it means that the system requires information. If you see a **<** or **>** symbol next to a Line Select Key, you can get to another menu by pressing that key - for example **<INDEX**, as shown above.

Dashed lines allow you to enter data that is specific to a flight, such as the departure and destination airports.

If there is not enough space on the display, you may see an indication on the top right of the page number you are on out of how many, as in 1/2, meaning page 1 of 2 available. The previous and next page buttons above the number pad on the CDU will cycle you through them.

The alphanumeric keys on the MCDU are used to make entries to the *scratchpad*, which is actually the bottom line of the display that behaves rather like a one-line wordprocessor, in that the contents of the line can be edited in the normal way (it's also where you might get messages from the computer):

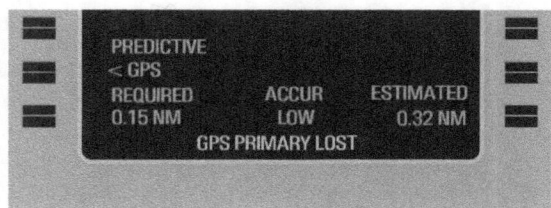

It is a working area where you can enter and/or verify data before it goes into the system. For example, if you wanted to go direct to a waypoint called ANKAR you would type:

    DIR TO ANKAR

Otherwise, enter information on the scratchpad then press the relevant LSK to get that information into the system.

Tip: Lat & Long figures are typically shortened in the main display. Pushing the button next to them brings them into the scratchpad (down-selection) so you can see the full readout. Up-selection is transferring data into the system by pressing the relevant LSK having entered it into the scratchpad.

Information in the scratchpad does not affect the FMS until it is moved to another line on the display. Data remains in the scratchpad over mode and page changes.

The FMS starts its power up sequence after you switch it on. The data on the **IDENT** page does not change regularly but still needs to be checked.

It will change according to the machine, but typical entries are shown.

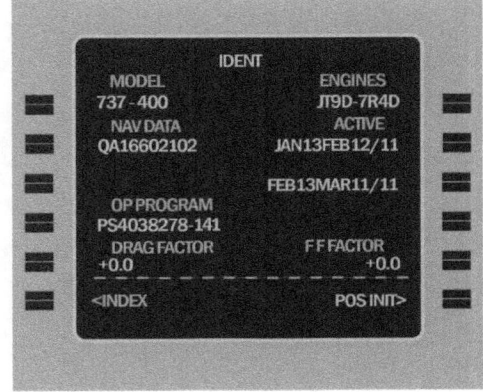

You then have to tell it where you are.

Press LSK 6R next to where it says POS INIT.

You might then get a selection of positions, such as the last known one, etc. (at the top right).

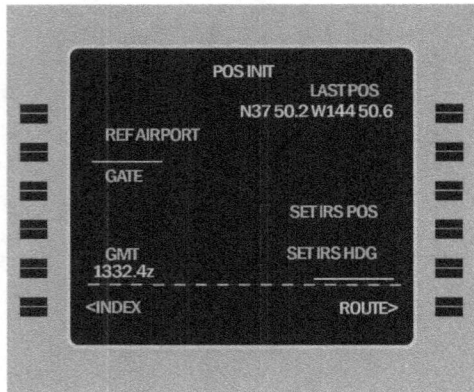

LAST POS refers to the last recorded position when the aircraft was powered down, or when the brakes were last set. If you want to accept it, push LSK 1R to downselect the information into the scratchpad, then press 4R to set the IRS position.

You can also use the Lat & Long of an airfield as a reference position, which is what the **REF AIRPORT** selection is for. Enter the ICAO code into the scratchpad, press LSK 2L, the 4R. You can also use the **GATE** position in the same way.

To enter a flight plan, the machine needs to know the destination, the route you propose to take, the alternate, the departure and the expected arrival procedure (all this should be in the database). The **ROUTE** page is the primary page for route construction, and you get there by pressing the LSK right next to where you see **ROUTE>**.

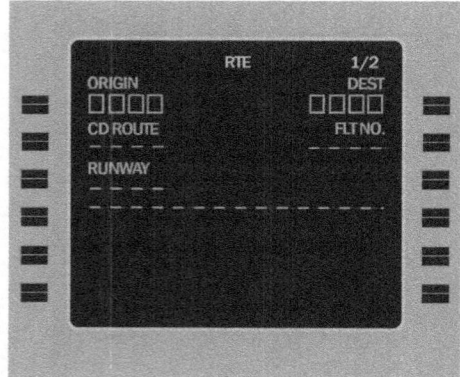

LSK 1L will have some empty boxes to the side. Enter the ICAO code into the scratchpad and push LSK (1L) to fill the boxes (empty boxes indicate required entries).

Do the same for the Destination with LSK 1R.

CD ROUTE refers to a previously saved flight plan. If there is a flight plan for the route in the database, it will be presented for your approval. Just press LSK 6L next to **<ACTIVATE** when it appears. This will also make the light on the **EXEC** key come on. This should be pressed to confirm your actions.

Another button that appears occasionally is **REVERSE**, which is a quick way of entering a return flight. If there is no flight plan, you can enter your own route. Generally, you follow established airways until you reach a specific waypoint where you can leave the system. More often than not, this is the first waypoint associated with an approach procedure (you join the system in the first place at the last waypoint associated with a departure procedure). With just that information, the system will deal with intermediate waypoints automatically.

Once the information required on page 1 has been entered, the page indicator at the top right will show that there are now 2 available. You can get to page 2 with the **NEXT PAGE** key on the CDU. The left hand side is essentially one column labelled **VIA**, and the right hand side is another labelled **TO**, which is where individual fixes are entered. The **VIA** column indicates how to get to them. Thus, you type the fix information into the scratchpad, then upselect it with LSK 1R. The information will be checked, and if the fix name is not unique, you can choose from a selection. the closest one to your present position will be first on the list. Press the LSK next to your choice.

The FMS will assume a direct routing, so the word **DIRECT** will appear next to LSK 1L. If you want to choose a particular airway, enter its name into the scratchpad, then press the relevant LSK on the left side to change the **DIRECT** indication. If it is a long route it will not be unusual to go through several pages.

If you want to save the route and not have to type it all in again, go back to page 1 and push the LSK next to **<SAVE**.

Eventually, you will reach the **PERF INIT** (*Performance Initialisation*) page. Performance data is used for many purposes, such as vertical navigation (VNAV), setting target speeds, fuel calculations, etc. Although we know the route, until the aircraft's weight is known, climb or descent profiles cannot be constructed. Neither can the optimum cruise altitude or any speeds be calculated, which is quite important on a machine like the 777 that can calculate those required for any manoeuvres in real time, which helps greatly with fuel consumption, because the flaps can be deployed at the most appropriate times. The data entered into the PERF INIT page must be correct and crosschecked!

The gross weight of the aircraft is entered using LSK 1L. 2L shows the calculated fuel (from the Fuel Quantity Indication System) in thousands of pounds and 3L shows the ZFW (normally you get this information from the loadsheet that comes from the dispatch office, but these days it comes over a datalink). 2L and 3L together make up the gross weight of the aircraft, and the sum of their values must match that in 1L.

Also on the left hand side will be the entry for the fuel reserves and the Cost Index - operating costs depend not only on how much fuel you burn, but also time - it might cost a lot less if you fly slower, for example. The cost index is a measure of how time affects costs - that is, *direct* operating costs (insurance, etc. are fixed costs) divided by fuel costs, which are expressed in cents per pound. If you fly slower or faster than the speed indicated by the index for that leg, costs will increase. The 777 (and probably others) has a sliding scale of 0-9999. The higher the number entered, the higher the speed will be and the more fuel will be used - you will get maximum range by using 0! It is very rare to find an entry into an FMS of more than around,500, on the 777, at least. This is because higher speeds will be very close to some structural limits. A good average starting value might be in the 250 range. It is possible, of course, to override the set speed for timing on approaches, etc.

On the right hand side of the **PERF INIT** page you can enter the **CRZ ALT** (cruise altitude) and the **TRANS ALT** (transition altitude).

In flight, you will use the **FPL** or **PROG** page while the FMS continuously computes your position from the IRS, VOR, DME and ILS as required. The priority for the most accurate fix is a DME/DME crosscut, then DME/VOR, then VOR/VOR, and IRS last. It will tune DME frequencies in sequence according to route information in the navigation database (if it cannot decode the morse identifier, it would show the frequency instead). Despite all that, you should still monitor your position carefully.

The **FLIGHT PLAN** or **LEG** page displays distance, true track, time prediction, plus waypoint elevation and distance relative to flight plan legs or waypoints. When two waypoints are entered here, the track between them is computed and displayed on the ND as a great circle arc.

There is a lateral offset function which allows you to fly along a leg with a constant offset distance to the right or left. The amount is manually entered on the CDU.

The FMS cross track (XTK), shown on the navigation display, is the abeam distance error (to the left or right) from the desired track to the position of the aircraft, or the distance between the actual position and the great circle track between active waypoints.

The Flight Director

The Flight Director's job is to reduce your workload by indicating the manoeuvres to execute, achieve or maintain a flight condition in pitch and roll, particularly when things are happening quickly, as they do when close to Decision Height on the ILS (assuming you are not using the autopilot). It uses a **computer** and **command bars** to presents data as control commands to show you the **optimal way to achieve your flight path**, using bank angles of 25° for intercepting desired tracks. In other words, the FD provides directions about *how to position the controls* - you get no information about the flight path, for which you need a separate display.

Thus, if the F/D is in G/S mode on approach, the horizontal bar will indicate the pitch corrections needed to join and follow the glide slope. If it is deviating upward, you are not necessarily below the glideslope, but must increase the pitch attitude. The vertical bar informs you about the direction and amplitude of the corrections to be applied on banking the aircraft (in LOC mode, simply the correction to join and follow the localiser axis.

Command bars may be displayed when flying manually or with the autopilot engaged. The FD will be in a display mode that is a combination of the artificial horizon, localiser & glideslope, radio altimeter for your Decision Height and warning flags for instrument failure, so it also tells you which way up you are.

The visual guidance can come in the shape of a V-bar:

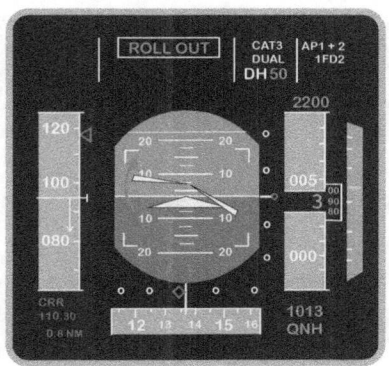

A two-cue system might use command bars. In fact, the original FD was Sperry's Zero Reader, which was a cross-pointed indicator like the modern ILS display: The horizontal bar is for the pitch channel, and the vertical bar for roll, in terms of information about the direction and amplitude of the corrections

to be applied to the controls. They will centralise once the inputs required are enough, so the bars can be centred even when you are not straight and level. Command bars may be displayed when flying manually or when the autopilot is engaged, so the essential components of a flight director are a *computer* and *command bars*. You engage the *heading select* mode (HDG SEL), once a heading is selected, after which the vertical bar will be centred if the bank angle is the same as the computed angle.

EFIS

Conventional instruments can go wrong, and tend to spread themselves out around the cockpit, so you need three pairs of eyes in a big machine to keep track of them all. They also have to be continually monitored. The *Electronic Flight Instrument System* replaces the traditional ones with CRT or LCD displays, or at least flat computer panels, hence the occasional reference to the *Glass Cockpit*. These have no moving parts, and can be switched to show different instruments, or duplicate information, which is helpful if one fails. In emergencies, you can isolate some instruments for closer scrutiny.

With the glass cockpit, a lot of information can be concentrated into a small space, and the associated computers can take on some monitoring tasks, so you only need to pay some of them any attention when something actually goes wrong (see *Warning & Recording*, later).

The heart of the EFIS is the symbol generator, of which there are 3 in a standard system, which receives input from the sensors around the aircraft. A third (centre) SG may be involved if the left or right unit fails. If two are used and one fails, the remaining one can supply both sides, but the information would be the same. Switching is pilot controlled. Once brightness is selected, it is automatically controlled by light sensors. Other information that can be displayed includes graphics of the aircraft systems, checklists, maps from the GPS, etc.

INSTRUMENTS
Flight Management Systems

The technology involves small computers using solid-state (no moving parts) 3-axis gyros and accelerometers to derive altitude, magnetometers to find heading, and pressure transducers to find air data (airspeed & altitude), all displayed on flat screens, through suitable software. Because of the potential problems with software, any EFIS system will be backed up by a selection of traditional instruments, or another, separate, EFIS system.

The benefits of using EFIS include:

- Increased reliability
- The output of many instruments can be combined into one, improving situational awareness
- You can put other information on, such as checklists and weather
- Colour

EADI/PFD

The *Electronic Attitude Direction Indicator* (EADI) or *Primary Flight Display* (PFD) can combine a lot of information in one small space.

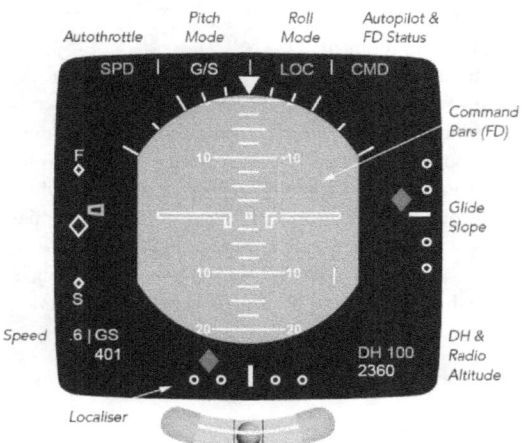

The above is the basic display. In the improved version, the Fast/Slow bar on the left is replaced by a speed tape.

On the left below is a typical takeoff display, in the middle is one for the cruise, and landing is shown on the right.

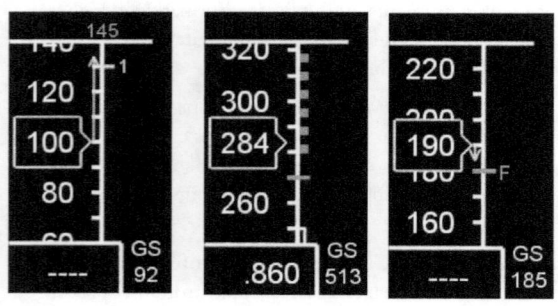

The attitude information could come from the IRS, if there is one, or more traditional gyroscopic sources (sideslip information will come from the inertial system). When the right equipment is switched in, you could also get ILS localiser/glideslope information, groundspeed, flight director commands, radio altitude, etc.

Between 1,000-2,500 ft AGL, radio altitude is shown digitally in white, with the Decision Height in green.

Below 1,000 ft, it changes to an analogue presentation, namely a white circular scale in 100-ft increments which unwinds as you descend and erases above the present height. The DH is a magenta marker on the circular scale, and is set through the EFIS control panel. Radio altitude is shown digitally in the middle. At DH, the scale and marker change to amber and flash for a few seconds. There is a reset button to fix that.

If you go beyond localiser and glideslope limits during an approach, and when below, 500 ft agl, the deviation pointers turn from white to amber and start to flash.

The **Flight Path Vector** (FPV) materialises the instantaneous flight path angle (FPA) and track (TRK) flown by the aircraft. It may be used by itself or in association with the flight path director (FPD).

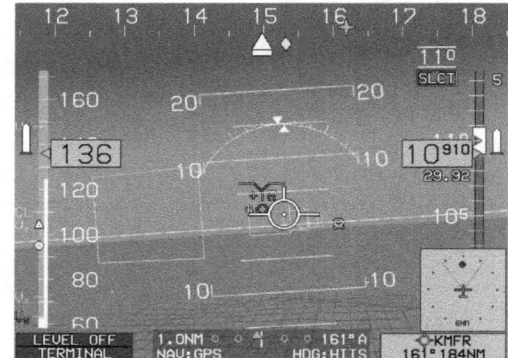

Picture: Courtesy, Chelton Systems, Inc.

It is a circular symbol that is superimposed on the AI part of the PFD when the FPV button is pressed. The symbol represents the aircraft's axis in relation to the vertical and lateral movement referenced to the Earth's surface. On the ground, the circle would be on the horizon line and centred in the display. In the picture, it is just below and to the right of the miniature aeroplane, indicating that the flight path is down and to the right.

The FPV provides an almost instantaneous display of flight path angle and drift. For example, if you took off in a 15 kt crosswind the Flight Director would register the pitch while the FPV would be above the horizon and to one side. The lateral deviation provides a visual indication of the drift from the crosswind, while the vertical deviation shows the attitude or pitch.

EHSI/ND

The *Electronic Horizontal Situation Indicator* (EHSI) or *Navigational Display* (ND) tells you where you are in one of three modes that have different capabilities.

If the signal from a VOR is lost, the deviation bar and pointer is removed from the display.

MAP

MAP mode is used for general bread-and-butter enroute navigation. It shows your position as a relationship between the current heading, navaids and actual track.

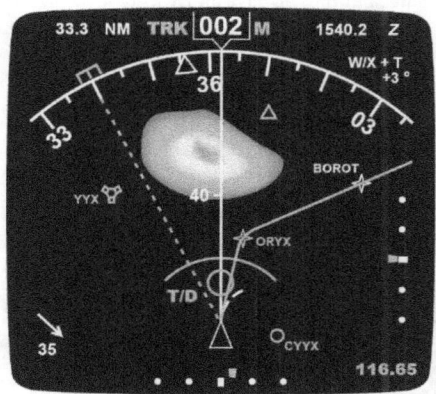

It is oriented to the aircraft heading or track, which can be shown in True or Magnetic (True is automatically selected above 73°N and below 65°S). In expanded (ARC) mode, the arc can cover between 30-60° either side of the track. Heading information comes from the IRS.

Your (FMC) position is at the apex of the white triangle (the aircraft) at the bottom of the screen and the track is a white line extending vertically away from it (see the Expanded version). Range markings are selected through the control panel. It normally points to 12 o'clock, except in heading mode where it will only do so in nil wind conditions.

In the picture above:

- The selected Course is 010°.
- The track is 002°.
- The heading is 356°, and the selected heading is outside the visible rose (dotted line).
- The aircraft is to the left of track and on the vertical profile.
- The W/V is 330/35 knots. Wind speed and relative direction are in the bottom left hand corner, shown according to the compass rose. It can be found on Map, Expanded ILS, Full ILS and Full VOR modes. When the track line coincides with the desired track, wind influence is compensated for.
- The ETA 15:40 and the distance to go is 33.3 nm.

The green circle ahead of your position is the Top of Descent (or Climb, as in T/C). The green arc behind it (the range-to-altitude ring, or banana bar) is where the selected altitude will be reached at the current vertical speed. The white arc extending away from the triangle is a trend vector with each dash representing 30 seconds ahead. The scales on the bottom and right that look like a localiser and glideslope show you deviations from LNAV and the VNAV descent path. A magenta line represents the active route, and the *active waypoint* is the one the system is currently navigating to. If you want a different heading than that chosen by the FMS, you must use the magenta heading select marker. When the track line coincides with the desired track, the influence of the wind is compensated for.

Fix information is a dashed green line. A dashed blue circle is a clean energy management circle. A dashed white one is a drag circle for extended speed brakes.

ETOs and ETAs as calculated by the FMC are naturally correct when the actual winds match the forecast winds and the FMC Mach number is the actual one. Magnetic heading is shown, but True is available via the IRS.

If a VOR receiver fails, the associated magenta deviation bar and/or pointer is removed from the display.

PLAN

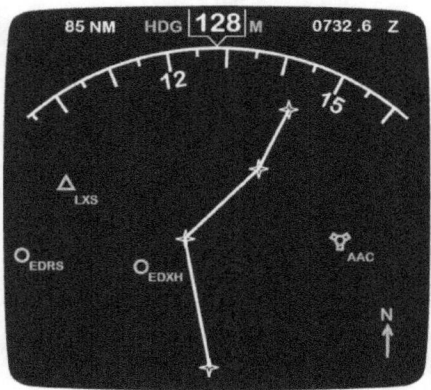

The PLAN display provides an overview of the whole or parts of the route, but is not displayed in real time, except for the information at and above the expanded rose.

You cannot normally display wind and weather in this mode (depends on the manufacturer). You might use it to see the effects of changes in the route before entering them into the FMC. Plan mode is always expanded, and oriented to True North (i.e. North up - watch for the arrow bottom right, though on some systems the arc may be set to N). There is also no aircraft symbol.

VOR/ILS

In full mode (also known as *centred*), you get an electronic representation of the traditional HSI. You will get wind, but not weather, information. In expanded mode, weather information is available on both EHSIs.

The full rose will change for the VOR and ILS according to the frequency selected. The full deflection is 20° for the VOR and 5° for the ILS.

DEAD RECKONING

DR mode is a backup for when the other navigation sensors are not working. It computes heading, airspeed, wind data, groundspeed and time.

OVERFLY FUNCTION

This makes the aircraft fly specifically over a waypoint, of which there are two types.

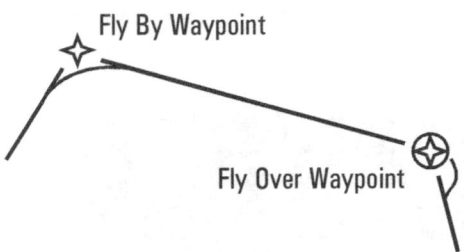

A *flyover waypoint* is one whose lat & long position* must be flown over before you can turn onto the next leg, typically used on standard departures to ensure that you don't make excessive bank angles that will interfere with performance calculations. You can fly *direct-to* any waypoint, or *direct/intercept*, where you can select a desired course to reach it. Waypoints can also have speed, altitude and time constraints (*not before*, etc.)

*Waypoints can be entered into all INSs as lat & long.

👍 **Rule Of Thumb:** Anticipate the turn by 1 nm for every 30° change.

SYMBOLS AND COLOURS

Active flight plans and waypoints are *magenta* in MAP mode. Otherwise, general colours are:

- **GREEN**: Present situation, low priority info, light precipitation.
- **WHITE**: Static information, turbulence, current and armed data values (cyan can also be armed).
- **MAGENTA**: Command information (i.e. FD bar), weather radar, turbulence, selected heading, active routes or waypoints.
- **CYAN**: Non-active and background information, can also be armed mode.
- **RED**: Warnings (flight envelope or system limits).
- **YELLOW**: Caution or abnormal sources.
- **BLACK**: Off.
- **BLUE**: The sky.
- **TAN/BROWN**. The Earth.

The extensive use of yellow for other than caution/abnormal information is discouraged. In colour Set 1, magenta should be associated with analogue parameters that constitute *fly to* or *keep centred* information.

EICAS

The *Engine Indicating and Crew Alerting System* (EICAS) shows you what all the systems around the aircraft are up to. EICAS & ECAM, from Boeing & Airbus, respectively, are well known monitoring systems, but they all have an EFIS-type display at the front end.

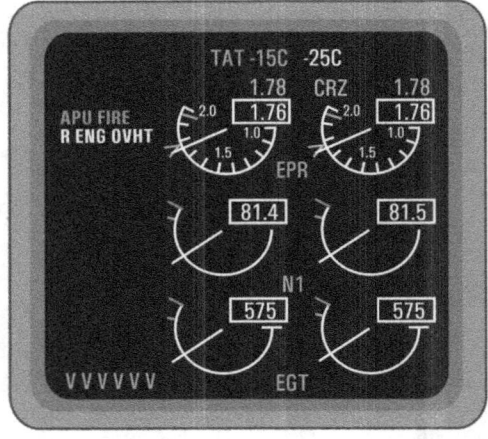

Although it primarily shows engine indications, it also acts like a central warning panel. The upper screen is the primary display, and the lower is the secondary.

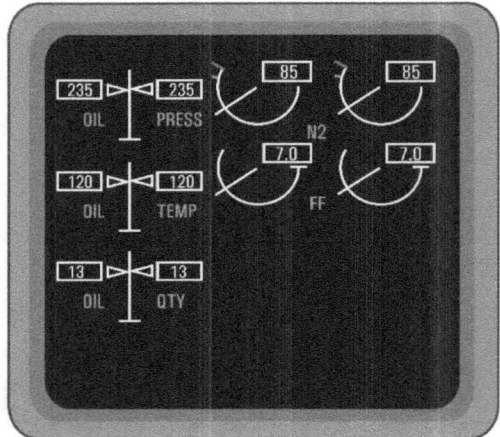

The downward pointing arrows at the bottom left of the upper screen tell you that there is information on the lower screen - if you can't see anything, it is not working.

You only get a warning light if the ECAM display fails.

INERTIAL NAVIGATION

Inertial systems can provide continuous information on your position, true track, heading, groundspeed and height without any outside help, allegedly first designed for the V2 rocket, but also extremely useful for submarines. With TAS information from the ADC, they can calculate wind velocity - being self-contained, they can work anywhere and, as a bonus for the military, are undetectable.

Although they can operate in True at any latitude, inertial systems can apply local variation (between 73°N - 60°S*) from a lookup table in a database, so a flux detector is not required, although there is an area between 90°W to 120°W and 70°N to 72°N (in Canada) where the variation table cannot update the output from true to magnetic. Some sets show HDG FAIL in that case and need manual switching to TRUE, which others can do automatically. This is because it is too close to the North magnetic pole.

*At higher latitudes the variation is either unusable, unreliable, or has too high an annual rate of change.

Tip: INS/IRS navigation uses great circle tracks (i.e. the shortest distance between any two points - see *Navigation*), because they orient themselves in space (against the stars) and their data is converted into latitude & longitude through a mathematical model, typically WGS 84. When you see IRS/INS in a question, you know it involves a Great Circle. The differences between WGS 84 and the proper shape of the Earth are why Schuler tuning is needed, discussed later.

The data provided and the equipment used can be made available for other systems - the high quality gyros will typically drive the artificial horizons and allow for accurate heading maintenance, which is the real trick - once the initial heading is calculated from the Earth's spin rate, no corrections should be required.

The principles are simple enough. Starting from a known (usually precisely surveyed) point, your present position is calculated from the directions and speeds you have used since then, so you have a continuously running **dead reckoning** position that will drift in proportion to the elapsed time. The drift should be around 1 nm per hour for a strapdown system, but it could be 3 nm for the older stable platform. A drift of 0.1° per hour over 15 hours at,500 knots would mean a position error of around 6 nm. The main causes of cumulative distance errors come from wander in the levelling gyros and integration errors in the second stage of integration. The accuracy of any computed altitude decreases exponentially with time.

All this sounds wonderful, but as the accuracy degrades over time, you must supplement it with navaids or GPS, where it becomes subject to *bounded* errors based on the other system. Otherwise, in the dynamic situation (exam speak for *in flight*) the error normally continues to build, at differing rates as the velocity error varies, but it will never cancel itself. As the system error keeps growing, it is *unbounded*, and readings will therefore be inaccurate to some extent, especially at the top of the descent, because it has had the whole flight to drift off. It will also be inaccurate just after takeoff, because no updating takes place while you taxi (although the FMC position can often be updated on takeoff with the TO/GA button).

As a fix is obtained (say by being overhead a navaid), you can place the system on hold and tell it where it really is, or at least reset the drift to zero (*Map shift* occurs when the moving map changes position to show the updates).

However, manual updating is only allowed within 25 nm of a co-located VOR/DME, or above a visual fix below 5,000 feet. Auto updating can take place within 200 nm of 2 DMEs or 140 nm of a single DME. GPS, described elsewhere, is a lot more accurate, although it is actually a low bandwidth system, meaning that its update rate is very slow and will resemble a straight line between the start and end points of a journey. IRS and INS are high bandwidth systems that update a lot more often and will show a truer picture. Combining INS/IRS with GPS can therefore provide an accurate, drift-free system, by combining the short term accuracy of INS with the long term accuracy of GPS. The two can also provide redundancy, as INS can keep things going if GPS conditions are not ideal, say when less than 4 satellites are in view, or those that are badly positioned (if GPS data is less than optimal, its signals are verified for accuracy before being incorporated into the system, which is why there are two receivers, but this is only possible with a strapdown system). The GPS can be used for alignment (10 minutes) or navigation. The two systems can be *uncoupled*, *loosely* or *tightly coupled*.

There will normally be at least three INS/IRS systems on most modern aircraft to guard against error, working through the FMS. In the early days, they were standalone, so the only way to check for errors was to inspect each one against a position fix or your DR position (or readings from another aircraft), if you didn't have GPS. Errors would not necessarily be seen until the system pumped out the codes, from which you could tell which one it was. Now, each one's output is compared in a voting system, from which inaccuracies are detected. Having said that, on a triple-fit IRS system, the displayed present positions may differ as the information comes from different sources - and, having said that, a 10 nm difference or one of 8° drift could mean at least one is drifting.

Inertial systems have their own (28v DC) batteries which run for 20-30 minutes, or they may use the hot bus. *If power is lost, you cannot realign for the rest of the flight*.

Older systems were called Inertial *Navigation* Systems because that was their main function, but more modern versions are fully integrated with other parts of the aircraft, hence the name Inertial *Reference* Systems.

Note: All INS/IRS systems depend on the right information being inserted in the first place, which is why it is so important in the checklist. *Both* pilots must check the entries (see *Flight Management Systems*).

ACCELERATION

Newton's first law of motion is the basis behind inertial navigation. Very loosely, it states that bodies at rest or in motion tend to retain their current state unless acted upon by an external force. Put another way, if you want to change the inertial state of a body, you must use a force. All that is obvious to us, probably, but apparently not so to Aristotle and other great thinkers before Newton. After Newton, however, Mr Einstein added his own views in his Special Theory of Relativity, which are relevant here.

In the wider scheme of things, it would appear that nothing is at rest! At least, a book on a table is "at rest" with regard to the table, but the book, table and the observer are actually sharing (curved) velocities in space, which brings us to Newton's second law which, in brief, states that the rate of change of velocity (acceleration) is directly proportional to the force making the body accelerate, and inversely proportional to the body's mass.

Acceleration is therefore a measure of how fast the speed of something is changing, being the time rate of change of velocity, or the time rate of change of the time rate of distance. That is, it is measured in feet (or metres) per second, per second. We know that velocity involves changes of distance over time, and acceleration involves changes of velocity over time. If you have a record of its history, an aircraft's accelerations in the vertical, horizontal and lateral planes in space can be integrated* over time to find the changes in its velocity, then again for how long it has been travelling at that velocity to find the distance travelled up, down or sideways. We use accelerations because we cannot measure velocity directly without external aids, which is not the point of the exercise.

*If you know how fast something is changing, you can find out by how much it has changed, in the same way that a fuel flow meter can work out how much has been used from the rate of flow, based on the measurement of infinitely small components. Thus, if you know by how much your speed has changed, you can find out what your speed is now, and from that deduce the distance travelled.

The data from the various integrations is used to calculate track and groundspeed and resolve distances into changes of latitude and longitude. Starting with speed, which is the rate of change of distance with time:

$$S = \frac{D}{T}$$

It is also called the *differentiation* of distance over time. Acceleration is the differentiation of speed with time:

$$A = \frac{S}{T}$$

Since we know that S = D over T (see first formula), the above can be written as:

$$A = \frac{\frac{D}{T}}{T} \text{ or } A = \frac{D}{T^2}$$

Working backwards, you integrate acceleration once for your initial speed, then integrate speed for distance.

SYSTEM CONTENTS

A typical (early) system consists of:

- *Inertial Navigation Unit* (INU). In it, the Inertial Sensor System contains the stable platform, accelerometers and a computer to integrate the information and provide a value for distance travelled. The ISS is turned into an INS by the ability to manipulate waypoints and find the time and distance to go to reach them.
- *Mode Selector Unit* (MSU).

- *Control Display Unit* (CDU), or *Inertial System Display Unit*, ISDU, below) with a multi-line keypad. It is used for inputting information, such as your starting position and waypoints, as lat & long.
- *Battery Unit* (BU) as a backup.

The MSU and CDU are on the flight deck, and the INU and BU in the depths of the aircraft, where only engineers touch them. The MSU (shown below) is used to switch the thing on in the first place, and select the mode of operation, such as STBY, ALIGN, NAV, ATT, etc.

There are also a couple of warning lights. You get a red one when the battery is flat. An ALERT light may come on 2 minutes before a turn. The HOLD button freezes the display. You turn the system on by moving the switch to SBY (if present), so the oil in the gyros can warm up to a specific viscosity, then ALIGN after you have entered your present position, time and date.

Note: The aircraft must remain stationary!

During alignment, the direction of North can be detected from which way the Earth is moving, and the rate of movement provides the latitude. In other words, North alignment uses inputs from the accelerometers and the East gyro.

This process takes at least 2.5 minutes at the Equator and up to 10 minutes at 70° N or S. During initial alignment, an INS will not accept a 10° error in initial latitude, but will accept one in initial longitude. Once everything is aligned, and before moving off, you must switch to NAV, which is the normal flight mode. At this stage, the outputs include acceleration (N/S & E/W), attitude and true heading.

ATT mode is a backup which retains just attitude and heading information while realignment takes place, so if the navigation computer fails, you can still use the artificial horizon, etc. Once a stable platform INS loses power in flight, it loses its level and alignment references and cannot be re-aligned, because it cannot discriminate between motion of the aircraft and rotation of the Earth, although a strapdown IRS (below) might be able to provide attitude and heading information - the procedure then is to switch to ALIGN and fly straight and level for a minute or two. If the FAIL flags disappear the system may be used for attitude information. If you then input the aircraft heading it may be used as a heading reference.

Picture: INS CDU & MSU for a twin system

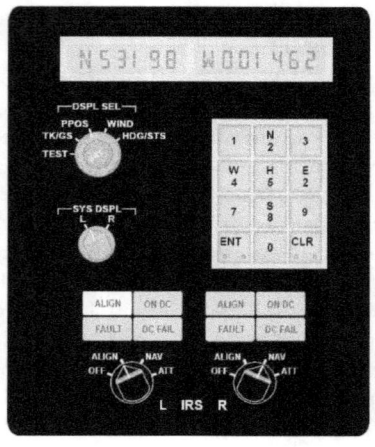

INSTRUMENTS
Inertial Navigation

In the picture above, if the ALIGN light is steady, the IRS is in ALIGN mode, ATT mode, or is shutting down. If it is flashing, alignment cannot be completed due to a Code 3, 4 or 8 error. If it is not on, alignment may be complete (if the selector is at NAV) or the system may be off.

If ON DC is illuminated, the IRS is working from the battery bus rather than AC. The right IRS is limited to 5 minutes. On the ground, a horn in the nose wheel well sounds, to indicate a possible battery drain.

STABLE PLATFORM

The *platform* (or *stable element*) is a gyro-stabilised cluster of linear accelerometers, in three circular gimbals (for the x, y and z axes), to keep them in the right position.

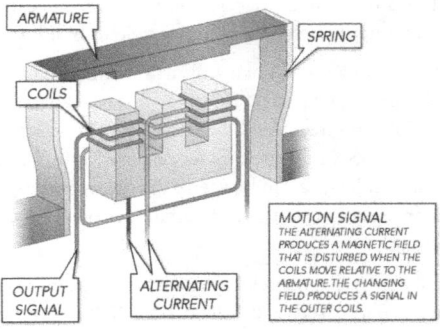

The basic system contains:

- **2 linear accelerometers** in the x and y axes (for LNAV sensing), with possibly another for the z axis. E & I bars may be used because they have minimal friction, otherwise some systems use pendulums. As with the arms on the flux detector, the bars are highly permeable, so a high flux density in proportion to the inducing field can be provided, with a rapid response to changes. The central arm is fed with 400 Hz AC, so the outer legs pick up a secondary induced AC voltage, which is affected by the gap between the bars. If there is no acceleration, the legs have the same voltage, but with opposite polarity. However, as the I bar moves away from the vertical (in the opposite direction to the acceleration), the secondary induced voltage is amplified, phase detected and rectified (to DC) so that a torque motor can try to restore the accelerometer to the null position - the amount of current involved is proportional to the acceleration experienced. The same signal also goes to the integrators.

  Phase detection ensures that the DC is of the right polarity so the I bar can be moved the right way.

- A **stable platform** that keeps the x and y axes oriented N-S and E-W and the z axis aligned with local gravity, so that the x and y accelerometers do not mistake gravity for acceleration. This isolates the aircraft's movements from the Earth's.

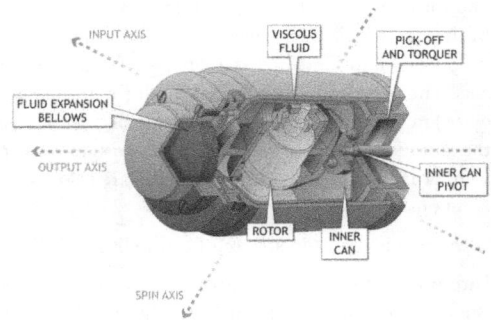

- **3 Rate Integrating Gyros** (for VNAV sensing, above) that measure and use changes in aircraft vectors to orient the stable platform (these have nothing to do with navigation - they are just there to keep the platform level). Rate integrating gyros provide a much higher output response for a given input than displacement gyros do. Their output also increases as a function of their rate of displacement, but they only act about a single axis, so three 3 are needed to cover all bases. They are surrounded with warm oil to eliminate friction and reduce bearing torques, and to stop the gyros precessing or toppling, as opposed to using a spring. They are mounted inside two cans, one inside the other. The outer one is fixed to the INS platform and the inner one is free to rotate within it, behaving like a gimbal.

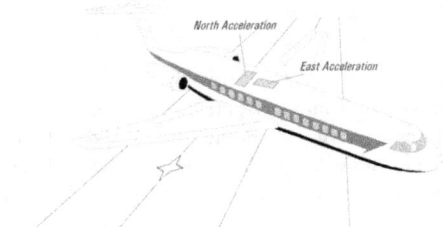

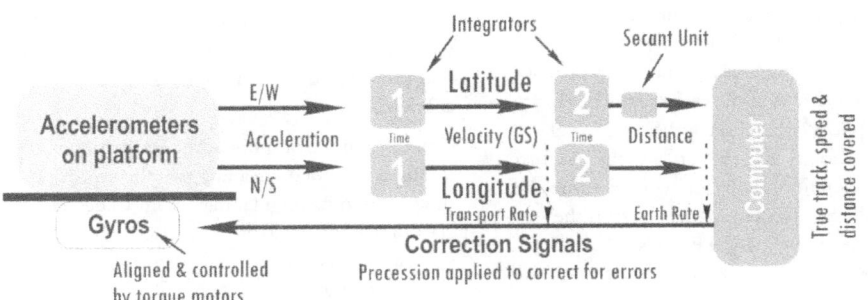

When a tilt from the level position occurs, the gyro spin axes remain fixed in space, but their cases move, and an error signal is measured to find the rate of movement, which is applied to the platform. Corrections are so quick that the platform does not rotate for more than 10 arcseconds before it is moved back to its original reference position. This also compensates for the local gravity vector being mistaken for an acceleration, which is what Schuler tuning is for (below).

The RIG that senses the N/S axis is the *North Gyro*, the one for E/W is the *East Gyro*, and the vertical axis gyro (if there is one) is the *Azimuth Gyro*, the drift of which is proportional to time. Gyros are named for the sensitive axis. The platform is also forced to tilt (by torquing the gyros) in proportion to the Earth's rate of turn, based on the latitude. Transport wander is dealt with in the same way, and Coriolis and centrifugal force are also compensated for.

Gyro drift is the main source of error with an INS.

- **Integrators** to convert the acceleration data into velocity and distance information. The signals from the accelerometers go to the *1st stage integrators* which produce velocity information by multiplying the acceleration against time. The *2nd stage integrators* multiply the resulting velocity against time to work out a distance. For N/S, as each minute is 1 nm, this is easily converted into change of latitude which can be added to the start point to find the present latitude. The E/W distance, where a nautical mile is not always a minute of longitude, has to be calculated with the aid of a secant unit.

- A **computer** to sort it all out and provide position information. Accelerometer signals are analogue, so there must also be an analogue-digital converter for the computer and displays.

Schuler Tuning

If an INS is not moving, it assumes it is falling towards the centre of the Earth. If it isn't actually doing that, to register a zero change in position, gravity must removed from its calculations (you need it to measure acceleration).

However, the value of gravity changes with your position and height, what you are flying over, and even the weather. Only the latest systems can use a geometrically correct model of the Earth and its gravitational fields, so the INS must distinguish between the proper shape of the Earth and the mathematical one in its memory (WGS 84).

If the platform is only slightly away from the horizontal, there could be major errors in distance figures as gravity is mistaken for acceleration. If an accelerometer is out by just 1/100th of G, the error on a 1-hour flight would be 208,000 feet, or over 34 nm. Even when you are not moving, misalignment can produce similar effects, but as the velocity is in the system, the platform overcorrects, tilts in the opposite direction and senses a real acceleration to reduce the velocity back to zero. As the platform continues to apply the deceleration, the velocity increases in the opposite direction to produce correcting signals to stop the deceleration, and the increase in velocity. The process starts again as the system is now in full swing back to where it started.

The time taken for the disturbance to go from one extreme to the other (a pendulum effect) is the *Schuler period* of 84.4 minutes, named after Dr. Maximilian Schuler, who showed in 1923 that a pendulum whose length is the same as the radius of the Earth could help eliminate inadvertent acceleration errors because it will always point to the vertical (he was trying to figure out a way of stabilising sea compasses). Put another way, if you could build a pendulum the length of the Earth's radius, with its bob at the centre of the Earth, it would still point to the vertical wherever you moved the point of support (in our case, an aircraft).

If the aircraft accelerates, the bob should stay where it is and the pendulum "cord" should stay vertical for all motions of the pivot point (the aircraft). Schuler determined that, if the bob were disturbed, the pendulum would oscillate over 84.4 minutes, so if a system is built with an identical period, it would indicate the local vertical regardless of any acceleration of a vehicle carrying it. It is ironic that he thought it was impossible to build an INS!

An INS platform behaves just like an Earth pendulum in that, when it is disturbed, it takes 84.4 minutes to settle down again, during which time you may be a bit off course. The Earth wobbles, not the INS, but it appears to, relative to the Earth. In other words, it wanders, as can be seen in crosstrack readouts which may increase, then return, in a certain period. The wobble is the Schuler cycle.

The relationship between a circle's angle in radians and its circumference is $1/R$ (based on 2π divided by $2\pi R$)*. Multiplying this by V (from the first stage integration) gives you an angular velocity over a surface distance, or the transport rate, which is used to torque the gyro and make the platform precess at the same rate that it is being moved over the Earth's surface.

Schuler tuning provides an undamped closed-loop corrective action to stop tilt errors, oscillating around a zero value over 84.4 minutes.

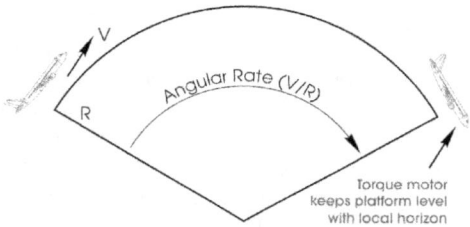

*To make allowances for altitude, $1/{R+H}$ is used.

Note: Although Schuler tuning prevents the accumulation of errors which would be caused by platform tilt and treating gravity as an acceleration, it will not compensate for errors from the precession of the steering gyro.

The Schuler tuned platform produces its maximum error at 21.1 and 63.3 minutes through each 84.4 minute cycle. The magnitude of the maximum error depends on the size of the disturbance that caused it, but the mean error remains at zero (assuming no accelerometer error).

Any error in the outputs of the accelerometers caused by Schuler tuning is bounded, meaning that the error does not increase with time beyond its original maximum value. The output of the first stage integrator (velocity) will also be bounded. Strapped down systems are also considered to be Schuler tuned, and to suffer similar bounded errors.

INSTRUMENTS
Inertial Navigation

ALIGNMENT

You cannot use the system until two tasks are accomplished. The platform (or rather the accelerometers) must be levelled*, then lined up with True North, also known as *gyrocompassing*. This is done over about eleven minutes by motoring the (level) platform until there is no topple output from the East gyro (when stationary on the ground, the only cause of topple would be the rotation of the Earth, so if there is none, the axis is assumed to be aligned N/S). The topple output of the North gyro should now equal the Earth rate, which is 15° x cos latitude, so this is impossible at high latitudes because of the torquing rates. Also the cosine value would be near zero. However, the INS cannot do this unless it has a latitude input.

*With coarse levelling, the pitch and roll gimbals are driven until they are at 90° to each other. The platform is then levelled to ± 10° against the aircraft frame or gravity using the horizontal accelerometers or gravity switches. Coarse azimuth alignment (± 2°) is achieved by turning the platform in azimuth until the heading output agrees with the aircraft's best known heading, normally obtained from the gyro-magnetic compass. This is followed by fine levelling, which is done by motoring the platform until no acceleration from gravity is sensed by the x and y accelerometers - this does not need lat & long input. It takes about 6 minutes. Fine levelling uses the accelerometer null technique - with the aircraft stationary there should be no output from the horizontal accelerometers if the platform is level. Fine levelling normally takes about 1.5 minutes.

Alignment is only done once, before the flight, because the outputs from the accelerometers and gyros are used differently, hence the separate ALIGN mode on the MSU (although alignment can be done in ALIGN or NAV mode). It takes about 17 minutes overall for a stable platform. However, with such a North pointing system, things get interesting when you go over a Pole, because the platform would have to turn through 180° almost instantly (in fact, the problems start several hundred miles away). A workaround is to keep the platform level, but not worry about aligning it to North necessarily - just detect how far out of alignment it is, and include it in future calculations. In this case, the accelerometers would be offset by the *wander angle*. Yet another is not to bother levelling (or aligning), but figure out how far out the accelerometers are at initialisation and monitor changes.

During alignment the aircraft must remain stationary. If there is excessive movement, the ALIGN annunciator will flash and the fault indicator will come on. Switch the Mode Select switch off for at least 3 seconds then put it back to ALIGN. The ALIGN light will also flash if you do not enter the present position within the normal alignment time. Once aligned, the platform will be level, pointing along True North, and you can switch to NAV mode. If it is level, and the aircraft is not, the difference is measured and displayed as Pitch and Roll. The yaw difference between the longitudinal axis and the platform (North) is *Heading*. During alignment, most systems start passing attitude information to the FMS before being fully set up.

ERRORS

Bounded errors are constant over time, such as track or groundspeed errors that start off at a fixed rate, but these can lead to unbounded errors that get larger with time. Otherwise, accelerometers cannot tell the difference between gravity and acceleration, hence levelling errors.

The estimated local gravity (from a database) can be subtracted from vertical accelerations to compensate. The usual stuff also applies, like Earth rate and transport wander, which are predictable, because the computer knows your position. Thus, Coriolis effect and centripetal acceleration can also be calculated, and Schuler corrections applied to compensate for Transport rate (using the velocity signal from the first integration).

Real wander is compensated for on the ground, but can occur in turbulence, etc.

STRAPDOWN

The *strapdown system* is strapped directly to the aircraft structure. It has no gimbals, because it uses ring laser gyros (at least 3, with 3 accelerometers), so the outputs are *rate* sensitive, as opposed to being *displacement* sensitive. The "spinning mass" therefore follows the airframe and its alignment to true North is *calculated*. As there are no moving parts, the "stable platform" is maintained mathematically*, rather than mechanically. This provides more accuracy and reliability.

*The strapdown has a bias signal to compensate for Schuler drift applied to the readouts. You may notice position variations of about 1 nm between systems when they are not on the same points of the Schuler cycle. Other potential errors, such as Coriolis, are allowed for, but not mentioned here.

The IRS contains:

- two **Air Data Inertial Reference Units**, with:
    - a **power supply**
    - an **Inertial Reference** (IR). This senses and computes linear accelerations and turning rates around each axis, to feed pitch and roll displays and navigation calculations. The only other information needed is your start position, barometric altitude and TAS, which is obtained from the ADR, together with other useful information. Barometric altitude provides a reference for vertical navigation, and stabilises the vertical velocity and inertial altitude outputs. As an IRS doesn't need a platform, it needs three "accelerometers".
    - an **Air Data Reference** (ADR), which is separate on some aircraft.
- a **display unit**
- a **mode select unit**

Rotation about an axis can be sensed with fibreoptic or ring laser gyros, as described earlier.

ALIGNMENT

This is a much faster process than with the stable platform, because the system moves with the Earth, although levelling and alignment are still done while stationary, because the only acceleration is from gravity and the only angular movement from the Earth's rotation. From its direction and magnitude, the position of True North can be sensed and the latitude can be estimated.

However, you have to enter your whole position because present longitude cannot be worked out (the latitude input is used as a crosscheck for the calculated figure. Your longitude input is compared to the last stored one). Put more in exam speak, *you need to position the computing trihedron with reference to the Earth*. Well, of course you do.

Without Earth rate compensation, the system would also think it is upside down after 12 hours at the Equator. Elsewhere, there would be pitch, roll and heading errors. If you put in the wrong latitude, the Earth rate calculations will be wrong and you won't be able to align to True North properly (if the ALIGN lights are flashing this is what has happened).

As with other systems, you must switch to ALIGN to set things up, although Boeing recommend selecting NAV directly if you're between the 70°S and 70°N latitudes (there is no STANDBY setting as there are no gyros to warm up). Alignment varies with latitude - 5 minutes at the Equator, 10 minutes at 70°N and 17 minutes between 70- 78°. Although, during turnarounds, it is best to turn the system off and allow it to realign completely, if time is tight (it usually is), a fast re-alignment can be done. Just switch to ALIGN and enter a new gate position. Reselect NAV once the ALIGN lights go out.

In NAV mode, the gyros measure the Earth's movement with respect to space, and your movement with respect to the Earth, in the form of Transport rate, because any movement over a sphere involves some sort of rotation.

Automatic Calibration

- **Auto cal** maintains the calibration of the gyros and the longitudinal and lateral accelerometers to improve performance and reliability.
- **Gyro autocal** measures the position error after the flight and estimates the gyro errors that would have caused it.
- **Accelerometer autocal** picks up lateral bias errors found during taxi, because movement is generally forward.

Errors

A strapdown system suffers from lock-in errors caused by imperfect mirrors, which are reduced by wobbling, or vibrating with the *dither motor* and *spring*.

Otherwise errors include:

- **Schuler Tuning**. Platform oscillations cause errors to be propagated over a 84.4 minute cycle.
- **Levelling & Azimuth Gyro Drift**. Real Wander possibly 0.01°/hour - the largest errors in the system, distance error unbounded.
- **Initial Levelling** (Tilt). The accelerometers sense gravity - velocity and distance errors unbounded.
- **Initial Alignment**. Accelerometers misaligned N/S & E/W - velocity error bounded, distance error unbounded.
- **Accelerometer Errors**. Small random errors throughout the system.
- **Earth Shape**. The computer's spherical trigonometry is in error.

- **Altitude**. Earth rate/transport wander gyro corrections are calculated for ground level, giving small unbounded errors on long flights.
- **Coriolis** (Accelerometer). Earth rotation and transport wander cause a curved track in space - very small random errors.
- **Centripetal Acceleration** (Accelerometer). A constant altitude creates a curved track in space and acceleration towards the centre of the Earth.

As the readings from the INS/IRS drift over time, you need to check that the system is working within certain limits. For this reason, after the flight, you check your real position with where the system thinks it is. The idea is to check the *radial error rate*. For this you divide the distance off by the time the system has been in navigational mode.

The error rate history can be checked on the *IRS Monitor* page of the Flight Management System. A probable error of 1 nm/hour is the maximum that is commonly accepted (0.3 nm/hr is considered normal), in addition to initial input errors, although you will usually see a spread of up to ½ nm. Vertical position is potentially not so accurate as horizontal position. If the end position is put in, some units can use it to self-correct for future flights (limits are 10° for base latitude and 30° base longitude).

```
Dist out (nm)
Time (hours)
```

Although the system uses spherical trigonometry, the departure formula (see *Navigation*) can be used to find your distance E-W. Combine that with your N-S distance in a normal Pythagoras calculation to find the distance you are out, which is the hypotenuse:

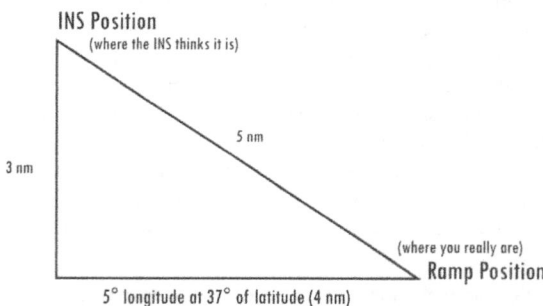

In the picture, the INS thinks you are 5 nm away from your real position, having flown for 2 hours. Your radial error rate is 2.5 nm per hour (the cosine of 37° is 0.8).

Example

1. With an azimuth gyro drift of 0.03° per hour, what will be the lateral position error after 5 hours at 500 knots?

After 5 hours (2,500 nm), the error is 0.065° (0.13/2) for a 2.7 nm error, using the 1 in 60 rule.

AHRS

An AHRS (*Attitude and Heading Reference System*) replaces traditional gyros* and their problems, such as topple, drift or gimbal lock in aircraft that don't have a full IRS. It is a combination of inertial sensors in one package that can output attitude, heading and flight dynamics information to flight deck displays and other systems. A flux valve and Air Data Computer will be involved, and 3D orientation is obtained by integrating the gyroscopes with accelerometers and magnetometers (for the magnetic field vector). An AHRS also converts the raw data into standard units like feet or metres, etc., although it will not necessarily provide a True heading output, as this is associated with commercial and military inertial reference and flight management systems. Thus, an AHRS requires less power, less wiring, weighs less and has a smaller footprint, but it will probably cost a lot more.

*While fibreoptic or laser gyros provide very stable angular rate measurements, *Micro Electro-Mechanical System* (MEMS) gyroscopes have the advantage of low power requirements and costs by using Coriolis Effect to measure an angular rate. They are used in solid state accelerometers, rate sensor gyroscopes and magnetometers. Most use a tuning fork configuration, where two masses oscillate and move constantly in opposite directions.

In any case, the AHRS is smaller, lighter, more accurate, more reliable and cheaper than traditional mechanical instruments.

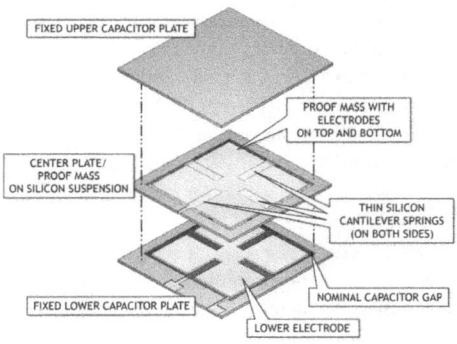

During linear acceleration, the two masses move in the same direction, so no change in capacitance will be detected. However, when angular velocity is applied, the Coriolis force on each mass produces a change in capacitance that is proportional to the angular velocity, which is then converted into output voltage for analog gyroscopes or LSBs for digital gyroscopes.

The magnetometer will usually be mounted remotely from the AHRS, where magnetic disturbances are minimal.

WARNING & RECORDING

Warnings should be attention-getting without being startling, while informing you of what is going on (or not). They should also guide you to the correct actions.

For example, if you need to be aware of something, but maybe have to take action afterwards, you will get an advisory message, which may be any colour except red, and preferably not amber.

Red (warning) lights indicate hazards that require immediate corrective action. Amber lights signify that action is required, but not immediately.

Systems should be reliable, meaning they should respond to genuine problems without generating false alarms.

Alerting for important failures should be done with audio warnings. There should be a single one to alert the crew and direct attention to a single central warning panel that announces the nature of the problem with a suitably illuminated caption.

Otherwise, the standard methods of bringing unusual occurrences to the notice of pilots include:

- **visual** (lights, gauges, displays)
- **aural** (bells, sirens, and sometimes voice)
- **tactile** (stick shakers)

The three levels of alerting are:

- **Warnings** (Level A) - Red, could be flashing
- **Cautions** (Level B) - Amber
- **Advisory** (Level C) - White

Off flags signify whether an instrument is working properly. They might come on if:

- electrical power is lost.
- a gyro is at too low a speed.
- the signal received by a navigation instrument is non-existent or too weak.

GPWS

CAT.OP.MPA.290

A major cause of accidents is Controlled Flight Into Terrain (CFIT).

GPWS

The first attempt at stopping CFIT was the *Ground Proximity Warning System*, which is supposed to be able to give warning of your impending approach towards Terrain Impact Mode in five areas of flight, whereas the radio altimeter relies on the crew looking at it, although it does have an adjustable height bug which acts as a rudimentary warning, if your attention is not diverted. This is why an urgent-sounding audio low height warning was considered necessary (apart from a scream from the other pilot!)

Neither, however, provide a look-ahead function, so would not help if you were about to hit a mountain. The GPWS might get its information from the radio altimeter, the ADC, the Captain's ILS receiver, and gear and flap indicators, over a range of 50-2,450 feet. When fitted, *a GPWS system should be switched on and used throughout the flight*, unless it is unserviceable, *and the MEL allows it to be so.*

The GPWS should have at least one sound alarm to which a visual alarm can be added.

The GPWS will warn you in case of (amongst others):

- dangerous proximity to the ground
- loss of altitude during takeoff or missed approach
- wrong landing configuration
- descent below the glidepath

The basic installation has five modes of operation:

- **Mode 1** - *excessive* (barometric) *rate of descent*, which operates when the barometric ROD is more than 3 times greater than the radio height or the clearance available. It uses two different warnings: an advisory, or soft warning, *Sinkrate, Sinkrate*, and a hard warning of **Whoop Whoop Pull Up**, repeated twice. Both stop outside the warning envelopes of between 50-2450 feet radio altimeter (the usual operating range of GPWS). The aural alert goes off when passing the first boundary.

- **Mode 2** - *excessive closure rate*, from a reducing radio altitude. This can be confused with Mode 1, but this means the ground is coming up rather than the aircraft going down, so it may even go off in level flight. Mode 2a is sounded if the flaps are not in the landing position, and 2b if they are. If the radio altitude, speed and rate of closure are within the warning envelope, the words **Pull Up, Pull Up** after a whooping sound are heard, which cannot be inhibited. Otherwise, the warning is *Terrain*.

- **Mode 3** - *negative climb rate* (for radio altitude), or *sinking after a takeoff or go-around* (i.e. height loss). If the barometric altitude lost is around 10% of radio altitude gained, the **Don't Sink, Don't Sink** aural warning will sound, with a second advisory of **Too Low Terrain** if the original radio altitude is over 150 ft AGL, then decreases by more than 25% of it. If you get a *Don't Sink* warning during takeoff or on a missed approach, you have started to lose altitude. Mode 3 activates between 30 and 667-1,333 feet radio altitude.

- **Mode 4** - *approaching too close to the ground with flaps or gear up*, so this is only active during the landing phase. There are two sub-modes (4a and 4b) and three alerts, depending on the phase of flight and aircraft configuration. Aural warnings will be either *Too Low Gear, Too Low Flap,* or *Too Low Terrain* (depends on aircraft speed).

- **Mode 5** - *going too far below the glideslope* (more than 1.3 dots), assuming you have tuned the correct ILS frequency. You may hear *Terrain, Too Low Glideslope, Glideslope* and *Pull Up*.

- **Mode 6** - *Miscellaneous* stuff like automatic height callout and bank angles, usually company-specific.

- **Mode 7** - *Windshear Mode*. A two-tone siren, plus the words **Windshear Windshear Windshear,** given once only, with a warning light, which are triggered if the predicted aircraft energy level falls below a safe threshold. Windshear warnings have a higher priority than other GPWS modes.

Alerts and warnings in Modes 1 and 2 are only given when you are less than 2,500 ft above local terrain, because this is in the normal operating range of the radio altimeter. Both modes are active in all flight phases.

A GPWS must generate at least one sound alarm, for which a visual alarm can be added. You can expect:

- An **alert**, which is just a caution, or
- A **warning**, which requires *immediate action*, because verifying warnings takes so long you may as well not have the device in the first place, and it takes a few seconds to get over the denial that you could be in the wrong position. Warnings could be:
  - *genuine*
  - a *nuisance* (when in a safe procedure), or
  - *false* (outside the validity area of a glideslope)

However, there are those who think that modes 1-5 have been "adjusted" so much to try to eliminate nuisance warnings that they have become ineffective. For example, to get a Mode 1 alert you need to exceed 3,000 feet per minute at,500', 1,200 fpm at 200' and 900' fpm at 10' - very high and very close, so the problems may well arise before the warnings! Typically, this will be for between 5-30 seconds beforehand, if at all over exceptionally rugged ground. Also, once an aircraft with GPWS has been configured for landing, there is very little protection against inadvertent proximity to terrain or water.

In summary, GPWS takes into account the aircraft's height as well as its descent rate and configuration. It has no terrain display or map, no predictive capability, and is radio altimeter based but, for all that it was a first generation attempt, GPWS marked a substantial decrease in hull loss rates in the 80s. Around 40% of fatal accidents were in aircraft without it.

TAWS

Terrain Awareness and Warning System is the generic term for altitude alerting systems of varying complexity, which includes GPWS and radio altimeters. The term therefore includes EGPWS, or Enhanced GPWS.

ENHANCED GPWS

This system is linked to all the instruments and can be updated with software. You get the basic GPWS modes but, in addition:

- **FLTA** (*Forward Looking Terrain Avoidance*), which checks for the absence of anything in the way within a preset search area (or volume, since it is vertical as well as horizontal). The search volume is curved in the direction of any turns

- **PDA** (*Premature Descent Alert*). Normally, after the gear is lowered, if there is no ILS signal, an aircraft would be unprotected, so the internal database can be used to provide a protected area around each runway, which enhances Mode 4, described below.

To provide the FLTA function, the details in a **world terrain and obstacle database** are compared with your GPS vertical and horizontal position, but radar helps as well, if you have it. The system also takes account of barometric altitude and the predicted flight path, so a side benefit is improved situational awareness from the advanced warning of the terrain.

As it happens, EGPWS has 32 modes, including *Terrain Clearance Floor* (TCF), *Terrain Look Ahead Alerting* and *Terrain Alerting and Display* (TAD). TAD is affected if the computed aircraft position gets less accurate. The system first identifies the stage of flight, then selects the appropriate one, with the airborne value stored in memory and kept immune from power interruptions. A system will typically go *In Air* when the weight on wheels switch indicates that you are airborne.

Note: Since the system relies on databases, they must be kept up to date! This means internal company procedures for ensuring that this is done in a timely fashion!

Note also that, to save memory space, the terrain database is only high resolution within about 16 miles of an airport - areas between them are low resolution. Beyond 60 miles, it is typically an eighth (you should be in the cruise by then). So, EGPWS is a terrain based map system, which has a predictive capability that can determine your position and flight path based on information from the FMS/GPS, Air Data System, Radio Altimeter and VOR/ILS (plus flaps and the angle of attack), comparing your altitude with its internal database and, if there is a potential threat of hitting the ground, can generate warnings well before the classic GPWS could do.

It uses the same colours as weather radar, namely green, amber, red and magenta.

In spite of the above benefits, there are still limitations. First of all, as mentioned above, the system requires an up to date database, which may have errors and will, by definition, not know anything about mobile obstacles.

Secondly, protection will be limited if your navigational accuracy is degraded - there are still areas in which GPS reception is poor. There may also be delays in alerts being given, or even unwanted ones.

BITE

Built In Test Equipment is a press-to-test function used to do part of the prestart checks. When pressed, the GPWS system lights come on in sequence with audio alerts and warnings. If the system is not functioning, they will not be complete (pushing the **PULL UP** light tests the system and illuminates all the lights). An **INOP** light will come on if the system fails or it loses a source of input.

Radio Altimeter

A radio altimeter is a self-contained on-board safety device that indicates the *true height* of the *lowest wheels* (with oleos extended) above the ground. Data supplied includes the distance between the ground and the altimeter. Radio altimeters (with audio) are required equipment over water. Low altitude radalts are used for precision approaches, with accuracy of ±2 ft between 0-500 feet or ± 1.5%, whichever is greater, and are only active below about 2,500 ft. High altitude ones work up to 50,000 feet above the surface.

A *continuous wave* FM radio beam in the SHF band (4200-4400 MHz)* is directed towards the ground in a 30° cone fore and aft, and 30° athwartships. The signal is reflected back to the aircraft. As the time delay for a pulsed signal is too small to measure properly (and the antennae cannot switch between transmit and receive that quickly), CW (as opposed to pulse) radar eliminates minimum range problems. You need separate transmit and receive aerials.

*Centimetric - see *Radio Navigation*. High altitude radalts use decimetric.

It takes around 6.1 microseconds for a wave to be reflected back from an object around 10,000 m away. With CW radar, we can arrange for a frequency change for that time period - say from 1,000 MHz to 1006.1. The difference of 6.1 MHz therefore represents 10,000 yards. You only have to measure the difference in frequency to find the range, so the system is frequency modulated. Although the frequencies change, the difference between them remains constant.

The transmitted frequency sweeps up and down through about 200 MHz either side of 4300 MHz. Compensation is made for aerial (residual) height and wiring, and to account for signal processing time, so the altimeter reads zero when the wheels touch down (placing the aerials near the gear means the radalt will also read zero when the nosewheel is on the ground). For most radio altimeters, when a system error occurs during approach, the height indication is removed.

In any case, below 1,000 feet, on an EFIS display, the readout changes to analogue.

When a system error occurs on approach, the height indication is usually removed.

Slope changes on a radio altimeter operating area should be avoided or kept to a minimum, being as gradual as practicable, with no abrupt changes or sudden reversals. The rate of change between two consecutive slopes should not exceed 2% per 30 m.

TCAS/ACAS

CAT.OP.MPA.295
ICAO Annex 10

If SSR can provide information to ground stations about aircraft carrying transponders, the same information can be provided to airborne stations.

Airborne Collision and Avoidance Systems (ACAS) provide you with an independent backup to your eyes and ATC by telling you if you are likely to hit another aircraft. The system was developed after the increased use of Area Navigation systems which allowed more direct routings away from specific airways.

An aircraft with such equipment is surrounded with three concentric envelopes of airspace that are monitored by radar. As the envelopes are defined by flight time, their size depends of the relative speeds of the aircraft involved. The space immediately around the aircraft is the **collision area**, then there is a **warning area** that represents 20-25 seconds of closing time. The largest envelope is the **caution area**, which expands outwards to allow for 45 seconds of response time.

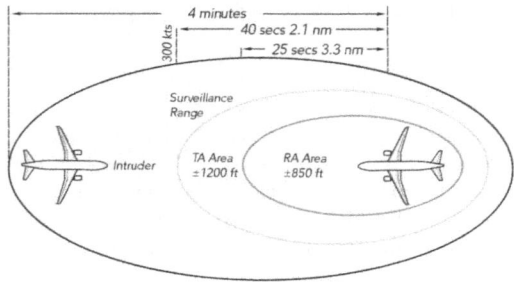

TCAS (the T stands for *Traffic*) is actually the system developed by the FAA, whilst ACAS is the generic name used by ICAO. Your aircraft's ACAS capability is not normally known to ATC, unless you mention it on a flight plan. Basic systems (TCAS I) just provide warnings of traffic without guidance.

However, TCAS II, the current equipment (version 7.1*), provides advice in the *vertical* plane, as a:

- **Traffic Advisory** (TA), or a warning, telling you where nearby *transponding aircraft* are, or a...
- **Resolution Advisory** (RA) which suggests avoiding action *in the pitch plane only*.

This is because all systems depend on azimuthal accuracy, which is not all that good, and why TCAS II makes you climb or descend to avoid traffic (TCAS I leaves any avoiding action up to you).

*For RVSM. A *Level Off* RA replaces the *Adjust Vertical Speed* one in version 7.0.

In view of the above, TCAS I can be regarded as a VMC aid, and TCAS II as an IMC aid, although it is possible, though not advisable, to use TCAS I in cloud. The system interrogates other aircraft, independent of ground aids, using four antennae, a computer *and a transponder* to continually survey the airspace around you and predict the flight paths of likely intruders, based on Mode C (TCAS I) or S (TCAS II) transponder signals from other traffic. If both aircraft have TCAS II, the bearing of the intruding aircraft is determined with a specific directional antenna.

It will not see obstacles or non-transponder equipped aircraft. Without Mode C, you will just get Traffic Advisories. The anti-collision logic of TCAS I is based on time. TCAS II will use inputs from the radio altimeter to inhibit RAs close to the ground.

The equipment scans a small amount of airspace around your aircraft in which it thinks a collision is possible. The range of intruding aircraft is determined by measuring the time lapse between the transmission of an interrogation signal and the reception of a reply from the intruder. Relative heights are measured by comparing Mode C transmissions.

An *intruder* will show up on the display with a symbol representing the grade of threat, plus numbers for their relative height above or below you in hundreds of feet (+ or - signs). An up or down arrow provides a vertical trend (over,500 fpm).

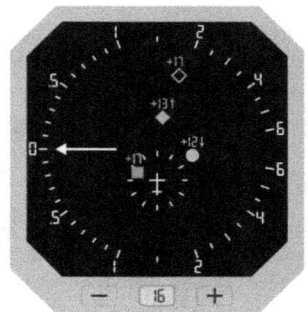

A hollow diamond (white on EFIS) indicates **non-threat** (other) traffic over 6 nm away horizontally. A shaded (solid) diamond indicates **proximate traffic** within 6 nm horizontally and 1 200 feet vertically.

A Traffic Advisory (TA) is given when an intruder comes with 30 seconds of your aircraft (45 seconds for TCAS II), as a *potential* threat, when the symbol changes to a solid amber circle.

A Traffic Advisory (TA) is given when a close traffic intruder comes with 30 seconds of your aircraft (45 seconds for TCAS II), as a *potential* threat, when the symbol changes to a solid amber circle. When it becomes a red square (RA) the intruder is an *immediate* threat - red for danger and a box, because if you don't follow an RA that's where you will be. An RA would normally come about 20 seconds after the TA.

A *corrective advisory* calls for a change in vertical speed (or something different to what you are currently doing) and a *preventive* advisory restricts it. All RAs are corrective except MONITOR VERTICAL SPEED, which is a *preventative* RA, during which you should avoid deviation from the current vertical rate, but no changes should be made to that rate.

Note: RAs do not take stall margins into account!

An RA voice message CLIMB CLIMB NOW repeated twice is generated after a DESCEND RA when a reversal is needed.

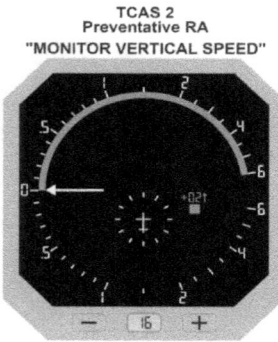
TCAS 2 Preventative RA
"MONITOR VERTICAL SPEED"

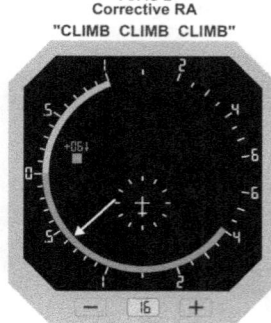
TCAS 2 Corrective RA
"CLIMB CLIMB CLIMB"

INSTRUMENTS
Flight Recording

TCAS MANOEUVRES

A TCAS manoeuvre is a valid reason for the inability to comply with a clearance. They should be reported to ATC, even after the action has been taken and the original clearance has been resumed (although ATC may issue a revised clearance).

A response should be initiated immediately (not in the opposite direction), and crew members not involved should check for other traffic.

Because of past confusion when responding to a TCAS RA, the only radio call you now make includes your call sign followed by TCAS RA. When you are clear of conflict, you report back to ATC, but maintain the new altitude until ATC tells you otherwise. Do not resume the previous altitude without ATC clearance.

An RA may be disregarded only when you visually identify conflicting traffic and decide that no deviation is necessary. If an RA and ATC conflict, the RA wins.

If an aircraft approaches from below, you would get an aural warning (CLIMB CLIMB CLIMB) and a visual one showing red for negative rates up to 15 fpm and green from 1500 fpm onwards (see right, above).

Nuisance or false advisories should be treated as genuine unless the intruder has been positively identified and shown visually to be no longer a threat.

TCAS II can display on its own screen, on weather radar, EFIS, a variometer (VSI) with an LCD display, and others. It uses two antennae, the upper one of which is directional.

POINTS TO WATCH

TCAS II can handle multiple intruders, and you could get multiple advisories when your workload is very high, which is why you can turn RAs off. Another time when you might want to do this is when operating with one engine inoperative (OEI), because a climb RA could demand a higher ROC than that available. Descent RAs are inhibited anyway when below 700 ft AGL, to avoid Controlled Flight Into terrain, or CFIT.

FLIGHT RECORDING

Flight data must be recorded over at least 25 hours, and cockpit voice and sound warnings at least 30 minutes.

Cockpit Voice Recorders
CAT.IDE.A.185

CVRs are required for:

- aeroplanes with an MCTOM **over 5 700 kg**. When the individual C of A has been issued **on or after 1 April 1998**, it must record the following for the past 2 hours (if issued before, 30 minutes):
  - Voice communications transmitted from or received on the flight deck by radio
  - The aural environment of the flight deck
  - Voice communications of flight crew members on the flight deck using the interphone system
  - Voice or audio signals identifying navigation or approach aids introduced into a headset or speaker
  - Voice communications of flight crew members on the flight deck using the public address system, if installed
- multi-engined turbojets with an MCTOM of 5 700 kg or less, an MOPSC of more than nine and first issued with a C of A on or after 1 January 1990. It must record the preceding 30 minutes.

A CVR must start to record automatically before the aeroplane moves under its own power* and continue until the termination of the flight when the aeroplane is no longer capable of so doing.

*As early as possible during the cockpit checks before engine start until the cockpit checks immediately following engine shutdown at the end of the flight.

A CVR must have a device to assist with locating it in water.

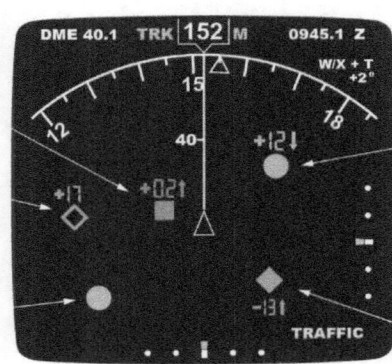

Resolution Advisory (RA)
30 Seconds From Collision
300-600 ft Vertical Separation
200 ft Above, Climbing

Non-Threat Aircraft
1700 ft Above
Less Than 500 fpm Change

Traffic Advisory (TA)
No Mode C
Altitude Unknown

Threat Aircraft
Traffic Advisory (TA)
1200 ft Above
Descending >500 fpm

Proximate Aircraft
Within 1200 ft & 6 nm
1300 ft Below
Climbing

Flight Data Recorders
CAT.IDE.A.190

- Aeroplanes with an MCTOM of more than 5 700 kg and first issued with a C of A on or after 1 June 1990
- Turbojets with an MCTOM of more than 5 700 kg and first issued with a C of A before 1 June 1990*
- Multi-engined turbojets with an MCTOM of 5 700 kg or less, with an MOPSC of more than nine and first issued with a C of A on or after 1 April 1998

require a digital FDR with a method of readily retrieving its data, positioned as far to the rear as practicable.

*For the previous 25 hours.

The FDR must start to record **before an aeroplane is capable of moving under its own power** and shall stop after it is incapable of so doing. It must be located as far to the rear of the aircraft as practicable.

Pushing the EVENT button on the control panel sets a mark on the recording, so it can be found quickly at the subsequent Board of Inquiry.

The FDR must have a device to assist locating it in water.

Air Law

This section covers the ICAO Annexes, except 6 and 18, which are dealt with in *Operational Procedures*. Annex 10 is covered in Communications. However, there is some crossover with the questions.

Governments often have to make laws about subjects they know nothing about, or cannot keep up with, or which are strictly for a local area (i.e. bye-laws), so a suitably qualified person or authority (such as the CAA) may be granted the power to make laws on their behalf, which saves a lot of time. This is known as *subordinate legislation* (or more commonly, and wrongly, as *delegated legislation*). The Canadians call it *Administrative Law*. In the UK, it is mostly brought to the notice of the public by *statutory instruments*, which is how the Air Navigation Order, and many other laws that affect your professional life, have been made (the ANO is a Statutory Instrument and an Order in Council).

INTERNATIONAL AIR LAW

One idea behind this concept is to reduce a phenomenon called *conflict of laws*, and the confusion arising where, say, a claim for damages is brought in a French court in respect of injury to a Canadian travelling on a ticket bought in Holland for a journey from Germany on an Italian plane. Another intention is to foster international trade.

010 01 04 01-04

International Air Law has mainly evolved through various International **Conventions** or **Treaties** which form the basis of Public International Law, which can be incorporated into the law of individual states, as with the **Chicago Convention of 1944**, which, through ICAO, described below, established **International Standards** and **Recommended Practices** for aviation (with which, over the high seas, you must comply, and inform ICAO if you don't). SARPs are developed by technical experts from the various countries, and each country adapts them for their own use.

You can tell the difference between the two - Standards tend to use the word *Shall*, and Recommended Practices the word *Should*.

A *Convention* is an agreement that many nations are at liberty to enter into (multilateral) and the word *Treaty* indicates agreements between two (or more) States that bind only themselves (bilateral). For example, there is a bilateral agreement between Canada and the USA that allows SAR aircraft of either country to cross each others' borders without the normal formalities.

As you will see later, conventions can cover many subjects, including standards for navigation equipment, but they can also create governing bodies, such as the *International Civil Aviation Organisation*, established by.........

The Chicago Convention 1944

This is arguably the most important legislation that affects aviation, because most of the countries in the world subscribe to it and adopt it as all or part of their own aviation legislation. Otherwise known as the *Convention on International Civil Aviation*, the parties to the Chicago Convention recognised that, after World War II (which ended in 1945), the future development of international civil aviation would help in creating and preserving friendship and understanding among the nations and peoples of the world, while recognising that its abuse can become a threat to general security. Not only that, the air transport industry was considered to be at risk, because there were thousands of surplus aircraft on the market, plus their pilots, and fatal crashes were the norm, due to the lack of regulation.

The idea was to avoid friction and promote cooperation between nations and peoples to foster peace, by agreeing to develop international civil aviation in a safe and orderly manner, establishing international air transport services based on equality of opportunity and sound, economic operation. In essence, the Chicago Convention grants the signatories (Contracting States) certain rights *against* other States in exchange for meeting certain obligations *towards* them. These could include the mutual recognition of licences and assistance with accident investigation, terrorism, etc.

Unfortunately, it wasn't that successful in some key areas, such as traffic rights, tariffs and capacity, and it does depend on the States following the rules so, since World War II, other agreements (some mentioned later) have been generated as workarounds. Some countries (and airlines) actually made their own arrangements, one result of which was the *International Air Transport Association* (IATA), formed by the airlines to establish uniformity for fares and ticketing arrangements, amongst other things, including Dangerous Goods. Although IATA* is a private organisation, it has strong links with ICAO and governments, and is often used as an agent for inter-airline cooperation. IATA has many committees, but the most significant is *Traffic*, which negotiates arrangements between states and airlines.

*And IACA, for charter operators.

One of the most important results of the Convention, as it is called, was the formation of ICAO in April 1947, under Article 43, whose standards and practices are used all over the world, with the odd difference here and there (these will be described in the *Aeronautical Information Publication* (AIP) of the country concerned).

The Chicago Convention has 96 articles and 18 Annexes (see Article 90):

ARTICLE 1 - SOVEREIGNTY

States have complete and exclusive sovereignty* over airspace above their territory, although this was actually established in 1919 at the Paris Peace Conference. Scheduled services may not operate over or into the territory of a Contracting State without first obtaining permission, although this is hardly ever refused, as the States concerned need it for their own aircraft.

*Sovereignty means having supreme, independent authority over a territory.

 The term *Scheduled Flight* is a legal definition describing services that run at predefined times with certain conditions imposed on them, such as being open to all classes of passenger and the flights always running, even though they may be empty (which means that whoever runs them are *common carriers*, but that is outside the scope of this course). This would mean that, although holiday flights and oilfield helicopters move at predefined times, they are not subject to the other restrictions and are not, technically, Scheduled Flights.

ARTICLE 2 - TERRITORY

Territory means nearby lands and waters under a State's sovereignty, suzerainty**, protection or mandate. Under the UN Convention of the High Seas, *territorial waters* are coastal waters of a State which may go out to 12 nm.

**Suzerainty occurs where regions or peoples are tributaries to more powerful entities which control their foreign affairs while allowing limited domestic autonomy.

ARTICLE 3 - CIVIL & STATE AIRCRAFT

The Convention applies only to civil aircraft - state aircraft (e.g. military, customs and police) are excluded. State aircraft must be authorised anyway to fly over the territory of another State, or land on it. Regulations for state aircraft must have due regard for the safety of navigation of civil aircraft.

ARTICLE 4 - ABUSE

Civil aviation should not be abused, that is, used for purposes inconsistent with the Convention.

ARTICLE 5 - NON-SCHEDULED FLIGHT

Aircraft of other contracting States *not* on scheduled international air services (i.e. general aviation aircraft) may, subject to the Convention, make flights into States (or non-stop in transit), and to stop for non-traffic purposes (refuel, emergency) without prior permission from the State concerned. However, they may have to follow prescribed routes for safety or security reasons. Assuming they are engaged in such services, they may also take on or discharge passengers, cargo or mail, subject to State regulations (see Article 7, *Cabotage*).

ARTICLE 6 - SCHEDULED AIR SERVICES

These need special permission or other authorisation, as there are commercial implications. See the *International Air Services Transit Agreement* and the *International Air Transport Agreement*, below, as these cover the "five freedoms".

ARTICLE 7 - CABOTAGE

This concerns airlines from one state performing internal flights within another, to protect domestic traffic of contracting States, so they can refuse aircraft permission to take on passengers, mail and cargo carried for hire, destined for another point within its territory. They also undertake not to grant exclusivity to any other State or airline, or to obtain it for themselves.

ARTICLE 8 - PILOTLESS AIRCRAFT

Special authorisation is required for these. Flight of such aircraft near civil ones must not be a danger to them.

ARTICLE 9 - PROHIBITED AREAS

States may, out of military necessity or public safety, restrict or prohibit aircraft of other States from flying over areas of its territory, with no distinctions being made. The areas must not interfere with air navigation, and be communicated to interested parties as soon as possible.

Any aircraft entering the areas above may be required to land as soon as practicable at a designated airport.

ARTICLE 10 - LANDING AT CUSTOMS AIRPORTS

Except when crossing without landing, aircraft entering State territory must, if required, land at customs airports and depart from them. See also Article 24.

Contracting states shall accept an oral declaration of baggage from pax and crew.

ARTICLE 11 - APPLICABILITY OF REGULATIONS

State laws and regulations apply to all aircraft engaged in international air navigation, without national distinctions, and must be obeyed by them while inside State territory.

ARTICLE 12 - RULES OF THE AIR

Aircraft inside a State's territory or carrying its nationality mark (wherever they may be), must obey its regulations, which will be uniform, as far as possible, with ICAO. State rules take precedence over ICAO where they conflict, but the Authority in the State of registration will need to be informed. However, over the high seas, the Convention applies. Each State also undertakes to ensure the prosecution of anyone violating regulations.

ARTICLE 13 - ENTRY AND CLEARANCE

Regulations about entry, clearance, immigration, passports, customs, and quarantine, and the admission to or departure from State territory of passengers, crew or cargo of aircraft, must be complied with.

The obligation (of a carrier) to transport any person away from the territory of a Contracting State terminates when they have been *definitely admitted* in another Contracting State of destination.

ARTICLE 14 - SPREAD OF DISEASE

Effective measures to prevent the spread (by air navigation) of cholera, typhus, smallpox, yellow fever, plague, and other communicable diseases, as applicable, will be taken, without prejudice to conventions to which States may be parties.

ARTICLE 16 - SEARCH OF AIRCRAFT

The appropriate authorities of each State may, without unreasonable delay, search aircraft of other States when landing or departing, and inspect documentation, which must be produced within a reasonable time.

ARTICLE 18 - DUAL REGISTRATION

An aircraft cannot be registered in more than one State at a time, but its registration may be changed from one State to another.

ARTICLE 19 - NATIONAL LAWS - REGISTRATION

Registrations or transfers must be made under State regulations. The Certificate of Registration must be carried at all times. See also Article 29.

ARTICLE 20 - DISPLAY OF MARKS

Aircraft engaged in international air navigation must bear the appropriate nationality and registration marks.

ARTICLE 21 - REPORT OF REGISTRATIONS

States undertake to supply to other States, or ICAO, information concerning the registration and ownership of aircraft registered there, including those habitually engaged in international air navigation. ICAO may then make it available to States.

ARTICLE 22 - FACILITATION OF FORMALITIES

States agree to adopt all practicable measures, through special regulations or otherwise, to facilitate and expedite navigation by aircraft between the territories of contracting States, and to prevent unnecessary delays, especially in administration of the laws relating to immigration, quarantine, customs and clearance.

ARTICLE 24 - CUSTOMS DUTY

Subject to Customs regulations, aircraft on flights to, from or across the territory of another State are admitted temporarily free of duty. Fuel, oil, stores and spares, etc. on board and destined to be leaving again are exempt from duties, inspection fees or similar charges, but this does not apply to any quantities or articles unloaded, except under customs regulations, which may require that they be kept under customs supervision. Spares and equipment imported for aircraft of other States engaged in international air navigation shall be admitted free of duty, but they may need to be kept under supervision.

ARTICLE 25 - AIRCRAFT IN DISTRESS

States must provide assistance to aircraft in distress in their territory as far as practicable, and permit, subject to control by their own authorities, the owners of the aircraft or authorities of the State of registration to provide such assistance as necessary. Each State, when searching for missing aircraft, will collaborate.

ARTICLE 26 - INVESTIGATION OF ACCIDENTS

If an accident happens in the territory of another State, involving death or serious injury, or serious technical defects (in aircraft or navigation facilities), the State in which the accident occurs shall institute an inquiry, under ICAO procedures, as far as its own laws permit. The State of registration will be able to appoint observers, and the State holding the inquiry shall communicate the report and findings to that State.

ARTICLE 28 - AIR NAVIGATION FACILITIES

States undertake, as far as practicable, to provide, in their territories, airports, radio and meteorological services, and other air navigation facilities for international air navigation, under standards and practices in this Convention (i.e. an appropriate aviation infrastructure). They also undertake to adopt and put into operation communications procedures, codes, markings, signals, lighting and other operational practices under this Convention, and to collaborate in international measures to publish aeronautical maps and charts.

ARTICLE 29 - DOCUMENTS CARRIED

Before entering the sovereign airspace of a foreign State with the intention of landing there, an aircraft must be airworthy, with all relevant documents on board:

- Certificate of Registration
- Certificate of Airworthiness
- Flight Crew Licences
- Journey Log Book
- Aircraft Radio Station Licence
- Passenger List (names, places of embarkation and destination)
- Cargo Manifest and detailed declarations of cargo

ARTICLE 30 - AIRCRAFT RADIO EQUIPMENT

In or over the territory of other States, aircraft may only carry radio transmitting apparatus that is licensed to be installed and operated by the State of registration. Its use shall be under the regulations of that State.

Radio apparatus may only be used by flight crew with appropriate licences, issued by the appropriate authorities of the State of registration.

ARTICLE 31 - CERTIFICATES OF AIRWORTHINESS

Aircraft on international navigation must have a certificate of airworthiness from (or rendered valid by) the State in which it is registered.

ARTICLE 32 - LICENCES OF PERSONNEL

Pilots and other members of the crew of aircraft engaged in international navigation must have certificates of competency and licences issued or rendered valid by the State of Registration. However, States may refuse to recognise, for flight above its territory, such certificates and licences, although this appears to contradict 33.

ARTICLE 33 - RECOGNITION OF CERTIFICATES

Crew licences must be issued by the State of registration. They can be recognised by others as long as they exceed ICAO requirements (this also applies to Certificates of Airworthiness).

ARTICLE 40 - VALIDITY OF CERTIFICATES

People or aircraft with inadequate licences or certificates must have permission from the relevant States to participate in international navigation over them. Registration or use of such aircraft or part, in any State other than that in which it was originally certificated, shall be at the discretion of the State into which it is imported.

ARTICLE 43 - ICAO

The *International Civil Aviation Organization* is formed by the Convention (in 1947). It is a specialised agency of the UN, and is made up of an *Assembly*, which overlooks a *Council*, which in turn overlooks such bodies as the *Air Transport Committee*, *Finance Committee*, or the *Air Navigation Commission*, as necessary. Its HQ is in Montreal, Canada. Working languages include English, Arabic, French, Russian and Spanish.

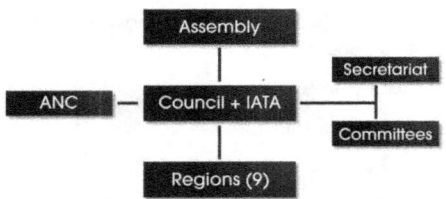

In 1944, there were 52 member states. Now there are 190.

The Assembly is the main policy-making body, which should meet once every three years, and on which all States have equal representation. One of its duties is to appoint the *Council*, which is a more consistent body consisting of 33 elected State representatives for the day-to-day work (in other words, it is the executive arm). The CEO's official title is *Secretary General*. The Council is elected by the Assembly every three years.

The *Air Navigation Commission* (ANC) considers and recommends **Standards and Recommended Practices** (SARPs) and **Procedures for Air Navigation Services** (PANS) for adoption or approval by the ICAO Council.

It has 19 members, with "suitable qualifications and experience in the science and practice of aeronautics" Although ANC Commissioners are nominated by specific ICAO Member States, and appointed by the Council, they do not represent the interest of any particular State or Region. They act independently and utilise their expertise in the interest of the international civil aviation community.

ICAO controls 9 regions, and 7 of them have a Regional Office. Regions include Africa - Indian Ocean (AFI), Caribbean (CAR), Europe (EUR), Middle East/Asia (MID/ASIA), North America (NAM), North Atlantic (NAT), Pacific (PAC) and South America (SAM).

ARTICLE 44 - OBJECTIVES

To develop the principles and techniques of international air navigation and foster the planning and development of international air transport so as to:

- Ensure safe & orderly growth of international civil aviation throughout the world
- Encourage the arts of aircraft design and operation for peaceful purposes
- Encourage the development of airways, airports, and air navigation facilities for international civil aviation
- Meet the needs of the world for safe, regular, efficient, economical air transport
- Prevent economic waste caused by unreasonable competition
- Ensure that the rights of contracting States are fully respected and that they have a fair opportunity to operate international airlines
- Avoid discrimination between States
- Promote safety of flight in international air navigation
- Promote development of all aspects of international civil aeronautics

ARTICLE 90 - ANNEXES

This gives the Council permission to adopt Annexes, which contain *Standards and Recommended Practices* (SARPs), which the various countries adopt as the framework (i.e. source documents) for their legislation. There are 18:

- *Annex 1* - **Personnel Licensing**
- *Annex 2* - **Rules of the Air**
- *Annex 3* - Meteorological Services for International Air Navigation
- *Annex 4* - Aeronautical Charts
- *Annex 5* - Measurement (Dimensional) Units
- *Annex 6* - **Aircraft Operation**
- *Annex 7* - Nationality and Registration Marks
- *Annex 8* - **Airworthiness**
- *Annex 9* - **Facilitation** (entry and departure for passengers and baggage)
- *Annex 10* - Aeronautical Telecommunications
- *Annex 11* - **Air Traffic Services**
- *Annex 12* - **Search and Rescue**
- *Annex 13* - **Investigation of Accidents**
- *Annex 14* - **Aerodromes**
- *Annex 15* - Aeronautical Information Services
- *Annex 16* - Environmental Protection 1 - Noise
- *Annex 17* - **Security**, for a program at each airport serving international civil aviation, by each contracting state
- *Annex 18* - **Dangerous Goods**

ARTICLE 96 - DEFINITIONS
For this Convention the expression:

- *Air service* means any scheduled air service performed by aircraft for the public transport of passengers, mail or cargo.
- *International air service* means an air service which passes through the air space over the territory of more than one State.
- *Airline* means any air transport enterprise offering or operating an international air service.
- *Stop* for non-traffic purposes means a landing for any purpose other than taking on or discharging passengers, cargo or mail (fuel, tech stop).

ICAO Publications
In addition to Annexes and SARPs:

PROCEDURES FOR AIR NAVIGATION SERVICES
PANS are procedures that have been adopted by the Council for worldwide use. They can contain new procedures or those which are complex, or which are not quite suitable for SARPs. In other words, they are detailed guidance documents issued by ICAO, containing operational practices that are beyond the scope of SARPs, but which are nevertheless subject to some uniformity.

PANS do not carry the same legal force as Annexes, but they are just as strictly observed. For example, the ICAO document about Aircraft Operations is DOC 8168-OPS, affectionately known as PANS-OPS, in which Vol I describes flight procedures (i.e. approaches, etc), and Vol II is for people who develop them, so the working pilot will only be bothered about Vol I. PANS-RAC (now PANS ATM) covers Rules of the Air and Air Traffic Services. They are both discussed later.

They come in three sections:

- **PANS-ABC** - ICAO abbreviations and codes
- **PANS-OPS** - Aircraft Operations
    - *Volume 1* - Flight Procedures
    - *Volume 2* - Construction of Visual & Instrument Procedures
- **PANS-ATM** - Air Traffic Management

At least 42 days' notice is needed before changes can take place. The effective date is Day 1 (Thursday) of a 28-day cycle.

REGIONAL SUPPLEMENTARY PROCEDURES
SUPPs contain stuff that is too detailed, or changes too much, for Annexes. They augment PANS and modify the SOPs in them, but must not be in conflict with Annexes or PANS.

TECHNICAL MANUALS
These amplify SARPS & PANS.

AIR NAVIGATION PLANS
Requirements for facilities and services for international air navigation.

ICAO CIRCULARS
Information of specific interest.

Freedoms Of the Air
The freedoms of the air are commercial aviation rights that allow airlines to enter and land in the airspace of another country, in an attempt to reduce potential domination by US airlines. They are put into practice as a result of bilateral agreements between pair of countries. They are commonly known as the *five freedoms*, although there are actually up to eight or nine, the remainder not being subscribed to by all States.

INTL AIR SERVICES TRANSIT AGREEMENT
The first two were established by this agreement. Being technical rights, they have no commercial implications.

- **One** - to fly across territory without landing (i.e. innocent passage)
- **Two** - to land for non-traffic purposes (such as technical stops, refuelling, etc.)

INTERNATIONAL AIR TRANSPORT AGREEMENT
The other three freedoms, however, do have commercial implications. Most air traffic is 3rd or 4th freedom, i.e. carried between States by airlines from those States.

- **Three** - put down passengers, mail and cargo taken on in the owning State.
- **Four** - take on passengers, mail and cargo destined for the owning State.
- **Five** - take on passengers, mail and cargo destined for any other Contracting State, and put them down (nothing to do with *cabotage*, in number 8).

SUPPLEMENTARY FREEDOMS
These are not so widely accepted, as they are workarounds for some minor problems arising from the fifth freedom:

- **Six** - start in another State, and go through the State of Registry to a third (combination of 3 and 4).
- **Seven** - revenue traffic between two States, neither being the State of Registry (i.e. by the carrier of another State). A variation of the fifth freedom.
- **Eight** - operate an internal service within another State (*consecutive cabotage*). That is, carriage of revenue traffic between two points in one State by the carrier of another State. Rare outside Europe.
- **Nine** - Code sharing, or stand-alone cabotage. Carriage of passengers by airlines other than the one booked. 2 or 3 airlines are often shown as operating one flight.

Suppression Of Unlawful Acts

THE TOKYO CONVENTION 1963
Offences committed on board, but not by, aircraft (penal law). It was an attempt to unite against threats to security, like hijacking or terrorism, but was later improved upon by the Hague Convention 1970. It covers damage caused in the territory of a

contracting state, or in a ship or aircraft registered therein, by an aircraft registered in another contracting state.

- **Article 3** says that the State of *Registry* has jurisdiction over offences and acts committed on board, and should take measures to prevent it
- **Article 4** says that other States may not interfere with aircraft in flight to exercise criminal jurisdiction over an offence committed on board, except when it has an effect on its territory, has been committed by or against one of its residents, is against its security, is a breach of its aviation rules, or such exercise is necessary under an international agreement

The Tokyo Convention also describes the authority and responsibilities of the PIC, who has final authority as to the disposition of the aircraft while in command.

If a person commits, or is about to commit, an unlawful act on an aircraft, the commander may impose reasonable measures, including restraint, to:

- protect the safety of the aircraft, persons and property on board.
- maintain good order and discipline.
- enable handover to the authorities by removal or refusal to allow the people on board.

Other crewmembers and passengers may be nominated to assist as necessary.

In a **hijacking** situation, the obligation of a State is the:

- provision of navigation aids
- ATC Services
- landing clearance

Contracting States must take measures for the safety of passengers subject to unlawful interference until their journeys can be continued safely.

Isolated parking positions must be established for aircraft subject to unlawful interference. The minimum distance from other aircraft, buildings, etc. is 100 m.

When an aircraft subject to unlawful interference must depart from its assigned track or level, the PIC must *attempt to broadcast warnings on the VHF emergency frequency.*

THE HAGUE CONVENTION 1970

This concerns the suppression of unlawful seizure of aircraft, and the rules for establishing jurisdiction.

THE MONTREAL CONVENTIONS

The 1971 version dealt with unlawful acts against the safety of civil aviation (air rage, etc.), particularly sabotage, but mainly acts **other than hijacking**. The 1998 version concerned unlawful acts of violence at international airports, and the 1991 version was about the international marking of plastic explosives.

International Private Law

THE WARSAW CONVENTION 1929

This relates to liability and its limitation for death, personal injury, or loss of or damage to baggage or cargo (if it didn't exist, airlines would soon go bankrupt). It applies to the international carriage of passengers, luggage or goods by aircraft for reward, but includes free carriage by an air transport undertaking. The carrier is liable for damage sustained on board, including during embarkation and disembarkation (except if the passenger's health was the cause). The liability for baggage or cargo exists when it is in the carrier's charge, so the claimant does not have to prove negligence by the airline. Claims must be brought within 2 years (Article 29).

Having said all that, in 1995, the *Airline Liability Conference*, under IATA modernised the Warsaw Convention. Essentially, it laid down that compensation for international passengers would no longer be limited by it.

Other previous modifications took place under the *Hague Protocol, 1955* and the *Montreal Agreement, 1966*. The former doubled liability and the latter widened it, on top of removing it from the gold standard.

TICKETS (ARTICLE 3)

The carrier must issue a document indicating departure and destination points, including stopping places (the same applies to luggage, covered in Article 4).

The absence, irregularity or loss of a ticket does not affect the contract of carriage under the Convention, but if a passenger is accepted without a ticket, the carrier cannot rely on limited liability.

LUGGAGE TICKET (ARTICLE 4)

One ticket for checked baggage is issued for the passenger, and one is kept by the airline.

AIR WAYBILLS (ARTICLE 5)

The equivalent of a ticket for cargo is the *air waybill*, which must be in 3 parts. The first must be marked "for the carrier" and be signed by the consignor, as must the second part, which must be marked "for the consignee". The third must be signed by the carrier and handed to the consignor after goods have been accepted. The carrier must sign before the cargo is loaded, and may ask for more than one if there is more than one package.

If the paperwork isn't done properly (or, more correctly, the consignor isn't warned about liability), the carrier cannot rely upon it.

Financing

Countries such as Iceland and Greenland provide many air traffic services across the Atlantic for aircraft that will not land there. There are arrangements to compensate them.

Liability For Damage & Injury

THE ROME CONVENTION 1933

To cover damage caused by foreign aircraft to third parties on the ground. There was a subsequent protocol signed in Brussels in 1938, and a *Protocol of Amendment* signed in Rome in 1952 and in Montreal in 1978. There was another Convention signed in

Rome in 1933, to do with the *precautionary arrest of aircraft*, for example, for debt.

People who suffer damage only need to prove that it was caused by an aircraft in flight, or anything falling from it, to get full compensation, but not if the damage did not arise as a direct result, or if it results from mere passage through airspace under existing regulations. The liability for compensation lies with the *operator*, but only up to a sum in line with the weight of the aircraft (they must insure themselves anyway). Although compensation is limited, it may not be if the damage was caused by intent or theft of the aircraft.

- **Article 15** allows States to require insurance for foreign-registered aircraft in terms of liability.
- In **Article 17**, the carrier is liable for damage if a passenger dies, is wounded or otherwise injured, if the root accident took place on board the aircraft, or during embarkation or disembarkation.
- **Article 18** is as above, but for baggage while in charge of the operator.
- **Article 19** covers liability for delay.
- **Article 20** allows the operator to weasel out of liability if it can be proven that all necessary measures were taken to avoid damage, or it was impossible to avoid it anyway.
- Under **Article 29**, rights to damages are lost if action is not brought within 2 years from:
  - The date of arrival at the destination
  - The date the consignment should have arrived
  - The date on which carriage ceased

World Organisation

WTO/GATS

Services, including air transport, are the largest and most dynamic component of economies, as well as providing support for the production of most goods. The *General Agreement on Trade in Services* (GATS) was ratified in Uruguay to make services the subject of multilateral trade negotiations. More negotiations began in early 2000, which are now part of the Doha Development Agenda. As far as air transport is concerned, traffic rights and directly related activities are excluded from GATS coverage because they are handled by the bilateral agreements described above. However, GATS does apply to aircraft repair and maintenance services, air transport marketing and computer reservation services.

The *Agreement on Trade in Civil Aircraft* came into force on 1 January 1980. Now with 30 signatories, it eliminates import duties on all aircraft, other than military ones, as well as on all other products covered by the agreement, such as aircraft engines, sub assemblies, flight simulators, and their parts and components.

European Organisations

Europe was originally formed from 12 countries, and now consists of over 15 (with more to come). They include Belgium, Denmark, France, Germany, Greece, Ireland, Italy, Luxembourg, the Netherlands, Portugal, Spain, UK, Austria, Sweden and Finland. The main administrative bodies are the *Council*, the *Parliament*, the *Commission* and the *Court of Justice*.

AIR TRANSPORT POLICY

The EU operates on free movement of goods, people, services and capital, which is reflected in its air transport policy. Objectives include enhancement of commercial competition, mutual acceptance of licences and qualifications, ensuring high levels of safety with common laws (*not* common law!) and learning from accidents.

ECAC

In 1953, ICAO convened a European conference on Coordination of Air Transport, which recommended a more permanent body, so the *European Civil Aviation Conference* was formed in 1955. It is a forum at which States meet to determine policy. It has 38 members. JAA was an associated body, with 34 members, being the only organisation to deal with security.

All members of ECAC could have joined the JAA.

JAA/JAR

The JAA ceased operation on June 30 2009, having been formed in 1990 at the *Convention of Cyprus*. The original name was Joint *Airworthiness* Authorities, since the idea was initially to harmonise certification of aircraft between States, but other subjects have since been added and the name is now Joint *Aviation* Authorities, soon to be overrun by EASA.

JAR stands for *Joint Aviation Requirements*, which work on the premise that aviation is the same in most civilised countries, and can therefore be standardised to a certain extent. Essentially, back in 1970, certain European countries agreed upon common procedures to help with importing and exporting aircraft, and type certification and maintenance, based on existing European regulations and FARs (from the FAA in the USA), where acceptable. In fact, the maintenance side of JAR, 145, is directly drawn from FAR Parts 43 and 145, and the bottom line was making it easier to use foreign aircraft. Naturally, there's a committee somewhere that jollies things along, which is somewhere in Holland. Documentation tends to follow ICAO Annexes - JAR OPS 1, for example, concerns transport in aeroplanes by JAA member states, and is based on ICAO Annex 6 (and is the equivalent of FARs Part 121).

Others include JAR 25, for large aeroplanes, based on Annex 8, and is the equivalent to FARs Part 25, and so on:

- **JAR 23 & 25** - regulations for small and large aircraft, respectively
- **JAR 145** - requirements for Approved Maintenance Organisations (AMOs)
- **JAR FCL** - Flight Crew Licensing between member states with minimum formality, based on ICAO Annex 1, with suitable amendments:

- **FCL 1** - aeroplanes
- **FCL 2** - helicopters
- **FCL 3** - medicals
- **FCL 4** - flight engineers (one day)
- **FCL 5** - balloon and glider licences
- **JAR OPS** - Commercial Air Transportation
  - **JAR OPS 1** - Aeroplanes
  - **JAR OPS 3** - Helicopters
- **JAR FTL** - Flight Time Limitations (not ready yet)

In other words, the JAR *rules* are a layer of paperwork that sits between ICAO and national laws. As such, they must be given recognition by the national legal process and are not necessarily the law of the land. EASA *laws*, however, are a different story, and override national legislation, assuming they have been ratified.

EASA

Although JAA was essentially European-based, other countries, such as Nigeria and the United Arab Emirates, have adopted the standards as well (they are called CAR OPS in the UAE). However, just to confuse matters, the JAA was replaced by EASA, or the *European Aviation Safety Agency*, which is the European Community's answer to the FAA, that is, a "real" aviation authority, which is set to try to bring things further back to ICAO standards.

EASA's mission is to promote the highest common standards of safety and environmental protection in civil aviation, monitoring the process through inspections and working with national authorities.

EASA formally started work on 28 September 2003, taking over airworthiness and maintenance issues within the EU Member States. During 2003, airworthiness and maintenance JARs were transposed or converted into EASA regulations, with some, such as JAR 21 and 145 becoming *Implementing Rules* (IRs) through *Commission Regulations*, and others becoming AMCs and *Certification Specifications* (CS) through Agency decisions. As they get converted, they arrive on EASA's website.

EUROCONTROL

Eurocontrol is a civil and military organisation formed from 38 member states across Europe which integrates air navigation services in Europe uniformly, for the best economic and environmental impact. Plus, of course, extracting as much money from you as possible.

It is supposed to be responsible for the safety of air navigation, but is more commonly known as a centralised place for filing flight plans, which saves you filing for every country you cross over. The *Central Flow Management Unit*, or CFMU, receives flight plans, checks them, and redistributes them as required over an area called the IFPS Zone, which consists of forty states and is slightly larger than Eurocontrol itself.

You can access the CFMU through the Network Operations Portal on the Eurocontrol website, where you will also find information (updated daily) on planning restrictions, etc., plus much reference information.

The CFMU evaluates traffic demand to ensure that the flow rate is not over the capacity of the airway.

When there is heavy demand, you may have to wait on the ground until a departure slot is available (filing a flight plan is also a request for a slot).

A slot is a 15 minute window, lasting from 5 minutes before the Calculated Takeoff Time (given in the Slot Allocation Message) until 10 minutes after. If you can't meet the slot, you must send a delay message to IFPS. There are many other messages concerning the improvement or otherwise of slots.

1 - LICENCES & RATINGS   010 04

You need a licence to fly as a crew member in any aircraft. When exercising its privileges during flight time, you must also carry a medical certificate and a document containing your photograph.

Part FCL

You must have a valid licence and rating that complies with Part FCL to fly as crew in an EASA-registered aircraft. The licence may have either been issued by an EASA member state, or come from another ICAO one, and been validated (licences issued by one EASA State are accepted without formality by others). Validations last up to one year, *if the base licence remains valid*, and further ones are subject to agreements within EASA. Users of such licences must otherwise comply with Part FCL. You need permission from a Contracting (ICAO) State if you fly in or over it in an aircraft from another and your licence does not meet full specifications.

You may not act as a pilot, except for tests or instruction, without an appropriate class or type rating (and medical), which essentially means that you can't hold a licence just by itself - there must be some sort of type rating on it (in fact, the ratings are what give you permission to fly - the licence gives you permission to hold ratings). Licences must be kept current and bear a valid *certificate of revalidation* for any ratings you wish to use. The holder must also have undertaken *differences training* under paragraph 2.235 of Part FCL, if there is a need to fly an aircraft within the variations allowed on a type rating, but which has significant differences, with particulars in the personal flying log book under the relevant paragraph.

Licences are valid for life, and there is no limit to the number of ratings on them (although not all of them can be used at any time), but *licences are not valid without the signature of the holder in ink*. An EASA licence may be transferred to another state if you are employed there or have established *normal residence*, which means you live there for at least 185 days in the year, with personal or occupational ties.

If you are over 60, you need dual controls and a second pilot qualified as PIC who is under 60. That is, you can only engage in commercial air transport in a multi-crew environment, and you must be the only one. If you're over 65, forget it. The minimum and maximum ages for an ATPL are 21 and 59.

If you fail a test, you cannot use the privileges of the relevant rating, even if there is time left on the original.

Skill Test

A skill test is a demonstration of skill for licence or rating issue, including oral exams.

Recent Experience

To carry passengers, you must do at least 3 takeoffs and landings (with circuits) in an aircraft of the same type, or approved simulator, in the previous 90 days. Without an IR, one of those landings must have been at night, if you want to fly at night.

Recording of Flight Time - 2.080

Normally, flight time to be credited towards a licence must be flown in the same category of aircraft as the licence (or rating) sought. All solo, dual or PIC flight counts in full towards the requirements for a higher licence. 50% of P2 (co-pilot) time is also counted, but Part FCL counts it in full on machines which require more than one pilot (must be countersigned by the PIC). SPIC time must be countersigned by the instructor. Examiners may log PIC if the test is passed.

Flight time is the total time from when an aircraft first moves under its own power with the intention of taking off until it comes to rest after the flight, so it includes taxi time. This is what goes in your log book and on customer invoices. *Air time*, on the other hand, is between wheels off and when they touch the Earth again. This is what goes in the Tech Log.

A number of flights on the same day, returning to the same departure point, with intervals between them of less than 30 minutes are counted as one flight.

Courses

You can have modular or integrated training (full time ground and flight training from an approved organisation). You need a minimum knowledge of maths, physics and English, which the school has to ensure you have, and they have to certify that you have done the ground school.

MODULAR

This route is for people with a PPL, who wish to stagger their training over a longer period. Any variations from the requirements (you may have non-ICAO licences) are dealt with by the training organisation, but such decisions are always subject to CAA approval.

Medicals

Flight Crew Licences, other than radio licences, are not valid without a medical certificate, which is renewed from time to time. *Currency begins on the date the medical assessment is issued.* EASA medicals are only issued for professional and private pilot licences for aeroplanes and helicopters. Flight Engineers have different arrangements.

You may not act as flight crew if you know or suspect that your physical or mental condition renders you unfit to do so. In other words, you may not exercise licence privileges once you are aware of a decrease in your medical fitness that makes you unable to exercise them safely. *Medicals are only valid if you meet the initial issuing requirements.* A Board of Inquiry or insurance company may interpret the words "medically fit" a little differently than you think if you fly with a cold or under the influence of alcohol or drugs. In any case, you should talk to a medical examiner as soon as possible in the case of:

- admission to a hospital or clinic for over 12 hours
- surgery or other invasive procedures
- regular use of medication
- regular use of correcting lenses

In addition, you should inform the authorities in writing of significant personal injuries involving your capacity to act as a member of a flight crew, or illness that lasts for more than 20 days (on the 21st day), or pregnancy. In these cases, your medical is suspended, but it can be reinstated after an examination, or if you are exempt from one. It can be given back directly after pregnancy.

You can spend up to 12 hours in a clinic or hospital before having to inform the authorities. A holder of a medical certificate must seek advice from an AME before medical treatment commences.

Exceptionally, a medical can be deferred for a single period of up to 6 months for flight crew members engaged in non-commercial operations.

CLASS 1

Although intended for professional licences, a PPL holder may hold one of these at any time. It is valid for 12 months if you are under 40 and 6 months if you are over (but 12 months when multi-crew). When a license holder with a Class 1 Medical certificate passes 40 years of age, the validation period changes from 12 to 6 months, unless you are multi crew.

CLASS 2

Required for the PPL. The initial issue can be done by any aviation medical examiner. If your national licence does not meet Class 2 standards, you can still exercise the privileges of that licence. The validity is 60 months until you are 30, 24 months until you are 50 and 12 months until 65. It is 6 months thereafter. Thus, a Class 2 medical for a 44-year old is valid for 24 months.

Commercial Pilot Licence

You can exercise all the privileges of a PPL.

You can be PIC or P2 of any machine for which you have a type rating on non-public transport flights, PIC for public transport on machines certificated for single pilot operation, or P2 of any type included for any purpose.

You need an IR to fly aeroplanes over 2300 kg on CAT, except flights beginning and ending at the same aerodrome, inside 25 nm. You also need one for IFR in, B or C airspace.

You can do PPL instructing or testing (with appropriate FI rating), in an aeroplane owned, or operated under a flying club where you and the student are members.

You can only do the above in an aeroplane that you can fly as PIC on a private flight, on aerial work or a public transport flight as above.

AGE

You must be at least 18. The maximum validity is 5 years.

MEDICAL FITNESS AND VALIDITY

You must have a Class 1 Medical, which is valid for 12 months under 40 and 6 months over that, but you may exercise PPL privileges until the end of the PPL period. The licence is maintained by a Class 1 Medical.

KNOWLEDGE

Modular or integrated training, as appropriate.

EXPERIENCE

For the CPL course, 80 hours dual, 100 PIC, to include 50 cross-country, with a flight over 300 nm, stopping at two different aerodromes. Also, 5 hours night (3 dual, with 1 cross-country), with 5 solo takeoffs and landings, and 10 on instruments, 5 of which can be done in a simulator. A PPL holder may be credited with up to 50% of any hours flown before the course (up to 40, or 45 if you have a night rating). For the CPL/IR course, as above, but with 100 hours on instruments, 50 being instruction, with up to 25 on the ground or 40 in a sim. The other 50 as SPIC.

ATPL

PRIVILEGES

As for the CPL, but you can be PIC on big aircraft (over 5700 kg). To carry passengers, within the previous 90 days, you must have done 3 takeoffs and landings as sole manipulator of the controls of a similar aircraft. In any case, the total number of persons is 4.

AGE

You must be at least 21.

MEDICAL FITNESS AND VALIDITY

You must hold a Category 1 Medical, which is valid for 12 months if you are under 40 and 6 months when over, but you may exercise PPL privileges until the end of the usual PPL period. The Medical Certificate maintains the licence.

EXPERIENCE

1500 hours, with 500 multi-pilot, 250 PIC (can include 150 PIC U/S), 200 cross country (100 PIC or PIC U/S), 75 on instruments (30 ground) and 100 at night (PIC or PIC U/S). You can do 100 hours in a simulator and 750 in an aircraft.

Flight Radio Telephony Operator Licence

You must be at least 16, although you can operate a radio under the supervision of an FI below that. The maximum validity is 10 years, if standalone, otherwise use the validity of an associated licence. It is normally issued for VHF, unless you pass a separate HF exam, or hold a CPL/ATPL (H), where you have passed the radio nav exams and are exempt. An exemption is also in place to operate without an FRTO licence for aircrew under training.

PRIVILEGES

You can use the radios in any aircraft with automatic frequency control, using external switching devices.

Flight Instructor

The minimum age is 18. You may act as an FI for PPL issue with CPL theory passed and an FI rating. You can instruct for the CPL with 500 hours plus 200 hours of instruction. You must have completed 15 hours on the relevant type in the preceding 12 months. 3 year validity.

Ratings

A *rating* is an entry in a licence stating special conditions, privileges or limitations pertaining to it. Although all the nonsense concerning the *issue* of your licence must have been done in *one* EASA state, you can obtain a rating in *any* EASA state. However, the details will be entered into your licence by the State that issued it. There is no limit to the number of ratings you can have. An examiner's rating lasts for up to three years.

MULTI CREW

Successful completion of the training is required before obtaining the first multi-pilot type rating.

CLASS RATINGS

Class Ratings cover *groups* of aircraft, such as single-engined, multi-engined, land, water, etc. They mostly apply to aeroplanes, where your licence can be issued, for example, for *single-pilot, single-engined aeroplanes* (helicopters are licensed by type). Such ratings are valid for two years.

TYPE RATINGS

Type ratings apply to any aircraft needing 2 pilots, any helicopter, and *any considered necessary*. To obtain one, you must pass a *skill test*.

Your licence will be issued with one type on it. Subsequent type ratings will theoretically need 5 hours each, but Part FCL allows this to be reduced to 3 hours by the ATO, *if* the ATO considers you to have enough time on a similar enough type, *and* if this discretion is written into their training manual. A first turbine type will need 5 hours. Type ratings are valid for 1 year *from the date of issue*.

NIGHT QUALIFICATION

For aeroplanes, you need 5 hours overall night training (3 dual, and 1 hour dual navigation) and 5 takeoffs and landings as PIC at night. The course is 5 hours ground instruction and 10 hours by sole reference to instruments, on top of any beforehand, plus 5 at night (3 dual and 5 solo circuits), all inside 6 months.

INSTRUMENT RATING

You must hold at least a PPL with night rating, or a CPL, and a radio licence. You also need 50 hours cross country, with 10 in the appropriate class. For multi-engined machines, you must have 55 hours instruction, 10 of which must be in multi-engined machines. 20 or 40 may be done in FNPT 1s and FNPT 2s, respectively. The IR is valid for 12 months.

2 – RULES OF THE AIR   010 05

Aircraft bearing the nationality and registration marks of a Contracting (ICAO) State must obey these Rules of The Air (Annex 2), wherever they may be, but **local state rules take precedence**. However, over the high seas, the Rules apply without exception, except where a State has supplied "an appropriate ATS authority", in which case the ICAO rules become subordinate to it.

Compliance & Authority

In flight or on aerodromes, you must comply with:

- The *General Rules*

plus, when in flight, either of:

- The *Visual Flight Rules* (VFR), or
- The *Instrument Flight Rules* (IFR)

according to the flight conditions (you can fly IFR in VMC). It is the responsibility of the PIC to comply with them, whether at the controls or not, but the Rules may be departed from *when absolutely necessary* for safety reasons.

Before starting a flight, the PIC must become familiar with *all appropriate information*. This should include (when not near an aerodrome, and when IFR), current weather reports and forecasts, allowing for fuel requirements and alternative courses of action. The PIC has final authority as to the disposition of an aircraft *while in command* - for aeroplanes, this is between when the doors are first closed and opened again at the end of a flight.

Intoxicating Liquor, Narcotics or Drugs

You may not act as pilot or flight crew while under the influence of intoxicating liquor, or any narcotic or drug, by which your capacity to act as such is impaired.

PSYCHOACTIVE SUBSTANCES

People whose functions are critical to safety (e.g. safety-sensitive personnel) must not act as such while under the influence of psychoactive substances that impair human performance.

Trivia: Coffee and tobacco are excluded from the Annex 1 definition of psychoactive substances, but Coca Cola, Pepsi, Tea, and others containing caffeine, are not.

Protection Of Persons & Property

NEGLIGENT OR RECKLESS OPERATION

Aircraft shall not be operated in a reckless or negligent manner that may endanger life or the property of others.

MINIMUM HEIGHTS

ICAO Annex 2 Paragraph 3.1.2

You may not fly over any congested area of a city, town or settlement, or over open-air assemblies of people, below a height that allows you to safely make an emergency landing (that is, without undue hazard to persons or property on the surface), except when taking off or landing, or with permission. IFR and VFR restrictions have their own headings, below.

CRUISING LEVELS

Refer to *Instruments*.

TRANSITION ALTITUDE

Refer to *Instruments*.

Aircraft Restrictions

The following must be done under conditions prescribed by the appropriate authorities and with clearances from the relevant ATS unit.

- Dropping Or Spraying
- Towing. A glider and whatever is towing it are *one aircraft* under the towing PIC
- Parachute Descents (aside from emergency descents)
- Aerobatic Flight

Formation Flight

This must be done by pre-arrangement with the PICs concerned. In controlled airspace, it must also be done under conditions issued by the relevant ATC, which shall include:

- operating as a single aircraft for navigation and position reporting
- separation between aircraft is the responsibility of the flight leader and the PICs, including when they are joining up and breaking away
- aircraft must be at least 1 km (½ nm) horizontally and 30 m (100 feet) vertically from the flight leader

Unmanned Free Balloons

Their operation must minimise hazards to persons, property or other aircraft, as per Appendix 4.

Avoiding Collisions

There are rules about how aircraft should be flown around other traffic, such as *not in such proximity to other aircraft as to create a collision hazard*.

RIGHT OF WAY

Even when you have right of way, you must take any necessary action to avoid collision (in other words, even with clearance, commanders are responsible for not hitting other machines). Another aircraft with an emergency gains priority over you.

GIVING WAY

If you must give way, you must not pass over or under, or cross ahead of, the other aircraft unless you are far enough away not to create a risk of collision, taking due note of wake turbulence. Aircraft with right of way should maintain course* and speed.

*ICAO says *heading and speed* - you might see both.

Approaching Head-On
If there is a danger of collision, each must alter course to the right.

Convergence
If a steady relative bearing is kept between two aircraft at the same altitude, they will eventually collide.

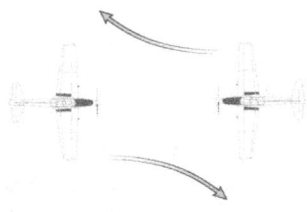

When two aircraft are converging in this way, the one coming from the right has the right-of-way, except that:

- power-driven, heavier-than-air aircraft (flying machines) give way to airships, gliders and balloons.
- airships give way to gliders and balloons.
- gliders give way to balloons.
- power-driven aircraft give way to aircraft that are seen to be towing or carrying loads.

When two balloons converge at different altitudes, the higher one must give way.

The rules do not state which way you have to turn.

Overtaking
You are overtaking when approaching another aircraft from behind *at less than 70° from the longitudinal axis*, which means that, at night, you should not be able to see its port or starboard navigation lights. **Aircraft being overtaken have right of way**, and the overtaking aircraft, whether climbing, descending or in horizontal flight, must keep out of the way by altering course to the right (*well clear* on the ground) until well past and clear, even if relative positions change. Gliders in UK may go right or left.

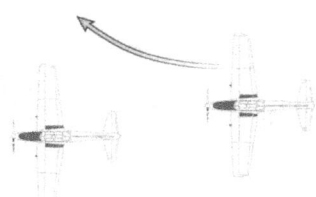

Landing
Except where ATC dictate otherwise, or in an emergency, aircraft landing or on finals have right of way over others in flight or on the ground or water. Where several are involved in landing, *the lowest has right of way*, as long as it does not cut in front of another on finals, or overtake it. However, power driven heavier-than-air aircraft must give way to gliders. *An aircraft whose pilot is aware that another is compelled to land shall give way to it.*

Taking Off
Aircraft taxying on the manoeuvring area must give way to those taking off or about to take off.

Surface Movement
If there is a danger of collision between two aircraft taxying on a manoeuvring area:

- when approaching head on, or approximately so, each shall stop or, where practicable, alter course to the right to keep well clear
- when converging, the one with the other on its right shall give way
- aircraft being overtaken shall have right of way, and overtaking aircraft shall keep **well clear**

Aircraft taxying on manoeuvring areas must stop and hold at all runway holding positions unless authorised by the Tower. They must also stop and hold at all lighted stop bars, and may proceed further when the lights are switched off. Aircraft landing and taking off must be given priority over emergency vehicles.

Details of position markings and signs are in Annex 14.

Lights & Signals
If more than one light is needed to comply with the Rules of the Air, only one should be visible at a time. Where a light must show through specified angles horizontally, it should be visible from 90° above and below. Lights showing in all directions must be visible horizontally and vertically. You may switch off or reduce the intensity of flashing lights if they *adversely affect the performance of your duties*, or *subject outside observers to harmful dazzle*.

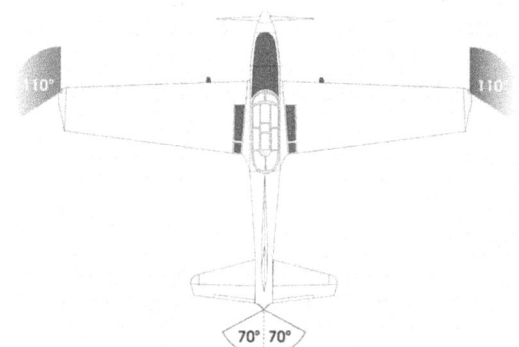

Anti-collision lights are there to attract attention, and are seen from all directions. **Navigation lights** are intended to show your relative path to an observer, and are set up so that only one can be seen by another aircraft at any time. Other lights may be displayed if they cannot be mistaken for either.

Between sunset and sunrise, you must show anti-collision and navigation lights. On the manoeuvring area, in addition, aircraft must display lights that show extremities of their structure (unless they are stationary and otherwise lit up adequately), and engine running lights (a red one must be displayed when the engine is running in any case). By day, anti-collision lights must be used in flight.

AIR LAW
2 - Rules Of The Air

Simulated Instrument Flight

Fully functioning dual controls must be installed and a fully qualified pilot must occupy the other seat (presumably trained to fly from there) with suitable vision forwards and sideways. If not, an additional observer in full communication with the safety pilot must be carried to fill in the gaps.

Operations Near Aerodromes

Aircraft on or near an aerodrome must, whether or not in an ATZ:

- observe other traffic to avoid collisions
- conform with or avoid the traffic pattern
- make all turns to the left on approach or takeoff
- unless otherwise instructed, land and take off into wind, unless the runway configuration or ATC dictate otherwise

Water Operations

Aircraft or vessels coming *from the right* have the right-of-way. If you are approaching another aircraft or vessel head-on, you must alter heading to the right to keep well clear. Aircraft or vessels being overtaken have the right of way, and overtakers must alter heading enough to keep well clear. Aircraft landing on or taking off from the water shall, as far as practicable, keep well clear of all obstacles and avoid impeding their navigation.

At night, lights conforming to the *International Regulations For Preventing Collisions At Sea* (Revised 1972) must be shown, unless it is impractical, in which case lights conforming as closely as possible must be shown.

Flight Plans   010 05 03
                     033 05

ATC clearance is needed before operating a controlled flight (in controlled airspace), or a portion of one. You get the clearance by filing a flight plan. A *controlled flight* is any flight subject to ATC clearance, which is *authority to proceed only as far as known traffic is concerned*.

There are many reasons for doing so - first of all, they help get you into the system, even if it isn't quite the route you asked for. Next, they help with radio failures, as, once you're in, everyone knows where you're supposed to be (more or less) and can act accordingly. Then there are forced landings, where an educated guess may be made as to your position, followed by statistics, and, finally, because the law says you must, before any flight:

- within controlled airspace under IFR
- in advisory airspace
- in designated areas or along routes where ATC provide flight information, alerting and SAR services, and where they liaise with military units and ATC from other States to avoid interception for identification
- across international borders
- under Special VFR if you wish the destination aerodrome to be notified
- over 40 km when MTOM exceeds 5700 kg

Tip: You can file a flight plan at any time - this also ensures that your destination is notified of your timings.

They are also *recommended* for flights over water more than 10 nm from the coast and/or over sparsely populated or remote areas.

 A filed flight plan has no changes. A *current flight plan* is a filed flight plan plus amendments and clearances.

Plans are filed with the ATSU at the departure aerodrome, but if there isn't one, you can do it by telephone or radio (in that order) to the unit serving the aerodrome. It can be done on line in some areas.

REPETITIVE FLIGHT PLANS

These are electronic flight plans on file for **IFR flights** operated regularly on at least ten consecutive occasions or days, to save you refiling over and over. Such plans must have a high degree of stability or similarity. However, on 25 December, individual plans must be filed for all flights. If you can't use an RPL (change of ID, etc.), you must cancel it and file an individual flight plan. Permanent changes require at least 7 days' notice. Temporary ones, no later than 30 minutes EOBT. See PANS-ATM, Part 11.

ADVANCE NOTICE

You should always file a plan as far in advance as possible, but at least 60 minutes before EOBT (*Estimated Off Blocks Time*)* is preferable for IFR (30 VFR). In any case, the time in advance should never be less than 30 minutes.

*When an aircraft moves under its own power in UTC.

The time in advance comes from the times before radar, when procedural separation was used, involving the use of paper strips containing the details of your flight. Based on your TAS, ATC would work out your ETA at the reporting points in your flight plan with a flight computer.

Flights subject to Air Traffic Flow Management (ATFM), must file at least **3 hours** in advance. A modification message must be sent if there is a delay of more than 15 minutes to the EOBT.

If there is a delay of more than 30 minutes for a *controlled flight*, or an hour for an *uncontrolled* flight (VFR), you should either amend the plan, or cancel it and submit a new one.

 You can file a flight plan up to 5 days in advance, but if you do not notify the date in Box 18, the takeoff time you specify is assumed to be the next time it occurs. You must include the date if you file over 24 hours ahead.

In flight, a plan must be received at least 10 minutes before the service is required, except for abbreviated flight plans and. RPLs.

Below are the details for each slot in the flight plan form (shown overleaf). Boxes with hyphens in front of them have sub-boxes. Refer also to Jeppesen, page 144.

AIRCRAFT ID

Without a company callsign, use the registration. Hyphens are not used.

AIR LAW
2 - Rules Of The Air

FLIGHT RULES & TYPE OF FLIGHT

The former goes in the first part of Box 8. V=VFR, I=IFR, Y=IFR/VFR, Z=VFR/IFR (the changeover point goes in the route section). Next is the *type* of flight. G=General Aviation, S=Scheduled, N=Non-scheduled, M=Military, X=Other. A Bell 206 would use G.

NO & TYPE OF AIRCRAFT, WAKE TURBULENCE

Box 9 is also in two parts. The first is the number of aircraft, and the second the ICAO code for the type (e.g. BH06 for Bell 206, but the full list is in ICAO Doc 8643). You would only fill in the first part if there are more than one aircraft, so the minimum number to be inserted would be 02. For the Wake Turbulence Category, H=Heavy (above 300,000 lbs), M = Medium (15500-300000 lbs) and L = Light based on *maximum certified takeoff mass*.

EQUIPMENT

Box 10, for comms, nav and transponder, in that order (COM, NAV, SSR). N=None or U/S. S=Standard, that is, VHF, ADF, VOR and ILS. C=LORAN, D=DME, F=ADF, G=GPS, H=HF RTF, I=INS, J=Data Link, K=MLS, L=ILS, M=OMEGA, O=VOR, R=RNP certified, T=TACAN, U=UHF, V=VHF, W=RVSM certified, X=MNPS certified, Y=8.33 KHz*, Z=other.

For SSR, N=Nil, A=Mode A, C=Mode C, X=Mode S without ident and PA, P=Mode S with PA & no ident, I=Mode S with ident & no PA, S=Mode S with ident & PA. For example, SD/C is commonly used for standard equipment with DME and Mode C transponder.

*Required above FL 195 in the European region.

DEPARTURE AERODROME

In Box 13, use the ICAO code or ZZZZ with an entry in Box 18 (Other Information) if there isn't one.

DEPARTURE TIME

Anticipated **off-block time** in hours and minutes UTC, preferably over 30 minutes ahead. Any delays more than that must be notified to ATC.

 Clocks must be within ±30 seconds, or 1 second when using Datalink. You need a time check (usually from ATC) before operating a controlled flight.

CRUISE SPEED, ALTITUDE, ROUTE

Box 15 is for the flight planned TAS. **N=Knots, M=Mach Number, K = Km**. Changes in speed of more than 5% of TAS or M0.01 must be indicated.

For cruising level, A=*Altitude* in hundreds of feet ASL (e.g. A050). F is for *Flight Level*. Under *Route*, include speed and altitude changes, airway numbers and waypoints on the route. DCT (*Direct*) is assumed unless they are included. IFR routes should be used when available, as per IFR charts. For EASA purposes, you are at the correct level within ±300 feet of the assigned level. In UK and Canada, and for ICAO, it's 200 ft for Mode C verification and level occupancy. Under ICAO, a shift of 300 ft is required to confirm that an aircraft has vacated or passed a level, but then it must be consistently within 200ft for level flight.

 You should report level when the altimeter reads exactly the desired level, and not try to get clever by leading it within the tolerances above because the controller's job is to validate that the readout is within 200ft (or 300ft EASA) of that level. Otherwise you will be asked to switch off Mode C or squawk 0000 (assuming the problem is with encoding and not the altitude you are at). That's why, before getting that far, the controller will ask you to confirm your altimeter setting and altitude (or FL). Standby altimeter(s) should rule altitude error out.

 Do not use odd symbols in the ROUTE section. No symbols or words are needed between checkpoints when the route is direct. If it is an airway, just name it.

From Eurocontrol:

- The tolerance value used to determine that Mode C-derived level information displayed to the controller is accurate shall be ±60 m (±200 ft) in RVSM airspace
- The criterion used to determine that a specific level is occupied by an aircraft is ±60 m (±200 ft) in RVSM airspace
- An aircraft cleared to leave a level is considered to have commenced its manoeuvre and vacated the previously occupied level when the SSR Mode C-derived level information indicates a change of more than 90 m (300 ft) in the anticipated direction from its previously assigned level
- An aircraft in climb or descent has crossed a level when the SSR Mode C-derived level information indicates that it has passed this level in the required direction by more than 90 m (300 ft)

DESTINATION, EET, SAR, ALTERNATE

In Box 16, use the ICAO code. For VFR, the EET is from takeoff until overhead the destination (including intermediate stops, although these are naturally rare with IFR). For IFR, it's to the IAF. Use your own SAR time, up to 24 hours after ETA. A takeoff alternate is required when the weather at the departure aerodrome is at or below landing minima, or you cannot return to it for other reasons. If you need one that doesn't have an ICAO ID, use ZZZZ, with the details in Box 18 after /ALTN. If you land at another destination, you must inform the planned destination within 30 minutes of the planned ETA.

OTHER INFORMATION

Use 0 if there is nothing to add. RMK/ means *Remarks*.

SUPPLEMENTAL INFORMATION

Fuel endurance (total usable fuel) in hours and minutes goes in Box 19. You can use TBN if you don't know how many passengers you will have. Place an X through the U and V if you don't have the VHF and UHF emergency frequencies (243 & 121.5 MHz). Cross out the survival equipment you don't have, and add with whom the arrival report will be filed. Finally, include your name and licence number, and the person to be notified if SAR is initiated.

AIR LAW
2 - Rules Of The Air

FLIGHT PLAN

PRIORITY	FF	
ADDRESSEE(S)		
FILING TIME		
ORIGINATOR		

SPECIFIC IDENTIFICATION OF ADDRESSEE(S) AND/OR ORIGINATOR — N = GA Commercial

- **3 MESSAGE TYPE**: (FPL) — Blank if only one
- **7 AIRCRAFT IDENTIFICATION**: GPACO — No Hyphens
- **8 FLIGHT RULES**: V (Y = IFR/VFR, Z = VFR/IFR)
- **TYPE OF FLIGHT**: G
- **9 NUMBER**: (blank)
- **TYPE OF AIRCRAFT**: BH06
- **WAKE TURBULENCE CAT**: L
- **10 EQUIPMENT**: SD/C
- **13 DEPARTURE AERODROME**: EGLL
- **TIME**: 0600 — Estimated Off-Blocks Time (EOBT) in UTC — A for Altitude, F for Flight Level
- **15 CRUISING SPEED**: N0100
- **LEVEL**: A015
- **ROUTE**: DCT — <200 nm (60 in Europe), Include SID & STAR numbers
- ROUTE from where you level out: **EGGW 0130 EGGW** — Intermediate Stop
- N for Knots, K for Km — Points included should not normally be more than 30 mins or 370 km apart
- **EGGW/N0120/A030** Speed & Altitude Change
- VFR - overhead destination airfield. IFR - initial approach fix
- **16 DESTINATION AERODROME**: ZZZZ (See 18)
- **TOTAL EET HR. MIN**: 0115 — Brake release to arrival inc intermediate stops
- **ALTN AERODROME**: EGGW
- **2ND ALTN AERODROME**: (blank)
- **18 OTHER INFORMATION**: DOF/071112   DEST/5201N00002W   WAYPOINT/N0120F085
  - Date Of Flight (5 days ahead)
  - Over Waypoint at 120 kts FL 85

SUPPLEMENTARY INFORMATION (NOT TO BE TRANSMITTED IN FPL MESSAGES)

- **19 ENDURANCE** — Total endurance (excluding taxi fuel) to dry tanks
- **E/** HR MIN: 0230
- **PERSONS ON BOARD**: P/003 — Cross out what you don't have
- **EMERGENCY RADIO R/**: UHF ✗ | VHF ✗ | ELT ✗
- **SURVIVAL EQUIPMENT**: ✗ / POLAR ✗ | DESERT ✗ | MARITIME ✗ | JUNGLE ✗
- **JACKETS**: ✗ / LIGHT ✗ | FLUORES ✗ | UHF ✗ | VHF ✗
- **DINGHIES**: ✗ / NUMBER (blank) / CAPACITY (blank) / COVER ✗ / COLOUR (blank)
- **A/ AIRCRAFT COLOUR AND MARKINGS**: WHITE WITH RED/BLUE STRIPES
- **REMARKS**: ✗
- **C/ PILOT IN COMMAND**: SMITH
- FILED BY / SPACE RESERVED FOR ADDITIONAL REQUIREMENTS
- Please provide a telephone number so our operators can contact you if needed

CHANGES

Changes must be notified as soon as practicable. If there is a delay of 30 minutes over the estimated off-block time (for a controlled flight) or 1 hour (uncontrolled), you should either make an amendment or cancel the old plan and issue a new one. A significant change includes fuel endurance and number of persons on board.

CLOSING A FLIGHT PLAN

An arrival report for a flight plan that covers the whole route, or the remainder of a flight, should be made in person, by radio or datalink, as soon as possible after landing. Where a flight plan is only in force for a portion of a flight (other than the remainder), you can report to the appropriate ATS unit. If there is no ATS unit at the arrival aerodrome, the report should be made to the nearest ATS unit as quickly as practicable after landing.

If the facilities at the arrival aerodrome are known to be inadequate, you can transmit the equivalent of an arrival report to ATC just before landing.

An arrival report should consist of:

- Aircraft ID
- Departure aerodrome
- Destination aerodrome (for diversionary landings)
- Arrival aerodrome
- Time of arrival

Signals

LIGHTS & PYROTECHNIC SIGNALS

Sent from the Tower to an aircraft. Acknowledge by rocking the wings or flashing the landing lights once.

Signal	To Air	To Ground
Steady Red	Give way to others, keep circling	Stop
Red Flashes	Airport unsafe do not land	Clear landing area
Green Flashes	Return for landing	Cleared to taxi
Steady Green	You may land	Cleared to take off
White Flashes	Land after continuous green. After green flashes, go to apron	Return to start point
Bursting Red/Green Stars	You are in or near a danger area; push off	
Blinking Runway Lights		Ground staff clear areas

A red pyrotechnic means - *Regardless of previous instructions, do not land for the time being.*

Refer to *CAP 637 - Visual Aids Handbook* for full details.

VISUAL GROUND SIGNALS

Refer to *CAP 637 - Visual Aids Handbook* for full details.

MARSHALLING SIGNALS

Refer to *CAP 637 - Visual Aids Handbook* for full details.

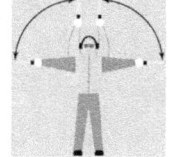

Time

Time is expressed in UTC, in hours and minutes, and seconds if required, starting at midnight.

You need a time check (usually from ATC) before operating a controlled flight.

 Clocks must be within ±30 seconds, or 1 second when using Datalink.

Air Traffic Control Service

Controlled flights must maintain continuous air-ground voice communication with the appropriate ATC on the appropriate channels, reporting the times and levels of passing compulsory reporting points, or others as requested, plus any other required information. If using Datalink, you only need to provide voice position reports when requested.

 This requirement is satisfied by SELCAL or similar automatic signalling devices. This requirement remains in effect after CPDLC has been established.

Clearances, Instructions, etc

You must comply with any clearance received and acknowledged. If you don't like it, you should say so at the time, since an acknowledgement without further comment is taken as such. You must also comply with *instructions* in the same way, unless safety is a factor. An instruction will be identifiable, but the word "instruct" may not be included. Information about flight conditions is assistance or reminders.

Clearances are valid only in controlled airspace, and there will be some form of the word "clear" in the text to identify them. *Clearances must always be read back*. They are passed slowly and clearly, since you will need to write them down, and preferably before startup, since you will not want to be bothered when taxying or hovering. They will contain the aircraft identification (as per the flight plan), the clearance limit (usually the destination) and the route, levels, changes and any other instructions, especially about departure manoeuvres. Control is based on *known traffic only*, so you are still responsible for safe procedures and good judgement - clearances do not constitute authority to violate the rules! If a clearance or an instruction is not suitable, you may request and, if practicable, obtain an amended one. Having accepted clearance for an approach, you may not deviate without further clearance. If a specific approach is not mentioned, tell ATC which one you are doing. Clearance to land, or any alternative, received from a non-radar controller should normally be passed to the aircraft before it reaches 2 nm from touchdown.

A flight plan may cover only that part of a flight that is subject to ATC, and only that part may need a clearance, as indicated in a clearance limit or reference to specific manoeuvres such as taxying, or taking off. If you think you might go to a different destination (say, for fuel planning reasons) and may have to re-clear in flight, this should be indicated in the flight plan.

Aircraft operating on controlled aerodromes shall not taxi on the manoeuvring area without clearance from the tower and shall comply with any instructions given.

For a departure, you will get the route clearance, and possibly additional instructions to provide separation:

Continue runway heading until 3000 feet, then route direct to X

When joining an airway, if you haven't already done so, you must file an airborne flight plan with the FIR before you enter. It is very unlikely you will get a clearance straight away, but will receive an *Expected Joining Time* for when they've processed the paperwork, and a place, which may be a compulsory reporting point or a navaid.

A visual approach on an IFR flight is one where only part of an instrument procedure is flown, the rest being flown visually with reference to the terrain. **It is an IFR manoeuvre**. Aircraft moving to control areas within 30 minutes of each other must be coordinated before departure clearance is issued.

The conditions affecting a controlled aircraft that is cleared to maintain its own VMC separation during a climb or descent are:

- Daylight only in VMC
- Below 10 000 feet
- The request must be made by the pilot
- ATC must issue alternative instructions if VMC conditions are lost

If you don't land at a controlled aerodrome, you must advise ATC once you stop being subject to ATC service.

ILS PHRASEOLOGY

The ICAO phrase *Cleared ILS Approach* is not routinely used in UK. Instead, unambiguous phraseology is used that includes a positive descent instruction to ensure that it takes place only when safe, that is, when the aircraft is clear of other traffic patterns (otherwise, you could descend to the altitude of the final approach point at any time after receiving the clearance).

ATC will say *Report Established On The Localiser*, which, if you recall from the Instrumentation section, is within half scale deflection. Only when established will you be given the instruction to *Descend On The ILS*. Both may be combined when things are busy.

LAND AFTER

A landing aircraft may be allowed to touch down before a previous aircraft that has already landed has cleared the runway *in daylight hours* if:

- The runway is long enough and there is no evidence that braking will be adversely affected
- The landed aircraft is not required to backtrack
- The controller is satisfied that the crew of the landing aircraft can see the landed aircraft clearly and continuously until it vacates the runway
- The flight crew of the following aircraft is warned

Responsibility for separation lies with following aircraft.

ADHERENCE TO FLIGHT PLAN

You must stick to the flight plan unless a request has been made for a variation and a *clearance obtained*. In an emergency, of course, you can do what you need and sort it out afterwards. For inadvertent changes:

- **Deviation from track** - regain track as soon as practicable
- **TAS variations** - you must inform ATC if the average variation of your TAS is expected to be more than ±5% from that given in the flight plan
- **ETA changes** - if the ETA for the next applicable reporting point, FIR boundary or destination aerodrome (in that order) is going to change by more than **2 minutes**, you should inform ATC. For VFR, the ETA is overhead the destination airport. For IFR, at the first associated fix.

Requests for *intentional* changes must include:

- **Change of cruising level**: aircraft identification; requested new cruising level and cruising speed at this level, revised time estimates (when applicable) at subsequent flight information region boundaries
- **Change of route:**
    - **Destination unchanged**: aircraft identification; flight rules; description of new route of flight including related flight plan data beginning with the position from which requested change of route is to commence; revised time estimates; any other pertinent information
    - **Destination changed**: aircraft identification; flight rules; description of revised route of flight to revised destination aerodrome including related flight plan data, beginning with the position from which requested change of route is to commence; revised time estimates; alternate aerodrome(s); any other pertinent information

If VFR flight is no longer possible and you do not have an Instrument Rating, you may have to leave controlled airspace and land ASAP if a new clearance or SFVR is not possible. Unless otherwise authorised or directed by ATC, you must, so far as practicable, keep to the centre line of any ATS route, directly between the navigation facilities and/or points defining that route. When using VORs, you should change over as close as possible to the change over point (usually half way).

VFR FLIGHTS - WEATHER BELOW VMC

When it becomes evident that flight in VMC under the current flight plan will not be practicable, a VFR flight operated as a controlled flight shall:

- request an amended clearance to allow continuance in VMC to the destination or to an alternate, or to leave the airspace, or
- if no clearance can be obtained, continue in VMC and notify ATC of the action being taken (either to leave the airspace concerned or to land at the nearest suitable aerodrome), or
- if within a control zone, request authorization to operate as a special VFR flight, or
- request clearance to operate IFR

POSITION REPORTS

An aircraft on a controlled flight must maintain two-way communications and make position reports. Those at compulsory reporting points require the time and level and usually the ETA of the next position. Additional reports must be made at additional points when requested. If there are no designated reporting points, position reports must be made at intervals prescribed by ATC.

AIR LAW
2 - Rules Of The Air

The *standard position report* contains the:
- aircraft identification
- position, time
- flight level/altitude
- next position and time over
- ensuing significant point

in that order.

 EUR SUPPs impose additional restrictions. See SUPPs Section 3.2. Controlled flights using Datalink only need to provide voice position reports when requested.

 SSR Mode C transmission of pressure altitude may satisfy the requirement for level information in position reports - see PANS-ATM, Part II (Doc 4444).

In controlled airspace, you must report to ATC the time, your position and level at whatever reporting points or intervals of time as may be established, or as directed.

COMMUNICATION FAILURE

If two-way communication is lost, a controller can check if you are receiving by giving instructions and watching you obey them. The instructions can be given out over any frequency they think you might be listening on.

If an aircraft experiencing radio failure is not identified, separation shall be applied between identified and unidentified aircraft along the expected route until it is known, or can be safely assumed, that you have passed through the airspace, landed or gone elsewhere.

Generally, you should report malfunctions (including navigation aids and transponders) under IFR in controlled airspace immediately to ATC.

Otherwise, if you are in, or have received a clearance to enter, controlled airspace, you must listen out on the appropriate frequency for messages or further clearances, set the transponder to 7600 and try to establish communications with ATC any way you can.

Tip: You can leave controlled airspace by descent as well as sideways.

UNDER VMC

If your radios fail in VMC, you are assumed to:
- continue under VMC
- land at the nearest suitable aerodrome
- report your arrival to the appropriate ATC

UNDER IMC

In general, continue under the current flight plan to the designated navigation aid serving the destination aerodrome, until the Expected Approach Time* (EAT) last acknowledged and received. If no EAT has been received, start your descent at, or as close as possible to, the ETA on the current flight plan. You must land within 30 minutes of the ETA, or the last EAT, whichever is later.

*EAT, or *Expected Approach Time*, is when ATC **estimates** that an aircraft, after a delay, can start an approach from the holding fix (sometimes known as a *Timed Approach Procedure*). It is issued if it is *known* that there will be a delay of 10 minutes or more, or if a hold for 30 minutes or more is *anticipated*. It is not a clearance as such, but when ATC expects to be able to grant one. Changes of over 5 minutes from the original time should be communicated by ATC as soon as possible. The *Onward Clearance Time* is when you can expect to leave a fix other than the IAF.

DEPARTURES

If your flight plan has been filed and accepted, and your initial clearance is to a flight level below your flight planned level:

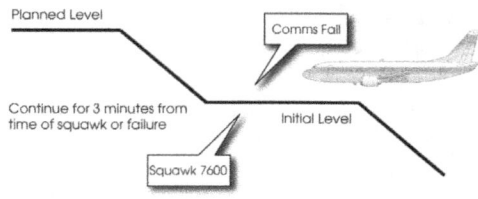

Squawk 7600 and maintain the last assigned level for 3 minutes, then climb in accordance with the flight plan.

If your flight plan has been filed and accepted, and you are being vectored away from your flight planned route:

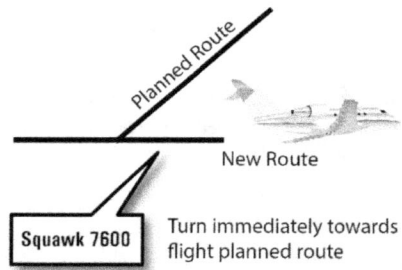

Squawk 7600 and turn immediately towards the flight planned route.

EN ROUTE

If your flight plan has been filed and accepted and radar is not being used:

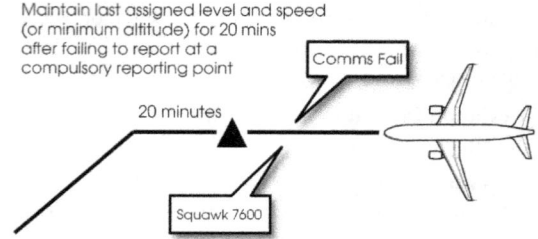

Maintain the last assigned speed and level (or minimum flight altitude, if higher) for **20 minutes** after your failure to report your position over a compulsory reporting point. Then follow the filed flight plan.

AIR LAW
2 - Rules Of The Air

If radar is being used:

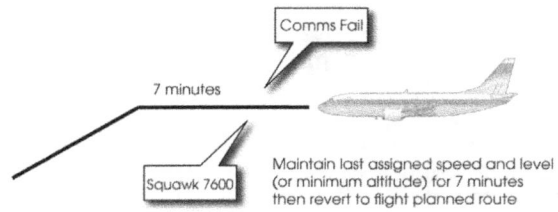

- Maintain the last assigned speed and level (or minimum altitude if higher) for **7 minutes** after:
  - Selecting 7600
  - The last assigned level or MSA is reached
  - Failure to report over a compulsory reporting point

  Then adjust speed and level as per the filed flight plan.

- when being radar vectored, or when directed (by ATC) to use RNAV offset without a specified limit, rejoin the flight planned route no later than the next significant point, allowing for MSA.

- proceed according to the current flight plan route to the appropriate navaid for the destination, and hold until required to descend

- start descent from the navaid at, or as close as possible to, the last EAT received and acknowledged or, if there isn't one, at, or as close as possible to, the filed ETA

- Complete a normal instrument approach

- land, if possible, within 30 minutes of the times above

Descent & Landing

If you have received and acknowledged an EAT:

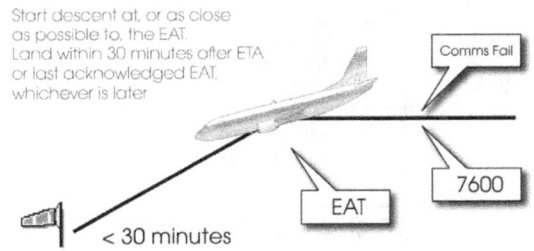

If you have NOT received and acknowledged an EAT:

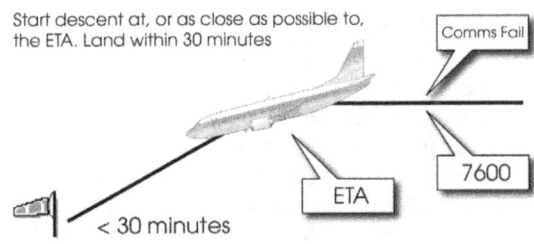

Termination Of Control

A controlled flight shall, except when landing at a controlled aerodrome, advise ATC as soon as it ceases to be subject to air traffic control service.

Unlawful Interference

ATC must be informed if unlawful interference occurs on a flight, especially with respect to changes in the flight plan. If this cannot be done by the PIC, the hijackers must do it (joke). See also *Annex 11*, below.

Interception

Under Article 9 of the Convention, states reserve the right to stop aircraft from other states flying over their territory. As a result, aircraft may need to be led away from an area or be required to land at a particular aerodrome.

If an aircraft assumes a position slightly above and ahead of you (normally on the left), rocks its wings, then turns slowly to the left in a level turn, you have officially been intercepted. Your response should be to rock your own wings and follow (the interceptor will normally be faster than you, so expect it to fly a racetrack pattern and rock its wings each time it passes). After interception, try to inform ATC and make contact with the intercepting aircraft on 121.5 or 243 MHz. You should also squawk 7700 with Mode C, unless otherwise instructed. If the intercepting aircraft's instructions conflict with those from ATC, you should obey the interceptor.

If the aircraft performs an abrupt breakaway manoeuvre, such as a climbing turn of 90° or more without interfering with your line of flight, you have been released. If it lowers its gear and descends to a runway (or helipad), you are expected to land there (the accepted phrase is *Descend*). However, you can make an approach to check the area, then proceed to land. Lowering your gear or showing a steady landing light means you acknowledge the instruction. Flashing the landing light means the area is unsuitable, as does overflight with the gear up somewhere between 1000-2000 feet. At night, the substitute for rocking wings is irregular flashing of navigation lights.

Here are some pertinent phrases:

Phrase	Meaning
Callsign	My callsign is....
Can Not	Sorry, can't do that.....
Am Lost	Where the hell am I?
Wilco	Your instructions will be complied with
Mayday	Help!
Hijack	Have been hijacked
Land	I would like to land at....
Descend	I require descent
Repeat	Say that again
Follow	Follow me
	From Intercepting Aircraft
Callsign	What is your callsign?
Recleared	Ignore last clearance, receive a new one
Descend	Descend for landing
You land	Land here
Proceed	You may proceed

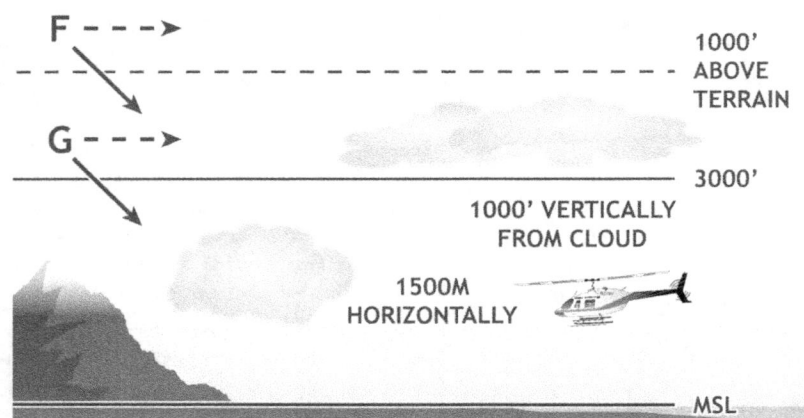

VMC Visibility & Distance From Cloud

A VFR flight must be operated in conditions of visibility and distance from clouds equal to or greater than those given in the table below.

OVERWATER

Flight shall not be conducted overwater out of sight of land when the flight visibility is less than that for the appropriate airspace, and in any case when it is less than 1500 m. The minimum cloudbase shall be 600 feet.

CLASS A AIRSPACE

This is the most restrictive, requiring the most experienced pilots. Except for gliders, all flights are IFR - you may not convert to VFR.

CLASS B AIRSPACE

You must be clear of cloud, with visibility at least 8 km (5 km below 10,000' AMSL). In UK, Class B airspace only exists above FL 245.

CLASS C, D OR E AIRSPACE

You must be at least 1500 m horizontally and 1000 feet vertically from cloud in visibility of at least 8 km (5 km below 10,000' AMSL). Class C airspace does not as yet exist in UK.

CLASS F & G AIRSPACE

Above 3,000 ft AMSL, or 1,000 AGL, whichever is higher, you must be at least 1500 m horizontally and 1000 feet vertically from cloud in visibility at least 8 km (5 km below 10,000' AMSL*).

Airspace	A	B	CDE	FG	
				Above 3000 ft AMSL or 1000 ft above terrain whichever is higher	At & below 3000 ft AMSL or 1000 ft above terrain whichever is higher
Distance From Cloud	No VFR	1500 m horizontally 1000 ft vertically			Clear of cloud Surface In Sight
Flight Visibility		8 km at and above 10,000 ft AMSL* 5 km below			5 km, but 1500 m by day**

VFR FLIGHT PLAN AND ATC CLEARANCE

Except for gliders, and unless otherwise authorised by ATC, before entering Class B, C or D airspace during notified hours of watch, you must file a flight plan and get clearance beforehand. During the time in there, you must keep a continuous listening watch on the appropriate frequencies and comply with any instructions.

Gliders flying by day in controlled airspace must remain at least 1500 m horizontally and 1000 feet vertically from cloud in visibility of at least 8 km. The same applies for mechanically driven aircraft without radios, but visibility becomes 5 km, *with previous permission*.

Visual Flight Rules (VFR)

Although the airspace you fly in comes in several varieties, it is, essentially, controlled or uncontrolled, although it's fair to say that, in Europe, once you are above 3000 feet, most airspace is controlled in one form or another. As the names imply, in the first you do as you're told (by ATC), and, in the second, you, as pilot, are responsible for the safe conduct of the flight, which means avoiding obstacles and other aircraft, which you can only do if you can see them. The official definition of a flight under VFR is "one conducted under Visual Flight Rules", conveniently leaving out what the Rules are.

The Visual Flight Rules govern flight in *Visual Meteorological Conditions* (VMC). A flight may only be conducted under VFR if the conditions exist all the way along the route. When the weather gets so bad that you can't see where you are going, *Instrument Meteorological Conditions* (IMC) apply, and you must fly under *Instrument Flight Rules* (IFR), described below, although you can fly IFR at any time, even in VMC (you just have to obey tighter rules for obstacle clearance, etc., since you're not supposed to be looking out of the window). The definition of IMC is actually a negative one, being "weather precluding flight in compliance with Visual Flight Rules", and where this happens could depend on the type of airspace, as well as the weather.

Class A airspace is always IFR, for example, as are some control zones. Normally, it's the pilot's responsibility to determine visibility and judge whether to accept a clearance but, when taking off from or approaching to land at aerodromes within Class B, C or D airspace, the visibility reported by the relevant ATC is the visibility *for the time being*. In other words, ATC do not usually declare airspace under their control as IMC or not.

VFR flights shall be operated at a level appropriate to the track, as per the Tables of Cruising Levels when above 3000 ft MSL.

Unless authorised, VFR flights shall not be operated above FL 290, or at transonic and supersonic speeds. However, no clearance shall be given above FL 290 in RVSM airspace.

SPECIAL VFR

Except when clearance is obtained from ATC, a VFR flight cannot enter or leave a CTZ when the ceiling is less than 1500 feet, or the visibility is less than 5 km.

Special VFR is used when you want to enter a Class A CTZ or any other type of CTZ at night or in IMC or when the weather isn't good enough for VFR (there is no VFR at night, except Special VFR in a control zone). It's a legal technicality, to allow VFR aircraft to go where the law says only IFR-equipped aircraft may fly. The aircraft *must be IFR-equipped*.

You must be clear of cloud and in sight of the surface, and get clearance from ATC, which means radios (except in Class E airspace, but there must still be a way of informing ATC of flight termination). You are absolved from the 1500-foot rule, but not being able to glide clear of a built-up area in emergency.

LOW FLYING

Except when taking off or landing, or with permission, you may not fly over congested areas of cities, towns or settlements, or over open-air assemblies of people below 1,000 feet above the highest obstacle within 600 m (2,000 feet). Otherwise, not less than 500 feet AGL or water.

Instrument Flight Rules (IFR)

Generally, all flights in IMC must be conducted under IFR, although you can actually fly IFR at any time, even if the weather is clear - for example, you must obey IFR rules at night. The essential difference between IFR and VFR is that tighter margins are applied for avoiding obstacles and choosing your altitude according to your direction. To start a flight under IFR, the weather must be *equal to or better than* specified minima at the destination or its alternate. In Class A, B, C, D, E or F Special Use Advisory airspace, you must also have ATC clearance, and observe any conditions included. You also need a minimum instrument and navigation equipment level.

IFR clearances can be received in plain language, or as a *Standard Instrument Departure*. They must be read back, except where a SID is in force and you got the clearance on the ground before departure, or by electronic means. However, ATC may request a read back at any time. You may deviate from clearances and instructions as far as necessary to avoid a collision, if you are responding to an advisory from ACAS or TCAS, or GPWS. As soon as possible afterwards, however, you must carry on with the last clearance or instruction, and inform ATC.

MINIMUM LEVELS

Unless you are:

- taking off or landing
- on a route that allows it
- otherwise authorised

You must be above the minimum altitude established by the State or, if none:

- over high terrain or in mountainous areas, at least 2000 ft above the highest obstacle within 8 km of your estimated position
- elsewhere, at least 1000 ft above the highest obstacle within 8 km of your estimated position, taking into account the navigational accuracy that can be expected in the conditions.

IFR TO VFR

If a flight plan was filed, tell ATC that you are cancelling IFR and the changes you require. In VMC only, you must use the words *Cancel IFR*.

You may not cancel IFR unless you expect to be in VMC for a reasonable period of time.

WITHIN CONTROLLED AIRSPACE

You must use these IFR levels in controlled airspace.

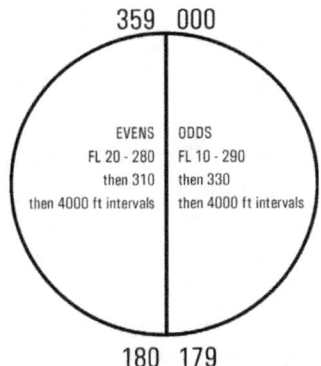

Magnetic tracks are used, or in polar areas above 70° of latitude, grid tracks.

OUTSIDE CONTROLLED AIRSPACE

Above 3000 ft amsl, or above the appropriate transition altitude, whichever is higher, you must fly at a semicircular level appropriate to your magnetic track, using 1013.2 hPa or 29.92 inches, or whatever the competent authority dictates, unless otherwise instructed by ATC or in an established traffic pattern.

3 - METEOROLOGICAL SERVICES

Aireps

Air-reports from aircraft follow this format:

Section 1	Section 2	Section 3*
Aircraft ID	ETA	Air Temperature
Position	Endurance	Wind direction
Time		Wind speed
FL/Altitude		Turbulence
Next position/ Time over		Icing
Next significant point		Humidity (if available)

*To be transmitted as follows:

- *Temperature Plus* or *Temperature Minus*, followed by the corrected air temperature in 2 digits in °C
- *Wind Direction*, in °T
- *Wind Speed* in km/hr or knots
- *Turbulence*:
  - *Light*, or less than moderate.
  - *Moderate*, more severe, but you are still in control. ICAO definition: *Moderate changes in attitude and/or altitude but the aircraft remains in positive control at all times. Usually, small variations in air speed. Changes in accelerometer readings of 0.5 to 1.0 g at the aircraft's center of gravity. Occupants feel strain against seat belts. Loose objects move about. Food service and walking are difficult*
  - *Severe*, with abrupt changes, and being temporarily out of control
- *Icing*:
  - *Light*, or less than moderate
  - *Moderate*. Change of course and/or altitude desirable
  - *Severe*. Change course and/or altitude now
- *Humidity* - Relative Humidity in %

Aircraft outside the Alger, Cairo, Casablanca, Tripoli and Tunisia FIRs are exempt from routine requirements except on parts of routes crossing the Mediterranean.

Aircraft without navigation equipment that can produce an instantaneous wind readout are also exempt.

A special observation report must be made if the temperature changes by over 2°C from the latest report.

4 - AERONAUTICAL CHARTS

Refer to Jeppesen for the symbols, and *Airspace Classification*, below, for Danger Area specifications.

7 - REGISTRATION MARKS

Registration marks are assigned by the *state of registry* or a *common mark registering authority*. The common mark is selected from the series of symbols in the radio call signs allocated to ICAO by the ITCU.   010 03

The nationality mark is the one that tells you what country the aircraft belongs to, as assigned by ICAO (e.g. *G* for UK, *N* for USA), and registration marks are combinations of letters or numbers assigned by the State of Registry, which should not be confusable with the five-letter combinations used in the International Code of Signals, or other common groupings used in aviation, so any containing the word PAN or the letters XXX or TTT should not be used. When the first character of the registration is a letter, it must be preceded by a hyphen.

Otherwise, marks must be in Roman characters, displayed to their best advantage, after the features of the aircraft, and be clean and visible. They must also be on a fireproof metal plate in a prominent position on the fuselage, wing (microlight), or basket or envelope (balloon).

Position and Size of Marks

On heavier than air aircraft (including kites), the first choice for marks is on the lower surface of the port wing, unless they stretch across both, if possible equidistant from the leading and trailing edges, with the tops towards the leading edge. They must be at least 50 cm, or as large as possible, either on the outboard sides, between the wings and tail, or on the vertical tail surface, at least 30 cm tall, or as large as possible, with a margin of at least 5 cm along each side. If there's a choice, use the largest area for the 30 cm letters.

Width, Spacing and Thickness

The width of standard letters (e.g. other than *I*, *M* and *W*), and the length of the hyphen must be two thirds of the height. *M* and *W* must be somewhere between two thirds and the height itself. *I* must be one sixth of the height. The lines making up letters and hyphens must be one sixth of the height of the letters. Spaces must be equal to a quarter or half the width of a standard letter, all being equal.

8 - AIRWORTHINESS   010 02

Annex 8 prescribes the minimum standards for aircraft that overfly or land in State territory (the *international* carriage of passengers and cargo). Standards apply to the complete aircraft, including power units, systems and equipment. Any assessments of airworthiness must take into account the ratio of the specified load to the weight of the aircraft in terms of aerodynamic and inertia forces, or ground reactions.

Airworthiness operation limitations (that is, publishings for each aircraft) must include *all limiting mass, C of G position, mass distribution and floor loading information*.

Certificate Of Airworthiness

The certificate of airworthiness is required by Article 31 of the Chicago Convention, issued (or rendered valid) by the State of Registry, whose responsibility it is to develop and adopt requirements to ensure continued airworthiness.

Airworthiness certification varies between countries. For example, an aircraft that is considered to be airworthy in Canada is also airworthy in the USA (by agreement), but not in Europe (under EASA). Similarly, an aircraft that is airworthy in one European country is airworthy all over Europe but not in the US or Canada.

The term *Airworthy* means that the aircraft is in the same state as it left the factory (aside from accumulated grime), so when you are replacing parts, you are bringing an aircraft back to its factory state (it must comply with the flight manual, any placards, and the ICAO Airworthiness Technical Manual). The airworthiness state of any aircraft must also be reported back to the authorities every year. The registered owner does this on a suitable form. The *captain* is responsible for ensuring airworthiness before flight (engineers sign for their work, not the aircraft).

The Certificate of Airworthiness is known as a *flight authority*. It states that the aircraft concerned must be operated and maintained in accordance with the Type Certificate Data Sheets, which are the basis for the Limitations section of the flight manual. A copy of the C of A must be kept in the aircraft when it is being operated. It is also possible to fly the aircraft if it is not airworthy by issuing another type of flight authority, called a *Permit To Fly*, which is used by engineers to get an aircraft back to base if it needs work done on it. **You may not carry passengers with a Permit To Fly!** There will be other limits if the aircraft has been built for a particular purpose and may be dangerous.

When an aircraft is no longer airworthy, permission can be obtained from the State to fly without fare-paying passengers on board to where it can be restored to an airworthy condition.

Only an aircraft maintenance engineer may certify an aircraft for a flight authority, so his task is to determine to what standard any maintenance has been done.

Maintenance

Hard Time Maintenance exists when known deterioration is limited to an acceptable level by maintenance actions at certain periods. For example, a part might be changed every 2 years regardless of the hours it has flown.

On-condition Maintenance is a preventive process in which an item is monitored continuously or at specified periods. Its performance is compared against an appropriate standard to see if it can stay in service. In other words, as long as an item meets the standards, it will not need maintenance.

Otherwise, maintenance can be *Scheduled* or *Unscheduled*, which basically speak for themselves. Both are supposed to ensure that an aircraft is kept at an acceptable standard of airworthiness. Depending on the performance category and its maximum authorised weight, there will be different schemes covering this, but the nature of General Aviation means that aircraft are very often not seen by an engineer from one check to the next (but the owner/pilot may be able to do some elementary tasks, as described below).

Types of check include 50-hour and 100-hour, which can be extended by 5 or 10%, respectively, for scheduling, but this should not be used as part of normal operations (lack of planning on your part doesn't justify an emergency on an engineer's part). In between, there will be times when components need to be changed, either on a planned or emergency basis.

The *Maintenance Schedule* contains the name and address of the owner or operator and the type of aircraft and equipment fitted. It lays down the periods when every part will be inspected, together with the type and degree of the inspection, including periods of cleaning, lubricating and adjustment. They are written for each aircraft, and are subject to CAA approval before moving to a new one.

Repaired components are certified as serviceable with a *Maintenance Release* (there is one for every removable component). Such a document must accompany every part coming from storage. If it comes directly from another airworthy aircraft, a maintenance release document is not required.

Only two signatures apply to certification, those of:

- an **Aircraft Maintenance Engineer** (AME)
- an **Aircraft Maintenance Organisation** (AMO), which is a group of AMEs and/or specialists who may either perform "normal" maintenance or specialised work on propellers, engines, etc

Where parts of an aircraft are too large to be moved, the technicians are brought in to do the work, as part of an AMO, using *field service standards*, meaning that after a certain point the work must be done by the manufacturer.

Parts may be used from other manufacturers, if the *original manufacturer* says so. Thus, to use non-Lycoming pistons in a Lycoming engine, you need permission from the aircraft manufacturer, not Lycoming. This is because the same engine may need to be run differently in another aircraft because of airframe vibration, or whatever.

If there is no information from the manufacturer, the most recent "standard industry practices" and materials should be used. The common reference for standard practices is a 500-page manual of methods that have been tested over time called FAA Advisory Circular 43.13.

After work is done, an *Aircraft Maintenance Engineer* (AME) signs a *Certificate of Maintenance Review*, which means that the work done meets applicable standards and the aircraft is released back into service (it may be just a box on the Tech Log page). However, you are still responsible for ensuring that the aircraft is airworthy. Not being an engineer, the only way you can find this out (aside from a thorough preflight) is to check the Technical Log before flight, in which you should find an alert card which shows when the next servicing is due. Simply subtract the current aircraft hours from that figure to see how many hours' flying you can do before the next check.

After an abnormal occurrence (such as a lightning strike or a heavy landing), the aircraft must be inspected (and not flown until it has been done). If nothing has to be taken apart, the inspection can be done by the PIC.

Maintenance is recorded into a Technical Log.

DUPLICATE INSPECTIONS

A duplicate inspection is first made and certified by one qualified person and subsequently made and certified by another. One is required when stuff like engine or primary flight controls have been modified, repaired, replaced or disassembled. Away from base, this may be carried out by a pilot qualified on type.

ELEMENTARY WORK

This is technically maintenance, but as some tasks are not subject to Maintenance Review, an AME is not required to do them (but not with public transport). A licensed pilot, who also owns or operates an aircraft, may do elementary work on it, normally limited to those under 2730 kg with a Private or Special Category C of A. This might include changing spark plugs or tyres, batteries, or bulbs, etc. (the key is that no special tools are required, or that the structure is not affected). Details of the work must be entered into an appropriate log, and certified. As stated above, elementary work needs no maintenance release.

AIRWORTHINESS DIRECTIVE

ADs are mandatory repair instructions from an aircraft manufacturer, sent directly to the aircraft owner. The verification of its completion is done by an AME, but the responsibility always lies with the owner.

Defects

MINIMUM EQUIPMENT LIST

The company will hold permission for you to operate with some equipment unserviceable for a limited time, subject to the *Minimum Equipment List* (MEL), which is based on the Master MEL produced by the aircraft manufacturer (there are none approved for aircraft less than a certain weight). A Master MEL will not necessarily apply to everyone, as circumstances differ, so operators must prepare their own, which may not be less restrictive than the Master. It will be found in the Ops Manual, Part B, *Type Technical Information*.

MELs are lists of systems and equipment installed on an aircraft, showing how many of them can be defective and for how long. In other words, they are changes to the type design that do not require recertification. In some cases, additional restrictions are applied - for example, you may have to troubleshoot, inspect or secure items as conditions to be met before takeoff. As the MEL is a detailed list, it follows that *any item related to airworthiness that is not on it must be working* at the time of dispatch. However, MELs are usually black-and-white and only address operation (or not) and not degraded performance, such as unusually slow landing gear or excessive fuel consumption, which means that not every possible combination is allowed for, or the additional workload from multiple defects. You still therefore need to exercise some professional judgment, but there are circumstances where operation is definitely not permitted and, although you are given the authority to operate with specified equipment unserviceable, you don't have to if you don't think it's safe (which is a point you may have to argue sometimes with your employer). When in doubt, consult an engineer, but remember that their signature in the log book only guarantees their work, so the responsibility is still yours. Once an MEL is approved, compliance is mandatory. They are not transferable between operators.

If you have a problem before taxying out (actually, until the machine is moving under its own power for the purpose or preparing for takeoff), you would refer to the MEL. After that point, try the Emergency Procedures section in Part B of the Ops Manual (which has the MEL in it anyway), which should contain Emergency Checklists from the Flight Manual.

CONFIGURATION DEVIATION LISTS

CDLs are the structural equivalent of MELs, allowing operation with minor bits missing.

DEFERRED DEFECTS

These are defects which will not prejudice the safety of a flight, but should be rectified as soon as practicable after it. For example, the minimum navigational equipment for IFR operations in most areas is 2 VOR + 1 ADF or 1 VOR + 2 ADF, ILS, DME, Transponder, Marker and 2 720 channel VHF Comms. However, you can fly when one of the above is unserviceable if it is not reasonably practical to effect repairs or replacements before taking off, especially as outside maintenance should not be used without approval. If you, as commander, are satisfied that the forecast weather, latest route information, regulations, etc. allow your flight to be safely made, you may complete one flight to a place where repairs may be effected.

 The idea is to get you to a place where a defect can be fixed, or to fly while awaiting spares - it's not for skimping on maintenance.

As a general rule, a defect is allowed for a *return* to base; you should not normally *depart* with one (see *MEL*, above). Defective equipment should be isolated from the remainder of the relevant system by removing fuses, blanking pipelines, locking selectors, or anything else that will promote safety, including labelling the equipment as defective (on gauges, the label needs to be placed so that no readings can be taken). Because you must be aware of the condition of an aircraft to exercise proper judgement, all defects should be entered in the relevant part of the Technical Log. The aircraft should not then fly until they are either cleared or deferred, which means that it can be scheduled for a more convenient time, such as the next service, when the machine is in the shop anyway. Details of deferred defects should also be recorded on the *Deferred Defects Sheet*, which is carried with the Tech Log. A new page must then be started, but if the same one must be used (you might have run out), the defect(s) must be clearly identified by numbering. When a deferred defect is finally cleared, the entries are made on the current Log page and DD Sheet (not the originals), with suitable cross-referencing.

9 - FACILITATION   010 10

This concerns the ease with which passengers and cargo can come and go between countries with the minimum of paperwork (see Article 37 of the Convention, as amplified by Articles 22 and 23). It therefore deals with such subjects as customs & immigration, and anything dealing with the *safety*, *regularity* and *efficiency* of air navigation:

> States agree to adopt all practicable measures, through special regulations or otherwise, to facilitate and expedite navigation by aircraft between the territories of contracting States, and to prevent unnecessary delays, especially in administration of the laws relating to immigration, quarantine, customs and clearance.

Aircraft *not* engaged on scheduled international air services flying to or through any designated international airport under Article 24 are admitted temporarily free of duty, and may remain there without security or customs duty being required.

No more advance notice than that required for ATC purposes and the authorities concerned is required, meaning that filing a flight plan is enough. *The minimum notification required for a non-scheduled flight from one State to another is the information in a flight plan at least two hours ahead of its arrival at a previously designated international airport.*

Documentation

You need the same documentation when arriving by air as if you had come by ship.

Under 3.19, contracting states should not require exit visas from their own nationals wishing to tour abroad nor from visitors at the end of their stay. Where passengers do not require visas, no identification other than a passport may be requested.

When a transit passenger has to stay until the next flight for lack of facilities or whatever reason, visas are not required before arrival when the passenger is to leave that state within two (2) days from the day of arrival.

Documents for entry and departure of aircraft are accepted in hand-written block lettering, in ink.

GENERAL DECLARATION

This is a customs form, used when inbound or outbound from a country. It consists mainly of information about the route and date of flight, the aircraft and the state of health of the crew on board. However, if the same information is available in other ways, it should not be required. It is signed by the PIC (who is responsible for its completion), or an agent. You need two copies outbound, and three inbound.

INBOUND AND OUTBOUND AIRCRAFT

Document	Outbound	Inbound
General Declaration	2 copies	3 copies
Cargo Manifest	2 copies	3 copies
Simple Stores List	2 copies	3 copies

Embarkation/Disembarkation cards may be required by some States. These must be available free of charge and completed by passengers in legible handwriting unless block lettering is specified. Inadmissible passengers will be transported away from the State of arrival *by the operator*, who may recover costs from them (the phrase is *shall not be precluded from recovering from such person any transportation costs arising from his (her) inadmissibility*).

Inspection of crew members and their baggage must be done as expeditiously as possible. States must accept oral declarations of baggage from passengers and crew.

CREW MEMBER CERTIFICATE (CMC)

The CMC is an ID card for crews (flight and cabin), which is valid for the term of employment. It is an alternative to a licence, which doesn't have a photo, and therefore isn't enough for identification purposes. The CMC may be used for temporary admission to a State, and does not require a passport or visa, if you stay within the bounds of the relevant city and depart on your next scheduled flight.

Passengers/Baggage/Cargo

There should be no mixing or contact between passengers who are and are not subject to control once past the security barrier. If it does occur, passengers and baggage must be re-screened before boarding the aircraft.

Unaccompanied baggage must be cleared by a simplified procedure distinct from that normally applicable to cargo.

The handling, forwarding and clearance of mail shall comply with the relevant procedures from the Universal Postal Union.

Where a Cargo Manifest is required, apart from the information included in the standard format, only the following three items are required in addition:

- Air waybill number
- Number of packages related to each number
- Nature of goods

10 - TELECOMMUNICATIONS

You can only use English, but French is the alternative language in English-speaking countries. See *Communications* for more.

11 - AIR TRAFFIC SERVICES

Whether you need ATC or not depends on the *type of traffic* and its *density*, with due allowance for the weather and "other factors". Once that has been sorted out, the airspace is carved up and designated according to the services provided.

`010 07`

ATC's mission in life is to *prevent collisions* (between aircraft in flight, and between aircraft, vehicles and obstructions on the manoeuvring area) and *expedite traffic*. They also help with rescues and provide advice and information, which is disseminated through various offices, including area control centres, terminal control units, etc.

There are three services provided:

- **Air Traffic Control Service,** including:
  - *Aerodrome Control Service*
  - *Approach Control Service*
  - *Area Control Service*
- **Alerting Service**
- **Flight Information Service**

All are covered in more detail later in this section.

PANS-ATM (Doc 4444)

PANS-ATM stands for *Procedures For Air Navigation Services - Air Traffic Management*. Previously known as PANS RAC, its procedures specify in greater detail than Annexes 2 and 11 the procedures to be followed by ATS units, so are of passing interest to pilots. They are complementary to those Annexes, so they do not have to be followed.

 ATC objectives in Annex 11 do not include stopping you hitting the ground, except when an IFR flight is being radar vectored or you are given a direct routing which takes you off an ATS route.

Emergencies & Contingencies

An aircraft in a state of emergency gets every form of assistance that a controller can provide, such as higher priority and service.

STRAYED OR UNIDENTIFIED AIRCRAFT

A *strayed aircraft* is one that has deviated significantly from track *or which has stated that it is lost*. An *unidentified aircraft* has been observed or reported to be operating in a given area, but whose identity has not been established.

AIRPROX

A situation in which, in the opinion of a pilot or controller, the distance between aircraft as well as their relative positions and speed have been such that the safety of the aircraft involved was or may have been compromised (ICAO).

AIR TRAFFIC INCIDENT REPORT

An Air Traffic Incident Report should be filed by a PIC whenever he considers that a serious occurrence involving air traffic occurred:

- aircraft proximity (airprox), or
- serious difficulty resulting in a hazard to aircraft caused by:
  - faulty procedures
  - non-compliance with procedures, or
- failure of ground facilities

The initial report should be made by R/T to the ATS unit with which the aircraft is in communication at the time of the incident, or by telephone to the appropriate controlling authority soon after arrival.

SYSTEM CAPACITY & FLOW MANAGEMENT

The various parts of ATC must be able to cope with the anticipated traffic demands, or the maximum number of aircraft that can be accepted over a given period of time. Flow management comes into force when traffic demand exceeds the nominated capacity. However, certain flights may be exempt, or given priority.

GENERAL PROVISIONS FOR AIR TRAFFIC SVCS

Flight information and alerting services are provided:

- *Within a FIR* - by a Flight Information Centre, unless delegated to another unit with adequate facilities.
- *Within controlled airspace* (and at controlled aerodromes) - by the relevant ATS units

Airspace Structure

Airspace can be restricted in certain ways, according to its density of traffic, the nature of the operations, the level of safety required and the National interest.

AIR LAW
11 - Air Traffic Services

To fly under IFR in controlled airspace, you need an Instrument Rating.

FLIGHT INFORMATION REGION (FIR)

This is a (generally large) area, within which flight information and alerting services are provided. It goes up to, but not including, FL 245 in UK, which has the *Upper FIR* above it. Examples are *London* and *Scottish*, for the Southern and Northern halves of the UK. The procedures in an *Upper Flight Information Region* (UIR) need not be the same as in the underlying FIR.

The bottom limit of a UIR must be the same as the upper limit of the FIR, to coincide with a VFR cruising level.

The minimum ATS service inside a FIR is a Flight Information Service and Alerting Service.

CONTROL AREAS & ZONES

These are part of an FIR, and are areas in which ATC service is provided to IFR flights.

- **Control Zones** (CTRs) are areas around busy airspace in which IFR traffic is controlled (VFR traffic may or may not be, depending on airspace notification*). They are typically Class D airspace, starting at the surface and going up to specified levels of controlled airspace above, or the height on the map (or in the AIP). Lateral limits extend to at least 5 nm (9.3 km) from the centre of the aerodrome(s) from where approaches are made.

*A CTR may be Class A (IFR only) or B, C or D if VFR aircraft become involved.

In a CTR, ATC provides separation between Special VFR and IFR flights.

- **Control Areas** (CTAs) extend upwards from at least 700 feet (200 m) above the surface.

They do not touch the ground as Control Zones do. Aerodromes underneath a CTA use the same QNH. In the above picture, the Gatwick CTR (Control Zone) is inside the CTA.

AIRWAYS & ROUTES

An airway is a *control area* in the form of a *corridor of protected airspace equipped with navaids*, serving popular routes between centres. Ground (ATC) controllers assume responsibility for the safe separation of the flights within them, as they will be Class A airspace (see below).

For airways defined by VORs, the width starts 5 nm either side of the centreline, diverging at 4° for 70 nm, until 20 nm wide. The width remains constant between 70-140 nm, where it diverges again at 4° until a width of 40 nm is reached at 280 nm out, at which point it remains constant (see below). For NDBs, the corridor starts 5 nm either side, diverging at 7° until a width of 20 nm is reached at 40 nm out, remaining constant between 40-80 nm out, thereafter diverging at 7° until 60 nm wide at 245 nm, then remaining constant.

Controlled flights should, when on an ATS route, operate along its defined centre. On any other route, they should operate directly between navigation facilities, and change over for primary navigation from the facility behind to that ahead when on routes defined by VOR.

Changeover points are established by reference to VORs, and should normally be the midpoint of segments of 110 km (60 nm) or more, except where routes are complex.

ROUTE DESIGNATORS

These make sure that routes have unambiguous references (saves you using Lat & Long all the time), and relate to levels of navigation performance or aircraft. The basic designator consists of a letter and a number (1-999), with a prefix (*K* for Helicopters, *U* for Upper Airspace, *S* for Supersonic) and a supplementary letter for the type of service. *Y*, for example, indicates RNP 1 route at and above FL 200, where turns must be made within a certain tolerance. Here are the figures:

- **Y** - at and above FL 200, where all turns between 30° and 90° must be within a radius of 22.5 nm
- **Z** - at and below FL 190, where all turns between 30° and 90° must be within a radius of 15 nm.
- **F** - where only advisory service is provided
- **G** - where only FIS is available in Class G airspace

There should not be up to 5 characters, and not more than 6. Type letters are:

- A, B, G, R for non-RNAV routes that are part of a regional network, and L, M, N, P for RNAV routes
- H, J, V, W for non-RNAV routes that are not part of a regional network, and Q, T, Y, Z for RNAV routes

TERMINAL MANOEUVRING AREAS

A TMA is a CTA that accepts several routes inbound and outbound and is intended to protect aerodromes that are near to each other. TMAs are usually Class A airspace.

CONTROLLED AERODROMES

These exist where it is deemed that ATC service should be provided to aerodrome traffic. A Tower is involved.

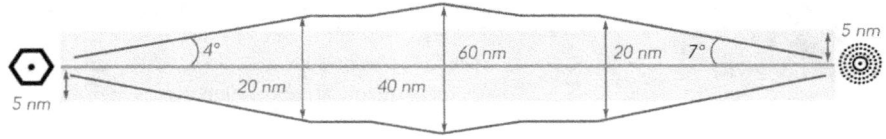

AIR LAW
11 - Air Traffic Services

AERODROME TRAFFIC ZONE (ATZ)
These protect aircraft operating near aerodromes. The symbol on a map looks like this:

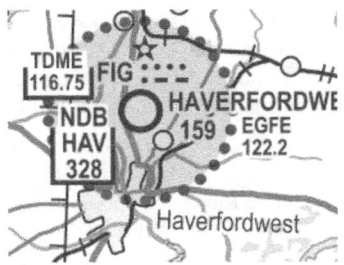

Being a zone, the vertical dimensions start from the surface and go up to the top level of 2,000 feet. The circle is centred on the mid-point of the longest runway - if this up to 1850 m long (inclusive), the radius will be 2 nm, or 2.5 nm if the runway is longer. Naturally, these dimensions will change, so check the AIP.

ATZs are only active during notified hours of watch.

You may not fly in an ATZ without the permission of the relevant ATS unit. Even if it is out of the notified hours, there may still be traffic.

PROHIBITED, RESTRICTED & DANGER AREAS
A **Prohibited Area** extends from ground level to a specified altitude, within which flight is prohibited.

A **Restricted Area** extends to a specified altitude, within which flight is restricted under certain conditions.

A **Danger Area** extends to a specified altitude. Inside one, activities dangerous to aircraft may take place. You are not prevented from flying through danger areas but it would be a rather silly idea, especially as you would be endangering your aircraft, which is illegal anyway.

Identification includes the nationality letters (such as EG for UK) of the State which has established the airspace, plus the letters *P*, *R* or *D* for *Prohibited*, *Restricted* or *Danger* area, respectively, followed by a number.

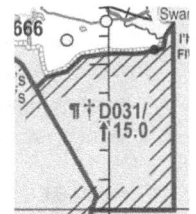

The picture represents a UK **scheduled** danger area (it has a solid outline) number 031, extending to 15 000 feet, active during published hours in the AIP.

A **notified** danger area is only active by NOTAM. It has a dashed outline:

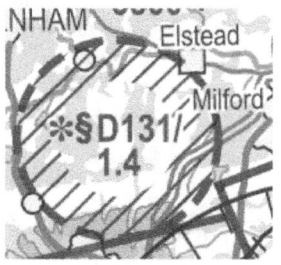

Danger area activity is notified by NOTAM and AIP. There may be a radio service that allows you to cross them, details of which will be in the AIP. Also in the AIP will be details of danger areas not on the map (below 500 feet), such as rifle ranges.

ICAO AIRSPACE CLASSIFICATIONS
European airspace comes in 7 varieties, namely Class A, B, C, D, E, F & G. The first 6 are known as *controlled airspace*, in which air traffic controllers have certain duties and responsibilities and where certain rules apply. Class G is *uncontrolled*, where only the Rules Of The Air apply. Controllers will only refer to controlled or uncontrolled airspace, not the classifications below.

CLASS A
This means most airways, and main control zones and control areas, providing the highest protection for aircraft. Separation is provided for *IFR aircraft only,* as VFR is not allowed*, from 18,000 ft to FL 600. Since clearance to enter is required, you need continuous two-way radio communication, a flight plan, a Mode C transponder and TCAS if you have 19 or more seats.

*But see *Special VFR*.

CLASS B
Separation is provided between all aircraft, IFR or VFR, from 12,500 feet (or MEA, whichever is higher) to 17,999 feet. Class B airspace may contain a control zone and TCA. Clearance is required for IFR and VFR aircraft (before entering), and position reporting is required, so you need a minimum level of radio equipment for continuous two-way radio communication. Unless you can get Special VFR, you must leave when conditions demand IFR. In UK, Class B airspace only exists above FL 245 (Upper Airspace), where there are no airways, only straight line Air Traffic Service Routes between navigation points or geographical positions known as Name Code Designators. Aircraft flying outside the routes, which have no defined width (with permission) are still in protected airspace. Visibility must be 8 km above 10,000 feet and 5 km below that, *clear of cloud*.

Class B has the same rules as for Class A except that, in theory, VFR is allowed, but not with reduced vertical separation.

CLASS C
This is very similar to Class B, but the rules concerning VFR are a little more relaxed.

Separation is between IFR aircraft, with VFR separated from IFR. VFR aircraft only receive traffic information in respect of other VFR aircraft and they require clearance to enter, so they also need a 2-way radio. If there is no ATC, Class C airspace reverts to Class E. There are no speed restrictions when IFR, but the VFR limit is 250 KIAS, below 10,000 feet (does not yet exist in UK). Visibility must be 8 km above 10,000 feet and 5 km below, plus 1500 m horizontally and 300 m vertically from cloud.

CLASS D
Most airport control areas and zones, and areas of lesser importance, so IFR and VFR traffic is allowed, but separation is provided only between IFR aircraft. However, they are informed about VFR flights (VFR traffic details are also given to VFR flights, but there is still no separation). The maximum speed is 250 kts IAS for IFR and VFR up to 10,000 feet. For VFR, visibility must be 8 km above 10,000 feet and 5 km below that, 1500 m horizontally and 300 m vertically from cloud. Two-way

radio communication is required, as is clearance to enter, so *minimum radio equipment* is *VHF comms*.

Class E

Anything that is still controlled airspace, but not meeting the requirements above, like low level airways, control area extensions, transition areas or control zones without a control tower. IFR and VFR flights are permitted, but separation is only between IFR aircraft. All flights receive traffic information as far as is practical - information is only given to VFR flights on request. The maximum speed is 250 kts IAS for IFR and VFR up to 10, 000 feet.

For VFR flights, visibility must be 8 km above 10,000 feet and 5 km below that, 1500 m horizontally and 300 m vertically from cloud. Two-way radio communication is required for IFR flights, as is clearance to enter.

Class F

Advisory Routes, where some limitations are imposed. Separation is between IFR aircraft as far as practicable (with advisory service) and all flights get flight information on request. Clearance is not needed to enter, but IFR flights need two-way radio equipment. For VFR, visibility must be 8 km above 10,000 feet and 5 km below that, 1500 m horizontally and 300 m vertically from cloud. At and below 900 m, or 300 m above terrain, whichever is higher, 5 km vis, clear of cloud, in sight of land or water. Maximum VFR speed is 250 kts IAS for IFR and VFR up to 10, 000 feet.

Class G

Anything not designated as A, B, C, D, E or F, where ATC has no authority, so it's free airspace. There's no separation service, but Flight Information Service may be provided.

For VFR, visibility must be 8 km above 10,000 feet and 5 km below that, 1500 m horizontally and 300 m vertically from cloud. At and below 900 m, or 300 m above terrain, whichever is higher, 5 km vis, clear of cloud, in sight of land or water.

Airspace Summary Table

Class	Type	Separation	Service	Speed	Radios	Clearance?
A	IFR	All	ATC	Not Applicable	Cont 2-way	Yes
B	IFR	All	ATC	Not Applicable	Cont 2-way	Yes
	VFR	All	ATC	Not Applicable	Cont 2-way	Yes
C	IFR	IFR from VFR/IFR	ATC	Not Applicable	Cont 2-way	Yes
	VFR	VFR from IFR	ATC separation from IFR VFR/VFR traffic info plus traffic avoidance on request	250 KIAS below 3050 m (10 000 ft) AMSL	Cont 2-way	Yes
D	IFR	IFR from IFR	ATC plus VFR traffic info & traffic avoidance on request	250 KIAS below 3050 m (10 000 ft) AMSL	Cont 2-way	Yes
	VFR	Nil	IFR/VFR & VFR/VFR traffic information & traffic avoidance on request	250 KIAS below 3050 m (10 000 ft) AMSL	Cont 2-way	Yes
E	IFR	IFR from IFR	ATC and VFR traffic info as far as practicable	250 KIAS below 3050 m (10 000 ft) AMSL	Cont 2-way	Yes
	VFR	Nil	Traffic information as far as practicable	250 KIAS below 3050 m (10 000 ft) AMSL	No	No
F	IFR	IFR from IFR if practicable	Air Traffic Advisory Service Flight Information Service	250 KIAS below 3050 m (10 000 ft) AMSL	Cont 2-way	No
	VFR	Nil	Flight Information Service	250 KIAS below 3050 m (10 000 ft) AMSL	No	No
G	IFR	Nil	Flight Information Service	250 KIAS below 3050 m (10 000 ft) AMSL	Cont 2-way	No
	VFR	Nil	Flight Information Service	250 KIAS below 3050 m (10 000 ft) AMSL	No	No

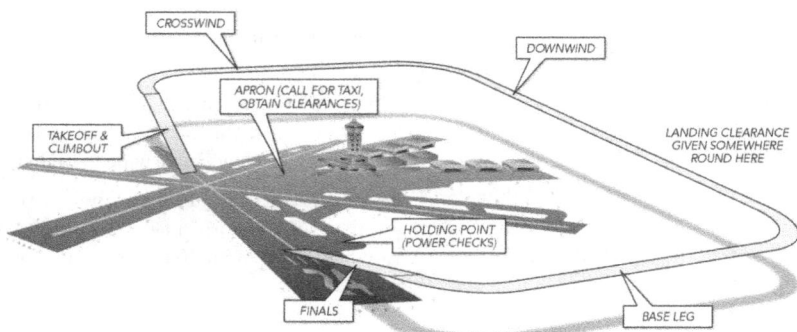

REQUIRED NAVIGATION PERFORMANCE

Navigation performance standards are classified as to how much accuracy is maintained 95% of the time, in nautical miles, for example, RNP 5 means *5 nm 95% of the time*.

Only RNAV equipped aircraft with a navigation accuracy of RNP 5 may plan for operations under IFR on ATS routes in certain European FIRs/UIRs. Equipment must:

- use accuracy equal to, or better than, 4.6 km (2.5 nm) for one standard deviation with a 95% containment value of 19.26 km (5 nm), thereby meeting RNP 5, and
- an average continuity of service of 99.99% of flight time, unless also carrying VOR/DME

Aircraft without RNAV but still with a navigation accuracy of RNP 5 will be restricted to operations on ATS routes which States may designate within their lower airspace.

Air Traffic Control Services

AERODROME CONTROL SERVICE

This occurs between control towers and aircraft and vehicles. The callsign is *Tower* or *Ground*, as appropriate.

- The **Ground Controller** handles all movements on the manoeuvring area, including aircraft and vehicles, and possibly start clearances (departure clearances given by Ground are *not* clearances to takeoff!) Typically, you would talk to Ground up to the holding point, and afterwards when landing - this helps ATC with planning and keep the tower frequency clear. It also reduces fuel waste from delays.

  Movement of vehicles and pedestrians on the manoeuvring area require authorisation from the Tower. Two-way communication facilities are normally required, except when the vehicle is only used occasionally and it is accompanied by vehicles who have them.

- For traffic close to the aerodrome, including the circuit, you talk to the **Tower**. After takeoff, you may be asked to change to Approach, but, more typically, you will stay with the Tower until clear of the area.

  Control towers issue information and clearances to aircraft under their control to achieve a safe, orderly and expeditious flow of traffic on and near an aerodrome with the object of preventing collisions between:

  - Aircraft in the traffic circuits around an aerodrome
  - Aircraft and vehicles on the manoeuvring area
  - Aircraft landing and taking off
  - Aircraft on the manoeuvring area and obstructions on it

In control zones, the Tower provides separation between Special VFR and IFR flights. In low visibility, ground movements are kept to a minimum, with protection for ILS sensitive areas.

Control towers are also responsible for alerting and must report any equipment failures. In addition, they report (to the area control centre or flight information centre) any aircraft which:

- Does not report after handover to a tower
- Having reported, ceases to maintain contact
- Fails to land 5 minutes after expected landing time

Surface wind directions given by the tower are magnetic.

The aerodrome control service will give landing clearance to an aircraft that has entered the traffic circuit without permission, if it is expedient.

SUSPENSION OF VFR

VFR operations on and near the aerodrome may be suspended by the following for safety reasons:

- The responsible area control centre
- The aerodrome controller on duty
- The appropriate ATS authority

All departures are held (except IFR ones with flight plans and approval), and all local flights are recalled or given Special VFR clearance.

MOVEMENT OF AIRCRAFT & VEHICLES

The term *runway in use* indicates the one considered to be most suitable by ATC for the prevailing conditions and traffic. You may request another runway at any time.

Above is a picture of a typical circuit, even though it is right handed. Takeoffs will normally be into wind, unless safety or conditions dictate otherwise.

The circuit is *part of* an aerodrome traffic pattern, and not *the* traffic pattern (which starts when you enter a control zone and ends in the downwind leg). The ICAO definition is: *specified paths to be flown by aircraft operating in the vicinity of an aerodrome.*

Such paths include the *crosswind leg*, which is at right angles to the runway, and is turned onto after takeoff. The *downwind leg* is parallel to the runway, and goes the opposite way to the runway in use - you make the "downwind" call just after turning on to it. The *base leg* is also at right angles, but in the opposite way and at the opposite end to the crosswind leg, from which you turn onto *final approach* (between 4-8 nm, it is a *long final*). Again, you make "base" and "final" calls just after the turn. On an instrument approach, you might call *Beacon* rather than *Final*.

In the UK, you normally make all turns to the left (but check the signals square), arriving **overhead** the landing point at 2000' AGL and at 90° to it, in a position to make a descending 180° turn over the *dead side* to arrive at circuit height over the other end of the runway, going the other way, tight crosswind. Then you join the downwind leg in the normal way, all the while looking for other traffic.

You can also join at 45° to the downwind leg, at the height published in the AIP (all circuit details will be in there, too). Only join directly downwind if there is no conflict.

WAKE TURBULENCE CATEGORIES
Aircraft are grouped as follows:

Category	ICAO & Flt Plan (kg)	UK
Heavy (H)*	136,000 or more	136,000 or more
Medium (M)	7,000-136,000	40,000-136,000
Small (S)	Not ICAO	17,000-40,000
Light (L)	7,000 or less	17,000 or less

ICAO does not split the Medium category nor do they recognise Small as a category. For timed approaches (non-radar), minima for **landing** aircraft:

- MEDIUMS behind HEAVY aircraft - 2 mins
- LIGHTS behind HEAVY or MEDIUM - 3 mins (6 nm)

For takeoff, it's 2 minutes behind anything, or 3 from an intermediate part of the same or a parallel runway separated by less than 760 m. For displaced thresholds and opposite direction runways, separation is 2 minutes. If an arriving aircraft is making a straight in approach, a departing one may take off in any direction which differs by at least 45° from the reciprocal of the direction of approach, if the takeoff is made at least 3 minutes before the arriving one is estimated to be over the instrument runway. Or in any direction 5 minutes before the arriving.

Super Heavy Aircraft is a standard ATC term that is used to alert pilots and others that the plane so designated needs additional separation. The A-380 is a super heavy.

SEPARATION METHODS & MINIMA
Since the crews in IFR aircraft by definition cannot (usually) see outside the cockpit, there must be ways of making sure they don't hit each other, which is why procedures have been established, especially when airways cross each other - the procedures perform the same function as traffic signals.

The word **clearance** means that an approved route is clear, or with no conflicting traffic but, in busy airspace, this won't be the case. If you have IFR departures every minute or so, with the "clearances" being copied down by pilots 10-15 minutes beforehand, you would have all sorts of conflicts because all those clearances would technically be in conflict. Although the Tower controller does not issue IFR clearances*, the procedures used by them below ensure that, when the airspace is clear, you can be sure that you won't hit anything inside the given limits. Once airborne, you will be handed over to Departure, who will maintain them. In other words, the Tower controller establishes the required separation by spacing the departures correctly.

*Thus, if you want to change a clearance, it has to be done by other means.

Anyhow, clearances issued by ATC must provide vertical and horizontal separation between:

- all flights in Class A and B airspace*
- IFR flights in Class C, D and E airspace*
- IFR and VFR flights in Class C airspace*
- IFR and Special VFR flights
- Special VFR flights

*Except in daylight when flights are cleared to climb or descend maintaining own separation in VMC (a pilot on an IFR flight in Class D and E airspace (by day, in VMC) may request to maintain "own separation in VMC", if the other pilot agrees). ATC provides separation between all IFR flights in Class E airspace.

Aircraft can be separated:

- **Vertically**, by assigning different levels from a table of cruising levels, or a modified table above FL 410. Aircraft flying East generally occupy odd flight levels, and those flying West occupy even ones (known as the semicircular rules), which is fine in the cruise, but can become awkward when you want to climb or descend, especially near busy airspace, which is why one-way systems have been devised, such as SIDs and STARs, described later, or even preferred routings.

  Systems such as RVSM (*Reduced Vertical Separation Minima*) make use of technology to reduce vertical separation to the lowest safe criteria.

  The criteria that determine that a specific level is occupied may be reduced by ATC, but never to less than 200 feet (it's usually 300 - a level is *occupied* within ±300', or at least 200'. Once the Mode C readout shows a difference of 300', the level is considered to be vacated).

- **Horizontally**:
  - **Longitudinally**, with time or distance intervals between aircraft along the same, converging or reciprocal tracks
  - **Laterally**, with different routes or areas
- **Composite**, or combinations of vertical and horizontal, under regional agreement. Such minima may be lower than, **but at least half** of, those applied individually. Standard radar separation is 5 nm, which may be reduced to 3 nm, equipment permitting, or even 2.5 nm.

Separation may be increased whenever wake turbulence or other circumstances (e.g. hijacking) call for it.

VERTICAL SEPARATION

Here, you must use prescribed altimeter setting procedures to operate at different flight levels or altitudes. What height you fly at is first of all determined by the direction in which you are going, for which, unless told otherwise, you use magnetic track (see Instrument Flight Rules). If vertical separation does not exist, the minimum separation between departing aircraft, if one will fly through the level of the preceding aircraft and both propose to follow the same track, is 5 minutes.

Separation in designated airspace (under a regional air navigation agreement) below FL 410 is 1,000', and 2,000' above. Within other airspace, 1,000' below FL 290 and 2,000' above. The lowest usable flight level corresponds to, or is immediately above, the established minimum flight altitude, which is determined by an ACC for its area.

Aircraft going to the same destination should be assigned cruising levels according to the approach sequence. Aircraft already at a level should be given priority over others desiring it, and others behind at the same level. A level is assigned after a previous aircraft has reported leaving it. If there is severe turbulence, the leaving aircraft should reach a level appropriate to the separation.

HORIZONTAL SEPARATION

ATC separate aircraft laterally by treating each procedure or navaid as being inside a little pocket of "protected airspace", taking into account the skills and equipment of an average pilot. If the areas do not overlap, separation is assumed. In low level airspace, the width of the airway is protected. Your equipment must be calibrated regularly, and you must keep to the centreline.

On approach, the basic horizontal dimensions of intermediate, final and missed approach areas are protected, and should not overlap with aircraft holding or en route, or on an adjacent approach. It is your responsibility to remain within the areas when cleared, and tell ATC when you can't, so they can allow more space for aircraft following.

Horizontal separation provided by radar and/or ADS-B should be at least 9.3 km (5 nm), which can be reduced to 3 nm if the radar system is capable, and the aircraft is within 40 nm of the radar head and below FL 245.

The reduction can be as low as 4.6 km (2.5 nm) between succeeding aircraft on the same final approach track within 18.5 km (10 nm) of the runway end if:

- the average runway occupancy time of landing aircraft is less than 50 seconds.
- braking action is reported as good and runway occupancy times are not adversely affected by contaminants such as slush, snow or ice.
- a radar system with appropriate azimuth and range resolution and an update rate of 5 seconds or less is used with suitable radar displays.

If the primary ground radar fails, horizontal separation is increased to 10 nm using SSR (transponder) information.

LATERAL SEPARATION

This is supposed to ensure that the distance between aircraft at the same level is never less than an established distance, allowing for navigational inaccuracies, plus a safety margin, geographically, with position reports and fixes, or by track.

Lateral separation at the same level is obtained by:

- using different routes
- using different locations from visual observation
- using navigation aids or RNAV equipment*

If an incoming aircraft is making a straight-in approach, a departing one may take off in any direction within the 5 minutes before the arriving one is estimated to be over the instrument runway.

*Separation between aircraft on specified tracks using the same navigational aid based on VOR is at least 15° and 15 nm or more.

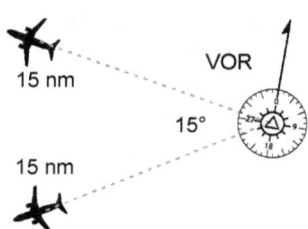

Minima from the same NDB are at least 30° and 15 nm from the facility:

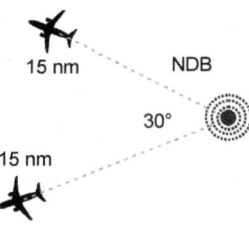

For dead reckoning, the minima are least 45° and 15 nm from the facility.

For RNAV operations, both aircraft must be established on tracks which diverge by at least 15° and the protected airspace associated with the track of one aircraft must not overlap with that for the other aircraft.

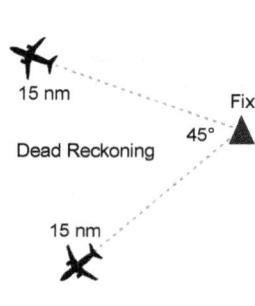

For aircraft using different navaids or methods, account is taken (by ATC) of the accuracy of the aids and the protection areas.

LONGITUDINAL SEPARATION

This is based on time. Aircraft may be required to:

- depart or arrive at specified times
- lose time, by slowing down or holding. Speed changes are not issued once you are inside 4 nm from the threshold on finals. You don't have to accept any changes if they are unsafe, of course, and once a clearance is issued, the adjustment is normally cancelled. There is no speed limitation below 10,000 feet in Class B airspace.

Aircraft at the same level and **on the same track** should be 15 minutes apart, or 10 minutes, where navigation aids permit frequent determination of position and speed:

May be reduced to 5 mins if lead aircraft is at least 20 kts faster or 3 mins if 40 kts faster

This could be further reduced to:

- 5 minutes if the lead aircraft is at least 20 kts (30 km/h) TAS faster
- 3 minutes if the lead aircraft is at least 40 kts (74 km/h) TAS faster

This applies if both departed from the same aerodrome, or have reported over the same reporting point, or the preceding reports a fix confirming 5 minute separation.

When an aircraft will pass through the level of another on the same track, they must be 15 minutes apart at the time the level is crossed. Aircraft on crossing tracks at the same level should be 15 minutes apart, or 10 minutes, where navigation aids permit frequent determination of position and speed.

Aircraft climbing or descending **on the same track** should be 15 minutes apart at the time the level is crossed.

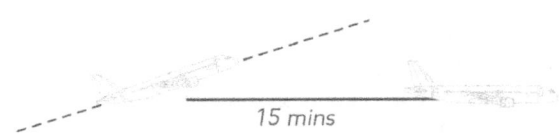

This may be reduced to 10 minutes in the climb, where navigation aids permit frequent determination of position and speed. In the descent, the time can be 5 minutes (at the time the level is crossed) if the level change starts within 10 minutes of when the second aircraft has reported over an exact point. Aircraft on **crossing tracks** when climbing or descending should be 15 minutes apart at the time the levels are crossed or 10 minutes, where navigation aids permit frequent determination of position and speed.

For traffic on **reciprocal tracks**, where lateral separation is not provided, vertical separation is provided for at least 10 minutes before and after the time the aircraft are estimated to pass, or are estimated to have passed. This does not apply if they have already passed each other.

For DME distances, for aircraft on the **same track**, the separation is 20 nm, or 10 nm if the lead aircraft is at least 20 kts faster. DME stations must be on track. **Crossing aircraft** have the same limits. The shortest DME distance for climbing or descending, for aircraft on the same track, is 10 nm, if each aircraft is using on-track DME stations.

On reciprocal tracks, using DME, clearance to climb or descend through levels occupied by other aircraft may be given if it is positively established that they have passed each other and are at least 10 nm apart. Both aircraft must be using on-track DME.

RNAV distance-based separation may be applied between RNAV-equipped aircraft on designated RNAV routes or on ATS routes defined by VOR (if it is working!).

When using RNAV, direct controller-pilot communication must be maintained. Position reports should be referenced to a common waypoint ahead of both aircraft.

An 80 nm (150 km) RNAV distance may be used instead of 10 minutes on tracks with the same direction, if the same on-track waypoint ahead of the aircraft is used. The Mach Number technique means that the lead aircraft should maintain a Mach Number equal to or greater than that of the following aircraft.

The same limits may be used for aircraft climbing or descending on the same track, but one aircraft must maintain a level while vertical separation does not exist.

SPEED ADJUSTMENT

Aircraft under radar control may occasionally be asked to increase or decrease speed to help traffic flow (with due regard for fuel reserves), in multiples of 10 kts IAS, except for aircraft entering or established in holding patterns. Very often, you can be slipped in before an approaching aircraft if you open up the throttle a bit. On the other hand, you may be catching up with one that is a little slow.

Only units of 20 kts may be used for intermediate and final approach, and not within 4 nm of the threshold.

PARALLEL RUNWAYS

Why have them? To increase capacity! There are many ways of doing it, described below. Normal IFR avionics, plus full ILS are required. When simultaneous approaches are in progress, the vector to intercept the ILS should enable interception of the localizer inside 30°, as only straight-in approaches are allowed. During simultaneous parallel approaches, the final radar vector should allow the aircraft to be established on the localizer for at least 2 nm before intercepting the glidepath. Radar monitoring is not terminated until the aircraft is visually separated, or until 1 nm from touchdown.

The *Normal Operating Zone* (NOZ) is airspace that extends either side of an extended ILS centreline, but only the inner half is taken into account.

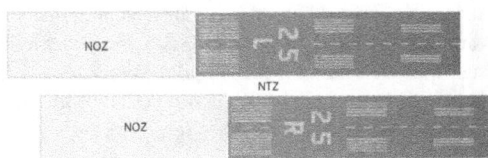

At least 1000 feet vertical or 3 nm horizontal radar separation is required until established inbound on the localiser and/or MLS final approach. The *No Transgression Zone* is a corridor of defined airspace located centrally between the two extended centrelines. For independent parallel approaches it must be at least 610 m (2 000 feet) wide between the extended runway centre lines, and it is to be depicted on the radar display. Penetration of it requires controller intervention to separate threatened aircraft. Officially, the NTZ extends from where 1000' separation becomes reduced to the threshold of the nearest runway:

Independent parallel approaches require surveillance radar equipment capable of identifying aircraft within 1 nm (2 km) of the end of the runway.

Subject to the capabilities of the system, at least 5.6 km (3.0 nm*) of radar separation must be provided between aircraft on the same ILS localiser or MLS final approach track, unless a greater distance is required for wake turbulence or other reasons. Such aircraft are separated from other aircraft on adjacent parallel course provided neither penetrates the NTZ.

*This can be reduced to 2.5 nm in some circumstances.

Missed approaches from the two runways must diverge by at least 30°, as must departure tracks diverge from missed approach tracks of the other aircraft.

- **Mode 1** - Independent. Where radar separation minima are not prescribed.
- **Mode 2** - Dependent. Where radar separation minima are prescribed.
- **Mode 3** - Simultaneous Departures. *Independent* - aircraft go in the same direction. When the minimum separation distance between runways is less than that required for wake turbulence, they will be treated as one runway, which cannot be used for simultaneous departures.
- **Mode 4** - Segregated. Where one runway is used for departures and one for approaches.
- **Mixed**. *Semi-mixed* operations mean that one runway is used for approaches, while the other has approaches (Mode 1 and 2) or departures (Mode 4). Or one could be used for departures and the other for approaches (Mode 4) or it could be for departures (Mode 3). Anything is possible!

SEPARATION NEAR AERODROMES

Essential Local Traffic includes aircraft, personnel or vehicles on or near the runway to be used, or traffic in the takeoff and climbout area or final approach area, that may collide with a departing or arriving aircraft. If ATC offer a takeoff direction that is not into wind, you may elect to take it or wait until a better one arises.

VISUAL APPROACHES

Separation must be provided between aircraft making visual approaches and others arriving and departing. A controller may initiate a visual approach for an IFR flight, if the crew agree, and there is no reason to believe that they are not familiar with the aerodrome, taking account of the weather and traffic.

If the crew is not familiar with the instrument approach being carried out, only the final track must be forwarded to them by ATC if they are making a straight-in approach. In all other cases, the other details of the approach must be specified.

HOLDING

Normally, the first aircraft to arrive over a holding fix or visual holding location should be at the lowest level, with following aircraft at successively higher levels.

APPROACH SEQUENCE

The sequence is supposed to ensure the maximum arrivals with the least average delay. A pilot may hold for weather improvement, but if other aircraft want to make an approach, that aircraft must be moved to a nearby fix to make way for them, or to the top of the sequence.

EXPECTED APPROACH TIME

An EAT is determined for an arriving aircraft that is subject to a delay of 10 minutes or more. If that changes by more than 5 minutes, a revised EAT is given. An EAT is also given when an aircraft is expected to hold for 30 minutes or more.

MISCELLANEOUS SEPARATION PROCEDURES

Essential Traffic is controlled traffic to which separation is applicable, but which do not meet required minima. Essential Traffic Information is issued by ATC during VMC climb or descent.

ARRIVING & DEPARTING AIRCRAFT

When takeoff clearance is given based on the position of arriving aircraft, these rules apply.

If the arriving aircraft is making a complete instrument approach, the departing aircraft may take off:

- in any direction until an arriving aircraft has started its procedure or base turn leading to final approach
- In a direction which is different by at least 45° from the approach reciprocal after the arriving aircraft has started a procedure or base turn leading to final approach, if the takeoff will be made at least 3 minutes before the arriving aircraft is estimated to be over the beginning of the instrument runway

If the arriving aircraft is making a straight-in approach, the departing aircraft may take off:

- in any direction until 5 minutes before the arriving aircraft is estimated as over the instrument runway
- In a direction which is different by at least 45° from the approach reciprocal:
  - until 3 minutes before the arriving aircraft is estimated to be over the beginning of the runway, or
  - before the arriving aircraft crosses a designated fix (as agreed between ATC and the operator) on the approach track

Before taxying for takeoff, you should get the following information, in this order, unless already received:

- Runway in use
- Current surface wind direction and speed
- QNH and possibly QFE
- Air temperature, for turbines
- Current visibility for the direction of takeoff and climb, if less than 10 km, or current RVR
- The correct time

Before takeoff, you should be advised of any significant changes to wind*, temperature and visibility, plus any significant weather in the takeoff and climbout area.

AIR LAW
11 - Air Traffic Services

*Significant changes includes a mean headwind component of 10 knots, a mean tailwind component of 2 knots and a mean crosswind component of 5 knots.

Departures are normally cleared in the order in which they are ready for takeoff, but this may vary.

Departing aircraft may not normally start to take off until:

- the preceding aircraft has crossed the end of the runway in use
- the preceding aircraft has started a turn
- until all preceding landing aircraft have cleared the runway in use

The above minima may be lowered, but not at night or between a departing and a preceding landing aircraft.

Aircraft **landing** or in the final stages normally have priority over those departing. Landing aircraft can not normally cross the threshold of the runway on final approach unless the preceding departing aircraft has:

- crossed the end of the runway in use
- started a turn, or
- until all preceding landing aircraft have cleared the runway in use

The above minima may be lowered, but not at night or if braking action may be affected by contamination, or if the pilot cannot make an early assessment of traffic conditions on the runway due to weather.

An aircraft subject to unlawful interference or which otherwise requires isolation may be cleared to a designated isolated parking position.

An **arriving aircraft** should be handed over to aerodrome control when:

- it is near the aerodrome and the approach and landing can be carried out visually
- it has uninterrupted VMC
- it has landed

A **departing aircraft** should leave the tower when:

- In **VMC** - the earlier of leaving the vicinity of the airfield or entering IMC
- In **IMC** - immediately before entering the runway in use for takeoff, or immediately after airborne

APPROACH CONTROL SERVICE

Radar allows the best use of airspace by *reducing separation between aircraft*, and the *provision of information*, such as traffic and weather. If SSR is available without primary radar, it will not be possible to detect all aircraft. Approach control covers arriving and departing flights outside the circuit. The callsign is *Approach*, although it might also be *Radar*, or *Talkdown* for PAR.

Approach controllers sit in a darkened room in front of radar screens, so they have no visual contact with the traffic they are dealing with (don't worry, they are fed frequently). They guide the aircraft during its approach or departure to or from the airport.
Mostly, arrivals and departures are handled by a single unit but, at busier airfields they may be separate, with different controllers, callsigns and frequencies.

An ATSU (*Air Traffic Services Unit*) consists of a combined radar unit and tower.

Before providing a service, ATC need to identify to whom they are talking. With SSR, ATC can recognise your aircraft's label on their screen, and issue you with:

- a code
- Mode S recognition
- transfer to another unit
- squawking ident

 Squawking ident is the only stand-alone method of identification. Transfers from one ATC unit to another are done by agreement with the receiving unit.

For PSR (i.e. no SSR), you can be recognised in relation to a known landmark or as an aircraft that has just departed, within 1 nm of the end of the runway used. In addition, you can be identified on transfer, or by observation of your track or a manoeuvre, such as a turn of more than 30°. However, a backup method is required, such as:

- correlation of position (particularly within 1 km of the end of the runway)
- transfer from another controller
- VDF bearing

Thus, ATC know which aircraft they are talking to with *position reports*, *identifying turns* or *transponders*. You will be told of any change in the identification status. Before providing ATC service based on radar information, a controller must radar-identify the aircraft *and inform the pilot*. Normally, turns requested by a controller should be executed as *standard rate turns*.

 Radar identification does not stop you being responsible for the disposition of your aircraft, including collision avoidance and obstacle clearance, although ATC accept responsibility for the latter when *vectoring* IFR flights (see below) enroute and on approach until within the final approach area.

DEPARTING AIRCRAFT
An ATC clearance will specify:

- The direction of takeoff, and turn afterwards. If the takeoff direction is not into wind (perhaps to expedite traffic), the PIC must decide if this is satisfactory
- Any track to be made good before proceeding on to the desired heading

- The level to maintain before continuing the climb to the assigned flight level
- The time, point and/or rate at which a level change shall be made
- Any other manoeuvres consistent with safe operation

A clearance may be given for an aircraft to depart in VMC, maintaining its own separation. Aircraft departing on long distance flights should be given as few turns and climb restrictions as possible. Delayed flights will normally be cleared on their ETD.

Significant changes in weather conditions in the takeoff and climbout area, and changes in the operational status of essential visual and non-visual aids must be transmitted to an aircraft without delay, unless the information has already been received.

ARRIVING AIRCRAFT

These may be required to report when:

- Leaving or passing a reporting point
- Starting a procedure or base turn
- Any other information that will help a controller expedite departing aircraft

An IFR flight is not cleared for an initial approach below minimum altitude unless:

- The pilot reports passing an appropriate point defined by a radio aid
- The pilot reports that the aerodrome is and can be maintained in sight
- The aircraft is conducting a visual approach. An IFR flight may cleared for a visual approach if the underlying terrain is in sight and can be maintained in sight, and:
    - the reported ceiling is at or above the approved initial approach level
    - The pilot reports at the initial approach level (or at any time during the approach) that the weather allows a visual approach and landing to be made
- The aircraft's position has been positively determined with radar

Separation must be provided between aircraft executing a visual approach and other arriving and departing aircraft.

A clearance may be given for an aircraft to descend in VMC, maintaining its own separation.

Pilots unfamiliar with an instrument approach may be given the following information:

- initial approach level
- the point (in minutes from the appropriate reporting point) at which a procedure turn is carried out
- the final approach track (for a straight-in approach only this item need be specified)

If visual reference is established before the procedure is complete, it must be finished unless visual is requested.

Significant changes in windspeed must be reported to aircraft on finals:

- Crosswind - 5 kts
- Tailwind - 2 kts
- Headwind - 10 kts

Speed adjustments must not be above ±20 kts, and no changes should be requested within 4 nm.

TERMINAL CONTROL SERVICE

This is from IFR units (ACCs) or *Terminal Control Units* (TCUs) for IFR and VFR flights in specified control areas.

TERMINAL RADAR SERVICE

From IFR units to VFR aircraft in Class C airspace.

RADAR ADVISORY SERVICE

This can be requested at any time, but is usually used in IMC, so you should not accept vectors if they take you there and you are not qualified. This can be time wasting, especially if it's a clear day and you're continually given vectors downwind that take ages to catch up on; although you are not obliged to accept the advice, you must inform the controllers, as you must if you change heading or altitude. Once advice is refused, you become responsible for traffic separation, although you are always responsible for obstacle avoidance and obtaining clearances. This can also be expensive, as you become subject to Eurocharges, 100% in UK (but only 25% in France). If you choose not to receive advisory service, you should still submit a flight plan and notify ATS of any changes.

RADAR INFORMATION SERVICE

For informing pilots of the bearing, distance and level of conflicting traffic. Controllers do not offer avoiding action, and updates are only done at pilot request if there is a definite hazard. The responsibility for separation is that of the pilot. RIS is normally only available within 30 nm of an Approach radar head.

RADAR VECTORING

This is achieved by giving you *specific (magnetic) headings* to maintain desired tracks. It may be used when separation is necessary, for noise abatement, when requested or if an operational advantage would be gained. You should be vectored along routes or tracks that you can easily monitor (in case the radar fails), but you will be told where you are being vectored to, and when it stops (although this can be assumed if you are on a final approach or traffic circuit and are given clearance). Otherwise, it continues until you leave the coverage area, go into controlled airspace or are transferred to a unit that doesn't have radar. You should not be vectored into uncontrolled airspace.

The *minimum radar vectoring altitude* is the lowest one that still clears obstacles and does not trigger GPWS, and is used to make the transition to an approach easier, but it may be lower than the minimum altitudes on your chart. If you are cleared to a lower altitude, ATC are responsible for obstacle clearance until you can start an approach (i.e. terrain clearance is with the controller). If the radio fails, be prepared to get back up to at least flight planned altitude or MSA in a hurry. When IFR in controlled airspace, and advised that radar service is terminated, you should *resume normal position reporting*.

Radar vectoring should not should not allow an intercept to a localiser of more than 45°.

AIR LAW
11 - Air Traffic Services

GROUND RADAR
A typical long range coverage will be up to 250 nm, with a preferred frequency of 600 MHz and a 50 cm wavelength. Shorter range coverage is provided by.....

As mentioned, the primary duty of a unit providing radar control is to *separate traffic*. To this end, one function of radar control in approach areas is to provide **surveillance radar approaches**. An SRA normally terminates 2 nm from touchdown, except when, as determined by ATC, the accuracy of the equipment allows a lesser distance. In that case, distance and level information must be given every ½ nm. When SRAs continue to the threshold, transmissions can only be interrupted for up to 5 seconds while the aircraft is within 4 nm from touchdown.

A go-around must be ordered by the controller if you are not visible for the last 2 nm.

Precision Approach Radar (PAR) is primarily used by the military, which is high-definition in nature, because it uses the 9-10 GHz range and has a 3 cm wavelength, similar to weather radar, so weather clutter can be a problem (meaning you may be denied its use when you need it most!) It uses two radars (and antennae) to give horizontal and vertical guidance to aircraft on final approach up to about 10 nm within 20° of final track and 7° of elevation (i.e. relatively narrow beams). It's supposed to be a landing aid, not for sequencing or spacing aircraft. As the range is 10 nm, PAR is limited to the final stages of approach. The display is described in *Radio Navigation*. Most PAR decision heights are around 200 ft agl.

PAR's usefulness lies in the fact that navaids are not required and neither is a compass, since the controller tells you to turn left, right, descend, etc. Also, as acknowledgements are not required, you can listen to instructions over an ADF or VOR.

While surveillance radar can be used for GCA applications if the update rate is quick enough, PAR doesn't really have the ability. There is also a PAR Azimuth Only Approach, using the PAR centreline for a non precision approach more accurate than SRA.

Otherwise known as *Airport Surface Detection Equipment* (ASDE), Aircraft Surface Movement Radar operates in the SHF band (16 GHz), using an antenna that rotates at around 60 RPM. It is sometimes possible to determine the type of aircraft from the return on the radar screen.

VISUAL CLIMB & DESCENT
If you are being vectored and can see where you are going (that is, you can avoid obstacles yourself and maintain visual reference), you can request permission to climb or descend visually, which may allow you a more direct track. Of course, this means that the responsibility for clearing them is transferred to you, although the proper separation intervals will be maintained.

AREA CONTROL SERVICE
From *Area Control Centres* (ACCs) for flights in control areas. Their callsign is *Control*, and they are supposed to achieve separation between controlled flights.

Alerting Service
This must be provided for aircraft using ATC, on a flight plan or otherwise, or which are the subject of unlawful interference (officially, the service notifies appropriate organisations about aircraft needing SAR, and to assist as required - usually done by a *Rescue Coordination Centre*, or RCC), which must have means of *rapid and reliable communication* with other RCCs, rescue services, met offices, alerting posts and relevant satellite systems.

Alerting is done by the ATS unit responsible for the aircraft at the time (exam question), and the decision to initiate it is the responsibility of the *flight information or control organisations* (another). Alerting Service and FIS are often provided by the same unit (yet another). The states of emergencies are in three phases, which are:

- **Uncertainty** (INCERFA), which exists after 30 minutes with no communication, or appearance after ETA, whichever is later
- **Alert** (ALERFA) exists if apprehension exists about the safety of an aircraft or its occupants after failed attempts to get in touch, it fails to land within 5 minutes of ETA or a clearance, it is believed to be subject to unlawful interference, or other data implies trouble short of a forced landing
- The **Distress** phase (DETRESFA) exists where there is reasonable certainty that an aircraft and its occupants are threatened by grave and imminent danger or require immediate assistance, such as with *fuel exhaustion* or a forced landing

Flight Information Service
Officially, FIS is for all aircraft that are likely to be affected by the information they have, and which already have an ATC service, or are otherwise known to them. More practically, it is there to supply pilots in *C-G airspace* with information about such things as *navaid unserviceability* or *hazardous conditions*, e.g. volcanic ash, etc., especially that which might not have been available on takeoff or have developed since then. Their callsign is *Information*.

OPERATIONAL BROADCASTS
ATC can provide some continuous broadcasts:

- **ATIS** (*Automatic Terminal Information Service*) is a repetitive broadcast on available VHF frequencies, VOR and NDB (not the ILS) at major aerodromes, to reduce congestion on VHF frequencies, although it may have its own channel. You should listen and take down the details before you contact ATC. ATIS broadcasts should be updated whenever a significant change occurs, and should not last over 30 seconds.
- **OFIS** (*Operational Flight Information Services*) are also on VHF and HF.

AIR TRAFFIC ADVISORY SERVICE
The idea behind this is to provide a service that is more effective with regard to collision hazard avoidance than a mere Flight Information Service (below). For example, it may be used by aircraft on advisory routes (Class F airspace). Because it is not a *control* service, and therefore does not have the same traffic information to hand, it does not offer the same degree of safety, hence the use of phrases like *advise* and *suggest*. IFR flights using this service should behave the same as controlled flights, except that flight plans (and changes) are not subject to clearance.

12 - SEARCH & RESCUE 010 11

SAR facilities must be provided on a **24-hour basis**, with no overlap on coverage areas. Areas where sovereignty is not determined are covered under Regional Air Navigation agreements. Each SAR region must have a *Rescue Coordination Centre* (RCC). SAR assistance is given regardless of nationality. SAR information, although not normally in an Operations Manual, is nevertheless required by it to be on board.

Procedures

AT THE SCENE OF AN ACCIDENT
The PIC should:

- keep any craft in distress in sight until no longer required
- determine his own position
- be able to report as many details as possible to the RCC, including:
    - type of craft in distress, identification and condition
    - position, time in hours and minutes UTC
    - number of people observed, and if they have abandoned the craft
    - number of persons observed afloat
    - apparent physical condition of survivors
- act as instructed by the RCC

The first aircraft on the scene should take control, until the first SAR one arrives. If it cannot communicate with the RCC, it should hand over to an aircraft that can.

INTERCEPTING DISTRESS TRANSMISSIONS
Distress transmissions are normally given out on the frequency in use at the time, but when over the high seas, say when flying offshore, you will typically be guarding one of the distress frequencies, either *121.5 MHz, 243 MHz* or *2182 KHz* for merchant shipping. ELTs operate on 121.5 MHz and 406 MHz.

If you hear a distress transmission, you must:

- Record the position of the craft in distress (take a bearing)
- Inform the appropriate ATS unit or RCC
- At your discretion, whilst awaiting further instructions, proceed to the position given

If you need to direct another craft to the scene, circle it at least once, fly low just in front and rock the fuselage, then fly off in the direction you want them to go.

You can use the same signals when they are finished with, but fly behind instead. In theory, they should hoist the *Code Pennant*, which is a flag with vertical red and white stripes, close up, or flash a series of *Ts* in Morse Code with a lamp. On the other hand, they could just turn in the direction requested. A blue and white chequered flag means *NO*, as does a series of *Ns* in Morse.

GROUND-AIR VISUAL SIGNALS
Survivors can communicate with SAR aircraft visually by making signals on the ground. They should be at least 8 feet high (or as large as possible) with as large a contrast as possible between the materials used and the background.

Need Assistance	V
Need Medical Help	X
No	N
Yes	Y
Going This Way	←

Rescue units can use these (mostly double symbols):

Operation Complete	LLL
All Well	LL
Found all personnel	LL
Found some personnel	++
Cannot continue - going home	XX
Split into different groups in directions indicated	← →
Aircraft in this direction	→ →
Nothing found but continuing	NN

AIR-GROUND VISUAL SIGNALS
Indicate your understanding of the ground signals above by rocking your wings in daylight or flashing your landing lights twice at night (or nav lights if you haven't any landing lights).

DROPPABLE CONTAINERS & PACKAGES
Those containing survival equipment should be coloured (with streamers):

Red	Medical Supplies/First Aid
Blue	Food and Water
Yellow	Blankets/Protective Clothing
Black	Miscellaneous (stoves, shovels, etc.)

Use a combination if the goods are of a mixed nature.

SEA SURVIVAL EQUIPMENT
This must be carried for passengers and crew:

- on multi-engined aircraft more than 50 nm (93 km) from shore*
- on single-engined aircraft beyond gliding distance from shore**
- when taking off or landing over water where, if there is a mishap, you may ditch

*At the lesser of over 120 minutes at cruising speed, or 400 nm (740 km) from a suitable emergency landing spot, you must carry life rafts and flares. **This is reduced to 30 minutes or 100 nm (185 km) for single-engined aircraft.

13 - ACCIDENT INVESTIGATION

An *Aviation Occurrence* is any accident or incident associated with the operation of aircraft, or a situation that could lead to one. After any occurrence, in UK, the AAIB must be told as soon as possible, by the commander or the operator, in that order. You can make reports in confidence under the *Confidential Aviation Safety Reporting Program* (CASRP).

Under ICAO, however, *investigation* of accidents or incidents is instituted by the State of *Occurrence*, who must forward notification of accidents or serious incidents by the quickest and most suitable means to the States of *Registry*, the *Operator*, of *Design*, of *Manufacture*, and ICAO when the aircraft weighs more than 2250 kg. However, when the State of Occurrence is not aware of a serious incident, the States of Registry or the Operator must forward the information to the others.

Upon receipt of the notification and request by the State of Occurrence for participation, the States of Design and Manufacture shall:

- for accidents or serious incidents to aircraft with a maximum mass of over 100,000 kg, inform the State of Occurrence of:
    - the name of its official representative
    - whether that person will be present at the investigation and, if so, any arrival dates
- For other aircraft, whether it will appoint an accredited representative, in which case, the above information must be provided

Preliminary reports shall be submitted in *one of the ICAO working languages*.

Aircraft Accident

A reportable one occurs when:

- anyone is killed or seriously injured from contact with the aircraft (or any bits falling off), including jet blast or rotor downwash
- the aircraft sustains damage or structural failure
- The aircraft is missing or inaccessible

between the time any person boards it **with the intention of flight**, and all persons have disembarked (ICAO). This does not include injuries from natural causes, which are self-inflicted or inflicted by other people, or to stowaways hiding in places not normally accessible to passengers and crew. So if someone is seriously injured by walking into the back of a wing during disembarkation, that is an accident. *Significant* or *Substantial Damage* in this context is essentially damage or failure affecting structure or performance, normally meaning major repairs.

Under ICAO, a *fatal injury* involves death within 30 days. A *serious injury* involves:

- more than 48 hours in hospital within 7 days
- more than simple fractures of fingers, toes & nose
- lacerations causing nerve or muscle damage or severe haemorrhage
- injury to any internal organ
- 2nd or 3rd degree burns or any more than 5% of the body
- exposure to infectious substances or radiation

In UK, the *Aircraft Accident Investigation Branch* (AAIB) is separate from any other authority - the Chief Inspector of Air Accidents is responsible to the Secretary of State for Transport. As its name suggests, it investigates aircraft accidents, and has teams of investigators on 24-hour standby to go worldwide. The authority to do so derives from the *Civil Aviation Act*, but ICAO also imposes the obligation not to apportion blame, and investigate accidents impartially, to ensure that they *don't happen again*.

POST ACCIDENT PROCEDURES

The legal responsibility for notification of an accident (or incident) lies with the pilot, then the operator if the pilot cannot do so. If it happens near an aerodrome, the aerodrome authority must also report it. However, in practice, the AAIB usually get told by the police, since they must also be informed by the people mentioned above. Normally, accidents to gliders, hang gliders, paragliders and parachutists are investigated by the relevant Associations, who have their own safety organisations, which are supervised by the AAIB, who will not attend unless the circumstances are weird enough. As for microlights, balloons or airships, the AAIB will only investigate if there is a fatality.

SITE SECURITY

An accident site could be quite large, especially when an airliner spreads itself all over the countryside. Only an authorised person (AAIB, a constable or Customs) may normally have access to an involved aircraft, and the aircraft and contents *may not be moved* except under the authority of the Secretary of State. If you do move anything (say for survival purposes, or to provide a marker in a remote area), make sure you note *exactly* where it was before. The police are responsible for guarding the site.

Incident

Any happening other than an accident which hazards or, if not corrected, would hazard any aircraft, its occupants or anyone else, not resulting in substantial damage to the aircraft or third parties, crew or passengers.

EXAMPLES

Precautionary or forced landings, due to engine or tail rotor control failure, an external part of the aircraft becoming detached in flight, contaminated fuel, forced, unscheduled, changes of flight plans from the failure of aircraft instruments, navigation aids or other technical failure, obstructions on rig landing platforms or other landing sites, loss of an external load, with no third party claim, bird strikes, Airprox, in-flight icing, incapacitation. The ICAO bird strike information system is *IBIS*.

SERIOUS INCIDENTS

These are nearly accidents, or have serious potential technical or operational implications, or may result in disciplinary action against aircrew or engineers. The 'Serious' classification is normally made by the senior person on the operation as soon as possible after the event and before the crew or aircraft fly again, mainly to preserve their recollection of the incident or to ensure their fitness for duty rather than for disciplinary reasons. Away from base, you should load a replacement CVR or CVDR and return the others to base. Both should be disabled after shutdown to prevent data being overwritten when power is re-applied. A near-collision needing an avoidance manoeuvre is a serious incident, as is fire or smoke in the passenger cabin.

AIRPROX

Aircraft **Prox**imity incidents (near misses). The class of risk depends on the *risk of collision, safety not assured, no risk of collision*, or *risk not determined*.

14 - AERODROMES & AIRPORTS

An aerodrome is generally any place for landing aircraft that fits the official definition, which is, broadly, being set apart for the purpose, including any necessary buildings. Offshore oil rigs are also covered by Annex 14.

010 09

An aerodrome or airport listed in the AIP that does not need previous permission is for public use. Where permission is required, you either need to get it first, or just provide prior notice, so they can get the sheep off the runway. *Aerodrome Traffic* is all traffic on the manoeuvring area of an aerodrome, and flying in its vicinity.

Aerodrome Data

Accuracy requirements for aerodrome data are based on a 95% confidence level.

The *aerodrome reference temperature* should be the monthly mean of the daily maximums for the hottest months averaged over many years.

AERODROME REFERENCE POINT

This is the designated geographical location of an aerodrome. It is near the initial or planned geometric centre of the aerodrome and normally remains where it is first established.

DECLARED DISTANCES

Certain distances are "declared" by the Airport Authority (to the nearest foot or metre for runways used by international commercial air transport) and published in the AIP, although they can be found in many other publications, such as Jeppesen. These include:

- **TORA** - Takeoff Run Available
- **TODA*** - Takeoff Distance Available
- **ASDA** - Accelerate-Stop Distance Available
- **LDA** - Landing Distance Available

*Any areas at the end of a runway unsuitable to run on, but still clear of obstacles, are called *Clearways*, which start at the end of the TORA, for up to half the length of the TORA. Clearways should extend to at least 75 m either side of the centre line.

The TODA is TORA + Clearway.

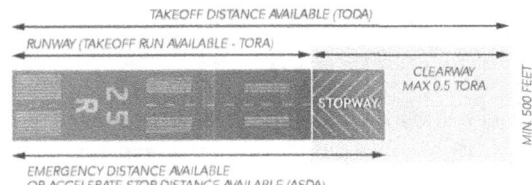

Part of the Clearway that can support an aircraft while stopping, although not under takeoff conditions, is declared as *Stopway* which may be added to the TORA to form the *Emergency Distance Available* (EDA), which is marked with yellow chevrons. This is the ground run distance available for an aircraft to abort a takeoff and come to rest safely - the essential point is that Stopway is ground-based and clearways are not, but they can be included in performance calculations. Stopways are the same width as the runway, and are included in the ASDA.

If a runway does not have a stopway or clearway (meaning that the threshold is right at the end), the declared distances above would normally equal the runway length.

AERODROME REFERENCE CODES

Aerodromes are assigned reference codes to make it easier to judge their suitability for aircraft using them, which consist of a number and a letter, such as 2B. The number is *Element 1*, and is based on the reference field length. *Element 2* is the letter, which arises from wing and outer main gear wheel span, or the distance between the outer edges of the main gear wheels:

Code 1	Field Length	Code 2	Wingspan	Wheelspan
1	< 800 m	A	< 15 m	< 4.5 m
2	800-1199 m	B	15-23.99 m	4.5-5.99 m
3	1200-1799m	C	24-35.99 m	6-8.99 m
4	> 1800 m	D	36-51.99 m	9-13.99 m
		E	52-64.99 m	9-13.99 m
		F	65-79.99 m	14-15.99 m

Pavement and aircraft classifications are in AGK.

RUNWAY WIDTH

The width of a runway for any code should be at least:

	Code Letter				
Code	A	B	C	D	E
1	18 m	18 m	23 m	-	-
2	23 m	23 m	30 m	-	-
3	30 m	30 m	30 m	45 m	-
4	-	-	45 m	45 m	45 m

Precision approach runways should be at least 30 m wide where the code is 1 or 2.

Instrument runways should have a graded area either side of the centreline and extended centreline for aeroplanes running off. The area should extend for 75 m (either side) where the code number is 3 or 4, and 40 m where the code is 1 or 2.

AIR LAW
14 - Aerodromes & Airports

WIDTH OF TAXIWAYS
The width of straight parts of taxiways should be at least:

Code Letter	Taxiway Width
A	7.5 m
B	10.5 m
C	15 m if the wheelbase is less than 18 m
	18 m if the wheelbase is more than 18 m
D	18 m if the outer main gear span is <9 m
	23 m if the outer main gear span is >9 m
E	23 m

Runways
Runways can be:

- Non-instrument (visual)
- Instrument
  - Non-precision
  - Precision

The end of a runway is called the *threshold*. If a runway has a displaced threshold, the LDA is reduced by the amount of displacement.

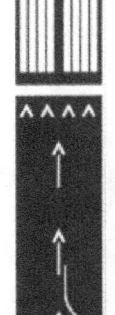

Displacement is marked by large arrows pointing towards the new threshold - a white painted transverse stripe across a runway indicates a temporarily or permanently displaced one (see left). The threshold will be relocated if part of the runway is closed (and crosses will be used instead of arrows). A displaced threshold affects only the LDA for approaches to it - reciprocal directions are not affected.

DER means *Departure End of Runway,* the end of the area declared suitable for takeoff.

For a 2500m landing distance, from the threshold to the aiming point is 400m, with 6 pairs of touchdown markings. The distance from the threshold to the fixed distance marking when the runway is 2000 m long is 300 m. Only paved runways need centreline markings. There should be 12 stripes in the threshold markings of a 45 m wide runway.

RUNWAY DIRECTION
Runways are named after the direction they are facing in, without the last number. For example, one facing West, or 270°, would be called Runway 27. In fact, the naming is to the nearest tenth degree, so one facing 067° would actually be Runway 07. A T after the number (as in 07T) would be a True direction. Clearances to enter, land on, take off from, cross and back track on runways must be read back.

Parallel runways will be known as Left or Right, but if there were 3, they would be Left, Centre or Right, for example 22L, 22C, 22R. Where no runways are available, takeoff and landing areas will be marked with pyramidal or conical markers, painted orange and white for airports, or just orange for aerodromes.

The reason that touchdown is made into the runway or helipad is that, if you sink, at least you are likely to hit a suitable surface.

RUNWAY STRIPS
The combination of the paved area and the stopway is also called the *runway strip*. It should extend from before the threshold and beyond the end of the runway or stopway for at least 60 m when the Aerodrome Reference Code is 2, 3 or 4, and 60 m for a Code 1 instrument runway. For a non-instrument runway, (Code 1) the strip should extend for 30 m.

If a strip includes a precision approach runway, it should extend laterally either side of the centreline by:

- 150 m where the code is 3 or 4
- 75 m where the code is 1 or 2

There should also be a graded area either side of the centre line for aircraft to run off:

- 75 m where the code is 3 or 4
- 40 m where the code is 1 or 2

A *Runway End Safety Area* (RESA) is for minimising risks when overshooting or overrunning. RESAs should extend as far as possible, but at least 90 m, and be at least twice as wide as the runway.

RADIO ALTIMETER OPERATING AREA
This provides a smooth area within which slope changes are kept to a minimum from which to obtain information for the autoflare (the radio altimeter feeds information into the system just before the threshold). If slope changes cannot be avoided, there should not be a rate of change more than 2% per 30 m.

The area should extend at least 300 m into the pre-threshold area, and 60 m either side of the extended centreline, which may be reduced if safety is not compromised. Obstacles interfering with the glideslope may need the threshold to be displaced, but the area behind it can still be used for taxying and takeoff runs, even if it cannot be used for the LDA.

Matters Affecting Performance
The operational status of the movement area and related facilities should be continuously monitored, especially:

- construction or maintenance work
- rough or broken surfaces
- snow, slush, ice or water on surfaces, or snow banks or drifts nearby
- anti-icing or deicing chemicals on a surface
- other temporary hazards, such as parked aircraft
- failure of a power supply

Contamination
A runway is contaminated when 25% of its surface area is covered by:

- more than 3mm of water or deep slush/snow
- snow compressed to a solid mass
- ice, including wet ice

WATER DEPOSITS

When there is water on a runway, the surface conditions in the centre half of the width are described (with depth) as:

- *Damp* - there is a change of colour due to moisture
- *Wet* - the surface is soaked, but there is less than 3mm of water without significant areas of standing water. Wet runways need factoring by 115% for performance purposes
- *Water patches* - significant patches of standing water*
- *Flooded* - there is extensive standing water visible*

*You might get aquaplaning.

Slippery When Wet means that surface friction characteristics as measured by a continuous friction measuring device are below minima. See also *Performance*.

FROZEN WATER

The three states to be reported are:

- *Dry Snow*. That which can be blown if loose or, if compacted by hand, will fall apart on release. The specific gravity is up to, but not including, 0.35.
- *Wet Snow*. That which, if compacted by hand, will stick together and form a snowball. SG is from 0.35 up to, but not including, 0.5.
- *Slush*. Snow that has been compressed into a solid mass that sticks together and resists further compression. SG is 0.5 and over.

BRAKING ACTION

Code	Estimated Action	Measured Coefficient
1	Poor	equal to or < 0.25
2	Medium-Poor	0.26-0.29
3	Medium	0.30-0.35
4	Medium-Good	0.36-0.39
5	Good	0.40 and above

Parking Bays

Those used for aircraft subject to unlawful interference must be at least 100 m from other bays (the term *parking bay*, by the way, is not really a recognised term).

Taxiways

When the cockpit remains over the centre markings, the clearance between the outer main wheel and the edge of the straight portion of a taxiway should be at least a distance based on the wingspan - 7.5 m for aeroplanes under 15 m span, and up to 23 m for those under 65 m. Both should be maintained when the taxiway curves.

Centre markings *must* be present on paved taxiways with an aerodrome code of 3 or 4 (runways at least 1200 m long), and *should* be provided on shorter ones (1 or 2).

A taxiway connected to the runway at an acute angle that allows turning off at higher speeds is a *rapid exit taxiway*.

Visual Aids For Navigation

Refer to *CAP 637 - Visual Aids Handbook* for full details.

The Signals Area provides basic information about an aerodrome to aircraft in flight without needing a radio. It is a small square surrounded in white that contains relevant symbols, situated next to the control tower.

The principal requirement of a signals area is that it must be visible from the air (obvious, really - it should actually be visible from above 10° above the horizontal from 300 feet). It should be on an even horizontal surface and be at least 9m square. Its colour should contrast with those of the panels used, and it should be surrounded by a white border at least 0.3 m wide.

 An aerodrome must have at least one wind direction indicator (*windsock*), which must be visible from aircraft in flight or on the movement area, and free from the effects of air disturbances from nearby objects.

A *landing direction indicator* (which should be in the form of a letter T) must be in a conspicuous position, typically in the signals area (see below). It should be white or orange, depending on which provides the best contrast, and be lit at night. A white T with a disc above (for airborne machines) and a single black ball suspended from a mast (for those on the ground), mean that the directions for takeoff and landing are not necessarily the same.

A white dumb-bell means *land and taxi on runways and taxiways only*. A black bar across each circular part of the dumbbell perpendicular to the shaft means you must still take off and land on runways, but other manoeuvres need not be on runways and taxiways.

There must be a *signalling lamp* in the control tower, capable of producing red, green and white signals which can be aimed at the target. It should be able to transmit Morse signals at up to four words per minute.

Markings & Signals

Runway surface markings must be white. Taxiway and aircraft stand markings must be yellow. Apron safety lines need only be conspicuous, that is, in a contrasting colour.

Two or more white crosses (with arms at 45° to the centre line) along a section or at both ends of a runway or taxiway mean the section between them is unfit for aircraft movement.

APRONS

Those used must be a contrasting colour to those on taxiways.

HOLDING POINTS

A non-instrument runway will have a yellow single solid and a single dashed line across the taxiway (the dashed line is on the runway side). An instrument runway has a double set of each (an

A Pattern) going to the runway (on the way back, they tell you when you are clear, when *all* of the aircraft has crossed the line).

A *B Pattern* looks like a ladder (left), and is used to protect ILS/MLS signals, so it is not so much a holding point, but a boundary line. An *intermediate* holding position has a single broken line.

There may also be a red marker board either side of the taxiway:

When a runway is 2000 m long, and taxi holding positions have not been established, aircraft shall not be held closer to the runway in use than 50 m.

Aeronautical Ground Lighting

This is the generic term for the various ways of making the airfield and runways more visible at night and in poor visibility. What you can expect for individual airfields is described in the AIP in AGA2, AGA3 and the relevant approach charts. An airfield will only be licensed for night if lighting is up to standard.

Lighting at unlicensed and military airfields is not inspected by the Authority, so expect the unexpected!

Aeronautical Ground Lighting is usually white, and steady, but variations are given below. Their brilliancy can be varied by ATC to suit the conditions, or at your request.

Approach lights (and their supports) must be frangible for the last 300 m before the threshold. Any beyond that over 12 m high must be frangible for the top 12 m. Supporting structures surrounded by non-frangible objects only need the bit above them to be frangible.

Aeronautical ground lights must be operated:

- continuously during darkness after the end of evening civil twilight until the beginning of morning civil twilight
- when required for the control of air traffic
- at any time when their use, based on weather, is considered desirable for the safety of air traffic

Lights on and near aerodromes that are not intended for enroute navigation may be turned off if no likelihood of regular or emergency operation exists, as long as they can be turned on again at least *one hour before an expected arrival.*

Tip: One trick for remembering what lights do is to remember that *omnidirectional lights* are for use when circling. Runway end lights should be unidirectional, as they must be seen down the runway.

APPROACH LIGHTING

Approach lighting uses cross bars and centreline lighting, with strobes for when background lighting is high.

Runway lighting works backwards from the threshold. It has a purpose other than to show you the way in at night - it's also meant to help you transition to the visual after emerging from the murk during an approach. There are various designs for various purposes, shown below.

SIMPLE

These are for non-precision runways, but they can be used for precision runways when it is impractical to fit a Cat I system. They can also be used for Code 3 or 4 non-instrument runways intended for night use. Simple systems can be single source or barrette (a *barrette* is 3 or more ground lights closely spaced).

The simple system is a row of lights on the extended centre line for at least 420 m from the threshold, with a row as a crossbar 18 or 30 m long, 300 m from the threshold, starting up to 500 m before the threshold.

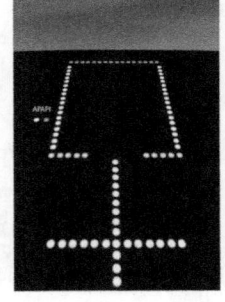

PRECISION CATEGORY I

Here, a distance coded centreline lighting system consists of single lights for the innermost 300 m, then 2 for the next 300 and 3 for the outer 300, plus 5 crossbars at 150, 300, 450, 600 and 750 m, so the distance between crossbars is 150 m - the minimum length is 900m. In exam speak, *a Cat I (Calvert) lighting system consists of 5 crossbars, a centreline with 3, 2, and 1 lamp per light unit.*

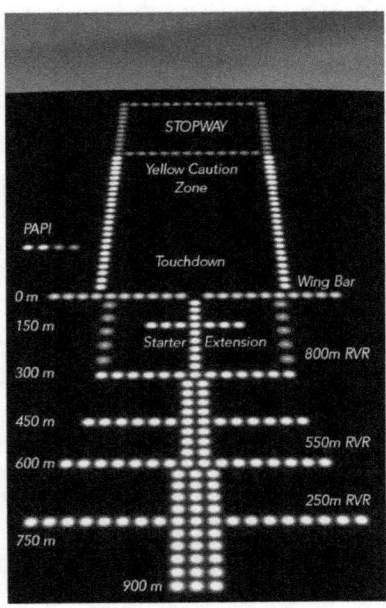

The above centre and crossbar lights can be replaced with a barrette at least 4 m long.

Another system has a row of lights on the extended centre line, over 900 m from the threshold, with a crossbar at 300 m.

Otherwise, centreline lights should be 30 m apart, fixed showing variable white, with the innermost one 30 m from the threshold. None should be screened from approaching aircraft, except possibly central ones.

The only thing that should be sticking up through the plane of the lights within 60 m of the centreline is an ILS or MLS azimuth antenna, which should be treated as an obstacle and marked and lighted accordingly.

RVR minima are determined by the class of approach lighting, as described in *Operational Procedures*.

Meanwhile:

- **Runway Visual Range** the range over which a pilot of an aircraft on the centreline of the runway can see the surface markings or the lights delineating it, or identifying its centre line. It may be measured by an observer, but typically is provided by automated instruments, and sometimes referred to as IRVR (Instrumented RVR). If the RVR less than 1500 m, it will be reported in the METAR, not the TAF. If no RVR is in the METAR, it is over 1500 m and you must convert the visibility for planning purposes.
- **Visibility** is the greater of the greatest distance at which a black object of suitable dimensions, near the ground, can be seen and recognised when observed against a bright background, and the greatest distance at which a lights of around 1000 candelas* can be seen and identified against an unlit background.

    *Not very bright at all.
- **Flight Visibility** is judged from within the cockpit.
- **Ground visibility** is the visibility at an aerodrome, as reported by an accredited observer, often referred to as *met vis*.

Whereas RVR is measured in one direction, visibilities are measured in a circle round the observation point. The other difference is the standard of lighting - that used for RVR is very much brighter.

Under **ICAO Annex 6**, paragraph 2.2.4.1, you may not continue towards the aerodrome of intended landing, unless the latest available information indicates that, at the ETA, a landing can be effected there, or at least one destination alternate, under the minima in 2.2.2.2.

An instrument approach shall not be continued beyond the outer marker (on a precision approach), or below 300 m (1 000 ft) above the aerodrome (non-precision approach), unless the reported visibility or controlling RVR* is above the specified minima.

*The controlling RVR is the latest provided by ATC on a tower or approach frequency. For CAT I operations, the touchdown value is the controlling one - if that is not available, use the mid-point.

If, after passing the outer marker*, the reported visibility or controlling RVR falls below the specified minima, the approach may be continued to DA/H or MDA/H. In any case, you may not continue an approach beyond a point at which the limits of the aerodrome operating minima would be infringed. This is an **approach ban**. The cloud ceiling is not a factor.

*In Europe, where no outer marker or equivalent position exists, a height of 1 000 feet above the aerodrome is used.

You may commence an instrument approach regardless of the reported RVR/VIS, but if it is below minima, the approach shall not be continued below 1 000 ft above the aerodrome, or into the final approach segment if the DA/H or MDA/H is more than that. If RVR is not available, you can convert the reported visibility. The touchdown zone RVR shall always be controlling.

If the reported RVR/VIS falls below minima after you pass 1 000 feet, you can continue to DA/H or MDA/H, and further (completing the landing) if the relevant visual reference is established and maintained at the DA/H or MDA/H and maintained.

Precision Category II/III

There should a row of lights on the extended centreline, over 900 m from the threshold, wherever practical. There should also be two side rows, extending 270 m from the threshold, and two crossbars, at 150 m and 300 m from it. Centreline lights should be 30 m apart, fixed showing variable white, the innermost one 30 m from the threshold.

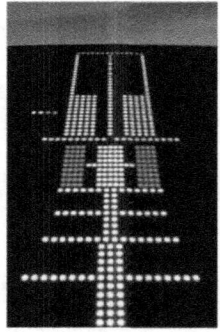

Side row lights should have the same spacing. The most common is the Calvert above.

RUNWAYS

Runway **end** lights should show *unidirectional red* (at least 6) in the direction of the runway. Runway **threshold** lights should show *unidirectional green* in the approach direction. Threshold *identification* lights are flashing white (it might be displaced). You should not land before the green lights or carry on the landing roll after the red lights.

Centreline lighting is white from the threshold until 900 m from the runway end, alternating red and white for the next 600 m, and those for the last 300 m should be red.

Touchdown zone lighting is used on ILS Cat II/III runways. It is two extra rows of white barrettes, extending from the threshold to the lesser of 900 m or the midpoint of the runway.

 Touchdown zone lighting normally determines the length of the Obstacle Free Zone that protects Cat II & III approaches below DH on a go-around. What this means is that a go-around beyond the TZ lights is not likely to be contained in the obstacle free zone.

Runway **edge** lights are fixed and (variable) white, except:

- **Caution Zone Lighting** - For ILS runways without centreline lighting, yellow omnidirectional lights can be used for the upwind 600 m or one third of the lighted length available, whichever is less. This is so you can see the end of the runway looming up. These lights are omnidirectional for circling
- **Pre-Threshold Lighting** - used when a threshold is displaced, but still available for a takeoff run. You will see red edge lights up to the green threshold (because you can't use the area for landing), then normal white edge lights. Blue edge lights mark the boundary of a *starter extension*, narrower than its associated runway. Approach lights may be used for centreline guidance if the whole of a runway is used for takeoff when it has a displaced threshold (but they shouldn't dazzle you)
- **Runway Exit Lighting** - One or two omnidirectional blue lights may replace or supplement the normal edge lights. Centreline lights on *rapid exit taxiways* are alternating green/yellow
- **Stopway Lighting** - red edge and end lighting, showing only in the direction of landing

Runway Lead-In Lighting

Groups of at least 3 white lights in a cluster or linear configuration, flashing in sequence towards the runway. They are supposed to define the desired approach path. The distance between groups should be up to 1600 m.

TAXIWAYS

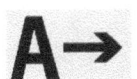

Taxiway edge lights* are fixed omnidirectional blue, although some may be shielded to prevent confusion.

Paved taxiways should have yellow centre line markings, for continuous guidance between runways and aircraft stands, but alternating yellow/green ones indicate an ILS sensitive or critical area (the nearest to the perimeter is yellow).

*For a taxiway that is not used often, reflective markers may be used instead of lights. On unpaved areas, the blue lights may be portable or reflective.

A **stopbar** across a taxiway shows red lights 3 m apart. They are linked with green lead-on lights in that, when one is off, the other is on. They act in this way like traffic lights, and **you should not taxi past a red stopbar**. Stopbars are used when RVR is less than 350 m, and must be controllable by ATC. If the RVR is less than 550 m, and there are no stop bars, runway guard lights should be used.

Guard lights are pairs of alternately flashing yellow lights, one on each side of the runway, to warn you that the runway is nearby.

Taxiway **intersection lights** are rows of at least 3 steady yellow lights symmetrically about the taxiway centreline. Here, you should give way to crossing traffic.

AERODROME BEACONS

A beacon is required if aircraft navigate mostly visually, or reduced visibility is frequent, or it is hard to see the aerodrome, especially at night.

- **Identification beacons** (*pundits*) are green for civil aerodromes, and yellow for those on water, used where many other aerodromes are nearby and identification could be difficult. Military aerodromes have a flashing red one. All show a two-letter Morse group
- **Aerodrome location beacons** are for smaller, more remote, aerodromes, with no problem as to identification. They are white and flashing, if they are well away from background lighting, or white & green where there is a lot of background lighting, like near a city (again, yellow for water)

OBSTACLES

Those less than 45 m high should have *low intensity steady red* lights. Between 45-150 m, *medium red, flashing simultaneously*. Over 150 m, *high intensity white flashing lights* (Type A) by day and night, flashing simultaneously. For towers or pylons supporting cables, etc., high intensity white flashing (Type B).

VISUAL APPROACH SYSTEMS

When approaching visually to a runway, it's useful to have a visual aid to help get the glideslope right (lateral guidance is provided by the runway lights). Those described here use different coloured light patterns to show whether you are on a glideslope, too high or too low. They will be to one side of the runway threshold and visible up to about 5 nm by day and 20 nm or more by night. Their sphere of influence is ±10° of the extended centreline, up to 4 nm.

VASIS

The *Visual Approach Slope Indicator System* is a group of four lights (2-bar), which provide an aiming point about 1,000 feet into the runway, based on a glideslope of 3° (usually).

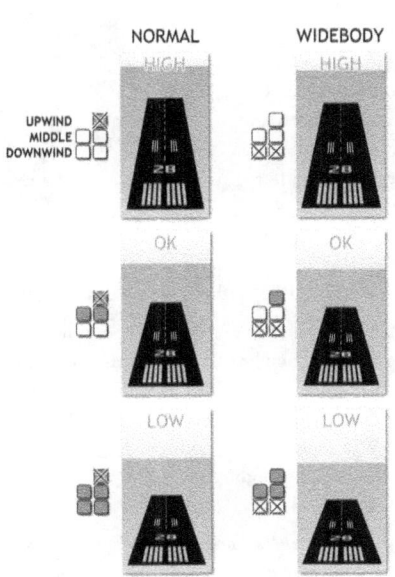

The light bars are *upwind* and *downwind*. The most common are the 2-bar version with a set of lights near the runway threshold and another about 20 feet further down the runway. If you view them from above a specific angle you see two white lights (too high), and from below, two red lights (two low). If you see red on the far set and white on the near set, you are on the glideslope.

In the 3-bar version, normal aircraft use the middle and downwind sets, and widebodies (high-cockpit) use the middle and upwind (far) ones. This gives an aiming point further in, so the gear clears the threshold. *Normal* means an eye-to-wheel height of up to 25 feet. Widebodies have up to 45 feet.

A *Tri-Color VASI* uses red, green and amber to indicate low, on the glideslope and high, respectively. Their range is around ½ to 1 mile during the day and 5 miles at night.

A *Pulsating VASI* (PVASI) uses a single light source to project a two-colour approach indication. When very low or very high, the light pulsates more in relation to your distance away, red or white, respectively. Otherwise it is steady white for on the glideslope when using one system, and alternating red and white on another.

A *T-VASIS* uses 20 lights, with 4 horizontal ones in the middle and the other 6 as 3 vertical groups above and below, which only appear when you are low or high. If you do things properly, you will arrive at the threshold at 45 feet. All lights are white, except where a gross undershoot is involved, when they turn red. Lights above the horizontal 4 are the fly down lights, whereas those appearing below are the fly up ones.

PAPI

The *Precision Approach Path Indicator* does the same thing as VASIS, but with 4 sharp transition multi lamp units in a row, on the left side of the runway.

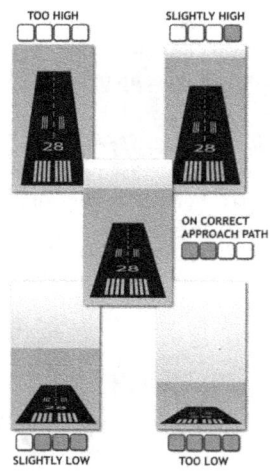

When on the correct slope, two lights show red and two show white. Three whites and a red mean slightly high, and three reds and a white means slightly low. Four of each is too much. When the approach is correct, you will be clear of obstructions within 6-9° either side of the centreline up to 4 nm, with safe wheel clearance over the threshold. PAPIs should not be used beyond 15° either side of the centreline.

An APAPI is an Abbreviated PAPI with only two lights for aircraft with an eye-wheel height of 10 feet. It is used when there is no ILS present. There should be a correlation between the PAPI and ILS glideslopes, assuming that your eye level is above the ILS antenna. Where it is above your eye level (as with the Shorts 330), the indications might read slightly low as compared to the ILS.

The *Minimum Eye Height over the Threshold* (MEHT - see AGA 2 or 3 in the AIP) is the lowest eye height over the threshold at which an onslope indication will be seen.

Signs

A *mandatory instruction* sign has white text on a red background, found at holding positions, etc. *Information* signs have black text on a yellow background (the other way round for a location sign, and a yellow border if it is stand-alone).

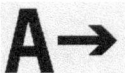

A *runway vacated* sign would be at the end of the ILS/MLS sensitive area.

Signs must be lit at night (for instrument runways, or non-instrument runways of Code 3 or 4), or in bad visibility (with RVR below 800 m).

Marking Of Objects

Objects within a 15 km radius of an aerodrome that are considered to be obstacles (in flight* or on the ground) are normally lit by night or otherwise marked in contrasting colours during the day.

*An object will be an obstacle to an aircraft in flight above 150 m in height.

MARKERS

Fixed objects that need to be marked (including buildings) should be coloured, preferably with a chequered pattern (orange and white or red and white), or have markers or flags displayed on or above them, except that conspicuous objects don't need it. Mobile objects must be coloured or display flags.

Bad ground markers, for example, are orange and white: Markers on or near objects must be in conspicuous positions that retain the general definition of the object, in order to be recognisable in clear weather from 1000 m away from the air and 300 m from the ground in every likely approach direction. Markers must be frangible and low enough not to be hit by propellers, engine pods, etc.

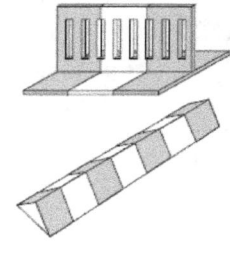

OVERHEAD WIRES

Overhead wire markers should be round, at least 60 cm in size, of one contrasting colour, at the level of the highest wire. Although the balls should be of one colour, they should alternate with different ones, such as red and white.

FLAGS

Flags should be near the highest edge of the object, at least every 15 m. Flags should be orange, or a combination of triangular sections of orange or red and white. For example, on the right is a bad ground marker flag: Mobile objects should be marked with a chequered flag, such as the usual red or orange and white, except where they will merge with the background.

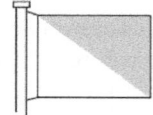

LIGHTING

Fixed obstacles up to 45 m high, wide or long usually have a steady red light at the highest practicable point. Bigger obstacles have more red lights that bring out the shape of the object. Red lights are also used to mark unserviceable parts of the manoeuvring area or surface objects.

Mobile obstacles (i.e. vehicles) will have flashing yellow lights. Emergency vehicles have flashing blue lights. The flashing should run at 60-90 per minute.

Emergency & Other Services

FIRE & RESCUE

The idea is to *save lives* during emergencies on airports or aerodromes, so the main task is to get passengers and crew out of dangerous situations which, of course, doesn't mean they can't deal with others at the same place. How many firefighters and how much equipment you need is based on the longest aeroplanes using the airfield and their width, that produce an *aerodrome category*, determined from a table in Annex 14. The most important factors are training, effectiveness of equipment and speed of response. Normal response time should be 2 minutes (not more than 3) to each end of the runway in optimum visibility and surface conditions.

APRON MANAGEMENT

Depending on the level of traffic, an apron management service must be established to:

- regulate movement to prevent collisions between aircraft and obstacles
- regulate entry and exit to and from the apron
- ensure safe and expeditious movement of vehicles

Control is usually done by the Tower, but the service may be run by another department.

Vehicles on aprons must:

- give way to emergency vehicles, aircraft taxying, about to taxi or being pushed or towed
- other vehicles, under local regulations

GROUND SERVICING OF AIRCRAFT

Fire extinguishing equipment suitable for at least initial intervention in a fuel fire, and personnel trained in its use, must be readily available during the ground servicing of an aircraft, plus a means of quickly summoning the rescue and firefighting service if there is a fire or major fuel spill.

15 - AERONAUTICAL INFORMATION

Aviation needs a huge flow of information to run smoothly - technically for its *safety*, *regularity* and *efficiency*, as wrong information can be dangerous. Many accidents have happened because crews have input wrong data. As with all computers, if you put garbage in, you get garbage out. The role of such services became more important with *RNAV* (Area Navigation), *RNP* (Required Navigation Performance) and *Computer-based navigation systems* (INS/IRS), which need accurate information for their operation, from the publications issued by *Aeronautical Information Services*, such as NOTAMS, etc. To ensure uniformity and consistency, States are urged to *avoid Standards and Procedures other than those established for international use*.

010 08

States are required to either provide such services themselves, or in conjunction with another, or through non-government agencies which meet the standards. The responsibility, however, still lies with the State, and information published on its behalf must show where the authority comes from, as well as being accurate, timely and of the quality expected by ICAO. States must share information, in English, with place names spelt as per local usage, and any translations in the Latin alphabet. Published coordinates must conform to WGS-84.

Aeronautical Information Publication

The AIP is a summary of the rules and regulations that affect aviation (all countries issue them) or, in other words, a publication containing aeronautical information of a *lasting character essential to air navigation*. As such, it is not the final authority for the rules you have to obey, but the law that backs it up is. A clue as to what is or isn't supported by law is given by the word "shall". The AIP should be easy to use in flight, and it is split into three parts:

PART 1 - GENERAL (GEN)

- **GEN 1** - *National Regulations & Requirements*. Entry, transit and departure of aircraft and cargo, Aircraft instruments, Summary of national regulations and differences from ICAO SARPS.
- **GEN 2** - *Tables & Codes*. Measurements, Aircraft markings, Holidays, Abbreviations, Chart symbols, Navaids, Conversions, Sunrise & sunset tables, Location indicators.
- **GEN 3** - *Services*. AIS, Charts, ATC, Met, SAR.

PART 2 - EN-ROUTE (ENR)

- **ENR 1** - *General Rules & Procedures*. VFR, IFR, Airspace Classes, Procedures, radar services, Flight Planning ATC flow management, Interception, Unlawful interference, ATC incidents
- **ENR 2** - *ATS Airspace*. FIR, UIR, TMA, etc.
- **ENR 3** - *ATS Routes*
- **ENR 4** - *Radio Navigation Aids & Systems*.
- **ENR 5** - *Navigation Warnings*. Danger areas, Military stuff, Obstacles, Bird migration, Sports
- **ENR 6** - *En-Route Charts*

PART 3 - AERODROMES (AD)

- **AD 1** - *Aerodromes/Heliports*. Index, Availability, Services
- **AD 2** - *Aerodromes*. Names, Hours, Facilities, Markings, Obstacles, Runways and distances, Communications, Noise abatement
- **AD 3** - *Heliports*. As above

The above sections should be the same from country to country (but, it would seem, not Canada) so you can find the information easier. When airspace is *notified*, its details are published in the AIP so you can take notice of them. Charts relating to aerodromes must be included in a specific order.

Permanent changes are issued as *AIP Amendments*. Temporary changes of long duration (3 months) and those of short duration containing extensive text or graphics are issued as *AIP Supplements*. Supplement pages are coloured, so they stand out, preferably in yellow.

AIRAC

The initials stand for *Aeronautical Information Regulation And Control*.

The AIP is amended regularly, and you should always make sure yours is up to date. Operationally significant changes are published through the AIRAC system, in Parts 1 and 2, which is aimed at advanced notification based on common effective dates of circumstances that necessitate significant changes in operational practices. So there. AIRAC information must be distributed at least 42 days ahead of the effective date, so the recipients get it 28 days ahead. The information should not change for another 28 days, unless it is of a (very) temporary nature.

AIRAC happens at 0001 every fourth Thursday, so changes to navigation databases, FMS and charts can be done at the same time. Every country issues a circular with AIRAC changes, which are usually new waypoints on airways and updates to SIDs and STARs. If there is nothing new, they state "no AIRAC changes".

AIRAC PART 1

This contains information concerning the establishment, withdrawal of, and premeditated significant changes to:

- Limits (FIRS, Control Areas, Control Zones, etc)
- Positions, frequencies, call signs, etc. of navaids and comms facilities
- Holding and approach procedures, arrival and departure, noise abatement and other ATS procedures
- Meteorological facilities
- Runways and stopways

AIRAC PART 2

Information concerning the establishment, withdrawal of, and premeditated significant changes to:

- Position, height and lighting of obstacles
- Taxiways and aprons
- Hours of service
- Customs, immigration and health
- Temporary Prohibited, Restricted and Danger areas, military stuff

NOTAM

A *NOTice to AirMen* is a warning or notice about anything that might affect a flight that is either temporary or happened too late to be in charts, etc., such as changes to frequencies or serviceability of navaids. They are in the list of items to be checked before flight and can be obtained by telephone, from ATC or over the Internet.

NOTAMs do not amend the AIP, but they may affect the information it contains - for example, a permanent danger area will have its hours of operation published in the AIP, and variations published by NOTAM. A temporary danger area, on the other hand, may be *activated* by NOTAM (where a permanent danger area has two upper limits, the higher one is raised by NOTAM). In fact, a NOTAM is generated and issued when its information is:

- *Temporary* and of *short duration*, or of *long duration* made at *short notice*. If it contains *extensive text and/or graphics*, it becomes an *AIP Supplement*
- *Permanent*, but operationally significant

Operationally significant means the establishment, closure or significant changes in the operation of aerodromes or runways, or the operation of aeronautical services, electronics, aids to navigation (frequencies, ID, etc), visual aids, fuel, SAR facilities, fire fighting, hazards to air navigation (obstacles), and the like.

CONTENT

```
B2385/16 NOTAMN
Q) EUAD/QMRXX/IV/NBO/A/000/999/
   5129N00028W005
A) EUAD
B) 0408231540
C) 0810310500 EST
E) RWY 08R/26L DUE WIP NO
   CENTRELINE, TDZ OR SALS
   LIGHTING AVBL
```

- **B2385/16** - a letter for the series, a 4-digit NOTAM number then a stroke and two digits for the year.
- **NOTAMN** - NOTAMs are issued in three categories to addressees for whom the information has direct operational significance, if they would not otherwise have 7 days prior notification (exam question). *N* means a new NOTAM. *R* means a replacing NOTAM, and *C* is a cancelling NOTAM.
- The **Q** or qualifier line contains details about the issuing FIR, relevance codes, etc. It is not examined under EASA.
- **A) EUAD** - ICAO indicator of the aerodrome or FIR. It can include more than one.
- **B) 0408231540** - Date/time group (UTC) when this NOTAM becomes effective.
- **C) 0810310500 EST** - Date/time group (UTC) when the NOTAM ceases to be effective. EST means *estimated* - NOTAMs remain in force until cancelled or replaced.

- **E)** RWY 08R/26L DUE WIP NO CENTRELINE, TDZ OR SALS LIGHTING AVBL - this is the text of the NOTAM using ICAO abbreviations.

In plain English, this means: "For runway 08/26, due to work in progress, there is no centreline, touchdown zone or simple approach lighting available"

These items are *not* covered by NOTAM:

- routine maintenance work on aprons and taxiways which does not affect safe movement of aircraft.
- runway marking, when operations can safely be conducted on other available runways, or the equipment can be removed when necessary.
- temporary obstructions near aerodromes that do not affect the safe operation of aircraft.
- partial failure of lighting where it does not directly affect aircraft operations.
- partial temporary failure of air-ground communications when suitable alternative frequencies are known to be available and working.
- the lack of apron marshalling services and road traffic control.
- the unserviceability of location, destination or other instruction signs on the movement area.
- parachuting in uncontrolled airspace under VFR, when controlled, at promulgated sites or within danger or prohibited areas..
- other information of a similar temporary nature.

A checklist of valid NOTAMs is distributed over the AFTN at regular intervals of up to a month, to the same distribution list as the NOTAMs themselves.

SNOTAM (SNOWTAM)

Tam

A small white Scottish terrier (see left). Seriously, a NOTAM about *snow, ice and standing water on aerodrome pavements*, valid for up to 24 hours, but reissued if there is a significant change in conditions, including the coefficient of friction or the type or depth of deposit, available width of runway or conspicuity of lighting.

The relevant form has *17 sections* (see ICAO Annex 15, Appendix 2). If the cleared length of runway is less than the published length, it would be displayed in Box D, with the cleared length in metres.

ASHTAM

A NOTAM about operationally significant changes in volcanic activity. Codes are:

- *RED*. Volcanic eruption in progress or likely. Ash plume/cloud reported/expected above FL250
- *ORANGE*. Volcanic eruption in progress or likely. Ash plume/cloud not reported/expected above FL250
- *YELLOW*. Volcano known to be active or activity increased or decreased from Red or Orange. Not currently dangerous but exercise caution
- *GREEN*. Volcanic activity has ceased or returned to normal state

Aeronautical Information Circulars

AICs contain operational and safety information that does not qualify for the AIP or NOTAMs. They contain amendments to the AIP, but not officially (this is done by replacing complete pages occasionally). *Pink* AICs concern safety matters which should be brought to everyone's attention (they are Very Important).

The others are:

- *White* - Admin
- *Yellow* - Operational
- *Mauve* - Airspace restrictions
- *Green* - Maps and Charts

AICs have serial numbers, based on the year and number, such a 27/2003, but they will also be called something like *Pink 27* or *Yellow 42*, in brackets afterwards. A checklist of valid AICs is issued once a year.

SUP

AIC SUPs contain temporary items of operational significance and comprehensive text and/or graphics (e.g.: major air exercises or aerodrome work) that make them awkward for NOTAMs, although a NOTAM may be used to indicate changes to the validity (which should normally be in the SUP itself) or cancellation. They are issued every 28 days, and should be kept in the AIP while valid.

Pre-Flight Information

The Integrated Aeronautical Info Package is preflight information, which consists of:

- AIP, plus supplements
- NOTAMs and Preflight Information Bulletins
- AICs
- Checklists and summaries

17 - SECURITY   010 12

The aim of aviation security is to safeguard civil aviation against acts of unlawful interference, achieved by a combination of human and material resources.

ICAO

Annex 17 requires each ICAO State to designate an appropriate authority within its administration to be responsible for the development, implementation and maintenance of a national aviation security program, which should apply to all international civil air transport, including cargo aircraft, and to domestic flights at the discretion of the State:

- Stopping unauthorised weapons and explosives being carried on board (the PIC must be notified of those used by air marshals).

- Not to mix transit pax or baggage with people not subject to screening - screened passengers must not mix with unscreened ones before boarding, otherwise they must be rescreened.
- Carriage of people subject to proceedings (potentially disruptive passengers, like deportees, inadmissible persons and those in lawful custody). These must be boarded before other passengers.
- Not transporting baggage for passengers not on board without extra security. Unaccompanied baggage carried by air must be cleared under procedures applicable to accompanied baggage, or under another simplified customs procedure distinct from that normally used for other cargo.
- Adequate measures against hijacking.

When a State allows police officers, security staff, bodyguards and other agents of foreign states to carry weapons in their territory to protect aircraft in flight, permission for such carriage should be conditional upon prior notification to the state in which the weapons will be carried, plus notification to the PIC.

UNLAWFUL SEIZURE

State assistance to aircraft subjected to unlawful seizure include the *provision of navaids, air traffic services* and *landing permission*, as may be required under the circumstances.

Measures must be taken, as far as practicable, to detain such aircraft on the ground, unless there is an overriding duty to protect human life, with due consultation between the State of the incident and the State of the operator. The State must take adequate measures for the safety of the passengers and crew until their journey can be continued. The States of Registry and of the operator must be informed, together with all States whose citizens have been harmed or detained as hostages, and who remain on board, not forgetting ICAO.

If 7500 is selected on the transponder, absence of a reply to a request for confirmation is taken as confirmation. Naturally, you must make a full report afterwards.

> *"If there is unlawful interference with an aircraft in flight, the PIC shall attempt to set the transponder to Mode A Code 7500 in order to indicate the situation. If circumstances so warrant, Code 7700 should be used instead."*

Following unlawful interference, try to keep the track and level until at least able to tell ATC what's going on. Otherwise, try to broadcast warnings on 121.5 MHz or use 7500.

The minimum isolation distance on the ground from a hijacked aircraft is 100 m, away from normal activities.

ECAC

This stands for *European Civil Aviation Conference*, an intergovernmental organisation which works only within Europe, and the only one to deal with security.

The PIC

The PIC may take any reasonable measures, including restraint, against anybody on reasonable grounds that they have committed, or are about to commit, an unlawful act on board.

Reasons might include protecting the safety of the aircraft, maintaining good order and discipline, enabling delivery of such people to the authorities, or disembarking them. Other crew members and passengers may be "volunteered" to assist. In this respect, the aircraft is "in flight" all the time the doors are closed but, in a forced landing, the PIC's authority continues until State authorities take over.

PANS-OPS (DOC 8168)   010 06

PANS-OPS is one of three documents issued by ICAO that supplement the Annexes. They do not have the same legal force, but are still widely used as working documents.

PANS OPS (Aircraft Operations) is in two sections:

- **Volume 1** - *Flight Procedures*, for the guidance of flight operations staff.
- **Volume 2** - *Construction of Visual & Instrument Procedures*. This is more specialised, for people who design approaches, to ensure that procedures are as uniform as possible around the world

Thus, much of PANS OPS concerns IFR flight, but there are some items of interest to the VFR pilot. To put it another way, instrument procedures are designed according to ICAO PANS OPS document 8168. The idea is to provide safe clearance from obstacles and the ground both horizontally (using a procedure) and vertically (with a Minimum Obstacle Clearance). The horizontal clearance is based on the radio aid being used and your distance from it. As you get further away, the protected area splays, or gets wider. A fix tolerance is also involved, as described in *Accuracy Of Fixes*, later. The minimum obstacle clearance is 984 ft (300 m) up to the Initial Approach Fix, and reduces during the Approach and Missed Approach, to at least 98 ft (30 m).

 Flying a published procedure does not guarantee obstacle clearance if an engine fails, as normal operations with all engines operating are assumed, so you must limit the weight of your aircraft to clear all obstacles *after* a failure of the most critical engine. Some companies produce their own procedures for this purpose. However, some procedures may allow them to be avoided laterally* which may include a turn (or a series of turns) based on specific headings or tracks.

Procedures also assume that you do not compensate for wind when being radar vectored, and that you do for routes expressed as tracks to be made good.

*The wind can help you obtain excellent gradients, but it can easily take you out of the protected Takeoff Flight Path, which starts at 90 m from the runway centre line at the end of TODA, then expanding at 12.5% to form a corridor of 300m from the runway extended centre line (with proper navaid accuracy). As go-arounds are typically done before the threshold, straying out of the protected area is quite easy.

It is the operator's responsibility to examine all relevant obstacles and ensure that the performance requirements of Annex 6 are met, with contingency procedures for abnormal and emergency operations, even to producing internal departure procedures for an engine failure (contingency procedures should follow the normal procedure as much as possible). It is the State's responsibility to make available the obstacle information described in Annexes 4 and 6, and any additional information used in the departure design.

Otherwise, you should, as part of any risk assessment specify the actions to be carried out if an engine fails.

Aircraft Categories

Performance affects the airspace and visibility needed for the manoeuvres required. The most significant factor is speed, because going too fast in a procedure turn can take you away from protected airspace. Five categories of aircraft have been established for approach purposes:

Category	Threshold Speed
A	< 91 kts IAS
B	91-120 kts IAS
C	121-140 kts IAS
D	141-165 kts IAS
E	166-210 kts IAS

The speed used is the IAS at the threshold, based on 1.3 times the stall speed (V_{SO}) in the landing configuration at Max Certified Landing Mass (V_{AT}), which is a computed number. Some countries like you to use the actual approach speed instead.

Most light aircraft use A or B, although GPS databases generally only use C & D. You may be asked to go a little faster when things are busy.

ARINC 424

Since the 1970s, the ARINC 424 standard has been used in addition to charts to allow IFR procedures to be stored and managed in electronic databases.

Essentially, paths (heading/track) are terminated by beacons and waypoints, and IFR procedures are based on 23 variations of them. Each leg type has a two-letter name based on the path/terminator combination.

Procedure Design

The design of instrument procedures includes the construction of routes, as well as those for arrivals, departures and approaches.

Each contracting state is responsible for ensuring that all published procedures can be flown safely by the relevant aircraft. It is not enough just to design such procedures - quality control and monitoring are involved as well.

Conventional designs are used for traditional navigation systems, which means that they depend on the location of those aids, and may therefore involve longer routes, and the fact that their accuracy degrades with distance.

With RNAV, on the other hand, there is no dependency on navaids, and much more flexibility, depending on the characteristics of the aids involved. However, there were still issues with individual system performance, which was unpredictable, so obstacle clearance limits were not improved

much. The Performance Based Navigation approach, described in *Radio Navigation*, allows for more predictable flight tracking and smaller obstacle clearances. Put more simply, given the accuracy involved, it is possible to introduce more complex procedures.

Departure Procedures

The departure procedure is there to get you safely from the takeoff point into the enroute environment, which necessarily means that you will be below the MSA while you do it. To make sure that you don't hit anything during a departure, procedures may be published as:

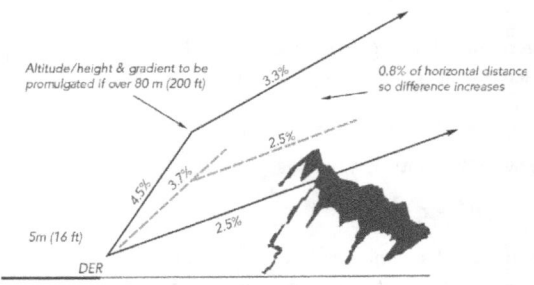

- specific routes to be followed, avoiding obstacles.
- omnidirectional departures, with minimum gradients to ensure you go over specified significant obstacles, although the gradients used (see below) are not intended to be an operational limitation.

Of course, sometimes you have to make it up as you go along if you are taking off from an airfield with no procedures at all (sometimes known as *unassessed*).

The simplest procedure is to climb visually* up to the MSA/MEA, which is not such a good idea if the weather is poor and you are in a fast jet trying to avoid mountains.

If things are a little tighter, you could climb visually to the Missed Approach Point relating to any of the approaches for that airfield, which will usually be at the threshold of a runway and may involve a tight turn, or go backwards up the approach, because approaches provide terrain clearance as well, albeit with steeper gradients.

*Don't forget to tell ATC, as they will have to provide separation.

Remembering that you need adequate performance for the *entire* flight, including when an engine fails, there are several aspects you have to consider - you must calculate the weights for takeoff, cruise, landing, HOGE and all the above without one engine, using the lesser weight.

In the climbout, the required performance is expressed as a minimum percentage gradient.

PROCEDURE DESIGN GRADIENT (PDG)

The PDG is the gradient needed to clear obstacles and provide the reserve divergence in height to ensure that you will achieve the 1,000 ft (2,000 ft in mountains) clearance from obstacles. A gradient is used (as opposed to a rate of climb) to enable any aircraft to apply the requirements.

A 2.5% slope is used to determine obstacles shown on the chart. Special procedures are required if any obstacles penetrate it. If not, a 3.3% gradient provides at least 48 feet of obstacle clearance for each nautical mile. The PDG is either the default (3.3%), or one that has been specified by the procedure designer. Unless otherwise published, a PDG of 3.3% is assumed, starting with 2.5%, or that based on the most critical obstacle, whichever is higher, plus 0.8%, but this may differ on the departure plate. The first part of the departure may have a steeper gradient to a specified height, after which 3.3% can be resumed. Aircraft are assumed to climb on the extended centreline to 120 m (394 ft) before turning. The gradient is calculated by:

```
ROC = Groundspeed x %
```

When determining limiting gradients on takeoff, the rate of climb to achieve a certain gradient is found by:

```
FPM = G/S (kts) x % Gradient
```

So to achieve a 3% gradient at 80 kts, your ROC must be:

```
270 = 80 x 3 (%)
```

There will be an OEI climb graph to tell you under what conditions you can expect to maintain that. If obstacles cannot be cleared, the use of minima ensures that they can be seen and/or avoided. In fact, if the slope is penetrated by obstacles, the procedure designer can use a combination of:

- Increasing the climb gradient
- Increasing takeoff minima
- Making you use a specific route (see *Standard Instrument Departure*, overleaf)

STANDARD INSTRUMENT DEPARTURES (SIDS)

Standard charts showing routes in and out of busy terminal areas are published to speed up a safe and orderly flow of IFR traffic. They provide obstruction free flight paths (if their conditions are observed) and clear instructions about what to do if communications fail. Noise abatement procedures may also be included.

A SID (DP, or Departure Procedure, in the USA) is a pre-planned departure route, used for:

- noise abatement
- ATC separation
- obstacle clearance

 SID (and STAR) charts are not drawn to scale, because there is simply too much information to fit into a small space! They merely tell you at what point to be at what height as you depart for the first airway joining point. Thus, the time taken for the departure cannot be assessed with accuracy.

The best you can do is take the total distance and apply the TAS and wind velocity at the mean altitude, rounded to the nearest minute.

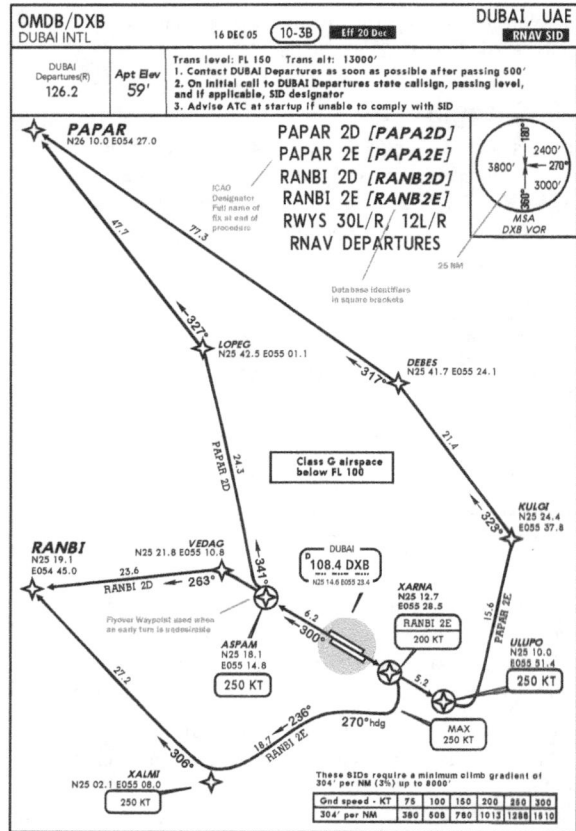

Another benefit is the reduction in pilot and controller workload, because not so many radio calls are needed. Misunderstandings are therefore reduced (assuming the charts are current), and flight safety is increased. Details of all the approaches will be in the navigation database of your FMS.

SIDs are normally designed to cope with as many aircraft categories as possible - those that are limited to specific ones are shown as such. SIDs terminate at the first fix, facility or waypoint of the enroute phase.

When filing for a flight plan that includes a SID, you should use the ICAO route code. The Database Identifiers (in square brackets) are used for the FMS.

 A climb gradient may be established for reasons other than obstacle clearance, such as to meet an ATC climb requirement or early or immediate turns after departure. They may also be needed for DME/DME reception when using RNAV based procedures.

AIR LAW
PANS-OPS (DOC 8168)

OBSTACLE CLEARANCE
To guarantee obstacle clearance, minimum performance is shown in a table that converts the climb gradient (in ft per nm) to the climb rate (in ft per min) for specified groundspeeds.

These SIDs require a minimum climb gradient of 304' per NM (3%) up to 8000'

Gnd speed - KT	75	100	150	200	250	300
304' per NM	380	508	780	1013	1288	1510

The obstacle free glide path is based on a climb rate of 200 ft per minute after crossing the end of the runway at least 35 ft above the ground. You must also be able to climb to 400 feet above the airfield elevation before needing a turn.

There are essentially two types of departure, *straight* or *turning*.

STRAIGHT DEPARTURES
Straight departures keep the initial departure track within 15° of the centreline, with guidance acquired within 20 km (10.8 nm) from the DER, from a suitably located VOR/NDB or RNAV. Where obstacles exist, steeper gradients may be specified, after which the minimum gradient of 3.3% is considered to prevail. Gradients to 200 ft for close-in obstacles are not specified.

The Splay (the angle by which an area expands) for a straight departure with no track guidance is, at DER, 150 m to each side of the centre line, going to Area 1, which extends 1.9 nm straight ahead. The angle of expansion is 15° to each side, parallel to the centreline. There is no Area 2 for a non-track guidance departure, but there is if guidance exists, starting after 1.9 nm from DER. If the track guidance is a VOR or NDB, the area decreases toward the aid by 7.8 or 10.3° respectively, measured parallel to the centreline. On passing the aid, the area will expand by the same figures. The area continues past the aid for another 2 nm (VOR) and another 2½ nm (NDB).

TURNING DEPARTURES
Turning departures are constructed if you go past 15° to avoid an obstacle before or after the turn - turns may be specified at specific altitudes, fixes and facilities, but straight flight is assumed until 394 ft (120 m) above the DER anyway. Guidance information from a VOR or an NDB must be available within 10 km of completing the turn. A turning area is constructed as shown overleaf.

For a turning departure, Area 1 is as above, but Area 2 is affected by the amount of course change. If a turn of 30° to the right is initiated in Area 2, the left side splay will continue as in Area 1, depending on fix and flight technical tolerance, after which it will make a right 30° turn. After this, it increases by 15° relative to a line parallel to the new centreline (the fix and flight technical tolerances are safety factors for ensuring the aircraft is overhead the turning fix and to allow it to initiate the turn). The right splay will increase by 15° measured from the new centreline until intersecting track guidance splay which is as above: that is, a fix on the centreline from which an obstacle clearance area is calculated. The splay is still 7.8 (VOR) and 10.3° (NDB).

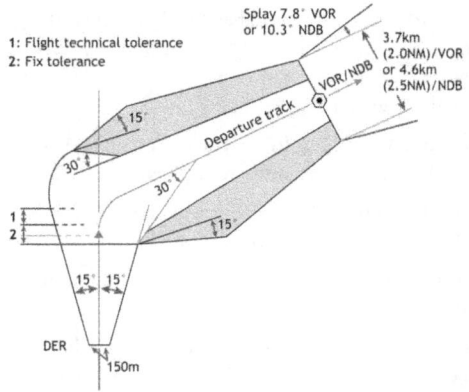

Obstacle clearance in the primary area of an initial approach segment is at least 300 m (984 feet). For an intermediate segment, it is 150 m (492 feet). The Minimum Sector Altitude (MSA) provides 300 m obstacle clearance within 25 nm of the navigation facility on which a procedure is based.

In summary:

- The splay in Area 1 is always 15°
- The splay in Area 2 for a straight departure is 7.8° (VOR) and 10.3° (NDB). Past the fix, the splay becomes positive
- The splay for a turning departure is nearly the same, except for the fix and flight technical tolerance, after which the outside boundary turns by the same amount as the centreline and thereafter expands by 15° outward until intersecting with the fix splay as in Area 2 for a straight departure. The splay is calculated to the sides of the track guidance aid, not overhead

OMNIDIRECTIONAL DEPARTURES
Where there is no track guidance for a departure, the omnidirectional method* is used, in which a 3.3% PDG is assumed, with a straight climb on the extended runway centreline until reaching 120 m (394 ft) above the aerodrome elevation. At least 90 m (295 ft) of obstacle clearance must be provided before turns greater than 15° can be specified.

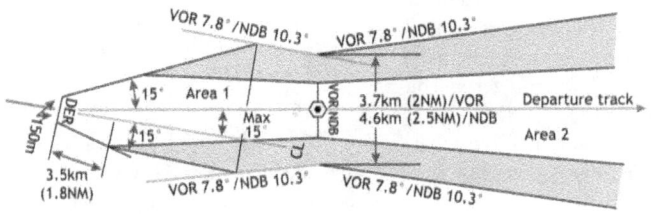

DER: Departure End of Runway   CL: Extended Runway Centre Line

*Despite the term *omnidirectional*, departures are based on runway headings. When this is not practical, maybe due to obstacles, there should be a departure route or increased minima to ensure that you can see them.

There are four types of omnidirectional departure, starting at the DER, assuming that turns are not initiated before 600 m from the threshold:

- **Standard** - climb straight ahead to 394 feet (120 m), using a 3.3% climb gradient, then turn in any direction, assuming no obstacles penetrate the 2.5% OIS and there is 90 m of clearance
- **Specified Turn Height** - if you can't turn at 394 ft, the 3.3% climb gradient continues until you can
- **Specified PDG** - climb gradient may be more than 3.3% to clear obstacles before a turn
- **Sector Departures** - sectors may have minimum specifications

Restrictions will be expressed as sectors to be avoided, or with minimum specifications. Where omnidirectional procedures cannot be used, you must either fly a departure route or see and avoid obstacles.

PUBLISHED INFORMATION

This will include:

- Significant obstacles that penetrate the OIS, including the position and height of close-in ones
- The highest obstacle in the departure area, and any significant obstacle outside the area affecting the design of the procedure
- The altitude/height where gradients over 3.3% are no longer used
- Navigation facilities, fixes or waypoints, radials and DME distances depicting route segments

The published minimum gradient will be the highest in any sector expected to be overflown. The altitude to which it is specified allows an aircraft to continue at 3.3% through that sector, a succeeding one, or an altitude authorised for another phase of flight. A fix may also be used to mark the point where gradients over 3.3% are no longer required.

RNAV PROCEDURES

Departure routes are only labelled as RNAV when that is the primary means of navigation used.

Approach Procedures

An approach procedure may have five separate segments, shown later. They are based on *tracks*, which you should try to maintain by adjusting heading for the known wind. The segments begin and end at designated fixes, or other specified points where fixes are not available. Whenever possible, a *straight-in* approach will be used, which is aligned with the runway centreline (a non-precision approach is considered to be "straight-in" if the angle between the final approach track and the runway centreline is 30° or less).

Minimum Sector Altitudes are established for each aerodrome, which provide at least 300 m (984 feet) obstacle clearance within 46 km (25 nm) of the homing facility for that approach.

The MOC for the final segment is a fixed margin of 90 m (295 ft) without a FAF, and 75 m (246 ft) with a FAF.

MINIMUM ALTITUDES

An obstacle clearance altitude/height (OCA/H) is calculated in the development of a procedure for each aircraft category. OCA/H is:

- for a **precision approach****, the lowest altitude (i.e referenced to MSL) or lowest height (above the elevation of the relevant threshold), at which a missed approach *must be initiated* for compliance with obstacle clearance criteria
- for a **non-precision approach****, the lowest altitude (OCA) or the lowest height above aerodrome elevation or that of the relevant threshold, if the elevation is more than 2 m (7 ft) below the aerodrome elevation (OCH), *below which the aircraft cannot descend* without infringing the appropriate obstacle clearance criteria
- for a visual (**circling**) procedure, the lowest altitude (OCA) or the lowest height above the aerodrome elevation (OCH) below which an aircraft cannot descend without infringing appropriate obstacle clearance criteria

**Approaches are either *precision* or *non-precision* - the former includes vertical guidance, technically being *direct approaches with bearing, elevation and distance information*. Good examples are an ILS or PAR, or even MLS. A non-precision approach is basically anything else, such as VOR or ADF, or a *Localiser Only* ILS, where the descent has to be judged by the pilot. The difference between the two is easy - *Decision Height* (DH), used on precision approaches, is *height-based*, in that you go directly down to it, and go-around if you don't see the ground. In other words, the vertical element is started at a precise point, and you likely have the runway in sight at the decision altitude, rather than looking for it in a visual manoeuvre, and reconfiguring the aircraft in a hurry. It is the point at which a decision is made to go around, so you may dip below it while you make your mind up. Obstacle clearance is also based on the runway threshold.

Minimum Descent Height (MDH), on the other hand, is time-based, in that you set the stopwatch on leaving the fix and look up to see if you can see the ground at the time you calculated from your groundspeed, having reached the MDH. For this reason, non-precision approaches *must be flown accurately* with regard to speed, otherwise your calculations will be out. *MDH is a height below which you must not descend without the required visual reference.*

In general, minima are developed by adding the effects of a number of operational factors to OCA/H to produce a DH or MDA/H. There

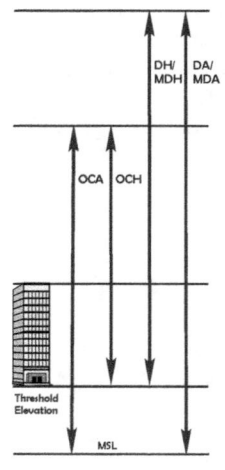

may well be further restrictions, based on experience,. in your Company's Operations Manual. The DA/H for a precision approach is found by adding OCH to the *threshold* elevation. That for a non-precision approach or circling uses *airfield* elevation.

In between the two is the APV approach, which is satellite based. APV stands for *Approach with Vertical Guidance*. Although it can have the same minima as an ILS, it is not a precision approach under ICAO rules.

STATE MINIMA

Minima set by the State have a tolerance of -0 feet, as signified by the term *not below*. They may be underlined on some charts. If in doubt, Intermediate and Final approach segment heights or altitudes as State minima.

APPROACH PROCEDURE DESIGN

The design of an approach procedure is generally influenced by:

- Terrain
- The type of operation
- The type of aircraft

Protection areas assume that turns are made at 25° or bank angles that provide a 3° per second turn rate, whichever is lower.

INSTRUMENT APPROACH AREAS

Where there is track guidance, segments have a specified volume of airspace, symmetrically about the centreline, with the vertical cross section divided into 1 primary and 2 secondary areas, which are half as wide and a quarter as wide, respectively, as the total width (the primary area surrounds the aeroplane, with secondaries outside.

Minimum Obstacle Clearance is provided for all of the primary area, and from the inner edge of the secondaries, reducing to zero at the outer edges (in other words, they slope upwards from the primary).

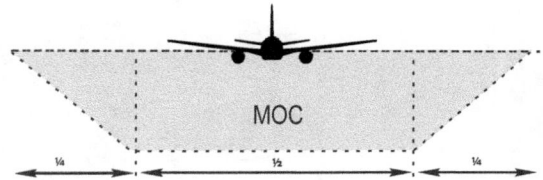

The MOC in the initial approach segment primary area is 300 m (600 m in mountains). On the intermediate approach segment it decreases from 300 m to 150 m.

For more than 15° (turning departures), the MOC is at least 90 m, or 295 ft, or even more in mountainous terrain.

ACCURACY OF FIXES

All navigation aids have limitations as to their accuracy:

	VOR	NDB	DME	LOC
System Tolerance	4.5°	6.2°	0.25 nm +1.25% of DME distance	1.4°
Flight Tolerance	0.7°	0.7°		1.0°
Total Tolerance	5.2°	6.9°*		2.4°

*Overhead, ±5°. Approach tracking accuracy is within ±10° of the published approach track.

Picture Below: Standard Arrival Route (STAR)

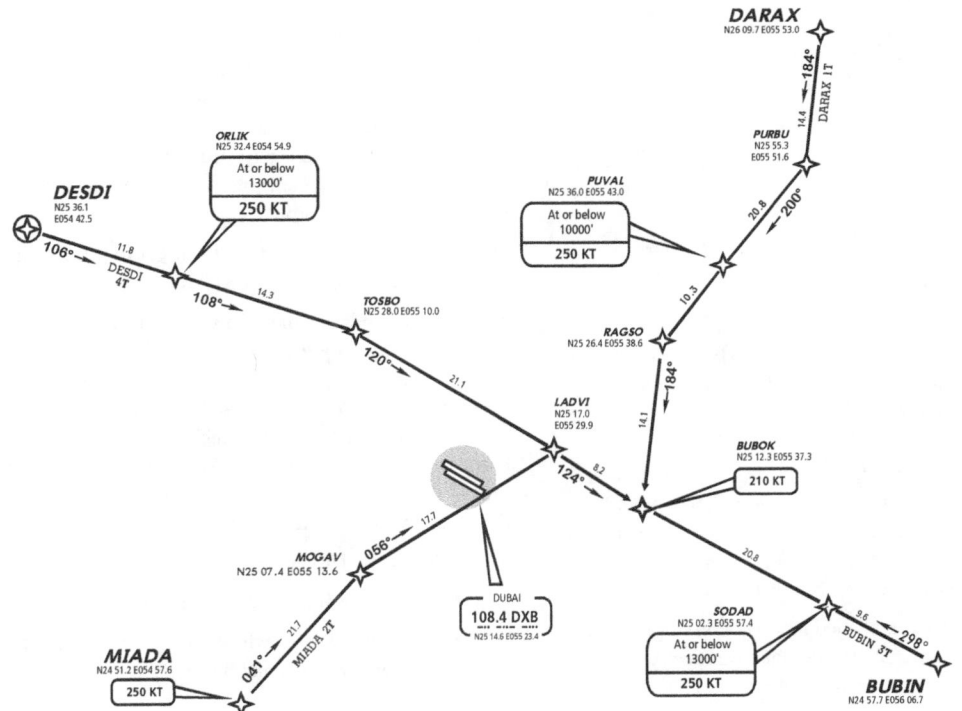

AIR LAW
PANS-OPS (DOC 8168)

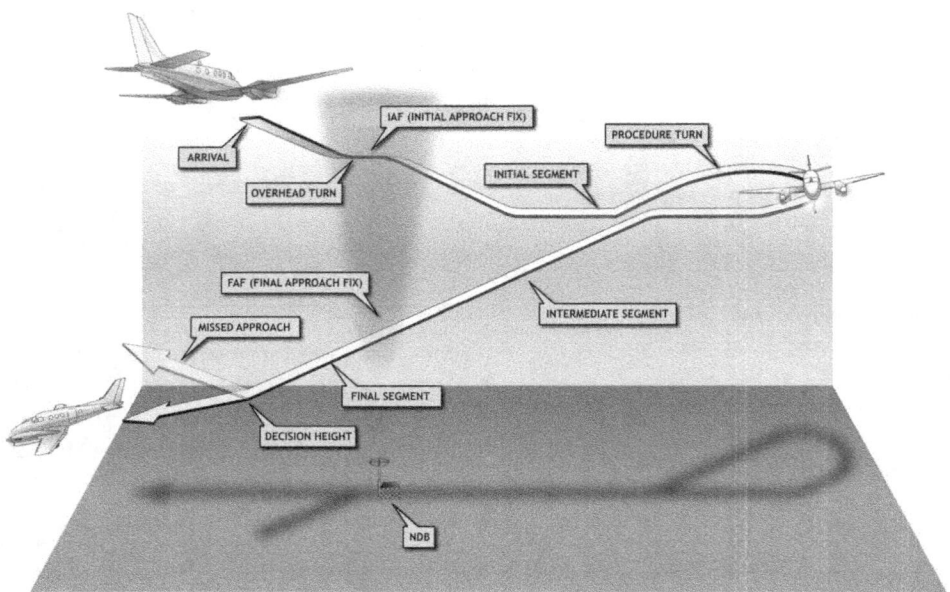

Values are based on *Root Sum Square* (RSS) of system errors. Others include:

- Terminal Radar within 20 nm - ±.8 nm
- Enroute Surveillance Radar within 40 - ±1.7 nm
- DME - ±0.25 nm, + 1.25% of the distance from the antenna
- Marker - 0.2 nm at 1000' (it increases with height)

To cope with these, fix tolerance areas are established, within which you are allowed to be and still be protected.

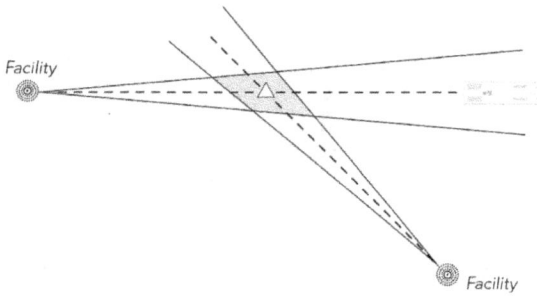

DESCENT GRADIENTS

In the final approach of a procedure with a FAF, the optimum is 5%, or around 300 ft/nm, for a 3° glidepath. The minimum is 4.3% (2.5°) and maximum 6.5% (3.5°).

STANDARD ARRIVAL ROUTE

A STAR is used like a SID, but for going *to* an aerodrome. It terminates at the first fix for the approach. The correct chart (in date!) should be available well before you get near the destination, so an effective briefing can be carried out.

 Until you are established in a recognised procedure, you are responsible for terrain clearance!

APPROACH SEGMENTS
ARRIVAL SEGMENT

Where you transfer from the enroute phase, up to the *Initial Approach Fix* (IAF). An IFR flight shall not be cleared for initial approach below the appropriate minimum altitude unless either:

- the pilot has reported passing an appropriate point defined by a radio aid
- the pilot reports that the aerodrome can be maintained in sight
- the aircraft is conducting a visual approach
- the aircraft's position has been positively determined with radar

INITIAL APPROACH SEGMENT

This portion runs from the Initial Approach Fix (IAF) to the Intermediate Fix (IF), if there is one. If not, some sort of reversal or holding pattern is required. You might not need this segment if the Intermediate Fix is part of the route structure*, in which case you can skip a bit and start the procedure at the IF, and intermediate criteria apply.

*You may get to the IAF directly, or get to it through a more complex procedure such as a STAR.

There is no standard length for the initial approach segment, but it must be at least long enough to allow for any required altitude changes, with the optimum descent gradient being 4%, but the maximum is 8%. You might use a racetrack procedure for descents where there is not enough distance in a straight line and entry into a reversal procedure (see below) is not practical. The outbound time should be 1-3 minutes to allow for increased descent, which may vary according to aircraft category.

The width of the IAS consists of:

- A primary area 2.5 nm either side of the track, and
- A secondary area which adds an extra 2.5 nm to the primary area, making 5 nm

In the primary area, minimum obstacle clearance of 984 feet (300 m) is provided within 25 nm. In the secondary area, this reduces linearly to zero at the outer edge.

You can make an initial approach along a VOR radial, NDB bearing, radar vector or a combination, or DME. Angles of interception should not exceed 120°, and when they exceed 70°, there should be at least a 2 nm lead.

Descent patterns and procedures are considered to be in the initial segment until you are established on the intermediate approach track. If you need to hold before entering the Initial Approach Segment, the holding fix and IAF should coincide, or the IAF should be at least within the holding pattern on the inbound track. You can use dead reckoning up to 10 nm, but otherwise track guidance will be required.

Procedure Turn (45/180)

This is a reversal mechanism, designed to turn you round through 180° in a controlled manner, so you come back in on the same track you went out on. The official definition is *a turn made away from a designated track followed by a turn in the opposite direction to intercept and proceed along the reciprocal of the designated track*.

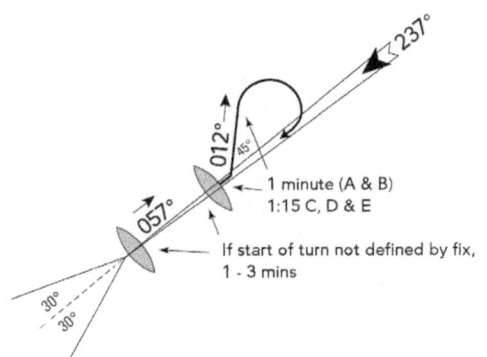

The procedure turn involves timings, based on speeds, that should keep you inside a safe area (from obstacles, that is). The basic one, as above, is to fly outbound for whatever time it says on the chart, turn left 45° (takes 15 seconds at rate 1), fly a straight track for 45 seconds or so (with wind allowance), turn right 180° until you can intercept your original track going the other way. If you got it right, you should be able to intercept it at 30° *without overshooting* (watch out for tailwinds). The turn is designated left or right according to the first turn.

Entry into a reversal procedure should be from a track within ±30° of the outbound track. If those conditions are satisfied, you must request a Procedure Turn approach.

The first straight leg may be timed or limited by a radial or DME distance. The second one (after the 45° turn) does not have track guidance but may be timed.

The maximum rate of descent in a reversal (or racetrack) procedure (or even holding) is as follows:

Track	Outbound		Inbound	
Category	A/B	C/D/E	A/B	C/D/E
1 minute	804 ft	1197 ft	492 ft	755 ft

 NThe rates are different for inbound and outbound segments - you can go down faster when outbound.

Maximum speeds for racetrack or reversal procedures are:

- Category A - 110 KIAS
- Category B - 140 KIAS

80/260° turns are popular, too, which are more circular (useful for aircraft with a wide sweep):

A specified 80/260 turn is mandatory. Since it occupies less space along the track, you will return to the final approach track around 1 nm closer to the FAF, although this is allowed for if the turn is specified.

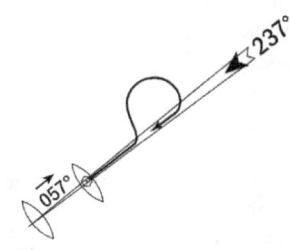

Base Turn

The *base turn* is more or less the same thing, but you turn at the fix:

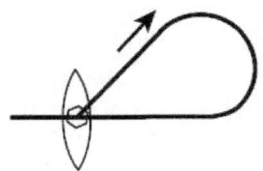

It officially consists of a specified outbound track and timing or DME distance from the facility, followed by a turn to intercept the inbound track where tracks are not reciprocal, or a turn executed during initial approach between the end of the outbound track and the beginning of the intermediate or final approach track.

The turn from the facility is 60° if you go outbound for 1 minute, or 70° if you go outbound for 2 minutes.

A base turn may not be substituted for a procedure turn and *vice versa*. Europe mostly uses base turns. Stornoway (in Scotland) is one of the few that uses a procedure turn.

Racetrack Procedure

A racetrack is similar to a holding pattern (see below), but used when a reversal procedure is not practical, or you might want to lose altitude during the initial segment, where there may not be enough distance to accommodate the normal rate of descent, or there may be something in the way that affects the turn. In effect, all you do is establish a hold and extend the outbound leg for 1, 2 or 3 minutes, then turn inbound (the turn may be based on a DME distance instead of timing).

Entry into the racetrack is similar to that of a hold, but on the parallel entry you must intercept the inbound QDM instead of flying direct to the facility having turned inbound, and on the offset entry, the time on the 30° offset track is 1 minute

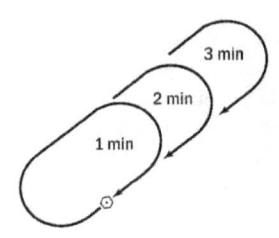

30 seconds, after which you are expected to be on a heading parallel to the outbound track for the remainder of the outbound time. If the outbound time is only 1 minute, the time on the 30° track shall also be 1 minute.

For outbound legs that are longer than one minute, use triple drift for the first minute, then single drift for the remainder. Multiply the timing correction you planned for the outbound leg by the number of still air minutes outbound. The glideslope needle should indicate about half-fly up at the end of the extended outbound leg.

DME Arc

DME arcs are used for transitions to the approach. As such, the aircraft has left the en route phase and is setting up to enter the intermediate or final segment, which may be DME arcs in their own right, although they are rare as final approach segments. The obstacle clearance depends on the approach segment. For an initial segment, 1,000 feet is required in the primary area, which exists 4 nm either side of the arc. For an intermediate segment primary area, try 500 feet. Viewed from above, the end result looks more like a polygon consisting of several short straight lines than an arc, and the bigger the "arc" is, the easier it is to fly, since the turns will be flatter.

 The DME arc is not part of the IR test, but is increasingly being used in the real world.

A line tangent to a circle is always 90° to the radius, so you need to keep the needle near the abeam position for the best results. Thus, the first turn should be made at 90° to the track, making allowance for the wind. That is, you start with an RB of 90° (left or right, as convenient), then allow the RMI needle to stray 5-10° behind. Your DME distance will increase slightly. Then turn enough to bring the needle the same number of degrees ahead of the abeam point, carrying on this way to keep the arc, cross-checking with the DME distance. In theory, with nil wind, you could describe a perfect circle by keeping the RB at 90°, but it almost never happens.

For example, if you need a 10d arc, once you have your starting heading, turn by 10° every time the DME ticks up by 0.1d. If it keeps increasing, turn 20° next time, and if it decreases too much, only turn 5°.

INTERMEDIATE SEGMENT

Preparing for final approach, from the inbound track of the procedure turn to the *Final Approach Fix* (FAF)*, when a final segment is available. Where no FAF is specified, the inbound track is the final approach segment. Any descent here is kept as shallow as possible, because it is where speed and configuration are adjusted, and obstacle clearance reduces to 150 m (492 feet) in the primary area.

*The FAF is usually at the same beacon as for the IAF, only going the other way. It should not be more than 19 km (10 nm) from the landing surface. Where you can gain an operational advantage, an ILS procedure may include a DR segment from a fix to the localiser. This will intersect the localiser at 45° and will not be more than 10 nm long, optimally 5.

An IAF that is at or near the airfield cannot be used as a FAF because it must be along the extended centreline (within 10 nm). It can, however, be used as a Missed Approach Point, in which case the rate of descent for the final segment (for Category A & B aircraft) should be between 394 - 655 feet per minute. During the intermediate and final segments, you may be asked to make minor speed changes adjustments of ±20 kts. However, speed control should not be applied within 4 nm of the threshold on final approach.

There may be alternative procedures, which will not be shown pictorially, but described in words somewhere. They should be used with ATC permission.

FINAL SEGMENT

This covers alignment and descent for landing, in between the FAF MDA/DA, or MAP (*Missed Approach Point*). Optimum and maximum distances for the *Final Approach Fix* (FAF) are 5 and 10 nm, respectively. For ILS or MLS approaches (i.e. precision approaches), the segment starts at the *Final Approach Point* (FAP), which is where the altitude for the intermediate segment intersects the glidepath or elevation angle (MLS). For non-precision approaches, it starts at the Final Approach Fix.

A *Straight-in Approach* (along the runway centreline) will be used as much as possible, which means, especially for non-precision approaches, within 30°, for Cat A and B aircraft, or 15° for others. Otherwise use a *Circling Approach*. The Outer Marker is a fix or facility (usually a 75 MHz beacon) that allows verification of the glide path/altimeter relationship. In other words, you should be at a certain height when you pass it (if asked, the marker performs two functions, as the IAF and FAF).

An SRA must be terminated at 4 km (2 nm) before the threshold unless, with approval, it may be continued to the threshold if the radar is accurate enough. Distance and level information should then be passed each ½ nm.

Landing Minima

There are weather conditions under which you're not allowed to land, attempt to land, or take off. A minimum cloud base and visibility is laid down, based on the navaids available, terrain, obstacles, type of aircraft, crew experience and State legislation. The unfortunate part is that Part OPS requirements are sometimes different from the ICAO ones. The lowest safe height an aircraft may descend to (system minima) depends on what guidance is being used, and the accuracy of the approach aid.

You don't have to do all the hard work; airway manuals should have all the calculations done for you. In any case, you are responsible for ensuring that before takeoff you've got the weather minima for the relevant times at every destination and at least one suitable alternative (this can mean up to 8 airfields if you include takeoff alternates).

Minima that apply to you will be the highest of:

- Those established by the State where you are flying
- Basic minima from your Company, which must not be lower in any case

They may be exceeded in emergency (refer to *Operational Procedures* for details of absolute minima).

The responsibility for establishing minima and their calculation lies with the operator, taking into consideration the adequacy and provision of ground aids, the runways, the skill and experience of flight crews, and obstacles in the missed approach, to mention a few. While you're not allowed to reduce the limits given, you are actively encouraged to increase them if necessary. As they're calculated for fog with little or no wind, you should make allowance for rain and/or crosswinds. Naturally, minima are not valid if anything affecting their calculation has been changed through NOTAMs, or by ATC.

The term *Low Visibility Operations* refers to lower than Standard Category I, other than Standard Category II and III approaches and low visibility takeoffs.

MISSED APPROACH

A Missed Approach must be initiated if you don't see the ground (or the required visual reference) by the time you either reach DH/MDH or the Missed Approach Point, whichever is earlier, otherwise you might hit something. It is quite an urgent procedure - you have just tried to get as close to the ground as the height of a small apartment block, which is a pretty fine tolerance, given the velocities involved, and you don't want to be there if you can't see where you're going, particularly when you are busy altering the aircraft's configuration, altitude and attitude. This is why Missed Approach procedures are kept as simple as possible - there's a lot to do in a short space of time!

 The Missed Approach Point is simply the point from where the Missed Approach criteria become definable - it is NOT the last point from which you can make a safe approach!

In addition, to be picky, the Missed Approach is a navigational process, in that you initiate a go-around but follow the Missed Approach procedure.

Procedure designers must consider obstacle clear gradients and areas in the missed approach, for which the term *segments* may be used - these have nothing to do with takeoff segments. They are meant to provide a reasonable terrain clearance for AEO missed approaches. Procedures are normally based on a minimum gradient of 2.5%, although 2% may be used if suitable precautions are taken. Even 3, 4 or 5% may be used (with approval) if an operational advantage can be obtained. Non-standard gradients are shown on the approach chart, as will the OCA/H for both types.

When under radar control, you will be directed to execute a missed approach if:

- your aircraft appears to be dangerously positioned on final approach
- traffic conflictions
- if no clearance to land has been received from the non-radar controller (i.e. Tower) by the time you reach 4 km (2 nm) from touchdown or some other agreed distance

You will be *advised to consider* a missed approach if, on a radar approach:

- your position means that a successful approach cannot be completed
- your position or identification becomes doubtful
- You are not visible on radar for significant intervals during the last 2 nm

The point when the Missed Approach is initiated depends on the type of procedure, but possible examples are:

- Overhead a navigational facility
- A specified distance from the FAF
- A fix (such as using DME)
- The point of intersection of an electronic glide path with DH

A standard missed approach procedure is based on a nominal missed approach gradient of 2.5% and is divided into 3 phases:

- **Initial.** This begins at the MAPt and ends at the start of climb (SOC). It requires a lot of crew concentration and attention, so no turns are specified in this phase.
- **Intermediate.** After the SOC the climb is continued, normally straight ahead to the first point where 50 m (164 ft) obstacle clearance is obtained and can be maintained. The track is assumed to change by up to 15°.
- **Final.** The final phase begins where 50 m (164 ft) obstacle clearance is first obtained (for Category H procedures, 40 m (131 ft)) and can be maintained, extending to where a new approach, holding or a return to en-route flight is initiated. Turns may be prescribed in this phase.

The Missed Approach is assumed to be initiated above (or not lower than) DH or MDH. If you go-around before reaching the MAP, it is expected that you will go to the MAP first, to keep you in protected airspace. From a circling manoeuvre, you are expected to make an initial climbing turn toward the landing runway and overhead, to establish climbing on the missed approach track.

Sometimes, the MAP will be a fix or a specified point, which is useful for timing.

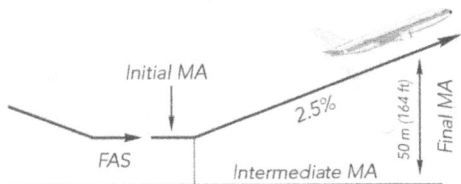

If no instructions have been received from ATC, follow the published ones. If you still don't get any by the time you reach the Missed Approach Holding Fix, hold there in a standard pattern on the inbound track. If you have to leave the circling procedure, one suggestion is to go to the centre of the airport, and follow the procedure for the approach you just did as closely as possible.

AIR LAW
PANS-OPS (DOC 8168)

CIRCLING (VISUAL MANOEUVRING)

Circling is *visually* manoeuvring to a runway after an Instrument Approach to another one, or the same one if the approach is not straight in (more than 30° off, in fact). You could also be going to an airfield that is very close to high ground, and to keep the required clearance you must arrive at the threshold too high for a proper approach. Minima for this will give the necessary obstacle clearance but, in mountainous areas, account will also be taken of height and effect on turbulence. The circling area is constructed by drawing an arc from *each threshold*, and joining them with tangents. It might be related to aircraft category, speed, wind (25 kts) and bank angle (average 20° or Rate 1, whichever is less). If you have to bank more than 30°, consider setting yourself up again. It also helps to keep a little above the MDA, say 50 feet, but remember you are also below normal circuit height. Since, by definition, the weather is bad (or you wouldn't be using it), set your radios and machine up for the missed approach before you reach MDA, in case you get clag on the downwind leg.

Some sectors may be prohibited to avoid obstacles.

 Circling is *part* of an instrument approach, not a separate procedure after one, so the minima (*visibility* is used for circling, not RVR) are limiting for all pre-flight and in-flight planning and approach ban purposes, if circling is required.

Circling height will be in the Airway Manual, precalculated to a standard formula; otherwise, just add 300 feet to the highest obstacle within 5 nm of the airfield (provided the result is above 500 feet agl). Descent below MDA/H should not be made until either visual reference can be maintained, you can see the threshold and you can avoid obstacles once in a position to carry out a landing (it is assumed that you keep all these in sight). If you lose visual reference, you must initiate a Missed Approach - make an initial climbing turn toward the landing runway and overhead for the track.

You can get a reasonably accurate circling visibility in metres by multiplying the circuit speed in knots by 20, that is, if speed = 120 knots, visibility must be 2400m.

However, here is a more accurate table:

A/C Cat	Max IAS (kts)	Obstacle Clearance	Lowest OCH	Min Vis km (nm)
A	100	90 (295)	120 (394)	1.9 (1.0)
B	135	90 (295)	150 (492)	2.8 (1.5)
C	180	120 (394)	180 (591)	3.7 (2.0)
D	205	120 (394)	210 (689)	4.6 (2.5)
E	240	150 (492)	240 (787)	6.5 (3.5)

You should not descend below minima until aligned with the runway, except to 500 feet agl on base leg at your discretion if you have the whole of the runway continuously in sight.

RNAV & VOR/DME

RNAV procedures are non-precision approaches. Those based on VOR/DME are assumed to use one facility with a VOR and co-located DME.

Approved RNAV systems may be used if the RNAV equipment and facilities are working, and the pilot knows how to operate the equipment.

A disadvantage is that humans have put the information into the system, and there may be data input areas, which result in errors in the computed position.

Navigational accuracy depends on:

- Ground station tolerance
- Receiving system tolerance
- Flying technical tolerance
- System computation tolerance
- Distance from reference facility

USE OF FMS/RNAV EQUIPMENT

When this equipment is available, it can be used to fly conventional non-precision approaches if the procedure is monitored with the basic display normally associated with the procedure, within the normal tolerances.

Holding

Holding is a procedure that keeps you more or less in one place if you have to wait for the weather to clear, for example, or for ATC scheduling purposes, or you have something to sort out. Technically, it is *a pre-determined manoeuvre which keeps an aircraft in a specified airspace while awaiting further clearance.*

Tip: The hold is your friend if you have a problem!

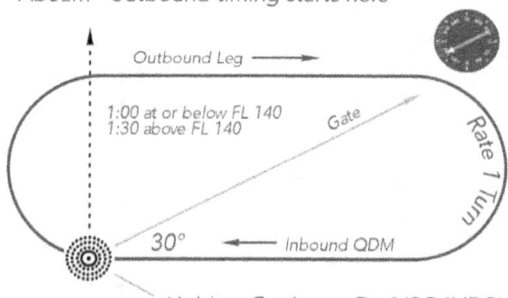

Holding was a routine requirement before radar came along, and still is in remote places without radar or a procedural service.

Patterns are usually right-handed racetrack patterns (known as *standard* patterns), but they may occasionally go to the left (*non-standard*) or have a different outbound leg time, which is usually up to 1 or 1½ minutes, depending on your height. In other words, the standard hold should take four minutes (although ICAO don't specify a total time - it's a good exercise for meeting EATs, and it is a matter of professional pride to many pilots to arrive over the holding point precisely on time).

The basic tolerances for timing are within 20 seconds of the required holding time (e.g. an EAT), having established timing and drift within three holds.

You should only *reduce* timing to keep you within protected airspace.

Tip: In a flight test, the primary goals are to establish and track the QDM, and time the outbound leg for one still air minute. The QDM relates to the inbound leg**.

A **holding fix** is usually a VOR or NDB, but it can also be an airway intersection*, an RNAV waypoint or a DME fix. However, they cannot be established within cones of confusion, or at an intersection where the radials cross at angles of less than 45° or are cross bearings from NDBs.

*Where you perform intersection holds, which are quite common on STARs, almost always with a direct entry.

**The inbound track is the only bit where you actually use radio navigation. VOR holds are often given in terms of radials so remember to calculate it the right way round!

OBSTACLE CLEARANCE

The *holding area* includes the *basic area*, which allows for speed, wind effect, timing errors and fix characteristics, and entry areas, for clearances of at least

- 300 m (984 ft) above obstacles in the holding area for non-mountainous areas, rounded up to the nearest 50 m or 100 ft. A mountainous area (terrain rise of 3 000 feet over 10 nm) requires 600 m (1969 feet) to cater for the possible effects of turbulence, downdraughts and other phenomena concerning the performance of altimeters.
- a value (in PANS-OPS) providing obstacle clearance in the buffer area.

A *buffer area* extends 9.3 km (5 nm) beyond the holding area, within which the height and nature of obstacles are taken into account when determining the minimum holding level*, providing a decreasing obstacle clearance margin the further you get away (zero at 5 nm).

*The *Minimum Holding Altitude* (MHA) is the lowest altitude prescribed for a holding pattern that provides for obstruction clearance and ensures good reception of radio and navaid signals. It provides a clearance of at least 1000 ft (300 m) above obstacles in the holding area, and is rounded up to the nearest 100 ft, or 50 m, as appropriate.

If no MHA is prescribed, minimum IFR altitudes apply:

- In a designated mountainous area, 2000 ft above the highest obstacle within a horizontal distance of 5 statute miles from the course to be flown.
- In other than mountainous areas, 1000 ft above the highest obstacle within 5 statute miles from the course to be flown.
- In other cases, as authorized by ATC (air traffic control) or by the operator.

BANK ANGLES

In a standard pattern, the bank angle should be the lesser of 25° or that for a turn rate of 3° per second, or Rate 1 (10% of your IAS +7 kts). This means that your speed should be reduced in the hold, for two reasons. One is that you cannot keep to 25° bank if you are going too fast (over 180 kts), and you need endurance speed anyway to stay there for the maximum time. If you cannot conform to a holding pattern, you should inform ATC as soon as possible and request a revised clearance.

Tip: When holding on a VOR, bug the outbound heading, and set the CDI on the inbound QDM. Start turning on station passage (after the flag has moved to FROM), and time the outbound leg when the flag appears after the cone of confusion, or at wings level, whichever is later.

You must fly accurately on the outbound leg, and note the time when passing over the facility at the end, which should be three minutes after the abeam. This routine (which should be done at every waypoint) should help:

- **Time**. Punch the clock as soon as you are overhead or get station passage, as even a second will affect the outbound in a hold. In the hold, check the timing and restart the time when abeam. In the cruise, write the time on your nav log.
- **Turn**. Get moving in the direction desired. Rate 1 to the outbound heading in the hold.
- **Twist** the OBS if using a VOR and set the heading bug before you start turning. **Tip:** To save writing down headings, just set the heading bug.
- **Throttle**. Adjust power for descent or climb or if a change in altitude is required.
- **Tune**. Make sure the navaid is still working (flags, or audio for NDBs).
- **Track** - If you did not choose a suitable heading above, start intercepting.
- **Talk** - To ATC **after** you have done the above.

CORRECTING FOR WIND

The outbound timing is corrected for wind velocity to keep you inside the primary holding area, especially when you are using an NDB. In the UK, at least, it should take you 3 minutes from the abeam position to the overhead.

You adjust the *outbound* leg for wind direction and speed so, if the inbound leg is into wind, you cut the outbound short by whatever amount is appropriate (usually 1 second per knot), plus double the drift correction you would use inbound. If the inbound leg has a tailwind, on the other hand, you add the time to the outbound leg.

The reason for using double drift outbound (and single drift inbound) is that you only have the one leg to make the correction on - if you were flying inbound with no correction, you would have to apply three times the drift on the outbound leg, but this could involve drift angles over 45°, and larger turns, which are not recommended. The hold will also not be correctly shaped, as you will be inside the normal path as you start going outbound, and outside it as you finish, so expect the relative bearing to be up to 45° just before you start to turn inbound (it's normally 30°). One suggestion is to use triple drift if the wind is compressing your hold, and double drift if the wind is expanding your hold. If the outbound time is less than 1 minute, you will be using more than triple drift anyway (and less if the outbound time is more).

You need more than 1 minute with a heavy crosswind.

For timing, one rule of thumb with an inbound headwind is to subtract $1/3$ of the time inbound from the outbound leg. Otherwise, add $1/3$. If the tailwind is more than $1/3$ of the TAS, you will be doing a 360° turn at the fix as the outbound time will be zero! If the headwind is more than $1/3$ of the TAS, the outbound time will be 2 minutes.

Another one is to reduce the outbound time by one second for every knot of headwind - 10 kts would give you 50 seconds (by now, the wind has taken you past the abeam point anyway). Yet another is that if it takes 45 seconds from the overhead to the abeam position, take a further 45 seconds for the bit between the abeam position to end of the outbound leg.

Rough Guide: Use either 0°, 5° in light winds, 10-15° in moderate breezes or 20-30° in strong winds. If it gets to howling gale or storm force then just be glad you got back over the aid in time! As a reminder, the outbound timing below FL 140 is 1 still air minute.

In addition to starting the timing when abeam the fix (or wings level, if the abeam point cannot be determined), it's a good idea to note the timing from wings level inbound as well, so you get a better idea of how to adjust the outbound. Another good clue as to how the outbound leg is doing is to keep an eye on the relative bearing of the beacon - it should be around 30° from behind if you are anywhere near the correct position (known as the Gate).

If you are inside the hold, the tail of the ADF needle will be at the 30° point ahead of time, so correct to that heading (fly the gate) until the end of the outbound leg time, then turn inbound (you might se a lesser rate of turn). For example, if your outbound QDR is 274 your gate in still wind will be 124 (304). If you reach your gate at 50 seconds, fly 304 for 10 seconds.

If the reading is more than 30°, you are too wide or too slow and can expect to increase the rate of turn to recover your timing. If all is going well during the turn inbound, 30° after turning (say at 60° to go), you should be within 10° of the QDM. Also, carry out 90°, 60° and 30° checks on the turn inbound - at 90 to go you should see +5 of the QDM, with 60 to go you should see the QDM, and with 30 to go, -5 of the QDM. If not, you need to roll out early if you are tight or keep rolling if you are wide.

DME HOLDS

DME holds are actually between two distances - the inbound fix is at the smaller one, and you start turning inbound when you reach the larger (that is, the outbound leg terminates as soon as you get to the limiting DME distance - no timing is involved).

They are more often than not given to turbine aircraft, with the leg length given with the clearance.

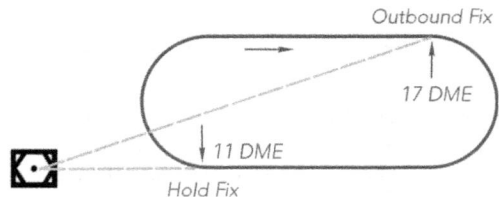

ENTERING THE HOLD

There are 3 ways of doing this, *direct*, *parallel* and *offset* (or *teardrop*), all according to the *magnetic heading* you are using when you approach the facility. Which you use depends on the direction the fix is approached from, and where the inbound heading lies. In short, your position.

Within 5° of two, you can use either, although momentum will make you overshoot on a direct entry when you are close to the parallel entry limit (worse with a tailwind). The almost vertical line in the diagram below is actually offset by 20° from North. Using the correct entry procedure (and speed) keeps you in the safe area. A 6-second delay is assumed between reaching the fix and initiating the entry.

The sectors concerned are created by extending the QDM through the facility and drawing a line at 70° through it (subtract 70° from the QDM for a right hand hold, and add 70° for a left hand hold). A non-standard hold simply has all the entry sectors reversed.

DIRECT

Approaching from **Area 3** close to the inbound QDM, or on the holding side, adopt the pattern straight away.

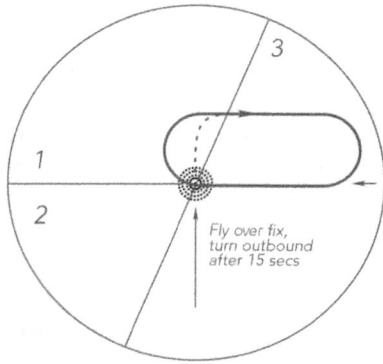

However, using the direct entry at more extreme angles will affect the spacing of the outbound track and take you too close to the inbound track.

If you cross the fix displaced from the QDM by more than 30° on the non-holding side (lower part of Area 3 above), you should maintain the heading for 5 seconds for each 30° of displacement before turning to the outbound heading so, if you were approaching at 90° to the QDM, you would wait for 15 seconds, then fly outbound for 40 seconds as you have just taken a major short cut.

This is the overshooting situation mentioned above.

On the holding side (upper part of Area 3), you initially fly outside the pattern, stopping the turn at 90° to the QDM for the same 5 seconds for each 30° of displacement, so if your inbound heading is 210°, you would use 10 seconds.

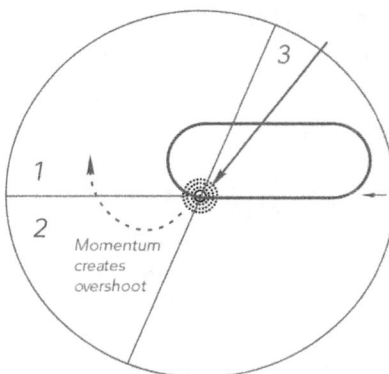

Alternatively, you could add or subtract 10° on top of the drift allowance.

Parallel

From **Area 1**, the parallel entry requires you to go overhead the fix, fly **parallel** to the inbound QDM a short distance away (that is, going the wrong way, and *not* backtracking) for 1 still air minute, then make a turn in the *opposite* direction to the holding pattern into the holding side to fly directly to the fix (if you were a perfectionist, you might turn a little more to the left and intercept the proper inbound QDM, making the subsequent hold more accurate for a better idea of your timing). Start timing at wings level to get a reasonable separation from the beacon before turning back.

Offset

An approach from **Area 2** requires the *offset* (or *teardrop*) entry. In this case, after the fix, turn to an angle which is 30° less than the QDR on the holding side. Continue across the hold for 1 still air minute until you're in the area of a normal turn in, then turn *in the same direction as the pattern* to join the inbound QDM.

The VOR

The only real difference is what happens at the overhead, which is difficult to assess because of the cone of confusion. At the heights normally used by light aircraft, this should last for about 10-15 seconds, so you should assess station passage as being 5-7 seconds after the OFF flag appears (start the turn for the outbound leg at the time of the first reversal of the TO flag). As you pass the overhead, you will need to twist the OBS for the abeam position, and again for the gate and the inbound QDM.

Shuttling

Climbing or descending in the hold is called shuttling.

Shuttling is generally used for approaches in mountainous areas. It may also be used where a descent of more than 2,000 ft is required during the initial or intermediate approach segments.

It can also be required during a missed approach or departure procedure from certain airports, or when the required descent rates for a procedure exceed the design rates for racetrack or reversal procedures shown previously. When shuttling, you can start a descent when cleared rather than waiting to reach the fix.

Leaving the Hold

When given the hold in the first place, you will also be given a time at which you can expect to leave it, in case your radio fails, and the aim is to adjust the patterns to leave the holding fix as near as possible to it. In fact, the holding clearance will include that to the fix itself, the direction to hold from it, the inbound track, DME distances (if holding over one), the altitude or flight level to be maintained and the time to *Expect Further Clearance* or *Expect Approach Clearance*.

If you are proceeding nicely through an approach, but do not receive further clearances when expected, hold on the inbound track at the point you are cleared to until the clearance time, all turns to the right unless published otherwise. If you cannot contact ATC, carry out the communications failure procedures (squawk 7600, etc.) discussed elsewhere in this chapter.

Some holds are on the charts, and therefore "published". If you are cleared to depart one at a particular time, you can either go there and hold till that time, reduce speed to make the departure time, or use a combination of both.

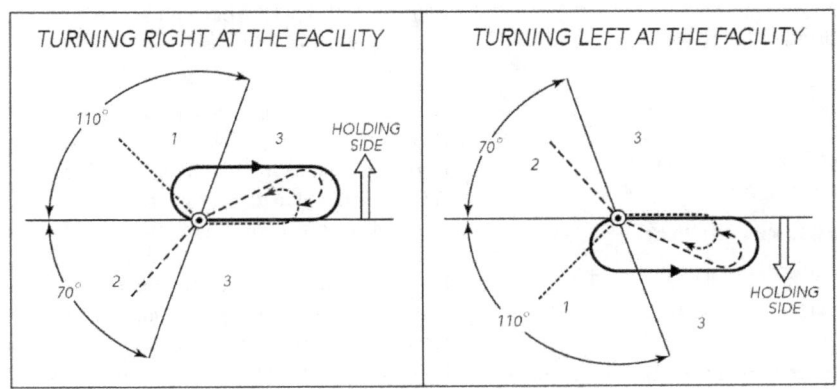

Altimeter Setting Procedures

For details of how altimeters are used in flight, refer to *2 - Rules Of The Air,* above.

Vertical separation en-route at and below the Transition Altitude is by means of *altitude*. Above the Transition Altitude, you use *Flight Levels*. At and below FL 290 the separation is 1 000 ft, and **2 000 feet above that**, except in RVSM airspace, where it may be reduced up to FL 410.

PRE-FLIGHT CHECKS

Rotating the altimeter setting knob through ±10 hPa must produce a corresponding height difference of about ±270 ft in relevant directions. At a known elevation on the aerodrome, vibrate the instrument by tapping, unless mechanical means is available:

- Set the scale to the current QNH. The altimeter should indicate the elevation, plus the height of the altimeter above it, within ± 20 m or 60 ft for altimeters with a test range of 0-9 000 m (0-30 000 ft) and ± 25 m or 80 ft for altimeters with a test range of 0-15 000 m (0-50 000 ft).
- Set the scale to the current QFE. The altimeter should show the height of the altimeter in relation to the QFE reference point, within the same tolerances as above.
- Both should be set to the aerodrome QFE and should indicate within ±60' of zero, within 60' of each other. Thus, they can misread by up to 120 feet between them and still be "serviceable"
- With No 1 on QFE and No 2 on aerodrome QNH, the difference should equal the aerodrome altitude AMSL, to within 60 feet.
- With both on aerodrome QNH, indications should be within ±80 feet of aerodrome elevation, and 60 feet of each other.

 No 1 is the handling pilot's primary instrument and No 2 the secondary.

According to CS 25 the tolerance for an altimeter at MSL is ±30' per 100 kts CAS.

TAKEOFF & LANDING

At least one altimeter must be set to aerodrome QNH before takeoff.

APPROACH & LANDING

Before descending below Transition Level, you must obtain the latest aerodrome QNH.

MINIMUM ALTITUDES

Within 20 nm of ground over 2000 ft amsl, increase MOCA/MORA by these amounts, against windspeed:

Elev (ft)	0-30 Kt	31-50 Kt	51-70 Kt	+ 70 Kt
2-8000	+ 500'	+1000'	+1500'	+2000'
+ 8000	+1000'	+1500'	+2000'	+2500'

This is because the venturi effect over a ridge makes the altimeter misread, on top of causing turbulence and standing waves. All this, plus temperature errors (see below), can make one over-read by as much as 3000'.

When the surface temperature is well below ISA (below -15°C), correct MSAs by:

Surface Temp (ISA)	Correction
-16°C to -30°C	+ 10%
-31°C to -50°C	+ 20%
-51°C or below	+ 25%

Transponder Operation

When a serviceable transponder is carried, it must be operated at all times during flight, regardless of whether a transponder is required for that airspace (SSR is required above FL100, and when IFR below that).

Normally, unless you have an emergency, communications failure, or are subject to unlawful interference, you must operate the transponder in Mode A as directed by ATC or as prescribed by regional air navigation agreements. In the absence of both, squawk 2000.

In an emergency, squawk:

- 7500 - Hijack*
- 7600 - Communications failure
- 7700 - Emergency

*Absence of a reply is confirmation that the selection is not accidental.

You cannot set the number 8.

Transponder codes must always be read back.

When unlawful interference is suspected, and where *automatic distinct display* of 7500 and 7700 is not provided, the controller can verify his suspicions by setting the SSR decoder to 7500 then 7700.

Mode C must be operated continuously, unless otherwise directed by ATC. You must read back the mode and the code. The tolerance level for Mode C level information is within ±300 feet of the assigned level (you must report it within ±100 feet, under Mode C).

When asked to *squawk ident*, your return becomes temporarily brighter, so you can be positively identified. *Do this only when requested.* If the ident doesn't work, a controller can ask you to switch to standby to avoid a turn for identification. The term *recycle* means reselect the assigned code. Modes and codes must be read back.

If a transponder fails during flight in a mandatory area (i.e. *after departure*), you may go to the next planned destination, then complete an itinerary or go to a repair base, as permitted by ATC. It is possible to enter controlled airspace without the required equipment, but ATC must be asked first. Permission is always subject to traffic. If your transponder is unserviceable before departure and you can't fix it, you can take off for a place where repairs can be done. Again, ATC must be informed, preferably before the flight plan is submitted (put an N in Section 10 of the flight plan form, or whatever character represents partial serviceability).

AIR LAW
PANS-OPS (DOC 8168)

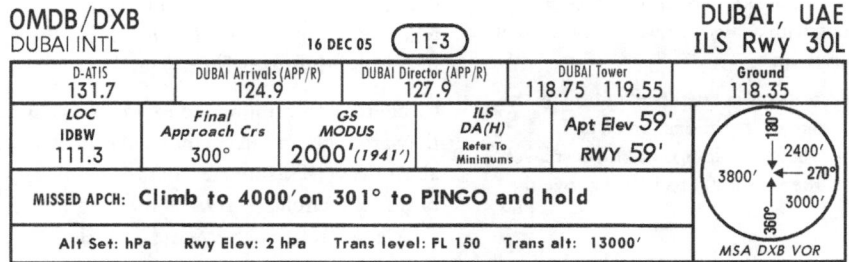

For more about transponders and how they work, refer to *Radio Navigation*.

ACAS

If your flight path has to be altered because of ACAS advisories, the deviation must be limited to the minimum extent necessary. You must promptly revert to the terms and conditions of any clearances previously issued once the conflict is resolved, and notify ATC as soon as practicable of the scope of the deviation, including its direction and when it ended.

Approach Charts

These are designed under ICAO PANS OPS procedures, although some countries, like the USA, use their own. Either way, they are graphical representations of government regulations.

 Charts not produced by government authorities are not legal documents!

Below is a typical approach chart, representative of those from many manufacturers. At the top is the procedure name - check that you're using the right navaid (it sounds silly, but mistakes do happen). Also check the place and the date, which should not only be current, but should also be the same as the one the copilot is using.

Jeppesen charts use an index number enclosed in an oval at the top of the chart (see next page). The first number refers to the principal airport for a city - for example, for London, Heathrow uses 1 and Gatwick uses 2. It does not refer to whether an airport is better than another.

The second number refers to the approach, and the one with the greatest precision gets the lowest number - e.g. 1 means an ILS, 3 means a VOR.

The third digit is used for sorting approaches of the same type.

There is also other useful information, such as the final approach course and the elevation of the field, so you can cross check your altimeter settings. A comparison with the Touchdown Zone Elevation will give you an idea of whether you have to cope with an up- or downslope.

The next box down, the largest on the page, is the plan view of the procedure, including the feeder routes from the enroute structure, drawn to scale, usually 1 inch to 5 nm. It is important to note where you are if ATC give you different routings, particularly if, for example, they give you extended downwind legs that take you off the chart.

The localiser front course is a tapered arrow, pointing to the airport. The right side is shaded, to represent the blue sector. The inbound magnetic course is in bold numbers. You will only see the back course at the other end of the runway if it is used for a missed approach or part of a transition, or as a back course approach. A thick line ending with a large arrowhead means that route can be flown as a transition.

On Jeppesen charts, ground features are depicted in brown, because that colour makes them more serious (green is apparently too friendly). The darkest colour is the highest level and the first contour level is the first 1,000 feet level above the airport elevation.

PROFILES

Underneath the plan view is the side view of the procedure. Although its size is small, it is arguably the most important one on the chart, since it gives you the heights to be at every stage. Naturally, it should be read in conjunction with the plan. Underneath all that might be a list of the appropriate Decision Heights or Minimum Descent Altitudes, based on the aircraft groups above.

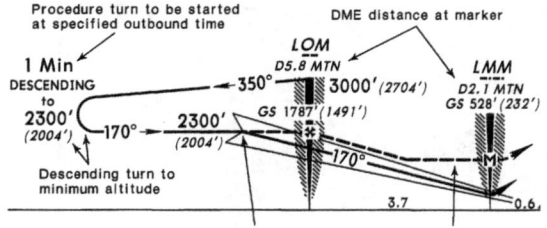

Of course, all this twisting and turning is no good without descending. Above is how an approach might look from the side on a typical approach chart.

In this case, you have to stay level at 2200 feet outbound (the *platform height*), and remain there until you have completed the procedure turn (that is, within 5° of the inbound track, or intercepted the glideslope, having been cleared for descent). On a Jeppesen chart, the Final Approach Fix is shown in the profile view with a Maltese Cross. The Missed Approach is shown with a dashed line. A related holding pattern will be drawn with a light line (instead of thick), on the plan view.

All altitudes in a Jeppesen profile view are minimum altitudes, except when otherwise stated.

The minima box is at the bottom of the page, with the lowest to the left. At the top is a mention of the only runway to which straight-in minimums apply. On the right are the circle-to-land minima which apply to all other runways, or for when straight-in is not authorised.

Performance affects the airspace and visibility needed for the manoeuvres required. The most significant factor is speed, and five categories of aircraft have been established for approach purposes, described elsewhere. Minimum altitudes for landing are laid out across the top of the box. They are shown as:

DA(H) **215'** *(200')*
MDA(H) **480'** *(465')*

The bold numbers are the Decision/Minimum Descent Altitude, and the ones in brackets are the Decision/Minimum Descent Height, depending on whether you are using QNH or QFE. MDA(H) is used when you don't have a localiser, and the approach becomes a non-precision one.

Circle to land minima are expressed as MDA, although they are higher than the normal one, because they apply to all runways. This means that the number in the brackets beside the circling MDA is the height above the airfield (HAA) as the Touchdown Zone Elevation does not apply.

The conversion table relates your ground speed to the recommended descent rate and time from the FAF to the non-precision Missed Approach Point (MAP)

Gnd Speed - Kts		70	90	100	120
GS	3.00°	379	487	542	650
CASSE to MAP 6.3		5:24	4:12	3:47	3:09

COMMUNICATIONS & RADIO NAVIGATION

Communications frequencies and call signs for various agencies will be found in many places. On a map, look for the small box next to the facility (if there is no box, it does not form part of an airway).

```
  DUBAI
108.4 DXB
--- --- ---
N25 14.6 E055 23.4
```

Weather information frequencies, including ATIS, may also be found around the side of the map.

Operational Procedures

Although it might seem that this section could suitably be combined with Air Law, it actually covers Annexes 6 and 18 and EASA requirements, which are often different from ICAO, plus other matters not covered there. Much of it will be found in the Company Operations Manual, when you finally get into one.

To emphasise the point, this chapter has been written in more or less the same subject heading order as a typical Operations Manual, together with background material.

REGULATIONS

The basic enabling regulation covers several areas, one of which is Air Operations, which in turn is divided into 5 subject Annexes (not to be confused with ICAO ones):

- **I - Definitions**
- **II - Part ARO**, which concerns *Authority* Requirements for Air Operations, such as what can be approved, and how.
- **III - Part ORO,** which concerns *Organisation* Requirements for Air Operations, as in how the organisation may comply with Part ARO, including terms of approval, privileges, responsibilities, etc.
- **IV - Part CAT**, for Commercial Air Transport, or what **you** have to do to comply.
    - Subpart A - general requirements
    - Subpart B - operating procedures
    - Subpart C - performance and limitations
    - Subpart D - instruments, data and equipment
- **V - Part SPA**, or Specific Approvals, for:
    - performance-based navigation
    - MNPS operations (See NAT, later)
    - operations in RVSM airspace
    - low visibility operations
    - the transport of dangerous goods (DG)
    - ETOPS

Air Operations is actually Commission Regulation (EU) No 965/2012, dated 5 October 2012. It lays down technical requirements and administrative procedures related to air operations pursuant to Regulation (EC) No 216/2008 of the European Parliament and of the Council.

It is based on ICAO Annex 6, and lays down detailed rules for commercial air transport operations, including ramp inspections of aircraft under the safety oversight of another State when landed at aerodromes in the territory.

Annexes III & IV (of 965) concern operators with principal places of business in EU States using civil aircraft on commercial air transport operations. They do *not* apply to:

- CAT operations starting and ending at the same aerodrome with performance class B aeroplanes.
- Aircraft in military, customs, police and SAR service.
- Parachute dropping and firefighting, and associated positioning and return flights, carrying people who would normally be carried on them.
- Flights immediately before, during, or immediately after aerial work if connected with that activity and, excluding crew members, no more than 6 persons indispensable to the activity are carried.

The relevant documents are in two parts. There are the basic rules, and to amplify them, additional material in the form of *Acceptable Means of Compliance* (AMC) is available. If a paragraph does not have an AMC, supplementary material is not required.

Their relationship is as follows: The rule tells you *what* is to be done (or gives you permission to do it), whereas an AMC tells you *how* it is to be done, that is, what you need to do in order to comply. In other words, AMCs illustrate one way, or several alternative ways, but not necessarily the only ways, by which requirements can be met.

To help you find your way around them, paragraphs will be numbered like this:

```
CAT.OPS.100
```

Meaning Commercial Air Transport, Operations, paragraph 100. The rule numbers are next to the subject headings in this section.

COMMERCIAL AIR TRANSPORT

There are three types of flying, *Commercial Air Transport*, *Aerial Work* and *Private*. As a professional (well, potentially, anyway), you are only concerned with the first two:

- **Commercial Air Transport** exists where payment is given for the use of an aircraft, which in this context means like a taxi or a bus, as opposed to self-drive car hire (but single seats cannot be sold on charter flights without special arrangements).

    A commercial air transport (CAT) operation means an aircraft operation to transport passengers, cargo or mail for remuneration or other **valuable** consideration. The word *consideration* actually means money, or something of money's worth that is more than merely nominal. It is legal expression referring to something that is used to bind a contract, even the chocolate wrappers sent in to a manufacturer to obtain a free gift. But EASA use the word *valuable*........

The definition is in Article 2 of Reg. 965/2012:

commercial air transport (CAT) operation means an aircraft operation to transport passengers, cargo or mail for remuneration or other valuable consideration.

Despite the above, training flights are not treated as CAT operations because of Article 5 of the Air Ops regulation, which directs training flights to be conducted under the rules for non-commercial operations (Parts NCC or NCO, depending on the aircraft being flown).

- **Aerial Work** covers other situations where payment is given, but in specialised areas like aerial photography. You can also take up to 6 "essential persons" in the machine to, during and from a job. However, UK legislation only defines *passengers* or *flight crew*, so you can't carry anyone on aerial work.

The definition of specialised operation in Article 2 (as amended by Reg. 379/2014) includes aerial work and can be conducted commercially or non-commercially:

Specialised operation means any operation other than commercial air transport where the aircraft is used for specialised activities such as agriculture, construction, photography, surveying, observation and patrol, aerial advertisement.

Specialised operators do not therefore need to hold an Air Operator Certificate. They need to follow either Part-NCO (if flying non-commercially in non-complex aeroplanes, non-complex helicopters, sailplanes, balloons) or Part-SPO (for any commercial specialised operation or for non-commercial operations flying complex aeroplanes/helicopters).

Military, police, SAR, customs etc. operations are excluded because of the Basic Regulation's Article 1(2) (Reg. 216/2008):

2. This Regulation shall not apply to:

(a) products, parts, appliances, personnel and organisations referred to in paragraph 1(a) and (b) while carrying out military, customs, police, search and rescue, fire-fighting, coastguard or similar activities or services. The Member States shall undertake to ensure that such activities or services have due regard as far as practicable to the objectives of this Regulation.

- **Private flying** speaks for itself, its most distinguishing feature being that no payment exists, other than by the pilot, for the right to use the aircraft in the first place (but you can take money for some 'private flights').

Within the above limits, the companies you could get involved with will also fall (broadly) into three categories, in the shape of *Scheduled*, *Charter* or *Corporate Flying*.

Scheduled

"Scheduled Flying" is a legal definition describing services that run at predefined times with certain conditions imposed on them, such as being open to all classes of passenger and the flights always running, even though they may be empty. This would mean that, although holiday flights and oilfield helicopters do indeed move at predefined times, they are not subject to the other restrictions and are not therefore "scheduled", but the difference is mostly transparent, as a scheduled journey is also one of a series between the same two places which amount to a systematic service. *Non-scheduled services*, in contrast, exist where the time of takeoff and destination are negotiated just before takeoff between the operator and the charterer (who must charter the whole machine, not single seats). In other words, scheduled services are planned for set times (that is, established in advance) in a continuous sequence (to a timetable). They are normally done with large aeroplanes by what people would normally think of as airlines, but have been done with small helicopters (with a list of exemptions as long as your arm). Another distinguishing feature of a scheduled service is the sale of single seats to the public, as charter aircraft must be sold as one unit to one person or entity.

Scheduled Flying is said to be boring (it is), but it does have the advantage of being organised anything up to 4 weeks in advance, so you can at least have some sort of planning in other areas of your life; this is strictly enforced by the authorities, and is covered under *Flight Time And Duty Hours* regulations. Well, at least you know when you're going, even if you're not sure when you'll be coming back!

Charter

If scheduled flying is like bus driving, then charter flying is a taxi service, which means you are on call twenty-five hours a day with everything geared to an instant response to the customer, leaving you unable to plan very much. This can be fun with plenty of variety and challenge in the flying, but this is also where other personal qualities come into play, as you will be very much involved with your passengers, who are more than just self-loading freight! Thus, while you can move relatively easily from Charter to Scheduled, it's not so straightforward the other way round. As an airline pilot, you rarely see your passengers, and the flying is very different. Charter (or Air Taxi) is intensive, single-handed and stressful work in the worst weather using the least accurate instruments.

As a pilot, therefore, you can have two types of working day, depending on the flying you do. In Scheduled, there is relatively little to do before departure, as a lot is done by others - for example, ground staff check-in and weigh the passengers whilst engineers look at the aircraft, although you still need a working knowledge of what they do, because the buck stops at the bottom. A day flying charter, however, is a different story. You could be working at almost any time, provided the Duty Hour limits are not exceeded, and departures are inevitably very early, as businessmen need to be where they're going at approximately the start of the working day and return at the end of it, so some days can be very long.

Corporate

Corporate flying, where you run the Flight Department for a private company, is similar to Charter, but not Commercial Air Transport, so the requirements (and paperwork!) are not so strict. Having said that, most corporate Flight Departments are run to Commercial standards, or better, and there is, naturally, no excuse for letting your own standards slip. One distinguishing feature is the way the Corporate world regulates itself - high performance intercontinental aircraft follow essentially the same rules as single-engined General Aviation ones, and it's a credit to the people in it that things run so well.

Operator Certification
ORO.AOC.100

AIR OPERATOR CERTIFICATE
Regulation (EC) No 2042/2003

If you charge to carry people or freight, you need an *Air Operator Certificate*, or AOC, which is granted by the relevant National Aviation Authority (NAA) and renewed annually. Governments must follow the rules, too, which is why Police forces have AOCs, so they can carry people from outside the organisation. Private aircraft do not need an AOC, and neither does aerial work.

You must operate safely, i.e. with a decent organizational structure, operational control system, and training and maintenance programs. The management must be full-time, and the aircraft must have a standard C of A issued by an EASA member state.

Applicants for an AOC must:

- Not hold one from another Authority unless approved by those concerned.
- Have his principal place of business and, if any, registered office in the AOC State.
- Have registered the aircraft in the AOC State, although an operator may operate, with the mutual agreement of the AOC Authority and another, aircraft on the national register of the other.
- Satisfy the Authority that he can operate safely. An AOC will be varied, suspended or revoked if the Authority is no longer satisfied of this.

The application form itself is quite easy to fill out. If the Operator is an incorporated body (a company), you will need to know the directors' names, addresses and nationalities and, if not, the same information with regard to the partners. If there is a trading name separate from the Company name, that will need to be given as well. This is quite important, because the AOC is issued to the parent organisation - the authorities will want to know which trading names are to be adopted. You will need a description of the management organisation, major post holders and their accountability, plus qualifications and experience as described below. The form and the fee should be sent to the relevant authority at least six weeks before you plan to start. On top of all that, you will need a copy of your proposed Operations Manual (see below), which will contain some of the above information anyway.

OPERATIONS MANUAL PART A

This is a document that is similar to the *Standing Orders* issued by any military unit, hospital or other type of large organisation. It's a book of instructions that are constant, so that Company policy can be determined by reference to it, containing information and instructions that enable all Operating Staff (i.e. you) to perform their duties. Its purpose is to promote *safety* in Company flying operations.

It's also there to save you constantly pestering Those On High, for when you can't speak to them anyway and need information with which to make decisions. As part of the Operating Staff of a Company, you are subject to the rules and requirements in it, and it's your responsibility to be fully conversant with the contents at all times. You will be expected to read it at regular intervals, if only because it gets amended from time to time.

The *operator* must supply flight operations personnel with an operations manual and the amendments to keep it up to date. The Ops Manager or Chief Pilot (see later) will usually be responsible for the contents and amendment policy. Amendments consist of dated and *printed* replacement pages on which the text affected is marked, ideally by a vertical line in the margin. On receipt of an amendment list, those responsible for copies of the manual incorporate the amendment in theirs and record it on the form in the front.

Although ops manuals are supplemented by statutory instructions and orders, not all of them will be mentioned. It doesn't mean that you should ignore them, but being acquainted with regulations, orders and instructions issued by whoever, is all part of your job. Naturally, references made to publications mean the current editions, as amended. When mentioned in the Ops Manual, they acquire the same legal force.

There will be several copies around, the numbers issued differing with the size of the Company, but the typical distribution list below should be regarded as a minimum; each person should have their own copy, or parts relevant to their duties.

Copy	Who Has It
1	Master Copy - Operations Manager
2	Authorities
3	Chief Pilot
4	Training Captain
5	Maintenance Organisation
6+	One per person, where relevant

A large company will likely have its own print shop just to produce operations manuals.

As the authorities are involved, the ops manual is compiled in accordance with the law (in fact, as far as you are concerned it is the law - it has the force of subordinate legislation) and all flights should be conducted to the standards set out in it. Usually in several parts, it can be a single volume with a small operator, or several in the average airline. They will consist of:

- **Part A - General/Basic**. Non type-related operational policies, instructions and procedures.

- **Part B - Aircraft Operating Matters** (SOPs). Type-related instructions and procedures, taking due account of differences between types, variants or individual aircraft.
- **Part C - Route and Aerodrome Guide**. Instructions and information about navigation, communications and aerodromes, including minimum flight levels and operating minima.
- **Part D - Training**. Training syllabuses and checking programs for all people concerned with the preparation and/or conduct of flights.

All are described more fully in the following pages.

0 - Administration & Control

This section covers how the ops manual is amended and revised, and who is authorised to do it.

COMPETENCE OF OPERATIONS PERSONNEL
ORO.GEN.110(c)

1 - Organisation & Responsibilities

ORO.GEN.110 - Operator Responsibilities

The operator is responsible for the operation of aircraft under Annex IV to Regulation (EC) No 216/2008, the relevant requirements of Annex III and its certificate (AOC). To this end, a system for exercising operational control over any flight operated under the terms of its certificate shall be established and maintained.

- All flights shall be conducted under the provisions of the operations manual.
- Aircraft must be equipped and crews qualified as required for the area and type of operation.
- All personnel assigned to, or directly involved in, ground and flight operations must be properly instructed, have demonstrated their abilities in their duties and be aware of their responsibilities and their relationship to the operation as a whole.
- Procedures and instructions for safe operation may not require crews to perform any activities during critical phases of flight other than those needed for the safe operation of the aircraft.
- All personnel must comply with the laws, regulations and procedures of those States in which operations are conducted and that are pertinent to the performance of their duties. The PIC must submit a report (normally within 10 days) if local regulations are violated while saving life or preventing damage to the aircraft.
- The operator shall establish a checklist system for each aircraft type to be used by crew members in all phases of flight under normal, abnormal and emergency conditions to ensure that the operating procedures in the operations manual are followed (Part B). The design and utilisation of checklists shall observe human factors principles and take into account the latest relevant documentation from the aircraft manufacturer.
- The operator shall specify flight planning procedures to provide for the safe conduct of the flight, considering aircraft performance, other operating limitations and relevant expected conditions on the route to be followed and at the aerodromes or operating sites concerned. These procedures shall be in the operations manual.
- The operator shall establish and maintain a dangerous goods training program as required by the Technical Instructions (later) which is subject to review and approval by the competent authority. Training programs shall be commensurate with the responsibilities of personnel.

The responsibility for *operational control* and *maintenance of Flight Safety and Accident Prevention programs* lies with the *operator*, as well as ensuring that employees know the rules and regulation, and how to behave in general.

Operators must ensure that flight crews demonstrate the ability to speak and understand a common language (CAT.GEN.MPA.115), and that used for radiotelephony in ICAO Annex 1 (English). *ORO.MLR.100(k)*.

Operators must establish a flight safety documents system, for the use and guidance of operational personnel, as part of its safety management system.

Information for pilots and flight operations personnel on flight and operational procedure parameters is in PANS-OPS (Doc 8168), Volume I. Criteria for the construction of visual and instrument flight procedures are in PANS-OPS (Doc 8168), Volume II.

Below is a typical company setup showing the relative positions of personalities described in the following pages.

COMPANY PERSONALITIES

An effective management structure is essential, especially in Operations. The Company will have appointed certain people to undertake particular tasks, and you will find them described below. Naturally, some will change, depending on your setup, and one person's functions may be combined with another's, but most companies will be laid out as follows:

NOMINATED POSTHOLDERS

These are people with direct responsibilities to the Authority which override any others they may have within the Company. As such, they are subject to approval before appointment, since they are the first people interviewed if there is a problem. Nominated postholders are required for Flight Operations, Ground Operations, Crew Training, and Maintenance but, curiously, not the Chief Pilot. They should have:

- Practical experience and expertise in the application of aviation safety standards and safe operating practices
- Comprehensive knowledge of:
  - EASA regulations, requirements and procedures
  - Operations Specifications
  - The need for, and content of, the Ops Manual
- Familiarity with Quality Systems
- Appropriate management experience in a comparable organisation

OPERATIONAL PROCEDURES
Operations Manual Part A

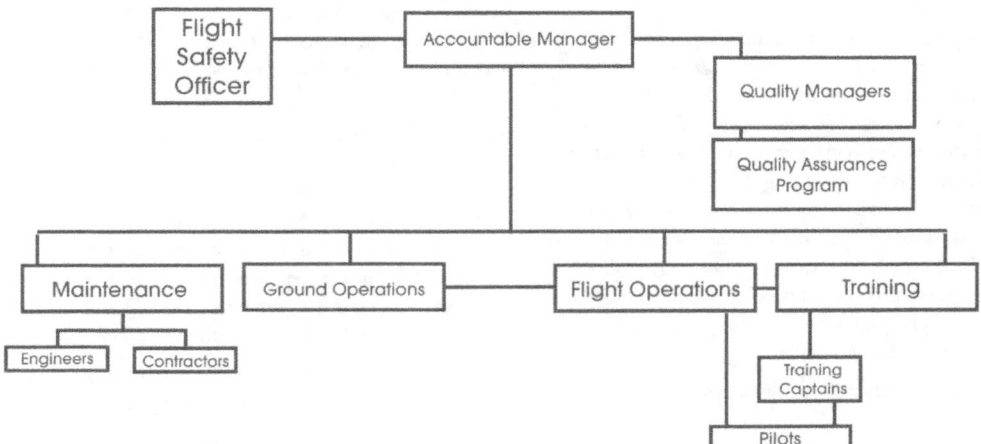

The Flight Operations postholder, or his deputy, should hold, or have held, an appropriate Flight Crew Licence.

The Crew Training postholder or deputy should be a current TRI for a type operated under the AOC and have a thorough knowledge of the training concept, as should the Ground Operations postholder or deputy.

The Maintenance postholder should have a relevant engineering degree, or acceptable experience, thorough knowledge of the CAME*, knowledge of maintenance methods and the aircraft.

*The *Continuing Airworthiness Maintenance Exposition* is a long-winded ops manual for engineers.

ACCOUNTABLE MANAGER
This person has the ultimate responsibility for the efficiency, organisation, discipline and welfare of the Company, ensuring that all activities are safe and legal and that the Company is commercially viable (he should have the authority to make financial decisions). This will include marketing and projection of the Company image.

THE CHIEF PILOT
Next in line is the Chief Pilot, who is the main point of reference that Inspectors and other officials will relate to, and they will expect to see him with some measure of control of the day-to-day happenings of the Company, although technically the job is just to keep things legal. However, to do that, there will have to be some involvement in the more commercial aspects, because the Sales Department generally won't have a clue.

The Chief Pilot is responsible to the Managing Director for the overall safety, legality, efficiency and economy of flying operations by the establishment of proper drills and procedures*, and for ensuring that people (well, pilots, anyway) are properly qualified, so he will be responsible for hiring and firing, in conjunction with the HR department, if there is one.

*ORO.GEN.110(f)

Whilst the MD handles the administrative acceptability of work, the Chief Pilot has the technical side of things to worry about, like keeping control of the Flight Time and Duty Hours Scheme (sometimes by random inspection of returned flight documentation) in addition to supervising aircrew currency, maintaining aircrew records, compiling and updating the Ops Manual, raising occurrence reports and Flying Staff Instructions.

Randomly inspecting returned flight documentation is a real chore, and is done for three reasons; the first is that it's part of the Company's Compliance Scheme (see elsewhere), and the second is to ensure that you're doing your job properly. The third, and most important, is to eliminate nasty surprises when the Inspector drops in for coffee. You will greatly endear yourself to your Chief Pilot if you make sure that *all* boxes on *all* forms are filled in *neatly* (whether or not you think they're relevant), especially on the Technical Log, Loadsheet and Navigation Log (Plog), and not at the end of the day, because you might get ramp-checked before then.

Digression: When ramp-checking, Inspectors are looking for (amongst other things), altimeter settings, holes in the dashboard, approach plates out (or not), the general condition of the aircraft, cleanliness, etc. and *scruffy paperwork*, with parts not filled in. They will especially be interested in weight and balance calculations, and might ask some searching questions on subjects such as where you would find performance information or limitations, or explain your way through a letdown plate.

With regard to the above items, where a signature is required, produce one, and always ensure that your departure fuel in the Tech Log agrees with the fuel load in the Load Sheet (all tanks) and the Nav Log, and that fuel usage throughout the flight is consistent with time, that is, that you're not using mysterious amounts of fuel that would indicate somebody's fiddling the books. Especially make sure that the fuel loads on the Tech Log and Loadsheet are *above* that required for the trip as specified on the Nav Log. The same rules apply to passenger and freight loads, and you should *always* check your figures, especially when adding up in hours, minutes and seconds - many engineers don't let pilots add up because it messes up the paperwork - they do all the entries themselves.

Lastly, don't write defects down on the Nav Log and forget to put them in the Tech Log at the end - that's a dead giveaway to your Inspector, as almost every aircraft goes unserviceable when it gets back to base (and not when it actually happens) as if programmed.

The Chief Pilot also liaises with Maintenance on airworthiness matters, and may designate a suitable person within the Company to carry out, or be responsible for, any of the above duties. That person would be directly responsible to the Chief Pilot (as is everybody else).

Flight Safety Officer/Safety Manager

The FSO operates any Mandatory Occurrence Reporting Scheme (MORS) and maintains a *vigorous Flight Safety policy*, which means collecting information from various sources, and spreading it around, with lectures and meetings, under the Compliance System; this may also involve internal investigations after an accident. The reason for spreading things around is part of the reason for accident investigation, i.e. *that it doesn't happen again!* Safety management involves plenty of communication, so an FSO must encourage people to speak up. Thus, personality is quite important. This person has direct access to management and should have the one job. Under AMC1.ORO.GEN.200(a)(1) the functions of the Safety Manager include:

- facilitate hazard identification, risk analysis and management
- monitor the implementation of actions taken to mitigate risks, as listed in the safety action plan
- provide periodic reports on safety performance
- ensure the maintenance of safety management documentation
- ensure that safety management training is available and that it meets acceptable standards
- provide advice on safety matters
- ensure initiation and follow-up

The Chief Training Captain

This person sorts out flying training, arranges periodical checks and examinations, selects training staff, and ensures that flying training meets statutory requirements, by liaising with the Authorities, in addition to compiling and maintaining flying training records. Where Training Captains are thinly spread between companies, meaning that you don't see them from day to day, the Chief Training Captain may simply be the Chief Pilot wearing another hat, for consistency.

 If an examiner, this person will be both an agent of the Company, and of the Authorities.

Fleet Manager

A pilot with management responsibilities, reporting to the Chief Pilot, in charge of a fleet of the same type of aircraft.

The Maintenance Department

The Maintenance Department (who may be an outside contractor) maintains and valets Company aircraft in accordance with directions and laid down procedures or, more simply, mends what you bend. If your Company does its own maintenance, you will find a Maintenance Manager and Chief Engineer, who will order spares and schedule maintenance in a timely fashion, together with other stuff to run an efficient organisation. The approval standard is Part 145, and the Compliance System (see below) ensures that it is kept running properly. Maintenance programs will be written for each aircraft *by each operator*, so be careful when leasing - aircraft should be as identical as possible for ease of administration.

 The engineers keep you up in the air, and it's not a good idea to upset them. They start work when you stop, often late in the night so you look like a hero next day. Not only that, they have no duty hour regulations, so anything you can do to help them is greatly appreciated, particularly cleaning aircraft. In fact, engineers also do a lot of stuff in the field, and a good one is worth his weight in gold (more valuable than a pilot, except that someone needs to fly the aircraft!)

The Operations Manager

Although the Operations Manager may be technically under the Chief Pilot, in practice, they have more or less equal status and, in some companies may have one person occupying both positions. Where the Ops Manager has more experience than the Chief Pilot, you may find that he is well and truly in charge and the Chief Pilot a few steps down in the pecking order. Look for this situation in larger companies, where you will also find *Flight Operations Officers* doing most of the work described below.

 Despite being in charge, Ops have to acknowledge your ultimate authority as aircraft commander.

Operations will provisionally accept work and, in liaison with the Chief Pilot, confirm it. As a result, they organise the flying program, including pilot duty and rest days, so you want to keep on their good side. Ops will ensure that duty times are in limits by keeping a record of flight crew flying and duty hours, and are supposed to ensure that you receive a written briefing (including NOTAMs, etc.) before going anywhere, and that all passenger and cargo manifests and tickets are completed as required.

The Ops Manager ensures scheduling for maintenance, forwarding completed Tech Log sheets and other relevant documents to them at the end of each flight. This is not the same as mentioned for the Chief Pilot, who does it on a more lofty level - all the Ops Manager does is monitor the aircraft hours so that nothing gets behind, and everything gets serviced on time. This is usually done by circulating coloured copies of the Tech Log after a flight.

Operations will also maintain carnets and aircraft documents (collectively referred to as *aircraft libraries*), an up to date stock of maps, route guides and aeronautical charts covering all areas of Company operations, Flight Information Publications (such as NOTAMs, Air Pilot, AICs, Royal Flights, the Landing Site Register, etc.), and arrange exemptions and clearances for particular tasks.

 Although Ops should ensure the validity of all licences, checks, etc., you must still keep your own valid.

The Ops Manager also ensures that Company accident and incident procedures are followed, processes amendments of the Operations Manual, assesses landing sites, categorises airfields, calculates specific weather minima, obtains met forecasts for planned routes and destinations, and arranges overnight accommodation for night stops, amongst other things. Most important is the arrangement of an accurate and up to date flight watch of all company aircraft movements and a standby telephone coverage outside normal working hours.

A company that actually gets the Ops Manager to do all that is setting quite a high standard. Naturally, the above duties may be delegated.

Flight Operations Officer (Despatcher)

This person is responsible for the supervision of flights, and to the operator for initiating ops manual procedures in emergencies, if they do not conflict with other ATC procedures, or the weather or communications services.

COMPLIANCE MANAGER

The Quality Manager ensures that the company's compliance system is established and implemented, in this respect assuming the role of "management representative", or a focal point for staff to refer to. Duties include the issue and withdrawal of all compliance documents and forms, and maintaining a list of them, together with the aforementioned regular checks of documentation, etc. Routine flights should also be accompanied occasionally to confirm that normal procedures are being followed, but this will be a Training Captain doing a Line Check.

CREW MEMBERS IN GENERAL
CAT.GEN.MPA.100

Crew members are responsible for the proper execution of all duties related to the safety of the aircraft and its occupants, as per the operations manual. They shall:

- report to the commander any fault, failure, malfunction or defect that may affect the airworthiness or safe operation of an aircraft including emergency systems, if not already reported by another crew member.
- report to the commander any incident that endangered, or could have endangered, the safety of the operation, if not already reported.
- comply with the relevant requirements of the operator's occurrence reporting schemes.
- comply with all flight and duty time limitations and rest requirements applicable to their activities.
- when undertaking duties for more than one operator, maintain individual FTL records and provide them to each operator.
- *not* perform duties on an aircraft:
  - under the influence of psychoactive substances or alcohol or when unfit from injury, fatigue, medication, sickness, etc.
  - until a reasonable time period has elapsed after deep water diving or blood donation.
  - if medical requirements are not fulfilled.
  - if in any doubt of accomplishing their duties.
  - if they know or suspect that they are suffering from fatigue or feel otherwise unfit, if the flight may be endangered.

PIC
CAT.GEN.MPA.105
CAT.GEN.MPA.110

As an aircraft commander, you are first and foremost subject to any aviation regulations that may be in force*. Inside the Company, you are responsible to just about everybody else (but especially the Fleet/Base Manager or Chief Pilot) for ensuring that aircraft are flown with prime consideration for the safety of passengers and persons on the ground; not negligently or wilfully causing an aircraft to endanger persons or property while ensuring it is operated under performance requirements, Flight Manuals, checklists, State regulations, the Operations Manual, Air Traffic Regulations, The Air Pilot, Aeronautical Information Circulars and NOTAMs.

*Between arriving on board the aircraft and leaving at the end of the flight, you are responsible for the safety of all crew members, passengers and cargo on board. From when the aircraft is ready to taxi for takeoff until it finally comes rest at the end of the flight, and the engine(s) used for its primary propulsion have been shut down, you are also responsible for its operation and safety. For this purpose, you have full authority to give necessary commands and take any appropriate actions. You may disembark any person, or any part of the cargo, that may represent a potential hazard, including persons under the influence of alcohol or drugs, or inadmissible passengers, deportees or persons in custody. The operator must take all reasonable measures to ensure that all persons carried in the aircraft obey such commands.

Seems a bit much, doesn't it? Hang on.......

It's also up to you to keep your licences and logbooks up to date, and to ensure that you are medically fit for your duties. You must keep customers and the Company informed of accidents, incidents and alterations caused by bad weather or other reasons.

Yours is the final responsibility for supervising the loading, checking and refuelling of your aircraft and making sure that *all* passengers are briefed on Emergency Exits and the use of safety equipment, although you also have the right to exclude persons, such as drunks, etc.

You must check that the aircraft is serviceable with a current Certificate of Release to Service (or equivalent) and with previously reported defects in the Technical or Journey Log as being rectified or transferred to the Deferred Defects lists by a person so qualified. Defects must be as per the MEL or CDL.

You must ensure that no weight limitation is exceeded, that the C of G will remain inside the envelope *at all times*, and that performance is sufficient to complete the flight, as well as leaving a duplicate copy of the Operational Flight Plan with a responsible person before each flight, and ensuring that all documents are correctly completed and returned to Ops at the end (all documentation must remain valid throughout the flight).

You should not permit crew members to perform activities during takeoff, initial climb, final approach and landing that are not required for safe operation, and take all reasonable steps to ensure that, before takeoff and landing, the flight and cabin crew are properly secured in their allocated seats (cabin crew during taxi, except for essential safety related duties).

Whenever the aircraft is taxying, taking off or landing, or whenever you consider it advisable (like in turbulence), you should ensure that all passengers are properly secured in their seats, and cabin baggage is stowed. In an emergency situation* (that is, requiring immediate decision and action), you should take any action considered necessary under the circumstances, which means you can break all the rules in the interest of safety. You can apply greater margins to minima at any time.

*Annex 6 paragraph 4.2.12.3: In an emergency during flight, passengers shall be instructed in such emergency action as may be appropriate to the circumstances.

You should ensure that a continuous listening watch is maintained on appropriate radio frequencies at appropriate times, which is whenever the flight crew is manning the aircraft for commencing and/or conducting a flight, and when taxying.

You should not permit a Flight Data Recorder or Cockpit Voice Recorder to be disabled or switched off during flight. After an incident or accident that is subject to mandatory reporting, they should not be intentionally erased and must be deactivated immediately the flight has completed. Reactivation may only take place with the agreement of the investigating authority.

Although it's part of Ops' job to get a met forecast, it's your responsibility, so you may as well do it yourself.

Finally, here's a gem, from 1919, which comes from *Recollections of an Airman*, by Lt Col L A Strange. Nothing changes!

> "...*As a pilot of a machine, you are responsible for that machine all the time, and it is always your fault if you crash it in a forced landing occasioned by any failure, structural or otherwise, of the machine or its engine. It is your fault if, in thick weather, you hit the top of any hill that has its correct height shown on your map. It is entirely your fault if you run out (of petrol) when coming home against a headwind after four or five hours (of flying), or if you fail to come down on the right spot after a couple (of) hours cloud flying. It is your fault if you have nowhere to make a landing when the engine fails just after you have taken off; in a forced landing, your machine is a glider that should take you down safely on any possible landing place.*
>
> *It is your fault - well, it is a golden rule to assume that whatever goes wrong is your fault. You may save yourself a lot of trouble if you act accordingly.*"

THE FIRST OFFICER

First Officers will more than likely find themselves preparing and maintaining the navigation and fuel logs in flight, because they should be fully aware of the intended route, weather, etc. that may affect it. Constant briefings from the Commander are essential, as the FO naturally must know the game plan if there is going to be a takeover at any stage. This even extends to the routes to be flown, minimum safety altitudes, overshoot action, etc. All this "interaction" is part of Crew Resource Management (see *Human Factors*). In addition, First Officers carry out checks (the Commander reads them, or *vice versa*), make radio calls, cross-check altimeters and other instruments and *monitor each flight continuously*. In particular, they are supposed to advise the Commander of apparently serious deviations from the flight path, such as specific warning if, on an instrument approach, the rate of descent exceeds 1000 feet per minute or the ILS indicator exceeds half-scale deflection, or of any abnormal instrument function.

First Officers have possibly the most difficult time, because, on top of their flying skills, and being the busiest people on the flight deck, they need tact and diplomacy, and the flexibility to satisfy the whims of the Captain, because each one you fly with will do things differently, even when there is supposed to be standardisation. For this, a good sense of humour, or at least the ridiculous, is high on the list, together with the ability to accept criticism without necessarily taking it personally. Good FOs are like good surgery nurses, who have the scalpel ready and waiting when the surgeon reaches for it. In particular, they:

- Know what they are doing, and know their company SOPs (without being *too* picky!)
- Interact well, by discussing checklists rather than just narrating them, or not operating items, such as crossfeed, that should normally be discussed.
- Are one step ahead of the aircraft, by setting up radios or navaids or getting the charts out early, rather than leaving them until they are needed.
- Communicate well, and are good social mixers.
- Control the aircraft, rather than allowing it to control them, or keep abreast of radio calls, with a good grasp of the air traffic picture.
- Learn quickly and are not afraid to ask questions.
- Continually monitor the flight, with no newspapers being read on the flight deck! Autopilots can go wrong, as can any electrical equipment, and the Captain relies on the FO to pick up things that might have been missed. Although the Captain carries the responsibility, FOs are still part of a team.
- Speak clearly and loudly. Cockpits are noisy.
- Turn up on time so the Captain doesn't have to do the paperwork in a rush.
- Can take over the flight if the Captain keels over!
- Do the preflight check when it's raining.

CABIN ATTENDANTS

These are needed when you have more than a certain number of passengers (1 for every 50).

Hash-slingers are responsible to the Purser, or No 1, or Cabin Manager, who is responsible in turn to the Commander for ensuring that catering is ordered for flights to which they are allocated, and that it is correctly used in cabin service.

It's their job to make sure that all passengers are briefed before takeoff on the items in the Passenger Briefing Card (or video), which includes being seated with safety belts fastened for takeoff and landing or any other times in flight as and when instructed. They must also ensure that doors and emergency exits are kept clear of obstructions during takeoff and landing, and that loose articles are in lockers or underneath a seat, if applicable.

2 - Operational Control & Supervision

This section describes how the company supervises its operations, in terms of flight following, etc. *Flight following* means monitoring a flight's progress, based on information from the crew, and the notification of the appropriate authorities if it is overdue or missing.

In small companies, operational control is typically delegated to the commander by the Chief Pilot (or a flight dispatcher if one is needed). As such, the commander has the sole authority to make decisions as to initiation, continuation, delay, diversion or re-routing of a flight when conditions make such decisions necessary (this does not absolve flight crews from ensuring that they stay within their capabilities). This means that, once tasked with a flight, it is the pilot's responsibility to organise everything, including authorising the flight. Otherwise, the Company should allocate crews to tasks as per qualifications and experience, with due regard to restrictions imposed by Training Captains.

A **flight release** is given under the conditions in *Flight Preparation (CAT.OP.MPA.175)*, later.

TAKEOFF CONDITIONS
CAT.OP.MPA.265

Before commencing takeoff, you must be satisfied that, according to the information available, the weather at the aerodrome and the condition of the runway to be used would not prevent a safe takeoff and departure, and that established operating minima will be complied with.

METEOROLOGICAL CONDITIONS
CAT.OP.MPA.245

For IFR flights, you may only commence takeoff (or continue beyond the point from which a revised ATS flight plan applies after in-flight replanning) when information indicates that the expected weather, at the time of arrival, at the destination and/or alternate(s) are at or above the *planning* minima.

You may only *continue* towards the planned destination when the latest information available indicates that, at the ETA, the weather conditions there, or at least one destination alternate, are at or above the *operating* minima. In addition, you may only continue beyond the decision point when using the reduced contingency fuel procedure, or the pre-determined point when using the pre-determined point (PDP) procedure, when information indicates that the expected weather conditions, at the time of arrival, at the destination and/or required alternate(s) are at or above the operating minima. On VFR flights, you may only commence takeoff when the appropriate weather reports and/or forecasts indicate that the meteorological conditions along the part of the route to be fl own under VFR will, at the appropriate time, be at or above the VFR limits.

ACCIDENT PREVENTION & FLIGHT SAFETY
ORO.GEN.200

The flight safety system, as fostered by the Flight Safety Officer, consists of a reporting system and a general awareness program, typically done by circulating safety information and holding safety meetings.

ICE & OTHER CONTAMINANTS
CAT.OP.MPA.250 , CAT.OP.MPA.2505

You may only commence takeoff if the aircraft is clear of any deposit that might adversely affect its performance or controllability, except as otherwise permitted and in accordance with the flight manual. You may only commence a flight or intentionally fly into expected or actual icing conditions if the aircraft is certified and equipped to cope with such conditions.

If icing exceeds the intensity for which the aircraft is certified, or if your aircraft (not certified for flight in known icing conditions) encounters icing, you must depart from the conditions without delay, by a change of level and/or route, if necessary by declaring an emergency.

POWER TO INSPECT
ORO.GEN.140

The Company will be assigned an Inspector, who is authorised to fly in Company aircraft during normal operations. Although arrangements for such flights will normally be made in advance, the inspector may board Company aircraft without prior notice, which can only be refused for flight safety reasons. Inspectors carry an authority and certificate of appointment that can be produced on request.

Inspectors may:

- require the production of documents and records
- direct the operator or commander not to permit an aircraft to make a flight and take necessary steps to detain the aircraft
- enter and inspect aircraft for the above purpose
- have right of access to aerodromes and other places where an aircraft has landed

COMPANY RESPONSIBILITY
The Chief Pilot shall:

- give any such authorised person access to any documents and records related to flight operations or maintenance.
- produce* all such documents and records, when requested to do so by the Authority within a reasonable period of time.

*The word *produce* does not mean *surrender*.

COMMANDER'S RESPONSIBILITY
CAT.GEN.MPA.190

The Commander shall, within a reasonable time of being requested to do so by an authorised person, produce to that person the documentation required on board.

3 - Compliance System
ORO.GEN.200

Life these days is complex, and operating aircraft is no exception. Indeed, the rate of change is such that legislators can hardly keep up with avionics, and Inspectors are even further behind, so the onus is on companies to self-regulate, which is where the Compliance System comes in. Operators must establish one to ensure *safe operational practices* and *airworthy aircraft*.

The Authority keeps an eye on your company by assessing the effectiveness of the compliance system. In theory, if this is well managed and proactive, their involvement can be reduced without compromising safety. To achieve this, the system is documented and inspected periodically by an auditor who uses a series of checklists to detect non-compliances, which are reported back to the Compliance Manager (see *Commercial Air Services*) for rectification. In short, a chap with a trilby hat goes round with a clipboard and checks out how you do things, and tells the boss if he finds anything untoward.

Although a certain amount of documentation already exists, in the form of Operations Manuals or MMEs, for example, the Compliance System extends things by introducing *compliance monitoring* and a *feedback system* to provide confidence that the system is working. In fact, it was Virgin's Quality Assurance system that prevented igniter components from a 747 that was destroyed in Kuwait from being used on their machines, that had come to them via the USA. However, aside from checking their own paperwork more, about the only thing the average pilot would notice is that, if anything untoward happens, a form has to be filled in.

Anything affecting goods or services delivered to customers is subject to the Compliance System, based on ISO 9000 (or 9002, the latest version), which is supposed to ensure that the Company product is of the "required quality" or, officially, is "assured as conforming to specified requirements and is supplied in accordance with the Company's quality policy and procedures". It is an internationally recognised standard for quality systems, where "quality" is defined as satisfying the customer's needs - as far as ISO is concerned, a product or service is of the required quality if it performs the function it was designed for. Well, a cheap watch performs a function, but I think Rolex would have something to say about it being "quality"! The truth of the matter is that the system was designed for manufacturing, to produce low return rates, which doesn't always translate well to service industries. The *International Standards Organisation* is Geneva-based, and 9000 has been around since 1987. It's a generic management system standard which doesn't have much to do with the end product, except for ensuring its production under sound management procedures, leading to efficiency and consistency, and, ultimately, cost reductions. Side benefits are improved employee motivation, customer relations and better perception of the Company image. Certification, by the way, is not actually done by ISO, but by "consultants" appointed by it.

The requirement to establish and document a Compliance System and employ a Compliance Manager applies to all operators, but complex systems are inappropriate for *small* (6-20 full time* staff) or *very small* (5 or less full time staff) operators and the clerical effort required to draw up manuals and procedures may stretch their resources, so they are allowed to tailor their systems to suit the operation.

For very small operators, a checklist may be used, with all items completed within a timescale, with a statement acknowledging completion of a periodic review by top management. An occasional independent overview of the checklist content and achievement of compliance should be undertaken.

The small operator, on the other hand, may use an internal or external system, or a combination. External specialists and/or qualified organisations may manage the system on behalf of the Compliance Manager. Whatever arrangements are made, the operator retains the ultimate responsibility.

Full-time here means employed for at least 35 hours per week, excluding holidays.

4 - Crew Composition
ORO.AOC.135
ORO.FC.100

The minimum flight crew should never be less than that in the Operations Manual, based on the Flight Manual or other document with the Certificate of Airworthiness.

Carrying 2 qualified pilots is not an airworthiness issue, as many machines that need 2 pilots for commercial flights can be flown single-pilot on a private basis.

Flight crew members must naturally hold appropriate licences, and be suitably qualified and competent (the *operator* must ensure this, especially for part time or freelance crews). Crew members may be relieved by other suitably qualified people - procedures should prevent inexperienced crews being rostered together.

DESIGNATION OF PIC
One pilot will be nominated as PIC so that the Subsequent Board of Inquiry can pin the blame on the right person. A commander must have:

- An ATPL, or
- A CPL, with 700 hrs for IFR (including 300 PIC and 100 IFR). When VMC at night, without an IR, 300 hours (including 100 PIC and 100 night).

but they can only be PIC if they have:

- the minimum experience in the operations manual.
- initial familiarisation training and adequate knowledge of the route or areas to be flown, and aerodromes, including alternates, facilities and procedures to be used, which shall be maintained by operating at least once on the route or area or the aerodrome within 12 months*.
- for multi-crew operations, completed a command course if upgrading from co-pilot.

*Not Performance Class B aeroplanes under VFR by day.

IFR
ORO.FC.200

You need 2 crew on turbo props with an MOPSC of more than 9, and all turbojets, but see also ORO.FC.202 for the conditions under which you can fly single pilot.

CABIN CREW
ORO.CC.100

Aircraft with an MOPSC of more than 19, when carrying one or more passengers, must have the greater of one cabin crew member for every 50, or fraction, passenger seats on the same deck, or the number established during the certification process.

Minimum Requirements
ORO.CC.110

Cabin crew must be at least 18 years old, and have passed an initial medical examination or assessment to be found medically (and remain) fit and competent to discharge the duties described in the Ops Manual.

Senior Cabin Crew
ORO.CC.200

A senior cabin crew member must be nominated when more than one is assigned, being responsible to the PIC for the conduct and co-ordination of normal and emergency procedure(s) in the Ops Manual. Senior cabin crew members must have at least one year's experience and successfully complete the courses. There must be procedures to select the next most suitably qualified cabin crew if the nominated one becomes unable to operate, taking account of operational experience.

More Than One Type Or Variant
ORO.CC.250

Crew members may not operate on more than three types except that, with approval, they may operate on four, if safety equipment and emergency procedures for at least two are similar.

Flight Engineer
ORO.FC.110

When there is a flight engineer's station, there must be a suitably qualified person in the flight crew.

5 - Qualification Requirements

A description of the minimum qualifications that personnel employed by the Company shall have.

6 - Crew Health Precautions
CAT.GEN.MPA.170

You may not act as a member of the crew of a company aircraft if your physical or mental condition could endanger its safety or that of its occupants (and presumably anybody or anything outside). The Company must be informed of any treatment or medication that may affect your fitness. Aircrew may not carry out any duties under the influence of:

- **Anti Depressants**
- **Alcohol and other intoxicating liquids** at least 8 hours before standby or reporting for duty.
  - **Blood Level**. You may not start a flight duty period with a blood alcohol level in excess of 0.2. mg per ml (milligrams per millilitre).
  - **Standby Duty**. You may not consume alcohol during standby or the flight duty period.
- **Narcotics**. Their use is expressly forbidden.
- **Drugs**. Using drugs that have not been prescribed is expressly forbidden. However, even prescribed drugs may have a detrimental effect on performance, so you should seek advice from qualified aviation medical practitioners.
- **Sleeping Tablets**. You may not undertake flight duty while taking any form of sleeping aid.
- **Pharmaceutical Preparations**. You may not undertake flight duty when taking any medication containing antihistamine, narcotic or stimulants.
- **Immunisation**. You may not undertake flight duty within 6 hours of receiving an immunisation, in case of allergic reaction.
- **Diving**, involving underwater pressure breathing devices. Crew members whose sporting activities include deep water diving over 10 metres deep may not fly within 48 hours of completing such activity
- **Blood/Bone Marrow Donation**. Crews should not normally act as blood donors. Flight crew members may not undertake flight duty within 72 hours of a loss of 200 cc or more of blood (but in no case will personnel fly within 72 hours of excessive loss of blood, and subsequently only with the concurrence of an aeromedical examiner).
- **Meal precautions** should be taken to avoid the risk of food poisoning (e.g. from shellfish of dubious freshness). When meals are taken or uplifted en route, pilots operating together should select different items from the menu.
- **Sleep And Rest**. Crew members shall not perform duties in flight if they know or suspect that they are suffering from fatigue, or feel unfit to the extent that the flight may be endangered. See also Section 7, *Flight Time & Duty Limitations*, below.
- **Surgical Operations**. Aeromedical advice should be sought before returning to flying duties after any surgical procedure. Crews should not fly for at least 12 hours after a local anaesthetic injection for dental treatment and at least 72 hours after a general anaesthetic.

7 - Flight Time Limitations

CAT operations with aeroplanes* are subject to Subpart FTL of Annex III, but air taxi, emergency medical service and single pilot CAT operations (by aeroplanes) are subject to Article 8(4) of Regulation (EEC) No 3922/91 and Subpart Q of Annex III to Regulation (EEC) No 3922/91 and to related national exemptions based on safety risk assessments carried out by the competent authorities.

*CAT operations with helicopters, balloons and sailplanes are covered by national requirements, as are non-commercial operations, including specialised operations with complex motor-powered aeroplanes and helicopters, as well as commercial specialised operations with aeroplanes, helicopters, balloons and sailplanes.

In short, the regulations only (at the moment) apply to Part-CAT aeroplane operators, including cargo operations and 2-crew aeroplanes with an MOPSC of more than 19. Air Taxi (19 seats or less), EMS, and single pilot operations are currently covered by national regulations.

For the purpose of flight and duty time regulations, **flight time** is the total time from when an aeroplane moves under its own power until it comes to a stop at the end of a flight. The time when propellers are kept running between sectors is included.

You have a maximum working day, to ensure that you are rested enough to fly properly. It's similar to truck drivers' hours, except that there's no tachograph; companies and pilots are trusted to stick to the ops manual and the authorities reserve the right to spot check the paperwork at regular intervals, mainly looking to see that flights are planned within the Company's scheme.

Put simply, your basic working day may be longer or shorter, depending on the time you start and the number of crew you have; the earlier you start, the less time you're allowed, as can be seen in the table below, for the maximum daily FDP (without extensions) for acclimatised (fixed wing) crew members.

It would appear that the maximum FDP without extension at the most favorable time of day (whatever that is) is 13 hours.

	Sectors								
FDP Start	1-2	3	4	5	6	7	8	9	10
0600-1329	13:00	12:30	12:00	11:30	11:00	10:30	10:00	09:30	09:00
1330-1359	12:45	12:15	11:45	11:15	10:45	10:15	09:45	09:15	09:00
1400-1429	12:30	12:00	11:30	11:00	10:30	10:00	09:30	09:00	09:00
1430-1459	12:15	11:45	11:15	10:45	10:15	09:45	09:15	09:00	09:00
1500-1529	12:00	11:30	11:00	10:30	10:00	09:30	09:00	09:00	09:00
1530-1559	11:45	11:15	10:45	10:15	09:45	09:15	09:00	09:00	09:00
1600-1629	11:30	11:00	10:30	10:00	09:30	09:00	09:00	09:00	09:00
1630-1659	11:15	10:45	10:15	09:45	09:15	09:00	09:00	09:00	09:00
1700-0459	11:00	10:30	10:00	09:30	09:00	09:00	09:00	09:00	09:00
0500-0514	12:00	11:30	11:00	10:30	10:00	09:30	09:00	09:00	09:00
0515-0529	12:15	11:45	11:15	10:45	10:15	09:45	09:15	09:00	09:00
0530-0544	12:30	12:00	11:30	11:00	10:30	10:00	09:30	09:00	09:00
0545-0559	12:45	12:15	11:45	11:15	10:45	10:15	09:45	09:15	09:00

The maximum daily FDP may be extended* by up to 1 hour, but not more than twice in any 7 consecutive days. In such cases, you can either increase the minimum pre-flight and post-flight rest periods by 2 hours, or increase the post-flight rest by 4 hours.

*The use of extensions shall be planned in advance and limited to 5 sectors when the WOCL is not encroached, or 4 sectors when the WOCL is encroached by 2 hours or less, or 2 sectors when the WOCL is encroached by more than 2 hours.

YOUR RESPONSIBILITIES

These stem from various provisions of the regulations (try CAT.GEN.MPA.100). It's also up to you to make the best use of any opportunities and facilities for rest provided, and to plan and use your rest periods properly - you should inform Operations if you can't sleep properly, who may arrange a specialist.

COMPANY RESPONSIBILITIES

These go beyond making sure you stick within minimum and maximum limitations. The intent is that operators, through the SMS, demonstrate the management of fatigue.

Duties must be scheduled within the Company's approved scheme, and rostering staff must be given adequate guidance. Work patterns must be realistic with the intention of avoiding, as far as possible, over-running limits. As a result, they must avoid such nasties as alternating day and night duties and positioning that disrupts your rest. Not that they ever do.

Unless you're in a large company, it's obviously difficult to schedule much in advance, but companies must advise you of work details as far ahead as they can (though not less than 7 days), so you can make arrangements for adequate and, within reason, uninterrupted pre-flight rest. Away from base, it's normally the Company's job to provide rest facilities (the legal definition is "satisfactory in respect of noise, temperature, light and ventilation"), but they may lumber you with finding them, as you're on the spot - they are allowed to claim that short notice precludes them doing it.

MAXIMUM DUTY PERIOD (FDP)

A **Duty Period** is any continuous period through which you carry out tasks associated with Company business, including any FDPs), positioning, ground training, ground duties and standby duty. A **Flight Duty Period** (FDP), on the other hand, is any duty period during which you fly in an aircraft as crew, being the period between reporting to operate a flight or series of flights and the on-blocks time of the last sector operated.

It includes positioning immediately before or after a flight (say in a taxi or light aircraft) and pre/after-flight duties, so the start will generally be at least 30 minutes before the first scheduled departure time and the end at least 15 minutes after engines last stopped time, though these may vary between companies.

The maximum flight duty time, excluding extensions, is 13 hours.

DISCRETION TO EXTEND AN FDP

There are always delays in aviation, and a Flying Duty Period may be extended if you think you can make the flight safely and have consulted the other members of the crew about their fitness. However, the normal maximum is based on the original reporting time, and calculated on what *actually* happens, not what was *planned* to happen. Sometimes you may have to exercise discretion if a lower performance aircraft is used, and takes longer to get round the route. This discretion is yours (as Commander), but some Companies make the decision for you before the first flight of the day, which is not when it should be used. Whenever discretion is exercised, it should be reported to Ops on the Discretion Report Form (in the Ops Manual).

FDP extensions must be pre-planned and rest periods around the extended duty increased, either by 4 hours post FDP or 2 hours pre- and post FDP (the maximum planned extension for **augmented** flight and cabin crew is **3 hours** above the scheduled FDP limits in ORO.FLT.205(e). This cannot be combined with split duty (below) and may not occur more than twice in 7 consecutive days.

An **Augmented Flight Crew** is one that comprises more than the minimum number required and in which each flight crew member can leave their assigned post and be replaced by another appropriately qualified person for the purpose of in-flight rest - *ICAO Annex 6*.

Commanders may, for unforeseen circumstances occurring at or after reporting time, at their discretion, increase maximum flight duty by up to 2 hours. After takeoff on the final sector, the flight may continue to the planned destination or alternate.

EASA also allows for the commander to reduce allowable flight duty periods by an unlimited amount on behalf of all crew. More than 2 hours gets the duty pilot involved.

MINIMUM REST PERIODS

As well as having a maximum number of hours on duty, there's also a minimum rest time between duty periods. A Rest Period is time before a Flying Duty Period which is intended to ensure that you're adequately rested before a flight. It doesn't include excessive Travelling Time (over 90 minutes or so) or Positioning. During it, you should be free from all duties, not interrupted by the Company and have the opportunity for a minimum number of consecutive hours sleep in suitable accommodation*, plus time to travel there and back, and for meals, etc.

*For the purpose of standby and split duty, a quiet and comfortable place not open to the public, with the ability to control light and temperature, equipped with adequate furniture that provides a crew member with the possibility of sleep, with enough capacity to accommodate all crew members present at the same time and with access to food and drink. The term *suitable accommodation* means, for the purpose of standby, split duty and rest, a separate room for each crew member, in a quiet environment, with a bed, sufficiently ventilated, with a device for regulating temperature and light, and access to food and drink.

You should have your rest periods rostered enough in advance to get your proper rest. Minimum rest periods should be at least as long as the preceding duty period, and at least 12 hours (in UK), except when away from base* and accommodation is provided by the Company, in which case the minimum may be 11, subject to any exemptions you have. Rest starts from the end of the Duty Period and not the Flying Duty Period.

*When away from home base**, EASA requires 10 hours plus total travelling time above one hour or the length of the previous duty, whichever is greater.

**The location, assigned by the operator, from where the crew member normally starts and ends duty periods and where, under normal circumstances, the operator is not responsible for the their accommodation.

EASA also adds the concept of the "Recurrent Extended Recovery Rest Period," or RERRP, a rest period of 36 hours including 2 local nights* with a maximum separation of 168 hours (7 days), and at least twice a calendar month must include 2 local days, a local day being a 24 hour period starting at 00:00L. EASA also factors in Time Zone Differences. If an FDP involves a change of 4 hours or more, see EOMA 7.1.11.6.

*A **local night** consists of 8 hours between 22:00 - 08:00 local time. A **day off** is at least 36 hours including 2 local nights. Two consecutive days off must have 3 local nights.

In a typical airline, you might get 10 days off in 28, 3 of which could be the final three. A duty block may consist of up to 5 FDPs, although a sixth may be allowed to return to home base after unforeseen circumstances. A single day off may only be followed by up to 4 FDPs, then at least two days off. Two consecutive days off should be planned within any 10 consecutive days.

 In UK, *The Civil Aviation (Working Time) (Amendment) regulations 2010*, also apply.

DISCRETION TO REDUCE A REST PERIOD

You can reduce Rest Periods below the minimum but, like extending Duty Time, it's at your discretion.

 Use of discretion for reducing rest is considered exceptional and shouldn't be done to successive rest periods (it's very much frowned upon). In general, you're better off extending an FDP than reducing a rest period if at all possible. Also, at no time should a rest period be reduced if it immediately follows an extended duty period, or *vice versa* (this is even more frowned upon).

In short, commanders may, in response to unforeseen circumstances occurring at or after reporting time, at their discretion, reduce the minimum rest requirement to at least 12 hours at home base and 10 hours away from base. At most, 2 reduced rest periods can occur between two RERRPs. Any reduction must be deducted from the subsequent maximum FDP, and must be appended to the next minimum rest period.

An added EASA twist is that a commander can increase required rest without limit on behalf of all crew. More than 2 hours gets the duty pilot involved. EASA also uses Rostered Reduced Rest. A crew member must be notified at latest prior to undertaking the immediately preceding non-reduced rest period. After roster publication, only one such reduced rest period may be rostered between two RERRPs.

SPLIT DUTIES

You can extend a duty day by other means than discretion, though, and you can do it before taking off on duties with a long time gap between flights. Technically, a Split Duty is a Flying Duty Period with two or more sectors separated by less than a minimum Rest Period, typically being a situation where you deliver people to a place and wait for them to come back. That is, you can claim half of the period spent hanging around in the middle as "rest" and tack it on to the end of the basic working day. What's more, you can plan to do this from the start, extending the FDP by half of the "rest" taken if it's between 3-10 hours (inclusive, providing the hours are consecutive).

Tip: The normal time spent on the ground is at least 6 hours. If your passengers are late, don't get in a panic - simply try to increase the delay to the length of a minimum rest period and start a new duty.

A split duty cannot follow reduced rest.

POSITIONING

Positioning means non-operating crew members being transferred from place to place as passengers in surface or air transport, usually before or after a FDP, but also at any time as required by the Company (this shouldn't be confused with normal travel from home to work, or *Travelling Time*, which is accepted as up to 90 minutes). Many airlines use taxis for this, but you may be lucky and get a comfortable bus or a light aeroplane. All time spent on positioning is classed as Duty, and when it comes immediately before a Flying Duty Period is included in it, so the subsequent rest period must account for (and be at least as long as) the total FDP and positioning. Positioning is not, however, counted as a sector, and in case I haven't mentioned it before, a sector is the time between an aircraft first moving under its own power until it next comes to rest after landing.

CONSECUTIVE NIGHTS, EARLY STARTS, LATE FINISHES

If any part of a duty falls between 02:00 - 04:59 local time (in the time zone in which you are "acclimatised*"), it becomes a night duty.

*Reporting in a place where the local time is no more than two hours different from local time at home base. A crew member is considered to be acclimatised to the time zone of the reference time for the first 48 hours. After 48 hours of the rotation has elapsed, the crew member is considered to be in an unknown state of acclimatisation. The crew member only becomes acclimatised to the destination time zone if they remain in the first arrival destination time zone (either for rest or any duties) for the time established in the table in ORO.FTL.105(1).

Consecutive refers to two night duties that are only separated by a rest period. Two night duties would not be consecutive if there is recurrent extended recovery rest between them or they are separated by rest periods surrounding a non-night duty.

Consecutive night duties are only allowed with these restrictions:

- Up to 4 sectors per duty
- If two consecutive night duties are scheduled, the preceding duty must finish by 23:59 local time.
- If three consecutive night duties are scheduled, the preceding duty must finish by 21:00.
- No more that three consecutive night duties can be scheduled.

EASA uses Disruptive Schedules*, a late type of which describes an Early Start Duty Period as starting between 02:00L- 06:59L, and a Late Finish as a duty period finishing between 00:00L - 01:59L.

A Disruptive Duty is one where any part occurs between 01:00L - 06:59L. The classification is only possible when a crew member is acclimatised and depends on:

- The local time at the point of departure if the point of departure is within the acclimatisation zone, or
- The local time of the previous departure time zone (as long as the crew is considered to be acclimatised there) if the point of departure is outside the acclimatisation zone.

Consecutive duties are defined as separation of less than 34 hours between disruptive duties of a given type.

If a crew performs 4 or more disruptive duties between 2 RERRPs, the second RERRP is further extended to 60 hours (2½ days).

4 or 5 consecutive Early Start duties are allowed if:

- 2 days off precede 4 consecutive Early Starts and 3 days off precede 5 consecutive Early Starts.
- Only 1 FDP starts between 02:00 - 04:59, which has a maximum of 2 sectors.
- 72 hours off follow.

Otherwise, up to 3 consecutive disruptive duties are allowed, and up to 4 in any 7 day period. Groupings of 10 Early Start duties must be separated by at least 5 days free of such duties.

If individual crew members have violated the 21:00 finish time before 3 consecutive night finishes by less than 3 hours, if they are "willing" (yeah, right), the published roster may continue. This does not appear to need the use of commander's discretion.

Under EASA, there does not appear to be a specific authorisation for a commander to exercise discretion to allow violation of any of the consecutive disruptive duty limits. The closest to one is in FRMS Appendix B paragraph 1, which allows a commander to "modify the limits on flight duty, duty and rest periods in the case of unforeseen circumstances in flight operations, which start at or after the reporting time." The Appendix then goes into detail for other forms of commander's discretion, but omits consecutive disruptive duties.

FLIGHT TIME & DUTY PERIODS
ORO.FTL.210

The total **duty periods** to which a crew member may be assigned shall not exceed:

- 60 duty hours in any 7 consecutive days
- 110 duty hours in any 14 consecutive days, and
- 190 duty hours in any 28 consecutive days, spread as evenly as practicable throughout that period.

The total **flight time** of the sectors on which an individual crew member is assigned as an operating crew member shall not exceed:

- 100 hours of flight time in any 28 consecutive days
- 900 hours of flight time in any calendar year, and
- 1 000 hours of flight time in any 12 consecutive calendar months

In UK, under *The Civil Aviation (Working Time) (Amendment) regulations 2010*, also apply. An employer shall ensure that in any month no person employed by him shall act as a crew member during the course of his working time, if during the period of 12 months expiring at the end of the month before the month in question the aggregate block flying time of that person exceeds 900 hours, and no crew member employed by him shall have a total annual working time of more than 2,000 hours during the 12 months expiring at the end of the month before the month in question.

8 - Operating Procedures

Flights shall not be started unless an operational flight plan is completed under *Flight Preparation*, below *(CAT.OP.MPA.175)*.

Flight paperwork must be retained by the operator for at least 3 months.

MINIMUM FLIGHT ALTITUDES

CAT.OP.MPA.145
CAT.OP.MPA.270

Minimum altitudes may not be less than those specified by the State for the same route. Where minimum altitudes have not already been established, those calculated may not be below any specified in Annex 2 (Rules Of The Air). The following factors should be considered:

- Accuracy and reliability of positioning methods
- Accuracy of altimeters
- Characteristics of the terrain
- The probability of unfavourable weather
- Accuracy of charts
- Airspace restrictions

In any case, you should fly at a suitable altitude for the task, and with due regard to performing a safe forced landing after an engine failure. In other words, you may not fly below specified minimum altitudes except when necessary for takeoff or landing, or descending under approved procedures.

AERODROME OPERATING MINIMA

CAT.OP.MPA.105
CAT.OP.MPA.110, (a)
CAT.OP.MPA.300
CAT.OP.MPA.320

There are weather conditions under which you're not allowed to land, attempt to land, or take off. A minimum cloud base and visibility is laid down, based on the navaids available, terrain, obstacles, type of aircraft, crew experience and State legislation (HUDs can increase the limits with approval). In fact, before commencing an approach to land, you must be satisfied that, according to the information available, the weather at the aerodrome and the condition of the intended runway or FATO should not prevent a safe approach, landing or missed approach, having regard to the performance information contained in the operations manual. The unfortunate part is that EASA requirements are sometimes different from the ICAO ones.

For example, here are the EASA VFR requirements:

Airspace	ABC D E	F	G (Open FIR)
		Above 3000 ft AMSL or 1000 ft above terrain (higher)	At or below 3000 ft AMSL or 1000 ft above terrain (higher)
Dist From Cloud	1500 m horizontally, 1000 ft vertically		Clear of cloud and in sight of the surface
Flight Visibility	5 km below 10,000 ft AMSL		1500 m by day 5 km by night

There are limits for Class A airspace, where no VFR is allowed under ICAO!

You don't have to do all the hard work; Airway Manuals should have all the calculations done for you. In any case, you are responsible for ensuring that before takeoff you've got the weather minima for the relevant times at every destination and at least one suitable alternative (this can mean up to 8 airfields if you include takeoff alternates). Minima which apply to you will be the highest of:

- Those established by the State where you are flying
- Basic minima from your Company, which must not be lower in any case

They may be exceeded in emergency.

The responsibility for establishing minima and their calculation lies with the *operator*, taking into consideration the adequacy and provision of ground aids, the runways, the skill and experience of flight crews, and obstacles in the missed approach, to mention a few. As they are calculated for fog with little or no wind, you should make allowance for rain and/or crosswinds. Naturally, minima are not valid if anything affecting their calculation has been changed through NOTAMs, or by ATC.

Minima are not valid if anything affecting their calculation has been changed through NOTAMs, or by ATC.

The term *Low Visibility Operations* generally means lower than standard ILS approaches. The **operator** must ensure that the minimum equipment that must be working at the start of an LVO is included in the operations or procedures manual, as applicable. The **PIC** or **commander** must ensure that the status of the aircraft, and relevant airborne systems, is appropriate for the specific operation to be conducted.

 The minimum RVR for a visual approach is 800 m, to guard against shallow fog obscuring an approach. Responsibility for separation from other aircraft during a Visual Approach is with ATC, because a visual approach is still an IFR manoeuvre. There must be no operations below 800m without RVR information provided.

Aircraft Categories

A certain amount of airspace and visibility is needed for obstacle avoidance. The most significant factor is speed, and five categories of aircraft have been established for approach purposes. The speed used is the IAS at the threshold, or V_{AT}, 1.3 times the stalling speed (V_{SO}), or 1.23 times $V_{S\,1G}$ in full landing configuration at max weight. If both are available, use the higher resulting V_{AT}.

The speed categories are:

Category	Threshold Speed
A	< 91 kts
B	91-120 kts
C	121-140 kts
D	141-165 kts
E	166-210 kts

OPERATIONAL PROCEDURES
Operations Manual Part A

Takeoff
AMC1 CAT.OP.MPA.110

Takeoff minima are there to make sure that the aircraft can be controlled during a rejected takeoff in adverse circumstances and a continued takeoff after the critical engine fails. They should be expressed as visibility or RVR limits, taking into account the relevant factors for each aerodrome planned for use and the characteristics of the aircraft. Where there is a specific need to see and avoid obstacles on departure and/or for a forced landing, additional conditions, e.g. ceilings, should be specified.

- Takeoff should not be started unless the weather conditions at the aerodrome of departure are equal to or better than applicable minima for landing at that aerodrome unless a weather-permissible takeoff alternate aerodrome is available.
- When the reported meteorological visibility (VIS) is below that required for takeoff and RVR values are not available, a takeoff should only be started if the commander can determine that the visibility along the runway used for takeoff is equal to or better than the required minimum.
- When no reported meteorological visibility or RVR is available, a takeoff should only be started if the commander can determine that the visibility along the runway used for takeoff is equal to or better than the required minimum.

At night, ground lights should be available.

For multi-engined aeroplanes that can either stop or continue to 1,500 ft above the aerodrome while clearing obstacles by the required margins, the minima should be expressed as RVR/CMV as detailed below for aircraft **without** LVTO approval.

Facilities	RVR/VIS(m)
Day only: Nil.	500
Day: at least runway edge lights or runway centreline markings. Night: at least runway edge lights and runway end lights or runway centreline lights and runway end lights.	400

For multi-engined aeroplanes that **cannot** perform as above, there may be a need to re-land immediately and to see and avoid obstacles in the takeoff area. Such aeroplanes may be operated to the following minima if they can comply with obstacle clearance criteria, assuming engine failure at the height specified. The takeoff minima specified should be based upon the height from which the OEI NTOFP can be constructed.

For a light twin, this would mean:

- From 50 feet to 1500 feet above the runway, the flight path must clear obstacles by 50 feet vertically or 90m laterally, with a maximum bank of 15°.
- The 2-engine climb gradient should be 77% of the flight manual figure, up to the engine failure point.
- The single-engine climb gradient may be 100% of the figure from the flight manual.

Below this minimum height, you will need enough forward visibility to attempt a safe emergency landing so, the higher the minimum height, the greater the RVR. For suggestions, refer to the approach tables below.

When RVR or meteorological visibility is not available, takeoff should not be commenced unless the commander can determine that the actual conditions satisfy the applicable minima.

System Minima (NPA, AV, Cat I Approaches)
AMC3 CAT.OP.MPA.110

The **Decision Height** (DH) for a non-precision approach (NPA) under the **Continuous Descent Final Approach*** (CDFA) technique, **Approach Procedure with Vertical Guidance** (APV) or **Category I ILS** operation should be at least the highest of...

- the minimum height to which the approach aid can be used without the required visual reference.
- the relevant Obstacle Clearance Height (OCH).
- the published DH for the procedure.
- the system minima in table below.
- the minimum DH in the flight manual or equivalent.

The **Minimum Descent Height** (MDH) for an NPA flown **without** CDFA should be at least the highest of...

- the OCH for the category of aircraft.
- the system minima in the table below.
- the minimum in the flight manual or equivalent.

*A technique, consistent with stabilised approach procedures, for flying the final segment of a non-precision approach as a continuous descent, without level-off, from an altitude/height at or above the FAF altitude/height to around 15 m (50 ft) above the landing threshold (or where the flare begins), depending on the type of aircraft flown.

The size and weight of transport aircraft does not suit the traditional profile of an NPA, where you could either drop down to MDA at the last minute, or do so early, then drag in for some distance with full flaps and the gear down.

NPAs must be flown using the CDFA technique, unless a specific exemption is obtained. Jeppesen approach plates generally only depict CDFA profiles and NPA minima are usually labelled CDFA and DA(H) rather than MDA(H).

 Jeppesen NPA minima labelled DA(H) are generally identical to the old obstacle clearing MDA(H) minima, meaning that an allowance has not been added for the dip below decision height.

The DH is the limit to which you are protected from hitting anything when you can't see outside. If you have a visual reference at DH, the RVR minima below are considered to be enough to make a safe landing from.

OPERATIONAL PROCEDURES
Operations Manual Part A

Approach Aid	Minima (ft)
ILS/MLS/GLS	200
GNSS/SBAS (LPV)	200
GNSS (LNAV)	250
GNSS/Baro VNAV (LNAV/VNAV)	250
LOC with or without DME	250
SRA (terminating at ½ nm)	250
SRA (terminating at 1 nm)	300
SRA (terminating at 2 nm or more)	350
VOR	300
VOR/DME	250
NDB	350
NDB/DME	300
VDF	350

APPROACH LIGHTING SYSTEMS
AMC5 CAT.OP.MPA.110

RVR minima are determined by the approach lighting. At a 200-foot Decision Height, you are around 900 m from the threshold (assuming a 3° glideslope and 50 feet over the threshold), but you must not go down further without appropriate visual references. If you only had an RVR of 150 m, you would not be able to make a safe landing. RVR minima therefore supplement the DH minima, which determines the distance from the threshold at which a visual reference is *required*, so you can see far enough ahead not to hit anything.

Facility	Length, Configuration & Intensity
FALS	CAT I lighting system (HIALS ≥720 m) distance coded centreline, Barrette centreline.
IALS	Simple approach lighting system (HIALS 420 – 719 m) single source, Barrette.
BALS	Any other approach lighting system (HIALS, MALS or ALS 210 - 419 m).
NALS	Any other approach light system (HIALS, MALS or ALS <210 m) or no approach lights.

The key property is the *length* of a system, the class of which determines how far back from the threshold they are *available*. RVR minima are the shortest sight picture with which you can safely complete a CAT I landing.

PRECISION APPROACH MINIMA (CAT 1)

The DH for a CAT I ILS is the higher of the 200 foot system minima and the OCH, on the basis that, if an obstacle penetrates the vertical and lateral protected airspace, the increase in DH helps you avoid it visually.

The table below shows the lowest RVR/CMV allowed as a function of the DH/MDH and lighting system:

DH(ft)	Facilities (RVR - metres)			
	FALS	IALS	BALS	NALS
200-210	550 m	750 m	1000 m	1200 m
211-240	550 m	800 m	1000 m	1200 m
241-250	550 m	800 m	1000 m	1300 m
251-260	600 m	800 m	1100 m	1300 m
261-280	600 m	900 m	1100 m	1300 m
281-300	650 m	900 m	1200 m	1400 m
301-320	700 m	1000 m	1200 m	1400 m
321-340	800 m	1100 m	1300 m	1500 m

The full table goes right up to 1200 ft DH.

CONVERTING REPORTED MET VIS TO RVR

The 1000 candelas mentioned in the definition of visibility is about as bright as an ordinary light bulb, so RVR is, in effect, visibility adjusted for the greater intensity of the runway lights. Thus, when visibility is converted to an equivalent RVR figure for a runway with HI lighting, the visibility figure is higher by 1.5 by day and by 2 at night.

Lighting Elements in Operation	RVR = Met Vis X	
	Day	Night
HI Approach and Runway Lighting	1.5	2.0
Any Lighting Other than Above	1.0	1.5
No Lighting	1.0	N/A

VFR EN-ROUTE MINIMA

SINGLE-ENGINED AEROPLANES

If an engine fails, you must be able to continue at or above MSA to 1000 feet above a place on land where you can make a safe forced landing. Since you will be gliding, flight above cloud extending below MSA is not a good idea. You need a cloudbase of 1000 feet agl (1500 over water or at night) and 3 km visibility at all times.

MULTI-ENGINED AEROPLANES

Categories A and B can operate under VFR between 3-5 km visibility in Class G airspace if the IAS is below 140 kts. Special VFR flights shall not be commenced when the visibility is less than 3 km, and not otherwise conducted when less than 1½ km.

APPROACH FLIGHT TECHNIQUE
CAT.OP.MPA.115

Approaches shall be stabilised unless otherwise approved for a particular approach to a particular runway.

NON-PRECISION APPROACHES

The CDFA technique must be used for all non-precision approaches. However, with approval, another method may be used for a particular approach/runway combination. In such cases, the minimum RVR must be increased by 200 m for category A and B aeroplanes and by 400 m for C and D. Where there is a public interest to maintain current operations and the CDFA technique cannot be applied, the RVR must be established and regularly reviewed by the competent authority.

INSTRUMENT DEPARTURE & APPROACHES
CAT.OP.MPA.125

Instrument departure and approach procedures established by the State of the aerodrome must be used, although others may be used with approval. However, a commander may accept an ATC clearance to deviate from a published procedure if obstacle clearance criteria are observed and full account is taken of the operating conditions. In any case, the final approach shall be flown visually* or in accordance with the established instrument approach procedures.

*A visual approach is still an IFR procedure if it is to do with an approach.

COMMENCEMENT & CONTINUING APPROACHES
CAT.OP.MPA.305

You may commence an instrument approach regardless of the reported RVR/visibility* but, if it is less than the minima, you may not continue below 1,000 ft above the aerodrome, or into the final approach segment when the DA/H or MDA/H is higher than that.

*When RVR is not available, the reported visibility may be converted.

The touchdown zone RVR is always controlling but, if reported and relevant, the midpoint and stop end RVR shall also be controlling. The minimum RVR value for the midpoint is 125 m or the RVR required for the touchdown zone if less, and 75 m for the stopend. For aircraft with a rollout guidance or control system, the minimum RVR for the midpoint shall be 75 m. If, after passing 1,000 ft above the aerodrome, the reported RVR/visibility falls below the minima, you may continue to DA/H or MDA/H, and below that (and the landing completed) if adequate visual reference for the type of approach and intended runway is established at that point and is maintained. To qualify as visual reference, the following must be distinctly visible:

- Elements of the approach light system
- The threshold
- The threshold markings
- The threshold lights
- The threshold identification lights
- The visual glide slope indicator
- Touchdown zone or touchdown zone markings
- The touchdown zone lights
- FATO/Runway edge lights; or
- Other visual references accepted by the Authority

FUEL, OIL & WATER METHANOL CARRIED

CAT.OP.MPA.150(b) requires your Company to have a fuel policy for flight planning and in-flight replanning, to ensure that every flight carries enough fuel for the planned operation, plus reserves for any deviations. Such planning must only be based upon procedures and data in or derived from the Ops Manual or current aircraft-specific data (e.g. the Flight Manual), and the conditions under which the flight is to be conducted.

Under CAT.OP.MPA.260, you may only commence a flight or continue when in-flight replanning when you are satisfied that at least the planned amount of usable fuel and oil to complete the flight safely is carried, taking into account the expected operating conditions.

CAT.OP.MPA.280 requires management of that fuel, including declaring an emergency when you have less than final reserve fuel. *Fuel management* means you must check and record the contents regularly in flight, to ensure that the actual consumption compares with the planned consumption, and that the remaining usable fuel is enough to complete the flight.

If the expected usable fuel remaining at the destination is less than required alternate plus final reserve fuel (or just final reserve if no alternate is required), you must divert to where a safe landing can be made, with final reserves.

You must declare an emergency (i.e. make a PAN* call) when usable fuel on board is less than final reserve fuel. This does not mean that you cannot use it, but the rules are there to ensure that fuel management is carried out, as mentioned above. However, the intent is clear - in general, you *should* always land with at least final reserve fuel (the word *shall* may be used in your Ops Manual), and preferably more - proper planning should ensure that you don't get down that far, but stuff happens sometimes. Declaring an emergency may allow ATC to bring you in with the reserves intact, by providing a more direct routing.

*It's a PAN call when the current fuel consumption and routing are likely to take you below the Final Reserve. It could escalate into a Mayday.

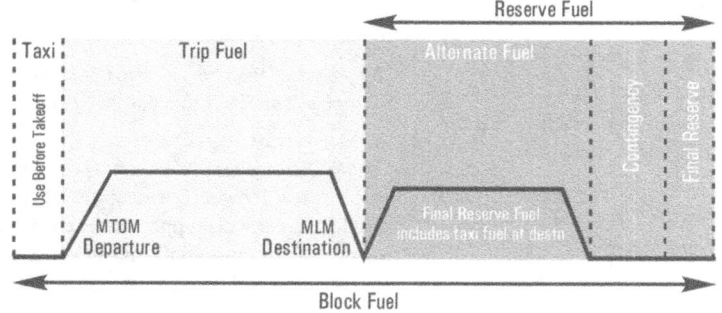

Pre-flight Calculations

For Annex 6, when you need to nominate an alternate, you should have enough fuel to be able to arrive over the destination in a position to make an approach, overshoot (carry out a missed approach) and fly to an alternate, and still have enough to **hold for 45 minutes** (plus 15% of the planned cruise time), or 2 hours, whichever is less, at the alternate, at which you must still be able to carry out an approach and landing. Just in case, 5% is required for contingencies as well, such as errors in forecast winds, navigation, ATC restrictions and individual variations from standard consumption. A turbojet only needs to be able to **hold for 30 minutes** at 1500 ft above the alternate.

The pre-flight calculation of usable fuel (i.e. *total block fuel*) must include:

- **Taxy Fuel**, at least what you expect to use before takeoff, including start, taxi and run-up, allowing for local conditions, APUs, icing equipment, etc. It's often a standard figure, such as 250 kg, but you can alter it on the day if conditions warrant it. Taxi fuel is not included in endurance figures!

- **Trip (Sector) Fuel**. That required for the trip as planned, including climb, cruise and descent. The difference between the takeoff and landing masses* must be at least equal to this:
  - Takeoff and climb from aerodrome elevation to initial cruising level or altitude, for the expected departure procedure
  - Top of climb to top of descent (e.g. the cruise), including steps
  - From top of descent to where the approach is initiated, for the expected arrival procedure
  - Approach and landing at the destination

- **Reserve Fuel**, which must be on board at takeoff, but is not necessarily used. It consists of:
  - **Contingency Fuel***. The greater of:
    - The highest of:
      - 5% of trip fuel (or the remainder when replanning in flight).
      - 3% of planned trip fuel (or the remainder) if a suitable alternate is available.
      - Enough for 20 minutes' flying, based on planned trip consumption, if a consumption monitoring program for using valid data is in force.
      - Fuel based on approved statistics to cover deviations from planned to actual trip fuel.
    - Enough for 5 minutes at holding speed at 1500 feet above the destination, in standard conditions.

    However, if you have a lot of trip fuel, the contingency fuel requirement will also be high, taking up space that could be occupied by fare paying passengers. There are ways of reducing this below the basic 5% minimum without reducing safety, which includes messing with the alternate fuel. For example, if you have a nice large airfield within 20% of your flight planned route distance (with the centre of the circle up to 25% away from the destination) at which you can make a tech stop pick to up more fuel, you can reduce the contingency fuel to 3%.

    If the above airfield is nearer the halfway point, you can use the Reduced Contingency Fuel procedure, which involves a Decision Point and a refuelling point. You still need 5% contingency fuel (for each leg), but you are now working with reduced distances, from the destination to the tech stop (via the DP) or from the DP to the original destination (you take the greater figure).

    Contingency fuel is based on fuel requirements to the destination so, in theory, if you have any left it could be used from the destination to the alternate. You don't have to use it at the cruise rate. This will increase the contingency time.

    For planning purposes, the Landing Mass should include the contingency fuel.

  - **Alternate Fuel**, if a destination alternate is needed* (you can use the departure point). If you need two, use the one that needs the most fuel. Otherwise, enough for:
    - Go around.
    - Climb to cruise.
    - Cruise from top of climb to top of descent to alternate.
    - From top of descent to where the approach is initiated, through the expected arrival procedure.
    - Approach and landing at the alternate.

    *At least one destination alternate is needed unless the flight is less than 6 hours or 2 separate runways are available and the weather forecast for one hour either side of the ETA indicates that the visibility will be greater than 5 km and the ceiling at least 2,000 feet, or 500 feet above the circling minima. If a destination alternate is not used, you must carry additional fuel as described below.

    You can burn in to the alternate fuel if the airfield you are holding over passes an EAT.

  - **Final Reserve Fuel**. This is sometimes called *holding fuel*, and should not be part of the fuel plan, as it is a final safety margin - although you can use it, you cannot *plan* to land with less than final reserve. It is calculated for a holding speed at 1,500 ft (450 m) above aerodrome elevation in standard conditions:
    - For **reciprocating engines**, enough to fly for 45 minutes.
    - For **turbine aeroplanes**, fuel to fly for 30 minutes, calculated with the estimated mass at

the alternate (or the destination) when no alternate is required.

- Minimum **additional fuel**, to allow (depending on the operation):
  - Holding for 15 minutes at 1,500 ft (450 m) above the aerodrome elevation in standard conditions without a destination alternate.
  - Following possible failure of a power unit or loss of pressurisation (at the most critical point), the aeroplane to descend as necessary and proceed to an adequate aerodrome, hold there for 15 minutes at 1,500 ft (450 m) above aerodrome elevation in standard conditions, and make an approach and landing, although additional fuel is only required if the minimum amount is not enough.
  - For ETOPS, enough to land at an alternate with 15 minutes fuel in the tanks in the worst case emergency (usually depressurisation, as flying at FL100 takes more fuel) at the worst-case location.
- **Extra Fuel** as required by the commander or other commercial reasons (it might be more expensive where you are going). While this is not mandatory, it might include fuel that is deemed so in an operations manual for certain routes or destinations, or even departure airports (taxi times at some can be way longer than expected!) Extra fuel is carried for delays at the destination, not the alternate, so flights arriving to a common alternate are in the same boat.

  Some Captains take about 10 minutes' worth of extra fuel for weird emergencies, like stuck flaps, although it might help to get the checklist time down to 5 minutes! In some business jets, you need to land with about 5,000 lbs of fuel on board, because otherwise the machine would be unstable on the ground. You can mostly have a substantial amount in your back pocket anyway because you don't have the commercial restrictions.

For planning the landing weight, it is assumed that only taxi and trip fuel are burnt, and the rest will be in the aircraft for landing. It is however perfectly acceptable to burn extra fuel and contingency fuel along the flight if needed (that is what it is for). At takeoff, therefore, you should have at least Minimum Reserve and Trip Fuel on board. *Minimum Reserve Fuel* is Reserve without the Extra Fuel. *Block Fuel* is Trip Fuel plus Taxi and Reserve Fuel.

Under CAT.OP.MPA.151, class B aeroplanes may use:

- taxi fuel, if significant.
- trip fuel.
- reserve fuel, consisting of:
  - contingency fuel of at least 5% of the planned trip fuel or, for in-flight replanning, 5% of the trip fuel for the remainder of the flight, and
  - final reserve fuel for an extra 45 minutes for reciprocating engines or 30 for turbines.

- fuel to reach the destination alternate via the destination, if one is required, and
- extra fuel, if specified by the commander.

IN-FLIGHT REPLANNING

The procedures do not include taxy fuel, and the trip fuel would be for the remainder of the flight. This would be used, for example, where fuel uplift is limited and you have to juggle alternates to make it all fit. So, instead of filing for Prestwick as an alternate to Glasgow when coming from London, you use Manchester as a destination. This is now legal, and you may well have enough to start a new flight to Glasgow when near to Manchester. Since you're up there anyway, you don't have to worry about the taxi and takeoff stuff. Mind you, it is pushing the legal envelope!

DECISION POINT PROCEDURE

This is a technique for increasing the Traffic Load by reducing the minimum fuel required. You reduce the contingency figures by using it only from the Decision Point to the destination.

For destinations reached via a decision point, fuel should be the greater of:

- The sum of taxy and trip fuel via the point, contingency fuel (at least 5% of estimated consumption from there to the destination), alternate, final reserve, additional and extra fuel.
- The sum of taxy and trip fuel to an alternate via the point, contingency fuel (at least 3% of estimated consumption from there to the alternate), final reserve, additional and extra fuel.

ISOLATED AERODROME PROCEDURE
CAT.OP.MPA.106

An isolated aerodrome is one for which the alternate and final fuel reserve required to reach the nearest adequate* destination alternate aerodrome is more than:

- for aeroplanes with reciprocating engines, fuel to fly for 45 minutes plus 15% of the flying time planned to be spent at cruising level or two hours, whichever is less, or
- for aeroplanes with turbine engines, fuel to fly for two hours at normal cruise consumption above the destination aerodrome, including final reserve fuel.

Thus, where the nearest diversion is so far away that you would need more fuel than you can carry to get there, you might be able to carry holding fuel instead, assuming that the worst weather will go through in under half an hour. With approval, the operator must ensure that:

- The flight does not depart unless the weather can *reasonably be expected* to be above limits at the ETA (typically 1 hour either side)
- Fuel is monitored

The departure fuel therefore includes enough for taxi and start up, the trip, contingencies and isolated airfield reserve. The commander may take extra fuel if required.

You can also expect special navigation procedures, such as PNR/CP calculation, or at least Last Point Of Diversion, or ETOPS (see below).

*An aerodrome is considered to be "adequate" if, at the expected time of use, it is available and equipped with necessary ancillary services such as ATS, lighting, communications, weather reporting, navigation aids and emergency services.

Pre-Determined Point Procedure

This is for those situations where the destination and its alternate are so far apart that you don't have enough fuel to fly from the departure point to the destination, then on to the alternate so, at some point on the journey, you must make a decision to go to one or the other. In this case, you don't need alternate fuel, but you do need holding fuel.

Where the distance between the destination and its alternate means you can only go through a predetermined point, the fuel loaded should be the greater of:

- The sum of taxy and trip fuel via the predetermined point, contingency fuel (see above), additional fuel, but at least, for reciprocating engines, fuel to fly for 45 minutes plus 15% of the time to be spent at cruising level, or two hours, whichever is less or, for turbine engines, fuel to fly for two hours at normal cruise consumption after arriving over the destination, including final reserve and extra fuel.

- The sum of taxy and trip fuel to an alternate via the predetermined point, contingency fuel (see above), additional fuel, but at least, for reciprocating engines, fuel for 45 minutes or, for turbines, 30 minutes at holding speed at 1,500 ft (450 m) above the aerodrome elevation in standard conditions, including final reserve and extra fuel.

ETOPS/EROPS/EDTO

SPA.ETOPS.100
CAT.OP.MPA.140
Annex V Part SPA Subpart F

Extended Range Twin Operations (ETOPS) is also known as *Extended Diversion Time Operations* (EDTO). It should be noted that engines are only 30% of the reasons for diversion.

Twin-engined Performance Class A aeroplanes with an MOPSC of 20 or more or an MTOM of 45 360 kg or more may not fly further from an adequate aerodrome*, under standard conditions in still air, than the distance flown in 60 minutes at OEI cruising speed.

For performance class A aeroplanes with an MOPSC of 19 or less and an MTOM of less than 45 360 kg, the distance flown increases to 120 minutes, or 180 minutes (with approval) for turbojets.

*For ETOPS alternates (see below) the term *suitable* is used as weather minima apply (they do not apply to "adequate" aerodromes).

For performance class B or C, the distance flown is 120 minutes at OEI cruise speed or 300 nm, whichever is the less.

The OEI speed is based on TAS (but not over V_{MO}) under ISA conditions in level flight at FL 170 (for jets) or FL 80 (for props) or the maximum, whichever is less, with max continuous power on the remaining engine and at least the takeoff mass at sea level.

The range of rule times above 60 minutes includes ETOPS 75, 90, 120/138, or 180/207*. The number specifies the furthest distance that can be flown from a suitable alternate. For example, ETOPS 90 approval permits an aircraft to follow a route that will allow it to reach a diversion within 90 minutes if one engine fails. For 180 minute approval, a twin turbojet must be able to divert or continue where the flying time is no more than 180 minutes from a suitable alternate, in still air, at OEI TAS. All ranges are calculated as NAMs.

*The numbers after the slash refer to areas where the number before it don't work - that is, 138 minutes (instead of 120) removes a no-go area over the North Atlantic that does not have a suitable alternate within 120 minutes.

Higher maintenance standards are naturally needed for all this (the crews need training as well), and despatch of an ETOPS aircraft must be carried out only by authorised people. Engines must be segregated, and no mechanic, inspector, tools or parts can be used on both engines. Aerodromes must allow you to stop within the landing distance available inside normal limits. Services and facilities must also be adequate, as must minima for the expected runway. For an hour either side of ETA, the latest forecast weather conditions must equal or exceed the planning minima for alternates, and the forecast crosswind component, including gusts, must be less than the maximum for landing, with one engine out.

Aircraft must conform to ditching requirements* over water when a suitable landing field is more than 120 min or 400 nm away. One of the requirements is *fuel system isolation* (no crossfeed) which is something the authorities missed when they allowed the Air Transat Airbus that ran out of fuel over the Atlantic to fly.

CAT.GEN.MPA.150

You must have relevant parts of the ops manual on board.

ETOPS Alternates
SPA.ETOPS.110

Before conducting an ETOPS flight, an ETOPS en-route alternate must be available, within either the approved diversion time, or one based on the MEL-generated serviceability status of the aeroplane, whichever is shorter.

An ETOPS en-route alternate is "adequate" if, at the expected time of use, it is available with necessary ancillary services such as ATC, lighting, communications, weather reporting, navigation aids and emergency services and has at least one instrument approach procedure available.

Planning Minima
SPA.ETOPS.115

An aerodrome may only be selected as an ETOPS en-route alternate when the weather reports or forecasts, or combinations, indicate that, between the anticipated time of landing until one hour after the latest possible time of landing, conditions will exist at or above the planning minima shown below.

OPERATIONAL PROCEDURES
Operations Manual Part A

Methods of calculation must be in the operations manual.

Approach	Minima
Precision	DA/H + 200 ft RVR/VIS + 800 m
NPA or Circling	MDA/H + 400 ft RVR/VIS + 1500 m

MASS & CENTRE OF GRAVITY

Aircraft are weighed:

- Before entering service (which includes after being manufactured and when coming into the EASA system from a non-EASA operator)
- Every 4 years, for individual aircraft, if no major modifications have taken place
- Every 9 years for fleet masses
- Every time a modification takes place

The commander must ensure that the loading, mass and centre of gravity of the aircraft comply with the limitations in the flight manual.

DETERMINING THE MASS OF PASSENGERS

Normally, actual mass values should be used for crew and passengers, ideally being weighed before flight. However, where this is not practical or desirable, for aeroplanes with less than 10 passenger seats, individual passengers may make a verbal statement as to their mass, in which case a constant should be added for clothing of at least 4 kg (10 lbs), and 6 kg (14 lbs) for hand baggage.

Personnel boarding passengers on this basis should assess their stated mass, with clothing, for reasonableness.

STANDARD MASS VALUES

When the total number of passenger seats is 20 or more, use the standard male and female masses in Table 1 for convenience. If the total number of passenger seats is 30 or more, use the *All Adult* mass values.

Using standard masses depends on statistical probability, which doesn't work under 20 passengers, which is why you must use actual weights below that.

PASSENGERS, 20 SEATS OR MORE

Seats	20 +		30 +
	Male	*Fem*	*Adults*
Non- charter	88 kg	70 kg	84 kg
Holiday charters	83 kg	69 kg	76 kg
Children (2-12)	35 kg	35 kg	35 kg

Holiday charter: part of a holiday package, with destinations outside the departure country, with accommodation.

PASSENGERS, 19 SEATS OR LESS

Seats	1-5	6-9	10-19
Male	104 kg	96 kg	92 kg
Female	86 kg	78 kg	74 kg
Children 2-12	35 kg	35 kg	35 kg

With no hand baggage, or if separate, deduct 6 kg (not overcoats, etc).

CHECKED BAGGAGE 20+ SEATS

Flight	Bge Std Mass
Domestic	11 kg
Within Europe	13 kg
Intercontinental	15 kg
All Other	13 kg

With 19 passenger seats or less, use actual mass. Here, *domestic flight* means one with origin and destination(s) within the borders of one state, *within Europe* means flights, other than Domestic, whose origin and destination are within the EEC, and *Intercontinental flight*, other than within Europe, means with origin and destination in different continents.

MASS VALUES FOR CREW

Crew Position	Std Mass inc Hand Bge
Flight Crew	85 kg
Cabin Crew	75 kg

ATS FLIGHT PLAN
CAT.OP.MPA.190

This has already been described under *Air Law*, but if one is not required, adequate information must still be deposited for the alerting service. The ATS flight plan is *not* the same as.....

OPERATIONAL FLIGHT PLAN

The Operational Flight Plan is a document that is completed as the flight progresses, listing passengers added and dropped off, fuel uplifts, weather, clearances, etc. - similar to a Nav Log, but more for admin purposes rather than flight planning. It can also be a simple message on a white board telling people where you've gone for the day, depending on the size of the operation. One must be completed for every flight, signed by the commander and flight despatcher. A copy must be left with the operator, or at least the airport authorities.

The plan must contain information such as registration, type and variant, date of flight, route and timings, etc.

TECHNICAL LOG

This is a system for recording defects and maintenance between scheduled servicing intervals, as well as information relevant to flight safety and maintenance. In other words, it is the formal instrument of communication between flight crews and engineering. It can be a paper or computer system, or any combination.

OPERATIONAL PROCEDURES
Operations Manual Part A

Tech logs must be carried in the aircraft, with copies of the entries above kept on the ground, except for helicopters and aeroplanes weighing less than 2730 kg, where they may also be carried on board in an approved container, if it is not reasonably practicable to do otherwise. They must be preserved for 24 months after the date of last entry. The tech log **must be filled in at the end of every flight**, by the commander, specifically noting takeoff and landing times, known defects that affect airworthiness or safe operation, and anything else needed.

 Your signature for the preflight means that you accept responsibility for the machine's condition. At the end of your flight, it is your obligation to enter any unserviceable items in the defect report.

FLIGHT PREPARATION
CAT.OP.MPA.175

Otherwise, *flights should not be started* unless an operational flight plan is complete* (based on performance and conditions en route) and you are satisfied that:

- the aircraft is airworthy with paperwork in order
- the aircraft's configuration is as per the CDL
- the instruments and equipment required are available and working, except as under the MEL
- those parts of the operations manual required for the flight are available
- the documents, additional information and forms required by CAT.GEN.MPA.180 are on board
- current maps, charts and associated documents or equivalent data are available for the intended operation, including diversions which may reasonably be expected
- ground facilities and services are available and adequate
- the provisions in the operations manual in respect of fuel, oil and oxygen, minimum safe altitudes, operating minima and availability of alternates can be complied with, together with additional operational limitations
- the load is properly distributed and safely secured
- the mass of the aircraft at takeoff will be such that the flight can be conducted in compliance with performance requirements

*Not required for non-complex motor powered aeroplanes taking off and landing at the same aerodrome under VFR.

DOCUMENTS TO BE CARRIED
CAT.GEN.MPA.180

The following must be originals unless specified:

- Certificate of Airworthiness or equivalent flight authority*
- Certificate of Registration*
- Noise Certificate, including an English translation, where one has been provided by the Authority responsible for issuing it.
- Radio Station Licence*

**Required by the Chicago Convention, Article 29*

- Air Operator Certificate (certified true copy) plus relevant operations specifications.
- Flight Crew Licences*, valid, with ratings, to include radio and medical certificates
- Third Party Insurance Liability Certificate
- Operations Manual and SOPs, if operating under an AOC - over water you must carry relevant parts of the Ops manual
- Flight Manual (or relevant parts in Ops Manual)

INFORMATION AND FORMS
These may be carried in forms other than printed paper:

- Technical Log, with Maintenance Release (Journey Log*). See Annex I (Part-M) to Regulation (EC) No 2042/2003.
- Route Guides and Charts
- Aircraft Weight Schedule, or Mass and Balance documentation
- Flight Plan (including the operational plan)
- Passenger list, or Cargo Manifest, as applicable, with notification of special classes of passenger (prisoners, deportees, etc.) and special loads
- Current and suitable aeronautical charts for the proposed route and all routes along which it is reasonable to expect a diversion.
- NOTAMs and other AIS briefing material
- Weather Information
- General Declaration
- Procedures and visual signals information for use by intercepting and intercepted aircraft.
- Information concerning search and rescue services for the area of the intended flight, which shall be easily accessible in the flight crew compartment.
- Current parts of the operations manual that are relevant to the duties of crew members, which shall be easily accessible to them.
- The MEL (should be in part B of the ops manual).
- the operational flight plan, if applicable.
- notification of special categories of passenger (SCPs) and special loads, if applicable.
- any other documentation that may be pertinent to the flight or is required by the States concerned.

For VFR by day with non-complex motor-powered aircraft taking off and landing at the same site within 24 hours, or remaining within a local area specified in the operations manual, the following may be retained at the aerodrome or site instead:

- noise certificate
- aircraft radio licence
- journey log, or equivalent
- aircraft technical log
- NOTAMs and AIS briefing documentation

- meteorological information
- notification of SCPs and special loads, if applicable
- mass and balance documentation

If the documents above are lost or stolen, the operation may continue until the flight reaches its destination or a place where replacements can be provided.

INFORMATION KEPT ON THE GROUND
CAT.GEN.MPA.185

At least for the duration of each flight (or series of flights), information relevant to the flight and type of operation must be left on the ground, as part of the evidence at the subsequent Board of Inquiry (in fact, your company will typically have to keep a file on each flight - see below). This will include a copy of the operational flight plan and weight and balance sheet, copies of the journey (tech) log, any relevant NOTAMs and details of special loads, such as Dangerous Goods Shipper's Declarations.

The information must be retained until it has been duplicated at the place at which it will be stored or, if impracticable, carried in a fireproof container in the aircraft.

PRESERVATION OF DOCUMENTATION
ORO.MLR.115

Original documentation, or copies, to be preserved, must be kept for the required period (below) even if ceasing to be an operator of an aircraft. When crew members move on, their records must be available to the new operator.

FLIGHT PREPARATION & EXECUTION

Item	Period
Operational Flight Plan	3 months
NOTAMs and AIS if edited	3 months
Mass & Balance Documentation	3 months
Special Load Notification	3 months
Journey Log	3 months
Flight Reports	3 months

FLIGHT CREW RECORDS

Item	Period
Licences	Period with operator
Crew training, checking etc	3 years
Recent Experience	15 months
Route/Role/Area Competence	3 years
Dangerous Goods Training	3 years

OTHER OPERATIONS PERSONNEL

Item	Period
Those for whom an approved training program is required	Last 2 records
Flight Data Recordings	60 days after an accident

FUELLING PROCEDURES
CAT.OP.MPA.195

Naturally, only competent and authorised personnel should operate fuelling equipment, who must also be fully briefed by their Company. In practice, of course, refuellers know very well what they're doing, but you should still be in full communication with them because you can never be really sure, especially in remote places.

In general, the following precautions should be taken:

- Documentation must reflect the fuel's origins and its correct handling.
- Vehicles must be roadworthy and inspected.
- Fire extinguishing equipment must be available and crews familiar with it.
- A clear exit path must be maintained for the removal of equipment in emergency.
- The aircraft, fuelling vehicle, hose nozzle, filters or anything else through which fuel passes should be electrically bonded *before* the cap is removed.
- Don't refuel within 100' (30 m) of radar equipment that is operating.
- Only essential switches should be operated, and observe radio silence.
- Avoid fuelling during electrical storms, and don't use bulbs or flash equipment in the fuelling zone. Non-essential engines should not be run, but if any already doing so are stopped, they should not be restarted until fuel has ceased flowing, with no risk of igniting vapours.

Fuel can burn you. High vapour concentrations will irritate the eyes, nose, throat and lungs and may cause anasthaesia, headaches, dizziness and other central nervous system problems. Ingestion (like when siphoning) may cause bronchopneumonia or similar nasties, including leukemia and death. If you get it on your clothes, ground yourself before removing any and rinse them in clean water. Fuel spills on the ground must be covered with dirt as quickly as possible. Otherwise, everyone not involved should keep clear - at least 50m away.

Fuel density changes with temperature - on a hot day, you won't get as much in, and will get less endurance. So, the colder it is, the heavier the fuel.

FUELLING ZONES
These should be 15 m from buildings, with no ignition sources within 6 m (20 feet), and no radar within 30 m.

AT BASE
Confirm with Ops that the fuel ordered is enough, and during the pre-flight, confirm that:

- The correct grade is used.
- Fuel drains are checked for water, and left properly closed.
- A visual check of tank contents, or a dipstick check, reveals the correct amount of fuel on board within reason.
- Fuel caps are secured.
- Fuel gauges indicate the required levels, and

OPERATIONAL PROCEDURES
Operations Manual Part A

- Details are correctly entered in the Journey Log and a gross error check carried out.

EN ROUTE

A flight crew member should normally be present, and as well as confirming the above requirements are met, should ensure that:

- The refuellers are advised of the type, grade and fuel quantity, especially units of measurement.
- The bowser (or whatever) is earthed to the aircraft before the hose is extended, and remains so until refuelling is complete.
- No smoking within 15 m.
- The correct quantity of anti-freeze is added.
- The bowser readings at the start and finish reflect the uplift as on the aircraft gauges, and a gross error check is carried out; particularly important in some countries, where they try and swindle you.

PASSENGERS ON BOARD

As a general rule, fuelling with passengers on board is not allowed when fuelling with AVGAS, or with wide-cut fuel, or in any aircraft with less than 20 seats, especially with engines running, or passengers embarking or disembarking (CAT.OP.MPA.195 & 200). However, in real life, in certain circumstances (i.e. casevac, bad weather, no transport) it may be permitted, if:

- Passengers are warned that they must not produce ignition by any means (including electrical switches). They must remain seated, with belts/harnesses unfastened.
- "Fasten Seat Belt" signs are off, and NO SMOKING signs on, with sufficient interior lighting to identify emergency exits.
- Qualified cabin staff able to direct an immediate evacuation are around, preferably at each main door, which should be open and unobstructed. One must be the entry doors through which the passengers embarked.
- Fuellers are notified if vapour is smelt in the cabin.
- Ground activities do not create hazards: the bowser or fuel installation should not stop people leaving in a hurry.
- ATC and the Fire Authority are informed.
- Fire extinguishers are nearby.

On-board APUs discharging into the zone must not be started after filler caps are removed or fuelling connections are made. If an APU is stopped during fuelling it must not be restarted until the flow of fuel has ceased and there is no risk of igniting fuel vapours, unless the flight manual dictates otherwise.

Electrical power supplies must not be connected or disconnected, and equipment likely to produce sparks or arcs must not be used, including combustion heaters in or near the aircraft and photographic equipment within 10 feet (3 m) of the fuelling equipment or the fill or vent points of the fuel systems. Smoking is not permitted either. Suspend fuelling when lightning is within 8 km of the aerodrome. Known high energy equipment like HF radios and weather-mapping radar must not be operated, unless the flight manual contains proper procedures.

PASSENGER BRIEFING & SAFETY

CAT.OP.MPA.165
CAT.OP.MPA.170
CAT.OP.MPA.240 - *Smoking On Board*

The regulations impose on you (as commander) the responsibility for the safety and well-being of your passengers. You are supposed to brief them before every flight, or at least take all reasonable steps to do so.

The operator is responsible for ensuring that the safety brief is carried out.

Passengers come in three groups:

- **Those likely to assist evacuation** - reasonably fit and strong people, who should be the only ones next to self-help (type III and type IV) exits - an exit door on a jet may weigh up to 53 lbs. They should be able to understand instructions.
- **Those likely to impede evacuation**, otherwise called **Special Categories Of Passengers** (SCPs - see CAT.OP.MPA.155). These are persons that require special conditions, assistance and/or devices when carried on a flight, seated where they will not obstruct emergency equipment or exits, or otherwise get in the way, such as:
  - **Persons of Reduced Mobility**, due to physical incapacity, intellectual deficiency, age, illness, etc. Their totals must not exceed those able to assist with evacuation.
  - Physically or mentally handicapped people who would have difficulty in moving quickly
  - Those with impaired sight or hearing
  - Children and infants, whether or not with an adult (< 12)
  - Those in custody and/or being deported (i.e. in handcuffs)
  - Those whose physical size prevents quick movement
- **Those unlikely to affect evacuation** - with no seating restrictions except as above

Multiple occupancy is only allowed when one is an infant under 24 months and the other is a responsible adult over 12.

Passengers should be either taken to the aircraft in approved transport, or escorted by a crew member, company or handling agent employee. Once there, they should be guided to their seats in a way that keeps the aircraft stable. Once seated, a flight or cabin crew member should close the door(s) and/or confirm it by inspection. At the destination, passengers should remain on the aircraft until the engines have been shut down, and they can proceed to the terminal by vehicle, or with an escort. If propellers are turning, competent people must escort them away by a safe route. They must remain in a unified group, refrain from smoking, and keep well clear of jet engine intakes and exhaust danger areas while on the movement area. If you have deportees or persons charged with criminal offences, special arrangements, including escorts, should be made and full details included in your flight brief (CAT.OP.MPA.155(b)).

Aircraft should be parked to avoid exposure to hazardous conditions, to which passengers must be alerted. There must be guidance and escorts along safe routes, smoking restrictions must be enforced and entertainment system headsets that decrease awareness of other traffic or limit reception of audible direction or warning signals should not be worn. Passengers must be briefed on how to safely get on and off when engines are running, and those on float planes must be alerted to their unique hazards.

Anyway, as I said, you, as commander, are responsible (on behalf of the *operator*, who bears final responsibility) for ensuring that all passengers are briefed, or have equipment demonstrated, as outlined below. One member of the flight or cabin crew should be responsible for cabin safety from the time the aircraft is accepted for flight, until all the passengers have been offloaded at the end of it.

Pre-Flight

Whoever it is should confirm that the passenger compartment contains emergency equipment in appropriate stowage(s), seatbacks are in the upright position and lap straps and/or harnesses are ready (neatly arranged seatbelts always give a good impression, or, rather, untidy ones don't). Tables should be folded and stowed, and catering secured. Unless weight and balance allows random seating, passengers should be shown, or conducted to their seats. Once they are seated and you have their attention, give them a briefing in a calm and authoritative manner. Some passengers may be experienced, others may not. The idea is to ensure they will retain enough to react sensibly in an emergency which, it should be emphasised, is unlikely.

Before takeoff and landing (and whenever you deem it necessary, e.g. during turbulence), they also need to be told about the dangers involved in various aspects of aircraft operation, in particular the location of all exits and the use of safety equipment required to be carried, but also:

- Your authority as aircraft Commander.
- Methods of approaching the aircraft, in particular avoiding exhausts. Children should be kept under control. Take off loose objects, clothing, hats, etc.
- Dangerous Goods and hazardous items that must not be carried. No objects above shoulder height - carry equipment horizontally. Long items should be dragged by one end. Do not throw cargo.
- Methods of opening and closing cabin doors (inside and outside) and their use as emergency exits. Where not to step and what to hold on to.
- When they can smoke (not when oxygen is in use!)
- Avoidance of flying when ill or drunk - it is this dangerous to themselves, and if they are incapable next to an emergency exit, others could suffer too.
- How to use seat belts and when to fasten them.
- What not to touch in flight.
- Loose articles, their stowage (tables, etc.) and the dangers of throwing anything out of the windows (CAT.OP.MPA.160).

- Use and location of safety equipment, including a practical demonstration (passengers must be briefed on the location and use of lifejackets when they are required to be carried). When oxygen needs to be used in a hurry, adults should fit their masks before their children.
- The passenger briefing card, described below.
- The brace position (including rear-facing seats). If you ever have to give the order to adopt it, don't do it too early, otherwise the passengers will get fed up waiting and sit up just at the point of impact
- How long the flight will be, how high, the weather.

In-flight and pre-landing briefings may be given by a crew member, or with illuminated cabin warning signs. In an emergency during flight, passengers must be briefed on relevant emergency action. The following items must be demonstrated:

- the use, fastening and unfastening of safety belts/harnesses.
- use of oxygen masks when appropriate.
- location and use of lifejackets,. This can be done before boarding.

Before Takeoff

- When, where, why and how carry-on baggage is stowed.
- Fastening, unfastening, adjusting and use of safety belts or harnesses.
- The requirement to obey crew instructions about seat belts or smoking.
- When seat backs must be upright & tables stowed.
- Emergency exits, and, for passengers near them, how they work.
- Location and advisability of reading safety cards
- Location and use of emergency equipment, e.g. ELT, fire extinguisher, survival gear (including access if locked away), first aid kit and life raft.
- Using portable electronic devices (see below).
- The location and operation of the fixed passenger oxygen system, including masks and the actions to obtain and use them and activate the flow of oxygen. This must include a demonstration.
- Location and use of life preservers, including removal from stowage/packaging and a demo, when to inflate.
- After takeoff, if not already done, that smoking is prohibited, and the advisability of using safety belts or harnesses during flight, and in-flight for turbulence, when seat belts are required and stowing of carry-on baggage.
- Before getting off, the safest route away and relevant dangers, such as pitot tubes, propellers, or engine intakes.

If no more passengers have boarded for subsequent takeoffs on the same day, the pre-takeoff and after takeoff briefing may be omitted if a crew member verifies that all carry-on baggage is properly stowed, safety belts or harnesses are fastened, and seat backs/tables are secured.

PREPARATION FOR EMERGENCY LANDING

Where time and circumstances permit, this must consist of instructions about safety belts or harnesses, seat backs and tables, carry-on baggage, safety features cards, brace position (when to assume, how long to remain), and life preservers. In short, as per Annex 6, instructions concerning any necessary emergency actions.

SAFETY FEATURES CARD

Something to read for passengers, not that they will ever do so. It may look something like the picture shown, and must contain applicable information, including that smoking is prohibited, each type of safety belt or harness (when to use, how to fasten, tighten and release), when and where carry-on baggage must be stowed and any other related requirements, plus correct positioning of seat backs for

takeoff and landing. The card must bear the name of the operator and the type, and contain only accurate safety information for the type and configuration, with clear separation between each instructional procedure (no words!) All actions for multi-action procedures must be in the right sequence, clearly identified and depicted.

ALTIMETER SETTING PROCEDURES

Covered in *Instruments* and *Meteorology*.

CREW MEMBERS AT STATIONS

CAT.OP.MPA.210

Flight crew must be at their stations for takeoff and landing. Otherwise, they may leave in the performance of their duties, or for nature breaks. Flight crews must remain alert - if a lack of alertness is encountered, appropriate countermeasures shall be used. If unexpected fatigue is experienced, a controlled rest procedure, organised by the commander, may be used if workload permits.

 Controlled rest taken in this way is not considered to be part of a rest period calculating flight time, nor may it be used to justify extensions to the duty period.

TAXYING

CAT.GEN.MPA.125

Aeroplanes may only be taxied on the movement area of an aerodrome if the person at the controls is an appropriately qualified pilot, or has been designated by the operator and has been suitably trained.

CABIN CREW

During critical phases of flight, cabin crew members shall be seated at their assigned stations, and shall perform only those activities required for safe operation of the aircraft.

USE OF SAFETY BELTS

CAT.OP.MPA.225
CAT.IDE.A.205

There must be:

- a seat belt on each passenger seat and restraining belts for each berth, except for aeroplanes with an MCTOM of less than 5 700 kg and with an MOPSC of less than 9, which require a seat belt with upper torso restraint on each passenger seat and restraining belts on each berth.
- a child restraint device (CRD) for each person on board younger than 24 months.
- a safety harness for each flight crew seat (and any alongside), and each observer seat, that will automatically restrain the occupant's torso in a rapid deceleration*.
- a seat belt with upper torso restraint on each seat for the cabin crew.*.

*Such safety harnesses and belts must have a single point release. Flight crew seats, or any alongside a pilot's seat, and for the cabin crew, must include two shoulder straps and a seat belt that may be used independently

CREW MEMBERS

During takeoff and landing, and whenever decided by the commander for safety, crew members shall be properly secured by all safety belts and restraint systems provided. During other phases of flight, flight crew members in the flight crew compartment shall keep the assigned station safety belt fastened while at their stations.

PASSENGERS

Before takeoff and landing, during taxying, and whenever deemed necessary for safety, the commander must be satisfied that all passengers occupy a seat or berth with their safety belts or restraint systems properly secured.

Multiple occupancy may not occur other than by one adult and one infant who is properly secured by a supplementary loop belt or other restraint device.

ENDANGERING SAFETY

CAT.GEN.MPA.175

People may not recklessly or negligently act, or omit to, as to endanger an aeroplane or person in it, or to cause or permit an aeroplane to endanger any person or property.

WEAPONS & MUNITIONS OF WAR

CAT.GEN.MPA.155

Approval for their carriage must be granted by all States concerned*. Weapons of war & munitions of war must be:

- Inaccessible to passengers during flight
- Unloaded, unless, before flight, approval has been granted by all States concerned

The commander must be notified before a flight begins of the details and location of such items.

There is no internationally agreed definition of weapons and munitions of war, although some States may have one for their own purposes or national need. It should be the responsibility of the operator to check.

*States that may be concerned with approvals are those of origin, transit, overflight and destination of the consignment, and the State of the operator.

SPORTING WEAPONS & AMMUNITION
CAT.GEN.MPA.160

Sporting weapons intended to be carried by air must be reported to the operator. Operators accepting their carriage must ensure that they are:

- Inaccessible to passengers during flight, unless compliance is impracticable and other procedures can be applied*.
- For firearms or other weapons that can contain ammunition, unloaded. Ammunition for sporting weapons may be checked baggage, subject to certain limitations under the (IATA) Instructions.

*Other procedures may need to be considered if there is no separate compartment where weapons can be stowed, as in a typical small aircraft. These should take into account the nature of the flight, its origin, destination, and unlawful interference. As far as possible, weapons should be stowed so that they are not immediately accessible to passengers (e.g. in locked boxes, or in checked baggage stowed under other baggage).

Again, there is no internationally agreed definition of sporting weapons. In general, they may be any weapon which is not a weapon of war or munition of war, but they might include hunting knives, bows and similar articles. For example, an antique weapon, such as a musket, may now be regarded as a sporting weapon. A firearm is a gun, rifle or pistol firing a projectile. A firearm, not a weapon or munition of war, should be treated as a sporting weapon for carriage on an aircraft.

In the absence of a specific definition, the following are generally regarded as being sporting weapons:

- Those for shooting game, birds and other animals
- Those used for target shooting, clay-pigeon and competition shooting, if they are not standard issue for military forces
- Airguns, dart guns, starting pistols, etc.

CARRIAGE OF AUTHORISED PERSONS

An Authorised Person (as far as the Company is concerned) is normally a fare paying passenger on a properly arranged trip, or a non fare-paying passenger flying with the permission of Management or Operations - however, when going foreign, nobody is authorised until they have passed through Customs. You can refuse to carry anyone who seems unfit for any reason.

Flight Operations Inspectors are Authorised Persons and will occasionally wish to fly in Company aircraft to check on operational procedures, unless you think the safety of the flight will be compromised. This is normally arranged in advance, but the right is reserved for them to turn up without notice. Inspectors carry authority/identity cards which will be produced on request.

UNAUTHORISED CARRIAGE

Operators must take all reasonable measures to ensure that people do not secrete themselves or cargo on board aircraft (i.e. no stowaways).

METHOD OF CARRIAGE OF PERSONS
CAT.GEN.MPA.165

No person may be in any part of an aircraft during flight that is not designed for their accommodation, unless temporary access has been granted by the commander:

- For taking action necessary for the safety of the aircraft or of any person, animal or goods in it, or
- Where cargo or stores are carried, if designed to enable access during flight.

ADMISSION TO FLIGHT DECK
CAT.GEN.MPA.135

Only flight crew members assigned to a flight may be admitted to, or carried on, the flight deck unless that person is:

- An operating crew member.
- AA representative of the Authority on official duty
- Permitted by, and carried under, the Ops Manual.

The commander must ensure that, for safety, admission to the flight deck does not cause distraction and/or interfere with the flight's operation, and that all persons on the flight deck are familiar with relevant safety procedures. Final decisions about admission to the flight deck are the responsibility of the commander.

However, in small aircraft, the second pilot's seat may be occupied by a person who is not part of the operating crew (e.g. a passenger) if they do not cause distraction or interference with operation of the flight and:

- the person is embarked or disembarked when propellers and engines are running with an escort.
- the person is briefed on the use of the full harness, the requirement to keep it fastened, plus safety procedures and equipment, and the necessity for avoiding contact with controls and switches.
- the person remains strapped in with the safety harness locked when propellers are turning, to avoid fouling of the controls when incapacitated.
- the person is able to remain clear of all flying controls while seated in a normal position.
- when appropriate, the passenger wears a lifejacket.
- dual controls are removed.

Despite the above, the commander has an absolute right to refuse a second pilot's seat for passenger use if dual controls are installed.

MINIMUM EQUIPMENT LISTS
CAT.IDE.A.105

Certain items of equipment may be unserviceable without adversely affecting an aircraft's fitness for a particular flight, or the required safety for commercial air transport.

Refer to Part B of the ops manual for each aircraft type.

CONFIGURATION DEVIATION LISTS
CDLs are the structural equivalent of MELs, allowing operation with minor parts missing, like access panels.

PORTABLE ELECTRONIC DEVICES
CAT.GEN.MPA.140

Transistor radios, tape recorders and the like should not be operated in flight as they may interfere with navigation equipment (or even the fly-by-wire systems). If you don't believe me, tune to an AM station, as used by ADF, on a cheap radio and switch on an even cheaper calculator nearby - you will find the radio is blanked out by white noise. In fact, the radiations from TVs and radios come within the VOR and ILS regions as well. Although cell phones are cleared for use near heart monitors (in hospitals), they do so at low power when inside the range of a cell. Once in an aircraft, and a long way away from a transmitter, they put the power up and then become dangerous - a couple of hundred phones searching for their cells in an aircraft can therefore create havoc. In fact, one passenger using a mobile phone on a Super Puma during finals blanked out the EFIS display for a second.

A study by Carnegie Mellon University researchers in the Department of Engineering and Public Policy (EPP) has found that cell phones and other portable electronic devices, like laptops and game-playing devices, can disrupt normal operation of key cockpit instruments, especially GPS receivers.

Here are some other examples:

- On an MD 87, failures in flight mode annunciator No 2 occurred while two video cameras were being used in the cabin. On another one, an uncommanded change of modes in the flight management system occurred when a CD player was used.
- On a DC 10 (as it was then), there were ADF bearing discrepancies when two Gameboys were being used.
- On a 727, coming down the ILS, between 2000-3500 feet, the flight director vertical bar and localiser needle both moved to the left when some clown used a cellular phone.
- On an MD 80, the wrong flight level was captured when another idiot used an FM digital receiver.

PROHIBITED DEVICES
Any transmitting device intentionally radiating RF signals.

PERMITTED DEVICES WITHOUT RESTRICTIONS
Hearing aids, pacemakers, electronic watches and properly installed equipment.

PERMITTED DEVICES WITH RESTRICTIONS
Personal life support systems may be operated during all phases of flight, if they do not interfere with systems or equipment. Portable two-way radio devices may be used only when the engines are not running, except the APU. They may not, however, be used during the passenger briefing. Other PEDs may not be used during takeoff, climb, approach and landing.

Lithium Ion batteries, as found in most modern laptops and Portable Electronic Devices, can overheat and burst into flame, as the charging circuitry works on battery heat. In 2004, they were banned in the US as cargo on passenger planes, but, due to the combination of the manufacturing process, where even a nano-sized particle of dust can cause a problem, and the falling quality control due to the economic climate, the incidents have been increasing, so be wary about putting such devices in a remote and inaccessible baggage compartment.

Such fires must be cooled as quickly as possible to stop them from intensifying - with soft drinks, or water, despite it being an electrical fire. In addition, the item concerned should not be moved until this has been done, because of the possibilities of jets of fire being ejected when the cells get overheated.

9 - Dangerous Goods & Weapons
Annex 18
CAT.GEN.MPA.200

For our purposes, the term *Dangerous Goods* includes anything that poses a significant risk to health, safety, property or the environment *when transported by air*, including aerosols, solvents, paints, chainsaws, matches, stoves, car batteries, gas tanks and even magnets or perfume under the right circumstances - in other words, mostly stuff that anyone may have at home, but subjected to the adverse forces involved in transportation, such as expansion and compression, or simply being handled differently (fuel evaporates more quickly at altitude). Even a 9-volt battery can generate enough heat to start a fire when its terminals are shorted out. Dangerous Goods could be toxic, flammable, corrosive, infectious, radioactive or explosive, or a combination, and the rules apply regardless of the reason for their movement, commercial or private. Many items already carried in an aircraft are hazardous, including fuel, ethylene glycol, methyl alcohol, halon, hydraulic fluid, carbon monoxide, etc., but they will be exempt from the regulations to a certain extent, because they will be needed for airworthiness purposes, or for sale to passengers (perfumes, or alcohol).

The carriage of dangerous goods by air may only be done with the approval of the relevant National Aviation Authority, as per ICAO Annex 18, which is otherwise known as the *ICAO Technical Instructions for the Safe Transport of Dangerous Goods by Air*, and what becomes incorporated into national laws to give them effect (permanent approval is given in your company's AOC, so check your Ops Manual).

Airlines use another document called the *IATA Dangerous Goods Regulations* (referred to as the *Regulations*, described below), which is compiled from Annex 18, but much easier to use, and sometimes more restrictive, due to industry practice and other operational considerations. Because of this, although it has no official force, the Book is accepted as a *working*, or *field document* for non-airlines, even though it says clearly in the front that it does not apply to them (1.2.1). In a legal dispute, the ICAO Technical Instructions will prevail.

The Technical Instructions are supposed to provide the basis under which Dangerous Goods can be transported safely by air, at a level that ensures no additional risk to the aircraft or its occupants (in other words, an *incident* is not supposed to lead to an *accident*). The classifications inside it are determined by a UN sub-committee of experts.

Everyone in the transport chain (including passengers) needs to be aware of the dangers, and their responsibilities, and your company has a legal responsibility to ensure that employees are trained properly. As a working pilot, flight attendant, or a member of the ground staff, you really only need an awareness of the subject, since you have no authority to change any paperwork or play around with packaging, but if you are a *shipper*, your knowledge needs to be much more extensive (it's very easy for you to change roles, because, out in remote places, your passengers may well turn up with dangerous goods and expect you to handle all the details). The information fed to passengers must at least consist of warning signs or placards displayed prominently where tickets are sold, or where passengers are checked in, boarding areas and luggage check in areas.

Sometimes, there will be two labels, where a substance or material comes with more than one risk, in which case, one will be a *primary* and the other a *secondary* label (secondaries do not have classifications). The primary one is on top. *Handling labels* ("This Way Up") are rectangular.

Packing Groups indicate degrees of danger within classes, which leads nicely to one key to the safe transport of Dangerous Goods, which is packaging, described later. If you need it, approved packaging can be obtained from various manufacturers (refer to the IATA regulations), but it will be relatively expensive, since they have some hold on the market. However, if you ship the goods in *Limited Quantities*, specialised packaging may not be needed, though it should still be of good quality. *Salvage Packaging*, which is not usually seen, is not for shipping, but recovering Dangerous Goods after an incident.

The safest way, of course, is not to transport Dangerous Goods at all, but you still need to recognise them in order to exclude them, and there is often a commercial demand to move such cargos to remote places, where air transport provides the only way in, aside from walking, and passengers, bless them, will hardly ever tell you what's in their baggage anyway. In other words, we need to get the job done with an element of risk management. If risk cannot be eliminated, then those goods are likely prohibited anyway, or at least subject to severe restrictions (the IATA Regulations list around three thousand items by name and quantity allowed).

CLASSES & LABELLING

Packages containing dangerous goods must have diamond-shaped labels that indicate their characteristics by class or division (the numbering is for convenience, and does not mean that Class 1 is more dangerous than Class 9). These are:

- 1 - **Explosives** (Black on Orange) - normally forbidden
    - 1.1 - Mass explosion hazard - REX
    - 1.2 - Projection hazard - REX

- 1.3 - Minor blast or projection hazard - REX/RCX/RGX
- 1.4 - No significant hazard - REX
- 1.5 - Very insensitive - mass explosion - REX
- 1.6 - Extremely insensitive - no mass explosion - REX

- 2 - **Gases**
    - 2.1 - Flammable (White on Red) - RFG
    - 2.2 - Non-flammable non-toxic (White on Green) - RNG/RCL
    - 2.3 - Toxic Gas (Black on White) - RPG

- 3 - **Flammable Liquids** (White on Red) - RFL

- 4 - **Flammable Solids**
    - 4.1 - Solids (Black on Red/White stripes) - RFS
    - 4.2 - Spontaneous (Black on White, Red lower) - RSC
    - 4.3 - Water reactive (White on Blue) - RFW

- 5 - **Oxidising Substances**, Organic Peroxide
    - 5.1 - Oxidising substances (Black on Yellow) - ROX
    - 5.2 - Organic peroxides (Black on Yellow) - ROP

- 6 - **Toxic & Infectious Substances**
    - 6.1 - Toxic substances (Black on White) - RPB
    - 6.2 - Infectious substances (Black on White) - RIS

- 7 - **Radioactive**
    - Category I - (Black on White) - RRW
    - Category II or III (Yellow with White lower half) - RRY

- 8 - **Corrosives** (Black on White) - RCM

- 9 - **Miscellaneous** (Black on White) RMD

You may see other labels from other hazardous alert systems, such as WHMIS, or even household, or consumer labels, on domestic products.

This one means Cargo Aircraft Only:

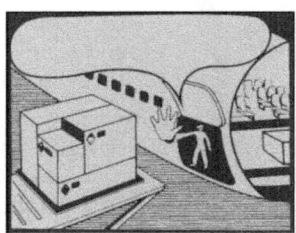

10 - Security

For programs at each airport serving international civil aviation, by each contracting state. See *Air Law*.

11 - Accidents & Occurrences

Company accident procedures, etc. See *Air Law*.

12 - Rules Of The Air

Various extracts from local legislation, including Annex 2. See *Air Law*.

13 - Leasing

ORO.AOC.110/ARO.OPS.110

A lease is legal custody and control of an aircraft for a short time, typically 2 weeks. The Certificate of Registration (for the proper owner) remains in force, but the authorities will still want to know where the machine is and who is operating it, and for what purpose. The registration can be cancelled if you lend the machine to anyone without telling them.

A *Dry Lease* exists when aircraft are operated under the AOC of the *lessee*. A *Wet Lease* exists when the aircraft remains under the AOC of the *lessor* (the terms used to indicate whether fuel was supplied or not). An EU operator is one certified by an EU State.

OPERATIONS MANUAL PART B

Technical information about the aircraft flown by the Company, intended for quick reference in flight and containing information from the flight manual:

- 0 - General Information & Units of Measurement.
- 1 - Limitations.
- 2 - **Emergency Procedures**. Used after takeoff.
- 3 - Normal Procedures.
- 4 - Performance.
- 5 - Mass and Balance.
- 6 - Loading.
- 7 - Flight Planning.
- 8 - Configuration Deviation List.
- 9 - **Minimum Equipment List**. *ORO.MLR.105*. A list of systems and equipment that may be defective, and for how long, before despatch. That is, they are changes to the type design that do not require recertification, but which maintain acceptable safety by using alternative procedures, equipment or instruments, and are applicable before any flight. Once a failure or unserviceability becomes apparent after starting a flight, any decision to continue is subject to checklists, pilot judgment and good airmanship, although you can still use MEL.

  MELs are based on, but are not less restrictive than, the **Master MEL** from the manufacturer, but they do not include items that are required for airworthiness (such as propellers or engines), or by legislation, or which are present merely for passenger convenience that do not affect the operation of the aircraft. Thus, anything required for airworthiness that is **not** in the MEL is **automatically required to be working**.

  However, MELs only cover operation of equipment, and not degraded performance, such as excessive fuel consumption so, although you have the authority to operate with unserviceable equipment, you do not have to if you still think the aircraft is not safe.
- 10 - Survival & Emergency Equipment, Oxygen.
- 11 - Emergency Evacuation Procedures.
- 12 - Aircraft Systems.

OPERATIONS MANUAL PART C

Route Guides & Charts

You need a route guide so you can get around the airways without messing things up for anybody else. Any used must be the current ones, as amended, and must be incorporated by reference in Part C of the Ops Manual, if they are not completely incorporated. Although the symbols and keys are generally printed on maps, it is still a good idea to know at least the basic ones for use in flight in a hurry. Because they are included on the maps, they have not been reproduced in this book. The ultimate Airways Manual is the AIP, being the source from which others get their information. The commercially available ones are really as good as each other, whichever one you get started on probably becoming your favourite. The best known is from Jeppesen, which is used in the exams.

ROUTES AND AREAS OF OPERATION

CAT.OP.MPA.135

Except for operations under VFR by day by non-complex motor-powered aircraft on flights departing from and arriving at the same aerodrome or site, operations may only be conducted along routes, or within areas, for which:

- ground facilities and services, including meteorological services, adequate for the planned operation are provided.
- the performance of the aircraft enables compliance with minimum flight altitude requirements.
- the aircraft equipment meets the minimum requirements for the planned operation.
- appropriate maps and charts are available.
- Operations must also be conducted under any restriction on the routes or the areas of operation specified by the competent authority.

Single-engined aeroplanes may only fly along routes, or within areas, with surfaces that allow safe forced landings.

OPERATIONS MANUAL PART D

Training & Checking

A training folder will be opened for you, in which will be a personal sheet with details of your licence, qualifications, previous experience, Next Of Kin (the usual stuff), plus the training forms that get filled in as you go along. The Training Captain gets to look at it before he gets his hands on you, and adds to its contents with reports, etc.

After a Type Rating or command course, and associated line flying under supervision, you are considered to be inexperienced until you get 50 hours on type and/or in the role within 60 days, or 100 hours on type and/or in the role (no time limit). Fewer hours may be OK when a new operator is starting up, or a new type is introduced, or crew members have previously done a type conversion course with the same operator (re-conversion), subject to other conditions imposed.

Under ORO.FC.A.250, to fly as commander on single pilot commercial air transport operations, a CPL(A) holder must:

- Hold an IR when under VFR over 50 nm from the departure point, or have at least 500 hours on aeroplanes (not for Performance Class B).
- On multi-engined aeroplanes under IFR, have at least 700 hours flight time on aeroplanes, to include at least 400 hours PIC, although this may vary under an approved program of supervision, in which case 2 hours of P2 is the equivalent of 1 hour as P1. Such hours shall include 100 hours under IFR and 40 on multi-engined aeroplanes.

INITIAL TRAINING

As a minimum, this could include:

- Fire and smoke training
- Emergency and Survival Equipment
- Ground Training (handling, etc.)
- Medical/First Aid
- Passenger Handling
- Communication
- Discipline and Responsibilities
- Crew Resource Management
- Specialised tasks (aerial survey, etc.)
- Dangerous Goods

CONVERSION TRAINING
ORO.FC.120

This is required for the transition from one aircraft type (or class) to another. It should be done by an Air Training Organisation (ATO). You must complete an approved course, and an operator's conversion course (which may be combined) before starting unsupervised line flying when changing to an aircraft which needs a new type or class rating, or when changing operators (this includes any installed equipment).

Conversion training must be conducted by qualified people under a syllabus in the Ops Manual, taking note of previous training. Minimum standards of qualification and experience before conversion training must be in the Ops Manual

Once a conversion course has been started, you may not fly another type until the course is completed or terminated, unless otherwise approved (if you only fly Class B aeroplanes and are converting to another Class B type, you can still fly Class B aeroplanes to the extent necessary to maintain the operation). CRM training must be incorporated. A conversion course is deemed to have started when the flying or STD training has begun. The theoretical element may be done before the practical.

Conversion courses should follow this format:

- **Ground training** covering all systems and emergency procedures.
- **Emergency and safety equipment training** and checking (done before flying starts). Training should take place whenever practicable in conjunction with cabin crew doing similar training with emphasis on co-ordinated procedures and two-way communications.
- **Flying training** (flight simulator and/or aircraft). Should be structured and done by suitably qualified TRIs and/or TREs. For multi-crew aircraft, emphasis should be placed on LOFT and CRM. Co-pilots should get the same as Captains. Training should include all elements of an IR if you are likely to operate under IFR, and proficiency training on aircraft, including at least 3 takeoffs and landings, except with an approved STD.
- **Line flying under supervision**. Unless already covered above, before being assigned to line duty, you should have successfully completed an OPC with a TRE. You should operate a minimum number of sectors and/or flying hours under the supervision of a nominated flight crew member. On completion of sectors and/or flying under supervision, a line check should be done.

DIFFERENCES & FAMILIARISATION TRAINING

Differences training requires additional knowledge and training on an appropriate device, when operating a variant of an aircraft currently operated, or when introducing a significant change of equipment and/or procedures on types or variants currently operated. It is a specific course, possibly from a third party.

Familiarisation training requires only the acquisition of additional knowledge, when operating another aircraft of the same type, or when introducing a significant change of equipment and/or procedures on types or variants currently operated. It is not a specific course, but may only be an ops manual entry. No test is required for either check.

RECURRENT TRAINING & CHECKING
ORO.FC.130, ORO.FC.230

Recurrent training is that needed to maintain a level of knowledge and expertise. You members must undergo recurrent training and checking relevant to the type or variant that you are certificated to operate.

A recurrent training and checking program must be in the Ops Manual, as approved. Recurrent checking must be done by:

- **OPCs** - by a TRE or, if the check is done in an STD, a TRE or SFE (flight crews must undergo OPCs as part of a normal crew). For Performance Class B aeroplanes, the check may be conducted by a suitably trained commander.
- **Line Checks** - by commanders nominated by the operator, as acceptable.

There are two things to note about checks; firstly, there is a written element, and secondly, if you take a renewal and fail it before your previous check expires, the first one expires as well! You can also take a renewal within 3 months of an expiry and still keep the original expiry date. As far as keeping your licences current is concerned, you will find yourself subject to the following checks on top of those needed for normal licence upkeep:

EMERGENCY & LIFESAVING EQUIPMENT
This is the one you do *before any flying training takes place* (or at least the paperwork should be dated that way!), and there are two; one done every year and another every three. The annual one is valid for 12 months, plus the remainder of the month of issue. It requires knowledge of the use and location of emergency equipment, with a written element. Usually, for small aircraft, a simple plan with boxes to put the location of any emergency equipment in will do.

Emergency training should cover a range of subjects from First Aid (appropriate to the aircraft) to fire and smoke drills and water survival training. Practical experience is necessary, so expect to cover the actual donning of a lifejacket and protective breathing equipment, actual handling of fire extinguishers, instruction on the location and use of all emergency and safety equipment and exits and security procedures.

Every three years you can expect the actual operation of all types of exits, actual fire-fighting with aircraft equipment, experience the effects of smoke in an enclosed area, with actual use of all relevant equipment in a simulated smoke-filled environment, handling of pyrotechnics, real or simulated, and demonstration in the use of the liferafts, where fitted.

OPERATOR PROFICIENCY CHECK (OPC)
Otherwise known as the *Base Check* to older hands, this is a look at your ability to carry out emergency manoeuvres at your normal flight station, plus IFR procedures. It's valid for 6 months*, plus the remainder of the month of issue. It's not necessarily type-specific and, although the statutory requirement is to assure your continued competence, it's also used for training, as it's a good time for practising drills and procedures that rarely arise normally. It also includes an element of CRM, as do many other checks. The OPC must be undertaken before commencing commercial air transport operations.

*For operations under VFR by day of performance class B aeroplanes conducted during seasons not longer than eight consecutive months, one OPC is enough.

Some items will be covered by touch drills (which are normally best attended to on the ground), as well as a general discussion of operating procedures, emergencies, recognition and diagnosis of aircraft system faults, pre-flight briefing, etc. Additional precautions may be considered if you operate in extreme weather. Some companies may have separate VFR & IFR checks.

LICENCE PROFICIENCY CHECK (LPC)
The LPC, which is type-specific, is required to maintain currency on a particular type. It has the same frequency as the OPC, so for convenience it is done at the same time.

LINE CHECK
This is valid for 12 months plus the remainder of the month of issue, but (as with any check) if you take it in the final three months, you can extend to 12 months from the previous expiry date. It's a test of your performance of *normal duties* (i.e. no emergencies) at your crew station, so will be done on a standard commercial flight, or at least the final line check will. It covers a flight from pre-flight preparations to completion of post flight duties and normally must be carried out on each type flown, although it may be done alternately where types are similar. It's not supposed to represent a particular route, but must be an adequate representation of the Company's work. Line Checks may be carried out by fully qualified Line Captains.

Although the stipulated frequency is once every 12 months, you might find a Training Captain hopping in on an empty seat once in a while before that. It's nothing personal, just part of compliance monitoring, and better than leaving things to the last minute and risking you being off-line because a check hasn't been done.

Line training, leading up to the check, is supposed to familiarise you with the routes over which you will operate, for which you will be supervised by experienced training staff. Before you can do this with passengers, you must have passed an initial line check, followed by some supervised flights, then a final line check before they let you loose on the unsuspecting public.

Supervised flights will have passengers on, so you will now become aware of commercial pressures, and are as much a hurdle to some pilots as other training is, because you will probably also have Flight Director systems to use - you normally don't get to use them in training.

GROUND & REFRESHER TRAINING
You need some sort of brush up if you have been absent from flying duties for more than 6 months.

OPERATIONAL PROCEDURES
Emergencies & Equipment

CREW RESOURCE MANAGEMENT
ORO.FC.115
ORO.FC.215

Before operating as flight crew, you must have received appropriate CRM training, as per the ops manual, in any case, before commencing unsupervised line flying.

If you have not previously received theoretical Human Factors training to ATPL level, initial CRM training must include a course at that level from the operator.

Otherwise, you must complete elements of CRM training every year, with the major parts of a full course over a 3 year recurrent training cycle. CRM should be included in all type, class or recurrent training, including checks.

OPERATING IN EITHER PILOT'S SEAT
ORO.FC.135
ORO.FC.235

This is only needed if you fly in any other seat than your normal one; you might become a Line Training Captain, where you need to be able to fly the thing home or get it on the ground if your examinee fails en route. Also, you may be a Commander who occasionally is a co-pilot.

For whatever reason, if done, it will likely coincide with a Proficiency Check. Commander's checks must be valid and current (see ORO.FC.230).

This training must include at least an engine failure during takeoff (simulated), an OEI approach and go-around, and an OEI landing.

COMMAND COURSE
ORO.FC.205

Pilots upgrading to commander must complete an appropriate command course, which must be specified in the Ops Manual and include at least:

- Flight simulator and/or flying training including a proficiency check as commander.
- Operator command responsibilities.
- Line training in command under supervision. At least 10 flight sectors is required.
- Completion of a commander's line check and route/role/area competency qualification.
- Suitable CRM training.

RECENT EXPERIENCE
Part OPS 1.970

Pilots may not operate aircraft unless they have carried out at least three takeoffs, circuits and landings as PF in an aeroplane or simulator of the same type, in the preceding 90 days (this may be extended up to 120 days by line flying under supervision of a nominated commander).

For night VMC, a pilot without an IR must do at least three takeoffs, circuits and landings at night in the preceding 90 days (may be done in an STD). A pilot with an IR satisfies the night recency requirement with at least 3 instrument approaches in the preceding 90 days (may be done in an STD).

INSTRUMENT RATING

This is completed at 13 month intervals by an Instrument Rating Examiner and may be completed as part of a Base Check, or at least tagged on the end, as you're in the air anyway. The IR's purpose is to establish whether you're maintaining the standards necessary for safe operations in controlled airspace under IMC

ROUTE/ROLE/AREA COMPETENCE
Part OPS 1.975

The Company must ensure that en route and destination facilities are such that a safe operation is run. Part of this is achieved by the this qualification (it is not a check), which is renewed every twelve months, plus the remainder of the month of last operation on the route. It tests your knowledge of specific route(s) or particular areas.

MORE THAN ONE TYPE OR VARIANT
ORO.FC.140
ORO.FC.240

Flight crews may not operate more than one type or a variant unless they are competent, and suitable procedures are included in the Ops Manual. In practice, you should generally not fly more than two types, having achieved at least 3 months and 150 hours experience before the conversion course. 28 days and/or 50 hours flying should then be achieved exclusively on the new type or variant, and you should not be rostered to fly more than one type or significantly different variant of a type during a single duty period.

For a combination of helicopter and aeroplane, you may only fly one helicopter type or variant and one aeroplane type, irrespective of MCTOM or passenger configuration.

EMERGENCIES & EQUIPMENT

CAT.IDE.A.100, 105

Flights may not start when the aeroplane's instruments, items of equipment or functions required for the intended flight are inoperative or missing, unless it is operated under an MEL, or you can operate within the MMEL. The following do not need an equipment approval:

- Spare fuses (see below)
- Independent portable lights
- An accurate time piece
- Chart holder
- First aid kits
- Megaphones
- Survival and pyrotechnic equipment
- Sea anchors and equipment for mooring
- Chjld restraint devices

Equipment to be used at your station during flight must be readily operable from there. When a single item needs to be used by more than one flight crew member, it must be readily operable from any station where it's needed. Indications must be seen readily, with the minimum practicable deviation from the position and line of vision normally assumed when looking forward along the flight path. Single instruments in multi-crew aircraft must be visible from each applicable flight crew station.

Spare Electrical Fuses
CAT.IDE.A.110

10% of spare fuses of each rating must be carried, with a minimum of three for each rating.

Operating Lights
CAT.IDE.A.115

Aeroplanes require, for day VFR, an anti-collision light system, plus lighting from the electrical system to provide adequate illumination for instruments and equipment essential to safe operation, illumination in all passenger compartments, and an independent portable light for each crew member, readily accessible at their stations.

In addition, when IFR or at night:

- Navigation/position lights.
- Two landing lights, or a single light with two separately energised filaments.
- Lights to prevent collisions at sea if the aircraft is operated as a seaplane.

If more than one light is needed to comply with the Rules of the Air, only one should be visible at a time. If a light must show through specified angles horizontally, the light should be visible from 90° above and below. Lights showing in all directions must be visible horizontally and vertically. You may switch off or reduce the intensity of flashing lights if they *adversely affect the performance of your duties,* or *subject outside observers to harmful dazzle.*

Anti-collision lights are intended to attract attention to your aircraft, and are seen from all directions. **Navigation lights** are intended to show your relative path to an observer, and are set up so that only one can be seen by another aircraft at any time (see *Air Law*). Other lights may be displayed if they cannot be mistaken for either.

Between sunset and sunrise, you must show anti-collision and navigation lights. On the manoeuvring area, in addition, aircraft must display lights that show extremities of their structure (unless they are stationary and otherwise lit up adequately), and engine running lights (a red one must be displayed when the engine is running in any case). By day, anti-collision lights must be used in flight.

Equipment To Clear Windshields
CAT.IDE.A.120

Aeroplanes with an MCTOM of more than 5 700 kg must have a means of maintaining a clear portion of the windshield during precipitation at each pilot station.

Communication & Navigation Equipment
CAT.IDE.A.330

This must be approved and installed as required, under minimum performance standards and operational and airworthiness requirements, and be working, except as under an MEL. The failure of any single unit must not result in the failure of another.

Equipment must be readily operable from any station at which it may be used.

APPROVAL AND INSTALLATION

- *Approved* means that compliance with the applicable design requirements and performance specifications, or equivalent, in force at the time of the approval application, has been demonstrated.
- *Installed* means that the installation has been demonstrated to comply with the applicable airworthiness requirements of CS 23/25, or the relevant code for Type Certification, and any Part OPS requirements.

RADIO EQUIPMENT

Where two independent (separate and complete) radio systems are required, each must have an independent antenna except that, where rigidly supported non-wire antennae or equivalent are used, only one is required.

Radio communication must provide 121.5 MHz.

AUDIO SELECTOR PANEL
CAT.IDE.A.335

Aeroplanes under IFR must have audio selector panels accessible to each flight crew member.

VFR
CAT.IDE.A.340

Under VFR over routes that can be navigated by reference to visual landmarks, radio equipment must allow communication with appropriate ground stations and ATC from any point in controlled airspace within which flights are intended, and receive weather information.

IFR OR VFR WITHOUT VISUAL LANDMARKS
CAT.IDE.A.345

Radio communication and navigation equipment for ATS requirements in the area(s) of operation is required.

Aeroplanes on short haul operations in NAT MNPS airspace and not crossing the North Atlantic must have at least one long range communication system, if alternative communication procedures are published for the airspace. There should be enough navigation equipment to ensure that, if one fails at any stage, the remaining equipment must allow safe navigation under the flight plan.

Where landing in IMC is intended, there must be suitable equipment for guidance to a point from which a visual landing can be performed for each relevant aerodrome and designated alternate.

OPERATIONAL PROCEDURES
Emergencies & Equipment

TRANSPONDER
CAT.IDE.A.350

Aeroplanes must have a pressure altitude reporting SSR transponder and any other SSR transponder capability required for the route being flown.

Flight & Navigation Instruments & Associated Equipment

DAY VFR
CAT.IDE.A.125

In addition to means of indicating when the power supply to the flight instruments is not adequate, aeroplanes must have a means of measuring and displaying:

- Magnetic heading
- Time in hours, minutes, and seconds
- Pressure altitude*
- Indicated airspeed*
- Vertical speed*
- Turn and slip* **
- Attitude* **
- Heading* **
- Outside air temperature**
- Mach number whenever speed limitations are expressed in terms of Mach number

*When two pilots are needed, the 2nd pilot's station must have these separate. When duplicates are needed, there must be separate displays and selectors for each pilot.

There must also be a means for preventing malfunction of the airspeed indicating systems due to condensation or icing for aeroplanes with an MCTOM of more than 5 700 kg or an MOPSC of more than nine, and aeroplanes first issued with an individual C of A on or after 1 April 1999.

**Single engine aeroplanes first issued with an individual C of A before 22 May 1995 are exempt if the compliance would require retrofitting.

IFR OR NIGHT
CAT.IDE.A.130

Aeroplanes must have means of measuring and displaying:

- Magnetic heading
- Time in hours, minutes and seconds
- Indicated airspeed
- Vertical speed
- Turn and slip, or for aeroplanes with a standby means of measuring and displaying attitude, slip
- Attitude
- Stabilised heading
- Outside air temperature
- Mach number whenever speed limitations are expressed in terms of Mach number
- Two means of measuring and displaying PA

Plus:

- A means of indicating when the supply of power to the flight instruments is not adequate.
- A means for preventing malfunction of the airspeed indicating systems due to condensation or icing, with an indication of failures to the crew if the aeroplane was issued with an individual C of A on or after 1 April 1998, or before 1 April 1998 with an MCTOM of more than 5 700 kg, and with an MOPSC of more than nine.
- Except for propeller-driven aeroplanes with an MCTOM of 5 700 kg or less, two independent static pressure systems.
- One static pressure system and one alternate source of static pressure for propeller-driven aeroplanes with an MCTOM of 5 700 kg or less.

When two pilots are required, the second pilot's station must have separate instruments as follows:

- Pressure altitude
- Indicated airspeed
- Vertical speed
- Turn and slip
- Attitude
- Stabilised heading

Aeroplanes over 5 700 kg or with an MOPSC of more than 9 must have an additional, standby means of indicating attitude, capable of use from either pilot's station, normally powered continuously, but automatically for at least 30 minutes, taking other loads into account, from an independent source after the normal generating system fails. It must be appropriately illuminated during all phases of operation, except for aeroplanes of 5 700 kg or less. It must be clear when it is on emergency power, or when it own system is in use, if it has one.

There must also be a chart holder in an easily readable position that can be illuminated for night operations.

SINGLE-PILOT IFR
CAT.IDE.A.135

There must be an autopilot with at least altitude hold and heading mode.

Altitude Alerting System
CAT.IDE.A.140

Turboprops with an MCTOM of more than 5 700 kg or an MOPSC of more than nine, and turbojets, must have an altitude alerting system that can alert the flight crew when approaching a preselected altitude and when deviating from a preselected altitude, except aeroplanes with an MCTOM of 5 700 kg or less, with an MOPSC of more than nine, first issued with an individual C of A before 1 April 1972 and already registered in a Member State on 1 April 1995.

TERRAIN AWARENESS WARNING SYSTEM
CAT.IDE.A.150

Turbine-powered aeroplanes with an MCTOM of more than 5 700 kg or an MOPSC of more than nine must have a Class A TAWS. Reciprocating-engine-powered aeroplanes with an MCTOM of more than 5 700 kg or an MOPSC of more than nine may have a Class B TAWS.

ACAS
CAT.IDE.A.155

Unless otherwise provided for, turbojets with an MCTOM of more than 5 700 kg or an MOPSC of more than 19 must have ACAS II.

De- or Anti-icing Equipment
CAT.OP.MPA.250

If icing conditions are reported or forecast, your aircraft must be adequately equipped, unless current weather or pilot reports indicate that icing conditions no longer exist. *Anti-icing* systems prevent ice forming, and *de-icing* systems remove it afterwards. Refer to *Meteorology* for information on icing in general and de-icing fluids.

ADDITIONAL EQUIPMENT AT NIGHT
CAT.IDE.A.165

Aeroplanes operating in expected or actual icing conditions at night must have a means of illuminating or detecting the formation of ice that does not cause glare or reflection that would interfere with the performance of crew duties.

Airborne Weather Radar
CAT.IDE.A.160

Required in all pressurised aircraft at night or in IMC where thunderstorms or other potentially hazardous weather conditions (regarded as detectable with radar) may be expected to exist along the route. This also applies to unpressurised aircraft above 5 700 kg with an MOPSC of more than 9.

Flight Crew Interphone
CAT.IDE.A.170

Aircraft requiring a flight crew of more than one must have a flight crew interphone system, including headsets and microphones (not handheld), for their use.

Crew Member Interphone System
CAT.IDE.A.175

Aeroplanes with an MCTOM of more than 15,000 kg, or an MOPSC of more than 19 must have a crew member interphone system, except for aeroplanes first issued with an individual C of A before 1 April 1965 and already registered in a Member State on 1 April 1995.

Fasten Seat Belt & No Smoking Signs
CAT.OP.MPA.240
CAT.IDE.A.210

Aircraft in which all passenger seats are not visible from the commander's seat must have a means of indicating to all passengers and cabin crew when seat belts must be fastened and when smoking is not allowed.

Flight Crew Compartment Security
ORO.SEC.100A

The flight crew compartment door (if fitted) must be capable of being locked. There shall be a means by which the cabin crew can notify the flight crew of suspicious activity or security breaches in the cabin. Passenger-carrying aeroplanes with an MCTOM over 45,500 kg, or with a MOPSC of more than 60 engaged in commercial air transport, must have an approved flight crew compartment door that can be locked and unlocked from either pilot's station and designed under applicable airworthiness requirements. The door must be closed before engine start for takeoff and locked when required by security procedures or by the PIC until engine shut down after landing, except when deemed necessary for authorised persons to gain access or egress under national civil aviation security programs.

A means must be provided for monitoring from either pilot's station the entire door area outside the flight crew compartment to identify persons requesting entry and to detect suspicious behaviour or potential threats.

INTERNAL DOORS & CURTAINS
CAT.IDE.A.215

Aeroplanes must be equipped with:

- for those with an MOPSC of more than 19, a door between the passenger and crew compartments, with a placard indicating *Crew Only* and a locking means to prevent passengers from opening it without permission from the flight crew.

- a readily accessible means for opening each door that separates a passenger compartment from another compartment that has emergency exits.

- a means for securing open any doorway or curtain separating the passenger compartment from other areas that need to be accessed to reach any required emergency exit from any passenger seat.

- a placard on each internal door or near to a curtain used for access to a passenger emergency exit, to indicate that it must be secured open during takeoff and landing.

- a means for any crew member to unlock any door that is normally accessible to passengers and that can be locked by passengers.

Cockpit Voice Recorders
CAT.IDE.A.185

CVRs are required for:

- aeroplanes with an MCTOM **over 5 700 kg**. When the individual C of A has been issued **on or after 1 April 1998**, it must record the following for the past 2 hours (if issued before, 30 minutes):
  - Voice communications transmitted from or received on the flight deck by radio
  - The aural environment of the flight deck
  - Voice communications of flight crew members on the flight deck using the interphone system
  - Voice or audio signals identifying navigation or approach aids introduced into a headset or speaker
  - Voice communications of flight crew members on the flight deck using the public address system
- multi-engined turbojets with an MCTOM of 5 700 kg or less, an MOPSC of more than nine and first issued with a C of A on or after 1 January 1990. It must record the preceding 30 minutes.

A CVR must start to record automatically before the aeroplane moves under its own power* and continue until the termination of the flight when the aeroplane is no longer capable of so doing.

*As early as possible during the cockpit checks before engine start until the cockpit checks immediately following engine shutdown at the end of the flight.

A CVR must have a device to assist with locating it in water.

Public Address System
CAT.IDE.A.180

Aeroplanes with an **MOPSC of more than 19** shall be equipped with a public address system.

Flight Data Recorders
CAT.IDE.A.190

- Aeroplanes with an MCTOM of more than 5 700 kg and first issued with a C of A on or after 1 June 1990
- Turbojets with an MCTOM of more than 5 700 kg and first issued with a C of A before 1 June 1990*
- Multi-engined turbojets with an MCTOM of 5 700 kg or less, with an MOPSC of more than nine and first issued with a C of A on or after 1 April 1998

require a digital FDR with a method of readily retrieving its data, positioned as far to the rear as practicable.

*For the previous 25 hours.

The FDR must start to record **before an aeroplane is capable of moving under its own power** and shall stop after it is incapable of so doing. It must be located as far to the rear of the aircraft as practicable. Pushing the EVENT button on the control panel sets a mark on the recording, so it can be found quickly at the subsequent Board of Inquiry.

The FDR must have a device to assist locating it in water.

Crash Axes & Crowbars
CAT.IDE.A.255

Aeroplanes with a maximum certificated takeoff mass over 5700 kg, or with an MOPSC of more than 9, must have at least one crash axe or crowbar on the flight deck. If the aircraft has an MOPSC of more than 200, an additional crash axe or crowbar must be in or near the most rearward galley area. Crash axes and crowbars in the passenger cabin must not be visible.

Megaphones
CAT.IDE.A.270

Aeroplanes with an MOPSC of more than 60, and which are carrying at least one passenger, must have portable battery-powered megaphones readily accessible by crew members during an emergency evacuation, as follows:

FOR EACH PASSENGER DECK

Pax Seats	Megaphones
61-99	1
100 or more	2

MORE THAN ONE PASSENGER DECK

When passenger seating configuration is more than 60, at least 1 is required.

Emergency Lighting & Marking
CAT.IDE.A.275

There must be an emergency lighting system with an independent power supply to provide a source of general cabin illumination to facilitate evacuation, and illuminated emergency exit marking and locating signs.

Passenger-carrying aeroplanes with an MOPSC of more than 9 must have emergency lighting systems with independent power supplies for evacuation. The power must last at least 10 minutes, and the system must include:

MORE THAN 19 PASSENGERS

Sources of general cabin illumination, internal lighting in floor level emergency exit areas and illuminated emergency exit marking and locating signs.

CERTIFICATE BEFORE 1 MAY 1972 AT NIGHT
Exterior emergency lighting at all overwing exits, where descent means required.

CERTIFICATE AFTER 30 APRIL 1972 AT NIGHT
Exterior emergency lighting at all emergency exits.

CERTIFICATE AFTER 31 DEC 1957
Floor escape path marking in passenger compartments.

LESS THAN 19 PASSENGERS, CS 23/25
Sources of general illumination, internal lighting in emergency exits and illuminated emergency exit marking and locating signs.

LESS THAN 19 PASSENGERS
When operated at night, general cabin illumination.

OPERATIONAL PROCEDURES
Emergencies & Equipment

Marking of Break-in Points
CAT.IDE.A.260

Designated areas of the fuselage suitable for break-in by rescue crews in emergency must be marked as shown.

The markings must be red or yellow, and, if necessary, outlined in white for contrast. If the corner markings are more than 2 m apart, intermediate lines 9 cm x 3 cm must be inserted so that there is no more than 2 metres between adjacent marks.

Means For Evacuation In Emergency
CAT.IDA.A.265

Passenger emergency exit sill heights must not be more than 1.83 m (6 feet) above the ground with the aeroplane on the ground and gear extended (or which would be after the collapse of, or failure to extend, one or more legs of the landing gear and for which a Type Certificate was first applied for on or after 1 April 2000) unless equipment or devices are available at each exit to enable passengers and crew to reach the ground safely.

Such equipment or devices need not be provided at overwing exits if the designated place on the structure where the escape route terminates is less than 1.83 m (6 feet) from the ground with the aeroplane on the ground, the landing gear extended, and the flaps in the take off or landing position, whichever is higher from the ground.

In aeroplanes needing a separate emergency exit for flight crew, under the conditions above, there must be a device to assist all members to reach the ground safely in an emergency. If the passenger capacity is more than 20, one exit must be provided on each side of the flight deck, or a top hatch.

First Aid Kits
CAT.IDE.A.220

Aircraft must have first-aid kits, distributed evenly and readily accessible for use. They must be inspected and replenished periodically, under instructions on their labels, or as circumstances warrant.

The distribution should be:

Passengers	Kits
0 - 100	1
101 - 200	2
201 - 300	3
301 - 400	4
401 - 500	5
501 or more	6

Flight Over Water
CAT.IDE.A.285

LAND AEROPLANES

When over water more than 50 nm from shore, or when taking off or landing at an aerodrome where there could be a ditching, aeroplanes must have easily accessible life jackets with a survivor locator light for each person. Persons under 24 months old may use equivalent flotation devices with a survivor locator light.

Aeroplanes operating over water, away from land suitable for an emergency landing, more than to 120 minutes at cruising speed or 400 nm, whichever is the less (if they can reach an aerodrome OEI) or, for all other aeroplanes, 30 minutes at cruising speed or 100 nm, whichever is the less, need liferafts big enough for all persons on board, stowed for ready use in an emergency, and large enough to accommodate all survivors if one raft of the largest rated capacity is lost.

There must also be life-saving equipment that can provide the means for sustaining life, as appropriate for the flight to be undertaken, and at least two survival ELTs.

SEAPLANES AND AMPHIBIANS

In addition to lifejackets as above for each person on board, seaplanes operated over water must also have:

- a sea anchor and other equipment necessary to facilitate mooring, anchoring or manoeuvring on water, appropriate to size, weight and handling characteristics, and
- equipment for making the sound signals as prescribed in the International Regulations for Preventing Collisions at Sea, where applicable.

Emergency Locator Transmitters
CAT.IDE.A.280

If an aircraft crashes, the severe G-forces can be used to trigger a G-switch that activates a battery-powered transmitter (assuming the batteries are kept up to scratch and are checked regularly). In theory, the transmitter's siren-like tone, on 121.5 and 243.0 MHz, and latterly 406 MHz*, should be heard by aircraft passing overhead, who "guard" these frequencies when the radio isn't needed for something else (when flying over wide open spaces, for example, the second radio is routinely tuned to 121.5 MHz). The hearing of an ELT signal should be reported to ATC who should then instigate a search.

*The ELT must be able to transmit on the distress frequencies in ICAO Annex 10 for at least 48 hours.

In fact, a distress signal is sent out on 406 MHz, and a homing signal on 121.5 MHz. The transmission will include the aircraft type, the callsign, GPS position and a SAR request.

An obvious limitation is that another aircraft must be within range and listening to receive the signal, which was one reason why the international COSPAS-SARSAT SAR satellite (SARSAT) network was developed in 1985 - it is a better system for receiving signals. Another reason was to find the location of each activation, which overflying aircraft were unable to do. The 121.5 MHz system uses Doppler to analyze a received signal and locate the beacon, which is only accurate to within 12 nm, so a circle with that radius would cover 452 square nautical miles. In addition, there is a 97% false alarm rate and they only activate properly in only 12% of crashes.

406 MHz ELTs dramatically reduce false alerts, have a higher accident survivability success rate, and decrease the time to reach accident victims by an average of 6 hours. An ELT that uses 406.025 MHz can punch through overhead cover such as leaves, aside from allowing better Doppler accuracy to within 2 nautical miles, which is equivalent to an area of about 13 square nautical miles. Every 50 seconds a 5-watt signal is sent in a 0.05-second coded location-protocol message which has the aircraft's registration and serial number, along with the beacon identification code and country of beacon registration.

To minimise the possibility of damage in crash impact, the ELT should be rigidly fixed to the aircraft structure as far aft as practicable, with antenna and connections arranged to maximise the probability of the signal being radiated after a crash.

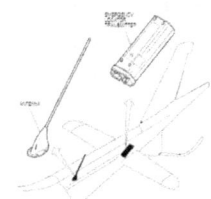

Batteries used in ELTs should be replaced (or recharged) when the equipment has been in use for more than 1 cumulative hour, and when 50% of their useful life (or charge) has expired. This does not apply to batteries (such as water-activated ones) that are essentially unaffected during storage intervals.

Types of automatic ELT are as follows:

- **Automatic Fixed** (ELT (AF)). To be permanently attached before and after a crash and designed to aid SAR teams in locating a crash site.
- **Automatic Portable** (ELT (AP)). To be rigidly attached before a crash, but readily removable after one, so it can be tethered to a survivor or a liferaft, functioning during the crash sequence. If the ELT does not use an integral antenna, the aircraft-mounted one may be disconnected and an auxiliary (on the ELT case) attached.
- **Automatic Deployable** (ELT (AD)). To be rigidly attached before the crash and automatically ejected and deployed after the crash sensor determines a crash has occurred. It should float in water.
- **Survival** ELT. Removable, stowed for an emergency and manually activated by a survivor, or automatically, such as on contact with water.

A PLB is a personal locator, smaller, with its own antenna.

MOPSC More Than 19
At least:
- two ELTs, one automatic, for aeroplanes first issued with a C of A after 1 July 2008, or
- one automatic or two ELTs of any type, for aeroplanes first issued with a C of A on or before 1 July 2008.

MOPSC 19 Or Less
At least:
- one automatic ELT for aeroplanes first issued with an individual C of A after 1 July 2008, or
- one ELT of any type for aeroplanes first issued with an individual C of A on or before 1 July 2008.

Use Of Headset
CAT.OP.MPA.215
CV AT.IDE.A.325

Flight crew members required to be on duty in the flight crew compartment must wear a headset with boom microphone or equivalent, in a position that permits its use for two-way radio communications. The headset is the primary device for voice communications with ATS:

- **When on the ground**:
  - when receiving the ATC departure clearance via voice communication, and
  - when engines are running.
- **When in flight**:
  - below transition altitude, or
  - 10,000 ft, whichever is higher.
- **Whenever deemed necessary** by the PIC.

Aeroplanes operated under IFR or at night require a transmit button on the manual pitch and roll control for each flight crew member.

Survival Equipment
CAT.IDE.A.305

Aeroplanes over areas in which SAR would be especially difficult must have signalling equipment for distress signals, at least one ELT(S) and additional survival equipment for the route to be flown taking account of the number of persons on board*.

*This does not need to be carried when the aeroplane remains within 120 minutes at OEI (for aeroplanes that can continue OEI), or 30 minutes at cruising speed an area where search and rescue is not especially difficult.

Oxygen Equipment and Supply
CAT.OP.MPA.285

You must use oxygen when the cabin pressure is lower than 10,000 feet (see also *Human Factors*). Pressurised and non-pressurised aeroplanes above 10,000 feet must have supplemental oxygen equipment that can store and dispense supplies. The amount is determined on the basis of cabin pressure altitude, flight duration and the assumption that a pressurisation failure will occur at the most critical pressure altitude or point of flight, and that, after the failure, the aeroplane will descend under emergency procedures in the Flight Manual to a safe altitude for continued safe flight and landing.

After a rapid decompression in an emergency descent, oxygen should be used until 10,000 ft, or the MSA, whichever is greater. A lack of oxygen will affect performance at 14,000 ft - the maximum altitude without oxygen at which flying efficiency is

OPERATIONAL PROCEDURES
Emergencies & Equipment

not impaired is 8,000 ft. After decompression and descent, there should be enough supplementary oxygen for the flight crew for all the time above 13,000 feet.

In fact, flight crew members engaged in performing duties essential to the safe operation of an aircraft in flight must use supplemental oxygen continuously whenever the cabin altitude exceeds 10,000 ft for more than 30 minutes and whenever the cabin altitude exceeds 13,000 ft.

Decompression can be slow, or rapid, or explosive, which is more likely to be the result of an airframe failure. Slow decompression is probably a leak somewhere. Depressurisation drill must be completed from memory within about 40 seconds - pick up your oxygen mask from its adjacent stowage in a one-hand action. Its head-harness inflates, making the fitting very quick, then deflates, pulling the mask firmly over your mouth and nose. Crew communication via the in-mask microphone is checked, then cabin altitude is verified on the overhead panel to ensure the warning is not false. If it is real, the pressurisation outflow valve is set to "manual", and the monitoring pilot closes it. The seatbelt sign is switched on and the emergency descent procedure follows, to MSA or 10,000ft (3,000m), whichever is higher. In case you don't think the drills are serious, in two cases of depressurisation, the captain lost consciousness, leaving only the first officer flying. In both cases, a flight attendant collapsed in the cockpit. In one incident the mask got tangled up with the captain's spectacles and in the other there was simply a delay.

The current recommendation from Airbus and Boeing is:

- Immediately don the nearest oxygen mask
- Sit down fasten your seat belt or grasp a fixed object
- Hold on

As the insidious nature of hypoxia causes a subtle decrease in individual performance, followed by incapacitation, the symptoms may not be identified until it is too late.

NON-PRESSURISED AIRCRAFT

Above 10,000 feet you need supplemental oxygen:

- for the flight crew above 10,000 feet PA
- for the cabin crew above 13,000 feet PA and over 30 minutes between 10,000-13,000 feet
- for all passengers above 13,000 feet PA
- for 10% of passengers after 30 minutes between 10,000-13,000 feet.

PRESSURISED AEROPLANES
CAT.IDE.A.235

Aeroplanes operating above 10,000 feet, that maintain cabin pressure below that.

Supply For	Duration & Cabin Pressure Altitude
Occupants of flight deck seats on duty	Time above 13000 ft PA and between 10000-13000 ft after first 30 minutes, but at least 30 for aeroplanes certificated up to 25000 ft (Note 2) or 2 hours for aeroplanes certificated to more (Note 3).
Cabin Crew	Time above 13000 ft PA, but at least 30 mins (Note 2), and all between 10000-13000 ft after first 30 mins
100% of pax (Note 5)	Time when cabin PA exceeds 15000 ft but not less than 10 minutes. (Note 4)
30% of pax (Note 5)	Time cabin PA between 14000-15000 ft.
10% of pax (Note 5)	Time cabin PA is between 10000-14000 ft after 1st 30 mins.

- **Note 1**: The supply must take account of the cabin pressure altitude and descent profile.
- **Note 2**: For a constant ROD from the maximum operating altitude to 10,000 ft in 10 mins, followed by 20 mins at 10,000 ft.
- **Note 3**: For a constant rate of descent from the maximum certificated operating altitude to 10,000 ft in 10 minutes then 110 minutes at 10,000 ft.
- **Note 4**: The quantity for a constant ROD from the maximum altitude to 15000 ft in 10 minutes.
- **Note 5**: For this table "passengers" means those actually carried, including infants. If all occupants of the flight deck use the crew supply, they are flight crew on flight deck duty. Otherwise, they are passengers. The crew must have oxygen masks within immediate reach at the duty station. Supplemental oxygen must be used continuously after 30 mins when cabin pressure is above 10,000 feet, and at all times above 13,000 feet.

Except for supersonic aeroplanes, above FL 410, at least one pilot at his station must always wear an oxygen mask.

Above 25,000 ft PA, the following are required:

- quick donning types of masks for flight crew, and enough supplemental oxygen for the entire time the cabin exceeds 13,000 feet, but at least 2 hours.
- enough spare outlets and masks or portable oxygen units with masks distributed evenly throughout the passenger compartment, to ensure immediate availability for each cabin crew member.
- an oxygen dispensing unit connected to oxygen supply terminals immediately available to each cabin crew member, additional crew member and occupants of passenger seats, wherever seated, and
- a device to provide a warning to the flight crew of any loss of pressurisation.

For pressurised aeroplanes first issued with a C of A after 8 November 1998 at pressure altitudes above 25,000 ft, or below 25,000 ft where a safe descent to 13,000 ft within four minutes cannot be undertaken, the individual dispensing units referred to above must be automatically deployable. The total number must exceed the number of seats by at least 10%, and be evenly distributed throughout the passenger compartment.

However, in aeroplanes not certified above 25,000 ft, the requirements may be reduced between 10,000 and 13,000 ft cabin pressure altitudes for all required cabin crew members and for at least 10% of the passengers if the aeroplane is always able to descend safely within four minutes to a cabin PA of 13,000 ft.

FIRST AID OXYGEN
CAT.IDE.A.230

Pressurised aeroplanes above 25,000', when cabin crew are required, must have undiluted oxygen for passengers who might need it after depressurisation. The amount is calculated with an average flow rate of at least 3 litres *Standard Temperature Pressure Dry* (STPD) per minute per person for the entire flight after depressurisation at cabin pressure altitudes of more than 8000' for at least 2% of passengers carried, but never less than one. There shall be enough units, but never less than two, with a means for cabin crew to use the supply. The amount of first-aid oxygen for a particular operation is determined from cabin pressure altitudes and flight duration, consistent with the procedures established for each operation and route.

The equipment must generate a mass flow for each user of at least 4 litres per minute, STPD, which can be decreased to at least 2 litres per minute at any altitude.

CREW PROTECTIVE BREATHING EQUIPMENT
CAT.IDE.A.245

Aeroplanes with an MCTOM over 5700 kg, or an MOPSC of over 19, must have equipment to protect the eyes, nose and mouth of flight crew members on flight deck duty, and to provide oxygen for at least 15 minutes, which may come from the supplemental oxygen required above. In addition, with more than one flight crew member, and when cabin crew is not carried, portable PBE must be carried to protect the eyes, nose and mouth of one member of the flight crew and all cabin crew, and provide breathing gas for at least 15 minutes.

PBE for flight crew must be on the flight deck and be accessible for immediate use at assigned stations. PBE for cabin crew must be installed next to each crew station.

An additional, easily accessible portable PBE must be provided and located at, or adjacent to, the required hand fire extinguishers in CAT.IDE.A.250, except that, where the extinguisher is in a cargo compartment, the PBE must be outside, but next to the entrance.

A PBE while in use shall not prevent the use of the means of communication referred to in CAT.IDE.A.170, CAT.IDE.A.175, CAT.IDE.A.270 and CAT.IDE.A.330.

Fire Extinguishers

See also *Fire Detection*, in *Airframes, Engine & Systems*. If there isn't actually an extinguisher in the engine, at the very least there should be a firewall shutoff, operated from the cockpit, that will stop the flow in fuel and hydraulic lines (PA 31, etc). If there isn't, try for a fuel valve that stops the flow to the engine. An engine-based system will have CO_2 or Halon in cylinders. Otherwise, you can use CO_2 on Class A, B or electrical fires. The recommended extinguisher for wheel assemblies is dry powder.

HAND FIRE EXTINGUISHERS
CAT.IDE.A.250

Hand fire extinguishers must be provided for crew, passenger and cargo compartments, and galleys after the kinds of fires likely to occur and, for personnel compartments, must minimise toxic gas concentration. At least one hand extinguisher containing Halon 1211 (BCF), or equivalent, must be on the flight deck for use by the flight crew., and in, or readily accessible for use in, each galley not on the main passenger deck and each Class A, Class B and Class E cargo compartment accessible to crew members in flight.

This chart describes seats against minimum numbers of extinguishers:

Seats	Extinguishers
7-30	1
31-60	2
61-200	3
201-300	4
301-400	5
401-500	6
501-600	7
601 +	8

Add at least one for the flight deck. Portable extinguishers must be in the pilot's compartment, and each one not readily accessible by the crew. When two or more extinguishers are required, they must be evenly spread around the passenger compartment.

Extinguishers are colour coded:

Water	Red (A)
Dry Powder	Blue (A, B, C & D)
Foam	Cream
CO_2	Black (A, B & C)
Halon/BCF	Green

Fuel Jettison

When you have to land in a hurry and your aircraft is too heavy, you are allowed to dump some of your fuel, under certain conditions*. You need a jettison system if your maximum landing mass exceeds your maximum takeoff mass by more than 15 minutes' flying time, consisting essentially of one circuit in the landing configuration, plus a go-around.

*The trend is to move away from jettisoning fuel, especially if the machine is on fire, because it can simply take too long. It must be dumpable within 15 minutes, and should ideally be done over the sea or above 10,000 feet AGL, but may be done above 7,000 in winter and 4,000 in summer. You can dump it anywhere if the need exists, but ATC must be informed, before and after. No Smoking lights must be on, with minimum electrical switching.

PERFORMANCE

CAT.POL.A.100
CAT.POL.A.105

Refer too the *Performance* chapter for compliance rules.

Runway Contamination

A "contaminated" runway has over 25% of its surface area covered with standing water or slush (or loose snow) more than 3mm thick, or compressed snow and ice anywhere along the takeoff run or accelerate-stop surface. However, your flight manual may have different ideas. The 3 states of frozen water from ATC are *snow, ice* and *slush*. Just 13 mm of slush can produce enough drag to equal 35% of a 747's total thrust. At 25 mm, it is equal to 65%. Your takeoff distance can therefore increase from anywhere between 30-100%.

In 1968, tests found that an average runway (that is, not porous or grooved), when wet, has a 2:1 wet:dry stopping ratio - in other words, the landing roll *doubled*. This could increase to 6:1 if there were significant rubber deposits, or the runway was otherwise worn. The important factors are loss of friction when decelerating, and displacement of (and impingement drag when accelerating through) whatever is on the surface, so it may be difficult to steer, and takeoff and accelerate-stop distances may increase due to slower acceleration, as will landing distance because of poor braking action and aquaplaning (see *Hydroplaning*, below), which is a condition where the built-up pressure of liquid under the tyres at a certain speed will equal the weight of the aircraft. In fact, slush drag increases until you get to around 70% of hydroplaning speed, after which it diminishes to zero when total hydroplaning is achieved. Slush's influence depends on fluid depth and density, and the square of forward velocity - half an inch will increase takeoff distance by 15%. At one inch, it's 50%. 2 inches' worth will stop acceleration completely.

When operations from contaminated runways are unavoidable, *do not* attempt to take off in depths of wet snow or slush over 15 mm, or try to grease it on when landing, or land too far in. *Do* lower the nosewheel as soon as possible, and use reverse thrust, or at least aerodynamic braking. Also, ensure the speed is safe before turning off the runway - the greatest tyre cornering effort occurs with no braking. The responsibility for assessing runway surface conditions lies with the operator of the airfield, and not ATC, who merely pass it on.

WATER DEPOSITS

A **dry runway** is one neither wet nor contaminated, including paved runways specially prepared with grooves or porous pavement and can retain effectively dry braking action with moisture present.

Surface conditions are described (with depth) as:

- **Damp** - there is a change of colour due to moisture. A runway is damp when the surface is not dry, but the moisture on it does not give it a shiny appearance. You can call a damp runway a dry one, if braking action is good.

- **Wet** - the surface is soaked, but there is *no standing water*. Over 25% of the surface is covered with water (or the equivalent in loose snow or slush) more than 3mm deep, or when there is enough moisture on the surface to make it appear reflective, without significant areas of standing water. *Any* compacted snow or ice counts as well. Without a shiny appearance, it is only damp. A wet runway, regardless of braking action, always affects minimum TODR/LDR. If the runway is wet, but the graphs are for dry runways, multiply the graph result by 1.15 (15% - exam question). This will likely mean reducing weight.

- **Water patches** - significant patches of standing water*

- **Flooded** - there is extensive standing water visible (you might get aquaplaning).

Slippery When Wet means that surface friction as measured by a measuring device is below minima.

FROZEN WATER

The three states to be reported are:

- *Dry Snow*. That which can be blown if loose or, if compacted by hand, will fall apart on release. The SG will be up to, but no including, 0.35

- *Wet Snow*. That which, if compacted by hand, will stick together and form a snowball. SG is from 0.35 up to, but not including, 0.5

- *Slush*. Snow that has been compressed into a solid mass that sticks together and resists further compression. SG is 0.5 and over

WHEN TAXYING

On the ground, you may need slower taxying speeds and higher power settings to allow for reduction in brake performance and the increase in drag from snow, slush or standing water, so watch your jet blast or propeller slipstream doesn't blow anything into nearby aircraft.

Try not to collect snow and slush on the airframe, don't taxi directly behind other aircraft, and take account of banks of cleared snow and their proximity to wing- and propeller-tips or engine pods.

GRASS

For dry short grass (under 5"), the TODR will increase by 20%, a factor of 1.2. When it's wet, 25% - a factor of 1.25. For dry, long grass (5-10"), TODR will increase by 25%, and 30% when wet (it's not recommended that you operate when the grass is over 10" high).

For dry short grass (under 5 inches), the LDR will increase by 20%, a factor of 1.2. When it's wet, 30% - a factor of 1.3. For dry, long grass (5-10 inches), LDR will increase by 30%, and 40% when wet. For other soft ground or snow, the increase will be in the order of 25% or more for take-off and landing.

COEFFICIENT OF FRICTION

This is the difference between braking action on wet and dry runways, for the same aeroplane at the same speed and mass. As groundspeed increases, so does the difference, so action can only get better if you start higher than 0.4 and decelerate.

OPERATIONAL PROCEDURES
Planning Minima

BRAKING ACTION

It is worth noting that certification testing may be done with new brakes and tyres - worn ones, as found on most aircraft, probably won't be capable of a high-energy RTO.

Coefficient	Action	Code
0.4 +	Good	5
0.39-0.36	Medium-Good	4
0.35-0.30	Medium	3
0.29-0.26	Medium-Poor	2
0.25 and below	Poor	1

HYDROPLANING

This occurs when liquid on the runway creeps under the tyres and lifts them completely, leaving them in contact with fluid alone, with the consequent loss of traction, so there may be a period during which, if one of your engines stops on take-off, you will be unable to either continue or stop within the remaining runway length, and go water-skiing merrily off the end (actually, you're more likely to go off the side, so choosing a longer runway won't necessarily help). The duration of this risk period is variable, but will vary for to weight, water depth, tyre pressure and speed. It only needs a tenth of an inch to do this.

Dynamic hydroplaning is the basic sort, arising from standing water (*lift off speed* is the important consideration here). It comes with as two subtypes, *partial* and *full*, both more likely when water depth is over 6 mm. *Viscous hydroplaning* involves a thin layer of liquid on a slippery surface, such as the traces of rubber left on the landing area of a runway which fill in the small holes (one reason why it's dangerous to drive after a rain shower in Summer). In other words, it is caused by a *smooth* and *dirty* runway surface, at a lower speed than dynamic hydroplaning, and you should particularly watch out for the white markings - it can almost be like landing on ice. *Reverted Rubber Hydroplaning* happens when a locked tyre generates enough heat from friction to boil the water on the surface and cause the resulting steam to stop the tyre touching the runway. The heat causes the rubber to revert to its basic chemical properties, i.e. black and runny.

Although there are many contributory factors, the most important is tyre pressure. A rough speed at which aquaplaning can occur is about 9 times the square root of your tyre pressures (see the formula below), 100 pounds per square inch therefore giving you about 90 kts (7.7 times if the tyre isn't rotating) - if this is higher than your expected take-off speed you're safer than otherwise. The point to note is that if you start aquaplaning above the critical speed, you can expect the process to continue below it, that is, you will slide around to well below the speed you would have expected it to start if you were taking off.

Most factors that will assist you under these circumstances are directly under your control, and it's even more important to arrive for a "positive" landing at the required 50 feet above the threshold at the recommended speed on the recommended glideslope than for normal situations (the positive landing helps the wheels break through the water). Under-inflating tyres doesn't help - each 2 or 3 lbs below proper pressure will lower the aquaplaning speed by 1 knot, so be careful if you've descended rapidly from a colder altitude. Naturally, you should try not to use the brakes, but as much aerodynamic braking as you can, after lowering the nose as quickly as possible to reduce the angle of attack and place weight on the wheels.

The (rotating wheel) formula is:

$$Vp = 34.5 \sqrt{(p)}$$

Vp is the ground speed in knots and p is the tyre pressure when using bars (for PSI, use 9 instead of 34.5. The stationary wheel formula uses 7.7, so you might get partial hydroplaning while the wheels spin up).

PLANNING MINIMA

Selection Of Aerodromes
CAT.OP.MPA.180
CAT.OP.MPA.185

Aerodromes selected as destinations or alternates* must be adequate and suitable for the types of aircraft that may use them, in terms of performance, obstacles and conditions, for the intended masses at takeoff and landing.

*An **alternate aerodrome** is one to which you may proceed when it becomes impossible or inadvisable to proceed to or land where you originally intended, where the necessary services and facilities are available, performance requirements can be met and which is operational at the expected time of use. This includes:

- **Takeoff Alternate**. One where you can land if it becomes necessary shortly after takeoff, where it is not possible to use the aerodrome of departure.
- **En-route Alternate**. One where you would be able to land after experiencing an abnormal or emergency condition en route.
- **ETOPS Alternate**. For ETOPS alternates the term *suitable* is used (as opposed to *adequate*) as weather minima apply.
- **Destination Alternate**. One to which you may proceed if it becomes impossible or inadvisable to land at the point of intended landing.

 You can use the departure point as an en-route or a destination alternate.

TAKEOFF ALTERNATE

An aerodrome may only be used as a takeoff alternate when the appropriate weather reports and/or forecasts indicate that, for 1 hour either side of the ETA, the weather will be at or above the minima in CAT.OP.MPA.110. The ceiling shall be taken into account when only non-precision approaches and/or circling operations are available, as must any OEI limitations.

When you cannot return to where you took off from (for weather or performance reasons), you need an alternative:

- For twin-engined aeroplanes:
  - Within one hours' flight time at OEI cruising speed, based on actual takeoff mass, or
  - Two hours, or the approved ETOPS diversion time, whichever is less, at OEI cruising speed
- For 3 and 4 engined aeroplanes:
  - 2 hours' flight time at OEI cruising speed, based on actual takeoff mass
  - If there is no such speed in the flight manual, use whatever you can get with the remaining engine(s) at max continuous power.

DESTINATION (NON ISOLATED)

A destination aerodrome shall only be selected as such (by the operator) when appropriate weather reports and/or forecasts indicate that, for 1 hour either side of the ETA, the weather will be at or above the minima under CAT.OP.MPA.110 and, for an NPA or a circling operation, the ceiling is at or above MDH. 2 destination alternates may be selected instead.

DESTINATION ALTERNATE

You need at least one destination alternate for each IFR flight unless:

- The planned flight is not over 6 hours (but see also CAT.OP.MPA.150(d) about in-flight replanning).
- There are two separate runways at the destination and the approach and landing can be made, for an hour either side of the ETA, in a ceiling of at least 2,000 ft or circling height + 500 ft, whichever is greater, with a ground visibility at least 5 km.
- The destination is isolated, with no alternate.

You need 2 destination alternates when:

- The weather for 1 hour either side if the ETA will be below applicable minima, or
- There is no weather information available

Destination alternates, isolated aerodromes, fuel en-route alternates (fuel ERAs) and en-route alternates (ERAs) shall only be selected as such (by the operator) when appropriate weather reports and/or forecasts indicate that, for 1 hour either side of the ETA, the weather will be at or above the minima below:

Approach Available	Planning Minima
CAT II & III	CAT I RVR
CAT I	NPA RVR/VIS Ceiling at or above MDH
NPA*	NPA RVR/VIS + 1,000 m Ceiling at or above MDH + 200 ft
Circling	Circling

*The next highest minima that apply in the prevailing wind and serviceability conditions, including localiser only approaches, if published. For APV operations, use NPA or CAT I minima, depending on the DH/MDH. For LTS CAT I, use CAT I minima, and for OTS CAT II operations, use CAT II minima.

Emergency & Precautionary Landings

These include any landing that is not at a normal landing site (i.e. an aerodrome or heliport). Some factors to be considered are:

- The size of the landing site.
- The facilities at the landing site.
- The time available.

DEFINITIONS

- **Ditching**. An emergency landing on water, deliberately executed, with the intent of abandoning the aircraft as soon as practicable. The aircraft is assumed to be intact before entering the water, with all controls and essential systems, except the engines, working properly.
- **Precautionary Landing**. One planned in flight to overcome unforeseen circumstances, which does not immediately endanger the safety of the aircraft. Alternatively, one that is necessitated by an apparent impending failure of engines, systems or components that makes further flight inadvisable.
- **Precautionary Forced Landing**. An inevitable landing or a ditching in which it can be reasonably hoped that no injuries will be suffered by the helicopter's occupants or people on the surface.
- **Emergency Landing**. A landing made as soon as possible to cope with an in-flight occurrence that endangers aircraft safety.

On the high seas, it is best to ditch parallel to and on top of the primary swell system, except in high winds*. The primary swell is easier to see from higher up. Secondary systems may only be visible lower down. In addition, the effects of wind may only be discernible at a much lower altitude from the appearance of the white caps.

*The primary swell system may disappear from view at lower altitudes when it becomes hidden by secondary systems and the wind chop. In strong winds it may be a good idea to ditch more into the wind and slightly across the swell (*Transport Canada AIM*). In ideal conditions, such as when the surface of the water is flat, or if the water is smooth with a very long swell inside which the aircraft will come to rest, landing into wind will provide the slowest impact speed (*FAA*).

The decision to ditch should be made as early as possible so that power (if available) can be used to achieve the optimum impact conditions. This would allow a stabilised approach at a low rate of descent at the applicable speed.

MAINTENANCE

Regulation (EC) No 2042/2003

Aircraft must be maintained and released to service by Part 145 organisations, except for preflight inspections (see below), which need not necessarily be done by them (reference to aircraft includes components). De- and anti-icing activities do not need 145 approval. An engineer's signature certifies that maintenance work on an aircraft has been done correctly so that other people (i.e. pilots) can determine that it is fit for service.

STOP Work defined as "maintenance" does not necessarily include servicing (depends on the country).

An engineer's licence grants the privilege to sign a maintenance release* for any work performed on an aeronautical product, either theirs or that of others, but if the others are unlicensed, their work must be supervised. It is not a licence to do the work, but to evaluate it and sign for it. Naturally, in order to do this, they must have had some sort of training, and be performing the job full-time (that is, they must be "current").

ICAO Annex 6 Part I Chapter 8.8. A maintenance release shall be completed and signed to certify that the work performed has been completed satisfactorily and in accordance with the approved data and procedures in the maintenance organisation's procedures manual. It shall contain a certification including:

- basic details of the maintenance done, including detailed reference of the approved data used
- the date such maintenance was completed
- when applicable, the identity of the approved maintenance organisation
- the identity of the person or persons signing the release

Airworthiness certification varies. For example, an aircraft that is considered to be airworthy in Canada is also airworthy in the USA (by agreement), but not in Europe (EASA). Similarly, an aircraft that is airworthy in one European country is airworthy all over Europe but not in the US or Canada. So it will need to be recertified.

"Airworthy" means that the aircraft is in the same state as it left the factory, so when you are replacing worn and broken parts, you are bringing an aircraft back to its factory state. The airworthiness state of an aircraft must also be reported back to the authorities. The registered owner does this every year on an appropriate form.

The Certificate of Airworthiness is known as a *flight authority* (see *Documents & Records*, overleaf). A copy of it must be kept in the aircraft when it is being operated. It is also possible to fly the aircraft if it is not airworthy by issuing anther type of flight authority, called a *Permit To Fly*. This is used by engineers to get an aircraft back to base if it needs work done on it. You may not carry passengers with a Permit To Fly! There may be other limits, especially if the aircraft has been built for a particular purpose and may be dangerous.

Only an aircraft maintenance engineer may certify an aircraft for the purpose of obtaining a flight authority, so his main task is to determine to what standard any maintenance has been completed.

Repaired components are certified as serviceable with a Maintenance Release. If there isn't one, the component must come directly from an airworthy installation, and not from storage. Anything sent for an overhaul must have an Airworthiness Approval Form attached to it. If the parts are too big and you have to use mobile technicians, the work is done under Field Service Standards. Major repairs must use information from the manufacturer (blueprints). Parts used but not made by the manufacturer must still be certified by the aircraft builder (where there is any conflict, the aircraft builder's recommendations are used).

Where the manufacturer does not specify any maintenance methods, "standard industry practice" is to be followed. The most often used reference for this is the FAA's Advisory Circular 43.13 which has over 500 pages. People who perform work on aircraft must use the most recent methods, techniques, part, materials, etc.

Preflight Inspection

The definition means all the actions necessary to ensure that the aircraft is fit for the intended flight, which should typically include but are not necessarily limited to:

- A walk-around inspection for condition including, in particular, obvious signs of wear, damage or leakage. In addition, the presence and condition of emergency equipment should be established
- Inspection of the Tech Log to ensure that the intended flight is not adversely affected by outstanding deferred defects and that no required maintenance in the maintenance statement is overdue or will become due during the flight
- That consumable fluids, gases, etc. uplifted before flight are of the correct specification, free from contamination, and correctly recorded
- That all doors are securely fastened
- Control surface and landing gear locks, pitot/static covers, restraint devices and engine/aperture blanks have been removed
- That external surfaces and engines are free from ice, snow, sand, dust, etc.

Tasks such as oil and hydraulic fluid uplift and inflation may be part of the preflight. Related instructions should address procedures to determine where the necessary uplift or inflation results from an abnormal consumption and possibly requires additional action by AMO.

Maintenance Responsibility

Airworthiness and serviceability must be accomplished by:

- Preflight inspections (see above)
- Rectification of defects and damage, as in MELs and CDLs
- Maintenance under approved programs
- Operational directives, ADs and other requirements made mandatory
- Modifications.

The requirement means that the *operator* is responsible for determining what maintenance is required, when it has to be done, by whom and to what standard, to ensure continued airworthiness.

Maintenance Management

Operators must be approved under Part 145 to carry out the requirements except when the Authority is satisfied that maintenance can be contracted out.

Operators must employ acceptable people to ensure that maintenance is done on time to an approved standard. The senior person is the nominated postholder. The NMP is also responsible for corrective action from quality monitoring. The NPM should not be employed by a Part 145 AMO under contract, unless specifically agreed.

When an operator is not Part 145 approved, arrangements must be made with such an organisation.

NOISE ABATEMENT

CAT.OP.MPA.130

Except for VFR operations with non-complex motor-powered aeroplanes, operators must establish appropriate departure and arrival/approach procedures for each type, taking into account the need to minimise noise. Such procedures must ensure that safety has priority, and be simple and safe with no significant increase in crew workload during critical phases of flight.

Noise is a function of the power used and the distance from people listening, so you want to use as little power as far away from people as possible.

Noise standards were originally issued by ICAO in 1981 as Annex 16, and relaxed in 1985, then amended many times after that. Currently, ICAO DOC 8168 refers, which lists procedures that have been developed for turbo jets. They may include:

- Using **particular runways** and **routes** to keep the noise away from sensitive areas. Runways selected must have suitable glide path guidance (e.g. VASIS, PAPI), but noise abatement should not be a factor if the runway is contaminated, in low visibility (ceilings less than 500 ft on landing, vis below 1900 m on takeoff), high crosswinds (15 kts) and tailwinds (5 kts), or when windshear or thunderstorms are around. When it comes to routes, turns should not be initiated below 500 ft, and bank angles should not exceed 15° (needs more power). No turns for noise abatement should be made when power reductions are required for noise abatement.

  Naturally, there should be enough navigation aids to help pilots keep to the procedure.

- Using **procedures** on takeoff and landing to keep the noise down when flight over such areas cannot be avoided, always allowing for flight safety. The *minimum* height for power reduction is 800 ft. Procedures for any particular type of aircraft must apply to all aerodromes. You must be in landing configuration after the outer marker or 5 nm from the threshold, whichever is earlier.

  Excessive rates of descent or turning should not be required, because you will need a period of stabilisation before landing.

  Noise abatement procedures do not stop you using reverse thrust on landing.

The worst combination of atmospheric conditions for noise is a windless, cold, overcast morning, since temperature and air movement have their effects. An inversion reverses the normal sound propagation curve because it turns quite a bit back towards the ground.

Procedure 1 produces noise relief in the early stages of takeoff (i.e. near the aerodrome), and *Procedure 2* is for the latter stages (further away). Both require an initial climb under full power at $V_2 + 10$ kts to $V_2 + 20$ kts, but Procedure 2 starts the flap retraction under full power at a minimum of 800 feet (Procedure 1 reduces thrust early and has the flaps retracted at 3000 feet).

In VMC, a runway should not be chosen if it has no ILS or visual approach slope guidance. At takeoff, the aircraft mass must be under that which would enable compliance with noise abatement procedures. The choice of runway, however, should come first, depending on whether it is clear and dry, the cloud ceiling is less than 500 feet, visibility less than 1.9 km (1 nm), the crosswind component, including gusts, exceeds 15 kts, or tailwind components, with gusts, exceed 5 kts, when windshear is reported or forecast, or thunderstorms are around.

You should be in the final landing configuration 5 nm from the threshold, or after the outer marker, whichever is earlier. However, reduced power/drag techniques, where flap and undercarriage extension is delayed until the final stages, are OK. There is no limit on using reverse thrust.

WAKE TURBULENCE

For timed approaches (non-radar), these minima are applied to **landing** aircraft:

- MEDIUMS behind HEAVY aircraft - 2 mins
- LIGHTS behind HEAVY or MEDIUM - 3 mins

For takeoff, it's 2 minutes behind anything, or 3 minutes if you are taking off from an intermediate part of the same or a parallel runway separated by less than 760 m. For displaced thresholds and opposite direction runways, separation is 2 minutes. If an arriving aircraft is making a straight in approach, a departing one may take off in any direction which differs by at least 45° from the reciprocal of the direction of approach, if the takeoff will be made at least 3 minutes before the arriving one is estimated to be over the instrument runway.

BIRD & WILDLIFE HAZARDS

The concern is not only for aircraft, but also the birds, as they can pollinate flowers and remove insect pests from commercial food crops and forest species. Notifications of permanent or seasonal concentrations are found in NOTAMs, but birds are *mostly* attracted by open refuse tips and *least* attracted by long grass. Otherwise, you can expect them at bird sanctuaries or along shorelines or rivers in Autumn or Spring - migratory birds use line features for navigation as well, but they don't necessarily keep 300m to the right (joke). Migration routes typically follow mountain ranges or coastlines, and may utilise updrafts and other wind patterns or avoid barriers like large stretches of open water. In fact, routes out and back are often different. Groups of birds will usually break away downwards from anything hazardous, so try to fly upwards if possible (i.e. *climb safely*). You could also use landing lights to make yourself more visible, especially where two are flashing alternately. Avoid freshly ploughed or harvested fields, and beware of updraughts in mountains areas, where birds will be trying to get some free lift. Birds are most active at dawn and dusk.

Noticeably fewer birdstrikes occur at height, so try to fly as high as possible, certainly above 1500 or even 3000 ft (40% of strikes occur on the ground, or during takeoff and landing. 15% occur up to about 100' agl. One of the highest so far hit a DC-8 at FL 390). Speed is also a factor (*Niering* 1990) because half the speed means a quarter of the impact energy. Since the highest risk occurs under 500 m, the lower you go, the slower you should be. A short delay on the approach could mean the clearance of a group of birds, as they do move in waves. The observations and studies conducted on the behaviour of birds on the ground, ahead of an aircraft taking off and having reached an average speed of 135 kt, show that birds fly away about two seconds beforehand.

The most efficient bird scaring technique generally available is broadcasting recorded distress calls, but pyrotechnics can be used as well.

Windshields

The force from a bird impact increases with the square of the speed - at 110 kts, the impact from a 1 lb bird can exceed 1200 lbs sq/inch (the force is actually determined by the square of your speed multiplied by the mass of the bird). The problem is that, below a certain weight, the windshield will only be designed to keep out rain and insects. However, a hot windshield is more pliable and less likely to shatter if it gets hit - some aircraft need these on for take-off and landing, but if there is nothing in the flight manual, use 15 minutes. Overheating is as bad as underheating, so be wary if your aircraft has been left in the sun for a long time.

LONG RANGE OPERATIONS

SPA.RVSM.100

There are still many parts of the world that have no ATC and/or radar. This would include large parts of Africa and the North Atlantic routes between Europe and North America, amongst others. However, there still needs to be some sort of control, to make best use of the airspace when lots of aircraft want to use it. For example, the normal vertical separation above FL 295 used to be 2000 feet, until it was possible to reduce this safely to 1,000 with altimeters and height-keeping systems under **Reduced Vertical Separation Minima** (RVSM), below.

Such procedures must be strictly observed by all concerned. That is, do not expect to change levels in oceanic airspace (including initial descent at the destination) unless you have an emergency, such as engine failure or decompression. Certainly not VFR! Instead, ask for clearance at the highest level you can possibly achieve on entering so that, as you burn off fuel, you will be at theoptimum flight level about half way across.

Another requirement is the standard of navigational equipment. As proper use of the airspace depends on it, you must tell ATC immediately if any of it fails, or you are "uncertain of your position*". Continual cross-checking, especially on entering the airspace, is therefore necessary.

*A *gross navigation error* is a track deviation of more than 25 nm - in fact, you should remain within 3 nm of your intended track for 95% of the time.

Navigation Equipment

Generally, you need at least two independent long range area navigation systems meeting certain specifications (i.e. a **Minimum Navigation Performance Specification**, or MNPS). With only one as long range, you may still be able to use the airspace, but your routes may be restricted. If both systems are short range, you may be approved for routes that do not require long range RNAV capability (if your final LRNS fails, contact ATC and wait for a reply within a reasonable time). TCAS is also required.

MNPS airspace across the Atlantic, for example, lies between 27°N to 90°N and FLs 285 and 420, so the effective cruising levels (with 1 000 foot spacing) are between FLs 290 and 410.

To join it, you (and the aircraft) need approval from the State of Registry or that of the operator. Such approvals cover everything, including crew operating procedures. The full reference is ICAO NAT Doc 001. Operators must ensure that crews follow NAT MNPSA Operations Manual procedures (ICAO Doc 7030 NAT/RAC-2 3.2.3).

If you do not meet MNPS standards, you will be kept below FL 280*, above FL 410 or South of 27° North, and separation will be according to the older rules, namely 120 nm (2°) laterally and 20 minutes longitudinally.

*If you wish to fly between Shannon and Gander without MNPS certification, you must fly at FL 280 or less.

All turbine-engined aeroplanes with an MCTOM over 5,700 kg or with an MOPSC of more than 19 passengers must carry and operate ACAS II in the NAT Region. Pre-flight procedures for any NAT MNPS flight must include a UTC time check and resynchronisation of the aircraft master clock.

OCEANIC CLEARANCE

It is recommended that oceanic clearance is obtained at least **40 minutes before the ETA** at the entry point. If the ETA for oceanic entry changes by **3 minutes or more**, a revised estimate should be passed to ATC.

When requesting an oceanic clearance, you should notify the OAC* of the **maximum acceptable flight level** at the boundary, allowing for the climb before entering, normally while you are within radar coverage. You should also notify them of any required change to the flight planned level, track or Mach

OPERATIONAL PROCEDURES
Long Range Operations

number as early as practicable after departure. The clearance request should also include the next preferred alternative track.

*Communication with OACs is done via aeradio stations staffed by communicators who have **no executive ATC authority**. SATCOM calls should be made to them rather than ATC, unless urgency dictates otherwise. Messages are relayed from the ground station to the controllers in the relevant OAC for action. You should state the HF frequency in use on initial contact.

An example of a request for oceanic clearance could be:

"ACA 865 request Oceanic Clearance. Estimating PIKIL at 1131. Request Mach decimal eight zero, Flight Level 350, able Flight Level 360, second choice Track Charlie".

 Having arrived at the point of entry into MNPS airspace, if you have not received oceanic clearance, you should enter into a holding pattern. The clearance, by the way, will include the **Mach number*, route and flight level** (covering the three basic elements of separation) and should have been requested 40 minutes beforehand, unless the airport is on the boundary, in which case get it on the ground.

After leaving oceanic airspace pilots must maintain their assigned Mach number in domestic controlled airspace unless and until ATC authorises a change.

If an aircraft, which would normally be RVSM and/or MNPS approved, encounters, en route to oceanic airspace, a critical in-flight equipment failure, or at dispatch is unable to meet the MEL requirements for RVSM or MNPS approval, ATC must be advised when initially requesting oceanic clearance, although this appears to be contrary to ICAO Doc 7030.

You should pay particular attention when the issued clearance differs from the flight plan. If the entry point of the route on which you are cleared differs from that originally requested and/or the oceanic flight level differs from the current flight level, you are responsible for requesting and obtaining the necessary re-clearance.

Some aircraft may be required to report MET observations of wind speed and direction, plus outside air temperature (the phrase *Send Met Reports* will be included in the clearance). Turbulence should be included.

Vertical separation is covered with....

RVSM AIRSPACE

As the altimeter is less accurate at higher altitudes there are only 7 usable flight levels between FL 290 and FL 410 where 2000 feet vertical separation is used. Technology has allowed this to be reduced down to 1000 feet, which not only allows for 13 usable flight levels, but also allows aircraft to operate closer to their optimum altitudes. The separation between Non-RVSM and any other aircraft (RVSM approved or not) remains at 2000 ft.

Even levels are used for Westbound traffic and odd ones for Eastbound traffic, but you would use whatever is in the track message for the day.

To fly in RVSM airspace, the aircraft needs certified equipment* on board (by the State of Registry), particularly with regard to altitude measurement. Pilots also need a short training course and must receive a certificate of completion before using RVSM procedures.

*That is, 2 independent altimeters, an autopilot, an altitude deviation alerting device and a transponder with Mode C. If you have RVSM equipment, regardless of whether you use it or not, put the letter W in item 10 of the flight plan, or item Q of a repetitive flight plan. MNPS approval is indicated with the letter X. If you want to enter RVSM airspace from non-RVSM areas, you must also include in item 15 the entry point and requested level, talking of which, you only put the track in Item 15 if you intend to fly the entire length of it (e.g. NATG). The planned Mach number and flight level at the start of the track must be specified at the start point and for each point where a change of Mach number or level is requested.

Non-certified aircraft must file above or below RVSM airspace, although they can climb through RVSM levels.

OPERATING PROCEDURES
AMC2 SPA.RVSM.105

Conditions that may affect operation in RVSM airspace include, but may not be limited to, verifying that the airframe is approved for RVSM operations plus the minimum equipment requirements for height-keeping and alerting systems (i.e. making sure that the static & pitot ports are clean).

The maximum acceptable differences between altimeters should not exceed 23 m (**75 ft**).

Any required equipment should be working before takeoff, however, before entry into RVSM airspace, at least the following should be working normally:

- 2 primary altitude measurement systems.
- 1 automatic altitude-control system
- 1 altitude-alerting device with a tolerance of ±300 ft
- operating transponder with Mode C

Should any required equipment fail before entering RVSM airspace, a new clearance should be requested to avoid entering it. In flight. The following practices should be incorporated into crew training and procedures:

- Comply with aircraft operating restrictions, if required for the specific type, such as limits on indicated Mach number, given in the RVSM airworthiness approval.

- Emphasis should be placed on promptly setting the sub-scale on all primary and standby altimeters to 1013.2 hPa / 29.92 in Hg when passing the transition altitude, and rechecking for proper altimeter setting when reaching the initial cleared flight level.

- The aircraft should be flown at the cleared flight level, so ATC clearances should be fully understood and followed. There should be no intentional departures from cleared flight levels without a positive clearance from ATC unless contingency or emergency manoeuvres are involved. You must report to ATC immediately on reaching any new cruising level.

- When changing levels, the aircraft should not be allowed to overshoot or undershoot the cleared level by more than 45 m (**150 ft**). The level off should be accomplished with an altitude capture feature.

- An automatic altitude-control system should be working and engaged during level cruise, except when retrimming is required or turbulence requires disengagement. In any event, adherence to cruise altitude should be done by reference to one of the two primary altimeters. Following loss of the automatic height-keeping function, any consequential restrictions will need to be observed.

- The altitude-alerting system should be working.
- Cross-checks between primary altimeters should be made around every hour. At least two must agree within ±60 m (**±200 ft**). Otherwise, the altimetry system should be reported to ATC as defective (the usual scan of flight deck instruments should be enough on most flights).
- In normal operations, the altimetry system being used to control the aircraft should be selected for the input to the altitude reporting transponder transmitting information to ATC.

If ATC notifies a deviation from an assigned altitude over ±90 m (**±300 ft**), return to cleared flight level as quickly as possible.

Traffic

There are three major traffic flows:

EUROPE (& MIDDLE EAST) - N AMERICA

Not Alaska

Much of NAT HLA traffic, i.e. that between Europe and North America flies here, in two traffic flows per day, according to passenger preference, time zone differences and night-time noise curfews at major airports. Around 6 approximately parallel tracks (each way) are established (under the *Organised Track System*), running between entry and exit points on the coasts of UK and Ireland, and Canada. The tracks are selected twice daily by computer, trying to avoid strong head winds on routes A-F from Europe, and to get the best winds on routes U-Z the other way. As the prevailing Westerlies typically lie between 50-55°N, Westbound traffic will be North or South of there. You choose routes that provide the best flight time, subject to availability.

Most of the Westbound flow leaves European airports in late morning to early afternoon and arrives at Eastern North American coastal airports typically 2 hours later in local time*. Most of the Eastbound flow leaves North American airports in mid/late evening to arrive in Europe early to mid morning.

*Flights used to take place at night as HF communications were better and astro navigation was useful.

Because the rules over the high seas are different, and separation standards are important, there are several FIRs for the region:

- Bodø Oceanic (Norway)
- Gander Oceanic
- New York Oceanic
- Reykjavik (Iceland)
- Santa Maria Oceanic (Azores)
- Shanwick Oceanic (Shannon and Prestwick)
- Søndre Strømfjord (Greenland)

Santa Maria controls areas South of 45°, and Reykjavik the areas North of 61°N.

If your preferred track lies within the OTS boundaries, you must use an OTS track, unless you fly above or below the system. Where part or all of the preferred track is clear of the OTS, you can nominate a *random track**, for which you must use great circle tracks joining successive significant points that are defined by whole degrees of latitude intersecting meridians spaced 10° of longitude apart. If your flight is completely clear of the OTS you can choose your own optimum level. If any part of your flight uses the OTS, you must use one of the published levels.

*Flights wishing to leave or join an organised track, or change from one to another, are considered to be random aircraft and full details must be in the flight plan (that means use full coordinates, and not mentioning the track letters). You may only join or leave the outer tracks.

If you need to divert across the main OTS traffic flow, but cannot maintain your assigned flight level and cannot get ATC clearance, you should start descent in the turn to acquire a track separated laterally by 30 nm from your assigned route, then descend quickly to below FL 285 before turning on to the track needed for the diversion.

If you are planning a route through MNPS but do not intend to use the NAT tracks, you should stay clear of them by at least 1°. You can fly above the tracks, and you can use their coordinates outside the OTS times.

 Flights North of 70°N should use waypoints at 20° intervals, because the meridians are closer together and the ground distance is shorter.

The OTS times of operation are:

- East or at night: 01:00 - 08:00 UTC
- West or during the day: 11:30 - 18:00 UTC

The times refer to the crossing of the 30°W meridian, which is the boundary between Shanwick and Gander, through whose areas most N Atlantic flights travel. Eastbound traffic tends to concentrate at around 04:00 UTC and the Westbound at 15:00.

Flights in the relevant direction should use the tracks and flight levels in the daily NATS message, which is issued via AFTN to all interested parties at 23:00 UTC (Westbound, from Shanwick) and 14:00 (Eastbound, from Gander). As the tracks change twice a day, your flight planning is done on the day.

The **Track Message Identification** (TMI) number starts from January 1st, with that day being number 1. Latitudes and longitudes are shown as 49/10, meaning 49° North, 10° West.

The track you choose depends on your points of departure and destination - you don't want one too far North if you are departing from a more Southerly airfield. For example, the Northerly tracks (A or U) are typically used for Central and Western American destinations due to the great circle requirements. Similarly for arrival.

The middle track is generally most popular (due to the winds), so it can be busy. You should however, look at the big picture and consider the distances involved for the whole flight. It might be that V or X may reduce them.

OPERATIONAL PROCEDURES
Long Range Operations

On the other hand, favourable winds may be a factor, as may the easiest NAT to join or leave. Here is a typical example, taken from a list running from U-Z:

```
Track W -- COLOR RONPO 47/50 49/40
51/30 52/20 LIMRI DOLIP
```

It starts at a waypoint called COLOR (near Gander) and ends at DOLIP (near Shannon). To get to the start and from the end, you have to use domestic airspace and airways, so you need two types of clearance - those for Canadian and UK domestic airspace and one for the oceanic trip, which in this case is obtained from Gander, at least 30 minutes before your planned ETA at COLOR (also squawk mode C(S)/2000).

 Although the NAT W track starts at COLOR, Oceanic's airspace does not start till just before 49N050W.

In the Track Message, tracks are referred to by letter, as in NAT B, meaning NAT Track Bravo. **North American Routes (NARs)** are also mentioned, which are preferred routes from the end of the oceanic track to a standard fix in N American airspace, as in NAR512C.

The designators can be found in the Jeppesen manuals, the Canada Flight Supplement and the US Airport Facility Directory. The European equivalents are in the Route Availability Document on the Eurocontrol website.

The NAT track and daily code should be entered on the flight plan if the whole flight is in MNPS airspace on the OTS. If the radios fail before leaving the region, maintain the last revised and acknowledged oceanic clearance, including level and speed, to the last route point (normally on land), then continue with the filed flight plan route. Cruising speed is stated as a Mach number on the flight plan. You may like to file a supplementary flight plan for an alternative route if you don't get the one you want.

Chart Extract: Copyright Jeppesen, Inc. Not for navigation.

Most of the airspace in Oceanic FIRs/CTAs is *high seas airspace* within which ICAO has resolved that rules relating to flight and operations of aircraft apply *without exception*. The majority of the airspace is also controlled airspace, and instrument flight rules (IFR) apply to flights in oceanic airspace when at or above 2000 ft (600 m) above ground level (AGL), whichever is higher, even when not operating in IMC. This means that the pilot and aircraft must be rated for IFR operations, as it is extremely unlikely that you will be VMC for the entire flight.

The North Atlantic system is based on ICAO Doc 7030. For any transoceanic flight, in a single, or underpowered multi (that is, unable to maintain flight if an engine fails), you must have an IR, an HF radio covering at least two international air-ground frequencies, hypothermia protection for each person and enough fuel (plus at least 10% as contingency) to get to the destination. You must also have the equipment for IFR and *a copy of the current track message*. Aircraft must have 2 Long Range Navigation Systems, which could be an INS or GNSS, for example, capable of giving a continuous display of position relative to track, with steering guidance preferably coupled to the autopilot. The rules apply between FLs 285-420, between 27°N and the North Pole, the Eastern boundaries the Santa Maria, Shanwick and Rekjavik CTAs, and Western boundaries of Rekjavik, Gander and New York CTAs, except West of 60°W and South of 38° 30'N.

Cruising speed is stated as a Mach number on the flight plan. You may like to file a supplementary flight plan for an alternative route if you don't get the one you want.

Most of the airspace in Oceanic FIRs/CTAs is *high seas airspace* within which ICAO has resolved that rules relating to flight and operations of aircraft apply *without exception*. The majority of the airspace is also controlled airspace, and instrument flight rules (IFR) apply to all flights in oceanic airspace when at or above FL060 or 2000 ft (600 m) above ground level (AGL), whichever is higher, even when not operating in IMC.

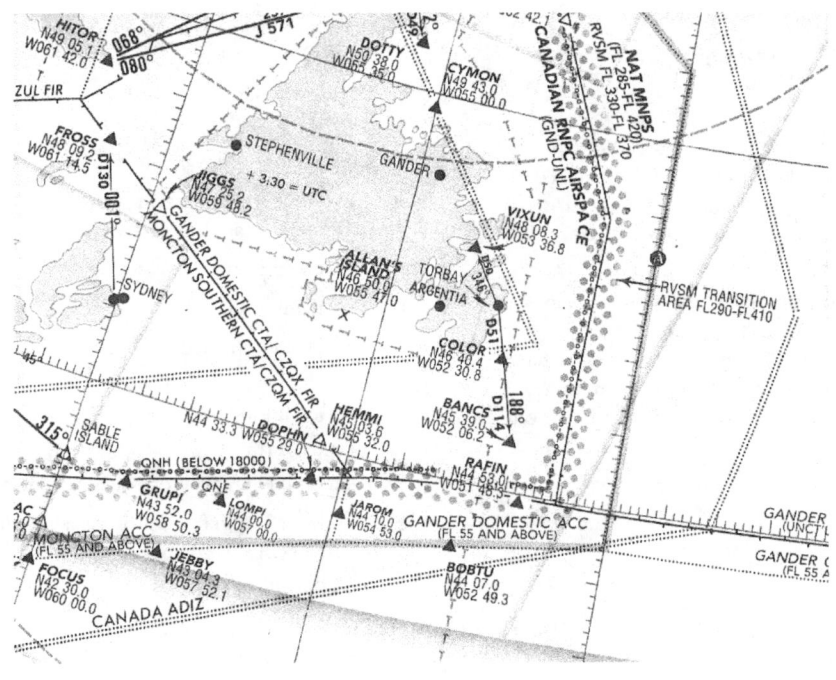

OPERATIONAL PROCEDURES
Long Range Operations

This means that the pilot and aircraft must be rated for IFR operations, as it is extremely unlikely that you will be VMC for the entire flight. Over the high seas, you must comply with the Rules of the Air in Annex 2 and the Regional Supplementary Procedures in Document 7030/4 of ICAO.

The North Atlantic system is based on ICAO Doc 7030. For any transoceanic flight, in a single, or underpowered multi (that is, unable to maintain flight if an engine fails), you must have an IR, an HF radio covering at least two international air-ground frequencies, hypothermia protection for each person and enough fuel (plus at least 10% as contingency) to get to the destination. You must also have the equipment for IFR and *a copy of the current track message*. Aircraft must have 2 Long Range Navigation Systems, which could be an INS or GNSS, for example, capable of giving a continuous display of position relative to track, with steering guidance preferably coupled to the autopilot. The rules apply between FLs 285-420, between 27°N and the North Pole, the Eastern boundaries the Santa Maria, Shanwick and Rekjavik CTAs, and Western boundaries of Rekjavik, Gander and New York CTAs, except West of 60°W and South of 38° 30'N.

Radio Communication

Radar coverage is not available in most of the NAT Region. Outside areas of radar coverage, ATC monitors flight progress with position reports between 30 and 50 minutes apart.

HF is used because VHF range is limited, but even that can be unreliable, so you must make position reports on coming within 200 nm of a VHF facility. Because of high noise levels and other difficulties, HF communications are conducted through a third party to relay communications for controllers. Satellite comms are used now, anyway. Use 131.8 MHz for air-to-air communications, and squawk 2000 from 30 mins after entry until 30 mins before leaving. If the HF fails, use 123.45 MHz.

If you cannot maintain your assigned FL in MNPS airspace, and you can't contact ATC, descend and turn off track for 30 nm separation. Above FL 410, climb or descend 1000' while turning to your alternate. When leaving MNPS airspace, you should select your cleared Mach Number.

VOR information in North Canadian airspace is referenced to True North.

Contingencies

The general concept of in-flight contingency procedures is, whenever operationally feasible, to offset* from the assigned route by 15 nm and climb or descend to a level that differs from those normally used by 500 ft if below FL 410 or by 1000 ft if above FL 410.

*The *Strategic Lateral Offset Procedure* SLOP) allows aircraft to offset the centreline of an airway or flight route by a small amount, normally to the right, so that collision with opposite direction aircraft becomes unlikely. Along a route or track there will be three positions that an aircraft may fly - centreline or one or two miles to the right.

Factors that may affect the direction of turn include:

- direction to an alternate
- terrain clearance
- levels allocated on adjacent routes or tracks and any known SLOP offsets used by nearby traffic.

Contingency procedures inside RVSM airspace are:
- Notify ATC of contingencies (equipment failures, weather) that affect the ability to maintain the cleared flight level and coordinate an appropriate plan of action. Examples include:
    - failure of all automatic altitude-control systems
    - loss of redundancy of altimetry systems
    - loss of thrust on an engine necessitating descent
    - anything else that affects the ability to maintain a cleared flight level
- Notify ATC of greater than moderate turbulence

If unable to notify ATC and obtain clearance before deviating from a cleared flight level, the pilot should follow any established contingency procedures for the region and obtain ATC clearance as soon as possible.

An aircraft in MNPS Airspace that cannot continue under its ATC clearance, and cannot obtain a revised one, but is able to maintain its assigned level above FL 410 should leave its assigned route or track by 90° to the right or left, then turn to acquire and maintain in either direction a track laterally separated by 30 nm from the assigned route while climbing or descending 1 000 feet. If the aircraft is at FL 410, climb 1000 ft or descend 500 ft. Below FL 410, climb or descend 500 feet.

So, if you need to divert en-route across the direction of the prevailing traffic flow, and if you cannot get prior ATC clearance, if you can maintain your assigned flight level you should:
- at FL 410, climb 1000 ft or descend 500 ft while turning towards the alternate.
- above FL 410, climb or descend 1000 ft while turning towards the alternate.

If you cannot maintain your assigned FL in MNPS airspace, and you can't contact ATC, descend and turn off track for 30 nm separation.

When leaving MNPS airspace, you should select your cleared Mach Number.

 VOR information in North Canadian airspace is referenced to True North.

If a revised clearance is not obtained:
- Establish communications with and alert nearby aircraft, broadcasting, at suitable intervals:
    - identification
    - flight level
    - position (including ATS route designator or track code)
    - intentions
  on the (VHF) frequency in use and on 121.5 MHz (or even on the inter-pilot frequency 123.45 MHz).
- Watch for conflicting traffic visually and with ACAS/TCAS (if equipped).
- Turn on all exterior lights.
- For deviations of less than 10 nm, remain at the level assigned by ATC.

OPERATIONAL PROCEDURES
Long Range Operations

For deviations of **greater than 10 nm**, when around 10 from track, initiate a level change. If deviating towards a Pole, descend 300 ft. If deviating toward the Equator, climb 300 ft (follow the tropopause).

ETOPS
Many NAT crossings are conducted under ETOPS rules, which are discussed elsewhere in the book. Enroute alternates must be named before dispatch, and flights monitored. The only suitable alternates are in The Azores, Bermuda, Greenland and Iceland, and they must be open, with the relevant facilities!

EASTERN N AMERICA WITH CARIBBEAN, S AMERICA & BERMUDA
This has a fixed track structure tied to NDB and VOR/DME navigation aids. You need long range systems when out of range of these, although this is not yet designated as MNPS airspace.

EUROPE TO CARIBBEAN AND SOUTH AMERICA
Along the Southern Atlantic. Occasionally, the optimum route for to these areas takes aircraft across the OTS in their early stages. Such flights should stay below the published levels until clear of the most Southerly track.

POLAR TRACK SYSTEM (PTS)
Polar flights should stay below the published OTS flight levels until clear of the most Northerly track.

There are 10 fixed tracks in Reykjavik CTA and 5 in Bodo OCA, which are continuations. They are not mandatory, but recommended for flights on the Europe/Alaska axis at FL 310-390. In the flight plan, you can use the abbreviation PTS plus the track identifier if you use the whole length of the track only, but the whole route must be detailed if you only use part. The last assigned transponder code should be kept for 30 minutes after entering the NAT region, using 2000 on leaving. To change levels, you must turn off the assigned track by 90° left or right, establish a 15 nm offset, then climb or descend as required. If you are above the NATS, you should offset 15 nm from the closest track, then descend as required.

Be aware of your performance, because ISA+ days are common and aircraft frequently fail to reach their assigned flight level. The fact that you are in far North latitudes does not mean that it is cooler! A good ploy is to flight plan for ISA +15 to cover yourself.

Separation
Separation minima for the NAT region are specified vertically, laterally or longitudinally.

VERTICAL
Vertical separation is obtained by requiring aircraft to operate at different flight levels or altitudes. In the same direction, under RVSM, flights must be 2000 feet apart, and 1000 feet apart in opposite directions.

While a single flight level is normally used, cruise climbs between two levels (or above one) may also be employed for efficiency reasons, in which case aircraft are considered to be occupying all levels in the clearance. Aircraft at cruising levels normally have priority over other aircraft desiring that level. When two or more aircraft are at the same cruising level, the preceding (leading) aircraft normally has priority.

The minimum separation between aircraft, airspace reservations, and between airspace reservations and other aircraft is:

- 2000 feet at or above FL 290 between a formation flight and any other aircraft, or
- 2000 feet at or above FL 290, or
- 1000 feet from FL 290 to FL 410 inclusive between RVSM aircraft, or
- 1000 feet below FL 290

Non-RVSM aircraft may be cleared to climb or descend through RVSM flight levels if they do so continuously through all levels. Aircraft must also be MNPS approved for this to apply within MNPS airspace.

Non-RVSM aircraft may also be granted exemptions to operate in RVSM airspace (formation flights* are non-RVSM). They shall be vertically separated from other traffic by the non-RVSM separation minimum of 2000 feet. Aircraft must also be MNPS approved for this to apply within MNPS airspace.

*Two RVSM approved aircraft with station-keeping equipment operating as a formation flight on the same route, at the same altitude with less than 4000 feet of longitudinal separation are considered to be one aircraft for the purpose of separation.

ATS units may temporarily apply increased vertical separation (such as with greater than moderate turbulence).

LATERAL
ICAO Doc 4444 (PANS/ATM) states in paragraph 5.4.1.1.1 that "lateral separation shall be applied so that the distance between those portions of the intended routes for which the aircraft are to be laterally separated is never less than an established distance to account for navigational inaccuracies plus a specified buffer."

Lateral separation exists between the segments on which aircraft are operating, independent of their location along those segments (which is a longitudinal consideration). That is, lateral separation is measured between the routes and segments along which two aircraft fly, not between the aircraft themselves.

3 lateral separation minima are published for the NAT region:

- 120 nm or 2°
- 90 nm or 1½°
- 60 nm or 1°, although this may reduce to 30 nm.

where the Earth's coordinate system is used to define tracks and effect separation. To bridge this gap between the formal specification and the real world (which is round), there are "gentle slope" rules that ensure that the actual separation never falls below distances which vary with latitude but never fall short of 50.5 nm.

Lateral separation on NAT tracks can now go right down to ½° of latitude (25 nm) between some waypoints, to create more tracks at higher altitudes, where fuel efficiency is better. Otherwise, most aircraft would be flying at less than their optimum altitudes. This is called *Reduced Lateral Separation Minima* (RLatSM).

OPERATIONAL PROCEDURES
Long Range Operations

LONGITUDINAL

Longitudinal separation for aircraft along same and/or intersecting tracks ensures that, throughout the period where lateral separation does not exist, they are separated by a time interval equal to or greater than:

- 60 minutes between moving airspace reservations, or
- 30 minutes between other than turbojet aircraft and any other aircraft, or
- 20 minutes between other than turbojet aircraft and any other aircraft in the WATRS area, or
- 15 minutes between turbojet aircraft, or
- 10 minutes between turbojet aircraft if the Mach Number Technique is applied in level, climbing or descending flight, under certain conditions

MACH NUMBER TECHNIQUE

When two or more turbojets operating along the same route at the same flight level maintain the same Mach number, they are more likely to maintain a constant time interval between each other than when using other methods.

Turbojets must keep to the Mach number approved by ATC and request their approval before making changes. If you need to make an immediate (temporary) change in the Mach number (e.g. due to turbulence), ATC must be notified as soon as possible.

You must ensure that any required corrections to the indicated Mach number are taken into account when complying with the true Mach number specified in the ATC clearance.

If you cannot maintain the last assigned Mach number during en-route climbs and descents, you must advise ATC at the time of the request.

 Since for practical purposes, the value of Mach 0.01 remains constant at a given temperature, the rate of closure between two aircraft operating at speeds differing by Mach 0.01 will be the same at high or low Mach numbers. One minute of flight at a low speed, however, produces fewer miles of additional separation than does the same minute of flight at a higher speed.

The potential for loss of separation is compounded by the fact that the slower aircraft takes longer to fly 600 miles and the closure will therefore act over a longer time.

POSITION REPORTS

Position reports are essential. They are done:

- At every waypoint you fly over, or 45 minutes after your last report, which ever is earlier.
- Whenever you wish to change speed or altitude.
- If the ETA for your inbound waypoint changes by more than ±3 minutes from the previous reported time.

Position reports must include:

- the reported position.
- the next reporting point and estimated time.
- the reporting point after that as per the cleared route.

If the ETA over the next reporting point is out by three minutes or more, a revised ETA must be transmitted as soon as possible to ATC. All times shall be expressed in UTC, giving both the hour and minutes.

"Avro 190, passed 48N 50W at 02:46Z, FL 360, Mach 0.81, estimating 48N 40W at 03:29Z, next is 51N 30 W."

VOICE CLEARANCE

Gander can be found on 128.450 (primary), or 135.450 (secondary) - their callsign is Gander Center. If they are not open, get the clearance from Gander Radio or Gander Domestic, in that order (i.e. the radar controller you are already talking to). ATC will not initiate communications - you must call them.

Coming Westbound, if you are at an airport West of 03°W you get your oceanic clearance on the ground, after the normal airways clearance. East of 03°W, you will get it passing 03°W.

This is what you put in the route section of the flight plan:

```
J509 YQY DCT COLOR/M080F370 NATW
DOLIP/N0490F390
```

In English: Taking airway J509 to Sydney VOR then direct to COLOR, after which a speed of Mach 0.8 will be used at FL 370 until reaching DOLIP, where the speed will be 490 knots at FL 390. Don't forget the Track Identification Number (TMI) in the remarks box (RMK/TMI079).

There is no special procedure for leaving the NAT, as you will just be handed over to the appropriate ATC, in this case Shannon control, who will assign a squawk and identify you. Position reports are not needed as this is a radar service.

To use the OCK2F arrival via BEDEK, use the available airways: UN523 CRK UL607 NUMPO Y3 BEDEK OCK2F.

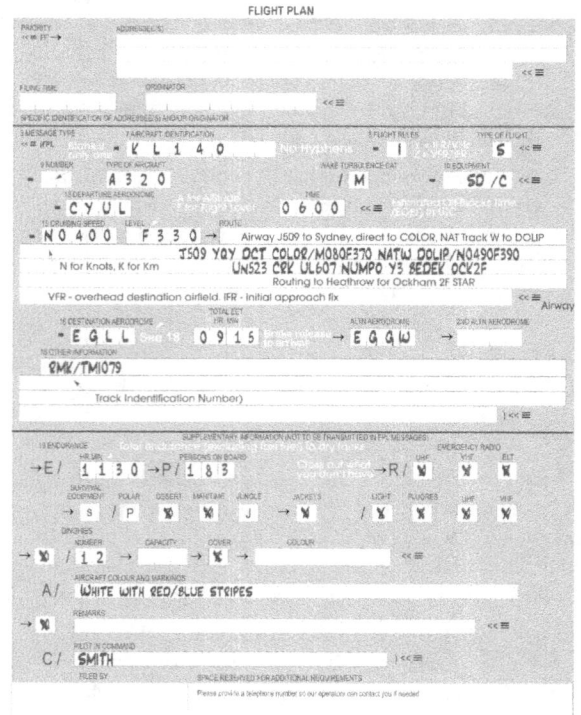

Other Routes In The NAT HLA

- **Blue Spruce Routes** are special routes for aircraft with only one serviceable LRNS. State approval for NAT HLA operations is required.

- Routes between Northern Europe and the Spain/Canaries/Lisbon FIRs (see *Tango Routes* below).

- Routes between the Azores and the Portuguese mainland and between the Azores and the Madeira Archipelago.

- Routes between Iceland and Constable Pynt on the east coast of Greenland and between Kook Islands on the West coast of Greenland and Canada.

- Special routes of short stage lengths where aircraft with normal short-range navigation equipment can meet the NAT HLA track-keeping criteria (G3 and G11). State approval for NAT HLA operations is required in order to fly along these routes.

TANGO ROUTES

Even though it means an extra 100-150 miles on the trip, many airlines choose to fly over the Atlantic West of France, Spain and Portugal to avoid their airspace and having to pay fees (especially when the French controllers are on strike!) There should be less delays as the airspace is quieter, but these routes become interesting to international operators, especially three very useful North-South routes within Shanwick's airspace, called The Three Sisters, which are permanent and go both ways:

- **Tango 9 LASNO-BEGAS**. The most popular, often full of holiday traffic between Northern Europe and the Canaries. You need an HF radio* (one is enough), plus an oceanic clearance**. You also need at least one LRNS and HLA Approval if you want to fly above FL285.

  *Required for Shanwick Airspace.

  **From Shanwick at least 30 minutes before you arrive at the boundary, or Santa Maria if you're going North on T16. 60 minutes is the best target time. Use Data-link (ACARS), Clearance delivery – 127.65 VHF, 123.95 VHF or HF (try 5598). Also relay on 123.45, or Sat Phone EGGX 423201 or EIAA 425002. Shanwick and Santa Maria are outside the IFPS zone, so copy flight plans to EGGXZOZX and LPPOZOZX, otherwise oceanic clearance will be delayed.

- **Tango 213 TAMEL-BERUX**. You need an HF radio (one is enough), plus an oceanic clearance. You also need two LRNS and HLA Approval if you want to fly above FL285.

- **Tango 16 OMOKO-NAVIX**. You need an HF radio (one is enough), plus an oceanic clearance. You also need two LRNS and HLA Approval if you want to fly above FL285.

You likely won't get the level that you want – either because the airway itself is busy, or because you're crossing East-West NAT Traffic. If the rest of your Flight Plan shows FL380, plan FL320 for most of the Tango portion – especially T9. If you get a low Flight Level for the Oceanic Route, check in again closer to the boundary and see if anything is available.

On entering Oceanic Airspace, make a full position report: Position and time /flight level/Next position and estimate for that point/Following position. However, don't make a full exit position report when you enter domestic airspace, just the callsign and "Approaching LASNO, FL370" (although Santa Maria likes one).

 Due to the risk of two aircraft using the same squawk leading to a mis-ident, Northbound traffic entering SOTA via T9, LASNO or T213, TAMEL should squawk 2000 at least 10 minutes prior to the Irish boundary.

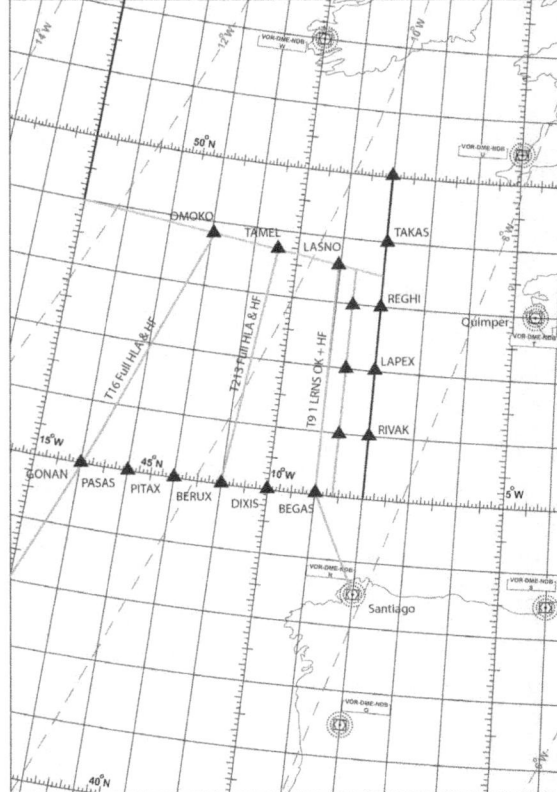

Because of the limited time spent in HLA airspace, on Tango 9, the change to the last assigned squawk to 2000 should be made Northbound 10 minutes after passing BEGAS and Southbound 10 minutes after passing LASNO. Otherwise, unless otherwise directed by ATC, pilots flying in NAT FIRs shall squawk Mode A/C 2000 continuously, except that the last assigned code should be kept for 30 minutes after entry into NAT airspace or leaving a radar service area.

© Phil Croucher, 2018

OPERATIONAL PROCEDURES
Long Range Operations

Flight Performance & Planning

The regulations (discussed below) require your aircraft to have adequate performance for any proposed flight, meaning, with regard to safety, its ability (in terms of engine power, at least, when one fails) to get off the ground in the first place, to maintain certain rates of climb against distance, and land, so you can avoid hard objects (obstacles), particularly when you can't see them. More commercially, based on the combined effects of thrust and drag, the term includes the ability to carry heavy loads for long distances at high speeds with the least fuel, which are often contradictory, and are more the subject of the *Flight Planning* section. The smaller the landing site, and the hotter and higher it is, the more thrust you need, and the lower the wing loading should be.

REGULATIONS & COMPLIANCE

There are two sets of regulations involving this subject:

- **Certification Standards**, which are set out in two documents, CS 23 for small aircraft, and CS 25 for big ones, based on similar FAA documents, called FAR23 and FAR 25 (CAR 523/525 in Canada).

    These are *airworthiness standards* that involve a Certificate of Airworthiness and minimum standards of construction and safety. They deal with what happens *when* an engine fails, as per takeoff speeds and distances.

- **Operating Regulations**, like *CAT.POL.A.100 & 105* (see *Operational Procedures*), that cover what happens *after* an engine fails with regard to not hitting anything on the way. These must be considered when establishing takeoff weight limits.

The above form the basis of a broad and uniform level of safety for performance purposes. Aircraft are *certificated* to an airworthiness standard and *operated* in a class (A, B or C), depending on their weight and the number of passengers carried.

Transport aircraft are less restricted operationally, because they tend to like landing in bad weather on contaminated runways. Light aircraft, on the other hand are more tightly controlled, as they have lower airworthiness requirements. This is why single-engined aeroplanes cannot do commercial air transport flights at night, or in IMC.

- **Class A** includes:
    - all multi-engined turbojet aeroplanes.
    - multi-engined turboprops with an MOPSC of more than 9 or that weigh more than 5,700 kg.

        Class A aeroplanes can suffer an engine failure (sometimes more than one) **at any time** and still have enough power to carry on or stop under control without damaging objects or people inside or outside. A forced landing should not be necessary. They can also operate from contaminated runways and with bits missing without compromising safety. In short, there is a **guarantee** that, if you follow the instructions on the tin, the required levels of safety will be achieved.

- **Class B** includes all propeller driven aeroplanes with an MOPSC of 9 or less which weigh 5700 kg or less (single- or multi-engined), for which there are no performance figures during the takeoff and initial climb, and late in the approach, so a (safe) forced landing *may* be necessary. A Class B aircraft that can get off a short runway in a strong headwind does not automatically enter Class A!

- **Class C** includes piston-engined aeroplanes with an MOPSC of more than 9 or which weigh more than 5700 kg (old stuff, like DC 3s).

If your aircraft cannot comply with the rules, perhaps due to design characteristics, an equivalent level of safety must be provided by the operator. Common sense mostly applies, in that the mass of an aeroplane at the start of the takeoff or, when in-flight replanning (from where the revised operational flight plan applies) must not be greater than the mass at which the above requirements can be complied with. Allowance may be made for reductions in mass as the flight proceeds, and for fuel jettisoning.

In addition, takeoff and landing masses shall not exceed the maxima in the flight manual, and distances required must not be more than those available, taking into account the pressure altitude and ambient temperature, the runway condition and the type of surface*, the slope in the direction of takeoff or landing, **up to 50%** of the reported headwind or **at least 150%** of the reported tailwind component, plus any loss of runway length due to alignment before takeoff.

*For performance purposes, a damp runway, other than a grass runway, may be regarded as dry.

The approved data in the flight manual must be used to comply with performance requirements, supplemented with other data as prescribed (this other data must be specified in the operations manual). However, account may be taken of any operational factors already in the flight manual to avoid duplication.

Adequate allowance must also be made for the effect of bank angle on operating speeds and flight path including the distance increments from increased operating speeds. That is, you need special requirements if you intend to bank or change track by more than 15°. Weather reports and/or forecasts must indicate

© Phil Croucher, 2018

that safe takeoffs and landings can be accomplished at the estimated times.

Finally, it is assumed that no limits will be exceeded, and that aeroplanes will use the most favourable runways, in still air, and those most likely to be assigned, considering the probable wind speeds and directions, ground handling characteristics and other conditions such as landing aids and terrain.

POWERPLANTS

For now, however, powerplant performance concerns:

- The **basic thrust available**, which is more or less constant for jets.

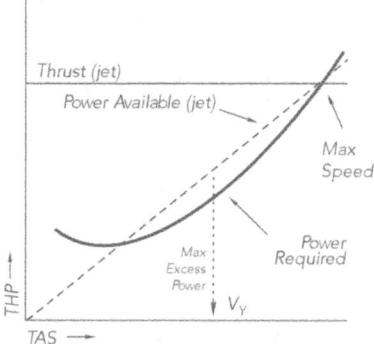

- The **horsepower available**, which is proportional to thrust multiplied by the velocity of flight. The excess power over that needed to overcome drag allows for climbing or accelerating (Thrust - Drag).
- **Specific Fuel Consumption** (SFC), or how many pounds of fuel might be used to produce a horsepower for an hour but, for jet engines, where the mass flow changes a lot with the environment, the thrust-specific SFC is a more useful figure which shows how much fuel you need to maintain unit thrust per hour.

To achieve the performance required, an aircraft must respond properly to the controls, and be able to recover from various disturbing influences, for which stability is important, as described in *Principles Of Flight*.

Otherwise, many accidents are performance-related, particularly those that happen during takeoff and landing, especially in hot air at high altitudes (an inversion at 1,000 feet could really ruin your day). As you are trying to get a large, heavy object into or out of a relatively small place at some speed, the point of performance calculations is to ensure that the space *required* is not more than the space *available*, taking account of an engine failure right when you don't want it. You must ensure, *before* it takes off, that an aircraft can do the *whole* of a planned flight safely, and the only thing you have any real control over is its weight (plus flaps, antiskid and thrust, etc. to a lesser extent, but weight reduction should be considered last).

The despatch weight is the most important factor because, if it is correctly determined, it will be unlikely* (i.e. a remote probability) that pilots will need to worry about such things when they are under pressure.

*Performance matters are based around probabilities:

Definition	Meaning	Value
Frequent (probable)	May occur many times (minor)	
Occasional	May occur sometimes (reasonably probable)	10^{-3}
Remote (improbable)	Unlikely but possible (major).	10^{-6}
Improbable (hazardous)	Very unlikely (extremely remote)	10^{-7}
Extremely Improbable	Virtually impossible (catastrophic)	10^{-9}

In other words, you don't just plan for the takeoff - you check out the whole route and the factor that is most limiting dictates your *Regulated Takeoff Mass* (RTOM). A Regulated Mass is the lowest of any mass that is limited for performance (and other) reasons and the structural maximum in the flight manual.

How heavy you can be is partly down to speed - the faster you go, the more lift you create and the more payload you can take, but various factors work against this, such as the length of the runway, as described below. Once you know what the weight of the aircraft should be, you can work out all the relevant speeds.

For performance reasons, flights are split into four phases:

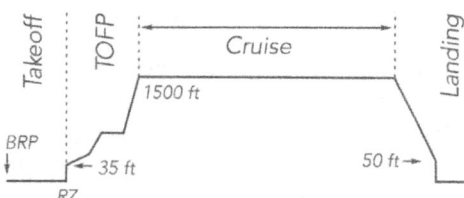

- **Takeoff**, which runs from the brake release point to a *screen height* of 35 (jets under CS 25) or 50 feet (light twins under CS 23). *Reference Zero* is the horizontal plane on the ground underneath the screen height at the end of the Takeoff Distance Required (OE) from which all distance measurements are taken. Takeoff is the most complex aspect of performance, and both the all-engines operating (AEO) and one-engine inoperative situations must be considered. This is because the aircraft is close to the ground and, on takeoff, has maximum fuel on board and the engines are operating at high thrust levels.
- **Takeoff Flight Path**, which starts at the screen height and ends at 1,500 feet, over 4 segments.
- **Enroute**, from 1,500 feet above the departure point to 1,500 or 1,000 feet above the destination.
- **Landing**, from 1500 or 1,000 ft to a complete stop. There is also lots of kinetic energy here, and using the brakes is still the main way of stopping (helped by flaps, etc.) As kinetic energy depends on V^2, even a small reduction in landing speed will decrease the energy absorbed by the brakes.

Of course, in the old days (when the trains ran on time), having enough engines to lift the load was all that mattered and no priority was given to reserves of power. Now if an engine fails you must be able to either fly away (keeping above all obstacles) or stop without damaging people or property (and the machine).

Trivia: The screen is based on the height of a double decker bus, as used in the original trials at Croydon.

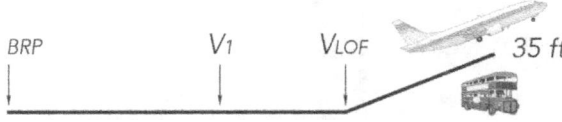

 The other engines are not necessarily spares, in the sense that you can carry on normally. In a light twin, you don't lose 50% of your climb capability if an engine fails, but more like 70 or even 90%! The whole point of having two engines is to carry more traffic load. Things are better than before, certainly, but safety is still secondary, as you will not get far on the other engine. Absolute safety would mean not flying at all, so a level of risk management (see *Human Factors*) is involved to maximise it, using probabilities.

It is your responsibility to decide whether or not a safe takeoff (and landing) can be made under the prevailing conditions, although the *operator* must also ensure that the performance claimed in the flight manual can be achieved. There will be a series of graphs in the Performance section showing you how well the machine will behave under various conditions.

The manufacturer only supplies data in the form of such tables and graphs, which must be matched with the operating environment and declared distances from the aerodrome operator. Declared distances have to be declared as such for performance purposes in the AIP or a NOTAM under the criteria for Licensing of Aerodromes.

Declared Distances

In static or unaccelerated flight, $F = ma = 0$. This is more or less assumed even in the climb or descent, because the cosine of the angles involved is very close to 1. During takeoff and landing, however, you have to cope with acceleration and deceleration. As acceleration comes from dividing Mass by Thrust, during takeoff, the rate of acceleration will decrease because there is a reduction in excess thrust (on all types). The end result is that, for example, a 10% increase in takeoff speed increases the TOR by more than the roughly 20% you would get if acceleration were constant. This is why flaps, etc., are used to keep takeoff (and landing) speeds as low as possible. Therefore, an increase in mass which reduces the acceleration and increases the takeoff speed (due to the increased lift requirement) will increase the TODR to the point where it exceeds the TODA. The **Field Length Limited Takeoff Mass** (FLLTOM) is the heaviest an aircraft can be for a given runway length.

The following are "declared" by an airport so that you have the required information for your flight planning:

- The **TORA** extends from the brake release point to the nearest point in the direction of takeoff where the surface cannot support the aircraft. Usually, the runway, less a bit for lining up.

- The **ASDA** (*Accelerate-Stop Distance Available*) is the distance from the brake release point to the nearest point in the direction of takeoff where the aircraft cannot roll over the surface and stop. Accelerate-stop (also called a *Rejected Takeoff*, or RTO) arises where an aircraft is accelerated from zero speed to where the pilot decides to abort the takeoff and stop on the runway using all available deceleration devices, which may include the brakes, spoilers, airbrakes or thrust reversers.

    This used to be called the *Emergency Distance Available*, and is TORA + Stopway. The Stopway is an area that can support the ground roll of an aircraft after an aborted takeoff, but not during takeoff (or landing!) It is of no less width than the associated runway and is marked with yellow chevrons. The greater the ASDA, the higher the speed you can accelerate to before reaching V_1.

- The **TODA** consists of the TORA + the clearway or 150% of TORA, whichever is less.

With no clearway or stopway, the above will all normally be equal to the runway length. When ASDA equals TODA (i.e. the stopway and clearway are the same size or not there anyway), you have a *balanced field*.

The distance needed to get to the screen height is the *Take-off Distance Required*, which should not be more than the TODA*. Landing Distance Available must similarly not be less than Landing Distance Required.

*Factors must be applied to all distances to provide a safety margin. For example, unless the Flight Manual states otherwise, for turboprops, the LDR can only be 70% of distance available, with no allowance for wet runways (factor by 1.43). Turbojets can only plan to use 60% of the landing distance available. In other words, the distance required is factored by 1.67.

For all aircraft, LDR must be increased by 15% if the runway is expected to be wet, unless the flight manual contains specific data - just multiply the dry graph result by 1.15. For a takeoff on a wet runway, CS 25.113 allows the screen height to be reduced to 15 feet. The use of reverse thrust to determine the ASD is allowed under CS 25.109. You can obtain higher takeoff weights off a wet runway, but CAT.POL.A.205 (b)(5) states that you can only use the mass permitted for a dry runway.

The screen height for landing is 50 feet, or 35 feet if the approach is steep.

AIRCRAFT WEIGHT

The factors to be considered when working out the Regulated Takeoff Mass include:

- The **maximum structural weights**, which are in the flight manual, and which may be modified to suit the conditions of the day, as with temperature and altitude (density). In this respect, we must look at the MTOM, MZFM and MLM and use the most limiting one (you should not arrive heavier than the landing mass, so a lot depends on how far away your destination is and how much fuel you use to get there. If it's the first destination, the prudent pilot would also check out the gradient on the way out after an abandoned landing).

- The **length of the runway**, or **Field Length Limited TOM**, based on declared distances in the AIP for the departure, destination and alternate aerodromes, including slope. These may be become *effective* lengths from various losses, including those from lining up, but the runway may also be contaminated, or sloping (or out of wind). You need enough room to stop if you lose an engine before you reach a certain speed, and to carry on if it happens at, or after that. If your **brakes** or **tyres** cannot cope with the speeds involved, the weight of the aircraft must be reduced until they can.

- **Climb gradients** - the basic ability to comply with the minimum requirements for an aerodrome are usually restricted by the second segment of the OEI takeoff climb path. This limits the climb-limited TOW (CLTOW), which was once known as the Weight-Altitude-Temperature (WAT) limit. You may also have to comply with noise limits. **Departure and approach charts assume that all engines are operating.** As this requirement must be met for all takeoffs, it is nothing to do with....

- **Obstacle clearance.** This should be based on OEI values. Although the takeoff flight path ends at 1,500 feet above the airfield elevation, in mountains you may have to go much higher than that (a twin-engined aircraft needs to achieve a gross gradient of 2.4% in the second segment of the takeoff flight path, but an obstacle may need more, for which you will have to reduce the takeoff weight). You may even have to avoid an obstacle over 25 miles away if you are hot and high! Commercially available charts are not perfect, so airlines tend to have large operations departments that can list relevant obstacles for the airports they are involved in (see the AIP), but charter pilots don't have that luxury.

- **Enroute Capability** (drift down, or how much distance you travel over land as you lose height).

- **Approach & Landing Climb**, for go-arounds, sometimes to do with returning in an emergency, but mainly for manoeuvrability.

The chart below does not mention drift down considerations in the cruise, which is a routing consideration, or noise abatement, which is not strictly a performance issue anyway.

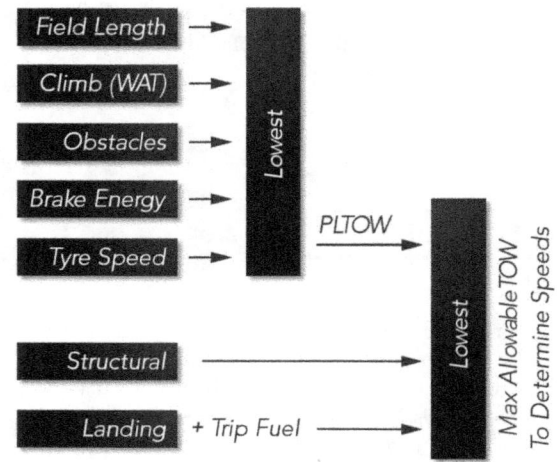

TYPES OF PERFORMANCE

Individual machines perform differently due to such variables as the age of the airframe and its engines, the standard of maintenance, or crew skill and experience, which means that what you can do on one day may not be possible at another time. The original testing is done with new aircraft and experienced test pilots, to provide **measured performance**, which is the average performance of an aeroplane (or a group of aeroplanes) tested by acceptable methods under specified conditions.

The figures are then analysed statistically to provide **gross performance** graphs, which are also known as *unfactored*. Gross performance figures are an estimated fleet average, where subsequent machines off the production line are assumed to be the same as the first. It is the standard that could be expected from an average pilot* flying an average aircraft under flight manual conditions. However, as gross performance is an average, there is a fair chance that it will *not* be obtained for 50% of the time, so you need a way of making sure that you can consistently get the performance you need or, put another way, a standard below which there is only a **remote chance** (10^{-6}) that a fleet aircraft will fail, if it is operated within its limitations.

*OK, the worst pilot in the company.

There is usually not enough data to determine the complete gross path, as the emphasis is on **net** (or *factored*) **performance**, which is lower due to a fudge factor, so there is a safety margin for tired engines or pilots, or operational contingencies that cannot reasonably be foreseen.

A safety margin is required if there is at least a remote probability of an untoward event - the greater the probability, the greater the margin must be. However, that for landing (67% for a turbojet) is much greater than it is for takeoff (15%) because you need to make sure that you can get down on the ground again, and there are too many variables involved - takeoffs are much more predictable.

The *Net Takeoff Flight Path*, for example (see later), is the actual or Gross Takeoff Flight Path decreased by a margin of 0.8% for twin-engined aircraft, 0.9% for 3-engined aircraft and 1% for 4-engined ones.

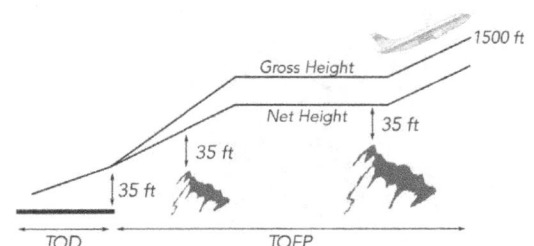

 Net performance is the legal minimum for Commercial Air Transport operations, and is what is in the flight manual. It means less weight!

FACTORS INVOLVED

Before getting into detail, it's worth looking at a couple of rules of thumb from NATS AIC 127/2006 (Pink 116):

Variable	T/O Distance	Factor
Weight	20% increase per 10% increase of weight	× 1.2
PA	10% increase per 1 000 ft above 0 ft pressure altitude	× 1.1
Ambient Temperature	10% increase per 10°C above +15°C	× 1.1
Tailwind	20% increase for tailwind component of 10% V_{LOF}	× 1.2
Uphill Slope	10% per 2% of uphill slope	× 1.1
Dry Grass	20% when under 8 inches	× 1.2
Wet Grass	30% when under 8 inches	× 1.3
R/W Surface Snow	25% for soft ground or snow coverage	× 1.25
Safety Increment	33% of TODA safety factorisation	× 1.33

Variable	Landing Distance	Factor
Weight	10% increase per 10% increase of weight	x 1.1
PA	5% increase per 1 000 ft above 0 ft pressure altitude	x 1.05
Ambient Temperature	10% increase per 10°C above +15°C	x 1.1
Tailwind	20% increase for tailwind component of 10% V_{REF}	x 1.2
Downhill Slope	10% per 2% of downhill slope	x 1.1
Dry Grass	15% when under 8 inches	x 1.15
Wet Grass	35% when under 8 inches	x 1.35
R/W Surface Snow	25% for soft ground or snow coverage	x 1.25
Safety Increment	43% of LDA safety factorization	x 1.33

Pressure Altitude

An increase in altitude means a reduction in temperature, pressure and air density. This leads to a higher TAS for a required IAS, which increases the takeoff run.

Pressure altitude is the starting point for any performance calculations. It is taken to be the altitude that is shown with 1013 hPa (or 29.92") set on the altimeter - if you set 1013 on the subscale and the needles read 6,000 feet, the PA *of the aircraft* is 6,000 feet. If the sea level pressure is less than standard, the air is less compressed, and your engine (and wings) think they are at a higher altitude and will not perform so well. Thus, when the sea level pressure is *less* than it should be, you are at a *higher* pressure altitude, or the equivalent of a greater height (a high pressure altitude means a higher *altitude* rather than higher *pressure*).

All aeroplane performance graphs are based on pressure altitude. To use them effectively (discussed later), you must find the Pressure Altitude you are really at then modify it for temperature by finding the..........

Density Altitude

This is also covered in *Meteorology* but, for performance purposes, particularly for piston engines, if the air is hot before it goes into the engine, the combustion process is much less efficient. In a turbine, you can get near the temperature limits of the engine. Air density affects Lift, Thrust, fuel flow and speed conversions.

Normally, the air density will reduce by 3% between sea level and 1,000 feet due to pressure changes, and increase by 0.66% due to temperature changes, so the overall result is that air density will reduce by 2.34%.

Density Altitude cannot be measured directly, but you can find pressure altitude with your altimeter and the OAT with the thermometer, and calculate it with this formula:

```
DA = PA ± (118.8 x ISA Dev)
```

but multiplying the ISA deviation by 120 is usually good enough. In simple terms, for every degree below ISA, subtract 120 feet. The effects are as valid at sea level as they are in mountains when temperatures are high - for example, 90° (F) at sea level is really 1,900 feet as far as your machine is concerned. In extreme circumstances, you may have to restrict your flying to early morning or late afternoon.

Anyhow, the idea is that the more the density of the air decreases, the higher your aircraft thinks it is, and the less efficiently your engine and propellers will perform. As mentioned, variations in air density can arise from temperature, pressure and humidity.

In the lift formula, you will see that the lift from an aerofoil is directly dependent on air density, as is drag.

$$L = C_L (\tfrac{1}{2}\rho V^2) S$$

If the density reduces, the angle of attack must increase to compensate, which means there is less surplus available. In the engine, the power margin is reduced.

The chart below is a typical Density Altitude chart which compares Pressure Altitude against temperature:

°F/C	60/15.6	70/21.1	80/26.7
1000	1300	2000	2700
2000'	2350	3100	3800
3000'	3600	4300	,5000
4000'	4650	5600	6300
5000'	6350	6900	7600
6000'	7400	8100	8800
7000'	8600	9300	1000
8000'	9700	10400	11100
9000'	11000	11600	12400
10000'	12250	13000	13600

It shows that, at 6,000 feet and 21°C, for example, you should be thinking in terms of 8,100 feet. On a 42°C day in Dubai, at sea level, the density altitude is 4,100 feet.

However, piston engines work on a fixed volume, and are affected only by density altitude. Turbine engines, being thermodynamic, depend on pressure altitude and air temperature **as separate items**. 5,000 ft DA can come from either 9,000 feet with -40°C or 2,000 feet and +40°C, but the power available in each case (from a turbine) will be wildly different.

To find DA on the flight computer, set the aerodrome elevation or Pressure Altitude against the temperature in the *airspeed* window.

In the picture, the temperature is -20°C at 10,000 feet P.A. The Density Altitude is 8,000!

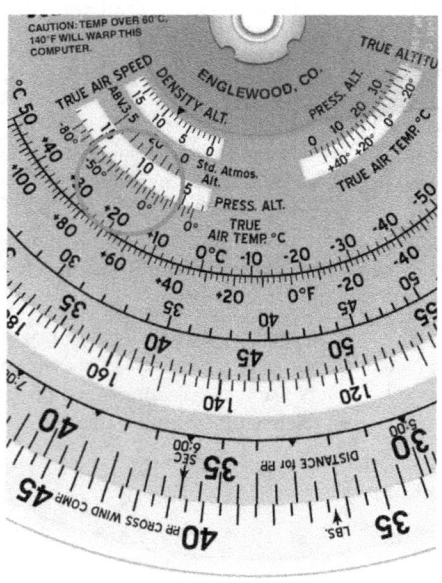

This is the sort of graph you might see in a flight manual:

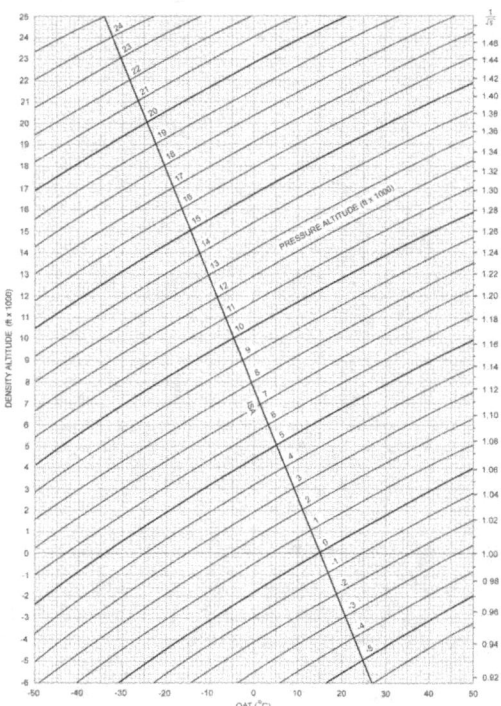

ALTITUDE

Air density drops off by 0.002 lbs per cubic foot (i.e. 2½%) for every 1000 feet in the lower atmosphere.

HUMIDITY

Adding water vapour to air makes it less dense because the molecular weight is lower (dry air is 29 - water vapour is 18). On cold days, humidity is less of a problem because cold air holds less vapour. A relative humidity of 90% at 70°F means twice as much than at 50°F. Fortunately, jet engines are not affected much by humidity as most of the air that goes through them (80% or so) is for cooling.

TEMPERATURE

As heat expands air, it becomes thinner. Thinner air is less dense (*Boyles law*). On the surface, an increase in temperature will decrease density and increase volume, with pressure remaining constant. At altitude, however, pressure reduces more than temperature does, and produces an apparent contradiction, where temperature will decrease from the expansion.

PRESSURE

Air density reduces with atmospheric pressure (*Charles law*). When you compress air, its density increases.

Runway Length

Getting the wheels off the runway is only part of the story. You must also be at a certain height (35 feet) at the end of the *Takeoff Distance Required* (TODR), which must not exceed the *Takeoff Run Available* (e.g. the runway) + the *Clearway*, which is a virtual runway at the end that is unsuitable to run on, but still clear of obstacles (above a 1.25% plane), so you can fly over it and include it in your calculations.

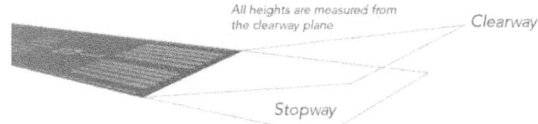

As it is air-based, you can fly over the sea, and its length is limited by the first non-frangible obstacle*, or a frangible one that is more than 0.9 m above the ground. In any case, the clearway may not be longer than 50% of the runway (TORA). It must be at least 150 m (500 feet wide), or 75 m (250 feet) either side of the centreline. *The clearway plane is regarded as the takeoff surface, and is used to determine the accountability of obstacles within the area.* That is, all heights are measured from it.

*A frangible obstacle is one that will distort or break so as to create a minimal hazard.

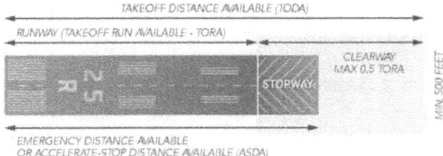

LOSSES DUE TO LINING UP

Unless you can line up on the runway having taxied straight in from over the threshold, you will lose some of the available length when entering it and lining up from an intersection, or even performing a 180° turn having backtracked. Although the FAA do not require it, EASA rules (CAT.POL.A.205(c)(6)) require any runway lost when lining up to be taken into account.

For example, a 737-800 needing a 90° turn to line up from the holding point loses 10.8 m from the TODA and 26.4 m from the ASDA, depending on its geometry and access to the runway.

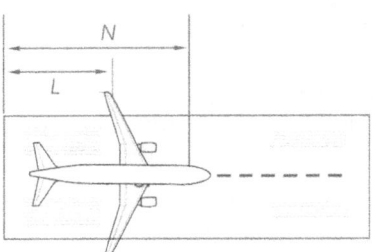

The "runway available" is actually the overall length less the distance to the main gear, which is where the distance to reach screen height is measured from. The ASD adjustment is based on the initial distance from the beginning of the runway to the nose gear. Two distances must be considered:

- The minimum distance of the main wheels from the start of the runway for determining TODA and TORA (*L* above).

- The minimum distance of the most forward wheel(s) from the start of the runway for determining the ASDA (*N* above).

BALANCED FIELD LENGTH

If an engine on a multi-engined aircraft fails early in the takeoff, there should be enough space to slam on the brakes and come to a stop on the runway. If the engine fails at a late stage, you should have enough speed to stagger into the air. Somewhere in the middle, the decision is not so clear cut, so a speed called V_1 is calculated before flight which is discussed more fully under *V-Speeds*, later. It is represented on the PFD by the green 1 in the picture. In simple terms, if an engine 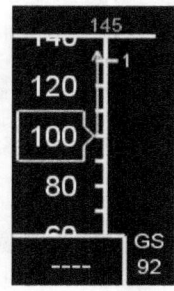 fails below this speed, the aircraft is certified as being able to stop within the ASDA. At or above it, the aircraft is certified to reach the screen height within the calculated distance. V_1 is *not* a decision speed, as described in many books, but an *action speed* - the first point of doing something about the situation (the first braking action). At V_1, you are committed to taking off.

 It is important to use the proper actions to retain the safety margins - there should be no delay in applying the brakes and using the airbrakes. High speed Rejected Takeoffs (RTOs) are a leading cause of accidents. The small margin allowed for pilot reaction time is *not* extra time that allows a reject above V_1.

Normal category aircraft (CS 23) may not be able to continue takeoff after V_1, so plan to reject up to (and often beyond) V_R. Put another way, for aircraft that are not certified for engine out climbs, the continued takeoff decision is normally made at V_R.

A *Balanced Field Length* exists where the distance required (from V_1) to stop is the same as that required to get to takeoff speed.

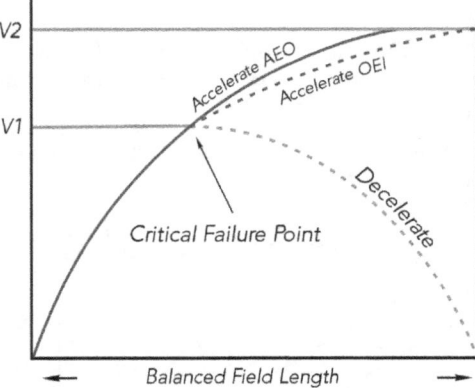

If the engine fails, the same space is available to either come to a stop or carry on to V_2 and the screen height*. Although this allows for simpler calculations, it may not be the best way to operate because unbalanced fields allow takeoff weights to be higher than the runway will support, which is actually more useful to airliners than small jets, as only major airports have clearways, and long runways make them redundant anyway.

*The speed at screen height is usually equal to the minimum velocity plus a safety factor. V_R is then set so it is reached at the screen height if an engine fails. Because engine failure is not accounted for below 300 feet in Class B operations, V_{EF}, V_1 &

FLIGHT PERFORMANCE & PLANNING
Factors Involved

V_2 do not apply, except for commuter aircraft. V_2 provides the best angle of climb for the weight.

When the runway available is much greater than the balanced field, and V_1 is significantly less than V_2, you may be forced to take off if an emergency happens after V_1, even though you have lots of runway left. You can increase V_1 markedly in this case, even up to the rotation speed and, if anything happens up to V_R you can abort for any emergency.

Changing the value of V_1 will change the takeoff distance (required) or the ASDR, and may require more runway. For example, reducing V_1 will obviously reduce the ASDR, because you shorten the distance required to get to V_1, and the distance required to stop (you are slower), but the TODR gets longer because the acceleration to V_2 within the TODA must be done without an engine and you have increased the difference between the two speeds, so you need more distance to cover it.

Put another way, reducing V_1 increases the part of the takeoff that must be done at a reduced rate of acceleration, so the TODR is increased. If you increase the V_1, on the other hand, the ASD will increase and the TODN-1 and TORN-1 (OEI) will be reduced (see picture below). This is because the AEO acceleration phase is longer if V_1 is higher so, if an engine fails at V_{EF} (i.e. with the worst timing) you can achieve the same V_2 at 35 feet in a shorter distance. Thus, you can obtain a balanced field just by changing the V_1.

TODN and TORN, on the other hand, are independent of V_1 as there is no engine failure, and no effect on the acceleration phase or the distance needed to reach 35 feet.

In fact, for a given takeoff weight, any increase in V_1 increases ASDN-1 (OEI) *and* ASDN (AEO). The acceleration segment from the BRP to V_1 is also longer, as is the deceleration segment from V_1 to the complete stop, and the 2-second segment at constant V_1.

The picture below shows the takeoff/rejected takeoff distances as a function of V_1, and that a minimum distance is achieved at a particular V_1 (point D).

This is called *Balanced V_1*, and the corresponding distance is the *Balanced Field*.

For a given runway (with a fixed ASDA and TODA), the V_1 value depends on the weight of the aircraft. Equally, for a given takeoff weight, ASDR and TODR are influenced by the chosen V_1. The maximum takeoff weight will be achieved when the V_1 corresponds to an equal ASDR & TODR (it will also be maximum when TODR = TODA).

The Accelerate/Stop Distance Analysis below shows the safe area that V_1 must be within for a given FLLTOM:

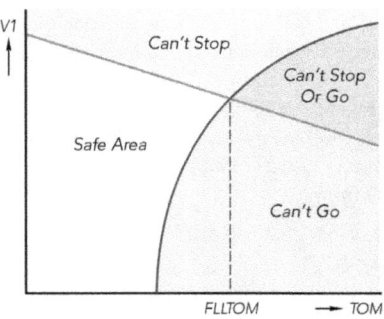

The red line shows the relationship between TOW and V_1 for a given ASDA, for a discontinued takeoff. To limit the energy required when you make the decision to stop, a high takeoff weight requires a low V_1, so you can stop within the ASDA.

The blue line shows what happens if you decide to carry on with the takeoff. To limit the OEI acceleration between V_1 and V_2, a higher takeoff weight requires a higher V_1 so that V_2 can be reached at the screen height.

Because of the dangers of stopping in a hurry, and the potential damage to the undercarriage, V_1 can often be reduced, as it is often safer to carry on than to stop.

As mentioned, for a given takeoff weight, an increase in V_1 reduces TOD_{N-1} and TOR_{N-1} (OEI), and increases ASD, but there is no effect on TOD_N and TOR_N (AEO).

For a given runway, therefore, there will be an increase in the OEI MTOW, and a reduction when it comes to the ASD, but there will be no effect on the AEO MTOW.

The graph below shows the runway-limited accelerate-go/stop takeoff weights as a function of V_1. If the runway is longer than the balanced field length, a range of V_1 speeds is available, as it is any time the actual TOW is less than the FLLTOW.

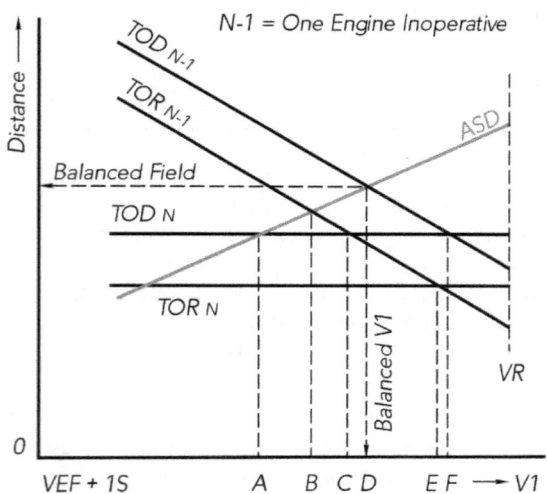

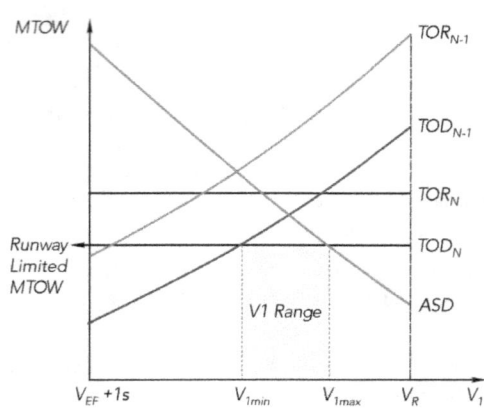

Put another way, a maximum TOW can be achieved within a range of V_1 speeds, or a range exists when the actual TOM is less than the OEI FLL TOM either when:

- the OEI FLL TOM is less than the AEO FLL TOM, and therefore limiting, or
- the AEO FLL TOM is limiting, in which case a range exists at the limiting TOM and lower masses.

In either case a higher V_1 than normal can be selected within the range available without changing FLLTOM. The OEI FLLTOM is TODA and ASDA limited, whereas the AEO FLLTOM is only TODA limited.

If a V_1 closer to the upper limit of the permissible range is selected and the engine is assumed to fail at V_1 (so the takeoff is continued), the TODR decreases because the speed range required to be accelerated through to reach V_R and ultimately V_2 without an engine is reduced. In theory, the TODA limited TOM could be increased in these circumstances. Selecting a higher V_1 will affect the stopping distance so, theoretically, the ASDA-limited TOM would reduce.

If the clearway is greater than the stopway, V_1 must be lowered, because the machine must still be able to stop within the unchanged ASDA. Conversely, if the stopway exceeds the clearway, V_1 needs to be increased, because you still need to get to V_2 within the unchanged TODA.

If you have a reduced *stopping* capability, you need a lower V_1. If you have a reduced *acceleration* capability, you need a higher V_1.

Altitude & Temperature

The higher you are, the less dense the air is and the less able are the wings and engines to "bite" into it, thus requiring more power and longer take-off runs to get airborne. Humidity has a similar effect, but it is usually allowed for in the graphs (it doesn't affect jets much anyway as most of the air going through the engine is used for cooling). TODR will increase by around 10% for each 1,000-foot increase in aerodrome PA above 0 feet (factor by 1.1) and 10% per 10°C increase in temperature above +15°C (factor by 1.1). LDR increases by about 5% for each 1,000-foot increase in aerodrome PA above 0 feet (1.05) and 10°C increase per 10°C above +15°C (factor by 1.1).

Aircraft Weight

Greater mass means slower acceleration or deceleration and longer distances. TODR will increase by about 20% for each 10% increase in weight and LDR by around 10% per 10% increase in weight (factor by 1.2 and 1.1).

Aircraft Configuration

Using flaps will reduce the ground roll during the takeoff, but also the still air climb gradient due to the increase in profile drag. In addition, the increased lift will decrease the efficiency of the brakes by reducing the weight on the wheels, and they just about cancel each other out, particularly with Airbus machines. Bleed air from the engine used for air conditioning or anti-ice also reduces the thrust available. Any contamination increases drag and weight while decreasing lift.

ENGINE FAILURE
This is rumoured to cause a drastic reduction in thrust.

POWER SETTINGS
If you are not using the maximum takeoff weight, you won't necessarily need to use full power for the takeoff*, which saves wear and tear on the engines (particularly at the turbine inlet). The technique can only be used when the available distance "greatly exceeds" that required. In any case, the maximum reduction is 25%.

*Noise abatement procedures also involve reduced thrust.

There are two ways of obtaining reduced thrust (assuming your weight is low enough to permit its use), *derating* and the *assumed temperature* method.

- **Derating** is just like using a less powerful engine, with each lowered thrust level having its own set of performance charts in the flight manual, and lower speeds, such as V_{MCG}. Treat the derate level as a new engine whose limits should not be exceeded.
- The **Assumed Temperature Method** uses a temperature that meets all of the takeoff performance requirements for the expected weight for a given runway (essentially, a red line is drawn across the graph for the worst situation). You simply put a higher figure into the FMS than the ambient temperature. One example would be taking off from Dubai in Winter, but programming the FMS with a temperature more suited to Summer.

CONTAMINATION
This is anything on the aircraft skin which should not be there, such as ice, snow, dirt, insects, birds, grease, deicing fluid, etc. The effects are increased weight and drag (skin friction), reduced lift, and higher stall speeds.

Runway Slope (Gradient)

Going uphill when taking off delays acceleration and increases the distance before V_{LOF} is reached.

👍 **Rule Of Thumb:** TODR increases by around 10% for each 2% of uphill slope, and *vice versa* (factor by 1.1). ICAO standards recommend a maximum slope of 2%. In the graphs, slopes are factored up to ± 2%.

When landing, an uphill slope aids stopping, thereby reducing LDR (any gains from landing upslope or taking off downslope should not be used for planning). Runway slopes are expressed like climb gradients, being either positive (uphill) or negative (downhill). Another way to look at them is the difference in elevations at either end of the runway, divided by the length, multiplied by 100. If the slope is unknown it can be calculated by taking the altimeter setting at each end of the runway and finding the height difference.

Tip: Compare the Touch Down Zone Elevation with the airfield elevation from the approach plate.

A couple of things to watch for with slopes:

- If the slope is over one part of the runway (say the first 400 m), the takeoff roll will be even longer.

- Upslope ahead causes a visual illusion, leading to a higher than normal nose attitude on rotation, which increases the angle of attack and drag, and reduces acceleration.

Surface Winds

Headwinds will reduce the distances required and improve the flight path after takeoff. Tailwinds have reverse effects and crosswinds may even exceed the ability of the tyres to grip the runway. Aside from handling, crosswinds may also increase the TODR if you need to use the brakes to keep you straight. Forecast winds should be factored by **up to 50%** for a headwind and **at least 150%** for a tailwind. TODR and LDR will increase by 20% for each tailwind component of 10% of the lift-off and landing speed (factor by 1.2). The flight manual will state maximum crosswinds (try *Limitations*).

Surface

A dry, hard (paved) surface provides the best braking coefficient. Wet grass means an increased TODR. This has already been covered in *Operations*.

The Takeoff

Taking off is the transition from being a ground-based vehicle to a flight-based one, and the process should be as short as possible, so the distance used is very important, given that there are additional elements trying to slow you down (on top of the normal drag) in the shape of the friction from the tyres on the runway (wheel drag) and any slope. The distance you need to do this is the *Takeoff Distance Required (TODR)*, which could be made smaller if you can reduce the stall speed (with flaps, etc.)

The takeoff begins at the brake release point (BRP) and ends when the lowest point of the aircraft clears a screen height of 35 feet (50 for Class B aircraft). It has a ground-based element and an airborne bit (the flare distance, from rotation) up to the screen height. Both of them together represent the Takeoff Distance.

The ground roll is divided into segments that are defined by velocities:

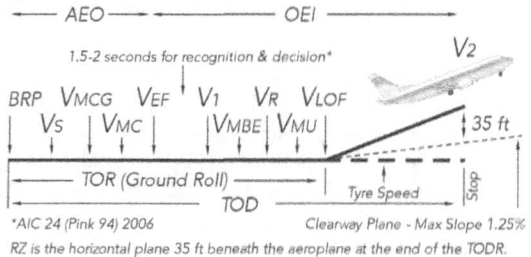

The speeds shown are based on IAS or CAS, depending on whether an Air Data Computer is being used, in which case any errors are corrected automatically.

Thrust is the only positive accelerating force. In the range of speeds used for takeoff, it will decrease initially due to intake momentum drag (where the acceleration across the engine reduces). It will then steady, then decrease a little more, even though ram air effect is building up. The overall effect is that, at around M 0.4, the ram effect recovers the thrust loss and overcomes intake momentum drag, to restore the static thrust value. On this basis, the thrust is considered to be constant. For a low bypass engine, the ram effect will increase mass flow (and thrust) above about 250 kts.

As the weight of the aircraft is taken up by the wings, there is a reduction in wheel drag, but also an increase in parasite and induced drag, which is highest just after rotation and lift off (it is as high just before landing).

With thrust reducing slightly during the takeoff roll, the result is that the net acceleration force reduces, especially at the rotation point, and so does the *rate* of acceleration. The rotation speed should therefore be as low as possible, because a small increase in it requires a disproportionate amount of runway to be made available. V_R, or the rotation speed, is the point when back pressure is applied to the control column to raise the nosewheel at around 3° per second*, but the rest of the aircraft does not follow until Liftoff speed (V_{LOF}).

*The same V_R is used whether an engine fails or not.

However, V_R must be greater than the stalling speed, for obvious reasons, and above V_{MCA} (below) so you can keep the thing under control once airborne with an engine out. BUT - the 5° of bank permitted for V_{MC} cannot be applied at V_{LOF}, which is *higher* than V_R, and is *after* it.

Anyhow, from the Brake Release Point, the aircraft accelerates past V_{MCG}, or the minimum velocity at which the vertical fin and the rudder (by themselves) can generate enough aerodynamic force to steer the aircraft (within 30 feet of the centreline) if an engine fails. In the air, a slightly higher speed is needed, namely V_{MC}, which is reached while the aircraft is on the ground. Its position in the diagram above depends on the aircraft.

The rotation angle of attack should naturally not exceed the stalling angle of attack, or the angle at which the tail will hit the ground. All Airbus aircraft are geometrically limited this way.

If there is a problem with ground clearance, the aircraft must continue the ground roll until reaching the *Minimum Unstick Speed* or V_{MU} (for safety, the angle of attack after rotation is slightly less than the maximum allowed for tail clearance). The value of V_{MU} is not in flight manuals.

Since V_{LOF} is not normally calculated, V_R is taken as being at least 1.05 V_{MC} (i.e. 5% above) to allow for the difference (see also *V-Speeds*, below). The OEI V_{LOF} is lower than the AEO version.

Tyres fitted to large aircraft are subject to high centrifugal forces at high speed (even more so at high altitudes), and are usually rated to 210 or 225 mph. This affects V_R indirectly, as the MTOM becomes the limiting factor, which will affect V_R in turn. However, you have to make some calculations because the tyres are running at a true groundspeed (they are literally on the ground) and V_R is an airspeed, and therefore affected by pressure altitude and temperature. The maximum tyre speed is the upper limit of the liftoff speed.

V_{EF} is the speed at which the critical engine is assumed to fail. It may not be less than V_{MCG}. The speed at which the first braking action must be applied, V_1, may not be less than V_{MCG}*, and the speed gained between the critical engine failure and the reaction to it. It may also not be higher than V_R and V_{MBE} (the maximum value of V_1).

*The minimum value of V_1 is equal to V_{MCG}, or V_{1MCG}.

V_2 is the Takeoff Safety Speed, or the target speed (in the takeoff configuration) to be achieved *when an engine fails* during the takeoff. If they all keep working, the aircraft will reach at least V_2 at the screen height and will continue to a fixed, steady climb speed (typically +10 kts). V_2 must be at least 13% above V_{SR} and 10% above V_{MC}. It is around 10 knots more than V_1.

FUEL JETTISON

In an emergency soon after departure, a transport aircraft will almost certainly be over the maximum landing weight. Fuel can be burned off in the hold, but to reduce this time and, especially if the emergency needs a quick landing, many aircraft can dump fuel overboard.

There are tables for fuel dumping. Usually, you find the intersection between the starting and ending fuel weights to find the time required, but don't expect a question in an exam to be so simple - expect to use Zero Fuel Weight.

The time limit for jettisoning fuel (down to safe reserves) is 15 minutes. You must be free from hazards, the discharge must be clear of the aircraft, and controllability must not be affected.

CLASS A LIMITATIONS
CAT.POL.A.200, 205

The data in the flight manual must be supplemented as necessary if reasonably expected adverse operating conditions such as contaminated runways cannot be covered, and engine failure in all flight phases. For wet and contaminated runways, data determined in accordance with certification standards of large aeroplanes or equivalent shall be used.

- a single value of V_1 must be used for the rejected and continued takeoff, and
- on a wet or contaminated runway, the takeoff mass may not exceed that for a dry runway under the same conditions.

CLASS B LIMITATIONS
CAT.POL.A.300, 305

At the planning stage for a Class B aircraft, the minimum climb gradient is 300 ft/minimum climb speed AEO. A single-engined aeroplane may not be operated at night in IMC, except under special VFR.

 Twin-engined aeroplanes that do not meet the climb requirements of CAT.POL.A.340 must be treated as single-engined aeroplanes.

The takeoff mass shall not exceed the maximum in the flight manual for the pressure altitude and ambient temperature at the aerodrome of departure. The unfactored takeoff distance may not exceed:

- when multiplied by a factor of 1.25, the TORA, or
- when stopway and/or clearway is available:
  - the TORA
  - when multiplied by a factor of 1.15, the TODA, or
  - when multiplied by a factor of 1.3, the ASDA.

CLASS C LIMITATIONS
CAT.POL.A.400

For aeroplanes with takeoff field length data in their flight manual that do not include engine failure accountability, the distance from the start of the takeoff roll required to reach 50 ft above the surface with all engines operating within the maximum takeoff power conditions specified, when multiplied by a factor of either:

- 1.33 for aeroplanes with two engines
- 1.25 for aeroplanes with three engines, or
- 1.18 for aeroplanes with four engines

shall not exceed the TORA at the aerodrome at which the takeoff is to be made.

If the flight manual includes engine failure accountability, the requirements for Class A shall be met.

The Climb

Almost as important as the cruise performance is the climb performance because, if you take too long to get to the optimum altitude were specific range is maximum, you will lose much of the advantage of being there.

 Instrument departures assume that all engines are working, so obstacle clearance is not guaranteed if an engine fails (it is an emergency and not a normal event). You must therefore limit the aircraft weight to clear all obstacles during takeoff, after a failure of the most critical engine. Many companies create their own Standard Departures to be used in such situations.

Takeoff requirements (for A and B) need you to vertically avoid obstacles along the takeoff path which cannot be avoided visually by 35 feet (50 if you bank by more than 15°, because part of the aircraft will then be below the rest) within an obstacle domain which ends at 1500 feet. Refer to *Net Takeoff Flight Path*, later. There are no obstacle requirements for single-engined aircraft as, if the engine fails, you are going nowhere but down.

The (ICAO) horizontal requirements for identifying obstacles are shown below:

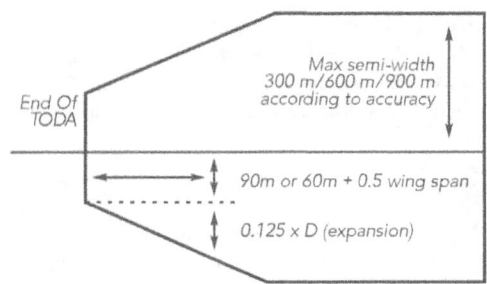

If your aircraft has a wingspan of less than 60 m, use half the wingspan plus 60 m, plus 0·125 x D* (*D* is the horizontal distance travelled from the end of the TODA, or the end of the TODR if a turn is scheduled before the end of TODA).

*D divided by 8.

For example, a twin piston has a wing span of 8m. At 3,936 ft from the end of the TODA, within what maximum distance would an obstacle have to be from the runway extended centre line to be regarded as a takeoff obstacle?

The answer is 64 + 150 = 214 m.

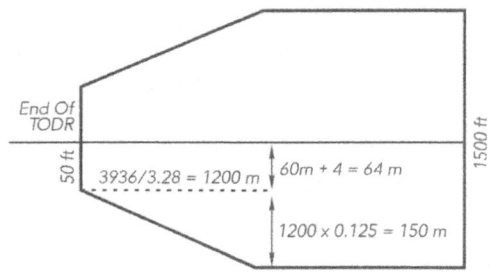

Obstacles must also be cleared by 200 feet horizontally within the airfield boundary or 300 feet outside.

 A 10 knot crosswind at 150 knots will push you nearly 350 feet of your intended track within 5,000 feet. The above diagram is for zero wind conditions!

Below maximum speed (down to the minimum point), the spread between the power required and power available curves becomes greater, and your rate of climb is determined by how great the spread is for a given speed. In other words, power that is not required for level flight is available for climbing - this is sometimes called the *power differential*. The rate of climb is proportional to it, and inversely proportional to weight.

The best Rate of Climb speed is obtained when there is the greatest difference between the power required for level flight and that available from the engines. For turboprops, this will coincide with the speed for the best lift/drag ratio, since power output is relatively constant. Turbojets, however, produce more engine power with speed, which is enough to overcome the extra drag, so the maximum differential between power required and available happens at a higher speed, and best ROC occurs above L/D_{MAX}. There will be performance tables to find time and fuel required for climbs. Remember that headwind and tailwinds will change the distance figures. To cope with this, work out the groundspeed with no wind and apply the corrections then. You can use the flight computer to find out the distance and time.

If a graph is used to show compliance with obstacle clearance requirements, the gradient from 50 feet to the assumed engine failure height is to be the average all-engine gradient x 0.77, which is equivalent to the distance travelled with all engines operating x 1.3 or 1.23 V_{S1g}.

GRADIENTS

The **net climb gradient** for Class A aeroplanes is the actual OEI climb gradient reduced by 0.8% for twins, 0.9% for three-engined aeroplanes and 1% for four-engined ones as an additional safety margin for obstacle clearance. It must meet the required gradient(s) of the departure procedure and clear all obstacles by 200 ft horizontally or 35 ft vertically within the aerodrome boundary and 300 ft horizontally outside.

Where an aircraft has multiple takeoff configurations and flap retraction schedules, climb gradients must be calculated to account for the drag from various stages of flap, plus each period of acceleration. If the net climb gradient after engine failure is not enough for the terrain clearance required by a SID, there may be restrictions on departure from that aerodrome, which is then categorised as Category B, or even C. The briefing might include emergency turns to avoid terrain if an engine fails, and for Class B aircraft might restrict the cloud ceiling and visibility as engine failure need not be accounted for until the altitude that visual terrain separation will be lost. The climb angle (air mass related*) increases if the nose is pitched up and *vice versa*.

*The flight path angle is ground related.

Rule Of Thumb: As climb gradients are hard to visualise, convert them to rates of climb by multiplying by the TAS - 180 kts x 3% produces 540 feet per minute.

TAKEOFF & LANDING CLIMB REQUIREMENTS
CAT.POL.A.340

The operator of a twin-engined aeroplane shall fulfil the following takeoff and landing climb requirements.

TAKEOFF CLIMB

With **all engines operating**, the steady gradient of climb must be at least 4% with takeoff power set on each engine and the gear extended (if the gear can be retracted inside seven seconds, it is assumed to be retracted). The flaps must be in the takeoff position(s), with a climb speed of at least the greater of 1.1 V_{MC} (minimum control speed on or near ground) and 1.2 V_{S1} (stall speed or minimum steady flight in the landing configuration).

With **one engine inoperative**, the steady gradient of climb at 400 ft above the takeoff surface must be measurably positive with the critical engine inoperative and its propeller in the minimum drag position, the remaining engine at takeoff power, the gear retracted, flaps in the takeoff position(s) and a climb speed equal to that achieved at 50 ft. Alternatively, the steady gradient can be at least 0.75% at 1,500 ft above the takeoff surface, with the critical engine inoperative and its propeller in the minimum drag position, the remaining engine below maximum continuous power, the landing gear and wing flaps retracted, and a climb speed of at least 1.2 V_{S1}.

LANDING CLIMB

With **all engines operating**, the steady gradient of climb must be at least 2.5% with not more than the power or thrust that is available eight seconds after starting to move the power controls from the minimum flight idle position, the gear extended, the flaps in the landing position, and a climb speed equal to V_{REF} (reference landing speed).

With **one engine inoperative**, the steady gradient of climb must be at least 0.75% at 1,500 ft above the landing surface, with the critical engine inoperative and its propeller in the minimum drag position, the remaining engine below maximum continuous power, the gear and flaps retracted, and a climb speed of at least 1.2 V_{S1}.

TURNS

As climb data is lacking for the 1st and 3rd segments of the takeoff flight path, because the aircraft is changing its configuration, turns are usually performed in the 2nd and 4th segments. Having said that, instrument departures usually allow up to 15° banked turns in the 1st and 2nd segments of a climb and 25° in the 3rd and 4th segments.

FARs do not consider additional vertical margins during turns, as the bank angle is limited to 15° anyway. EASA requires any obstacles to be cleared by 50 feet if the bank angle is greater than 15° (1.495), because one wing will encroach on the clearance area underneath. On Airbus fly-by-wire aircraft, the OEI bank angle on takeoff is limited to 15°. If the departure procedure needs more than that, the aircraft must be flown manually.

👍 **Rules Of Thumb:** The angle of bank for a standard rate turn is 15% of the TAS. Roll out from the turn at half the bank angle before the target heading. For heading or track adjustments less than 60°, half the change in heading required so, for a 10° change of heading the bank angle would be 5°.

CLASS A OBSTACLE CLEARANCE
CAT.POL.A.210

The net takeoff flight path must allow the aeroplane to clear all obstacles vertically by at least 35 ft or horizontally by at least 90 m plus $0.125 \times D$, which is the horizontal distance you have travelled from the end of the TODA (or the end of the TORA if you turn before the end of the TODA). For aeroplanes with a wingspan of less than 60 m, a horizontal obstacle clearance of half the aeroplane wingspan plus 60 m, plus $0.125 \times D$ may be used instead (see *The Climb*, below).

Track changes are not allowed up to where the net takeoff flight path achieves a height equal to half the wingspan (but at least 50 ft) above the elevation of the end of the TORA. Thereafter, up to 400 ft, bank angles up to 15° are assumed. Above 400 ft height bank angles between 15-25° may be scheduled. Any part of the net takeoff flight path in which the aeroplane is banked by more than 15° shall clear all obstacles within the horizontal distances above vertically by at least 50 ft. See CAT.POL.A.240 for operations with increased bank angles of up to 20° between 200-400 ft, or up to 30° above 400 ft.

When track changes of more than 15° are not required, you need not consider obstacles with a lateral distance greater than:

- 300 m, if navigational accuracy can be maintained through the obstacle accountability area, or
- 600 m under all other conditions.

With track changes of more than 15°, the distances increase to 600 m and 900 m, respectively.

Operators must establish contingency procedures to satisfy the requirements above and to provide a safe route, avoiding obstacles, to enable the aeroplane to either comply with CAT.POL.A.215, or land at either the aerodrome of departure or at a takeoff alternate.

CLASS B OBSTACLE CLEARANCE
CAT.POL.A.310

The aeroplane must clear all obstacles vertically by at least 50 ft, or horizontally by at least 90 m plus $0.125 \times D$, where D is the horizontal distance from the end of the TODA (or the end of the takeoff distance if a turn is scheduled before the end of the TODA). For aeroplanes with a wingspan of less than 60 m, a horizontal obstacle clearance of half the aeroplane wingspan plus 60 m plus $0,125 \times D$ may be used. It is assumed that:

- the takeoff flight path begins 50 ft above the end of the TODR (see CAT.POL.A.305(b)) and ends 1,500 ft above the surface.
- the aeroplane is not banked before reaching 50 ft above the surface, and then not more than 15°.
- failure of the critical engine occurs on the AEO takeoff flight path where visual reference for avoiding obstacles is expected to be lost.
- the gradient of the takeoff flight path from 50 ft to the assumed engine failure height is equal to the average AEO gradient during climb and transition to the en-route configuration, multiplied by 0.77
- the gradient of the takeoff flight path from the height reached above to the end of the takeoff flight path is equal to the OEI en-route climb gradient shown in the flight manual.

With no track changes of more than 15°, you do not need to consider obstacles with a lateral distance greater than:

- 300 m, if navigational accuracy can be maintained through the obstacle accountability area, or
- 600 m under all other conditions.

When track changes of more than 15° are involved, the distances increase to 600 m and 900 m, respectively.

CLASS C TAKEOFF OBSTACLE CLEARANCE
CAT.POL.A.405

The OEI takeoff flight path must allow the aeroplane to clear all obstacles vertically by at least 50 ft plus $0.01 \times D$, or horizontally by at least 90 m plus $0.125 \times D$, where D is the horizontal distance from the end of the TODA. With a wingspan of less than 60 m, a horizontal obstacle clearance of half the wingspan plus 60 m plus $0.125 \times D$ may be used.

The takeoff flight path begins 50 ft above the end of the TODR, and ends 1,500 ft above the surface.

Track changes are not allowed before reaching 50 ft. Thereafter, up to 400 ft, bank angles up to 15° are assumed. Above 400 ft bank angles between 15-25° may be scheduled. Adequate allowance must be made for the effect of bank angle on operating speeds and flight path, including the distance increments resulting from increased operating speeds.

When track changes of more than 15° are not required, you need not consider obstacles outside:

- 300 m, if navigational accuracy can be maintained through the obstacle accountability area, or
- 600 m under all other conditions.

When track changes of more than 15° are involved, the distances increase to 600 m and 900 m, respectively.

The Cruise

This extends from the top of the climb (TOC) to the top of the descent (TOD), when the Captain wakes up. The idea is to use the least fuel, if only because some airlines increase your pay packet, but sometimes, you must get somewhere as quickly as possible, with maximum TAS. This is covered in *Flight Planning*, but the performance considerations for Class A include Drift Down, plus Load Factor and Manoeuvre Capability.

The obstacle clearance requirements are 2000 feet clearance within 5 nm of track.

👍 **Rules Of Thumb:** To convert the Mach number to an approximate groundspeed in nm per minute, multiply the Mach number by 10. Then multiply by 60. To determine TAS within 1 or 2%, divide the flight level by 2 and add the result to the IAS.

RECIPROCATING ENGINES

In the cruise, you should reduce power and lean the mixture, which will reduce the fuel consumption and wear on the engine. Generally, the higher the RPM, the greater the speed, but at the expense of fuel economy, range and endurance. The lower the RPM, of course, the fewer number of times the engine goes round, and the less fuel is used. Calculating the Specific Air Range (the fuel used per Nautical Air Mile) can help you compare the various options. That is, find out how far you can go for each pound of fuel. Note that twin-engined aeroplanes have higher power and fuel consumption, so there will be a significant difference in fuel required for descent.

In a non-turbocharged aircraft, the TAS increase between 5,000-12,000 is hardly discernible, so you would only go that high if you were getting a good tailwind or the MSA (or weather) forces you there - fuel consumption will be more or less the same at either altitude and the climb will take up more fuel than you save. Turbocharging increases TAS, so you can decrease power to reduce fuel consumption and engine wear, and increase range.

EN ROUTE DIVERSIONS

You must be capable of continuing the flight from any point of engine failure at or above MSA to a height above a suitable airfield (within the landing-climb gradient and runway limits with suitable weather), where you must be able to maintain a positive rate of climb. Consideration must therefore be given to height loss, and the likely drift down rate with engine(s) out is established from the flight manual. The charts will indicate how quickly you can descend, based on weight, temperature, altitude, etc. If terrain is restrictive after drift-down, emergency routing might need to be considered during the planning stage.

CLASS A LIMITATIONS
ENROUTE — ONE ENGINE INOPERATIVE

You must, if a critical engine fails, be able to continue to an aerodrome without flying below the minimum flight altitude. The net flight path must have a positive gradient at 1,500 feet above the aerodrome, taking account of icing equipment, or at 1,000 feet above terrain and obstacles on the route within 5 nm either side of track*.

From cruising altitude, the net flight path must clear vertically, by at least 2,000 feet, all terrain and obstacles along the route within 5 nm either side of track*. See also CAT.POL.A.225 or 230 (Landing), below.

 The engine is assumed to fail at the most critical point along the route, and winds must be taken into account. Fuel jettisoning is allowed if you can reach the aerodrome with the required fuel reserves, if a safe procedure is used, and the aerodrome where the aeroplane is assumed to land after engine failure must meet the performance requirements at the expected landing mass.

*These must be increased to 18.5 km (10 nm) if the navigational accuracy does not meet at least RNP 5.

Under CAT.OP.MPA.180, if the flight manual does not contain a cruising speed for OEI, use whatever speed you get with the remaining engine(s) at **maximum continuous power**. Note, however, that this rule relates to selecting takeoff alternates when you can't use the departure aerodrome, and is not necessarily a general rule, although it might be regarded as such in questions.

*After an engine failure, the power selected on the remaining engine(s) will depend on what's going on. For example, if an engine fails in a 4 engined machine, with no other implications, it would not be considered a major emergency, and you might continue as planned. The throttle setting on the remaining engines could be MCT to start with (for obstacles), but a 3-engine cruise setting would be used as per the ops manual.

ENROUTE - TWO ENGINES INOPERATIVE
CAT.POL.A.220

Naturally, this applies to aircraft with three or more engines, which must be able to fly to a suitable alternate, and not be more than 90 minutes away from a suitable aerodrome unless it can fly to an aerodrome and land with the engines out, clearing by at least 2000 feet, all terrain and obstacles within 5 nm (10 if navigation accuracy does not meet RNP 5). The effect of icing equipment must be taken into account.

The two engines are assumed to fail at the same time at the most critical point (i.e. more than 90 minutes from a suitable aerodrome), there must be a positive gradient at 1,500 feet over the aerodrome, and enough fuel to fly level for 15 minutes. Fuel jettisoning is allowed, if you keep the required reserves and use a safe procedure.

CLASS B LIMITATIONS
MULTI-ENGINED AEROPLANES
CAT.POL.A.315

If one engine fails, the aircraft must be able to fly to 1000 feet above a suitable aerodrome, assuming a rate of climb of 300 feet per minute can be maintained, and the enroute gradient with one engine out must be the gross of descent or climb increased or decreased by 0.5%, respectively.

SINGLE-ENGINED AEROPLANES
CAT.POL.A.320

You must reach a place where a safe forced landing can be made (land planes must do this on land), assuming a rate of climb of 300 feet per minute can be maintained, and the enroute gradient is the gross of descent increased by 0.5%.

CLASS C LIMITATIONS

ENROUTE ALL ENGINES OPERATING
CAT.POL.A.410

An aeroplane must be capable of climbing at 300 feet per minute at max continuous power and at the minimum altitudes for safe flight and engine-out conditions (see CAT.POL.A.415 and 420).

EN-ROUTE — OEI
CAT.POL.A.415

An aeroplane must be capable of continuing to an aerodrome clearing obstacles within 5 nm* either side of track by at least 1000 feet, or 2000 with a rate of climb of less than zero (i.e. descending) with the operating engines set to maximum continuous power. The flight path must have a positive slope at 1500 feet above the aerodrome, with all calculations based on a ROC 150 ft/min less than the gross. Safe fuel jettisoning is allowed.

*18.5 km (10 nm) if the navigational accuracy does not meet at least RNP5.

ENROUTE - TWO ENGINES OUT
CAT.POL.A.420

Naturally, this applies to aircraft with three or more engines, which must be able to fly to a suitable alternate, and not be more than 90 minutes away from a suitable aerodrome unless it can fly to an aerodrome and land, clearing by at least 2,000 feet, all terrain and obstacles within 5 nm*. The two engines are assumed to fail at the same time at the most critical point (i.e. more than 90 minutes from a suitable aerodrome), there must be a positive gradient at 1500 feet over the aerodrome, with enough fuel to fly level for 15 minutes. Fuel jettisoning is allowed, as long as it is safe. The rate of climb is 150 ft/min less than that specified.

*18.5 km (10 nm) if the navigational accuracy does not meet at least RNP5.

Safe fuel jettisoning is allowed.

Descent

This is where the power developed is less than required. As the rate of sink is proportional to the difference between power required and power available, it is lowest where the power required is lowest, that is, at the bottom of the curve. In the glide, where either no power is available (engine failure in a single) or idle power is set (commonly used for the descent in jet aircraft), the minimum rate of sink gives the greatest time in the descent, not the best range in the glide. This is found by drawing the usual tangent to the curve from the origin, to find the minimum rate of sink relative to forward speed. The ratio of greatest horizontal distance flown for a given amount of altitude is the *glide ratio*. The net descent path is *steeper* than the gross descent path.

👍 **Rule Of Thumb:** To find the TOD from the destination, divide the change in flight level by 3, adding a bit for deceleration. From the threshold, divide the height AGL by 300.

The obstacle clearance requirements are to be able to maintain a positive gradient at least 1000 feet above such obstacles and 1500 feet above the landing aerodrome.

Landing

Final approach is normally done at 1.3 V_{S0} for the weight (30% above stall speed) or 1.23 V_{RS0} (23% above the reference stall speed for large jet aircraft). This is because flying the approach at stall speed (for minimum distance) makes the short final too dangerous and because speed is unstable closer to the stall, so extra landing distance is sacrificed for safety. As this is an indicated airspeed, the groundspeed may be different - high aerodrome pressure altitudes and temperatures increase it, as do tailwinds. Brakes are the most used way of stopping once on the ground because aerodynamic braking is not very good for large aircraft, and reverse thrust is best at high speeds.

Performance Class A aircraft must be at 50 feet and 1.3 V_{S0} at screen height on landing.

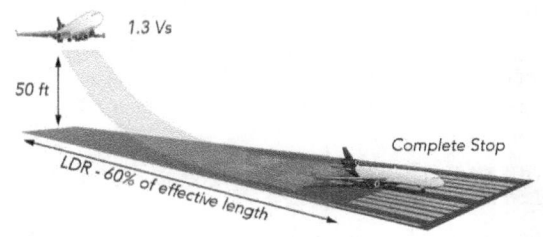

SPEED

Peculiar to landing is speed - a higher one requires a longer distance, not only for slowing down, but the FAA have also determined that being 5 knots too fast over the threshold is the same as being 50 feet too high. Aircraft are classified according to IAS at the threshold (V_{AT}), equal to Stalling speed (V_{S0}) x 1.3:

Category	Threshold Speed
A	< 91 kts
B	91-120 kts
C	120-141 kts
D	141-166 kts
E	166-210 kts

Balked Approach Flight Path

An instrument approach is designed with a Missed Approach Point and MDA or DA, then a standard missed approach that is designed to keep you away from sharp pointy bits of ground. This is why there is a minimum climb performance for the approach - to keep you clear of ground if you have to go around. This might place a restriction on the landing mass.

A balked approach is a go-around in the landing configuration (gear and flaps down, etc.). It is similar to Net Flight Path, and commences at DH above the upwind end of the LDR. Once you have entered a low-energy landing configuration, you might get a runway-assisted go-around, because your flaps and gear would be set for landing and producing high drag, you might be below 50 feet, in the descent, with the throttle in the idle range and with decreasing airspeed. This is accepted for a late go-around decision on a Cat III approach, and if you rotate too urgently to try and avoid it the aircraft might stall if you try to climb before your engines have spooled up.

FLIGHT PERFORMANCE & PLANNING
V-Speeds

CLASS A LIMITATIONS
CAT.POL.A.225, CAT.POL.A.230

The landing mass (see CAT.POL.A.105(a)) may not be more than the maximum for the altitude and ambient temperature expected for the estimated time of landing at the destination and alternate aerodromes.

DRY RUNWAYS
Turbojets must plan to use 60% of LDA, and turboprops 70% from 50 ft above the threshold. For **steep approach** operations*, the landing distance must be based on a screen height of between 35 - 60 ft, and CAT.POL.A.245 must be complied with.

*Glideslope angles of 4.5° or more. See *CAT.POL.A.245*.

For **short landing** operations, the operator must comply with CAT.POL.A.250.

The altitude at the aerodrome, up to 50% of the headwind component or at least 150% of the tailwind component; and the runway slope in the direction of landing (if greater than ±2%) must be taken into account.

WET & CONTAMINATED RUNWAYS
CAT.POL.A.235

If the runway at the ETA may be wet, the LDA shall be at least 115% of the required landing distance, determined as per CAT.POL.A.230. If the runway at the ETA may be contaminated, the LDA shall be at least the landing distance above, or at least 115% of the landing distance under approved data or equivalent, whichever is greater.

A landing distance on a wet runway shorter than that required above, but at least that required by CAT.POL.A.230(a), may be used if the flight manual includes specific additional information about landing distances on wet runways.

CLASS B LIMITATIONS
As for Class A, except:

DRY RUNWAYS
CAT.POL.A.330

From 50 feet, aeroplanes must use 70% of LDA, slope must be taken account of and there is no exemption to allow an aircraft to launch even if it cannot land in still air at its destination, as there is for Class A. For steep approaches, the landing distance data must be factored as above, for a screen height between 35 - 60 ft, complying with CAT.POL.A.345.

The same for short landings, but complying with CAT.POL.A.350.

CONTAMINATED RUNWAYS
CAT.POL.A.335

The factor for landing on *wet* runways is 115% - the LDA must equal or exceed the required landing distance, factored by 1.15.

LDR must not exceed LDA on *contaminated* runways.

A landing distance on a wet runway shorter than that required above, but at least that required by CAT.POL.A.330(a), may be used if the flight manual includes specific additional information about landing distances on wet runways.

CLASS C LIMITATIONS
Destination & Alternates - CAT.POL.A.425

DRY RUNWAYS
CAT.POL.A.430

The landing mass under CAT.POL.A.105(a) for the estimated time of landing must allow a full stop landing from 50 ft above the threshold within 70% of the LDA.

WET & CONTAMINATED RUNWAYS
CAT.POL.A.435

For *wet* runways, the LDA shall be equal to or exceed the required landing distance under CAT.POL.A.430, multiplied by 1.15. For *contaminated* runways, the landing distance required may not exceed the LDA.

V-SPEEDS

As turbine aircraft operate with wide variations in weight and configurations, a wide range of speeds is needed to cope with them. However, you cannot remember them all, so a range of terminology has been developed for turbine aircraft. V-speeds are significant speeds, on large aircraft, calculated for every takeoff, and varying with weight (or mass), that is, they increase as you get heavier. Often, as with the DC-9, you have to find the basic speeds first, then apply the above parameters.

Sometimes, as with the DC-9, you have to find the basic speeds first, then apply the above parameters.

Here are some:

Speed	Explanation
M_{MO}	V_{MO} for higher altitudes, in Mach numbers (the red line on the airspeed/Mach indicator). The changeover altitude is in the POH.
V_A	Design manoeuvring speed. The max speed you can make abrupt, full scale deflections of the controls without damage (about twice V_S). Not always the best speed for entering turbulence (see below). Valid only at gross weight. A 20% decrease in weight needs a 10% reduction in manoeuvring speed. Flying just above this speed may cause permanent deformation of the aircraft structure if the elevator is fully deflected upwards.
V_{APP}	Minimum approach speed.
V_B	Maximum gust or turbulence penetration speed for turbines, at least 10 kts below V_A, compensating for the power used delaying the stall and for windshear. Lighter aircraft should be flown slower, as stall speed decreases in line with weight.
V_{BE}	Best Endurance, or the greatest airborne time per unit of fuel, around 75% of V_{BR}.
V_{BG}	Best power-off glide (for greatest distance per unit of height). Distance affected by windmilling prop.
V_{BR}	Best Range, or best L/D, and greatest air distance per unit of fuel, decreasing with weight.
V_C	Design cruise speed, for the most velocity per unit of fuel. Around 1.3 x V_{BR}

FLIGHT PERFORMANCE & PLANNING
V-Speeds

Speed	Explanation
V_{CL}	Minimum climb speed above acceleration height.
V_{CEF}	The airspeed at which the critical engine is assumed to fail, not less than $1.05\ V_{MC}$. See V_1.
V_D	Design dive speed, normally at least 25% higher than cruise speed ($1.4 \times V_{NO}$).
V_{DF}	Demonstrated diving speed.
V_{EF}	The point at which it is assumed that the critical engine fails for Performance Class A aircraft.
V_F	Design flap speed.
V_{FE}	Max speed Flaps Extended - the top of the white arc.
V_{FO}	Max Flap Operating speed.
V_{FRI}	Flap retraction initiation speed, given for each flap setting.
V_{FTO}	Final takeoff climb speed. The speed to attain the minimum permissible gradient in the final segment of the NFP
V_{GA}	Minimum Go Around speed.
V_H	Max level speed at max continuous power.
V_{LE}	Max speed, gear extended.
V_{IMD}	Minimum drag speed (Indicated). It is used in range and endurance calculations, being approximately the best range cruise speed for a piston engine aircraft, and approximately the best endurance speed for a turbo jet.
V_{IMP}	Minimum power speed, attained at the lowest point on the power required curve. The best endurance speed for piston engined aeroplanes.
V_{LO}	Max gear operating speed.
V_{LOF}	Lift-Off speed. About 10% above V_{MU}. The speed where the aircraft first becomes airborne, or where lift overcomes the weight. The upper limit is the maximum tyre speed.
V_{MBE}	Max Brake Energy speed, or the maximum speed on the ground from which you can stop within the capabilities of the brakes. As they turn kinetic energy into heat, it is affected by mass, PA, temperature and slope, so it is most limiting at high masses, temperatures, pressure altitudes and downhill slopes. Certification is done with worn brakes.
V_{MC}	Minimum Control Speed in the air - the minimum speed at which the aeroplane is controllable up to 5° of bank when the critical engine becomes inoperative with the remaining engines at takeoff thrust (i.e. your rudder does not have enough push). It is not connected with stalling speed, and on bigger twins your approach speed can be less - thus, if an engine goes after the point where you can gain speed and reconfigure, you are committed for landing. V_{MCA} decreases with increase in PA, and increase with aft C of G. There is no guarantee that you can maintain altitude, let alone climb - you can only expect to maintain heading. V_{MCA} is marked with a red line on the ASI. The maximum rudder force needed is 150 lbs.

Speed	Explanation
V_{MCG}	Ground Minimum Control Speed - the minimum calibrated airspeed on the ground (using only rudder to correct yaw) where takeoff can be safely continued, when the critical engine becomes inoperative and with the remaining ones at takeoff thrust (it is assumed the aircraft has just been rotated, the nose wheel is no longer in contact with the runway, but the main wheels are still on the ground). The distance between where the engine is assumed to fail and the aircraft becomes parallel with the centreline may not be more than 30 ft from the centreline. It decreases as elevation and temperature increase, as there is less yaw from the critical engine (it is producing less thrust from the less-dense air). V_1 must not be less than V_{MCG} because, if an engine fails below V_{MCG}, throttles must be closed to maintain directional control. Although no account is officially taken of nosewheel steering, in practice, it should be available too. Factors that reduce V_{MCG} include temperature, density altitude (also V_{MCA}), reduced thrust on takeoff, large tail fin or rudder area, forward C of G and engines closer to the fuselage.
V_{MCL}	Approach and Landing Minimum Control Speed - The minimum speed with a wing engine inoperative where it is possible to decrease thrust to idle or increase thrust to maximum takeoff without encountering dangerous flight characteristics. Up to 5° of bank is allowed and only 150 lbs of rudder force is needed. The minimum rate of roll of 20° towards the live engine should be achievable within 5 seconds.
V_{MD}	Minimum Drag TAS - induced drag equals profile drag. It increases with weight and lift. Also means Minimum Descent, or the lowest rate of sink in a power-off glide, which occurs at minimum drag x velocity. The time in flight is affected by a windmilling prop.
V_{MO}	Max operating speed (at lower altitudes), to prevent excess damage from dynamic pressure, relevant to high speed aircraft (same as V_{NE}). Varies with altitude.
V_{MP}	Minimum power TAS, lower than V_{MD}. It is close to V_S.
V_{MU}	Max Unstick speed, or the minimum speed you can fly off the runway without hitting it with the tail (actually, that point is the limiting speed for geometrically limited aircraft - the actual limit is the angle of attack at which you reach the maximum coefficient of lift). As it is established as the basis for V_1 and V_R during manufacturer testing, you don't normally have to deal with it, but it is useful where you just want to get the wheels off a dodgy surface and stay in ground effect until V_{TOS}.
V_{NE}	Never Exceed speed, around 90% of Dive Speed (V_D). On a turbine, the equivalent is V_{MO} or M_{MO}.
V_{NO}	Normal Operations in still air, with caution.

FLIGHT PERFORMANCE & PLANNING
V-Speeds

Speed	Explanation
V_R	Rotation Speed, or the IAS at which the aircraft is rotated to the takeoff attitude, whether the engine has failed or not. It is at or just above V_1 (On the 727, they are the same), but must not be less than that, or $1.05 \times V_{MC}$ or V_{MU} when OEI. V_R must also be high enough to get to V_2 before screen height. It is a speed that, if maximum rate of rotation was applied, V_{LOF} of at least $1.1 \times V_{MU}$ with all engines operating could be attained, or at least $1.05 \times V_{MU}$ with one engine out. When taking off from a contaminated runway, use V_R for an uncontaminated runway. Must be greater than V_{MCA} because you need to control the aircraft.
V_{RA}	Maximum speed in rough air.
V_{REF}	Reference (touchdown) speed, used on the approach, derived from $1.3 \times V_{S0}$ or $1.23 V_{SR}$, so it increases with weight.
V_S	Stall speed, or minimum steady controllable speed in flight. An increase in altitude has no effect on it.
V_{SL}	As above, for a specific configuration.
V_{S0}	Stall speed in landing configuration - the bottom of the white arc, decreasing with weight.
V_{SR0}	Reference Stall speed, equal to $1.06 V_S$.
V_{S1}	Stall speed, clean, power off - the bottom of the green arc on the ASI. It decreases with weight (and unloading manoeuvres). That is, the conventional stall, with a load factor of less than 1. Officially, The stall speed (minimum steady flight speed) in a specific configuration.
V_{S1g}	Stall speed, corresponding to max lift coefficient (just before lift starts decreasing).
V_T	Threshold Speed - V_{REF}. Where you should aim to cross the threshold to ensure the scheduled landing field lengths are consistently achieved. The speeds at the threshold are V_{T0} - all engines operating, V_{T1} - a critical engine out and V_{T2} - two critical engines out. Maximum threshold speed is described below, but the minimum speed is determined by V_{MCL}.
V_{TMAX}	Max Threshold Speed - speed at the threshold above which the risk of exceeding scheduled landing field length is unacceptably high. Go-around action should normally be taken if this will be exceeded. It is normally 15 knots more than all-engines operating target threshold speed.
V_{TMIN}	Minimum Safe Threshold speed - the lowest to be maintained at or before the threshold. It is the higher of VIMD + 5 kts or VS1g + 20%. Approaches made below this speed may result in loss of control.
V_{TIRE}	The maximum ground speed at which the tyres may remain in contact with the runway surface, which may limit the maximum takeoff weight. Exceeding this speed cause the fuse plug to melt and the tyre to deflate.
V_{TOS}	Minimum speed to attain a positive climb in the takeoff condition, one or more engines out.
V_X	Best angle of climb, or the most height in the shortest distance. It decreases with weight, but the angle of attack remains the same. As V_{S1} increases in a turn, the safety gap between it and this speed will be eroded if you attempt a climbing turn. It does not change with altitude, but increases with mass for a jet, and decreases with flap.
V_{XSE}	Best s/e angle of climb.
V_Y	Best rate of climb, or the most height in the shortest time. It occurs with the greatest difference between power available and power required. For a jet, it is quite high, and because the graphs are relatively flat against each other, it can vary widely from the optimum and not affect things much. For a prop it is quite low, however, and very low climb rates are achieved below it.
V_{YSE}	Best s/e rate of climb, represented by a blue line on the ASI.
V_{ZRC}	Zero ROC - you cannot accelerate, climb or turn, so must reduce drag.
V_1	So-called Takeoff Decision Speed (old terminology), at or above which the takeoff is supposed to be continued, and below which abandoned, if an engine fails. It used to be called the critical engine failure speed, also called V_{CEF}, but it is actually the maximum speed at which you take the first actions to abort, or the minimum speed to continue after an engine failure. Put another way, the speed at which takeoff can no longer be aborted, based on the length of the runway, your current speed and how good your brakes are. It is the speed at which you are committed to takeoff since, if you get a problem at V_1, you cannot initiate a Rejected Takeoff (RTO) quickly enough to stop within the planned Accelerate-Stop Distance. According to Boeing, if you reach this speed accelerating, you have already made the decision to continue. Thus, it is a performance speed, as the decision to abort must be made beforehand. In other words, it is the speed at which an engine failure is recognised, not the speed at which it occurs.
	A basic V_1 can be calculated for a balanced field, based on weight, flaps, altitude and temperature (nothing to do with runway length),. Raising any one of these variables will raise V_1, and vice versa.

Speed	Explanation
	If runway length is not performance limiting, V_1 can be varied for operational reasons. A high V_1 gives you better obstacle clearance, but you need a larger ASDR to cope with the acceleration to get there and the stopping afterwards. The TODR reduces because you spend less time with one engine out of use. A low speed means you don't abuse the tyres and brakes. Compared to a balanced field, if stopway is longer than the clearway, V_1 will be higher at performance-limited take-off mass. If clearway is longer than stopway V_1 will increase at the performance limit. Engine failure having been recognised, V_1 is the speed at which the continued TODR will not exceed the TODA, the continued Take-off Run Required will not exceed TORA and the Accelerate-Stop Distance Required will not exceed that available. You cannot determine V_1 accurately until you know your takeoff weight, which is sometimes not found until you are taxying out and the information transmitted to you over a datalink so, for planning, you work with an approximation, with standard weights. If you end up waiting a long time for takeoff, you may have to recalculate it as some fuel will have been burned off.
	You may see the odd table with a correction for very strong winds, but wind otherwise has no significant effect. Treat slope in the same way (a headwind or an upslope will mean an increased V_1). When asked whether a condition increases or decreases V_1, think about committing to flight at a higher or lower speed - for example, if stopping distance must be increased, or antiskid doesn't work, or you have a tailwind, decrease it, and vice versa. V_1 must not be less than V_{MCG}, or greater than V_R or V_{MBE}. V_1 must be greater than V_{MCG} because you need to control the aircraft. It may not be faster than V_R or the weight must be reduced. If V_1 is less than V_{MCG}, you cannot take off from a wet runway. V_1 is not scheduled for a contaminated runway. When the calculations are done for finding V_1 it is assumed that it takes 2 seconds to recognise an engine failure. The stop/go decision cannot be taken until you are sure what has happened so your continued acceleration is calculated as from the time at V_{EF} plus 2 seconds for the "go" case. In the "stop" case you have more to do - close the throttles, select reverse, get on the brakes - so there are 2 seconds more before applying stop data. A V_1 cut is a practice engine failure at V_1. If you try to take off with a wet V_1 as opposed to the dry version, the TODR will increase and the obstacle clearance will be degraded.

Speed	Explanation
V_2	Takeoff Safety Speed, or minimum safe flying speed if you lose an engine after takeoff, to be achieved before screen height (35') to provide a safe margin above stalling speed for manoeuvring to flap retraction speed. It must be at least 20% more than stall speed and 10% above V_{MC}. Weight is the main factor. Calculate for each landing for go-arounds. Because V_X is low for prop-driven aircraft, V_2 will be close to the speed for best angle of climb, and well below for a jet (for which it is an initial target speed - V_4 gives a better climb angle and manageability). On the PFD it is a magenta triangle on the speed scale. The lower limits for V_2 are $1.2 \times V_S$ and $1.1 \times V_{MC}$. The difference between V_2 and V_R for lightly loaded and heavily loaded aircraft can be significant. A lightly loaded Dash 8 can rotate at 102 knots, while a heavy one may need 133, which is a lot of runway to be covered. For all engines, a jet is usually accelerated to V_2 +10kt (V_4) after rotation because it gives a better angle of climb, a more manageable pitch attitude and, if an engine fails later, the climb gradient will be better. You can only do this if the declared distances exceed those required and if there are no obstacles in the takeoff path. That is, when your TOM is only limited by the gradients, making due allowance for tyre speeds and brake energy.
V_{2MIN}	The lowest takeoff safety speed is based on the higher of $1.08 V_S$ and $1.1 V_{MC}$ for 4-engined turboprops and the higher of $1.13 V_{SR}$ and $1.1 V_{MC}$ for 2- or 3-engined turboprops.
V_3	Flap retraction speed in the US. In Europe, it is the speed at which the aircraft is assumed to pass the screen height of 35 ft with all engines operating on takeoff. Not used in reality, as it is usually just blasted through.
V_4	Steady Initial Climb Speed. The AEO takeoff climb speed used to the point where acceleration to flap retraction speed is initiated. You should get to V_4 by a gross height of 400 feet. It is never less than $1.2 V_{MC}$ or $1.3 V_{MS1}$.

EASA Regulations have specific definitions for terms such as V_{MCG}, V_{MC} and V_{MCL}, none of which include crosswind so, although a crosswind may make it more difficult to stay on the centre line after a critical engine failure, it will not change the value of V_{MCG}. A similar problem arises with C of G position and V_{MC}. Forward C of G movement reduces the minimum speed at which you can maintain control in the air after a critical engine failure, but the definition of V_{MC} says "with the C of G at the most unfavourable position". Thus, the actual C of G position does not affect the value of V_{MC} as defined.

FLIGHT PERFORMANCE & PLANNING
Charts

CHARTS

The flight manual contains the limitations affecting the aircraft, such as those concerning takeoff, obstacle clearance, enroute, climb and landing. As the certification process addresses the worst case scenarios, most charts will reflect engine-out conditions. Put another way, you won't find much information about working normally.

 Because you may not operate at weights over those in the performance charts, they are just as limiting as the information in the Limitations section of the flight manual, which is normally the only legally binding part. As well, performance information could also be in documents that may not have been involved in the certification process.

Anyhow, performance charts may look complex but, once you've used one, you can usually use them all. The best tip is to read the small print around the graph itself, as this is where you will find the conditions on which it is based, like "generator off", or "anti-icing on".

Accuracy is essential (to within one small square) - very often you have to interpolate between figures or lines, and it's a good idea to get used to paralleling lines between the several graphs that may be on one chart. Study the examples in this section carefully and always read the associated conditions on which they are based.

Essentially, performance charts are combinations of several graphs in one, each feeding off the other. Usually, you start with something like your weight against Pressure Altitude, go from their intersection to temperature deviation, then runway slope, then the wind component to find your answer. You also have to work backwards, or at least go through the process several times.

When using a chart for the purpose it was designed, travel to the reference line first, then follow the grid lines to the relevant data point. Then move to the next grid. Otherwise, travel to the data point first, then follow the lines to the reference line before moving to the next grid.

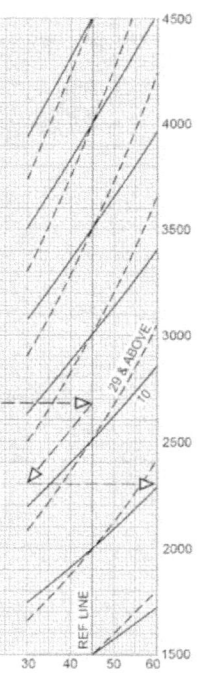

Three types of aircraft are covered in this section, but others may be used to illustrate different points:

- a Class B single-engine piston, based on the Beech Bonanza. This is a six-seater with retractable undercarriage and a normally-aspirated engine (it has no turbocharger or supercharger).
- a Class B piston twin based on the Piper Seneca V (the Seneca III, a more common commercial aircraft, uses the same graphs). This is a six-seater with twin turbo-charged piston engines.
- a Class A Medium Range Jet Transport (MRJT) based on the Boeing 737-400.

Using Charts

With performance matters, there are some principles that remain constant:

- Don't expect to use all the runway - you will lose some of its length from lining up. Turbojets can only plan to use 60% of the LDA (70% for piston- and turboprops) - factor by 1.67 and 1.43, respectively. For Performance Class B aircraft, the TODR may only be 80% of the TORA for departure unless a stopway or clearway is available, in which case the maximum unfactored takeoff distance is the TORA. Factor by 1.25.
- Distances from the graphs when factored for slope and surface are *gross* distances. They become *net* distances when the CAT safety factor is applied, which must not exceed the distance available.
- You can only *plan* to use **up to** 50% of any expected headwind component, and *must* use **at least** 150% of any tailwind. This is to cover any uncertainties in judging the expected wind from reports and forecasts - remember that the winds reported from the Tower are magnetic and there can be great differences between them! Except for obstacle clearance, the graphs already take this into account*, which is why the tailwind lines have a far greater gradient than the headwind ones.

  *CAP 698 does not give much help as to whether you should use the forecast wind component or factor it first, aside from a single piece of information in the MRJT section above Figure 4.1 (paragraph 1.4 - item f). All graphs for **takeoff and landing calculations** are presented with the wind grids already factorised. Use the forecast wind value as shown in the examples. As that used for obstacle clearance does not have to be factorised, these graphs do not allow for it.
- You must account for the climb-limited landing weight and brake energy for the destination as well.
- You must account for runway surface condition, type and slope.
- Distances *required* must not be more than distances *available*.
- The aircraft mass must not be more than that in the flight manual for the conditions.
- Use airfield pressures and temperatures.

Wind Component

There is a graph at Figure 4.1 of CAP 698 for figuring out head- and tailwind components, and crosswinds, for takeoff and landing, as referenced to runway headings.

Find the intersection between the actual wind speed (on the left) and relative wind angle (to the longitudinal axis), then look to the left for the head/tail component (negative values are tailwinds) and down for crosswind.

However, it's just as easy to use the Jeppesen CR-3:

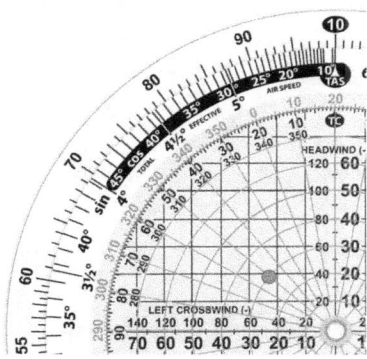

The example (from CAP 698) is set up for runway 02 and a wind velocity of 330°/30 kts. The crosswind component (by 50° from the left) is 23 kts, and the headwind component is 19 kts.

Pressure Altitude

Performance calculations are based on pressure altitude.

Figure 4.2 contains a table for calculating the PA from QNH. Enter it with the QNH (right hand side for hPa) and apply the correction in the centre column to the airfield elevation.

Total Air Temperature

Figure 4.3 is a table that gives you the expected TAT in ISA conditions. Of course, the gauge in your aircraft will read something different, and any differences between the gauge and the table can be taken as ISA deviation.

Start on the left with your pressure altitude, and get the ISA figure underneath the relevant Mach number. If you want the actual OAT, apply the temperature deviation to the figures in Column 2.

SINGLE ENGINE PISTON

For commercial air transport, the SEP is operated under Performance Class B. Single engined aircraft may not fly for commercial air transport purposes at night or in IMC* (except under Special VFR) or without surfaces enroute that will allow a safe forced landing.

*Some states allow single-engined aircraft to be used for commercial cargo transport under these conditions.

Takeoff

Use the lowest of 3 takeoff masses:

- **Max Structural** (MSTOM). 3,650 lbs.
- **Mass, Altitude, Temperature** (MATTOM).
- Category B requirements for **Field Length Limited Takeoff Mass** (FLLTOM), also 3,650 lbs. This is the maximum weight at which you can meet the operational requirements in terms of stopways and clearways. With neither available, TODR, when multiplied by 1.25, must not be more than TORA.

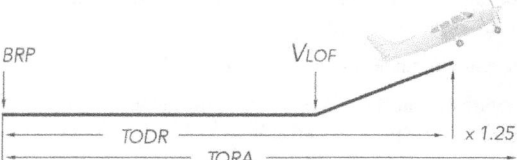

In English, this means that, if you need 2,000 feet to take off, you need a runway at least 2,500 feet long. The takeoff distance available must be longer than that required. You should therefore reach the screen height with 25% of the runway to go. This covers the remote probability that you might need all 2,500 feet.

Factors must be applied before the distances are used to establish takeoff weights.

With a stopway and/or clearway, TODR must:

- not exceed (be within) TORA.
- when multiplied by 1.3, not exceed ASDA (within 77%).
- when multiplied by 1.15, not exceed TODA (within 87%).

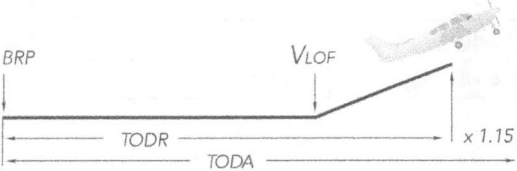

CAP 698 2.1 says that the only one to consider is the field length, but the other two make sense as well!

Takeoff distance is increased by 5% for each 1% of upslope. There is no factorisation for downslope.

Takeoff finishes at the screen height of 50 feet.

Below is the TODR chart (Figure 2.1), for **flaps up**, for the maximum climb angle after takeoff. Instructions are overleaf.

You work forward to find the ground roll, to which various safety factors are applied to get the TODR which, naturally, must be less than or equal to the declared distances available by the airport authority.

Backward working (to find the maximum allowable takeoff weight, for example, or a head- or tailwind) involves going from left to right to the weight block, then entering from the right with the shortest available de-factored distance, considering slope, surface, condition and regulation (see table below). *Stop at the value first, then follow the guides to the reference line.*

FLIGHT PERFORMANCE & PLANNING
Single Engine Piston

Although there are two graphs (for flaps up and flaps down), their parameters are the same, namely full power against the brakes, mixture rich, landing gear retracted after a positive rate of climb is established, and the cowl flaps open. The difference is in the rotate and 50-foot speeds, because the flaps reduce the stalling speed. If you go straight across the last block, you just get the ground distance without clearing the 50-foot obstacle - to do that, you have to follow the lines.

You can see that increases in pressure altitude, temperature, weight or tailwind will increase the takeoff distance, due to the higher TAS or groundspeed.

To determine the takeoff distance from the chart:

- Start with at the OAT. Move vertically up to the aerodrome pressure altitude.
- Travel horizontally right to the mass reference line. Parallel the grid lines to the takeoff mass input.
- Continue horizontally right to the wind component reference line. Parallel the grid lines to the wind component input.
- Proceed horizontally right to the obstacle reference line. Continue right to read ground roll distance or proceed parallel to the grid lines to read total distance to the 50 ft obstacle (TOD).
- Factorise for surface and slope.

To find the most limiting runway length, construct a table:

	TORA	ASDA	TODA
Length	4050	4600	4350
Slope	1.05	1.05	1.05
Surface	1.3	1.3	1.3
Regulation	1	1.3	1.15
Factored Length	2967	2592	2771

The ASDA is limiting here. Use it as a reverse entry in the Takeoff Distance graph to find the FLLTOM.

WORKED EXAMPLE

Pressure Altitude:	5,653 ft
Ambient Temperature:	+15°C
Takeoff Mass:	3,650 lbs
Wind Component:	+10 kts (headwind)
Runway Slope:	1.5% Uphill
Runway Surface:	Grass
Runway Condition:	Wet

SOLUTION

Graphical Distance:	3,450 ft
Surface Factor*:	x 1.3
Slope Factor*:	x 1.075
Take-Off Distance	**4,821 ft**

*If the surface is not dry or paved, use the following table:

Surface	Condition	Factor By
Firm grass up to 20 cm long	Dry	1.2
	Wet	1.3
Paved	Wet	1

Increase TODR by 5% for every 1% of upslope. No factoring is allowed for downslopes.

Figure 2.2 in CAP 698 is for flaps down (the approach setting), for the shortest takeoff run. Use it in the same way as 2.1.

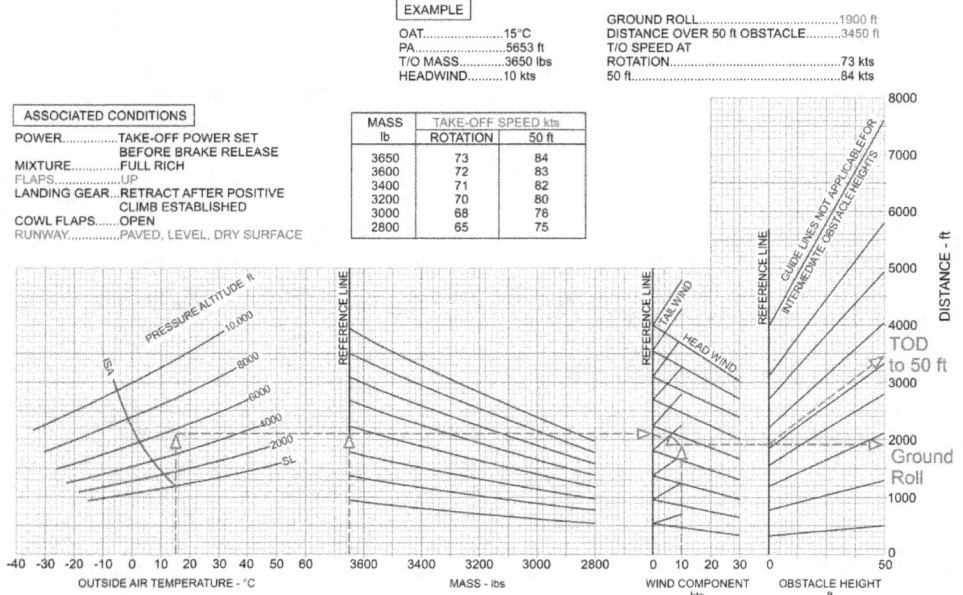

FLIGHT PERFORMANCE & PLANNING
Single Engine Piston

Climb

Below is the climb graph (2.3) Again, instructions are below. No obstacle limits or climb gradients are required, although there are rumours that it should be 4% (the worked example suggests that this is easily attainable).

 The still air gradient concerns climb limits, and is nothing to do with performance, which deals with the rate of climb. The graphs output a rate of climb that is *not affected* by winds.

To determine the climb gradient and rate of climb:

- Find the TAS.
- Enter the graph at the ambient temperature, then move vertically up to the pressure altitude.
- Proceed horizontally right to the mass reference line. Parallel the grid lines to the mass input.
- Continue horizontally right to the first vertical axis to read the rate of climb.
- Continue horizontally to the TAS reference line.
- Parallel the grid lines to intersect the TAS input, then travel horizontally to the right vertical axis to read the climb gradient.

Be prepared to use the flight computer to find the TAS, and to compensate for wind to get a percentage gradient relative to the ground if asked for the ground distance covered - then use the ground speed to multiply whatever time it takes to climb from the screen height to the altitude concerned, convert the time value to hours (divide by 60), then multiply the result by the groundspeed for the distance in nautical miles.

EXAMPLE

Pressure Altitude:	11,500 ft
Ambient Temperature:	-5°C
Weight:	3,600 lbs

SOLUTION

Graphical ROC:	515 fpm
TAS:	120 kts
Climb Gradient:	4.2%

To find out how heavy you can be to achieve a particular gradient (using the same graph):

- Enter the graph at the ambient temperature and move vertically up to the Pressure Altitude.
- Travel horizontally to the right to the weight reference line and make a mark.
- Calculate the TAS.
- Enter the right vertical axis at the gradient and go left horizontally to intercept the TAS above. Then follow the grid lines to reach the reference line and draw a horizontal line through the weight grid.
- From the mark you made, parallel the grid lines to intersect the horizontal line you drew. Drop vertically to read the climb-limited takeoff weight.

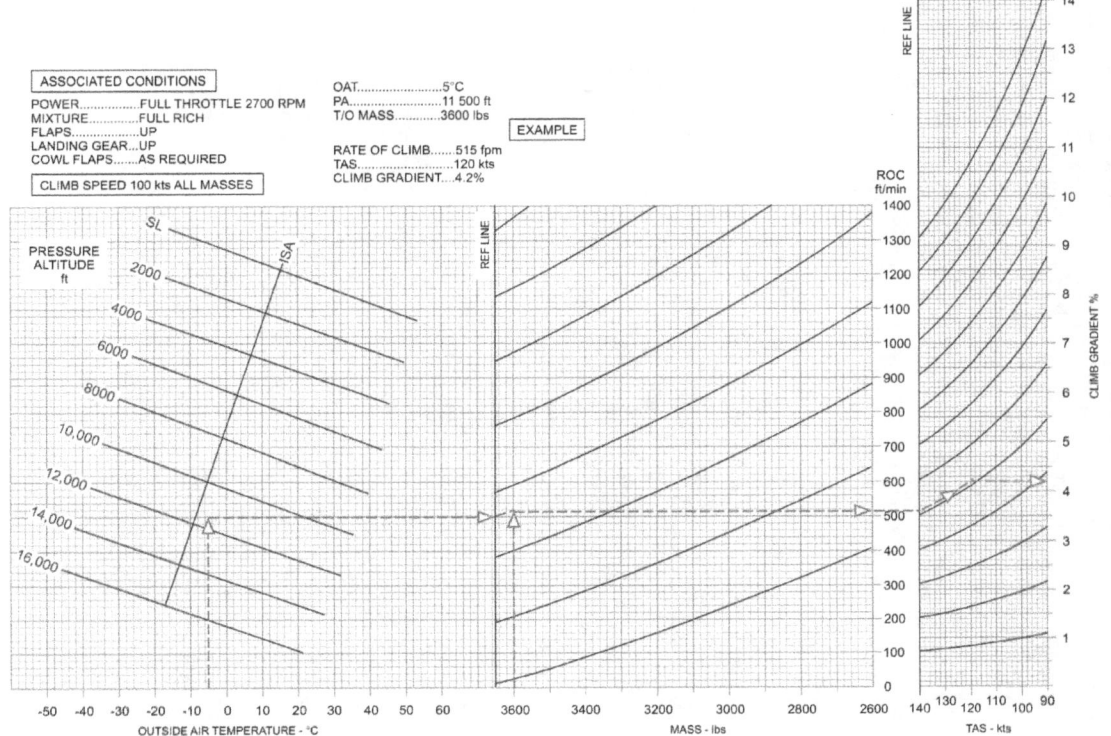

© Phil Croucher, 2018

FLIGHT PERFORMANCE & PLANNING
Single Engine Piston

En Route

The aeroplane may not be assumed to be flying above the altitude at which a rate of climb of 300 ft/min is attained.

In other words, drift down calculations (assessing the range to a safe landing area) are taken from a maximum altitude where the ROC becomes 300 ft/min, at maximum continuous power, using Figure 2.3 above - in the case of the SEP1, this will be well over 13,000 feet.

The net gradient of descent, if the engine fails, shall be the gross gradient increased by 0.5%.

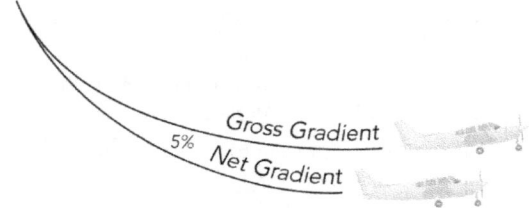

Thus, if you have an 8% gradient, for planning purposes, you should use 8.5% to figure out how high you must be to reach landing sites within a certain distance of your track. To find the horizontal distance required, divide your height by the gradient, then multiply by 100. Or just use the flight computer.

You should then not fly more than that distance away from a landing site.

Landing

You must take the lowest of three landing masses:

- **Max Structural** (MSLM). 3650 lbs.
- **Field Length Limited** (FLLLM).
- **Mass, Altitude, Temperature** (MATLM).

Landing is achieved from the screen height of 50 feet until the aircraft comes to rest. The approach speed must be at least 1.3 x the stall speed in the landing configuration. If the landing surface is grass up to 20 cm long on firm soil, or it may be wet at the ETA, the landing distance should be multiplied by 1.15. It should also be increased by 5% for each 1% downslope, with no allowance for upslope.

Below is Figure 2.4 from CAP 698 (keep parallel after the kink in the middle section). To calculate landing distance:

- Enter at the ambient temperature and proceed vertically to the pressure altitude.
- Move right horizontally to the landing mass reference line. Parallel the grid lines to the appropriate landing mass input.
- Continue to the wind component reference line and parallel the grid line to the wind component.
- Travel right horizontally to the ground roll reference line, then either continue horizontally to the right vertical axis to read the ground roll distance, or parallel the grid lines to the right vertical axis to read the graphical distance.

Apply the surface and slope factors above to the graphical distance to obtain the landing distance, then the regulatory factor to obtain the landing distance required.

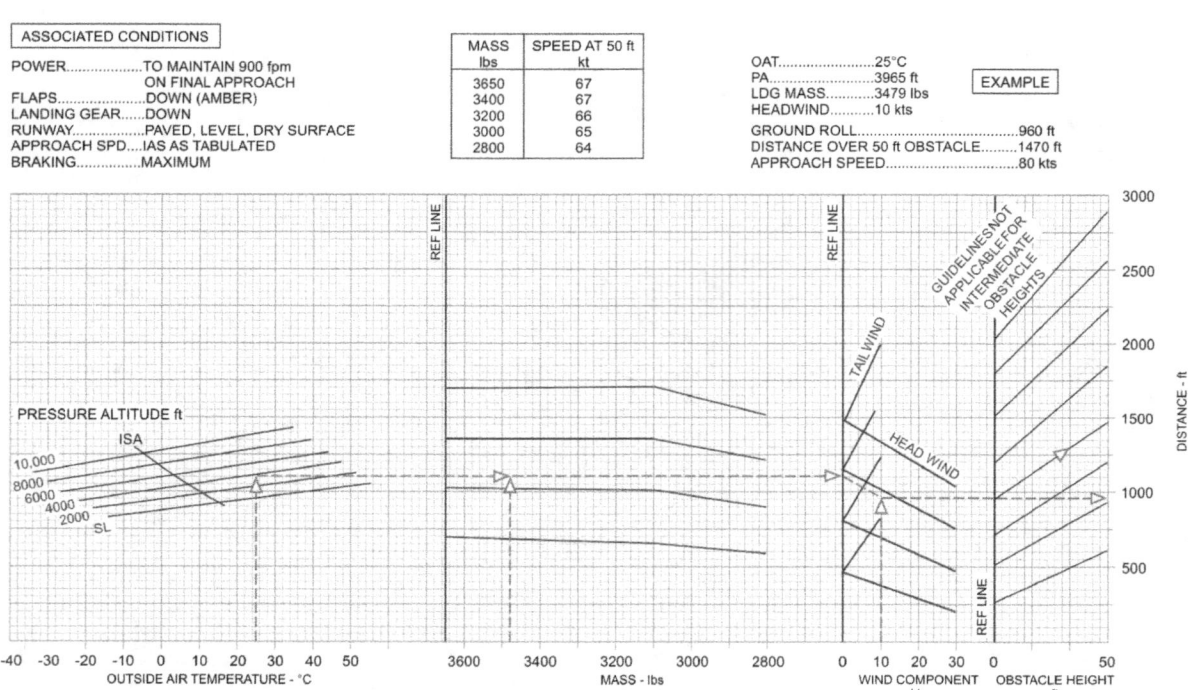

MULTI-ENGINE PISTON

As this is a Class B aircraft, for takeoff obstacle clearance purposes, the engines are assumed to be working up to 300 feet. Before then, you are on your own!

Takeoff

As with the SEP 1, there are two requirements:

- **Minimum Field Length** (MLL). As for SEP 1.
- **Minimum Climb Gradient** - at least 4% AEO with:
  - Takeoff power on each engine.
  - Landing gear extended, but you can assume it is retracted if it comes up within 7 seconds.
  - Flaps set for takeoff position.
  - A climb speed of at least the greater of 1.1 V_{MC} and 1.2 V_{S1}.

With One Engine Inoperative, the climb gradient at 400 feet must be measurably positive, with the failed engine's propeller in the minimum drag position, the remaining engine at takeoff power, the landing gear up, and the flaps set for the takeoff position. The climb speed must also be equal to what it was at 50 feet. At 1500 feet above the takeoff surface, the gradient must be at least 0.75% in the conditions as above, but with the flaps up and the operating engine at max continuous power. The speed must be at least 1.2 V_{S1}.

If the surface is not dry or paved, use this table:

Surface	Condition	Factor By
Firm grass up to 20 cm long	Dry	1.2
	Wet	1.3
Paved	Wet	1

Increase TODR by 5% for every 1% of upslope. Do not account for downslope.

Winds in the graphs are already factored in. There are 2:

- **Normal** - zero flap. Although acceleration is faster because profile drag is less, but the higher rotate speed increases the takeoff run.
- **Maximum effort** - 25° flap

Acceleration is faster during the normal takeoff because there is less profile drag as the speed increases, but the higher rotate speed increases the takeoff run. Aside from different rotate and barrier speeds, the associated conditions are the same for both techniques, namely power at 40 ins Hg, and a dry level runway.

Use of the graphs is similar to the SEP 1.

FLIGHT PATH PROFILE

This will depend on whether you can see where you're going up till 1500 feet.

CLEAR VISIBILITY (NO CLOUD) TO 1500 FEET

You can go direct to 1500 feet for flap retraction.

- Determine the TOD
- Determine the AEO net gradient (gross x 0.77)
- Divide the height gain (minus the screen height) by the gradient to find the distance travelled in feet.

CLOUD BASE BELOW 1500 FEET

You will need two segments. the first will extend from the screen height to the cloud base where visual reference is lost, in which case the distance travelled will equal the height of the cloud base minus the screen height divided by the net gradient then multiplied by 100.

In the second segment, use the OEI gross gradient.

Climb

The climb graphs output a *rate* of climb* that is not affected by winds, so there is no wind input. As with the SEP1, the examples include 50/150% factorisation.

*Times, distances and gradients need to be calculated.

The process starts at the screen height of 50 feet and ends 1500 feet above the aerodrome.

 The 5 minute takeoff power limit starts at screen height, then max continuous power is used.

If visual references are lost, assume the critical power unit has failed (i.e. use single-engine data once in cloud), but not below 300 feet.

All obstacles within the accountability area must be cleared by 50 feet. There should be no turns before the end of the TODR, then a maximum bank angle of 15°.

The minimum climb gradients are:

- 4% at the screen height.
- Positive at 400 feet with an engine failed.
- 0.75% at 1,500 feet with an engine failed.

Reduce the weight as necessary.

For obstacle clearance, you need time, distance and gradient, which is determined from one of three graphs, all shown overleaf:

- 3.5 - Gear extended with takeoff power
- 3.6 - Gear up with takeoff power
- 3.7 - Gear up with Max Continuous Power

FLIGHT PERFORMANCE & PLANNING
Multi-Engine Piston

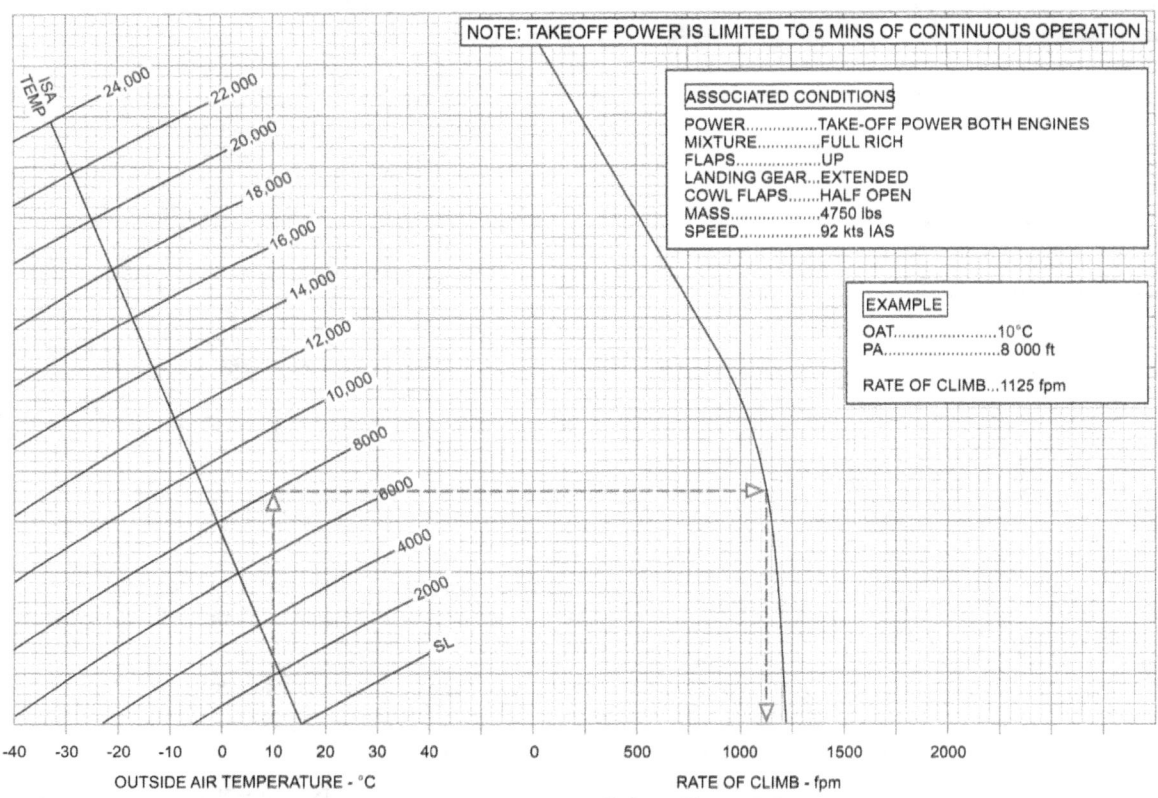

Figure 3.5

Below: Figure 3.6

Note the shaded area.

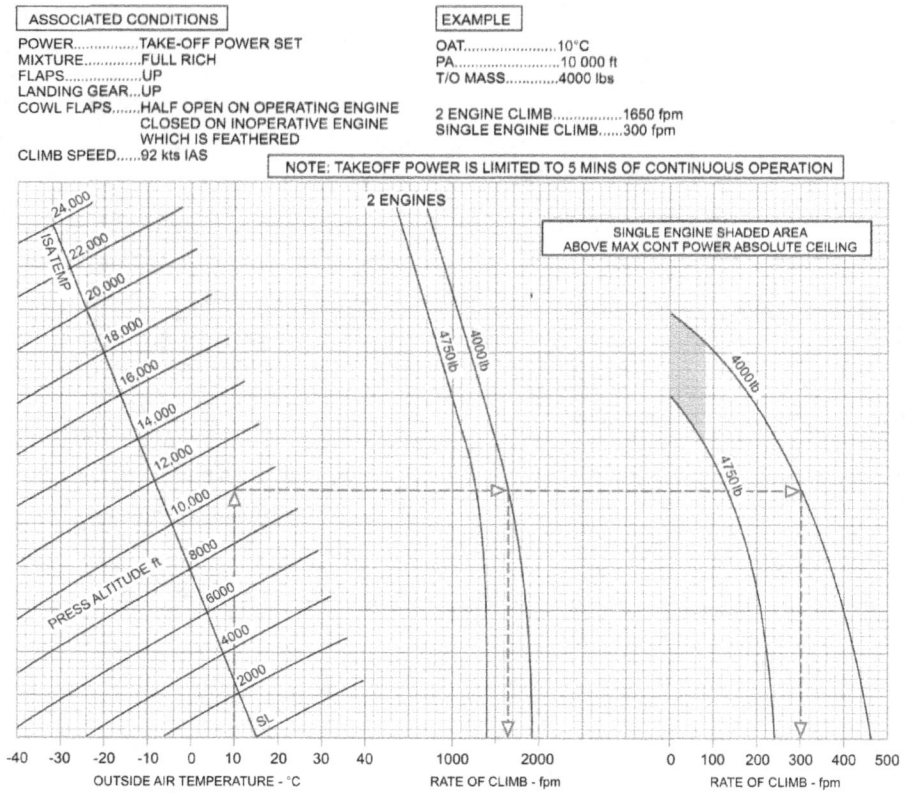

FLIGHT PERFORMANCE & PLANNING
Multi-Engine Piston

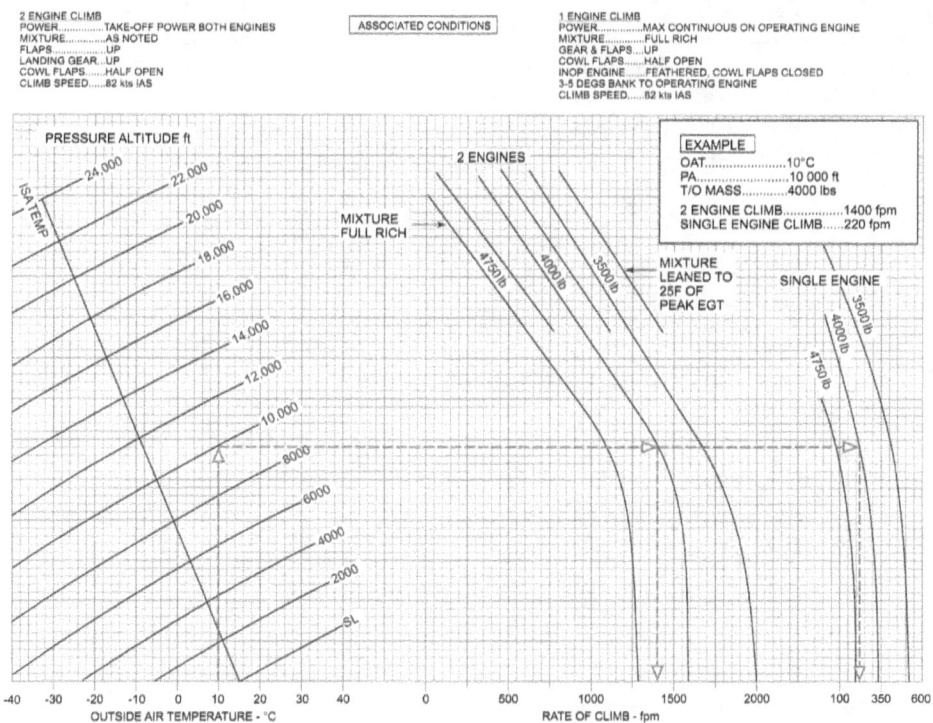

Above: Figure 3.7

Worked examples are given in the pictures, but note that 3.6 has a shaded area on the single-engine part. If you reduce the power to Max Continuous in this area, you don't have enough power to maintain altitude and will have to descend out of the shaded area.

Also, on the two-engined part of 3.7, there are extra lines for the rate of climb if the mixture has been leaned. The adjustment is made to rich of peak by 25°F.

Enroute

The enroute stage lasts from 1,500 feet after departure to 1,000 feet on the approach. If an engine fails:

- Carry out the appropriate drills
- Set MCP on the remaining engine
- Adjust to drift down speed, then drift down to one-engine stabilising altitude
- Continue above MSA, land at a suitable airfield

The MEP must be able to continue flight after an engine failure, so you need to know the descent range as well as the OEI cruise range. then you need to ensure that an airfield is always within the total OEI descent distance. To comply with this, the maximum altitude (as with the SEP 1) is where the rate of climb would be 300 fpm. The climb gradient is reduced by 0.5% while the descent gradient is increased by 0.5%.

The problem is that the descent gradient for a twin is always changing, because the air density increases lower down, and the thrust from the working engine increases, which means you can reduce the angle of descent until you reach an altitude where you can level off.

To work out the limiting altitude for drift down purposes, use Figure 3.7 and work backwards from 300 fpm ROC on both engines to the aircraft weight, then back across the temperature to find the maximum pressure altitude. The one-engine level-off altitude can be calculated by going back through the graph from the OEI section and zero fpm ROC (but try 100 fpm). This is the 1 engine service ceiling and the maximum altitude that can be used for the MSA.

Landing

The landing procedure starts at 1,000 feet on the approach, with a screen height of 50 feet. The landing criteria are essentially the same as for the SEP1, in that the LDR must be within 70% of the LDA - a factor of 1.43.

The landing distance graphs (3.9 & 3.10) are used in the same way as those for SEP 1. 3.9 is for a normal landing and 3.10 is for a short field landing, both with 40° of flap. The barrier speed depends on weight, and is calculated by going vertically upwards from the actual weight.

You also need to consider:

- a **balked landing**, where the gradient must be at least 2.5%, with the power set in 8 seconds (both engines operating), the gear down, the flaps at the landing position and speed at V_{REF}. Figure 3.8 is used in the same way as 3.5.

- a **missed approach**, where the gradient must be at least 0.75% at 1,500 feet above aerodrome elevation with the critical engine inoperative and feathered, MCP on the good engine, gear and flaps up. The speed must be at least 1.2 V_{S1}.

MEDIUM RANGE JET TRANSPORT

This is a Performance Class A Transport Category aircraft based on the 737-400, under CS/FAR 25. Certified engine thrust is used, minus the usual losses, like bleed air. Temperature is fully accounted for in the graphs, except for the landing ones.

Limitations

A quick sample for the graphs:

Item	Value
Maximum Relight Altitude	25,000 feet
Maximum Crosswind	33 kts
Over water speed	380 kts
MSTOM	62,800 kg
MSLM	54 900 kg
MZFM	51 300 kg
Maximum Power Use	5 minutes

Flap Settings

At least 5° must be used for takeoff, so that leading edge devices are deployed (they do this for any flap setting). 15° is the optimum*. There is a 4° transition setting. For approach, you normally use 22°, and 15°, 30° or 40° for landing. A smooth, hard surfaced runway is assumed.

*The climb gradient also depends on excess thrust. Increasing the flap setting to the optimum may allow an increase in mass for the available runway length, but the drag involved reduces its ability to climb.

Takeoff

As mentioned, the following influence the takeoff weight, and will give you the *Regulated Take Off Mass:*

- **Maximum Mass** in the flight manual.
- **Length of runway** (contaminated or otherwise).
- Altitude & Temperature.
- Tyre Speeds.
- Brake Energy.
- Obstacles.
- Noise Abatement.
- Reduced Thrust Procedures.

The lowest figure is used to determine your takeoff speeds (V_1, V_R & V_2). If your actual weight is below them, you have adequate performance. If not, you will either have to kick a couple of passengers off or change a parameter (maybe choose a longer runway).

MAXIMUM STRUCTURAL MASS (MSTOM)

62,800 kg.

FIELD LENGTH LIMITED (FLLTOM)

Our task is to find the Limiting Mass (and its associated V_1/V_R) based on the runway length, as affected by temperature, PA, slope, wind* and flap settings.

Figure 4.4 is based on a balanced field where TORA, TODA and ASDA are equal, that is, the stopway and clearway are not accounted for so, if either is available, the FLLTOM will be lower than necessary. That is, as the minimum V_1 is assumed to be equal to V_{MCG}, if a stopway or clearway is available, you will lose some payload.

*Winds are factored in. Having obtained a weight, keep it until the others can be compared with it. The example in CAP 698 gives you a FLLTOM of 63,000 kg, which is over the maximum weight anyway, so it is not limiting.

Takeoff Distance Required

The TODR is the greatest of:

- **AEO**. 115% of the horizontal distance to reach a screen height of 35 ft. In other words, when you reach 35 feet, you should have 15% of TODA remaining.

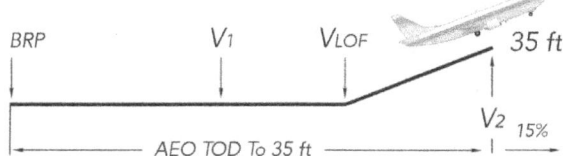

- **OEI**. For a dry runway, the distance to accelerate from BRP to V_{EF}, plus the distance to accelerate OEI (N-1) to the screen height (35 ft), or 15 ft* on a wet or contaminated hard surface.

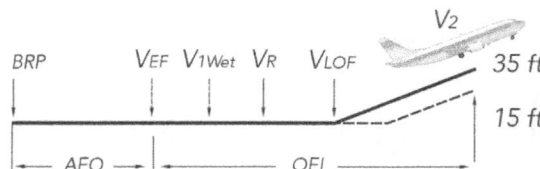

This is normally more limiting for twin aircraft.

*The reduction in takeoff weight for a wet runway is quite marked, so it was considered that the abandoned takeoff deserved the greater consideration, in return for a relatively small reduction in safety for the continued takeoff, in the shape of a reduced screen height of at least 15 feet, assuming lift off at the end of the TORA. Due to the reduced screen height, you cannot use a clearway on a wet runway, although it seems that you can on a contaminated runway.

Takeoff Run Required

If a clearway is available, the TORR is the greatest of:

- **AEO** (dry & wet runway). 115% of the gross distance from BRP to V_{LOF}, plus half of the gross distance from V_{LOF} to the screen height*. This must not exceed the length of the TORA.

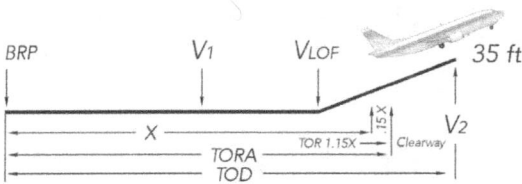

*Only up to 50% of the airborne distance between lift off and 35 feet can be over the runway.

The factors must be applied before the distances are used to establish takeoff weights.

- **OEI** (dry runway). The horizontal distance from BRP to halfway between V_{LOF} and screen height (i.e. half the flare distance) with the critical power unit inoperative.

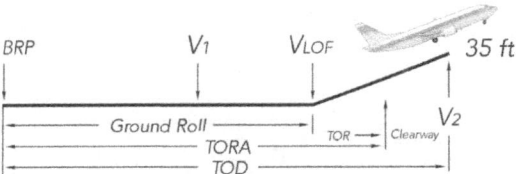

- BRP to 15 ft above the takeoff surface, achieved in the same way that you would get to V_2 by 35 ft, assuming the critical power unit stops at V_{EF}, which must not exceed the length of the TODA.

No factorisation is required for OEI distances.

A runway is considered to be wet as soon as it has a shiny appearance, but with no risk of hydroplaning from standing water. The water depth is assumed to be less than 3mm.

The wet runway engine failure point is determined by reducing the dry V_1 speed by 5-10 knots.

 The weight needs to be adjusted for non-standard conditions, such as the power management computer or air conditioning not being on, or engine anti-icing being on.

Acceleration and climb gradient are both reduced when an engine fails, which may affect obstacle clearance.

ASDR (Wet Runway)

ASDR must not exceed the length of the ASDA and is the greatest of the following distances:

- **OEI**. The sum of the distances needed:
  - to accelerate from BRP to the highest speed reached during the rejected takeoff, assuming the critical engine fails at V_{EF} and the first reject action is taken at V_1, and to decelerate to a full stop on a dry hard surface with one engine inoperative.
  - plus a distance equal to 2 seconds at V_1, to allow for recognition of the failure, the decision to do something about it and the transition to the stopping configuration.
- **OEI**. As above, but on a wet runway.
- **AEO**. As above, but with all engines operating.

Figure 4.4

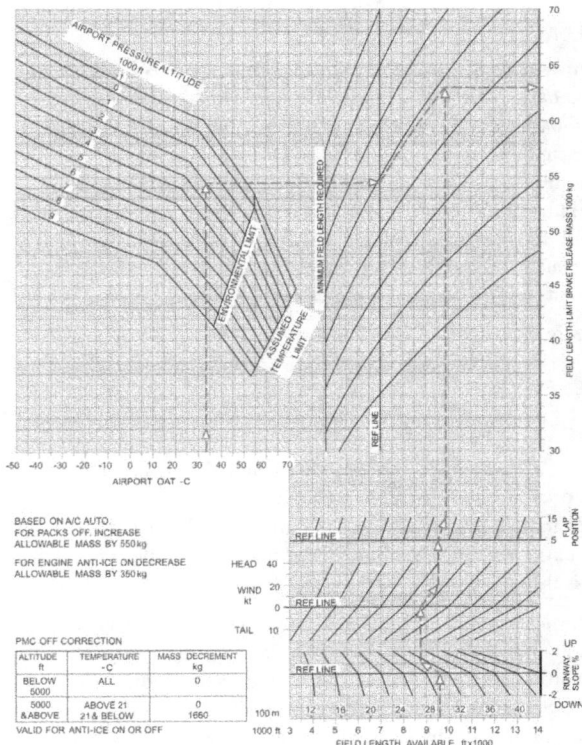

Method of Use

- Enter with Field Length Available (TORA). Move vertically to the runway slope reference line.
- Parallel the grid lines to the runway slope then the grid lines to the appropriate wind component and flap reference lines.
- If flap is 15°, parallel the grid lines then draw a vertical line through the weight grid. If flap is 5°, draw a vertical line from the reference line through the mass grid.

- Enter at the ambient temperature and proceed vertically to the aerodrome pressure altitude and proceed right to the mass grid reference line.
- Interpolate and follow the grid lines to intersect the vertical line drawn above. From this intersection draw a horizontal line to read the Field Length Limited TOM (63,000 kg in the example below).
- Apply any corrections necessary.

EXAMPLE SHOWN:

Field Length Available (TORA):	9,600 ft
Runway slope:	1% Uphill
Wind Component:	20 kts Head
Flaps:	15°
PMC:	On
Ambient Temperature:	+33°C
Pressure Altitude:	2,000 ft

MASS, ALTITUDE, TEMPERATURE (MATTOM)

The climb-limited TOM used to be known as the **WAT Limits** (*Weight-Altitude-Temperature*), or the atmospheric conditions under which the takeoff is conducted. An engine's output will normally be restricted by the maximum compressor RPM or the temperature on hot days (normally anything above ISA +15°C). Temperature limits can be reached at lower RPM, so the mass flow and thrust available will reduce. On the other hand, the thrust available will increase in colder temperatures, because the RPM limits will be higher, for a greater mass flow.

See Figure 4.5 below.

 CLTOM is based on a still air climb gradient using *Pressure Altitude* and is **not affected by wind**. It also has nothing to do with obstacles.

This graph shows the climb limited takeoff mass for a given pressure altitude and temperature. This is the heaviest an aircraft can be to just achieve the minimum required climb gradient after takeoff. The more thrust there is available, the higher is the CLTOM.

Normally speaking, there would be more thrust available at sea level than at altitude, due to the difference in temperature. In other words, a reduction in pressure altitude reduces the thrust available. Sometimes, however, you can get the same value of thrust at any altitude, typically within range of a particular ISA deviation.

The graph shows that, at temperatures above ISA +15°C, less mass would be available but, at temperatures lower than that, the temperature will not affect the mass (the pressure altitude lines are almost horizontal (yellow box). The others (full rated thrust) are parallel to the TIT limit.

This is known as being **flat rated**, in this particular case below ISA +15°C. As the engine RPM limit is reached first (jets are limited by their internal pressures, then by the LP RPM, the HP RPM, then the EGT), within the range of temperatures affected by it, the engine temperature does not affect the thrust available (RPM is limited electronically on modern aircraft). This is to protect against excessive pressure inside the engine.

In other words, flat rated engines can produce 100% thrust up to a given temperature at standard sea level pressure, after which they behave like standard engines, rather like using a supercharger in a piston engine. Above the flat rating limit, the EGT limiter reduces thrust by governing fuel flow to the engine.

Using flaps reduces the CLTOM because the L/D ratio is reduced, so the 5° setting for the MRJT is best.

Figure 4.5 guarantees meeting the most severe gradient requirement of the takeoff flight path, but it does not guarantee obstacle clearance.

Figure 4.5

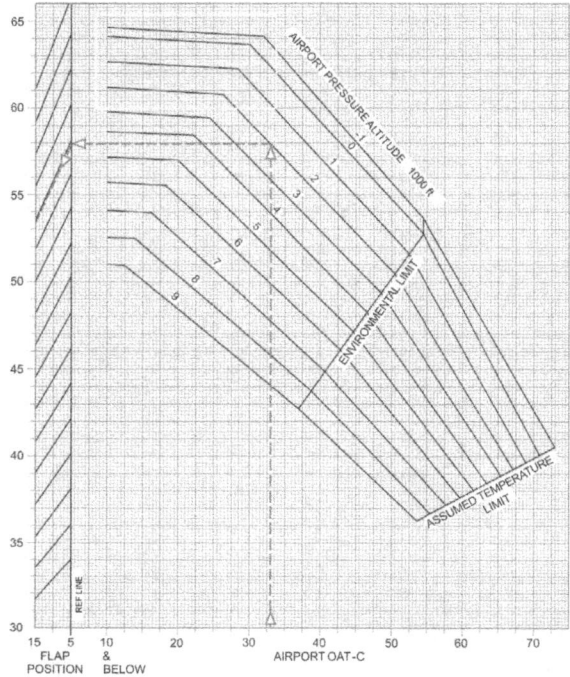

METHOD OF USE
- Enter the graph at the ambient temperature.
- Move vertically to the aerodrome pressure altitude.
- Travel left to the flap reference line and apply the appropriate setting to read climb limit mass.
- Apply any corrections necessary.

The example shows a Climb Limited TOM of 53,400 kg:

Field Length Available (TORA):	2,000 ft
OAT:	+33°C
Flaps:	15°

FLIGHT PERFORMANCE & PLANNING
Medium Range Jet Transport

TYRE SPEED (TYRETOM)

How well the tyres can cope with speed, affected by high ground speed, as when hot and high or with a tailwind and a small flap setting. See Figure 4.6 below. It is for 225 mph tyres, which is not normally limiting until you start using V_2 overspeed departures to get airborne with an increased payload, based on the fact that the manufacturer's figures are conservative anyway, certainly below the optimum climb gradient speed, or V_X. Increased V_2 may be considered if the second segment climb gradient limits the takeoff weight, meaning that you won't need all the runway, so V_1 and V_R must also be increased.

METHOD OF USE

Enter the graph with aerodrome OAT. Proceed vertically to the pressure altitude, then left to read the tyre speed limit. Correct as necessary - for 210 mph tyres and/or 15° flap, apply the correction below the graph.

OAT:	+ 33°C
Pressure Altitude:	2000 ft
Flaps:	15°
PMC:	On
Tyres:	210 mph
Uncorrected limit:	80400 kg
Correction:	-1500 kg

The Tyre Limit Mass is 78900 kg.

Figure 4.6

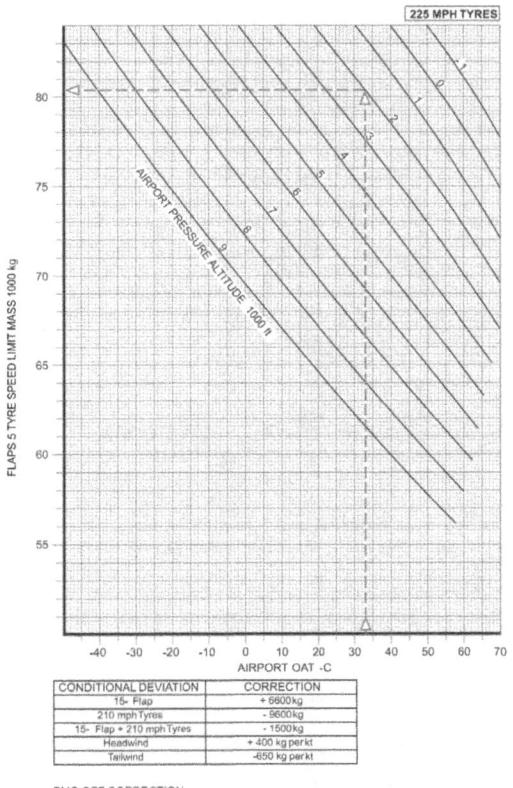

MAXIMUM BRAKE ENERGY (VMBETOM)

How good the brakes are at stopping you if you have to stand on them. This is not normally a problem, as the manufacturer will have built them to a high specification, but it can be occasionally. In fact, CAP 698 says that, in general, V_{MBE} will not be limiting except at hot, high aerodromes or with a tail wind.

The graph gives you a speed (not a weight) which must be equal to or greater than V_1, or you must reduce weight (if V_1 exceeds V_{MBE}, apply the correction below the graph). Aside from high ground speed (see TYRETOM, above), this is also affected by slope. See Figure 4.7 below.

METHOD OF USE

Enter the graph with aerodrome pressure altitude. Travel horizontally to the OAT, drop vertically to the takeoff mass, then horizontally right to V_{MBE}.

Take-Off Mass:	64,000 kg
Airfield Pressure Altitude:	5,600 ft
Ambient Temperature:	-10° C
Runway Slope:	1.5% Uphill
Wind Component:	10 kts Head
PMC:	On

From the worked example above, the V_{MBE} = 165 + 3 + 3 = 171 kts.

Figure 4.7

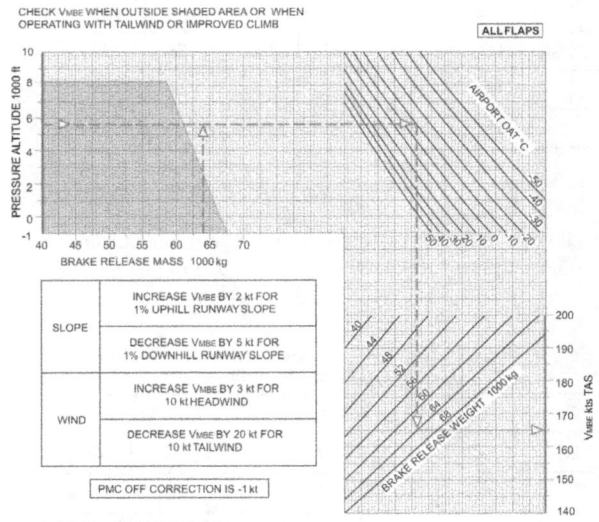

Speeds

Having sorted out the takeoff weight, you now need to find out at what speed you can leave the runway.

Reminder: V_1 must not be less than V_{MCG}, and must be equal to or less than V_R and V_{MBE}.

To calculate the V speeds, use the tables at Figure 4.8 (5° flap) or 4.9 (15°) as follows:

- Enter the density sub-graph (below) with pressure altitude and ambient temperature to find which columns in the tables should be used. For example, at 3,000 feet and 20°C, you need column B.

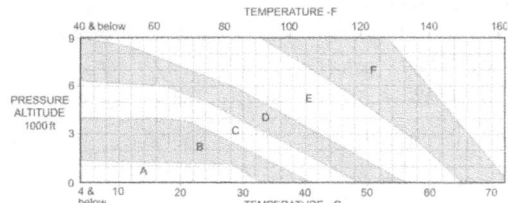

- Select the tables appropriate to the flap setting.
- Enter the with the actual takeoff mass and extract V_1, V_R and V_2 from Column B:

Flaps 5°	A			B		
1000 kg	V_1	V_R	V_2	V_1	V_R	V_2
70	158	163	168	158	164	169
65	151	155	161	152	156	162
60	144	148	155	145	148	155
55	137	139	149	138	140	149
50	129	131	142	130	132	142

- To correct V_1 for slope and/or wind component, enter the table at the top of Figure 4.8 or 4.9 at the actual takeoff mass and interpolate the correction.

Flaps 5°	Slope/Wind V_1 Adjustment					
PMC On	DN	Slope %	UP	T	Wind kts	H
1000 kg						
70	-3	0	4	-3	0	1
60	-2	0	2	-3	0	1
50	-2	0	1	-4	0	1
40	-2	0	1	-4	0	1

- Apply the corrections to V_1.
- To determine the V_{MCG}, enter the left column at the ambient temperature, then proceed right along the row to the aerodrome pressure altitude (interpolating if necessary). Extract V_{MCG}.

OAT	PA x 1000 ft				
°C	0	2	4	6	8
55	104				
50	107	103			
40	111	107	103	99	94
30	116	111	107	104	98
20	116	113	111	107	102
10	116	113	111	108	104
-50	118	115	112	109	105

If V_1 is less than V_{MCG}, takeoff is not permitted.

A V_1/V_R range becomes available when:

- The aircraft is lighter than the FLLTOM and/or the climb limited TOM, or both exceed the MTOM.
- The climb limited weight is less than the FLLTOM.
- The AEO TODR is limiting.

Engine failure at the low V_1 would need full use of Distance D if the takeoff is continued, and you would need less than the full emergency distance. The opposite would apply if you used the high V_1.

Below is how the speeds table might look in the FCOM:

FLAPS	WT 1000 KG	A			B			C			D		
		V_1	V_R	V_2	V_1	V_R	V_2	V_1	V_R	V_2	V_1	V_R	V_2
5	70	158	163	168	158	164	169						
	65	151	155	161	152	156	162	153	157	162			
	60	144	148	155	145	148	155	146	149	155			
	55	137	139	149	138	140	149	138	141	148	140	143	148
	50	129	131	142	130	132	142	131	133	142	132	134	141
	45	121	123	136	122	124	135	122	125	135	124	126	135
	40	113	114	130	113	116	129	113	116	128	113	117	128
15	70	150	152	158									
	65	143	145	152	145	146	151						
	60	137	139	146	138	140	146	139	140	146			
	55	130	131	141	131	132	140	131	133	140	134	134	140
	50	122	124	135	123	125	134	124	125	134	126	126	134
	45	114	116	128	116	117	128	116	118	128	118	119	127
	40	104	107	122	104	109	122	104	110	122	109	111	121

In the shaded areas, check the V_{MCG} for the actual temperature.

%N1 VALUES

%N_1 tables may be used for engine anti-icing on and off. However, correction is necessary if the air conditioning packs are off. Use the following procedure:

- Select the table appropriate to PMC on or off.
- Select the table for the phase of flight (takeoff, climb or go-around - the extract below is for takeoff, but they all work the same way).
- Enter the left column with either aerodrome ambient temperature or TAT, then read %N_1 in the aerodrome pressure altitude column.

OAT	PA				
°C	-1000	0	1000	2000	3000
54	93.3	94.1	93.6		
52	93.6	94.2	94.2	93.7	
50	93.8	94.3	94.3	94.3	93.9
48	94.0	94.5	94.4	94.4	94.4
46	94.1	94.7	94.6	94.5	94.5
44	94.3	94.8	94.8	94.7	94.7
42	94.5	95.0	95.0	94.9	94.9

ABNORMAL TAKEOFFS

These include:

- **Contaminated runway** (see tables in Figure 4.14). There is more drag and the brakes won't work properly, so you must reduce weight and/or V_1. The maximum contamination depth is 13 mm.

  You cannot use an increased V_2 or reduce your thrust. If the anti-skid isn't working, you cannot take off. To calculate the correct weight:

  - Find the normal takeoff mass limit.
  - Select the right table for the depth of contaminant (interpolate as required). the table shown below is for 2 mm slush depth.
  - Enter the table with the RTOM.
  - Find the mass and V_1 reductions for the mass and pressure altitude (if you end up in the shaded area, try the table on the right).
  - Calculate the new limiting takeoff mass.
  - Calculate the V speeds.
  - Apply the V_1 reduction from the table.
  - Check that V_{MBE} is within limits, although this won't normally be a problem as a reduced weight is being used.

Figure 4.14

Mass 1000 kg	Mass & V1 Reductions			
	PA ft	0	4000	8000
40	1000 kg	2.9	3.4	4.0
	KIAS	22	21	19
44	1000 kg	3.7	4.2	4.9
	KIAS	22	21	18
48	1000 kg	4.3	5.0	5.8
	KIAS	21	19	17
52	1000 kg	4.9	5.7	6.5
	KIAS	20	18	15
56	1000 kg	5.6	6.3	7.0
	KIAS	18	16	14
60	1000 kg	6.1	6.8	7.3
	KIAS	16	15	12
64	1000 kg	6.6	7.2	7.6
	KIAS	16	13	10
68	1000 kg	6.9	7.5	8.2
	KIAS	13	11	8

- **Increased V_2**, or **Improved Climb** Technique. This extends the second segment and is used to enhance the takeoff weight and climb performance when you are limited by the gradient or obstacles*, but otherwise have too much runway available (especially on hot days, in places like Dubai). The improved climb performance is converted into a relatively small weight increase on the CLTOM. You use the extra runway to get up to a higher speed, which means a longer takeoff run, but a better angle of climb with V_X. In other words, the higher the speed, the better the climb gradient.

*An obstacle cleared on this basis must be the last one in the TOFP.

The technique cannot be used with a contaminated runway or if the anti skid is not working, or if you are not using full power. This is because V_2 is not always aerodynamically efficient on takeoff, being based on stall speed ($V_2 = 1.2\ V_S$).

Although the standard safety factors are maintained, this procedure makes the aircraft field length or tyre speed limited. In the former case, use Figure 4.15. For the latter, use Figure 4.16. Both work in similar ways.

Figure 4.16

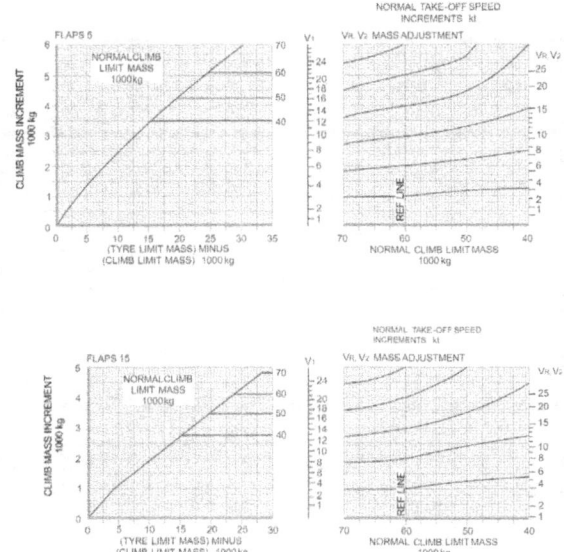

The above table is used in the same way as Figure 4.15 for the Field Length Limit.

- **Reduced Thrust Takeoff** (Figure 4.17). If you are not otherwise limited (i.e. when your actual Takeoff Mass is lower than the Field Length Limited Mass), you can use less power on takeoff to save engine wear and reduce noise at the expense of a longer takeoff run, as used for most departures. It is accomplished by confusing the FMS with a higher temperature than the ambient one.

The most limiting factors for variable thrust are:

- Field Lengths.
- Climb limit.
- Maximum thrust reduction (25%).
- NTOFP obstacle clearance (least limiting).

Thrust may be reduced until the first one of the above becomes limiting.

Reduced thrust **may not** be used:

- on contaminated runways.
- if the anti-skid is not working.
- if reverse thrust is not working.
- if increased V_2 is used.
- when PMC is off.

- **Anti Skid Inoperative**. The ASDR is increased because the braking action is reduced, so V_1 must be reduced and so must the RTOM. The extra time spent on one engine also reduces obstacle clearance. Not to be used if:

- The runway is contaminated.
- Increased V_2 procedure is used.
- Reduced Thrust Takeoff is used.

FLIGHT PERFORMANCE & PLANNING
Medium Range Jet Transport

OBSTACLES (OBSTTOM)

Hard objects to be avoided by at least 35 feet within an obstacle domain, which starts at 1500 feet, at the end of the takeoff stage. Its vertical direction takes the shape of the Net Takeoff Flight Path, discussed later. Graphs are provided for Flaps 5° and Flaps 15° (Figures 4.20 and 4.21). They are meant to be used when a detailed airport analysis is not available. Detailed analysis for the specific case from the aeroplane flight manual may result in a less restrictive weight and can account for the non-use of the air conditioning packs.

These graphs are not valid for A/C packs off or for take-offs using the improved climb technique.

- Select the appropriate graph.
- Adjust the obstacle elevation to account for runway slope to determine obstacle height as shown.
- Enter the bottom left vertical axis at the adjusted obstacle height.
- Travel horizontally right to intersect the horizontal distance of the obstacle measured from the BRP, then move vertically up to the ambient temperature reference line, then parallel the grid lines to the temperature.
- Continue vertically to the aerodrome pressure altitude reference line. Parallel the grid lines to the appropriate pressure altitude before continuing vertically to the wind component reference line.
- Parallel the grid lines from this point to the value of the wind component then continue vertically to read the obstacle limited take-off mass.

EXAMPLE SHOWN BELOW

Flap Setting:	5°
Pressure Altitude:	1,000 ft
Ambient Temperature:	+ 37°C
PMC:	ON
Wind Component:	20 kts Head
Runway Slope:	2% down
Obstacle Distance from BRP:	18,000 ft
Obstacle Elevation:	1,160 ft
Take-Off Distance Required:	10,000 ft

Obstacle Height = 1160 - [1000 - (10000 x 2%)] = 360 ft

Obstacle Limited TOM = 51,700 kg

Figure 4.20

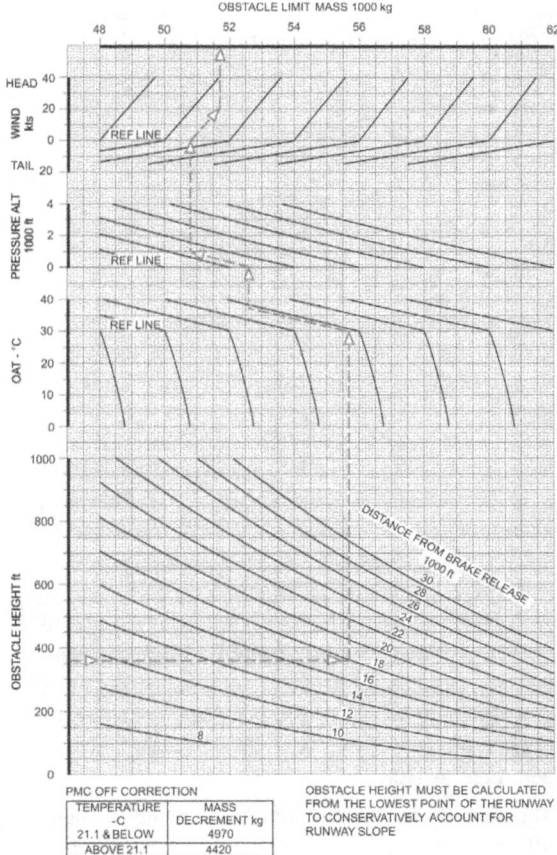

NET TAKEOFF FLIGHT PATH

This covers the relationship between height and the distance needed to clear obstacles during takeoff, when the critical engine has failed is based on net performance. The gross figures are decreased by a 0.8% margin* for two-engined aircraft, 0.9% for 3-engined aircraft, and 1% for 4-engined machines.

*You can find the vertical distance between the net and gross flight paths by multiplying the distance from Reference Zero by 0.008 (0.009 for 3-engined aircraft).

These represent a very low probability factor of 10^{-1} for the rare event of continuing after an engine failure so close to V_1 that there is hardly any AEO benefit from a delayed engine failure, which is a remote probability anyway (for 10^{-7} you would need a gradient nearer 3.2%).

The takeoff flight path is divided into several segments, each representing a change in configuration, thrust and/or speed, according to the most critical condition, and without the benefit of ground effect (in general, an aircraft is considered to be out of ground effect at a height equal to its wing span).

All the data you need to construct the NTOFP will be in the flight manual, but there may be no information at all in some areas. For instance, a Class B aircraft is assumed to have all of its engines working until it gets above 300 feet, under which height there is no data for landing or takeoff (which is why the takeoff minima should not be below this, because you must be visual to avoid any obstacles should an engine fail*). Sometimes, there can be no specific provision for engine failure at all, especially for going around after an extended approach with the gear and flaps down, or dragging in straight and level on a non-precision approach (hence continuous descent paths).

*The net takeoff path for a Class A aeroplane assumes the failure of the **critical engine** at V_{EF}.

The various stages of the NTOFP for CS 25 are:

- The **first segment**, from screen height, which is 35 ft at the end of the TODR, 15 feet when wet, or 50 feet if turning until the gear is up and locked. This is the only configuration change allowed below 400 feet. This segment is quite variable and may not exist in some aircraft. It is a balance between varying climb performance and a constant retraction time. The gear is assumed to be down at the end of the TOD, but if it happens to be retracted at screen height, the 1st segment is dispensed with. Transport category aircraft must at least be able to climb positively during this segment. The rotation speed must be selected so that V_2 is achieved by 35 feet.

 The 35 feet clearance net flight path is straight ahead. An escape will be based on a turn involving 15° of bank with an extra 15 feet for the engine pod or flap depression.

The **first segment** requires a positive climb gradient (out of ground effect) for 2-engined aircraft, 0.3% for 3-engined aircraft and 0.8% for 4-engined aircraft. No descent is possible.

- The **second segment** lasts from gear up until levelling off for the cleanup (*at least* 400 feet AGL*, having gone through V_2, V_3 and V_4 with flaps and power at takeoff and the propeller of the failed engine feathered). This is normally the most limiting because its relatively high gradient (flaps out) helps you clear close-in obstacles.

*As there must be no change in configuration, except for the gear, until 400 feet, this is the *minimum* altitude for retracting high lift devices, which must satisfy several requirements. The larger the flap setting, the more you can lift off the runway, but this will limit the climb, and vice versa. Most manufacturers use a higher figure.

The **second segment** requires 2.4% for 2-engined aircraft, 2.7% for 3-engined aircraft and 3% for 4-engined aircraft. This is usually the most limiting.

The minimum climb gradient is defined by:
- Gear Up
- Flaps in takeoff position
- Engines (N_1) at takeoff thrust
- Speed equal to V_2

- The **third** (transition or acceleration) **segment** is the horizontal distance needed to accelerate at a constant altitude to aid with flap or slat retraction and acceleration to final takeoff climb speed (V_{FTO}), which is typically V_2 +60 or 70 kts (level off height). It is usually a level burst at a minimum height of 400 feet*, during which V_{climb} (or V_{YSE}**) is achieved, flaps are retracted and power is reduced to Max Continuous (there is usually a time limit for engines above this). This is the worst configuration as there is a lot happening. The end of this segment often coincides with the end of the 5 minute limit for takeoff thrust, but most aircraft now have a 10 minute limit. If this time limit is reached before this segment is complete, you need to set maximum continuous power and rethink its length or use a steeper 2nd segment climb, higher than dictated by obstacles, to reach the 3rd segment quicker and leave enough Takeoff Power/Thrust available.

*Although you must be *capable* of achieving the minimum gradients required by the fourth segment, the third segment is flown level to reduce the time and distance taken for acceleration.

**V_{YSE} is the Class B Normal category aeroplane's version of V_2 and the enroute climb speed, V_{climb}. It normally relates to the climb configuration (gear and flaps up), so you are not configured for it on takeoff.

The third segment can go on for a while - a light twin can take many miles to get to 1500 feet.

- The **fourth** (and final) **segment** is a climb to 1,500', or higher if there are obstacles or you have not reached the single engine en-route climb speed. The aircraft is clean with Max Continuous Power on one engine, and the other secured. The gradient here is lower due to the reduction in thrust in the third segment. For aeroplanes certified for engine-out climbs, the optimum speed for a single-engined climb is known as V_{climb}.

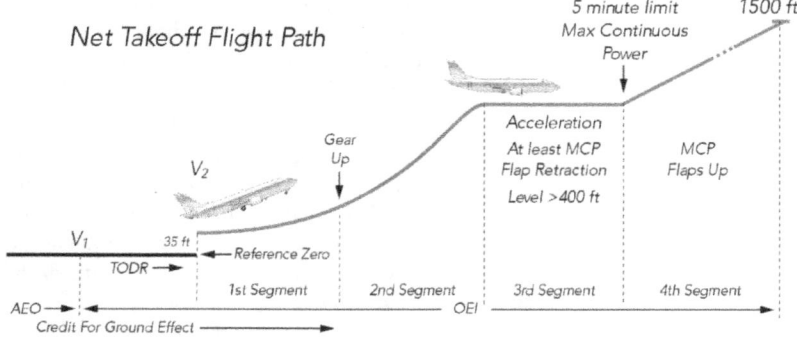

The **third** and **fourth segments** require a 1.2% gradient for 2-engined aircraft, 1.5% for 3-engined aircraft and 1.7% for 4-engined aircraft. This is because the available gradient in the third segment must be at least equal to that for the final segment.

Acceleration from V_{FTO} to final en-route climb speed is done at the end of the fourth segment, as is done with some British aircraft.

The NTOFP should clear all obstacles vertically by 35 feet and 300 feet horizontally (200 feet within the airport boundary). In determining this, the lowest point of the aircraft is used, hence the limiting bank angle of 15° in turns, because the wing will become the lowest point.

The relevant chart in CAP 698 is Figure 4.5. It gives you the limiting CLTOM (without having to calculate the NTOFP) for various temperatures and pressure altitudes. Any weights above those given mean the aircraft will not meet the gradients.

If an obstacle (including a frangible one) intrudes on the Net Flight Path, the takeoff weight must be reduced until it's cleared by the relevant margin, so this may be a determining one in calculating *Restricted Takeoff Weight*. You can make gentle turns to avoid obstacles (not more than 15° in the 2nd and 4th segments only) without adjusting takeoff weights, and there will be graphs in the Flight Manual allowing you to calculate radii and procedures for it. However, for Class B aeroplanes, you will need to be visual, so you need a minimum cloud base.

 Distances for flight planning purposes are taken from the end of TODR, while on charts they are taken from the end of the clearway, so the actual distance to the obstacle is greater than that reported by the difference between TODR and TODA.

The Climb Limited TOM graph shows the maximum TOM at which the MRJT can achieve the minimum legal **still air** climb gradient. Wind therefore plays no part in the process and is not an input to the graph, so there is no compensation.

Here is a quick reference for minimum climb gradients:

	1	2	3	4
2 Engines	Positive	2.4%	1.2%	1.2%
3 Engines	0.3%	2.7%	1.5%	1.5%
4 Engines	0.5%	3.0%	1.7%	1.7%

Under CS 25.121(b)(1), the minimum steady climb gradient of twin engined aircraft during the 2nd segment shall not be less than 2.4%. At the same time, CAT.POL.A.210(a) & (b)(5) requires that, if an engine fails during takeoff, the net flight path must clear all obstacles by at least 35 ft, taking into account loss of gradient during the turn due to the bank angle. The net flight path is obtained by reducing the actual (gross) climb gradient by 0.8% for twin-engined large aeroplanes (CS 25.115(b)(1)). From the certification point of view, the minimum gross (actual) climb gradient before entering a turn of more than 15° turn shall be 2.9% to achieve the minimum required gradient in the 2nd segment, under CS 25.121(b)(1). It arises from 2.4% as the minimum + 0.5% that will be lost during the turn due to bank.

Enroute (Cruise)

Fuel consumption, range and endurance are covered in the *Flight Planning* section.

The enroute phase lasts from 1500 feet on departure to 1500 feet on the approach, during which you must stay above the safety altitude. However, if the MSA is quite high (say over the Rockies at 14,000 feet), you're obviously going to be pushed to get there in some aircraft with two engines, let alone one. This means that you will have no choice but to descend until you reach a height at which you can keep flying on one engine, with a small climb capability available (all terrain within 10 nm must be cleared by 2,000 feet during the descent, or 1,000 if you have a positive rate of climb). The problem is that the mountains are in the way, so you will have to make an emergency turn as well to get clear. This procedure is called Drift Down. The maximum height for the procedure is the same as the maximum height for relighting the engines. What you do is establish a point one side of which performance is OK and the other side of which, if you have an engine failure, you make an emergency turn to get yourself away from the area and (hopefully) out of trouble, drifting down to the MSA. The charts will indicate the rate of descent and the distance flown. Just make sure you don't go further into the mountains than that distance. If you can't comply with this, you may have to reduce your weight until you can.

The drift down procedure is designed to minimise loss of range, but it requires Maximum Continuous Thrust (MCT) from the working engines. You also need a descent speed that will allow the safe clearance of obstacles.

V_{MD} would provide the greatest tradeoff due to the very shallow descent gradient, but using the single engined climb speed means that the machine will at least be speed stable while you sort the problem out. See Figures 4.24 - 4.27 (below). However, when terrain or obstacles are not a factor, and for simplicity, most aircraft manufacturers recommend drifting down at high speed or Turbulence Penetration Speed to increase the range.

Figure 4.27

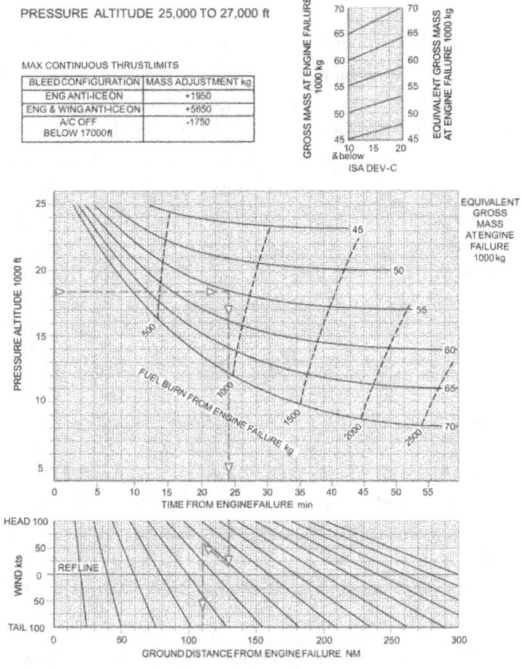

If an engine fails, the procedure is to:
- Set max continuous power* on the other one(s)
- Maintain altitude until you reach drift down speed
- Descend at that speed until you reach the stabilising altitude, where the air is dense enough to support the aircraft

The net drift down path is 1.1% less than the gross path.

 In CAP 698 this is given as a negative figure which is added to the drift down gradient.

*The tables on page 39 of CAP 698 give you the $\%N_1$ you need to get max continuous power. The next one provides the gross level off altitude for a given weight and temperature correction, plus the drift down speed** for given weights, which reduces as weight decreases.

**Just above V_{MD}, for speed stability.

Figure 4.23 contains the net level off altitude with varying temperatures. The line at 17,000 feet assumes that air conditioning packs are off at that altitude. If they are on, subtract 2,500 kg (see table). Also check adjustments for anti-icing systems. The net drift down flight path from various heights is on the next four pages.

You have to alter the weight to an equivalent weight to account for changes in temperature. Above ISA + 10 in the temperature deviation graph, adjust as necessary.

Descent

The point at the end of the cruise where descent is normally initiated is called the Top Of Descent, or TOD. The descent ranges from TOD to the touch down.

Due to the fuel consumption, you must stay as high as possible until you know that a landing can be made shortly after the descent. Fortunately, most modern aircraft will calculate that for you. When planning for the descent, you have to take into account any expected (or unexpected!) radar vectoring.

 Track distance is the actual distance over the ground until touchdown. It is *not* the same as the more direct DME distance!

The descent from high altitudes always starts with a constant Mach number, for the same reasons that such a climb schedule is used in the climb.

The basic rule is to divide the FL by 3 and add 10 nm for the deceleration from descent speed to initial approach speed. You would therefore need 120 nm if you started from FL 330. The DME at this range will also be 120 nm.

You could also multiply the distance by 3 and subtract 3000 feet for deceleration to get the correct flight level. From a distance of 60 nm, you should be at FL 150.

On top of the above, add or subtract 3 nm for each 10 knots of tailwind or headwind, respectively.

Landing

Landing weights can be climb or field-length limited.

The approach extends from 1,500 feet down to the screen height of 50 feet, and the landing itself is carried out from that point until the aircraft comes to a stop. It must naturally do so within the landing distance available, and you need to consider the go-around. The velocity of the aircraft at 50 feet should be V_{REF}. The flare is the transition from the straight approach to the horizontal ground roll. The distance measured from the 50 ft point to where the flare is initiated is the approach distance. Touchdown occurs when the wheels touch the ground, and the velocity at that point should be 1.15 V_S. After touchdown, there is a free roll before the brakes and/or thrust reversers are applied. The ground roll is the distance between the touchdown and the point where the aircraft velocity is zero.

As with the takeoff, you have to take the most limiting of a number of masses, in this case 3.

MAXIMUM STRUCTURAL (MSLM)
54,900 kg.

FLIGHT PERFORMANCE & PLANNING
Medium Range Jet Transport

FIELD LENGTH LIMITED (FLLLM)
Use Figure 4.28.

For go-arounds, the minimum gradients are:

	Approach	Landing
2 Engines	2.1%	3.2%
3 Engines	2.4%	3.2%
4 Engines	2.7%	3.2%

Under normal circumstances, climb limits for landing should not be a problem, because if you can satisfy them within 15 minutes of takeoff (which is what they are for), you can make them at the destination after you've used all the trip fuel. However, it is something to watch for when flying from a low altitude airport to one at a high altitude.

Figure 4.29

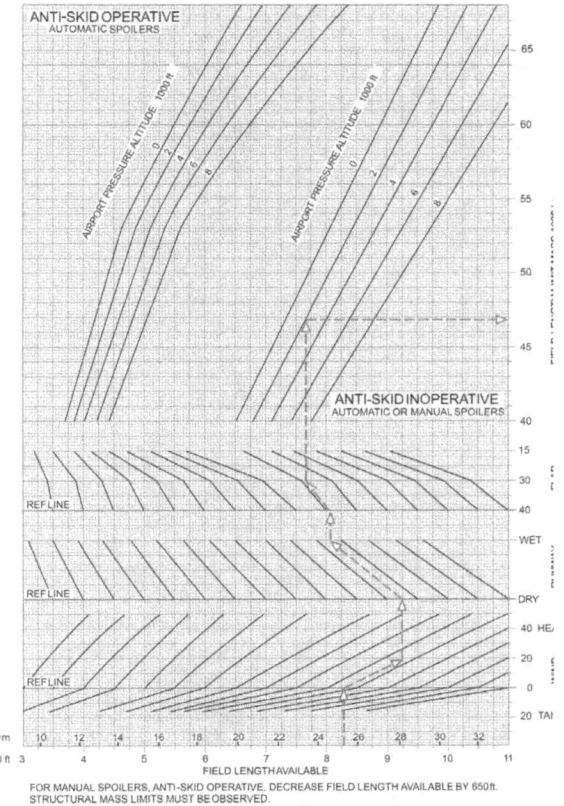

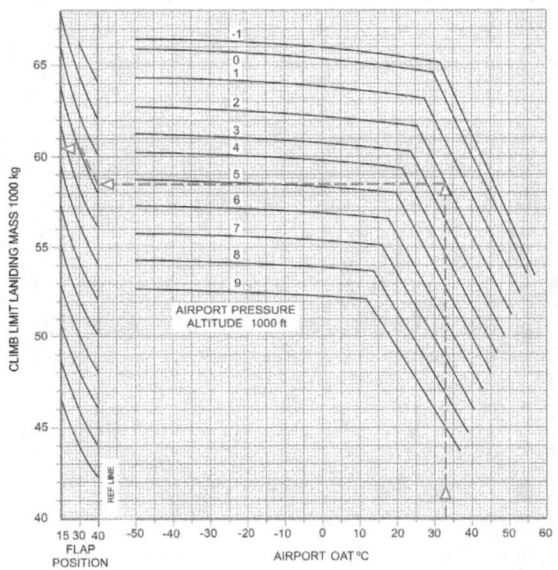

The weight of the aircraft may not be more than that which will allow it to be stopped within certain percentages of the effective length of the runway, according to whether it is a turboprop or turbojet and whether the runway is wet or dry.

Slope and temperature are ignored (slope is only a factor when it is over 2%).

MASS, ALTITUDE, TEMPERATURE (MATLM)

The need to abandon the approach or reject a landing and climb away is assumed, so there is a distinction between going around in the approach or landing configuration. Figure 4.29 enables the calculation of the missed approach climb-limited weight. The graph for the configuration of the balked landing climb weight has not been provided in CAP 698.

- **Balked Landing**, in the landing configuration with all engines operating and full power applied.
- **Missed Approach**, with gear up, flaps at the go around position, one engine failed and the other at go-around power.

QUICK TURNAROUND LIMIT

The tables on page 48 allow you to find out the maximum weight at which you can land and be able to take off again without having to wait for 53 minutes for the brakes to cool down (don't forget to check the thermal plugs in the tyres). You can then land with a reasonable fuel load and not waste time sitting on the ground. If the landing weight is less than that from the graph, there are no restrictions.

The Brake Cooling Schedule (Figure 4.31) is used *after* landing or an aborted takeoff. The brakes are affected by *groundspeed*, which can be obtained from the INS/IRS, or using the flight computer. If you are using IAS, use 50/150% factoring for the wind.

The graph enables due allowance to be made for a single stop and provides advice on the procedure to be adopted and the minimum cooling time. Separate sub-graphs are for determining the stop distance with manual braking.

ABANDONED TAKEOFF

- Enter the top left vertical axis at the Regulated Take-Off Mass and travel horizontally right to V_1, minus 50% of headwind or plus 150% of tailwind.
- Drop vertically to the first reference line then follow the gridlines to correct for PA then OAT.
- Continue vertically downward to read the Brake Energy per Brake in millions of foot pounds. To this value add one million foot pounds for each taxi mile to obtain the total energy.
- Continue vertically down to determine the advised cooling schedule and recommended cooling time.

LANDING

- Enter the left vertical axis at the estimated landing mass and travel horizontally right to a speed of $(V_{REF} - 3)$ kts corrected for wind component minus 50% of a headwind or plus 150% for a tailwind.
- From this intersection, drop vertically to the first reference line then follow the gridlines to correct for Pressure Altitude then OAT.
- Continue vertically downward to the Braking Configuration reference line.
- Follow the gridlines to the appropriate braking configuration.
- Continue vertically downward to read the Brake Energy per brake in millions of foot pounds.
- To this value, add one million foot pounds for each taxi mile to obtain the total energy.
- Continue vertically downward to determine the advised cooling schedule and recommend cooling time.

BRAKING DISTANCE

For a manual braked landing with no reverse thrust or for a manual braked landing with normal thrust #2 detent, select the appropriate sub-graph in Figure 4.31, then enter the sub-graph at the Brakes ON IRS Ground Speed KIAS and travel vertically up to intersect the equivalent autobrake setting. From this intersection travel horizontally left to the vertical axis to read the stopping distance in thousands of feet.

 The maximum level of energy that brakes can safely absorb is reduced as they wear. Brake energy is typically limiting in high/moderately hot conditions, on long runways, with less deflected takeoff flap settings.

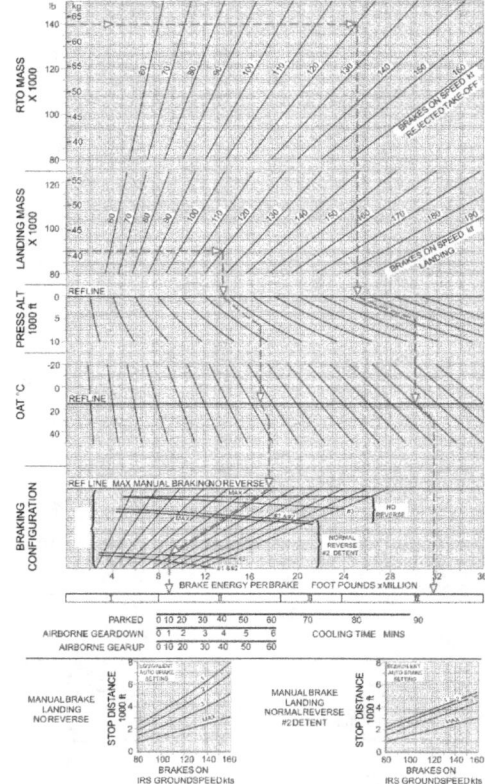

Figure 4.31 - Brake Cooling Schedule

Mass & Balance

This must follow the Flight Manual, to ensure that an aircraft is safely loaded. As the Flight Manual forms part of the Type Certificate, if its conditions are not met, the flight becomes illegal, and any insurance is invalidated.

In fact, the loading, mass and C of G of an aircraft must comply with the *more restrictive* of the Flight or Ops Manuals (your company may impose their own restrictions). The Mass & Balance limitations for any aircraft are found in the Flight Manual and should be repeated in Part B of the Ops Manual. The details for a particular aircraft, after being weighed, will be in the *Weight & Balance Schedule*, found en either the Technical Log, the Flight Manual, or the aircraft document folder.

A large range of C of G is needed on transport aircraft in order to get the various loads of passengers and freight comfortably loaded. The loading of fuel is not normally a problem with piston-engined machines, but jets need a larger range to play with, firstly because, when the fuel is taken from the wings, which are usually swept, the C of G will move forward as the fuel is used up (it will move aft if the fuel comes from the centre tank). Also, when fuselages are longer, the effects of changes can be exaggerated.

The effects of having the C of G in extreme positions are the same for all aeroplanes, mainly in terms of stability and controllability in the longitudinal plane. If it is too far forward, the aircraft is harder to fly, and if it is too far aft, the static and manoeuvre margins are smaller, albeit lighter on the controls (and some aircraft can pitch up markedly when the spoilers are activated on landing).

The C of G will move around during flight as fuel is used from various tanks.

For the exams, you will need to complete a Load & Trim sheet to find the C of G position and the Taxi and Zero Fuel weights. The taxi weight C of G is needed to set the horizontal trim stabiliser properly for takeoff.

For example, as fuel is less dense than water, a typical SG value (found in most flight manuals) for jet fuel is 0.79, meaning 7.9 lbs per gallon. As a rule of thumb, for Jet A, take the weight in lbs, add half, then divide by 10 to get US gallons. 2,000 lbs is therefore approximately 300 US gallons, at the usual fuel weight of 6.76 lbs/gal. The precise figure can then be calculated with a flight computer.

Alternatively, the Operations Manual will give a standard figure for the conversion to be used with a calculator.

The figures may vary with fuel temperature - although fuel might be delivered in litres, the invoice will give a calculation for the equivalent volume at a fixed density.

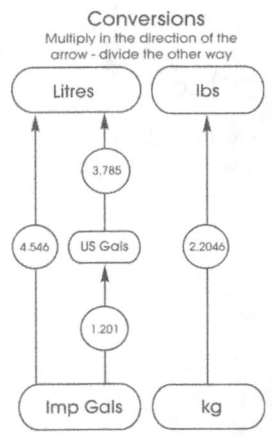

UNITS & CONVERSIONS

The *weight* of the fuel in your tanks determines your range - each pound of it has a specific value of heat that creates horsepower or thrust so, the denser your fuel is, the further you can fly (check the specific gravity). This is why pounds or kilograms are often used for calibrating fuel quantity gauges. Unfortunately, fuel is delivered to you in gallons or litres, so correct conversion is important.

Tip: You get more fuel in the tanks in cold temperatures.

Units of volume in general use are Imperial Gallons, US Gallons and Litres. Units of mass (weight) are pounds (lbs) and kilograms (kg). To convert from one to the other (that is, from volume to weight and *vice versa*), you need to know the *specific gravity* of the liquid concerned, based on that of pure water, which is taken as 1, since 1 Imperial Gallon of it weighs 10 lbs.

The Captain is responsible for checking, before flight, that the loading, mass and C of G of the aircraft complies with the limitations in the flight manual, the flight can safely be made, and that any cargo is properly distributed and secured.

THE CENTRE OF GRAVITY

The Centre of Gravity of an object is a point where its weight (or gravitational attraction) passes through, or where its mass is concentrated, so all the forces involved act parallel to the gravity vector (OK, they actually point towards the centre of the Earth, but that is so far away you may as well regard them as being parallel). For the exam: *When stationary on the ground, the total weight of an aircraft will act vertically through the Centre of Gravity.*

MASS & BALANCE
The Centre Of Gravity

The C of G could also be described as the average location of an object's weight force, or its point of balance, around which an autopilot will control an aircraft. It is normally referenced to the longitudinal axis.

The location of the C of G depends on an object's shape, density and the external gravitational field. If a vertical line through the C of G lies outside the base on which the object relies for support, it will overturn, unless you counterbalance the force:

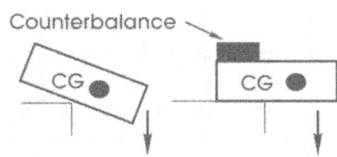

A lighter weight than the one shown above, but further away from the CG (if there were room) will have the same restraining effect. In the diagram below, the beam is balanced even though different weights are suspended from it - the difference is compensated for by each one's distance from the fulcrum:

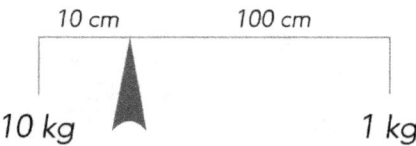

Loads in aircraft work the same way. A smaller value of lift at the tail has the same effect as a large one near the Centre of Gravity.

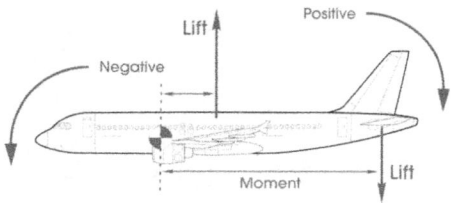

If the Centres of Pressure and Gravity are in different locations, you will get a pitching moment which must be corrected with a force from the elevator if you want to maintain level flight. You will be nose heavy if the C of G is forward of the C of P and *vice versa* - although stability may be increased in the former situation, a down force from the elevator is required to balance the pitching moment, which simply adds to the load that the wings have to carry. Ultimately, you will have more drag and higher fuel consumption, reduced range and rates of climb, and the stalling speed will be increased.

Fuel efficiency is best when the C of G is near the aft limit*, which is normally at, or just in front of, the Centre of Pressure. The forward limit is established to cope with higher stalling speeds and stability requirements.

*If it is too far aft, especially behind the C of P, the aircraft will be dynamically unstable, and the nose may even pitch up before you rotate. The forward limit will move to the rear, and the rear limit will move forward as the weight of the aircraft increases.

Distribution & Loading   03 1 03 04

The requirements for an aircraft to be stable and balanced place restrictions on its Centre of Gravity. Incorrect loading can also affect performance, as described below. The limitations to be considered include:

- **Limiting mass** (how heavy the aircraft can be)
- **C of G position**
- **Mass distribution**
- **Floor loading.** The structure will be stressed for a certain weight per area with the load in position.

Weight

 The word *mass* is used by EASA to signify what everyone else calls *weight*, which can end up in a kind of circular definition - e.g. weight is the effect of the force of gravity on a mass, which itself is weight multiplied by acceleration. Since acceleration is normally 1g, for the purposes of mass and balance, the two words can usually be used synonymously.

It's well known that every aircraft has a Maximum Takeoff Weight (sorry, Mass), which is the heaviest with which you may get airborne (although you may not always be able to use it - see below). It's also well known that aircraft will fly overweight to a certain extent, if only because there's a tolerance range in the performance figures - ferry flights frequently do so (with approval), with the extra weight being fuel, but having the ability to do so doesn't mean that you should. You will at some stage be under some pressure to take an extra bit of baggage or top up with that bit of fuel that will save you making a stop en route, but consider the implications. Firstly, any C of A (and insurance cover) will be invalid if you don't fly within the limits of the flight manual and, secondly, you will be leaving yourself nothing in hand for turbulence and the like, which will increase your weight artificially. The designer will have allowed for 60° turns all the way up to MAUW (i.e. 2g - see *Load Factor*), but not heavier than that, because you simply won't have the power to overcome that weight and stay airborne. Even worse, your engine-out capabilities will be less than expected.

If an aircraft is heavy (see also *V Speeds*, in *Performance*):

- V_{MCG} will remain the same, as it is a function of air density.
- V_{STOP} will decrease.
- V_R will increase for given flap setting, so it will occur later in the takeoff run as you need a higher speed to generate the extra lift required. The stick force required for rotation will increase with weight but reduce with airspeed.
- V_1 occurs earlier.
- Stalling speed will increase. This is because, for a given speed, a heavier aeroplane needs a higher angle of attack. The result is a smaller pitch range up to the stall angle, and a smaller amount by which you can trade pitch for forward speed to maintain level flight.
- V_{2MIN} (safety speed at the screen) will increase.

MASS & BALANCE
The Centre Of Gravity

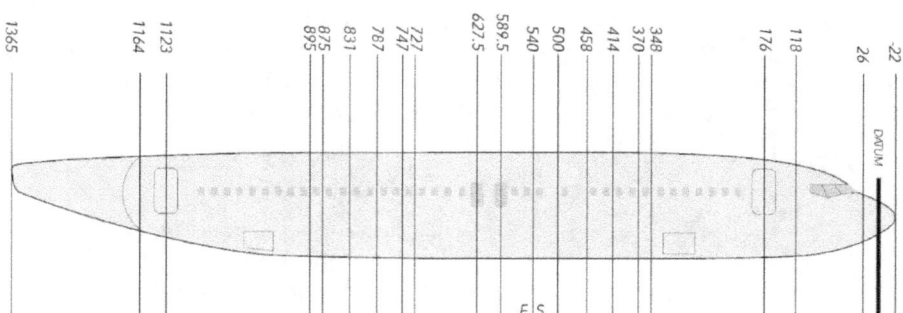

- The climb gradient will decrease, despite the higher takeoff speed. Watch those obstacles!
- The rate of climb will decrease. The ROC derives from the difference between the power available from the engines and that required to overcome drag. A heavier aircraft creates more drag and requires more power, but the power available reduces during a climb due to air density.
- The difference between minimum and maximum speeds will decrease. As mass increases, so does the drag and the thrust requirement from the engines, so the thrust available for acceleration is reduced, as is the maximum attainable speed, at the same time as the stalling speed increases.
- The absolute and service ceilings will reduce because the excess power needed to climb reduces.
- Range and endurance decrease. As the power required increases, so does the fuel consumption.
- The rate of descent in the glide will increase.
- Approach and landing speeds increase.
- Landing loads will increase due to the increased momentum.
- Braking energy increases, as does tyre wear.
- There may be structural damage
- Longitudinal stability increases.

Station Numbers

The position of an item on or in a fuselage is given by a station number, which is expressed as a distance (usually in inches) aft from a position in front of the aircraft (the nose of the 737 is at Station 130). As the datum for moment (balance) arms is 22 inches aft of the nose, its station number is 152, not shown in the above diagram.

Longitudinal C of G

The *reference datum* (set by the manufacturer and found in the flight manual) is an imaginary point in a convenient location from which all measurements and calculations start and where some C of G ranges are expressed (e.g. *106 inches aft of datum*).

The influence (*turning moment*) of an object on the aircraft is found by multiplying its weight by its distance from the datum. If the turning moment is clockwise (nose up), it is seen as positive, and if it is anticlockwise, as negative. If the datum is at the nose, all moments will therefore be positive.

The formula is:

```
arm = moment
      force
```

The *moment arm*, or *balance arm*, is the distance from the reference datum to the C of G of a mass. To get the longitudinal C of G of an aircraft, you multiply the weight of each item in it by the *lever arm* of the location it occupies to get the *moment*, or the amount of leverage that item contributes. Then you add the moments and divide their total by the total weight. Because you might end up using very long numbers, sometimes you use a *moment index*, the result of dividing the moment by 10,000 or a similar large number (a constant) to make the figures more manageable, especially in a drop-down trim sheet, which is described later.

The aircraft itself will have a weight and a moment from when it was last weighed, which is where you start. You can find it in the *weight and balance schedule*, and it may be varied if you add or remove various items of equipment. Here is a simplified typical calculation (the principles are exactly the same for larger machines, just with more seats):

Item	Wt	Arm	Moment
Aircraft	1881	116.5	219137
Front Pax	185	65	12025
Rear Pax	185	104	19240
Baggage	50	147.50	7375
Zero Fuel CG	2301	112.45	257777
Fuel	310	110.7	34273
Total	2611	111.85	292050

The total C of G for takeoff is 111.85, obtained by dividing the total moment figure (292050) by the total weight, or mass (2611).

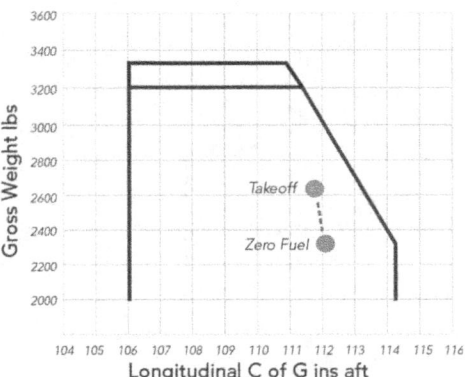

You calculate the takeoff and zero fuel positions to make sure that the C of G remains within limits throughout the flight, assuming the fuel is used in the correct sequence. An example is given later.

To recap - the distance of any object on the aircraft from the fulcrum (or datum) is the *lever arm*. The lever arm multiplied by the object's weight is the turning effect around the datum, or the *moment*. The total moment divided by the total weight of the aircraft provides an average figure which is the centre of gravity.

Next, refer to the flight manual to see if the figure fits into an authorised range on a graph similar to the one above - simply take the all-up weight you end up with, and the final C of G, and line them up horizontally and vertically. If they are inside the envelope, you are OK, but don't forget you have to land again! Your C of G may be fine for takeoff, but check again after fuel has been used!

CHANGES

Calculating how much mass to be moved from one place to another will always produce a smaller answer than adding or removing a mass to obtain the same change in C of G, which will change the total moment and gross weights. This is because the mass to be shifted is already part of the load, so the total won't change. The C of G will always move towards where you are moving the load to, or any additional load.

The top part of each fraction described below is the same in any such problem, only the denominators change.

MOVING MASS

The formula starts off like this:

$$\frac{m}{M} = \frac{d}{D}$$

where:

	m	Weight to be moved (mass change)
	d	Distance the C of G is out (C of G change)
	M	Total mass of the aircraft
	D	Distance moved by the mass concerned

You can see it's a ratio problem and therefore solvable by the flight computer.

1. If an aircraft weighing 3000 lbs has its C of G 48½ inches aft of the datum, but the aft limit is 47 inches, how much weight must be moved from the baggage compartment to the rear seats which are 34 inches away?

$$132.35 = \frac{3000 \times 1.5}{34}$$

On the flight computer, divide how much the load is out by the distance it must move and the answer is opposite the total weight.

Another way to solve the problem is to first find the current situation of the aircraft, such as:

$$3000 \times 48.5 = 145500$$

Then the desired situation:

$$3000 \times 47 = 141000$$

The desired moment shift is 4500, and we know the rear seats are 34 inches away, so:

$$\frac{4500}{34} = 132.35$$

In reality, there are many possibilities - in this case we had a fixed distance, but in an aircraft with a large hold (and plenty of room), you could shift half the load for twice the distance and vice versa. It doesn't matter where the load is, just move it the required distance.

2. On an aircraft weighing 4500 lbs, the aft C of G limit is 69 inches aft of the datum, but the present C of G is 71 inches aft. There is 200 lbs of freight at 85 inches aft. By how many inches must it be moved to bring the aircraft C of G within limits*?

$$4500 \times 71 = 319500$$
$$4500 \times 69 = 310500$$

The desired moment shift is 9000. Divide by the weight concerned to get 45 inches.

*Just bring it to the limit line.

3. The current C of G of an aircraft is at Station 25, and its mass is 3750 lbs. What is the effect on the C of G if you move 75 lbs from Station 15 to Station 19?

$$\frac{m}{M} = \frac{d}{D}$$

changes to:

$$d = \frac{m \times D}{M}$$

or:

$$d = \frac{75 \times 4}{3750}$$

The C of G moves aft by 0.08.

MASS & BALANCE
The Centre Of Gravity

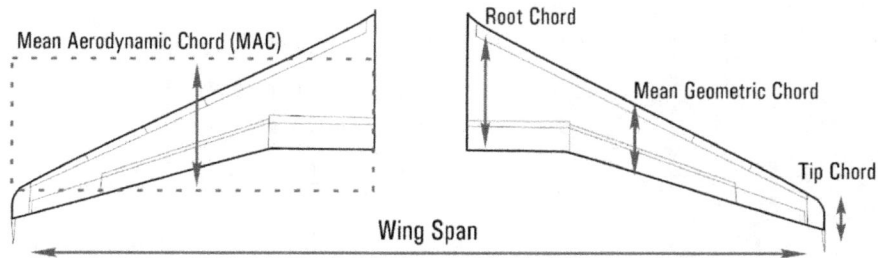

ADDING MASS

In the formula, M is the new mass, having added the extra (but see the example below), and D the distance between the added mass and the desired C of G.

EXAMPLES

1. Your aircraft has its datum at the nose, the front seats are 75 inches aft of the datum, the passenger seats are 100 inches aft and the separate baggage compartment is 140 inches aft. Two passengers are in the rear seats, with the baggage compartment full, and the front seat is empty.

However, you only weigh 120 lbs, and the Centre of Gravity of the aircraft is 4 inches behind the aft limit, which is 143 inches aft. The maximum takeoff mass is 3200 lbs, and the current mass is 2850 lbs. How much extra ballast must be secured in the front seat to bring the C of G to the rear limit?

Here, we cannot use a new mass, because we do not know what the ballast will be, so we would have two unknowns. So, if m = ballast, M = old mass and D = distance from the new location (the ballast) to the desired C of G:

$$\frac{x}{2850} = \frac{4}{68}$$

$$x = \frac{4 \times 2850}{68}$$

167.65 lbs, rounded to 168 lbs.

Using the alternative method:

```
2850 x 147 = 418950
```

The desired moment is:

```
2850 x 143 = 407550
```

Subtracting:

```
418950 - 407550 = 11400
```

The distance between the desired C of G (143) and the front seat where the ballast will be (75) is 68 inches. Divide the difference in moments by it:

```
11400 = 167.65, or 168 lbs
  68
```

The only thing to remember is that you either use the old mass and new C of G (if you don't know the new mass) or the new mass and the old C of G (if that is unknown).

2. A loaded aircraft weighs 3200 lbs with its C of G 8 inches aft of the datum. An extra 100 lbs is loaded 30 inches forward of the datum. What is the new C of G position?

The mass has to move 38 inches (30 + 8).

$$\frac{100}{3300} = \frac{x}{38}$$

$$x = \frac{100 \times 38}{3300} = 1.15$$

8 - 1.15 = 6.85 inches aft of datum. It will only be forward of the datum if the mass is moved by more than 8 inches.

REMOVING MASS

This is just the opposite of adding mass, so use OM (Old Mass) instead of NM.

LEMAC

The position of the Centre of Pressure in relation to the Centre of Gravity is useful to know for aerodynamic, performance, stability and controllability reasons. As the C of P is usually expressed with reference to the chord, the C of G could be expressed in the same way.

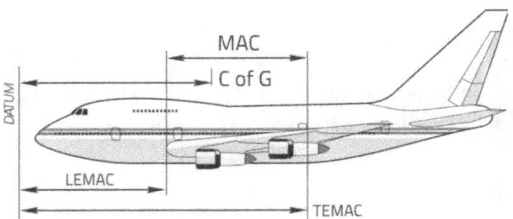

Because the chord length of a swept wing is difficult to measure (they have a variable chord), a *Mean Aerodynamic Chord* (MAC) is used instead, with the allowable C of G range expressed in percentages of it (%MAC). It is drawn through the centroid of the planform (it is not an average!), being an equivalent rectangular wing with the same chord and span that produces the same pitching moments. As with the "normal" C of G, it can be used to predict handling characteristics, which are normally acceptable at the 25% average chord point.

The aerodynamic centre can usually be found near the 25% MAC point, with the allowable C of G range either side of it - typically between 10-30% or 10-40%.

Some jets have their horizontal stabiliser trim settings marked in %MAC (the figures are a product of the C of G and flap setting).

Others, like the 737, have them marked in units of nose up trim, and you must look in the trim tables to get the settings for a given C of G.

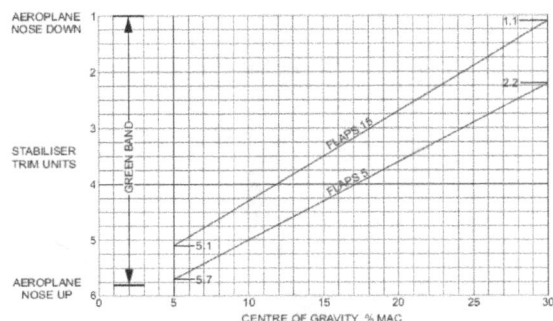

LEMAC is the distance from the datum to the leading edge of the MAC, at the front, and TEMAC is the distance to the trailing edge, at the back. LEMAC is therefore 0% MAC (TEMAC is 100%) and may also be expressed as a distance aft of the datum, so the C of G will lie somewhere between LEMAC and TEMAC, depending on the weight and configuration. This formula calculates the %MAC (use the same units):

$$\%MAC = \frac{CG-LEMAC}{MAC} \times 100$$

Find the conventional C of G first, then divide its distance aft of LEMAC by the MAC (TEMAC minus LEMAC).

For example, if the C of G is 16.36 m aft of datum, and the MAC is 3.416 m with a LEMAC 15.89 m aft of datum, what is the C of G position as a % of MAC?

$$13.76\% = \frac{16.36-15.89}{3.416} \times 100$$

To convert %MAC figures back to an arm (for C of G changes), first convert the C of G as %MAC to C of G in ins aft of LEMAC:

$$CG\ (aft\ LEMAC) = \frac{CG\%MAC \times MAC}{100}$$

Then just add the figure obtained above to the distance from Datum to LEMAC.

 %MAC is the result of a calculation from aircraft mass and the dry operating index, or the C of G position and MAC. It is different for each flight, so it is not in the aircraft documents. Instead, you will find the arm of the leading edge and the length of the MAC.

EXAMPLES

1. The planned takeoff mass is 190,000 kg, with a C of G at 29% MAC. Just before starting the engines, some passengers have gone missing, so their baggage must be offloaded. This weighs 4,000 kg, and it is in Cargo 4 (23.89 m aft of the reference point).

If the distance from the reference point to the leading edge is 14 metres, and the length of the MAC is 4.6 m, what will the new C of G be?

We use the regular formula, which works just as well with large numbers:

$$\frac{m}{M} = \frac{d}{D}$$

where M is the old total mass.

Converting the C of G at 29% MAC:

$$\frac{29 \times 4.6}{100} = 1.334\ aft\ of\ LE$$

The Leading Edge (LE) is 14m aft from the reference point, so the C of G is 14 + 1.334 = 15.334 aft of the reference point. The baggage is removed from Cargo 4 which is 23.89m aft of the reference point, so the distance between there and the C of G is 23.89 - 15.334 = 8.556.

The change of C of G is therefore:

$$\frac{4000}{190000} = \frac{x}{8.556}$$

$$x = \frac{4000 \times 8.556}{190000}$$

The C of G will shift 0.18m forward from its last position, as the mass removed was behind it, so the new C of G will be 1.334 - 0.18 = 1.154m aft of the leading edge, or:.

$$\frac{1.154 \times 100}{4.6} = 25\%\ MAC$$

2. On an aircraft weighing 4500 lbs, the aft C of G limit is 69 inches aft of the datum, but the present C of G is 71 inches aft. There is 200 lbs of freight at 85 inches aft. By how many inches must it be moved to bring the aircraft C of G within limits?

```
4500 x 71 = 319500
4500 x 69 = 310500
```

The desired moment shift is 9000. Divide by the weight concerned to get 45 inches.

THE AIRCRAFT

Aircraft are weighed in an enclosed building with the air conditioning off:

- Before entering service (which includes after being manufactured and when coming into the EASA system from a non-EASA operator). New aircraft are normally weighed at the factory and may be used without reweighing if the records have been adjusted for alterations or modifications (an *equipment list* is used to name which items are included in the process).
- Every 4 years, for individual aircraft
- Every 9 years for fleet masses
- Every time a modification takes place (when equipment is installed or uninstalled)

The individual mass and C of G position must be re-established periodically, with the maximum interval between two weighings being defined *by the operator* as per the regulations. In any case, they must be re-established either by weighing or calculation whenever cumulative changes to the DOM exceed ± 0.5% of the maximum landing mass. Weighing equipment must be calibrated every 2 years. The empty weight is usually determined by

MASS & BALANCE
The Centre Of Gravity

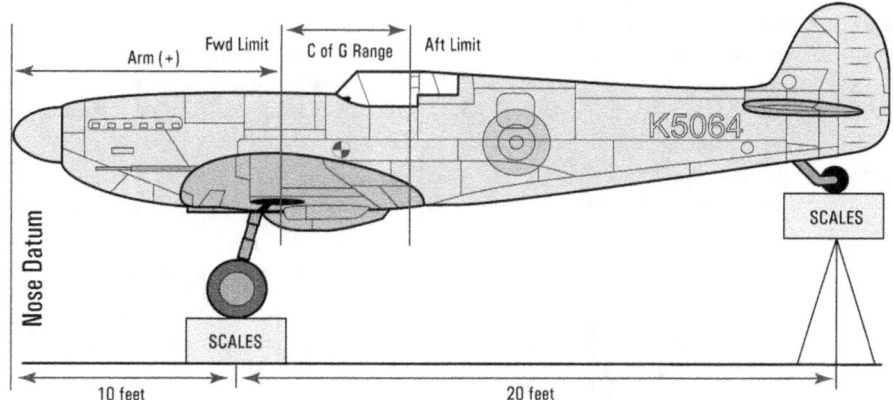

measuring the downward force at each wheel. As their station numbers are known, you just need to combine the figures to get a weight & balance figure.

Each part weighed is called the *reaction mass* (a reaction to the upwards thrust from the Earth) - so the sum of them all is the total mass. The *reaction moments* for each *reaction point* are added together and divided by the total mass to get the ship's C of G.

For example, after weighing a Spitfire (above), the following values are noted:

Weight on port wheel: 2500 lbs

Weight on starboard wheel: 2500 lbs

Weight on tail wheel: 1500 lbs

What is the longitudinal C of G? See the table below.

All the arms are positive, so the calculation is relatively easy but, on modern aircraft, the numbers can get so large that negative numbers can be a benefit, as the fewer zeroes there are, the less chance there is for making mistakes - for large aircraft, it is common to divide them all by a constant number (typically 1,000) to make them more manageable. This number is called an *Index*. It is also usual to use a graphical solution with a dropdown trimsheet, later.

Item	Weight	- Arm +	- Moment +
Port wheel	2500	10	25000
Starboard wheel	2500	10	25000
Tail wheel	1500	30	45000
Totals	6500	14.62 feet aft of datum	95000

TRICYCLE UNDERCARRIAGE

In the picture overleaf, the nosewheels are bearing 20,000 kg and each mainwheel assembly is bearing 50,000 kg.

To find the C of G:

```
20,000 x 6 = 120,000 kg/m
100,000 x 24 = 2 400,000 kg/m
Total Mass = 120,000 kg
Total Moment = 2 520,000 kg/m
2 520,000
─────────  = 21 m aft of datum
 120,000
```

The C of G could also be expressed as 3 m forward of the main wheels.

Now you have the basic C of G of the aircraft (found in the Weight & Balance Schedule), you can add the various loads, calculate their moments and determine the C of G for takeoff.

Item	Mass (Kg)	Arm (m)	Mom/1000
BEM	120,000	21	2520
Fuel	60,000	23	1380
Freight	30,000	12	360
Total	210,000		4260

$$\frac{4260 \times 1000}{210,000} = 20.29 \text{ m}$$

The new C of G is 20.29 m aft of datum.

The strength of the main gear can be a limiting factor with regard to the aft position of the C of G at higher takeoff weights. Similarly, the strength of the nose gear limits its forward position.

Up till the start of the takeoff, when the speed is not enough for the rudder to be effective, you can only control the aircraft on the ground with the nosewheel, which needs friction for this purpose, and enough weight over it. Friction can be reduced during the takeoff when full power is applied, because of the pitch up moment (when the engines are below the C of G of the aircraft, as they are with most jets, you get a couple).

THE LOAD

Generally, actual weights must be used, meaning that you must physically weigh your passengers* and cargo, but, under some circumstances, you can use *Standard Masses* for convenience, described in *Operational Procedures*.

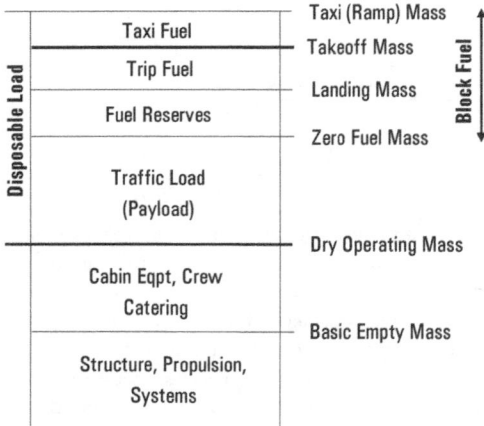

*Weighing machines used for this purpose must have a capacity of at least 150 kg, displaying at minimum graduations of 500g.

Here are the relevant definitions:

- The **Basic Empty Mass** *(or Standard Empty Mass)* is that in the Weight and Centre of Gravity Schedule (done by the company), which is established by weighing before the machine is used for commercial air transport. It is the mass of the empty aircraft, plus integral equipment (fire extinguishers, emergency oxygen equipment) and fluids in closed systems (unusable fuel and full operating fluids). *The operator* must re-establish the C of G after operational items are added, removed or otherwise modified. This is the starting point for light aircraft.

- The **Dry Operating Mass** is the BEM plus operator's items for a specific type of flight, excluding usable fuel and traffic load, but including the *Variable Load*, which is the crew, their baggage, unusable fuel and oil, emergency and catering stuff, paperwork, etc. (the DOM used to be the *APS Weight*). The mass of all items in the DOM must be determined by weighing or using standard masses (by the operator), and their influence on the C of G must also be determined. This is the starting point for large transport aircraft, as established by the operator.

- **Operating Mass**. DOM plus takeoff fuel (or max weight without passengers and cargo).

- **Area Load** or **Floor Load**. The load (or mass) distributed over a defined area

- The **Disposable Load** (or *Useful Load*) includes freight, passengers and usable fuel and oil (e.g. *Traffic Load* plus *Usable Fuel*)

- The **Traffic Load** is the payload, or Disposable Load without fuel, oil and consumables. It can be:
  - The total mass of passengers, baggage and cargo, including non-revenue stuff
  - Zero Fuel Mass minus Dry Operating Mass

- The **Zero Fuel Mass** is the weight of an aircraft, above which, any increase in weight must consist entirely of (usable) fuel. It is there to prevent the wings being stressed from having too much weight in the cabin (the fuel tanks are in the wings and the weight of the fuel in them is supposed to balance the lift and reduce the bending moment at the wing root. This is why the wing tanks are the first to be filled and the last to be emptied). The ZFM is equal to Traffic Load plus the DOM. If you are only needing a small amount of fuel (say on short sectors), this may well limit your takeoff weight.

- The **Maximum Taxi** (Ramp) **Mass** is the maximum weight at which the aircraft may be moved, under its own power or otherwise, to protect both itself and the hard standing at the apron. It is officially the sum of the Maximum Takeoff Mass plus any fuel for taxi and runup, so it can be higher than MTOM, and you should be able to burn off the difference before takeoff. It is the maximum weight to which an aeroplane may be loaded before starting engines.

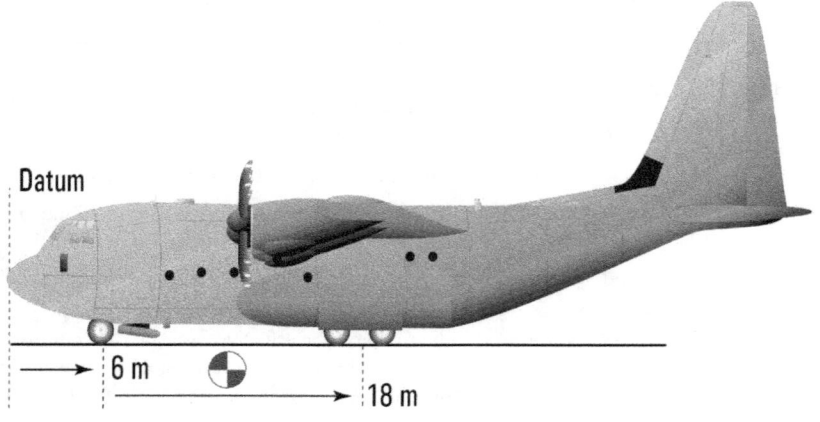

MASS & BALANCE
The Centre Of Gravity

- The **Takeoff Mass** is of the actual mass of the aeroplane, including everything in it, at the start of the takeoff run. That is, the DOM, plus the Disposable Load (or ZFM plus fuel), which must not be over the maximum for performance reasons, or that in the Flight Manual. **This is a fixed value!**
- **Maximum** (Structural) **Takeoff Mass** (MTOM). The maximum allowable total mass at the start of takeoff. A structural limitation in the flight manual that may not be exceeded.
- **Performance Limited Takeoff Mass** (PLTOM). The mass resulting from performance restrictions at the aerodrome.
- **Regulated Takeoff Mass**. Sometimes called *Maximum Allowable* Takeoff Mass, this is the lower of the MTOM and PLTOM.
- **In-Flight Mass**. Mass in flight at a specified time.
- **Landing Mass**. The mass at landing, under normal circumstances
- **Maximum** (Structural) **Landing Mass** (MLM). The maximum permissible total mass on landing under normal circumstances. A flight manual restriction that may not be exceeded at any time. It helps to prevent the impact with the ground being transmitted through the undercarriage to the rest of the aircraft, which can only happen if the weight is kept within limits (it also assists in reducing downward velocity). This weight may very well be restricted performance-wise in a similar way to Takeoff Mass, and could equally be a factor in further reducing your payload at the *start* of a flight. It's actually the Zero Fuel Mass, plus reserve and alternate fuel (i.e. no trip fuel).
- **Performance Limited Landing Mass** (PLLM). The mass allowing for performance restrictions at the aerodrome.
- **Regulated Landing Mass**. The lower of the MLM and PLLM.
- **Passengers**. *Adults* are aged 12 years and above. *Children* are 2 years and above, but less than 12. *Infants* are less than 2 years old. Standard mass values are given in *Operational Procedures*.
- **Useful Load**. Traffic Load plus usable fuel.

The Maximum Takeoff and Landing Masses are there because of *structural and performance limits*, plus *aerodynamic reasons* and *weather*. They will be affected by such things as:

- Pressure Altitude
- Temperature
- Space available. If you have to perform a steep climb or descent, you will need more power and maybe have to reduce weight

 When calculating traffic loads for Mass & Balance purposes only, if contingency fuel is not specified, ignore it. If it is, include it as part of the fuel on board for takeoff and landing, and ramp mass calculations.

BASIC PROCEDURE

First, you need to determine the Maximum Takeoff Mass, which may need to be adjusted for the conditions under which the aircraft has to operate. For example, the normal max weight might be 3200 lbs, but on a hot day, at high altitude, it could drop to 3100 lbs (see *Performance*). Write this on a piece of paper for now. Then you need to find the DOM, which is derived from the aircraft's Basic Mass, plus that of the crew. The Basic Mass will be found in the Weight & Gravity Schedule, in the aircraft's technical documentation. It will have been written out by the maintenance department, and may include weights and arms for various configurations, such as dual flight controls fitted, etc. Subtract the DOM from the MTOM to find the Disposable Load. For example:

```
3150   (MTOM)
2060   (BEM of 1875 + Crew)
1090   (Disposable Load)
```

You must fit the fuel and passengers in the Disposable Load, so subtract the fuel required for the trip to find the Traffic Load, or what the customer is paying for (passengers, baggage and/or cargo, including non-revenue). If the Traffic Load available is not enough, you must either reduce it, or the fuel, which means you must stop en route to pick up some more.

Zero Fuel Mass should still be within C of G limits.

To find out how much Traffic Load you can carry, the calculation is therefore:

```
TL = AUM - (Fuel + DOM)
```

If you know the AUM at any time you can quickly find out how many passengers you can carry by taking away the sum of the fuel and DOM from it. The trouble is, that the maximum AUM can vary, so you constantly need to be aware of the conditions under which you are flying. For example, on a hot day, you can carry less, so the MAUM will be less for performance reasons. There may also be structural reasons.

The minimum fuel is the subject of the flight planning chapter. The **maximum fuel** allowed is the lowest of:

- Max TOW – Actual ZFW (DOM + TFC)
- Max LW - Actual ZFW + Trip fuel
- Max fuel capacity

Note that the Empty Mass and the payload will not change during flight, but the fuel load will, and may change the C of G as it reduces, of which more later.

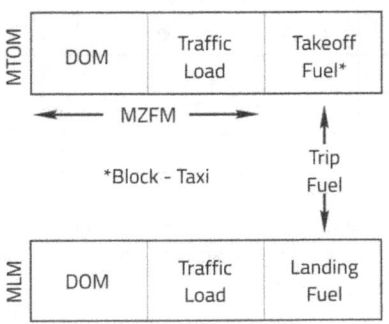

© Phil Croucher, 2017

MASS & BALANCE
The Centre Of Gravity

The picture above shows that the only difference between MTOM and MLM is the trip fuel. The takeoff mass must not be so much that, having burned the trip fuel, you will be over the Maximum Landing Mass (a problem with small journeys). This means that you must begin by finding the maximum takeoff mass that will not exceed one of three limits, for takeoff, landing and with zero fuel, with the help of a small table:

RTOM	RLM	MZFM
	+ Trip Fuel	+Takeoff Fuel*
TOM 1	TOM 2	TOM 3

*Block fuel minus taxi fuel.

The RTOM (Regulated Takeoff Mass) is the lower of the maximum structural mass and the performance regulated mass - similarly for landing. You take the lower of the three potential TOMs because:

- If TOM 1 is the lowest you will otherwise exceed the takeoff mass.
- If TOM 2 is the lowest you will otherwise exceed the landing mass.
- If TOM 3 is the lowest you will otherwise exceed the maximum zero fuel mass.

 The mass of the fuel must be determined with the actual density or, if it is not known, the density calculated under a method described in the Ops Manual.

EXAMPLE
Find the maximum fuel load, given:

MTOM: 64,400 kg
MLM: 56,200 kg
MZFM: 53,300 kg
DOM: 35,500 kg

Traffic Load: 14,500 kg
Trip Fuel: 4,900 kg
Minimum T/O Fuel: 7,400 kg

Find the allowed takeoff mass first:

	RTOM	RLM	MZFM
Max	64 400	56 200	53 300
Fuel		4 900	7 400
ATOM	64 400	61 100	60 700
DOM			35 500
Traffic Load			14 500
			10 700

The only relevant column is the MZFM as that is the lowest figure. Subtracting the DOM and Traffic load results in a max fuel figure of 10,700 kg.

THE LOADSHEET
A new loadsheet is required for every takeoff, and each one must satisfy certain legal requirements (meaning that it must contain certain information, such as registration, commander's name, etc.) The original goes with the aircraft documentation (and must be kept after the flight for three months), but a copy must be left on the ground.

Loadsheets for small aircraft can be simple, and many examples are given later in this section. They may be called load manifests when they contain passenger names and other details. Larger aircraft will use something more complex, again, described later.

LAST MINUTE CHANGES
Aviation is a flexible industry, meaning that there are always Last Minute Changes (LMCs) - just when you're all set to go, more passengers turn up! The 1090 lbs payload above can also be referred to as the *underload*, or spare capacity, which will affect the size of the Traffic Load. There should be a maximum LMC in the ops manual after which you have to redo the paperwork.

EXAMPLES
1. Given the following:

Maximum Take-off Mass: 62 800 kg

Maximum Zero Fuel Mass: 51 250 kg

Maximum Landing Mass: 54 900 kg

Maximum Taxi Mass: 63 050 kg

Trip fuel: 1 800 kg

Alternate fuel: 1 400 kg

Holding fuel (final reserve): 1 225 kg

Dry Operating Mass: 34,000 kg

Traffic Load: 13,000 kg

Catering: 750 kg

Baggage: 3 500 kg

What is the takeoff mass?

(a) 51 515 kg

(b) 55 765 kg

(c) 51 425 kg

(d) 52 265 kg

There are some red herrings! Baggage is part of the traffic load, and catering is part of the DOM!

The DOM plus the traffic load (i.e. pax and baggage) is 47000. Add the fuel (4425) to get 51425. You may need to consider contingency fuel, which is 5% of the trip fuel (i.e. 90 kg), to get 51 515 kg.

MASS & BALANCE
The Centre Of Gravity

2. Given:

MTOM: 60,000 kg

MLM: 44,000 kg

DOM: 30,000 kg

MZFM: 42,000 kg

Fuel at takeoff: 15,000 kg

Fuel at landing: 4,000 kg

What is the maximum Traffic load?

60,000 - (15,000 + 30,000) = 15,000 kg

44,000 - (4,000 + 30,000) = 10,000 kg

42,000 - 30,000 = 12,000 kg

The answer is 10,000 kg, as it is the lowest figure, and your flight is governed by the landing conditions.

If the customer has already weighed the passengers and has an actual Traffic Load, you can quickly work out how much extra fuel you can carry by subtracting it from the maximum. In the case above, you can take an extra 6,000 kg of fuel if the actual Traffic Load is 4,000 kg.

Floor Loading

If the weight of the aircraft is not distributed evenly, the longerons under the floor structure (and ultimately the fuselage) will be deformed, with the largest distortion being where the largest weight is.

On top of the maximum mass or volume in a compartment, the floor will not be able to take more than a certain amount of weight for a given area as a static figure (meaning when the load is not moving), usually expressed in pounds. This referred to as the area load or maximum load intensity and is expressed in pounds per square foot, kg per square foot or newtons per square metre. For example, a typical **floor loading** is 100 lbs per square foot.

The more floor space a load occupies, the less weight per square foot it will exert (*load spreading*), so a flattish box on its thinner side is likely to have a higher floor loading. The **Running Load Limit** (*per metre run, or linear load*) is the maximum that the under floor structure can take when using something like a conveyor system for loading - it ensures that the weight of the cargo does not exceed the limit of the structure between cross beams. Put another way, the load per metre run limitation (839 kg in the 727) is the maximum load that can be placed over any one metre of linear measurement, and it is assumed that the longest side is parallel with the fuselage centreline. In this case, instead of using the area, divide the weight by the length of the load along the fore and aft axis of the aircraft. It uses the SI units of newtons or kg per metre.

Area and running load limits are in the flight manual.

Tip: The longest side has the least running load.

Uniformly distributed loads as mentioned above are the general rule, but concentrated loads may need spreaders to make them more acceptable, both in terms of loading and protecting the aircraft.

To find the floor area taken up, find what it is in square inches, then divide by 144, so a pallet 37" x 39" will take up 10.02 sq ft

(refer to the *Limitations* section in the Flight Manual). To find what the floor can hold in that area, multiply it by the floor load limit, then subtract the weight of the pallet and fixings to find what you can put on it.

In the real world, however, you more often have to find an area that will take a particular pallet, since it will be inconvenient to break it down. As above, you first find the area from the dimensions, then divide it into the total weight of the item - the limit must be above this weight.

For example, you have a compartment with a maximum floor loading of 750 kg per square metre, into which you want to place a package weighing 600 kg, how large can the pallet be?

The calculation is:

$$\frac{750}{1} = \frac{600}{X}$$

Which can easily be set up on the flight computer.

Shuffling the formula around instead, we end up dividing 600 by 750 to get 0.8 square metres.

TIEDOWNS

Passenger seats occupy the whole floor space evenly; this load-spreading principle needs to be borne in mind with freight (cargo is best distributed like passengers would be), which makes it easier to provide decent restraint on each pack, because access areas to exits above and around the cargo are needed for *when the load has moved* after an emergency stop. Loads should be restrained with nets or straps (or a combination) and must distribute the load over the available fixtures, such as seat attachments. In emergency, you can use seat belts.

Some aircraft have a proper cargo fit, but problems arise where one that normally carries passengers is used without modification, which is why you may need to be certificated on your training forms as being cleared to change the aircraft layout. Naturally, in small aircraft where the emergency exits are obvious, this really only involves removing the seats, because the aim is just to substitute loads that use the same fixtures and locations, but where you get involved in removing galleys and otherwise converting the cabin in larger ones, the exercise becomes a little more difficult (just because a Flight Manual contains details of freight loading limitations, don't assume that any modifications you make are permitted - those figures may only have been used for basic certification).

When loading cargo, it is important to use the tiedown points provided, since they have been designed to provide restraint in the usual attitudes of flight. However, very often, cargo is loaded onto passenger seats, but it should still be restrained, using at least the passenger seat belts. This is because it may move in flight, and in doing so, it will affect the C of G.

As to when a shift of cargo becomes important has not officially been defined, but a common-sense interpretation would be "when it changes the C of G of the aircraft" to quote one inspector. Even if it doesn't change the C of G. it could still cause changes in pitch and trim.

One example was the early morning newspaper run from Bournemouth to Jersey with an F27. When the pilot selected landing flap at Jersey the whole load of newspapers moved forward making the aeroplane uncontrollable. It unfortunately crashed, killing the crew.

SEP 1

The first few pages of the SEP 1 section contain general details of the aircraft, but some points should be noted.

The aft C of G limit is fixed, but the forward limit varies with the gross weight:

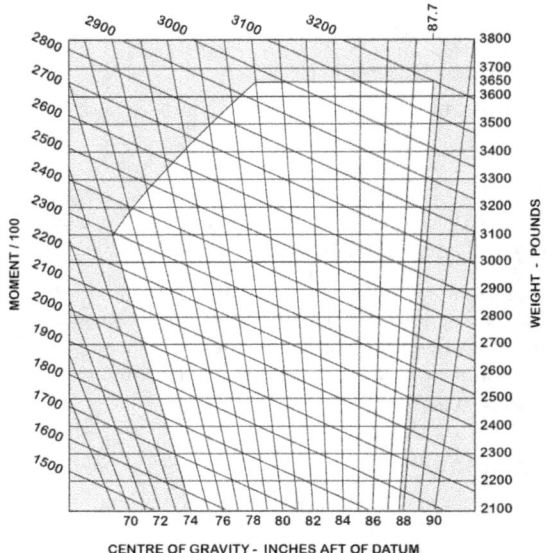

Also, the max takeoff and landing weights are identical, which is typical of light aircraft in general.

The loading configurations are as follows:

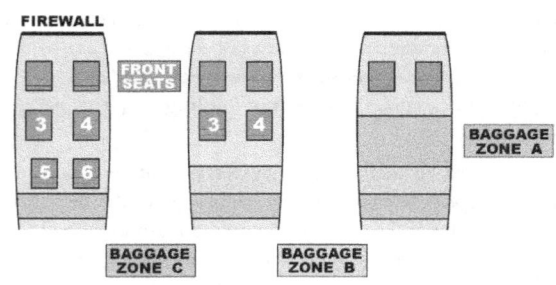

Picture: SEP1 Location Diagram

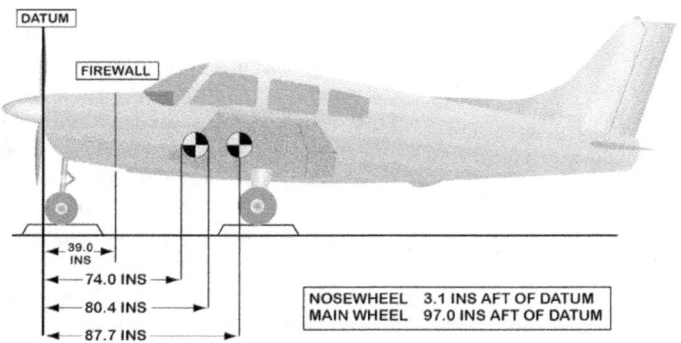

The arm lengths for seats 3, 4, 5 and 6 are shown below in the example calculation. Loading details for the fuel are:

Leading Edge Tanks		
US Gals	Wt (lbs)	Moment
5	30	22.5
10	60	45
15	90	67.5
20	120	90
25	150	112.5
30	180	135
35	210	157.5
40	240	180
44	264	198
50	300	225
55	330	247.5
60	360	270
65	390	292.5
70	420	315
74	444	333

EXAMPLE CALCULATION
You are going to carry:

- Pilot, with gear: 200 lbs
- 2 pax in the 3rd and 4th seats, total 370 lbs
- 50 lbs of baggage in zone B
- 175 lbs of freight in zone C
- 50 gallons of fuel (at start)

Item	Mass	Arm	Mom
BEM	2415	77.7	187646
Front	200	79	15800
3 & 4	370	117	43290
Zone A		108	
5 & 6		152	
Zone B	50	150	7500
Zone C	175	180	31500
ZFM	3210	89.01	285736
Fuel	300	75	22500
Ramp Mass	3510	87.82	308236
Taxi Fuel	-13		-10
TOM	3497	88.14	308226
Trip Fuel	-210	75	-15750
LM	3287	88.98	292476

You are just about on the margin at Ramp Mass, but otherwise out of limits. How would you adjust the weights? (Hint: There is a lot of baggage in Zone C).

Picture Below: MEP 1 Location Diagram

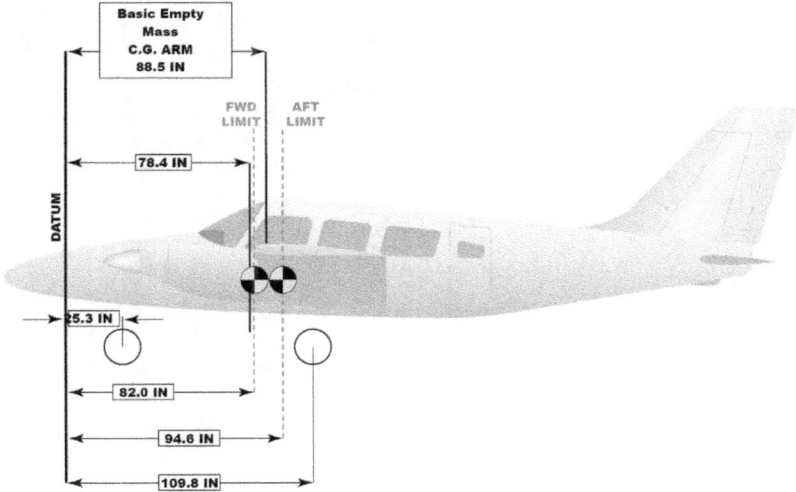

MEP1

A Performance Class B twin-engined aircraft with a retractable undercarriage:

- the datum is not at the nose (see diagram below).
- the aft C of G limit is fixed at 94.6 inches, but the forward one varies with the gross mass between 82 - 90.8 inches (see envelope overleaf).
- the BEM and its arm are 3 210 lbs and 88.5 inches.
- weight limitations are:
    - MTOM: 4750 lbs
    - MLM: 4513 lbs
    - MZFM: 4470 lbs
- the gear position has little effect.
- there is no standard fuel allowance for start, taxi and runup - check the question for it. The example below uses 4 US gallons, or 24 lbs, at 6 lbs/gallon.
- the maximum floor limit is 120 lbs/sq ft.
- the maximum zone weights are:
    - Zone 1 - 100 lbs at 22.5 inches
    - Zone 2 - 360 lbs at 118.5 inches (with centre seats removed)
    - Zone 3 - 400 lbs at 157.6 inches (with rear seats removed)
    - Zone 4 - 100 lbs at 178.7 inches

Otherwise, the procedures are similar to SEP 1.

EXAMPLE

Item	Mass	Arm	Mom
BEM	3210	88.5	284085
Front	340	85.5	29070
Centre (Zone 2)	236	118.5	27966
Rear (Zone 3)	340	157.6	53584
Zone 1	100	22.5	2250
Zone 4		178.7	
ZFM	4226	93.9	396955
Fuel	545	93.6	51012
Ramp Mass	4771	93.9	447967
Taxi Fuel	-23	93.6	-2153
TOM	4748	93.9	445814
Trip Fuel	-450	93.6	-42120
LM	4298	93.9	4036.94

Picture Below: Loading Envelope For Above

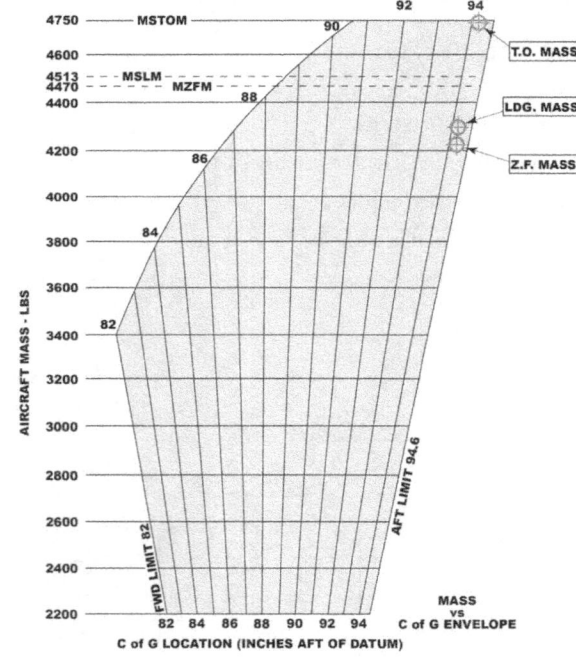

MRJT

A Medium Range Jet Transport certified under FAR/CS 25 in Performance Class A.

 Watch Out! Standard masses are used!* Refer to *Operational Procedures* for the figures.

*The figures in CAP 696 for standard masses are different than those in Part OPS - RTFQ!

The datum point is 540 inches forward of front spar (FS).

The Mean Aerodynamic Chord (MAC) lies at 134.5 inches, and the MAC Leading edge is 625.6 inches aft of the datum.

Landing gear retraction or extension has a negligible effect the Centre of Gravity, but flap retraction is different, as can be seen from this table:

From	To	Moment Change (kg-ins x 1000)
5°	0°	-11
15°	0°	-14
30°	0°	-15
40°	0°	-16

Figure 4.4 in CAP 698 shows the stabiliser trim settings for takeoff for various flap settings against the C of G (the setting of the flaps affects the lift, and therefore the Centre of Pressure).

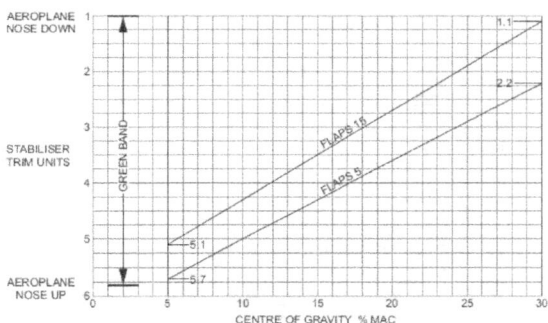

Enter the graph at the %MAC setting on the bottom line, move vertically up to the relevant flap setting, then horizontally to the stabiliser setting on the vertical line. The result should be in the green band mentioned on the left of the graph, i.e. the acceptable range for takeoff shown by markings next to the elevator trim wheel.

Mass Limitations

Maximum structural limits are as shown below:

	Structural Mass (kg)
Maximum Taxi Mass	63,060 kg
Maximum Takeoff Mass	62,800 kg
Maximum Landing Mass	54,900 kg
Maximum Zero Fuel Mass	51,300 kg

C of G Limitations

The C of G Limitations fall into Figure 4.11:

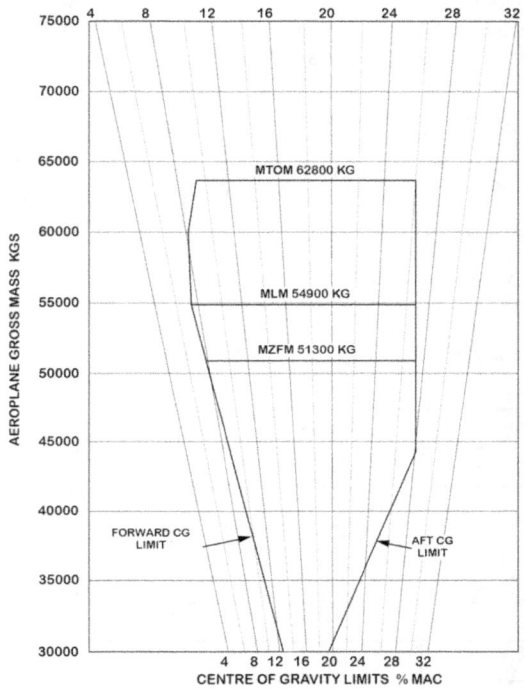

Fuel Usage

The fuel tanks are located as follows:

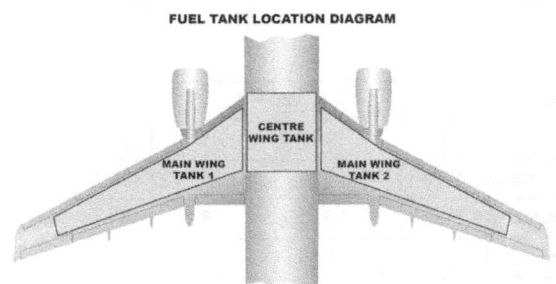

Fuel in the fuselage is not counted towards the Zero Fuel Mass. Fuel in the centre tank is used first.

If the centre tank contains more than 450 kg, the wing tanks MUST be full.

Tank	BA (Mom)	Volume	Mass
L Main 1	650.7 (599)	1 499 (4.6)	4 542 (14)
R Main 2	650.7 (599)	1 499 (4.6)	4 542 (14)
Centre	600.4 (600.9)	2 313 (7.9)	7 008 (24)
Max	628.8	5 311	16 092

The volume is in US Gallons, and the Mass is in kg. The conversion factor is 3.03 kg per US Gallon. Figures in brackets are unusable values.

Passenger Distribution

The cabin is zoned from A to G, which is easier than counting individual seats. Passengers are distributed thus:

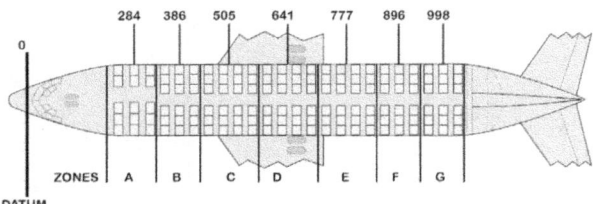

The maximum figures are:

Zone	Number	BA
A	15	284
B	18	386
C	24	505
D	24	641
E	24	777
F	18	896
G	18	998

Unless otherwise stated, the standard passenger mass is assumed to be 84 kg (including a 6 kg allowance for hand baggage). This is also the EASA value for non-charter flights with 30 or more seats.

Seats	20 +		30 +
	Male	Fem	Adults
Non- charter	88 kg	70 kg	84 kg
Holiday charters	83 kg	69 kg	76 kg
Children (2-12)	35 kg	35 kg	35 kg

Unless otherwise stated, you can use a baggage allowance of 13 kg per passenger.

The crew allowances, on the other hand, are non-standard (for EASA, at least):

Location	No	BA	Mass
Flight Deck	2	78	90
Cabin Fwd	2	162	90
Cabin Aft	1	1 107	90

Cargo

There are two cargo compartments, fore and aft. Each one is divided into three sections.

Forward Cargo Compartment (Cargo Hold 1)

	BA - in	228	286	343	500
Maximum Compartment Running Load (kg per inch)		13.15	8.47	13.12	
Maximum Distribution Load Intensity (kg per ft²)			68		
Maximum Compartment Load (kg)		762	483	2059	
Compartment Centroid (BA - in)		257	314.5	421.5	
Maximum Total Load (kg)			3305		
Fwd Hold Centroid (BA - in)			367.9		
Fwd Hold Volume (cu. ft)			607		

Aft Cargo Compartment (Cargo Hold 4)

	BA - IN	731	940	997	1096
Maximum Compartment Running Load (kg per inch)		14.65	7.26	7.18	
Maximum Distribution Load Intensity (kg per ft²)			68		
Maximum Compartment Load (kg)		3,062	414	711	
Compartment Centroid (BA - in)		835.5	968.5	1,046.5	
Maximum Total Load (kg)			4187		
Aft Hold Centroid (BA - in)			884.5		
Aft Hold Volume (cu. ft)			766		

You can see that, between balance arms 286 - 343, the maximum running load is 8.47 kg/inch, while the maximum floor loading is 68 kg per square foot (this actually applies to the whole compartment).

Examples

1. To find the C of G expressed as %MAC for takeoff and landing, given the following data:

   DOM: 35,500 kg

   BA: 655 inches

   PAX: 72 Adults (at 84 kg each) seated as follows:

   A5, B4, C19, D21, E12, F10, G10

   Cargo: 600 kg in hold 1, 2,750 kg in hold 4.

   MSTOM: 62,800 kg

   PLTOM: 64,000 kg

   MSLM: 54,900 kg

   PLLM: 55,000 kg

   MZFM: 51,300 kg

   TOF: 12 300 kg

   Fuel in tanks 1 & 2: 9,500 kg

   Fuel in centre tanks: 5,500 kg

   Taxy fuel: 250 kg

   Trip fuel: 8,750 kg

   Trip fuel moment: -5947 inches

Item	Mass (kg)	BA (ins)	Moment
DOM	35 500	655	23252500
Pax Zone A	420	284	119280
Pax Zone B	336	386	129696
Pax Zone C	1596	505	805980
Pax Zone D	1764	641	1130724
Pax Zone E	1008	777	783216
Pax Zone F	840	896	752640
Pax Zone G	840	998	838320
Cargo Hold 1	600	367.9	220740
Cargo Hold 4	2750	884.5	2432375
Additional			
Zero Fuel Mass	45654	667.31	30465471
Tanks 1 & 2	9500	650.7	6181650
Centre Tank	5500	600.4	3302200
Taxi Mass	60654	658.64	39949321
- Taxy Fuel	250	600.4	150100
Takeoff Mass	60404	658.88	39799221
- Trip Fuel	8750		-5947
Landing Mass	51654	770.38	39793274

It's just the same as any other C of G calculation, only with more ~~seats~~ zones. The trip fuel moment is given in the example, but if it isn't, you will need to work out the split between the centre and wing tanks and apply their separate values.

To find the %MAC, subtract the LEMAC (625.6) from the BA for takeoff (658.88) to get 33.28 inches aft of the LEMAC, which translates to 24.74%. The landing BA is 770.38, which is 144.78 inches aft of the LEMAC and 10.28 inches aft of the TEMAC.

2. Determine (see load and trim sheet overleaf):

   (a) The maximum Last Minute Change (LMC)

   (b) The C of G in MAC% for takeoff and landing

   (c) The trim setting for takeoff with 5° of flap

Given the following information:

   DOM: 36 800 kg

   DOI: 40

   MSTOM: 62 800 kg

   PLTOM: 64,000 kg

   MSLM: 54 900 kg

   PLLM: 55,000 kg

   MZFM: 51 300 kg

   TOF: 12 300 kg

   Flight Fuel: 6 700 kg

   PAX: 120 Adults seated as follows:

   A5, B10, C24, D24, E24, F18, G15

   Baggage: 120 Items in CPT 4

   Cargo: 860kg in CPT 1

SOLUTION

The Traffic Load is:

   Pax: 120 x 84 kg = 10 080 kg

   Baggage: 120 x 13 kg = 1 560 kg

   Cargo: 860 kg

   Total: 12 500 kg

Takeoff Fuel Index: -7.5

Landing Fuel: 12 300 kg - 6 700 kg = 5 600 kg

Landing Fuel Index: -6.0

LMC: 0 kg

Takeoff C of G %MAC: 20.5%

Landing C of G %MAC: 21.2%

Takeoff Flaps 5° Trim: 3.5

The top part of Section 1 is just to do with administration, and mostly airline specific. For example, such things as the flight number and aircraft registration, the relevant date for the form, the number of flight crew members and flight attendants (2/4). Note the phrase *All Masses In Kilograms*. The next bit is more interesting.........

The first step is to enter the maximum masses into the top line ❶, which is used to establish the maximum payload. The takeoff fuel goes under the DOM and MZFM ❷, and the trip fuel under the MLM ❸. All are added to each other ❹.

MASS & BALANCE
MRJT

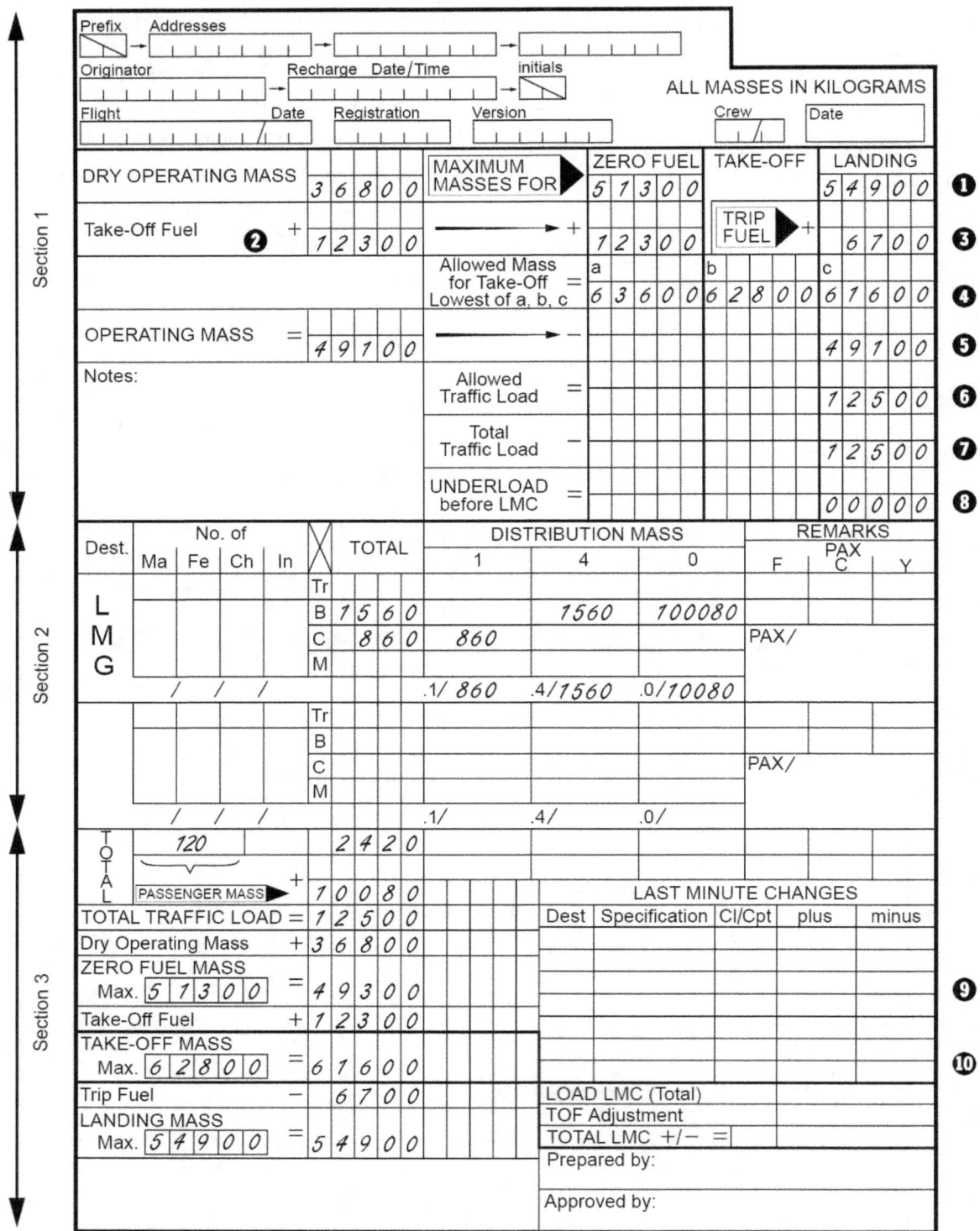

MASS & BALANCE
MRJT

The Takeoff and landing masses (column b) are the regulated values.

Subtract the wet operating mass (49100) from the *lowest* value of Allowed Takeoff Mass in boxes a, b and c (in this case, c) ❺, for the allowed traffic load of 12500 ❻.

The other two columns stay empty as they are not needed.

The underload value shows how much extra you can take in terms of fuel or payload before you violate the limiting mass - zero in this case. You need to use the next section before you can calculate it.

Section 2, the middle section, concerns load distribution. It is in two identical parts so you can identify loads for different destinations with intermediate landings (the letters **Tr** mean transit pax, or passengers that stay on board for the second leg).

You can break down the mass by males, females, children and infants, if required. Cargo is inserted as well. Add the masses in Hold 1, Hold 4 and the passenger cabin (Hold 0) to get the Total Traffic Load ❼. Enter it into Section 1, and subtract it from the Allowed Traffic Load to find any underload before LMCs are carried out ❽.

Part 3, the lowest part, is a summary that allows for Last Minute Changes (within certain limits, or you have to do a new trim sheet).

Enter the number of passengers at the top (120) then multiply it by the standard mass of 84 kg to get the total mass, in this case 10080. Add that to the total of the dead loads (baggage, cargo - 2420) from section 2 to get the total traffic load.

Add the Traffic Load to the DOM to find the ZFM, ensuring that is does not exceed the maximum (there are handy boxes in which to put the maximum limits for quick reference). Subtract it from the Allowed Traffic Load to get the underload. If the value is negative, the aircraft is too heavy.

Add the takeoff fuel to get the TOM, again checking that it is not over the limit ❿.

Subtract the trip fuel to get the Landing Mass.

At the top of the drop down trim sheet, there is an overview of how the passenger compartment is laid out, divided into sections from a to g. Each section has 3 or 4 rows of seats, with the number of seats available show.

To use the drop down trim sheet, you need a Dry Operating Index (DOI), which is given in the examples and inserted under the overview.

- The **DOI** (Dry Operating Index) indicates the position of the C of G at the DOM. It's reduced to a smaller workable number by multiplying with a constant. This makes calculations easier as you can just add indexes to each other.

- The **LIZFW** (Loaded Index ZFW) is the C of G at ZFW, which can be translated into a MAC%.

- The **LITOW** (Loaded Index TOW) is the C of G at the takeoff weight, which can be translated into a MAC%.

- The **LILAW** (Loaded Index LAW) is the C of G at the landing weight, which can be translated into a MAC%.

In this case, 40 is entered in the top right hand side. The DOI represents the C of G position that relates to the DOM, and is where you start on the first line. The index shift due to the loads in compartments 1 and 4 is done graphically on the next two.

Next, enter the masses of baggage and mail, and the number of passengers in each compartment (there is no way to distinguish between males, females, etc.) The maximum masses are shown.

Move down according to the disposition of the load (each large tick mark stands for 1000 kg - small ones are for 100 kg). The scale in the passenger sections is for the number of passengers, as we are dealing with standard masses.

Two lines are used from the fuel index, to cater for zero and full fuel situations. Ignoring the fuel index, drop a line from the last passenger row down to intersect the horizontal line for the ZFM, and read the %MAC.

The fuel index accounts for the amount of fuel on board, for which use the table overleaf. Do not interpolate, but use the next higher mass, which will create a difference from calculated figures. Write the figure into the box on the left hand side.

Move along the required number of divisions for the index obtained above, then go down to the C of G envelope. Drop straight down until you cross the TOM (horizontal).

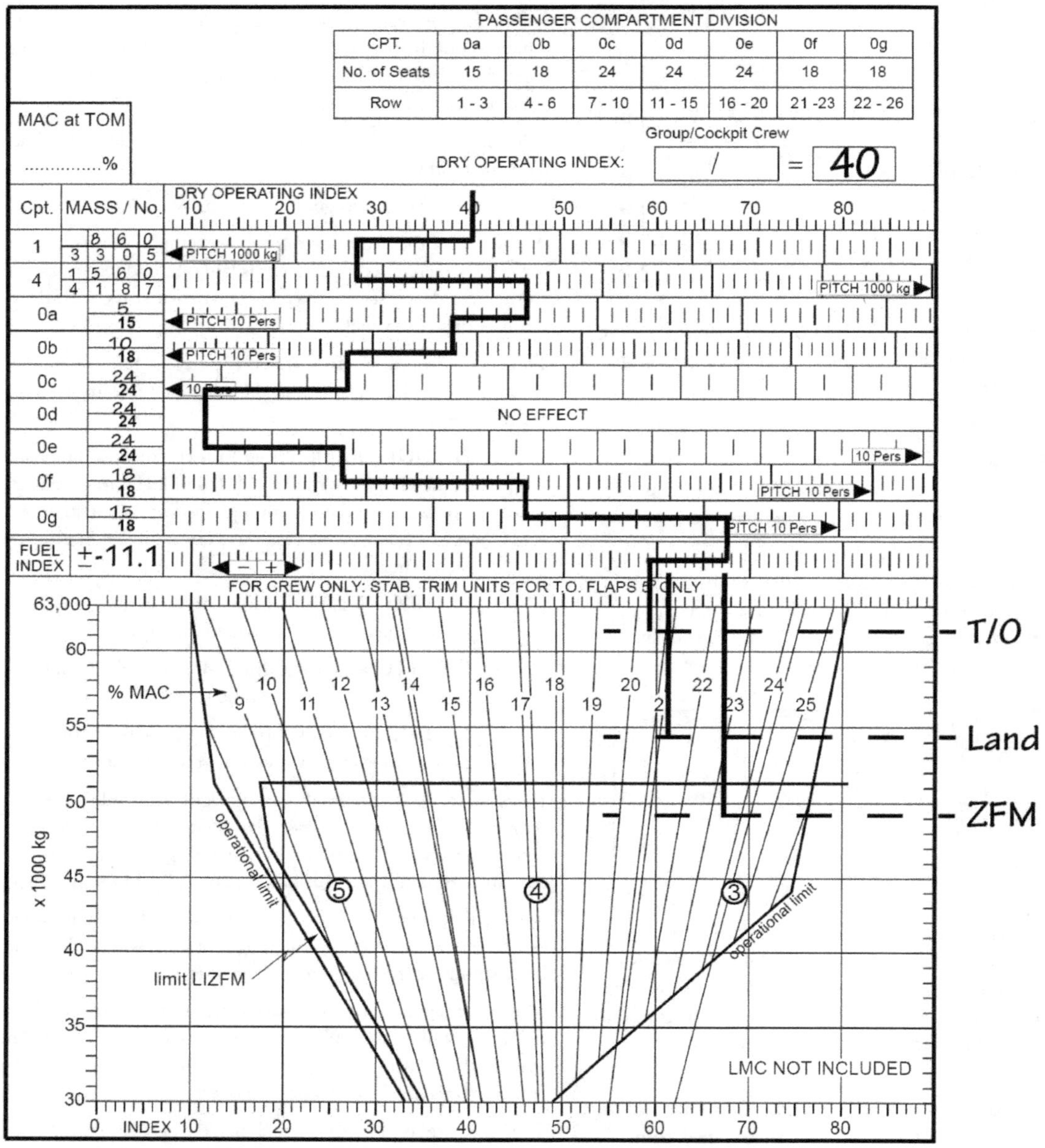

MASS & BALANCE
MRJT

The %MAC can be read (with interpolation) as can the stabiliser setting (numbers 5. 4 and 3 in circles). If you need 15° of flap, you need to use this table.

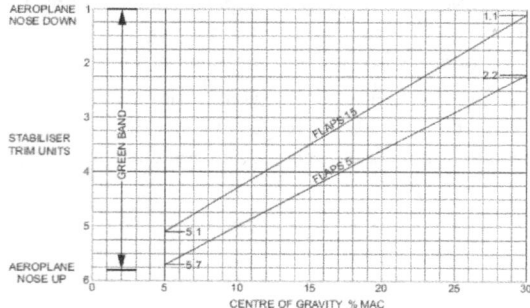

For landing, work out the landing fuel, (i.e. no trip fuel) find the index, move along the required number of divisions and drop a line to the LM to find the landing %MAC.

You can break down the mass by males, females, children and infants, if required. Cargo is inserted as well. Add the masses in Hold 1, Hold 4 and the cabin to get the Total Traffic Load ❼. Enter it into Section 1, and subtract it from the Allowed Traffic Load to find any underload before LMCs are carried out ❽.

Part 3, the lowest part, is a summary that allows for Last Minute Changes.

Add the Traffic Load to the DOM to find the ZFM, ensuring that is does not exceed the maximum (write the maximum value in the box to the left).

Add the takeoff fuel to get the TOM, again checking that it is not over the limit ❿. Subtract the trip fuel to get the Landing Mass.

The fuel index is taken as follows:

Mass (kg)	Units	Mass	Units
500	-1.0	9330	-0.3
750	-1.5	9580	-0.9
1000	-1.9	9830	-1.5
1250	-2.3	10080	-2.1
1500	-2.6	10330	-2.7
1750	-3.0	10580	-3.3
2000	-3.3	10830	-3.9
2500	-3.7	11080	-4.5
3000	-4.3	11330	-5.1
3500	-4.7	11580	-5.7
4000	-5.1	11830	-6.3
4500	-5.4	12080	-6.9
5000	-5.7	12330	-7.5
5500	-5.9	12580	-8.1
6000	-6.0	12830	-8.7
6500	-6.1	13080	-9.3
7000	-5.9	13330	-9.9
7500	-5.0	13580	-10.5
7670	-4.6	13830	-11.1
7830	-4.1	14080	-11.7
8000	-3.7	14330	-12.3
8170	-3.2	14580	-12.9
8330	-2.6	14830	-13.5
8500	-2.1	15080	-14.1
8630	-1.6	15330	-14.8
8750	-1.1	15580	-15.4
8880	-0.6	15830	-16.3
9000	-0.1	16080	-17.1
9080*	+0.3	16140**	-17.3

*Tanks 1 & 2 full. **Centre tank full.

LRJT

LRJT stuff follows the same procedure as the MRJT, but fuel tankering deserves some attention (graphs overleaf).

The Fuel Price Ratio (FPR) is obtained by dividing the fuel price at the departure point by the price at the destination. If it is less than 1, the fuel at the destination is more expensive, so you might want to tanker some fuel. There are graphs that enable you to calculate an optimum departure mass, after calculating the sector distance in NAM and lining it up with the FPR.

Dry Operating Mass: 110,000 kg

C of G: 31% MAC

Deviation or adjustment: +100 kg in Zone F

Total cargo: 11 500 kg, as:

    Cargo 1: 2 500 kg

    Cargo 2: 3,000 kg

    Cargo 3: 3,000 kg

    Cargo 4: 2,000 kg

    Cargo 5: 1,000 kg

Fuel: 72,000 kg

There are 240 passengers with standard weights of 75 kg. 20 are in cabin 0A, 120 are in 0B, 100 are in 0C.

PROCEDURE

Enter the Master Data in ❶, then calculate the dry (meaning no fuel) operating weight index with the formula at ❷. The results go in ❸, in this case 119.1.

Enter the weight deviation in ❹ and read the corresponding index in ❺: -0.51. Calculate the corrected index and place it at ❻: 118.6. Enter the cargo weights and passenger numbers at ❼.

Enter the index scale at ❽ with the corrected index and work your way through the passengers and cargo as shown at ❾.

From the final point (Cabin 0C) draw a vertical line down to the zero fuel line at ❿: 139 600 kg.

Check that the intersection with the zero fuel line determined in table ⓫ is within the maximum zero fuel weight and zero fuel operational limits. If not, rearrange the cargo.

MASS & BALANCE
LRJT

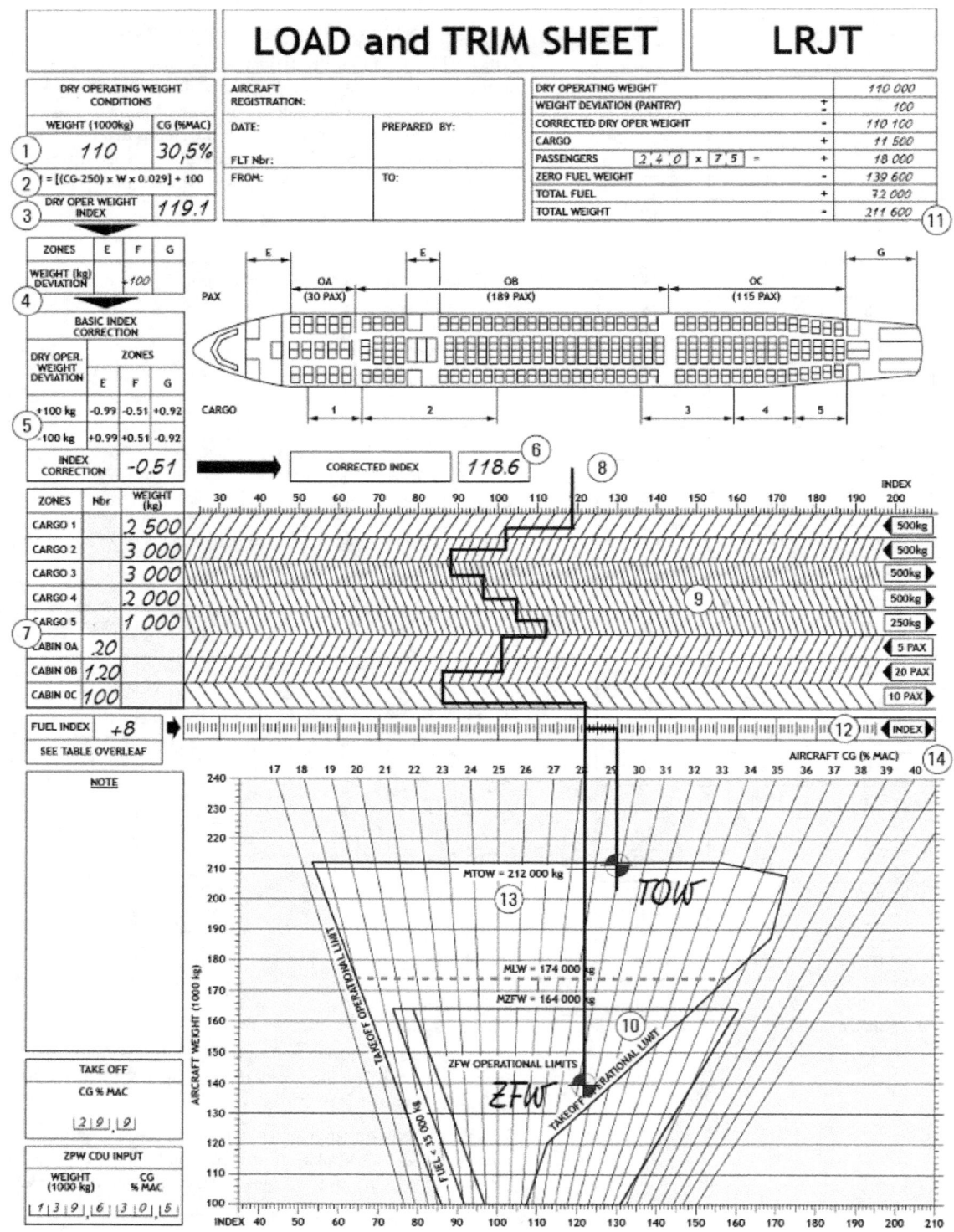

The fuel on board is 72,000 kg at a density of 0.78. The fuel index correction is +8 (see table).

Carry in scale ⑫, then draw a vertical line down to the takeoff weight line ⑬ at 211 600 kg.

Check that the intersection with the takeoff line determined at table ⑪ is within maximum takeoff weight and operational limitations. If not, rearrange the cargo.

Read the takeoff C of G on the C of G scale ⑭: 29.9%.

Radio depends on the movement of electric and magnetic waves, which depend on the movement of electricity, which ultimately depends on the activities of electrons inside an atom. If you are wondering why you need to know this stuff as a pilot, it is because it is also part of the syllabus for an amateur radio licence, of which a pilot's radio licence is a cut-down version.

RADIO NAVIGATION

Alternating current is also the basis of radio waves, which we use to convey information or find our way. The sound of a rotor blade slap from 1100 feet will take one second to reach your ears, but air travelling at that speed would be ten times more powerful than a hurricane, so the sound you hear is not *in* the air - it changes the characteristics of the air instead.

The effect is like the example of electrons moving down a cable. One pushed in at one end affects the others in line until one falls out at the other, so it is easier to imagine a wave of compression pushing air particles in front of it before it affects your eardrums. If this is done too slowly, though, the air particles have a chance to get out of the way, so the effect is not noticeable below a certain rate of vibration, or *frequency*.

WAVE MOTION 062 01

A wave is a progressive disturbance in a medium that itself is not displaced permanently, although electromagnetic waves do not need a medium. Either way, waves can be transmitted without affecting matter.

The usual example is dropping a stone into water, where the water only moves up and down, but there is forward movement of energy, which comes in the first place from the loss of kinetic energy as the stone hits the water.

Making electrons move along an antenna can set an electromagnetic wave in motion in the air in the same way.

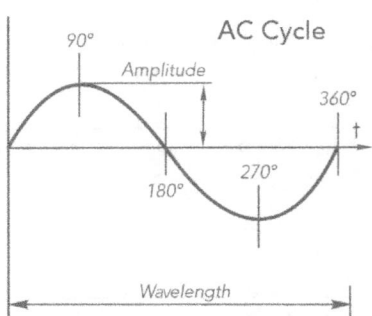

The qualities associated with any type of wave motion are:

- **Velocity**.
- **Frequency**. The rate of oscillation, or the number of waves that pass a fixed point in one second, measured in Hertz (Hz).
- **Wavelength**. The least distance between two consecutive points on two consecutive waves with the same displacement and velocity, represented by the symbol λ.
- **Period**. The time between successive waves.
- **Amplitude**. The maximum displacement of a moving particle from its mean position, labelled positive or negative. Loosely termed *volume*.

Radio waves were originally classified by wavelength, but it is more convenient to use frequency (see table overleaf).

Where the particles of the transmitting medium move at right angles to the direction of propagation (say up and down on the surface of water), you have a *transverse* wave. Where particles move back and forth in the same direction as the propagation (sound), you have a *longitudinal* wave.

Polarisation

Electromagnetic radiation is made up from E and H fields, which stand for *electric* and *magnetic*, respectively. In other words, radio waves have electrical and magnetic axes, acting at right angles to each other. The electric field arises from voltage, and the magnetic one from current.

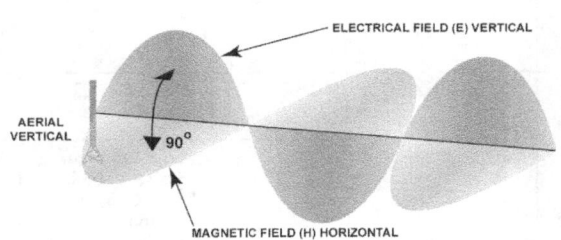

A wave's polarisation is noted with reference to the electrical field, which is parallel with its antenna, so a vertically polarised wave has a vertical electric field, which will come from a vertical aerial (for efficiency, the receiver must have the same orientation). For example, NDBs (and weather-based static) are vertically polarised, whilst VORs and ILS Localisers are horizontally polarised.

With such linear polarisation, the plane of oscillation is fixed in space, whereas with circular polarisation, the plane is rotating - the electrical and magnetic components of the wave spin about the axis of the advance at a rate equal to the frequency. Circular polarisation is often used (with helical antennae) where the relative orientation of the transmitting and receiving antennae cannot be easily controlled, as with GPS, or where the polarisation of the signal may change. It can reduce rain clutter with radar.

In general, polarisation does not change over short distances, but over long distances, especially at high frequencies, it can change drastically.

Calculations

In free space (or a vacuum), electromagnetic waves move at the speed of light, which is taken to be 300,000,000 metres per second, abbreviated as C. The number of waves that will arrive per second at a radio antenna (the frequency) depends on dividing C by the length of the wave concerned. Put another way, over 1 Hz (i.e. 1 cycle), a wave will travel for 300,000 km. For radar purposes, this is **300 m per microsecond**. In nautical miles, try 161,800.

Frequency and wavelength are related as follows:

$$\lambda = \frac{C}{F}$$

F is the frequency in cycles per second. Wavelength is in metres. So, to find the length of a wave with a frequency of 300 KHz:

$$\lambda = \frac{300{\cancel{000000}}}{3\cancel{00000}}$$

The answer is 1000 m, or 1 km.

Wavebands

The range of electromagnetic waves is quite large, but radio waves only occupy a small part of it, actually between about 3 KHz to 3,000 GHz.

This area is split up by International agreement between the people who wish to use it, and consists of frequency ranges, or bands, that share similar characteristics.

Trivia: Wavelengths below 100m (i.e. short wave, or HF) used to be thought of by scientists as useless for long distance communications until amateur operators proved them wrong!

Band	Frequency	Wavelength	Aids	Notes
VLF	3-30 KHz Kilo = Thousand	10-100 km Myriametric		This needs high power and large antennae, so it is used for long ranges, where no transmissions are required from the aircraft - the signal travels as a ground wave for several thousand miles and can penetrate the ocean. Has the least attenuation.
LF	30-300 KHz	1-10 km Kilometric	NDB, Decca, LORAN	Distances of around 1500 miles, with minor attenuation
MF	300-3,000 KHz	100-1000 m Hectometric		Can cover 100-300 miles over land, but the range increases at night as the ionosphere merges back into one layer. Fading and static are problems, so can be unreliable at night. Needs fairly high power and fairly large antennae.
HF Short Wave	3-30 MHz Mega = Million	10-100 m Decametric	HF/RT	Longer distances (100-2000 miles) but only after refraction from the ionosphere - it doesn't go as far by itself as LF can (i.e. 30-100 nm), but you can use a transmitter in the aircraft. This band also suffers from fading and static, and you need to choose the frequency carefully according to the time of day, season and direction of transmission. Severe attenuation. Affected by sunspots
VHF	30-300 MHz	1-10 m Metric	VOR, VDF, ILS Localiser, Marker	Line of sight, is meant for local services, say up to 50 miles. It gives more precise results, and is not really affected by static.
UHF	300-3,000 MHz	10-100 cm Decimetric	Radio Altimeter (High Alt), SSR, DME, GPS, Glidepath	Short range line of sight, but there is little interference and antennae are small
SHF	3-30 GHz Giga = Trillion	1-10 cm Centimetric	Radio Altimeter (Low Alt), MLS, Radar, AWR, Doppler	Short range line of sight, but there is little interference and antennae are small
EHF	30-300 GHz	1-10 mm Millimetric		

HOW IT ALL WORKS

A sound wave will only travel so far by itself, which is why it needs help, in the shape of a *carrier wave*, to move over longer distances (if you could transmit a sound wave, it would be so long that huge aerials and large coils and capacitors would be needed). The carrier wave is created at radio frequency (the RF carrier), and a sound wave (the AF signal) is added to it, so that an electronic copy of the original signal is made. In other words, we are transferring energy with an electromagnetic wave. The process of frequency shifting is called *modulation*, below.

Radio waves are the product of the changing fields that result from alternating current. The backward and forward flow of the electrons produces electrical and magnetic fields along the cable. If the cable forms a closed circuit, the fields tend to cancel each other out, but you can still induce AC in an open circuit that ends in a bare wire. If the frequency is high enough, the fields will propagate at 90° to it. If the wire, or antenna, has the right length (half the wavelength, or multiples thereof), the fields will resonate and send continuous alternating waves of energy (radio waves) outwards, at the same frequency as the AC.

If a wire of the same length as the transmitter is placed in the same orientation in space some distance away, the propagating fields will induce an identical alternating current along it.

The Transmitter

Radio transmitters are based around high frequency oscillators, but applying lots of power directly to an oscillator (above about 100 MHz) reduces its stability, so a relatively weak signal is used, then amplified for the later stages. The audio signal is treated the same way. A *modulator's* job is to combine the signals from the radio and audio amplifiers by superimposing the amplified speech signal on the RF carrier with a transformer.

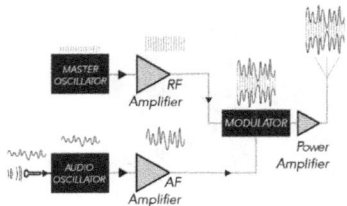

MODULATION

The process of imposing information on to a carrier wave by changing its characteristics is called modulation. That is, the information to be sent *modulates**, or varies, the carrier wave, although an unmodulated signal travels further than a modulated one for the same power, hence their use with long range NDBs.

*You can't just add the voltages together because the antenna would only transmit the radio signal.

The *Depth Of Modulation* is the extent to which a carrier wave is modulated by another frequency, as expressed by a percentage. Such modulation is actually done at just below 100% (typically 90% for voice) because there is a danger of over-modulation that will cause distortion. If the modulation is too low, the signal may be hidden by noise.

AMPLITUDE MODULATION (A3)

With AM, the amplitude, or power, of a carrier wave is varied according to the strength of an audio (or video) signal applied to it. Its shape changes as the AF signal distorts it.

The top part of the picture shows an RF carrier with alternating cycles above and below the line of nil current flow. The middle part shows a fluctuating DC waveform representing speech from a microphone (it is positive because it is all above the nil current line). When the two are merged together (in the bottom part) the RF carrier takes on the shape of the distorting AF signal.

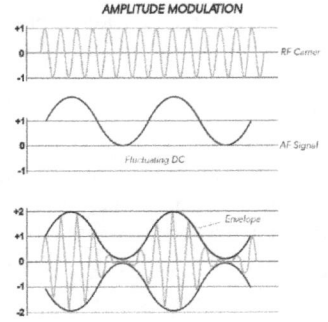

AM suffers from two practical defects, one being noise, and the other lack of quality. Almost all natural and man-made electrical disturbances, such as atmospheric static, or electrical equipment, radiate amplitude-disturbed energy. In addition, the air gets more positively charged as you climb higher, as described under *The Ionosphere*, later, especially when it is wet. This may cause sudden leaks or discharges that produce electromagnetic waves called *precipitation static*, that interfere with radio transmissions, which is a factor when you want reliability in bad weather.

A quick look at a rainfall map of the world will tell you where it is worst, namely the tropics.

The lowest frequency where freedom from static interference can be guaranteed is 30 MHz.

*This ionisation of the air creates a layer around the Earth called the ionosphere which has less resistance to the flow of electricity. It is useful for getting longer ranges with certain frequencies (HF) and is discussed later on.

AM transmissions can therefore be noisy because the receiver cannot distinguish between the signals you want to hear and the ones you don't. This has led to the use of systems such as SELCAL (*Selective Calling*), which mutes the receiver until a special code is sent, so you don't have to listen to the background noise all the time.

Also, for a quality signal, you need to transmit all the audio frequencies in the range of human hearing. AM channels are not wide enough to do that, for historical reasons. This is why a contralto female voice is used for VOLMET - it fits the frequency spectrum better than a soprano does.

SIDEBANDS 062 01 01 03

When a carrier is modified by a frequency lower than itself, you get a band of frequencies either side of the carrier. The boundaries are effectively two extra frequencies, being the equivalent of the *sum* and *difference* frequencies of the carrier and the modulator, so you get three in total, from the carrier *plus* the audio and the carrier *minus* the audio (there are way more with FM transmissions). The extras are called *upper* and *lower sidebands*, which are exact mirrors of each other, in terms of the information carried, with half the original strength.

A receiver would normally need to pick up all the frequencies involved, but this can waste bandwidth (and power) as you are transmitting two identical sidebands and the carrier, which is there even if nothing is being transmitted - it is simply something to hang the sidebands on. In addition, the efficiency is limited to 33% to prevent distortion in the receiver when demodulating.

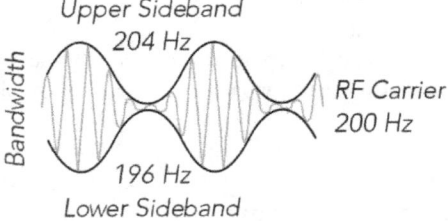

Because 80% of the power of an AM signal is in the carrier wave, which is essentially wasted, a neat trick is to suppress the carrier and one sideband, to transmit just the other one, *adding what was taken away at the receiver*. This means that you need less than half the power to transmit* (for the same distance), and the signal doesn't take up so much space, so you get to use more channels, although your receiver now needs an oscillator. In effect, you can transmit with narrower bandwidths. This is *Single Sideband Transmission*, or SSB. As there is no carrier, there is no transmission unless information is being sent.

*SSB can do with 250 watts what AM requires 1000 watts for, so the ratio is 4:1, or 16 times more efficiency.

Traditionally, the upper sideband is used above 10 KHz, and the lower one below (it is a modified form of A3). HF upper sideband is used for aeronautical voice communications over the N Atlantic - now replaced with satellite communications or ADS-B. HF VOLMET signals are also single sideband, as are HF two-way communications.

FREQUENCY MODULATION

Here, the frequency is changed instead of the amplitude, so FM does not suffer from man-made interference. As well, because the signal to noise ratio for FM is lower than it needs to be for AM, you don't need as much power for the same quality of reception (it is also more steady), although FM receivers are more complex to produce.

The whole audio range is covered because they were able to allocate a wider bandwidth to FM transmissions.

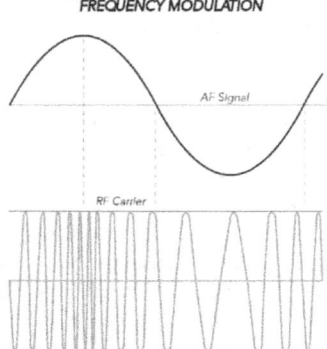

When the amplitude is positive, the frequency increases above the mean carrier frequency, and *vice versa*. The amount of change is called the *deviation*. The maximum limit is ±5 KHz for speech.

PULSE MODULATION

This is used for radar, where the superimposed information is the time of transmission. See *Radar*, later.

FREQUENCY SHIFT KEYING

For data, as used with satellites, where the carrier frequency is shifted above and below the mean (as 1 and 0) to represent bits of information.

Input is in FM with a very small deviation.

RESONANCE (TUNED CIRCUIT)

Radio waves must oscillate at a frequency high enough to excite the air molecules surrounding an antenna. This needs *inertia* and *elasticity*, so that energy can be stored and released. A capacitor and inductor (coil) in parallel is the simplest kind of electrical oscillating system, which behaves in a similar way to a weight on a spring, or an electrical pendulum. The problem is that, left to itself, the energy dissipates over time and the oscillations will stop, so we need a way of making sure that they keep going. With a weight on the end of a spring, all you need to do is pull the weight at its lowest point by just enough to cover for the losses caused by friction. In a watch, the main spring is timed to release just enough energy to the balance wheel to keep it moving.

In our case, friction is replaced by resistance, and we have to produce undamped (continuous) oscillations. Because of their ability to amplify, transistors are very good at doing this - the amplification creates energy that can be fed back into the system at the right moments to keep it going (otherwise called regenerative feedback).

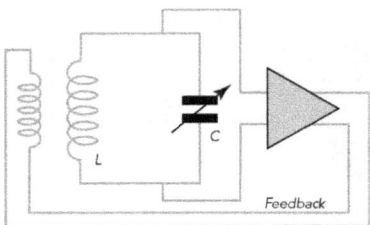

A *tank (LC) circuit* (so called because it stores energy) consists of a capacitor and inductance coil (see above). Depending on their electrical values, an alternating current can go back and forth between them in a periodic cycle.

The capacitor discharges through the coil as the excess electrons try to move from one of its plates to the other. However, back emf from the coil slows this down, and keeps the movement of the electrons going, where it would normally die away (the polarity reverses each cycle).

Current in a capacitor leads the applied voltage by 90°, while through an inductor it lags by 90°. With both in a circuit, the current flowing through the capacitor leads that in the inductor by 180°, so they cancel each other out, and only a little current is needed to keep things going. The resonant frequency is the one where reactance is zero, meaning that the circuit is operating on pure resistance. This provides a significant rise in voltage.

The coil and capacitor between them therefore behave like a flywheel and a spring. The energy is alternately stored in the electric field of the capacitor and the magnetic field of the coil, and we have an oscillator.

The Receiver

As the signal at the receiving antenna is very weak, a receiver must not only provide gain, but also be selective. The antenna picks up all the waves that are passing it, but the tuner makes the radio respond to the one you want to listen to.

To get audio output from a direct conversion receiver, the signal is mixed with one from a Beat Frequency Oscillator.

BEAT FREQUENCY OSCILLATOR

To hear a signal, it must naturally be inside the audio range of between 300 - 3000 Hz. Beat notes are created when any waves of different frequencies are mixed.

On the ADF (later), the BFO produces a small AC current which differs from the IF by around 2 KHz. The IF and BFO outputs are fed to the frequency mixer (heterodyne), where they are subtracted from one another to produce four frequencies, only one of which can be heard - the *difference* or *beat* frequency, which is amplified and fed to a loudspeaker which produces a steady AF of 2 KHz, within the human hearing range. If the incoming RF stops, no sound is heard from the loudspeaker. On modern aircraft the BFO is activated automatically.

The **squelch circuit** eliminates background noise when nothing is being transmitted. It is automatic on modern sets above a certain noise level.

DEMODULATION

Demodulation involves using a rectifier to ensure that only signal pulses moving in one direction get through.

In practice, the circuit will be sensitive to a *range* of frequencies, due to the ratio of resistance to inductance, so the less resistance there is, the better the spike of voltage impressed upon the circuit. The antenna circuit can be decoupled to send its current into the circuit via a transformer, so that resistance is reduced to make the circuit tune more sharply. Notice that a step up transformer is used to give the signal a boost.

Finally, the audio-only signal goes into an audio amplifier for a quick boost before an exact copy of the original speech comes out of the loudspeaker.

Bandwidth

The "width" of any signal is known as its *bandwidth*, but a transmission medium also has a bandwidth, and here, the term is twisted slightly to mean the width it is *able to provide*, rather than the *width it occupies*. The aim, when matching signals to media, is to ensure that the signal bandwidth does not exceed that of the intended link, or that your car is not too wide for the road. So officially, the bandwidth is the difference between the highest and the lowest range of frequencies that a signal occupies. As an example, 3,000 Hz is a wide enough spread to carry voice, and if you used it to modify a carrier wave of 3 MHz (3,000,000 Hz), your bandwidth will range from 2,997,000-3,003,000 Hz (see *Sidebands*, above). Unofficially (and more commonly), the term defines the amount of information that can be carried by any media, or signal, (that is, capacity) in a given time.

Emissions

The simplest method of transmitting information is to turn a signal on and off in a recognisable code, as used by older NDBs which break the carrier wave in a pattern matching the Morse Code ID of the station, called *Telegraphy*, or CW (or even *keying*). This is an A1 transmission, whereas a carrier wave only would be A0.

Otherwise, we use *telephony*, or ordinary speech, where an audio signal modifies, or modulates, a carrier wave. Sending Morse as an audio signal creates an A2 signal.

When describing the emissions from a station, three symbols are used. The first is a letter describing the type of modulation, the second is a number for the nature of the modulation signal, and the third is a letter for the type of information transmitted.

For example, the VOR, discussed later, is A9W, because its carrier wave is frequency and amplitude modulated.

Table: Types Of Emission

Code	Modulation Type	No	Nature Of Modulating Signal	Code	Information Type
N	Unmodulated	0	Unmodulated CW	N	None
A	AM double sideband	1	Keyed CW (Morse)	A	Telegraphy (aural)
J	Single sideband, suppressed carrier	2	Modulated CW	B	Telegraphy (automatic)
H	Single sideband, full carrier	3	AM Modulated	E	Telegraphy (inc sound)
F	Frequency modulated	7	2 or more channels, Digital	D	Data
G	Phase Modulation	8	2 or more channels, Analogue	W	Combinations of the above
P	Unmodulated Pulse	9	Composite (digital/analogue)		
K	AM Pulse				

EXAMPLES

Class	Aid
N0NA1A	NDB (BFO on)*
N0NA2A	NDB (BFO on for tuning only)
A2A	NDB
J3E	HF (Communication)
A3E	VHF/VDF
A8W	ILS
A9W	VOR
P0N	DME, SSR
N0X/G1D	MLS (DPSK)

*Produces peak power all the time for better range.

Propagation

Although undisturbed waves travel through space in straight lines at a constant speed, the Earth is an uneven mass of solids and liquids surrounded by gases with varying densities and electrical charges, all of which affect the propagation of radio waves, or the means by which they travel between a transmitter and a receiver. They normally take the scenic Great Circle route (see *Navigation*), but they can be helped along by the weather - because of a rapidly rising pressure tendency at both ends, for example, in August 2013, NDBs in Canada were received in

Europe. The trouble is that propagation is not an exact science, which doesn't help when you are trying to talk to a base station from a remote place. The fact that you can get through on one day does not mean that you can do it on another.

The Earth has a rhythm called a Diurnal cycle, meaning a pattern that recurs every 24 hours. It is also a factor in Meteorology, which is handy, because propagation is affected by what the Sun does. In fact, it is the driving force behind much of HF propagation, simply because more energy and particles arrive on the surface of the Earth during the day. The more illumination there is, the easier propagation will be. There is less in the morning and evening than there would be at noon, which is easily proven with a lightmeter. The complication is that more energy arrives per square mile at the Equator than anywhere else.

THE IONOSPHERE

This is a region surrounding the Earth where the Sun's rays dislodge electrons from the gas molecules, making them ionised (and positively charged) and creating several conductive layers a couple of hundred miles thick around the Earth, starting about 60 miles up (but lower during the day) and varying with the seasons (they are not spheres, but change their shape constantly).

This is because the gases involved have different densities, so the molecules will settle out at different heights, as described below.

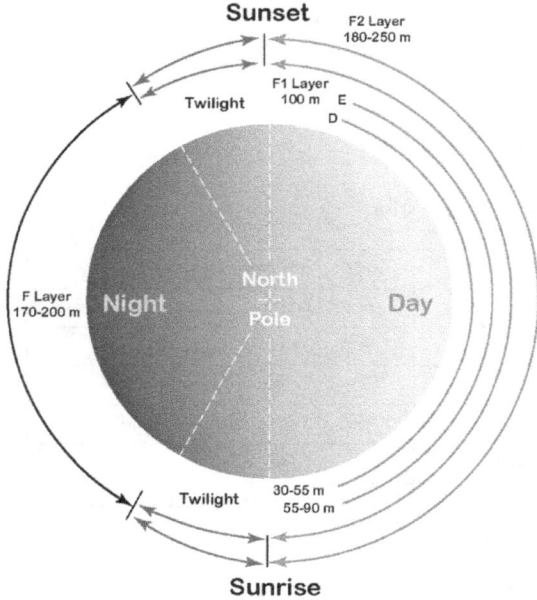

The ionisation stops the Sun's most violent radiation from reaching the Earth (ultraviolet light is dealt with by the production of ozone in the Stratosphere). It also makes the gases (nitrogen and oxygen) conductive. The nitrogen is ionised at the higher levels - lower down it is the oxygen. This happens mostly in daytime and is least just before sunrise, so air is a good insulator in the lower parts of the atmosphere, but ionisation makes it more conductive as you go up. *Recombination* is the process that gets electrons and atoms back together, starting in the late afternoon and early evening, and continuing overnight.

As the ionosphere depends directly on the Sun's radiation, the way the Earth moves around the Sun affects its characteristics.

As the ionosphere is warmed up, its ionisation level increases, so it will reflect signals better. Things are better towards the East in the mornings because that part of the world has been in daylight for longer (more about this in *Navigation*). Signals paths to the South tend to be stronger around midday, and those to the West stronger in the afternoons and evenings. Contrary to popular belief, the weather doesn't have much of an influence at all.

As an example, in Europe, you won't receive many transmissions from America in the morning because it is still dark there. The best time is late afternoon, before Europe gets so dark that the signals start to fade away. In the picture above, reception times are related to specific frequency bands.

Some ionospheric changes are predictable, and some are not, but all of them affect radio propagation. Regular variations can be 27-day, daily and 11-yearly (from sunspots), but the daily ones have most effect on aviation. As the atmosphere is bombarded by waves with different frequencies, 4 cloud-like layers of electrically charged gas atoms are produced between 50-300 km above the Earth: The D, E (Heaviside), and F1 & F2 layers (Appleton). The first was discovered by James Van Allen in 1957, hence its naming as the Van Allen belt. UV rays with higher frequencies can penetrate deeper into the atmosphere so they create the lowest ionised layers.

- The **D layer** sits between 50-100 km high **during daylight hours**, so it starts to form at dawn and fades away after sunset. Ionisation is low because fewer UV waves penetrate to this level. The D layer can **refract VLF,** if large antennae and high power transmitters are used, but it is mainly responsible for **absorbing and blocking** (or at least attenuating) **LF* and MF waves**, while being transparent to HF. As the D layer fades, MF (NDB) signals can reach the higher layers where they may be reflected back.

  *Although the sky wave may be blocked, if the transmitter is powerful enough to have one, and the frequency is low enough, a ground wave can still travel for hundreds or even thousands of miles. Between 700-1000 kHz would appear to be the upper limit for ground wave propagation.

- The **E layer** is higher, between 100-150 km. It returns **LF and HF bands**, or waves longer than 100m, and is normally transparent to VHF, but **Sporadic E** involves patches of strong ionisation that can return them.

- In daylight, the **F layer** splits into the **F1 and F2 layers**. It is responsible for most **HF long-distance** communication (waves below 100m). During maximum sunspot activity, F layer atoms can stay ionised all night because the process is a lot slower. For horizontal waves, the single-hop capability can be up to 3000 miles, and more with multiple hops.

TRANSMISSIONS

In a transmitter, the energy is alternately stored in the electric field of a capacitor and the magnetic field of a coil. An antenna connected to the circuit would therefore alternately radiate electric and magnetic fields. In fact, they surround the antenna at all times, as there is a crossover where each field builds up and dies down.

As electrons rush up and down the antenna (as alternating current), they form an electric field between the antenna and Earth, as the relationship between them is capacitive. The movement of the electrons also creates a magnetic field. Both radiate outwards and synchronise together about a quarter of a mile away. When a transmitter is feeding an omnidirectional antenna, the waves will spread out equally in all directions.

Picture: Typical Propagation from a vertical antenna

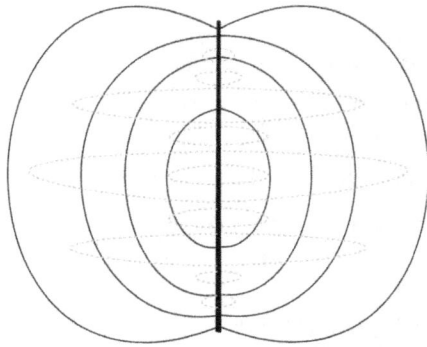

As the circumference of a wave front increases, its energy reduces per unit of length (see *Attenuation*, below). The signal strength at any point is called the *field strength*, and it is usually measured in volts.

Point B in the picture is 3 times the distance from the antenna than Point A is, and the circumference is three times larger, so the field strength at B a third of A's. Field strength in volts is therefore inversely proportional to distance.

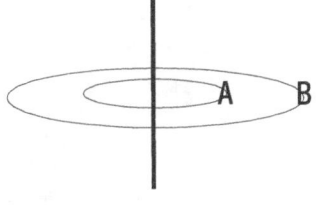

However, the signal also moves vertically and the signal has to spread out over the area of the resulting sphere. This measure of strength now is the *power* of the signal which is measured in Watts. As Point B is on the surface of a sphere with 9 times the surface area of the one at Point A, it will receive a ninth of the power. Thus, the power of a signal fades in an inverse square relationship, meaning that a signal 2 nm from its source will have a quarter of the strength of one only 1 nm away. Put another way, you need 4 times the power to double the range of transmission, as a radio wave is an expanding circle, so its area depends on the square of the radius.

This has important implications for radar, described later.

ATTENUATION

This concerns the loss of energy and velocity in various parts of a radio wave as energy is absorbed by the Earth and/or the atmosphere and ionosphere, on top of the normal decrease of power with range described above. If a signal's path is obstructed by rain, fog or a hill (for example), there will be a noticeable weakening of the signal behind the obstruction as a radio shadow is created.

The only way of combatting attenuation that we have any control over is with the frequency. The higher it is, the greater will be the attenuation.

- **Surface attenuation** increases with frequency.
- **Ionospheric attenuation** increases with a decrease in frequency.
- **Radar attenuation** increases with frequency, but is affected by water droplets which can also absorb and reflect the signal.

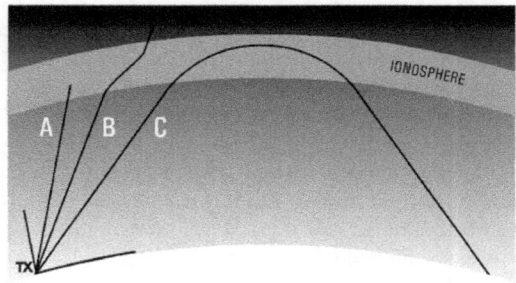

Radio waves generally travel pretty much in a straight line, but they may change direction because of:

- **Refraction (B)**, which is the change of speed and/or bending of a wave as it travels across different media, such as land or sea (as discussed under *ADF/NDB*, later). This also happens at the ionosphere, with HF, according to temperature, pressure and humidity. See *Sky Waves*, overleaf. The frequency does not change when refraction occurs.

- **Reflection (C)**, from a flat surface such as the Earth, or an aircraft (radar), like light off a mirror (where the initial and reflected waves have the same angle), but after reflection, a phase shift occurs, which will depend on the angle at which the surface was struck, and the wave polarisation.

- **Diffraction** (scattering). This is the spreading of a wave as it passes through a gap or round an edge, and is a problem when signals are transmitted in a narrow beam, but it is also one reason why a radio wave follows the shape of the Earth (see *Ground Waves*).

This means that, if you rely on radio waves for approaches to airfields, you should be aware that they bend at certain times of the day (e.g. dawn/dusk) and over certain terrain, such as mountains, where you could also get multipath propagation*, as signals are received from many sources and will be out of phase with each other at the antenna. Such waves can cancel each other out and you end up with no guidance at all.

*In the above pictures, signals being received off the ionosphere have been shown as single refractions for simplicity. In reality, as the ionosphere is not uniform in terms of thickness, density or altitude, it is quite common for signals to be reflected from more than one layer to arrive at one point at different times. In other words, they are out of phase with each other, which is a characteristic of AM, but it can happen with line of sight signals such as VHF as they bounce off mountains and other terrain.

It barely affects SSB, but it can badly affect the PSK modulation used by GPS satellites, although problems with accuracy tend not to occur at the mid-latitudes occupied by Europe.

GROUND (SURFACE) WAVES

Ground waves are sometimes called *Surface Waves*. They are associated with VLF and LF, and often MF, and may go directly to their destination (if it is close enough), or curve to follow the Earth's surface, depending on the frequency (they don't leave the lower atmosphere). The two factors involved in the curving are diffraction and scattering, and attenuation.

Radio waves tend to be reflected by objects that are larger than about half their wavelength. At centimetric wavelengths (SHF), this will involve reflection or absorption, and radio shadows behind the obstacles concerned but, at lower frequencies, the waves will curve round small obstacles, such as hills. The obstacles slows down the part of the wave that is closest to it, making the wave curve towards it as it passes. Similarly, the bottom surface of the wave is slowed down close to the surface and the wave will tilt into it.

As the H field cuts the Earth's surface, currents are created, the energy for which must come from the wave itself, so contact with the surface and the widening circumference of the wave eventually weakens its power (attenuation), causes it to curve downwards and eventually be absorbed. Once a ground wave starts to die away, it does so very quickly. Over 300 miles, for example, it may only die away in proportion for the first 200 miles - then it halves its strength for each hundred miles after that until it is undetectable.

The approximate lengths of LF/MF ground waves are 1000/500 nm, respectively, although MF suffers more from atmospheric attenuation. Ground waves must be vertically polarised to induce ground currents, and their range depends on:

- **Wavelength**. The lower the frequency (and the longer the wavelength), the better the reception over long distances. Put another way, the higher the frequency, the greater the attenuation. Below 500 kHz, you can obtain over 1000 miles just with a ground wave.
- **Type of ground**. The rate of attenuation of a surface wave is around 3 times greater over land than it is over the sea. Typical figures for maximum range are 100 and 300 nm respectively, with high power.
- **Polarisation**. Vertically polarised waves normally have the least attenuation.

A *ground-reflected wave* bounces off the ground on its way to the receiver (which is why Distance Measuring Equipment uses an echo protection circuit). As it is not subject to continuous absorption by the Earth, it travels further than the ground wave, but the phase can be reversed at the point of reflection.

DIRECT (SPACE) WAVES (A3E)

These are contained within the troposphere, and are otherwise known as *tropospheric, or space waves*. Being direct, they are known as *line-of-sight*, meaning that anything in the way, like hills or buildings, will affect the transmission (direct waves will not bounce like HF waves do).

VHF/SHF/UHF reception is line-of-sight and will not curve to follow the Earth's surface, so you have to be high enough to receive your selected station at a particular distance. As an example, when crossing the Irish Sea, you must be above 3000 feet to hear either Shannon or London Information. However, when using the VOR at high altitudes, you might get station overlap and erroneous readings, so don't use VOR bearing information beyond the published protection range (see the AIP).

Air-ground transmissions are limited to 25 nm in the UK, up to 4,000 feet for tower frequencies and 10,000 feet for approach. Such limitations also mean little interference from other stations.

The (theoretical) reception range for line of sight transmissions can be estimated with this formula:

```
NM = (1.23 X √H) + (1.23 X √h)
```

 Despite the fact that the value of 1.23 has been used since at least the 1950s, some questions in the EASA exams use 1.25.

H is the height of the aircraft antenna and h is that of the one on the ground. Do not be tempted to combine them into one calculation - the square roots won't work.

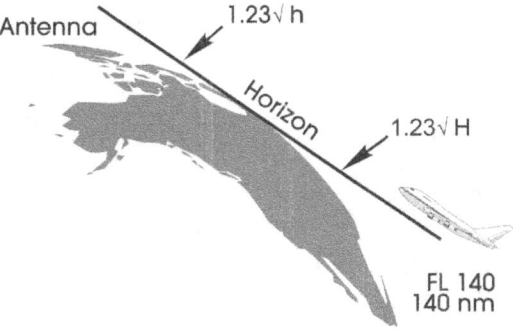

The short cut is to use Pythagoras and add a bit, or to multiply the square root of the flight level of the aircraft by 12. In real life, however, the results will vary if the transmitter is weak, there is something in the way, or the receiver is not working properly. The actual figure is greater by around 4/3 due to diffraction.

The actual figure is greater by around 4/3 due to diffraction. Here are some samples:

Height	Range (nm)
1 500	50
5 000	87
10 000	123

SKY WAVES (J3E)

A *sky wave* reflects off the ionosphere, where it might be reflected downwards again, if the angle is right, and reach further distances (on HF). The HF frequencies allocated to commercial aviation range from 2 - 22 MHz, but not all of it is used. Details about ATC units using it will be found in Flight Information Publications. Transmissions are AM and SSB, coded J3E.

REFRACTION/REFLECTION

Anyhow, HF waves that hit the ionosphere can be bent if the angle is right, as the side of the wave that hits one of its layers first starts to speed up, due to the reduced *dielectric constant from ionisation**, which makes it turn. This is similar to that of light refraction in water which makes an object appear to be displaced.

*The speed of radio waves in the atmosphere is determined by its dielectric property, which ultimately depends on pressure, temperature and relative humidity. As pressure and relative humidity decrease with altitude, so does the Dielectric Constant**, but it increases as temperature decreases. Their combined lapse rates make radio waves increase their speed with height, so that, when a radio wave moves away from the Earth at less than a 90° angle, its upper part moves faster than its lower part. In essence, as you climb, the refractive index decreases uniformly (as does the ISA lapse rate). Radio waves can therefore be bent, particularly in a downward curve towards the surface of the Earth.

**The *dielectric constant* is the ratio of the capacity of a condenser in a given medium, i.e. air, to its capacity in a vacuum. It can also be thought of as a measure of the resistance of the air to wave propagation, and vertical changes in the Dielectric Constant determine the path of a radio wave, typically following a curved path with a radius of 1.3 times the radius of the Earth. This makes the normal range of VHF/UHF (line of sight) transmissions 1.3 times the visual horizon.

The angle at which the bending of a wave first happens is the *critical angle*, or the smallest angle that will allow a wave to be reflected back to Earth. Any rays more vertical than this are *escape rays*, typically used for satellites. The *critical frequency* (at which bending occurs) depends on the density of the layer concerned. If a wave manages to pass through one, it can still be reflected from higher up if its frequency is lower than that layer's critical frequency. Thus, the ionosphere behaves like a pane of glass directly above, and more like a mirror towards the horizon.

The first wave to reach the ground after being refracted or reflected is called the *First Returning Sky Wave*, until the maximum range is reached. When a wave leaves an antenna, the ground wave will be detected until it fades, or attenuates. Between that point, and where the first sky wave comes back from the ionosphere, is an area where nothing is heard, called a *skip zone*, or *dead space*.

Note that the antenna will be radiating the above signals in all directions of the compass, so some will be going to the left of the diagram, as a mirror image.

The **skip distance** is the Earth distance taken by a signal after each reflection, or the distance covered by the first sky wave. 30 MHz signals do not return because they are too high in frequency, being at the bottom of the VHF band (15-25 MHz is more typical for bouncing).

You can reflect off the ionosphere and back off the ground several times for multiple hops (skip).

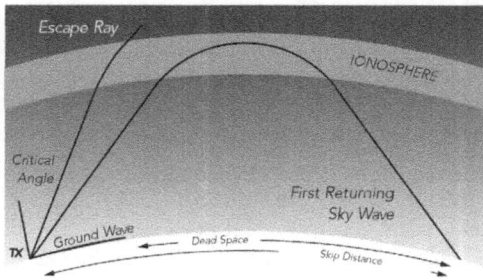

The size of the skip zone changes with frequency*, and it doesn't always stay constant, even when you are using only one. If the ionisation gets stronger, the ionosphere will behave more like a mirror, and you will get what is called Short Skip propagation, where the skip zone gets much narrower. If high angle signals reflect back very close to the transmitter, they could meet or overlap the ground wave and provide coverage out to a thousand miles or so.

*The lower the frequency of a wave, the longer its wavelength, the more rapidly it is reflected, and the larger will be its critical angle, but the less the distance it will travel. A 20 MHz wave will be detected further from the transmitter than a 5 MHz one.

The skip zone of HF transmission will increase with higher frequencies and higher reflecting ionospheric layers. At night, if you use the same frequency, the skip distance will increase. So what can you do if you are not getting through to a station but are receiving another from a greater distance away? Should you change to a higher or lower frequency? A lower one reduces the critical angle to make the skywave return at a shorter range and reduce the dead space.

Skip is usually best when the Sun is about halfway between you and the area you are transmitting to or receiving from. You will normally hear skip from the East in the morning and the West in the afternoon with that from the North or South at any time. *Long path skip* takes the long way round the Earth, usually because ionospheric conditions are better that way.

Thus, we depend on the ionosphere for all HF contacts beyond the ground-wave zone. It moves all the time, itself being dependent on the intensity of particle and wave emissions from the Sun, so propagation is affected considerably by the ionosphere's movement, which is why the ADF suffers from what is called *night effect* just after sunset and before sunrise when the needle swings erratically as the plane of polarisation changes after reflections (on the other hand, during the night is when you will receive distant stations best).

Generally, HF communication is always possible when the frequency is low enough to be reflected and high enough not to be attenuated. Unfortunately, the only information we have about the above changes usually comes from statistical sources. It's not something you can work out.

HF DATALINK

This uses the upper sideband of a selected frequency to send phase modulated digital information, or voice transmissions

RADIO NAVIGATION
How It All Works

having been converted to digital form. Once established, the link the link can be kept open without crew interaction.

ANOMALOUS PROPAGATION

Within the atmosphere, the velocity of a wave is less than it would be in free space, due to atmospheric conditions. Normal refractivity, which exists for around 50% of the time, will cause a wave to be bent downward from its usual straight line. It exists when moisture, pressure and temperature decrease with altitude.

However, when lapse rates depart significantly from normal, VHF, UHF and SHF waves (particularly radar) can follow different curved paths. A rapid increase of temperature with height (an inversion) and a rapid decrease of relative humidity (a steep lapse rate) can bend the wave more toward the surface of the Earth and increase propagation distances with little attenuation (although fading* can occur) for a condition of **super refraction**. This means that radar coverage, for example, can be extended for up to 50% above the normal range.

*During twilight.

Propagation distances can reduce (*sub refraction*) with opposing conditions. Radar can suffer from **ghosting**, or false echoes. A **shadow zone (radar hole)**, makes objecs invisible electronically.

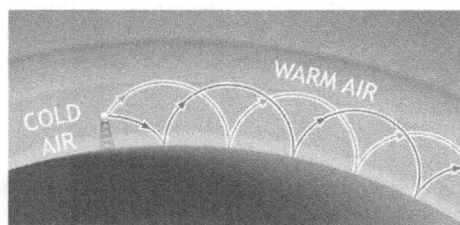

If the waves curve more than the Earth does, because conditions are more intense, radio waves can become trapped between the surface and the negative gradient causing the refraction. Because the waves also bounce off the surface, they can travel for much longer distances. Such **ducts** are associated with regions of high pressure, over flattish terrain and the sea - not normally over hilly ground. Semi-permanent ducts can be found around the Earth in the major areas of high pressure, usually in meteorological conditions associated with tropical and subtropical latitudes (i.e hot by day, and cool by night), near the Equator. In the Trade Winds, for example (see *Meteorology*), ducting over 3 000 miles can occur, off the surface and below about 5 000 feet.

The depth of the duct increases with the wavelength, such as 50 feet for wavelengths of 3 cm, and 600 feet for wavelengths of 1 metre, but they are normally less than 1 000 feet deep. Elevated ducts (between two layers of the atmosphere) can occur at height, so they may be present at more than one level, so if you are experiencing radio/radar reception difficulties, you can fly towards the destination, descend, or try a lower frequency.

With radar, ducting will increase ground clutter.

- More moisture means more refraction
- Higher temperatures mean less refraction

Pressure by itself has little effect.

VLF signals can travel long distances through a similar process involving the ionospheric layers and a *conduit wave*, which is *reflected* rather than *refracted*.

FREQUENCY SELECTION

With HF, frequencies need to be higher during the day or when you are at greater range from the station. Because the ionosphere is higher at night, you can use lower ones, generally about half (that is, use *Double During Day*), which is something to be aware of when you are operating at a remote base and you use HF to keep in touch with the Operations office. Generally, you might leave for camp with a selection of five frequencies you can use depending on the time of day.

Otherwise, for successful communication on HF between two given points, there is a maximum frequency, a lowest frequency and an optimum frequency.

OPTIMUM WORKING FREQUENCY

The *optimum* usable frequency, where attenuation is minimum for the range obtained, or where you have the least number of problems, is the best theoretical frequency that brings the skywave back to the receiver. It is the one that causes the first returning sky wave to fall just short of the receiving station, so that when it drifts, the station will still pick it up. This frequency should be high enough to avoid the disadvantages from multipath fading, absorption and noise, but not so high as to be affected by rapid changes in the ionosphere. It is about 85% of the ....

MAXIMUM USABLE FREQUENCY

The point at which refraction is no longer possible. As the level of ionisation is less in the ionosphere by night than it is by day, you have to lower the frequency to get the same type of refraction. Luckily, attenuation is reduced at night as well, so this is offset slightly. The MUF not only varies with path length and between day and night, but also with the seasons, meteor trails, sunspots, etc. This is why HF transmitters have to use a wide range of frequencies between about 2-20 MHz to get through.

LOWEST USABLE FREQUENCY

This is the point below which refraction cannot start.

Antennae   062 01 02

Aircraft radios use 760 channels that are spaced 25 KHz apart with a power rating of between 2-25 Watts, but power won't help without a good antenna.

An antenna is a conductor (or a group of them) that can radiate or collect electromagnetic waves. Put another way, it is a device that can convert electrical (AC) energy into electromagnetic energy and *vice versa*. The relationship between an antenna and the Earth is a capacitive one, with the air between them acting as a dielectric.

A certain length of straight wire will possess a natural amount of inductance and capacitance, which will correspond to a particular wavelength, as the length of a radiated wave depends on their product. For example, a half-wave dipole* for 18 MHz should be 8.33 m long (as the name implies, the optimum length for an antenna is half the wavelength, or multiples thereof). At higher frequencies, the antenna will be too long to be resonant, and will be inductive as well as resistive. At a lower frequency, it will be too short and will show capacitance (as a reminder, anything other than exact resonance will involve reactance and resistance, known collectively as impedance). An antenna tuning unit will tune out unwanted reactance - the classic way of making a piece of wire seem longer is to add a coil to it, but a lot of the energy is lost in heating the coil up, and it decreases the impedance anyway. Capacitive loading is a better solution that doesn't actually use capacitors, but just another piece of wire perpendicular to the original. The capacitance lies between them.

*A dipole is an antenna that is split at the centre, with each section a quarter-wavelength long. More correctly, two equal lengths of wire connected to a combined feedpoint in the centre and suspended horizontally above ground is called a doublet. Radio waves passing by will induce voltage and current along the wires equal in amplitude but opposite in phase to each other. At the frequency where half a wavelength forms on the two wires there will be a low impedance at the feedpoint and a dipole is formed. The impedance will always be high at the ends because the current is close to zero.

In practice, the wires are about 5% shorter than the correct length (pruned), to allow for electric current in a conductor being slower than a radio wave, and to remove unwanted inductance. The physical length is therefore shorter than the electrical length - as it is not practical to carry around a range of antennae, adding a capacitor or coil (inductor) to the mix (*loading*) will allow you to artificially adjust its natural wavelength to suit the circumstances. A coil increases the inductance of an antenna and reduces its natural frequency, while a capacitor in series reduces the capacitance and raises the natural frequency (the same as reducing the wavelength). As an example, a normal VHF antenna would be about 15 cm long, but using complex circuitry allows you to electronically shorten it.

However, airborne systems do not use dipoles, as they tend to be large and their energy is not directional. A unipole, on the other hand, is a quarter length conductor mounted vertically on the fuselage, which acts as the other half, so one used for VHF communications can be less than 60 cm long. Two unipoles can often be seen back to back on a vertical stabiliser to behave like a dipole with VOR or ILS transmissions.

At frequencies between around 2 - 30 MHz (HF), a dipole would be between 5 - 75 m long. As the aircraft itself is around that length, its fuselage can be used as the radiating or receiving element. A tuned notch or slot in the base of the vertical stabiliser with a large oscillating voltage applied across it can drive current through the fuselage, which then radiates. A slot aerial is a rectangular shaped hole resonant at half a wavelength long that works like a dipole. A notch is a hole cut into a rounded part of the aircraft skin, covered with insulating material to preserve the aerodynamic shape. RF energy is fed to both sides of the aperture to produce skin currents.

However, for frequencies between 10 - 100 kHz, even the largest aircraft would be too small, so capacitive antennae are more suitable, with one "plate" being the airframe, but the receive-only systems they would be used for are now largely redundant. The ADF uses an alternative, though, in the shape of the loop antenna, described later.

At much higher frequencies (3,000 MHz), a **waveguide** may be used, as described under *Radar*.

In summary, there are two basic types of antennae, the *Hertz* (half-wave) or *Marconi* (quarter wave). Hertz types are also known as *dipoles*, and are usually positioned well above ground, radiating horizontally or vertically (see *Polarisation*) for frequencies of 2 MHz and above. Marconis are perpendicular to the Earth and have one end grounded to it, used for frequencies below 2 MHz.

DIRECTIONALITY (DIRECTIVITY)

Most people know they have to turn a domestic radio round in order to get the best signal. This works the other way round as well - it is possible, with simple procedures, to transmit radio waves in certain directions, which can be useful if the wave attenuates quickly, as the power can be concentrated - using a directional aerial can boost transmission in a particular quarter and increase the gain in that direction for longer range. Some directionality can be achieved with just two elements, or dipoles.

A rod slightly shorter than an antenna placed just less than a quarter wavelength away from it will strengthen the signal in that direction. Similarly, a slightly longer rod placed a bit further away will strengthen it in the opposite direction, effectively reflecting the signal. Thus, if a second rod, not fed with power, and slightly longer, is placed a quarter of a wavelength behind a **driven element** (the one radiating all the power) it behaves like a resonant coupled circuit which has oscillatory currents induced in it. The currents re-radiate, and the quarter-wave spacing causes it to be in such a phasing as to cancel out the original radiation on that side, and to reinforce it on the opposite side, so the second dipole has the same effect as a reflector (see *Radar*), and gives you a marked gain in signal strength in one direction. The more the number of dipoles in an array, the narrower and more intense will be the beam of radiation.

A shorter antenna called a *Director* in front of the driven element will behave like a lens which concentrates the energy. Directors and reflectors are called *parasites*, but a series of them is generally known as a Yagi array (like a TV aerial). It can create spurious side beams (or lobes) as well as the main beam.

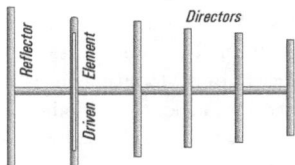

The Yagi is used with radar instead of parabolic arrays.

THE LOOP

Before metric and centimetric waves came on the scene, direction finding was based on the simple loop aerial, or vertical ones spaced apart (the Adcock).

Remembering that there must be a *difference* in electrical pressures between two points for electrons to flow*, the maximum signal is found when the loop is in line with the transmission (i.e. sideways-on), when the points of contact are out of phase, so a current is generated, which drives an electric motor to continually seek the null position, when the loop is square (across the signal). As the vertically polarised signal now reaches both sides of the loop at the same time, no signal is detected.

The null signal point is used for direction finding because it is easier to detect (it is much more sharply defined).

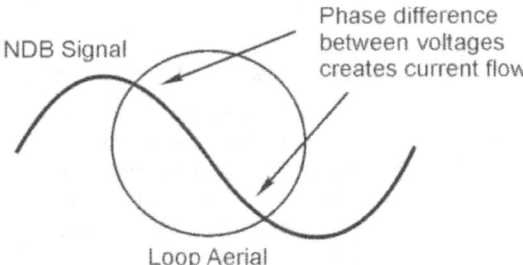

Various stages of magnification inside the receiver help this along, but they need not concern us here. Because the current flows in the opposite direction depending on the position of the loop, you also need some way of determining which end is what, otherwise you could be 180° out. A single vertical aerial called a *sense antenna* helps here - the signals are combined algebraically and the magnitude and polarity of the sense aerial arranged to be identical to the loop. The result is a polar diagram* called a *cardioid*, with only one null point:

*A polar diagram shows what happens to a signal after it leaves an antenna, as a map. It shows the position of points around it where the signal has reduced to (in general) half of its original strength. For most aids, a polar diagram is designed to be a particular shape, as with the cardioid, above, or the limacon with the VOR. The strength of a transmission in a particular direction is shown by a vector drawn from the antenna to the edge of the polar diagram. Thus, loop aerials receive a signal, but the sense aerial is there to resolve ambiguities. It is placed vertically in the middle of the loop. By using a transformer, the electrons flowing in the sense aerial set a second stream flowing in one of the vertical parts of the loop.

So, on one side of the loop, the polar diagrams are positive and combine, but on the other, one is positive and the other negative, so they cancel out, hence the null point on one side. The modern (and more stylish) equivalent of the loop antenna is a small housing with two coils at right angles to each other, wound on ferrite cores, one fore and aft and the other athwartships. The sense aerial resolves the two null points. There is another pair with a search coil in the middle that reacts to its influence and drives a needle as it searches for the null point.

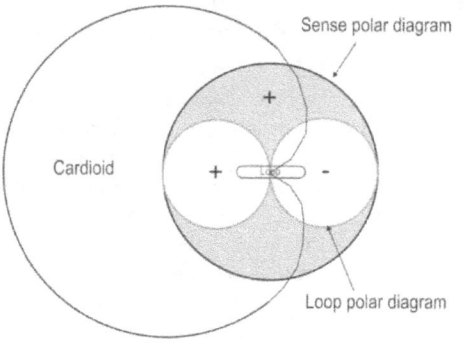

THE HELICAL ANTENNA
A helical antenna, as used with GPS, allows you to use smaller equipment.

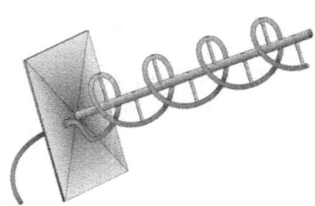

It can be used like a normal antenna, with maximum radiation at right angles to the axis of the helix. The radiation is linearly polarized parallel to the axis.

In the axial mode, however, the radiation comes out of the end (i.e. along the axis), and it works as a directional antenna radiating circularly polarized waves.

PARABOLIC
Parabolic dishes are used with radar systems and are described in that section.

THE SLOTTED PLANAR ARRAY
As used with most modern weather radar systems:

It is flat (i.e. a plane), with slots that act as waveguides (in fact, they have the same effect as a dipole antenna). By stacking them, as shown, the beamwidth of the E plane can be reduced. This gets round a problem caused by slotted waveguides which are long but thin, creating a wave that is wide in the E (vertical) plane but narrow in the H plane. Sidelobes are also reduced.

GAIN
The ratio between the amount of energy propagated in a particular direction and that which would be propagated if the antenna were not directional is called antenna gain. An antenna with a gain of 3 decibels, for example, could put out around double the power of a quarter wave antenna, which has no gain (referred to as *unity*). An antenna with a gain of 6 db hooked on to the back of an amplifier pushing 4 watts into it would put out the equivalent of 16 watts, or 80 if the gain were 13 db.

The gain control for Airborne Weather Radar adjusts the sensitivity of the receiver for optimum target acquisition.

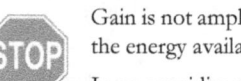 Gain is not amplification, but making the best use of the energy available.

In an omnidirectional antenna, the gain can come from spreading the RF energy closer and flatter to the ground, creating stronger ground waves, as is found by using a five-eighths antenna, for a 3-4.5 db gain (i.e. the power is taken from the higher angles).

The increase in range can be up to 10 km or more.

RECIPROCITY
This is the ability of an antenna to be used for transmitting and receiving.

RADIO NAVIGATION
Radio Navigation

TRANSMITTING SIGNALS

When an alternating current is applied to one end of a straight antenna, the wave travels to the other end, where it can go no further. This is a point of high impedance, so the wave bounces back towards where it came from. Although there is some loss from resistance, the wave is reinforced at the start point with more energy, which results in continuous oscillations that are sustained with suitably timed impulses. There is also a high voltage at the *start* point, meaning the centre of the wire has minimum voltage. The maximum movement of electrons is also in the centre, so it has a low impedance there. The meeting of these two stresses sets up a standing wave which makes the particles oscillate all the time. Standing waves can be kept going with the minimum expenditure of energy.

The length of the antenna must allow the wave to travel from one end to the other and back within one cycle, and the wavelength is the distance travelled within that cycle.

RECEIVING SIGNALS

In simple terms, the antenna catches a radio wave and a small electrical current with the same waveform as the incoming signal is induced in it through an electronic tide. In practice a *selection* of frequencies is captured because an antenna is cut for the middle of the frequency band you want (half wavelength is good, but a quarter is often used).

The signal passed on to the radio set after being received is at the resonant frequency of the antenna, with a few on either side for good measure. This signal is amplified and selectivity improved with a tuned circuit, where capacitive reactance cancels out the inductive reactance. Some other signals do get through however, so filters eliminate them in later stages. In the end, all radio frequencies will finally be extracted, leaving only a low-level audio signal to be amplified and sent to your headset.

A receiver's ability to reject signals outside the relevant bandwidth is called its *sensitivity*.

Doppler

The Doppler effect is a change of frequency that comes from relative motion between the sender and receiver. It works on the principle that radio waves compress when directed to a station and elongate when going away (in other words, as two objects get closer together, the frequency of any radio wave between them will increase artificially because of their relative speed). The usual example given is listening to the change in the noise of a train approaching you, and passing by. The pitch is higher than normal at first, and becomes lower than normal when it has passed.

Picture: Doppler Effect

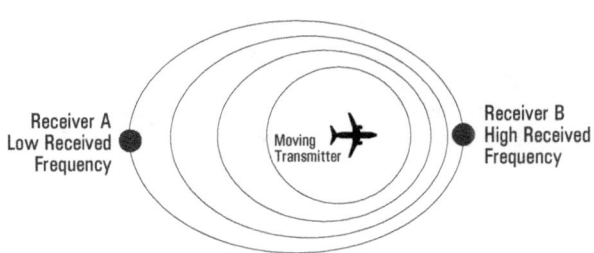

This is because the forward speed means that the sound waves have to fit into a smaller space, and therefore have shorter wavelengths, and a higher pitch, so the receiver will intercept more waves in a given time.

The opposite is true after the train passes - they have more room to fit into, and the wavelength becomes longer, to produce the lower sound. Apply that to radar, since both sound and radio travel as sine waves, and you have the basics of a good navigation system that can compute groundspeed and drift - in helicopters, it can provide auto-hover capabilities, amongst other things, although it has almost entirely disappeared, except for its use with GPS. The change in frequency is called *Doppler Shift*, which is given a positive (+) quality when a closing relative velocity produces an increase in frequency, and a negative quality when otherwise.

Discharge Detectors

Otherwise known as *Stormscopes*, after one manufacturer, these detect lightning discharges and display them on a green screen in the cockpit. They work in a similar way to an ADF with its needle pointing towards a storm.

RADIO NAVIGATION

Most radio aids just give you information about your position - only landing aids tell you what to do with it. Your position can be given in four ways:

- As a relative bearing *to* a radio station relative to the longitudinal axis of the aircraft (ADF, VOR)
- As a radial *from* a station (VOR)
- As a distance from a station (DME)
- As an actual position (GPS, RNAV, INS)

For the first three, you need a chart with which to compute your position.

 As a point of airmanship, equipment not directly required for navigation should be tuned to ground stations to check accuracy or ground speed, so errors can be detected and the equipment be available in an emergency. Also, **do not rely on a beacon until it has been identified**.

VOR   062 02 03

Very High Frequency Omnidirectional Range is a ground-based short range navigational aid that broadcasts two signals on VHF, using the *phase difference* between them to signify your direction from the transmitting station as one of 360 radials *from* it*. The usable frequency range is between **108-117.975 MHz** (metric), which is just below aviation voice channels.

*An infinite number of tracks is theoretically available, but 360 is easier to manage.

RADIO NAVIGATION
VOR

Low-powered VORs (as used near terminals) and ILS localisers occupy the space between 108-112, with 50 Hz spacing, so there is room for 40 ILS and 40 VOR channels. The VORs usually use even decimals, plus even tenths to prevent confusion with the ILS, which uses odd tenths. For example, an ILS might use 108.1, while a Terminal VOR might use 108.2.

Higher powered VORs, as needed for aircraft at higher altitudes, operate between 112-118 (112-117.975) on odd and even tenths, for another 120 channels. They can be received up to 100 nm away.

In total, there are 40 ILS and 160 VOR channels.

VORs represented on maps have a compass rose round them, aligned with Magnetic North. They are a pain to shut down and realign, which is why a VOR's variation will often be different from its aerodrome.

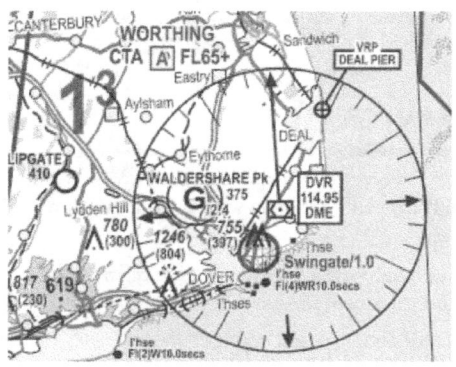

VORs are not sensitive to heading, as is the ADF (below), because they show *track*, although most pilots set the OBS to the heading anyway for neatness so that the left/right needle reads correctly. Neither do they suffer from many of the other problems associated with the ADF, especially night effect.

The *Station Identifier* is transmitted in Morse every 15 seconds (4 times a minute), and you must confirm the frequency and ID before using a VOR for navigation. If there is no ID, but behaviour is otherwise normal, the system is on maintenance (you may sometimes hear a Morse test code of ▬ ••• ▬).

Theory Of Operation

The equipment electronically measures an angle, having transmitted a signal with three components. There is a 30 Hz FM omniphase signal, received by all stations at a constant phase, and a variable phase (variphase) signal whose phase changes according to its bearing from North. The variphase signal is a 30 Hz tone that modulates the amplitude of the carrier, and its sidebands are used to make the phase angle of the modulation equal to the azimuth angle.

To make separation easier (or to detect which signal is which), the reference signal frequency-modulates a sub-carrier (at 9960 Hz), because the carrier is already modulated by the variphase signal. The result is that an apparently AM signal (rotating at 30 Hz or 1800 RPM) is eventually seen by the aircraft in terms of varying *power* (amplitude) levels. After demodulation, the signals have their phases compared to derive a bearing.

There is also a voice/ID channel that can carry 1020 Hz Morse and voice signals.

So, both signals are in phase when the "rotating" signal passes Magnetic North, but they get more out of phase by the number of degrees you go round the circle so, if the phase difference is 30° at your receiver, you are on the 030° radial from the VOR.

Thus, your receiver picks up the reference signal first and the maximum point of the variphase signal a little bit later so, for an aircraft on a 230° magnetic bearing *from* a station, the variable phase will lag the reference phase by 230°. The time difference is indicated in degrees.

However, the information presented in the cockpit is the bearing *to* the station rather than from, in this case 050°.

 As the radial information depends only on the phase difference between the modulating signals, and is independent of the aircraft heading, you may fly the long way round without heading information.

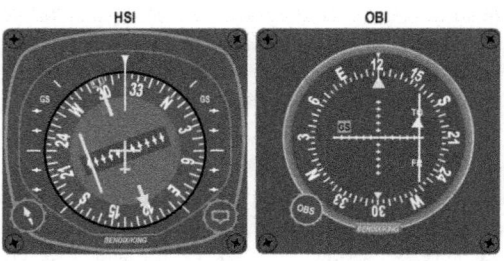

As an example, above is a comparison of the HSI against the OBI - you are heading 320°, and both have a setting of 120° *inbound*. Notice how the HSI presents the information clearly, but the OBI says something quite different - With no heading information, you could be going either way!

Thus, to get the best results, the heading should approximately follow the OBS setting. In any case, you need to set the desired track according to the TO flag.

The situation shown above is typically found during a procedure turn - it's not a normal tracking scenario.

If the reference phase is shifted by the selected course, then compared with the variable phase, you will get a fly-right indication if R + C lags behind V and, if R + C leads V, fly left. R + C + 180 will either cancel part or all of V to get a TO indication, or reinforce it, for a FROM.

All this produces a polar diagram called a *limacon*, which has been inherited from an earlier navigation system, and is similar in shape to the cardioid used by the ADF (later), but without an absolute null point, rotating electrically at 30 times/second. There is no null point because transmission is momentarily interrupted when the maximum point of the limacon passes through North. If it were otherwise, you would get a false North indication.

Because the signal is frequency and amplitude modulated, it is classed as an A9W signal (Doppler VOR, mentioned later, has its modulations the other way round).

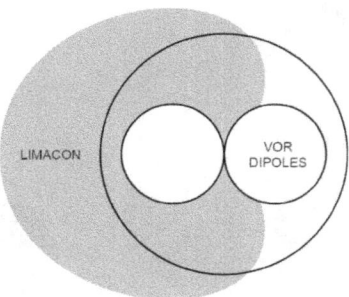

In your aircraft, the signals are received by a horizontally polarised V-dipole antenna, then mixed, converted to an intermediate frequency, amplified, detected and demodulated. Then the audio part of the signal is fed into a low-pass filter which allows the reference signal to enter one part of the circuit and the rotating one to enter another, through a 10 KHz bandpass filter, eventually to become 30 Hz AC.

The rotating signal is also fed into a calibrated phase shifter which is controlled by the OBS on the front of the instrument in the cockpit. It is turned until the two signals are in phase and the Course Deviation Indicator (CDI) is in the centre.

The TO indicator is driven by another phase shifter and phase detector operating in parallel. Because of the nature of VOR transmissions and the way they are used for direction finding, there is a 180° ambiguity, so the CDI is equally sensitive to signals coming from either of two opposite directions (i.e. two radials, 180° apart, from the same VOR). To resolve this an additional circuit indicates TO or FROM with a flag. The reference signal is shifted by another 90° and compared again to the rotating one, to tell whether it is leading or lagging the rotating signal, to make the indicator show the relevant direction.

The TO indicator moves when the difference between the selected course and the measured radial passes 90° in either direction. Over the beacon, you will be in a *cone of confusion,* the same as you would be with any antenna - this is an area where no signal is received, so the TO/FROM flags disappear and the alarm flag comes up. The ICAO limit for the cone is 100° across, and the width can be worked out by finding the tangent of the angle and multiplying it by your height, to get the answer in feet (FL 360 = 6 nm). During this *station passage,* just ignore the signal or use something else.

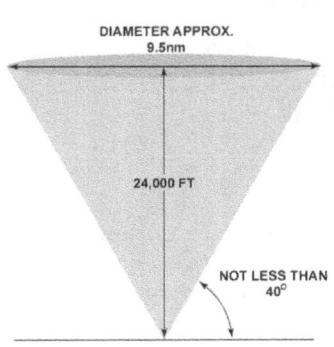

There are also ambiguities *abeam* the beacon - 90° either side of the selected radial there is a *zone of ambiguity* up to 10° across where the flag will not show at all, and the indications should therefore not be relied upon.

In the bowels of the aircraft will be a large black box, connected to a *remote indicator* in the cockpit, that might also double as an ILS display.

This one is a 5-dot display, using 4 dots plus a circle, so each one is 2°, for an overall width of 10°. For 3 dots plus a circle, each is 2.5°.

Once you select a radial by turning the *Omni Bearing Selector* (the knob under the dial), the *Course Deviation Indicator* (CDI) needle will be in the centre, or either side of it.

When the needle is in the middle, you will be on the selected radial, which is *from* the station when on the same side, shown by TO/FROM Flag, which, on later instruments, will be a small white triangle pointing in the relevant direction*. If the indicator shows *TO,* you are on the *reciprocal,* or going the other way. In the example above, the radial selected is S, or 180°, because the *To* flag is showing (as the needle is showing you are three dots left, you are on the 186° radial). Thus, when holding *inbound* on the 240 radial, your heading should be 060°. This is a common trap in exam questions (and check rides) - if you are tracking inbound on a radial, set the reciprocal at the top of the display, as radials go *from* a station.

*The changeover sector is within 10° either side of the abeam position. The TO/FROM indicator is independent of the heading. On the side of the radial you have selected, FROM is displayed. On the other side, you get TO.

All you have to do then is watch the needle - if the needle is pointing left, then you fly left until it centres.

The thing to remember is that the needle always points to *where the radial is,* which has *nothing to do with the heading of the aircraft* (on the RMI, the tail of the needle shows the radial*), and you do not necessarily turn that way to get to it - sometimes, having the needle on the left means turn right! *Only if your heading is the same direction as the OBS will it be on the correct side.*

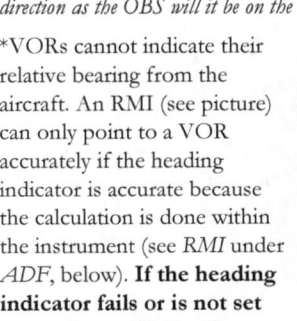

*VORs cannot indicate their relative bearing from the aircraft. An RMI (see picture) can only point to a VOR accurately if the heading indicator is accurate because the calculation is done within the instrument (see *RMI* under *ADF,* below). **If the heading indicator fails or is not set correctly, an RMI will not**

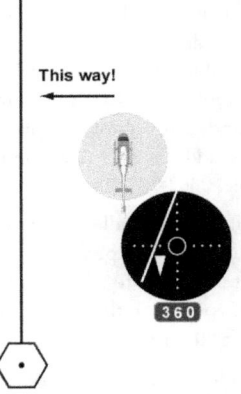

point to the VOR, but will just show you the radial you are on (watch the tail of the needle*). The ADF, on the other hand will always point to the station, so you can still get to it even if the heading indication is not working.

*The pointer indicates the radial plus 180°.

For any radial, there are boundaries formed by the CDI and the TO/FROM indicator, creating quadrants around the station (that is, four distinct areas). You will be in one of them. In the picture below, which displays would the pilot see, and in what order, for a helicopter moving from A to B?

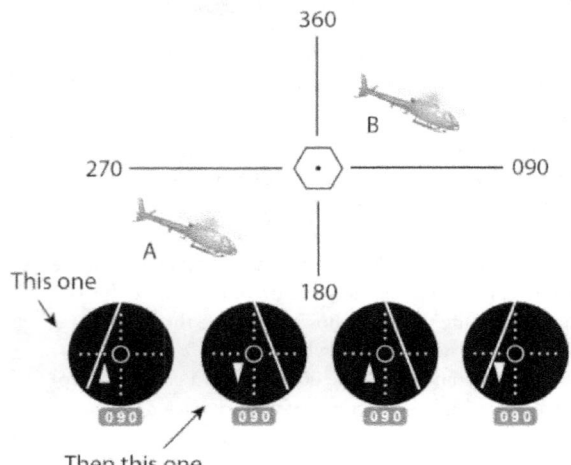

To intercept a radial inbound, tune and identify the VOR station, then select the reciprocal of the desired radial by turning the OBS until you get a TO reading. Fly to whichever side the needle is displaced, turning the shortest way to a heading 90° away from it, until the needle starts to move, at which point reduce the intercept angle to 45° (rather like 2-3 above). As the needle centres, reduce the intercept angle again and maintain the track with suitable adjustments for drift. Do the same outbound, except look for a FROM reading. A good rule (inbound and outbound) is to subtract the intercept angle if the needle goes left, and add if it goes right to find the heading to steer. For example, 280°-90°=190°.

Thus, if a VOR needle is centered when 200 is selected, with TO indicated, to intercept a radial of 100° inbound at 90°, the aircraft must turn to a heading of 190°. As you are going to the station, you are on the 080° radial*, so you must turn left. Subtract 90 for the intercept to get 190°.

*Read the radial from the bottom of the instrument. With a FROM flag you read it from the top.

With a heading of 140° and the needle centered with a TO indication when 120° is selected on the OBS, what heading should be steered to in zero wind conditions to intercept the 240° radial outbound at an angle of 45°?

The TO flag means that the aircraft is on the 300° radial, or NW of the VOR. To intercept the 240° radial it must move South, so to cut the 240° radial by 45°, subtract 45 from 240 to get 195° as a heading.

Here are the needle movements and responses of an aircraft drifting off to the left and coming back on course:

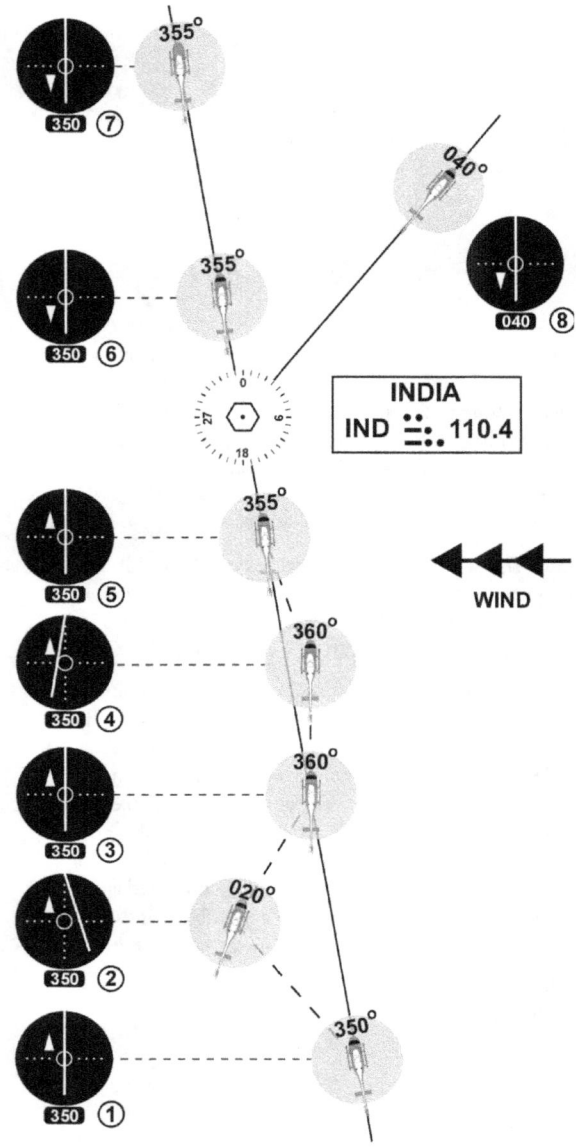

To bracket for drift, turn onto a zero wind heading and see what the drift actually is. Make a large correction the opposite way and see what happens. Then half the original correction. Keep going until the correct heading is found.

When tracking along an airway, tune and identify the station you are going from, track the selected radial until near the mid-point, then tune and identify the next station. The TO/FROM flag should change over.

If you have to use another VOR for a fix as a reporting point along the airway, select the required radial, and when the needle is centred you are over the fix:

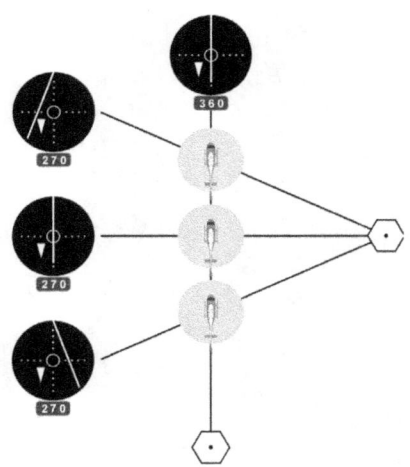

Range
As for standard VHF.

Time to Station
You often need to know the time (and distance) it will take to get to a station (well, you will in the exam, anyway), which is simply found by turning abeam the station and noting the time taken to go through a number of radials. For example, if it takes 13 minutes to fly from A to B, how long will take to get to the VOR?

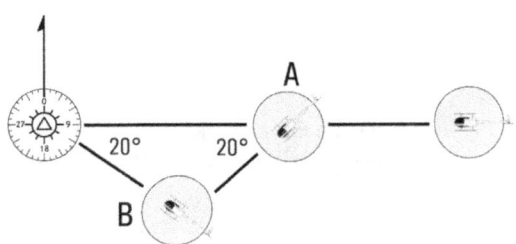

Rotate the OBS 20° to the right, turn left 20° and note the time. Keep the heading constant until the CDI centres. The time to the station is the same as the time just elapsed. There is no need to calculate anything, because we are simply working with an isosceles triangle.

Tip: If you use a station between 10-45° off the nose, the time taken to fly until the angle doubles is the same as the time to the station.

All you need do then is use the groundspeed (or TAS in an emergency) to find your distance. It is a variation of the 1 in 60 rule, as explained in *Navigation*. In short, for every 1° left or right of track, you will be 1 nm off track for every 60 travelled or, conversely, if you are 2 nm left of track having travelled 60 nm, you have drifted by 2°.

The logic behind finding the time to a station by measuring the number of degrees you pass through lies with radians, which are a scientific method of measuring angles.

A radian is an angle that subtends an arc of the same length as the radius of a circle (360° = 2π radians).

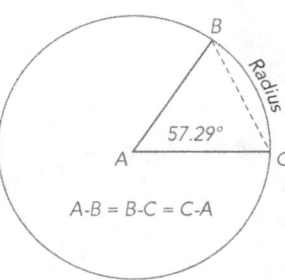

There is an equilateral triangle inside the circle, except that one side of it is an arc, which sweeps through 57.29°, or 60° for government work (the difference is less than 5% anyway). As the arc is the same length as the radius of the circle, the time taken to fly the arc is the same as it takes to fly to the centre.

If you set up any proportion of distance over time on the flight computer, as in the example below, the speed at which you fly round the arc is shown against the 60 marker, and therefore is the time to get to the station.

For example, your relative bearing to a fix is 315°, which 3 minutes later is 270°.

The formula is:

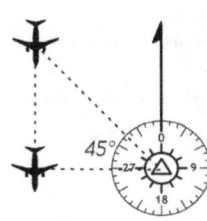

```
Time (mins) =
               Seconds
               Degrees

       4 = 180
           45
```

Or working with minutes:

```
Time (mins) = 3 x 60
              45
```

On the flight computer, just set up a ratio of time over degrees passed through ($^3/_{45}$) and look for the answer (4 minutes) against the 60 marker:

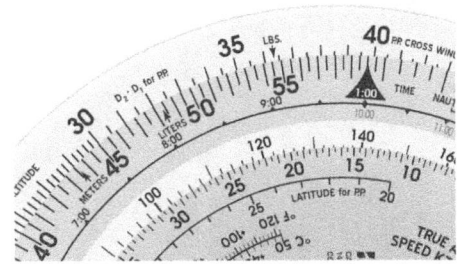

4 minutes is the time it would take to fly the straight line between B and C above, although the accurate answer is 3.8 minutes if you look opposite 57.29.

The front face of the Jeppesen CR-3 can give you the time to fly the arc, which can be handy with approaches:

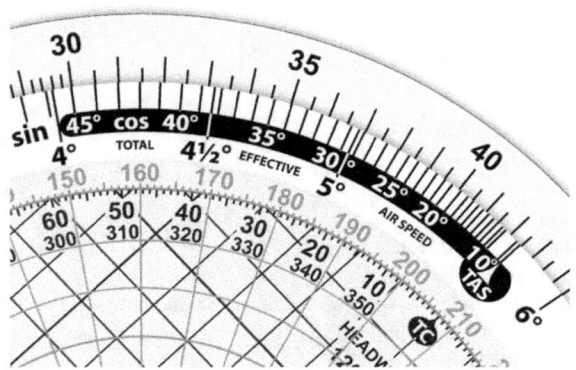

The Lead Radial (where you start turning) of an arc based procedure is 2 nm before intercepting the final approach course. Of course, it is printed on the approach chart, but if you want to work it out yourself, remember that 57.29° of arc is equal to the DME value which, for the sake of argument, we will take as 7 nm. So, set up $7/57.29$ on the flight computer and look opposite 2 on the outer scale to find the amount to add to or subtract from 16.4. The answer would have been 17 had you used $7/60$.

You can use the same logic to find the point at which you might want to slow down and collect your thoughts. If you want to start preparing 5 nm away, just use that instead.

However, it is more logical to want to know the distance to a station, as it is a handy way of finding out whether you are inside an airway as you fly along it, where no crosscuts are available and the DME isn't working (or there isn't one), as you might find in the open spaces of Canada.

You need to know the groundspeed for this one:

$$\text{Distance} = \frac{\text{Mins} \times \text{GS}}{\text{Degrees}}$$

Using the situation above, how far West of the VOR would you be with a ground speed of 180 knots? 12 miles.

Again, on the flight computer, set up the $3/45$ ratio and look for the answer (12 miles) against the grounsdpeed.

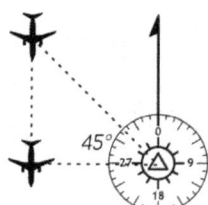

Logic check: 4 minutes at 3 miles per minute is 12 miles.

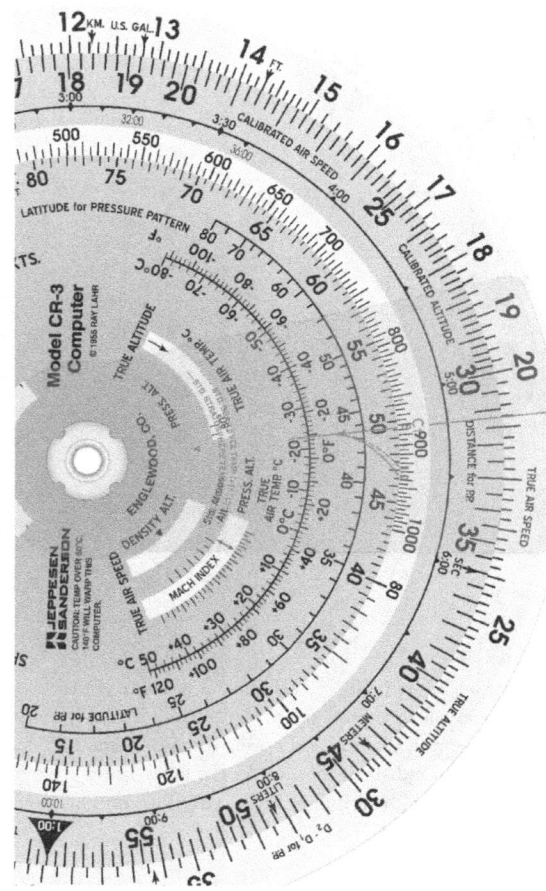

Airways

Question: If you are 100 nm from a VOR, and if 1 dot = 2°, how many dots deviation from the centreline of the instrument represent the limits of the airway boundary?

Airways are normally 5 nm wide either side of the centreline, so, applying a variation of the 1 in 60 rule:

$$\frac{5 \times 60}{100}$$

The answer is 3°, or 1.5 dots deviation.

At 200 nm you would be 3.5 nm off track, with a 1° error.

Question: An airway 10 nm wide is defined by two VORs with a bearing accuracy of ± 5.5°. To ensure accurate track guidance within the airway, what is the maximum distance between the transmitters? **Answer:** About 109 nm.

Tip: You change over halfway so there are two triangles.

The greatest acceptable cross track error is 5 nm off the airway centreline. If you fly out of one beacon and switch over halfway, the greatest error occurs at the halfway point, where the maximum distance off track is 5 nm, and the track error angle is 5.5°, so:

$$\frac{5 \times 60}{5.5}$$

Multiply by 2 to get 109 nm. Use this formula as well:

$$\frac{\text{airway width} \times 60}{\text{accuracy}}$$

Testing

Some airfields have low power test equipment (2 watts) transmitting on 114.8 (usually, but you might get 108.0 from a repair station), identified with the ATIS, so have a pen ready to save you writing it down again later (the ID may just be a series of dots). The VOT is intended for ground use, although it can be used when airborne (there will be certified airborne check points), but you could always get to a position on a known radial and check the readings. As you move the OBS, you can expect the usual indications relating to the bearing selected (which is why two transmitters are used, to save you moving the aircraft to the radials). With the needle centred, the instrument should read 000° FROM or 180° TO at any point in the airport, with an accuracy of ± 4° (± 6° when airborne).

In fact, propagation error (or FM/AM synchronisation, at least) should be within ±1°. The system should shut down automatically if it gets outside that (the monitor will remove the ID once the measured bearing changes by more than 1°). Phase comparison (equipment) error should not be more than ±3°, and station (site) errors should be within ±1° (at 200 nm this is 3 nm). The nominal accuracy is ±5° within the published protection range, based on a 95% probability rate.

Problems

Although the VOR is less subject to static and other interference than an NDB (there is no night effect), and it is more accurate, the transmissions depend on line of sight, and there are suspect areas at 90° to a radial (zones of ambiguity), and overhead (cone of confusion), as mentioned above. In addition, certain rotor or propeller RPM settings can cause fluctuations up to ±6° (change them slightly before saying the instrument is not working!) Transmissions may be adversely affected by uneven propagation over irregular ground surfaces (scalloping), and if bearing information is used beyond published ranges, you may get interference from other transmitters.

If the transmitting station cannot stay within required limits, the identification is suppressed and the navigation components from the carrier wave will cease.

Doppler VOR

Using Doppler allows the frequency of a signal to decrease when the distance between the beacon and aircraft increases, and *vice versa*. It removes site errors and allows you to use a VOR in hilly country (it also needs less of a clear radius around the station). Range is also improved.

The reference signal is AM and the FM variphase signal rotates **anticlockwise**. A wide-aperture antenna averages out the local distortions that would normally be much more noticeable with the more narrowly focussed CVOR antenna (which uses about half a wavelength as opposed to about 5), so a theoretical tenfold reduction in site errors is possible (something to do with space diversity).

The Doppler shift comes from the relative motion of the antenna and the receiver. It is used because the wide aperture system needs Doppler to work properly, in that it creates the direction-dependent **FM signal** which allows you to detect a frequency change (in proportion to the azimuth) as the antenna rotates.

Thus, the Doppler shift makes the transmitter look as if it is advancing and retreating 30 times a second. The aircraft sees a varying frequency rather than varying power. The end result is signals that are the opposite way round to a normal VOR, but the equipment in the aircraft doesn't notice because the signals still have the right phase and they are rotating the other way.

ADF/NDB 062 02 02

An *Automatic Direction Finder* (ADF), also known as a *radio compass*, is a device in an aircraft that picks up vertically polarised signals broadcast on the Medium wave band (LF/MF) by *Non Directional Beacons* (NDBs), so called because they radiate in all directions, using mainly surface waves as modified by indirect waves*. Medium frequencies are used because their range is good, and the aircraft dimensions are not similar to the wavelength. Th term *automatic* means that you do not physically have to turn a loop antenna.

*You can only depend on the range when the ground wave is dominant, as with low powered beacons that cannot manage a space wave. At higher powers, sky waves can reach the E layer of the ionosphere and make the readings inaccurate. If the needle is hunting and the signal gets louder and fades away, the ground wave is being contaminated by sky waves.

Although there are a few problems (see the next column), you can get 1,000 nm range over the sea and 300 nm over land if the power is high enough, but NDBs tend now to be used as *Locators*, or enroute navaids on airways, homing beacons for instrument approaches and markers for the Instrument Landing System (ILS), with a typical power of 15W and a range of about 10-25 nm.

A long range (LF) NDB could put out 200 watts for a range of between 50-60 nm. To help with the range, they could be **N0NA1A** (the most common), which uses less power but will need the BFO to be selected because the information will be keyed Morse. The problem is that, during the breaks when the ID is transmitted, there is no navigation signal, and the needle will wander around.

A N0N A2A transmission remains a carrier wave for most of the time, but the ID is amplitude modulated when required. The BFO is needed only for initial tuning. Plain A2A transmissions that are continuously modulated do not need a BFO.

The approved ICAO frequency range for aeronautical NDBs is between **190-1750 KHz** (hecto- or kilometric), but that part of the radio spectrum includes commercial radio stations, whose use in IFR work is not allowed because of the problems involved with quality control, and there are no guarantees of consistency of service. If there is no ID, but the system otherwise appears to behave normally, it is undergoing calibration or maintenance.

The minimum signal to noise ratio is 3:1. ICAO also requires ±7° accuracy for 95% of the time by day. Bearings in the published protection range should be accurate to within ±5° **by day**.

The tracking accuracy for an NDB approach is within ±5°.

NDBs are dual systems, meaning that they have main and standby transmitters, plus two monitors to ensure continuous service. If the power falls by more than 50%, or a monitor or the ID fails, an automated telephone message creates an alarm. Standby transmitters have an E at the end of their identification so you know it is a standby. The ID is not transmitted when the system is being tested - instead you will hear T or TST (in Morse).

Errors

The most common error is failing to recognise *station passage* - if you are directly over the beacon, it will swing around all over the place and be confused with one of the above, or failure of the instrument, where the needle just rotates to the right. This is the same cone of confusion effect that VOR has (above).

Limitations*

Limitations of the system include:

- **static**, including local thunderstorm activity, which is likely to cause the greatest inaccuracy and make the needle point towards a storm.
- **night effect**, where the needle swings erratically, at its strongest just after sunset and before sunrise. The loop is designed to receive surface waves - any sky waves will be out of phase and distorted, because they energise the horizontal parts of the loop (waves change their polarisation when reflecting off the ionosphere). If the ionosphere is not parallel with the Earth's surface, they will also arrive from different directions. Low power beacons are virtually unaffected by this as they can only produce a ground wave. Check for an unsteady needle and a fading audio signal.
- **station overlap**, when NDBs have the same frequency. This is more pronounced at night, so it can be confused with *night effect* (promulgated ranges are not valid at night for this reason). **This will have the greatest effect on ADF accuracy, particularly at night.**
- **mountain effect**, or variations caused by **reflections** from high ground, where two signals might be received at once from different paths.
- **quadrantal error**, or variations from the aircraft itself, in the same way as it might affect a compass. The signal is reradiated by the airframe and the receiver gets an additional (much weaker) signal to contend with. The greatest error lies at 45° to the fore and aft axis, hence

*This is useful knowledge for an NDB approach to a coastal aerodrome in mountains as the sun is setting!

the term *quadrantal*. Modern systems have corrector boxes for this.

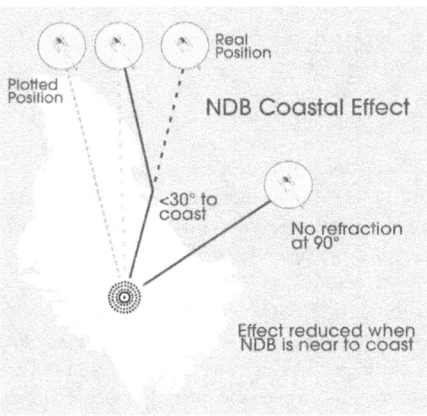

- coastal refraction (diffraction), from radio waves in transit from land to sea, because they travel slightly faster over water, which makes your aircraft appear closer to the shore. This effect is most noticeable at less than 30° to the coastline (i.e. an acute angle), and at lower frequencies, so expect errors if you are using an NDB inland directly in front of or behind you. With two NDBs, one 20 nm, and the other 50 nm inland from the coast, and if the coastal error is the same for both, the error seen by an aircraft will be greater from the beacon that is further away. Your altitude has an effect.
- **Identification**. As there is no flag indication of failure, as there is with the VOR, you should continuously monitor the station ID when relying on the instrument. Aside from that, the only way of knowing about problems is seeing the needle rotate to the right if the signal is not received.

Use

The ADF is normally tuned with the function switch in the ANT position (it stands for *antenna*). This removes the needle from the loop (that is, receiving is done through the sense antenna) and saves wear and tear as it tries to point at every station you tune through - here, the sense antenna is used by itself to obtain the ID. Once there, return the switch to the ADF position.

As always, check - in this case, ensure that the needle points vaguely where you expect it to.

The TEST button spins the needle 90° from its tuned position, and back, to indicate a good signal. The BFO switch also uses the sense aerial by itself to detect the modulated Morse identifier.

While most NDBs use a modulated continuous wave, some use a plain carrier wave, which may be interrupted. The giveaway on a chart is an underlined frequency:

395

This requires the BFO (Beat Frequency Oscillator) to identify the station (it is used for A1A transmissions), but this is automatic on modern aircraft.

N0NA2A transmissions amplitude modulate the carrier for identification.

The fixed card display (*goniometer*) has a compass rose with 0° representing the nose of the aircraft at the top of the instrument, and a needle that points to where the signal is coming *from*, in this case a QDM of 165° (including thunderstorms if they are stronger than what you are tuned into).

Thus, if a station is ahead, the needle will point to 0°, or 180° if it is behind. However, if you made no allowance for wind, and just pointed the nose of the aircraft at the station (*homing*, as opposed to *tracking*), you would actually follow a curved path of pursuit towards it (also known as *bird-dogging*).

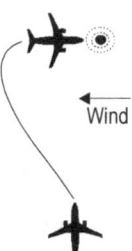

Allowing for drift lets you keep a straight track, which is needed for airways (see *Tracking,*), and which is why homing is unacceptable for IFR work (it takes you away from the centreline of an airway). If you are heading to a beacon with a relative bearing of zero, and the magnetic heading decreases, you have some right drift, and *vice versa*. Unfortunately, working with fixed cards involves maths!

First of all, though, some definitions:

- **Magnetic Heading** - the angle between the aircraft's longitudinal axis and magnetic North
- **Relative Bearing** - the angle between the longitudinal axis and the NDB, which is what you read directly from a fixed card ADF
- **Magnetic Track** or **Bearing** - the angle between the aircraft position and the NDB, To or From

Take note of this formula (you will need it in the exam):

    MH + RB = BTS (MB)

The magnetic heading plus the relative bearing gives you the bearing to the station.

Taking the example below, the formula would read:

    324 + 46 = 010

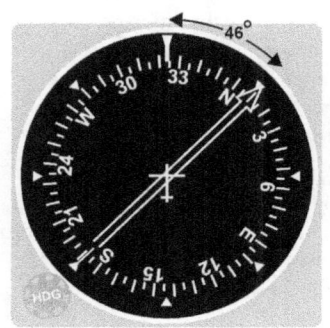

MB = MH + RB

My **B**uddy
Must **H**ave
Red **B**lood

You can get the relative bearing like this:

    BTS - MH = RB

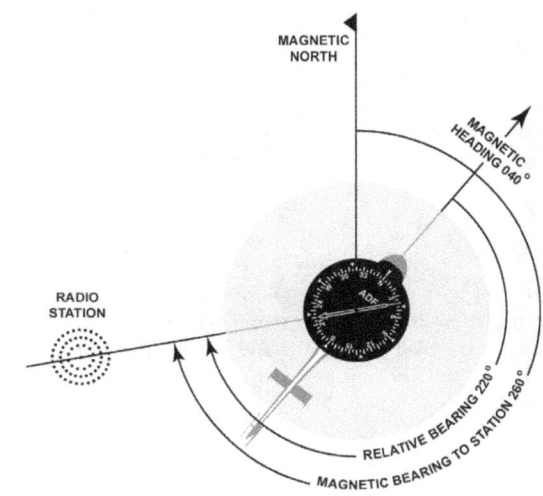

RMI

The *Radio Magnetic Indicator* is a combination of ADF indicator and slaved compass. The top of the instrument represents the aircraft's compass heading (which includes deviation) and the needle points to the QDM (or QDR, if you look at the other end), which saves you doing the calculations above in your head. In other words, it always displays the present heading and bearing, and does some of the work required by a fixed display. There may also be a repeater needle from the VORs giving you the same information relative to the stations they are tuned to.

In the picture, the heading is 139°, and the ADF QDM is 077°. The VOR needle is pointing to a QDM of 210°. The RMI does not need a TO/FROM flag, as there is no 180-degree ambiguity. With the VOR, the tail of the needle on the RMI shows the radial. Change it to True by using the variation at the VOR.

As a point of interest, the VOR needle on an RMI will always read correctly if any deviation occurs, but headings and ADF readings will be in error by the deviation. This is because the ADF needle will naturally point towards the transmitting station, regardless of what the compass rose does. The VOR QDM, on the other hand, is created *within the instrument* by subtracting the aircraft heading from the QDM and applying the difference clockwise round the dial from the lubber line. Deviations are automatically applied because the number cruncher ensures that the VOR needle moves in the same direction for the same amount as the compass rose.

Put another way, the tail of the VOR needle always points to the radial even if the heading indication is wrong. The ADF needle always points to the station, so you will be on the wrong course if the Heading Indicator is not accurate, although you will always be able to find the station.

For either needle, however, if it is off to the left, you fly left, and *vice versa*.

Position Fix

For a fixed card ADF, find the relative bearing to each station and add them to your heading to get the tracks to the stations. Then find the reciprocals and plot them outwards (using variation at the aircraft). Along an airway, to find where you are in relation to an intersection, you will already know the bearing to station (BTS), because it will be on the map.

Time to Station

As with the VOR.

Tip: If, while flying along, you wait until you double the original relative bearing, your distance to the station will be the same as the distance just travelled (that is, A-B and B-C in the picture below will be two sides of an isosceles triangle), which you can work out with your groundspeed.

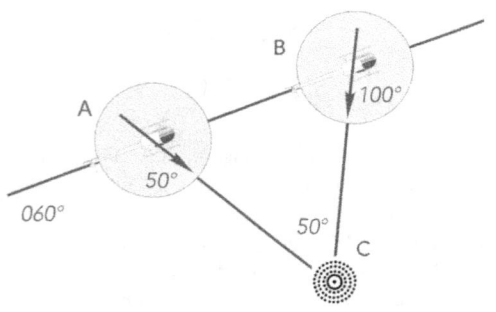

Tracking

When drifting, the needle will always point to the side of the aircraft the wind is coming from, so corrections should always be made that way, ensuring that the needle goes to the *other* side of the lubber line* once a corrected heading is established.

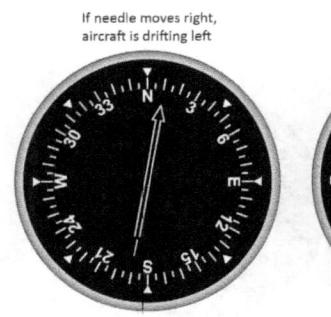 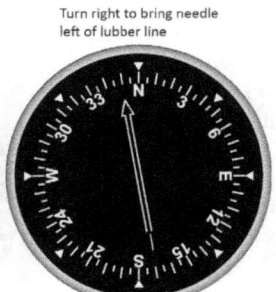

*When tracking inbound.

For example, if the wind is coming from the left, you need the heading to be an equal amount of degrees the other side of the lubber line as the needle is, such as a heading of 350° (*minus* 10 of the lubber line), looking for a 010° relative bearing (*plus* 10 of the lubber line). If you just turned left enough to point the nose to the beacon, you would follow the curve of pursuit described above. Taking the needle across the lubber line means that you 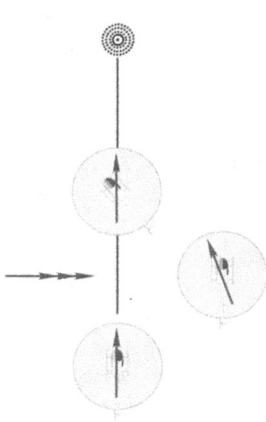 can make an attempt at regaining track as well. In other words, you are adding the drift to the track correction. If you were off track on the windward side, it may be possible to just turn to a heading that is equal to the track and let the wind do the work.

In other words, the relative bearing of the NDB should be equal (in magnitude and sign) to the angle of drift.

How far you are away from the beacon determines how large the intercept angle can be. It should be smaller as you get closer to the beacon. As you probably won't know how far away you are, the trick is to watch the speed of the needle as it moves - it rotates faster when you are close. In fact, it gets very sensitive in the overhead - you should not be correcting by more than 10° in that area, if any.

A good ploy is to allow the drift to happen until you get a positive reading, say 10° port, double it the other way (go 20° starboard), and when you are back on track, reduce it by half (10° in this case) to hold it. This is *bracketing*, and the process may have to be repeated several times in smaller amounts until you get it right. *Do not chase the needle* - hold it steady so you can see the effects of adjustments.

In fact, bracketing can be done simply with as few as two heading changes, and you should rarely need more than six. It is essentially a game between you and whatever needle you are using. Starting with your heading matching your track, at some point you will start to drift off if there is any wind at all. If you were heading 270°, your next heading could be 250° or 290°, according to the direction of the drift. Now you wait for the results, and your next heading change will be 10°. So, had we encountered left drift and turned onto 290°, if the needle moves to the right again, you would now select 300°, or if it moved left, you could select 280°. You should rarely need to go down to 5° changes.

Anticipation is the key! Do not wait until you have passed through your track until turning back on to it. Using 5° as a lead angle is good enough. The closer you are to the beacon the greater that angle will be.

When tracking *outbound*, you need the needle on the same side as the wind, so, although you are still looking for the plus 20, minus 20 equation, the needle would be pointing at 160° RB (when you make your initial turn, the needle looks like it's going the wrong way, but you get used to it).

If needle moves right, aircraft is drifting left

Turn right to bring tail further left of lubber line

In short, if the pointy end moves to the right of a line between 0° and 180°, fly right, as drift is to the left, and *vice versa*. This is true going to or from an NDB.

If you split the display into two halves, on a line between 0° and 180°, and call the right half plus, and the left minus (if going to a station), you can use the needle's position to find the track to a station. For example, if the needle is in the right half (the + segment), add the heading to the relative bearing to get the track. If it is in the left, take it away (work the needle back from zero). Whilst turning right, the aircraft heading will increase while the relative bearing decreases, and *vice versa*. If you remain on the same bearing, the heading change will always equal the change of ADF indication. When outbound, reverse the signs.

EXAMPLES

1. An NDB bears 279° relative from an aircraft whose heading is 209°. If deviation is -7° and variation is 18°E, what is the bearing (M) of the aircraft from the NDB?

```
C = 209°C  D = -7°  M = 202°M
```

HDG(M) + RB = QDM:

```
202°M + 279° = 481° (-360°) = 121°M
```

QDR from NDB to aircraft = 121°M + 180° = 301°M. For a True Bearing:

```
C = 209°C
D = -7°
M = 202°M
```

```
V = 18°E
T = 220°T
```

HDG(T) + RB = QUJ

```
220°T + 279° = 499° (-360°) = 139°T
```

The QTE from NDB to aircraft = 139°T + 180° = 319°T

2. If the magnetic heading is 120°, and variation is 17°W, and there is an island 15° to the left, what is your True bearing from the island? The heading is:

```
120 - 17 = 103
```

And the relative bearing of the island is 345°:

```
103 + 345 = 448 - 360 = 088
088 + 180 = 188
```

AIRWAYS

The information from navaids becomes less reliable the further away you get from them, so corridors are defined, within which the signals can be counted on.

For VORs, the corridor width starts 5 nm either side, diverging at 4° for 70 nm, until 20 nm wide. The width remains constant between 70-140 nm, where it diverges again at 4° until a width of 40 nm is reached at 280 nm out, at which point it remains constant.

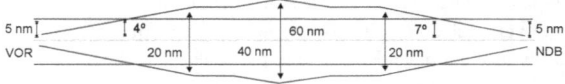

For NDBs, the corridor starts 5 nm either side, diverging at 7° until a width of 20 nm at 40 nm out, remaining constant between 40-80 nm out, thereafter diverging at 7° until 60 nm wide at 245 nm, then remaining constant.

TACAN

This is a pulse-based military navigation system operating in the UHF band (*Tactical Air Navigation*), which can be used by the DME in your aircraft (*not* the VOR - military aircraft have a display which is not compatible). When a TACAN is co-located with a VOR, the VORTAC will show DME readouts automatically when you tune the VOR, as the frequencies are paired. Of course, a military machine can pick up the complete TACAN signal, which provides range, radial speed and bearing information.

The maximum distance between VOR and DME/TACAN ground installations if they share the same Morse ID is 600 metres.

FANS

Future Air Navigation Systems relate to developing the necessary equipment and procedures to manage air traffic in a more efficient manner, using new technology, although much of it has already arrived.

Improvements relate to:

- **Communication**, and the use of data links rather than voice communications to transmit complex ATC clearances, plus 8.33 kHz spacing for radios. This can be done automatically by the FMS, using HF, VHF, Mode S transponders, ADS-A & B and satellite links.
- **Navigation**, and the use of GPS with other aids to improve accuracy and make better use of airspace. This would include Performance Based Navigation, using RNP and ANP, plus RVSM, WAAS, the ILS and MLS, all discussed below.
- **Surveillance**, and the use of datalinks to signal the position of aircraft and the intentions of their crews to the ground and other users.

All are commonly referred to as CNS.

RNAV   062 05

Airways normally use ground-based navigation aids, but these days you don't necessarily need them to maintain an accurate track.

Area Navigation is a generic name for systems that allow navigation over wide areas - it was originally coined for a way of electronically moving navaids, VORs in particular, to other places enroute (they became *phantom waypoints*), which implies that you must be within range of the navaids concerned in order to use them. If the system does not receive radial or distance information, it goes into *Dead Reckoning* mode.

For example, you could tell the black box the distance and bearing of your house from the nearest VOR and it would present all the signals as if the aid was at your house.

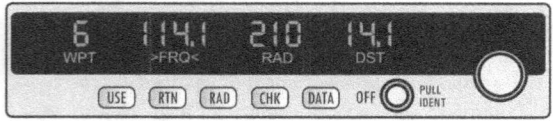

In the above case, waypoint 6 in the device's memory has been programmed with the frequency 114.1, and the VOR concerned has been offset by 14.1 nm on the 210 radial. When in range of the VOR, the readings would base themselves around the new location, and you can fly directly to it.

On a direct route with no specific navaids to aim for, you could shift all nearby ones to fit on your direct track for a series of phantom waypoints, typically displaying cross-track and along-track distance with reference to the phantoms, and not the navaids on which they are based. The concept is illustrated in the picture below, where the direct route is 24 nm less than using the airways.

You could also fly parallel to a track at a chosen offset distance*, or fly approaches involving turns that do not depend on the location of navigation aids.

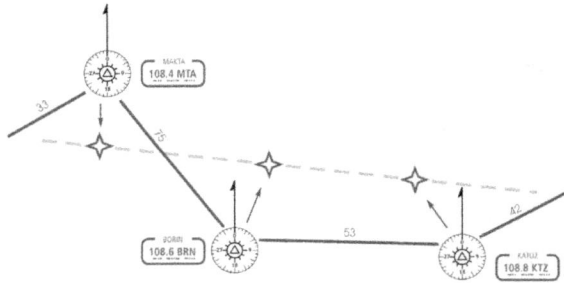

*If a fast aircraft is following a slow one on the same track, an instruction to *fly offset by X nautical miles* can allow it to overtake and climb/descend through the level of the slower aircraft, an alternative to radar vectoring.

Strategic Lateral Offset Procedures (SLOPs) provide for emergencies that require immediate descent, including avoiding wake turbulence.

Thus, RNAV describes ways of flying directly across country without doglegging all over the place, or having to pass over radio fixes, which saves fuel and makes better use of airspace, as you don't pack more aircraft into a relatively small portion of the airspace, i.e airways. You can also eliminate procedure turns because you don't care where the ground-based aids are (indeed, straight-in approaches can often be the norm, with arrival at the threshold in a specific time window). Lower minima and increased capacity are also available.

The FMS can also provide ideal vertical flight paths for climb and descent to arrive over positions at particular altitudes. The FMS, using the autopilot, can fly the whole route in three dimensions, and even airspeed adjustments can be made to achieve arrivals at required times.

As far as pilots are concerned, RNAV means a reduction in workload and increased safety, as the navigation is undertaken by accurate and sophisticated equipment, and the reliance on navigation aids that lose their effectiveness over distance (splay areas) is lessened. ATC can also use straighter routings and use them instead of radar vectoring, which reduces their workload as well - parallel route systems are a characteristic of airspace in which RNAV or RNP systems are being used.

ICAO Annex 11 defines Area Navigation (RNAV) as "a method of navigation which permits aircraft operation on any desired flight path within the coverage of station-referenced navigation aids or within the limits of the capability of self-contained aids, or a combination." An RNAV waypoint could be a geographical position derived from a VOR radial and DME distance but, in the USA at least, RNAV is no longer VOR-based. Otherwise, RNAV can use VOR/DME and/or GPS to update an FMS position that was originally based on Inertial Reference Systems. It does not use ADF!

In RNAV mode, the horizontal dots on the instrument face represent not an angular displacement from a radial, but a distance to the side of a track. Each dot represents one nautical mile, so a full scale deviation on a 5-dot CDI in enroute mode means a deviation from the desired track of 5 nm. On a 2-dot display, the deviation per dot is 5 nm. In approach mode, it becomes 1.25 nm for a 5-dot display (1 dot represents 0.25 nm in approach mode on a 5-dot display) and 0.5° per dot for a 2-dot display.

Standards

There are nearly as many RNAV standards as there are varieties of airspace. For example, Basic and Precision RNAV are used in ECAC (Europe), MNPS* over the North Atlantic and RNAV 1 and 5 internationally (RNAV 1 = P-RNAV). RNP 4 (and RNAV 10) are used over oceanic and remote continental airspace - although both rely on GNSS, RNAV 10 does not need ATS surveillance. In the US, RNAV 2 is the basis of navigation in enroute continental airspace.

*MNPS tends to be excluded from these definitions due to its mandatory nature, and the fact that no changes are expected anyway. It is otherwise called RNAV 10.

 Under RNAV 10, aircraft operating in oceanic and remote areas must have at least two independent and serviceable LRNSs comprising an INS, an IRS FMS or a GNSS. Aircraft with dual INS/IRU installations have a standard time limitation. Operators may extend their RNAV10 navigation capability time by updating.

The above terms are used interchangeably here, especially as the ECAC specifications will migrate to RNAV 1 & 5. Note that P-RNAV does not have the same functionality as RNP 1, even though it shares the same accuracy.

Otherwise:

- RNAV 5 is used in the enroute and arrival phases.
- RNP 2 (RNP requires monitoring - see below) is used in enroute, and oceanic/remote phases.
- RNAV 1 and RNP 1 are used in the arrival and departure phases.
- RNP APCH and RNP AR APCH are used in the approach phase.
- RNAV 2 and RNP 2 are also used as navigation specifications.

There are no RNAV approach specifications.

In Europe, **B-RNAV** is the basic system, with an accuracy of ± 5 nm for at least 95% of the time, as for RNP 5 (see below). B-RNAV is needed for flights in Europe above FL 95, using VOR/VOR or VOR/DME fixing. The course line computer's job is to transform the information from a VOR/DME station into tracking and distance information to any phantom waypoint.

Precision Area Navigation (**P-RNAV**), used for SIDs and STARs, has the same accuracy as RNP 1, meaning ±1 nm on 95% of occasions*, and will be controlled by the FMS (the FMC will automatically select and tune stations based on their relative accuracy). You need P-RNAV to use DME/DME fixing, which gives you the best accuracy.

*P-RNAV requires a track-keeping accuracy of 0.5 nm standard deviation or better, referenced to WGS 84.

The aircraft will fly as accurately as it can, which is mostly down to around 0.02 nm (Actual Navigation Performance). The difference between systems is how happy the aircraft is to be off track, or how much its ANP can degrade before you get warnings. Thus, if the GPS fails and the ANP gradually rises to 2.0, the aircraft will still navigate in RNAV 5 airspace, but not RNAV 1.

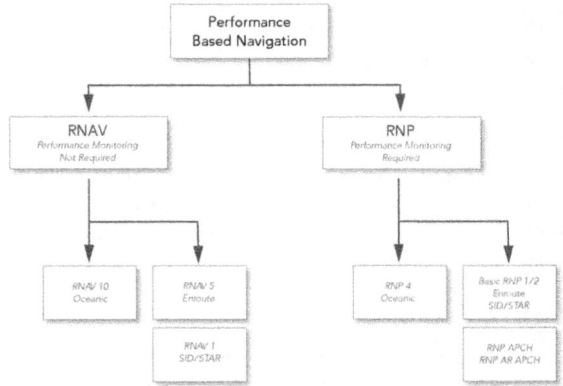

2D systems provide information in the horizontal plane only. 3D RNAV adds guidance in the vertical plane, and 4D has a timing function.

System Capabilities

RNAV equipment should at least be able to:

- Display the present position as latitude/longitude or a distance and bearing to a selected waypoint.
- Allow you to select or enter the required flight plan through the CDU.
- Allow review and modification of navigation data for any part of a flight plan at any stage of a flight and store enough to carry out the active flight plan.
- Review, assemble, modify or verify a flight plan in flight, without affecting the guidance output.
- Execute a modified flight plan only after positive action by the flight crew.
- Where provided, assemble and verify an alternative flight plan without affecting the active one.
- Assemble a flight plan, either by identifier or selection/creation of individual waypoints from the database, or defined by latitude/longitude, bearing/distance parameters or other parameters.
- Assemble flight plans by joining routes or route segments.
- Allow verification or adjustment of the displayed position.

- Provide automatic sequencing through waypoints with turn anticipation. Manual sequencing should also allow flight over, and return to, waypoints.
- Display cross-track error on the CDU.
- Provide time to waypoints on the CDU.
- Execute a direct clearance to any waypoint.
- Fly parallel tracks at a selected offset distance (offset mode should be clearly indicated).
- Purge previous radio updates.
- Carry out RNAV holding procedures.
- Make available estimates of positional uncertainty, either as a quality factor or by reference to sensor differences from the computed position.
- Conform to WGS-84.
- Indicate navigation equipment failure.

The airworthiness approval process assures that each item installed is of a type and design appropriate to its intended function and that the installation functions properly under foreseeable operating conditions.

NAVIGATION PERFORMANCE

Navigation performance is one factor used when determining minimum route spacing, but certain standards must be met before a system can be a sole navigation system for IFR:

- **Accuracy** in terms of *position error*, or the difference between estimated and actual positions.
- **Integrity** - the measure of trust that can be placed in the information supplied by the system.
- **Continuity** (Reliability) - the system's capability (as a probability) to perform. That is, there must be a high probability that the service will be available over a full approach procedure.
- **Availability** - the time during which the system can deliver for a specific phase of flight. Sole means navigation systems require 99% availability.
- **Coverage**.

Safety is contingent upon the accuracy, resolution and integrity of the data, which in turn depends upon the processes applied during its origination.

The Actual Navigation Performance of a system is represented by a circle defining its accuracy for 95% of the time, derived from the output all the navigation sensors and weighing them statistically. It is then compared with the Required Navigation Performance.

RNP is a measure of the standards needed to operate within certain airspace, or within which the ANP needs to be constrained. This commonly means the lateral accuracy in nautical miles that must be maintained for 95% of the time, relative to a desired flight path (technically, a Total System Error* of X nm or less for over 95% of total flight time). In practice, a system's capability is determined by the most limiting of the characteristics described above.

*TSE is the vector sum of:

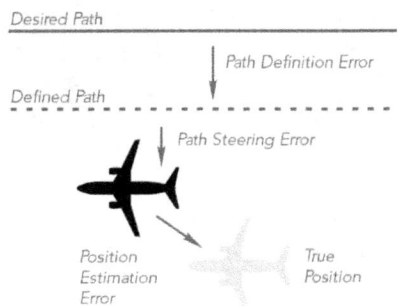

- **Path Definition Error**, or the difference between the intended path and the actual path. On board performance monitoring and alerting is managed by gross reasonableness checks of navigation data.
- **Path Steering Error**, from steering the course, either manually or by autopilot, not including human error (this is the biggest factor). In simple terms, the ability to follow the defined path. Also known as *Flight Technical Error*. On board performance monitoring and alerting is managed by on board systems or crew procedures.
- **Position Estimation Error**, the combination of system or sensor errors and computation error. Also known as *Navigation System Error*. On board performance monitoring and alerting is a requirement of on-board equipment for RNP.

Otherwise, the system accuracy takes after the specification - for example, RNP 4 means within 4 nm along or across track. This would typically be used en route, whereas you would need RNP 1 or 2 around terminals, which are busy. The lowest value is 0.10.

RNAV and RNP systems are essentially the same, but RNP requires on-board performance monitoring and alerting, so it can warn you if you are likely to stray outside airspace boundaries, which are equal to twice the RNP value - for example, RNP 4 has corridors 8 nm wide.

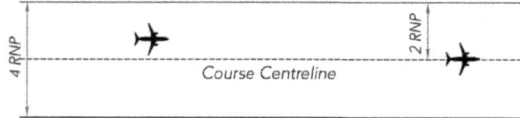

As monitoring is already incorporated within satellite systems, the distinction is essentially the requirement for GNSS, which can support very low RNP values, if you consider position accuracy alone*. So, with some exceptions (where you cannot monitor cross-track), RNP operations are satellite based.

*Accuracy also depends on Path Steering Errors, otherwise known as *Flight Technical Error*, or FTE, which is actually the most dominant factor. This term tends to be irrelevant for the PBN operations described below, as cross track errors are commonly managed by the system rather than by pilots moving the controls.

Thus, although many RNAV systems are very accurate, if they cannot provide assurance of their performance, they cannot be used in RNP airspace. Having said that, RNP 10 is inconsistent because it does not require monitoring, so it is often referred to as RNAV 10 as it is too much of a pain to change all the charts - it is not an RNP operation, but the term is already used in current documentation.

 Aircraft approved for higher standards are not necessarily approved in airspace with lesser standards. This is because lateral navigation accuracy is not the only criterion for approval. For example, to meet the RNAV 1 specification, you can usually use any of GNSS, DME/DME/IRU or simply DME/DME. However, one state may specify GNSS and another may disallow it.

At least two LRNSs, capable of navigating to RNP 4, and in the flight manual, must be operational at the entry point of the RNP airspace as well as ADS/CPDLC capability.

RNP is a measure of the probability that the aircraft (or at least the FMC) will think it is somewhere that it isn't. As a result, the term *performance* refers to the abilities of the complete navigational system, including satellite data accuracy, transmission accuracy, and the receiving component's ability to interpret the data properly.

Any breakdowns will create an alert that the ANP is not acceptable for whatever RNP you are trying to use so, if a satellite is missing, your flight plan may contain a warning of an ANP limitation around your ETA.

That is, with a satellite off line, if the ANP is within the RNP, the chances that the system is confused are within acceptable limits, although you could be half a mile off track during the approach and you will not get an ANP alert. The concept depends on average risk, where most pilot training is based on specific risks.

Advanced RNP (the successor to P-RNAV) incorporates RNAV 5, RNAV 2, RNAV 1, RNP 2, RNP 1 and RNP APCH, although it may be associated with other functional elements.

It can apply to all flight phases, and has a lower navigation specification than RNP AR, to which it is similar, but there are less stringent requirements for crew training, operational procedures and onboard equipment.

PERFORMANCE BASED NAVIGATION   062 07

Specific approval to use conventional navigation equipment such as VOR/DME on airways is generally not required, but you may sometimes need to use older equipment (even specific models, which may or may not be available), even though newer and better systems are around, which means unnecessary expense.

To help with this situation, the emphasis is now on performance capability, in that, as long as the equipment you propose to use meets the requirement of the airspace, it doesn't matter who made it, or where you got it, provided it passes the usual safety checks. In other words, PBN is **not sensor specific**, although it does require on-board performance monitoring and alerting so, instead of depending on the accuracy of the raw data from specific navigation aids, PBN systems integrate that data into a computed solution. Under PBN, navigation requirements are based on operational requirements*, and operators can select the most cost-effective option. Technology can then evolve as fast as it likes without slowing the system down.

*Communication, surveillance and ATM environments, the availability of navigation aids, and redundancy.

Two fundamental aspects of PBN are the requirements in the relevant navigation specification and the navigation aids available (the infrastructure). A navigation specification sets out the requirements to be met by aircraft and aircrew to support a navigation application* by defining the performance required from the RNAV systems as well as any specifics, such as the ability to fly curved paths or parallel offset routes.

*The application of a navigation specification and the supporting infrastructure, to routes, procedures, and/or defined airspace volume, in accordance with the intended airspace concept.

 When you meet the airspace requirements, you must include /R in Item 10 of the ICAO flight plan form. If you are not so equipped, ATC need to know so, in Box 18, insert STS/NONRNAV. Also mention it on your initial contact with them.

For RNP legacy reasons, in oceanic/remote, en-route and terminal phases, PBN is limited to operations with linear lateral performance requirements and time constraints. In the approach phase, PBN accommodates linear and angular* laterally guided operations.

*Approach and landing operations with vertical guidance for APV-I and APV-II GNSS performance levels, as well as ILS/MLS/GLS precision approach and landing.

In other words, PBN is a range of operations based on two types of navigation specification, RNAV and RNP. As such, it allows aircraft separation to be built in to the airspace design, on which hinges the *airspace concept*, or what you plan to do with it.

For example, Europe's current airspace concept, which extends well beyond PBN, has these characteristics:

- A parallel network of ATS routes, based on B-RNAV, across the continent.
- A system of feeder or link routes based mainly on B-RNAV which connect to P-RNAV or Conventional SIDs and STARs, starting at the nominal TMA boundary.
- An organised track system (OTS) in the North Atlantic based on MNPS, which is due to change to RNP 2 or RNAV 10.
- The use of RVSM between FLs 290 and 410.
- Class C airspace above FL195.
- Extensive use of the *Flexible Use of Airspace* concept.
- Some use of Free Routes.
- Evolution from State managed upper airspace to Functional Airspace Blocks (FABs).

Europe's Airspace Concept will eventually use Advanced RNP (discussed below) in en-route and terminal operations, and RNP APCH* on the Approach.

*The RNP APCH is known as an RNAV Approach even though the specification requires on-board performance monitoring and alerting. There are four versions:

- RNP APCH LNAV (LNAV only, relying on GPS).
- RNP APCH LNAV/VNAV (with VNAV added, relying on GPS and Baro VNAV). This is also referred to as an APV Baro.

- RNP APCH LP (Localiser Performance only, relying on GPS and EGNOS (see *Satellites*).
- RNP APCH LPV (with VNAV added, relying on GPS and EGNOS). Also called an APV SBAS.

In en-route operations, the European starting point was the European-wide 1998 mandate for B-RNAV, which is now known as RNAV 5. For terminal area operations, this was followed through with the 2001 introduction of P-RNAV, which is closest to RNAV 1*, and the subsequent introduction of RNP APCH - RNP APCH to LNAV and LNAV/VNAV minima from 2009 and RNP APCH to LPV minima since 2011.

*In Europe, the main difference between P-RNAV and RNAV 1 is that P-RNAV permits the use of VOR/DME in limited circumstances.

You cannot fly an approach if it is not correct as published on the charts (i.e. with a waypoint missing on the chart). You should request another type of approach.

Reading the official PBN manual (ICAO Doc 9613) is cruel and unusual punishment but, in summary:

- PBN needs an on-board RNAV or RNP system.
- You need airworthiness certification and operational approval to use RNAV in the airspace concerned.
- The RNAV system must not only be accurate within a certain range, but must also perform other tasks, such as BaroVNAV, RF, FRT, etc.

In short, aircraft and crew must be qualified for the airspace.

Conditions Of Use

Abnormal and contingency procedures must be used if PBN capability is lost.

 Unless otherwise specified in ops documentation or an AMC, the navigational database must be valid for the current AIRAC cycle.

SIDs or STARs based on RNAV1, RNAV2, RNP1 or RNP2 may not be flown unless they are retrievable by route name from the onboard navigation database, and conform to the charted route, which may subsequently be modified through the insertion (from the database) or deletion of specific waypoints in response to ATC clearances. The manual entry, or creation of new waypoints by manual entry, of latitude and longitude or place/bearing/distance values is not permitted, although manual data entry is acceptable for RNAV 5.

Advanced RNP

Advanced RNP (the successor to B & P-RNAV) is an ECAC-wide navigation specification used in enroute and terminal airspace, including the approach, missed approach and departure phases, which have gaps in them. For example, P-RNAV stopped at the FAF and started again at the MAP. Although RNP APCH covered the missing Final Approach, it only started just before the IAF and finished halfway up the missed approach.

A-RNP therefore can apply to all flight phases. It incorporates RNAV 5, RNAV 2, RNAV 1, RNP 2, RNP 1 and RNP APCH, although it may be associated with other functional elements.

One of the main requirements is the need for track repeatability and predictability in turns, which is why Radius to Fix (RF) functionality is required, with Fixed Radius Transition (FRT).

RF is a path terminator used for SIDs, STARs and Approach. FRT is a leg transition used when the FMS is in en-route mode. In PBN, both functionalities are associated only with RNP specifications.

Approaches

Most RNAV approaches default to 0.3, down to which you can hand fly - autopilots are needed below that.

An RNP APCH must not be flown unless it is retrievable by procedure name from the on-board navigation database and conforms to the charted procedure.

An RNP APCH to **LNAV minima** is a **non-precision** instrument approach designed for 2D operations. An RNP APCH to **LNAV/VNAV minima** is a 3D operation with lateral guidance based on GNSS and (certified) vertical guidance based on SBAS or BaroVNAV. The latter may only be conducted when the aerodrome temperature is within a promulgated range.

 The correct altimeter setting is critical for the safe conduct of an RNP APCH using BaroVNAV, as well as for LNAV and any other 2D operation.

An RNP APCH to **LPV minima** is a 3D operation that requires a FAS datablock.

An RNP AR APCH requires authorisation (the *AR* stands for *Authorisation Required*).

RNP AR approaches are designed with BaroVNAV capability in mind*. They are characterised by:

- RNP values of 0.3 nm.
- Curved flight paths before and after the FAF or Final Approach Point.
- Protection areas laterally limited to a value of 2 x RNP without additional buffers.

RNP AR operations may include missed approach procedures and instrument departures with reduced RNP (<1 nm).

*BaroVNAV is a function of the FMS that computes vertical guidance referenced to a specified vertical path, based on barometric altitude. This means that the Altimetry System Error (ASE) is also a component of the vertical Total System Error (TSEz). Aircraft operating in airspace where vertical performance is specified must have a TSE in the vertical direction (TSEz) that is less than the specified performance limit for 99.7% of the flying time. For example, the specified performance at or below 5000 ft in ED-75/DO-236 is 160 ft.

There is no integrity and continuity requirement for vertical navigation.

Flight Paths & Terminators

In its simplest form, the system will compute the track between two waypoints, but life is not that simple! More complex flight paths are needed, both lateral and vertical.

Combinations of path types and terminators (e.g. track and beacon, respectively) are used to describe around 23 path/terminators. They are described in ARINC 424 code, with the terminator (or end statement) providing the RNAV system with the information it needs to connect the current segment with the next.

In other words, the system uses a library of leg types to create your flight path. One of the most common is a series of **TF** legs (Track to/from Fix), or straight lines*, during which the system normally interprets the coding to fly by a waypoint with a curved flight path.

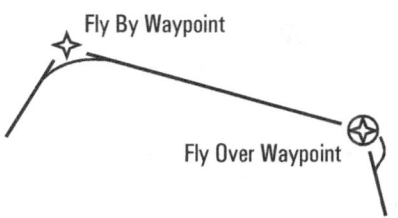

*Although they are regarded as straight lines, TF legs are great circle tracks over the ground between known fixes.

An **RF** leg (Radius to Fix) allows you to fly a circle with a specified radius **relative to the Earth's surface*** rather than the undefined curve shown above. RF segments provide a large amount of flexibility, especially when it comes to avoiding mountains or reducing noise footprints.

*The radius of the turn is now limited by the *groundspeed* and angle of bank, as opposed to the TAS. Thus, there will be a maximum tailwind limit. If the IAS is not managed properly, the limiting bank angle may be reached at less than that limit, so it is important to respect the guidance from the flight director. This is an RNP function.

The fix in path/terminator legs can be based on radio aids or be an RNAV waypoint.

A **CA** (Course to Altitude) leg allows you to follow a course until you get to a specified altitude, commonly used (if supported by the equipment) to specify the initial leg of a departure. It may then, for example, change to a DF (Direct to Fix) leg. The termination of a CA leg will be automatic if you have an integrated VNAV system, otherwise it must be terminated manually.

- **First Letter** (path): V = heading, C = course/track, F = course from a fix, H = hold, D = direct, P = procedure turn, T = track, I = initial, A = arc, R = radius.
- **Second Letter** (terminator): A = altitude, D = DME distance, I = intercept (next leg), R = radial, F = to fix/at fix, M = manual termination, C = distance from fix.

Terminators that may be used for PBN include:

- **VA** = Heading to an altitude (often used off parallel runways).
- **VI** = Heading to intercept next leg (used with Localisers).
- **VM** = Heading to a manual termination (e.g. end of STAR for radar vectors).
- **CA** = Course to an altitude (more accurate ground path than VA).
- **CF** = Course to a fix (the original path/terminator).
- **TF** = Track between fixes (most accurate leg type).
- **IF** = Initial fix (begins a series of path-terminators, used for some SIDs, and for all STARs/APCHs).
- **DF** = Track from present position direct to a fix.
- **RF** = Constant radius to a fix.
- **HM** = Hold to a manual termination.
- **HA** = Hold to an altitude (climb in the hold).
- **HF** = Hold to a fix (1 circuit in hold then continue).

OVERFLY FUNCTION

This function in the FMS makes the aircraft fly over a waypoint. Although they tend to be avoided because they are less controllable, *flyover waypoints* are those whose lat & long position* must be flown over before you can turn onto the next leg, typically used on standard departures to ensure that you don't make excessive bank angles that will interfere with performance calculations. You can fly *direct-to* any waypoint, or *direct/intercept*, where you can select a desired course to reach it. Waypoints can also have speed, altitude and time constraints (*not before*, etc.)

*Waypoints can be entered into all INSs as lat & long.

The start of the turn is based on the current groundspeed and a programmed bank angle, which will normally allow enough radius to provide a smooth interception. As such anticipation does not provide track guidance during the turn, the crosstrack error cannot be monitored, and crew intervention may sometimes be required.

The RNAV computer needs the heading and TAS input so it can work out the wind velocity.

Short Range Systems (2D RNAV)

Traditional instruments display only one position line, such as an arc from the DME, or bearing from a VOR, and you have to combine several to get any meaningful information. They can now be combined on one instrument for ease of interpretation, and interfaced with other equipment. Short range systems are typically based on line-of-sight navigation aids, such as VOR or DME. For best results, the area you fly over must necessarily have a reasonable density of them (the FMC will have a database, including their frequencies, and it will tune those required for you). In normal NAV mode, with at least four stations (and position lines), the accuracy will typically be around 2 nm.

VOR/DME (RHO-THETA)

Here, you can get a fix from only one position line, so with the proper computer (such as the original KNS-80), this is the simplest form of RNAV. One of the functions of the Course-Line Computer is to transfer the information from a VOR/DME station into track and distance indications to any chosen phantom waypoint.

As mentioned above, the VOR/DME station can be offset electronically to any desired position within its range of promulgation. A VOR does not have to be in range when its details are entered into the system, but must be when used, otherwise erratic indications may be experienced when flying towards a Phantom Station at low altitudes close to the limits of reception. In fact, the system will go into DR (*Dead Reckoning*) mode when receiving only one VOR, or if there is no bearing and distance information, using whatever TAS is coming from the ADC, the heading from the compass and the last computed wind velocity (to calculate the wind, the system needs radials and distances from various VOR/DMEs, heading and TAS).

Filters limit the rate of change of VOR bearings, where they arise from multi-path reflections (site error). Close to the beacon, DME range sets the maximum rate, as the bearings change fast anyway, and errors might occur. On approach, 1 dot's deviation is equal to ¼ nm, and 1 nm en route - 5 dots span half the airway.

Trivia: The Greek letter R (*Rho*) stands for range, and *Theta* is an angle, so a Rho-Theta fix involves a range and an angle, as you would get from VOR/DME.

DME/DME (RHO-RHO)

Also called *direct ranging*, DME receivers are used with a microprocessor to measure the distance from two DME receivers for a position fix. Some systems have their own tuners and can automatically set up DMEs, etc. according to signal strength for best position lines (the most accurate RNAV fixes come from DME/DME).

Long Range Systems

Long range systems do not rely on short-range navigation aids. These would include GPS, Loran, Decca, etc.

INERTIAL NAVIGATION SYSTEMS

These are long-range area navigation systems that have already been described under *Instruments*.

Global Navigation Satellite System

The original satellite systems were based partly on hyperbolic navigation aids such as Decca Navigator or LORAN, and Doppler. By measuring the distortions from Sputnik in 1957, it was realised that a satellite's position could be established with some accuracy. It wasn't too hard to reverse the situation.

062 06

There are two systems currently available, with another one coming. The USA one is **NAVSTAR/GPS** (GNSS is the generic ICAO term), and the Russian system is **GLONASS**, which is only just operational, so it is not approved even for B-RNAV, although smartphones can use it. Each can produce extreme accuracy at a much reduced cost compared to, say, Inertial Navigation, with better approach paths, etc.

These days, satellite signals are not only used for navigation, but also for specialised clock systems in various earthbound systems, such as cell phone networks and TV stations, since the satellites all have atomic clocks on board. ATC use it for this purpose as well (GPS is a legal source of accurate time).

A satellite system can calculate distance, track and speed from your changing position. It can also give your altitude, but such 3D readouts require 4 satellites. In any case, the datum for altitude information when under IFR or conducting approaches is **barometric altitude**, because the Earth is not a true sphere and there may be wide differences between its actual shape and the WGS 84 model inside the GPS receiver.

GPS reliability approaches 100%, within 100 m of the true horizontal position for 95% of the time and 300 m for 99%.

However, it can be affected by atmospheric interference, satellite positioning and tuning inaccuracies.

Each satellite has three sections, for timing, signal generation and transmitting.

GALILEO

Although the American GPS system is still usable, it is old technology and originally designed for military use so, for modern purposes, continual workarounds have to be employed, which often turn out to be more expensive than starting from scratch. *Galileo* is a European system whose first satellite was launched on the 28th December 2005. It will start with five types of signal - one being available to everyone, like the GPS C/A code, a more precise commercial signal, a *safety of life* service for critical applications, a *public regulated service* (PRS) for government use, and one combined with a distress signal, for rescues.

2 types of clock have been developed for it - a Rubidium Frequency Standard clock and a Passive Hydrogen Maser. In other words, they are non-identical atomic clocks.

Galileo should use **30 satellites**, with **9 and a spare** in each of **3 planes** in a near circular orbit at **23 222 km** inclined at 56° to the Equator. Orbits will take 14 hours. The signals will be transmitted on two bands, 1164-1215 MHz and 1559-1591 MHz. The overlap with GPS will use *spread spectrum technology* to unscramble the mess.

The frequency band is 1164 - 1215 MHz, 1260 - 1300 MHz and 1559 - 1591 MHz.

NAVSTAR/GPS

The Global Positioning System was originally set up by the US military in 1977 to help submarines get lost more accurately, based on Doppler Shift, as one of six satellites passed overhead, although how they received the signals beats me. Now the system is managed by an executive board that ensures that all users' needs, including civilians, are considered. This was after flight KAL 007 hit a Russian missile that was on a peaceful mission.

GPS is supposed to use 24 (21 + 3) satellites, in 6 groups of 4 (60° apart), with at least 21 operational at any time, although there are now over 31 on line, to allow for orbital manoeuvres and maintenance. The idea is that the transmissions from as many satellites as possible, but at least 4 for best results, are received by a device that is permanently tuned to 1575.42 MHz, although there is another frequency used by the military for precision positioning*. Satellite transmissions include atomic time in their signals so the receiver can calculate its distance from them. The phrase *Full Operational Capability* means that all 24 satellites are working. *All In View* means that a receiver is tracking all the satellites it can find (because it cannot find the ones that it wants), and can instantly replace a lost signal with another that is already being monitored. *Search The Sky* is a procedure that starts after switching on a receiver to check that no stored satellite data is available. It typically occurs after you move the GPS some distance since its last use. A pseudo satellite (*pseudolite*) is a ground beacon that transmits similar information to a satellite.

*The 95% position accuracy should be 30 metres horizontally under ICAO.

The centre of the Earth can be used in the same way.

The satellites fly high enough to avoid the problems encountered by other navigation systems. They operate (at 7500 mph) between **6 circular planes, 20 200 km above the Earth, with 4 in each plane**, optimised for wide coverage. Each should have a 28° view of the Earth, and at least 5 should be in line of sight from any point on Earth (in view), provided they are more than 7.5° above the horizon (satellites are *in view* when over 5° above). The most satellites are visible round the Equator, but this varies, according to the time and your location. A good combination would be 3 satellites with a low elevation above the horizon with a 120° spread between them, and a fourth directly overhead.

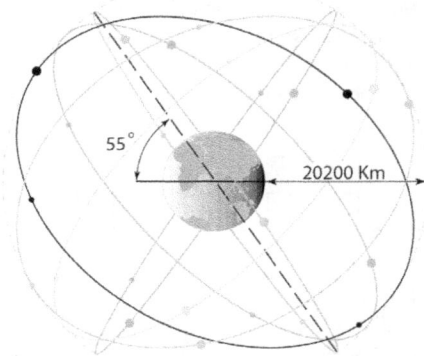

Any errors in satellite orbits are down to solar winds and the gravitational effects from the sun, moon and planets.

This does not affect polar service, because, at high latitudes, receivers can see satellites over the other side, so more can actually be visible than elsewhere (they never go right over the Poles). Where the satellite goes South to North it is in the *ascending node*, and vice versa. The *mask angle* is the lowest angle above the horizon from where a satellite can be used, due to possible range errors.

*The inclination is the angle between the orbital and Equatorial planes.

The satellites move once around the Earth, from W-E, every 11 hours 58 minutes (that is, twice a day, getting 4 minutes earlier each day, actually half of a sidereal day). That's 14 times faster than a 747! The height used gives the best coverage with the least number of satellites, though you could get a problem flying through the odd ravine, especially as their transmitting power is only around 50 watts, or rather less than the average light bulb, which allows you to use smaller antennae. The signals themselves have less strength than a Christmas tree light.

GLONASS, in contrast, uses 3 planes with 8 satellites equally displaced by 45° of latitude. To stop them hitting US satellites, they fly lower, in a near circular orbit at **19 100 km** at an inclination of 64.8° to the Equator. Each orbit is completed in 11 hours, 15 minutes. The time reference is UTC Russian time, and the datum is PZ-90 Earth-centred, Earth-fixed. Navigation signals are transmitted on two frequencies on the L band (UHF), L1 at around 1.6 GHz and L2 around 1.2 GHz. The navigation message is 2 seconds long, with "immediate" data relating to the satellite transmitting the signal and "non-immediate" data relating to the other satellites.

Although it is guaranteed to be kept running for the foreseeable future, in (US) National Emergencies NAVSTAR may be unavailable, which is why you still need radio-based navigation aids, at least under EASA*. As well, the satellites are not always in an optimal position, and interference can affect their signals, including jamming, which can be done with minimal equipment.

*If a position fix from GPS differs from conventional systems by an unacceptable amount, the flight may be continued with those systems, so prescribed IFR equipment must still be installed.

The system consists of three basic elements:

- The **Space Segment**, which contains the satellites, transmitting signals that are used by the receivers.

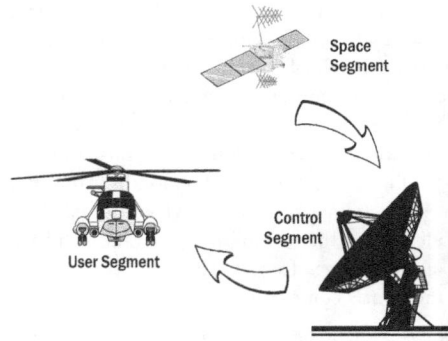

- The **Control Segment** has the ground stations and systems that track the satellites and monitor their status. It includes a **Master Control Station** in Colorado, its backup and 5 **monitoring stations** around the world, including their **ground antennae**. Their data is sent to and processed at the MCS, then used to refine and update satellite navigational signals, including the sending of new ephemeris and clock data to the satellites. Otherwise, its main tasks are:
  - to manage performance
  - to upload navigation data
  - to monitor satellites
- The **User Segment** includes the receivers that select satellites automatically, track their signals and calculate the time taken for them to reach the receiver. *Single channel* receivers move from one satellite to the next in sequence. Although this can be very quick, it is not fast enough for navigation. *Multi-channel* receivers (most suitable for aircraft) continuously monitor position data whilst locking on to the next satellites. *Continuous receivers*, with up to 12 channels, can eliminate GDOP problems (see *Errors*) by watching more than four satellites. GPS receiver antennae are semi-omnidirectional, and the active element is a quarter wavelength of 1.6 GHz, or approximately 2.5 cm.

GPS signals are line-of-sight, and will not pass through water, buildings or solid objects in general, although they do pass through clouds, glass and plastic (regardless of that, though, the best conditions for reception are in clear areas with open skies).

In simple terms, each satellite transmits a signal composed of a noise-like digital code (a Gold code) modulated on a microwave carrier frequency known as L1, whose timing is precisely controlled by an atomic clock. A GPS receiver can tune into a satellite signal by generating ts own copy of the Gold code and carrier, then matching their timings to the incoming signal. The differences are then converted to distance.

In more detail, satellites transmit a **Coarse Acquisition** (C/A) code, with a **navigation data message** encoded in it. Navigation data is transmitted every 30 seconds as frames, that contain 5 subframes.

Clock	Ephemeris	Ephemeris	Almanac	Almanac

Because even atomic clocks can drift, the first frame tells the receiver the difference between satellite and true GPS time, as defined by the ground stations. Subframes 2 and 3 include details of that satellite's exact orbital path for the next 4 hours or so, which is called the **Ephemeris**, and unique to that satellite (it is used to correct for small disturbances). The last 2 subframes make up the **Almanac**, which has less precise positioning details of the other satellites, valid for around 6 months. Thus, the receiver knows which ones should be in view and searches for their C/A codes. It can then establish the elevation and azimuth of a satellite and your range from it. The speed of light is assumed, as the signals come from space.

The C/A code is the ranging code used by the receiver to measure the distance (also called *Standard Positioning Service*, or SPS, as distinct from the military P code). It is a 1023-bit pseudorandom number (PRN) that is transmitted at 1.023 Mbits/second, so it is repeated every millisecond.

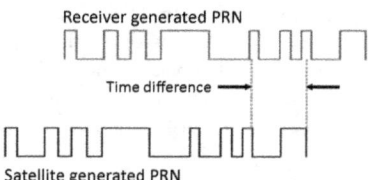

The receiver knows the PRN code of each satellite and can generate them internally. As the satellite includes a time tag (referenced to GPS time) in its signal, indicating when the PRN started, on reception, the receiver can compare when its own version started with the arrival time of the satellite's PRN. The difference in time (in nanoseconds) corresponds to the distance between the satellite and receiver, for a pseudo random range.

The system depends very much on precise timing between satellites and receivers. Although they generate time-codes together, satellite signals lag behind due to their distance. If they are out by 0.6 seconds, the satellite will be 11 160 miles away. 0.7 seconds will be 13 020 miles, and so on.

Time measurement therefore consists of:

- The transit time of the signal
- The time offset between transmitter and receiver

The timing accuracy is actually down to one billionth of a second. The General Theory of Relativity predicts that time runs slower with more gravity, and the atomic clocks in satellites indeed run slightly faster (2 seconds over UTC) than they would on the surface, so corrections have to be made continually. If you are off by even 1 millisecond, your position would be in error by over 300 km, so, for 1 m accuracy, time measurement must be accurate to within 3 nanoseconds. Satellites therefore use atomic clocks for high precision, and continuously transmit their positions, plus a code number in a set code, at exactly the same time. The signal is modulated with a pseudo-random code that allows the time of the transmission to be recovered by the receiver. Instead of trying to distinguish the signal from the Earth's background noise, it is sent as Pseudo Random Noise because it is not really as random as normal noise.

Although noise will change randomly, the GPS signal will have the same sequence. Over time, more matches will be found for the PRN than for the noise, so the GPS signal can be found. This technique allows all satellites to use the same frequency, with individual ones being identified by their Pseudo-Random Noise code (PRN).

The system works loosely like DME, except that is it passive - the time it takes for a signal to travel from a satellite to your receiver is multiplied by the speed of light for a distance, which gives you a *Line Of Position* (LOP). One, of course, is no good by itself, and you actually need 4 LOPs* to determine your position in terms of latitude, longitude and altitude.

*The job can actually be done with three satellites - the fourth is there to correct for timing errors by calculating the position a second time, and the results will differ by an amount equal to the timing error. As calculations are involved, and are therefore subject to receiver clock error, the distance is called a pseudorange.

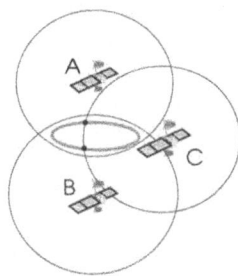

For example, you must be somewhere on the surface of a sphere centred on Satellite A, and similarly for Satellite B. In fact, you must be somewhere on the circle formed where they intersect. With Satellite C, the three spheres intersect at only two points, and you must logically be at one of them, which is where the fourth satellite comes in - there are techniques for deciding which one, using "bad mathematics" according to Garmin. Mostly the wrong one is discarded because it puts you somewhere weird, like 100 miles out in space.

The basic elements transmitted from a satellite are:

- clock offset from UTC
- ephemeris data
- almanac data
- ionospheric delays (see *Errors*, later)
- satellite health data
- satellite clock corrections

As each satellite contains **almanac** data for the entire constellation, a GPS receiver only needs to download it from one satellite to figure out the approximate location of them all. Almanac information is transmitted every 12.5 minutes and takes **12.5 minutes to download** (30 seconds per data frame), so it will take at least that time before accurate fixes can be determined (the initial setup is known as a *cold start*). This data becomes stale over time or if you move the receiver to another location more than several hundred kilometers away. The Almanac covers:

- Satellites that are operating normally
- The PRN codes of available satellites
- Predicted positions of satellites in their orbits

The receiver can then determine which satellites are in view and their relative geometry, then which are the four best ones to track for the best lines of position.

As each satellite transmits only its own **ephemeris** data, the receiver must get it from each one in view. Ephemeris data is transmitted every 30 seconds, and takes 12 seconds to download. It is valid for up to 4-6 hours.

Normally, when two PRNs are multiplied together, they give a value of near zero. A satellite's PRN is multiplied by the L1 carrier (described below) at different time shift intervals, until it finds a lock-on, when a particular time shift results in a high multiplication value. Thus, all the other satellites are filtered out and the time-shift required for the lock-on is used to calculate the satellite's range and extract the navigation message from the C/A code.

By decoding the navigation message, the receiver gets the data it needs to correct the pseudo range. When the two code patterns match, the satellite and receiver can be synchronised, which is the first step in finding an LOP (*initial acquisition*). The receiver in your aircraft can generate the same pseudo random code as the satellite because it has its own code book with them all in. The code sequence is started when the local clock says the satellite should have started transmitting its PRN.

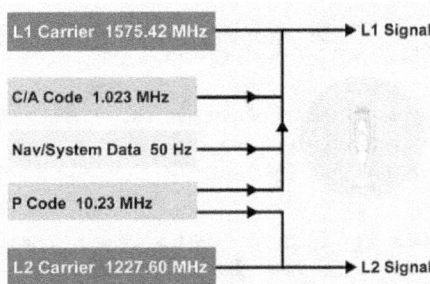

The x, y, z position from the centre of the Earth is translated into latitude and longitude using the WGS 84 model, and GPS time is translated into UTC. Your velocity is calculated with a combination of your rate of change of position and Doppler shift from the L1 frequencies of different satellites, compared to the receiver's L1 oscillation frequency.

In fact, two UHF frequencies are used, L1 and L2*. The (higher) L1 frequency is 1575.42 MHz and L2 is 1227.60 MHz. Both are multiples of a base frequency of 10.23 MHz (L1 is 10.23 x 154) which is generated by a crystal controlled by an atomic clock. All satellites transmit on both frequencies, but their outputs are multiplexed so they can share the same carrier.

The higher frequency transmits the C/A and P codes.

*L2C (and M for the military) was added in 2005 so that cheaper receivers could use proper signals instead of having to make do with the carrier, because they couldn't decrypt the military code. L5 is coming in 2015.

L5 is a civilian frequency that allows the avionics to compute ionospheric corrections without the need for a separate SBAS, like WAAS or EGNOS.

The (digital) information is superimposed on the carriers with BPSK modulation (*Binary Phase Key Shifting*), where code changes cause a 180° phase shift in the carrier (i.e. phase modulation reverses the carrier wave). Being digital, the data exists as strings of 1s and 0s, which are simpler to transmit, more reliable, and less prone to jamming because redundancy checking can be used. The P (Precise) code is transmitted on L1 and L2. As it runs at 10.23 MHz, it is ten times more accurate than C/A. It can be encrypted (as Y Code) and is therefore almost impossible to jam. Comparing the L1 and L2 frequencies at the receiver can compensate for ionospheric propagation errors. In other words, differences between the frequencies tell you what the ionosphere is doing - radio waves change speed as they pass through it. As the delay is inversely proportional to frequency, it can be calculated and virtually eliminated.

SIGNAL AUGMENTATION

 The majority of PBN operations can be conducted using unaugmented satellite signals.

GROUND BASED
Ground Based Augmentation Systems (GBAS) are the practical application of Local Area Differential GPS. Differential GPS was a workaround (by the US Coastguard!) for the intentional errors in the C/A code for unauthorised (non-military) users of the GPS system using a LORAN data channel. It uses a fifth signal from a precisely surveyed ground based transmitter whose position can be compared against that of the receiver. The difference is the intentional error. The nearer the receiver is to a DGPS ground station, the more accurate is the fix.

In other words, corrections are sent **directly to aircraft receivers** from ground stations at airports, typically within about 20-30 nm (the closer the better). The VDB signal provides error correction & integrity data, and approach data for more than one runway. The coverage is within 35° of the final approach path up to 15 nm from the landing threshold, and within 10° between 15 - 20 nm. When even that is not enough, extra GPS transmitters nearby (pseudolites) can increase the accuracy right down to less than the size of a manhole cover (GBAS + GPS is also called *Local Area Augmentation System* in the US).

In summary, GBAS can provide two services:

- Precision approach - down to 200 feet at Sydney.
- Horizontal Positioning for RNAV operations in terminal areas.

SATELLITE BASED
Here, Differential GPS is extended to cover a larger area. The idea is to measure the signal errors from the satellites and

provide separate corrections for ranging, ephemeris, clock and ionospheric errors. Correction data is then transmitted directly to **geostationary** satellites, and re-transmitted to the user (the frequency band of the data link is identical to that of the GPS signals). Pseudorange measurements to the geostationary satellites can also be made as if they were GPS satellites. SBAS regionally augments GPS and GLONASS by making them suitable (as a standalone navigation aid) for safety critical procedures such as landing.

The FAA's **Wide Area Augmentation System** (WAAS) allows GPS to be used throughout a flight, including a Cat I precision approach. Satellite signals are received by precisely surveyed ground stations, which detect errors and send them to a Master Station (WMS), which in turn adds correction information based on geographical area (which is fairly constant) and uplinks a correction message to geostationary satellites (around the Equator and way above the other satellites) for rebroadcast, from which pseudorange measurements can be made, as with normal satellites. This improves the 95% signal accuracy from 100m to 7m, but it can be better than 2 m. The term LPV stands for *Lateral Precision Vertical* guidance, with lateral accuracy as good as ILS, with vertical capability. Unlike BARO VNAV, SBAS vertical guidance is not subject to altimeter errors, non-standard temperatures or lapse rates.

When SBAS integrity messages are used, the additional satellites that would be required for RAIM are not needed, because the messages are available wherever the satellite signal can be received. WAAS currently uses two satellites over the Atlantic and Pacific Oceans.

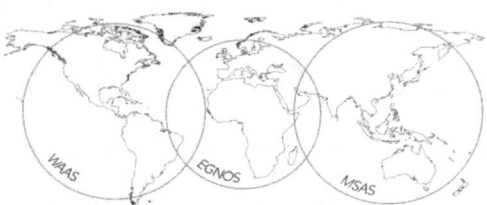

EGNOS, or the *European Geostationary Navigation Overlay Service* is the European equivalent to WAAS (there is also MSAS in Japan and GAGAN in India). It has INMARSAT satellites broadcasting GPS look-alike signals (on UHF), so the coverage is limited to between 80N and 80S (EGNOS has a primary service area further North than WAAS). It is designed to improve accuracy to **1-2 m horizontally** and **3-5 m vertically**. Integrity and safety are improved by alerting users within 6 seconds of a malfunction, as opposed to the normal 3 hours.

Aircraft Based (ABAS)

This uses redundant elements (i.e. excess information that is not otherwise needed) within the GNSS constellation to develop integrity control (ABAS does not improve positioning accuracy, as you get with GBAS and SBAS). ABAS using GNSS information only is RAIM (*Receiver Autonomous Integrity Monitoring*), described below. A system using information from additional on-board sensors is AAIM (*Aircraft Autonomous Integrity Monitoring*). Typical sensors used are barometric altimeters, clocks and inertial navigation systems.

Although the ground stations monitor satellites and detect faults, it can take up to two hours for an error to be corrected.

Receiver Autonomous Integrity Monitoring (RAIM) is a bit quicker than that. It is achieved within the receiver, which monitors satellites and verifies their signals, so an extra satellite is needed to detect corrupt information. For the bad signal to be isolated as well, you need one more. Without RAIM, accuracy is not assured, and you still need 4 satellites for a 3D fix. Thus, Basic RAIM (fault detection) needs 5 satellites in order to work, and 6 (with good positioning) to continue working after a failure is detected (*Fault Detection & Exclusion*, or FDE). If a satellite is excluded, the system works as Basic RAIM and can be used as an independent means of navigation.

If RAIM is available, the integrity limits are 4 nm for oceanic, 2 nm for enroute, 1 nm for terminal work and 0.3 nm for GPS approaches. If RAIM is not available, the GPS must be integrated with other systems, such as DME/DME fixing, with traditional equipment (VOR, etc.) as backup. If the GPS is the only equipment meeting the B-RNAV standards, RAIM availability must be confirmed before flight.

5 positions are calculated using 4 of the 5 visible satellites:

ABCD
ABCE
ABDE
ACDE
BCDE

The signal is assumed to be reliable if they all agree within a certain tolerance.

RAIM can be assisted with *baroaiding* (barometric aiding), which uses barometric information from the aircraft's altitude encoder to reduce the number of real satellites required by one. Barometric altitude is the datum for altitude information such as MDA. The idea is to convert the aircraft's altitude to a range from the centre of the Earth, which can then be used for consistency checks with the pseudo ranges from the satellites that are used to create the fix.

Another technique is *clock coasting*, which uses atomic clocks in the user segment to reduce clock bias (below).

ERRORS

The effects of the errors below are smallest when the satellites are directly overhead and greatest when they are near the horizon, as the signal is affected for a longer time. Having said that, the most accurate fix comes from 3 satellites with a low elevation above the horizon, 120° from each other and a fourth directly overhead.

- **Clock Bias**. As the receiver's clock is not as precise as the atomic clocks in the satellites, there can be a large difference in the measurements, which can introduce a ranging error. When a receiver starts up, its own code is inaccurate by an unknown error called clock bias, or clock offset, against GPS reference time. In addition, the size of the atomic clocks in satellites are necessarily smaller than ground-based ones would be. The receiver corrects by running a series of simultaneous equations. It must be aware of the satellite's position, which is where the ephemeris comes in. Signals are monitored by control segment ground stations and the corrections sent to the Master station, which makes the necessary corrections then relays them to the satellites.

- Satellite **clock drift**. Although the orbital paths of GPS satellites could theoretically be predicted under Kepler's laws of planetary motion, the assumption that the Earth is a perfect sphere of uniform density is not correct, and gravity from other heavenly bodies (e.g. the Moon and the Sun) have their own effects on top of Earth gravity. There is also very slight atmospheric drag, because satellites are not travelling in a perfect vacuum, plus the impact of photons of light emitted by the sun both directly and reflected off the Earth and Moon. This solar radiation pressure is a function of a satellite's size and orientation, distance from the sun, etc., but the end result is that satellites headed towards the Sun are slowed down, and accelerated when headed away. This *clock drift* is virtually impossible to estimate accurately, and is the largest unmeasurable source of error.

- **Ephemeris** (position) error. This error is caused by the satellite not being where the receiver thinks it is. That is, there are errors in the satellite's calculation of its own position due to the gravitational effects mentioned above from the sun, moon and other planets. Ground monitoring stations check satellite positions every 12 hours, so the maximum error is 2.5 metres. The computers at the master control station can predict the satellite's future position at a specific time, which is compared with its actual position from the monitor stations. Updated information on future positions is then uploaded.

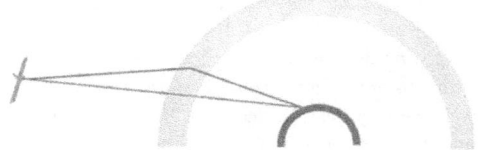

- **Ionospheric Propagation**. UHF signals are not normally refractable by the ionosphere, but even the very small amount that they suffer from increases the time taken for the signal to reach the receiver as it bends through a shallow angle, as shown above. The total distance covered by the red signal is greater than the (correct) green line, especially when they pass through the layers of the ionosphere at a shallow angle (this is less of a problem when the satellite is overhead the receiver). The signal is also subject to attenuation as it passes through the layer of ions, which is effectively thicker and therefore has more effect at a shallow angle. The combined error is called the *ionospheric group delay* which, when combined with the delay from other satellites can produce a total position error of around 5 m. Ionospheric group delay is inversely proportional to the square of the frequency so, if two frequencies are received, as with military systems, by noting the time delay between the L1 and L2 signals, much of the effect of atmospheric propagation can be removed internally by the receiver (as determined from the satellite navigation message). The corrections are imperfect, although they are slow and can be averaged over time. The model of the ionosphere is corrected by the ground stations every 12 hours, so the maximum position error is 5 metres. This is the worst natural error.

- **Receiver noise**. Internal noise within receiver circuits can cause position errors of up to 0.3 m.

- **Signal noise**. Similar to Receiver noise.

- **Tropospheric**. Water vapour in the atmosphere affects refraction. The maximum error from tropospheric propagation is between 0.3 - 0.5 m.

- **Multi-path reflection.** Antennae should be fitted on the upper fuselage near the Centre of Gravity, as shadowing by parts of an aircraft may stop signals from being received or cause them to come from different directions. Some frequencies, such as 109.5 MHz, have been known to cause the GPS not to work if the antenna is not sited properly. The maximum error is 0.6 m.

- **C/A Selective Availability**. Now discontinued, but it used to be done by dithering satellite clocks.

- **Manoeuvring Errors**. Caused by aircraft attitudes and similar to Multi-path reflection.

- **GDOP/PDOP.** When satellites are too close to each other, vertical and horizontal position accuracy is degraded, because the lines of constant range do not cut cleanly (the optimum is 60°) resulting in *Geometric (Position) Dilution of Precision*, where you end up anywhere inside a range of positions rather than just one. ICAO requires a PDOP/GDOP of less than 6 for en-route navigation, and 3 or less for non-precision approaches (4 is considered to be good). The normal accuracy of 100 m for 95% of the time assumes a PDOP of 3 and a range error of 33.3 m (range errors are multiplied by PDOP to obtain stated accuracies). GDOP is minimised by RAIM.

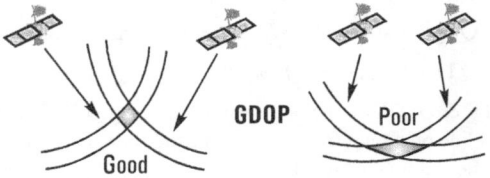

DIRECTION FINDING 062 02 01

Direction finding is the process of determining the straight line (Great Circle) along which a transmitter is located, so you need a chart that allows straight lines to represent Great Circles as closely as possible, so you can measure the angles correctly. For aviation purposes, this is normally a Lambert projection. By using more than one transmitter, you can get a series of position lines with which you should be able to determine where you are. The accuracy is not brilliant, but it is enough to be a supplement for dead reckoning navigation, so it is useful when the weather is bad and you can't see much, assuming that you identify the correct station.

RADIO NAVIGATION
Radar

The most basic method is to turn a directional antenna round until the signal disappears.

VDF

The purpose of *VHF Direction Finding* is to provide directional assistance in times of difficulty, rather than for general navigation, so a typical frequency it might be used on is 121.5 MHz (the full range is between **118-137 MHz**, or metric), although military stations tend to use UHF. One or more ATC stations can get a bearing for you to steer (QDM) to get to their location from your transmissions, so the minimum equipment is a VHF radio. On its own, a direction-finding station can only find your position in relation to itself - for an exact position, you need two or even three more, who will all report to a Master Station. As well, you must work out the headings needed from the information given.

Being based on VHF, VDF is subject to the usual limitations (line of sight, multipath, etc.), so the higher you are, the better the results you will get. You must transmit for a few seconds for a bright line to spread from the centre of a screen to the outside which is marked with compass bearings.

The full range of services available could include:

- Emergency Cloudbreak
- Emergency No-compass Homing
- Homing
- Fix - only on 121.5 MHz
- Track-out Assistance
- Time & Distance Estimates

However, ICAO only recognizes homing, with no compensation for wind, which is actually the only element that most pilots are aware of, receive training on, or use.

The following services are available, assuming no wind:

- **QDM** - magnetic bearing *to* (with no wind)
- **QDR** - magnetic bearing *from*
- **QUJ** - true bearing *to* (to be steered, with no wind)
- **QTE** - true bearing *from*

The QTE & QDM are the only serious ones - a QTE allows you to plot a line on a map from the station and the QDM gives you a magnetic heading to steer.

When a position is given in relation to another point, or in lat & long, it is a **QTF**. When positions are given by heading or bearing & distance from a known point that is not the station making the report, the point shall be from the centre of an aerodrome, a prominent town or geographic feature, in that order.

A series of bearings is a QDL (so QDL QDM means several QDMs). QGE is the distance from the relevant point. A VDF letdown exists where ATC give you QDMs, and you work out the headings to steer, so the responsibility lies with the pilot. A QGH is an approach based on VDF bearings, where a VDF unit is prepared

to give you assistance, based on VDF bearings (the responsibility lies with the controller). Older equipment uses a cathode ray tube on which the line appears (like a radar sweep) pointing to where your transmission is coming from. More modern digital equipment uses a circle of LEDs at 10° intervals, which will show the same information, with a digital readout in the centre (see left). The controller can store the last transmission, if busy with something else at the time.

Accuracy comes in these classes, in relation to bearing or position, and will be included in the transmission:

Class	Bearing	Position
A	±2°	5 nm
B	±5°	20 nm
C	±10°	50 nm
D	<C	<C

Multipath signals may result in bearing errors.

RADAR 062 03

Although technology has improved matters, radar is still quite a crude instrument which requires an understanding of how it works in order to understand its information correctly, especially when you consider the speed of the waves against the ranges involved. Very short intervals of time in the order of millionths of a second have to be measured with considerable accuracy for the best results.

Using radar improves aircraft spacing and safety - the word stands for *Radio Direction and Ranging*, but the system was called RDF (*Radio Direction Finding*) until 1943, when the name was changed to harmonise with the Americans (in those days it just about got the distance right). It works on the basis that microwave pulses can be reflected (or echoed) off suitable objects, and the time between transmission and reflection can be used to calculate the distance because the speed of transmission is known (the reflection of signals is called scattering. Reflections in the exact opposite direction are called *backscatter*). The "blips" representing the objects are displayed on a monitor and a controller can see the relative positions of reflecting aircraft.

The radar beam is rather like that from a lighthouse, as the antenna focusses the pulses in one direction with the most energy concentrated in the centre. VHF does not provide the bandwidth required for the short pulses that allow good target definition*, so SHF bands are currently used. Thus, radar is limited to line of sight.

*For accuracy, the leading edge of the pulse must be sharp, so it needs to jump to its maximum value suddenly. This is a serious matter when using longer waves, because radio waves with different frequencies have to be mixed, so the process is better done with very short (centimetric) waves.

In most countries, outside of terminal control areas, radar is used more as a monitoring device but, in others, you are more or less under radar control all the time and you may very rarely follow a flight planned route. You will be given details of other traffic according to the clock system, such as "fast mover at 6 o'clock".

The word *pulses*, mentioned above, means that short bursts of electromagnetic energy are mixed with relatively long periods of silence (*relatively long*, in electronic terms, means less than a thousandth of a second). *Continuous Wave radar* is used in radio altimeters and the Doppler system.

Pulses were used originally because early radar sets used thermionic valves as opposed to the transistors of today. A valve small enough to produce the short waves required would overheat when used continuously, so using pulses allowed them suitable periods to cool off.

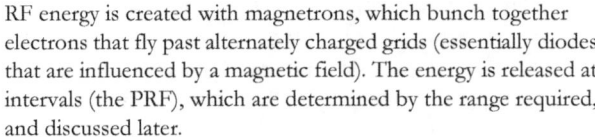

RF energy is created with magnetrons, which bunch together electrons that fly past alternately charged grids (essentially diodes that are influenced by a magnetic field). The energy is released at intervals (the PRF), which are determined by the range required, and discussed later.

The range of a target is determined by measuring the time taken for a pulse of energy to travel there and back. It takes around 3 microseconds for a wave to travel around 1 000 m, but it has to get back, so between transmission and reception there will be a time interval of around 6 m/s for every 1 000 m of (slant) range. This is *primary radar*.

Radio signals weaken over distance and, as the pulses must make two journeys (there and back), the range is necessarily limited. The blip on the screen is also quite large, and aircraft very close together cannot be told apart, unless the beam is narrow enough to pass between them (a 1 millisecond pulse takes up 300 m of space). Finally, radio waves can be bent by the atmosphere or screened by mountains or buildings, and different aircraft return signals differently, in terms of shape or surface (long wavelength is required to penetrate cloud).

The strength of an echo received back at a radar set varies with the size of the target and its distance. As the returning pulse is not reflected, but re-radiated*, it decreases in strength in the same way as it did on its way out, so the received signal in this case has one third of one third of its original strength, meaning one ninth. As power is proportional to the square of the field strength, echo power is inversely proportional to the distance of the target^4. So every time you double the range of a target, you reduce the power of its echo by 2^4 or 16 times (or, to double the effective range of primary radar, the power output must be increased by a factor of 16). Trebling the range reduces it by 3^4 or 81 times.

*Pulses make valence electrons ripple and release energy.

The transmitter has to:

- Generate very high power at high frequencies. The radio frequency (RF) energy is produced inside the **HF oscillator** by a *magnetron*, which is a piece of copper with cavities in surrounded by a strong magnet. The electrons are made to spin within the cavities and set up the microwaves, hence their use in microwave ovens.

- Be capable of being switched on and off rapidly to produce pulses. This is done by the **modulator**.

- Send out the pulses at regular intervals (as per the *pulse recurrence rate*) via the **synchroniser**, which regulates the rate at which pulses are sent (i.e. sets the PRF) and resets the timing clock for range determination for each pulse. Signals from the synchronizer are sent simultaneously to the transmitter, which sends a new pulse, and to the display, which resets the return sweep.

The generated pulses travel through either coaxial cable or a hollow, generally rectangular, metal tube called a *wave guide*, which prevents excessive power loss because it is tuned to the wavelength. The RF energy is injected into the waveguide by a probe, which is simply an antenna that only radiates into the waveguide.

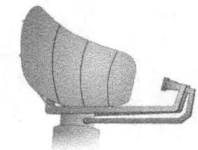

A waveguide is not required for weather radar because it uses slots on a flat (planar) array.

The clock drives the deflector plates of the screen used for the display. It oscillates at a very exact frequency, geared down by dividers. The clock also ensures that the spot of light that moves around the screen is cut off at appropriate moments to keep the screen clear (blacking out flyback - by making the grid (brilliance) negative, the fly-back is suppressed, meaning that you won't see the lines where the pulse flies back from the end of one line to the beginning of the new line). Range markers are displayed with a saw-tooth wave.

The problem is that the signals are very different - the transmitted signal is very strong, but the received one is very weak and the system must be sensitive enough to detect it. In

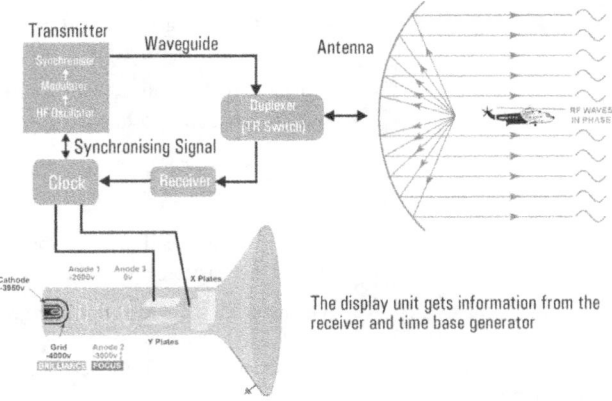

The display unit gets information from the receiver and time base generator

other words, the receiver circuits must be protected against the high energy from the transmitted signals, otherwise they would be fried when the system is switched on. The solution is not necessarily to switch between transmit and receive, but to route the signals to the appropriate places, which is where the **duplexer** comes in. It is a routing device that directs outgoing pulses to the antenna and incoming pulses from the antenna to the receiver. The speed at which it returns to the receive position helps to determine minimum range.

The antenna is a parabolic dish, shaped according to its function. For example, the orange peel produces a wide narrow beam. A parabolic dish produces a focussed beam, but it spreads with distance. A phase array has a series of conducting elements like small dipoles that are arranged in a line and fed with signals that are in phase with each other. The interference patterns produce a pencil beam.

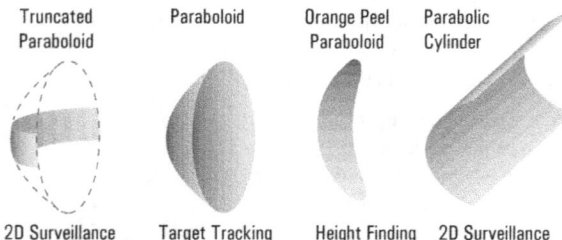

There is a protruding element (a probe) somewhere in the middle, which beams the signals to the face of the dish, to form the beam into the desired shape and go in the direction required.

The dish and element work in the reverse sense when receiving signals - the larger the dish, the more of the weak signal can be received. If the width of the main beam is taken from where the signal strength drops to half of what it is at the centre, you can find the beam width with this formula:

```
Beam Width° =  2 x wavelength in cm
               diameter (ft)
```

try also:

```
Beam Width° =  70 x wavelength
               diameter
```

So a reflector 4 feet wide using 3 cm waves would have a beam width of around 1.5°. Here are some common sizes:

Dish Size	Beam Width
10"	9.5°
12"	7.5°
18"	5°

Advantages of a narrow beam are:
- getting bearings more easily
- greater concentration of energy
- more range
- target definition

A *short pulse length* with a *narrow beam* gets the best picture.

As the antenna is expected to work with a transmitter (horizontally) and a receiver (vertically), it should be able to produce a thin beam, and receive a wide one, respectively. A perfectly directional antenna would be very large and unwieldy so, to use small ones, we have to live with unwanted radiations known as sidelobes, which can show multiple targets for one aircraft at close range.

The advantage of a slotted antenna is to virtually eliminate lateral lobes, and concentrate more energy in the main beam. The receiver converts the microwave returns into electrical signals that are amplified, because they have only a fraction of the power that was sent originally. Thus, the receiver should have a high overall gain, with little random noise in its circuitry. Because of this high amplification capability, no RF stage is required.

Finally, the signal is sent to the *Plan Position Indicator* (PPI), which is called that because it displays the returns as if you were looking from the top, as opposed to the original display, which showed the returns from the side.

The display's timebase (the frequency with which the picture is repainted) is linked to the antenna, in that when it passes through North, so does the beam painted on the display. As a pulse is fired off, a spot of light moves from the centre of the tube to the outside, reaching the

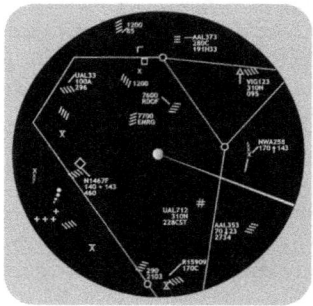

circumference before the next pulse goes. The effect is a line of light rotating round the screen.

When a return is received, the electron flow is increased and the intensity of the display increases to a spot which fades away slowly as the line moves on.

Calculations

You can calculate the distance between the transmitter and the target because the speed of the radio wave is known, and the direction the antenna is pointing at the time supplies the bearing. It takes 12.36 microseconds for a radio wave to travel out and back for each nautical mile of range (radar mile), or 123.6 microseconds for each 10 nm.

Given that radar speed is 300 m per microsecond, the leading edge of the average pulse is already several hundred metres on its way when the transmitting stops.

Put more mathematically, if the time delay is Dt, then you can find the range (R) with:

$$R = \frac{cDt}{2}$$

where c = the speed of light, and it is divided by 2 because the pulse train has to get to the target and back again.

The maximum unambiguous range* will be determined firstly by the *Pulse Repetition Frequency* (PRF)**, because pulses have to return to the transmitter before the next ones are sent, plus the *Pulse Interval* (PI).

*If an echo is received from a long range target after the pulse following the one it relates to, the radar uses the very much shorter time between the second pulse and the echo, and calculates a shorter range. Range ambiguity occurs when the time taken for an echo to return from a target is greater than the Pulse Repetition Time. For example, if the interval between pulses is 1000 microseconds, and the return time of a pulse from a distant target is 1200 microseconds, the apparent distance of the target is only 200 microseconds.

To increase the unambiguous range, you have to increase the PRT, which means increasing the PRF.

**It is more correct to say that the PRF is limited by range. To see targets up to say, 25 nm, the maximum PRF is around 3000 pulses per second. It can be determined by:

$$\text{Max PRF} = \frac{80\,000}{nm}$$

Simply replace the letters *nm* with the distance required. 80,000 represents half the speed of light in nautical miles. In fact, the range is determined by the time *between* pulses (the *Pulse Recurrence Period* or *Interval*), which must be long enough for a pulse to go out to the target and return. It follows that, if it is too short, this cannot happen. As the number of pulses per second depends on the length of the interval, we say that maximum range depends on PRF. As an example, the maximum range of Long Range Surveillance Radar is between 200 - 300 nm.

The number of pulses per second is the Pulse Repetition Frequency (PRF), so the further the target is away, the longer must be the PRP and, by extension, the PRF. A shorter PRP means more pulses per second and a higher PRF. The two are related:

$$\text{PRF} = \frac{1}{\text{PI (PRP)}}$$

With this formula, make sure you use the right numbers!

In between pulses, you also need some dead (rest) time.

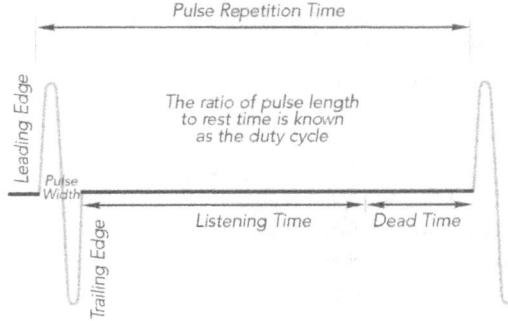

This is because a pulsed wave doesn't just stop when it hits a target, but carries on, and may be reflected from other objects way back. At 100 000 yards, for example, it would take around 610 microseconds to travel out and back from the target. If the time interval between pulses is only 610 microseconds, any reflected pulses from further away would be received after the next pulse and produce confusing results, such as a false echo near to the station.

Thus, the interval between pulses needs to be made a little bit wider to allow all possible echoes to be received. The sweep of the beam will still take 610 microseconds, but the spot on the screen will be held at the start during the dead time until the next pulse is ready.

MAXIMUM RANGE

Although it mostly affects the minimum range (see below), the pulse width can also affect the maximum detection range, as the energy depends on pulse width and output power (a long pulse has more energy and returns a stronger signal). *Maximum Theoretical Unambiguous Range* (MTR) in km is found by:

$$\text{MTR} = \frac{c}{2 \times \text{PRF}}$$

PRF (if you know the range) is found by:

$$\text{PRF} = \frac{c}{2 \times \text{Range (km)}}$$

Example: Assuming transmission power is enough, the maximum range of a ground radar with a PRF of 450 pulses per second is 333 km.

MINIMUM RANGE

This (or, more technically, the dead zone at close range) is set by the pulse width (plus the recovery time of the duplexer), because a long pulse could still be receiving part of an echo from one target while starting to get the information from a second, if they are close together (with continuous wave radar, the minimum range restriction is removed, so you can measure short distances, hence its use with radio altimeters). Put more simply, the receiver is switched off while the pulse is being transmitted.

The minimum range is around half the pulse width, as is range resolution. As a pulse width of a microsecond will cover over 300 m, two aircraft within 150 m of each other will appear on the screen as one, so the pulse width can also affect the ability to discriminate between targets that are close together. Based on the scale in the diagram above, if the duty cycle was 1:1000, and the pulse was 1 microsecond, the next one would be over 10 feet away. The transmitter is idle a lot of the time.

Moving Target Indication

Strong radar returns from stationary objects (e.g. terrain and buildings) can mask a primary radar return from an aircraft, especially if it is at low level. MTI uses Doppler to eliminate returns from fixed objects. That is, only returns that show a Doppler shift (moving targets) will be shown, but **targets at constant range will not show up**.

Secondary Surveillance Radar

This is a development of a system introduced during the Second World War called *Identification Friend or Foe* (IFF), which was supposed to distinguish between friendly and enemy aircraft. Friendly aircraft had a small transmitter that produced a longer blip on the screen, so anything shorter was an enemy. It was codenamed Parrot (or Canary) by the British, which probably has something to do with the current use of the word *Squawk* to mean *transmit the relevant codes*, which you dial up on the transponder and which will appear next to your blip with your height readout, depending on the type of transponder you have.

SSR improves on primary radar* by using double-pulse secondary equipment to provide more information, hence the name. An interrogating ground station sends a rotating beam of pulse modulated signals in all directions in a form that is recognised as a request for information. Participating aircraft carry a *transponder* (for *transmitter/responder*) that receives the interrogation pulse (1030 MHz ±0.2 MHz), superimposes information on it and sends it right back on another paired frequency (1090 MHz). Aside from being 60 MHz apart, this means, first of all, that the range of operation can be doubled (the power of the echoed pulse has nothing to do with range, so is only subject to normal radio range limitations) and that the blip on the screen can be made much smaller, together with information that makes it more easily identifiable to ATC, because the pulses can be coded. As well, there is no storm clutter, as the principle of echo return is not used. Computers can provide predicted tracks and collision warnings, etc.

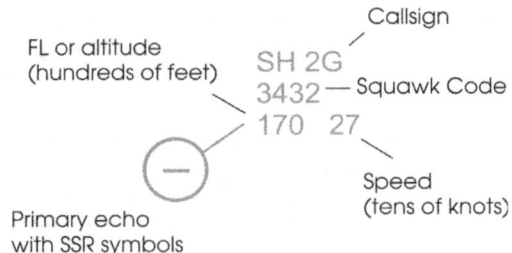

*Primary radar is more accurate in terms of bearing and distance.

The following can be presented on the radar screen:

- Squawk Code
- Flight Level
- Flight Number or Registration
- Groundspeed

You cannot set the number 8! Watch for this in questions that ask you to choose between valid codes

There are standard numbers to squawk, when not otherwise instructed, which are:

- 2000 - from non-SSR area
- 7000 - conspicuity code

In emergency, squawk:

- 7500 - Hijack*
- 7600 - Comms failure
- 7700 - Emergency

Absence of a reply is confirmation that the selection is not accidental

When making routine code changes, you should avoid inadvertent selection of 7500, 7600 or 7700 (**do not** switch the transponder to standby during the change to avoid it, as senior pilots often do, because this removes your display from ATC's screen and creates all sorts of alarms). For example, when switching from 2700 to 7200, switch first to 2200 then to 7200, not to 7700 and then 7200. This applies to 7500 and all discrete codes in the 7600 and 7700 series (i.e. 7600-7677, 7700-7777) which will trigger special indicators in automated facilities.

When fitted, transponders should be used **all the time**.

Elementary Surveillance provides a controller with aircraft position, altitude and identification. It is based on ground initiated Comm-B protocols and needs a Mode S transponder with Surveillance identifier (SI) code capacity and automatic reporting of aircraft identification, known as ICAO Level 2s. SI codes must correspond to the aircraft ID in the flight plan, or the registration mark. On the other hand, *Enhanced Surveillance* extracts additional information from the aircraft, known as *Downlink Additional Parameters* (DAP). Such information, being automatically extracted, reduces controller workload so that they can concentrate on safety. Because radio calls can be reduced, it also makes things easier for pilots.

MODES & CODES

Modes are used to ask questions, such as "Who are you?" (Mode 3/A) or "How high are you?" (Mode C) in the form of pairs of interrogative pulses and a control pulse (they are never sent together). The answer comes back as a code, of which there can be up to **4096** (8^4), but not Mode S, which has nearly 17 million.

The decoding of time between interrogation pulses determines the operating mode of the transponder (a spacing for transmission and reception is called a mode).

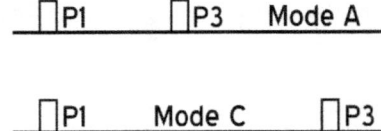

For modes 3/A and C, a pair of pulses called P1 and P3 are sent out to the aircraft (the interval between them decides which one it is). An omnidirectional antenna sends out another one called P2, which is weaker than the others but stronger than any sidelobes so, if the transponder sees P1 and P3, it knows it is receiving the main lobe. If it sees P2, it's a side lobe, so responses from aircraft near them are avoided (in fact, the transponder's responses will be suppressed for a short while). Mode S also uses a short P4 pulse. A long P4 pulse means that the interrogator is transmitting a Mode A/C/S all call.

A Special Position Identification (SPI) pulse is sent by using the IDENT switch.

MODE A/B

Mode A is the regular variety, based on the original IFF, which just displays the code you select in the aircraft - you get this just by turning the switch to ON. In other words, it is for basic identification (Mode B is occasionally used in place of Mode A in some countries, but has been superseded by Mode S).

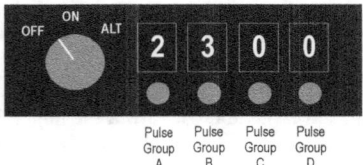

In answer to an interrogation, a Mode A transponder will transmit up to 14 pulses 8 microseconds apart (17 for B), the first and last ones being *frame pulses* (F1 and F2), which are always there and enclose the whole signal so it doesn't get confused with others. The 12 that are left can be there or not in up to 4096 (2^{12}) combinations, from 0000 to 7777. The *ident pulse* is transmitted for up to 20 seconds, 4.35 microseconds after the last frame pulse when you press the button.

Each number selection knob controls 3 pulses (pulse groups A, B, C & D). 2300 (for example) produces the binary codes of 010, 110, 000 and 000. 0 means Off, or no signal, so selecting 2 means that only pulse 2 of Pulse Group A is transmitted. Selecting 3 requires pulse 1 plus pulse 2 of the B group (refer to *Binary Arithmetic* under *Computers, Etc.* for more information). There would therefore only be 3 pulses between the frame pulses, which saves on transmission bandwidth.

Mode C

"Mode C" is selected by switching to ALT, after switching on for Mode A, so it is separate (being actually A + altitude reporting - it s not a mode in the proper sense). You should always use Mode C unless directed otherwise.

It will transmit altitude information alternately with the code information - a Mode C transponder is directly attached to an encoding altimeter (or, more precisely, an altitude digitiser, which selects a different code to that selected in the window), but only Pressure Altitude (or FL) information based on 1013.25 (or 29.92) information is sent from the aircraft (in **100-foot increments**) - the conversion to local pressure, if required, is done inside the ATC computer. **Moving the altimeter subscale does not affect ATC's display**. In Mode C an air traffic controller's presentation gives information regarding your indicated flight level that is accurate to within ±50 ft. The tolerance is ±300 ft. The pulses are 21 microseconds apart.

Mode S (Datalink)

S stands for *Selective*, using pulses 25 microseconds apart. It allows aircraft to have unique codes, and respond only to requests directed to them, as opposed to all requests, although broadcast transmissions of information to all Mode S aircraft can be made without needing a reply.

However, if the interrogator does not know that an aircraft has Mode S, it will not use its individual address, although there will be responses to the station's Mode A and C interrogations. The interrogator therefore sends out an occasional *all call* message, which contains an extra pulse that is a request for every Mode S equipped aircraft to respond with its address and basic information, such as the call sign, its transponder's capabilities*, and an altitude report in 25-foot intervals.

*Transponder capability is described in levels:

- **Level 1** has no data link capability but recognises an individual address - effectively a Mode C transponder with selective calling.
- **Level 2** permits standard data link communication in both directions.
- **Levels 3, 4 and 5** increase the data link capabilities beyond the standard flight information.

In a Mode S interrogation, the initial two pulses are followed by a long pulse containing a string of up to 112 bits, which are transmitted by making phase reversals in the long pulse. This string of bits forms a message, the first **24 bits** being a unique address for the aircraft allowing **nearly 17 000 000** possible codes. In this way, the problems of fruiting, garbling and over-interrogation are overcome. The transponding aircraft will reply with the information requested, in a similar phase modulated pulse. Either 112 or 56 bits may be sent, depending on what the interrogation has asked for.

The aircraft address is allocated by the registering Authority, and is transmitted in any reply except Mode S only all-call (the SI code must correspond to Box 7 in the ICAO flight plan). This reduces mistakes and allows more capacity and efficiency, because the transponder does not have to transmit so often. For example, Mode S transponders have 20-foot resolution of altitude data, while Mode C has 100-foot resolution. Mode A/C/S all-call consists of 3 pulses P1, P3 and the long P4. A control pulse P2 is transmitted following P1 to suppress responses from aircraft in the side lobes of the interrogation antenna. Mode A/C only all-call consists of 3 pulses P1, P3 and the short P4.

A Mode S transponder regularly delivers a *squitter*, which is a short transmission of basic data without receiving a request, simply to advertise your position for TCAA. *Extended Squitter* is additional data on the Mode S Squitter that carries position information from the GPS, so a device receiving the transmission knows the position of the transmitting aircraft without any bearing or range measurements. You can therefore have a pseudo radar service within range of a single mode S ground station (non-rotating antenna) simply by connecting a two-wire data cable from the GPS to the transponder.

Mode S can also provide a two-way data link on 1030 and 1090 MHz, used by TCAS for manoeuvre messages, but also as a backup for VHF voice.

Mode S equipped aircraft over 5 700 kg or with a max TAS over 250 kts must use *transponder antenna diversity*.

The two main design functions of Mode S are:

- air-ground and ground-air data link
- improved ATC aircraft surveillance capability

ERRORS & ACCURACY

Modes A and C can suffer from interference, otherwise known as *fruiting* and *garbling*. FRUIT stands for *False Replies Unsynchronised to Interrogator Transmissions*. Since SSR equipment uses the same frequencies for transmitting and receiving, any interrogator can trigger any transponder within range, so any ground station can receive their replies, which appear as interference, or fruit. Defruiting uses different PRFs, and comparator circuits only pass replies at the correct home PRF.

Garbling comes from other aircraft within line of sight range responding to the same interrogation.

Because the length of a transponder code train is about 20 microseconds, it is not always possible to decipher replies from aircraft within 2-3 miles of each other on a radial from the interrogator (you could get overlapping returns **within 1.7 nm**). The reply signals may garble and the decoder equipment can generate false targets between the aircraft or cause cancellation of all or part of either or both returns (this may occur even with altitude separation). Circuits in the decoder equipment cancel garbled replies, and controllers will often ensure that only one aircraft within a formation has a transponder operating.

Weather Radar

Although it shares the same name, this is not a good system for detecting other aircraft or ground returns because it is tuned to the average size of raindrops (when used for navigation, AWR is only a *secondary* means). In fact, the primary purpose of weather radar is to detect the sort of rainfall that would indicate thunderstorms and their associated turbulence. It therefore relies on your interpretation of the screen display for best results.

 Weather radar is required on aircraft that can carry more than 9 passengers (i.e. 10 and above) under IFR or at night when current weather reports indicate that thunderstorms or other potentially hazardous weather conditions, regarded as detectable with AWR, may reasonably be expected along the route.

Two frequency bands are used, such as *C band* (4000-8000 MHz), and *X band* (8000-12500 MHz). C band illuminates storms beyond nearby precipitation better, but X band has more resolution, although its higher frequencies are subject to absorption, and scattering from smaller raindrops. The wavelength is about 3 cm (at **10 GHz**, or maybe 9375 MHz), to detect a 1½ cm raindrop - ½ the wavelength is the optimum object size for detection (larger droplets give good echoes and you can have a smaller antenna). Weather radar can detect volcanic ash, sandstorms and smog, but it is **unlikely to detect snow or clear air turbulence** (except with the use of Doppler).

Cumulus clouds are most readily detected with the weather beam, but snow (or clear air turbulence) cannot be seen. At low altitudes, turbulence may be difficult due to ground returns.

 The antenna (scanner) is kept inside a *radome* in the nose of the aircraft, and there is an RT box containing the transmitter/receiver, together with a scope in the cockpit.

The antenna can be parabolic or flat, sweeping through 45-60° either side of the nose - the flat scanner reduces power demand and sidelobes. In *weather* mode, the beam is narrow, between 3-5° (pencil) and cone-shaped. For mapping, it is wide and fan-shaped (up to 50-60 nm), but for long range mapping, you should use weather mode anyway, because the narrow beam goes further with more power concentrated in it. The antenna is stabilised in pitch and roll, ±20° combined, using inputs from the attitude system. It is not stabilised in yaw.

Weather radar detects rainfall to *avoid* (not penetrate) severe weather, as many large raindrops in a small area are a dead giveaway for thunderstorms or, rather, their activity is - turbulence is proportional to the rate at which rainfall increases or decreases over a given distance. Whether you want to go towards the area concerned depends on the intensity of the echoes received, the spacing between them, your capabilities and those of the aircraft.

 A clear area on the radar screen (say between significant echoes) does not mean there is no cloud or precipitation, as minute droplets, ice, dry snow and dry hail have low reflective levels, if at all.

In fact, a clear area is more likely to indicate large water droplets, as they will totally absorb the energy as they approach the size of the radar wave, and the screen will not be able to display the remaining thunderstorm area behind the point of complete attenuation (absence of returns produces a use for the stray side lobes mentioned above, in that the downwards one produces a **height ring** on the screen at the same range as your height above ground, so you can at least check if the equipment is working). Thus, the greatest echoes come from rain, and drop size is more important than their number.

Because of attenuation, a weak return does not mean a less violent storm - you could just be too far away from it to get decent information. As well as the nature of the target, the strength of the returning signal depends on the range of the cloud. Sensitivity Time Control (STC), or swept gain techniques are used, where the receiver gain is lowered at the instant each pulse is fired, then progressively increased so that echoes from distant ranges are amplified more than closer ones.

Operation of weather radar is quite simple, but full use on the ground should be avoided (not below 500 feet, in fact, because the radiations will affect people or equipment). Naturally, you must check the equipment before departure, but most sets have an internal procedure for this. When you do switch it on, it should be set to *Standby* for at least 3 minutes first, to allow things to warm up. When not in use, the set should always be set to SBY to keep the (roll and pitch) stabilisation gyros running - it stops them crunching together as the aircraft moves. Ground testing requires *tilting up* in weather mode.

TILT

Once airborne, the tilt capability will point the antenna up or down so you can adjust for the aircraft attitude and get more detail about approaching storm cells, but don't expect to see the tops of a storm, because the crystals won't reflect the energy in the first place, and your beam focussing will be too narrow to include it (convective thunderstorms are much less reflective above the freezing level). The tilt control is an important key to a more informative display in moderate rain, and should be used often to get a better 3D picture. Tilt down until you see ground returns, then up until they disappear, then add 2° to cover for turns. The tilt should be higher at lower altitudes and lower at higher altitudes.

To see whether a cloud return on an AWR is at or above the height of the aircraft, subtract half the beam width from the angle of tilt - the tilt angle - beam width x 100 x range in nm equals the approximate height difference of the cloud tops (in feet) from your flight level. With a 5° beam width, the tilt control should be set 2.5° up.

The tilt setting should be lower if you climb to a higher altitude.

MAPPING

In the same way, you will also get ground echoes, which are good for detecting the enemy coast ahead, but only because water will absorb the echoes and you will see a big black hole instead. In fact, it will be very hard to distinguish between the edge of the ice and the real coast in polar areas.

Buildings and the like won't reflect properly at all - you might just see a mass of confusing colours (that's what the MAP selection is for, but that's not wonderful, either). MAP mode uses a *cosecant radiation pattern* with a *cosecant squared* antenna, so you can scan a large ground zone with echoes whose signals are practically independent of distance.

When looking at the ground for mapping purposes at fairly close range, the beam must be widened vertically as well as having its energy distribution controlled so that returns from longer range (the top of the beam) are of similar strength to those from shorter range (the bottom of the beam). The strength of the signal vertically within the beam depends upon the square of the cosecant of the angle of depression, so more energy is radiated in the upper part of the beam than the lower part.

You will have several scan ranges to choose from, possibly from 250 miles down to 5, but 80 is adequate, which is about what you would get with a 10 inch antenna, the usual fit in small aircraft. The smaller it is, the wider the beam and the dispersal of energy, which means that a lot of it will pass by whatever storm is around, giving you an indication very much less than the true hazard. You would be safe to assume that whatever you see on the screen is in reality one or two levels more severe.

MAP mode is effective up to 50 or 60 nm, but the pencil shaped beam is preferred for longer distances because more power can be concentrated in the narrow beam.

STORM PATTERNS

If you haven't got the luxury of colour and computer-controlled echo highlighting (and have to rely on steam), there are distinctive storm patterns to look out for:

- *The Hook*. These stick out from a cloud, suggesting strong wind circulations, like tornadoes, or hail, which has a wet surface and therefore reflects like a large raindrop. Both are found in thunderstorms with a marked windshear in the middle levels.
- *The Finger*. This is like a spur out from a cloud, not quite as curled as the hook, and usually in the next intense colour, such as yellow. The trick here is to look at the edges - sharp contours mean a growing storm, while fuzzy ones mean a dissipating storm.
- *The U-shape*. This is like a valley in a mountain, with strong updraughts surrounded on three sides by the sort of heavy precipitation associated with downdraughts.
- *Scalloped edges*. When round a cloud outline, particularly at the back end of a storm, they signify severe attenuation due to heavy precipitation.

Shapes can change quickly, so they need careful monitoring (hail shows up better when the gain is reduced). The heaviest precipitation, and the heaviest turbulence, will show up as black holes, or red when using colour, which is best detected in *Contour mode* (where high rainfall rates, or maximum cell activity, appears in Red).

Tip: Radar signals weaken, and might show the end of the weather falsely.

Iso-Echo (for mono screens) produces a hole in a strong echo when the returned signal is above a pre-set value. *It is used to detect areas of possible severe turbulence in cloud.* The edges of the hole that actually appears on the screen have the same rainfall rate, and is like a contour line, hence the name. When the lines are narrow, there is a strong intensity gradient, so avoid hooked echoes, especially rapidly changing ones. In fact, you should beware of thin lines of whatever colour.

In the picture below, the line along the centre is your intended track, and the curved lines are your range markings, so there's something nasty lurking 10 nm away slightly on your port side, with a little finger (or hook) in front of you which may or may not be producing some rainfall. The colour zones closest together (or nearest the edge of the cell) indicate the greatest turbulence. Note the colour progression from green to yellow to red, and possibly magenta for maximum severity (although the most severe turbulence is shown by a steep colour gradient). By changing the scale to 10 nm, the returns on the radar screen should increase in area and move nearer to the top of the screen.

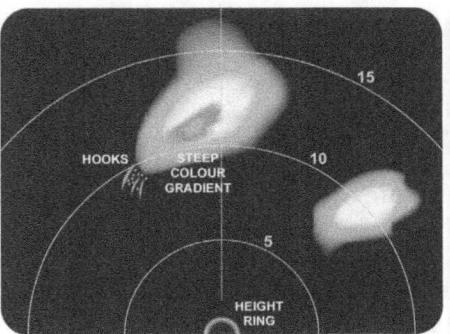

 Targets separated by a distance less than the beam diameter will merge and appear on the display as one. Avoid the brightest returns (i.e. those that are changing rapidly, or contouring, or coloured magenta or red) by at least 20 nm. Above the freezing level, make it 5 nm and 10 nm when below. If you see anything at all between 50-70 nm, keep well away from it. The minimum height above a storm should be 1,000 feet for each 10 kts of wind speed.

Ground Radar

Those used for longer range, such as those covering airways and larger airspace, tend to have lower frequencies and longer wavelengths, lower PRFs and larger pulses to get maximum range with as little attenuation as possible. Where shorter range is good enough, say, for use near an aerodrome, short frequent pulses provide better picture definition. In addition, antenna rotation will be higher because shorter range radar will be used when things are changing quickly.

A typical long range coverage will be up to 250-300 nm, with a preferred frequency of 600 MHz and a 50 cm wavelength. Shorter range coverage is provided by.....

AIRCRAFT SURFACE MOVEMENT RADAR

Otherwise known as *Airport Surface Detection Equipment* (ASDE), this operates in the SHF* band (16 GHz), using an antenna that rotates at around 60 RPM. Its definition is such that it is sometimes possible to determine the type of aircraft from the return on the radar screen.

*EHF is absorbed and scattered by moisture in the air.

DME 062 02 04

Distance Measuring Equipment is secondary radar, but in reverse. It measures the time difference between *paired pulses* being sent from an aircraft, and received back (on different frequencies). Then the distance is calculated.

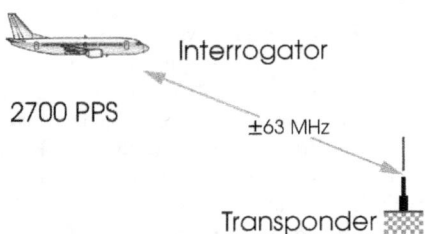

In other words, the aircraft is the first to transmit on UHF (decimetric), then the DME transponder on the ground returns the signal (with the same PRF and pulse spacing) after a 50 microsecond delay which is subtracted during the number-crunching. The delay reduces the chances of uncoordinated activity when the interrogating aircraft is near the station although, if the DME is part of an ILS installation, the delay is not present. The pulses are 3.5 milliseconds wide.

Two frequencies are used because, otherwise, the first pulse received would be the ground return from below (with normal radar, targets are relatively free from other objects. They are more difficult to distinguish the other way round). Similarly, the ground station could self-trigger from other sources, such as those being bounced off a building. *Jittering*, or deliberate random variation of the time interval between interrogations, is used to identify pulses. That is, only signals with the same jittering pattern (PRF) are replied to, because they are unique to each aircraft (the antennae are omnidirectional).

DME is UHF-based, between 960 and 1215 MHz, so a typical frequency is 1000 MHz.

The auto standby circuit does not allow interrogations to start unless signals are detected from the beacon, so there may be a situation where the beacon will not reply unless it is interrogated, and the interrogator will not do so unless it receives signals. Relying on the ident feature means waiting for up to 30 seconds, so the beacon transmits pulse pairs even without interrogations. These are called **squitter** pulse pairs.

Aircraft DME receivers do not lock on to transmissions reflected from the ground as they are not on the receiver frequency - that's why the interrogation and reply frequencies differ. Signal discrimination depends on *frequency separation* and *pulse spacing*.

The **Echo Protection Circuit** (EPC) prevents lock-on to signals from the ground transponder that are reflected off a surface before reaching the aircraft, or vice versa. Such a lock-on would cause an incorrect DME reading greater than the real slant range because the echo will arrive a short time after the line-of-sight interrogation. In the air, both replies will also have the same jittering pattern. To achieve echo protection, the interrogator searches outbound, from zero nautical miles. Reflections are prevented from confusing the equipment by having only the first signal at the receiver accepted, which will have travelled by the shortest path and therefore will not have been reflected. **The circuit detects whether the transmitter/receiver has been locked by pulse pairs.**

The DME ident is pitched higher than that of a VOR (at 1350 Hz), so you can identify it between VOR idents on the same frequency (it is transmitted only once to the VOR's four, within every 40 seconds). Instruments in the cockpit will not only show your distance to a station, but will calculate the rate of movement and display the groundspeed (just multiply the distance flown in 6 minutes by 10 if yours doesn't). The reason it's not completely accurate is because the distance is the *slant range* from the station, and not the equivalent position on the ground, just as with primary radar, although at long distances and lower altitudes, this is minimised. The groundspeed readout reduces at an increasing rate when overflying an aid, to zero at the overhead.

In practical terms, the difference is insignificant over 10 miles from the station, and the maximum error occurs overhead - at 12,000 ft, the instrument would read 2 nm, and 4 nm at 24,000 ft, and so on.

Simple Pythagoras will give you the real distance:

$$D = \sqrt{(S^2 - A^2)}$$

D is the ground distance, S is the readout (slant range) and A is your altitude in *nautical miles* (above the DME source).

The slant range itself is calculated by:

$$\text{Range} = \frac{\text{Time } (\mu s)}{12.4}$$

Don't forget to subtract a 50 m/s delay at the transponder.

Example: At FL 210, you will not receive any distance indication from a DME station approximately 220 nm away because you are below the line of sight altitude. If the time taken

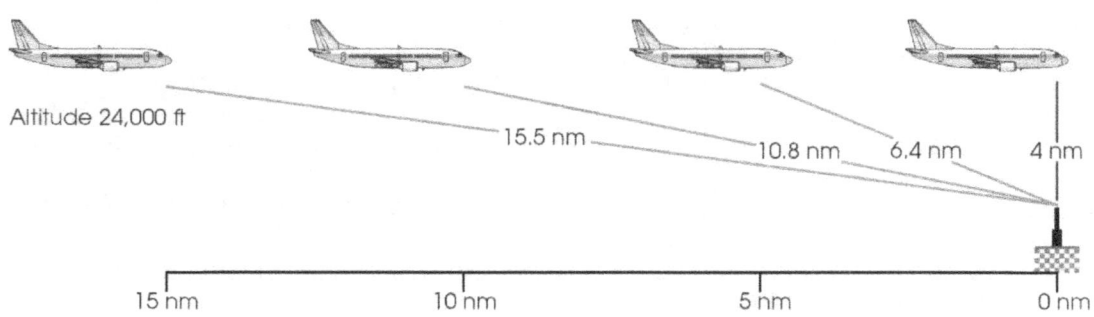

for an interrogation pulse to travel to the ground transponder and back is 2000 microseconds, the slant range is 158 nm (the ground transponder has a 50 microsecond delay, so total time is 1950 microseconds). The most accurate calculation of your ground speed will come from a DME on the flight route, meaning that you will be tracking directly to or from it.

The ground station can only respond to a certain number of interrogations in a given period of time. Normally, 30 pulse pairs are transmitted per second, but going up to 150 (for searching) allows up to 100 aircraft to interrogate the system before *beacon saturation* occurs - the ground station can only cope with 2700 pps. A DME experiencing difficulty with locking on will stay in search mode, but will reduce the PRF to up to 60 PPS after 15 000 pulse pairs have been transmitted.

X/Y Channels

DME stations use channels rather than frequencies because they are normally co-located* with a VOR or ILS. The channel is paired with a frequency.

Co-located means within 30 m and frequency paired within 600 m. *Associated* means that the DME callsign ends with a Z, and that they are more than 600 m apart or within 2000 feet of each other (the maximum distance between VOR and DME/TACAN installations with the same Morse ID is 600 m if used for enroute navigation).

X channels are the most common**, with the transponded signal 63 MHz higher than the received signal. Y stations reply at 63 MHz below, and the pulse pairs are differently spaced. The information should be on the chart, but if you only see the frequency, X channels are linked with VOR frequencies ending in 0 (116.70 = 114Y) and Y channels are for those ending in 5 (116.75 - 114X). In other words, X stations use whole number decimals (114.30), and Y beacons use halved decimals (114.35). In some places, the X is not shown after the channel, but the Y is, when relevant. There are 252 DME reply and 126 interrogation frequencies in the full TACAN range. Using X and Y Channels makes more efficient use of the bandwidth available and reduces interference.

**When the demand for VOR/DME stations increased and the frequency spacing between VORs was reduced from 0.1 MHz to 0.05 MHz, the number of DME channels naturally doubled, which is not a problem when channels and frequencies are paired but, for those people who could use DMEs separately (i.e. the military using TACAN) a workaround was required. They designated the old channels as X and the new ones as Y, reversing the 63 MHz interrogation and response frequencies.

DME is normally based with a VOR or TACAN and has a range of about 200 nm, ± 6, with an accuracy better than ½ nm or 3% of the distance, whichever is the greater (max range is determined by height). Thus, when the DME is co-located with a VOR, the two signals combined will give you a position based on a radial from the VOR and how far away on that radial you are.

Errors

Theoretically, 126 aircraft can use each station at a time, if none of them are scanning at the high rate. On average, however, we can assume that some aircraft will be attempting to lock on, so 100 aircraft is commonly accepted as the average number that can be handled at once. However, some RNAV systems alternate their DME interrogations between several stations, requiring a re-lock every minute or so, which means that they are interrogating at the high rate for much of the time. The ground stations will only reply to the 2700 strongest signals every second, so a large number of high-rate interrogations mean fewer aircraft can use each station.

If too many aircraft are interrogating it, the receiver will automatically be desensitised so it can hear and reply only to the strongest thus, busy airspace can result in shorter-than-normal DME reception range, particularly with lower-powered units. An aircraft DME in tracking mode that experiences a reduction in signal strength will switch to *memory mode* so it has something to work on until the signal gets better (display counters rotating mean that the receiver is conducting a range search).

Where the ground distance is less than or equal to 3 times the height, the inaccuracy is too much for the system. The difference is negligible for enroute navigation when the indicated distance in nm is more than the height of the aircraft above the DME in thousands of feet.

The accuracy of a position line, as required by ICAO at least 95% of the time, is ± 0.5 nm, or ± 3% of the aircraft's range if greater. As DME is the most accurate of the classic navigation aids, it is the preferred input for RNAV. Otherwise, assuming no saturation, the maximum range is limited by the line of sight formula. Most airborne equipment indicates a maximum of 200 nm, but some can reach to 300 nm, which is only really useful for Concorde (that's about 56,000 ft).

Range errors should not exceed **±0.25 nm plus 1.25% of the distance measured** so, at 100 nm, the maximum should not exceed **±1.5 nm**. The total system error for **DME-P** should not exceed 0.2 nm.

ILS 062 02 05

The Instrument Landing System is a pilot-interpreted *precision* approach aid because it includes tracking and slope guidance. It is currently the primary precision approach facility for civil aviation at all major airports, although no more will be installed in the US in favour of GPS approaches. The equipment is constantly monitored by ATC and calibration is carried out frequently by the authorities. If any limits are exceeded, transmissions will be stopped within 6 seconds The following components may be used to guide you down to a *Decision Height*:

- a **VHF transmitter** for **horizontal guidance** along the extended centreline (the *localiser*), with a 1.4° wide beam, at the far end of the runway (the upwind end), about 300m out, to stop it being an obstacle. The beam is about 700 feet wide at the threshold. If it does not go across the extended centreline within 30°, it is an *offset localiser*. The ILS frequency carrier is amplitude modulated.

- a **UHF transmitter** for **vertical guidance**, which usually produces a 3° *glideslope*, within about 120m of one side of the runway, typically about 300m from the threshold. The touchdown area is a little way in from the threshold so you have concrete to land on if you have a problem. The *Threshold Crossing Height* (TCH) is where the glideslope antenna should be to ensure that the wheels don't hit the ground if they hang too far below the cockpit, otherwise you will get a runway-assisted go-around. *Glideslope signals are only valid down to the lowest authorised DH*, so if you bust minima, you need to be aware that following the needles will just take you along the runway at that height.

- Up to three 75 Mhz **marker beacons**. The Middle Marker is typically 1000 m away from the threshold, and the outer marker 4 nm.
- high intensity **approach lights** for better visual guidance in the latter stages (typically 100 feet apart, up to 3000 feet from the end of the runway).
- radar monitoring.

Types Of Approach

Approaches are classified as to equipment on the aircraft and at the airport, plus pilot training and experience.

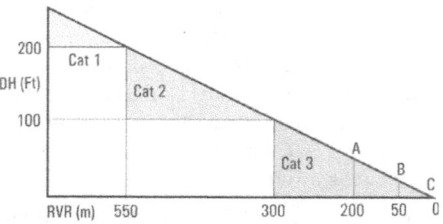

 This is the ICAO standard. PART OPS allows 75m for the Cat IIIb approach.

CATEGORY I

This is the least restrictive, and the one that most people in General Aviation will use. It uses a (barometric) Decision Height* of at least **200 feet** and an RVR of 550 m, with a high chance of success. Ceiling is not a factor.

*Where the localiser intercepts the glideslope.

CATEGORY II

This takes you further down, to 100 feet DH and 300m RVR. It needs special training under an approved syllabus in the Ops Manual. Qualifications are specific to type.

For Cat II (and III - see below), the aircraft must be certificated for Decision Heights below 200 ft, or none, and equipped as per regulations. A suitable system for recording approach and automatic landing success and failure must also be established and maintained to monitor safety. There must be at least 2 pilots, with **DH determined by radalt,** and the aerodrome must also be approved. Low visibility takeoffs in less than 150 m RVR (Cat A, B and C) or 200 m (Cat D) need approval.

You also likely need the following to be up and running:

- **Lighting**: approach, threshold, touchdown zone, centreline, runway edge and end lights
- **ILS**: localiser, glidepath and middle marker
- **RVR**: two transmissometers, one at the threshold, and at the mid-point
- **Power** - airport emergency power as the primary source for essential elements, with commercial power available within one second

CATEGORY III

A Cat III ILS glidepath transmitter provides reliable guidance information down to the surface of the runway.

- **IIIa** - A DH of less than 100' with 200m RVR
- **IIIb** - Below 50' DH (or none), and 75-200m RVR
- **IIIc** - Zero-zero

Any precision more than Cat II needs a high accuracy radio altimeter.

The Localiser

The localiser comes from two overlapping lobes of radio energy (notes) on VHF, the one on the left (yellow) during approach being A2 modulated at 90 Hz, and the other (blue) also A2 at 150 Hz, i.e. metric.

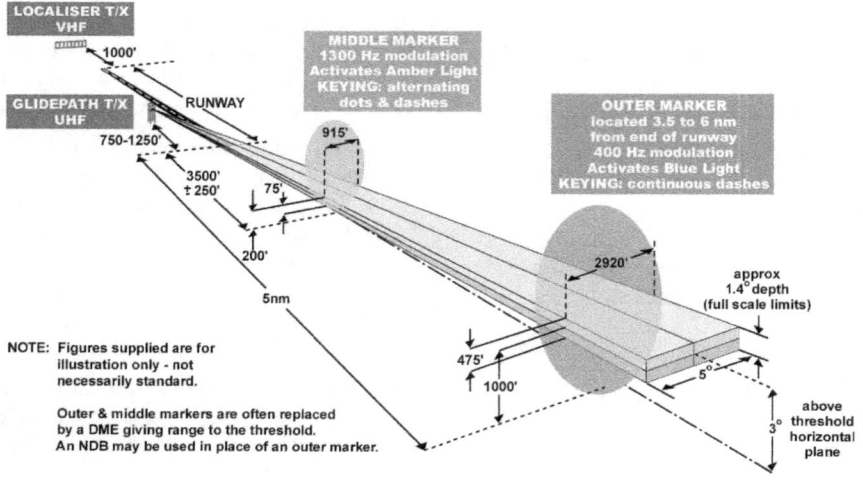

RADIO NAVIGATION
ILS

The principle of operation is that the *difference in depth of modulation*, or the ratio of the amplitude of the modulating waveform to that of the R/F carrier, determines the position of the needle. If the depth of modulation of both lobes appears to be the same, the receiver assumes you are on the ILS QDM in the centre, or following the *equisignal*. The greater the difference in modulation depths, the more the indicator needle is displaced. More 90 Hz than 150 Hz means fly right (and down).

Beam bends in the approach path are slight curves that can be followed by large aircraft.

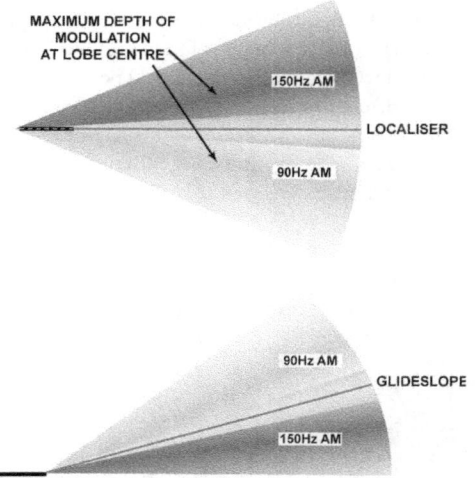

If the angular displacement of an aircraft doubles, so does the difference in Depth of Modulation.

 The impression given is that two narrowly focussed beams intersect to provide the guidance but the "beams" are created electronically *by the equipment in the aircraft* (that is, voltages are produced from the radio signals - they have to be at a minimum level to keep the Off flag away). This means you can get on-course or on-glidepath indications regardless of your position, as was found by an Air New Zealand 767 in July 2000, which got down to 400', *6 miles short of the runway* (check your distance and altitudes, and do *not* use equipment on test! In ILS test mode, you always get an on-glideslope indication without warning flags, irrespective of your position). The flags are operated by voltmeters in the indicator.

ICAO defines "established on course" as being within half full-scale deflection for an ILS or VOR/TACAN/RNAV/GPS procedure and within ±5° of the required bearing for the NDB. You are not established until you are within these limits.

Tip: When intercepting, double the track error, so if you are 4 dots off, turn by 4° until interception takes place, then turn on to the inbound track.

The frequency range for the localiser lies between 108.1-111.975 MHz (VHF), on *odd decimals* as this range is shared with the VOR, within which there will be 40 channels, so a typical frequency is 109.15 MHz. A three-letter ID is transmitted at regular intervals in Morse Code (at 1020 Hz). If the localiser alignment exceeds 3° of the runway heading, the first letter will be X. If it is 3° or less, the letter is I. The normal approach is called the *front course*, and is used with the other components of the system. The course line along the extended centreline in the opposite direction is called the *backcourse*. Unless your system has reverse-sensing capability (check for the B/C button on the autopilot), you have to do the opposite of what the needle says when inbound along the back course (as you would when outbound along the front course). On an HSI, the course arrow should be set to the front beam inbound course. Aside from the reverse sensing, backcourses are not used in UK because:

- There is no glideslope (so it is non-precision).
- It is less accurate.
- There are no markers.

In any case, you can't use them unless there is a published procedure.

Disregard glideslope indications on a backcourse, unless one is shown on the chart.

ILS is 4 times more sensitive than the VOR, so full needle deflection is 2½°, as opposed to 10° (½° per dot). One dot means you are 300 feet off course at the Outer Marker or FAF, and 100 feet off at the Middle Marker.

Tip: When coming down the glideslope, don't forget to adjust your heading as the wind slows down and backs nearer to ground level (on an airfield near the coast, you will also be affected by sea breezes. At Southend, for example, you can suddenly get a tailwind halfway down the approach, followed by a headwind). This is particularly important for helicopters because the ILS was originally based on fixed wing characteristics. When very slow, large drift correction angles make it hard to follow a localiser.

Localiser errors are due to ground reflections. *Scalloping* means that the beam direction varies from side to side of the intended approach path.

The Glidepath

Glidepath transmissions are done in a similar way, but on UHF (between 328.6-335.4 MHz), with the frequencies paired with localiser ones (i.e. the glidepath frequency is automatically tuned when the localiser frequency is selected). The upper lobe is the 90 Hz yellow one, but ground reflections from the lower lobe produce *side-lobes* which can give false indications*. These should be above the real glidepath, but you should still be aware of them. Watch for high rates of descent, and check altitudes against distances - full deflection is only 0.7°, and one dot means 50 feet at the Outer Marker (around 8 feet at the Middle Marker).

The glidepath is set to cross the threshold at 50 feet (the ILS Reference Point).

*The 150 Hz signal can be received above the intended glideslope, at twice the normal angle, i.e. 6° instead of 3°.

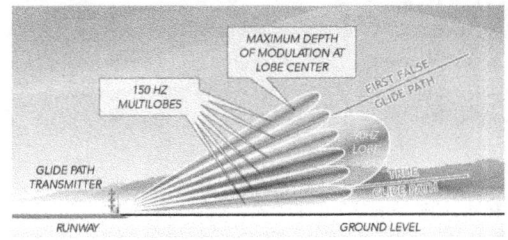

EASA Professional Pilot Studies 11-47

This is why the glideslope is captured from below (3-10 nm from the threshold) to avoid false readings.

The pattern is achieved through the interaction of directly radiated waves with those reflected from the ground. As the number of lobes increases with the height of an antenna above the ground, and the angle of elevation of the lowest decreases with height, two antennae, one above the other, are used to give the best effects. The lower one radiates at 90 Hz and the upper one 150 Hz. By adjusting the amplitude of the 150 Hz carrier, the lowest lobes of the two antennae can be made to intersect at the chosen glideslope angle (usually 3°). The first false equisignal should not be lower than 10°, so there should be a low risk of confusion. Because they are offset from the runway (to stop aircraft hitting them), suitable phase adjustments must be made to keep you on the glideslope. This is achieved by moving the lower antenna a few inches further away from the runway.

ILS transmitters are sensitive to vehicles, etc., around them, which is why there are *ILS Critical Areas*, in which no aircraft or vehicles are allowed to move during ILS operations. The same applies to *ILS Sensitive Areas* in low visibilities (Cat II/III). The reason why pre-takeoff holding areas are sometimes further from the active runway when ILS Category 2 and 3 landing procedures are in progress than during good weather operations is that aircraft manoeuvring near the runway may disturb the guidance signals. Look for the sign like the one left and below, and the *B Pattern* next to it on the taxiway:

 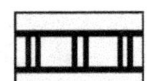

The signals received in the cockpit are translated onto an instrument like the one on the left, below. The vertical needle shows whether you are left or right of the localiser and the horizontal one tells you whether you are high or low in relation to the glideslope. In the example, you are on the glideslope and *left* of the localiser, so you "chase the cross" to get back on, in this case, fly level to the right.

On the right is a picture of a *Horizontal Situation Indicator* (HSI). Glideslope indicators are on the side.

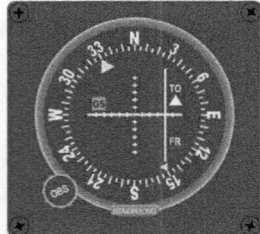 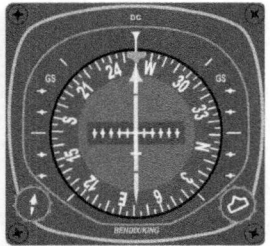

 The OBS doesn't work when the VOR instrument is used for the ILS, because it is only radiating one course, but it is usually set to the inbound course for neatness.

 Glidepath means any part of the glideslope intersecting the localiser.

Tip: When using an HSI, a smooth intercept can be obtained by keeping the top of the CDI bar next to the lubber line.

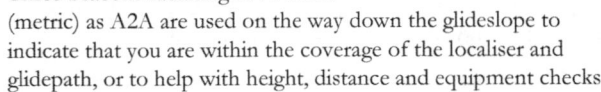

Markers & Beacons

Three beacons radiating at 75 MHz (metric) as A2A are used on the way down the glideslope to indicate that you are within the coverage of the localiser and glidepath, or to help with height, distance and equipment checks.

The Outer Marker is at about 4 miles (where you should be around 1500 feet, when the glideslope meets the minimum holding altitude), which often coincides with, or is replaced by, an NDB or DME. The Middle Marker is found at about ½ mile or 1050 m from the threshold (where you should be at around 200 feet), using a quarter of the power of the Outer Marker, and the inner marker is just before the threshold, at DH, if it is there (it's mainly for Cat II approaches). It uses a tenth of the Outer Marker power. Vertical beams are used to stop interference.

The markers don't have to be tuned, as they have their own identification.

 The outer marker produces a blue flashing light within a few degrees of the overhead. Each vertical dot is about 50 ft.

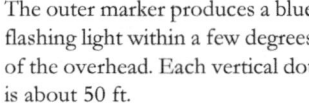 The middle marker is amber, where each vertical dot is equal to about 8 feet.

 The inner marker is white, if used.

 The markers beep as well as flash, using different tones (400, 1300 and 3000 Hz if you really want to know) in Morse. The OM uses two dashes per second, the MM dot-dash-dot-dash at two per second, and the inner marker four dots at 6 per second.

High allows you to pick up the signals a bit sooner, but *Low* is a bit more precise on positioning.

A DME installation at the threshold can replace the markers.

RADIO NAVIGATION
ILS

Lighting

This is meant to help with the transition from instruments to visual, although they are not actually a requirement for the system. However, if lighting is not present, the minima will be increased somewhat.

CATEGORY I

This is what you might see as you come out of the clag with a Cat I approach:

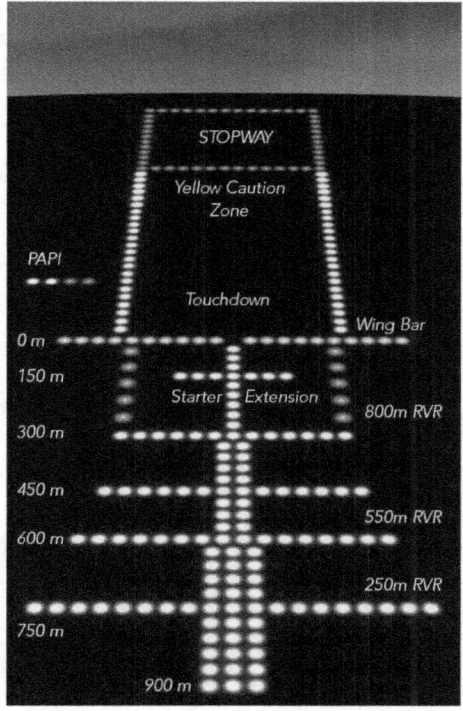

The lights begin 900 m from the threshold, with lateral bars at 150 m intervals. The figures on the right are what you might expect to see from the DH at 900 m with RVR values of 250 m, 550 m and 800 m.

Thus, an RVR of 900 m should let you (just about) see the threshold from the DH. One of 250 m would let you see just one bar of the ALS, which is hardly anything on which to base a visual glide path. In fact, it would be pretty much impossible to land safely.

If you perform a night ILS with an RVR of 550 m, you should get the minimum adequate visibility from the approach lights at the DH. However, it will be near zero outside of that, so taxying could be interesting.

Gradients, Etc

To guarantee obstacle clearance, there is usually a required climb (200 feet per nautical mile) or descent gradient (usually 320 ft/nm for a 3° glideslope) when leaving or arriving at an airfield.

The obstacle free path is based on a climb rate of 200 ft per minute after crossing the end of the runway at least 35 ft above the ground.

You must also be able to climb to 400 feet above the airfield elevation before needing a turn.

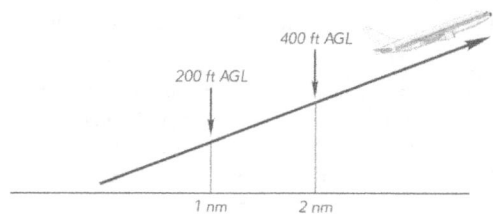

However, depending on the surrounding area, the required gradients may be different - you may well need a steeper one for a non-precision approach in the mountains.

These SIDs require a minimum climb gradient of 304' per NM (3%) up to 8000'						
Gnd speed - KT	75	100	150	200	250	300
304' per NM	380	508	780	1013	1288	1510

In the normal case, to find out the minimum safe altitude at the 5 nm point after takeoff (i.e. the height required to meet the gradient), set up the $^{200}/_1$ ratio on the flight computer and you will see the answer on the outside scale opposite the 5 on the inner scale - 1000 feet.

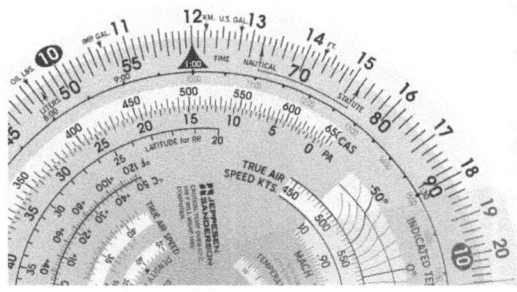

But what vertical speed might you need? At 60 kts in the above diagram, it is 200 feet per minute. Put another way, at 60 knots, **the climb rate equals the gradient** so, if you need to maintain 304 feet per minute, that is what the climb rate should be.

The table above converts the required gradient (in ft per nm) to the climb rate (in ft per min) for specified groundspeeds, but if you set up the relevant ratio on the flight computer, you can find the corresponding rates against vertical speed yourself.

For example, $^{60}/_{304}$ means 455 feet per minute at 90 kts.

If you know your groundspeed and vertical speed you can work backwards to find your gradient so, at 120 knots at 900 feet per minute, set up $^{120}/_{900}$ and look opposite 60 on the outside scale to find 450 feet per nm.

Having found that, you can find out the altitude at a specified distance - set up $^{450}/_1$ (in this case) and the answer is on the outside scale opposite the distance.

RADIO NAVIGATION
ILS

RATE OF DESCENT

Radar will give you a distance to touchdown so you can calculate a smooth rate of descent. You don't want to be making sudden drops at the last minute to make the glideslope and risk spilling the coffee.

Glidepath gradient calculations are variations on the 1 in 60 rule - the standard 3° glidepath is an ROD of 300 ft per nm, or 100 feet per degree. 3° slopes can be calculated by multiplying your groundspeed by 5, as derived from:

```
ROD = GS x 10
       2
```

At 60 kts, the ROC/ROD equals the gradient.

If the speed changes on the approach, a strong headwind causes a *decrease* in groundspeed and rate of descent, and a tailwind does the opposite. Every 10 kts decrease in groundspeed on a 3° glideslope means a decrease in ROD of 50 fpm, and *vice versa*.

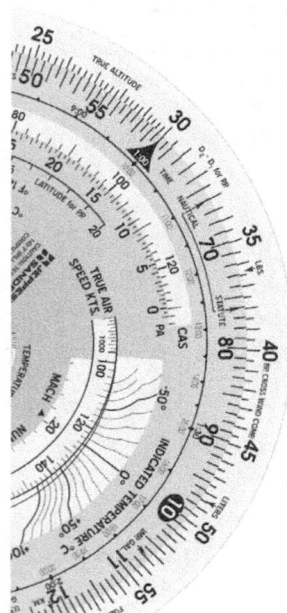

You can use the slide rule on the flight computer to solve these as a proportion problem. If you put the 60 kt index on the slide rule against 30 (3°) on the outer scale, you can read 450 fpm against 90 kts, and so on……..

For a 2.5° glideslope, just put the index against 25, or 35 for a 3.5° glideslope. The rate of descent required to maintain a 3.25° glide slope at a groundspeed of 140 kts is approximately 800 ft/min.

Range & Coverage

Outside the published range, you should not normally receive signals.

LOCALISERS

The localiser range and coverage is:

- 8° up to 10 nm
- 35° either side of the centreline up to 17 nm
- 10° either side of the centreline up to 25 nm

These may be reduced to 18 nm, 10° off the centre line if there is satisfactory alternate coverage within the intermediate approach area.

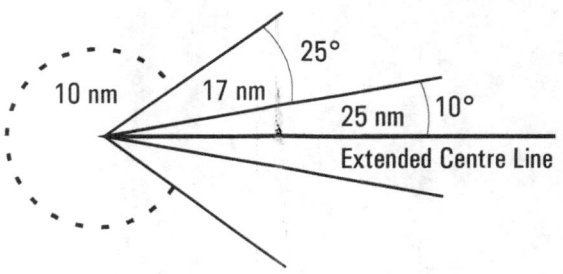

GLIDESLOPES

You should be able to receive the glideslope signal up to 10 nm. The approximate angular coverage of reliable navigation information for a 3° ILS glide path out to 10 nm is 1.35° above the horizontal to 5.25° above the horizontal and 8° each side of the localiser centreline. An aircraft tracking to intercept the localiser inbound on the approach side, outside the published ILS coverage angle may receive false course indications.

HEIGHT ON THE GLIDESLOPE

Use the formula:

```
Height = GP Angle x dist to go in ft
              60
```

The formula refers to the touchdown point. If the distance is quoted from the threshold (like with DME) add 50 feet because you will be at the screen height.

If the glideslope is published as a percentage, place the 10 index on the inner scale of the flight computer and against the percentage value on the outer scale, reading the degree value on the outer scale against the 60 index on the inner scale. In the picture above, the gradient is 5%.

The source of this material is the ICAO Manual of Radiotelephony, DOC 9432

COMMUNICATIONS 12

Pilots need a radio licence to use the airwaves, which lasts for life and requires no revalidation. Although your use of the airwaves is limited, you still need to know the rules so that other people don't suffer.

In Aviation, using non-standard phraseology can be fatal. The phrase:

"Advise ready for taxi, use caution, company pushing out"

is not a clearance to pushback, even though it might sound like one. Similarly, an instruction to conduct runup checks on the other side of a runway you would have to cross to get there is not a clearance to do so.

As further examples: The words *"request Federal Aid"* in one message were interpreted to mean that a hijack was in process, rather than the intended request for FAA clearance expressed in a joking fashion. The figures 210 by themselves could mean a Flight Level, a heading, or a speed to be maintained.

Communications should be restricted to what is required for the task in hand. Obscene language is prohibited, and using the air-to-air frequency to talk about personal matters is highly unprofessional. This is because anyone with an emergency can't send a MAYDAY until you have stopped talking. The only time you can interfere with another station is when you have to send a higher priority message (see *Categories Of Messages*, below). It is also an offence to use a callsign for a purpose other than that for which it is notified.

Within about 200 nm of an ATC station (depends on your height), VHF is normally used - over a 1 hour flight, it is easily possible to use over 10 frequencies. Unless there are relay stations along your route, or there are special arrangements to patch into the telephone system, as used in Canada, after that distance you will need to use HF. When even HF is no use (it is often drowned out by static), messages are often relayed between aircraft as a professional courtesy.

One of the main reasons for RTF congestion is having to send extra messages because people don't use the radio properly, which includes using *concise and unambiguous phraseology*. Controllers are also not supposed to transmit during takeoff, or on the last part of final approach or the landing roll, unless safety is a factor (you are working hardest at these times and don't need distractions). Luckily, most of them realise that you can't change frequency in the hover.

These points should be borne in mind:

- Always use standard phraseology
- Maintain radio discipline by not using the system unnecessarily and by using unambiguous language
- Monitor the frequencies being used
- Pass all information relevant to the phase of flight
- Wait and listen before transmitting on a new frequency
- If it's been quiet for a while, check the frequency
- Set the clearance given, not the one expected
- Note down any clearances
- **Check** if you are unsure!

You are bound to preserve the *secrecy of communications*. That is, you may not say anything about, or even the existence of, any transmissions received, transmitted or intercepted by a radio station, except to whoever is supposed to receive it in the first place, or a properly appointed official, which may be someone who operates a retransmission service (this does not apply to distress messages, or those relating to safety, such as severe weather, or addressed to *All Stations*). Messages should be as brief as possible, consistent with getting the point across. Thinking about what you are going to say before you speak will help with this - if it is a long message (say filing a flight plan), write it down first, and break frequently, in case anyone is trying to get an emergency message out.

Naturally, a continuous listening watch should be maintained at all times, for airmanship, but especially when transiting controlled airspace during notified hours of watch. You must report your position and height on entering and just before leaving an ATZ.

Due to licence restrictions, aircraft equipment is meant to have as little power (around 250 watts) and as few controls as possible, including displays, so some frequencies may not be completely shown - 122.075, for example, comes up as 122.07 (usually, you will pull one of the knobs to get the extra bit). In fact, everything should be preset.

The standard channel spacing is 25 kHz, so a 760-channel transceiver is necessary (if the last digit displayed includes 2 or 7, your equipment is capable of 25 kHz operations). In some areas of Europe, channel spacing has been reduced to 8.33 kHz, especially in upper airspace (above FL 245). This is an awkward channel spacing, so the frequencies don't fall into convenient round numbers, so they are referred to by a kind of shorthand.

COMMUNICATIONS
Definitions

Under CAP 413, all six figures shall be used when identifying frequencies irrespective of whether they are 25 kHz or 8.33 kHz spaced. Exceptionally, when the final two digits of the frequency are both zero, only the first four digits need be given. Technically, an 8.33 kHz frequency is a "channel", but the word "channel" is not used in RTF:

- To indicate 8.33 kHz capability: *AFFIRM EIGHT POINT THREE THREE*
- To indicate lack of 8.33 kHz capability: *NEGATIVE EIGHT POINT THREE THREE*

Note: *Decimal* is used when reading back a frequency, whereas *point* is used when describing a frequency spacing such as eight point three three.

The primary medium for aeronautical communications is VHF (AM) in the frequency range between 118 - 136.975 MHz. Its official classification is A3E.

The *Squelch* quietens down the output when no signal is being received, so you don't get continuous earfuls of white noise. A signal coming in cancels this and activates the audio (a variable squelch merely determines the signal level when this occurs). The correct procedure with the Squelch, therefore, is to rotate the knob until the hiss just stops, and leave it there, although it is true to say that this will also hide a weak signal, so lifting the squelch may help you hear it, if you are far away.

There are one or two points about radios that aren't often taught properly during training. The first is to wait a split second to speak after pressing the transmit button, which gives all the relays in the system a chance to switch over so your message can get through in full, that is, not clipping the first bit. Secondly, whenever you get a frequency change *en route*, not only should you write it down on your Nav Log (because of short term memory limitations), but change to the new frequency *on the other box*, so you alternate between radios. This way, you have something to go back to if you can't get through on the new one.

Primary reference documents for this subject are ICAO Docs 4444 (Air Traffic Management), Doc 9432, and Annex 10.

English must be used for air–ground communications unless an alternative has been arranged with ATC.

DEFINITIONS

- **Absolute Minima**. A theoretical value, calculated according to the approach and facilities available at the aerodrome, which will be equal to or less than the specified operating RVR for a category A aircraft carrying out that instrument approach.
- **ACARS**. *Aircraft Communications Addressing and Reporting System*. An onboard, computerised communications system that provides a digital, voiceless datalink between aircraft and their operating companies using VHF radios. It is typically linked to the FMC, so flight plans can be uploaded easily (takeoff parameters are typically transmitted en route to the runway, and clearances can also be transmitted).
- **ADS-B**. *Automatic Dependent Surveillance Broadcast* is a transponder based system that generates radar-like displays for pilots and controllers that show traffic, weather and terrain in real time. It is an advisory system that does not replace TCAS, but is useful for situations where nothing else would even be available.
- **Advisory Area**. A designated area where air traffic advisory service is available.
- **Advisory Route**. A designated route along which air traffic advisory service is available (ICAO).
- **Aerodrome**. Any area of land or water designed, equipped, set apart or commonly used for the landing and departure of aircraft, including those capable of descending or climbing vertically, but not including any area that has been abandoned for those purposes and has not been resumed.
- **Aerodrome Control Service**. Air traffic control service for aerodrome traffic.
- **Aerodrome Flight Information Service** (AFIS). A flight information service provided to aerodrome traffic.
- **Aerodrome Operating Minima** In relation to the operation of an aircraft at an aerodrome, the cloud ceiling and runway visual range for takeoff, and the decision height or minimum descent height, runway visual range and visual reference for landing, which are the minimum for the operation of that aircraft at that aerodrome.
- **Aerodrome Traffic**. All traffic on the manoeuvring area of an aerodrome and all aircraft flying in the vicinity of an aerodrome (ICAO).
- **Aerodrome Traffic Zone**. A 2 nm circular airspace round an aerodrome notified for Rule 39 (of the UK ANO), unless within that of a controlling aerodrome, with the longest runway less than 1850 metres, from the surface to 2000 ft agl or msl when offshore. If the longest runway is greater than 1850 metres, the radius of the circle becomes 2.5 nm. Offshore, it is 1.5 nm.
- **Aeronautical Mobile Service**. A mobile service between aeronautical stations and aircraft stations, or between aircraft stations, in which survival craft stations may participate; emergency position-indicating radio beacon stations may also participate in this service on designated distress and emergency frequencies (ICAO).
- **Aeronautical Station**. A *land* station in the aeronautical mobile service, that is, a transmitting or receiving node, on land, a ship or a platform at sea, or a satellite (one would logically include *in the air*, but it would appear not). Normally, control is exercised by the ground station (meaning that you must do what they tell you), except for distress calls, which are controlled by the station initiating the call. Between aircraft, the one *called* has control.
- **Airborne Collision Avoidance System** (ACAS). An aircraft system based on SSR transponder signals which operates independently of groundbased equipment to

provide advice to the pilot on potential conflicting aircraft that are equipped with SSR transponders.

- **Aircraft Station**. A mobile station in the aeronautical mobile service on board an aircraft.
- **Air-Ground Communications**. 2-way communications between aircraft and stations or locations on the surface of the Earth.
- **Air/Ground Communication Service**. One provided from an aerodrome to give information to pilots of aircraft flying near it by means of radio signals. The term *air/ground communications service unit* shall be construed accordingly (ANO).
- **AIRPROX**. A situation in which, in the opinion of a pilot or controller, the distance between aircraft as well as their relative positions and speed have been such that the safety of the aircraft involved was or may have been compromised (ICAO).
- **Air Traffic**. All aircraft in flight or operating on the manoeuvring area of an aerodrome (ICAO).
- **Air Traffic Control Clearance**. Authorisation for an aircraft to proceed under conditions specified by an air traffic control unit (ICAO).
- **Air Traffic Service** (ATS). A generic term meaning a flight information service, alerting service, air traffic advisory service, air traffic control service, area control service, approach control service or aerodrome control service.
- **Airway**. A control area or portion thereof established in the form of a corridor (ICAO).
- **Altitude**. The vertical distance of a level, a point or an object considered as a point, measured from mean sea level (ICAO).
- **Area Control Centre**. An air traffic control unit established to provide an area control service to aircraft flying within a notified flight information region which are not receiving an aerodrome control service or an approach control service.
- **ATS Surveillance Service**. One provided directly by means of an ATS surveillance system (ICAO).
- **Automatic Terminal Information Service** (ATIS). The automatic provision of current, routine information to arriving and departing aircraft throughout 24 hours or a specified portion thereof (ICAO).
- **Base Turn**. One executed by an aircraft during the initial approach between the end of the outbound track and the beginning of the intermediate or final approach track. The tracks are not reciprocal .
- **Basic Service**. A Basic Service is an ATS provided for the purpose of giving advice and information useful for the safe and efficient conduct of flights. This may include weather information, changes of serviceability of facilities, conditions at aerodromes, general airspace activity information, and any other information likely to affect safety. The avoidance of other traffic is solely the pilot's responsibility.
- **Blind Transmission**. A transmission from one station where 2-way communications cannot be established, but it is believed that the called station can receive it. The transmission should be preceded with the words "Blind Transmission" or "Transmitting Blind" and an indication of the time of the next transmission.
- **Broadcast**. Information relating to air navigation that is not specific to a station or stations
- **Clearance Limit**. The point to which an aircraft is granted an air traffic control clearance. A clearance limit shall be described by specifying the name of the appropriate significant point, or aerodrome or controlled airspace boundary (ICAO).
- **Control Area**. Controlled airspace which has been further notified as a control area and which extends upwards from a notified altitude or flight level (ANO).
- **Controlled Airspace**. That which has been notified as Class A, Class B, Class C, Class D or Class E airspace (ANO).
- **Control Zone**. Controlled airspace which has been further notified as a control zone and which extends upwards from the surface (ANO).
- **CPDLC**. Originally developed for use over the Atlantic and Pacific Oceans, *Controller-Pilot DataLink Communications* effectively allows pilots and controllers to text each other, as an addition to the more traditional VHF and HF methods, which reduces congestion and blocked frequencies, assuming they are available in the first place. Messages are received in the same way as ACARS - crews send a logon message to start things off.
- **Cruising Level**. A level maintained during a significant portion of a flight (ICAO).
- **Decision Altitude/Height**. In relation to the operation of an aircraft at an aerodrome means a specified altitude/height in a precision approach at which a missed approach must be initiated if the required visual reference to continue the approach to land has not been established (ANO).
- **Deconfliction Service**. A surveillance based ATS where, as well as the provisions of a Basic Service, the controller provides specific surveillance derived traffic information and issues headings and/or levels aimed at achieving planned deconfliction minima against all observed aircraft in Class F/G airspace, or for positioning and/or sequencing. However, the avoidance of other traffic is ultimately the pilot's responsibility.
- **Elevation**. The vertical distance of a point or level on, or affixed to, the surface of the Earth measured from mean sea level (ICAO).
- **Estimated Time of Arrival**. For IFR flights, the time at which it is estimated that an aircraft will arrive over a designated point that is defined by reference to navigation aids, from which it is intended that an instrument approach procedure will be commenced, or, if no navigation aid is associated with the aerodrome, the time at which the aircraft will arrive over the aerodrome.

For VFR flights, the time at which it is estimated that the aircraft will arrive over the aerodrome (ICAO).

- **Flight Information Service Officer** (FISO). A Flight Information Service Officer at any aerodrome or area control centre.
- **Flight Level**. One of a series of levels of equal atmospheric pressure, separated by notified intervals and expressed as the number of hundreds of feet which would be indicated at that level on a pressure altimeter calibrated under ISA and set to 1013.2 hPa (ANO).
- **Flight Plan**. Specified information provided to air traffic services units, relative to an intended flight or portion of a flight of an aircraft (ICAO).
- **General Air Traffic**. Flights operating under civil air traffic procedures.
- **Heading**. The direction in which the longitudinal axis of an aircraft is pointed, usually expressed in degrees from North (true, magnetic, compass or grid) (ICAO).
- **Height**. The vertical distance of a level, a point, or an object considered as a point measured from a specified datum (ICAO).
- **Holding Point**. A speech abbreviation used in radiotelephony phraseology having the same meaning as Taxiway Holding Position or Runway Holding Position.
- Identification. The situation which exists when the position indication of a particular aircraft is seen on a situation display and positively identified.
- **IFR Flight**. One conducted under Instrument Flight Rules (RoA).
- **Instrument Meteorological Conditions** (IMC). Weather precluding flight under Visual Flight Rules.
- **Known Traffic**. That which the current flight details and intentions of which are known to the controller concerned through direct communication or co-ordination.
- **Level**. A generic term relating to the vertical position of an aircraft in flight and meaning height, altitude or flight level (ICAO).
- **Level Bust**. Any deviation from assigned altitude, height or flight level in excess of 300 feet.
- **Minimum Descent Altitude/Height**. The altitude/height in a non-precision approach below which descent may not be made without the required visual reference (ANO).
- **Missed Approach Point** (MAPt). The point in an instrument approach procedure at or before which the prescribed missed approach procedure must be initiated in order to ensure that the minimum obstacle clearance is not infringed.
- **Missed Approach Procedure**. That to be followed if an approach cannot be continued.
- **Procedural Service**. An ATS service where, as well as the provisions of a Basic Service, the controller provides vertical, lateral, longitudinal and time instructions which, if complied with, shall achieve deconfliction minima against other aircraft in the Procedural Service. Neither traffic information nor deconfliction advice can be passed with respect to unknown traffic.
- **Procedure Turn**. A manoeuvre in which a turn is made away from a designated track, followed by a turn in the opposite direction to permit the aircraft to intercept and proceed along the reciprocal of the designated track (ICAO).
- **Radar Approach**. One in which the final approach phase is executed under the direction of a controller using radar (ICAO).
- **Radar Contact**. The situation which exists when the radar position of a particular aircraft is seen and identified on a situation display (ICAO).
- **Reporting Point**. A specified geographical location in relation to which the position of an aircraft can be reported (ICAO).
- **Runway**. A defined rectangular area on a land aerodrome prepared for the landing and takeoff of aircraft (ICAO).
- **Runway Visual Range**. The range over which the pilot of an aircraft on the centre line of a runway can expect to see the runway surface markings, or the lights delineating it or identifying its centre line (ICAO).
- **SAFETYCOM**. A common frequency (135.475MHz) made available for use at aerodromes where no other frequency is allocated, to enable pilots to broadcast their intentions to other aircraft that may be operating on, or in the vicinity of, an aerodrome.
- **Signal Area**. An area on an aerodrome used for the display of ground signals.
- **Significant Point**. A specified geographical location used in defining an ATS route or the flight path of an aircraft and for other navigational and ATS purposes (ICAO).
- **Special VFR Flight**. One made in a control zone that is designated as Class A airspace, or is in any other control zone in IMC or at night, in respect of which ATC has given permission for the flight to be made under special instructions given by that unit, instead of under IFR and, in the course of which flight, remaining clear of cloud and with the surface in sight (RoA).
- **Straight Ahead**. In departure clearances, the term means *track the extended runway centreline*. When given in Missed Approach Procedures, it means *continue on the final approach track*.
- **Terminal Control Area**. A control area normally established at the confluence of airways near one or more major aerodromes (ICAO).
- **Threshold**. The beginning of that portion of the runway that is usable for landing (ICAO).
- **Traffic Alert and Collision Avoidance System** (TCAS). See *Airborne Collision Avoidance System (ACAS)*.

- **Traffic Service**. A surveillance ATS where, as well as the provisions of a Basic Service, the controller provides specific surveillance derived traffic information to assist the pilot in avoiding other traffic. Controllers may provide headings and/or levels for the purposes of positioning and/or sequencing; however, the controller is not required to achieve deconfliction minima, and the avoidance of other traffic is ultimately the pilot's responsibility.
- **Vectoring**. Provision of navigational guidance to aircraft in the form of specific headings, based on the use of an ATS surveillance system (ICAO).
- **VFR Flight**. One conducted under the Visual Flight Rules (RoA).
- **Visual Meteorological Conditions** (VMC). Weather permitting flight under Visual Flight Rules (ANO).
- **Waypoint**. A specified geographical position used to define an Area Navigation Route or the flight path of an aircraft using it.

ATC Abbreviations

Note: Some abbreviations, such as ILS, RVR, QNH or CAVOK, may be used as read instead of being spelt phonetically. Those not listed here are either covered in the text or in the Glossary.

- **CAVOK**. Cloud and Visibility OK, or more than 10 K visibility and no cloud below 5 000 feet
- **RNAV**. Area Navigation
- **HJ**. Hours of operation - sunrise to sunset
- **HN**. Hours of operation - sunset to sunrise
- **HX**. No specific hours of operation
- **H24**. Hours of operation - continuous day and night service
- **IMC**: Instrument Meteorological Conditions
- **VMC**: Visual Meteorological Conditions
- **AIS**. Aeronautical Information Service
- **SELCAL**. Selective Calling. Allows aircraft to be contacted on VHF or HF frequencies that are not being monitored by the flight crew.
- **FEW** = 1 to 2 oktas of cloud
- **SCT**, or scattered = 3 to 4 oktas
- **BKN**, or broken = 5 to 7 oktas
- **OVC**, or overcast = 8 oktas)
- **SKC** = Sky Clear

Q CODES

These are a hangover from the old wireless telegraphy days when Morse Code was used, partly to reduce ambiguities between pilots using different languages, but also to reduce the transmission time. They are not officially for voice transmissions, but they are still used:

- **QFE** is used near an airfield, particularly in the circuit, and is the pressure read directly from the altimeter when on the ground at an airfield
- **QNH** is used for general transit elsewhere, below the transition altitude. It is the QFE converted to a pressure that would theoretically exist at sea level at that point - this is done because reporting stations are not all at the same level. You add the pressure change for elevation above sea level on a standard day. The QFE is reduced to MSL using ISA temperatures and lapse rates. It is forecast for one or two hours ahead over large areas
- **QNE** is the "standard" setting of 1013.2 hPa (or 29.92") for Flight Levels above transition altitude. Flight Levels are surfaces of constant atmospheric pressure related to a datum of 1013.2 hPa
- **QFF** is the QFE reduced to MSL using the *actual* temperature at the surface (between there and sea level it is assumed to be constant). QFF allows accurate surface charts to be drawn. It is equal to QNH at sea level, regardless of temperature. When above MSL and warmer than ISA, it will be less than QNH, and more when the temperature is colder than ISA (the opposite below MSL)
- **QDM** - magnetic bearing to
- **QDR** - magnetic bearing from
- **QUJ** - true bearing to
- **QTE** - true bearing from

To request a True Bearing, the correct phraseology is:

True Bearing, True Bearing, Callsign, Request True Bearing, Callsign

Accuracy Of Bearings

Class	Bearing	Position
A	±2°	5 nm
B	±5°	20 nm
C	±10°	50 nm
D	>10°	>50 nm

COMMUNICATIONS
Categories Of Message

CATEGORIES OF MESSAGE

Messages must be dealt with in this order:

- Distress
- Urgency
- Direction Finding
- Flight Safety (ATC messages, avoiding weather)
- Meteorological
- Flight Regularity (parts and materials)
- UN Charter
- Government messages
- Service communications
- All others

True Bearing, True Bearing, G-PACO, Request True Bearing

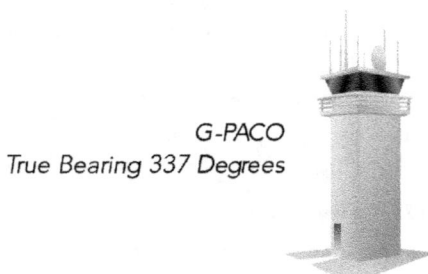

G-PACO True Bearing 337 Degrees

OPERATING PROCEDURES

A message consists of four parts: The *Callup*, The *Reply*, The *Message* and The *Acknowledgement*.

Note: An inexperienced pilot may use the word *Tyro* when speaking with a military controller, who will then speak slowly and carefully in words of one syllable.

Morse Code

Although the codes (see below) are printed on maps, etc., it's still a good idea to learn them, even if only to keep your job in an airline (many make it a requirement to have at least 6 words a minute). It also stops you peering at your map in the murk and moving your head around too much. Amateur radio clubs are a good source of training materials. Starting off at a high speed is best, with the simplest letters. E, for example, is one dot (*dit*). Listen to a stream of Morse, picking out that letter only, then add another, like T, which is a dash (*dah*), then I (2 dots), M (2 dashes) and so on. In a few days you can be up to 20 wpm.

Phonetic Alphabet

NUMBERS

Number	Speech	
0	ZERO	*The reason you might say *Two Thousand Four Hundred* rather than *Two Four Zero Zero* is that it can be construed as *To Four Zero Zero*, as in *Cleared To Four Zero Zero*
1	WUN	
2	TOO	
3	TREE	
4	FOWER	
5	FIFE	
6	SICKS	
7	SEVEN	
8	AIT	
9	NINER	

Numbers (as used for altitude, cloud height, visibility and RVR information) should generally be spoken individually, except for whole thousands (or hundreds) where they occur as round figures. 65 is therefore *six-five*, while 2000 is *two thousand*. Eleven thousand is *One One Thousand*. In other words, combinations of thousands and whole hundreds must be transmitted by pronouncing each digit in the number of thousands, followed by the word *Thousand*, followed by the number of hundreds, followed by the word *Hundred*. For example:

- Altitude 800 (Eight Hundred)
- 1,500 (One Thousand Five Hundred)*
- 6,715 (Six Seven One Five)
- 12,000 (One Two Thousand)
- 200 (Two Hundred)

Use the word *decimal (daysimal)* when you need a decimal point - *one one six decimal two* means 116.2 (the word *decimal* is an ICAO word, replaced with *point* in the USA).

Altitude above sea level is expressed in thousands of feet, plus hundreds, but flight levels use separate digits, thus 2500 is said as *two thousand five hundred*, but FL 100 is *flight level one zero zero*.* You would express a heading separately, e.g. *two five zero* for 250°.

Note: In UK, the word *To* is not used with flight levels:

Climb Flight Level 100

although the ICAO standard is to use it. This is to prevent it being mistaken for the number two. However, *To* is used with climb and descent instructions relating to heights or altitudes, followed by the relevant word.

*This ICAO standard is not used in UK. Instead, Flight Levels are expressed in hundreds, as in *one hundred, two hundred*, etc., as an effort against level busts. Flight levels below FL 100 are referred to as 2-digit numbers, e.g. *Flight Level Eight Zero*, to reduce the risk of confusion with a heading, which might be *Zero Eight Zero*.

COMMUNICATIONS
Operating Procedures

LETTERS

To make transmissions clearer, letters are pronounced in certain ways, as shown in the table below. Speak all words plainly and clearly, with none of them running together and no accentuation. Do not shout, or speak too quickly. Although the phraseology can be a bit longwinded (*day-si-mal* for decimal, for example), and you may feel a bit stupid pronouncing some of the words, remember they are that way to reduce ambiguity, which would have been handy in Tenerife when two 747s collided with each other because the clearances got confused (see *Human Factors*).

Letter	Word	Speech	Morse
A	Alpha	ALFAH	·—
B	Bravo	BRAHVOH	—···
C	Charlie	CHARLEE	—·—·
D	Delta	DELLTAH	—··
E	Echo	ECKOH	·
F	Foxtrot	FOCKSTROT	··—·
G	Golf	GOLF	——·
H	Hotel	HOTELL	····
I	India	INDEAH	··
J	Juliet	JEWLEEETT	·———
K	Kilo	KEYLOH	—·—
L	Lima	LEEMAH	·—··
M	Mike	MIKE	——
N	November	NOVEMBER	—·
O	Oscar	OSSCAH	———
P	Papa	PAHPAH	·——·
Q	Quebec	KEHBECK	——·—
R	Romeo	ROWMEOH	·—·
S	Sierra	SEEAIRRAH	···
T	Tango	TANGGO	—
U	Uniform	YOUNEEFORM	··—
V	Victor	VIKTAH	···—
W	Whiskey	WISSKEY	·——
X	X-ray	ECKSRAY	—··—
Y	Yankee	YANGKEY	—·——
Z	Zulu	ZOOLOO	——··

Transmission Technique

Assuming you are within the performance range of your equipment, and after listening out first, to make sure you don't interfere with another transmission, call ATC, using their name, and normal conversational tones (no need to shout!), followed by their function, as in *London Tower*. Then use the words *This Is*, followed by your own identifier (you should use the full callsign on initial contact with ATC, but you can subsequently use any abbreviations they make. See *Callsigns*, below). Normally, your callsign is the same as your aircraft's markings, unless you have applied to ICAO for permission to use a company name or a flight number. Include the frequency you are on, in case they are listening to several, so they know which button to push, then the word *Over*, as an invitation for them to respond:

"*London Approach, this is Golf Papa Alpha Charlie Oscar on one one eight decimal two, over.*"

You should maintain an even rate of speech, not above 100 words per minute, with a constant volume, avoiding hesitation.

ATC will reply with your full callsign, but may well shorten it afterwards, to the country letter followed by the last two of your registration, as in *Golf-Charlie Oscar*, if there will be no confusion with another aircraft. You can use it from then on. Don't be concerned if there is a short delay - the controller might be writing down your details first, or may even have to put down the coffee (in Canada, you may be on a remote link). If you receive no reply, wait ten seconds before trying again.

If the field has an ATIS (continual weather broadcasts, changed every half hour), obtain the information and include the code letter with your initial call:

"*with information Delta.*"

The format is the same if ATC call you first, but you can omit the word *over* if the reply is obvious and there will be no misunderstanding.

FREQUENCIES

The way to transmit and read back a frequency is to use all six figures, except when the last two figures are zero, when you can use four. For example, 120.375 MHz is:

One Two Zero Decimal Three Seven Five

However, in airspace where channels are separated by 25 KHz, and there is no operational requirement to use 6 figures, you can use the first five, except where the last 2 are zero, when you can use the first four.

Standard Words & Phrases

To make a correction, say the word "Correction" followed by the last correct word or phrase before continuing. To get something repeated, use the words *say again*. You can specify parts of a message by saying *say again all after....*

A message from ATC to all stations listening out on a frequency would be a *general call*, and be preceded with the words *All Stations*. A message to multiple stations can be done in any convenient sequence, but the replies must be in the order given.

Confirm Squawk means "What code is set on your transponder?"

Phrase	Meaning
Acknowledge	Confirm you received this message
Affirm	Agreement
Approved	Permission granted for proposed action
Break	Separation between parts of a message
Break Break	Separation between parts of a message when busy
Cancel	Annul previously transmitted message
Changing to	Going to another frequency
Check	Examine a system
Cleared	Proceed under the conditions specified
Confirm	Did I get that right?
Contact	Get in touch with....
Correct	That is correct

© Phil Croucher, 2017

12 COMMUNICATIONS
Operating Procedures

Phrase	Meaning
Correction	Oops - made a mistake
Disregard	Ignore my last
Go Ahead*	Proceed with message
How Do You Read?	What is my readability?
I say again	I repeat
Monitor	Listen out on (frequency)
Negative	No, or not correct
Out	This conversation is over - no reply is expected
Over	I have finished speaking and I expect a response
Read Back	Repeat the message back exactly as received
Recleared	Ignore your last clearance and receive a new one
Report	Pass me the following information (as in Report altitude).
Request	I would like......
Roger	The last messages has been received (if not understood!)
Say again	Repeat what you just said
Speak Slower	Reduce your rate of speech
Standby	Wait to be called (and do not assume a clearance)
Verify	Check and confirm
Wilco	Your instructions will be complied with (Will Comply)
Words Twice	Send (or will send) every word twice

*In the UK, the term *Pass Your Message* is used instead.

The correct phrase to use when abandoning a takeoff is *Stopping*, and *Runway Vacated* when clear.

PUSHBACK

Large aircraft are parked nose-in to the terminal to save parking space. They have to be pushed backwards by tugs before they can taxi for departure. Some aircraft can reverse from the terminal under their own power, known as powerback. Requests for pushback or powerback are made according to local procedures.

IFR DEPARTURE

Arrivals and departures are often handled by a single approach control unit. At busier airports, they may be handled separately.

Pilots of aircraft flying Instrument Departures (including those outside controlled airspace) shall include the following information on an initial call with the first en-route ATS unit:

- Call sign
- SID or Standard Departure Route Designator (where appropriate)
- Current or passing level, plus
- Initial climb level (i.e. the first level at which the aircraft will level off unless otherwise cleared. For example, on a SID that involves a stepped climb, the initial climb level will be the first level specified in the profile)

AIRWAYS CLEARANCE
That given before taxi, which must be read back exactly.

POSITION REPORTING
For traffic sequencing and to aid situational awareness, controllers may request a pilot to report when established on final approach track or to report at any other relevant point in the procedure, such as *G-CD, report established on final approach track*.

IFR ARRIVAL
Aircraft flying within controlled airspace will normally receive descent clearance to the clearance limit from the ACC prior to transfer to an approach control unit. On transfer to approach control further descent instructions may be given.

APPROACH BAN
In the UK, you may not continue an instrument approach beyond the outer marker or equivalent position, if the reported RVR or, where RVR measurements are not taken or available, the visibility, is below the minimum specified for that approach. Essentially, this means that you may not descend below 1,000 feet above the aerodrome when these conditions exist. This RVR/visibility is known as an absolute minimum.

Time

Time is expressed in terms of the 24-hour clock, based on UTC (*Universal Co-ordinated Time*), or what used to be called Greenwich Mean Time. The letter Z (for *Zulu*, meaning GMT - sorry, UTC) is used as shorthand in things like flight plans, etc. The first two figures of a 24-hour time represent the hour past midnight, and the second two the minutes past the hour, so 2345 means 45 minutes past eleven in the evening (take away 12), or a quarter to midnight. If you see a timegroup:

220345Z

It means a quarter to four GMT on the 22nd of the month. Usually, you only transmit the numbers for minutes ("arriving at 45"), but this only relates to the *current* hour, and if there will be no misunderstanding. If there is any possibility of confusion, or you mean another hour, include the other figures. Time is normally given to the nearest minute, except that control towers may state the time to the nearest half minute when issuing a taxi clearance to a departing aircraft.

You can *Request a Time Check* from ATC at any time.

Callsigns

You should use your full callsign until it is abbreviated by ATC, then you can use the shortened version. For example, XY-ABC can become X-BC or X-ABC. *Helicopter G-YABC* would become *Helicopter BC*. A6-GLC becomes A-LC. *Norjet 123* cannot be abbreviated (in general, you can shorten callsigns that contain registration marks).

Once satisfactory communication has been established, and there will be no confusion, you are allowed to abbreviate a ground station's callsign.

Note: The abbreviation of callsign XY-ABC to Y-BC is not an ICAO Standard. The relevant Standard is ICAO Annex 10, Vol. II, Para. 5.2.1.7.2.2 *Abbreviated Call Signs* (as of 6th E, Oct. 2001).

AERONAUTICAL STATIONS

ATS units are identified by the name of the location, then the service available:

Service	Suffix
Area Control	CONTROL
Radar (General)	RADAR
Approach Control	APPROACH
Aerodrome Control	TOWER
Approach Control Arrival/Departure	DIRECTOR/DEPARTURE (RADAR when combined)
Ground Movement Control	GROUND
MATZ Crossing	ZONE
PAR	TALKDOWN
Flight Information	INFORMATION
Air/Ground Communication Service	RADIO
Clearance Delivery	DELIVERY

The use of the calling aeronautical station's callsign followed by the answering aeronautical station's callsign shall be considered the invitation to proceed with transmission by the station calling. The phrase *Pass Your Message* may be used when considered to be appropriate.

Position Reports

This is the order of items in a position report:

- Callsign
- Position
- Time at position
- Level or altitude
- Next position
- ETA at next position

Talking to Air Traffic Control

You should comply with ATC instructions as soon as they are issued, but sometimes a climb or descent is left to your discretion, in which case the words *When Ready* will be used. You should report *leaving* your present level once you have departed from it and are maintaining a positive rate of climb or descent, because another aircraft above you may be given descent straight away. Control is based on *known traffic only*, so you are still responsible for safe procedures and good judgement - clearances are not an authority to violate the rules! Information about flight conditions is meant as assistance or reminders.

There are three main categories of aeronautical communications service:

- **Air Traffic Control Service** (ATC) which can only be provided by licensed Air Traffic Control Officers (ATCOs) who are closely regulated by the Authority
- **Flight Information Service** at aerodromes can be provided only by licensed Flight Information Service Officers (FISOs), who are also regulated by the Authority
- **Aerodrome Air/Ground Communication Service** (AGCS) which can be provided by Radio Operators who are not licensed, but who have a certificate of competency to operate radio equipment on aviation frequencies from the Authority. These operations come under the jurisdiction of the radio licence holder, but are not otherwise regulated.

Other categories of aeronautical communications service include VOLMET, SIGMET, Automatic Terminal Information Service (ATIS) or Aeronautical Information Services (AIS).

On a typical flight, you might talk to several ATC departments, loosely in the following order (some may be combined at smaller airfields). In general, the procedure for outbound aircraft is:

- Obtain the ATIS or current weather
- Request startup clearance, stating the ATIS version you have, but....
- Obtain taxi instructions (up to a limiting point - normally the holding point of the runway in use). Doing this while taxying is difficult in the hover, so maybe get it beforehand.
- Change to Tower for takeoff clearance, also difficult in the hover, so you will often taxi on the Tower frequency

On the way back in:

- Obtain the ATIS or current weather
- Request joining instructions, stating the ATIS version you have
- Report position in the circuit, such as downwind, finals, etc (the *finals* call is made within 7 km. *Long finals* is at 15 km)
- If ATC require you to *Go Around*, they will say so, at which point you climb away and start the circuit again. You can initiate a Go Around at any time by saying *Going Around*

GROUND CONTROL

The Ground Controller handles all movements on the manoeuvring area, including aircraft and vehicles, and possibly start clearances (departure clearances given by Ground are *not* clearances to takeoff!) Typically, you would be talking to Ground up to the holding point, and afterwards when landing - this helps ATC with planning and keeps the tower frequency clear (but a helicopter may taxi on the Tower frequency, as your hands are full in the hover). It also reduces fuel waste from delays.

It often helps if you say where you are, and include the current ATIS:

> *"G-PACO on Helipad 1 with Bravo, request start"*

Bravo is the latest ATIS. You will get an acknowledgment, with the current QNH.

TOWER

For traffic close to the aerodrome, including the circuit. After takeoff, you may be asked to change to Approach (below), but, more typically, you will stay with the Tower until clear of the area. Taxi instructions will contain a clearance limit, meaning a point beyond which you must not go without further permission. This will normally be the holding point of the runway in use (you are automatically cleared across those on the way, *holding short* when you get there), but may be elsewhere if they are busy. On a large airfield, taxiways to be used will be included:

"Taxi to the hold for 19, via taxiway Alpha, then Bravo."

THE CIRCUIT

In a standard overhead join at 2000 feet, you should call "Deadside Descending" on the dead side. In the circuit, a normal final approach is within 4 nm of the runway - *long finals* is between 4 and 8 nm. You can also call *Outer Marker* instead of *Finals* if there is one.

When landing, if told to *continue*, because of traffic on the runway, that is *not* a clearance to land - you still need permission. If the runway is long enough, in daylight, you may be allowed to *land after* whatever is on it already. The words "go around" mean "initiate a missed approach".

However, helicopter operations are a lot more informal at smaller airfields.

APPROACH

Sometimes known as *Radar*, these controllers sit in a darkened room in front of radar screens, so have no visual contact with the traffic they are dealing with (don't worry, they are fed frequently). Approach controllers guide the aircraft during its approach or departure to or from the airport. Mostly, arrivals and departures are handled by a single approach unit but, at busier airfields they may be separate, with different controllers, callsigns and frequencies.

Under IFR in controlled airspace, you will be given descent clearance to whatever limit is used by ACC before handover to Approach. Outside controlled airspace, do not enter until cleared to do so.

The phrase *Under RADAR Control* is only used when a radar control service is being provided, meaning that you must do what you are told, unless you are avoiding immediate danger. ATC will assume responsibility for separation and terrain avoidance.

A *Radar Advisory Service* is only provided under IFR, regardless of the weather. You will be given the bearing, distance and height of known conflicting traffic, plus *advisory* avoiding action, which should nevertheless not be ignored. If you do, you must advise ATC. You remain responsible for terrain avoidance.

You can get A *Radar Information Service* (RIS) under IFR or VFR. You still get information on conflicting traffic, but without avoiding action. You are responsible for separation from other aircraft and terrain avoidance.

A *Flight Information Service* is *not* a radar service. It is merely someone to talk to.

RADAR IDENTIFICATION

You can be identified by information from yourself (position reporting, or in relation to a prominent object), by making turns that can be seen on radar, or by identing with SSR. You should be advised if radar identification is lost, or about to be lost, and appropriate instructions should be given. **Note:** The only form of identification that does not require a backup (such as a turn) is squawking ident.

Heading information and instructions are in degrees magnetic.

RADAR VECTORING

You may be given specific vectors for lateral separation, and left to resume your own navigation when it is completed (they may be nice and tell you where you are). *Orbits* (complete turns) may be used for delaying purposes or for increasing separation.

AREA

Area controllers are not necesssarily at an airport, and control aircraft that are passing through the airspace without landing.

Clearances and Readbacks

You should start a transmission with the callsign of the service provider followed by the aircraft callsign. When a readback of an ATC message is required, you should terminate the read back transmission with the aircraft's radio callsign.

You must comply with any clearances received and acknowledged. If you don't like them, you should say so at the time, since an acknowledgement without further comment is taken as such. Clearances are valid only in controlled airspace, and there will be some form of the word "clear" in the text to identify them. Clearances must always be read back (although you don't need to read back the wind velocity). You must also comply with instructions in the same way, unless safety is a factor. An instruction will be identifiable, but the word "instruct" may not be included. All clearances should be read back, to ensure that they have been received and transmitted properly in the first place, to the right aircraft.

If a clearance or an instruction is not suitable, you may request and, if practicable, obtain an amended one. Use the words *Unable To Comply* if you have a problem with a clearance. Clearances are supposed to be passed slowly and clearly, since you will need to write them down, and preferably before startup, since you will not want to be bothered while taxying, hovering or when lining up for takeoff. They will contain the aircraft identification (as per the flight plan), the clearance limit (usually the destination) and the route, levels, changes and any other instructions, especially about departure manoeuvres.

These clearances should be read back in full, in the order given:
- Taxi instructions
- Clearances to enter, land on, take off from, cross, backtrack and hold short of the runway in use
- Heading, speed and level instructions, including Transition Levels
- Approach clearances
- Altimeter settings
- Transponder codes
- Airways or route clearances
- VDF information
- Frequency changes
- Type of radar service

Route clearances must be read back completely. Others (including conditional clearances) need only contain key elements and include sufficient detail to clearly indicate that they will be complied with.

Note: The word *Takeoff* is only used by a pilot when actually cleared for takeoff (in a separate transmission) - up until then, the word *Departure* is used. Similarly, with regard to runway movements, the word *Cleared* is only used in connection with a clearance to takeoff and land. Otherwise, the words *cross* and *approved* will be used.

CONDITIONAL CLEARANCES

A conditional clearance depends on the actions of another aircraft, such as when being given clearance to cross a runway after a taxying aircraft has passed. Correct identification of the aircraft involved is essential. Conditional clearances must be given in this order:
- Identification
- The condition (specify)
- The subject of the condition
- The instruction

For example: "G-PACO - Behind* the A 340, Line up". Your reply: "Behind the A 340, Line Up, G-PACO".

Note: This implies the need for you to identify the aircraft or vehicle causing the conditional clearance.

Readback must be in full and in the same sequence as given, with the condition first.

*In the UK, the word *After* is used because the ICAO one, *Behind*, has been misinterpreted.

Test Transmissions

Radio transmissions for test purposes should be as short as possible, and in any case not more than 10 seconds. Repeat testing shall also be the minimum necessary.

The test must be identifiable as a test transmission and must not be confused with other communications. To achieve this, the following format is used:
- the callsign of the aeronautical station being called
- the aircraft identification
- the words RADIO CHECK
- the frequency being used

The operator of the aeronautical radio station being called will assess the transmission and will advise the aircraft making it in terms of the readability scale described below, together with a comment on the nature of any abnormalities noted, such as excessive noise, using the following format:
- the aircraft identification
- the callsign of the aeronautical station replying
- READABILITY x (where x is a number from the table below)
- additional information with respect to abnormalities

Sometimes it may be necessary for the operator of an aeronautical station to reply with *STATION CALLING (frequency or 8.33 channel) UNREADABLE*.

READABILITY SCALE

To check a radio, call up another station (if they're not busy) and ask how they read you (don't take more than about ten seconds). They will reply with a readability grading on the following scale:
- 1 - unreadable
- 2 - readable now and then
- 3 - readable with difficulty
- 4 - readable
- 5 - perfectly readable

"Reading you Strength Three", for example.

Transfer Of Communication

When ATC want to hand you off to another ATS unit, they will say something like:

Contact Ground (or whatever) on (frequency)

Contact London on 118.75

TCAS Manoeuvres

A TCAS manoeuvre is a valid reason for the inability to comply with a clearance. They should be reported to ATC, even after the action has been taken and the original clearance has been resumed (although ATC may issue a revised clearance).

COMMUNICATIONS
Radio Failure

RADIO FAILURE

ICAO Annex 10, Vol II refers.

Try another frequency, or talk to other aircraft first. You will at least then know that your radio is OK. Make sure also that the facility is not closed, that you are not out of range, you have selected the right frequency, and that the volume is set! In case the set is transmitting, you can transmit your message twice, preceded by the words *Transmitting Blind*.

If all that fails, essentially, you must comply with the last clearance, which hopefully included permission to land, or clear the area. If you don't need to enter controlled airspace, carry on, maintaining VFR as necessary; don't enter it even if you've been previously cleared. If you must do so, divert and telephone for permission first. If you're already in controlled airspace, where clearance has been obtained to the boundary on leaving, or the field on entering, proceed as planned. If in doubt, clear the zone the most direct way as quickly as possible, avoiding airfields, and making blind transmissions, in case the transmitter is working. If you are in a circuit, and your radio fails, repeatedly switch the landing lights on and off.

In the open FIR, with unlimited visibility and no cloud, land at the nearest suitable aerodrome and inform the ATS unit.

Squawk 7600 for communications failure. If you can hear ATC they will likely ask you to push the ident button if you cannot transmit.

There is a system of flying a left or right-handed triangle pattern that can be seen on radar, although it's usually only used if you're lost as well as having a duff radio. If ATC recognise your problem, they will send up a shepherd aircraft to formate on you and bring you down, so remain VMC if you can, and as high as possible so radar can see you better. If you can squawk Mode C, do so, because that will give a height readout to work with. If you can only receive, fly in a right-handed pattern for a minute (over 300 knots, make it two). Fly at best endurance speed and make each 120° turn as tight as possible. If you can't transmit either, go to the left.

Receiver Failure

Make reports at scheduled times or positions (i.e. advise the time of your next transmission), preceded by the phrase "Transmitting Blind due to receiver failure".

Refer to *Air Law*.

DISTRESS & URGENCY

An emergency exists the moment you become doubtful about position, fuel, weather, or anything else that could affect the safety of your flight. The first transmission should be on the frequency in use at the time, then the international one of 121.5 MHz, followed by others (the auxiliary frequency is 123.1 MHz).

The first station receiving a Distress or Urgency call (see below) should *acknowledge it* and take immediate action to ensure that the necessary information is made available to ATC and the operating agency, and take control of communications if necessary, including imposing radio silence by saying *Stop Transmitting - MAYDAY*, after which everyone should keep quiet (this may also be done by the aircraft in distress). If and when the threat is over, the Distress call must be cancelled by notification on ALL frequencies on which the original message was sent.

Note: Distress/Urgency messages must include the nature of the emergency, fuel endurance and persons on board.

Fuel Emergencies

In UK, flight crews of aircraft short on fuel must declare a PAN or MAYDAY to ensure being given the appropriate priority. The phrase *No Delay Expected* means that holding will be less than 20 minutes before starting an approach.

Intercepting Distress Transmissions

Distress transmissions are normally given out on the frequency in use at the time, but when over the high seas, say when flying offshore, you will typically be guarding one of the distress frequencies, either *121.5 MHz, 243 MHz* or *2182 KHz* for merchant shipping. ELTs operate on 121.5 MHz and 406 MHz.

Under ICAO Annex 12, para 5.7, if you hear a distress transmission, you must:

- Acknowledge the transmission (if somebody else does that before you, then it may be a good idea to maintain radio silence)
- Record the position of the craft in distress, if given
- Take a bearing on the transmission
- Inform the appropriate ATS unit or RCC
- At your discretion, whilst awaiting further instructions, proceed to the position given. Once there, if a rescue is in progress, do not interfere without checking with whoever is in charge

If you need to direct another craft to the scene, circle it at least once, fly low just in front and rock the fuselage, then fly off in the direction you want them to go.

You can use the same signals when they are finished with, but fly behind instead. In theory, they should hoist the *Code Pennant*, which is a flag with vertical red and white stripes, close up, or flash a series of *Ts* in Morse Code with a lamp. On the other hand, they could just turn in the direction requested. A blue and white chequered flag means *Much Regret, Unable* (i.e. *NO*), as does a series of *Ns* in Morse.

COMMUNICATIONS
Distress & Urgency

Distress

The Distress call (MAYDAY) is used when threatened by *grave and imminent danger* and in *most urgent need* of *immediate assistance*. You can use the letters SOS in Morse Code (··· --- ···), or the spoken words MAYDAY, repeated 3 times, followed by relevant details, like your position, and what is happening:

> MAYDAY MAYDAY MAYDAY
> Name of station addressed
> Callsign (e.g. G-JLBI)
> Type (e.g. Helicopter)
> Nature of emergency (e.g. Total Engine Failure)
> Intentions of PIC
> Position (e.g. 20 Miles E of London VOR)
> Pilot qualifications*
> Any other information e.g. endurance remaining, number of people on board (POB), aircraft colour/markings, survival aids.

*There is no ICAO requirement to include pilot qualifications in a distress message, but this information should be included whenever possible in UK emergency messages as it may help the controller to plan a course of action best suited to the pilot's ability. Such information could include:

- *Student* - Solo student pilots shall prefix the aircraft callsign with STUDENT to indicate their lack of experience. Although intended primarily for *ab initio* students, the prefix shall also be used in other circumstances where, for example, the holder of a valid licence is returning to flying practice after a significant absence and is undergoing renewal training involving solo flight conducted as a student under supervision of a flight instructor.
- *No Instrument Qualification*
- *IMC Rating*
- *Full Instrument Rating*

Repeat as necessary. You can also fire rockets or red lights at short intervals, and parachute flares. Control of distress traffic is the responsibility of the aircraft in distress.

To cancel a MAYDAY:

- State MAYDAY once
- Say ALL STATIONS three times
- Aircraft ID
- Station called
- Time
- Name of station in distress
- DISTRESS TRAFFIC ENDED
- Station called
- OUT

You could also use CANCEL DISTRESS.

Distress frequencies are:

- 121.5 MHz - VHF Aeronautical Emergency Frequency
- 243 MHz - UHF Military Emergency Frequency
- 500 KHz - MF International Distress Frequency
- 2182 KHz - MF International Distress Frequency (this is officially in the MF band, but most HF radios can deal with it)

The squawk code for an emergency is 7700.

Tip: If you don't have time to change the squawk, keep pressing the Ident.

Urgency

The Urgency call (or "PAN") spoken three times, indicates a very urgent message concerning the safety of a ship, aircraft or other vehicle, or of some person on board or in sight, but immediate assistance is not required. It has priority over all other messages except Distress (above). If you just wish to mention that you are compelled to land, but don't need help right away, switch the landing lights and/or navigation lights on and off in an irregular pattern.

Include as much information as you can, but the format follows that of Distress:

> PAN PAN PAN PAN PAN PAN
> Name of station addressed
> Callsign (e.g. G-JLBI)
> Type (e.g. Helicopter)
> Nature of emergency (e.g. Total Engine Failure)
> Intentions of PIC
> Position (e.g. 20 Miles E of London VOR)
> Pilot qualifications*
> Any other information

The phrase *PAN PAN MEDICAL* means that the following message concerns a protected medical transport using aircraft assigned exclusively to medical transportation., as defined in the *Geneva Convention of 1949*, which also mentions something about conflicts.

TCAS

To notify ATC of a TCAS RA, state the callsign, plus TCAS RA.

ATC can only modify an altitude after you have reported TCAS CLEAR OF CONFLICT.

Simulations

You can simulate urgency incidents (but not the state of distress) on 121.5 MHz. Use the word PRACTICE in front of the keyword, such as PRACTICE PAN.

PROPAGATION & FREQUENCIES

Review the first part of *Radio Navigation*, particularly Emission Classifications, Attenuation, Frequency Allocations and the heights and distances at which you can receive transmissions.

INTERCEPTION

Already covered in Air Law.

IFR STUFF

Already covered in Air Law.

Navigation (General)

Navigation involves taking an aircraft from place to place without excessive reference to the ground, except, perhaps, for checking that you've got the right destination! To do this without radio navigation aids, a system of calculation called *Dead Reckoning* is used, which is actually short for *Deduced Reckoning*, based on solving a *triangle of velocities* with a flight computer, discussed later in this chapter.

The biggest mistake people make when starting to fly is to confuse navigation with map reading (or *pilotage*), which is used when you need to know your position more precisely, as when doing survey. As far as navigation goes, however, you only really need your location relatively vaguely, in terms of something like "10 miles SE of a radio beacon", or similar, because position fixes need to be quick - things can happen so fast that, by the time you have figured out where you are, you are miles away! This allows you to devote your attention to something slightly more useful.

In fact, there are many ways of keeping track of where you are:

- **Pilotage** (visual reference to landmarks), typically used under VFR with.......
- **Dead Reckoning**, or calculating a heading that will take you to where you want to go, allowing for forecast winds. It is used where pilotage is hard to deal with, such as over the sea or a desert, and is often combined with it.
- **Radio Navigation** (with radio beacons).
- **Astral Navigation** (not on the syllabus!)

Usually, combinations are used, with pilotage getting you started on a trip, and helping you end it (as soon as you see the destination, head directly towards it). Pilotage is certainly used to confirm your DR position.

The first step, however, is to get acquainted with .....

THE EARTH

The Earth is the third planet away from the Sun and the fifth largest in the Solar System. It is not round, but pear-shaped, with the greater of its mass in the Southern hemisphere. It is therefore a *geoid* (its actual shape), an *ellipsoid* (a smoother version, as a 3D ellipse) and a *sphere* (for convenience) in order of accuracy. It is also called an *oblate spheroid*.

The ellipsoid is easier to express mathematically, and the sphere will have the same volume. As it happens, the distortion caused by treating the Earth as a sphere is less than 5% in terms of distance and 12 minutes for direction.

As the Earth is not a perfect sphere, its "radius" can mean many things. It is the distance from the centre to the *mean sea level* at a point, which can vary quite a bit (it is around 12 miles from the top of the tallest mountain to the bottom of the deepest ocean).

The value of the radius *at the Equator* (the *major semi axis*) is **6378.4** km (around **12 700 km in diameter**) for an Equatorial circumference of 40 069 km (21 600 nm).

Between the Poles (the *minor semi axis*, around which the Earth revolves), it is **6356.6**, with a circumference of 39 943 km, so the Earth is larger round the Equator than it is through the Poles by just under 140 km, or 74 nm.

The difference is called the *compression ratio*, and the value for the flattening is $1/298$ (0.3%) or $1/297$.

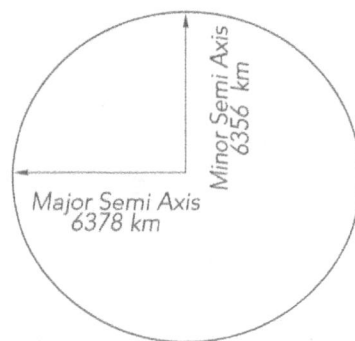

The difference in diameters is around 21,384 km.

So, if the major (Equatorial) radius is 6378 km (3444 nm), the minor (Polar) axis is 1/298 shorter, or:

$$6378 - \frac{6378}{298} = 6356.6$$

The assumed radius of the Earth (as a sphere) is 6371 km. As this is a constant figure, you don't need to include it in any calculations, which allows us to use a 2D coordinate system, as described below.

POSITIONAL REFERENCE

A Positional Reference System identifies any position* on the surface of an object. The following can be used:

- A graticule system (latitude & longitude or a grid)
- A known point (a position fix)
- The bearing and range from a known point

*The word *position* means a place that can be positively identified, and which may be qualified by such terms as *estimated*, *nil wind*, etc. The distance between two points, or axes, on a sphere, is measured by angles which can be related to physical distances. Positions are related to others by the differences in latitude and longitude between them.

Longitude

We can find our position on a straight line graph by using just two parameters, *x* and *y*, otherwise known as *Cartesian coordinates*. As the Earth is a sphere (well, nearly, anyway) with no obvious place to start, we have to use *polar coordinates*, using the angles λ and ϕ, also known as *latitude* and *longitude*, respectively. As a starting point for finding your position, a series of imaginary lines is drawn from Pole to Pole through the Equator, called lines of *longitude*. The Poles are points about which the Earth rotates. The North Pole is the one at the top.

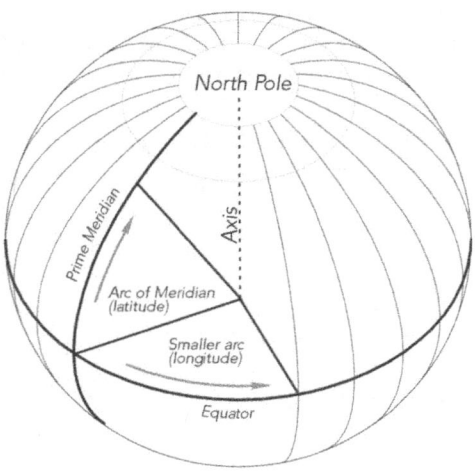

The lines are also called *meridians*, and by convention are drawn for every degree you go round the Equator, of which there are 360. Each meridian has its own antimeridian on the other side of the Earth. The two together form a Great Circle, described later. Also, by convention, they start at Greenwich, in London (with the *Prime Meridian* at 0°). Longitude is the distance East or West from the Prime Meridian up to 179° E or W (180° is just called 180° longitude as it is neither). Technically, it is the *smaller arc of the Equator between the Prime Meridian and the one through the point concerned*. The angular difference between meridians is the *Change Of Longitude* (ch long).

As the Earth takes nearly 24 hours to spin on its N-S axis, 15 lines of longitude represent 1 hour, and it is noon when the Sun is overhead (*transiting*) any particular meridian (the day starts when it transits the antimeridian). The spinning is anticlockwise at 15.04° per hour when viewed from the top of the Earth (from West to East), so the Sun and other heavenly bodies appear to move the other way, rising from the East and set in the West.

Latitude

Having only one vertical line, however, is not enough to find a position with, as you could be anywhere on it, so horizontal lines are also drawn, parallel to each other, North and South of the Equator, up to 90° each way, called *parallels of latitude*. The Equator is 0°.

Parallels go across lines of longitude, and indicate your position North or South of the Equator, up to whichever Pole. An aircraft travelling North in the Northern hemisphere and South in the Southern hemisphere is increasing its latitude, and *vice versa*.

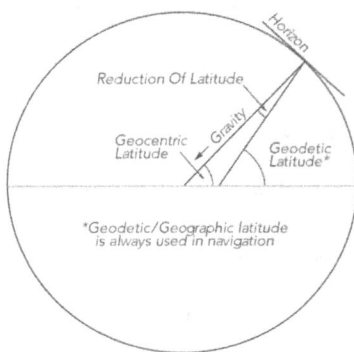

The latitude of any point is the *arc of the meridian between the Equator and the parallel through the point*, or that represented by the angle between the plane of the Equator and a line from the point of interest to the centre of the Earth. Just to confuse things, there's more than one way of defining this angle, because of the Earth's ellipsoid shape. The angle between a line from the centre of the Earth to a point on its surface and the Equator, measured along a Meridian, is called **Geocentric Latitude**.

If the Earth were a sphere, the story would end there, but it isn't, so such a line is not always vertical, and its angle from the horizon can vary. Put another way, the angle can change with latitude, and it is not always perpendicular to the surface. **Geodetic latitude** is the angle between the normal (right angle) to the geoid, and the plane of the Equator. Geodetic (or geographic) latitude is used in all navigation, and different geoids give slightly different geodetic latitudes, longitudes and times. Most charts use the WGS84 geoid, as used inside the GPS.

At the Poles and the Equator, a line from the centre of the geoid is normal to the surface anyway, so the geodetic and geocentric latitudes are both the same at those points.

The difference between the two (*Reduction of Latitude*), is greatest half way between, at **45°N or 45°S**, where it is about **11.6'** (nm), almost $1/5$ of a degree. Each degree of latitude represents 60 nautical miles, and each minute is 1 nautical mile, or 6080 feet*. The difference between parallels is *Change Of Latitude* (ch lat).

*This is the British version - the ICAO one is 6076 feet.

Lines of latitude are fixable by natural means - for example, the Tropics of Cancer and Capricorn represent the limits of the Sun's travel North and South as it rises and sets every day, based on the Earth's tilt.

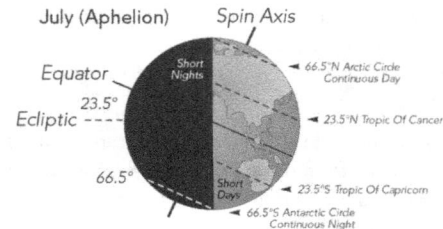

NAVIGATION (GENERAL)
Positional Reference

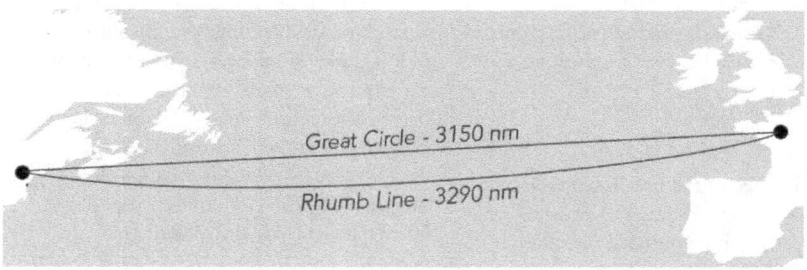

Important latitudes include the *Tropic of Cancer* (23° 27' N), the *Tropic of Capricorn* (23° 27' S), the *Arctic Circle* (66° 33' N), and the *Antarctic Circle* (66° 33' S).

Only between the two Tropics can the sun be at its zenith, and only North or South of the Arctic and Antarctic Circles, respectively, is the midnight sun possible.

Until the 1770s, however, when John Harrison invented a marine chronometer which only lost 5 seconds in two months, you could not fix longitude precisely, because time was measured by the cabin boy turning a glass with sand in it over and over. In other words, you only knew your longitude by calculation from when you left port, and if you knew what the time was. The Moon (against the fixed stars) was the only useful item in this respect as it orbited the Earth so quickly (13° of arc per day).

Ptolemy had plotted some sort of lat & long system by 150 AD, but he used the Canaries for the Prime (or zero) Meridian, which has also been at the Azores, Cape Verdi, Rome and Paris, to mention but a few (the Ancient Egyptians probably used the pyramids). It was placed at Greenwich in 1884 because the Royal Navy was the dominant naval power at the time, and there had been an observatory there since 1675 (Prince George was also a keen astronomer). It may also have something to do with being part of the shortest Polar circumference.

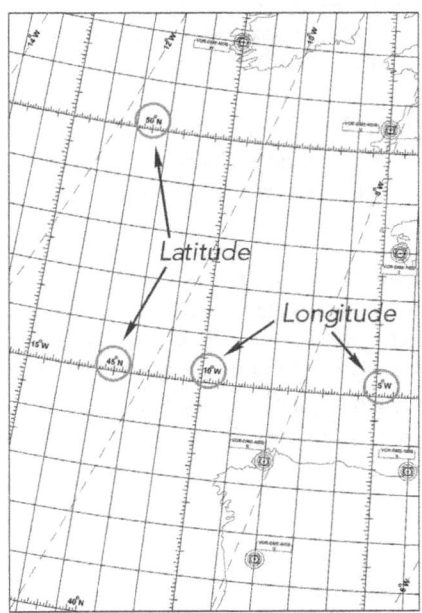

When giving position, latitude is always given first, as in 45°N, 163°W.

Great Circles (Orthodromes)   06 1 01 02

Great Circles have planes that go through the centre of the Earth, or, in other words, are circles whose centre and radius are the same as the Earth's, so they will divide it into two equal parts. The name comes from the fact that it is the largest circle you can obtain, so only one Great Circle can be drawn through two points on the surface of the Earth that are not diametrically opposed. *The shortest distance between any two points on the surface of a sphere is the smaller arc of the Great Circle joining them.*

Imagine a great circle as the path taken by a satellite, or a star over the Earth's surface. Radio waves follow Great Circle routes.

The definition includes lines of longitude and the Equator. As meridians are semi-great circles, a meridian and its antimeridian together make a Great Circle.

Although the shorter arcs of great circles are the shortest distances between two points on the Earth's surface, as you change meridians during your travels, your relationship to True North is changing by the amount of *Convergency*, which is discussed later.

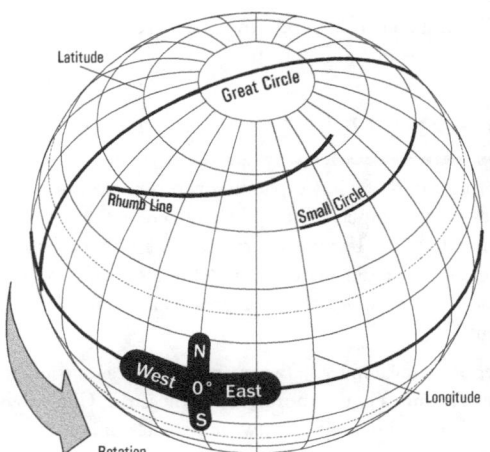

Thus, your track direction is defined by the local meridian, and you must keep altering track if you want to fly long distances along great circles. This, of course, is a pain, and there are solutions, discussed later.

Small Circles

These are circles on the surface of a sphere whose centre and radius are less than those of the sphere itself, so anything that is not a Great Circle is a Small Circle. You can have an infinite number of them between two points.

Parallels of latitude (except the Equator) are small circles constructed with reference to the Equator (they are also rhumb lines - see below). The angular distance between them along a meridian is *latitude*.

Rhumb Lines

Rhumb Lines are lines on the surface of the Earth that cross each meridian at the same angle, so they are lines of constant bearing. They are not straight (being concave to the nearer Pole), because meridians converge, so they are longer in distance than Great Circles between the same points. For example, over 2,000 miles a rhumb line may be 4 miles longer than a Great Circle at 20° latitude, 20 at 40°, and 100 miles longer at 60°. Over 500 miles, it is less than a mile longer, even at 60°, so long flights (say over the Atlantic) are usually plotted as Great Circles made up of a series of rhumb lines every 10° of longitude. At 60° latitude, this is only 300 nautical miles. Thus, the difference between rhumb lines and Great Circles is not worth worrying about below about 1,000 miles, for the convenience of steering one track, especially in low latitudes, and when they are close.

The difference between Great Circles and Rhumb Lines is greatest E/W, and increases with latitude - it could easily be 600 nm near the Poles, as described in *Grid Navigation*.

Rhumb lines (or *loxodromes**) spiral toward a Pole unless they are going East, West, North, or South, in which case they close on themselves to form parallels of latitude or a pair of meridians. That is, lines of latitude are rhumb lines, as are meridians, but the Equator and meridian pairs are also great circles. Because a rhumb line appears as a straight line on a Mercator chart (later), following one is often called Mercator flying, or following Mercator tracks.

*A rhumb line is a course, a loxodrome is a curve.

SPEED & DISTANCE   061 01 05

Distance is the length of a line separating two points, although this becomes more complicated on a sphere, where the line becomes curved. As the Earth is considered to be a sphere for our purposes, and its radius is "constant", the distance between places on the Earth's surface can be expressed as an angular measurement.

The number of nautical miles between any two places is equal to the number of minutes in the shorter arc of the Great Circle that joins them. We take the distance between parallels of latitude as 60 nautical miles, although the physical distance varies between the Poles and the Equator because the Earth is not a sphere. The length of a nautical mile at these points is 6108 and 6046 feet, respectively, but the UK value of 6080 is used for calibration and navigation in general, and is only correct at 48° latitude*.

*The syllabus is limited to where 1 degree of arc = 60 nm - two points on the same meridian, or on a meridian and anti-meridian, or two on the Equator.

One minute of longitude, however (i.e. along a parallel of latitude), will only be 1 nm *at the Equator*, because every point on it is the same distance from the centre of the Earth. The distance between meridians gets smaller toward the Poles.

You can find the true length of a degree at any latitude by multiplying the change of longitude (in minutes) by the cosine of the latitude, so at 60°N, the distance between meridians is only 30 nm, or half of what it is at the Equator (this is the *departure formula*, which is accurate along one parallel). The circumference of the 60°N parallel is around 10 800 nm.

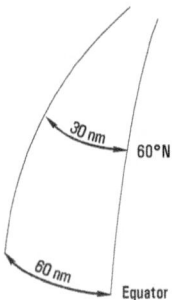

Horizontal distance is measured in kilometres or miles, and speed is a *rate of change of position expressed in those units* (per hour, minute, or whatever). For example, a **knot** is 1 **nautical mile** per hour. It was originally measured by allowing a rope with a log on the end to stretch out behind a ship. The rope had coloured rags tied in knots at regular intervals, which were counted over time. For aircraft, we need *airspeed, groundspeed* and *relative speed*, discussed later.

In navigation, a typical length can be expressed as:

- A **kilometre**, which is 1000 metres, and was originally 1/10,000 of the average distance between the Equator and either Pole on a meridian passing through Paris (thanks to Napoleon, although the Sumerians were there first). It is equivalent to 3280 feet, and 8 km equals 5 statute miles. As a rate, it is expressed in km/hour.

- 1 **nautical mile** (nm) is an angular distance taken in UK as an average of 6080 feet, or 1853 m. However, 6076.1 feet is used by ICAO, which equates to 1852 m (as a reminder, check out your calculator - see right).

- A **statute mile**, which is 5280 feet and an Imperial measurement introduced by Elizabeth I. In aviation, it is used only in visibility reports in some countries. 1 nautical mile is equal to 1.15 statute miles.

Relative Velocity

Subtract one speed from the other if aircraft are going the same way, or add them if they are travelling head-on.

BASIC EXAMPLES

1. At 12:00, an aeroplane flying at 105 kts is 30 miles behind a helicopter which is flying at 95 kts. When will the aeroplane overtake the helicopter? The difference in speeds is 10 knots, so it will take 3 hours to cover 30 miles. The answer is 15:00.

2. Two aircraft, each flying at 90 kts, are 120 nm apart and approaching head on. How much time is there for avoiding action? 40 minutes.

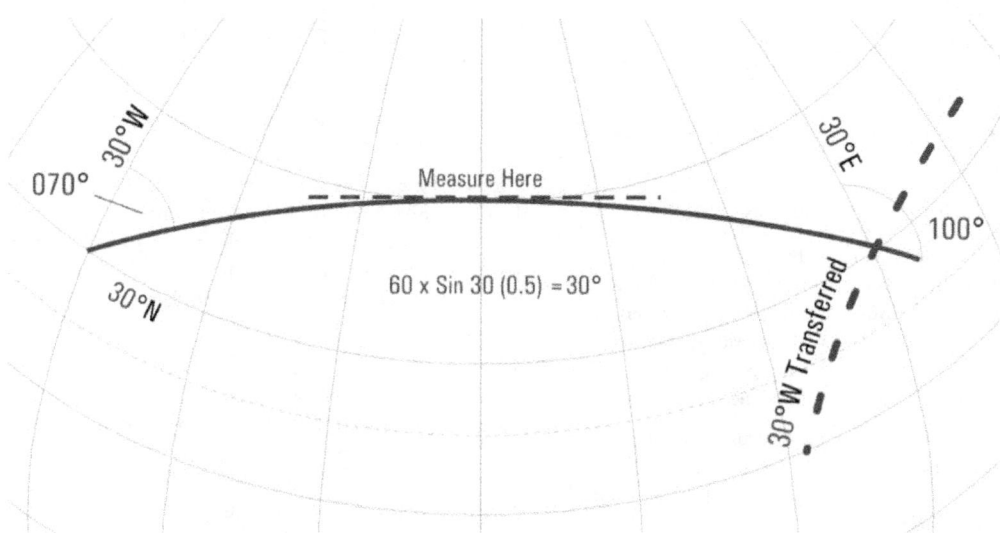

CONVERGENCY

Meridians are only parallel to each other when they cross the Equator. Elsewhere, they get closer (converge) as you go toward the Poles*. Convergency is the angle of inclination between two meridians at a given latitude, or the change in direction that a Great Circle experiences over its length, which can be calculated, and is often more accurate than measuring it. Finding the *distance* between two points on the same latitude, on the other hand, involves the **departure formula**, discussed later.

*The convergency angle at the Equator is 0°. At the Poles it is equal to the difference in longitude.

This means that, as you fly a great circle track to the East in the Northern hemisphere (and West in the Southern hemisphere), your true direction increases, as can be seen in the picture above, where you start off at 070° and end up at 100° if you follow the Great Circle route (remember, meridians point North).

Earth Convergency

This is the angle between the tangents to two meridians.

It is zero at the Equator, and is equal to the difference in longitude between them at the Poles - in general terms, Earth convergency is the difference in Great Circle bearings between two meridians, varying with the **sine** of the latitude because the maximum change is at the Poles.

On the right hand side of the diagram below, the 10°E meridian has been transferred from its original position, so we have the original direction of 090° plus a little bit.

The difference between A & B is the *Convergency Angle*.

The approximate formula for convergency is:

```
ch long x sin mean lat
```

where *ch long* means the change in longitude between the meridians. In the example given, the difference between 10°E and 30°E is 20°, and the sine of 60° is 0.866*, so:

```
20 x 0.866 = 17
```

Add 17 to the original direction to obtain 107°.

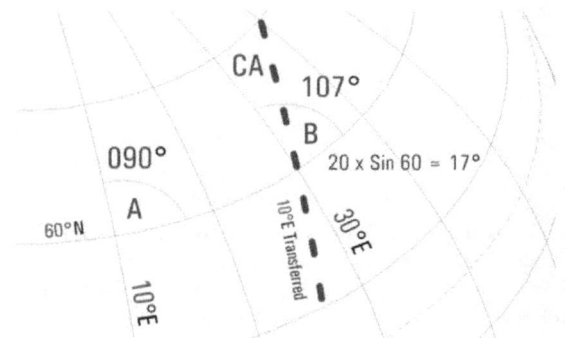

*Get used to this figure, it is used a lot. Also remember the cosine value, which is 0.5.

Chart Convergency

As charts are based on the Earth's surface, they suffer from convergency as well - chart convergency is the angle made between meridians *on a projection*. The convergency factor is the number of degrees change in track bearing per degree travelled. It, too, is zero at the Equator, and 1° at the Poles, and varies at the *sine* of the latitude, but as the meridians are straight, the value stays constant over the chart, instead of changing between latitudes, as it would on the Earth. This means you can use a factor for the whole chart instead.

On a Mercator projection, the chart convergency is zero everywhere because the meridians are parallel (towards the Equator, it is *greater* than that on the Earth, and *vice versa*). On a Lambert, chart convergency equals Earth convergency at the Parallel of Origin but otherwise remains constant everywhere. The sine of the PO is called the constant of the cone.

On a Polar Stereographic, chart convergency equals Earth convergency at the Poles and is constant everywhere.

NAVIGATION (GENERAL)
Convergency

Direction & Variation

These have already been covered in *Instruments*.

Departure

Distance along a parallel of latitude is also known as *departure**. Here is the formula:

```
α (nm) = ch long (mins) x cos lat
```

In English, it means that the distance between two points on the Earth's surface **in nautical miles** is equal to the difference in longitude between them **in minutes** multiplied by the cosine of the latitude. The cosine is used because the meridians converge towards the Poles and the distance between them gets shorter - in this case, the maximum change is at the Equator.

*Change of longitude (d´long) is an *angle* measured in minutes at the Equator, and departure is a *distance* in nautical miles elsewhere. More technically, *departure is the distance made good in an E-W direction along a rhumb line.*

If you are going N or S of track, you take the mid latitude, or the mean for short distances. This is because the departures above and below the track are of different lengths due to convergency.

To find a mid-latitude, add them, then divide by 2.

Once you know the positions of two places, you can work out the rhumb line direction and distance between them, approximately enough for our purposes. The trick is to divide the vertical distance by the horizontal distance, having worked out the changes in latitude and longitude, respectively. For short distances, these become the two (non-hypotenuse) sides of a right-angled plane triangle:

```
departure = tan (course)
  d'lat
```

For example, you have to fly from 54°N 100°W to 56°N 110°W. You can already see that you are going a little bit North and quite a bit West, judging by the angles (2°N, 10°W). To work it out more accurately, the mean latitude is 55°N, so the departure is:

```
α (nm) = 600 x cos 55
```

or:

```
α (nm) = 600 x 0.5736 = 344 nm
```

so:

```
344 = tan (course)
120
```

or:

```
344 = 2.868
120
```

This is 71°. Subtract from 360° to get 289° as a course to steer. The distance is the hypotenuse which can be found (accurately enough for our purposes) by dividing the departure by the sine of the course (0.9455) to get 375.5 nm, or dividing the d´lat by the cosine of the course (0.3256) to get 368.5. The accurate calculation is 374.74!

This is the kind of mental calculation you can get involved in all the time while flying. All you need to know is where you are in terms of lat & long (GPS!) and the cosine of your latitude, which won't vary enough to make a difference. Very often you can head more or less in the right direction straight away and refine it on the way.

Note: Always assume the shortest route. For a change of longitude between *different* hemispheres (one value is E and one W), just add the values. In the *same* hemisphere, subtract the lowest value from the higher. If the answer is more than 180°, subtract the result from 360° for the shortest route. If the longitudes equal 180°, the shortest way is over the Pole, as they make a Great Circle based on a meridian and its antimeridian.

Note: For Local Mean Time calculations (see later) you take the longest route.

On the Jeppesen CR-3, you can find out departure quite easily. Say from York (roughly 54°N), you need to find a ship just East of the Isle Of Man, which is more or less on the same latitude, but 3° to the West, or 180 minutes, which at the Equator would be 180 nm. The black band represents cosines, which stop at 45°, but the cosine of 54° is the same as the sine of 36° so, looking opposite, you have 106 nm to go.

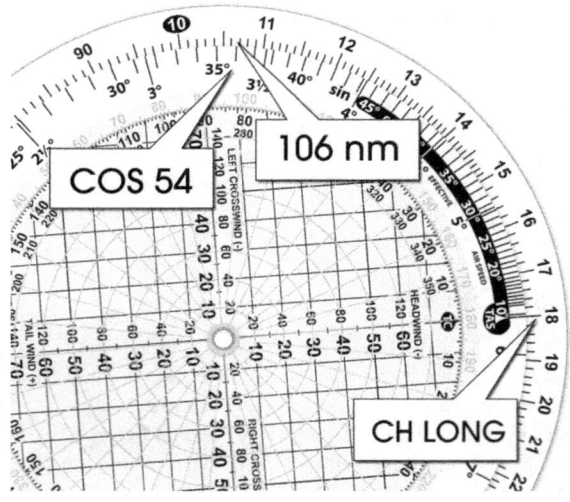

EXAMPLES

1. In what latitude will a d´long of 3°40´ correspond to a departure of 120 nm?

We know that the difference in longitude refers to the Equator, where 3°40´ (3 x 60 + 40) equates to 220 nm.

The other distance is 120 nm, so divide that by 220 to get 0.5455 for which the cosecant means 56°56.5´, N or S

2. What is the approximate rhumb line track between 45° 00'N 010° 00'W and 48°30'N 015°00'W?

  (a) 270

  (b) 245

  (c) 315

  (d) 350

Given the spread of the answers, this can easily be solved by just drawing a simple diagram, but the line from 45°N 010'W to 45°N 015'W is the base of a triangle, and the distance along it can be found with the departure formula:

```
212.132 = 300 x cos 45
```

From 010°W to 015°W is 5° x 60 = 300 minutes. The change of latitude is 3° 30' or 210', or 210 nm.

The tangent of the angle at 45°N 010'W is 210/212.132 nm, or 0.9899, or 44.71°. Adding this to 270° gives you 314.7°. The nearest answer is 315°.

3. What is the distance between 35°25'W and 28°53'W at 41°S?

The d'long is 6°32' or 392', multiplied by 0.7547 (the cosine of 41°), so the distance is 296 nm.

4. You fly North from a position at latitude 60°N for 90 nm. Then you fly another 90 nm to the East, South and West. How far away are you from where you started?

At the end of the first leg, you arrive at 61°30'N. You also go South for the same distance on the third leg, so you arrive right back at 60°. However, the distance at 61°30'N. gives you a larger d'long than the distance at 60°. The distance from where you started will simply be the difference in departures for the two latitudes, or 4.31 nm.

Tip: The North and South legs cancel each other out.

5. Two aircraft 45 nm apart at 40°30'S fly North at the same speed until the distance between them is 55 nm. How far did each one fly?

The d'long will be the same on both parallels. Working backwards, this is 59.1794' or 59 nm. Divided into 55, this gives 0.9294, the cosecant of 21° 40'.

6. At 24°N, with a departure of 32 nm, what is the change of longitude?

The cosine of 24 is 0.91. Divide that into the mileage to get 35 minutes.

7. If you fly on a track of 300° for 400 nm, what is the departure and change of longitude?

347 nm and 200 minutes to the North. **Hint:** 400 nm is the length of the hypotenuse.

8. A is at 40°N 120°E and B is at 60°N 086°E. The initial great circle track is 315°(T). What is it measured at B?

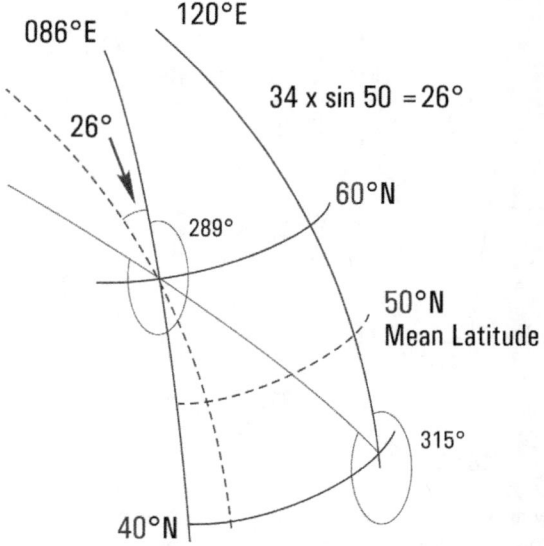

The change of longitude is 34°, and the sine of the mean latitude of 50° is 0.77, so the convergency angle is 26°, to be *subtracted* from the original track of 315° (see the transferred meridian of 120°E). The answer is 289°.

9. What is the final great circle track between 60°S 169°W and 40°S 173°E if the initial track is 290°(T)?

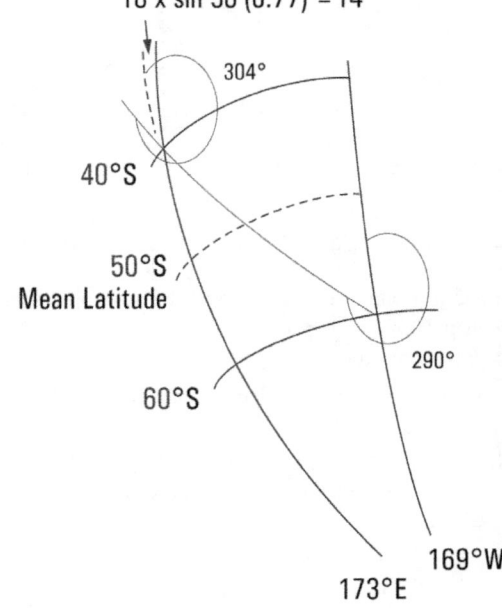

The ch long is 18°, so the CA is 14°. Added to 290°, we get 304°.

10. The initial and final tracks between A (30°N 18°W) and B (50°N) are 060°(T) and 082°(T). What is B's longitude?

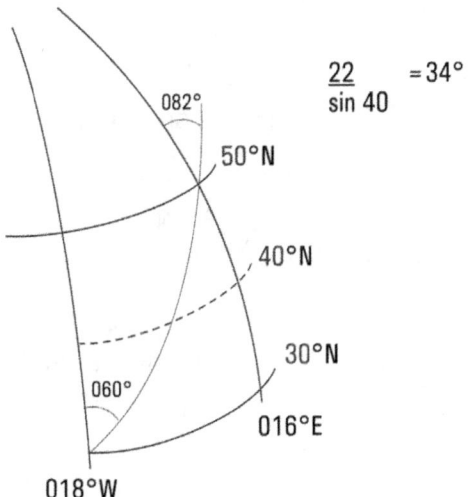

We know the CA (22°) so divide it by the sine of the mean latitude to get 34°. Subtract 18° (you are going past the Prime Meridian), and the remainder is 16°.

11. What is the distance and track between 58°N 13°W to 66°N 2°E?

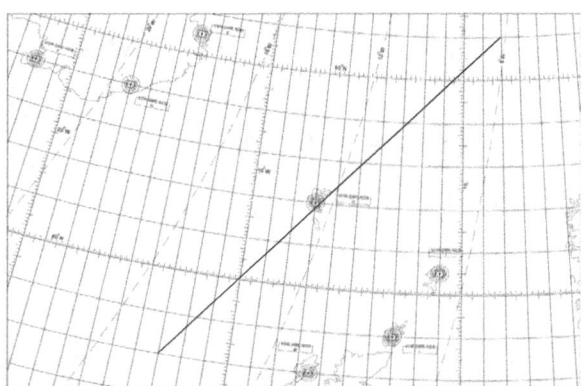

The track of 042° can simply be measured (at the mid point) if you have the map. However, it can also be calculated with the tangent value (opposite over adjacent).

The change of latitude can easily be figured out from 8° x 60 = 480 nm.

The change of longitude is 15° which, multiplied by 60 is 900 nm. The cosine of the mean latitude (62°N) is 0.4, so the departure is 423 nm.

You could now use Pythagoras and obtain the track distance of 639 nm, but you could also use the variation scale on the wind side of the CR-3:

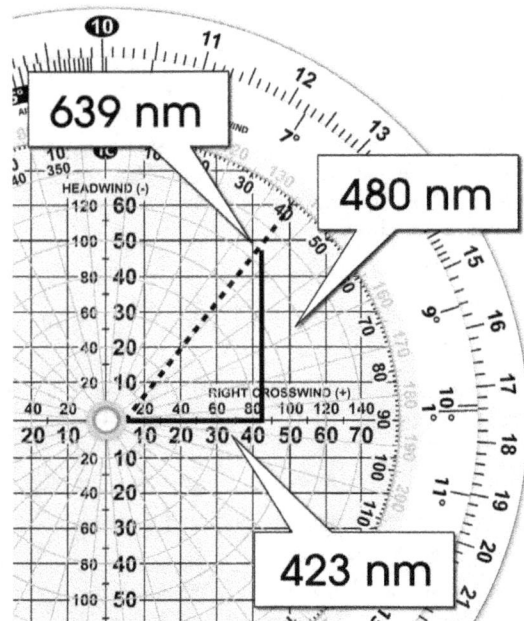

Apply the change of longitude horizontally, then go vertically for the change of latitude, according to scale. The average track direction (042°) can be read on the degree scale and the distance (639) just past the green line marked 60.

Conversion Angle

Sometimes, you need to convert between rhumb lines and great circles, especially when plotting radio bearings on Mercator charts. It may be best to come back here after having read about their properties, later.

The conversion angle is irrelevant close to the Equator, where it is almost zero, and only possibly of use to helicopters close to the Poles, in which case, the ranges involved are so short that, except in the highest latitudes, it is going to be very small.

Radio bearings take the Great Circle route, which is a curved line on a Mercator chart. As these are difficult to plot, you must convert them into rhumb lines, which are straight. Complications also arise from whether the plot is done at the aircraft (ADF) or the station (VOR/VDF), and where you apply variation and conversion angles.

The conversion angle is the difference between a rhumb line (or a Mercator track) and a great circle at each end of a line joining two points - it happens to be half the convergency because the difference between them would be full convergency. At the halfway point, the two lines are parallel, so the change must be half, and their bearings would be the same, so you should measure your track **at the mid-point** if you use a chart where straight lines are great circles (i.e. most flight planning charts). If the average true course of a great circle is 130°, for example, the true course of the rhumb line will be the same.

Conversion angle is applied to bearings at the point of measurement, towards the Equator.

Both variation and conversion angle must be applied wherever the bearing is measured. For example, the ADF measures the bearing, so both must be applied at the aircraft. A VOR signal gives the bearing measured at the VOR, so only variation needs to be applied at the VOR. See *Plotting*, below).

Plotting

A bearing from a VOR or NDB is called a *Line Of Position* (LOP). You need at least 2 LOPs to obtain a position fix.

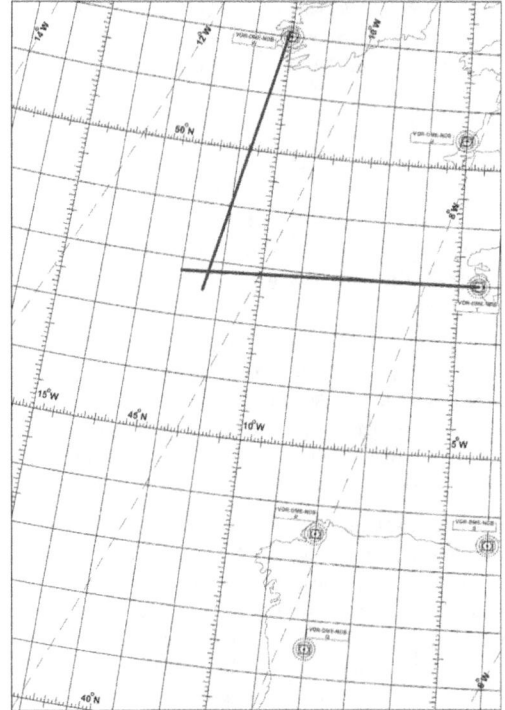

When plotting LOPs, you might have to use True bearings, so if the reading is from a VOR (which is normally aligned to Magnetic North, except in the Arctic), it must be converted to True before you draw the line.

In the chart above, two LOPs have been drawn from 2 VORs and where they cross is your position fix. The radial from the most Northern VOR is (for example) 195°, while the one from the most Eastern is 265°. Remember that the CDI must be centred with a FROM indication!

If required, you must apply the variation at the VORs first - but notice that each one is lying next to a different isogonal. Also make sure that one VOR is not in the Arctic, where its readings will be True anyway.

The Northerly VOR in this case must therefore be adjusted by 12° and the Easterly one by 8°. The process is similar for NDBs, but the bearings are not the same - both must be adjusted by 10°, which is the value of the isogonal at your position fix.

VOR EXAMPLE

A VOR is at 60°S 20°W, and the variation there is 10°E. The DR position of the aircraft is 62°S 9°W, sitting on the radial (QDR) of 145°. What true bearing would you plot from the beacon?

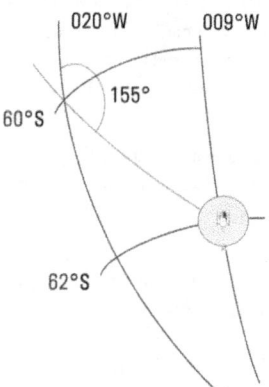

The lat & long figures are irrelevant when it comes to the VOR, because the variation is applied at the beacon. In this case, just apply the variation to get 155°.

ADF/NDB

An NDB is at 70°S 175°E, with a variation of 10°E. An aircraft is at 72°S 172°W, where the variation is 8°E. If the QDM is 325° and the sine of the Parallel of Origin is 0.75, what is the true bearing plotted from the beacon?

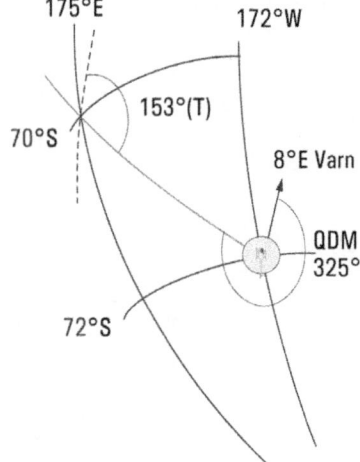

Things get more complex with NDBs, as you must apply the variation at the aircraft, then account for convergency, because you must transfer the aircraft's meridian (where the variation is measured), so the QDM now becomes 333°. The ch long (13°) x 0.75 = 10° for the CA, so 333 + 10 = 343 – 180 = 163° to plot.

MAPS & CHARTS 061 03

A map is a graphical representation of part of the Earth's surface drawn to a scale, as seen from above. On them, features found on the ground are represented by symbols, which are larger than the items they represent, so you can see them without a magnifying glass*. A map's purpose is to provide information on the existence and location of, and distance between, ground features.

*Not everything on a map is done to its scale; if it were, you would hardly see roads and railways, so they are artificially expanded to be visible. The centre of any object is its actual position.

Technically, a chart is a representation of a small part of the surface of the Earth on a plane, where distortion from any curvature of the surface is practically absent. In the marine world, a chart refers to the ground features underneath the sea. In aviation, the words *map* and *chart* are interchangeable, as an aviation chart will show parallels and meridians with minimal topographical features:

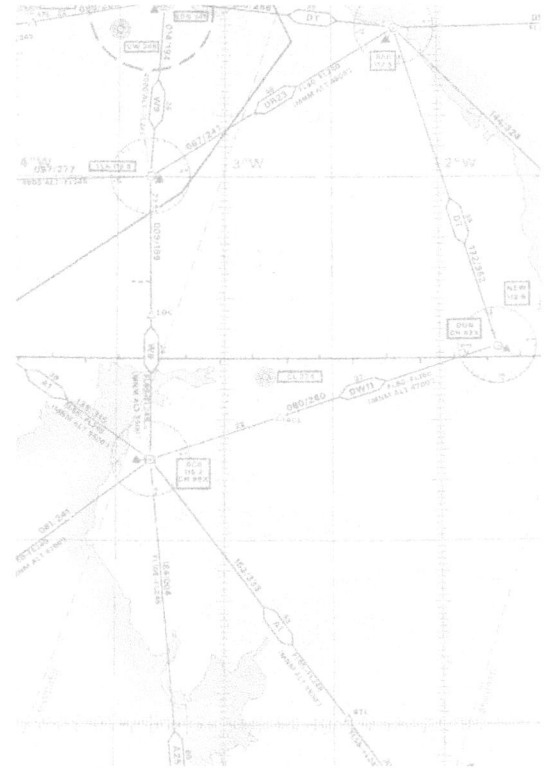

A map will show greater detail of the Earth's surface, so maps are for looking at, and charts are for working on!

You can use a chart as a map, but not necessarily the other way round.

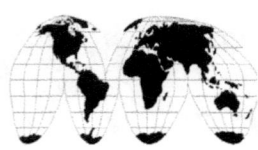

The point about them both is that they are small scale representations of the Earth's surface that are only accurate within a relatively small area, since you are trying to show a 3 dimensional object on a 2 dimensional surface. The further from the *centre of projection* you go, the more the distortion you get but, to all intents and purposes, it can mostly be ignored in its general area. You can see the problem if you try to flatten a globe, and it would be bad enough if the Earth were a real sphere, but it isn't. The Equator and poles pose special problems because their meridians are parallel and converging, respectively.

Distortion can be minimised, but not eliminated, and there are many ways of adjusting for it, each suiting a different purpose, so lines drawn on maps based on different projections will not necessarily cross through the same places (watch those danger areas!) When producing maps and charts, a reduced model of the Earth is used, which means that the compression factor is so small that it can be ignored.

Projections

The term *projection* means that an imaginary light is placed inside a model of the Earth and the shapes of the land masses are projected onto a *developable surface*, which is one that can be flattened without being torn, stretched or wrinkled. This does not include a sphere.

The type of surface primarily determines a projection's classification, but the source of the imaginary light is also a factor. The main ones used in aviation are *conical* (Lambert), *cylindrical* (Mercator) or *flat* (stereographic). All projections require sophisticated maths to be effective, in order to keep any distortions under control.

The quality of *orthomorphism*, or *conformality*, which is the more modern term, that all charts should strive for, means the scale is correct in all directions, or at least within a very small area if the scale varies, and bearings are correctly represented. That is, the scale at any point is independent of azimuth, so, for a short distance in any direction, it will be equal. The outlines of the areas must conform, or be free from angular distortion. As well, parallels must cross meridians at right angles. If a chart is not orthomorphic, compass roses would not be circular.

The scale on orthomorphic charts does not have to be the same all over - it only has to be constant in all directions at each point.

Otherwise, no chart is perfect, as you will find when you try to fold them!

Lambert's Conformal

Imagine the Earth with a light shining at its centre, then place a cone on top. If it could shine through the crust, an image of the Earth's surface will be projected onto the cone. Where the cone meets the Earth, the shadows of the land formations will be accurate, but will be out of shape the further North and South you go. This is the *conic projection*, and the latitude at which the cone touches the Earth is known as the *Standard Parallel*. All points on it are the same distance from the top of the cone, so distance is also the radius of the arc produced by the parallel when the cone is unrolled. The shape unrolled will be a circle with a wedge missing - the amount remaining (*n*) bears a direct relationship to the location of the Parallel of Origin.

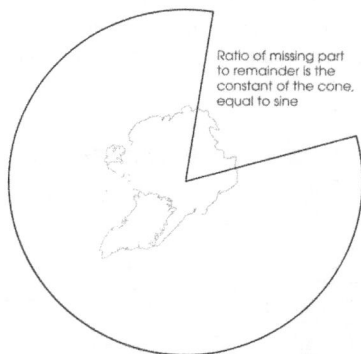

If the missing wedge is 25%, 75% (0.75) remains. This is the *Constant Of the Cone*, or the *Chart Convergence Factor (n)**. It is the same as the sine of the Standard Parallel, which is important for calculating convergency on Lambert Charts. The inverse sine of 0.75 is 48° 35', which is the Standard Parallel for this chart.

*The rate of change of a great circle track depends on the convergence factor (n) of a chart, which in turn depends on latitude. *n* is the number of degrees of change in track bearing for each degree of longitude travelled. 0.8 means that the change will be 0.8 for every degree.

In the simple conic projection with one parallel, the scale is correct only along that parallel and expands away from it, which limits the use of that chart in the N-S sense as it is not orthomorphic. Johannes Lambert improved things in the 18th century by mathematically pushing the imaginary cone into the Earth's surface, to cut it in two places instead of one.

This produces two *Standard Parallels*, where scale is correctly shown (and where the nominal scale is). The original SP now becomes the *Parallel Of Origin*.

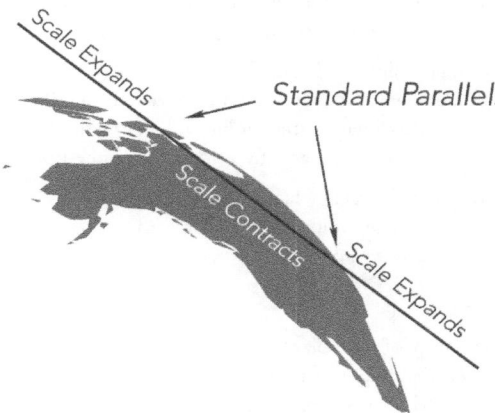

There is a slight contraction between them, but this is insignificant (1% or less) if two-thirds of the chart is between Standard Parallels that are less than 16° apart. The Parallel of Origin (or Parallel of Tangency) is almost midway between them (slightly closer to the Pole), where the scale will be smallest. Outside the standard parallels, the scale expands, and will be greatest at the top and bottom of the chart. Thus, although the scale is not constant, the chart is used as if it is, the variation being less than 1%.

The Lambert Conformal is what most of today's aeronautical charts are based on, as all latitudes apart from those close to the Poles can be represented fairly accurately with well-chosen Standard Parallels.

Great Circles drawn on a Lambert are (nearly) straight lines, so they are good for plotting radio bearings although, to be precise, Great Circles that are not meridians are curves concave to the Parallel of Origin. Rhumb lines will be curves concave to the nearer Pole (parallels are rhumb lines!)

Here is a good example of a Lambert Projection.

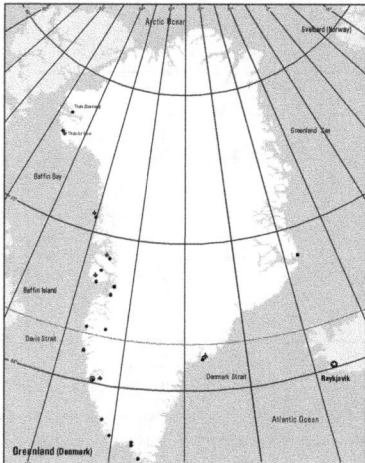

Note the converging meridians, and the curved parallels.

Remember:

- The sine of the parallel of origin is also the constant of the cone
- There are 2 standard parallels at which the *scale* is correct
- There is one parallel of origin where *convergency* is correct
- The scale is constant within 1% if the Standard Parallels are up to 16° apart
- Two thirds of the chart is between the Standard Parallels so the maximum spread of latitudes is 24°
- Great Circles are nearly straight, but are concave to the parallel of origin
- Rhumb Lines are concave to the Pole

Mercator

The Mercator projection does things differently. Instead of being capped by a cone, the Earth is imagined to be surrounded by a vertical cylinder, which touches it at the Equator (the chart is actually constructed mathematically).

Archimedes did it first, but Mercator varied the vertical scale inversely to the cosine of the latitude to make the chart orthomorphic. This is because the light projection becomes very distorted near the Poles. Mercator's trick was to figure out how to space the parallels to make rhumb lines appear as straight lines, which they will do if the meridians become straight.

Meridians on a Mercator chart are therefore *parallel, equally spaced, vertical straight lines* (compare this with those on the Lambert), and the distance between latitudes increases away from the centre. Up to around 600 m either side of the Equator, this can be ignored.

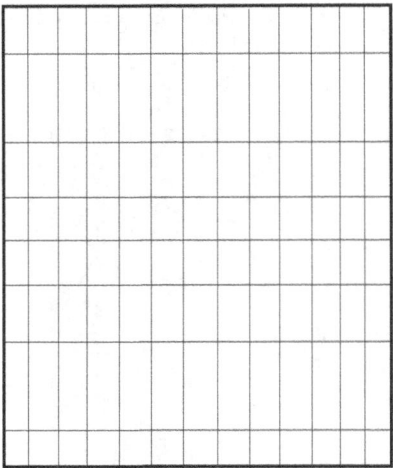

As the scale varies greatly away from central parts of the map (with the secant of the latitude), it does not show equal areas. An island at 60° latitude on a Mercator will have the same shape as it would at the Equator, but it will be twice the size, because of the scale expansion.

The Mercator is relatively accurate within about 500 nm (about 8° latitude) of the Equator because that is where the chart paper touches and is parallel to the reduced Earth. Scale there is roughly correct and great circles plot as almost straight lines. This is actually the only region a Mercator chart would be used for plotting these days.

As rhumb lines on this projection are straight lines, it follows that great circles must be curved, in this case, concave to the Equator, and convex to the direction of the increase in scale (except for meridians and the Equator itself). This curvature increases away from the Equator.

Note: The rhumb line is always nearer the Equator (rum comes from Jamaica!)

The rhumb line looks shorter than the great circle because of the scale expansion that occurs as you move away from the Equator.

MERCATOR PROPERTIES

- No convergence
- Rectangular graticule
- Scale correct at the Equator, expands with secant of the latitude
- Scale roughly constant within 8° N/S
- Rhumb lines are exactly straight lines
- Great circles are curves concave to the Equator

Polar Stereographic

These charts are used in polar regions (between 50°-90°), because the others cannot cope with convergency that well. To get the details correct, the paper is held flat over the top of the Pole and the imaginary light projected straight up from the centre or the other side of the Earth.

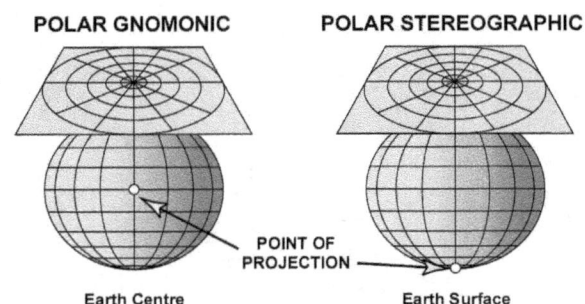

The theory is that, if an observer's eye is at the centre of the Earth, it is therefore within the plane of all great circles, so they should all project as straight lines as, indeed, they do on the gnomonic. They are not quite so straight on a stereographic.

Note: The Polar Gnomonic is only used for planning. It is not used in flight. Probably because you can't include the Equator if you project from the centre of the Earth.

The Parallel Of Origin is at the Pole.

PROPERTIES

Parallels of latitude are shown as concentric circles, and the spacing between them *increases* away from the Pole, so the scale expands, like it does with Mercator. As the scale and convergency are correct at the Pole, the chart is accurate in the Polar region, with its scale within 1% of the reduced Earth scale from the Pole down to about 78° of latitude, although the chart is often used beyond this. It is mostly used for general navigation and plotting in the polar region, or for trans-polar, long-haul flights.

Meridians are straight lines, radiating from the Pole. Great Circles, except meridians, are (very) slightly concave to the Pole but more closely approximate a straight line at higher latitudes. Rhumb lines, except meridians, are curves concave to the Pole.

As the value of the convergency factor is 1, convergency is always equal to the change of longitude. That is, there are no sines involved (see *Convergency*,).

CALCULATIONS

The simple geometry of the Polar Stereographic allows you to make calculations that might be more difficult on other charts. For example, parallels plot as circles, so a track with both ends at the same latitude makes an isosceles triangle with the Pole at the third apex, so we can calculate (as well as measure) the initial bearing of a track from A 80°N 070°W to B 80°N 040°E, plotted as a straight line.

Tip: When drawing diagrams, select the Prime Meridian for your North direction, so that the Western Hemisphere is on the left, and the Eastern Hemisphere on the right.

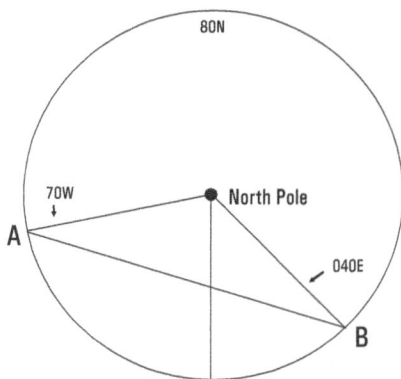

In the picture, the angle at the Pole between the 070°W and 040°E meridians is the same as chart convergency between the meridians, which is 110°. The angles in the triangle between these two and the track must add up to 180°, so the other two add up to 70°. As it is an isosceles triangle, and the angles are the same, each must be 35°.

In this case, the track from A to B, measured at A, is 35° right of North, or 035°T. Of course, this does not remain the same due to convergency, but the same figures can be used to find the track at B, which is 35° left of South, or 145°. The difference between the two is 110°T, which is the convergency between A and B. So, once you know one bearing, the one crossing any other meridian can be calculated with convergencey

Looking at the track, it reaches its most Northerly point, and is closest to the Pole, half way between A and B at 015°W. Given the convergency between A and 015°W, the track here is 090°T, which is hardly surprising as any track runs 090° or 270° at its Southern or Northern vertex.

POLAR NAVIGATION

At the Poles, it's darker for longer and there are fewer navaids (those that do exist are oriented towards True directions). The compass is unreliable because of the dip and the change in the rate of magnetic variation nearer the Poles, and there is increased deviation from the aircraft's own magnetic field, so realigning the DGI is also a problem, especially as it wanders in the long term (many pilots align it by flying down a runway or other feature with a known bearing).

Tip: Another way to determine true heading is to ask your GPS (if it is capable) for the true bearing to an NDB. Then subtract your relative bearing for the true heading.

Communications are difficult, as well, but that's part of another chapter. The two main problems are excessive compass dip, and the meridians converging at acute angles, where you cross them more rapidly, discussed under *Grid Navigation*, below.

Areas above 65° latitude are officially known as *high latitudes*. A *polar track* exists where part of it crosses an area where the horizontal component of the earth's magnetic field is less than 6 micro-teslas. Inertial Reference Systems are used to overcome these problems.

Tip: If an aircraft is at the North Pole itself, every direction is South, and every direction is North at the South Pole. This means that direction must be specified either as a grid direction (see below) or stating which meridian is to be followed. If a grid direction is given, measure bearings off the grid, which might not be straight up on the map. If a meridian is given, count around from the Prime Meridian, in the correct hemisphere.

GRID NAVIGATION

In higher latitudes, the difference between a rhumb line track and a great circle is very much greater than it is at low latitudes, as can be seen in the picture below:

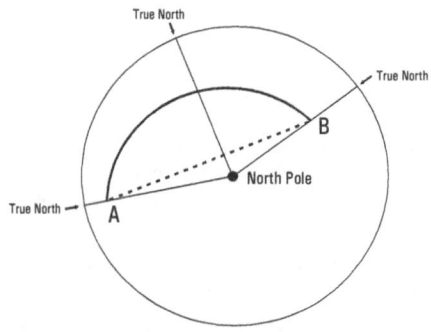

It is obvious that the shortest track lies near the pole on a great circle track that is nearly a straight line on a Polar Stereographic chart. However, the magnetic field is weak (so North is hard to detect), meridians converge greatly, and isogonals are very close together, so true track and magnetic variation are changing all the time. However, the transport drift is the same as convergence, so they cancel each other out and you can keep a constant gyro heading.

Note: Grid Nav requires a stable gyro (i.e. one with very little random wander), so your alignment with reference to Grid North can be maintained for as long as possible - for every degree of compass error, you will drift around 5 miles off per hour at 300 kts. This is where the high quality gyros in the Inertial Navigation/Reference System become useful.

The nearer you get to the poles, the quicker things happen. In the picture, you can see the angular differences in starting and ending points relative to the poles. At A, the initial True track is around 350°, whereas near the pole it is 270°. At B, it's around 190°. In other words, you start off nearly Northbound, but end up nearly Southbound in a very short space of time!

So how can you navigate under these conditions?

The answer is to use an artificial grid of parallel lines about 60 nm apart on a chart which can be aligned with any meridian (known as the *Datum Meridian*), although, in practice, it is almost always aligned with the Prime Meridian. This is called a *Standard Grid*. Anyone using the UK Ordnance Survey maps will already be familiar with using a grid over a UTM projection - see *Map Reading*, later.

Tip: The Douglas protractor has a useful grid that can be superimposed on a map.

Using a grid therefore compensates for massive changes in variation and convergency where the meridians disappear up their own orifice. Although the original purpose of grid navigation was to help with navigation at the poles, it can be used at any latitude, and the process can be illustrated on a Lambert*. You can see below that the transposed 0° line (which is also the grid) creates a greater angle to True North as you go West.

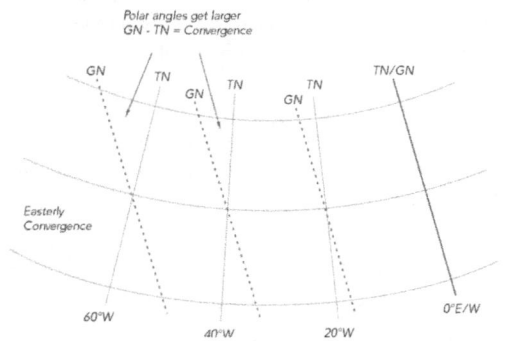

*Grid works best on Polar Stereographic and Lambert charts, because (nearly) straight lines on those charts represent great circles (you can use a Transverse Mercator as well). A grid track is therefore a great circle.

The angle between Grid and True North is governed by longitude and the convergence factor of the chart*. It is called *Grid Convergence**, or the *Convergence Angle*. With a CF of 1, it is equal to the convergence between the Datum and the local meridians, and it can be calculated with the normal convergency formula. For example, in the Northern hemisphere, at 30°W, GN is 30° West of TN, as adjusted by the convergence factor, if any.

*Convergency at the poles is equal to the change of longitude, but as you move away, the rate of convergency decreases. However, you could probably go down to as much as 80° of latitude before you noticed any real difference, so, over a whole Polar Stereographic chart, the convergence angle is taken to equal longitude.

**Convergency is the angular difference between any two meridians - convergence is that between the datum meridian and another. They therefore have the same numerical value as the change in longitude, as the angular difference is 1° for every degree of ch long. If your position is at 100E, that is your convergence angle.

If True North is pointing East of Grid North, you have Easterly convergence, and *vice versa*.

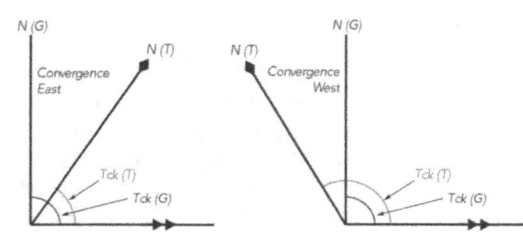

 Easterly or Westerly convergence does not necessarily mean that the aircraft is in the respective hemisphere. This will only be the case on a South Polar chart. In the Northern hemisphere, therefore, if the local meridian is West of the Datum Meridian (as in the picture), convergency is East.

The convergence angle is treated in exactly the same way as variation. When going from True to Grid, add Westerly convergence and subtract Easterly (and apply the convergence factor!). Do the reverse when going from Grid to True.

```
GH  =  TH  +W  -E
TH  =  GH  -W  +E
```

For example, in the diagram below, the True track to B is about 350°T at A which is 075°W. Adding 75° to 350° gives a grid track of around 065°.

At B, true track is around 190°, but B is at 125°E, and the grid track is still 065°.

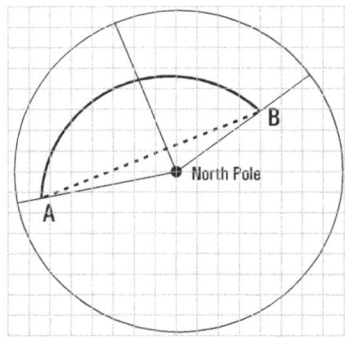

Note that, in moving away from the centre of the chart, although you are heading "Northwards" on the grid, you are actually going South as you move away from the pole.

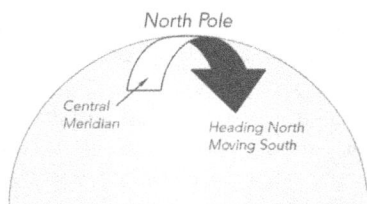

This visualisation is important! You set the DGI against Grid North instead of Magnetic North.

In the picture below, the Grid North line to the East of A is pointing to the left of the True North meridian at 40°W.

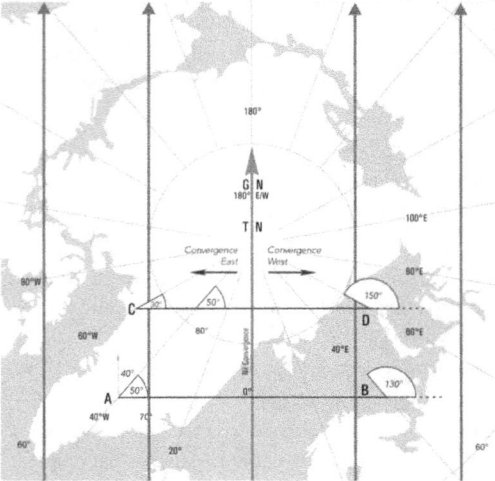

Grid direction is equal to the true direction plus the polar angle, which is measured clockwise from GN to TN. The grid track here is 090°G, based on 40 + 50. Grid and True tracks are the same at the alignment point.

A is at 40°W, so the Convergence is East, True track is least and the calculation becomes:

    090° - 40° = 050°T

At B, on the other hand, which is at 40°E, you get:

    090° + 40° = 130°T

It's a problem that is simply solved on the CR-3:

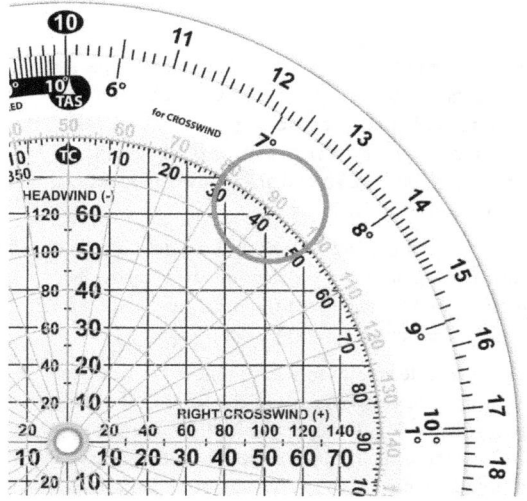

For A, simply set up the True Course against the TC index, and opposite the longitude* (40°W) you will find the Grid Track of 90°.

*On a Polar Stereographic, chart convergence is considered to be 1, so convergence = longitude. If you were using a Lambert, you would need to involve the convergence factor of the chart.

For B, place 90° against 40°E and you will find the True Course of 130° against the TC index.

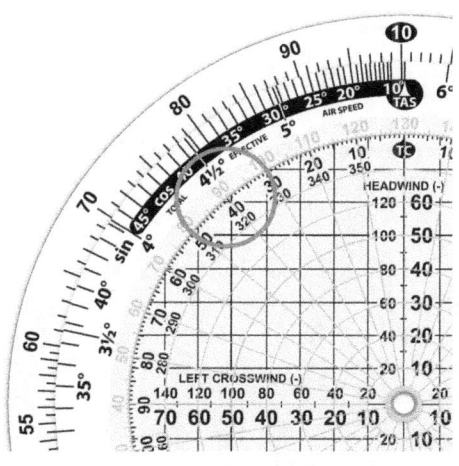

For a standard grid (North Polar chart) grid convergence is W for Easterly longitudes, E for Westerly longitudes, and the opposite for a South Polar chart.

If the grid is aligned with the Greenwich anti-meridian, meaning what they call a non-standard grid where the Grid Datum points down, work out the convergence for standard grid and subtract 180°. The result is negative which reverses E and W, but the figure is correct. Another option is to calculate with standard grid then take the reciprocal of the answer.

You can also subtract the longitude from 180° and work with the result as a standard grid. For example, if a grid is printed on a South Polar stereographic chart, with Grid North aligned with geographical North, aligned with the 180° meridian, the true track of an aircraft at 80°S 100°E flying on a grid track of 280° would be 000°.

    180° - 100°E = 80 + 280 = 360

Grivation

This is the difference between Grid and *Magnetic* direction or the sum of Grid convergence and variation. As the difference between True and Grid tracks is longitude, so Grivation is longitude + variation. Whereas normal

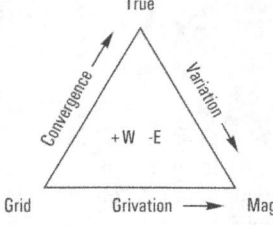

variations make the compass point along meridians, grivations make it point along the artificial grid lines (this is not needed if you have inertial navigation).

You can either convert Grid to True, then apply variation, or combine convergency and variation in one step.

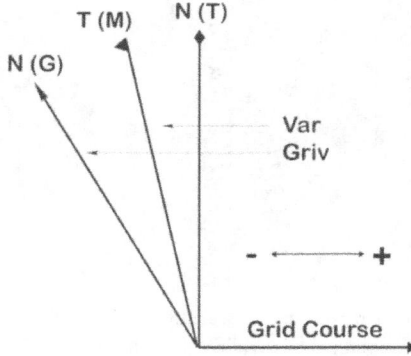

Grivation East, Magnetic Least

Grivation West, Magnetic Best.

So, if your Grid Heading is 90° and the Grivation is 30°E, the magnetic heading is 60°.

Isogrivs join points with the same value of grivation.

NAVIGATION (GENERAL)
Maps & Charts

Scale

Because a map is a representation of the Earth's surface, you need to know to what proportion it has been drawn to gauge distances accurately.

Assuming a constant scale, the ratio between distances on a map and the Earth's surface is expressed as a scale based on the map's size. For a scale of 1:500,000 (commonly referred to as a half-mil), one inch on the map is equal to 500,000 inches on the Earth:

Picture: CAA 1:500,000 map (small scale)

There are 63,360 inches to the mile, so an inch on a half-mil map is 7.89 statute miles. A "one-inch map" is one that uses one inch for one mile. A "quarter inch map" has 4 miles to the inch (about the length of the distance between the joint on your thumb and the tip, for quick reference).

Picture: CAA 1:250,000 map (larger scale)

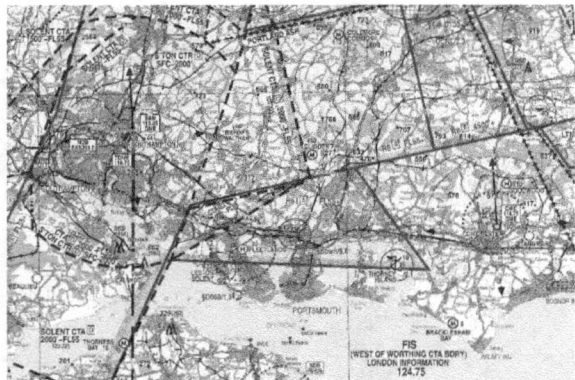

You can tell which chart has a larger scale by looking at the *representative fractions*, obtained by dividing chart distance by Earth distance. Thus, a chart distance of one inch divided by its Earth equivalent of 13.7 nm would be a 1:1000000 map, and of a smaller scale than a 1:500000 (the bigger the number after the colon, or under the dividing line, the smaller the scale is). The representative fraction is always written with the map distance (as the numerator, on top) as 1, regardless of the measurement units.

To find out what Earth distance is represented by a chart distance, multiply the chart distance by the scale so, taking the 1:500,000 scale above, 5 units on the map would be 2,500,000 units of ground distance. If asked what distance is represented by 25 cm on a 1/1,000,000 chart, multiply 25 x 1,000,000 to get 25 million centimetres. Divide that by 100 to get metres (250,000), then by another 100 to get 250 km.

To find the distance on the map, take the ground distance and divide by the denominator, or apply the line against a marking like this:

Tip: To find the scale at a particular latitude, multiply the scale at the Equator by the cosine of the latitude concerned. The RF at the Equator will be bigger!

MERCATOR

As the chart distance between parallels of latitude stays the same and the Earth distance reduces, the *scale* of a Mercator chart *becomes larger* at higher latitudes, expanding as the *secant* of the latitude, or the reciprocal of the cosine. This is not significant below about 300 nm, but you should always use the scale near the distance to be measured.

The easiest way to calculate the scale at different latitudes is to use the cosine of the latitude on the denominator (the large number, ignoring the 1 to the left of the scale ratio - so on a 1:5 000 000 chart the denominator is 5 000 000).

To convert from a scale at any latitude to that at the Equator, divide the denominator by the cosine of the latitude. To convert the Equatorial scale to that at the new latitude, multiply the denominator by the cosine of the latitude. Thus, if you have the scale at any latitude, it can be found for any other latitude.

For example, if the scale at 30°N is 1:5 000 000, what is the scale at 45°N?

$$\frac{5\ 000\ 000}{\cos 30} = 5\ 774\ 000$$

so the scale at the Equator is 1:5 774 000.

$$5\ 774\ 000 \times \cos 45 = 40\ 852\ 387$$

which means that the scale at 45°N is 1:40852387.

A quicker way is to use:

$$\frac{\text{Denominator} \times \cos B}{\cos A}$$

Note that it doesn't matter if the new latitude is North or South of the Equator.

EXAMPLES

- If the scale of a Mercator chart is 1:500,000 at the Equator, what is the scale at 15°N?

  The cosine of 15° is 0.97, so 500,000 x 0.97 = 482963. Since the scale will have expanded, the denominator should be smaller.

- If the scale of a Mercator chart is 1:600,000 at 30°N, what is the scale at the Equator?

  This time, divide the denominator by the cosine of the known scale, so: 600,000/0.87 = 689655.

- What is the chart distance between longitudes 179°E and 175°W on a direct Mercator chart with a scale of 1:5 000 000 at the equator?

  It's 6° (assume the shortest route) or 360 nm, or 26,265,600 inches. Divide by the scale for 5.25 ins.

- On a Direct Mercator chart at 15°S, a certain length represents 120 nm on the Earth. The same length on the chart will represent on the Earth, at 10° N, a distance of:

  The original line is at 15S, so to go to 10 (doesn't matter N or S) the distance represented will be slightly longer, for one thing (often you can see the answer just with this type of logic). Anyhow, 120 nm at 15S means 123.7 at the Equator (cos 15 = .97 - divide into 120 to get larger number). The cosine of 10 is .98, so multiply the new number by that to get 121.2 nm.

- If the chart distance between 150°W & 150°E on a Mercator at 25°S is 25 cm, what is the scale at the Equator?

  At the Equator, the distance between the meridians is the same (they are parallel lines). The Earth distance at 25°S is 60 x 60, or 3600 nm, so 1 cm = 144 nm or 266 km, or 26600000 cm. The scale is 1/26600000.

- If the scale of a Mercator at 50°N is 1/5000000, what is the chart distance between 150°W & 150°E at 20°N?

  The distance between 150°W & 150°E at 50°N is 60 x 60 x .64 (cos 50) = 2314 nm or 4300 km, or 430000000/5000000. The chart length is 86 cm.

Relief

Information about high ground is given in various ways. *Contours* are lines on a map joining points of equal height (or elevation) above sea level, so they are like isobars (the closer they are, the steeper the slope they represent).

Spot Heights show the elevation of prominent peaks with small dots, with the actual height shown next to them. The highest one will be distinguished in some way, possibly surrounded by a square, or printed in bold.

Tip: Add 300 feet to spot heights for obstacle clearance, because obstacles up to 299 feet can be built without lighting. Also, round up to start with, and add 1000 feet!

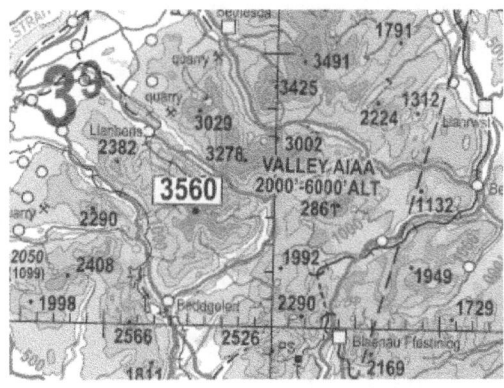

A bold italic figure next to an obstruction is the height AMSL of the top.

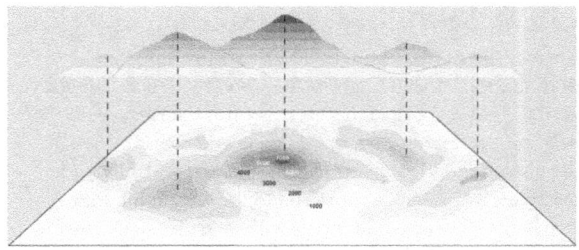

The smaller figure (often in brackets) is the height of the top of the obstruction above ground level. Subtract it from the bold figure to get the elevation of the ground AMSL.

Note: The Minimum Safe Altitude (MSA) will be at least 1800 feet in the UK. This is because ground lower than 499 feet is not shown on the charts, so we start at 500 feet. Add the theoretical height for obstacles of 299 feet, making 800 feet, rounded up. Then add the safety margin of 1000 feet to get 1800. The big blue figure 3^9 in the picture above is NOT an MSA value, it is a **Maximum Elevation Figure**, which is the maximum elevation of an obstruction within half a degree of latitude and longitude. You need to add 1000 feet to the MEF to get the MSA. Check the maps - in Germany, the big blue figure is an MSA.

Some maps may give different colours or shading to various layers to make things more obvious, known as *Layer* or *Hypsometric Tinting* (see below).

Otherwise, on a map, expect water to be blue, vegetation to be green, and railways and power lines to be black.

TIME & TIME ZONES 061 01 01/3

As it happens, the principles of modern time-keeping have evolved from the needs of navigation, in particular finding your longitude when at sea, as it is not fixable by natural means. The standard used is the interval between two transits of the same heavenly body over some place on the Earth, otherwise known as a **sidereal day**, or one which is related to the stars. All other methods of recording time (clocks, watches, eggtimers, etc.) reflect regular divisions between those transits. However, sidereal time is only used in observatories, because it doesn't fit naturally with the Sun's motion, which is what we base our lives on. The Solar day is longer than the sidereal day by about 4 minutes (it varies), and it is noon when the Sun is over the meridian you are on. This is *local time* unless you know when it is noon at a standard meridian, like Greenwich.

To recap, a sidereal day concerns one revolution of the Earth against a particular star. A solar day relates to one revolution against the Sun, and it is longest in February (+14 mins), and shortest in November (-16). This is the result of several circumstances, one being the *obliquity of the ecliptic*, and another being the Earth's orbit.

The Earth does not spin vertically, but is inclined at 23½° from the vertical over a 41,000-year cycle, so the Equator is not in line with the Celestial Equator (for the fixed stars). This obliquity of the ecliptic actually ranges over 22.1-24.5°, so the Earth, in this respect, behaves rather like a ship caught in the swell of the sea as it nods back and forth. When the inclination points towards the Sun, the Northern Hemisphere days are long and the nights are short - it's Summer. The day of the maximum value is the *Summer Solstice* on June 21 (Solstice is Latin for *Sun Stand Still*). In other words, the Sun sets further South each day, until, on December 21st, it stops, then starts moving North again about 3 days later. On June 21st, it stops going North to go South.

Only between the two Tropics can the sun be at its zenith, and only North or South of the Arctic and Antarctic Circles, respectively, is the midnight sun possible (66½° is the highest latitude at which the Sun will NOT set. That at which it will rise above the horizon and set each day is 64°). The highest latitude at which the Sun can be vertically overhead any place is 23°.

The Earth takes 365 days, 5 hours, 48 minutes and 45 seconds to orbit around the Sun.

Kepler's Laws Of Planetary Motion

We know that the Earth, with 8 other planets (making 9), revolves round the Sun although, to be picky, Pluto is no longer considered to be a real planet, because its orbit intersects with Neptune's - it is referred to by astronomers as a dwarf planet. There are also about 2000 minor planets and asteroids. 1 year is the time it takes a planet to go once round the Sun, in the Earth's case being 365¼ days (the odd quarters are consolidated every four years into one day in a leap year, and 3 leap years are suppressed every 4 centuries). While it is going round the Sun, the Earth spins on its axis once nearly every 24 hours, and the speed of the Earth's orbit is 66,600 mph, or 18.5 miles per second, much faster than a bullet. Because the Earth rotates from West to East, the heavenly bodies appear to revolve about the Earth from East to West.

Copernicus first proposed that the planets revolved around the Sun but, using 3 laws, Johannes Kepler (after Tycho Brahe) determined that:

- **1.** Each one moves in an ellipse*, with the Sun at one focus (it's an ellipse rather than a circle due to influences from outside the solar system).

  *But the Moon's orbit around the Earth is nearly circular.

- **2.** the radius vector (the straight line joining the Sun and any planet) sweeps **equal areas in equal time**, so planets speed up and slow down to compensate (they are fastest near the Sun).

- **3.** The squares of the periods of revolution of any two planets are proportional to the cubes of their mean distances from the Sun. That is, their orbital speed increases with distance away from the Sun. Essentially, the planets move in their orbits because they follow a mean line between two forces, and such a line is a curve. This is a corollary of Kepler's third law. True, the mean looks like a straight line, but the curve is so large that small segments would look like one.

The two forces are centripetal and centrifugal force, which could be regarded as attraction and repulsion. In fact, it was Kepler, and not Newton, who discovered that gravity varies inversely with the square of the distance between bodies (in simple terms, a phrase like "the square of the distance" just means that any attraction at two feet is a quarter of the attraction at one foot, etc.) Similarly, "the squares of the times as the cubes of the distance" refers to the square of repulsion being equal to the cube of the attraction. With only two bodies, you end up with a circle. With many, you get an ellipse, as with a typical planetary orbit, as per the second law, above.

The Earth's orbit, then, is the result of a balance between gravity (centripetal force, attraction) from the Sun, and centrifugal force (repulsion) due to the Earth's movement around it.

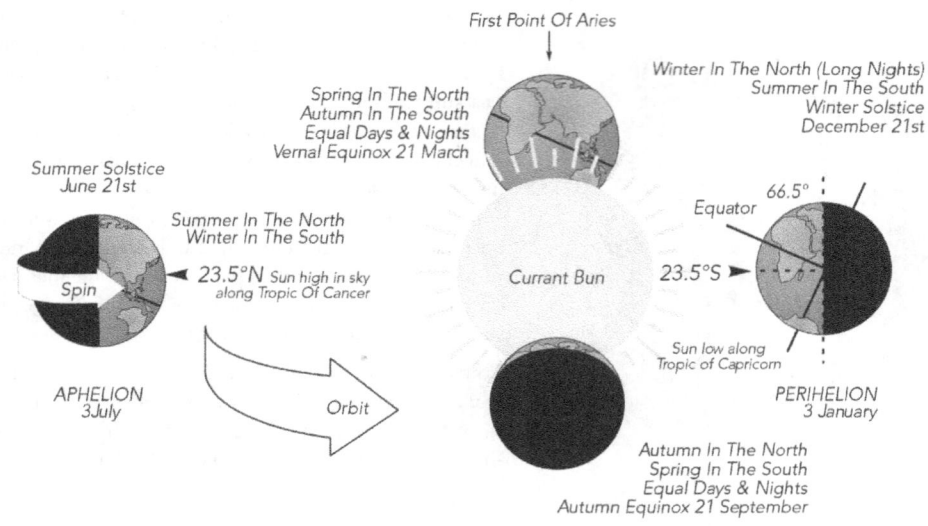

NAVIGATION (GENERAL)
Time & Time Zones

The *perihelion* (1-10 Jan) is where the Earth is closest to the Sun, and the *aphelion* (1-10 Jul) is where it is furthest away. Having said that, at perihelion, Earth is about 91 million miles from the Sun; it moves outward to around 95 million miles at aphelion, so the difference in distance is only about 3%.

The problem with the elliptical orbit and the different speeds is that the length of the apparent solar day varies. For example, in Summer in the UK, a sundial in Cornwall could be as much as an hour and a half away from the UTC value, so your watch must keep changing its speed to keep up with the real, or apparent (visible) Sun.

We use the *mean solar day* at 24 hours as the average between the longest and shortest Solar days. Thus, a (non-existent) Mean Sun actually transits any meridian at noon, hence the expression *Local Mean Time* (LMT), which is an averaged time at a particular meridian.

A sundial does, however, indicate the proper time of the upper transit of the real Sun over a meridian at *Local Apparent Noon*, and the lower transit on the other side of the Earth at midnight 12 hours before (the observer is considered to be in the upper branch of the meridian concerned - the lower branch is the anti-meridian).

Remember: The Mean Sun is a fictitious (or hypothetical) Sun moving at a uniform rate along the Celestial Equator at the *average (uniform) speed* of the real Sun's movement along the Ecliptic. It coincides with the Apparent Sun at the Spring Equinox (below).

The difference between solar and mean days less than a minute, but the results are cumulative - the real Sun is around 16 minutes **ahead of the mean Sun in November** and 14 minutes **behind it in February**. The difference between clock and apparent solar times (or between a clock and a sundial) is the *Equation Of Time* to be added to or subtracted from civil time for apparent time.

In summary, the word *transit* means the passage of a heavenly body over the meridian of a place on the Earth (actually across the face of the Sun) - the time difference between two transits is called a *day*, and we have to cope with transits of the Sun and the fixed stars, so we have two types of day. *Sidereal time* (star time) is kept with regard to the fixed stars, which appear to be fixed only because of their distance from us (it's actually time measured by the apparent diurnal motion of the vernal equinox*, which is very close to, but not identical with, the motion of stars. They differ by the precession of the vernal equinox relative to the stars, but you knew that already ☺).

*The word *equinox* is Latin for *equal night* - when the apparent path of the Sun round the Earth (Ecliptic) passes over the Equator on its way North or South (that is, it has a declination of zero), the days and nights are of equal length everywhere, at the Spring and Autumn Equinoxes, which are the times in the year when the relationship between the length of day and night, as well as the rate of change of declination of the Sun, are changing at the greatest rate in mid-latitudes. They are also points where the Sun rises and sets due East and West, respectively.

Because the position of the Sun on the longest and shortest days of the year shifts Westward amongst the stars, and some stars move relative to others anyway, the best point from which to locate stars with reference to East and West, and to start the year from, is the position of the Sun when the days and nights are of equal length, in this case the Vernal Equinox (the one that happens in Spring), also known as the First Point of Aries.

The Sun increases its declination (latitude) until it reaches the Solstice point, on June or December 21st, North or South of the Equator, respectively. The Solstice is the point where the Sun stops travelling and starts to go the other way. Having stopped going South on December 21st, for example, three days later, it starts North again.

To all intents and purposes, therefore, the Earth rotates by 360° in one *sidereal day*, which is regarded as a constant figure against the stars, even though, technically, it isn't. A sidereal day lasts 23 hours and 56 minutes (of solar time), which is about 4 minutes less than a solar day, because the Earth's direction of rotation and its orbit round the Sun are the same. To make up the time, the Earth must rotate an extra 0.986° between solar transits so, in 24 hours of solar time, the Earth will actually rotate 360.986°. In other words, during the course of one (solar) day, the Earth has moved a short distance along its orbit around the sun, and must rotate a little bit more before the Sun reaches its highest point again at any given place.

Using the sidereal day removes this anomaly.

The Earth spins slower every day, enough to be detected by the atomic clocks in satellites which must be resynchronised every 20 years or so (1000 weeks).

Time

In navigation, time can mean a specific hour of the day, or a time interval. After Einstein, the state of motion and location of the clock used to measure time became an important part of its measurement (see *Satellites*).

Days and nights are of equal length on the Spring and Autumn Equinoxes, March 21 and September 23 (*Equinox* is Latin for *Equal Night*), because the spin axis is vertical to the Earth's orbit. The Equinoxes are the times in the year when the relationship between the length of day and night, as well as the rate of change of declination of the Sun, are changing at the greatest rate. They are also where the Sun rises and sets due East & West.

Trivia: The Moon rises and sets at the same points as the Sun, but at opposite solstices. For example, it rises at midwinter at the same place the Sun does at midsummer. The Earth and Moon also rotate round each other, round some pivotal point, as they proceed on their way around the Sun. Even more strange is that the Moon fits exactly over the Sun when superimposed on it.

The beginning of the day at any location is when the Mean Sun is in transit with its anti-meridian, on the opposite side of the Earth to the point in question. This would be midnight, or 0000 hours *Local Mean Time* (LMT). Similarly, when the Sun is in transit with the meridian concerned, it will be Noon, or 12:00 hours. The angle between a meridian over which a heavenly body is located and where you are is the *Local Hour Angle*, or LHA. It serves a similar purpose to longitude.

In fact, the Hour Angle is measured Westwards (from the meridian to the celestial body), based on three datums, Greenwich, Local and Sidereal.

NAVIGATION (GENERAL)
Time & Time Zones

The *Prime Meridian* is the standard to which local mean time is referred - it is currently in the UK. *Greenwich Mean Time* (GMT) is now referred to as *Universal Coordinated Time*, or UTC, which is more accurately calculated, but can be regarded as the same for our purposes (GMT itself only came about because of the railways - previously, every part of Britain ran its own time scheme). The Greenwich day starts when the mean Sun transits the anti-meridian (180° away), and transits the Easterly ones before it reaches Greenwich. The local mean time in those places will therefore be *ahead* of UTC, and that of those West will be *behind*. When calculating, reduce everything to UTC first, and don't forget the date!

THE INTERNATIONAL DATE LINE

This is where a change of date is officially made, mainly the 180° meridian which bends to accommodate certain islands in the South Sea and parts of Siberia, but otherwise it over the sea. As you cross it, you can gain or lose a day, depending on which way you are going. When solving time problems, however, calculating in UTC usually sorts things out automatically.

Since we take (more or less) 24 hours to go round the Sun, in one hour we move through 15°, or we take 4 minutes to go through 1°. Similarly, in 1 minute we transit 15 minutes, or take 4 seconds to go through 1 minute (just to remind you, a degree is split up into minutes, which in turn are split into seconds).

STANDARD TIMES

To save you adjusting your watch constantly as you move round the Earth, some countries adopt standard times, as established by the US Navy in 1920. That is to say, legal authorities allocate a standard amount of time East or West of Greenwich, based on State borders. For example, Canadian time zones are:

Zone	Convert (UTC-)
Newfoundland	3.5
Atlantic	4
Eastern	5
Central	6
Mountain	7
Pacific	8

Picture Below: Time Zones across the USA.

They don't necessarily coincide with longitude lines, but are aligned with province boundaries, for convenience (some towns in Northern BC actually keep Alberta time). In theory, standard time is based on the LMT 7.5° either side of a regular meridian, divisible by 15°. There can be a 13-hour time difference between countries. To convert standard time to LMT, multiply the degrees distance from the standard meridian by 4 to get minutes, then subtract if you are West and add if you are East.

DAYLIGHT SAVING (DST)

This was originally set up in UK during the First World War (actually 1916) in an attempt to keep people out of pubs during working hours, or to save fuel in munitions factories (it depends on which book you read) and to get people up earlier so they could use the daylight.

Essentially, clocks go forward one hour for the summer - in *Spring* they go *forward*, in *Fall*, they *fall back* (Windows will tell you automatically!)

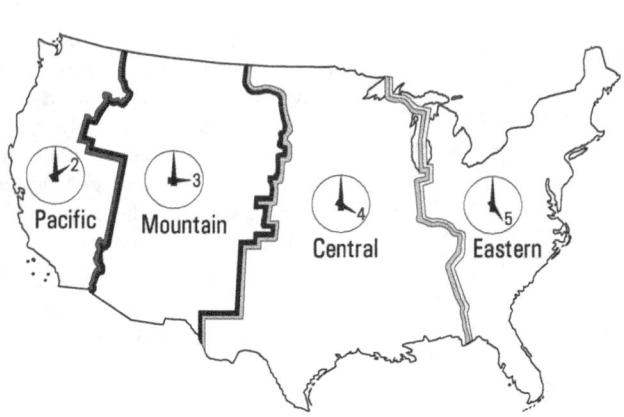

NAVIGATION (GENERAL)
Time & Time Zones

The Air Almanac

Standard times around the world are in three lists on pages A20-A23, *Fast on GMT*, *Slow on GMT*, and *Keeping GMT*.

List I - PLACES FAST ON G.M.T. (mainly those EAST OF GREENWICH)

The times given below should be *added* to G.M.T. to give Standard Time. *subtracted* from Standard Time to give G.M.T.

	h	m		h	m
Admiralty Islands ...	10		Estonia	03	
Afghanistan	04	30	Ethiopia	03	
Albania*	01		Finland	02	
Algeria*	01		France*	01	
Bangladesh	06		Iran‡	04	

*Summer time may be kept in these countries
‡ The legal time may differ from that given here

Check the footnotes!

List III - PLACES SLOW ON G.M.T. (WEST OF GREENWICH)

The times given below should be *subtracted* from G.M.T. to give Standard Time and *added* to Standard Time to give G.M.T.

	h	m		h	m
Argentina ...	03		Chile‡	03	
Azores	01		Colombia	05	
Bermuda*	04		Cuba*	05	
Canada			Ecuador	05	
Alberta*	07		Grenada	04	

At 105° 45' E, at noon LMT, what is the GMT?

105/15 = 420 mins, or 7 hours. 45 divided by 15' = 3 mins. Greenwich is least because the location is East, so 12 (noon) - 7 hrs 3 mins is 04:57 GMT

At 147° 28' W, at 1327 LMT, what is the GMT?

147/15 = 588 mins, or 9 hours 48 mins. 28 divided by 15' = 2 mins. Greenwich is best as the location is West, so 1327 + 9:50 23:17 GMT

SUNRISE, SUNSET

There are also tables for specific days and latitudes in LMT that tell you when the Sun rises and sets, varying with date and latitude (between 60°S to 72°N). There are no calculations involved - the tables have been made up from observations over hundreds of years. Sunrise or Sunset occurs when the Sun's upper edge is on the viewer's horizon, which will be affected by atmospheric refraction - when you see the Sun for the first time, it is still half a degree below the horizon, but this will not affect the figures as they are based on visible phenomena.

At the Equator, Sunrise is always 0600 and Sunset at 1800. Except in high latitudes, the times of Sunrise and Sunset vary only a little each day, so they may be taken as the same for all latitudes. Notice that the Sun rises later and sets earlier as latitude increases in Winter, but it rises earlier and sets later in Summer. However, outside the latitudes above, the Sun will not set in Summer, or rise in Winter. An open square box at the top of a column means the Sun is visible, and a filled in box means it isn't. 4 hash marks (////) means continuous civil twilight. This is representative of a Sunset table from the Air Almanac:

Lat	July							
	1	4	7	10	13	16	19	22
°	h m	h m	h m	h m	h m	h m	h m	h m
N 72	■	■	■	■	■	■	■	■
70	□	□	□	□	□	□	□	□
68	□	□	□	□	□	□	////	////
66	////	////	////	////	////	////	////	////
64	////	////	////	////	////	////	////	////
62	////	////	////	////	00 19	00 51	01 11	01 27
N 60	01 01	01 09	01 17	01 26	01 36	01 45	01 55	02 05
58	01 47	01 52	01 57	02 03	02 09	02 16	02 24	02 31
56	02 16	02 19	02 24	02 28	02 33	02 39	02 45	02 51
54	02 38	02 41	02 44	02 48	02 52	02 57	03 02	03 08
52	02 55	02 58	03 01	03 04	03 08	03 12	03 17	03 22

The readings depend on latitude and time only. To find the time of sunset at 55°N on July 12th in the table, first interpolate for the latitude, so you end up with 02 38 on the 10th, and 02 42 and a bit on the 13th. With 4 minutes between them, the answer is 02 40

If only one set of values for sunrise and sunset is given, the data is accurate enough, but may need adjustment for high altitudes.

NAVIGATION (GENERAL)
The Triangle of Velocities

The Almanac also has tables for Sunrise and Twilight, but the process is the same. It deals with the real Sun, but the times are in LMT.

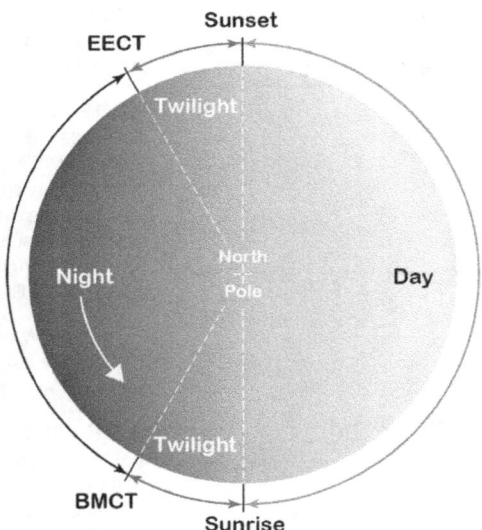

In fact, it is refraction that accounts for twilight (which is longer at higher latitudes). *Civil twilight* exists when the centre of the Sun's disk is within 6° of the horizon, during which you still have a distinct horizon. *Nautical twilight* exists when the Sun's centre is between 6-12° below the horizon (which cannot be distinguished).

Between 12-18° below, you get *astronomical twilight*. *Legal twilight* happens 30 minutes before sunrise and 30 minutes after sunset. Night exists between the end of evening civil twilight (EECT) and the beginning of morning civil twilight (BMCT).

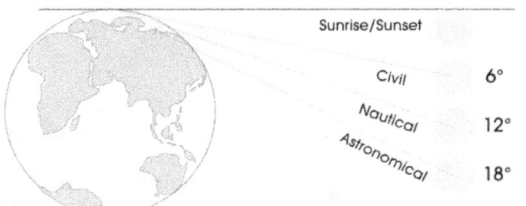

Remember that the figures are tabulated according to *local mean time*, which is based on the mean Sun, which doesn't exist, which is why twilight is shortest at the Equinoxes (the Sun's daily motion is fastest then). You will also have to interpolate, as not every day is shown, or every latitude.

Note: You have to be above 66° 33' N or S before the sun is above or below the horizon for a full 24 hours at some time during the year. However, the atmosphere plays tricks with light. In summer the midnight sun is actually visible at 66°. In winter, you need to go beyond 67° so as not to see the sun on the winter solstice. The onset of darkness is more sudden at the Equator because the Sun is setting perpendicular to the horizon, while at higher latitudes, it can set more obliquely, allowing it to remain close to the horizon for longer.

The Sun is also used, with other tables, to get a True Bearing, with which to set your DGI, which is very handy when up North. You could also use the heading of a known feature, such as a runway.

THE TRIANGLE OF VELOCITIES

An aircraft in flight is affected by the wind both along its axis and from the side, or, in other words, from a head/tail or abeam component.

In flying between point A and point B, you will only get there by just pointing the nose in the right direction if there is no wind or, if there is, it is exactly on the nose or tail. This is very rarely the case, so your aircraft would *drift* off course, according to the wind's direction, if you did nothing to correct it. In other words, you would end up a certain distance left or right of the original target if the wind were blowing across your track from the relevant direction (in the early days of the North Sea, when navaids weren't around, pilots would build in a slight error to their calculations, so that they would know which side of the rig they were in case it all went wrong).

The smart thing to do would be to make a heading correction towards the wind's direction to maintain a straight track. This, unfortunately, inclines the body of the aircraft more sideways to the track over the ground, which reduces the groundspeed, because some of the energy from the engine is used to keep it there. Thus, for various reasons, the speed of the aircraft through the air will not necessarily be the same as its speed over ground - if you are flying into wind, you will go slower relative to the surface, and faster if the wind is behind you:

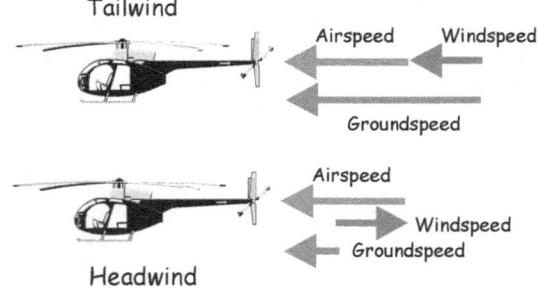

The result is the sum of two vectors in the same line.

You work out what the wind's effect on your trip will be by getting the forecast winds from the flight planning office, and working out a combination of three sides of a triangle, called the *triangle of velocities*, because a velocity expresses a combination of speed and direction, and we are concerned with those of your aircraft, the wind and the difference between them.

First of all, though, a few definitions:

- *Track.* Sometimes called *course*, this is the path the aircraft intends to follow over the ground, represented by the line on a map from one point to another (*Track Made Good* is the actual path - the difference between them is *Track Error*. Think of TMG as Track Made Bad, because it is where you don't want to be). Put another way, track

NAVIGATION (GENERAL)
The Triangle of Velocities

is the angle between the direction of a meridian (True or magnetic) and the longitudinal axis of the aircraft.

- *Heading*. The direction the aircraft is pointed in, according to its compass.
- *Wind Velocity*. The speed and direction of the wind. The faster your aircraft, the less its effect. Forecast winds are given as True.
- *True Air Speed* (TAS). The speed relative to the atmosphere, not necessarily the same as that indicated on your ASI, and not necessarily the same as.....
- *Ground Speed*, or the speed of the aircraft over the ground, due to wind effects.
- *Drift*. The difference between heading and track due to wind, measured *from* heading *to* track. In sailing, this is *leeway*. The *drift angle* is the difference between the airspeed and groundspeed vectors.
- *Air Position*. The position the aircraft would have reached without wind.
- *DR Position*. The calculated position of the aircraft.
- *ETA*. Estimated Time of Arrival.
- *Fix*. Definite confirmation of position by ground observation, radio aids or astro navigation.

The velocity of an aircraft in flight (i.e. through the air) will therefore consist of its heading and airspeed. In the diagram below, the heading is 270°(T) - the single arrow is the symbol for the heading vector, pointing the right way, of course.

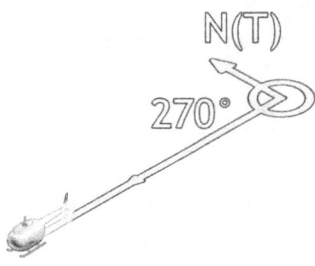

When plotting, a scale is used, so if the heading vector were 3 inches long, at 50 kts to an inch it would equal an airspeed of 150 kts, or the air position after 1 hour of flight. If we added the wind speed and direction to the heading vector, the resultant between them would represent track and groundspeed, also to scale.

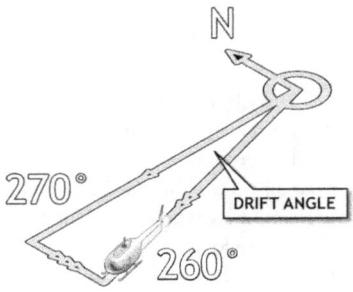

In this case, the wind vector is half an inch long, meaning 25 kts, coming from the North. Joining the ends would therefore show your ground position after one hour, and your track and groundspeed, after measurement (you will have deduced already that two arrows are used for the track and three for the wind - the track arrows always go in the opposite direction to the other two, and the wind always goes from heading to track). The *drift angle* (or track error) is measured *from* the heading *to* the track, in this case about 10°, so the track made good is 260°. It is the angle at which you will drift away from the desired track if the wind correction angle mentioned below is not applied.

The diagram above shows what would happen if you simply pointed the aircraft nose towards the West - you would drift to Port for the amount indicated. If you wanted to arrive over the intended destination, you would actually have to point the nose to the right (i.e. Starboard) enough to counteract the drift.

Just draw the wind vector on the *opposite* side of the line, and measure the length and angle of the new line joining it at the other end to find out what heading to steer (280°). The difference between heading and track is now called the *Wind Correction Angle*, or crab angle. It is the angle through which the aircraft must be turned into wind to maintain the desired track.

Note that the drift and wind correction angles are not the same - there may be a significant difference between them if the winds are strong. The WCA is always smaller than the drift angle, but at low wind speeds we ignore it.

Don't forget to work out the variation and deviation so that the compass heading is correct.

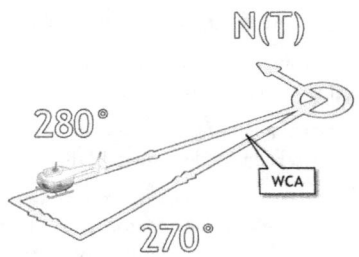

Dead Reckoning

As a navigator you need to know your present position, and how to get to another one, but the only information you have after some time in flight (if you're not looking out of the window) is your air position, based on the airspeed and heading(s) you used since you started. In theory, if you then add the wind velocity for the relevant period, you should get a ground position, which is called a *Dead Reckoning* (DR) position, because it has been deduced, or calculated, rather than being positively identified. To do this properly, you must keep an account (reckoning) of the course and distance run, and update things by using information from other sources, such as visual reference to landmarks (pilotage) or radio aids. Indeed, once the information chain has been broken, the other sources are required to re-establish your position - any errors with DR are cumulative, so the further you travel without an accurate position fix, the more the likelihood that errors will creep in.

Because you don't have room for a navigation table in your cockpit, various rules of thumb can be used in the form of *Mental Dead Reckoning*, successful use of which requires thorough flight planning and accurate flying (the 1 in 60 Rule is a good example).

NAVIGATION (GENERAL)
The Triangle of Velocities

DR involves the calculation of your best known position without navaids or visual fixes. In essence, it involves drawing the equivalent triangles of velocity you would create on your flight computer on a map, although it is important to grasp that the triangle's purpose is more to do with finding directions and speeds rather than a position. With no wind, your air position would be the same as your ground position. Dead Reckoning attempts to reconcile the two, having taken into account whatever the wind has gotten up to.

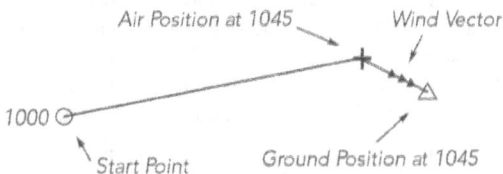

With DR, you know your TAS and the track you wish to fly, and you have a forecast wind, so you need a heading that will maintain the track, plus the ground speed so you know when you are going to get there.

Errors in DR are typically around 2-5%, usually from measurements of heading and speed. In fact any accuracy with Dead Reckoning depends on:

- The flight time since your last fix (the longer it is the less accuracy there will be)
- The accuracy of the forecast wind
- How accurately you maintain speed & heading

An air plot should be maintained constantly - every time the heading is changed, it should be recorded.

Note: There is usually a change of drift or grounsdpeed with a change of heading, which is ignored in mental DR.

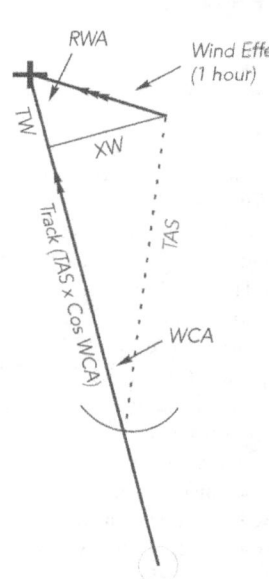

The traditional way for a navigator to do the job without a computer would be to draw the required track on the map, and an hour's worth of wind velocity from the start of that line, to scale. Then, with a pair of compasses opened out to the TAS, an arc would be described on the proposed track (the other point would be placed on the end of the W/V line). Joining the two points would produce the heading to steer to make good the track, and the length (along the track) would tell you the groundspeed, which consists of the TAS multiplied by the cosine of the Wind Correction Angle (WCA), plus the Tailwind (TW). The WCA can be assumed to be constant for long enough to draw a predictive series of lines for 6 minutes ahead.

As mentioned above, the lines you draw will be to scale, so one 3" long at 50 miles to the inch would represent 150 kts. When climbing and descending, take the mean TAS for the leg, and mean wind velocity.

 Tailwind, headwind and crosswind components are relative to the *track*, not the TAS.

As long as the WCA is small, there is not much difference between Track and Heading as the cosine of a small angle is almost one. You can therefore do a quick estimate of the groundspeed by adding the TAS to the TW.

Remember that these velocities go together:

- Heading & Airspeed
- Track & Groundspeed
- Wind Direction & Speed

The problem is that you have to find mixed pairs, such as heading and groundspeed, rather than the combinations mentioned above, because you start with a mix in the first place (you usually know the airspeed and track already). Given any four, you can figure out the others by measurement, but you can do it mechanically with the flight computer, discussed later. Although we can find the WCA and groundspeed with TW and XW, we can't do it the other way round unless we use the Relative Wind Angle (RWA), as created when the wind meets the track. This is what the Jeppesen CR-3 is especially good at.

However, in flight, you often need a mental calculation, for which you need to know the magnetic wind (upper winds are true, so don't forget the variation) and its relation to the aircraft. With the Track on the nose:

- If the wind is within 30° of the nose* or tail, 90% of it is HW and 50% is XW.
- If the wind is within 45° of the nose or tail, 70% of it is HW and 70% is XW.
- If the wind is within 60° of the nose or tail, 50% of it is HW and 90% is XW (the reverse of the 30° situation).

Nose in this sense does not represent Heading.

So, when the wind is on the nose, it is all HW or TW, and when it is abeam, then it is all XW.

Tip: Take the TAS of your aircraft, multiply it by pi, then divide it by 180. Remember the result, which is unique to your aircraft. You can then get an estimate of the WCA by dividing the XW by that number. This works for approach and other speeds as well. Thus, at 60 knots, with a 20 knot XW, the WCA would be 20°. At 220 knots, it would be 5°.

FIXES

If you happen to fly over an object that can be identified from a map, you have a *position fix*, which can be used to find what the real wind is, and your actual groundspeed. On the map, simply connect a line from your air position to the fix, and measure the resulting line between them (the wind vector). The line between your start point and the fix would be the *Track Made Good*, which could be used to solve the problem on the flight computer. The length of the wind vector is proportional to the length of time the plot has been running. Otherwise, the unit of measurement is the local nautical mile, conveniently obtained from the scale markings of the chart in use (for most purposes, use the mean latitude. Similarly, where meridians are converging, use the mid-longitude).

When obtaining a fix, VORs are more accurate than NDBs (remember to check line-of-sight in the exam), and a 90° cut is best, always being aware of coastal effect, or coastal refraction, as described under *ADF* in *Radio Navigation*. Unfortunately, multiple position lines never meet exactly, and your position is assumed to be in the middle of the resulting *cocked hat*.

Nowadays, since fixes are readily available, the *track plot* is the favoured method, that is, the wind direction is found from the known parts of the other two sides of the triangle, using the flight computer, as discussed below.

PLOTTING

The above activities with triangles are part of *plotting*, which is (usually) done on a Mercator chart, because it has a latitude scale on its vertical sides, and 1° always equals 1 nm. As the latitude scale expands from the Equator, you start with that part of it nearest to your track.

- A *bearing* is the horizontal direction of one point on the Earth from another, generally expressed as an angular distance from 000° (North) clockwise through 360°. If True North is used, the bearing is a *True Bearing*. If the reference direction is the aircraft heading, it is a *relative bearing*.
- A *visual bearing* is obtained visually.
- A *radio bearing* is obtained by radio (the reciprocal of the direction of propagation of the radio wave). A *radial*, being a line of sight, is one of an infinite number of directions of radio wave propagation **from** a VOR. Radials are independent of heading.

Before being plotted, relative bearings should be converted to True bearings by adding them to the true heading of the aircraft (when the bearings were taken), and subtracting 360° when the sum exceeds this amount. Thus, TB = RB + TH.

If a radio bearing line is to be plotted as a straight line on a Mercator chart, you need to use a conversion angle.

LOST PROCEDURE

Assuming you have flown as accurately as possible, and the wind velocity was accurately forecast, and you made no mistakes in your flight planning, you should find yourself pretty much on track throughout the flight. However, life is not always like that, and once in a while you may find yourself unsure of your position, the technical term for being lost. The *circle of uncertainty* is a way of trying to remedy this by allowing a percentage of error and drawing a circle of appropriate size centred on your destination. In theory, you should be somewhere inside it. The diameter will very rarely be more than 10% of distance flown.

You could also find the average heading, wind velocity and TAS to estimate your ground position. Averages are based on two observed fixes.

A useful method of a pilot resolving, during a visual flight, any uncertainty in the aircraft's position is to maintain visual contact with the ground and *set heading towards a line feature such as a coastline, motorway, river or railway*.

THE 1 IN 60 RULE

This is a rule of thumb that can solve many problems in aviation without getting the calculator out (as such, it shouldn't really be used in exams). It means that, for every 1 degree left or right of track, you will be 1 nm off track for every 60 travelled (or, in other words, with a hypotenuse of 60, the length of the opposite side equals the value of the angle in degrees).

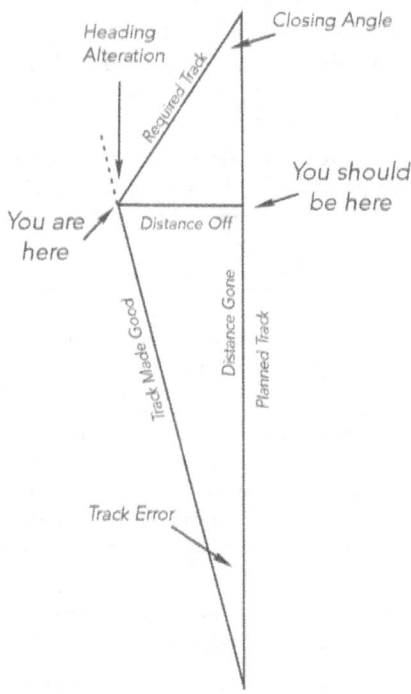

Picture: 1 in 60 Rule. Track Error + Closing Angle is equal to the Heading Alteration

The formula starts off like this:

$$\frac{\text{Error}}{60} = \frac{\text{Distance Off}}{\text{Distance Gone}}$$

It ends up like this:

$$\text{Error} = \frac{\text{Distance Off} \times 60}{\text{Distance Gone}}$$

Here are some quick reference figures:

- 6 nm off means 6° at 60 nm
- 6 nm off means 12° at 30 nm
- 10 nm off means 10° at 60 nm
- 10 nm off means 5° at 120 nm

It is a good idea to work out the maximum drift that you might encounter on a flight, which you get with a wind component at right angles to the track.

In this case, the formula becomes:

$$\text{MD} = \frac{\text{W/V} \times 60}{\text{TAS}}$$

If the estimated drift is more than 60°, use the full value. If it is around 45°, use 75%, at 30° use 50% and at 15° use 25%.

Of course, when you are off track, there is the potential for getting lost, so the first thing to do is parallel the original track. Now, at least, you shouldn't get any further off track while you work out how to get to the destination.

- To **parallel your original track**, alter course by the track error in the appropriate direction
- To **get back on the original track** (provided you haven't gone more than halfway), alter course by double the track error. Then apply the correction as a single figure to keep you there
- To **track directly to the original destination**, you would need an extra bit, called a *closing angle*, which you can find by altering the formula above:

```
CA = Distance Off x 60
     Distance To Go
```

Add the combination of closing angle and track error to the heading the appropriate way.

Notes: The time to regain track may be more than that used to create the error in the first place. Also, these rules are approximate, because altering heading changes the relationship of the wind to your machine. 1 in 60 is used for convenience - if the exact figures for π are used it should be 1 in 57. The Tan may be used up to 25°, and the Sine is accurate up to 40° (within 10% up to 70°).

Tip: If you have travelled ¼ of the way along your track, the heading alteration is 4 times the closing angle.

You can use the 1 in 60 rule to see if you are still inside an airway. If the centreline was 045°, and you were on the 040° radial, you would be off track by 5°. If the DME says you are 45 nm away, it's a simple calculation:

```
Dist Off = TE x Dist Gone
                60
```

The answer is 3.75 nm, so you are OK as airways are 5 nm either side of the centreline. It works for glideslopes, too:

```
Height = GP Angle x Range
              60
```

THE FLIGHT COMPUTER

The E-6B was developed in the United States by Naval Lt. Philip Dalton in the late 1930s. The name comes from its original part number for the US Army Air Corps in World War II. It is a device with a sliding scale, marked with drift angles and TAS arcs, with a frosted circular screen on which you can draw the business end of the triangle of velocities.

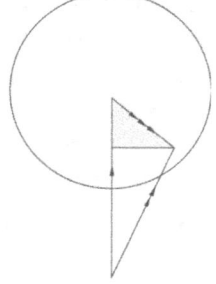

There is a dot in the centre of the screen on the vector face, around which is a compass rose that can be rotated to bring your heading or track under the lubber line at the top, labelled *True Index* in the picture below. To the left and right of the lubber line are variation/drift markings.

Note: The centreline of the slide is for heading and airspeed, and track and groundspeed is found along one of the angled drift lines after the wind has been applied.

Note: The LOs require you to use a flight computer and NOT trigonometry - some questions have the mathematically more precise trigonometrical solution as an incorrect option.

Picture: Vector Face of E6B Computer

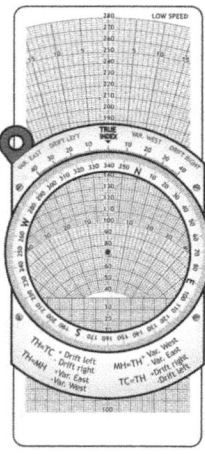

Note: Refer to the instruction book with your computer.

The main trap to watch out for is not matching the 2 drifts, that is, the drift against track on the compass rose must match that from the drift lines.

Helpful hints:

- If you know the wind, set it in first
- If you are not using a CRP-5, label the top index mark on the Dalton Computer "True Hdg"
- Except for the wind component (airfield wind and runway are magnetic) use true bearings

MISCELLANEOUS

Chart Symbols

1. VOR/DME (co-located)
2. DME
3. VOR
4. NDB
5. Non-specific navaid
6. TACAN
7. VOR/TACAN (colocated)

Meteorology

Weather is the sum total of the atmospheric conditions over a place over a short period of time (the *climate* of an area concerns its average weather over longer periods). Knowledge of the weather is important because we have to fly through it, and therefore have to cope with its various hazards.

If you understand the weather, you can avoid problems such as icing and turbulence, or use it to your advantage, say, by making use of tailwinds to speed things along.

We have weather (and seasons) because the Earth is heated unevenly as it rotates and the surface temperature changes. This is because the Earth is not vertical in space, but is tilted by 23½°, so different areas are exposed in turn to the Sun's rays during its orbit. Also, the atmosphere contains varying amounts of moisture that release and absorb heat when they change state from vapour to solid and back. This can be a major source of energy for thunderstorms and hurricanes. Essentially, the more heat and moisture there is in the air, the more energy it contains, with the more potential for rough weather.

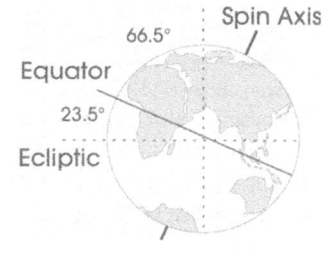

Tip: The temperature and dewpoint figures (and their relative closeness) in weather reports give the best clues.

In brief:

- **Differences in air temperature create the winds** - hot air rising from the surface creates an area of low pressure that allows air under a higher pressure to rush in and fill the space left behind. What happens next depends on where the air came from, and how it got there, plus its moisture content. For example, moving air that is heated from below becomes unstable, and may produce cumulus-type cloud and showers. Visibility will generally be good, except over deserts. On the other hand, moving air that is cooled from below becomes more stable, and may to produce stratus-like (layered) cloud, or even fog, or drizzle, so visibility will be relatively poor.
- **The Earth's spin twists the wind direction**.
- **Pressure decreases with height**, and subsequently the temperature under Charles' law.
- **Cooler air cannot hold as much water vapour**, hence clouds, which can tell you what's going on.

There is a net transport of heat from the Equator to the Poles that helps keep the average temperature of the Earth at around 14°C, which is varied by minor circulations as described in the *Wind* section.

The energy for all this originally comes from the Sun, and its effect on the atmosphere is explained in terms of basic physics, particularly the Gas Laws. The proportion of the Sun's energy that actually reaches the surface of the Earth can vary from place to place according to the area covered and how much is reflected back into the atmosphere, plus the surface it reflects from, but all this is discussed later.

THE SUN 050 01 02

The Sun's diameter is 865,000 miles, or 109 times that of the Earth (and 400 times that of the moon). Although its surface temperature may be high (5800 Kelvin), some scientists (like Herschel) have proposed that its *centre* is actually cold, like the middle part of a candle flame which won't burn anything. We feel its effects as heat and light, but it also throws out magnetic, or cosmic, rays, which vary in an 11.5-year cycle, signified by sunspots, that affect radio propagation, and radio amateurs pay close attention to them. Nobody really knows what sunspots are, but they could be gaps in the Sun's own atmosphere which allow us to see its dark centre. They were originally discovered by the ancient Chinese, and rediscovered in 1952. In 1982 it was also found that the Earth's magnetic field vibrated in sympathy with the bombardment of electrons and protons from the Sun, and is a better explanation of global warming, as the Earth's temperature changes match sunspot activity almost exactly.

The energy from the Sun is generated by a nuclear reaction, during which hydrogen is constantly changed into helium, which has a slightly smaller mass. As a result, the Sun reduces in size as energy is given off.

The Earth receives about 2 billionths of the Sun's total radiation, roughly 23 billion horsepower - more energy per minute than is used on the Earth all year. Energy from the Sun is received in three ways:

- **Ultraviolet waves** (9%), which have the highest frequency and are absorbed by oxygen and ozone.
- Waves from the **visible spectrum** (45%) which, mixed in equal proportions, produces white light.
- **Infrared waves** (46%), which have the lowest frequency and which are absorbed by CO_2 and water vapour. They can be seen by some animals.

The *Solar Constant* is an average value of 1370 watts/m^2.

Reflection & Radiation

The Sun's rays are depleted on their way through the atmosphere in the formation of ozone (O_3) at around 80,000 feet (where the highest concentration is), which acts as a screen to keep out ultraviolet rays. Water vapour absorbs most of the infrared.

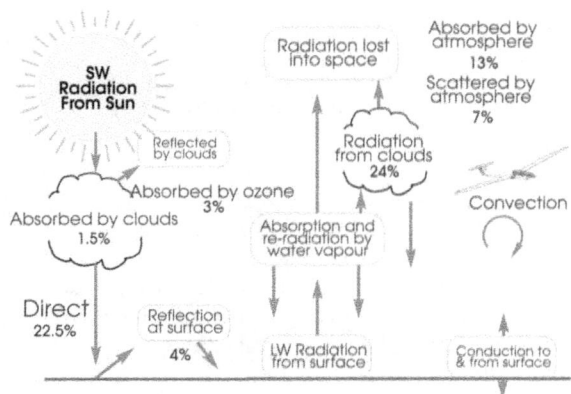

Very little visible radiation is absorbed, but small amounts are reflected back from clouds, leaving less than 50% to be absorbed by the Earth's surface. This is the credit side of the Earth's *solar budget*, which is the difference between solar energy received and reflected back (the two are only equal at 38° latitude). Clouds are important here, because they can stop a large amount of incoming radiation from the Sun by reflection, and they cut down losses from outgoing radiation by *absorption* and *re-radiation*.

Heat Exchange

Whatever radiation gets through from the Sun heats the Earth's surface by **insolation** (*in*coming *sol*ar radi*ation*). It is maximum at the local noon. **Radiation** involves the flow of heat from one material to another without affecting the temperature of the space between them. The atmosphere gains little or no heat from direct radiation.

The air in contact with the surface is heated by **conduction**, where heat can pass from a warmer to a colder body without the transfer of matter. As air is a poor conductor of heat, the air close to the ground usually ends up warmer than that above it, although the opposite can happen with an **inversion**, of which more later.

Convection exists where the body carrying the heat itself moves, usually vertically*, which is how warmth is spread through the rest of the atmosphere, until the temperature equalises with the surrounding air. Turbulence has a similar effect, and there is also the transfer of latent heat, which occurs when heat absorbed during evaporation at the surface is released during condensation. Finally, some direct transfer of heat is done when short wave radiation is absorbed by the ozone layer (see *Greenhouse Gases*).

***Advection** is the horizontal movement of air. If this happens with warm air in the upper parts of a layer, stability will increase in the layer.

For a given amount of sunshine, the rate at which the surface heats up depends on:

- The **angle of incidence** of the rays (see overleaf).
- **Dampness of the ground**, or moisture content of soil (as the moisture must be warmed up first, any output of heat is retarded).
- **Nature of the surface** - sandy surfaces warm up quicker, but granite keeps heat longer. Snow surfaces don't change much. Water is slow to heat, because the Sun's rays can travel far in, and are widely spread, which makes it a better storehouse of solar energy than land. As over two thirds of the Earth is covered by water, the oceans play a significant part in the generation of weather, especially as ocean currents can act the same way as winds do in balancing out the Earth's heat energy (e.g. the Gulf Stream). Water doesn't reflect much heat when the Sun is directly over it, but it reflects more when the Sun's rays are at an angle. Thus, for the same energy, land surfaces reach higher temperatures more quickly than water surfaces do. Land also cools more rapidly when the source of heat is removed, say at night, so land areas will have large daily and seasonal *ranges* of temperature, which are instrumental in the creation of land and sea breezes.
- **Colour of the surface** - the darker the area, the more absorption that takes place, and the more heat that is generated.
- **Foliage cover** - trees will absorb rays before they hit the ground during the process of evaporation from the leaves.
- **Reflection** from the ground.

The *albedo* of a surface is the ratio of global radiation from the sun and sky reflected by that surface.

As there is a time lag, the warmest months in UK are July and August instead of June, when the Sun gets to its highest altitude. In the same way, the warmest part of a sunny day is not noon, but a couple of hours afterwards.

THE GREENHOUSE EFFECT

The Earth is about 33° warmer than it would be without its atmosphere. The difference lies in the *Greenhouse Effect*, and the gases that help things along are the *Greenhouse Gases*. The primary heat-trapping gas is water vapour (it absorbs long wave radiation), with CO_2, methane and sodium dioxide among the secondaries. The atmosphere is largely transparent to short wave solar energy.

Bodies with temperatures above absolute zero (-273°C) radiate heat energy that travels as electromagnetic waves. The wavelength of such energy is inversely proportional to the temperature of whatever is emitting it. As the Sun is very hot, its radiations are of shorter wavelength than those from the Earth, which has a much lower temperature (in fact, around 99% of the Sun's energy is emitted in the shorter wavelengths). This is a similar (but not identical) effect to that produced by the glass in a greenhouse, that lets short wave radiation (light) in, but does not allow the longer infrared radiation out. Essentially, long wave energy radiated from the surface of the Earth is readily absorbed by water vapour and CO_2, and is reradiated back to the Earth.

Between the Equator and 35° of latitude, more energy is absorbed than is radiated, so there is a surplus. There is also a deficit between 35° of latitude and the relevant Pole.

The Seasons

At the Summer Solstice in June (longest day), the Sun is over the Tropic of Cancer at 23.5°N. In Winter, in December, it is over the Tropic of Capricorn at 23.5°S. It is overhead the Equator at the March and September Equinoxes, when days and nights are of equal length.

The paradox is that, in the Northern Hemisphere's Winter (on the right, overleaf), the Earth is at its *closest* point to the Sun (after Kepler's Laws), where you would expect it to be warmer, proving that the Earth's heat is self-created.

The reason for the paradox is that the Sun's rays are distributed differently. In Winter, they are spread over a wider area and are less effective because the days are shorter. They have also had a longer path through the atmosphere, with all its impurities.

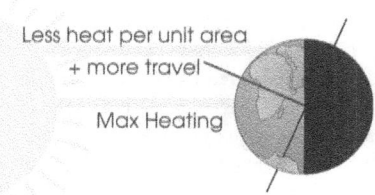

The distance of the Earth from the Sun can vary by as much as 3 million miles, as explained in *Navigation*.

Picture: Earth's Orbit Around The Sun

THE ATMOSPHERE

This has already mostly been mentioned in *Human Factors*, but there are a few points relating to meteorology that need to be made. Almost all weather happens in the troposphere, because it contains more than 75% of the mass of the atmosphere, which is drawn to the Earth by gravity. About half of that mass is below 18 000 feet, with no clear cut upper limit.

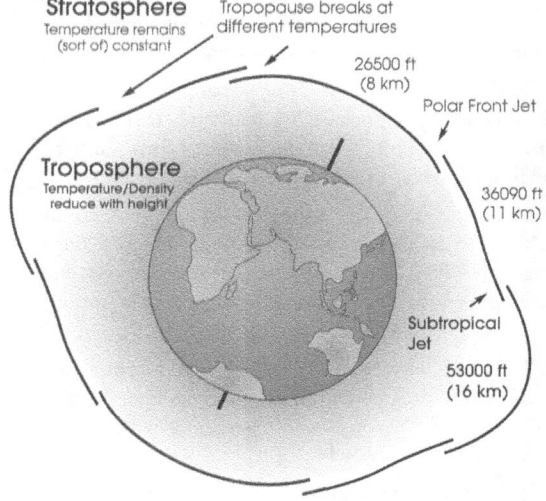

The tropopause is the "boundary" between the troposphere and stratosphere. It normally represents the maximum limit for winds and clouds, because that's where the temperature abruptly stops decreasing with altitude (the Sun warms up the ozone in the Stratosphere). Temperature *decreases* in the troposphere, at 1.98°C per 1000 feet. This is because, as pressure decreases, so does the temperature, resulting in *adiabatic cooling**.

*Adiabatic means that the air gets hot, or cold, all by itself, according to whether it is being compressed or expanded - no energy is added or taken away, or exchanged with the outside

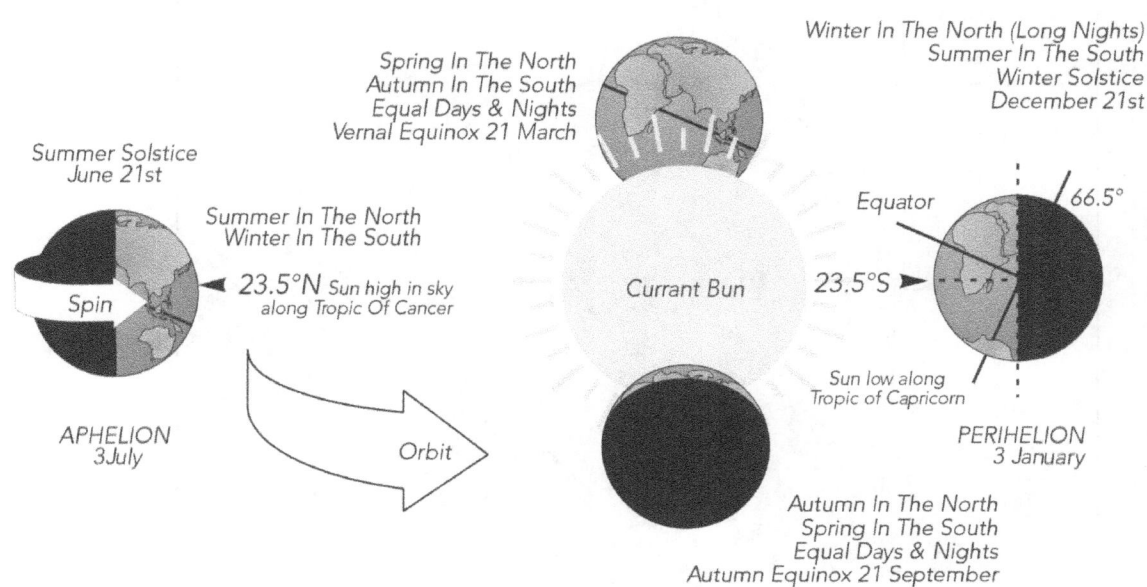

world. In other words, as air expands, the molecules have more room to move around in, so they slow down, which has the effect of reducing the temperature. Similarly in reverse. Thus, as a parcel of air rises into a region of lower pressure, which makes it expand, it cools adiabatically, through its own expansion, in the short term. Conduction between different sources of air takes quite a long time.

Although the stratosphere is generally not important for weather forecasting, there are pockets of warm air in the lower levels, called *warm sinks*, which are associated with strong upward motion in the troposphere, meaning that rising air can overshoot the tropopause.

Over the Equator, the tropopause lies at around 16-18 km, higher than it is at the Poles (8 km), because the air is warmer and has expanded, taking the tropopause with it.

North of 60°N in Winter, the tropopause will be found at about 29 000 ft. At 50°N, in the North Atlantic, at around 31 000 feet (the average is 36 090 feet, or 11 km). However, the height of the tropopause can be locally affected by the movement of various airmasses, so there can be sudden variations.

At 40°N, 55°N and between 60-70°N, it changes height quite abruptly, and can fold over, or even break, which is an instrumental factor in the formation of jetstreams which can affect the weather at lower levels.

Nearer to the Equator the tropopause is slightly higher in January than it is in July. So, the average temperature of the troposphere determines the height of the tropopause*, although the temperature of the tropopause itself is determined by its height. The *lowest* tropopause temperature is around -75°C at its *highest* point at 16 km around the Equator, otherwise it will be more like -56.5°C and -45°C at the Poles. The heights will vary by a couple of thousand feet between January-July.

Picture: Upper winds with jetstream. The heavy line starts and finishes where windspeeds of 60-80 knots are forecast.

*If the temperature distribution is uniform, the height of the tropopause can vary with pressure. Low pressure means a lower tropopause and vice versa. In the chart above (for upper levels), the L underneath a figure in its pointy box means that the tropopause is lower at that point. An H means that it is higher.

Turbine engines become more efficient in the low temperatures found at the tropopause, so it is where most jets operate, as there is no advantage to be found by climbing higher, but you won't see the height of the tropical tropopause in the flight paperwork because it will be well above the heights normally flown anyway.

Although oxygen may be important to pilots and engines, the proportion of gases making up the atmosphere has no relevance to meteorology, except that it holds water as:

- a gas (water vapour)
- a liquid (clouds or rain)
- a solid (ice)

Water vapour is important because it is invisible, and affects the humidity ratio of the air (discussed later). It is mostly formed by evaporation, when the Sun's rays strike moist ground or a water surface.

Because it weighs five-eighths of an equivalent amount of dry air, water vapour will also reduce the density of the air and your engine's punch, but that's the subject of the *Performance* chapter. The water vapour content on average is around 1%, but can get as high as 4%. The troposphere (the lower part of the atmosphere) contains more than 90% of all water vapour, but the correction is small and generally negligible. Its presence is expressed as relative humidity, described later, and its importance lies in the energy that is released and consumed as it changes from gas to liquid to ice and back.

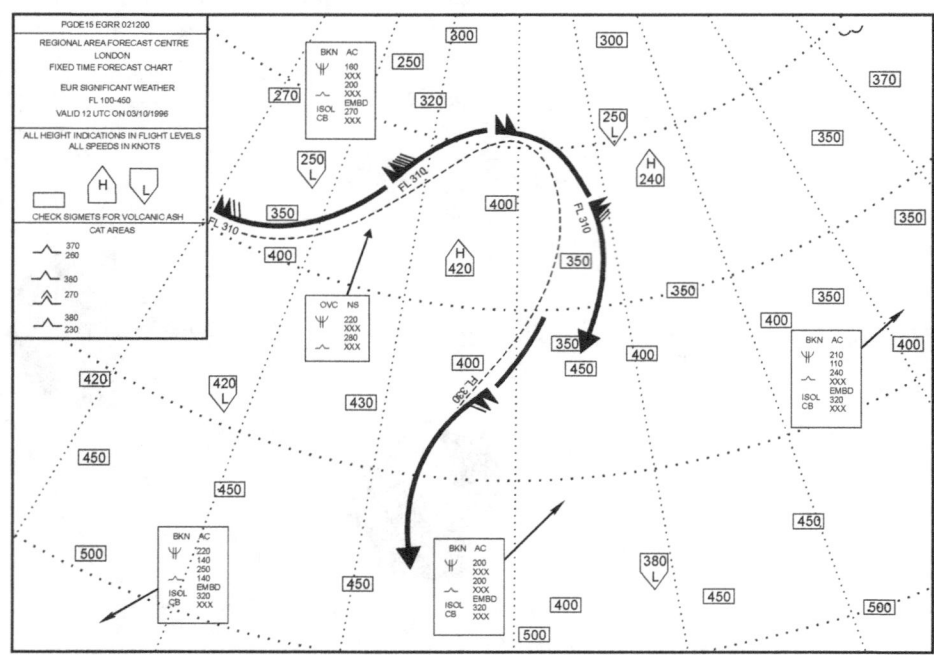

THERMODYNAMICS

The temperature of the atmosphere (and its variation) is the basis of all weather, and is intimately linked with pressure, and therefore wind. Temperature has already been covered in *Instruments* but, as a reminder, it is a measure of the kinetic energy of air molecules.

As mentioned above, most of the Earth's heat comes from the Earth itself, that is, from below. The Sun's rays do not produce heat (or light) until they hit something like the atmosphere (which is why it's cold and dark in space), so the air will get warmed by *conduction* from the ground. In other words, *terrestrial radiation* and *conduction* are primarily responsible for heating the lower atmosphere, followed by convection. Rising parcels of warm air are called *thermals*, or *convection currents*, which is what keeps gliders up in the air. Along with the type of surface, the latitude of a place has an effect on the local temperature. The standard for comparison is that for water, which has a specific heat value of 1. Smaller quantities warm up more rapidly.

The **virtual temperature** is the temperature that dry air (with no water vapour at all) would have at the same density as a given amount of "normal" air. The **potential temperature** refers to a parcel of air that is dried adiabatically to 1 000 hPa. It is an accurate way of comparing air temperatures at different levels.

Diurnal Variations

There is a rhythmic difference in temperatures between day and night over 24 hours, known as *diurnal variation*. The effect is less marked over water, which reacts more slowly to temperature changes. In fact, those over the sea are not much more than 1°C, whereas desert areas can vary by as much as 20°C. The maximum variations happen inland with clear skies over dry areas in calm conditions although, near the coast, the difference depends a lot on where the wind is coming from - it is greater if the wind is coming off the land.

As incoming radiation only occurs during daylight, the temperature begins to rise shortly after sunrise (after an initial dip*) when the Sun's radiation exceeds that of the Earth, and starts to fall mid-afternoon, when it falls below, carrying on through the night until the process starts again. The peak temperature occurs between 1400-1500 because the surface air is still warming by conduction. Essentially, the Earth's heat lags behind the Sun's passage by about 4 hours. The most significant difference between day and night is in the lower latitudes.

*With clear skies and calm winds, the minimum temperatures occur around half an hour after sunrise.

Clouds also absorb and reflect energy from the Sun during the day, and act as a blanket overnight to stop heat being radiated away. They can reduce the normal 50% insolation on a sunny day right down to 15% (the remainder being reflected back by clouds and the atmosphere). Windspeed and relative humidity will also have an effect.

Vertical temperature Distribution

A parcel of air rising through the atmosphere meets air at lower pressure, so it expands and reduces its temperature adiabatically. The standard reduction of temperature with height (lapse rate) is 1.98°C per thousand feet.

Temperature Measurement

Refer also to the *Instruments* chapter.

Air temperature at the Earth's surface is defined as the shade temperature as measured in a louvred screen about four feet (or 1.22 m) off the ground, because cold air can sometimes accumulate below this height. A *Stevenson Screen* is a louvred cabinet that allows air conditions to be monitored without being directly exposed to sunlight. Inside it, you will find a selection of thermometers, amongst other things, such as hygrometers, which will provide dry and wet bulb, maximum and minimum temperatures.

The louvres provide shade as well as free air flow and the white exterior reflects solar radiation. The doors face toward the Poles to reduce the risk of sunlight falling on the thermometers inside when they are opened. The cabinet is also positioned over grass to reduce insolation.

Inversions

Where the lapse rate remains constant, there is an *isothermal layer*. Where it *increases* (typical in anticyclonic conditions), you have an *inversion*. The end result is that cold air is underneath warmer air, which can happen during the passage of a cold front, or a cooler onshore breeze might be flowing over warm sea water. Cool air that is rising will lose its buoyancy and be stopped from rising further upon reaching its equilibrium level. In a thunderstorm, this happens just above the tropopause, where the cloud material settles into a layer that causes the anvil shape. Thus, conditions in an inversion are stable, because lifted air is always cooler than its environment.

However, aircraft performance is affected by variations in temperature, and inversions will make things worse. Large ones encountered shortly after takeoff can seriously degrade your climb performance, particularly when you're heavy. Even a small one in the upper levels can prevent you reaching a preferred cruising altitude. At lower levels, expect deteriorating visibility, as an inversion can keep the fog down for long periods until it is blown away by the horizontal movement of air (a change of air mass). Below a low level inversion, visibility is often moderate or poor because there is no vertical exchange to carry pollutants and haze into the free atmosphere (industrial pollutants, especially incinerated pesticides during the stubble burning season, collect at the base of an inversion).

You can find the top of an inversion (if the air below it is well mixed) by allowing 400 feet for every degree of difference (C) between the temperature and dewpoint.

Inversions can be caused by:

- **Overnight radiation cooling** of air at the surface, strongest at sunrise and a few hundred feet thick.
- **Katabatic winds** in mountains, settling in valleys.
- **Descending currents of air** near the centre of an older high in the mid-latitudes which can make the air warm up by compression, so the air at middle altitudes

becomes warmer than that at the surface. In other words, the top layer subsides more than, and warms more rapidly than, the bottom layer. This is a **subsidence inversion**, or a stable layer at some height (4,000-6,000 feet) which can trap thick haze and smoke in the lower levels.

- **Frontal** or **sea breeze** inversions that form when a wedge of cooler air forms under warmer air.
- **Turbulence**. Moderate winds at low level that may cause adiabatic expansion and cooling in the lower layers from mixing. If the lower layers become cooler, an inversion forms.

ISA Conversions

The ambient temperature is almost never standard, so we have to compare it against what it should be under ISA conditions. Although the reduction is technically 1.98°C per 1000 feet, 2° is often used for convenience, as is done with the *jet standard atmosphere*, which is used by engine manufacturers and which doesn't have a tropopause - a point to watch above 36,000 feet.

Actual atmospheric conditions are sometimes given in terms of *ISA Deviation*. For example, you might be asked what the temperature deviation is at FL 290 with an OAT of -47°C? First of all, find out what the temperature difference from sea level *should* be, so, using 2°C per thousand feet, we find it should be 58° lower (29 x 2). Given that the temperature at sea level is always 15°C in ISA, subtract one from the other to get -43°C (-58+15). As the OAT is -47°C, the temperature deviation is ISA -4°C (that is, 4° colder than it should be). Height changes by 4% for every 10° deviation.

The other way round, you could have to find temperature, given a deviation at a flight level. If it's ISA -7°C at FL 250, +15 (ISA) - 50 (25 x 2) gets us -35°C, normal ISA temperature. Applying the deviation, which is colder, we get -42°C.

ISA deviation is assumed to apply to the whole airmass. Calculate the correct PA first!

Latent Heat

A parcel of air at a certain temperature can hold a certain amount of moisture. It can hold more as it gets warmer, and less as it gets colder. The source of such water vapour is mainly evaporation from oceans, lakes, vegetation, etc. As particles of exposed water break off into the air, the *average* rate of motion of those left behind decreases, which is detected as cooling, thus, heat energy is used up as molecules break away, and is regarded as being hidden within the vapour as *latent heat*.

In the solid and liquid states, water molecules are bound strongly together but, as a gas, the bond is weak. Rather a lot of energy is needed in the form of heat to make it weak - 600 times more, in fact, than is required to raise the temperature of water by 1°C*. The heat energy that is used to break the bonds is absorbed by the water vapour, from which position it is used to keep the molecules apart, so the water vapour can remain as a gas. Because this energy is stored with the water molecules, it is known as *latent heat*, and it accounts for how water vapour is able to transport large amounts of heat, albeit hidden, around the globe. The heat is released again when it condenses, warming the surrounding air. As it is now less dense, the warmed air will rise further. In short, latent heat is added to a substance to make it change to a higher state, with no change in temperature. **Sensible heat**, by contrast, involves a temperature change with no change of state. The processes that absorb latent heat are melting, evaporation, and sublimation.

*The energy required to raise the temperature of 1 gram of water (or ice) by 1°C is 1 calorie. The latent heat of fusion (melting) of water is 80 calories per gram, but the water (or ice) remains at 0°C because the calories are being used to change its state. The latent heat of vaporisation, on the other hand, is 600 calories per gram at 0°C.

- **Condensation** occurs when moist air becomes saturated.
- **Evaporation** is liquid water turning into vapour.
- **Deposition** occurs when water vapour goes directly to the solid state (i.e. ice) without a liquid stage but, according to ICAO......
- **Sublimation** occurs when ice converts directly to water vapour. The latent heat of sublimation is 680.
- **Freezing** is the process of turning water into a solid. Zero degrees is when water becomes *capable* of freezing. A Supercooled Water Droplet is one below freezing, but not frozen, because of the absence of hygroscopic nuclei to bind to. They are found most often in warm fronts.
- **Melting** (or fusion) is the change of state of water from a solid to a liquid state.

The heat energy used to convert water vapour into a liquid changes the DALR to the SALR.

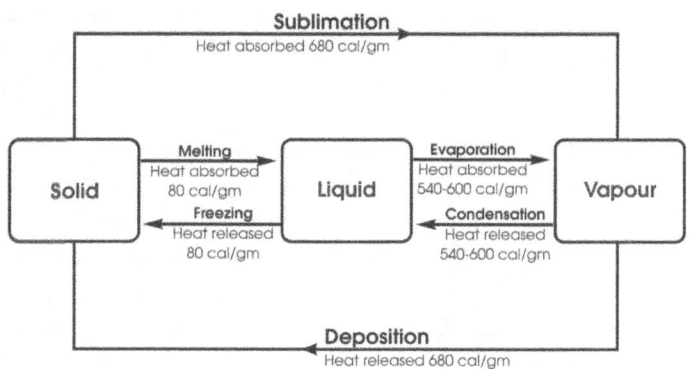

Humidity

Humidity concerns the invisible moisture (vapour) contained in a parcel of air. When the air cannot hold any more, it is saturated.

The **dewpoint** is the temperature at which cooling of air results in 100% saturation, or the point at which water vapour *begins* the process of condensation* into visible droplets, if pressure and moisture remain constant. As the atmospheric pressure only varies slightly on the surface, the dewpoint is a good indicator of how much water vapour is in the air, in that a high dewpoint indicates a high content. In other words, it depends only on the amount of water vapour in the air. The **dewpoint depression** indicates the number of degrees that the dewpoint temperature is below the actual temperature. Small values mean that they are very close together and the air is close to saturation.

*Condensation actually occurs below the dewpoint, but without hygroscopic nuclei for water particles to bind on to, it may not occur, even when air cools below its dewpoint (*supersaturation*).

If the temperature and dewpoint are the same, it will be very easy for clouds to form. When they are less than 1° apart, for example, fog or low cloud is likely - the smaller the gap between temperature and dewpoint, the lower the cloudbase will be. The further apart they are, the less likely you are to get cloud, and therefore icing if the temperature is low enough (however, the warmer the wet air is, the more likely is bad weather).

If the air is cooling (the Sun may be going down), or its moisture content is increasing (rain falling from a front), the dewpoint will increase. Conversely, if the air is heated, the temperature and dewpoint will separate, although sometimes fog can form after the Sun comes up, as with radiation fog. Katabatic winds will separate them. On the other hand, as the pressure reduces when air is lifted, the dewpoint reduces with altitude, and vice versa. The effects can be seen with lenticular clouds.

The **absolute humidity** is the actual mass of water in a parcel of air, expressed in grams per cubic metre (i.e. in a *volume*). Over the sea, it is usually minimum at dawn, and maximum shortly after noon, because of the temperature (opposite to *relative* humidity, below). However, if the volume changes, as it would when you climb, for example, so does the absolute humidity, which is why we can't use it as a standard to measure things by.

The **specific humidity** is the mass of water vapour divided by the total *mass* of air, expressed in grams/kg. Its average value is highest in the tropics, and is still high over deserts - the air over the Sahara desert contains more water vapour than Polar air.

MIXING RATIO

This expresses humidity as ratio of the mass of water vapour to the mass of **dry** (unsaturated) **air** in a given parcel, also expressed in grams/kg, or as weight rather than volume.

The HMR decreases at 5°C per 1000 feet.

The specific humidity and mixing ratio of an air parcel remain constant as long as no water vapour is added or taken away. Put another way, changes in the size of a parcel of air do not affect the specific humidity or mixing ratio, because the total number of molecules stays the same in both cases.

The **Saturation Mixing Ratio** is the theoretical maximum amount of water vapour that air at a specific temperature and pressure can hold. In fact, the HMR and SMR depend on temperature and pressure - the former is independent of temperature but inversely proportional to pressure, while the latter is directly proportional to temperature.

For any pressure level, the mixing ratio is read through the dewpoint and the saturation mixing ratio is read through the temperature.

RELATIVE HUMIDITY

The moisture content of the air can also be expressed in terms of pressure - the extra water exerts its own partial pressure* over and above atmospheric pressure, up to the **saturation vapour pressure**. The amount of vapour that the air can hold, and the SVP, increase with temperature.

*Humidity is also known as *vapour pressure*, or the pressure that would be exerted by water vapour molecules if the air was saturated.

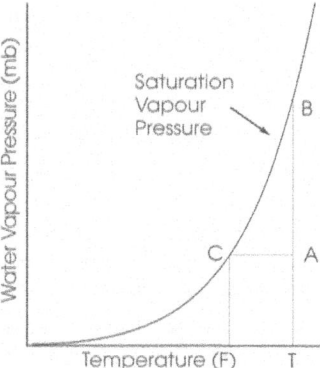

In the graph above, the line AT represents an actual value of humidity, and the line BT the maximum that the air can hold. The ratio between the two is **relative humidity**, which is officially defined as the vapour pressure (or HMR) divided by the saturation vapour pressure (or SMR), multiplied by 100, or a ratio of the amount of water vapour to the saturation value. It is *not* the dewpoint divided by the temperature! If you move to the left, the line BT will get shorter and closer to the length of AT, until you reach C, where they are the same and relative humidity would be 100%. This is the dewpoint temperature at which the actual vapour pressure becomes the saturation vapour pressure.

In other words, for a particular temperature, the relative humidity can tell you how close the air is to being saturated, as indicated by the relative closeness of the temperature and dewpoint. It is a measure of how much moisture an air parcel is holding against the maximum it *could* hold at that temperature (and pressure) or, in other words, the ratio of *content* to *capacity*. It can be changed by varying the amount of water vapour or the temperature, but the latter is more likely (including diurnally with the Earth's atmosphere), at least for our purposes.

On a typical day, RH is high in the morning (as it is cooler) and lower in the late afternoon (when it gets warmer). RH *decreases* if the air gets warmer, because it can absorb more moisture, as with the comparison of desert air against Polar air. Expect the relative humidity to be low when the temperature and dewpoint are far apart, and high when they are close together.

If they are the same in Polar air, the relative humidity will be 100%. Typical figures are:

Temp	Vapour
30°C	27 gms/kg
15°C	11 gms/kg
0°C	4 gms/kg

Relative humidity can also indicate the drying power of the air, since evaporation is most intense at high temperatures and low humidities, and *vice versa*.

MEASUREMENT

The *hygrometer* is an instrument that is used to measure how wet the air is. A piece of human (or horse) hair, which gets longer as it gets moister, is laid against a calibrated scale and a "suitable linkage" transmits its movements to show relative humidity.

Another method is to use two thermometers inside a Stevenson's screen*. One measures the temperature of the ambient air, and the other has its bulb surrounded with wet muslin, using distilled water. If the air is dry, the water in the muslin will evaporate and absorb latent heat, so the wet-bulb thermometer will indicate a lower temperature.

*Moisture can now be directly measured with controlled refrigeration of a mirror, producing condensation that is detectable by an infra red beam.

Thus, the drier the air is, the greater will be the difference between the readings. Relative humidity is then deduced with the use of tables, or a tephigram.

The *wet bulb depression* is the difference between the wet and dry bulb temperatures. When the air is saturated, the wet and dry bulb temperatures will be the same, not because the wet bulb is evaporating, but because the dry bulb is covered with moisture and both become wet bulbs, and there is no evaporation.

The wet bulb temperature is always between the dewpoint and dry bulb temperatures, except at 100% RH (saturation point) where they are all the same.

Mostly, air is made to reach its saturation point by force, such as being moved up the sides of mountains or over large areas of slower moving air (*large scale ascent*) and, if the right conditions, cloud will form. The ways of cooling air are many, including:

- Turbulence (not with thunderstorms).
- Convection.
- Orographic.
- Frontal.
- Convergence (as with low pressure).

Lapse Rates

A lapse rate is how fast an air sample cools as it rises, which varies as to whether the air is dry or saturated. The change of temperature with height is usually a decrease, which is positive - a negative lapse rate is a temperature *increase*, or an inversion. A layer of air which does not change with height is isothermal.

ENVIRONMENTAL LAPSE RATE

This is the actual measured change, which is about 6.5°C per 1000 m (1.98°C per 1000 feet), but it can vary from local conditions. Several factors may influence this:

- **Height**. Lapse rates depend on ground temperature, and are normally very high near the ground with strong insolation.
- **Time of Year**. Lapse rates are lower in Winter or during a rainy season.
- **Surface**. Lapse rates are lower over land than over the sea.
- **Air Masses**. Different air masses have different lapse rates.

ADIABATIC LAPSE RATE

The rate of change of temperature with height of air which is changing its temperature adiabatically There are two variations, which do not strictly follow the guidelines below, but do so accurately enough to provide something to work with:

DRY ADIABATIC LAPSE RATE

The DALR is the (constant, fixed) *decrease in temperature of unsaturated air with height* at around 3°C per 1,000 feet* or 9.8°C (10°C) per 1,000 m (*Dry* just means a relative humidity of less than 100%).

*In practice, there is an excess of around 1° near the ground, so the first 1 000 feet should really decrease at 4°C per 1,000 feet. This is called *super-adiabatic*, and it is not a factor for the exams, I'm just being picky.

The dewpoint temperature of unsaturated air decreases at around 0.5°C per 1 000 ft.

SATURATED ADIABATIC LAPSE RATE

The SALR allows for *latent heat*, or the energy that is released when water condenses. Converting water from one state to the other (without a rise in temperature) requires energy, which is stored with the vapour, as the water molecules must be kept apart with it. Condensed water molecules are strongly attracted to each other, and are balanced by equally strong repulsive forces. The energy that goes with the vapour is the *latent heat of vaporisation*. When vapour condenses back into a liquid, the latent heat is released into the surrounding air as *sensible heat* and affects the SALR. Warm saturated air liberates more latent heat.

The presence of latent heat means that the air will cool slowly. There can be so much heat released that flight in normally stable layer cloud can be quite bumpy, from internal eddying. Latent heat leads to the Chinook, which can raise the air temperature to over 20°C in Winter in the lee of the Rocky Mountains.

The SALR can range from 4°C to as high as 9°C per 1000 m, but the average (for lower levels anyway) is 6°C per 1000 m, or 1.8°C per 1000 feet, for Europe (the rest of the world uses 1.5°C per 1000 feet). The reason for the variation is simply that warm air can hold more moisture - and there is more latent heat with which to warm the air as condensation takes place. This also explains why high clouds are thinner - there is less moisture to condense out because the air is cooler.

The higher you climb, the closer the SALR will get to the DALR because the air is drier. They are nearly equal when the rising air is very cold, or in cirrus clouds.

Finding The Cloudbase

Knowledge of the cloudbase is important for many reasons, particularly when descending on approach (at least you will know where the turbulence is!) To find it, take the difference between the wet and dry bulb temperatures, and subtract it from the wet bulb temperature to get the dew point, where vapour will condense. Now take the difference between the dewpoint and the dry bulb temperature and multiply it by 352 (220 in °F) for the probable height of the condensation. An easier way is to take the difference (in °F) and double it. The answer is the altitude in hundreds of feet.

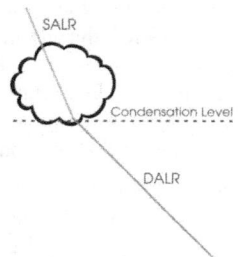

If the temperature and windspeed increase, so does the cloudbase. If the humidity increases, cloudbase decreases.

The Bradbury Rule

This is named after the glider pilot/meteorologist Tom Bradbury, but **it is only valid if cumulus actually forms**. It works on the basis that the Dew Point Lapse Rate is about 0.6°C per 1000 feet, so its rate of closure against the DALR is around 2.4°C per 1000 feet, or 1°C per 400*, so, when finding out a freezing level, first find the cloud base, then switch to the SALR. To find the cloudbase, multiply the difference between the surface temperature and dewpoint ($T_{dry}-T_{dew}$) by 400 for an approximate height. If you divide the difference by 2.4, the answer is in thousands of feet. For example, if the ground temperature is 10°C, and the dewpoint 7°C, the cloudbase should be at 1,200 feet (3 x 400). Then divide whatever the dewpoint temperature is by 1.8 and add the converted number in thousands of feet to the cloudbase to get the freezing level. Divide 7 by 1.8 to get 3.8889, which becomes 3889 feet, so the freezing level is at 5089 feet.

*The Dew Point Lapse Rate may not be needed if you know the dew point at the cloud base. In that case, just divide the difference between the surface temperature and the dewpoint by 3 (the DALR).

Normand's Theorem

This states that the DALR (through the dry bulb temperature), the SALR (through the wet bulb) and the Humidity Mixing Ratio (through the dewpoint) all meet at the condensation level. Well, more or less, anyway.

Stability

Remembering the previous mention of convection currents, you can see that air has vertical movement as well as horizontal, and it is often associated with turbulence and/or the formation of clouds. The less vertical movement there is, the more stable the air is, and the less bumpy, because it tends to resist vertical motion - a parcel of air in stable conditions will tend to return to its original level after rising or sinking. On the other hand, a parcel in unstable air will rise or sink more quickly - that is, it will continue accelerating.

Stability depends on the difference between atmospheric lapse rates and the temperature of the air being forced to rise. Air will rise if it is warmer than its surroundings, but not because of its temperature - it rises because warm air is less dense.

Thus, the amount of vertical motion in the air is largely determined by the stability of the atmosphere, which depends on the lapse rates of various parcels of air, and what happens to them after being lifted.

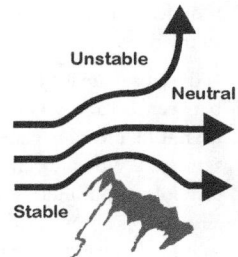

Instability arises when air is upset by small disturbances. A cold air mass moving over a warmer surface will be unstable because the lower layers will pick up moisture and temperature, which will be warmer than its surroundings. This heating from below steepens the lapse rate, and the moisture makes the air less dense. This will carry on into the night over the sea, as the water will keep its heat better than land will. On the other hand, a warm air mass over a cold one will have cooler lower layers, possibly as far as an inversion, which is about as stable as you can get.

Air may have been lifted in the first place by:

- convection.
- convergence.
- mechanical turbulence.
- orographic means (i.e. over geographic barriers, like a mountain range).
- frontal means.

The warmer it is when it starts, the more energy a given bubble of air has to keep going. As it rises, the air expands, and cools adiabatically, matching the air around it, until it eventually cools off quicker than the surrounding air, and stops, when it reaches a level of the same density. Once it becomes saturated, though (and cloud forms), cooling slows down and allows the ascent to continue further, because the condensation releases heat and gives the (now less dense) parcel of air a boost, so if the air is already hot and moist before it hits relatively cooler air, say from the Caribbean, thunderstorms are highly likely.

In addition, the air containing water vapour is less dense.

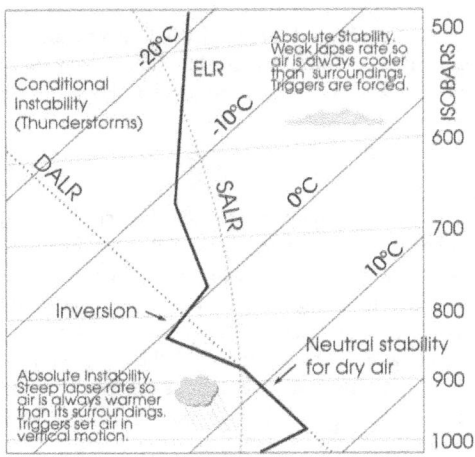

- An ELR that follows the DALR creates a condition of **neutral stability**.
- If the environmental lapse rate lies to the left of the DALR (being steeper), air is **absolutely unstable**, which is quite a rare condition, except near the ground on sunny days.
- If the lapse rate is between the DALR and SALR (that is, between 1.8 and 3°C per 1000 feet), it is **conditionally unstable**, meaning stable when dry, but unstable if saturated. When the air is dry, continued vertical motion can only occur under forced conditions - an unsaturated air parcel is always colder than its surroundings. When saturated, once the trigger is removed, the air will be warmer than its environment (ideal for thunderstorms).

The relative humidity of conditionally unstable air is unknown, otherwise it would be stable or unstable.

- To the right of the SALR (and the DALR), you get **ab,solute stability** from an inversion.

In flight you can estimate stability by the rate of change of temperature with height - the more rapid the change, the more instability there is. The average value of the ELR is around 2°C per 1000 ft. Also, as the pressure and volume of a rising parcel of air will change with the pressure found higher in the atmosphere, the temperature and dewpoint will change as well. If you know by how much they change, and whether that parcel will end up warmer or cooler than the ELR, you can figure out the amount of stability aloft.

A parcel of air will follow the dry adiabat until it meets the SMR line, where condensation occurs (at the *Lifted Condensation Level*). After that, it will follow the moist adiabat line. Where the parcel is cooler than its environment (to the right) there is a negative energy area because the air is sinking. Where it is warmer, the air is buoyant, with positive energy. When the air surrounding the parcel becomes warmer (typically in the stratosphere), it stops rising at the Equilibrium Level. Any rising after this point is due to momentum.

*The dewpoint rate of change at 0.6°C per thousand feet for unsaturated air.

In the picture below, the temperature at the surface is 15°C and the dewpoint temperature is 11°C.

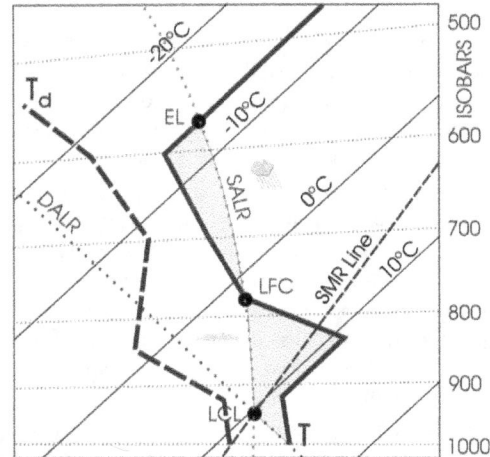

The bottom grey area is negative and tends to stability. The top one is positive and tends to instability.

In summary, stability affects the type of clouds and precipitation, visibility, wind strength and turbulence. Stable air can produce poor visibility at low levels, constant drizzle, light or calm winds with layer cloud, and no turbulence. Unstable air, on the other hand, tends to be associated with good visibility, heavy precipitation, heap clouds, strong winds, turbulence and storms.

In the radio soundings shown below, picture 3 shows that low stratus will form where the temperature and dew point lines meet at around 1 000 ft, for a grey overcast:

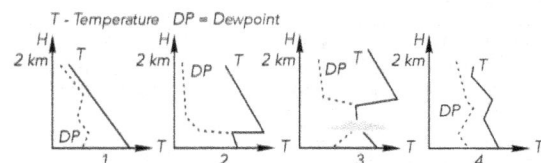

You would find ground fog in picture 2.

CLOUDS

Knowledge of cloud types is useful when interpreting satellite images, as they tend to be left out in automated weather reports. Such knowledge can also be used to analyse vertical air movement - you only need about 1 cm per second to produce clouds, which indicates that air has been cooled below its dewpoint, usually in rising air (rarely above the tropopause).

Thus, they are symptoms of the weather - in theory, if you know what clouds belong to what weather systems, you can deduce what weather is coming, and when, based on the known movement characteristics of those systems.

For example, if you see wisps of cirrus cloud like this approaching:

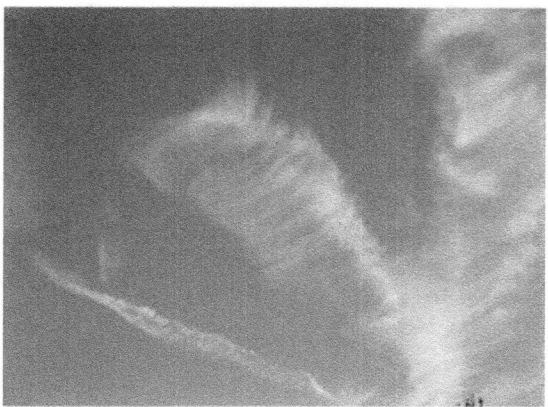

You know that in around 15-20 hours it will be raining continuously from low, grey cloud (nimbostratus), and you might encounter freezing rain, because that's what happens with a warm front, and they move at around 15-20 knots, assuming they are not blocked by something like a high pressure system. If you later notice that the wind has picked up and the altimeter setting has dropped a bit, you would know it is quite close. Similarly, if you see Cu or Cb clouds, you know the air is unstable.

Essentially, there are two types of cloud - those arising from the upward movement of air, such as cumulus, and those from the horizontal movement of air masses. Both are included in 10 basic cloud types.

The amount of cloud in the sky is reported in *Oktas*, or eighths of the sky area. *Opacity* is a function of cloud depth and droplet distribution. The *cloud base* is the height of the first available cloud above the official aerodrome elevation, although this may differ between countries (in the USA, for example, it is the height of the base of a cloud layer, of which there can be many). It can be measured by releasing a balloon which ascends at a known rate and timing its disappearance into cloud. At night, beams of a searchlight can be reflected, and the angles calculated with an *alidade*. In a *cloud base recorder*, a narrow beam of light continually swings from near the horizontal to the vertical. Inside, a photo-electric cell only receives light from the vertical, and for any cloud base, there will be only one angle that provides this. However, these are now largely obsolete, and the *laser beam ceilometer* is now in widespread use.

The *cloud ceiling* is the height above the aerodrome of the lowest layer of cloud that is more than 4 oktas in extent.

Cloud names were coined by an amateur meteorologist, Luke Howard, in 1803, who based them on the Latin words for *hair*, *heap*, *layer* and *rain-bearing* (*cirrus*, *cumulus*, *stratus* and *nimbus*) not to mention *middle* and *broken* (*alto* and *fracto*). Others, as modifications, were added by Kaemtz and Renou, whose work was followed by scientists at Upsala University - Hildebransson used height in a classification.

Clouds form in the first place because air contains water vapour. When air gets warm (unstable), it expands, becomes less dense, rises and cools. It stops rising (and becomes stable) when the temperature inside the parcel is the same as that outside. If the air is damp, at some stage, the water vapour it contains condenses out at the saturation point and binds onto *hygroscopic nuclei*, the official name for dirt, which can include pollen and particles of pollutants. As heat is released during this process, the temperature now falls more slowly so the air can carry on rising and cooling.

The most effective way to dissipate cloud is subsidence.

Air holds more vapour when it is warm, and it can become saturated in two ways - you can either add more water vapour, or reduce its temperature, as above. The excess vapour changes from gas to liquid, with the droplets *coalescing* into clouds as they collide. When they get heavy, they fall under gravity. The *Bergeron-Findeisen* theory says that some water droplets turn to ice and grow after sublimation of water vapour and collision with supercooled water droplets (see *Icing*). However, I have seen snow materialise out of the sky in Northern Canada (e.g. formating on nothing at all), and favour the coalescence theory, as Bergeron-Findeisen doesn't explain clouds in Summer with no freezing level.

The coalescence process depends on tiny cloud droplets being swept up by larger ones, where the various sizes of the droplets move at different speeds and often collide. In mid-latitudes, it will only produce drizzle or light rain.

 The two processes are not necessarily independent - they can often act together.

Cooling occurs when air expands as it is forced upwards:

- **Uplift** over a land or air mass, or a depression (orographic or frontal lifting). The exact type depends on the stability (or otherwise) of the air

- **Convection currents**, where air that is warmer than its environment becomes buoyant and rises (such as thermals rising from a heated surface). If condensation occurs, you get cumuliform cloud. If the air remains cooler than its surroundings, you get stratiform cloud.
- **Eddying** (at the surface, or at the boundaries of two layers of air).
- **Waves** in the lee of mountains.

Low (Strato)

From sea level to about 6 500 feet, mainly water:

- **Stratus** (St), thin and low, with a fairly uniform base, and associated with relatively stable air. Any precipitation is usually from other clouds, but there may be drizzle or snow grains (which can also be found in supercooled fog). At ground level, stratus is called fog or mist, and may also be called *scud* or *pannus* in poor weather. It arises from large areas cooling, rather than individual pockets of air, as with cumulus. When the sun is visible through it, its outline is clearly discernible. Sometimes it appears as ragged patches. A layer of stratus is most likely to be dispersed by *insolation resulting in the lifting of the mixing condensation level*.

- **Stratocumulus** (Sc). Like stratus, but cumulus-like, with small globules popping up here and there, and well-defined bases. Often formed in eddy currents which cause stratus to clump up, because the stratus tops will be cool from reflecting the Sun's rays and the bases warm from absorbing the Earth's infrared radiation. These can also form from cumulus joining up under an inversion. Sc can produce light rain or snow, and heavy showers will come from embedded cumulus. You might see clouds in patches, sheets or grey or whitish layers made from elements resembling large pebbles or rollers, together or not, and clear of the ground.

- **Nimbostratus** (Ns). Thick, dark, low rain cloud, typical in warm fronts, which may be found through all layers, but at least starts in the *alto* range. Moderate to heavy continual rain or snow.

Middle (Alto)

Between 6 500-23 000 feet, made of water, ice, or supercooled water droplets, depending on temperature:

- **Altocumulus** (Ac) is similar to Sc (above), but higher. The size of cloudlets is between one and three finger-widths, with noticeable shading (but not dark and gloomy, like stratus). Altocumulus Castellanus indicates upper level instability which may lead to the development of thunderstorms

- **Altostratus** (As), similar to stratus, but higher, medium sheet greyish or bluish cloud, of any thickness up to 10-12,000'. No ground shadow, made of ice crystals and water droplets.

High (Cirro)

Between 16 500-45 000 feet, made of ice crystals, so they have some transparency:

- **Cirrocumulus** (Cc) is high sheet cloud, made of small cloudlets (for want of a better word) which do not cast shadows, looking like a mackerel sky.

- **Cirrostratus** (Cs) translucent high cloud, very delicate, made up of ice crystals. When in front of the Sun, you may see a halo round it.

- **Cirrus** (Ci) is a high and fibrous filament. Otherwise known as *Horse tails*, or *Mares' tails,* they can produce precipitation which evaporates well before reaching ground level - the falling ice streaks form the distinctive filaments.

 The limits of each classification vary with latitude (and the troposphere). Low clouds do not have a prefix added to their name. *Nimbo* means rain-bearing.

Other

- **Heap clouds** (i.e. marked vertical extent):
- **Cumulus** (Cu), are small amounts of heap cloud at low and medium levels, looking a bit like small balls of cotton wool with flat bases.

It's actually *convection cloud*, which gives you a clue as to how it is made, and glider pilots seek out the thermals underneath them for lift (when a cumulus cloud is removed from its thermal, it can still grow from the latent heat released inside it, making it warmer than its surroundings and float upwards). The vertical extent of cumulus clouds in an unstable layer depends on how thick the layer is.

In strong winds, you might see them in long lines called *cloud streets*.

So-called "fair weather cumulus", as seen on a nice Summer's day, normally forms directly as such, but (less commonly) can develop from stratus or strato-cu that has broken up with morning heating (they can also spread out into strato-cu or alto-cu in the presence of an inversion). This would mean uneven heating of a land surface in a stable atmosphere. Fair weather cumulus is often an indication of turbulence at and below the cloud level. It is known as fair weather cloud because it produces no precipitation.

Over land, fair weather cu usually forms in the morning and reaches its maximum in terms of number and size by mid afternoon. It dissipates rapidly in the evening once the ground cools and convection currents die out. Over the sea, this is less marked and tends to be the reverse because the sea temperature stays the same while the air aloft cools.

Characteristics of cumuliform cloud include large water droplets, instability, turbulence, showers, and mainly clear ice. *Cumulus Congestus* has a large vertical extent. *Cumulus Castellanus* looks like the side of a castle (*AC Castellanus* may lead to the development of thunderstorms from the upper level instability). *Mediocris* are as tall as they are wide, and *Humilis* are the smallest, being wider than they are tall. *Cumulus Fractus* clouds are decaying, and appear ragged and woolly.

- **Cumulonimbus** is towering storm cloud. "Towering" means up to as much as 60,000 feet, with 12 km being the maximum height, and the anvil shape at the top is due to it meeting the tropopause, where temperature starts to remain constant, stopping the cloud's ascent. CBs are mostly found around late afternoon, and can project into the stratosphere. They are cumulus congestus until the upper regions turn into ice crystals. See also *Thunderstorms*

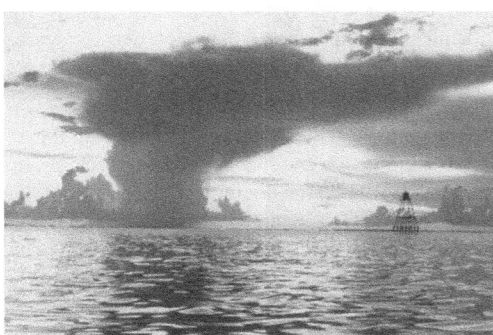

- **Lenticular**, found at the crest of standing waves formed in the lee of mountain waves

Lenticular clouds are a form of altocumulus that remain stationary against the ground, and will produce airframe icing. They are formed by orographic uplift in stable air over mountain tops.

Cloud Cassification Table

Genus	Species	Notes
Cumulus 2 000-3 000 ft	Humilis	Wider
	Mediocris	As wide as tall
	Congestus	Taller
	Fractus	Decaying - ragged, broken up
Cumulonimbus 2 000-60 000 ft	Calvus	Indistinct top
	Capillatus	Anvil shaped top
Stratus 0-6 500 ft	Nebulosus	Grey, generally featureless
	Fractus	Separate, ragged shreds
Stratocumulus 2 000-6 500 ft	Stratiformis	Clumps over a large area
	Lenticularis	Smooth lens shape
	Castellanus	Crenellated tops
Altocumulus 6 500-18 000 ft	Stratiformis	Form over a large area
	Lenticularis	Smooth lens shape
	Castellanus	Crenellated tops
	Floccus	Cumulus-like tufts
Altostratus 6 500-23 000 ft		Corona round Sun or Moon
Nimbostratus 2 000-18 000 ft		Thick, grey, featureless, lots of rain & drizzle
Cirrus 16 000-45 000 ft	Fibratus	Straight or curved filaments
	Uncinus	Hooks or commas
	Spissatus	Grey patches
	Castellanus	Small clumps with crenellated tops
	Floccus	Independent small round tufts
Cirrocumulus 16 500-45 000 ft	Stratiformis	Extensive layer
	Lenticularis	Smooth lens shape
	Castellanus	Crenellated tops
	Floccus	Cumulus-like tufts
Cirrostratus 16 500-30 000 ft	Fibratus	Fibrous or striated appearance
	Nebulosus	No variation in tone

AIR MASSES

A large body of air will have the characteristics of its origin (the *source region*), particularly with regard to moisture and temperature, in that a mass of air can originate from Tropical or Polar regions (i.e. be warm or cold) or be Maritime or Continental (wet or dry). The effects might be spread throughout the air mass by conduction, convection or turbulence. To acquire the characteristics to meet the classification, a mass of air must stay in one more or less uniform place for several days, so one definition of an air mass could be *a large body of air with uniform properties of temperature and moisture*. For the necessary stagnation, light winds are needed, so a source region is likely to be subject to high pressure. Air masses are basically *Arctic* or *Polar*, *Tropical* or *Equatorial*, *Maritime* (sea-based) or *Continental* (land-based). Arctic and Polar only really differ at the upper levels, otherwise they are much the same, especially at the surface.

There may also be an indication of whether the air mass is warmer or colder than the surface it is passing over (w for warm, k for kold, sorry, cold), so a mild maritime polar air mass passing over a frozen ocean would be mPw. This would give a very good indication of potential stability, or otherwise.

Thus, air masses vary as to moisture content and temperature. It's what happens when one moves away from its source region that is important, as well as what happens when it mixes with others - refer to *Tornadoes* to see the effects when N Westerly airflow meets S Easterly airflow over the USA. Air masses of the same type mix well, but others don't, and will produce problems at the transition zone between them, where frontal low pressures will form. Air from the Azores would be warmer and more humid than North Russian air, for example. Europe in Summer is affected by Tropical Continental air from the South Balkans and the Near East, but the main ones that affect the UK are:

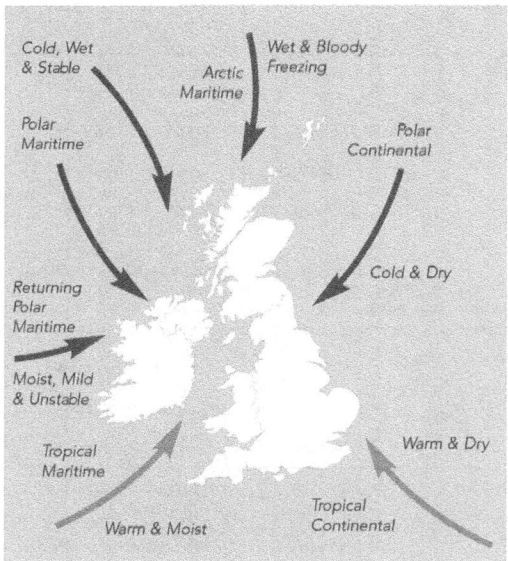

- **Polar Continental**, which is dry and cold because it comes from Polar land regions, such as Siberia or Canada. It has little energy and is only significant in Winter - in Summer it would be regarded as Tropical Continental. It produces the lowest temperatures in the UK. On its way there, it passes over the North Sea. If it has a short sea track, from Belgium or the Netherlands to the SE coast it remains dry, and produces cloudless skies and severe frosts. However, with a long sea track, it becomes unstable as it picks up moisture, and is warmed more in the lower levels (in Winter the sea is warmer than the land). It comes to resemble a Polar Maritime airmass, and give cumuliform cloud and showers on the East coast (cloud disperses inland). In Summer, the North Sea cools the air, and it gets more stable and can form low cloud and sea advection fog on the East coast.

- **Tropical Continental**, during Summer. As the source is North Africa (and the Sahara, mostly over land), it is warm and dry, and produces the UK's highest temperatures. As it is cooled from below as it tracks North, it stays stable, and will tend to give poor visibility, despite cloudless skies, due to collecting pollutants as it travels over Europe, and sand particles from Saharan dust storms. It affects UK the least.

- **Polar Maritime**, which is cold, moist and stable at its origin (the Arctic, or at least Northern Canada and Greenland), becomes warmer and more unstable as it comes South East across the North Atlantic, typically from East of Greenland (surface heating from the sea increases the temperature). It is therefore North Westerly in the UK, and moist from surface evaporation, producing convective cumuliform cloud after its long passage over the relatively warm waters of the North Atlantic - its temperature rises rapidly and it becomes unstable to a great depth. It produces showers all year round, and hail and thunder in Winter.

Returning Polar Maritime sweeps out wide into the Atlantic before turning round and going back towards the Pole. It travels well South of the British Isles and come back from the South West with Tropical Maritime properties at low level. After the initial warming over the Atlantic, the unstable elements are cooled in their lowest layers as the air goes North again. Over the British Isles, this will produce dull, overcast weather, maybe with drizzle, albeit still with showers and even thunderstorms.

- **Tropical Maritime**, moist and warm, from tropical oceans between the Azores and Bermuda, so the predominant wind direction over the UK is South Westerly. It picks up moisture on its travels, so it is warm and moist in its lowest layers. Relative humidity increases and the air mass becomes cooler and more stable as it moves North and the air becomes saturated. In Winter, you can expect stratiform cloud and drizzle, with poor visibility after the cloud has been heated away by the warmer land mass. In Spring and early Summer, you will get advection fog in Western areas, particularly Cornwall and Devon, and advection fog in the English Channel.

There are also *Arctic Continental*, *Arctic Maritime* (as for Polar, but colder and drier, due to the shorter sea track*), which only affect the UK in Winter.

*Arctic air is uncommon during Summer, but when it does occur it may bring heavy showers or thunderstorms and unseasonably low temperatures. Between October and May, the air is cold enough to produce hail showers or snow, which are most frequent over Scotland and along the coasts exposed to Northerly winds. Arctic Maritime has its origins over the North Pole and the Arctic Ocean.

There is also *Equatorial Maritime*, but no *Equatorial Continental* because there is no land mass in the region large enough to produce the required effects.

Prevailing Westerly winds mean that the UK is most commonly affected by maritime air masses.

The strongest winds close to the ground will be found in the transition zone between two air masses

Identification

First, determine the air mass's stability by asking whether it is warm air passing over a cold surface, tending to stability, or the other way round, for instability.

The *stability* of an air mass is affected by its *origin* and *how it got to where it is*, in terms of track and time. Apply Buys Ballot's law and follow the isobars back.

Next, determine the likely moisture content. Air coming from over the sea is likely to be clean. From a continent, it is likely to be polluted, with poor visibility.

FRONTAL SYSTEMS

A front is a line of discontinuity, or a narrow transition zone between air masses where they are forced to mix, even though they don't want to (air is very antisocial). Otherwise, the boundary between two air masses might cover several kilometres.

The process starts in mid-high latitudes, when low pressure systems form along the boundary between cold Polar air and warmer air from temperate zones.

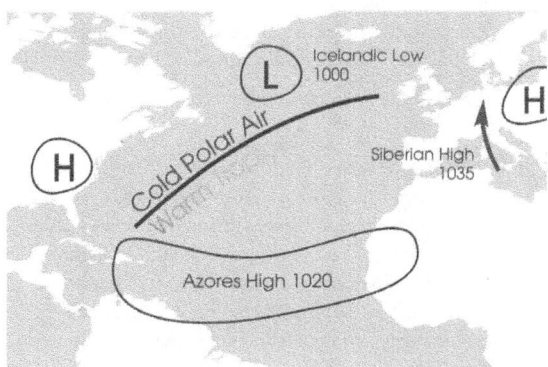

As some parts of the boundary are faster than others, they can catch up, with the end result being that warmer air is forced upwards. In fact, Polar air lows are usually formed by Polar Maritime air moving South East over the sea during Winter.

The associated weather on the air masses concerned and the way in which they interact - if the warm air that is forced upwards is dry and stable, for example, you won't necessarily see any clouds.

This is a plan view of a frontal system:

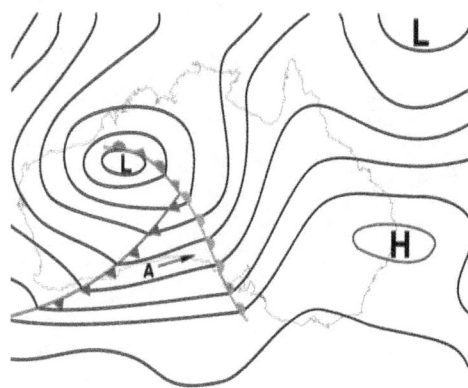

As air rises in a low pressure area, the wind blows into the centre, pulling in warm air from the South and cold air from the North, forcing them to mix and rotate. Warm tropical air could be forced over colder Arctic air, because it is less dense and, if moist, will form a typical cloud structure described overleaf.

A depression moves in the direction of the 2,000-foot wind in the warm sector (if there is one), so the system is moving in the direction of the arrow at A (the warm sector is the triangular area between the fronts).

Over Central Europe in the Summer, you can typically expect to see fair weather cumulus cloud, but isolated thunderstorms are possible. In Winter, expect stratus.

The red or blue lines signify the *ground position* of the warm and cold fronts, as their effects are felt for some distance either side. The difference is usually in temperature (which can be very small), but may be due to moisture content. A *dew point front*, or *dry line*, forms when two similar air masses with only a moisture difference between them meet. Other than that, there is little contrast across it.

Fronts are always associated with depressions*, which are sometimes referred to as *frontal waves*. They also tend to move towards the greatest falling pressure. If the gradient is weak, this could be against the geostrophic wind, described later.

*Fronts will rotate *anticlockwise* around a low.

The name of a front, that is, *warm*, or *cold*, comes from whichever air mass is overtaking the other, whereas the type of weather you get is determined by the stability and moisture content of the *warm air mass*. The actual temperature is less important than its relationship to that of the surface it is passing over.

The *Polar Front* is where South- and North-Westerly airstreams meet to form long series of depressions, starting off the Atlantic Coast of North America, generally lying between 40-70°N in the temperate latitudes, and similarly in the Southern Hemisphere. It is the boundary between Polar and tropical air (Polar Front depressions move along it toward the East, being most Southerly during Winter). In Summer, you can generally expect to see the Polar Front range from Newfoundland to the North of Scotland, and, in Winter, further South from Florida to South-West

England. It lies in a trough of low pressure with highs on each side - interaction between them can cause a bend, or wave, in the Polar front, and so the whole process starts.

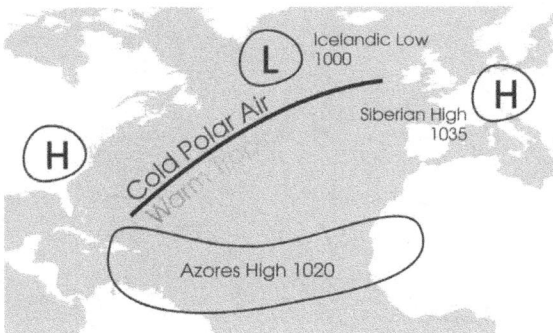

Frontogenesis means the formation of a front, and *frontolysis* means its dissipation. The cold air mass does not move at a *stationary front* (where surface winds tend to flow parallel to the frontal zone), and you get an *upper front* with any temperature gradient aloft. To try and find where a front might be on the surface, look at the temperature, pressure, dew point and wind velocity. On the ground itself, watch for the wind picking up a bit, and the altimeter dropping slightly. In fact, knowing the signs given out by an approaching front can be very useful when operating in remoter places. You need to watch these items:

- **Wind speed and direction**. Winds veer* as a front approaches, and back as it passes, so if you fly through one, expect some left drift and a change of heading to the right in the Northern hemisphere. For a cold front, winds will start from the South and end up Westerly or North Westerly - with a warm front, look for winds to start from the East (ish) and end up in the South (ish). Any farmer will tell you that the wind will reverse direction as a thunderstorm approaches.

    *Upper winds will back as polar front depression passes through.

- **Temperature**. The greater the temperature, the more active the front is, with more violent weather. It gets colder as a cold front passes, and warmer as a warm front goes by. The greater the temperature *difference*, the more violent the passage.

- **Humidity**. Humidity will be high, and the temperature and dew points will be close together with a cold front passage. If the temperatures are both high, there is more chance of thunderstorms, due to the energy in the air. The temperature and dewpoint spread will widen once the front has gone through, and humidity will decrease.

- **Clouds**. Cold fronts and warm fronts bring cumuliform and stratiform clouds, respectively.

- **Pressure trends**. Pressure always falls as a warm front approaches, because massive amounts of air are being lifted. The faster the rate of change, the more severe the weather is likely to be, and it may include thunderstorms and heavy rain. Pressure will rise again after the front passes by.

These items will change as a front goes by:

- Wind veers (clockwise change in arrow direction).
- Pressure drops as fronts approach, steadying after warm fronts, rising after cold ones.
- Temperature changes according to type of front.
- Weather will start with moderate continuous rain ahead of the warm front to drizzle in the warm sector, followed by heavier intermittent or continuous precipitation at the cold front, then nil (or showers) afterwards.
- Visibility improves behind the cold front.

 The EASA exams state an average slope of 1:80 for cold fronts, which move, on average, at about the speed of the geostrophic wind component normal to the front, and measured at it (*Source*: UK Met Office).

Passive (kata) fronts can slope up to 1:100 and active (ana) fronts up to 1:50.

The Warm Front

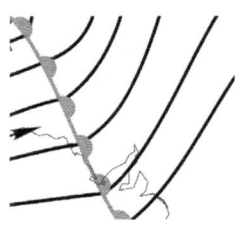 This exists where warm air overtakes a colder air mass and is forced upwards over it, meaning clouds. Its symbol on a weather map, resembling beads of sweat, is shown on the left. The frontal slope has a gradient in the order of 1:150 (run per rise), although the clouds themselves will be about 5 miles high, starting with Nimbostratus at more or less ground level, through alto-stratus to cirrostratus. When flying towards it, you would see the clouds the other way round, of course, so once you start seeing cirrus clouds, you know that a warm front is somewhere ahead, anywhere between 300-600 miles away, or nearly 24 hours at a typical speed of about 15 kts*, so have an overnight kit if you have to wait it out (rain will typically be 200 miles ahead). You can use the typical slope figure to work out the cloud base in front of the system. At 100 miles, it will be 2 640 feet, which comes from 1/200*100, or half a mile, multiplied by 5280 (feet).

*Actually two thirds of the speed found by measuring the isobars along the front.

Clouds will therefore appear in this order as you fly towards a warm front - cirrus, cirrostratus, altostratus, stratus and nimbostratus. The extensive cloud layers are caused by unstable warm air overrunning retreating cold air, with a high moisture content. Thus, the precipitation will change from steady rain to heavy showers. The shallow slope ensures that whatever is coming will last some time, and you can expect the pressure to fall, the cloud to get lower, the wind to back and increase in speed, rising humidity, bad visibility, drizzle and rain, though not necessarily in that order. The freezing level will be lower in front than behind, and the slope means that freezing rain will be falling on anything underneath, so if you are flying towards a warm front, or towards the rear of a cold front, in between their freezing levels and that in the warm sector, watch out!

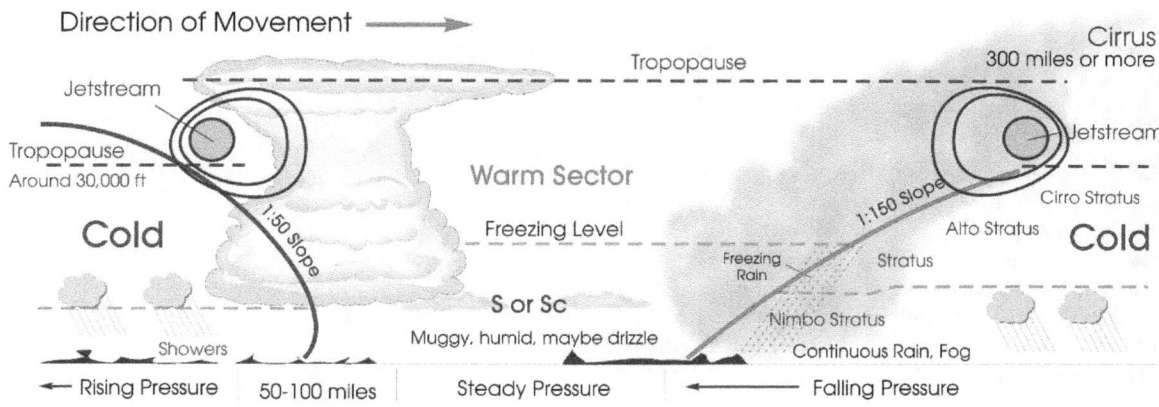

Picture Above: Cross Section Of A Frontal System, as represented by the line A-B in the picture below.

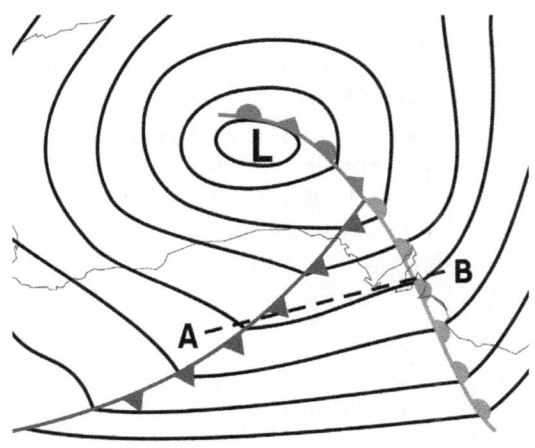

Supercooled water droplets from above will freeze onto your cold airframe. Once you see ice pellets, expect freezing rain next. If you are thinking of trying to descend out of it, remember that the cloud base lowers in precipitation.

As the front passes, you will experience *frontal fog* in front (from the added water), followed by advection fog afterwards. The rain will stop, then become drizzle under an overcast sky, and the wind will veer. As humidity rises to saturation point, visibility could be poor. You will then be in the warm sector, where conditions will be more settled for a few hours (the pressure will rise abruptly), with broken or overcast stratus, just a few hundred feet thick. The further you are away from the low centre, the more the cloud is likely to break up, but don't be fooled - high ground upwind could be holding the cloud back, giving a false impression that the system has passed on. The warm sector is called that because it has the warmest air of the whole system, stuck as it is between the warm and cold fronts.

After the warm sector comes......

The Cold Front

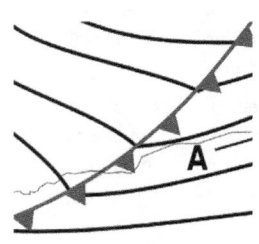

The cold front occurs when cold dense air moves towards the Equator (from the Poles) and undercuts warm air to force it aloft, usually along a trough of low pressure. A cold front has a much steeper slope (1:50) than a warm front, and brisker activity, with more of a chance of thunderstorms, because the convergence is typically stronger, providing a greater forcing mechanism. The rain becomes showery and the wind veers more, to the West or North West. (behind a cold front, winds veer and increase with height). Pressure gets higher, and temperature and humidity decrease. In temperate climates, large amounts of cumulonimbus are unusual, but not over continental land areas. The rain belt is relatively small compared to the warm front, and visibility will improve markedly.

The associated weather is actually determined by the stability and moisture content of the warm air mass, the speed of the front, and steepness of the frontal surface.

An **Ana-Front** (active cold front) is fast moving, with a steep frontal surface up which slower moving warm air is forced to rise, producing the convective cloud normally associated with cold fronts. Heavy rain occurs at frontal passage with a large drop in temperature and sharp veer and decrease in wind.

A **Kata-Front** is passive and slow moving, with a less steep frontal surface, and warm air moving forward faster than the front and forced down the frontal slope. Cloud is mostly thick strato cumulus. Light rain occurs at frontal passage, often with more rain 100 km ahead. A slight drop in temperature and a gradual veer and increase in wind also occurs at passage.

Movement Of Fronts

Upper winds blowing across them cause the rapid movement of surface fronts.

A cold front moves at about the speed of the wind perpendicular to it just above the friction level (i.e. about 2,000 feet, for 15-25 kts), but they are faster in Winter because the air is colder and exerts greater pressure. However, friction with the ground slows the lower levels, so there is a bulge effect along the leading edge. The friction, often coupled with strong heating from below as the cold air crosses warmer ground, often creates gusty wind conditions. The weather is generally colder after its passage, and with less cloud, because pressure is greater to the West and less to the East, limiting the inflow of air.

As warm air finds it hard to displace cold air, a warm front moves at about $^2/_3$ of the speed of a cold front, perpendicular to itself. To predict future positions of warm fronts (and the weather), use the isobar direction in the warm sector, as the system moves parallel to them. Depressions move in the direction indicated by the FIRST isobar of the warm sector, and at the geostrophic wind speed given by the distance between the FIRST and SECOND isobars.

(QUASI) STATIONARY FRONTS

These are non-moving (or stalled) boundaries between two air masses, neither of which is strong enough to replace the other. They tend to remain in the same area for long periods, usually moving in waves, and producing lots of rain. The weather usually consists of clouds and prolonged precipitation.

Stationary fronts either dissipate after several days or devolve into shear lines*, but they can change into a cold or warm front if conditions aloft change. Stationary fronts have alternating red half-circles and blue spikes in opposite directions, meaning no significant movement.

*When stationary fronts become smaller, degenerating to a narrow zone where wind direction changes significantly over a relatively short distance, they become known as *shear lines*, shown as a line of red dots and dashes.

Upper Fronts

These arise from any change of temperature gradient aloft. No change of air mass is recorded as stations detect no change.

Occlusions

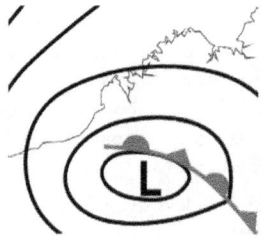

Cold fronts move faster than warm fronts. When they catch up with each other, the warm sector is lifted from the ground (shut off), leaving only one front on the surface, with another on top, although some scientists say that frontal occlusions occur when storms redevelop farther back into the cold air. In most cases, storms start to weaken after a frontal occlusion occurs. Whatever the reason, the essential point with an occluded front is that warm air is isolated as it is forced aloft to condense and form clouds. One danger is thunderstorms embedded in stratiform cloud.

The point where occluding starts is the *triple point*, because there are three air masses involved: that ahead of the occlusion, the warm air aloft, and the air behind the occlusion, or where the cold, warm and occluded fronts meet. It is the nearest location of warm air to the centre, and therefore the point of most lifting, so it is often a focus for a secondary low. It lies at the rear edge of the cloud band associated with the occluded front, within a sharp trough, but the air mass behind the boundary can be either warm or cold.

Occluded fronts are normally crossed by a jet stream.

COLD OCCLUSION

If the air behind the occluded front is the coldest, it will plough under both air masses to produce a cold occlusion.

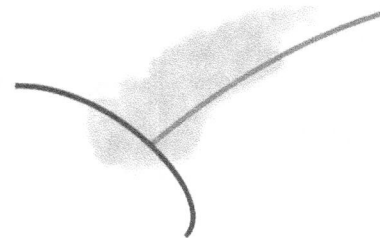

It is referred to as cold because the cold air is touching the surface. The greatest depth of warm air aloft is behind the occluded front, so there may be a trough behind.

The weather is initially like a warm front but, during the passage, showery weather similar to that of a cold front occurs. This kind of occlusion is common in Summer.

A cold occlusion is more or less the same as a Trough of Warm Air Aloft (**TROWAL**), again from a cold front catching up with a warm one. Trowals are parts of systems in their decaying state.

They are found on constant pressure charts above 700 hPa (10,000 ft), most frequently in Summer in Europe, and can severely affect surface weather.

WARM OCCLUSION

If the air is warmer than the air ahead, which is typical of Britain in Winter, it will ride over the colder air mass, because it is lighter, to produce a warm front occlusion, even though the air masses are cold.

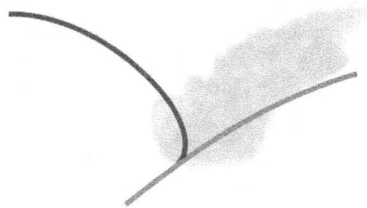

Here, the greatest depth of warm air aloft is ahead of the occluded front, so there will be a trough in front.

The weather is like a warm front, mostly occurring in Winter, and less common. In fact, a wide variety of weather can be found along occluded fronts. As they are associated with mature systems, the weather can be very unsettled with rain and/or snow likely and possibly (embedded) thunderstorms, potentially over prolonged periods. However, you do get more rain with a warm occlusion, plus a quicker transition from warm to cold front weather.

METEOROLOGY
Wind

WIND

Because the Earth is heated unevenly, air at the Equator becomes warmer than that at the Poles, so the atmosphere expands upwards around the middle of the Earth and contracts down to the surface higher up the latitude scale.

This general trend gives rise to regular patterns of air movement, in the shape of winds that were well known to navigators on the high seas, such as the trade winds. Because of the wind, we have to make adjustments to headings and calculate fuel flows.

Wind is the *horizontal* movement of air from high to low pressure, just like the air from a pricked balloon - the larger the pressure difference, the faster the wind will flow. Where isobars are closer together, there is a greater rate of change over a short distance.

Wind is expressed as a velocity, so it needs direction and speed to fit the definition. The wind always comes *from* somewhere, expressed as a *true bearing* in weather reports (*magnetic* from the Tower*), so a *Southerly* wind is *from* 180°. The speed is mostly in knots, or nautical miles per hour, as if you didn't know already, measured at 10 metres over open terrain as a ten-minute average.

*Anything that is printed is always True, just like the newspapers ☺. Any winds spoken by ATC/ATS are Magnetic. The only exceptions are VOLMET broadcasts which are basically transmitted METARS anyway.

Wind direction is measured with a *wind vane*, while speed is measured with an *anemometer*, which should be on a mast 6-10 m above the runway and calibrated after *Saint Venant* (to allow for compressibility) for best results. 10 m is used to make sure that the wind is not affected by small local obstacles. A *pressure tube anemometer* works in the same way as a pitot tube. A more common type has three cups on stalks that are driven round by the wind, and the speed of rotation gives the wind speed.

Obstacles interfere with the wind in different ways. A forest is like a large brush, slowing the air down and mixing it up. The wind will also build up before an obstacle and create turbulent eddies behind it. This is one effect that will result in *gusts* and *lulls* as the speed varies. *Gusts* are rapid changes of speed and direction that don't last long, while *squalls* do. They are sudden increases by at least 16 kts lasting at least 1 minute, reaching a top speed of 22 kts. A gale has a minimum wind speed of 34 kts, or is gusting at 43 kts or more. In Central Europe, the highest wind speeds are just below the tropopause.

Veering is a clockwise change in wind direction with height or time - backing is the reverse.

Winds affect runway distances, range and flight time.

Geostrophic Force (Effect)

Under normal circumstances, according to Hadley, air initially at rest would just move *across* the isobars, due to the *Pressure Gradient Force*, or PGF*, which makes it move directly from high to low pressure.

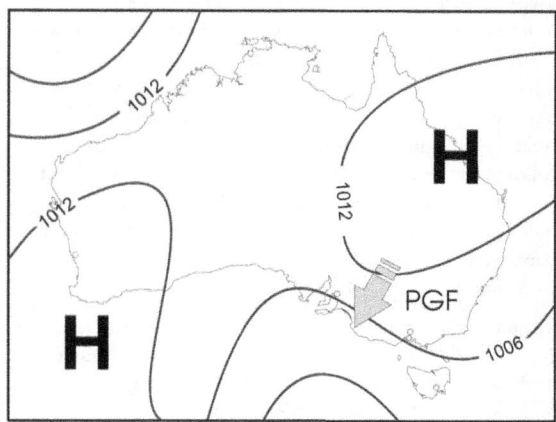

*After Buys Ballot, though, the pressure gradient has come to be regarded as the distribution of force that steers the wind rather than the force that causes it. In fact, the PGF could even be the result of the movement of air, rather than the other way round. For example, looking at the picture under Coriolis, below, the two flows of air would have a higher pressure between them due to their convergence, or a low pressure if they changed places.

However, in simple terms (for exams), the pressure gradient around a parcel of air is equal to the change in pressure per change in distance ($\Delta P/\Delta n$), perpendicular to the isobars.

Because the Earth is spinning, and deflects normal air movement, above about 15° of latitude, the wind will eventually blow *along* the isobars (instead of across) at around 2,000 feet, where there is no friction effect from the Earth's surface. Thus, an imaginary (Coriolis) force *appears* to cause a moving body to follow a curved path (in the Southern hemisphere, air is deflected to the left). Below 15° of latitude, the wind follows the PGF more.

CORIOLIS

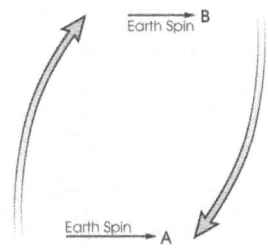
The Earth moves faster at the Equator than it does at the Poles (based on a cosine relationship) so, if you fire an artillery shell from the North Pole to the Equator (B to A, on the left), progressively more of the Earth's surface would pass under its track, giving the illusion of the object curving to the right (or West of A) as it lags behind - the Earth is moving slower towards the North. If you threw whatever it was the other way, it would "move" to the East of B, because you are adding the Earth's movement at both latitudes. That is, B will be moving slower relative to A. In other words, a bullet might fly in a straight line, but its target will move to the right.

This apparent movement (East or West) is often called the *Coriolis Effect*, after a Frenchman who noticed that a billiard ball tends to veer to the right in the Northern hemisphere, and to the left in the Southern hemisphere. It is actually *Geostrophic Force* (after Sir Napier Shaw) when it refers to air movement, although no "force" is involved, hence the use of the word *effect*. As the wind moves towards low pressure, its speed increases, and so does the deflection due to Coriolis, which is directly proportional to wind speed and the sine of the latitude. As latitude increases, geostrophic force increases, other things being equal, so it has a maximum value at the Poles. **The geostrophic wind is the theoretical** (i.e. imaginary) **wind that would result from an exact balance between Coriolis and the Pressure Gradient Force**, at higher latitudes than around 15° N/S. However, this would only occur in a straight line, with no centrifugal force or friction involved (above 2 300 feet or 700 m over land, but higher over mountains).

A **supergeostrophic wind** is faster than the geostrophic wind. The excess Coriolis force forces the air to flow towards higher heights until it loses kinetic energy and slows down again (typically around the exit region of jet streams). A **subgeostrophic wind** is slower than the geostrophic wind. Here, the PGF is dominant until the flowing air gains kinetic energy to restore the balance. This typically happens around the entrance to jet streams.

In the picture on the right, a parcel of air initially at rest starts to move under the PGF across the isobars towards the low pressure (from 1000 to 996 hPa in this case). Once movement starts, geostrophic force turns it to the right, the effect increasing with speed until, eventually, the PGF is balanced by Coriolis and there is no more deflection - the flow is along straight isobars, at right angles to the pressure gradient.

The wind direction is now stable - any tendency to flow towards the low pressure will increase the speed, and Coriolis, until the air is following the isobars again. Blowing away from the low pressure will decrease the speed and Coriolis until the wind is again with the isobars.

As always, there is a mathematical solution. Coriolis force is represented by **fv**, where *f* is equal to:

$$2\Omega\sin\theta$$

Ω is the rotational speed of the Earth, as modified by the sine of the latitude. *f* will therefore be zero at the Equator and will increase as latitude increases. *v* is the velocity of the parcel of air concerned, so Coriolis will be zero when the air is not moving. When it is moving, Coriolis will be directly proportional to the parcel's velocity. It will also increase in strength away from the Equator.

GRADIENT WINDS

However, there is another force, called *cyclostrophic force*, which operates outward (like centrifugal force*), at 90° to the instantaneous motion, to the left in the Northern hemisphere and the right in the Southern hemisphere when the isobars are curved, assuming no friction.

*The reaction to an imbalance between Coriolis and the PGF.

This combination of geostrophic and cyclostrophic effects is called the *gradient wind**. **Winds that blow at constant speeds parallel to curved isobars above the level of frictional influence are called gradient winds**.

*In lower latitudes, the sine value of the latitude is small, so the cyclostrophic effect will balance the PGF, rather than Coriolis (the geostrophic effect is minimal) and create a **cyclostrophic wind**, as found in tropical revolving storms and tornadoes. At higher latitudes, cyclostrophic force will only have a greater influence at higher windspeeds.

The actual wind is the gradient wind plus whatever force you get from friction, which reduces Coriolis and allows the PGF to deflect the air towards the low pressure. In other words, as you descend, friction with trees, etc. will lessen the geostrophic effect and give you an effective change of wind direction to the left (to the right in the Southern hemisphere). As this is enough to reduce the wind speed enough to stop it deflecting, it will tend to blow towards the low pressure, i.e. inwards, to contribute towards the lifting effect, as it is forced up, to cause adiabatic cooling, and precipitation.

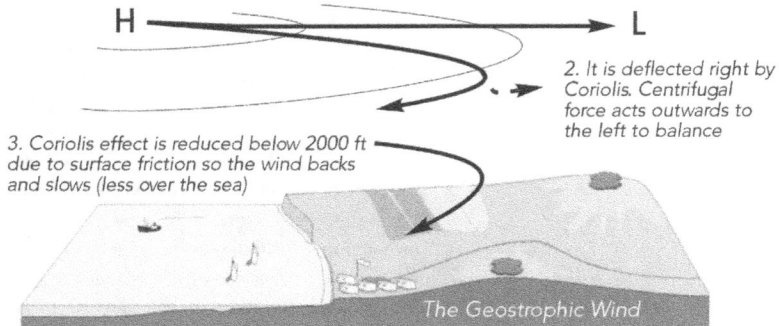

1. Pressure Gradient Force makes air move from High to Low Pressure
2. It is deflected right by Coriolis. Centrifugal force acts outwards to the left to balance
3. Coriolis effect is reduced below 2000 ft due to surface friction so the wind backs and slows (less over the sea)

The Geostrophic Wind

As the centrifugal force opposes the PGF, the PGF is reduced and the gradient wind will have a lesser speed. *Thus, around a low pressure system, the gradient wind is less than the theoretical value for a given latitude,* and the Geostrophic Wind Scale (below) will over-read. In the tropics, once a swirl develops around a low pressure area, the cyclostrophic effect may be enough all by itself to make it stick around and develop int something nasty like a cyclone.

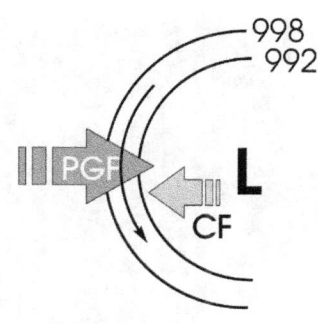

Around a high, the centrifugal force goes in the same direction as the PGF, is added to it, and the gradient wind has more than the theoretical value, so the wind scale will under-read. At low latitudes, where the cyclostrophic wind predominates, the winds will be slight and the high pressure area dissipate rapidly as mass is removed from it.

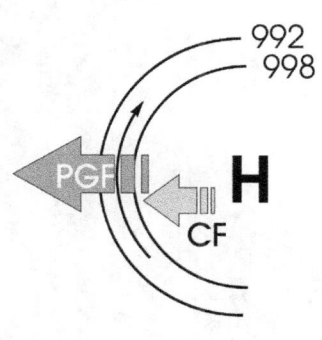

However, in high pressure areas, the combination of descending air and cyclostrophic force makes the winds blow outwards, which is offset by the pPGF in a low being much steeper, creating stronger winds anyway. This is known as the *isallobaric effect*, since lines joining places with an equal *rate of change* of pressure are *isallobars*.

Over the sea, the geostrophic effect will be less, giving about 10° difference in direction, as opposed to the 30° you can expect over land (the speed reduces to about 70% over water, and 50% over land). To use maths again:

$$GF = 2w\rho V \sin\theta$$

where w = the Earth's rotational velocity, ρ is density, V is the wind speed and θ is the latitude. You can see that, as latitude increases, so will the geostrophic force. All you need to do is swap GF for PGF and play with the formula:

$$V = \frac{PGF}{2w\rho \sin\theta}$$

The windspeed increases with height as density reduces, but it all breaks down within about 15° of the Equator, or you would have an infinite windspeed. Given the same pressure gradient at 40°N, 50°N and 60°N, the geostrophic wind speed is greatest at 40°N.

According to Professor *Buys Ballot's Law* (a Dutch meteorologist who lived in Utrecht in 1857), if you stand with your back to the wind in the Northern hemisphere, the low pressure is on your left (on the right in the Southern hemisphere), so if you fly towards lower pressure, you will drift to starboard as the wind is from the left. It's the opposite way round in an anticyclone.

GEOSTROPHIC WIND SCALE

The wind speed measured from a chart is the *geostrophic wind speed*. It approximates the actual wind speed, but not always. The measurements are taken across the isobars, and the speed is deduced from the spacing between them, allowing for density and latitude.

The inwards acceleration depends on the closeness of the isobars and inversely on the density of the air because, the denser it is, the more force you need to make it accelerate. Yet again with the maths:

$$\text{accel} = \frac{\text{closeness of isobars}}{\text{air density }(\rho)}$$

But Coriolis is equal to the windspeed multiplied by the sine of the latitude and, as the wind blows along isobars, the inwards acceleration must be equal to Coriolis, so:

$$V\sin\theta = \frac{\text{closeness of isobars}}{\text{air density }(\rho)}$$

so:

$$V = \frac{\text{closeness of isobars}}{\text{air density }(\rho) \times \sin\theta}$$

Thus, allowing for air density and latitude, you can find the windspeed just by measuring how close the isobars are, which is what the geostrophic wind scale does by assuming that the air has normal density at 2000 feet and by covering a limited band of latitude - if you lay the scale across the isobars, you can read the speed of the wind at 2000 feet. If there isn't a scale on the weather map, find the speed this way:

- Find something the same length as 5° of latitude.
- Lay it at right angles to the relevant isobars or contours and measure difference in height or pressure between the ends.
- Multiply the result by the factors in this table to get the wind speed in knots:

Table: Deriving Geostrophic Windspeed

Lat°	Isobars (hPa)	Contours (m)
70	2.1	0.25
60	2.3	0.27
55	2.4	0.29
50	2.6	0.31
45	2.8	0.33
40	3.1	0.37
35	3.4	0.41
30	3.9	0.47
25	4.7	0.56

A 10 hPa drop at 50° N or S gives a windspeed of 26 kts.

METEOROLOGY
Wind

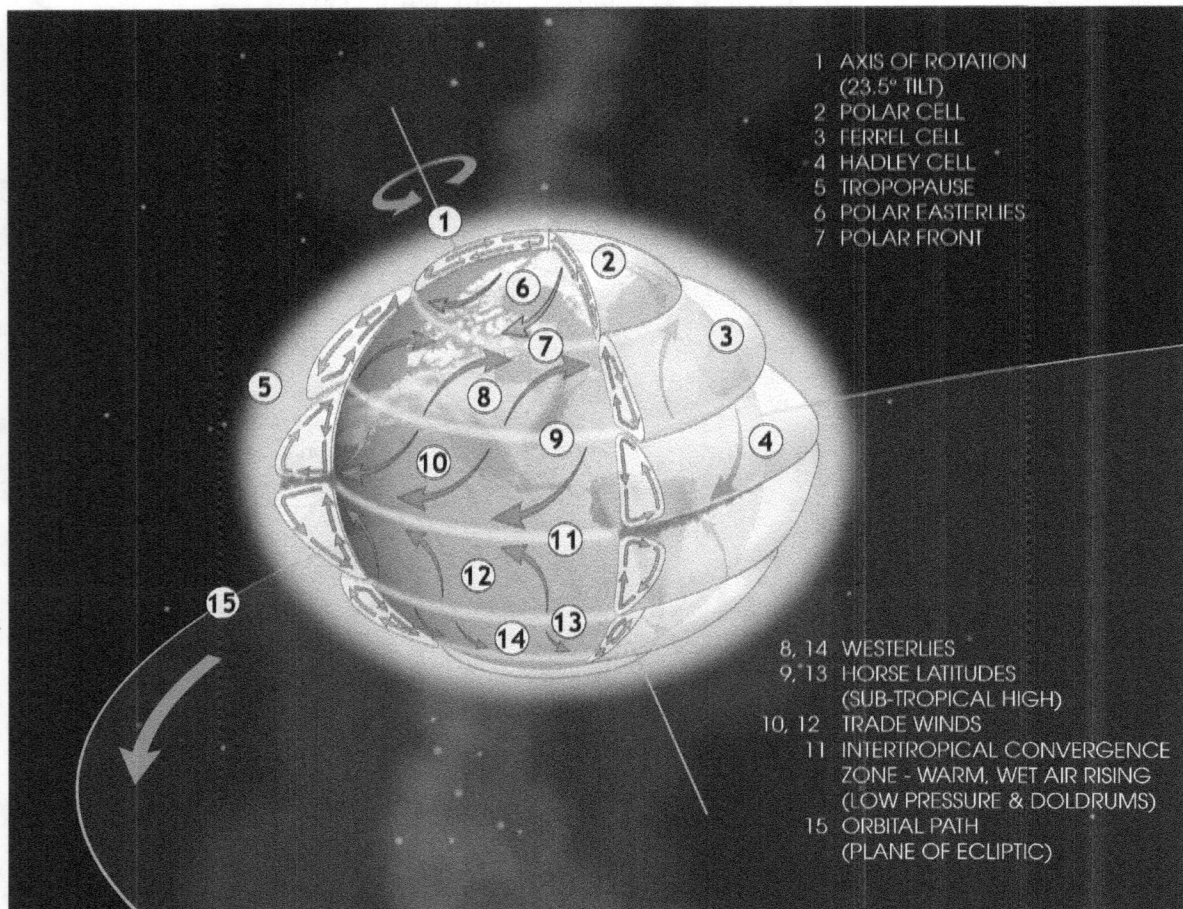

Picture: World Air Circulation. Rising air around the Equator/ITCZ provides the heat engine for the weather.

Prevailing Winds

Prevailing winds blow more from one direction than any other, and will be a characteristic of a particular region, so they are influential in the placement of runways. In desert and polar regions, they produce sand dunes and snowdrifts. The arctic and subtropical areas of the Northern hemisphere have a generally East to West movement of weather systems - Polar Easterlies carry storms, as do the NE trade winds. The prevailing Westerlies, typically at 50°N, but affecting the Polar regions, drive mid-latitude storms from West to East.

In fact, the Westerlies can have effects as high as 50,000 feet, fanning out above the Polar Easterlies and the trade winds. In the Northern Hemisphere, you can trace the Southern edge of the Westerlies by checking out the path of the Polar front jet stream. As such, they are the prime weather movers of the world.

In general, Easterly winds are found over the tropics and subtropics (the tropics cover the lower latitudes where most of the Sun's energy is received to create large scale currents in the oceans and weather systems that redistribute the excess heat towards the Poles.

Technically, they lie between the Tropics of Cancer and Capricorn (23.5° N & S) but, for meteorological purposes, they are on the Equatorial side of the belts of high pressure between 25-45° (see picture overleaf). High pressure belts in the mid-latitudes contain centres that mostly move from West to East, and there will be Westerly winds on their Polar sides, with embedded fronts and troughs that move West-East. There will be a high pressure area over either Pole that will be ringed by Easterly winds.

GLOBAL AIR CIRCULATION

There are three major parts to this. It all starts at the Equator, where warm, wet air rises and moves towards the Poles in the upper levels, generally forming thunderstorms in the process. However, it doesn't quite reach that far in one hop. The air that rushes in at the surface to fill the gap comes from the North and South, but is deflected Westward by the Coriolis effect to form the **trade winds**, which blow from the SE in the Southern hemisphere and the NE in the Northern hemisphere. They are powered by the difference in temperature between the Poles and the Equator and occur only in the lower part of the troposphere, being more pronounced over the oceans.

The deepest tropical air is usually within 15° of the Equator and referred to as the *deep Easterlies*. The *shallow Easterlies* are further North and South, and are between 10-20 000 feet deep. The air above usually has a Westerly flow from the Ferrell circulation but, due to its Polar origin, there could be a Trade Inversion.

Sir Edmund Halley deduced the causes of tropical trade winds and monsoons through observations made over two years off the West Coast of Africa. In 1735, George Hadley, a London lawyer, also deduced that the Westerly movement of the winds arose from the W-E rotation of the Earth. Instead of going straight to the North Pole, the warm air from the Equator is affected by the Coriolis force* that makes it accumulate in the subtropical (horse) latitudes and sink to the surface at around 30° latitude, creating a **subtropical high**. The sinking occurs because the air loses its heat at altitude, but it warms up again as it is compressed to form arid areas, going back to the Equator from NE to SW, courtesy of Coriolis.

*The air retains the speed it had at the Equator.

The resulting circulation, up at the Equator and down again at 30° N & S was called a **Hadley cell**. It effectively transfers concentrated heat energy from the Equator to higher latitudes and, combined with the Earth's spin, produces prevailing global wind patterns, such as the trades, or *tropical Easterlies* (warm sea water is also moved by wind-driven currents). Meanwhile, at the Poles, the radiation of heat into space creates an area of very dense air that sinks to the surface and creates an outflow towards the Equator. Coriolis kicks in at about 60° latitude, where the air accumulates and is forced to rise. Once it does, it diverges and flows back to the Poles. The **Polar cell** involves the Polar Easterlies. In between the Hadley and Polar Cells lies the **Ferrel* cell**, in which the sinking air from the Hadley cell at 30° flows Poleward and is deflected by Coriolis at 60°. In the Northern hemisphere, this produces a band of prevailing winds flowing from SW to NE called the prevailing Westerlies. There is no corresponding Easterly upper flow because the air does not actually rise at 60°.

*After William Ferrel, in 1856.

The high-level convergence is responsible for the formation of high pressure cells beneath the subtropical jet stream, on the Poleward margin of the tropical Hadley cell. The resulting highs are slow-moving, produce long spells of fine weather, and create some major deserts.

CLIMATOLOGY

This is the study of the average weather in various parts of the Earth (the various regions concerned are discussed at the end of this section). For this, an understanding of the idealised general circulation of the atmosphere (discussed above), modifications to it and the resulting weather are required, as well as the type of weather associated with the main air routes and upper level winds and jet streams likely to be met. Climatology therefore needs some knowledge of geography, the location of major cities and countries, particularly in relation to the Equator and the tropics of Cancer and Capricorn, major oceans and land masses.

Important features include:

- The **Equatorial Low** (Equatorial Trough). An area of low pressure into which the trade winds converge. Also known as the **Intertropical Convergence Zone** (ITCZ), and known to sailors as the *Doldrums*, it contains areas of complete calm either side of the Equator, where the only movement of air is up (although it slides horizontally North and South once it hits the tropopause). In fact, the only wind is caused by air getting sucked in from areas just outside to form the trade winds - as they converge, warm, moist air is forced upwards, to condense any water vapour as it rises and cools, resulting in a band of heavy precipitation (i.e. frequent and widespread cumulonimbus) around the Equator which moves seasonally towards the most intense solar heating, or warmest surface temperatures. The ITCZ is the "meteorological Equator", because it moves with the Sun, usually being found in whatever hemisphere is experiencing Summer. This movement is responsible for the monsoon rains, where winds blowing from one direction for part of the year switch round and blow in the other direction for the remainder.* It can produce extremely bad weather over a wide area, over two seasons - rainy and dry, which exist when the Sun is and is not present, respectively.

*As the ITCZ moves North in June, so do the Hadley cells. They bring warm, moist air and heavy rains (SE Monsoons) to the Indian subcontinent and parts of South East Asia. When it is further South, the Northern Hemisphere trade winds bring warm, dry air to the Indian subcontinent over the Himalayan plateau from the NE. This is the North-West Monsoon (again, see the end of this section).

The ITCZ tends to lag about four weeks behind the Sun's latitude, and particularly affects West Africa between 10° and 20° N, and the Northern coasts of the Arabian Sea in July, when it reaches its maximum Northerly position of 15° to 20° N (North China). Thus, it lies in the Northern hemisphere in July, and occupies both hemispheres in January, having moved South for the Winter (it does not lie completely in the Southern hemisphere). Winds at Equatorial latitudes flow more across isobars than along them, but they tend to be weak anyway, as they are created more by diurnal heating and cooling. This is towards the Southern Hemisphere between September to February, reversing direction in time for Summer in the Northern Hemisphere. However, in oceanic longitudes the ITCZ is stationary just North of the Equator, which means more rain as it gets hotter. In January in the Southern hemisphere, the maximum heating is over the land masses, which then become areas of low pressure, effectively moving the ITCZ well South of the Equator (see the picture below) but, over the Eastern Pacific and the Atlantic, it sits mainly 5-10° North of the Equator due to a warm ocean current in that latitude, whereas most of the SE Pacific is cold (between Dakar and Rio de Janeiro, the ITCZ can be found between 0°-7°N).

Otherwise, the ITCZ lies in over the Indian and the Western Pacific Oceans.

In July (the Northern hemisphere Summer), the ITCZ reaches its maximum Northerly position over China (around 45°N), rapidly moving back towards the Equator over the China Sea. It reaches 20°N over North Africa and Southern Arabia, and 30° over India, where the Himalayas form a natural Northern limit. Over the Atlantic and Pacific oceans, it lies mainly between 10°N and 15°N. Thus, if you go to Dakar from Marseille in July, expect to meet it near Dakar.

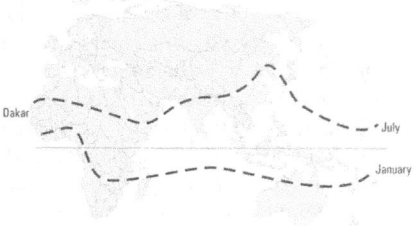

The weather in the ITCZ has wide variations and depends on local factors. Sometimes over land, a relatively narrow front is created when converging air masses have different characteristics, as with fronts in temperate latitudes. The ITCZ is 40 - 500 km wide.

At the beginning of the trade wind flow, the typical weather is scattered light cumulus cloud. Instability is shallow at this stage, limited by the inversion from the sub-tropical high which is carried along between 3,000 - 8000ft. Further progression to lower latitudes should lead to larger cumulus and CB development as instability and increased moisture content combine to break through the trade wind inversion. In the convergence zone itself, the weather largely depends on the degree of convergence but, even in the Doldrums where winds are light and variable, fair weather cumulus may be replaced by squalls and thunderstorms when instability develops.

Where winds are stronger, vertical development is likely, with frequent extensive cumulonimbus and thunderstorms. There may be violent turbulence and severe icing with cloud tops above 50,000 ft. On the other hand, with stable conditions at medium and high levels, the cumulus build-up stops and the cloud spreads out into large sheets of stratiform clouds.

The main idea is that warm moist air can converge to produce heavy cloud and rain.

- **Subtropical Highs**. These are anticyclones created by the upper level air flowing away from the Equator, between latitudes 20 - 40° N/S. As a result, high pressures occur over the oceans all year round - over land, they occur only in the local Winter, i.e. the dry season. Wide variations occur because the land heats up and cools down more rapidly than the sea. This *Continentality* means that Winters over the land are cold and Summers are hot, but the oceans reduce the differences in coastal areas and nearby land masses. The rainy seasons in Equatorial Africa are between March - May and October - November.
- **Trade Winds**. Belts of light winds (typically less than 15 kts) that blow from NE and SW into the ITCZ. They extend up to about 10,000 ft, but can be as low as 7,000ft or as high as 15,000ft, and are strongest in the Winter half of the year. The air masses concerned are initially relatively dry and stable, as the air starts off as subsiding air in the subtropical high pressure belts. Passage over warmer seas towards the ITCZ produces increasing instability (heating from below) and an increase in moisture content due to evaporation into the dry air at the lower levels. After a long sea track, the trade wind air mass will be humid and unstable.

Because they are essentially products of solar heating, the features of the idealized circulation change latitude with the seasonal movement of the Sun. For example, pressure zones produce climatic zones - low pressure means convergence and you get cloud and precipitation in the temperate and Equatorial belts of low pressure. On the other hand, at the Poles and in the sub-tropical belts of high pressure, due to subsiding air, it is mainly dry.

Polar Climate
High pressure is weaker than in the sub-tropical highs and often replaced by travelling depressions producing unsettled weather and snow. Below 0°C, the ground is permanently covered by ice and snow. Above 0°C, there is some growth of mosses and lichens, but the sub-soil remains frozen (permafrost).

Disturbed Temperate Climate
In the North Atlantic and across Northern Europe*, the weather is dominated by travelling frontal depressions and the odd high pressure system. Winds are mainly Westerly, with frequent gales. There is a lot of cyclonic precipitation with no dry season. Seasonal changes between Winter and Summer are small.

*As there are no pronounced N-S mountain barriers (such as the Rockies or Andes), North Atlantic depressions can penetrate well into Europe. In doing so, they tend to dry out, so the rainfall in the East is only about half that in the West, near the Atlantic Ocean, so the main weather feature is frontal activity associated with low pressure systems moving in from the Atlantic.

Mediterranean Climate (Warm Temperate Transitional)
This is a transitional climate, being disturbed temperate in Winter and dry subtropical in Summer. Winters are wet, cool and unsettled, and Summers are hot and dry.

Arid Subtropical Climate
These great desert areas are always under the influence of the sub-tropical highs. As a result, skies are clear, it is warm (hot in Summer) and practically rainless. Winds are notable for their trade wind consistency.

Tropical Transitional (Savannah) Climate
In Winter, the weather is governed by the dry trade winds and, in Summer, the belt of Equatorial rains which follows the seasonal movement of the Sun. The wet season gets shorter as latitude increases.

Equatorial Climate (Humid Tropical)
This zone, about 10° either side of the Equator, has two main rainy seasons as the Sun crosses the Equator, but there is no real dry season. There is a lot of convective activity with heavy showers and frequent thunderstorms. Temperature and humidity are both high and are almost uniform throughout the year. Winds are generally light, and over the oceans where the zone is narrower, the area is known as the Doldrums.

World Temperature Distribution
While temperatures in general decrease from the Equator to the Poles, surface isotherms (lines joining points of equal surface temperature) do not always line up with the parallels of latitude.

In **January**, the Sun is overhead in the Southern hemisphere, where the warm air over the continents creates low pressure at the surface and breaks up the subtropical high pressure belt between 20°S and 40°S.

In the Northern hemisphere, the subtropical high pressure belt is only really noticeable in the Atlantic and the Eastern Pacific Oceans at about 30°N. Over the land masses of Eurasia and North America, the subtropical high is masked by the cold anticyclones from the low land temperatures. The Siberian high is the dominant feature of the Eurasian land mass. The two mean low pressure areas in the North Atlantic (Icelandic low) and the North Pacific (Aleutian low) are not permanent, but seem so because of the many travelling depressions that pass through. The highest temperatures occur between 10°S and 20°S over the land - sea temperatures are below those of the land at the same latitude. The sun is overhead at about 20°S.

The Northern hemisphere land masses are coldest, being extreme in Siberia (NE Asia) and Northern Canada (God's frozen people). It is also cold over North America and Eurasia, with cold air well down towards tropical regions.

The warmer temperatures of the North Atlantic contrast the land temperature to the West and East, due to the outflow of warm water (the Gulf Stream) from the Caribbean Sea NE across the North Atlantic (the North Atlantic Drift) and into the Norwegian Sea.

In **July**, the sun is overhead in the Northern hemisphere and, over the oceans, the subtropical high pressure belt is well established. The Azores high is more intense than in January, extending from the SE United States through the Azores to SW Europe and well into the Mediterranean.

High pressure over Asia has been replaced by a large low pressure area over Northern India, extending West over the Persian Gulf. This is the monsoon low of India (or Asian Low) and is the dominant feature of Eastern Europe, Asia and the Far East. The mean pressure in the monsoon low in July is the same as that in the Icelandic low in January.

The Icelandic low is now a much weaker feature in the North Atlantic and the dominant low pressure area is over NE Canada.

In the Southern hemisphere, the pressure situations are much closer to the idealised circulation above. Relatively low continental temperatures encourage the formation of high pressure over land which, combined with the warm highs of the sub-tropical anticyclone, form a continuous belt of high pressure around the globe.

The highest temperatures are over land between 20°N and 40°N, with sea temperatures slightly lower. There is extreme heating over North Africa and SE Asia and India. The Sun is overhead at around 20°N and the large land masses get very hot. In tropical or Equatorial regions, average mean temperatures vary by only 5°C through the year, particularly over sea areas. In fact, the average ocean temperatures near the Equator are always very similar.

Large variations of temperature occur over large land masses, particularly in the Northern hemisphere. In Siberia, for example, the difference between average January and July temperatures is considerable. There are no such extremes in the Southern hemisphere.

The polar fronts between the Subtropical and Polar air in each hemisphere are less well defined in Summer. In the Northern hemisphere Winter, the mean position of the front in the North Atlantic lies from Florida to SW England, whereas in July its mean position is from Newfoundland to the North of Scotland.

WESTERLIES

Between the Hadley and Polar cells are *Ferrell Westerlies* in the mid-latitudes, where the outflowing winds from the polar side of each subtropical high clash to form frontal waves. They are named after the William Ferrel mentioned above, who found that the sinking air from the Hadley cell at the surface made its way Poleward, then deflected right at about 60°, to produce prevailing Westerlies that flow SW-NE.

The largest of the Westerly waves are called *long*, or **Rossby**, waves, which create an asymmetric wave pattern out of the major orographic features of the Rockies and the Tibetan Plateau in the Northern Hemisphere, and the Andes in the Southern Hemisphere. 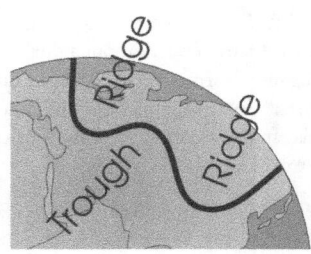 In other words, high mountains, running North/South in both hemispheres affect the flow of air which is also influenced by warm oceans in Winter and warm continents in Summer. This produces large-scale upper troughs and ridges, and the jetstreams. The 52% land mass creates the greatest pattern in the Northern hemisphere (19% in the South). The strongest winds occur in Winter when the thermal gradients are greatest.

Low heights indicate areas of low temperature, which can form cold pools. These are closed circulations of cooler air that have become cut off from their source regions in higher latitudes (they are also known as cut-off lows). Cold pools tend to be quasi-stationary, or slow moving, producing typically unsettled polar airmass weather. In Summer, over Western Europe, thunderous conditions are often associated with cold pools.

The winds that branch North and South in the upper regions above the Equator are called the *anti-trade winds*, and they divide again at about 25° latitude. One branch continues towards the Poles to form upper Westerlies.

The other descends to pile up in the lower levels at 30° latitude to create a zone of calm air with fair weather called the *Horse Latitudes*, which are apparently so named because the winds are relatively slack and horses used to be thrown overboard when fodder (or, more likely, water) got short. This descending air divides yet again to flow towards the Poles and the Equator, the latter creating the trade winds.

The air currents moving towards the Poles from the Horse latitudes are deflected Eastwards to merge with the cooler Westerlies between 30° and 60° latitude, which is why that area produces lots of weather fronts.

 There is a sharp temperature maximum somewhere between 6 000 - 10 000 feet called a *Trade Wind Inversion*, which damps down the rising air and prevents clouds forming to produce rain. This is why there are so many desert areas in this region.

The *Roaring Forties* are winds that come from the NW in the Souther hemisphere, between 40° - 60°S, that are able to blow at gale force across vast stretches of open sea because there is nothing in the way to stop them.

POLAR EASTERLIES

As cold air that accumulates at the Poles spreads out to move towards the Equator, it is deflected by the Coriolis effect to become the Polar Easterlies. These are lighter and more variable winds.

THE WALKER CIRCULATION

This is an E-W vertical circulation in the Australia-Pacific region. The Pacific Ocean covers about a third of the Earth's surface and is significantly warmer on its Western side, which produces a zonal circulation rising over Indonesia to the North West of Australia, and descending over the Eastern Pacific Ocean, near South America.

At intervals spanning several years, the temperature gradient across the Pacific is reduced and the seas North of Australia cool down as the warm water moves into the centre of the Pacific and the usually cold area in the East warms up by 5° or so. Thus, pressure becomes higher than normal in the West, and lower than normal in the East (this is called the *Southern Oscillation*). The rising side moves Eastwards to enhance the upward motion in the Central and Eastern Pacific, which suppresses the monsoon in the Australia-Indonesian area, otherwise known as *El Nino*.

Mountain Winds

The vertical distance to which a mountain range can influence air movement is around 3 - 5 times its height. The horizontal distance, on the other hand, is variable, and cannot be estimated correctly.

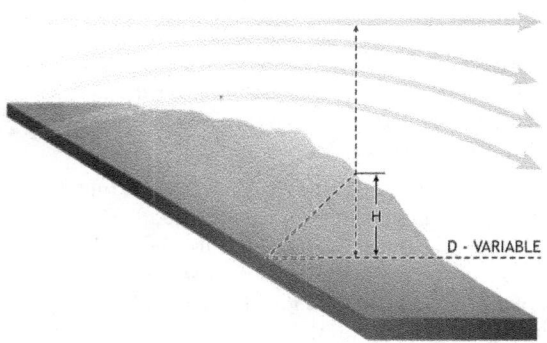

Experienced mountain pilots have rules that they will not deviate from under any circumstances. Some safety points to bear in mind include:

- Mountains don't care about you.
- Always be able to turn towards lower ground, which means approaching or crossing pretty much everything at 45°, from around half a mile away. This is called *dropoff*, meaning an escape route.

- Never go past the point from where you can make a 180° turn without power and without hitting anything, especially in box canyons. This means thinking ahead because, if you leave it too late, you will go past that point while you make a decision. Slowing down allows you make tighter turns.
- Make all turns away from rising ground.

Otherwise, keep clear of marginal weather* and avoid strong winds. Allow much more time for twilight, as it will be darker inside mountains sooner.

*Flying near the clouds keeps you further away from the ground, but it also gives poor visibility and you can get into trouble without seeing it, especially when updraughts force you into the cloud. It's best to fly in the lower third of the distance between the ground and the cloudbase.

The area of lift from high ground is greatest where the air is made to move sharply in a different direction, and, in line with Bernoulli, the greatest windspeed is found at the top of the crest, where it has to move a greater distance in the same time.

There can also be a drop in pressure. This will cause the altimeter to over read and, because the greatest windspeed is over the highest point of the mountains, that is where the greatest over-reading occurs.

The loss of altitude can be as follows:

< 30 kts	Nil significant
31 - 40 kts	add 500 feet
41 - 50 kts	add 1 000 feet
51 - 60 kts	add 1 500 feet
> 60 kts	add 2 000 feet

You are therefore lower than expected just when you need height to clear the mountain, so safety altitudes must be suitably adjusted.

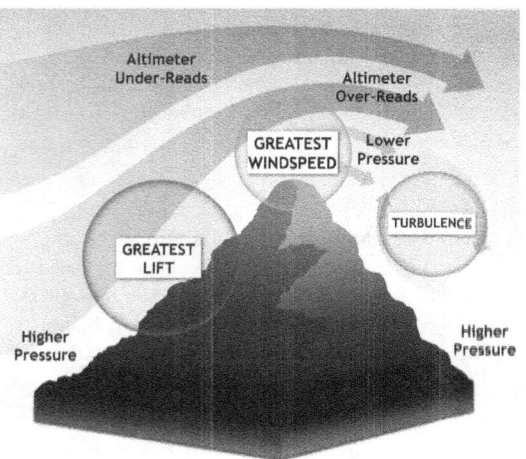

There are several types of wind in the mountains, which can loosely be grouped into:

- **Prevailing winds**, which are steady and fairly reliable, and start to affect you from about 6,000 feet AGL upwards. Indeed, upper winds can come in many directions at different levels, and are usually the opposite of lower winds. Where mountains are concerned, they also acquire a vertical element.
- **Local Winds**, on the other hand, have effects in more limited areas. They can be subdivided into other types, such as *valley*, *anabatic*, *katabatic*, etc., and which are infinitely variable.
  - **Valley winds** can be felt up to 2,500 feet above a valley floor, and reach peak strength around mid-afternoon. Inside mountains, the same venturi effect that causes a wing to fly or pulls fuel vapour into the throat of a carburettor will cause the wind to speed up as it passes through narrower channels or along valleys (the *Mistral* is a good example).

    Cool air that is generated overnight with radiation cooling will flow down a slope, because it is more dense, and therefore more subject to gravity, causing a **katabatic** wind. It's the same effect as in a closed room on a cold day, where there is a draught near a window even when nothing is open - the air next to the window is cooled, and flows downwards. The katabatic effect usually happens around sunset and overnight (when the heating effect of the Sun is lost), and its significance is not just that you might get wind from somewhere you don't expect (and downdraughts from severe slopes), but also that it slips underneath the air not in contact with the slope - if there is a river at the bottom of the valley, the extra moisture could also cause fog, so be careful when flying to valley airfields in the evening.

    Katabatic winds tend to stay within 500 feet of the surface, and can arise suddenly, even up to gale force. Glaciers have permanent katabatic winds.
  - An **anabatic** wind flows *up* a hill, due to ground heating and air expansion during the day. It is not a regular thermal movement, that is, the whole layer does not move vertically away from the slope, but is rather a *slide* of the layer up the hill, so, to get any benefit, you must fly close to the surface. Anabatic winds are quick to decline with cloud cover.

THE DEMARCATION LINE

The demarcation line is the point at which smooth air is separated from turbulent air around a peak, rather similar to that over an aerofoil.

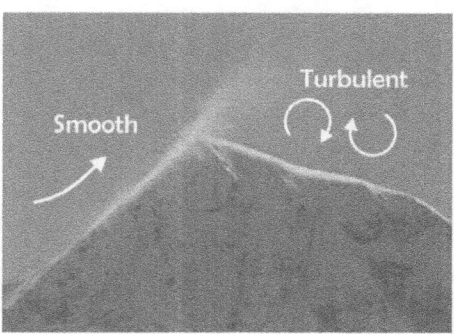

In the picture above, the snow follows the demarcation line. Above or to the windward side (on the left), air is relatively smooth and upflowing - below, or to the right, in the lee, it is downflowing and turbulent. The demarcation line steepens as wind velocity increases (and the severity of the slope), as does the area of downflow, and moves toward the top of the hill.

So, in general, air moving up is smooth (left of the line), and that moving down is turbulent (to the right). As a guide to wind speed, the snow in the picture is light and powdery, so it might be around 10-15 kts.

MOUNTAIN WAVES

When an obstruction such as a mountain range has stable air above it, air flowing over it at the 10,000 foot level at about 20 knots (depends on the size of the range), within about 30°, you can get standing waves for some miles downwind. These occur because the wind has enough momentum to bounce off the ground behind the mountain and push the air already there out of the way. That air will fall again when it reaches a peak. The Fohn, Mistral and Bora behave in a similar way.

Being standing waves, they do not move (the air flowing through them does), and the distance between them is constant. They are easily identified by the types of cloud associated with them, which also do not move, such as the lenticular shown below that can be found at the peak of each wave.

Although the waves as a whole can reach up several thousand feet, the air oscillates up and down about a central mean as it moves downwind.

The flowing air can be deceptively smooth, and only the VSI will tell you if you are going up or down. If you are flying parallel to a ridge on the downwind side in a smooth downdraught, as a result of the local drop in pressure associated with the wave, the

VSI and the altimeter will not indicate a descent until you pass through a layer equal to the error caused by the mountain wave (they may indicate a climb for a short while), so you may not recognise that you are in a downdraught until you pass through the original pressure level which is closer to the ground than before you entered the wave. Thus, in cloud, or at night, you could be in some danger*. There could also be turbulence with accelerations up to 20 G in extreme cases.

*This does not just apply to light aircraft! 747s have lost complete engines in mountain wave downdraughts, but the most common problems are severe reductions in rates of climb and excessive rates of sink.

The trapped lee waves are associated with marked adverse pressure gradients as they go up and down, sometimes dropping over 5 hPa through just a few kilometres. There could also be large vertical increases of temperature (inversions) in the order of 10°C over 200 metres.

The combination of mountain waves and non-standard temperature may result in your altimeter over-reading by as much as 3 000 feet! An aircraft affected by mountain waves can expect severe turbulence below any rotors, downdraughts that may be stronger than the rate of climb and greater than normal icing in associated clouds.

Downdraughts can be particularly dangerous when flying towards a range into a headwind, as the airflow follows the general shape of the surface, and you will experience a strong downdraught just before the ridge. In other words, when into wind, height variations are out of phase with the waves. They are usually in phase downwind.

 The wind speed and direction should be more or less constant up to about 18,000 feet, although it doesn't have to be particularly fast over the peaks. However, it must increase with height.

As the wind needs to be fairly straight in direction, warm sector winds and jetstreams can be very conducive to the formation of waves. They will be more dangerous in Winter because the wind speeds are stronger, and there will be a longer wavelength.

There can be several miles between their peaks and troughs, which can extend between 10,000-20,000 feet above the range and up to 200 or 300 miles downwind:

Watch for long-term variations in speed and pitch attitude in level cruise (the variations may be large). Near the ground in a mountain wave area, severe turbulence and windshear may be encountered, especially at the bottom of a rotor where you may get a performance decreasing shear if you are going in the same direction as the wind.

The potential loss of altitude is 500 feet if the wind is between 30-40 kts, 1000 feet between 40-50, 1500 feet between 50-60 kts and 2000 feet over 60 kts.

This is the real world picture of what is happening:

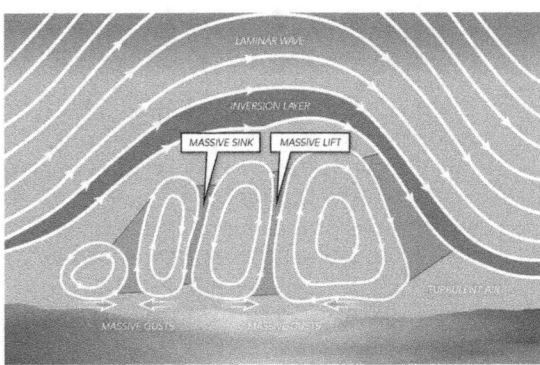

ROTORS

Rotors are ares of rotating turbulence found under the lenticular clouds that are a clue to the position of the peak of a wave. They are always in circular motion, constantly forming and dissipating as water vapour is added and taken away. They are dangerous, and the most turbulence will be found in them, or between them and the ground. Rotor clouds are formed in the same way as lenticular clouds, from air forced upwards and condensing, then dissipating as they proceed downwards in the wave.

Rotor streaming is a phenomenon that occurs when air flowing across a mountain is enough to create waves, but decreases in effect with altitude above the mountain - that is, they are only strong in the lower levels.

The air downstream of the mountain still breaks up and becomes turbulent, like rotors, but there are no lee waves, so the rotors travel downwind rather than stay in one place as they normally would.

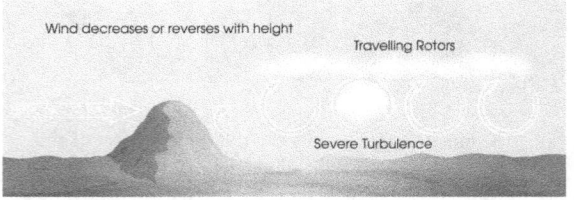

If the rotor forms in an inversion, warm air from above is rotated downward and heated further as it is compressed. On the other way up, cold air is expanding to cool further.

Thus, very cold air ends up lying over warm air and conditions are extremely unstable.

METEOROLOGY
Wind

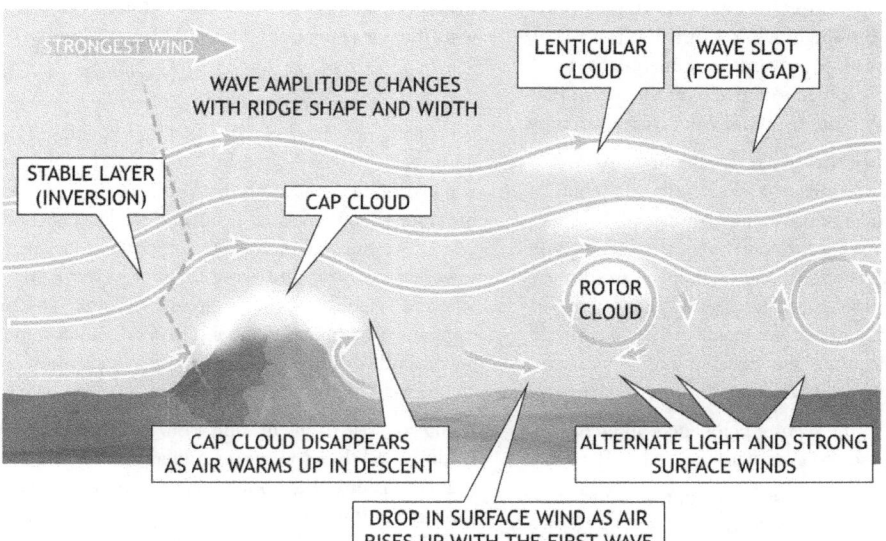

Other Clouds

A seemingly harmless *cap cloud* can sit over the top of the range, creeping down the *lee side* (downwind), as a downdraught, which can be as much as 5 000 ft/min.

It disappears as air descends and warms adiabatically.

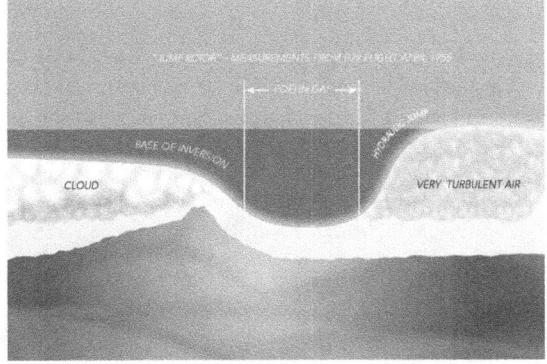

If you have mountain waves, but there are no clouds, the air is too dry.

Windshear

This is the name for sudden airspeed changes over about 10 kts resulting from sudden horizontal or vertical changes in wind velocity - more severe examples will change not only airspeed, but vertical speed and aircraft attitude as well. Officially, it becomes dangerous when variations cause enough displacement from your flight path for substantial corrective action to be taken; *severe* windshear causes airspeed changes greater than 15 kts, or vertical speed changes over 500 feet per minute. Expect it to occur mostly inside 1,000 feet AGL, where it is most critical, because you can't quickly build up airspeed. You can often tell the presence of windshear by clouds moving in different directions or plumes of smoke rising then going off at angles.

Although mostly associated with thunderstorms, where you have the unpredictability of microbursts to contend with, windshear is also present with wake vortices, temperature inversions, mountain waves and the passage of fronts, not forgetting obstructions near the runway, and can occur over any size of area. You can even get it where rain is falling from a cumulus cloud, as the air is getting dense from the cooling, and will therefore fall quicker. Helicopters, especially, can suffer from windshear above and below tree top level in forest clearings, when a backlash effect can convert any headwind to a tailwind.

All fronts are zones of windshear - the greater the temperature difference across them (over 10°C), the greater the changes will be. The surface wind speeds associated with a front, particularly over rough ground, can influence windshear production (friction + windspeed + instability = mechanical turbulence). Warm fronts tend to have less shear than cold ones, but as they're slower moving, you catch it for longer. In general, the faster the front moves (say, over 30 kts), the more vigorous the weather associated with it; if it goes slower, the visibility will be worse, but you can still get windshear even then and for up to an hour after its passage.

Warm air moving horizontally above cold air can produce turbulence at the point where they join, as would be typical with an inversion, at around 2,000-4,000 feet with a windspeed of 25 kts or more (low level windshear is likely to be greatest at the top of a marked surface-based **inversion**, or **near thunderstorms**). In a valley, in particular, when the moving warm air hits a mountainside, it will be forced downwards, but unable to penetrate the cold air, so it is forced to move over the top of that in the valley bottom, so watch out on those cold, clear mornings.

The most significant effect of windshear is, of course, loss of airspeed at a critical moment, similar to an effect in mountain flying, where a wind reversal could result in none at all! You would typically get this with a downburst from a convective type cloud, where, initially, you get an increase in airspeed from the extra headwind, but if you don't anticipate the reverse to happen as you get to the other side, you will not be able to cope with the loss. This has led to the windshear classifications of *performance increasing* or *performance decreasing* (*Microbursts*).

The helicopter on the left in the picture below gets an increased headwind, so power is reduced to compensate.

This takes effect just as the downburst is encountered, and the headwind becomes a tailwind, so IAS decreases.

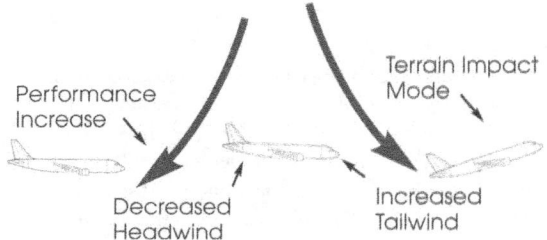

Coming down an ILS with the wind slightly off to the left, and decreasing in speed as you get lower, left to itself, the aircraft is likely to fly above the glide path with an increasing deviation.

Windshear is *occasional* if it exists for about a third of the time, *intermittent* between then and two thirds, and *continuous* over that. The alert is given when the mean surface wind is over 20 kts, and the difference between it and the gradient wind is over 40 kts. There also needs to be a temperature difference of 10° between the surface and 1,000 feet and CBs or heavy showers within 5 nm. Vertical windshear is expressed in kts/100 ft.

LLWAS is a North American system for the detection and warnings of low level windshear.

MICROBURSTS

These are small, intense concentrated downdraughts with high speeds and a lower temperature than the surrounding air that spread out in all directions when they reach the surface, commonly associated with thunderstorms in the mature stage. They are formed in rain clouds when evaporating raindrops create a pocket of cool, heavy air that falls as a heavy downdraught.

You are most likely to encounter them within 1,000' of the ground, that is, right on the approach. They are most dangerous where the vertical push converts to the horizontal, between the base of the microburst and the ground - you could get a vertical speed of over 6000 feet per minute and a horizontal one over 45 kts, with a 90-knot shear across the microburst. The diameter of any damage will be up to 4 km, and the duration from 1-5 minutes from first striking the ground, or more, though the maximum intensity is in the first 2-4 minutes. The vertical windshear is expressed in kts/100 feet.

A transit through a microburst involves a performance-increasing shear to start with, followed by a performance-decreasing one, because the downflow divides at the surface (although the burst might be "only" 45 kts, the complete shear will be double that). With the former, you get more airspeed and lift from either increased headwind or decreased tailwind, taking you above the glidepath - recovery involves reducing power and lowering the nose, and using a higher power setting than before when re-established, or the aircraft will sink. The latter is the opposite, of course - you lose airspeed, the nose pitches down and altitude decreases. Recover by increasing power and setting it to less than the original value.

Being so close to the ground, you are likely to be taking off or landing, and therefore more vulnerable. The angle of attack reduces inside a downburst, because induced flow increases, so power should be increased on entry, and reduced (quickly) on exit. Where the air is dry, the microburst will become more vigorous, because the dry air absorbs any moisture, cooling the air and making it more dense, so it falls faster. For more on Wake Turbulence, refer to the *Operations* chapter.

SQUALLS

A squall is a sudden increase of at least 16 kts in average wind speed to a sustained speed of 22 kts or more for at least one minute.

Upper Winds

Hurricanes blow themselves out as they reach the boundary of the Hadley and Ferrel cells, where huge volumes of air of wildly different temperatures are rising and falling against each other. Air masses tend to carry their own tropopause with them, so you could get height changes in the order of 10 000 feet in a single day. Because pressure in the upper levels depends on the mean temperature of a column of air, a low mean temperature produces low pressure aloft, and *vice versa*, producing a pressure gradient high up in the atmosphere, where air will flow. That is, air flows from high to low pressure, but the cause is temperature (more in *Upper Level Charts*, later on). With your back to the wind, the cold air is to the left in the Northern hemisphere.

JETS

A jet is a narrow band of strong winds in warm air, formed from temperature gradients. They might be near the tropopause or simply over the desert. In fact, there are two main jetstreams in the troposphere, the subtropical at the 200 hPa level at the Poleward limit of the Hadley cells, and the mid-latitude version, which is called the Polar Front jet because it is connected with the frontal zone. In the Northern hemisphere, jets can be West- and Easterly.

Polar Front Jet (Jetstream)

This is the most commonly known jet, otherwise known as the *jetstream*, or the *circumpolar vortex*.

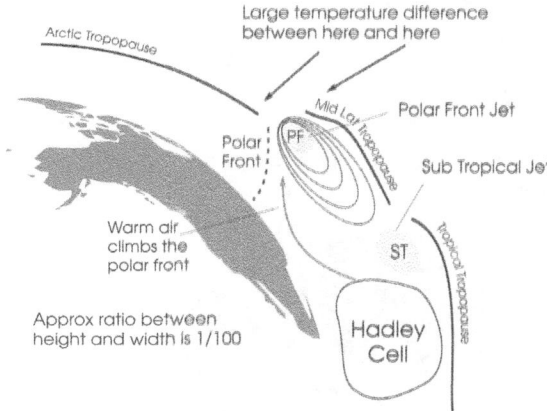

In both hemispheres, it is typically found between around 30,000 - 40 000 feet (200 hPa), where there is a marked contrast in temperature, just under one of the breaks in the tropopause, where it has been lowered after the Polar Front has moved towards warmer air at the Equator.

The Polar Front is where cold polar air meets warmer sub-tropical or temperate air in mid-latitudes, which means a rapid change in temperature over a short distance, known in the trade as a marked temperature gradient.

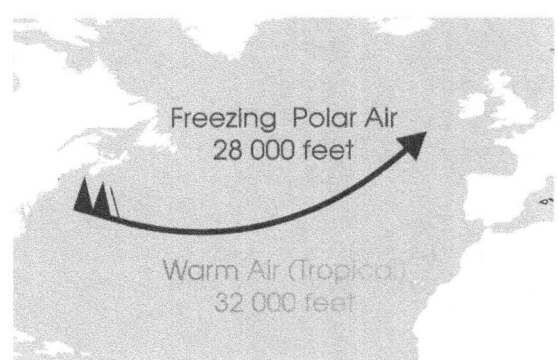

Thus, a jetstream will be found moving along an area of greatest temperature *contrast*, particularly between Polar and Tropical air, with the cold air on the left in the Northern Hemisphere and on the right in the Southern Hemisphere, looking downstream (the core is in the tropical air mass, at a height where there is no horizontal temperature gradient). The contrasts produce different thicknesses in the atmosphere above them, which serves to intensify any pressure gradients aloft, flowing from South to North, being deflected to the East by Coriolis force as they accelerate to form a river of air.

The PFJ will be found 50-200 nm behind a warm front and 300-450 nm ahead of a warm front.

Contrasts are greater in Winter, so winds will be stronger then. A Polar Front jetstream blows all the year round but, in Winter, will move South, and its speed will increase.

Such a jet is always below the tropopause and in the warm air, but on the cold air side. It will tend to follow the ground position of any fronts, since it is thought that frontal systems percolate downwards from jets rather than grow upward from the surface.

The winds in a jet change direction and speed constantly, at which points high and low pressures form, and either go with the flow or develop into something stronger - such positive and negative acceleration points are used by forecasters to predict frontal movement (they can be identified by long streaks of cirrus clouds).

A surface low is usually Equatorward of the jetstream, moving nearer the centre as it deepens, and it will cross at the point of any occlusion.

The wind gradient will be greatest between the surface and the tropopause, because the air above the tropopause is more or less isothermal. As the tropopause acts like a cap, the jetstream will be fastest just under it (it's actually fastest in the area between a trough and a ridge). With colder air to the left when looking downwind, the wind speed will increase with height while, with the colder air to the right, it decreases with height.

Turbulence will also be the worst - try to avoid the tropopause from below by about 4 000 feet. The higher temperatures above it will cause performance problems.

Because the cold air undercuts the warmer air, the interface is sloping, which makes the core look, to a ground observer, as if it were in polar air, although it is actually in the subtropical warm air mass, between the two tropopause levels. If you are flying North above the PFJ at, say, FL 400 in the Southern hemisphere, the temperature will decrease as you are moving from the stratosphere to the troposphere.

The core is a Westerly tubular ribbon of high-speed air with a circular rotation, when looked from behind or in front, with the rising air being tropical, so you might see cirrus on the Equatorial side, although clouds are not usually associated with jetstreams, which makes them more difficult to detect.

Because of the circulation, there will be low pressure above the cold air and high pressure above the warm air.

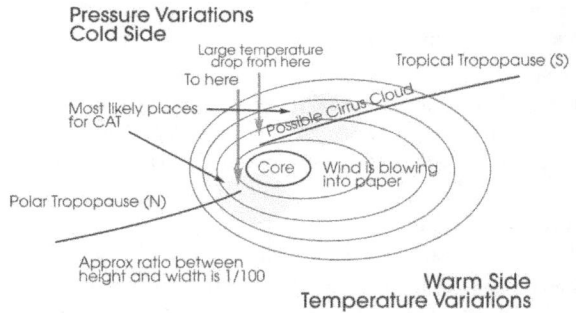

In Winter, in mid latitudes, (over the Atlantic) the PFJ moves South and its speed increases due to the larger thermal difference over the sea. When crossing a jetstream at right angles in Western Europe, 3 000 feet below the core, with decreasing OAT, the prevailing wind is from the left. If you proceed poleward through a Polar jetstream, the temperature will decrease, and *vice versa*.

Jetstreams are at least 60 kts in strength (more typically 100, or even 150 kts, but 200 kts is rare), and may only be around 200 miles wide (and 2 nm deep), but they can be a couple of thousand miles long, containing extreme turbulence, which can extend to around 15,000 feet below the tropopause, usually on the Polar side. The approximate ratio between height and width is 1:100. The length, width and height of a typical mid-latitude jet stream are respectively 1 000 nm, 150 nm and 18 000 ft.

Clear Air Turbulence* (CAT) is often found where the jetstream curves poleward from a rapidly deepening surface low, but it's most severe when curving near a deep trough. It's on the cold air side of the core anyway (the depression side) - the highest possibility is, looking downstream, to the left of the core. The most effective way to combat this is to change flight level. Jetstreams over 110 kts may have significant turbulence in the sloping tropopause above the core, in the front below the core and on the low pressure side. Maximum winds occur near a break in the tropopause, on the Polar side.

*Details will be in the **Significant Weather Chart**.

Maximum winds occur near a break in the tropopause, on the Polar side.

When jetstreams oscillate, they become slower (particularly in Summer) and can become semi-permanent and cause stagnation, which produces blocking highs. Jetstreams can also affect the positioning of the ITCZ.

SUBTROPICAL JET
The STJ arises from slight temperature contrasts along the Hadley and Ferrel cells in subtropical latitudes. As parts of it bulge North, the air flows through the axis at a higher velocity due to the increased angular momentum.

It is also thought to arise from the Earth's rotation, because the rising air from the Equator is moving faster than the Earth's surface underneath it, once it has fanned out at high levels.

It can usually be found between 25° & 35°, at the 200 hPa level (FL 400), extending almost continuously around the globe, except over Asia during the Summer. the maximum wind speeds are usually found in the tropical air, below the tropopause.

Its position only varies slightly with the seasons (it is a permanent fixture), whereas the PFJ is quite irregular.

Between Stockholm and Rio at FL 350 in July, you might encounter a Polar Front Jet, then 1 or 2 Sub Tropical Jets.

EQUATORIAL
As commercial flights are concerned with winds up to about 38 000 ft, the Easterly Equatorial jetstream is too high at the 100 hPa level (around 53,000 feet). It is seasonal, between June and August.

LOW LEVEL NOCTURNAL JET
A band of unusually strong Southerly winds between 700 and 2000 feet AGL, developing overnight on the Great Plains in the USA, or the Prairies in Canada, or over Southern Queensland or the Northern Territories during Winter in Australia. It occurs when a fast moving stream of air circulating round a high hits a mountain range and accelerates into a narrow stream along it. As a nocturnal inversion develops, the wind near the top can increase to speeds much higher than would be indicated by isobar spacing (say 30-40 kts). It starts at sunset, gets to a maximum a couple of hours after midnight and decreases as the inversion is destroyed.

These jets advect large volumes of warm, moist air Northward from the Gulf of Mexico into the central USA.

They are a major factor in the development of thunderstorms in the afternoon and evening.

Low level jets can also be found just ahead of fronts and along a physical barrier such as hills or escarpments (funnelling also creates them).

SUMMARY
This table summarises the common jetstreams in the Northern hemisphere:

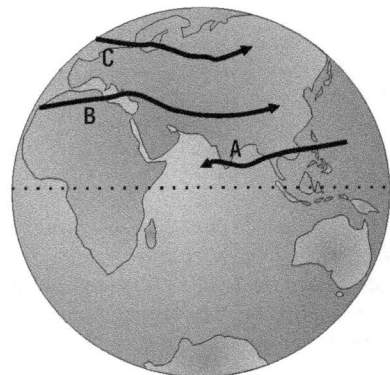

Name	Characteristics	FL
Arctic	Winter	15
Polar (C)	Westerly Permanent	30
Subtropical (B)	Westerly Permanent	40
Equatorial (A) Tropical	Easterly Summer	45-53

You will only find Easterly and westerly jets in the Northern hemisphere. Notice how the heights increase from the Poles towards the Equator.

Land & Sea Breezes
These arise out of a temperature difference between land and sea areas. Air over land warms up and cools down faster than that over the sea, because land has a lower specific heat and needs less heat to warm it up. Thus, temperature changes over land will occur a lot more frequently than they do over the sea.

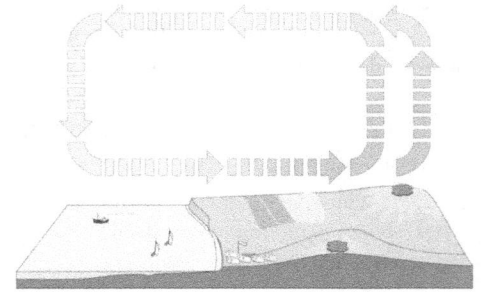

When the land is warmer than the sea, the air over it becomes less dense and the space left by the rising air is filled with an extra component coming from over the water (which is cooler, and does not rise) to produce a *sea breeze* which is added to any existing wind (in fact, a relatively high pressure is created at about 1000 feet over land, to produce a pressure gradient aloft).

With lower pressure at the same height over the water, there will be air movement towards the sea, at the upper levels (the column of warm air is taller, and the relative pressure is higher), which will subside to come back towards the land. At night, the process is reversed to get a land breeze, but land is a poor conductor of heat and will only be affected through a shallow layer.

Land breezes are weaker because the temperature differences are smaller and so is the local pressure gradient.

A prevailing wind can oppose a sea-breeze and delay its development, or go with it and increase its speed, although, at latitudes greater than about 20°, Coriolis can change the direction of a sea breeze by itself.

If a convergence is created, sea breezes can be strong enough to create their own cold fronts, well inland*, and even trigger thunderstorms, as the colder sea air undercuts the land air (look for small lines of cumuliform cloud). Below is a possible example for the UK.

*In Australia, sea breezes have been encountered 400 km away from the sea.

Knowing this is useful when you're going to a destination near the sea, and the wind (and landing direction) could be different to what you might expect, or you might be offshore and know that a tailwind will be around to help bring you home.

 Although land and sea breezes arise from temperature differences, they are not thermal winds because the geostrophic force does not achieve an eventual balance with the pressure gradient that make the wind flow parallel to the local isobars.

The sea breeze has some effect on temperature and precipitation in the tropics - see *Monsoon*, below.

Diurnal Effects

The pressure around the Earth varies up and down by about 2 hPa twice a day, at 10 and 4, am and pm. It is more detectable in the tropics because it is masked elsewhere by more extreme weather. In low latitudes (i.e. nearer the Equator), interruptions to this schedule may mean an impending tropical storm. As a result, the surface wind increases speed and veers during the day in the Northern Hemisphere, and *vice versa* by night. In the Southern Hemisphere, it increases and backs by day, decreasing and veering by night. Because of this effect, many local winds can be predicted with clock-like regularity.

 The *diurnal variation* actually refers to temperature differences, which is what is ultimately responsible for winds in the first place, although there are diurnal pressure variations, too. Refer back to *Temperature*.

There is a rhythmic difference in temperatures between day and night over 24 hours, known as *diurnal variation*. The effect is less marked over water, which reacts more slowly to temperature changes, and least in the tropics. In fact, those over the sea are not much more than 1°C, whereas desert areas can vary by as much as 20°C. The maximum variations happen inland with clear skies over dry areas in calm conditions although, near the coast, the difference depends a lot on where the wind is coming from - it is greater if the wind is coming off the land.

Other (Local) Winds

Local winds are those that do not arise from patterns of isobars or contours, but are controlled mainly by differences in surface heating. In fact, coastlines, mountains and valleys have quite an effect on local winds - so much so that the airflow is often across any isobars (they blow for too short a time for Coriolis to have much influence). Many local winds arise from diurnal, orographic or seasonal effects, and are so regular that they have their own names - so regular, in fact, that navigators could use them to tell direction.

One important place is Dakar, which is the capital of Senegal on the West coast of Africa. In July, the ITCZ is just North of it, so it is wet, with Southerly winds. Northerly winds arise in January, coming from the Sahara desert, so they are dry and dusty. This is the **Harmattan**, a dry sand and dust-laden NE trade wind, so expect dust and poor visibility.

THE MEDITERRANEAN

The Mediterranean lies in a **temperate transitional** climatic zone, between the **disturbed temperate** climate of NW Europe (to the North) and the arid **subtropics** of North Africa (to the South), so the weather has marked seasonal variations due to the changes in pressure distribution over Summer and Winter (the annual rainfall is significantly below 700 mm). It is almost completely surrounded by mountain ranges which produce many local winds, together with katabatic drainage off the high ground. Although local names are given to the winds, they are often the result of the general pressure distribution.

In Summer the Azores high moves North and, as the sea is colder than the land around it, the anticyclone is intensified, which makes for fine weather, with an occasional depression to the North West. Isolated Summer thunderstorms occur when colder air overrides warm air at low levels. Sea breezes can help the local convergence trigger thunderstorms.

In Winter, the Azores high is to the South to make way for the disturbed temperate weather of NW Europe. The waters are warmer than the surrounding land masses to the North, East and West, producing low pressure over the sea. The weather is now much more disturbed and squally. The depressions described below tend to move from West to East or SE through the region:

- Polar front depressions move in from the North Atlantic over France.
- Orographic depressions in the lee of the Alps or Pyrenees in the Gulfs of Lyons and Genoa, and the North Adriatic as a cold front advances from the North or with a broad Northerly airstream over NW Europe. Most Mediterranean depressions are formed like this.
- Depressions developing on trailing cold fronts near Gibraltar becoming intense as they move East into the Mediterranean.

Otherwise, the build up of high pressure over Siberia in Winter leads to outbursts of cold air at low levels that are funnelled across the Black Sea and down the Aegean and through gaps in the mountains of Turkey and the Balkans, creating thermal lows in the Eastern Mediterranean. Lee depressions form South East of the Atlas Mountains and move North East into the Mediterranean. Depressions near the Southern coasts give much less cloud and precipitation as the air in the warm sector is from the Sahara and is very dry. As they track Eastwards, the air ahead of the warm front near the surface is South or South Easterly and is often strong enough to create sand and dust storms there, and hot dusty winds over the Mediterranean. These are the Scirocco (Algiers/Tunis), Ghibli (Libya) and Khamsin (Egypt) and occur most often from December to May (they are mentioned below).

Warm Fronts

In the Northern Mediterranean, these give unusually intense precipitation. In the South, they tend to be weak. Near the coast of North Africa, the air will usually be so dry that there will be little or no cloud. Cold fronts moving South East across Western Europe are often retarded by the mountains in Spain and France, but burst through the Carcasonne Gap or the Rhone Valley to advance across Corsica, Sardinia, Sicily and Malta at high speeds.

Cold Fronts

These are very active in the Mediterranean and usually come with squalls and thunder. To the South, near the North African coast, cold air undercuts dry air drawn from the desert (the Scirocco), so there is a decrease in cloud and precipitation. However, there is still a lot of turbulence, and when these fronts reach North Africa they often cause severe dust and sand storms, with the dust being carried up to over 10,000 ft. Even well into the desert where the cloud has dried out completely, the cold front still creates dust or sand storms.

Behind cold fronts, the cold polar air becomes more unstable as it moves over the warmer sea, which means heavy showers and thunderstorms with hail. As the cold air penetrates further South East, the thunderstorms may become almost continuous and, with orographic lifting over Corsica, Sardinia, Sicily, and the Atlas mountains, conditions may become extremely difficult.

Further East, over the sea where there is no orographic uplift, conditions behind the cold front are less severe. Inland, conditions improve rapidly as the air dries out. However, there may still be convection and turbulence.

Winds

The **Khamsin** is a mainly Southerly wind that occurs in Egypt and the Eastern Mediterranean during late Winter and Spring, generally ahead of Eastward moving depressions. It is also hot and dry, and brings a lot of dust from the desert, but will produce stratus or stratocumulus if it picks up moisture. The name *Khamsin* is frequently given to the depressions with which the wind is associated and the hot dry dusty weather that they produce. Khamsins are most frequent from March to May.

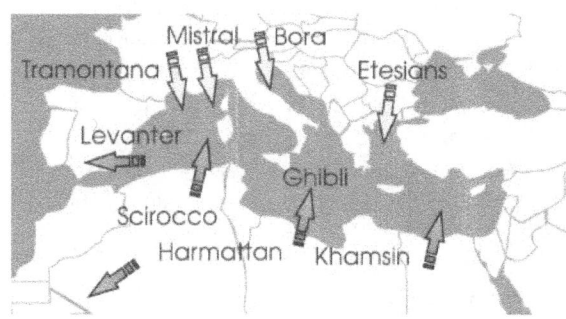

*As the Scirocco comes from the Sahara desert, it (predictably) reaches the North coast of Africa as a hot dry wind, having had its temperature increased by compression from the descent to sea level. By the time it reaches Malta, Sicily or other parts of the Mediterranean coast, however, it is warm and moist from the sea passage. Having said that, the word is often used for a warm, Southerly wind, dry or not. Many winds that are called Sciroccos are probably Fohn winds (below). The most favourable synoptic situation for their development is a low pressure in the Western part of the Mediterranean.

The **Vendevale** is a strong South Westerly wind that occurs in the Straits of Gibraltar and in the SW Mediterranean mainly between September - March (Winter). It is associated with depressions and rough weather that includes thunderstorms and violent squalls, during which the surface wind may veer suddenly to the NW, remaining strong.

The **Levanter** is an Easterly wind associated with the Straits of Gibraltar and the central areas of the Western Mediterranean. The funnel in the straits increases the wind speed, but it is usually light or moderate and seldom blows at gale force. It is a very moist wind that produces the characteristic banner cloud downwind of the Rock. It may occur at any season, but is most frequent from July to October (Autumn) and in March (Spring).

During Levanter conditions, violent eddies are formed in the lee of the Rock, the wind frequently blowing strongly in opposite directions at places only 50 yards apart. Turbulence extends for as much as two miles downwind and up to 5,000 feet.

The **Gregale** is a strong NE wind that occurs mainly in Winter near Malta. It usually blows behind a depression which has moved Eastwards over or to the South of Malta. The accompanying weather may be fine or showery with rain or hail.

The **Haboob** is a dust storm (with cumulonimbus clouds) that usually occurs late on Summer days in the Northern Sudan in the afternoons and evenings between May-September when the ITCZ is to the North, although they have been known to occur in the USA. You can see them as a wall of dust from 50 miles away, up to 10 000 ft high.

The **Etesians** blows from between NW and NE down the Aegean and is the prevailing wind there particularly during Summer (May to September). The weather is nearly always fine and clear.

The **Pamperos** comes from a marked advance of cold air in South America, flowing from South to North, originating in Argentina.

The **Fohn** occurs when saturated air is made to rise by the Alps. On its way up it cools at 1.5°C per 1000 feet, and when it descends on the other side, having dropped its moisture, it warms at 3°C, so you get a dry, warm, downslope wind with clear skies. In California, it causes fires. Being downslope, it is a katabatic wind.

The essential point is that the temperature on the lee side of the mountain is warmer, which is why you can grow grapes in the Okanagan valley in the middle of the Rockies.

Here are some sample figures:

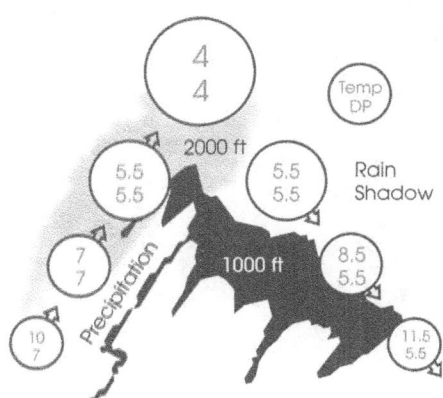

The cloudbase on the lee side is higher due to the precipitation on the windward side and the change in dew point. The temperature also increases through a greater depth than the cooling on the windward side.

The **Chinook** is a warm, dry, katabatic wind that comes off the Rockies, which are a huge physical barrier between the Pacific coast and the prairies on the Eastern side, from Canada to the USA. Although fohn-like, the air on the windward side of the mountains is so cold (and therefore stable) that it does not rise up the slope, and is blocked. A trough of low pressure that is created on the Eastern side draws the wind at higher levels down the lee slopes. As this air has very little moisture to start with, it descends at the DALR all the way, hence the warm and dry characteristics. Compression is also a factor.

The **Santa Ana** is like the Chinook, where air from the Mojave desert in California squeezes through the San Gabriel mountains to flow across Los Angeles. Again, compression helps.

A **Bora** is a strong, relatively cold and dry katabatic wind similar to the Mistral (below), that blows from high, cold plateaus onto the Eastern coasts of the Adriatic, particularly in the Trieste area from the mountains to the North-East, with the possibility of violent gusts. It was originally defined as a very strong, cold wind that blows from the NE onto the Adriatic region of Italy, Slovenia, and Croatia (the word is from the Greek *boreas*, meaning North). It is strongest and most frequent in Winter and occurs when cold air crosses the mountains from the East and descends to the coast, sometimes getting to gale force (it has been recorded at over 70 kts in Trieste with gusts over 110 kts). A famous one comes out of the Balkans and can stop shipping on the Adriatic and Dalmatian coasts. When humidity is a factor, you can expect dense cloud, icing, thunderstorms, heavy snow and rain. Although Boras can occur anytime, the peak frequency occurs in the cold season (November - March). In general, the frequency of gale force Boras varies from one day per month, or less, in Summer, to six days per month during Winter.

The **Mistral** is a bora-like valley wind (therefore katabatic) that blows down the lower Rhone valley between the Massif and the Alps ranges in Southern France, so its speed is increased as it flows through them, and beyond, into the Northern Mediterranean. A British Army Beaver flying against it once took nearly 5 hours to reach the next beacon. It is also heavily ionised - it is used as an excuse in court for weird actions.

The Mistral is often associated with high pressure over Western France and low pressure over the Gulf of Genoa where the wind is funnelled down the Rhone valley and may be reinforced by a katabatic flow from the mountains. The Mistral may last for several days.

As it is a cold dry wind, you normally get bright clear weather. Speeds vary between 20 - 40 kts, but speeds up to 80 kts have been recorded. The Mistral is most frequent and strongest in Winter but it can blow at any season.

MONSOONS

The word *monsoon* is derived from the arabic for *season*, originally referring to winds of the Arabian sea that blow for about 6 months from the North East and 6 months from the South west. However, these days, people use it to mean persistent seasonal winds that blow quite steadily for long periods near the ITCZ in the mid latitudes.

In simple terms, monsoons are large sea (and land) breezes that blow for very much longer than a day. They can be associated with dry and fine weather or heavy and wet weather, depending on their origin, continental or maritime. As a general rule, the monsoon is considered to exist below about 10,000 ft although it may vary from 7,000 ft in some areas to 15,000 ft in others.

The monsoon climates include West Africa, Ethiopia, NW Australia, the NW corner of South America, and the best known and largest areas, East and South Asia, including the East Indies and the Philippines. However, the biggest temperature variations are in North America and Asia. In North America, the mountain ranges run from North to South, which modifies the effect of Winter cooling and Summer heating, as tropical air can move North in Winter, and Polar air can come South in Summer. Over

Asia, on the other hand, the mountain ranges run mainly East - West and this, together with the fact that Asia is the largest land mass in the world, limits such movement, making seasonal contrasts much greater.

One "monsoon" is a seasonal wind that soaks India between June - September as the Sun changes its position and height and moves the ITCZ across the Himalayas. It blows for six months from the North East, then the South East, and can be predicted to the week. The monsoon low of India makes the SE trades that have crossed the Equator to become the SW monsoon to turn left in the Bay of Bengal to affect the coast of India.

The **Asian Monsoon** is a seasonal circulation that arises from 2 causes.

- In Winter, cold air from Siberia (which is snow-covered) strengthens the Siberian High, and its cold outflow produces Northerly winds and limited moisture across China, making it the driest season.
- In Summer, the Siberian High weakens as the land warms up, and a region of lower pressure forms over SE Asia. The ITCZ moves Northward and warm, humid air from the Indian and Pacific oceans is drawn inland over China.

In Summer in the Southern hemisphere, the Equatorial Trough (ITCZ) travels South to lie over **North Australia** which therefore gets a NW airstream that brings rain (the **NW Monsoon**). Again, it behaves like a large sea breeze and pulls in warm moist air from the ocean. In Winter, the direction changes to SE, from the trades, for drier weather. Refer to the *Indian Subcontinent* section (much later) for more about monsoons.

PRESSURE   050 01 03

The distribution of pressure at the surface does not remain constant, and has a major impact on the type of weather we get, in terms of the generation of wind and changes in weather. The variations happen because of the movement and intensity of the pressure systems described below, with some diurnal variation.

Variations in atmospheric pressure can be traced to variations in air density, which are often caused by temperature differences.

Pressure Systems   050 07

During the day, the pressure is measured at many hundreds of weather stations, converted to sea level pressure (using ISA) and marked on a map, with the points that have equal pressure being connected up. The lines that join the dots are called *isobars* (*iso* is Greek for *same*), and will be 4 hectopascals apart, counting up and down from 1000. The closer they are together, the more the pressure drops per mile and the more severe the pressure gradient* will be, for stronger winds (air moves from high to low pressure).

*The rate of change of pressure with distance.

Isobars are like contours, and make common patterns, two of which are the *low* or *high*, other names for *cyclone* and *anti-cyclone*, respectively (nothing to do with the cyclones that seem to damage trailer parks).

Another name for a low is a *depression*. The exact position of a system on a chart will be marked by an X.

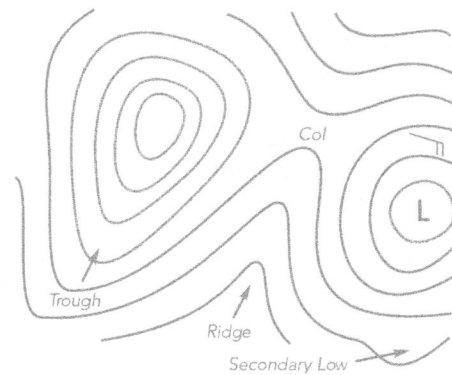

In the diagram above, the wind is flowing anticlockwise around a low pressure on the right (the clue is in the wind pennant). The air is going into the High at the top left, twisting to the right, and coming out of the low at the bottom right, twisting left. This makes the space between them a trough, and the system going away from the high pressure a ridge.

Thus, if you were flying from East to West, it would be best going South of a High and North of a Low, in the Northern Hemisphere.

 Isobars are based on readings corrected to a certain level, usually sea level. Contours, discussed more fully in *Upper Winds*, are illustrations of how the height of a pressure varies and would look like hills and valleys if you could see them in 3D.

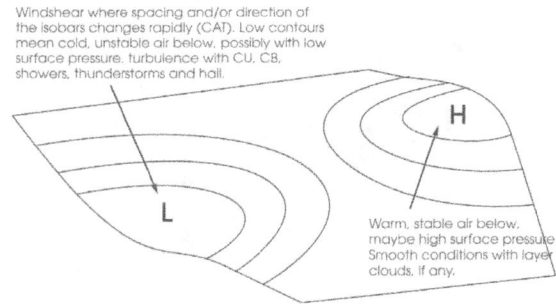

In tropical regions, especially nearer the Equator, isobars do not give an accurate indication of the wind, so they are replaced by *streamlines*, which resemble spirals.

RIDGES & TROUGHS

A ridge of high pressure is a wedge-shaped extension of an anticyclone or belt of high pressure, with similar characteristics to an anticyclone. In temperate latitudes as in the British Isles, ridges of high pressure often occur between two depressions and move with them. They give rise to intervals of fair weather between the cloud and rain of the low-pressure systems.

A *trough*, on the other hand, is an elongated region of relatively low atmospheric pressure, often associated with fronts and identified as an extension of isobars away from a low pressure center, with similar weather characteristics. However, the region between two high pressure centres may also assume the character of a trough when there is a detectable wind shift at the surface.

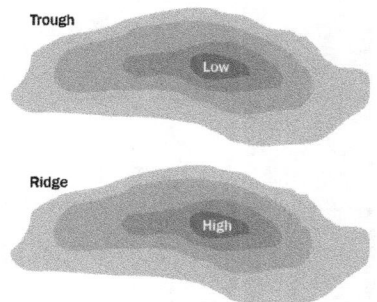

COLS

Areas of slack pressure between opposite low and high pressure systems. They can bring quiet weather or rain if traversed by fronts. In Winter they are generally associated with low cloud and fog. In Summer, thunderstorms are more frequent.

ANTICYCLONES

An anticyclone is an area of high pressure (on the Earth's surface) between around 1020-45 hectopascals (even up to 1060 hPa). Above every surface high pressure, there is a low pressure at altitude.

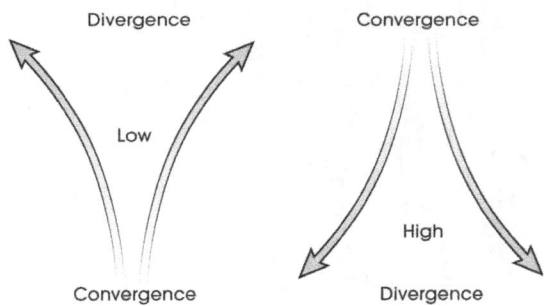

The *damping effect* is shown on the right, above.

The isobars around the centre are more or less concentric and are widely spaced, so winds are usually light and variable, although they normally blow clockwise and outwards (in the Northern Hemisphere), faster towards the outside of the system. As a result, weather conditions are mostly quiet, dry and settled but, just because cloud is mostly absent in a high, don't expect clear skies, as the descending air may trap haze or smoke, leading to *anticyclonic gloom* near industrial areas.

As air descends in a high, it gets warmed by adiabatic compression, which leads to low relative humidities, hence the absence of cloud. However, the descending air might not get to ground level, due to convection and turbulence, leaving a cool moist layer around 500-1500 m deep immediately above the surface. The boundary between this cooler air and the subsided air aloft is characterised by a subsidence inversion which limits the upward movement of convection currents, preventing extensive air cooling and cloud formation. Unfortunately, if the air is moist below the inversion, a dreary formless layer of cloud can form which becomes difficult to disperse due to the light winds. Such weather is common in Winter when the Sun's radiation is too weak to burn off the cloud layer.

In Winter, a short cloudless day can mean a long night with more radiation cooling than the Sun can cope with the next day, due to its low angle. The second night of cooling therefore starts with a lower air temperature than the first. This can mean successive nights of frost, which become progressively harder. When the air is particularly moist, cooling at night soon results in fog. Britain in particular can experience episodes of anticyclonic fog between September and May.

COLD ANTICYCLONES

These are shallow, often no more than 3000 m deep, forming over cold surfaces due to convergence aloft from the contraction of the cold low level air. Air in the centre is colder than in the surrounding air.

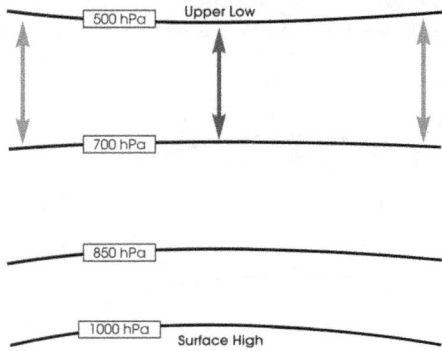

With increasing altitude, the high is less pronounced, or weaker (there is a flatter contour at 500 hPa level, or 18 000 ft), or a weak low may occur.

They may be found over Antarctica and the Arctic Ocean any time of the year, and over Northern Eurasia, Greenland, and North America during Winter.

As an example of the influence a high pressure area can have, a strong one commonly sits over Eastern Canada in late Spring because most of Hudson Bay is still frozen. It is very good at stopping the movement of other systems and weather. With such blocking highs (discussed below), the normal Easterly movement of depressions and fronts becomes more South-North, or meriodonal (in line with meridians).

Permanent cold anticyclones include the **Siberian High**, with an elongated section that stretches into NW Europe in April.

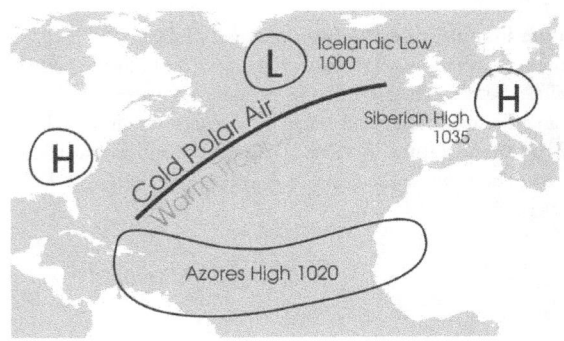

When this happens, the clockwise flow brings in warm moist Mediterranean air over Italy, up the Alps and into the upper atmosphere. This air takes longer to slow and cool down, so over NW Europe there is a high tropopause height in April with a cold temperature.

In the central region, the air is generally dry, with brilliant frosty weather. In the outer regions, the increased moisture content may be enough to form persistent fog or low stratus.

Temporary cold anticyclones include the **Polar High** (which is frequently subject to travelling lows) and mid-latitude ridges of high pressure between families of lows (between Polar front depressions – they appear to travel). The weather is generally brilliantly fine with radiation fog (or low stratus) where surface cooling occurs.

Warm Anticyclones

Warm highs result from convergence in the upper troposphere and subsidence beneath, producing relatively warm air throughout the troposphere above the subsidence inversion (the Azores High is a good example).

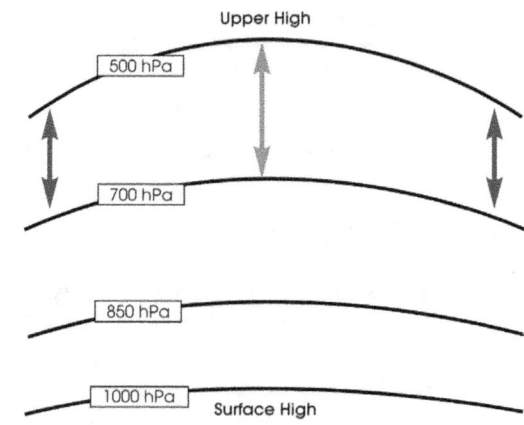

 "The Azores High" is really a succession of highs that are stagnating in that position, so it is called a *statistical low*. It gets smaller in Winter, which moves the fronts that normally progress between Scotland and Iceland further South over the UK.

Warm highs also form in temperate latitudes from convergence just ahead of a ridge in the upper Westerlies. They are either extensions of subtropical highs, linked to them by strong ridges of high pressure, or as persistent blocks that disrupt the more normal Westerly flow and prevent depressions from following their usual routes.

With increasing altitude, the high becomes more pronounced, more domed or with a bulging contour at the 500 hPa level (18 000 ft). The air in the troposphere is warmer than average and the high pressure arises from an excess of air at high levels. **Permanent** warm anticyclones include the sub-tropical high pressure belt, where the weather is usually fine with excellent visibility.

Temporary warm anticyclones include extensions of sub-tropical highs, such as the extended Azores high over the UK in Summer.

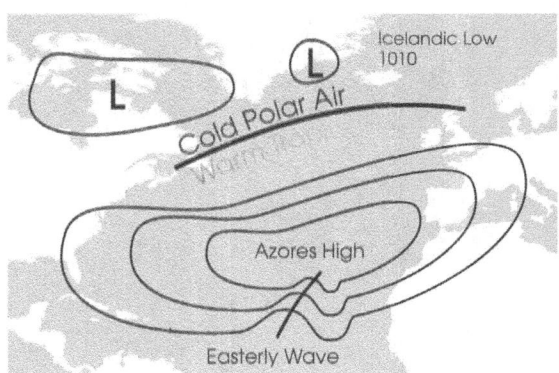

In summary, warm anticyclones may persist for weeks, bringing fine and warm weather over land in Summer. With surface cooling, radiation or sea fog may form below an inversion.

Blocking Highs

Quasi-stationary (often warm) high pressure areas between 50-70° of latitude that stop the progress of depressions and other systems.

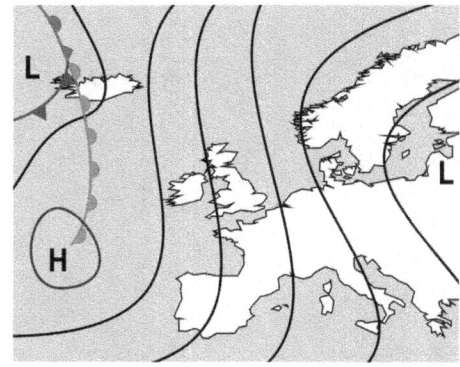

Blocking highs can also bring cold wintry Arctic air from the North to the UK, as shown above, but a good example is the Bermuda High, which can be responsible for thunderstorms, high density altitudes and low visibility in haze - the clockwise circulation sends warm, damp ocean air up the Eastern half of the United States, which destabilises during afternoon heating.

Air Mass Subsidence

This concerns the descent of larger masses of air over wide areas, typically found in the Earth's circulation at subtropical latitudes, where the deserts are.

NON-FRONTAL DEPRESSIONS

High level divergence produces areas of low pressure at ground level as air is lifted to fill the void (the chimney effect), which is why an approaching low can be detected by a falling barometer. Having said that, friction is involved with the convergence at the surface, plus the cyclonic curvature of the isobars.

Lows are generally found meandering around the Equator and in temperate latitudes, where they tend to dominate the scene with clouds and rain. On the other hand, a dry, sunny region can get very warm from intense surface heating, and create a *thermal low*, typically over land in Summer (monsoon lows are one example, that bring fine weather). Lows are often classed as *deep* or *intense*, *shallow* or *weak*, but these classifications are relative to each other.

An *Instability Low* is one that gets its energy from the release of heat from condensation.

Lows can move in almost any direction, but most often to the North East (SE in the Southern hemisphere), anywhere between 10-40 knots during the middle and most active stages of their existence. If there are two or more low pressure centres, the system is said to be *complex*, as mentioned below. If the central pressure is rising, the low is *filling*, and will slow down (see also *Occlusions*). The life of a low is between 4-6 days.

A low will usually have one or more weather fronts radiating from the centre, each one representing a belt of relatively bad weather, with the wind veering (backing in the Southern hemisphere) marking the change between air masses. In between the fronts will be a warm sector originating from the warmer air in the South - lows usually travel approximately parallel with the isobars (and the direction of the wind) in the warm sector.

Lows appear seasonally over land masses in Summer and over large lakes and inland seas in Winter.

Secondary Low

This is a smaller one inside a larger one, usually on the Equatorial side, or at the tip of the warm sector, in which the weather is more intense as it feeds on its bigger brother (at least, the winds can reach gale force on the further side from the parent low). A secondary low can also form in the cold air advection behind a cyclone, or at the triple point of an occlusion*, or when air moves across barriers and is lifted. In any case, it will move faster than the primary Low which makes it move cyclonically (anticlockwise in the Northern Hemisphere).

*A common point for a secondary depression to form is on the trailing end of a cold front when the primary system is well occluded.

Orographic (Lee) Trough

This is a low pressure area that lives in the lee of a range of hills after the air has gone over and round it, where it gets compressed as a ridge beforehand.

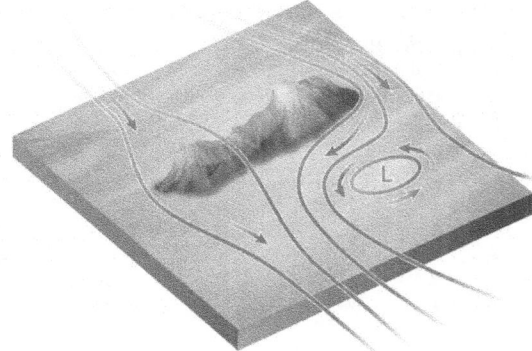

Within the depression, there can be good weather*, with no cloud or precipitation from the Föhn effect (below), but you can still get cloud and rain from the air being forced up the mountainside. If it is unstable cold air (polar maritime), as a cold front reaches the mountain range, the upper part of the front passing over it (and on top of the warm air) could result in widespread Cb with heavy showers and thunderstorms.

*On the lee side of the Alps, the downward flow combined with the Föhn effect can give clear skies.

The air going over the ridge reduces in height and spreads out horizontally, to resemble a high pressure, so the Coriolis effect is reduced, and the process is reversed further down the lee slope, to resemble a low (the air behind the barrier has not been compressed, so it has a relatively lower pressure anyway).

As the air sweeping around the ends of the obstacle flows towards this low pressure area, geostrophic force (below) causes the flow to become cyclonic. The end result is, if you are flying into wind, you will be lower than you think.

As you will see under *Mountain Winds*, the air flowing over the top also reduces in pressure due to the Venturi effect, which affects winds that flow through the valleys of mountain ranges (e.g. the Mistral). As they increase speed, there is a local decrease in pressure, returning to normal some distance away from the range. A difference of 2 or 3 hPa can mean your altimeter misreads by nearly 100 feet.

Another orographic situation arises when a cold front reaches a mountain range. At the surface, the front is effectively stopped, its slope gets steeper and the cold air at upper levels spills over the range. With cold air above and warmer air below, a state of severe instability exists in the lee of the range and heavy showers and thunderstorms may develop. This is a major cause of much bad weather in Northern Italy and the Northern Mediterranean in general. The weather can change very quickly.

Complex Low

A complex low is one with several fronts and air masses (discussed later) overlapping each other.

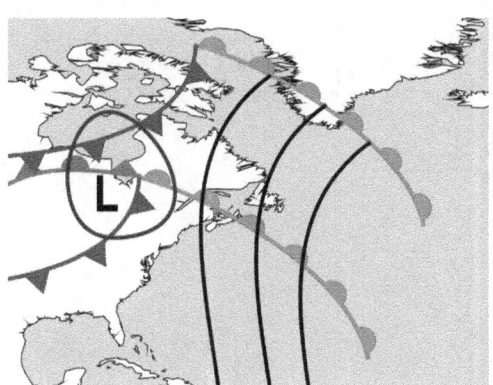

THERMAL LOWS

Surface heating and expansion results in high pressure and an outflow of air at higher levels. The resulting reduction in surface pressure creates an inflow of air which, due to geostrophic force, becomes a cyclonic circulation.

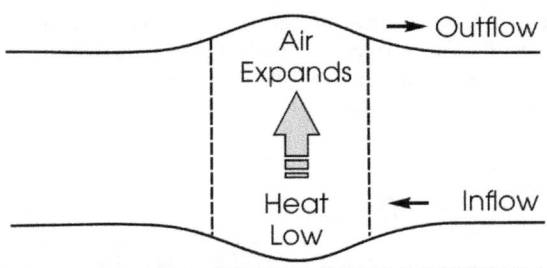

Hurricanes are the most extreme examples.

If thermal lows form in stable conditions, convergence can occur at low level with little weather activity. If enough moisture or instability is present, on the other hand, you can expect cumulus and cumulonimbus clouds. The low pressure belt around the Equator (the Doldrums) is a permanent heat low associated with seasonal movement of the ITCZ, or the meteorological Equator.

SHALLOW LOWS

Shallow depressions form in slack pressure gradients with surface heating overland in Summer. With vertical instability or old frontal zones, squalls, widespread rain or thunderstorms may result. They often appear in Central & Western Europe.

OVER INLAND WATERS

The temperature of inland waters in Winter is relatively high compared to the surrounding land mass. If polar air spreads over large inland seas the air becomes unstable and local depressions may develop with showers and squalls. The effects may be intensified or modified by local orographic or katabatic effects.

This affects the Mediterranean, Black Sea and US Great Lakes.

COLD AIR LOWS

These should not be confused with polar front depressions. They develop in temperate latitudes in large masses of polar air due to vertical instability (cold air over warm). There is an absence of fronts.

Those affecting the UK and Western Europe develop in N-NW airstreams in Polar air over the North Atlantic (possibly near Iceland or Greenland) with primary Polar front depressions over the Norwegian Sea or Scandinavia. Local showers with increasing instability may produce thunderstorms and continuous rain or lots of snow for areas of Scotland.

MONSOON LOWS

These develop over large continents in Summer (Asiatic Monsoon or Baluchistan Low). The weather largely depends on topography and characteristics of prevailing local air masses.

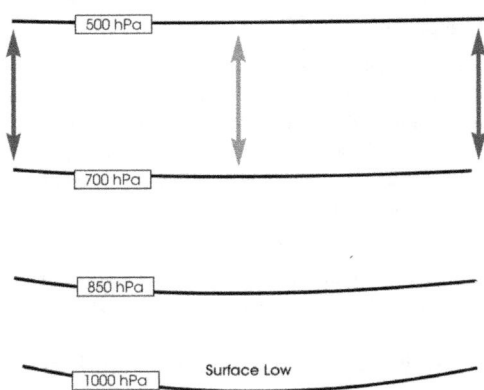

Although it is a warm depression, the low becomes less pronounced at higher levels and, at the 500 hPa level, gets much weaker.

HURRICANES (TROPICAL CYCLONES)

Severe tropical cyclones, or *revolving storms*, to give hurricanes their proper names, are non-frontal thermal lows (actually warm-core barotropic lows) that start over tropical oceans, in low latitudes*, around a core of very low pressure, intensifying from the widespread release of latent heat. They are typically the size of Scotland.

*Between 5-15° N or S of the Equator, but rarely within 5° due to the lack of Coriolis force to sustain the flow. They dissipate if they move over land (lack of moisture), weaken over cooler water (reduced vapour content) and/or to higher latitudes (reduced Coriolis). Around 12 per year form on average in the Atlantic (and 2 East of Darwin), but they don't form in the South Atlantic (or the South Pacific) because of the low temperature of the water. They have the highest frequency in the NW Pacific, South China sea and around the Philippines (Japan, Korea).

Hurricanes arise from small disturbances in the air over water within 300 nm of the Equator, so that Coriolis force is present, plus surface temperatures over 27°C to a depth of 70 metres (200 feet), where surface winds converge from different directions. As warm wet air is forced upwards, its water vapour condenses out and latent heat is released. The air is now much warmer and rises faster, which is the main source of energy. A high pressure is also formed above.

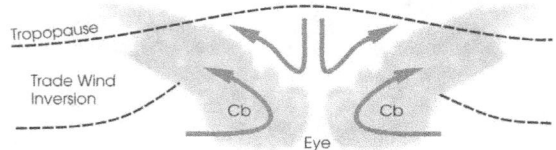

These unstable conditions, which will only exist over open oceans in the tropics (no land masses in the way), lead to thunderstorms which are pushed into line by uniform upper winds (if the winds are not uniform, the thunderstorm development is broken up).

The Coriolis effect starts rotating the small group of potential thunderstorms around the low pressure at their centre, anticlockwise in the Northern hemisphere. As the winds get faster and faster, you get a spiral structure.

Thus, a fully-fledged hurricane consists of a dense pack of individual thunderstorms that are spiralling round the eye, which is surrounded by a wall of cumulonimbus in a steep slope to the upper rim at 30,000 ft or more (the wall round the eye is the most dangerous place to be). Outside the cloud wall is the maximum speed ring, where the winds may exceed 150 kts and towering cumulonimbus clouds produce torrential rain and a lot of thundery activity.

Dense cirrus clouds are one indication of the presence of a tropical revolving storm.

The high pressure above is forced into the eye, which calms things down a bit in there.

- In the **formative stage**, a depression deepens, and windspeeds increase above gale force (34 kts).
- In the **immature stage**, the pressure falls below 1000 hPa and wind speeds reach hurricane force (65 kts) over a 30-50 km radius.
- In the **mature stage**, the pressure is steady.
- In the **dissipating stage**, pressure starts rising.

*The water's high specific heat allows the warm waters to persist long after Summer, so you can expect hurricanes to occur mostly in the NW Pacific, affecting the Eastern seaboards of Japan, Taiwan, Korea and the Chinese coastline, that is, in the Western parts of tropical oceans, because there is more humidity from the long sea passage of the trade winds (they are known as *typhoons* there). There are usually no hurricanes in the SE Pacific and S Atlantic because of the low water temperatures, although there was one in the South Atlantic in 2004 or 2005.

Hurricanes are classified as to their average one-minute wind speeds - a *tropical depression* or *cyclone* has sustained wind speeds up to 34 kts and a *tropical storm*, between 35-64 knots. Proper hurricanes, or *typhoons* in Asia, are over 65 knots, but in the centre, or the *eye*, the wind speed will be light - 10-20 kt winds are common, in descending air (the eye can be seen from a satellite).

The *Saffir-Simpson Hurricane Scale* divides hurricanes into five categories according to their sustained winds, officially, in the Atlantic and Northern Pacific Oceans East of the International Date Line. To be a hurricane, a tropical cyclone must have maximum sustained winds exceeding 74 mph (64 kts). The highest category, 5, is reserved for storms with winds over 155 mph (136 kts).

One dangerous part is in the wall of (mainly stratiform) clouds around the eye, which is formed in the first place because the air is descending and warming and drying at that point. Thick cirrus cloud is an indication of a Tropical Revolving Storm because air rises and spreads out against the Tropopause (there is no more vertical development as it reaches the isothermal layer). The most destructive part is in the front left quadrant due to the combination of windspeeds and the velocity of the system itself.

The intense low pressure around a hurricane will lift the sea surface up slightly, and the bulge will push water ahead of the hurricane into very large waves, enough to create a wall of water if it hits land. Hurricane movement is erratic and difficult to predict, but they tend to move to the NorthWest (in the Northern hemisphere) in the lower latitudes, and more to the North East once they get far enough North to hit the prevailing

Picture: Tropical Cyclone Distribution

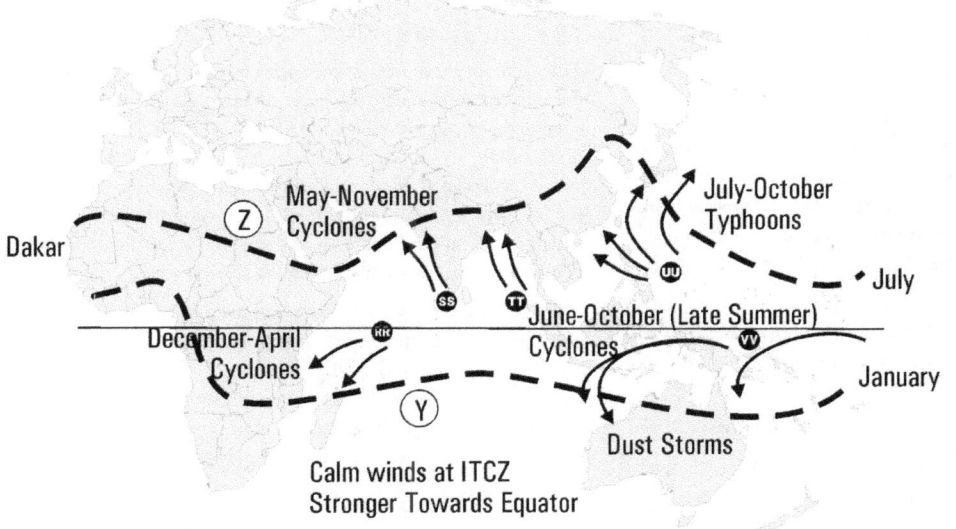

There is more air movement in the Northern Hemisphere because there are more land masses for the air to interact with.

Westerlies. However, a likely track in the Caribbean is West, turning North East.

Tropical revolving storms form only in the Southern hemisphere but, in the Northern hemisphere, those of the Caribbean, the South China Seas and the Bay of Bengal can occur as late as November.

The hurricane season is mainly between July-November (Summer & Autumn) but, in Australia, it is between November-April when the Equatorial Trough is around.

In the USA, they occur mostly along the SE coast (hitting the SE coast of almost anywhere that is affected by them).

Storms tend to move in a Westerly direction at first, at speeds below about 10 kts, then towards the Pole, then generally Easterly after reaching around 20 kts. This process is called *recurving*. Having said that, storm movement can also be unpredictable, but their violence calms down as they reach higher subtropical latitudes.

Tornadoes

One reason that squall lines are of interest is that they sometimes spawn tornadoes. These are rotating funnel-shaped clouds coming downwards out of convective clouds, usually cumulonimbus. Although most thunderstorms do not come with tornadoes, tornadoes do not form unless there are thunderstorms (ones that have been active a long time, having been capped).

A rapidly developing super-cell thunderstorm creates an intense local depression (50m – 250m diameter) underneath a cumulonimbus cloud. There is high instability as the ascending air cannot be replaced from below, and a pressure drop often to below 1000 hPa.

The resulting high pressure gradient creates a high speed rising spiral of air lasting up to 2 hours. The decrease in pressure also causes adiabatic cooling and condensation, resulting in a funnel cloud which becomes a tornado when it touches the ground.

To take Tornado Alley (Kansas - Oklahoma - Missouri) as an example, a layer of warm dry air flowing off the desert regions to the SW of the Great Plains starts the process off. As it lies between 3000-6000 feet, this creates an inversion, so the warm, moist air from the Gulf is stopped from rising until it gets powerful enough to break through to start a thunderstorm that is much larger and more violent than usual. It can rise as high as the jetstream, which can suck the air up more.

However, the storm must rotate for a tornado to form, and nobody really knows how the process starts, but a trough of low pressure with sharply inclined isobars is certainly involved. This leads to massive convergence with a rotational twist arising from the sharply different wind directions. The end result is that air along the outside of the tornado's funnel spirals upwards, while that on the inside descends.

Tornadoes can touch the ground, with a typical diameter of less than 100-150 m, and can lift very heavy items and transport them for several miles.

The typical range of movement is between 20 - 40 knots.

The pressure inside a tornado can be as low as 150 hPa. Such a vacuum can be effective - in St Louis, Missouri, in 1896, a pine plank was forced by the high winds that were created from the sharp pressure differentials through a solid iron girder that was supporting the Eads bridge.

The peak season for Tornadoes in this area is between March-June. Otherwise, they are most likely in the North Atlantic during Spring and Summer.

A *waterspout* is a gentler cousin of the tornado, coming from a weaker type of cloud, which doesn't mean they're not destructive. Waterspouts or tornadoes are most often found in the SW quadrant of a storm, during the mature stage, discussed later.

Similar in origin to tornadoes but the lower surface temperature of the sea means that they are not so intense or large. The lower section of the spiral of air may include a sea spray vortex.

PRESSURE VARIATION WITH HEIGHT

Pressure reduces with height, because there is less air above you as you climb. The air also gets thinner - at around 18 562 feet, it is 50% of its sea level density, so the hPa is worth about 50 feet (as opposed to 27 at the surface). Thus, the pressure at a place depends on its height, and the temperature and density. You can check the height change per hPa with a formula:

```
Height change per hPa (ft)= 96T
                            ───
                             P
```

where 96 is a constant (depends on the gas), *T* is mean temperature in Kelvin and *P* is mean pressure in hPa so, in ISA conditions, 1 hPa would be 27 feet at mean sea level:

```
27 ft = 96 x 288
        ────────
          1013
```

If your sea level pressure is 1010 hPa, and the temperature 16°C, at what altitude will the pressure be 990 hPa, if the temperature there is 14°C? The mean temperature is 15°C + 273°, which equals 288K (see *Temperature* later). The mean pressure is 1000 hPa. To apply the formula:

```
27.648 ft = 96 x 288
            ────────
              1000
```

The answer is 27.648, so:

```
27.648 x (1010 - 990) = 552.96 (553)
```

The Barometer

This is an instrument that measures atmospheric pressure, using mercury or an evacuated capsule, hence the *aneroid* (no fluid) barometer (*baros* is Greek for *weight*). The mercury barometer is quite simple - a long test tube with a vacuum inside is inverted and its end placed into a quantity of mercury. Air pressure makes the level rise or fall, and the height of its column in the tube is measured. You could actually use any liquid, but mercury is very dense, which means you can have a shorter tube.

Aneroid barometers are smaller and used in confined spaces, particularly instrument panels, but they are calibrated against mercury barometers. A device that measures pressure changes over time (with a moving pen over a moving paper drum) is called a *barograph*.

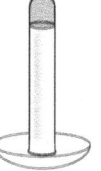

PRECIPITATION

This is the collective term for moisture that condenses into the atmosphere at a higher level before falling to the ground, but most people use it as a general term for rain or snow.

It comes from anything with *nimbo* in its name and is the end result of a chain of events that starts with the cooling through ascent of a parcel of dirty moist air ("dirty" meaning that it contains microscopic particles that water can bind on to). Once the saturation point is reached, condensation occurs and droplets coalesce to fall out as rain, snow, or whatever, according to temperature.

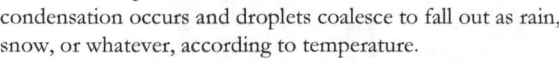

The vast majority of clouds from which precipitation falls have a sub-zero layer in which ice crystals and supercooled water droplets are present.

Precipitation includes rain, drizzle, snow and hail, but not drifting snow, sand or dust, because they are raised by the wind. Dew, hoar frost and rime are also excluded because they are surface condensation phenomena. The intensity of precipitation depends on the vertical thickness of cloud, the water content, the strength of updraughts and topography.

- **Rain** is liquid precipitation in the form of drops of some size, as opposed to **drizzle**, which is very fine, and appears to float down, because there is little vertical air movement (it also doesn't splash on reaching the ground). The intensity or rate of fall is the determining factor in classifying rain as slight, moderate or heavy, not the total fall over a period of hours. For example, slight rain accumulates at about 0.5 mm* per hour. Moderate rainfall fast enough to form puddles rapidly and heavy rain involves a downpour. Rain indicates significant layers of warm air in the atmosphere.

    *A good rule of thumb is that if the moisture in the air is descending (as opposed to drifting around), the droplet size is larger than 0.5 mm.

    The rainy period in the Northern hemisphere is around the 21st June, and the 21st December in the Southern hemisphere. In Equatorial areas, it is March and September.

- **Virga** is like a fine mist (from thin altostratus) that evaporates before reaching the ground, which looks like streamers just below the cloud base. It should be avoided because it is turbulent**, and may be coming from a microburst.

    **As rain changes from liquid to vapour, it removes heat from the air. The colder air can descend rapidly, creating a dry microburst.

Picture: Virga

- **Snow*** is a solid form of precipitation that consists of crystals of white ice, apparently opaque, generally in light, feathery flakes. While a drop of rain typically takes about forty minutes to reach the Earth's surface, snowflakes may take as much as an hour and a half. They are ice crystals which come from water vapour freezing directly to a solid, so they require a cold atmosphere. It will partially melt through a warm layer deeper than 600 feet, and it cannot turn back into snow again. Snow has the greatest effect on visibility.

    *Anything larger than 0.5 mm droplet size is freezing precipitation - and must be avoided, even if your aircraft is cleared for flight in icing (a dot from a pencil on a piece of paper is the largest size that would have been tested for an icing clearance).

- **Hail** forms from large water droplets forced above the freezing level, although there is an accretion and growth process as well. Raindrops in this situation can turn into small pieces of ice which may collide with supercooled water droplets and get larger, until they get so large that they fall out of the sky and cause damage. Hail is typically found coming out of thunderstorms over continents in mid-latitudes, up to FL 450.

- **Sleet** is half-melted snow (i.e. mixed rain and snow), that begins to unfreeze during descent below freezing level when it is quite high above the surface (in the US, the word refers to ice pellets). It freezes *before* striking the ground. Freezing rain freezes *after* striking the ground.

Continuity

Showers are local outbreaks of precipitation from detached heap clouds, however long its duration. They are caused by convective processes that are usually more vigorous than the frontal or orographic uplift with continuous precipitation, which falls from an extensive layer of cloud over a larger area, reported as:

- **Intermittent**, lasting less than an hour.
- **Continuous**, or prolonged, lasting an hour or more.

TURBULENCE

This is found in cloud and clear air (that is, *Clear Air Turbulence*, or CAT), and usually comes from friction when air currents mix, from various sources, such as *convective, orographic, windshear* and *mechanical*, and is reported as:

- **Light**, with small changes in height or attitude, near stratocumulus
- **Moderate**, more severe, but you are still in control. ICAO definition: *There may be moderate changes in aircraft attitude and/or altitude but the aircraft remains in positive control at all times. Usually, small variations in air speed. Changes in accelerometer readings of 0.5 to 1.0 g at the aircraft's center of gravity. Occupants feel strain against seat belts. Loose objects move about. Food service and walking are difficult.* Good indicators are cumulus-type clouds, which may also warn you about....
- **Severe**, with abrupt changes, and being temporarily out of control, indicated by cumulonimbus and lenticular clouds, if there are many stacked on top of each other. Expect the latter when winds across mountain ranges are more than 40 kts
- **Extreme**, impossible to control

If turbulence is likely, use turbulence speed, which will be less than normal. Advise the passengers to securely fasten their seat belts/harnesses. Catering and other loose equipment should be stowed and secured.

Vertical windshear consists of vertical variations in the horizontal wind It can be:

- **Convective**, in and below cumulus and Cb
- **Mechanical** - with wind blowing over and around surface obstructions
- Frontal

THUNDERSTORMS

The Earth has a surplus of electrons, and the ionosphere doesn't - if you take the air between them as a dielectric, you have a very large capacitor (see *Electricity* in *AGK*) with a potential difference between its "plates" in the order of 360,000 volts, reducing with height at about 100 volts per metre (the body's resistance is high, so you don't notice the 200 volts between your feet and your head). However, capacitors leak, and they break down when one plate gets overcharged and the dielectric becomes a conductor, having been ionised. The thunderstorm replenishes the Earth's negative charge through this mechanism, and it is estimated that, at any time over the planet, there are over 40,000 active thunderstorms, with the highest frequency in tropical areas. The power contained in a thunderstorm is more than 4 nuclear bombs put together (some say 10), which is a very good reason to avoid flying through them (penetrate the sides if you can't avoid it).

Lightning itself is a discharge of around a million volts with an associated current of between 10,000-40,000 amps, heating the air up to 30,000°C. This can fuse sand or start a fire.

Picture: Thunderstorm Display On Weather Radar

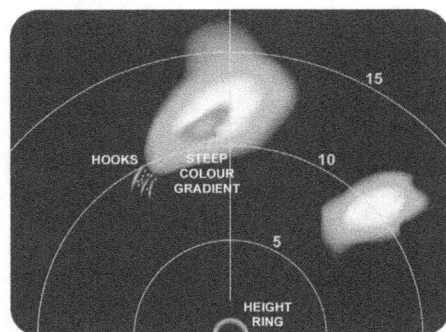

It is estimated that every airliner is struck by lightning at least once a year, on average (*Air & Space*). It attaches to entry and exit points almost at the same time, affecting the nose, wingtips, engine cowlings and tips of tails. The shapes of such items encourage electric fields to concentrate on them.

Composite materials require protection, such as lightning defrauders, which are thin metal strips that work as small lightning rods. A conductive mesh in the skin also spreads the current and keeps it on the outside of the fuselage. The hazards associated with thunderstorms include:

- **Electrical and Magnetic**. Lightning, obviously, plus damage to compasses and radios, exploding fuel tanks or ruined avionics. The temperature band for lightning is between +10° to -10°C.
- Severe **turbulence** from strong up- and downdraughts, which can be encountered up to 20 miles away and 5 000-10 000 ft above. Even over baby ones near to larger storms, you will need at least 5000 feet clearance - *sprites* have been known to go up 75 miles into space (for the exam, clear the top of a severe thunderstorm by 1,000 feet for each 10 kts of wind). The currents inside a thunderstorm will easily be enough to suck in the average light aircraft, or spit it out.
- Severe **icing** between 0°C and -23°C.
- Heavy **precipitation**, e.g. hail over ¾" across.
- Strong, variable **winds** (squalls and microbursts).
- Rapid **pressure changes.** Pressure usually falls rapidly as a thunderstorm approaches, then rises rapidly with the first gust. It returns to normal after it passes.

There are two main types of thunderstorm:

- **Air Mass** (non-frontal), triggered by convection (surface heating), so they are very common by day, over land, in Summer, forming in late afternoon and dissipating by the evening. They are often isolated and can usually be avoided, but are difficult to forecast and detect. Look for them in cols and weak lows where there has been enough time to heat the air by surface contact. Air mass thunderstorms can also be triggered by:

- **Orographic uplift** (i.e. after hitting the side of a mountain), so they can be found by night and day, and have more icing and turbulence, because the added updraughts can support more (and larger) water drops.
- **Cold stream**, over a warm surface, leading to instability over a deep layer.
- **Night Equatorial**. Cloud tops cool from radiation to create unstable conditions.
- **Shear**.

Mass Ascent, or frontal, thunderstorms are found at air mass boundaries under cold front (and occlusion) conditions, that is, where cold air undercuts warm air, in a line along or just ahead of a cold front* (in the warm sector), to form line squalls. These are more frequent in Winter, simply because there are more fronts, and can therefore form by night and day, over land and sea. They are difficult to avoid because they cover larger areas. The frontal conditions can also produce other types of cloud, so mass ascent thunderstorms can be embedded and not easily detected. Frontal thunderstorms move the fastest, and a cold front thunderstorm will have its base closer to the ground, so the winds underneath will be stronger.

*They can also develop on a warm front if the warm air is conditionally unstable. These would be embedded thunderstorms, which may look like something like this in the early stages:

You will only get thunderstorms from cumulonimbus clouds, but not every time (nobody really knows why). The airflow is greatly disturbed anywhere near them, usually noticeable by strong up- and downdraughts, together with heavy rain and lightning, or even tornadoes. Because of the inflow of warm air and the outflow of cold, the *gust front* can extend up to 15-20 miles ahead of a moving storm (a gust front is formed from the cold outflow). Best avoided.

To start a thunderstorm, you need:

- **moisture** (high relative humidity), particularly in the lower levels and throughout a deep layer.
- cloud tops above the 0° isotherm.
- a **steep** (conditionally unstable) **lapse rate**, over about 10 000 feet. A deep layer of instability can occur when a land surface is warmed up during the day at the same time as air is cooled above.
- a **lifting**, or *trigger*, **agent**, which could be orographic, convective (thermal), frontal or nocturnal, as occurs in the midWest plains after night-time radiation from the cloud tops, which would increase lapse rates (you could get two trigger actions, as when a front hits the Rockies). Turbulence is not a thunderstorm trigger because it is only instrumental in forming layer type clouds.

The instability and moisture content determine the severity of any storm, and a high temperature and dewpoint close together are a good early warning as the air is hot, and contains lots of water vapour. Convective activity over land in mid-latitudes is greatest in the Summer, in the afternoons, so you can expect local isolated thunderstorms arising from thermal triggering mostly in the mid-afternoon, from warm updraughts (thermal triggering depends on relatively light winds that allow high surface temperatures to develop).

Isolated thunderstorms of a local nature are generally caused by *unstable air, high humidity and a lifting force.*

Picture: Typical ELR Profile For Thunderstorm

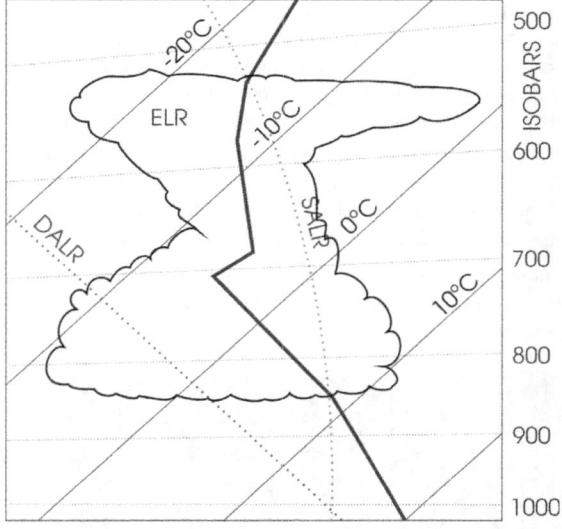

Structure

Although the clouds associated with a thunderstorm may extend for some distance, a thunderstorm is actually a collection of several cloud cells in varying stages of development, with varying diameters, a few hundred feet across. The different cells may be developing, maturing or dissipating at rates of their own, which could form their own trigger actions and make the storm self-perpetuating. You might find three variations on the theme:

Single Cell - active for less than an hour, with up and down draughts on the same axis. They move after 700 hPa winds.

- **Multi Cell**. Squall lines.
- **Super Cell**. Up and downdraughts exist side by side so convection has no restrictions. They can last for several hours if enough warm moist air is available. On top of the normal start conditions, super cell thunderstorms also require a lot of moisture and a change in wind vector aloft.

Essentially, however, a thunderstorm consists of updraughts and downdraughts, the former being what fuels the storm in the first place - it is warm, moist air that is buoyant and rises rapidly. Exceptionally strong updraughts can start to rotate, and form tornadoes and/or waterspouts. At the top of the updraughts, precipitation forms and starts to accumulate. Some coalesce, but others evaporate, chilling the air and making it sink. It can do this in the face of the updraught (which helps to calm things down), or to one side, slightly downwind. Downdraughts become **outflow** at the surface - the leading edge is the **gust front**.

SINGLE CELL

This is the simplest form of storm which, in reality doesn't exist, as the various types tend to share their characteristics. However, it is typical of the air mass type of thunderstorm found in Summer over the plains, and squall lines, which are long lines of single cell thunderstorms (in theory) that can be hundreds of miles long. Severe lines will prompt a SIGMET to be issued.

Squall lines occur under the same conditions as thunderstorms and can appear anywhere that air is moist and unstable, but often ahead of cold fronts in late afternoon or early evening, or before a "dew point front", which separates air masses that only have different moisture levels. They are the product of severe cold frontal conditions, where a cold front nudges under the warm sector (watch for an acute bend in isobars at the front, or low roll cloud across the advance). They can move so fast that they can get embedded into the warm frontal cloud. However, the normal propagation method comes from a line of updraughts along an outflow boundary from a thunderstorm, spreading out as they hit the ground and nudging air upwards to its dewpoint.

Precipitation falls behind the system, and a classic squall line has the updraught along the front (East) side and the downdraught on the back (West) side.

As the updraught is pushed along rather than being cut off, they can be sustained for many hours. Strong straight-line winds can be present as the storms march Eastward.

These clues will help you detect squall lines before flight:
- A well defined warm sector, with high dewpoints, especially ahead of and parallel to the cold front.
- Cold air aloft, where any warm air rising into it gets a buoyancy boost. Jetstreams can give air a similar boost as it gets sucked up from lower levels.
- Strong Southerly winds just ahead of the cold front.

DEVELOPMENT STAGE

It all begins with a single cumulus cloud which you could call the mother cell - it comes from a very strong updraught of warm air that rises so fast that it penetrates the ceiling where ordinary clouds stop. That is, instead of cooling from expansion, it gets into cold air faster than that, plus there is a lot of heat from the rapid condensation.

This starts off a chain reaction that keeps things going. By the time the mother cell is 4 nm across (and ten miles high), the updraught might well be above 150 knots or so (5 knots is 500 feet per minute).

During the development, or cumulus stage, which takes around **15-20 minutes**, several such cumulus clouds will begin to merge, where the system consists **mainly of updraughts** (up to 5000 ft/min), and will grow to around 4 miles wide at the base and 20,000 feet in height. That is, warm, moist unstable air is forced to rise because of the trigger agents mentioned above. Rapidly growing cumulonimbus clouds should be avoided by 10 nm.

Water droplets are merging as well, to form larger raindrops, which get to be a hazard once they get above the freezing level and become supercooled (see *Icing*, below). When they are big enough, they will fall, and pull cold air down with them (and drier air in from above), which is where the downdraughts come from. The drier air causes some evaporation, which absorbs latent heat and makes the air even colder, to fall faster.

Rain at the surface is an indication of the transition to ....

THE MATURE STAGE

This is distinguished by rainfall (or precipitation), but mostly by downdraughts and updraughts in the middle over about **30-40 minutes**.

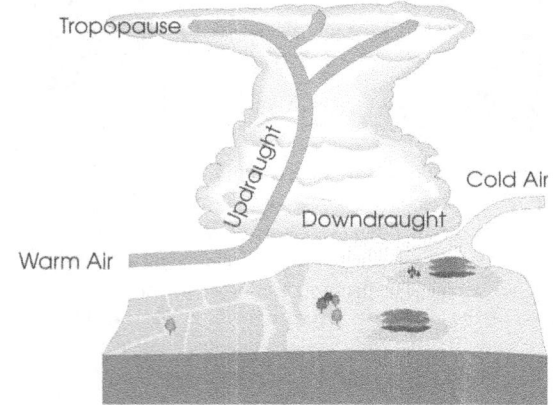

In the mature stage, rain falls through or immediately beside the updraught, inducing frictional drag to retard it and turn it into a downdraught. This will reduce the cell's life cycle to between 20 minutes and 2½ hours. In a Steady State thunderstorm, this will be several hours because the precipitation falls outside the downdraught. Tornadoes often form with steady-state thunderstorms associated with cold fronts or squall lines.

In the picture below, there is a positive charge in the anvil, a negative charge in the freezing layers, and a positive charge below. They naturally migrate towards each other, and when they meet, there is a sudden and intense flow of current, the natural resistance of the air is breached and you get a lightning discharge. There can be negative cloud base to positive ground strikes, and highly positive anvil cloud to positive ground strikes. Aircraft flying between oppositely charged regions can trigger lightning from within a cloud, between clouds, or from cloud to ground.

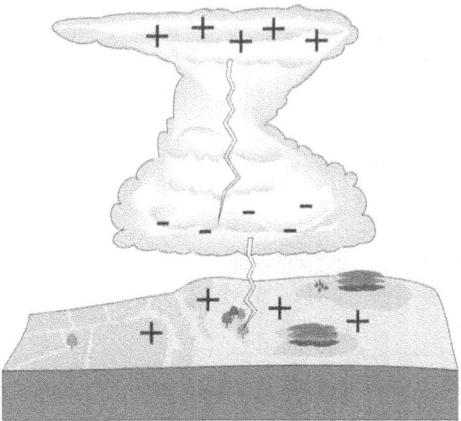

While some heating takes place in a downdraught, there is also a lot of evaporation which will cancel it out and increase cooling, so cool air ends up near the surface below the cloud, on top of turbulence in the shape of microbursts. This means that there will often be a roll of stratocumulus ahead of the storm caused by mixing of the descending cool air with a warm moist updraught.

The storm will move under the influence of the upper winds, with the average movement following the 700 Mb (10 000 ft) wind. It can produce lightning at this stage from large static discharges, with the most severe being within 5 000 feet of the freezing level.

THE DISSIPATION STAGE

This is the third stage, which starts after the updraughts cease*, around 2 hours after the development stage. It is distinguished by the presence of a well developed anvil, formed as the clouds at the top of the storm meet the tropopause, and therefore an inversion, where they spread out in the wind. Characteristics are downdraughts and disappearing cloud over around 1 hour.

MULTI CELL

This is the most common type of thunderstorm. The **cluster** type often appears as one larger storm with many updraughts and downdraughts in various stages of formation and decay. A cluster will usually start as a unicell, but the outflow forms new updraughts around the perimeter. This would be how the vast majority of Summer air-mass storms come into existence.

When there is high instability, with solar heating and strong vertical wind shear, a **line of multicells** may form, with the activity in a line around 10-30 miles long. Old cells die out on the Northern part as rainy downdraughts, and newer cells form to the South, composed of towering cumulus. This process of *backbuilding* tends to keep the storm going Eastward rather than to the North East. Such lines of multicells can produce weak tornadoes, large hailstones, torrential rains and strong winds.

SUPERCELL

This storm has achieved a steady-state updraught/downdraught life cycle, often containing a rotating updraught. It is the most dangerous type of thunderstorm, defined as a convective thunderstorm with a mesocyclone or mesoanticyclone. It is essentially a multicell that is self-propagating and concerns regeneration, where the cell feeds on itself rather than forming new cells or re-generating its neighbours.

It occurs with a marked change of wind velocity (direction or speed) in the deep band of unstable air within which the storm cell grows. The cloud becomes tilted out of the vertical and, at the active stage, much of the precipitation and downdraught tends to descend outside the cell boundaries. As a result, the updraught is not counteracted by the downdraught as it might be in a normal storm. The rapid ascent of air and subsequent fall in pressure can create a localised vortex that produces funnel cloud and possibly tornadoes at the mature stage.

They are common in the Mid-West of the USA. Warm, moist air from the Gulf of Mexico coming in at low level is heated over the land and rises rapidly into the cooler air above. The storms tend to follow a path which is either 20° to the right and slower than the mean tropospheric wind, or 20° to the left and faster than the mean tropospheric wind. Those travelling to the right are more common in the Northern hemisphere. The rotation of the cloud that coincides with this movement is connected with the development of tornadoes near to the updraught. In principle, a supercell storm passes through four stages - initial, supercell, tornado and dissipating.

There are actually three types of supercell storm:

- **Low Precipitation**. As the name implies, there is very little precipitation, so there is very little incentive for tornadoes to form - if they do, there are small ones, but there will still be a lot of hail.

- The **Classic** supercell produces moderate precipitation - just enough to help tornadoes. These rain curtains become involved with the mesocyclone circulation, as indicated by the hook echoes that can be seen on weather radar. As such, they can occlude any tornadoes that form.

- **High Precipitation** supercells are one of the most violent types, due to the weak shear that allows the precipitation to fall back into or just outside the updraught, which wraps the tornadoes with rain. If the shear is stronger, the rain will fall around the updraught and form a *bear's cage*, which hides the tornado inside a cage of rain.

Windshear

When wet-bulb cooling occurs in the middle and upper levels of a thunderstorm, the cooling of the air causes it to become negatively buoyant (i.e. it sinks), and accelerate toward the Earth's surface causing a *derecho*, a macroburst or a microburst. In other words, cold air from high altitudes is forced down to balance the powerful updraughts caused by the warm air rising inside the cells. The cold air spreads out when it hits the ground to form a cushion, or *cold dome*, ahead of which are more, called *downbursts*, which may themselves contain *microbursts*, which, technically, are concentrated inside a 4 km radius. Expect lightning as well at this stage, which comes from the friction between up- and downdraughts and between water and air molecules, so a well-developed line of thunderstorms pushes a mass of cold air in front of it, which forces warm air up, to form more storm cells. The leading edge of cold air becomes the windshift line, only sometimes marked by roll cloud. As the top of the cloud reaches the tropopause, inversions stop the ascent and strong upper winds produce the distinctive anvil shape.

Windshear reports are updated every minute.

Takeoff and Landing

Not if thunderstorms are overhead or within 5 nm, due to the risk of lightning strikes. The same goes for refuelling!

ICING

Ice on your airframe is dangerous because it makes the machine heavier, displaces the Centre Of Gravity, and distorts the lift-producing surfaces, to produce less lift and more drag. In addition, it can jam the controls, block instruments, vision, and cause interference with radios when it covers the antennae. In particular, with helicopter rotor blades, or with propellers, it may cause an imbalance which leads to severe vibration and asymmetric shedding (kinetic heating can create a difference of 5° between the roots and tips of rotor blades).

Ice will form on an airframe if there is water in a liquid state combined with either the air or the airframe temperature below 0°. Zero degrees is actually when water becomes *capable* of freezing, from which you can infer that it doesn't necessarily do so. A *Supercooled Water Droplet* is one below freezing, but not frozen. This is due to the absence of hygroscopic nuclei to bind on to, and they can be found in clouds, fog and precipitation.

When such a droplet strikes an airframe, however, just below 0°, some of it will freeze on impact, releasing latent heat and warming the remainder, which then flows back, turning into *clear ice* when the freezing is slow, which can gather without noticeable vibration. The time taken for this to happen depends on the temperature of the aircraft surface (lower temperature, quicker freezing), the initial temperature of the water drop (lower temperature, quicker freezing), and the size of the water drop (large drops, slower freezing). In other words, the airframe will act as one giant ice nucleus, and the freezing is *behind* the point of impact, and therefore behind the influence of deicing equipment, where it can pile up and distort the lift-producing surfaces. $1/80$ th part of a SWD will freeze on impact for each degree below zero, assuming a large droplet - small ones will form *rime ice* - mentioned below. The worst place to penetrate cumuliform cloud is between 0 to -10°C, where most SWDs are - you are most likely to find large ones in the lower levels of cloud that has formed in unstable air (cumulus), in temperatures only a few degrees below freezing, and you can expect clear icing from them. Ice is reported as:

- **Trace**, meaning slight, non-hazardous, perceptible
- **Light**, with occasional use of deicing equipment. Flights over 1 hour might be inadvisable, but *No change of course and altitude necessary* (ICAO)
- **Moderate**, where use of above equipment is necessary. Time to consider diversion. The ICAO phrase is *Change of course and/ or altitude desirable*
- **Severe**, where the equipment is useless and you must divert. ICAO: *Change course and/ or altitude immediately*

If you are getting light-moderate icing and you start seeing ice crystals, you can expect the icing intensity to decrease. Altocumulus and Altostratus are the most likely clouds to produce light to moderate icing, when not subject to orographic lifting. Moderate to severe icing is most likely to occur in Nimbostratus. You can virtually rule out icing in Cirrus cloud.

Types Of Icing

RIME ICE

This comes from *smaller* SWDs well below 0° (actually between -10° and -30°C in nimbostratus), when freezing is fast. It is opaque and granular and moves forward as it builds up on sharp surfaces like antennae. On a helicopter rotor blade, it is more likely to occur on the top rather than the leading edge. Below -40°C, you will likely only encounter ice crystals, which will not stick to the aircraft, or *very small* SWDs. However, ice accumulation is too unpredictable to assume anything - you can get severe icing in towering cumulus down to -25°C. It is worst at the top of CBs, but light to moderate amounts can be typically found in thin stratus at around -5°C.

CLEAR (GLAZE) ICE

Clear ice is transparent, with no trapped air, so it is very hard to get rid of. It is the most dangerous form of aircraft icing because it is very heavy and can affect controls and surfaces - the most serious risk is on the front surfaces of the aircraft, but because it can run back behind the effect of deicing equipment, it is dangerous to the rear as well.

It may be encountered above the freezing level in the cold sector ahead of a warm front, but most often in cumulus clouds and unstable conditions between **0 and -15°C**, where large supercooled water droplets are found, and where they freeze **relatively slowly**. It would also appear to be most likely to form when the ambient air temperature is between **-10°C and -17°C**.

MIXED ICE

A mixture of the above two types. It is often called cloudy ice, and it can be formed from large or small SWDs between -0°C and -20°C in layer and heap type clouds. In nimbostratus, it is most common between -7°C and -13°C.

RAIN ICE

This can be found when clear of cloud, above the freezing level, commonly just ahead of a warm front, where there is a freezing level above you and rain is falling from the overhanging cloud. It builds up quickly and immediate action is required. The best option is to climb or fly faster - do not descend unless you know where you are and that the freezing level is above the surface. Turning takes time and increases the chances of losing control.

FROST

Sometimes called *Hoar Frost*, this is a light crystalline deposit which forms away from clouds and precipitation. It is the only type of icing that occurs in clear air, typically forming after the process of **deposition** (ICAO say sublimation) a clear night when the airframe has been allowed to creep below 0°C and the surrounding air gets cooled below its dewpoint, proceeding directly from a vapour to a solid. It can also occur during rapid descents from high, cold levels into warmer (clear) moist air, or, rarely, after takeoff on a frosty morning as you fly through an inversion into warmer, moister air. Although it is technically light icing, it is similar to a bad paint job and can increase drag markedly. It increases the stalling speed, reduces visibility and impairs communication.

Avoiding Icing

Pitot head, static vent and fuel vent heaters should be on whenever you encounter icing, together with anything else you feel is appropriate. Otherwise, you need warmer air to get rid of it effectively - just flying around in clear air can take hours to shift it, but you could at least say you won't get any more. Aerodynamic heating comes from air friction, which may get rid of ice, but only at high speeds, so will not likely benefit helicopters, except for rotor blades, which may be warmer by 1° or so, from their speed. Climbing out is often not possible, due to lack of performance or ATC considerations, and descending has problems, too - if you're getting clear ice, it's a fair bet that the air is warmer above you, since it may be freezing rain, from an inversion, probably within 1,000 feet or so, as you might get before a warm front, or after a cold one. The most dangerous position to be in is in rain - it is quite common to fly above a freezing level (always being aware that there may be two!) if there is no moisture around.

In this position, landing on your first attempt becomes more important as you are unlikely to survive a go-around without picking up more. You basically have three choices, go up, down or back the way you came. Going up is a good first choice if you know the tops are nearby, if only because you won't have a chance to do so later, but you present more of the airframe to icing risk, which is why there is often a minimum speed for climbing in icing conditions, slightly more than normal. To keep out of trouble, before going, check that the freezing level is well above any minimum altitudes, which will help get rid of ice in the descent. Try to make sure the cloud tops are within reach as well, or that you have plenty of holes.

Deicing

De-icing is the process of removing ice from an airframe after it has formed. *Anti-icing* is the process of stopping it from forming in the first place. A one-step procedure does both at the same time using a combination fluid. The two step procedure involves de-icing, then anti-icing. De-icing fluid is hot, and anti-icing fluid is cold, because it increases its thickness and effective working time. Although heating a fluid increases its *deicing* properties, unheated fluids are more effective for *anti-icing*. The operator must establish procedures for its removal (including inspections), and a commander is not allowed to take off until the external surfaces of the aircraft are clear of any deposit that would affect performance or control of an aircraft, other than that in the Flight Manual. In addition, a commander may not take off into known or expected icing conditions unless the aircraft is certificated and equipped to cope.

When an aircraft is contaminated by ice on the ground, approved de-icing methods include:

- applying de-icing fluids (but see below)
- warming the airframe with hot air blowers
- placing the aircraft in a warm hangar
- sweeping surfaces with frost and light ice on them

DEICING FLUIDS

Although they are not generally used on helicopters, the main types of deicing fluid are:

- **Type I** (unthickened) with a high glycol content (80%) and low viscosity (they must be heated), and
- **Type II** (thickened) with a minimum glycol content of about 50% which, with a thickening agent (one or two teaspoons of corn flour), remains on surfaces for longer, but it has to blow off before you get airborne otherwise it will spoil as much lift as the ice it is meant to prevent
- **Type III** lies somewhere between the two.
- **Type IV** is similar to II, but with much longer holdover times*. It needs care to provide uniform cover, especially over Type I fluid already there

*The holdover time is how long the effects should last - it can be affected by high winds or jet blasts damaging the fluid film, and temperature, humidity, etc. It begins at the final application and expires when the fluid loses its effectiveness. Frost has the longest holdover time.

The idea (with fluids) is to decrease the freezing point of water but, as the ice melts, the fluid mixes with the water, both diluting it and making it more runny (what's left after repeated applications to combat this is of an unknown concentration, and may refreeze quickly).

VISIBILITY

This is defined as the greatest horizontal distance that a dark object (of known dimensions) can be seen and recognised against a light background, usually prominent objects from the tower, or a measure of the opacity of the atmosphere in a particular direction. The *prevailing visibility* is the greatest that is met or exceeded through at least half the visible horizon. This poses a problem at night, so *night visibility* really refers to how far you would be able to see in daylight. Visibility may be reduced by fog, mist, cloud, precipitation, sea spray, smoke, sand, dust and industrial haze, etc. but, generally, warm air gets cooled to its dewpoint and saturates.

You get the best visibility in haze down-sun and up-moon.

Bad visibility makes things look further away.

Measuring Visibility

If possible, pilot measurement is used, but machinery is often involved in remote places or where constant information is required.

METEOROLOGICAL VISIBILITY

Met vis is defined as *the greatest horizontal distance at which known objects can be seen and recognised by an observer on the ground with normal eyesight under conditions of normal daylight illumination*. Put another way, it gives information on the transparency of the atmosphere to a stationary ground observer, who will measure the distance in many directions and report the least one as the met vis. Other factors may determine whether the same object can actually be seen by aircrew.

Visibility is quoted in metres up to and including 5000 m (5 km) and in kilometres thereafter.

RUNWAY VISUAL RANGE

RVR is the maximum distance that a pilot 15 feet above the runway (in the touchdown area) can see marker boards by day and lights by night, when looking towards the touchdown or landing area. It will be less than met vis because runway lights are involved in its measurement.

RVR is reported when normal visibility is 1500 m or less, or when shallow fog is reported or forecast. The readings are valid *for the time being*, or every 30 minutes when traffic is continuous, or within 15 minutes if traffic is light. RVR is *never* forecast.

RVR is measured with a *transmissometer*, which is a device that uses a photoelectric cell to produce an equivalent to daytime visibility (the strength of current in the cell depends on the clarity of air between the transmitter and receiver). Because only a small portion of the atmosphere can be sampled, three are used - one at each end of the runway, and the middle, so you will get figures from ATC for the *touchdown zone*, *mid-point* and *stop end*. If you only get two figures, the first will be for the touchdown zone, and the other will be specified. Mid-point or stop end values are suppressed when they are equal to or above that of the touchdown zone, and are above 400 m, or 800 m or greater.

Fog

Fog is essentially cloud at ground level, which exists when you cannot see more than 1,000 metres (not inclusive) due to water droplets in the air (i.e. a relative humidity of 100%). It is not really cloud, because you cannot see anything at all in clouds, but the process of formation is the same, with the other difference being that fog forms downwards and clouds form upwards - therefore you cannot fly under fog. With *freezing fog*, the water droplets are **supercooled**. When only freezing fog occurs, there will be just about as much freezing of the fog droplets onto surfaces as there will be sublimation from the surface, so there is not much (rime) ice accumulation. There may also be freezing drizzle, in which case a film of ice will coat surfaces. *Ice fog* is composed of tiny ice crystals, where the temperature is becoming too cold for supercooling.

Ice fog will only be seen in cold Arctic/Polar air.

- **Radiation fog** forms over land, preferably low-lying, when temperatures approach the dewpoint with very slight winds (2-8 kts), with moisture present, so high relative humidity, long cooling periods and clear skies are relevant. It **doesn't form over the sea**, because the diurnal temperature variation is less. It is often found in the early morning after a clear night, since it likes high relative humidity, light winds and clear skies (and long cooling periods). Its vertical extent is typically **500 feet**, and it usually clears quickly, once the Sun's heat gets to work, often getting worse before it gets better. If the winds are just enough to stir things up (3-5 kts), fog will form. If there is no wind, you will get dew on the ground, and if the wind is too strong (greater than 10 kts) you will get low level stratus. Radiation fog disperses with wind, heat, or a drier air mass. You can expect the densest type the night after an afternoon of heavy rains, in low lying areas, which is where you find most airfields.

Picture: Radiation Fog In The Rockies

- **Valley Fog** is radiation fog found in valleys.
- **Advection fog** arises from warm air flowing over a cold surface, typically from an air mass moving inland from the coast in Winter, and can be found immediately after the passage of a cold front, but it can appear suddenly by day or night. Advection is the sideways movement of air in bulk - warm advection means warm air replacing colder air, and *vice versa*, as you would find with fronts. It is not the same as radiation fog because air movement is involved, and the coolness does not arise from diurnal variations, but longer periods, as with the sea, where this type of fog is commonly found. In the Atlantic

provinces of Canada, it occurs when moist air passes over the cold Labrador Current in Newfoundland during Spring time. It is also the type of fog that rolls in, for example, over the San Francisco bridge.

Winds over 15 kts will lift advection fog into a layer of low stratus or stratocumulus.

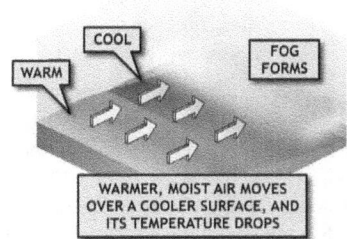

- **Orographic (Hill) Fog** is low cloud covering high ground, which may or may not have helped with its formation - if moist air is forced up the side of a hill, it will condense. This can happen by day or night. It is cleared with a change of airflow.

An observer on the ground sees low cloud - a person on the hill is in fog.

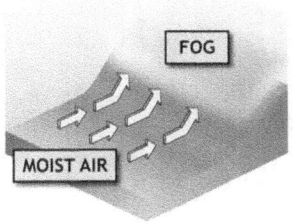

Icing here is likely to be more severe because more water is released as the air is forced to ascend.

- **Upslope fog** is a larger scale type of hill fog that forms from adiabatic cooling of moist, stable air as it moves up slopes, typically over the Canadian prairies when air is moving from East to West (Winnipeg is about 800 feet ASL, Regina to the West is about 1900, and Calgary, in the foothills of the Rockies, is about 3500 feet ASL).

- **Frontal fog** may simply be low cloud touching high ground, or come from rain falling through unsaturated air beneath:

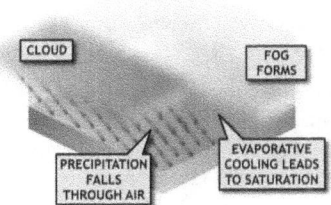

Also known as mixing fog, it occurs when very humid warm air meets with very humid cold air, most likely in advance of a warm front.

- **Steam Fog**, or **Arctic Smoke**, comes from the advection of cold air over warm water, so moisture is added, as opposed to being warm air that is cooled.

In the process, heat and moisture are transferred from the warm water to the cooler, drier air in a shallow layer near the lake surface. You now have an unstable situation with warm, saturated air at the lake's surface below cooler air which rises to form steam fog.

- In **shallow fog**, which only gets up around 2 m off the ground or 10 m above the sea, you may be able to see the whole of the approach and/or runway lights from a considerable distance, even though reports indicate fog. On descending into the fog layer, however, your visual reference is likely to drop rapidly, in extreme cases from the full length of the runway and approach lights to a very small segment, but typically about half. This may give the impression that you're pitching nose up, making you more likely to hit the ground when you try to correct it. *You should be prepared for a missed approach whenever you have the slightest doubt about forward visibility.* The minimum RVR to land from a visual circuit is 800m.

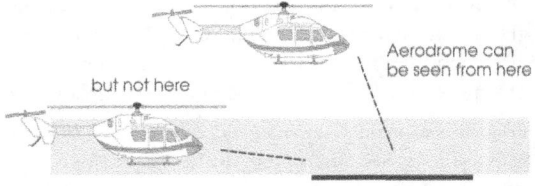

The types of fog just in front of and just after a passing a warm front are *frontal* and *advection* fog.

Mist

This is essentially, thin fog, except that the visibility is between 1 000 - 5 000 m, inclusive.

Haze

Small dry particles suspended in the air, with relative humidity below 95%.

Whiteout

This is defined by the American Meteorological Society as:

"An atmospheric optical phenomenon of the polar regions in which the observer appears to be engulfed in a uniformly white glow".

You cannot distinguish between the ground and the sky - the snow-covered surface cannot be detected by the naked eye because of the lack of normal colour contrast. Whiteout typically occurs over unbroken snow cover beneath a uniformly overcast sky, when the light from both is about the same. Blowing snow doesn't help, and it's particularly a problem if the ground is rising. In fact, there are several versions of whiteout:

- *Overcast Whiteout*, which comes from complete cloud cover with light being reflected between a snow surface and the cloud base. Perspective is limited to within a few feet, but the horizontal visibility of dark objects is not materially reduced.
- *Water Fog*. Thin clouds of supercooled water droplets contacting a cold snow surface. Horizontal and vertical visibility is affected by the size and distribution of the water droplets.
- *Blowing Snow*. Winds over 20 kts picking up fine snow from the surface, diffusing sunlight and reducing visibility.
- *Precipitation*. Small wind-driven snow crystals from low clouds with the Sun above. Light is refracted and objects obscured caused by multiple reflection of light between the snow covered surface and the cloud base. Spectral reflection from the snow flakes and obscuration of landmarks by the falling snow are further complications.

Once you suspect whiteout, *immediately* climb or level off towards an area where you can see things properly. Better yet (for a helicopter), put the machine on the ground before you get there. *Flat light* is a similar phenomenon, but it comes from different causes, where light is diffused through water droplets suspended in the air. *Brownout* comes from blowing sand or dust.

 If you are at maximum weight, you may not have the power to get out of a snow or dust cloud!

MET SERVICES & INFORMATION

The meteorological service operates a vast intelligence system that gathers information every half hour and transmits it to a central point for analysis. Even ships at sea contribute information. The reports are combined with the findings of a low-orbit satellite that flies round the world every 107 minutes, which measures wave-heights, amongst other things, whilst others might look at conditions in the troposphere and stratosphere. A Cray computer crunches the results and the information is used to try to forecast the weather.

The results (MET Reports* and operational information) can be listened to on ATIS (*Automatic Terminal Information Service*), which is broadcast on available VHF frequencies, VOR and NDB (not ILS) at major aerodromes (you can use it as an ID on instrument rides). This reduces congestion on VHF frequencies, although it may have its own channel. You should listen to it and take down the details before you contact ATC, inbound or outbound. ATIS broadcasts should be updated whenever a significant change occurs, and should not last over 30 seconds. See also *Air Law*.

VOLMET consists of long readouts of METARs (and SPECIs) in a sequence, so if you miss the aerodrome you want, just wait for it to come round again. Many airfields have it available over the telephone.

*MET Reports are not METARs (see *Communications*).

Tip: When looking at METARs, check for possible special requirements, such as an alternate aerodrome or holding fuel for when you arrive. In deciding whether you have good or bad weather for what you want to do, it's a good idea to apply a 30 minute safety buffer to the forecast time of change, to protect you from being caught out and running low on fuel. For example, if the weather is improving, assume that any changes will happen 30 minutes later than the forecast predicts. if it is getting worse, assume it weather happen 30 minutes sooner.

If you have what is known as an "operational requirement" (i.e. bad weather that's getting worse), there's no need for buffers. Only apply them when you are considering whether you have an OPR for the flight.

The term *arrival* means overhead the aerodrome, so if you are going to get there at 08:00, for exams, consider conditions that are due to start then (no buffers).

Variations occur when the forecaster expects deteriorations, with a subsequent return to the background conditions (i.e. afternoon showers). These will be indicated by INTER or TEMPO, and you could apply 30 minute buffers to the beginning and end of the period.

Changes (FM or BECMG) occur when one set of conditions will be replaced by another and the weather after the change will remain as described, as with the passage of a cold front. In such cases, apply a buffer to the beginning of the change if the weather is getting worse, and afterwards if it is getting better.

TEMPO doesn't occur in the main body of a METAR, but it can appear in the short TREND section, which is a forecast, where it just means temporarily, with no time qualification, just sometime inside the TREND time of 2 hours. However, you may see TEMPO followed by FM (from), TL ('til) or AT (at) and a four digit time. Because the whole trend only lasts 2 hours these will be in hours and minutes UTC.

In a TAF, which is a forecast, TEMPO has a specific meaning. The four time figures afterwards in a TAF are two different whole hours UTC.

World Area Forecast System

A *World Area Forecast Centre* (WAFC) provides real-time meteorological information broadcasts for aviation, supervised by ICAO. The WAFC provides meteorological messages with world-wide coverage for pilot briefing, particularly for upper air regions. They are usually part of the Pre-flight Information Bulletin (PIB). The WAFC provides various types of data, including OPMET information, T4 charts (which are obsolete but some portions are still distributed for legacy reasons), and GRIB and BUFR charts - these are Wind and Temperature charts and SIGWX charts (Significant Weather Chart) for SWH (high levels) and SWM (medium levels).

There are only two World Area Forecast Centres, each providing a backup for the other. These are the UK Met Office and Washington NOAA, working in duplicate so they can replace each other if one fails. Each of these two services operates its own satellite-based broadcast system to distribute data to airports all over the world. The UK Met Office is called SADIS (SAtellite DIstribution System) and mainly covers Europe, Asia, Indian Ocean and Africa. The U.S. NOAA broadcast system is ISCS (International Satellite Communications System) and mainly covers America and the Pacific Ocean.

Meteorological Offices provide aerodrome forecasts and briefing documents. *Meteorological Watch Offices* provide SIGMETs and AIRMETs*. *Aeronautical Meteorological Stations* observe pressure and temperature changes between land and sea based stations and provide METARs and MET reports. *Volcanic Ash Advisory Centres* give advice about volcanic ash.

*Area forecasts for low level flights exchanged between met offices for AIRMETs are in a standard format called a GAMET forecast when issued in plain language.

The World Meteorological Organisation (WMO) is a specialised agency of the United Nations, being their authoritative voice on the state and behaviour of the Earth's atmosphere, its interaction with the oceans, the climate it produces and the resulting distribution of water resources. It originated from the International Meteorological Organization (IMO), which was founded in 1873. Established in 1950, the WMO became the specialized agency of the United Nations in 1951 for meteorology (weather and climate), operational hydrology and related geophysical sciences. Its chief role is to establish and implement (with ICAO) a global regulatory framework for the national meteorological services.

Area Forecast

This covers several hundred square miles. Cloud bases are reported above sea level.

SIGMET

Warnings of dangerous meteorological conditions for all aircraft in the FIR, 60 minutes' flying time ahead. The normal life is 4 hours, before they must be cancelled or amended. Volcanic ash warnings last for 12 hours.

A SIGMET may be triggered by a special air report, and prepared by a **meteorological watch office**. Examples would be severe mountain waves, heavy dust storms or thunderstorm lines. A Convective SIGMET refers to thunderstorms obscured by massive cloud layers.

AIREP

Routine reports by pilots, commencing with *UA*. *UUA* is *urgent*. AIREPs are similar to position reports, except that they also include met information, such as temperature, wind, turbulence of any category, icing and other relevant information. Section 2 contains the ETA and endurance.

Air reports should be reported as soon as practicable.

PIREP

Special air report. One is required when encountering severe turbulence and other phenomena which affect the safety of aircraft, including thunderstorms, without hail that are obscured, embedded, widespread (but not isolated CB), volcanic ash cloud, heavy dust or sand storms.

Section 1 contains a position report, including the aircraft ID, height, position and time.

AIRMET

A telephone service for people without access to charts, etc. with information in plain language for certain areas. They are valid for 8 hours, and are issued 4 times a day, with an outlook of 6 hours:

0500-1300 UTC	to 1900
1100-1900 UTC	to 0100
1700-0100 UTC	to 0700
2300-0700 UTC	to 1300

Radar & Satellite

Radar or satellite images give a good real-time overview:

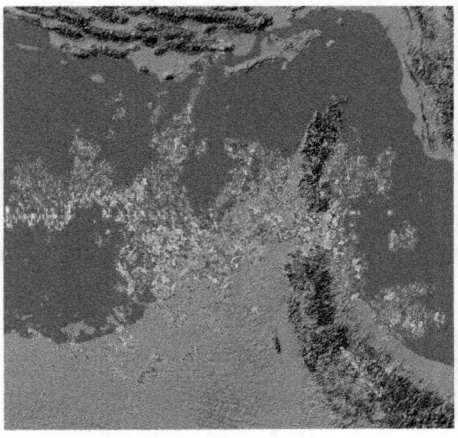

Remember that weather radar detects *raindrops* and *hail*, not cloud droplets, so you will generally only see precipitation, not clouds.

There are two main types of meteorological satellite:

- those that stay in one place (**geostationary**). The Meteosat series flies about 36,000 kilometres above the Equator, with an orbit time of exactly 24 hours, so they stay in the same place over the Earth's surface. They can take pictures every 15 or 30 minutes, but resolution is limited due to distance. The image is also distorted due to the angle from which it is taken.
- those that fly round the Earth from Pole to Pole (**Polar orbiting**). These fly 800 km above the surface, to provide higher resolution images than those from geostationary satellites. They make 14 orbits per day (around 102 minutes for each one), passing close to the Poles. Between one orbit and the next, the Earth rotates 25°, so they can take only four useful images per day of any particular place.

The main types of cloud image produced are *visible* and *infra red*, with the intention of locating fronts where there are few observation stations.

With visible images, the brightest and most reflective surfaces (ice, snow, thick cloud tops) are in shades of white, and the least reflective (land and sea) are in grey and black. Clouds, in general, appear as white objects, unless they are very thin (cirrus) or very small (less than 1 km across), when they likely won't be seen at all. Volcanic ash appears as a grey streak of cloud.

Infra red images detect heat from beyond the visible portion of the spectrum of light, and the brightness of the image depends entirely on the temperature of the radiating surface. Cold cloud tops (such as high cirrus) will appear as white, and the Earth's surface will be black.

Temperatures in between -30°C and +30°C will be in varying shades of grey.

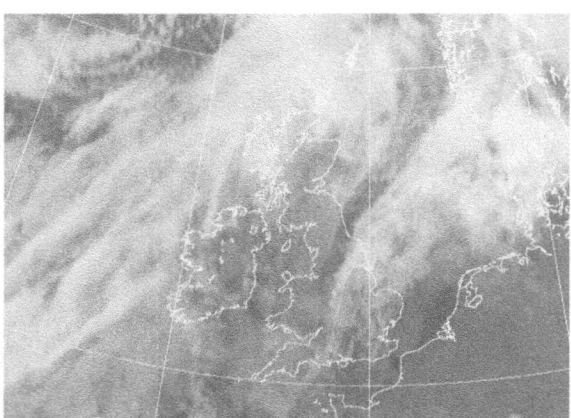

Thus, high, thick clouds will be seen on both types of image because they are both very cold and will reflect sunlight strongly.

As there is little contrast between the surface of the Earth and the tops of clouds, low clouds will be hard to detect with infra red. However, they are very reflective and will be seen best as visible images.

Satellites typically only sense the top features so, if a cloud layer is stable at lower levels and unstable aloft, for example, a surface observer would report stratiform cloud, while satellite imagery will show cumuliform. Thus, low level clouds are hard to detect.

To estimate the height of the top of cumuliform clouds using satellites, you need infra red and visual imagery.

ATIS

This is routine information for departing and arriving aircraft supplied (every 30 minutes) by a continuous and repetitive broadcast on discrete VHF frequencies and/or VOR, and possibly NDB (but not ILS) at major aerodromes. The *Automatic Terminal Information Service* reduces congestion on VHF frequencies, because it saves ATC saying the same stuff over and over, although they will still give you the QNH anyway. You should listen to it and take down the details before you contact ATC, inbound or outbound. On first contact with ATC, you should state the version you have received, such as "Information Golf", or whatever. ATIS broadcasts should be updated whenever a significant change occurs, and should not last over 30 seconds.

These are the items transmitted in the correct order:

- ATIS ID
- Time (24 hour clock)
- Wind Velocity (Degrees/Knots)
- Visibility (Metres)
- Low Cloud (oktas/feet)
- Medium Cloud (oktas/feet)
- High Cloud (oktas/feet)
- Temp/Dew Point (Degrees)
- Altimeter (hPA/Inches)
- Runway in use
- Anything else useful, such as runway missing, lights out, etc.

RVRs are not included, but IRVRs may be available when approved.

CAVOK means more than 10 km visibility and no cloud below 5000 feet. TEMPO means fluctuations of less than 60 minutes' duration

Visibility less than 5 km is reported in metres, and in km above that.

VOLMET

This is usually transmitted over HF for long-distance flights (North Atlantic and Arctic for Canada), but can be found elsewhere on VHF. It consists of long readouts of TAFs and METARs* in a sequence, so if you miss the aerodrome you want, just wait for it to come round again. Many airfields have it available over the telephone.

*VOLMET (VHF) is actually the equivalent of METARs and TRENDs. VOLMET (HF) also includes TAFs.

METEOROLOGY
Met Services & Information

A VOLMET broadcast includes:
- Aerodrome identification (e.g. Heathrow)
- Surface wind
- Visibility*
- RVR (if applicable)*
- Weather
- Cloud*
- Temperature
- Dewpoint
- QNH
- Trend (if applicable)
- *Non essential words such as *surface wind, visibility* etc. are not spoken.

SNOCLO indicates that the aerodrome is unusable for takeoffs or landings due to heavy snow on runways or snow clearance.

All broadcasts are in English.

TAFs

Terminal Aerodrome Forecasts describe forecast conditions at an aerodrome for between 9 and 24 hours. The validity periods of many longer ones may not start for up to 8 hours after the time of origin, and the details only cover the last 18 hours. 9-hour TAFs are updated and re-issued every 3 hours, and 12- and 24-hour TAFs, every 6 hours, with amendments issued as and when necessary. They are not available for offshore operations, and are only issued after 2 consecutive METARS (which will look suspiciously similar - in fact, many groups in METARs are found in TAFs, but differences are noted below). Check METARs overleaf for the full reference. A TAF may be sub-divided into 2 or more self-contained parts by the abbreviation FM (from) followed by the time UTC to the nearest hour, expressed as 2 figures.

 UK TAFs do not include temperatures, so be careful with freezing levels! Neither do they show RVR, vertical visibility, QNH or dewpoint, as they are hard to forecast. A landing forecast will come from a **METAR** with **TREND** information.

 On Nov 5th 2008, the format for TAFs changed slightly, although this will not affect exam questions until CQB 15 is introduced. Essentially, some larger airfields will have a 30-hour validity, there will be a day of the month added to some time fields, and a FM (from) prefix which will provide a full time figure. AIC 47/2008 refers.

MESSAGE TYPE
TAF or TAF AMD, for *amended*. The acronym AMD will be inserted between TAF and the aerodrome identifier, and will cover the remainder of the validity period of the original forecast.

STATION IDENTIFIER
4-letter ICAO indicator for the aerodrome.

DATE AND TIME OF ISSUE
A 6-digit code, with the date as the first two, then UTC.

VALIDITY PERIOD
A METAR reports conditions at a specific time, but the TAF has the date and time of origin, followed by the start and finish times of its validity period in whole hours UTC, e.g. TAF EGLL 130600Z (date and time of issue) 0716 (validity 0700 to 1600 hours UTC), normally 9 hours.

WINDS
To the nearest 10°, in knots, True. 00000KT is calm, VRB means variable, less than 3 kts. Gusts are in 2 digits. WS means windshear, when significant, with speed and direction at a height.

HORIZONTAL VISIBILITY
Minimum visibility. RVR is not included because it is *never* forecast.

WEATHER
If no significant weather is expected, this is omitted. After a change group, however, if the weather ceases to be significant, NSW (no significant weather) will be inserted.

Refer to METARS, below, for the tables of codes.

CLOUD
Up to 4 cloud groups, in ascending order of bases, and cumulative, based on the amount of the sky covered, in eighths, or oktas **AAL**. The cloud ceiling is the height of the first layer that is broken or overcast. The first group is the lowest individual layer; the second the next of more than 2 oktas and the third the next higher of more than 4 oktas. A group has 3 letters for the amount (FEW = 1 to 2 oktas, SCT, or scattered = 3 to 4 oktas; BKN, or broken, = 5 to 7 oktas, and OVC, or overcast = 8 oktas) and 3 for the height of the cloud base in hundreds of feet above ground level. For clear sky, expect SKC. VV means vertical visibility in hundreds of feet which, if you get it at all, means an obscured ceiling, where the height of the cloudbase cannot be measured (VV/// means that vertical visibility cannot be measured). CB means thunderstorms and is added as necessary. Clouds may cover the sky, but not conceal it if transparent, hence the term opacity.

SIGNIFICANT CHANGES
In addition to FM and the time, significant changes may be indicated by BECMG (becoming) or TEMPO (temporarily). BECMG is followed by a four-figure group indicating the beginning and ending of the period when the change is expected. The change is expected to be permanent, and to occur at an unspecified time within it, over the next 2 hours. TEMPO will similarly be followed by a 4-figure time group, indicating temporary fluctuations. TEMPO conditions are expected to last less than 1 hour each time, and collectively, less than half the period indicated.

PROBABILITY
Probability of a significant change, 30 or 40%*. The abbreviation PROB will precede the percentage, followed by a time group, or a change and time group, e.g.:

    PROB 30 0507 0800FG BKN004

or

```
PROB40 TEMPO 1416 TSRA BKN010CB
```

EXAMPLE

```
EGHH 0615 VRB06KT 9999 SCT 030
```

was issued at Heathrow for 0600-1500, with variable wind at 6 kts, visibility more than 10 km and 3-4 oktas of cloud at 3000 above the airfield elevation.

*In the real world (inside Company Operations Manuals) PROB 30 usually means Captain's discretion, and PROB 40 means you should assume the information to be valid.

EASA-SPEAK

The words *Most Likely* mean that you can discount TEMPOs. *lowest Forecast* or *lowest Expected* means include them. *Forecast, Expected, Anticipated* mean consider BECMGs and TEMPOs.

METARs

These are *Aviation Routine Weather Reports* that detail the weather *observed* at a station, compiled half-hourly (+20 or +50), and valid at the time of observation, not for any particular time period. The minimum interval is 20 minutes, but should not be more than an hour. At major airports, observations are made through the day and night - at minor airports, only during opening hours.

The METAR reports the prevailing weather over the ten minutes before the message was transmitted. Elements of the report are separated with spaces, except temperature and dewpoint which use /. Missing items have the preceding space and that element omitted, so you need to know the sequence to realise what has been left out.

METARS are reports, not forecasts, but you may see an outlook tagged on the end after the word TREND, representing a 2-hour period from the time of the observation. For example, NOSIG means no significant changes expected in the next 2 hours.

 Although similar to a METAR, the wind information in a **MET Report** refers to the **2 minute mean value** in the touchdown zone and the visibility information mainly concerns the approach sector. As well, a SPECI is made when the weather passes a significant limit between two normal reporting times. *A METAR would update the ATIS when a SPECI is issued.*

MESSAGE TYPE

METAR means a routine actual weather report. **SPECI** means a significant change off the hour (i.e between normal reporting times), normally because the weather has changed significantly since the last report. The METAR format is used.

STATION IDENTIFIER

The 4-letter ICAO indicator for the aerodrome.

DATE/TIME

Date and time of the observation. 6 numbers followed by Z, e.g. 231020Z = 23rd day, 1020 UTC clock time.

AUTOMATIC OBSERVATION

AUTO is inserted where the METAR contains fully automated observations with no human intervention. AUTO METARs are only disseminated when the aerodrome is closed or, at H24 aerodromes, when the meteorological observer is on a break.

Reports of visibility, present weather and cloud should therefore be treated with caution due to the limitations of the systems involved.

WINDS

5 numbers followed by the speed units used (KT, MPS or KPH), representing the mean heading and wind speed over the **immediately previous 10 minutes**. The first three numbers are the direction to the nearest 10° (**True**) and the next two the speed. If the wind direction changes by more than 60°, and the speed is over 3 kts, the extreme directions are given with the letter V in between them.

G before the speed reading means *Gusts*, when the average reading is exceeded by 10 kts (the maximum reading is given). 00000KT is calm, VRB is variable, less than 3 kts.

If it is gusting, the value is reported after the speed of the steady state wind, and if the wind is variable, the range in degrees is also reported.

A squall is an increment of at least 16 kts to a uniform speed of at least 22 kts, measured over a minute.

HORIZONTAL VISIBILITY

The minimum is in metres, followed by one of the eight points of the compass if there is a difference in visibility by direction, as with 4000 NE. If the minimum visibility is between 1500-5000 m in another direction, minimum and maximum values, and directions will be given, e.g. 1400SW 6000N. 9999 means 10 km or more, while 0000 means less than 50 m.

```
EGZZ 231020Z 02006KT 4000 0900NE
R27/0600U R32/0150D PRFG OVC007
12/11 Q1028
```

In the example above, 4000 is the prevailing visibility, which is the best figure that can be applied to at least 50% of the horizon (contiguously or otherwise), so if the visibility varies from 8 km down to 4000 m for at least half of the visible horizon, the prevailing vis is 4000 m.

If the visibility in a particular direction is less than 1500 m or is less than half of the prevailing figure, the lowest visibility observed (900 m above) is reported, with the direction (NE - NDV means *No Directional Variation* of visibility sensors). If the lowest value applies in several directions, the most operationally significant one is given. If the visibility is fluctuating wildly (such as with a rapid shower transition), only the lowest visibility is reported.

RUNWAY VISUAL RANGE (RVR)

RVR figures are assessed when the visibility gets below 1500m. If the touchdown visibility is less than 400m, all three parts of the runway are reported. Between 400-800m, the mid- and endpoints are only given if they are less than the touchdown zone. Above 800 m you only get them if they are lower than 800 m.

An RVR group has the prefix R followed by the runway designator, then an oblique stroke followed by the touch-down RVR in metres. If RVR is assessed simultaneously on two or more runways, it will be repeated; parallel runways are distinguished by L, C or R, for Left, Central or Right parallel respectively, e.g. R24L/1100 R24R/1150.

When the RVR is more than 1500m or the maximum that can be assessed, the group will be preceded by P, followed by the lesser value, e.g. R24/P1500. When less than the minimum, the RVR will be reported as M followed by the minimum value, e.g. R24/M0050.

PRESENT WEATHER

Any precipitation. A minus (-) means light, no sign is moderate, and + means heavy. **VC** means within 8 km, i.e. in the vicinity. It is described as per the tables below and you can blame the French for the illogical abbreviations (BR for Mist = Brille).

DESCRIPTORS

Symbol	Description
MI	Shallow
BC	Patches
BL	Blowing
SH	Showers
TS	Thunderstorm
FZ	Freezing (Supercooled)
PL	Partial (Part of the aerodrome)

OTHER

Symbol	Description
PO	Dust/Sand Whirls (Dust Devils)
SQ	Squall
FC	Funnel Clouds (Tornado/Waterspout)
SS	Sandstorm
DS	Dust Storm

PRECIPITATION

Symbol	Description
DZ	Drizzle
RA	Rain
SN	Snow
SG	Snow Grains
IC	Ice Crystals (Diamond Dust)
PL	Ice Pellets
GR	Hail
GS	Small Hail

OBSCURATION

Not shown if the visibility is below 5 000 m.

Symbol	Description
BR	Mist
FG	Fog
FU	Smoke
VA	Volcanic Ash
DU	Widespread Dust
SA	Sand
HZ	Haze

The abbreviation UP indicates when it has not been possible to identify precipitation using automatic observation. REUP should indicate that the automatic system has been unable to identify a recent precipitation.

CLOUD

Cloud bases in METARs are reported in steps of 100 feet up to 10 000 feet, and steps of 1 000 feet above that.

Up to 4 cloud groups may be included, in ascending order of bases. A group has 3 letters for the amount:

- **FEW** = 1 to 2 oktas
- **SCT**, or scattered = 3 to 4 oktas
- **BKN**, or broken = 5 to 7 oktas
- **OVC**, or overcast = 8 oktas)
- **SKC** = Sky Clear

There are also 3 for the height of the cloud base in hundreds of feet above ground level.

Apart from significant convective clouds (CB) cloud types are ignored. Cloud layers or masses are reported so the first group represents the lowest individual layer; the second is the next individual layer of more than 2 oktas; the third is the next higher layer of more than 4 oktas, and the additional group, if any, represents significant convective cloud, if not already reported, e.g.:

    SCT010 SCT015 SCT018CB BKN025

The cloud ceiling is the height above the aerodrome of the lowest layer of cloud that is more than 4 oktas in extent.

The symbol /// means that the automated station cannot detect the type of cloud group at this level. ////// is used in front of CB (or TCU) where the automatic system has detected a CB (or TCU) and where the coverage (or height) of these clouds has not been measured. With an automated system, NCD is used in place of the cloud code when none has been detected and the absence of CB or TCU cannot be detected. On the other hand, NSC means that the system can detect their absence.

CAVOK AND SKC

CAVOK replaces visibility, RVR, weather and cloud groups when visibility is 10 km or more, there is no cloud below 5000' or the highest MSA, whichever is greater, with no precipitation, thunderstorm, shallow fog or low, drifting snow. Otherwise, the cloud group is replaced by SKC (sky clear) if there is no cloud report. CAVOK is not used in Canada.

 Towering Cumulus Clouds (TCU) are regarded as significant so, if they are present, CAVOK cannot be reported.

AIR TEMPERATURE AND DEWPOINT

Rounded up to the nearest °C, separated by /. A negative value is indicated by an M in front of the appropriate digits, e.g. M10/03. A small spread between the two temperatures means that fog is more likely to form.

PRESSURE SETTING

QNH (or the **altimeter setting** in the US and Canada) is rounded down to the next whole number and reported as a 4-figure group preceded by Q. If less than 1000 hPa, the first digit will be 0, e.g. Q0993.

QNH is the **QFE*** (**station pressure**) reduced to MSL under ISA conditions**. Although the met office would correct for temperature and pressure, for our purposes, only pressure is used, at 27 feet per hPa at sea level through to 50 feet at 18,500 feet (if you want to include temperature, use the average below the aircraft).

*An altimeter set to QFE reads zero on the ground (being pedantic, the height of the altimeter above ground). If the airfield is below sea level, the QFE would be greater than the QNH, instead of the other way round.

**QFF is similar to QNH, but using isothermal conditions, i.e. the mean temperature of the column of air below the airfield. In cold and dense air, pressure changes more rapidly, so QFF will be more than QNH. In ISA conditions, QNH and QFF will be the same. Above MSL, if the temperature is greater than ISA, QNH will be greater than QFF, and vice versa. Below MSL, this is reversed.

If the QFF at an airfield 500 ft **above** sea level is 1004 hPa, in ISA +5°C conditions, the QNH will be more than 1004 hPa and the altimeter will read less than zero on landing (the column of air for the QNH is longer).

If the airfield is at sea level, i.e. zero feet, QFF will be the same as QNH anyway. Isobars are lines of equal QFF.

RECENT WEATHER

Significant weather after the previous observation, but not currently relevant, will be reported with the standard present weather code preceded by RE, e.g. RETS.

WINDSHEAR

Included if windshear is reported in the lowest 1600 feet, beginning with WS: WS TKOF RWY20.

RUNWAY STATE

For snow or other contamination, an 8-figure group may be added at the end:

1st 2 digits	Runway Designator
3rd Digit	Runway Deposits
4th Digit	Extent of Contamination
5th & 6th Digits	Depth Of Deposit
7th & 8th Digits	Friction Coefficient or Braking Action

TREND

For when significant changes are forecast during the next 2 hours or between the stated times.

- **BECMG** (Becoming) means a permanent change, and takes priority over.....
- **TEMPO**, which means a temporary change within the 2 hour period, if a single occurrence will last less than half the time period (i.e. not more than 59.999 minutes for a normal METAR). The sum of a number of occurrences must be less than half the time period.

BECMG or TEMPO may be followed by a time group (in hours and minutes UTC) preceded by FM (from), TL (until) or AT (at). These are followed by the expected change using the standard codes, e.g. BECMG FM 1100 250/35G50KT or TEMPO FM 0630 TL0830 3000 SHRA. Where no such significant changes are expected, the trend group will be replaced by NOSIG.

 A METAR with a TREND in the end will take priority over any forecast in the TAF, in that first 2 hour period that the TREND is valid for.

DENEB

Fog dispersal is in progress.

CHARTS

Weather information is issued in many ways, including the charts mentioned below. Those showing *expected* patterns are *prognosis* charts, but you can bet they won't be anything like what you see when you get there.

As the weather map tries to be a simple representation of weather that pilots can understand, it will not show all the weather that might affect your flight, particularly any local variations - for example, you will have to guesstimate many surface winds based on isobar spacing and the application of friction effects. For best results, they should be used in conjunction with TAFs and/or METARs.

Reported cloud bases are within 500 feet and fronts can be up to 95 nm away from their reported position.

All charts show expected conditions anyway!

FORM 214

This is a *spot wind chart* from the Met Office that shows you the winds you can expect at selected heights, *for a particular time*, so you will need to correlate its information with that on Form 215 (overleaf) to see how movement of pressure systems might change the winds for when you want to fly. Boxes are placed on certain intersections of latitude and longitude, with wind direction, speed and temperature between 1000-24000'.

The location of each wind box is shown at the top. The column on the left is the altitude in thousands of feet, the second the wind direction in °T, then the wind speed in knots, followed by the temperature in °C, which can give you important information as to atmospheric stability and other conditions.

```
57N 0230E
24 320 60 -35
18 310 45 -21
10 310 25 -08
05 310 20 +01
02 310 20 +07
01 300 20 +09
```

If the temperatures are dropping rapidly, for example, you can expect good visibility, as long as there are no fronts around, which is characteristic of an unstable atmosphere and a steep lapse rate (see *Stability*).

The less steep the lapse rate, the poorer the visibility. Thus, if you get an increase in temperature with altitude at lower levels, followed by a steep decrease, you can expect any early morning mist or fog to clear relatively quickly. Check the wind vectors to see how high the inversion might be, since wind direction usually changes significantly above them. Flight above that point will be in clearer weather.

For answers to exam questions, interpolate between the boxes and the figures in them, as you can guarantee that the level given will not coincide with any in it! For real world flight planning, as a gross error check, take the present wind, add 30°, double the speed and subtract 10% to see how the results compare against the 2000 ft wind. If they are wildly different, don't trust the chart!

FORM 215

The *Significant Weather Chart* (see below) is a low level forecast for the next 6 hours, graphically represented, so you can more easily detect CAT regions and jetstreams (well separated CBs are described as OCNL CB).

This chart provides information about icing - in the example below, the freezing level is given in the right hand column.

Scalloped lines do *not* represent cloud!

Upper Level Charts

These are also prognosis or analysis charts, but based on a particular pressure level*, so the real altitude represented will vary a great deal (they will be lower as you go North, because it gets colder there). The charts are based on the relationship between winds and temperature, in that a height of a pressure surface will increase as it gets warmer and *vice versa* (the same principle as with altimeter errors). The point of such charts is that they do not depend on air density, like isobar charts do.

*Pilots refer to heights - meteorologists refer to pressure levels because they work with physical interactions based on temperature, pressure and density (height is a man-made property that requires measurement). The height of a constant pressure surface varies with air density below.

Here are the approximate heights the charts represent:

hPa	FL	Purpose
200	FL 390	Summer jetstreams
250	FL 340	
300	FL 300	Winter jetstreams
400	FL 240	
500	FL 180**	Mid clouds
700	FL 100	Mid clouds
850	FL 50	Low level winds minimal friction

**18,000 feet is about halfway up the atmosphere in terms of pressure, meaning that near the midpoint of the troposphere, so 500 hPa charts give a good average view of what's going on. In fact, they show the broad scale of events at the higher levels, but some of the lower storm systems can also be visible. Forecasts are produced at six hourly intervals from 0000 UTC.

The difference in height between two pressure levels is called *thickness*, and a chart on which the same thickness values of a given layer are plotted is a *thickness chart*.

There is a mean temperature for any layer of the atmosphere. As the Earth's surface has varying temperatures, there will be corresponding differences in the **mean** temperatures of a layer of air covering a large area. These determine the PGF and hence the wind velocity in the upper levels. The greatest horizontal gradients occur at the boundaries between cold and warm air masses. Isotherms can represent the Thermal Wind Component, or TWC.

The chart will represent average temperatures in the layer, and will show where the regions of relatively cold and warm air lie. A centre of low thickness and therefore low mean temperature is known as a **cold pool**.

There is also a relationship between the thermal wind and thickness lines. It blows parallel to them and, in the Northern Hemisphere, the greater thickness lies to the right (to the left in the Southern Hemisphere).

Upper level features tend to lag behind those on the surface - that is, an upper trough associated with a surface front would lie further to the West. Winds will also tend to increase with height.

Because pressure in the upper levels is dependent on the mean temperature of a given column of air; a low mean temperature through a column of air in the troposphere produces low pressure aloft, and a high mean temperature produces a high, resulting in a pressure gradient high up in the atmosphere, where air will flow. You only need to know the temperature up high to get a good approximation of the wind, although they are generally Westerly anyway.

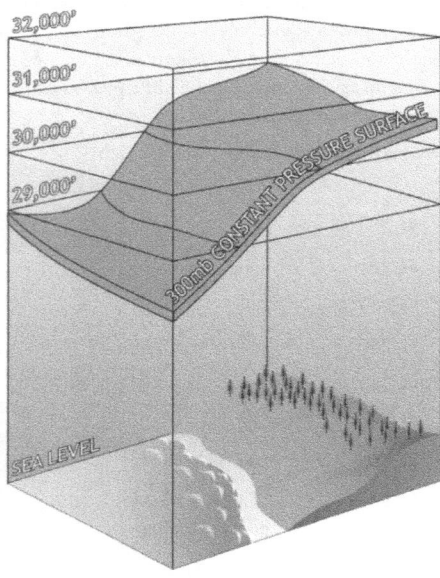

In other words, once a pressure level is high because of the air temperature, there will be a gradient between it and colder air, which will be lower - air will flow from high to low pressure, but the root cause will be temperature. Eventually, geostrophic force will make the wind veer to the right, to blow parallel to the imaginary isobars.

For example, if you are flying from a low pressure to a high pressure at a constant pressure level of 500 hPa, you will be at a higher true altitude in the high pressure area, although you have a constant *indicated* altitude. If true altitude is greater than indicated altitude, the air is warmer than ISA. If it is less than indicated altitude, the air is colder than ISA. The values used are direction relative to True North and speed in knots.

Windspeed is inversely proportional to density, so, as density decreases with altitude, windspeed will increase.

Buys Ballot's Law is still good - in the Northern Hemisphere with your back to the wind, the cold air will be to the left and the thermal wind will blow parallel to the isotherms, with low temperatures to the left. Speed will be inversely proportional to the distance between the isotherms, meaning that the strength of the wind will depend on how steep the slope is.

For example, two points with the same surface pressure of 998 hPa are 200 nm apart in the Northern Hemisphere. The mean temperature between the surface and 20,000 feet at A is -2°C and -10°C at B, to the South. What is the wind velocity at 20,000 feet halfway between A and B?

As the mean temperature changes by 8°C, the temperature gradient is 4°C/100 nm. The height of the layer is 20,000 feet, so the wind speed at that level is 80 kts (4 x 20). Since the points are N-S with respect to each other, Buys Ballot's law gives you an Easterly wind, or 090/80. As both points have the same surface pressure, there is no geostrophic wind at the surface, otherwise you would have to add it to the thermal wind to get the upper wind (just draw a diagram).

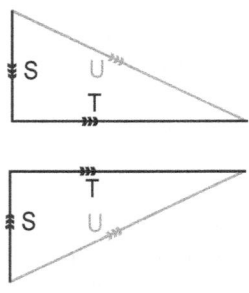

Isotherms of mean temperature are roughly parallel to lines of latitude, and the average thermal wind is Westerly outside the tropics. From this information, you can deduce the direction of the surface or upper wind, depending on which one you know already. For example, if the surface wind is Northerly, and the thermal wind is Westerly, the upper wind will be backed in relation to the surface wind (left, top). Similarly, a Southerly surface wind will veer to the thermal (bottom).

 The "thermal" wind does not flow independently of the pressure or contour gradients. It is just a name given to the vertical shear of the actual wind.

Westerly winds will increase their speed but keep their direction, while Easterly winds will decrease in speed, then veer or back to become light Westerly. In the tropics (between 0-20°), winds up to 40,000 feet will be Easterly.

*Although the contours look the same as isobars, and the wind will behave the same way, remember the surface chart is based on sea level pressure, and the ones here show the *altitude* of the pressure level, so a Low really is lower than a High, instead of indicating an area of rising air, as it would on a sea level chart. Also, there will be lines joining points of equal temperature (isotherms) and windspeed (isotachs), which are both dotted and easy to confuse with each other. *High level winds are the sum of the vectors of the low-level winds and thermal components.* Buys Ballot's law applies with temperature as well, except that you stand with your back to the thermal component, and closely spaced isobars still mean a high gradient and hence stronger winds (look for jetstreams around closely spaced isotherms and isotachs).

The height of any contour line depend on the surface pressure and the mean temperature of the air between the line and mean sea level. In practice, they follow isotherms (lines joining points of equal temperature) very closely. Contours can be used to assess likely upper wind speeds. Just as the spacing of isobars governs the wind speed, so does the contour spacing (contour gradient) on upper charts. Using an appropriate scale, upper wind speeds can be measured from the contour spacing, the direction being parallel to the contour lines. Winds are assumed to flow with low contour heights to the left in the Northern hemisphere and to the right in the Southern hemisphere.

Closely spaced and sharply curving contours, as found around upper troughs (low contour heights) or ridges (high contour height) indicate likely jet stream activity and associated areas of clear air turbulence.

You can detect CAT by comparing charts for vertical windshear gradient over 6 kts per 1,000 feet, and horizontal shear over 40 kts per 150 miles. Areas with strongly curved and closely packed isohypses, in particular, will produce moderate to severe CAT.

While an isobar connects points of equal barometric pressure normalized to sea level, an *isohypse* connects points of equal geopotential height (they are also called *height contours*). As well, isobars are plotted only on surface charts while isohypses are found on upper air charts. An isohypse, or *height contour*, represents the distance from zero geopotential meters (at about sea level) to the pressure level of interest (in decameters). Its value depends on the average temperature and moisture content of the air underneath.

Low isohypse values indicate colder air (troughs) while high isohypse values (ridges) indicate warmer air. Moisture has a minor effect on height as compared to temperature - moist air will have a little higher isohypse value than dry air at the same temperature because moist air is less dense. If an *isohypse* of the 500 hPa pressure surface is labelled as 552, it means that for all connected points, topography is 552 decameters above MSL.

The relevance of upper level charts is that they give you a better idea of the real movement of air masses and the sort of weather coming your way. Although the winds follow the contours, remember that the 500 and 850 hPa charts can often oppose each other. Upper winds are also stronger because the density is less. Half the density, say at 20,000 feet, is double the speed. Wind direction is given relative to True North, in knots. The best approximation of wind speed at FL 250 is obtained from interpolation between the 500 and 300 charts, taking into consideration the significant weather chart. Laying a temperature and humidity chart over them is helpful - if low level winds are warm and moist, expect instability and thunderstorms, particularly if upper winds are cool. If things are the other way round, expect an inversion and poor visibility (from industrial haze), albeit no clouds.

If it's very dry at higher levels, moisture will be sucked out from lower ones - with no saturation there will be no clouds, but good visibility. The idea is to get a 3D picture of what's going on upstairs - for example, the slope will always be downward, toward the colder air mass.

In the picture below, there is a ridge with a high contour height over the North Atlantic and a low contour trough over Ireland. Both are associated with warm and cold air, respectively. Contours are very close on the lower right.

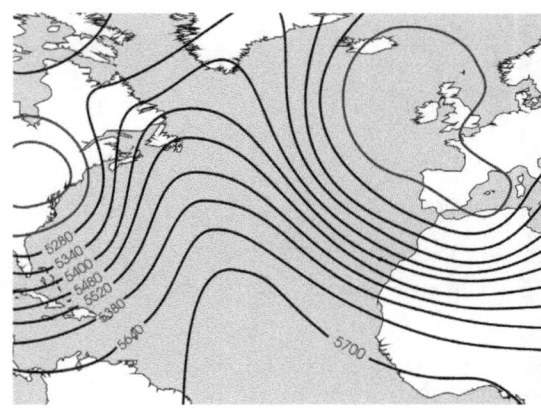

The upper winds are strongest in this area and may reach jetstream speed at higher levels. Clear air turbulence is likely where the contour direction is changing, such as South of Ireland and near to 50°N and 40°W.

ANALYSIS CHARTS

These come out at 00 and 12Z each day. The 850 hPa chart has contours at 60 m intervals, starting at 1500, with isotherms every 5°C. Fronts are usually shown in their surface position (but not shown on the 700 hPa chart).

PROGNOSTIC CHARTS

These cover between FL 100-250, based on 700-400 hPa pressure levels. They forecast moderate to severe icing, significant cloud layers, mountain waves, freezing levels at 10,000 feet and the surface position of highs and lows. Wind pennants are triangular for 50 kts.

Spot wind velocity arrows are drawn every 2½° of latitude and 5° of longitude. Temperatures are shown at each one.

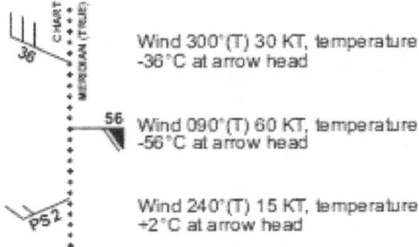

When finding the mean wind for a track, unless the winds either side are in the same direction, average the Westerly and Easterly ones, then interpolate (take the stronger one).

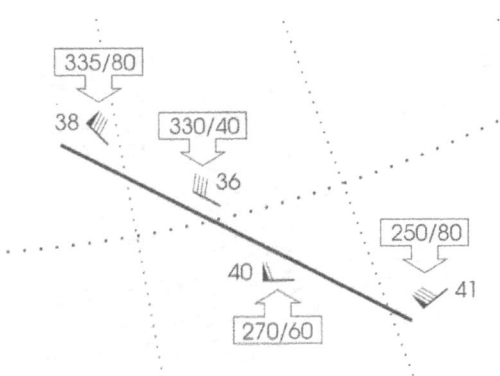

Taking the example above, we have:

335/80
330/40
270/60
250/80
―――――
1185/260

Dividing by 4, we end up with 296/65.

If the winds are hard to work with, draw a vector diagram:

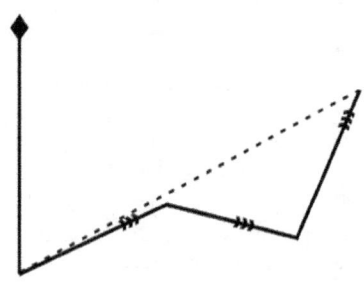

As three winds are involved, the resultant should be calculated over three hours.

MEAN TEMPERATURES
For mean temperatures, use a lapse rate of 2°C per 1000 feet. Given a temperature of, say, -35°C over a point on a 300 hPa chart, you may be asked to find the temperature at FL 320. As it happens, the 300 hPa chart equates to FL 300, so you would decrease the temperature above by 4°C, making the answer -39°C.

Weather Symbols

℟	Thunderstorm
6	Tropical Cyclone
,	Drizzle
∆	Hail
⌒	Moderate Turbulence
⌃	Severe Turbulence
○	Marked Mountain Waves
Ψ	Light Aircraft Icing
Ψ̄	Moderate Aircraft Icing
Ψ̿	Severe Aircraft Icing
∾	Freezing Precipitation
////	Rain
*	Snow
+→	Widespread Blowing Snow
∇̇	Shower
S	Severe Sand or Dust Haze
S·	Widespread sandstorm or duststorm
∞	Widespread Haze
=	Widespread Mist
≡	Widespread Fog
≣	Freezing Fog
∽	Widespread Smoke

Proper Planning Prevents Poor Performance

Well begun, half done

FLIGHT PLANNING & MONITORING   15

This may appear tedious in the early stages, but planning is actually around 75% of a trip - you're not just getting paid for the flying! The more planning you do, the more answers you will have when things go wrong and the better the trip will be conducted. Any plan you have spent time over is better than one cooked up on the spur of the moment.

If you get into a little routine, the process will become speedier as time goes by.

The flight planning exam consolidates a lot of facts from the rest of the syllabus. You will be expected to select a route and altitude based on the following criteria:

- **Airspace** you will fly through (controlled or uncontrolled). There might be several factors that affect your choice of route:
    - Routes inbound and outbound. For example, there are preferred routings within UK and Ireland going to or from oceanic waypoints for the North Atlantic routes, and many airfields have visual procedures, such as those shown on the chart for Alicante, below.
    - Restricted areas
- **Weather** (destination and alternates, including takeoff), plus enroute forecasts, weather and winds, etc., including Minima (when IFR)
- **Minimum safe altitudes,** plus the best levels for performance and comfort, and winds aloft. Can you actually fly that high?

You will also be expected to interpret ATC information (from the AIP, etc.) for departure, enroute, destination and alternates:

- Radio frequencies required
- Maps and preparation
- NOTAMs

On top of all that, a little admin:

- Fuel required
- Mass & balance
- Documents required to be carried
- Flight plans
- Aircraft serviceability
- Passenger comfort

As covered elsewhere. Note that flight planning in some companies will also include economic aspects, such as avoiding strong headwinds, ATC fees, etc.

Picture: Visual Routes At Alicante

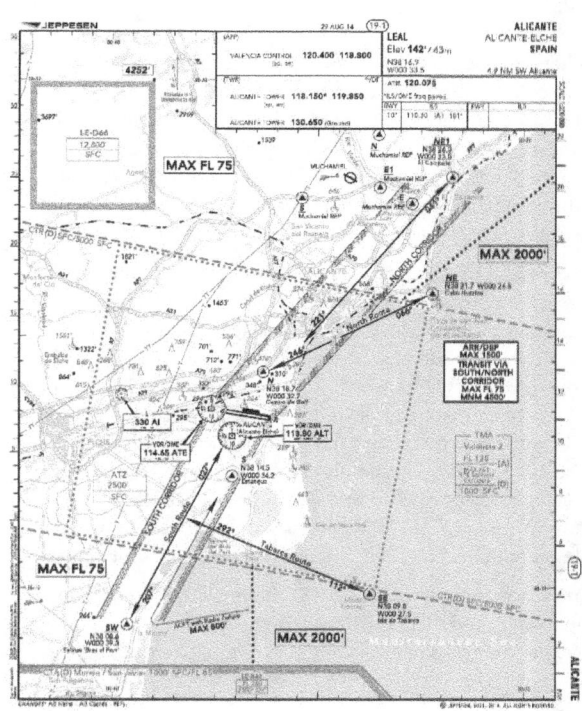

Chart reproduced with permission of Jeppesen Sanderson, Inc. NOT FOR NAVIGATIONAL USE © 2017

ATS FLIGHT PLAN

The reasons why you need a flight plan are in *Air Law*, as is what you put in it. See also *Jeppesen*, below.

EUROPEAN AIRWAYS

Depending on the distance you are going to fly, and the type of aircraft (and if there's anything wrong with it), you need to decide what type of airway to use. Very short sectors, for example, mean that there is little time to climb and descend, so a low level airway would typically be used to fly to an alternate from the original destination, even if you used a high level airway to get there.

FLIGHT PLANNING & MONITORING
Jeppesen Manual

There is a system called *City Pair Level Capping* which may impose a limit on you anyway. It states a maximum flight level between any two airports that are both in Europe. Limited details are given on Jeppesen charts and full details are in the Route (un)Availability Document on the Eurocontrol website, which contains details of all the current restrictions. One of its annexes defines the longest direct segment (i.e. off the airway structure) that can be flown between two points, in nautical miles, and which transition waypoints can be used at which airfields.

Generally, such RAD restrictions only apply to the direction specified. If they apply both ways, the other will be on a separate line. *Inclusive* restrictions mean that *all* the conditions must be met before a restriction applies. *Exclusive* restrictions apply when *any* of the conditions are met. The third type of restriction is *mandatory*. Often a restriction is there merely to stop creative flight planning.

As to whether an airway is high level or not is down to the individual country. In the UK, for example, high level airspace starts at FL195, as it does over most of Europe. However, in the past, there were different levels, with upper airspace starting at FL245 in the UK and FL285 in Sweden. The up to date values are on the aeronautical chart and, for exam questions the figure on the relevant chart should be used.

The Flexible Use of Airspace concept allows civil and military traffic to share airways at different times of the day. Jeppesen charts annotate airways with a conditional status by using the acronym CDR. The numbers 12 next to an airway designator means that it can be CDR1 or CDR2 according to conditions in the AIP. You can plan to use a CDR1 airway as a normal one during the published times, and filing the flight plan will activate it. On the other hand, you can only use CDR2 airways when they have been specifically opened in the Conditional Route Availability Message (CRAM), which is published daily and available through the Network Operations Portal at Eurocontrol.

CDR3 routes are only available on ATC instructions. You cannot therefore plan to use them in advance and should not be mentioned in the flight plan.

Radios

In Europe, two VHF radios with 8.33 KHz channel spacing are required above FL 195, or FL 245 if the State concerned has not implemented the lower level.

This equipment is signified by using the letter Y in item 10 of the ICAO flight plan form.

JEPPESEN MANUAL

To fly on airways and to get in and out of airfields safely, you need relevant and up to date information. There are many companies producing it, but Jeppesens (see right) are used in the EASA exam.

As there is little point in reproducing the information it contains here, the Jeppesen manual should be studied carefully, as most answers are in it. This especially means page 57 in the Introduction section for the symbols used on the charts. The VFR section at the back is for helicopter pilots - mostly involving Aberdeen.

 The student book is just that - for exam purposes only! **The charts are way out of date and must not be used for real navigation situations!**

 No pages are missing in the table of contents - as only pages relevant to the exams are used, and the original page numbers are retained, there are gaps. For example, the *Chart Glossary* runs from 1-14, and the next page is 41, *Abbreviations*.

Charts

Jeppesen en-route charts use the Lambert Projection, because the great circle routes taken by radio waves are pretty much straight lines, so you can plot bearings easily. They use code letters for the areas of the world covered, letters for the altitude, and a number relevant to the chart, such as E(LO)1A, for Europe, low level, number 1A in the series (see below).

The materials in the Jeppesen can be categorised as:

- **Enroute charts**, high or low altitude. The dividing line between the two varies, but is usually 17,999 feet. Because the concentration of navigation aids varies, enroute charts can use different scales. One inch may therefore mean either 5 or 10 minutes' flying time, depending on the chart.

- **Terminal charts**, such as approach charts, SIDs & STARs. The letter *T* next to the frequency of a facility indicates that it is for terminal use only.

Changes take place in line with ICAO recommendations, that is, with at least 42 days' advance notice, being effective from 0901Z on day 1 of a 28-day cycle, which is always a Thursday (see the effective date on the chart).

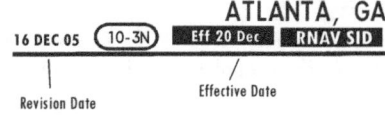

Each time a Jeppesen chart is revised, the change that caused the revision is noted at the bottom left of an instrument approach chart, or on the front page of an enroute chart.

Airways shown on charts are based on the positions of navigation aids such as VOR* or ADF, and the magnetic tracks between them are shown, as are the distances. You need clearance to fly on airways, and an instrument rating.

 *These are called Victor Airways in Canada, which have a number that is preceded by the letter V. ADF airways may use A, B, G or R. Hi level airways based on NDBs use the letter J for *Jet*.

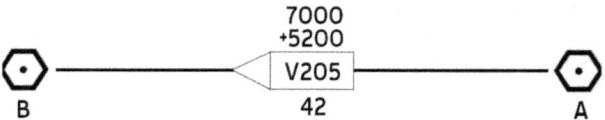

Also, in Canada, LO charts may also show air routes, which are similar to airways, but uncontrolled. They are established as an extra protection for aircraft that would otherwise have none, or for convenience.

LOW LEVEL IFR CHARTS

LO charts are used for enroute navigation within low level airspace, generally below 18,000 feet.

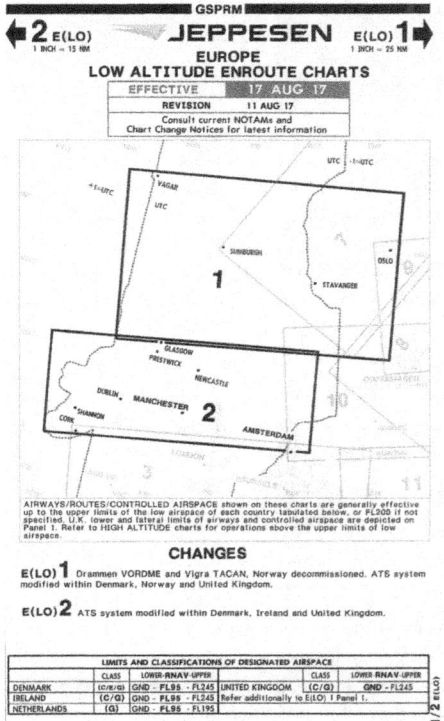

The box on the front of the chart shows a map of UK and part of Europe with smaller boxes covering separate areas and code numbers for the charts involved, so if you were going to Prestwick, you would use E(LO)2 (8 airfields are named inside the highlighted box). Classes of designated airspace are at the bottom of the page, with revision data (what's been changed) above.

Communications are shown on a panel on the back of the folded chart, or on the chart itself.

The top line gives the airfield name, country and ICAO identifier, to the right of which is a chart code. The lower line gives the identifying name in light text and the radio callsign in bold text with the frequency. An asterisk means that the airfield operates part time.

 Chart extracts reproduced with permission of Jeppesen Sanderson, Inc. NOT FOR NAVIGATIONAL USE © Jeppesen Sanderson, Inc. [2017].

At the top of the chart itself in the left hand corner is:

2 SUMBURGH/ABERDEEN

This refers to one of the place names on the front panel of the chart, plus the panel number, in this case panel 2.

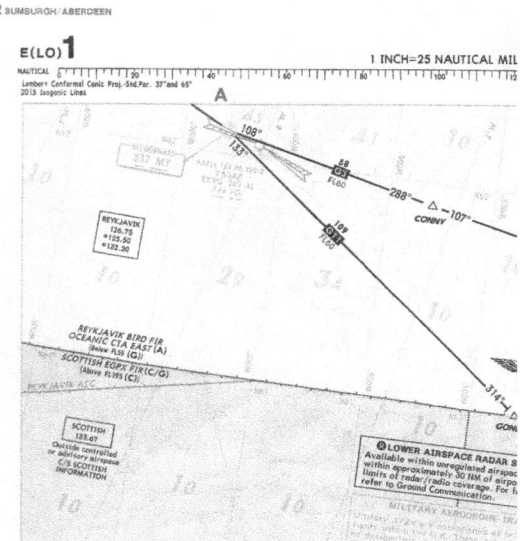

Other place names can be found along the top of the chart when it is fully opened, after their panel numbers.

Underneath the scale at the top, the letters A and B are repeated, and the letters C & D along the bottom. With a panel number, they provide a quick reference for finding the airfields on the front panel. Using Sumburgh, the chart code is p2B, or panel 2 and the top left panel, B.

IFR CHART SYMBOLS

Above is a representation of a typical Jeppesen IFR chart. You don't need to memorise the symbols, as that information is included in the Jeppesen manual - just remember where to find it (page 57!)

Tip: On high level charts, VORs and NDBs both use small circles to indicate their position (the VOR has a dot in the middle) - otherwise, the only way you can tell the difference between them is by looking at the frequency.

Airways are shown as bold blue lines, with magnetic radials, except in the Northern Domestic Airspace of Canada, where they are True (look for the letter T). The white space on either side of the line is the airway boundary and the rest of the chart has a blue tint so you can see it clearly. The airway designator is marked in a rectangle (e.g. B4). An open triangle is an on-request reporting point - a compulsory one is solid.

The directions between navigation aids are written right next to them. The shadow on the navigation aid box (TFN in the picture) indicates an enroute navaid and its location with respect to the box.

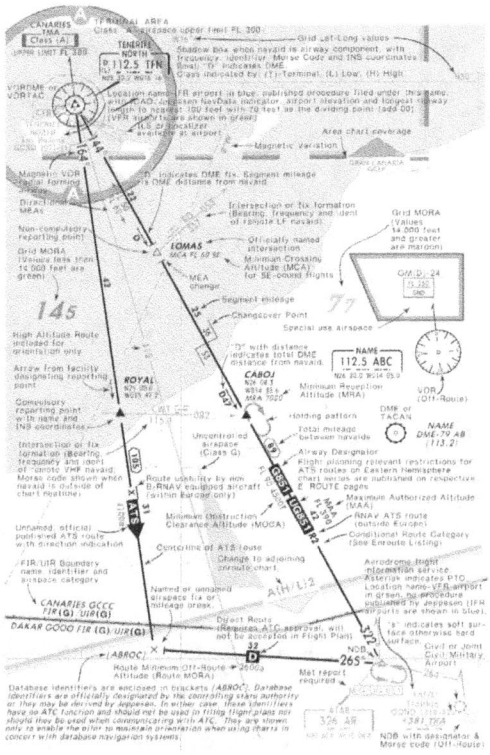

A complete flight will be broken down into legs, which are usually straight lines flown between waypoints. When using the FMS, the whole route is entered as a series of legs, with no breaks between them (you can select various types of leg from a menu). The distance between waypoints is shown as a small numerical figure.

An airway with either an **E>** or an **O>** symbol (such as N864 in the picture) shows that it does not comply with the semi-circular rule and indicates the flight level to be flown in the direction of the arrow. Thus, although the airway direction of 005°(M) would normally indicate an odd FL, in this case you would choose an even one, and vice versa.

HIGH LEVEL CHARTS

High level airways are shown on HI charts (all flight in high level airspace is IFR). There are 2 versions of chart number 4. Only the one labelled *To be used for ATPL and CPL requirements* should be used.

ED-4 & ED-6 6 VFR CHART

One chart used for VFR planning is the **ED-6**, covering part of Germany. The other is the ED-4 (extract shown overleaf). Both have a nominal scale of 1:500,000*. Elevations are given in feet with the highest (12,028 ft) at N47°07.4 E012°20.8.

```
SCALE - MASS-STAB         KILOMETERS    km
     1 : 500.000          NAUTICAL MILES NM
True scale - wahrer Mass-Stab
   at 48° N  1 : 515.000  STATUTE MILES  SM
```

Use the scale on the bottom of the chart - the actual scale of he ED-6 is 515,000 (503,000 for the ED-4) so there would be a 3 nm difference if you used a direct reading from a ruler from (for example) Regensburg aerodrome (49°08 N 012° 05E) to the one at Gerstetten (48°37N 010°01E). This is because the standard parallels at 37°N and 65°N are too far apart at 28° so the chart is almost at maximum distortion. You can also use the latitude figures at the side of the map.

The large red number in the centre of each half degree of latitude and longitude square is the *Minimum Grid Area Altitude* (MGAA). It provides for clearance from the highest obstacle in the grid square of:

- 1,000 ft to obstructions of 5,000 ft and below.
- 2,000 ft to obstructions above 5,000 ft.

For CAA UK charts, the large grid number is the highest obstacle elevation within the grid square to which the appropriate clearance value should be added to obtain the MSA. If an accurate en-route MSA is required, the elevation of the highest obstacle within 10 nm of the planned track should be used and the appropriate clearance added.

Tip: Mark points on the map with a pointed object such as a pencil - this saves you working out the lat/long figures all the time.

Some authorities (e.g. the UK) do not allow the use of pointy labels.

Otherwise, the information you need for the exam will be found around the sides (on the back of the ED-4), because the map is not officially part of the Jeppesen manual (it is there for convenience). For example, ATIS frequencies are shown in a small map at the bottom left (WX means VOLMET). All navigation aids are listed down the right hand side (or on the back).

AIRFIELD BLOCK

Each airfield has essential information next to it:

```
      EDRO
   Schweighofen
    492'  - 620m
    Info 123.00
```

FLIGHT PLANNING & MONITORING
Jeppesen Manual

The airfield designator is at the top (military airfields start with ET), then the name, the airfield elevation and length of the main runway and the main frequency.

Control Frequencies

The small black circles can be referred to a small table for control frequencies and airspace designators:

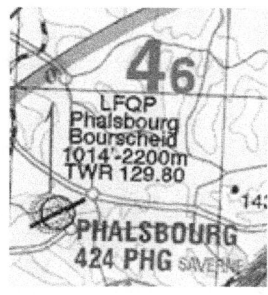

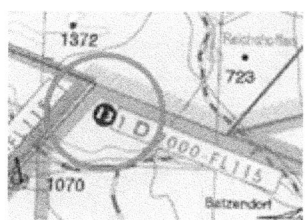

Minimum Altitudes

MINIMUM OBSTACLE CLEARANCE ALTITUDE

This is the lowest published altitude that meets the obstacle clearance requirements for route segments between radio fixes on airways, off-airway routes or route segments. It is meant to cover for the decreasing accuracy of navigation aids as you fly away from them. On a Jeppesen chart, it appears with a T suffix, as in **3500T**.

MOCA is the sum of:

- The elevation of the highest obstacle en route, between waypoints or navaids, plus
- An appropriate altitude increment from the table below, rounded up to the next 100 ft, plus
- Any additional requirements.

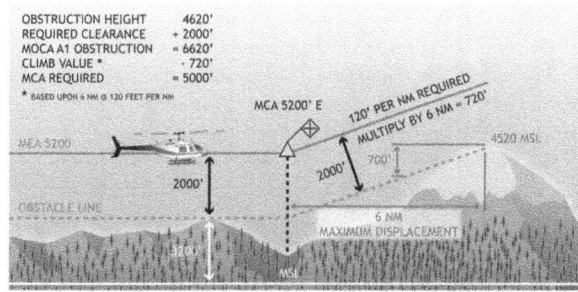

Picture Above: How MOCA is determined

MOCA Corridor		Altitude Increment	
Segment Length	Distance from track	Below 5000 ft	Above 5000 ft
Up to 100 nm	10 nm	1000 ft, to next 100 ft	2000 ft, to next 100 ft

MAXIMUM ELEVATION FIGURES (MEF)

These give the elevation of the highest known obstacle in a square created from a ½° of latitude and longitude (not Jeppesen). They are the highest figure from either:

- The highest obstacle, to the next 100 ft, or
- The highest ground + 300 ft, to the next 100 ft.

 MEF elevation is shown in thousands of feet by a large figure, and hundreds of feet by a smaller, superscript figure. The figure on the left shows a maximum elevation of 600 ft.

MEF is not a safety altitude, but one can be calculated from it by using the methods below.

MINIMUM SAFE ALTITUDE (MSA)

This figure must be in your navigation log, as an altitude that guarantees clearance from terrain or obstacles. It is made up from:

- The elevation of the highest obstacle within 5 nm of the track, rounded up to the next 100 feet.
- Plus 1000 feet for terrain at or below 5000 feet, or 2000 above 5000 feet.

The quick way is just to use the Minimum Grid Area Altitude shown in red within each ½° of latitude and longitude on a VFR chart, like this:

MINIMUM ENROUTE ALTITUDE

The lowest published altitude between radio navigation fixes that assures acceptable navigational signal coverage and meets obstacle clearance requirements between them. Only used in the USA, Canada and some other countries.

MINIMUM OFF-ROUTE ALTITUDE (MORA)

This is a safe altitude along the airway. Jeppesen MORAs give at least 1,000' clearance above terrain and man-made obstacles up to 5,000 feet, and 2,000' in mountains (5001 feet and above), rounded up to the next 100 feet.

- **Route MORAs** provide obstacle clearance within 10 nm (19 km) either side of an airway and around the ends.
- **Grid MORAs** provide an obstacle clearance altitude within a latitude and longitude grid block, usually 1° by 1°. They are presented in feet, omitting the last two figures.

Although MORA is a safety altitude, it may need to be increased.

ALLOWANCE FOR WINDSPEED

When operating within 20 nm of terrain whose maximum elevation exceeds 2,000 feet amsl, standard MORA must be increased by the amounts in the following table, according to the wind speed over the route:

Elevation	Wind Spd in Kts			
In Feet	0 - 30	31 - 50	51 - 70	Over 70
2,000 - 8,000 ft	+500	+1,000	+1500	+2,000
Above 8,000 ft	+1,000	+1500	+2,000	+2500

© Phil Croucher, 2018

FLIGHT PLANNING & MONITORING
Fuel

ALLOWANCE FOR LOW SURFACE TEMPERATURE

Surface Temperature	Correction To MORA/MOCA
ISA -16°C to ISA -30°C	+10%
ISA -31°C to ISA -50°C	+20%
ISA -51°C and below	+25%

You could, of course, also use the 4% correction formula given in *Instruments*.

MAXIMUM AUTHORISED ALTITUDE

The maximum usable altitude or flight level for an airspace structure or route segment. Above the MAA you could tune in to a station with the same frequency as the one you want.

MINIMUM CROSSING ALTITUDE

The lowest altitude at which a navigational fix can be crossed to clear all obstacles during a normal climb to an MEA that is higher.

WITHIN CONTROLLED AIRSPACE

You must use these IFR levels in controlled airspace.

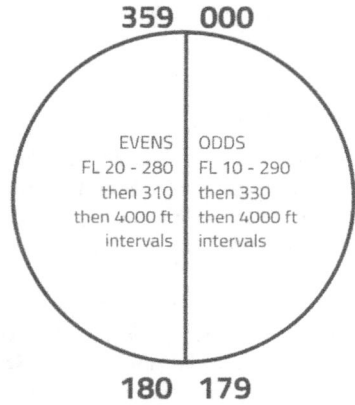

Magnetic tracks are used, or in polar areas above 70° of latitude, grid tracks.

FUEL

Fuel costs can account for more than 35% of the operating costs of an airline. Even a small rise can add millions of dollars to the bottom line. For example, a 1% increase could mean not selling a few thousand seats (according to Boeing, a 1% decrease in landing weight means a 0.75% reduction in trip fuel). A 747 can take up around 311,000 lbs of fuel, which is enough to fill a large swimming pool.

Thus, how much fuel you load can have quite an effect when multiplied over a fleet. Even departing on time is important - it is hard to recover more than 10 or 15 minutes when making up for lost time, and it would cost too much anyway (the trick is to tighten the turnaround).

Of course, nobody should ask you to take less fuel than is necessary for safety or legal reasons, but neither will you be encouraged to take too much either, as around 3-4% of fuel is burnt just to carry the rest of it, so it makes sense to carry as little as possible to make space for fare-paying passengers. However, the fuel at home base can often be cheaper than what you can get elsewhere, so some sacrifices may be necessary to save money in the long run (carrying extra fuel for economic or planning reasons is called *tankering**). Contrast this with the GA habit of filling up as often as possible. The main thing to bear in mind is that your weight at the end of a leg will be a lot different than that at the start of it, due to the usage of trip fuel, and so will the fuel flow, which will change in sympathy.

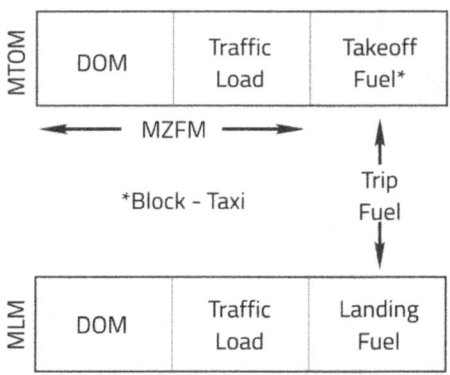

*Many companies allow an automatic figure, but too much extra fuel may have to be reported after the flight. Even then, your ability to tanker fuel can be restricted due to a high payload or the need for deicing. Carrying a lot of fuel on a long trip can create Cold Soaked Fuel Frost (CSFF) as the fuel cools at the high altitude. The 737NG is particularly prone to it because its tanks are closer to the skin of the wing, amongst other reasons.

Depending on how the fuel planning figures are tabulated, you might therefore have to get used to making educated guesses as to the mid-leg weight to get a mean fuel flow. For example, if the aircraft weighs 126,000 kg at the start of a leg, the associated fuel flow is 7,500 kg/hr, and the leg time is 35 minutes, you can immediately round the time up to 36 minutes for a mid-point time of 18 minutes. You could probably assume 7,000 kg/hr, which means just under 120 kg per minute. 18 minutes at that rate means you will burn off 2,160 kg, meaning that your approximate mid-leg weight is 124,000, which is what you enter the charts with. However, the tables used here take all that into account, based on the Beech Bonanza, Piper Seneca and the Boeing 737, all fairly common types.

With fuel planning, you are treading the fine line between taking the least fuel to carry the most passengers, but having enough on board to be safe. It's usual to keep an eye on the fuel contents to see if things are going according to plan, so checks are done at regular intervals (usually over each waypoint), so you can compare the actual consumption to the planned consumption (see *The Fuel Plan*, below). This allows you to find out if you are using too much too early, in which case you could reduce power, change altitude or divert (don't forget to tell the engineers the engines might be suspect), or make sure you have enough to finish the flight. The checks would either be noted on the fuel plan or plotted on a graph (a Howgozit, rare nowadays).

Very few aircraft will actually take a full load of passengers and fuel (in fact, one of the Learjets can do 6 hours on a full tank of fuel, but they don't tell you that you are overweight at that point and you haven't even loaded any passengers!), so you need to know how long it will take between two points, find out how much fuel is needed, *then fit the passengers in*. *Do not put the passengers in first and fit the fuel in afterwards!* Not unless you plan to stop on the way, at least. Of all the things there is no excuse for in aviation, running out of fuel is one of them! If you have to take less fuel, you will have to pick up some more on the way, or leave someone behind. If you take the same fuel anyway, you will be overweight, with not enough power in the engines to get you out of trouble, and *invalid insurance*.

You will need more fuel to counteract the effects of ice, and fuel flow must also be adjusted if you plan to use specialised equipment in flight, such as heaters, or not use anything essential, such as an engine.

The Fuel Plan

Every operator must have a fuel policy in the ops manual (CAT.OP.MPA.150(b) - see *Operational Procedures*), the intention of which is to ensure that you don't run out of fuel in flight. Realistic fuel consumption figures must be used, either from the manufacturer or some sort of monitoring system.

The fuel plan is a form that is filled in before takeoff that tells you what fuel is required for a trip, and during flight to tell you what is being used and what you theoretically have left. It may come to you directly from a computer, with an empty column so you can put your own figures in. Its purpose is to consolidate as much information as possible about a trip, particularly fuel requirements. Filling in the fuel plan is the reason why we need to use the graphs and procedures in this section (partially filled examples are used later). Once you've drawn your track on the map and put its details in the appropriate boxes on the plan, work out the wind, obtain your intended heading and groundspeed, apply the magnetic variation, calculate the fuel required, fill 'er up and you're ready to go.

Tip: If there's room, leave a line between each leg, in case of any changes, or you note any differences, such as wind velocity, and have to work out a new groundspeed.

There can be several types of leg:

- **Departure** (climb). These end when you set the heading, which may come before or after the Top Of Climb (TOC), or even be the same point. Such a Set Heading Point (SHP) could be the airfield (for an overhead departure) but, if there's a lot of traffic, or the airfield uses routes in and out, you might want to choose something clear of the zone (but enroute, of course), which may increase the distance used, so the mean values for planning purposes are those two thirds of the way up the climb. In short, you must allow for manoeuvring, etc. 99% of the time, the distance required to climb to the selected altitude will be more than that to the SHP, so the remainder of the first leg is usually for the rest of the climb. Check out the flight manual for charts covering time, fuel and distances* concerned. Also remember that the wind and speed values change as you climb.

   *Distance is the only one affected by the wind.

- **Enroute** (including to alternates). This is the largest group, running from waypoint to waypoint. The first one starts at the Top Of Climb (TOC). Each one should be of a manageable length, though not too short.
- **Arrival** (including to alternates). These end at the Initial Approach Fix (for IFR) or the circuit (VFR).

For most flights each type will take up one line, but they can stretch into two or even three.

TOP OF CLIMB

Figure out the times based on the rate of climb, then use the mean groundspeed* and work inwards from the start point of the journey for distance and time. For example, with a rate of climb of 500 feet per minute, it will take 20 minutes to climb to 10,000 feet. At 180 knots, you will travel 60 miles. Subtract that from the total distance and the remainder is the distance taken for the cruise.

*The average climb TAS (and W/V) are found at two thirds of the cruising altitude, certainly for light aircraft whose rate of climb drops off quickly (mid-time happens later than halfway up because the slope decreases with altitude, so you spend half the time below the two thirds point and the other half above it). For more powerful aircraft, use the groundspeed halfway up.

During the descent, the slope remains constant, so the wind and TAS can be regarded as average values at the mean point. If no elevation is given for the start of the climb, assume Mean Sea Level. A flight to an alternate should require no climb allowance.

Fuel Management
CAT.OP.MPA.280

For most trips, fuel management revolves around getting the maximum range for a given amount of fuel or, looked at another way, how little you can get away with over the distance flown. However, occasionally you are asked to hold, or patrol, and the question of how long you can stay airborne arises, namely endurance. The fuel burnt per unit of thrust, per unit of time, is called the *Specific Fuel Consumption*, or SFC, so it is a measure of the efficiency of an engine, and the lower the SFC, the better. Two engines with the same SFC value will have the same fuel flow if their thrust values are the same.

For jets, SFC usually reduces with altitude (up to the tropopause, where it remains constant) because it is proportional to temperature and turbine engines like running at 90% of the maximum RPM - you can't do that lower down. However, after a certain flight level, fuel flow increases, due to the increased drag penalty from the excessive angle of attack needed to create enough lift (if it goes high enough the machine will stall). There is an altitude above which climbing simply increases the time taken for the whole flight. This is the *optimum altitude*, discussed later, which is a function of fuel flow and TAS, which reduces as you climb at a fixed Mach number into colder air.

For prop driven aircraft, SFC is related to the fuel flow per unit of power. Again, it improves with altitude, but propeller tip speeds limit their altitude anyway. After full throttle height with pistons, SFC *increases* with altitude.

MINIMUM TIME

Here, maximum thrust is used to obtain the highest speed, or V_{MO}, if limiting. An altitude that provides the greatest groundspeed using forecast winds is chosen (taking into consideration varying speeds and winds), which is found by plotting the track for an hour or so over several altitudes, then repeated over the whole route. This is how the NAT track system works.

The MSC (Maximum Speed Cruise) schedule is normally flown up to 25,000 feet, where the resultant TAS is greatest.

MINIMUM COST

This considers fuel and airfield costs, which are represented as part of the cost index in the FMS. If fuel is cheap, you might be able to fly faster and save engine hours and maintenance costs. If it is more expensive, the big picture may require you to fly slowly.

MAXIMUM RANGE

Efficient performance in the cruise is required to maximise range and minimise operating costs.

Range (the sum of climb, cruise and descent distances) is the distance that an aircraft can travel with a given quantity of fuel and payload. The Bombardier Global Express can fly 6,500 nm at Mach 0.80 while carrying 8 passengers (1,600 lbs).

However, when too low at the wrong altitude, you could be burning uneconomical amounts relative to what you would burn when at a higher level. The increased fuel flow is exacerbated if the aeroplane is heavy. For example, an MD-11 burns 16,000 lbs an hour at FL 350, but *26,000* at 11,000 feet (it will also go a lot slower). The best range height for most jets is around 35,000 ft, although the BAe 146 apparently likes about 30,000 ft. On top of normal cruise, the flight manuals may quote other cruising speeds, *High Speed* (0.78 M for the 737-400) and *Economy* (0.74 M), and possibly Long Range Cruise (LRC) where Mach number varies with weight.

Assuming correct weights (i.e. not heavy), and ignoring winds, maximum range in any aircraft is achieved when the ratio between distance covered and fuel flow is maximum, meaning minimum fuel usage for a given distance, or maximum distance from a given fuel load. The common denominator between them is the **specific range**, namely the distance travelled per unit of fuel, as in miles per gallon, like you would use in your car but, with jets at least, we may use nautical air miles and kgs of fuel.

It comes from:

$$SR = \frac{V}{SFC \times BHP}$$

or, over a given amount of time (say, 1 hour):

$$SR = \frac{TAS}{Fuel\ Flow}$$

So, for a TAS of 450 kts using 2400 kg per hour, we can end up with 0.1875 NAM/kg, or 187.5 NAM per 1,000 kg, which is typical of an A320 or similar aircraft.

Both of the above indications can be seen in the cockpit. You can also use:

$$SR = \frac{Cruise\ NAM}{Fuel\ Consumption}$$

The total range is simply the amount of fuel on board multiplied by the SR.

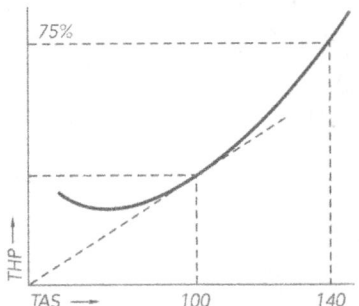

The first equation above includes the ratio of velocity to power (V/BHP)*. Multiplied by weight, this is the same as the L/D ratio, so you get maximum SR at the maximum ratio which, unfortunately, at 100 knots in the picture above, for example, is way below normal cruise speed, and only really useful if you are flying over somewhere not very nice, like a desert.

*THP only differs from BHP by prop efficiency.

With performance calculations for small aeroplanes, the weight of the aircraft tends to be regarded as a constant* which, in reality, is only true for gliders. Otherwise, it decreases as fuel is burned. This means that aerodynamic performance changes during flight, and is one reason why the FMS keeps a track of the fuel burn.

*Calculations are normally done at maximum gross weight, for a conservative or worst case scenario.

In other words, the power curve at the end of the flight will be different from that at the start because the weight reduces as fuel is used up.

This means that the speed for maximum L/D will be lower at the destination.

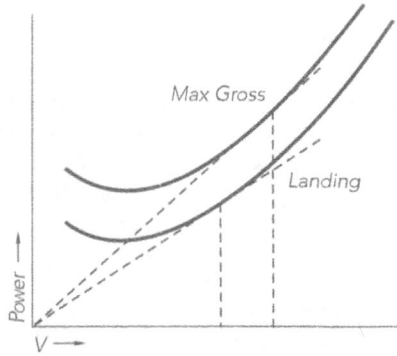

Light aircraft are not affected much by this because the fuel they carry is a small percentage of their total weight, and the difference in speed will be less than around 5 knots, but transport aircraft are affected a great deal.

Generally, the maximum range of a turbojet increases markedly with height because the SFC reduces* - it is typically twice as much at 30,000 feet than it is at sea level. Piston propeller aeroplanes, on the other hand, fly more efficiently for range at lower altitudes.

*In theory, fuel consumption is more or less constant with height because drag and thrust are constant but, in practice, the higher TAS increases propulsive efficiency. In a 50,000 kg 737-500, for example, you can get 345 kts TAS at FL 100, but 425 at FL 240, at a 300 KIAS cruise. This translates to a 5.2% increase in fuel flow and a 30% improvement in fuel mileage.

EFFECTS OF WEIGHT

In a typical jet, a weight reduction from 140 tons down to 100 tons can improve the specific range by 14% at 25,000 feet and by 38% at 39,000 feet (the optimum altitude).

EFFECTS OF SPEED

For every weight and altitude there is a speed for maximum range, the Maximum Range Cruise (MRC), achieved at the optimum altitude (discussed later), which will achieve maximum fuel mileage or maximum range. It increases with altitude, for a constant weight, and decreases with decreasing weight at constant altitude.

However, in practice, a slightly higher airspeed is used. *Long Range Cruise*, or LRC, provides a good compromise between fuel efficiency and flight time.

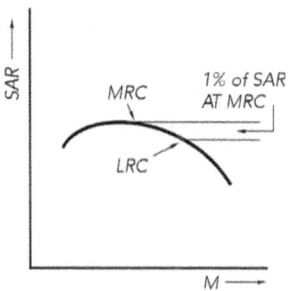

It provides 99% of maximum SAR, so 1% is sacrificed for an extra 3-5% of cruise speed. Given that fuel can be a relatively small cost of an operation relative to others, this is a good tradeoff. LRC also increases with increasing altitude, for a constant weight, and decreases with decreasing weight at constant altitude.

TEMPERATURE

Unless maximum cruise speed is used, temperature has a negligible effect on SAR and range. In order to maintain a constant thrust level at a higher temperature, the fuel flow increases, which is compensated for by the higher TAS obtained at the higher temperature. The effect on SAR is typically less than 0.1% for every degree of deviation from ISA conditions.

WINDS

Headwinds and tailwinds will also affect the speed for best L/D ratio, and hence SR. You can fly all day at 100 knots into a 100 knot headwind and still get nowhere!

Thus, the speed should be increased in a headwind because you can then use a lower angle of attack (for less drag), and your exposure to the headwind is less (lowering the nose for range is not intuitive, but it works).

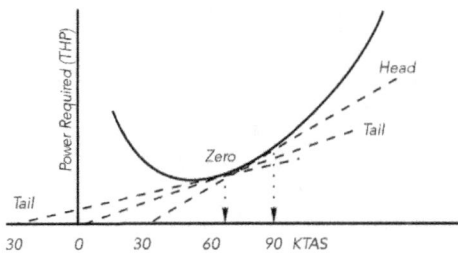

The origin is moved forward or back to take into account the effects of a head- or tailwind. If you have a 30-knot headwind, for example, you simply start the tangent line at the 30 knot point on the TAS line. Similarly, but in reverse for a tailwind.

INOPERATIVE ENGINES

With one or more engines inoperative, the maximum range at the optimum altitude will be less due to the drag from the dead engine. At low altitudes, however, the thrust required per engine is lower. The end result is that specific range is improved at low altitudes with one or two engines inoperative.

CLIMB

The initial climb will be at a constant IAS, which means an increase in TAS up to the changeover level. The climb thereafter is at a constant Mach No, which means a decrease in TAS. The change to Mach number in the climb is known as *Transition*. A good rule of thumb for climb winds is to use 50% of the cruise wind velocity.

The effect of increasing altitude is generally to increase the specific range but, at heavy weights, the thrust requirements are such that you will get a lower value. In other words, for every weight there is an altitude for maximum range, the *Optimum Altitude*, which increases as the weight of the aircraft reduces.

The cruise climb means climbing steadily to maintain the optimum altitude as fuel is used up.

The cruise climb means climbing steadily to maintain the optimum altitude as fuel is used up. That is, you climb initially to the most efficient level, and keep going up as weight reduces until you reach the TOD, but this is not always convenient for ATC, especially on NAT routes (in fact the only aircraft to do this was Concorde because it was up there by itself) so, in practice, a *stepped climb* is used, where you go up 4,000 feet at a time, having started 2,000 feet above the ideal starting altitude, and flown until you are 2,000 feet under the next one, for the Semi-Circular Rule (the North Atlantic is RVSM so this might be done in 2,000-foot steps).

In the picture below, Point A is an altitude above optimum by 2,000 feet. The weight decreases until reaching point B, when the altitude becomes 2,000 feet below optimum. A step climb has to be started to C at an altitude 2,000 feet above as the weight decreases further, and so on.

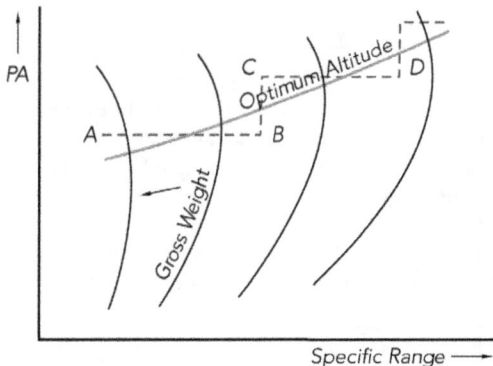

In general, large overshoots of the optimum altitude should be avoided*, as the specific range drops off rapidly above and below it. The procedure above keeps you within 1% of the optimum with your range about 95% of the maximum available.

*As well as providing 99% of the maximum range, flying at the optimum altitude also allows for a 1.5g (up to 48° of bank) load factor for most jets at LRC speed. Flying higher may have an adverse effect on safety because there will be a significant reduction in the load factor, and the ability to manoeuvre, which will be further aggravated with turbulence and gusts.

However, stepping should only be considered if it is going to use less fuel - doing it before the machine is ready costs fuel which cannot be recovered later (the climb itself takes fuel, as it is done at climb thrust rather than cruise thrust.

Another method is to set constant power and accept an increase in airspeed, but this makes ETAs harder to calculate, so you can set a target airspeed and reduce power as fuel is used instead. With TAS constant, drag reduces as weight decreases. With stepped climbs, your range will be 80-90% of the maximum available.

Power required in straight and level flight is *Drag x TAS**, and increasing TAS equates to increasing the rate of distance covered, so, for maximum range, you must fly at the speed at which the ratio of TAS to drag is maximum, i.e. where the TAS is higher, at altitude.

*Each unit of fuel allows the engine to deliver a certain amount of power for a certain amount of time. This product is a fixed quantity, in that if you vary power or time, the other quantity has to change - double the power, you halve the time, and so on. Thus:

```
Work Available = Drag x TAS x Time
```
or:
```
Power Reqd x Time = Drag x TAS x Time
```
Cancelling out Time on both sides, we get:
```
Power Reqd = Drag x TAS
```
Now, *TAS x Time* is the same as the air distance travelled so, if work available equals work required, you can rewrite the above to read:
```
Work Available = Drag x Air Distance
```
or:
```
Air Distance = Work Available
               ─────────────
                    Drag
```

Since Work Available is a fixed quantity, drag must be minimised to maximise the distance flown. Maximum Range speed is therefore the same as that for Minimum Drag, or V_{IMD}, which is not affected by height (it's an aerodynamic property, and is expressed in terms of IAS). TAS increases, of course, but so does power required, so the two effects tend to cancel each other out, and range obtainable is not much affected by height either.

DESCENT

Initial descent is done at a fixed Mach number, so the IAS and TAS will be *increasing with decreasing altitude*. After the descent changeover level, a fixed IAS value is used, so the Mach number and TAS *decrease with decreasing altitude*. Early descent from cruise altitude can result in a fuel penalty of around 30 kg per minute for some jets, not helped by incorrect selection of descent speed, which could add 10-20 kg on top. The normal descent point is roughly 3 nm from the destination for every 1,000 feet of descent for a turbojet. The ideal descent allows the crew to close the thrust levers at TOD and not advanced until levelling off to intercept the glideslope on approach.

WINDS ALOFT

For a headwind, speed up to minimise the time affected - 10% increase in airspeed gives more than a 10% increase in groundspeed (for example, at 100 kts, with a 40-kt headwind, adding 10 kts gives you a groundspeed of 70 kts, which is 16%). With a tailwind, slow down and let the wind do the work. As weight decreases with fuel usage, you could either increase altitude to improve SFC or decrease speed to keep the best L/D ratio (the optimum angle of attack will not change). However, although fuel usage decreases with height, so does the TAS, which offsets most of the advantage, so altitude is not always the answer, especially if the winds change. Thus, fuel calculations are also done by counting units of fuel per unit of distance over the ground (see *Specific Ground Range*).

TURBULENCE

EPR gauges become inaccurate in turbulent air, so you might have to use N_1 settings instead, from a *Turbulent Air Penetration* table. In severe turbulence, since the AI does not read correctly, you should set power for the recommended rough air speed (check the tables) and maintain a level attitude, regardless of altitude and air speed variations.

CENTRE OF GRAVITY

The C of G is usually forward of the Centre of Pressure because this will make the aircraft more stable (in pitch). However, this does involve a nose down element, which must be counteracted by the elevator, which in turn must be counteracted by extra lift from the wings, involving extra drag and fuel consumption, leaving aside higher stalling speeds. For fuel efficiency purposes, the best place for the C of G is near the aft C of G limit.

RECIPROCATING ENGINES

As fuel flow in a propeller aircraft is proportional to power*, maximum range will be achieved when the least power is used for a given distance covered. Because piston engines keep their RPM and internal temperatures more or less constant, the SFC won't change much, so fuel savings at altitude are minimal, except on very long flights.

*The power specific fuel consumption is the mass of fuel consumed per unit time per unit shaft power. The units are slugs per unit power per second in the English system, or kg per unit power per second in SI units. Similarly, the power units are horsepower and watts.

As with jets (thrust), there is often an alternate definition of specific fuel consumption in terms of the weight of fuel consumed instead of the mass. In dealing with propellers, the propulsive efficiency must be considered, which relates the shaft power from the engine to the power used by the propeller to transfer momentum to the air.

For a given specific fuel consumption and efficiency, the rate of fuel consumption is least when the power required (DV) is minimum, and the fuel consumption per amount of distance travelled is least when the drag is minimum.

Thus, minimum power required and minimum drag are conditions needed for optimum flight.

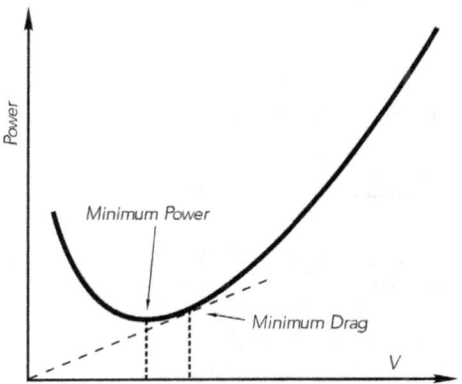

Maximum range for a jet occurs when D/V is minimum while, for a prop, it occurs in minimum drag conditions. The velocities for both cases can be determined by finding the point of tangency for a line drawn from the origin on either the drag *vs* velocity curve in the jet case or the power required *vs* velocity curve for the propeller.

This can be extended to find the speed for best range with either a head- or a tailwind.

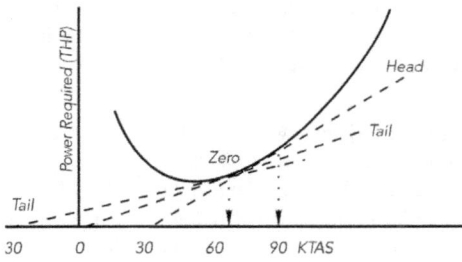

The origin is displaced to the left by a tailwind or to the right by a headwind. The point of tangency of a line drawn from the displaced origin locates the new velocity for optimum range with a wind. The magnitude of this new optimum range velocity is read with respect to the original origin (not the displaced origin). This speed is an airspeed, not a ground speed.

In the cruise, you should reduce power and lean the mixture, which will reduce the fuel consumption and the wear on the engine. Generally, the higher the RPM and MAP, the greater the speed, but at the expense of fuel economy, range and endurance. The lower the RPM, of course, the fewer number of times the engine goes round, and the less fuel is used. Lower MAP means lower charge weight in each four-stroke cycle.

Calculating the Specific Air Range (the fuel used per Nautical Air Mile - see below) can help you compare the various options. That is, find out how far you can go for each pound of fuel. Twin-engined aeroplanes have higher power and fuel consumption than single-engine aircraft of the same size and performance, so there will be a significant difference in fuel required. In a non-turbocharged aircraft, the TAS increase between 5,000-12,000 feet is hardly discernible, so you would only go that high if you were getting a good tailwind or the MSA (or weather) forces you - fuel consumption will be more or less the same at either altitude and the climb will take up more fuel than you save. Turbocharging increases TAS, so you can decrease power to reduce fuel consumption and engine wear. Thus, you increase range as well. Typically the optimum altitude is around 18,000 feet for TAS and range; unpressurised aircraft are generally limited to FL100, so are flown at this or FL90 depending on the semi-circular cruising rule.

SPECIFIC GROUND RANGE

Knowing the SGR is useful when IFR and planning on particular fuel consumption, but actually burning something entirely different. It also gives you an idea of the most efficient cruising altitude, allowing for winds. Thus, the best altitude for *range* will be what gives you the most SGR, and you need to find the groundspeed first.

Divide fuel flow by groundspeed to get lbs per nm, or the other way to get nm per lb of fuel, if those units are used, e.g. 600lb/hr at 120 kts is 5lb/nm or 0.2 nm/1lb fuel. Thus, if an aircraft at FL 320 has a TAS of 494 kts, a headwind component of 50 kts and a fuel flow of 7900 kg per hour, its fuel burn would be 17.8 kg/nm. At FL 350, with TAS 486 kts, head wind 55 kts and fuel flow of 7500 kg/hr, it might be 17.4 kg/nm. Other things being equal, the best FL for range would therefore be FL 350. If you had 21,500 kg in hand, you would get 1236 nm out of the old bus. To get the same at FL 320, the headwind would need to reduce to 40 kts. The reciprocal of the 17.4 kg/nm above is 0.057 nm/kg.

The reciprocal of the 17.4 kg/nm above is 0.057 nm/kg. Here are two handy formulae:

$$\frac{TAS}{G/S} = \frac{NAM}{NGM}$$

$$\frac{NGM}{G/S} = \frac{NAM}{TAS}$$

Where NGM = *Nautical Ground Miles*, NAM = *Nautical Air Miles*. Both are proportion problems and therefore solveable by the flight computer.

The relationship between Nautical Air and Nautical Ground Miles is the same as that between True Air Speed and Groundspeed, in that they will vary according to whether you have a head- or tailwind. For example, with a headwind, your NAM will be more than your NGM, because the TAS is higher than the ground speed and vice versa (this is a useful logic check).

 All charts in CAP 697 use NAMs, so you may have to convert NGMs first.

By shuffling the above formula, you can calculate the NAMs involved for specific range purposes in the cruise portion of a flight.

$$NAM = \frac{NGM \times TAS}{G/S}$$

For example, with a stage length of 1,000 nm and a 50 kt headwind against a TAS of 450 kts, the groundspeed would be 400 knots and you would need to do 1125 NAM to cover 1,000 NGM. Use that figure in the specific range formula to find the total fuel for the cruise portion.

ENDURANCE

Sometimes you just have to keep up in the air for short periods, possibly to wait for some radiation fog to burn off, or when holding (see below). Whereas flying for range is more concerned with *specific* fuel consumption (per nautical mile, for example), endurance flying is more to do with *gross* fuel flow, or how much is burned off per hour, in terms of weight. Fuel flow is least when thrust is least, so you are getting maximum (level flight) endurance at the IAS for minimum drag (V_{MD}), because, in level flight, thrust is equal to drag. You need to run the engines at max continuous RPM to get the required thrust most economically, which also means doing it at the right altitude, since jet engines are less efficient when lower (RPM must be severely reduced to get the lower thrust). The greater the power/weight ratio, the greater will be the optimum altitude.

Endurance calculations are not affected by wind.

EXAMPLES

1. Using the following extract from a computer fuel plan:

Wpt	ETA	ATA	Planned Fuel Kg Remaining	Actual Fuel Kg Remaining
A	01:07	01:07	3400	3400
B	01:27	01:27	3160	3120
C	02:02	02:02	2740	2630
D	02:37		2320	
S	03:07		1960	
M	03:27		1720	

Overhead C, you are given direct routing to M, which will take 1 hour 6 minutes. What fuel would remain at M?

You need the latest fuel flow to start with, so, looking at the column on the right, you have used 770 kgs of fuel, over 55 minutes (third column). This is 804 kgs/hr. Over the next 66 minutes, you will therefore use 924 kgs. Subtracting this from 2630 gives you 1706 kg.

2. Given:

Flight Time: 2 hrs 42 min
Block Fuel: 138 kg
Taxi Fuel: 8 kg

The reserve fuel should never be less than 30% of the remaining trip fuel. What minimum fuel should be in the tanks after 2 hours of flight?

This is a rather stupid question, as the trip fuel will be zero on landing (you will have used it all up), so 30% of it is also zero! As the final reserve is not mentioned, this is just an intellectual exercise. However, even after two hours the original 30% should still be sloshing around in the tanks.

Takeoff fuel is block fuel minus taxi, or 129 kg, which is the trip fuel plus 30% of the trip fuel, which is therefore an unknown quantity, and it is supposed to last for 2.7 hours, or 162 minutes.

$$129 = x + 0.3x$$
$$129 = 1.3x$$
$$x = \frac{129}{1.3}$$
$$99.23 \text{ trip fuel}$$

The 99 kg is supposed to last for 2.7 hours, so the fuel used over 2 hours is:

$$\frac{99.23}{2.7} \times 2 = 73.5 \text{ kg}$$

The remaining fuel after 2 hours is 25.73 kg (99.23 - 73.5), 30% of which is around 8 kg.

FLIGHT MANAGEMENT SYSTEM

This will control most flight profiles. The one in the 737 gives you four different speeds:

- **ECON** (used with a cost index in the database)
- **LRC** (Long Range Cruise - see below)
- **Manual**
- **RTA**, where that speed will be adjusted (by autothrottle) to meet a *Required Time of Arrival*

The FMS optimum altitude will be where 90% thrust produces 1.32 V_{MD}, as modified for the cruise wind and cost index. Most operations manuals require you to fly within 2,000 feet of it, so you might want to select a higher level at first so the optimum level climbs up as the weight reduces. Otherwise, the main cruise methods are:

- **Long Range Cruise**, where the TAS changes as a function of aircraft mass. LRC speed is 4% faster than best range speed in still air, but still provides 99% of the maximum, so it may often be better to use more fuel and save other costs. LRC is better for headwinds, and speed stability is better than with Maximum Range Cruise Speed (V_{MRC}).
- **0.74 Mach** (normal cruise) - a constant TAS for a flight level.
- **0.78 Mach** (high speed cruise) - a constant TAS for a flight level. The graphs show the maximum altitude of 37,000 feet for the 737.
- **Low Level cruise** at 300 kts IAS at a variety of pressure altitudes.

BUFFET ONSET BOUNDARY

The maximum altitude can be limited by the absolute or pressurisation ceilings, that specified in the flight manual or the buffet onset boundary, which is usually the most limiting, unless the aircraft is very light. The low speed boundary concerns the stall speed (10% above) and the high speed boundary lies around M_{MO}.

This is a typical Buffet Onset Boundary (BOB) chart.

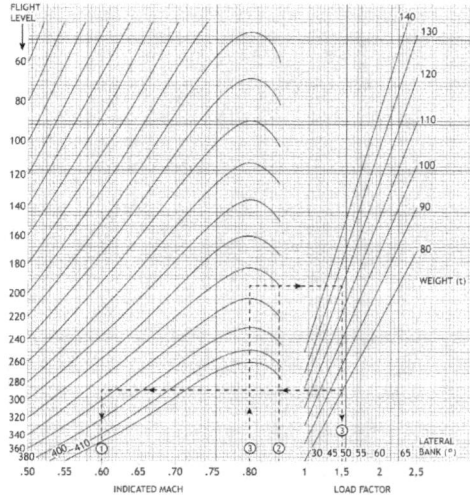

The curves on the right concern the weight of the aircraft and those on the left relate indicated Mach numbers to pressure altitude. For a given flight level, the speed range decreases with a forward C of G.

If an actual C of G greater than the default of 15% MAC is entered (on the PERF INIT page of the FMS), the maximum altitude will increase and the cruise buffet margins will get wider. In the picture on the right, the buffet boundary is indicated by the yellow marking above the Mach number. The black and red squares show the 1G limit.

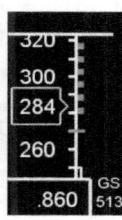

Critical Point

If you are flying across lonely places like deserts and long stretches of water, you often want to be able to land as soon as possible, which is where the Critical Point, or the Point of Equal Time (PET) comes in.

At some stage between the departure and destination, there is a point from which it will take the same time to return to where you came from as to carry on to where you were going in the first place, or to either of two airfields, not necessarily in front of or behind you, which is more like what you would actually do. For example, you could use the last suitable airfield before going over the water, and the first suitable one on the other side.

Also known as the *Point of Equal Time* (PET), or the *Equi-time Point* (ETP), this point is expressed in terms of time, assuming that the TAS, wind and fuel consumption are constant. In other words, it has nothing to do with fuel but, having said that, given that the same time is involved in going on or back, if the fuel flow doesn't change, then you will be using the same fuel in either case. The only difference would arise from the approach requirements at each end. You could get the odd situation where you are burning more fuel OEI, but you need less fuel if no approach fuel is required (in this respect a VFR flight could be more restrictive as the lower final reserve fuel would mean less.available with which to replan).

A lot depends on the type of emergency. If it's a medical one, for instance, or a disruptive passenger, your aircraft will have no change in performance and you won't lose any airspeed. However, if you lose an engine, it will all change drastically. Thus, there are two options to consider:

- **All Engines Operating** (AEO).
- **One Engine Inoperative** (OEI). Reduced airspeeds are used after the engine fails, of course, but full airspeed is used to calculate when you get to the PET. That is, you find the *position* (going from) with reduced speeds first, then when you will get there (going to) at full speed.

The simple formula to find the distance is:

$$\frac{D \times H}{O + H}$$

where D = total distance, H is the return groundspeed and O is the Onward. The Out (before the PET) and On speeds (after the PET) are technically different things (especially after an engine failure), but EASA do not seem to notice.

If a TAS* is given along with a wind component, simply add the wind component to the TAS to find the groundspeed. You might also have to assume that the wind home is simply the reverse of the wind out (which is not realistic, as this only happens for direct headwind or tailwind). A negative wind component implies a headwind, positive is a tailwind.

To calculate the time taken to arrive at the ~~critical point~~ PET, first find the distance, then divide by the outbound groundspeed (so in the engine failure case use the all-engines-operating airspeed) to find a time in hours.

Example: A flight is planned over a distance of 312 nm. The TAS is 162 kts and safe endurance is 2 hours 40 minutes. In still air the critical point would be half-way, 166 nm from the departure point. With a forecast tailwind of 20 knots out the groundspeeds can be calculated as 182 kts out and 142 kts home. The distance to the PET is now 137 nm. This is significantly close, because the wind will take the aircraft more quickly towards the destination.

The formula is derived from the fact that the *times* from the PET in the picture to A and B are the same, or x = y:

$$A \xleftarrow{\ x\ } CP \xrightarrow{\ y\ } B$$

But time is equal to distance divided by speed, so:

$$\frac{x}{H} = \frac{y}{O}$$

where O is the groundspeed *On* and H is the groundspeed *Home* (assuming you are travelling from A to B in the first place). Take D as representing the whole distance, DO as distance On and DH as distance back.

Therefore:

```
OX = HY
OX = HD - HX
```

FLIGHT PLANNING & MONITORING
Fuel

OX + HX = HD

$$X = \frac{D \times H}{O + H}$$

Another way of looking at it is to start with the total distance divided by twice the TAS, which gives you the midpoint, so:

$$\frac{Distance}{TAS \times 2}$$

Now you need a conversion factor, which is found by dividing the unknown distance to the PET by the return groundspeed, to end up with the formula above.

Either way, the problem can be set up to work as a proportion on the flight computer by placing the sum of the groundspeeds home and out on the inner scale against groundspeed home on the outer scale, due to shuffling the formula around:

$$CP\ (Distance) = \frac{D \times H}{O + H}$$

$$\frac{CP\ (Distance)}{D} = \frac{H}{O + H}$$

You have a total distance of 920 nm, with a groundspeed out of 240 kts and one home of 210 kts and a flight planned time enroute of 230 minutes. Find the time and distance to the PET.

First, line up the sum of the groundspeed home and out (450 kts) on the inner scale against the groundspeed home on the outer scale ❶. The corresponding times and distances will appear opposite each other, with the answers on the outer scale. The time to the CP (107.5 mins) is against the flight planned time of 230 minutes ❷ and the distance (430 nm) is against the total distance ❸.

Always add the totals up (there and back) to see if they are the same. **The CP will move into wind** from the halfway point, where it will be in nil wind conditions.

MULTIPLE LEGS

With multiple legs (say, on an airway route), you can work them out individually, add them all up and treat them as one distance. Alternatively, you can find out on which leg the PET is with a process of elimination, working from the outside inwards to find the unbalanced portion of the route, then use the standard formula.

It helps to draw a diagram, showing the turning points. Then mark the times between them outbound and inbound above the line.

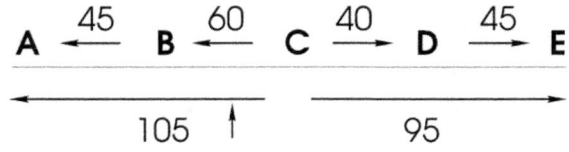

In the picture, they have been added up and noted underneath the line. The upwards pointing arrow shows where the two totals balance at 95 minutes, so the PET must be between the arrow and C, which will be the *D* value in the formula. The groundspeed On will be that between B and C, and the groundspeed Home that between C and B.

Tip: The distance from the arrow to C is equal to the time difference (105 – 95), i.e. 10 minutes, multiplied by the ground speed between C and B.

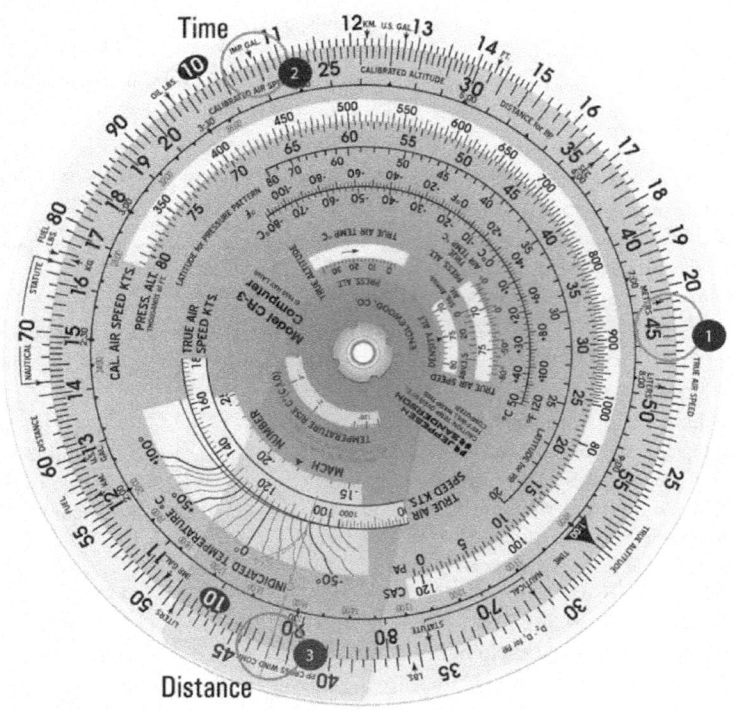

Point of Safe Return

You also need to know the point at which you cannot turn back at all, which is a calculation done every day for long flights over hostile terrain, or with no alternates.

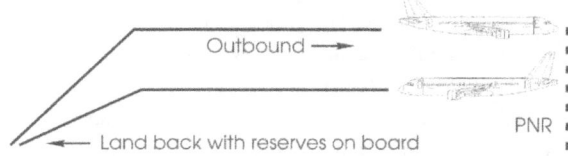

Originally known as the *Point of No Return*, this is the furthest point you can fly to and then return to a landing point behind you (usually your point of departure), based on a given amount of fuel, which usually, for obvious reasons, takes account of reserves. In other words, it is an on-track situation. The *Point of Safe Diversion* is for off-track problems, when alternates become involved.

Beyond the Point of Safe Return, you do not have enough fuel to return home safely, hence the name. It is purely a fuel (actually, an endurance) problem, having nothing to do with distance, again assuming that the TAS, wind and fuel consumption are constant (not the case if you have an engine failure). Because you are returning to the departure point, the operating limits at the original destination no longer apply, so you have more fuel to play with, which helps to compensate for the higher consumption if one engine has failed. The speed to the PSR is calculated at full value, and the return at the lesser speed.

 Given that you are returning to the destination, the safe endurance should be the original fuel at startup, less:

- Start/Taxi
- Final Reserve Fuel
- Approach and holding fuel at the departure point
- Contingency fuel

Then remove the climb fuel from the result.

The principles are good for other situations, too - your destination might get socked in underneath a warm front, so you would need to know the last position enroute that would allow you to go to an alternate where the weather is better. You would check the weather at the original destination and make the decision whether to abort or not when you start to approach the calculated value. With this in mind, another definition of PSR is **the greatest distance you can go past an airfield, and return to it with required reserves intact.**

Any tailwind outbound becomes a headwind homebound and, as the detrimental effect is experienced for longer than the beneficial effect, you will spend longer beating headwinds than the benefit gained from tailwinds. If you estimate the same fuel for each leg of an out-and-back trip, and assume that the head- and tailwinds will cancel each other out, you will run out of fuel not too far from home.

As soon as a wind gets involved, you need more fuel than you would in still air.

Example: Every day, you fly from Rainbow Lake (where there is no rainbow and no lake!) in N Alberta to Shekhili compressor station, where there is no fuel. The distance is 50 nm each way and the cruise speed is 100 kts. Fuel consumption is 29 US gals per hour. On a nil-wind day, therefore, it should be half an hour each way but, with 20-knot tailwinds outbound, you get there in only 25 minutes.

The journey back, on the other hand, takes 37.5 minutes, which is 62.5 minutes in total. This may not sound much, but with 60-knot winds, you would be flying for 35 minutes longer than expected, and the figures get worse with longer stage lengths. **The distance to the PSR is greatest with zero wind**, and reduces with the wind, regardless of its direction.

Otherwise, to get the simple (normal) PSR time in minutes, we start with the observation that the *distances* out to the PSR and back are the same. However, distance is equal to groundspeed multiplied by time, so:

$$O \times T = H \times (E-T)$$

Where E is the safe endurance (i.e. allowing for reserves), H the homebound groundspeed and O the outbound.

Moving on:

$$OT = HE - HT$$
$$OT + HT = HE$$
$$T \times (O + H) = HE$$

$$\frac{E \times H}{O + H}$$

All it does is find the ratio of the groundspeeds and apply it into the endurance, assuming normal TAS. For example, with 3 hours' endurance, and a 90 kt groundspeed outbound, with 150 home, the equation is:

$$\frac{180 \times 150}{90 + 150}$$

$$\frac{180 \times 150}{240}$$

$$\frac{27,000}{240}$$

The answer is 112.5 minutes. Again, this is a proportion problem, as the sum of the groundspeeds out and back to the total time (endurance) is to the return groundspeed against the time for the outbound leg. In this case, the ratio ends up as 5:8.

On the flight computer, you need to set the sum of the groundspeeds on the inner scale under the endurance (in minutes) on the outer scale, then against the return groundspeed (inner scale), read the time available for the outbound leg, before you have to turn back. To keep things consistent (because time is on the inner scale), just swap the figures around:

$$PSR\ (Time) = \frac{E \times H}{O + H}$$

$$\frac{PSR\ (Time)}{E} = \frac{Home}{O + H}$$

Take an endurance of 390 minutes, with a groundspeed out of 240 kts, and back of 210 kts, place the combined groundspeeds (bottom part of the formula) on the inner scale against the groundspeed home on the outer, and read the time to PSR (182 mins) against the endurance (390 mins) on the inner scale (see picture on the right).

As a gross error check, add the totals for the two legs together and check the total equals the endurance.

If an engine fails, use the full TAS to find out when you would get to the PSR, having used the reduced speed to find out where it is. For radius of action, mix the airspeeds (full TAS on, reduced back), so you know how long you can fly on a tank and still get back, even if an engine fails.

Just apply the groundspeed to get the distance if you want to mark it on the map, or work it out directly like this:

$$\frac{E \times O \times H}{O + H}$$

The endurance, however, is now in hours.

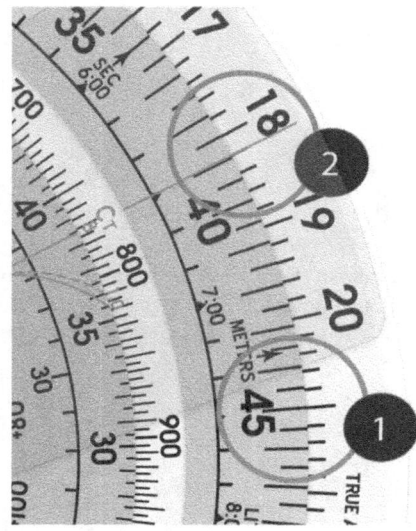

Another method is to divide the fuel available by the amount used out and back for each ground nautical mile:

$$\frac{\text{Fuel available}}{\text{Rate O + Rate H}}$$

To find the rates, divide the speed by the fuel flow.

IN FLIGHT REPLANNING

You may have to work out the PSR having already departed. The calculation is just the same as the standard PSR, but you work with the fuel on board rather than that on board at start up. That is, you don't need to remove the start/taxi fuel because you are already airborne. There is no climb fuel to worry about, either.

What we will be doing is working out the PSR from the present position and back to it, then adding the remainder home - so you need to find out how much fuel you will need to fly back from the present position back home, then subtract it from the endurance calculation or, put another way, add it to the safe reserve.

MULTIPLE LEGS

Here, you need to complete a full flight and fuel plan (see below) for the whole route, inbound and outbound. From the total endurance (or fuel available) subtract the sum of the fuel required for each leg, outbound and inbound, until you get to the point where you don't have enough fuel to complete the return leg. The fuel available from the last turning point to the PSR is then divided by the sum of the outbound and inbound gross fuel flows* to find out exactly where it is.

*The fuel flow in kilograms per hour divided by the ground speed in knots, or the number of kilograms of fuel used per nautical mile (see below).

CHANGES IN FUEL FLOW

Where the fuel flow changes for part of the flight, a more convenient solution would be to work out the fuel consumption per nautical mile (out and back), then divide that into the total endurance. This is similar to working out the Specific Ground Range, above, in that you divide the fuel flow by groundspeed both ways (i.e. Out + Home) to get the fuel used per nm. The result divided into the endurance provides the distance to the PSR.

You may need more fuel to fly OEI than AEO! In which case you may not make it to either your destination or departure point!

CHARTS

Once you've figured out the way to enter one chart, you can mostly use them all. The best tip is to read the small print around the graph, as this is where you will find the conditions on which it is based, such as "generator off", or "anti-icing on".

Accuracy is essential - very often you have to interpolate between figures or lines. Essentially, fuel planning and performance charts are combinations of several graphs in one, each feeding off the other. Very often, you have to work backwards, or at least go through the process several times to get what you need.

 Although pictures of the graphs used are given in the text, **t**he remainder of this chapter should be read in conjunction with CAP 697. **All speeds in it are given as TAS, and distances as NAMs.**

FLIGHT PLANNING & MONITORING
Charts

Single-Engine Piston

The flight planning graphs and tables are arranged in order of flight sequence, starting with the takeoff and climb graph, followed by the cruise tables and range and endurance. There is no graph for descent and approach.

TAKEOFF AND CLIMB

To fill out the flight planning log correctly, for this stage of the flight we need to consider the fuel required for stsrtup and pre-flight checks on the engine, taxy to the takeoff point, the takeoff and climb to the cruise. All this can be done on one graph.

Figure 2.1 (below) is for the time and fuel required to climb to a cruising altitude, and the distance covered.

If the departure aerodrome is significantly above sea level, it should be read twice, once for the cruise level and once for aerodrome pressure altitude with the difference between them being the actual climb. Note that the chart uses US gallons. Assumptions are noted on the chart.

As an example, find the time it takes to climb from an airfield at 2,000 feet PA to FL 90, the fuel used and the distance covered, given an average of 15 kts of headwind. The aircraft weight at takeoff is 3,400 lbs.

The temperature at FL 90 is expected to be -10°C and on the airfield the reported temperature is +30°C.

Enter the graph at -10°C and go up to halfway between the 8,000 and 10,000 ft PA lines. Follow straight across to the 3,400 lb fan line, and drop a line down to cross all three scales across the bottom. This gives 9 minutes, a fuel consumption of 3.5 USG over 18 NAM.

These figures are correct for a climb from zero pressure altitude to FL 90, so they need correcting for the airfield. Enter at the airfield temperature of 30°C and trace directly up to the pressure altitude of 2,000 ft. Follow along to the takeoff weight, 3,500 lb and down to cross the three scales.

You get a time of 2 minutes, using 0.9 USG over 4 NAM.

	Time min	Fuel USG	NAM
To FL90	9	3.5	18
To 2,000 ft	2	0.9	4
2,000 ft to FL 90	7	2.6	14

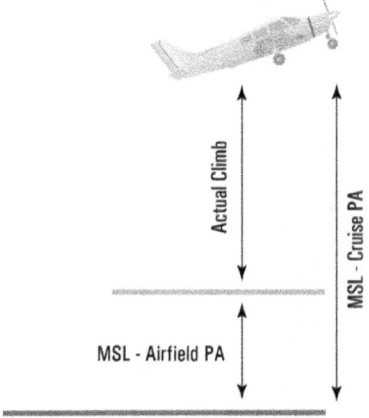

Picture Below: Time & Fuel To Climb

ASSOCIATED CONDITIONS:
POWER.....................FULL THROTTLE, 2500 RPM
FUEL DENSITY...........6.0 LBS/GALL
MIXTURE....................FULL RICH
COWL FLAPS.............AS REQUIRED

CLIMB SPEED 110 KTS ALL WEIGHTS

EXAMPLE:
OAT AT TAKE-OFF.............................30°C
OAT AT CRUISE.................................-10°C
AIRPORT PRESSURE ALTITUDE......2000 FT
CRUISE PRESSURE ALTITUDE........9,000 FT
INITIAL CLIMB MASS.......................3650 LBS

TIME TO CLIMB (9 - 2).......................7 MIN
FUEL TO CLIMB 3.5 - 0.9).................2.6 GAL
DISTANCE TO CLIMB (18 - 4)...........14 NM

Now apply the wind component to get the ground distance covered. All climb times include an allowance for takeoff and climb to 1,000 feet AGL. The only method that works for all SEP/MEP climbs and MEP descents is to use the mean PA (5,500 feet in this case) and mean ambient temperature (10°C) with a given TAS (110 kts on the graph), so we end up with 121 kts. The average headwind is 15 kts, so the groundspeed ends up as 121 - 15, or 106 kts. Over 7 minutes (0.15), you will have covered 12 miles in round figures.

CRUISE POWER, SPEED AND FUEL FLOW

Having climbed, you need to reduce power and lean the mixture. The table on the next page is used for fuel flow and expected IAS and TAS at many common power settings, pressure altitudes and temperatures. Table 2.2.3 (overleaf) is for 23 ins Hg and 2300 RPM, a typical cruising power for light aircraft.

 Details are given for ISA, +20° and -20° and every 2,000 feet of pressure altitude. Where full throttle is used, the table is shaded grey.

Let's find the fuel flow in PPH/GPH and expected airspeed at FL 90 if the forecast temperature is +7°C. The ISA temperature at FL90 should be -3°C, so +7° is ISA +10°. Figures are given for 8,000 feet and 10,000 feet pressure altitude, but not for 9,000 feet, so you must interpolate for temperature and pressure altitude. At ISA the fuel flow is 11.9 USG per hour (GPH) at 8,000 feet or 11.0 GPH at 10,000 feet. This is 71.1 lb per hour (PPH) and 66.2 PPH, respectively. At ISA +20° the figures are 11.4 GPH/68.5 PPH at 8,000 feet and 10.7 GPH/64.0 PPH at 10,000 feet. It is easiest to interpolate over two variables with a table, as shown below. First use one variable to find two results, then interpolate between them using the second variable.

In the table, the figures for 8,000 and 10,000 feet are interpolated to give figures for 9,000 feet, then the results for ISA and ISA+20° are interpolated to give an answer for ISA+10°.

	ISA	ISA +10	ISA +20
8,000 feet	71.1/11.9		68.5/11.4
9,000 feet	68.7/11.5	67.5/11.3	66.3/11.1
10,000 feet	66.2/11.0		64.0/10.7

The order of interpolation, temperature then pressure altitude or *vice versa* is not important in this case, because the temperature is halfway between ISA and ISA +20 and the pressure altitude halfway between 8,000 and 10,000 feet. However, if the temperature is less convenient to work with, start with altitude. In most cases, the fuel flow need only be calculated in PPH or GPH and not both, but the correct units should be chosen. A similar interpolation shown below can be used to calculate the likely airspeed, TAS or IAS (use the correct one!) The TAS is not strongly related to temperature.

	ISA	ISA +10	ISA +20
8,000 feet	145/160		140/160
9,000 feet	141/158	138/158	136/158
10,000 feet	137/157		132/156

FLIGHT PLANNING & MONITORING
Charts

Table 2.2.3: 23 Ins HG (full throttle) at 2300 RPM.

ISA DEV	Press Alt	Indicated OAT		MAP	Fuel Flow		Airspeed	
°C	Feet	°C	°F	Ins	PPH	GPH	KIAS	KTAS
-20	0	-3	26	23.0	67.6	11.3	152	144
	2,000	-7	20	23.0	69.7	11.6	152	149
	4,000	-11	13	23.0	72.1	12.0	153	154
	6,000	-15	6	23.0	74.4	12.4	153	158
	8,000	-18	-1	22.4	73.8	12.3	150	160
	10,000	-23	-9	20.7	68.4	11.4	143	157
	12,000	-27	-16	19.2	63.8	10.6	135	153
	14,000	-31	-23	17.8	60.0	10.0	127	148
	16,000	-35	-31	16.4	56.3	9.4	117	141
0	0	17	62	23.0	65.4	10.9	147	145
	2,000	13	56	23.0	67.4	11.2	147	149
	4,000	9	49	23.0	69.4	11.6	148	154
	6,000	5	42	23.0	71.7	12.0	148	159
	8,000	2	35	22.4	71.1	11.9	145	160
	10,000	-3	27	20.7	66.2	11.0	137	157
	12,000	-7	20	19.2	61.8	10.3	129	152
	14,000	-11	13	17.8	58.5	9.8	120	146
	16,000	-15	5	16.4	55.3	9.2	109	137
+20	0	37	98	23.0	63.2	10.5	142	145
	2,000	33	92	23.0	65.1	10.9	143	149
	4,000	29	85	23.0	67.1	11.2	143	154
	6,000	25	78	23.0	69.0	11.5	142	158
	8,000	22	71	22.4	68.5	11.4	140	160
	10,000	17	63	20.7	64.0	10.7	132	156
	12,000	13	56	19.2	60.0	10.0	123	151
	14,000	9	48	17.8	57.1	9.5	113	142
	16,000	-	-	-	-	-	-	-

RANGE WITH MAXIMUM FUEL

The range profile graph, Figure 2.4, below, provides the maximum range at different power settings. The curves show that range initially decreases with altitude but, at full throttle height, it increases again. They also show that range increases with lower power settings.

This is only for a takeoff with full fuel (check the top of the graph). Also, the range given takes into account 45 minutes of reserve fuel at economy cruise (i.e. low) power, which would equate to final reserve fuel.

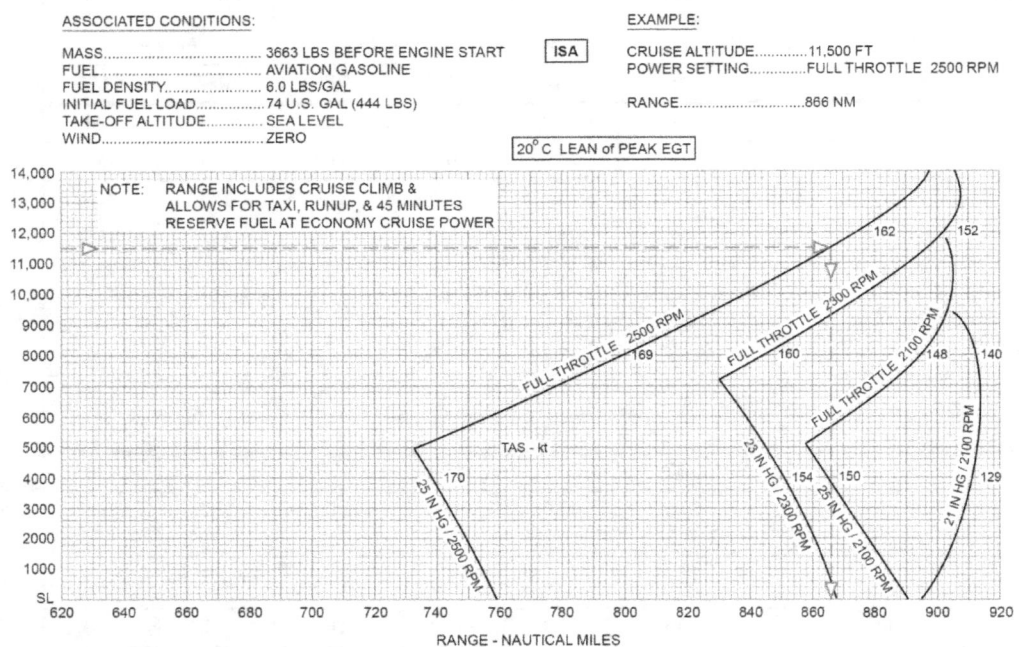

Picture Above: Figure 2.4

Picture Below: Figure 2.5 Endurance With Minimum Fuel

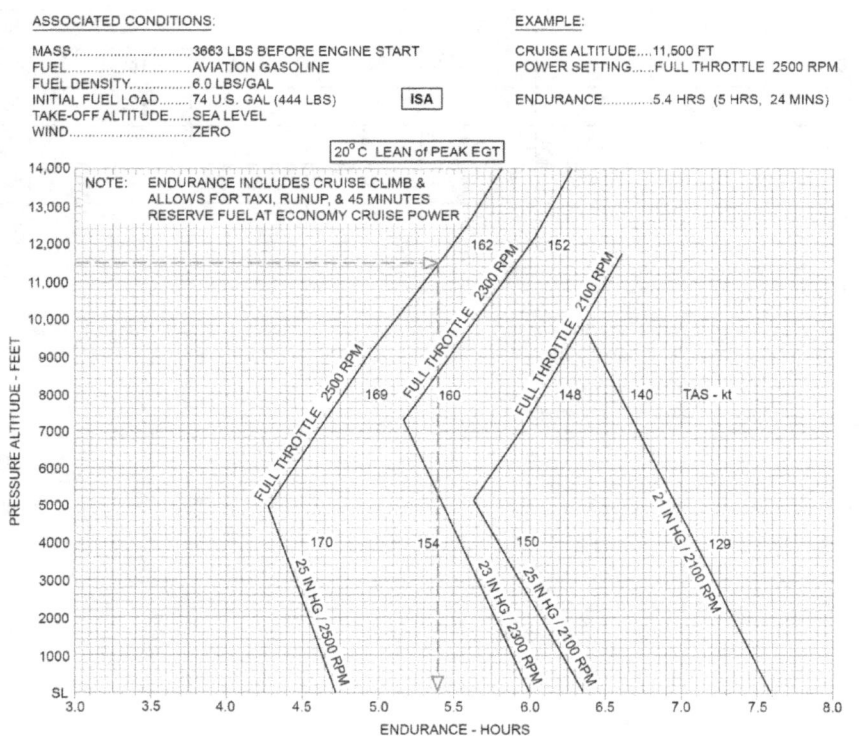

FLIGHT PLANNING & MONITORING
Charts

Stage		Temp °C	FL	ISA Dev °C	Wind		Tck °T	Hdg °T	TAS Kt	W/C Kt	G/S Kt	Dist	Time Min	F/Flow kg/hr	Fuel Usage		Fuel Reqd	Corr
From	To				Dir	Spd									Planned	Actual		
																Taxi		
A	TOC				270	15	270		120		105							
TOC	B		90		270	15	270		120		105	12	7		2.6			
B	C	7	90	10					158					11.3	11.3			
	TOD																	
TOD															Correction			
															Trip & Taxi			
															Contingency			
															Holding			
Alternate												30	30					
															Final Reserve			
															Block Fuel			

Picture: PLOG based on previous examples

For example, find the range of an aircraft cruising at FL 60 and 23 in. Hg at 2300 RPM in a 20 kt headwind. Enter the graph at 6,000 feet pressure altitude (temperature is not important) and trace across to the correct power line, then straight down to read off a range of 838 nm. This is the still air range, as wind has not been considered, so we need the TAS to correct for wind. On the graph, it is given as 154 kts at 4,000 feet PA and 160 kts at 8,000 feet, so at FL 60 it would appear that the TAS will be 159 kts*, so the groundspeed will be 139 kts.

*You cannot interpolate round a kink in the graph line, so refer back to the appropriate recommended cruise power table at the PA in the ISA sub-table.

The formula to calculate ground range (nautical ground miles, NGM) from still-air range (nautical air miles, NAM) in terms of groundspeed (GS) and true airspeed is:

$$NGM = \frac{NAM \times GS}{TAS}$$

$$733 \text{ nm} = \frac{838 \times 139}{159}$$

ENDURANCE WITH MAXIMUM FUEL

Figure 2.5 (above) shows the endurance with full fuel. It is used in the same way as the range graph in figure 2.4. The wind makes no difference.

 This table uses decimal hours.

DESCENT

Fuel consumption and time are the same as for the cruise, so ending the last leg over the destination is good enough.

FLIGHT PLANNING & MONITORING
Charts

Multi-Engined Piston

The graphs and tables are arranged in order of flight sequence, starting with takeoff and climb, then the cruise and range and endurance graphs. The final graph is for the descent and approach.

FUEL, TIME AND DISTANCE FOR CLIMB

Figure 3.1 is for the fuel used, time passing and still air distance covered during the climb to cruising altitude.

Like the SEP climb graph, the figures given relate to a climb from sea level, and can be corrected for a higher-level aerodrome by repeating the process with the airfield pressure altitude and air temperature.

 As with the Bonanza, the values of time and distance will lead to an incorrect TAS: Using the example in CAP 697, the extracted time of 24 minutes and air distance of 45 nm give a mean TAS in the climb of:

$$\frac{45 \times 60}{24} = 112 \text{ kts}$$

This is obviously wrong, as you should get a mean TAS of more than 120 kts as density reduces in the climb.

The moral: Use the flight computer with mean pressure altitude and temperature for MEP1 climb TAS.

Otherwise, the conditions for the graph are again at the top left; in this case the MAUW of 4 750 lbs is assumed.

	USG	Mins	nm
To FL 120	10.5	19	33
To 3,000 feet	2.5	5	8
3,000 feet - FL 120	8	14	25

For example, find the fuel and time taken to climb from an airfield at 3,000 feet PA to FL 120 if the temperature at the airfield is +10°C and the forecast temperature at FL120 is -20°C.

First, the climb from sea level to FL120. Follow up from -20°C to the 12,000-foot PA line, and across to each of the three lines fuel, time and distance, looking down to the scale from each. This should give a fuel of 10.5 USG, time 19 minutes and distance 33 nm (round the fuel up to the nearest sensible figure for safety). Use the same method to find the figures from sea level to 3,000 feet PA at +10°C, which should be 2.5 USG (this time round down for safety), 5 minutes and 8 nm. These figures must be subtracted from the climb figures to FL 120.

RANGE WITH FULL FUEL

Figure 3.2 is used to find the range of the aircraft with full fuel, including taxy take-off, climb, descent and landing. It is used in the same way as 3.5, overleaf. There are two sets of curves for various power settings. One set allows for 45 minutes reserves at

Picture Below: 3.1 - Time, Fuel & Distance To Climb

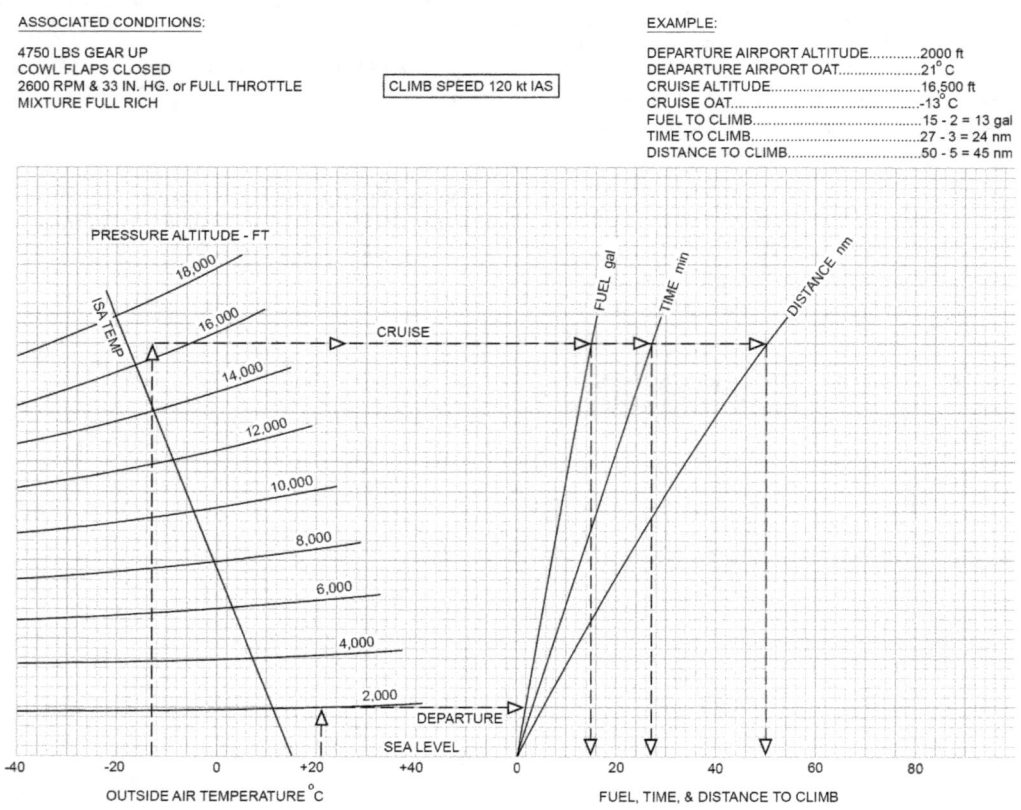

45% power* (45% is for minimum airborne power, so this gives final reserve fuel). The other set gives range to dry tanks.

*45% power only refers to the power setting for the 45 minutes' reserve. The power setting for the cruise is economy, given as 65% in the table at the top right.

Notice the top right corner, which gives the power settings for high speed, economy and long range cruise. These might be given instead of the percentage power setting. Also note that the range increases slightly for temperatures above ISA, and reduces for temperatures below and that there is no correction for wind; without the cruising TAS (see figure 3.4) the wind cannot be taken into account. For example find the range at FL120, at economy cruise with 45 minutes' reserve at 45% power if the temperature is forecast to be -20°C.

Following across from 12,000 feet to the 65% power line with 45 minutes' reserves at 45% power gives 765 nm range. ISA temperature at FL 120 is -9°C, so the COAT is 11° below ISA, and the range must be reduced by 11 nm. The range is therefore around 754 nm with 45 minutes' reserve fuel at 45% power.

CRUISE POWER SETTING AND FUEL FLOW

Figure 3.3 in CAP 697 is a table containing RPM and manifold absolute pressure (MAP) values to achieve certain power settings at various pressure altitudes and ISA temperature (a correction is given for temperature deviation from ISA - adjust by 1% for every 6°C). The most important part of the table is the second row, which gives the fuel flow at those power settings.

That fuel flow is independent of the RPM/MAP combination chosen to achieve the power and independent of altitude. For example at 65% power the fuel flow is always 23.3 U.S. gallons per hour. A minimum time flight would need more than this.

Cruise Manifold pressure must not exceed 34 ins.

TRUE AIRSPEED

Figure 3.4 gives the TAS expected at given pressure altitude, temperature and power setting.

For example the TAS at FL120 and -20°C given 65% (economy cruise) power is 176 kts.

ENDURANCE

Figure 3.5 gives the endurance of the aircraft with full fuel.

Like the range graph there are two sets of curves, one allowing for 45 minutes of reserves at 45% power, and the other giving total endurance. This is of more practical use than the graph of range with no reserves, as on the ATS flight plan endurance should always be given to dry tanks.

 Without Reserve exceeds *With Reserve* by 45 minutes only in the case of 45% power, as otherwise the power level is maintained above 45% during reserve time.

Picture Below: TAS Values (Figure 3.4)

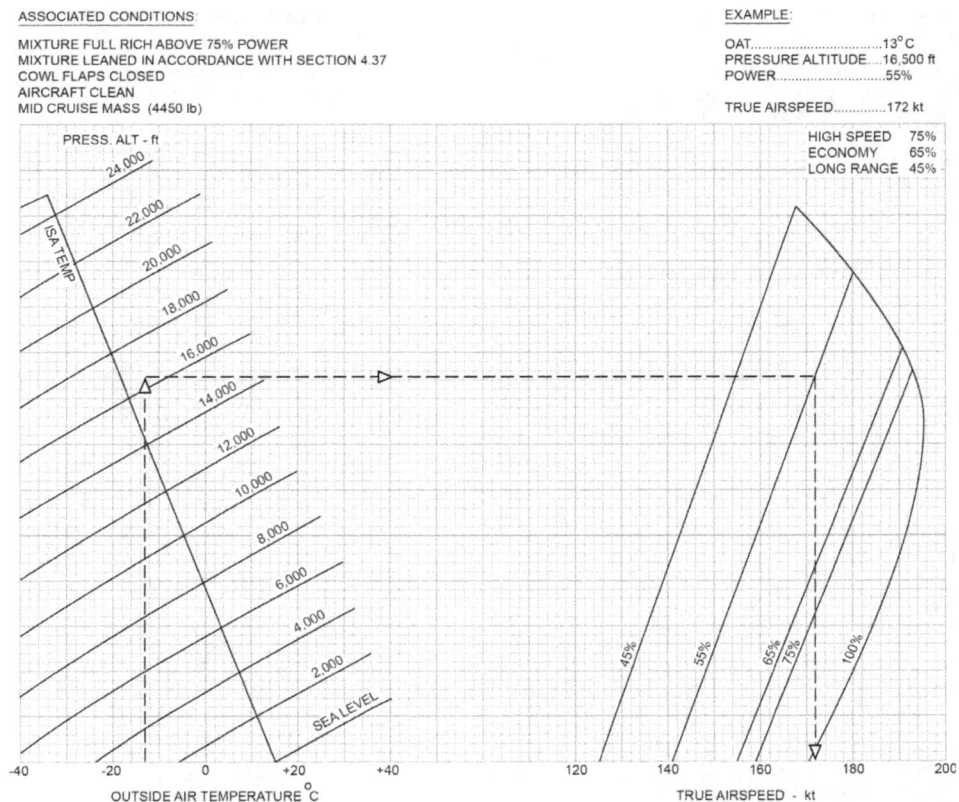

FLIGHT PLANNING & MONITORING
Charts

FUEL, TIME AND DISTANCE TO DESCEND

Figure 3.6 is for finding the fuel and time used for a standard descent to approach, and the distance covered.

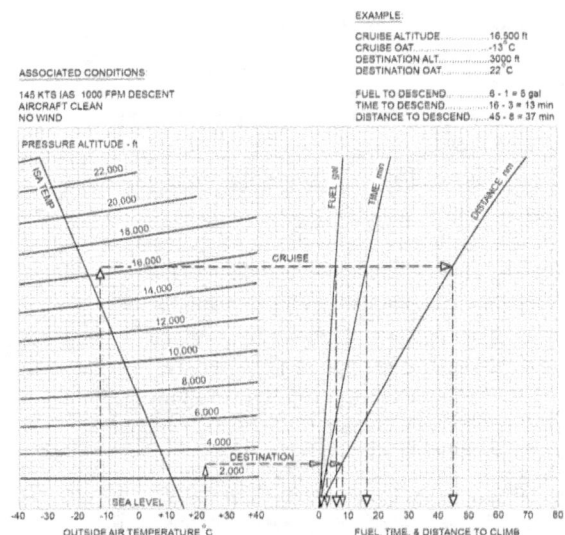

It is used in just the same way as figure 3.1 for the climb.

Medium Range Jet Transport (MRJT)

This is a medium-sized, twin-engined passenger jet with a range of around 3,000 nm (i.e. the Boeing 737-400).

 The figures on the first page of Section 4 of CAP 697 are for illustration. Although they are correct for the 737-400, the graphs extend beyond them and you can get answers that would be technically illegal or impossible. For example do not be surprised to find a fuel load greater than 16 145 kg, which is more than you can get into the tanks anyway!

OPTIMUM ALTITUDES

Each aircraft weight has an optimum altitude for the best fuel consumption, which can be found in Figure 4.1:

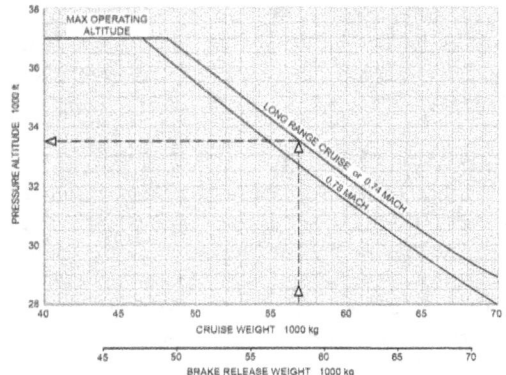

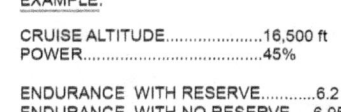

Below: Figure 3.5 - Endurance for MEP

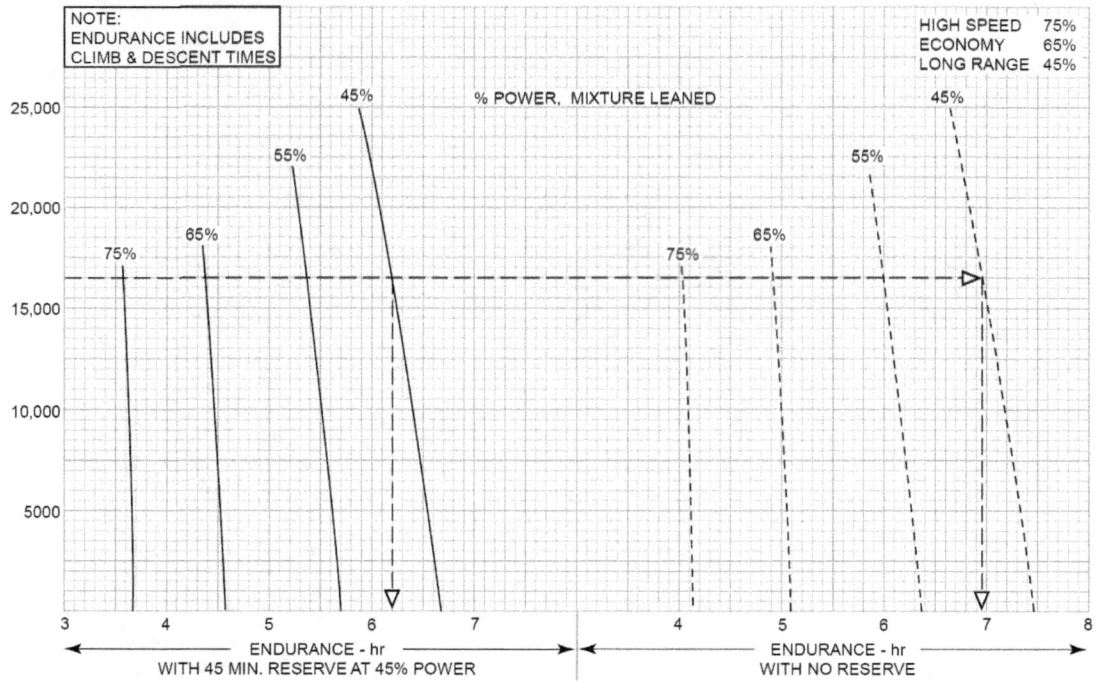

15-24 EASA Professional Pilot Studies © Phil Croucher, 2018

One curve covers the LRC and the normal cruise at 0.74M, and the second is for the high speed cruise at 0.78M. It also shows the maximum altitude of 37,000 feet. In either case, the optimum altitude increases as the aircraft weight decreases.

Going above the optimum reduces the buffet boundaries and flying below it increases the fuel burn and will result in a fuel mileage penalty as shown in Table 4.1:

Off-Condition	Fuel Mileage Penalty%	
	LRC or 0.74 M	0.78 M
2,000 ft above	-1	-1
Optimum	0	0
2,000 ft below	-1	-2
4,000 ft below	-4	-4
8,000 ft below	-10	-11
12,000 ft below	-15	-20

You will need to interpolate for odd amounts - for example, if you were 3,900 feet below the optimum altitude, you would deduct 1% for the first 2,000 feet, then take a proportion of the remainder. In this case, the answer would be 3.85%.

 There are two axes - the most commonly used is the bottom one, the Brake Release Weight, or Takeoff Mass. It is only marked at intervals of 5,000 kg so interpolate as accurately as possible.

To find the optimum initial cruising altitude at Mach 0.78 for an aircraft with a TOM of 62,000 kg, go from the bottom scale at that weight to the 0.78 Mach line, then across for the optimum PA, which is 31,300 feet.

Tip: Go for an initial cruising altitude above the optimum rather than below. As fuel is burnt (at around 2,500 kg per hour, depending on weight, altitude and speed) and the aircraft becomes lighter, the optimum altitude increases, so if you choose slightly higher one from the start, this soon becomes the optimum. Remember also that the semi-circular cruising rule might demand a flight level that is dependent on the magnetic track. In this example, the obvious cruising level is FL320 for Westerly tracks or FL 330 for Easterly ones. However, for non-RVSM airspace, FL 310 or 350 would be used to the East, depending on the expected flight time at that level - 350 will not become optimum for over 3 three hours, so there is no point being there for less than an hour and a half.

Short Distance Cruise Altitude

If the trip is too short to get to the optimum altitude anyway*, you might use more fuel in the climb than you might save over the time involved. The Short Distance Cruise Altitude chart (Fig 4.2) takes into account the weight reduction from using fuel over a whole journey, so you would choose the closest available flight level, whether it is above or below the optimum level:

This is the first graph that has a reference line crossing a set of fan lines. The simple rule is to trace to the reference line first, then follow the fan lines. This graph can be used in reverse for some questions so be careful!

*The 737 takes about 90 nm to go up and 90 nm to come down again.

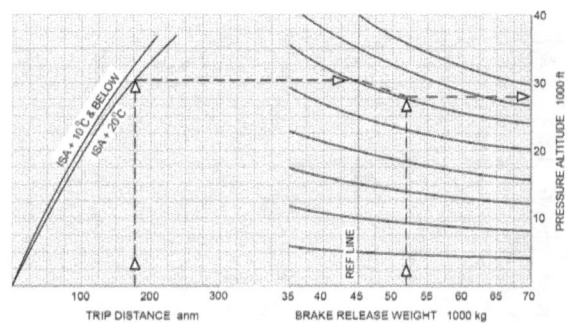

For a 120 nm flight in ISA conditions with a BRW of 55 200 kg, enter the graph at 120 nm, go up to the line for ISA + 10°C and below. Follow across to the reference line then follow the fan lines to a weight of 55,200 kg, then go straight across to read an optimum PA of 21,000 feet, which would be good for Easterly tracks. FL 200 or 220 would be used for Westerly tracks.

Note that the table uses air miles!

SIMPLIFIED FUEL PLANNING

Simplified tables allow you to get a fuel value for a whole flight in a hurry, at the expense of a small fuel penalty. There are several graphs and/or tables associated with this, relating to different trip distances, and two of them might often cover the same situation, in which case just use the one with the shortest maximum trip distance.

In CAP 697, graphs 4.3.1 to 4.3.6 are used for simplified fuel planning and trip times. 4.3.1 to 4.3.4 are the standard ones, compiled for various speeds. 4.3.5 is for a stepped climb, giving the greatest range. The technique is to climb to the next available level above optimum and then, as fuel burn brings the optimum level to half way between the current level and the next higher semi-circular one, to climb to that level, ensuring that the aircraft is always as close as practicable to the optimum level. The graph has no fan lines for level, as that is determined by weight. Instead the main fan lines are for brake-release weight.

Figure 4.3.6 for alternate planning is very similar, but instead of brake-release weight, it uses the landing weight at the alternate, which should include final reserve and contingency fuel. This table lists the fuel included as alternate fuel as missed approach, climb to cruising altitude, descent and straight-in approach. This is the operational requirement, with no allowance for a missed approach at the alternate.

This is the only graph that mentions the word alternate!

ADJUSTMENTS

If you plan to use the FMS in ECON Mode, adjust the **cost index** as follows:

Cost Index	Fuel	Time %
0	-1	+4
20	+1	+1
40	+2	-1
60	+4	-2
80	+5	-3
100	+7	-4
150	+10	-5
200	+14	-7

On the ground, the APU fuel flow is 115 kg per hour and you use 11 kg per minute while taxying.

Flying at a **non-optimum altitude** results in fuel penalties already discussed above.

In the **cruise**, increase trip fuel by 1% with the air conditioning at high flow. With anti-ice on the engines only add 70 kg/hour. For engines and wings add 180 kg/hour.

In the **descent**, simplified charts assume 0.74 M/250 KIAS and a straight-in approach. For every additional minute with the flaps down, add 75 kg fuel. if you use anti-icing, add 50 kg.

When **holding**, use this table (4.4 in full in CAP 697):

PA ft	WEIGHT x 1,000 kg				
	66	64	62	60	58
	FUEL FLOW kg/hr				
37,000					2740
35,000		3020	2820	2660	2520
3,0000	2840	2740	2660	2560	2480
25,000	2840	2760	2660	2580	2500
2,0000	2840	2760	2680	2580	2500
15,000	2880	2800	2700	2620	2540
1,0000	2920	2820	2740	2660	2580
5,000	2960	2860	2780	2700	2620
1500	3,000	2900	2820	2740	2660

It gives the fuel flow expected at minimum drag speed* in a racetrack holding pattern at various altitudes, which is useful for calculating final reserve fuel, in which case calculate the pressure altitude 1,500 feet above the alternate (or destination if no alternate is required). For the next lower altitude find the figure for the weight at the alternate, interpolating if necessary.

*210 KIAS is the minimum in any case.

For example, if the weight at the alternate is 51,000 kg and the aerodrome pressure altitude is 4 300 feet, then 1 500 feet above aerodrome elevation is 5 800 feet PA. Using the 5,000-foot line will give a figure that errs on the safe side. At 50,000 kg the fuel flow is 2 300 kg per hour and at 52,000 kg it is 2 380 kg per hour. Interpolating for 51,000 kg the fuel flow is 2 340 kg per hour. Of course final reserve fuel is 30 minutes, so half of this at 1 170 kg. Apply the holding time to the fuel flow to get the total required.

Reduce the figures by 5% if the hold is to be conducted in straight and level flight.

EXAMPLE

Using Figure 4.3.1a, find the fuel used and time taken over 500 nm at FL 290 with a 40-kt average tailwind with a planned landing weight of 58,000 kg and a temperature of ISA +20°.

Enter the graph (see overleaf) at 500 nm and follow straight up to the reference line for winds. Track the wind fan lines back down and left to 40 kts tailwind, then track straight up again to the fan line for FL290 and straight across to the landing-weight reference line. Trace the fan line up to 58,000 kg, Fuel required is 3 450 kg.

To find the flight time, trace through the wind in exactly the same way but carry on through the first set of PA fan lines to the second set (just two lines in this case), estimate an interpolation for FL 290 and trace across to the temperature-deviation reference line. Follow the guidelines to ISA+20°C to find a time of 1 hour, 12 minutes (each tiny square is three minutes).

The other simplified graphs work in much the same way.

EXAMPLE

Using the Jeppesen Route Manual chart E(HI)4 (just to make life interesting), for a flight from Paris (N49 00.9 E002 36.9) to Heathrow (N51 29.2 W,000 27.9) in a twin jet, with Manchester (N53 21.4 W002 15.7) as an alternate. The wind from London to Manchester is 250°/30 kts, over 160 nm. The estimated landing mass at Manchester is about 50,000 kg. Determine fuel and time to the alternate.

As mentioned, there is only one alternate planning graph for the MRJT, and it's on page 16 of the MRJT section. The only information that is missing is the track which can be measured from the Jeppesen chart as 330(T). Using the square section of the flight computer gives you a 5 kt headwind. A 50,000 kg landing mass from the graph gives you 1450 kg & 32 minutes' flight time.

EN-ROUTE CLIMB

Figure 4.5.1 has four tables, depending on the mean ISA deviation. Between ISA-6°C and ISA-16°C, use the first one. Each table gives values for time and fuel used to climb, distance covered and TAS at various brake-release weights, plus climb to various pressure altitudes. They assume the aeroplane to be instantaneously at the PA of the table at an AUW of 67,900 kg with a traffic load of 32,900 kg, which includes full tanks of 16,145 kg.

In each case, for a given weight and climb altitude, the box has all four pieces of information arranged as below.

Some interpolation might be needed for different weights, but only fuel is corrected for PA at the departure aerodrome.

	Time / Fuel Distance / TAS	

For example, find the time and fuel for a climb from 5,000 feet PA to FL 330 if the forecast for FL 330 is a COAT of -44° and the brake-release weight is 57,000 kg. ISA at FL330 is -50°C, meaning ISA+6°, so use the third table. Enter with your cruise altitude and BRW. Convert NAM to NGM as follows:

$$NGM = \frac{NAM \times GS}{TAS}$$

Adjust as necessary for field elevation.

Figure 4.5.1: Enroute Climb 280/.74

	ISA +6°C TO +15°C								
	BRAKE RELASASE WEIGHT (KG)								
PA ft	68,000	66,000	64,000	62,000	6,0000	58,000	56,000	52,000	48,000
37,000	Time/Fuel Dist/TAS			33/2350 212/409	27/2,000 169/404	24/1850 147/402	22/1700 132/400	18/1500 111/397	16/1300 95/396
36,000			30/2250 189/405	26/2,000 161/402	23/1650 143/400	21/1700 130/398	20/1600 119/397	17/1400 102/395	15/1250 89/393
35,000	35/2600 224/407	29/2250 180/402	26/2050 157/399	23/1900 141/397	21/1750 129/396	20/1650 119/395	19/1550 110/394	16/1350 95/392	14/1200 83/391
34,000	28/2250 173/400	25/2050 154/397	23/1900 140/395	21/1800 128/394	20/1650 118/393	19/1550 110/392	18/1500 102/391	16/1300 89/389	14/1200 78/388
33,000	25/2100 151/394	23/1950 138/393	21/1800 127/391	20/1700 118/390	19/1600 109/389	18/1500 102/388	17/1450 95/388	15/1300 84/386	13/1150 74/385
32,000	23/1950 136/390	21/1850 126/389	20/1750 117/388	19/1650 109/387	18/1550 102/386	17/1450 95/385	16/1400 89/384	14/1250 79/383	13/1100 70/383
31,000	22/1850 125/386	20/1750 116/385	19/1650 108/384	18/1550 101/383	17/1500 95/382	16/1400 89/382	15/1350 84/381	13/1200 74/380	12/1100 66/380
3,0000	20/1800 115/382	19/1700 108/381	18/1600 101/380	17/1500 95/379	16/1450 89/379	15/1350 84/378	14/1300 77/378	13/1150 70/377	12/1050 62/376
29,000	19/1700 105/376	18/1600 98/376	17/1550 92/375	16/1450 87/374	15/1400 82/374	14/1300 77/374	14/1250 73/373	12/1150 65/373	11/1,000 58/372
28,000	17/1600 95/371	17/1550 90/371	16/1450 84/370	15/1400 80/370	14/1300 75/369	13/1250 71/369	13/1200 67/369	12/1100 60/368	10/1,000 54/368

At FL330 the figures give 18 minutes using 1500 kg of fuel and covering 102 nautical air miles (NAM) at 58,000 kg and 17 minutes using 1450 kg and covering 95 NAM at 56,000 kg, at a mean TAS of 388 kts in both cases. For 57,000 kg then the time will be about 17.5 minutes, the distance covered approximately 98 nm using 1475 kg of fuel. However to correct for the initial elevation there is a sub-table at the bottom of the page. The adjustment for a climb from 5,000 feet is -150 kg, for a final fuel usage of 1325 kg.

Tip: If you cannot interpolate between the fan lines, follow them both to their logical conclusion and interpolate between the results.

INTEGRATED CRUISE

The integrated method of fuel planning breaks the flight down into components, so it can reduce the fuel penalty involved with the simplified method.

The figures in each column show the air distance that could be flown to dry tanks for each listed gross weight. They are listed at 100 kg intervals, although you should interpolate for the exact weight of the aeroplane. They represent the range that the aircraft would have to dry tanks at that level and speed if all the weight above 35,000 kg consisted of fuel, i.e. if the zero-fuel mass was 35,000 kg. That is why the value for 35,000 kg is zero. The fuel needed for a leg is determined by subtracting the end of leg weight from the start of leg weight.

To do this, given the length of the leg (in NAM) and the weight of the aircraft at the beginning, look in the table at that weight (thousands of kilograms down the side, then across the row to the appropriate hundreds). Note the start of leg air distance, then subtract the leg air distance to determine the end of leg air distance. Enter the table to find the leg air distance and the end of leg weight equivalent to the distance (some interpolation might be required). The difference between the two weights gives you the fuel burn.

EXAMPLE

Find the TAS and the fuel required over a distance of 500 NGM at Mach 0.74 at FL 290, with a 50 kt headwind and a temperature of ISA -30°C. The mass of the aircraft at the start of the cruise is 54,500 kg.

 The table (4.5.3.2, found after the next page) uses **Nautical Air Miles** (NAM). You must convert any NGM values in a question.

The steps are:

- **1. Find the TAS**. In Figure 4.5.3.2, as shown overleaf, this turns out to be 408 knots, which is derived from the figure at the top of the table* (438 knots) and the adjustments for non-standard temperature (see Note 2 at the bottom about adding or subtracting 1 kt per °C above or below ISA conditions). You have to subtract 30 knots.

  *The exception is for LRC, because the speed changes to reflect the weight of the aircraft. In those tables the speed is in the second column.

- **2. Find the NAM value**. The formula is:

  $$\frac{TAS}{GS} = \frac{NAM}{NGM}$$

  Which translates to:

  $$\frac{408}{358} = \frac{NAM}{500}$$

  The result is 570 NAM, give or take.

  It's a proportion problem, so it can easily be done on the flight computer.

  Tip: Figure 4.5.2 in CAP 697 converts NAM to NGM and vice versa, but it is hard to be accurate due to the closeness of the gridlines.

- **3.** Enter the table with the start weight of the aircraft to find the cruise NAM of 3,629 NAM. The extreme left column gives you the basic 54,000 and the value for the extra 500 is in the 6th column of the cruise distance.

- **4.** Subtract the NAM figure derived above to get the NAM at the end of the cruise of 3,059.

- **5.** Now you need to work backwards by looking for 3,059 in the tables. 3,053 can be found, which is 6 less than the end of leg value, or $^6/_{18}$ of 1100 kg, meaning 17 kg less for 51,217 kg at the end of leg.

- **6.** The difference between how heavy you were at the start of the cruise and the end is 3,283 kg (54,500 - 51,217), the fuel required. Under Note 2 at the bottom of the chart, this should be adjusted by 0.6% per 10°C above or below ISA conditions which, in this case, means reducing it by 1.8%. the corrected fuel required is 3,283 - 59 = 3,224 kg.

All Engines, A/C Auto, Max Cruise Thrust Limits.

Notes: At the bottom of the table in CAP 697, Note 1 can usually be ignored, but you **must** take note of the speed adjustments, of 1 kt per °C above or below ISA conditions in Note 2. Apply the fuel corrections (in Note 2) as well.

A variation to the usual questions about integration tables is to find the specific fuel consumption, or the fuel required divided by distance flown over the ground. Another is being given a straight temperature to be converted to an ISA deviation. A light and variable wind means that the NAM and NGM values will be equal. If you are given flight time, calculate distance as normal.

Planning a flight with a given load might mean that you know the weight at the end rather than the beginning of the leg. The fuel burn can be found in a similar way, except that the leg length must be *added* to the NAM figure in the table to calculate the figure for the start of the leg. This can be looked up, and again the difference between the two figures gives the leg fuel burn.

Examples

1. The gross mass at the TOC is 61,500 kg. The distance to be flown is 385 nm at FL 350 and the OAT -54.3°C. With a 40 kt tailwind, using the LRC procedure, what fuel is required?

Long Range Cruise at FL 350 means using Figure 4.5.3.1 in the MRJT section of CAP 697.

 The writers of some questions give an off-optimum altitude range penalty of 6%, then use the integrated range tables, and apply the 6% penalty again, apparently blissfully unaware that this is already accounted for in the table, which is the whole point of it!

The TAS is 429 kts (against the aircraft weight down the left hand side). Convert the 385 NGM into 352 NAM, as the tables work in air miles (there is a tail wind). TOC mass of 61 500 kg gives an air distance of 5313 NAM - 352 = 4961 NAM. Enter the table looking for 4961 (about half way between 4954 & 4971 which equates to 59 350 kg. 61 500 - 59 350 = 2 150 kg. Simples!

2. Find the fuel to fly a 440 nm leg at FL 310 in the long range cruise if the temperature is -26°C and the weight at the beginning of the leg is 56 200 kg.

The first thing to do is find how far the leg is in air miles. The TAS at around 56,000 kg is given in the second column as 437 kts. However -26° is 20 degrees above ISA so 20 kts must be added, to give a TAS of 457 kts. With a 50-kt headwind the groundspeed is 407 kts.

$$494 \text{ NAM} = \frac{440 \times 457}{407}$$

Looking up 56,200 kg on the table gives a distance of 4,169 NAM. Subtract the leg distance from this figure gives 3,675 NAM. Looking up 3,675 in the table gives a weight of 53,400. The difference between this and 56,200 kg is 2,800 kg, so this means that in flying that distance the aircraft became 2,800 kg lighter, i.e. it burnt 2,800 kg of fuel.

A correction of 1.2% must be made for the temperature being 20° above ISA, so the total fuel used is 2834 kg.

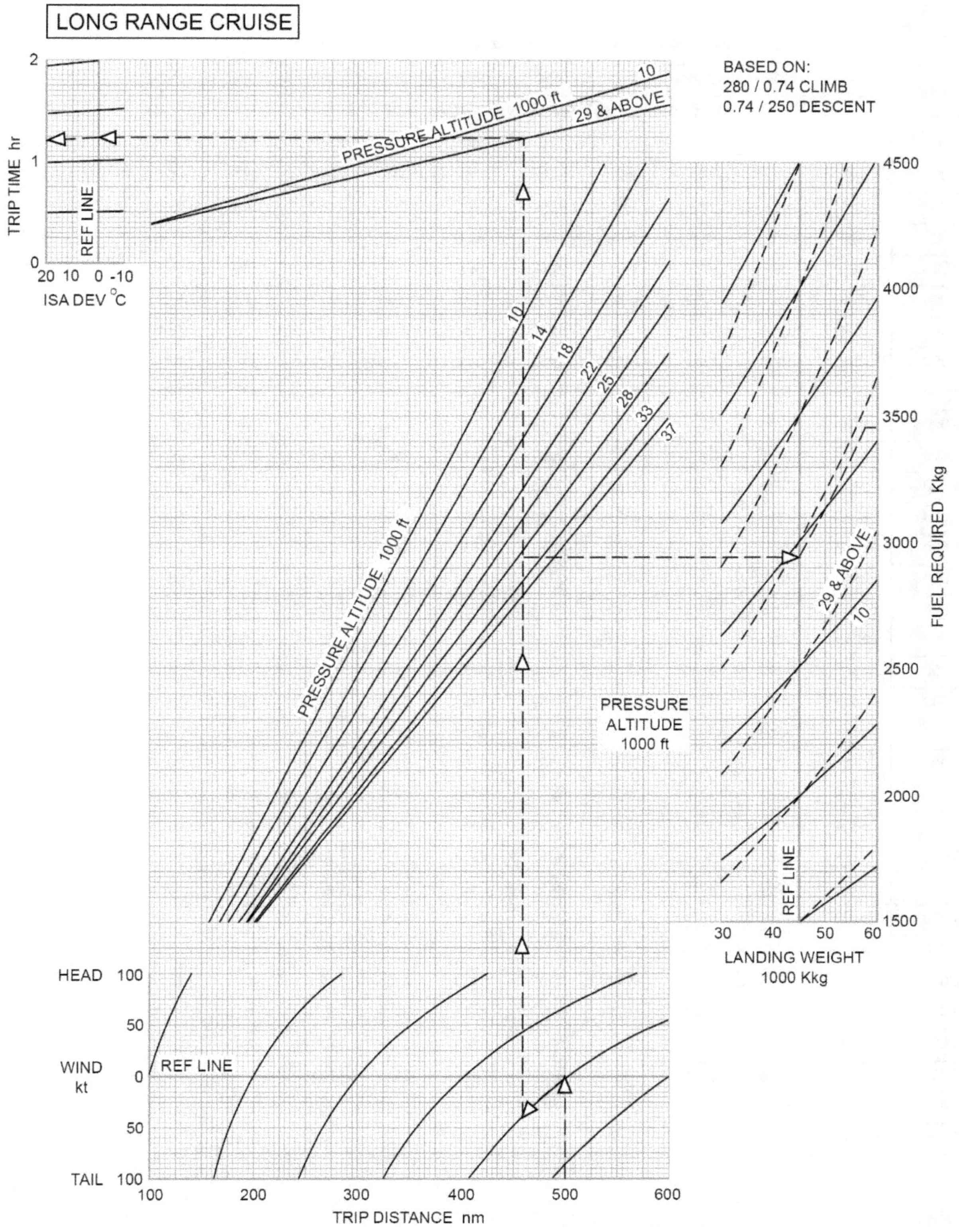

FLIGHT PLANNING & MONITORING
Charts

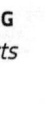

Figure 4.3.1a from CAP 697

Figure 4.5.3.2 from CAP 697

GROSS WT kg	0	100	200	300	400	500	600	700	800	900
PA 29,000 feet - Mach 0.74 Cruise - TAS 438 kts										
				CRUISE DISTANCE NAUTICAL AIR MILES						
35,000	0	19	39	59	79	98	118	138	158	178
36,000	197	217	237	256	276	296	315	335	355	375
37,000	394	414	433	453	473	492	512	531	551	570
38,000	590	609	629	648	668	687	707	726	746	765
39,000	785	804	823	843	862	881	901	920	939	959
4,0000	978	997	1017	1036	1055	1074	1093	1113	1132	1151
41,000	1170	1189	1209	1228	1247	1266	1285	1304	1323	1342
42,000	1361	1380	1399	1418	1437	1456	1475	1494	1513	1532
43,000	1551	1570	1589	1608	1626	1645	1664	1683	1702	1721
44,000	1739	1758	1777	1795	1814	1833	1852	1870	1889	1908
45,000	1926	1945	1963	1982	2001	2019	2038	2056	2075	2093
46,000	2112	2130	2149	2167	2186	2204	2222	2241	2259	2278
47,000	2296	2314	2333	2351	2369	2387	2406	2424	2442	2461
48,000	2479	2497	2515	2533	2551	2569	2588	2606	2624	2642
49,000	2660	2678	2696	2714	2732	2750	2768	2786	2804	2822
5,0000	2840	2858	2875	2893	2911	2929	2947	2964	2982	3,000
51,000	3018	3036	3053	3071	3089	3106	3124	3142	3159	3177
52,000	3195	3212	3230	3247	3265	3282	3300	3317	3335	3352
53,000	3370	3387	3404	3422	3439	3456	3474	3491	3508	3526
54,000	3543	3560	3578	3595	3612	3629	3646	3664	3681	3698
55,000	3715	3732	3749	3766	3783	3800	3817	3834	3851	3868
56,000	3885	3902	3919	3936	3953	3970	3987	4003	4020	4037
57,000	4054	4071	4087	4104	4121	4137	4154	4171	4187	4204
58,000	4221	4237	4254	4270	4287	4303	4320	4337	4353	4370
59,000	4386	4402	4419	4435	4451	4468	4484	4501	4517	4533
6,0000	4550	4566	4582	4598	4614	4630	4647	4663	4679	4695
61,000	4711	4727	4743	4759	4775	4791	4807	4823	4839	4855
62,000	4871	4887	4903	4919	4935	4950	4966	4982	4998	5014
63,000	5030	5045	5061	5077	5092	5108	5123	5139	5155	5170
64,000	5186	5202	5217	5233	5248	5263	5279	5294	5310	5325
65,000	5341	5356	5371	5387	5402	5417	5433	5448	5463	5479
66,000	5494	5509	5524	5539	5554	5569	5585	5600	5615	5630
67,000	5645	5660	5675	5690	5705	5720	5735	5750	5765	5780

DESCENT

Although you have to come down anyway, the descent should be properly planned, as you want to keep flying as high as possible for as long as possible. Coming down too early increases the fuel burn and coming down too late causes problems in the passenger cabin.

There are two tables for descent, one used on most flights for Mach 0.74 then 250 kts IAS, the other at turbulence-penetration speed, which is lower than the normal descent at Mach 0.70, with a higher IAS of 280 kts at the start. This is to keep a greater margin below M_{MO}, with a greater margin above stall speed.

The table gives time and fuel to descend from various levels, as well as distance covered at different weights.

For example, calculate the figures for a descent from the cruise at FL310 to FL50 if the landing weight is 50,000 kg at economy descent with an average 20-kt headwind.

From 31,000 feet the time would be 20 minutes, using 280 kg of fuel and covering 95 NAM. From 5,000 feet would be 6 minutes, 140 kg of fuel and 18 NAM.

Subtracting the figures for 5,000 feet from those for 31,000 feet:

	Mins	Fuel / kg	NAM
FL310	20	280	95
FL50	6	140	18
FL310 - FL50	14	140	77

However the notes state that figures have an allowance for landing of 2 minutes and 100 kg of fuel, so subtracting one from the other has removed the allowance. This needs to be put back in, giving 16 minutes, 240 kg of fuel and 77 NAM. The headwind has therefore affected the aircraft for 16 minutes, which at 20 kts will reduce the distance covered by 5 nm, giving 72 NGM.

NON-NORMAL OPERATION

Figure 4.6.1 concerns simplified flight planning for a ferry flight with gear extended. It works in exactly the same way as the main simplified flight-planning graphs.

CRITICAL FUEL RESERVES

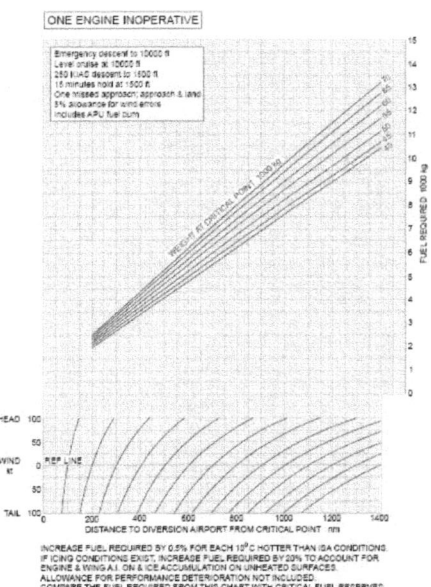

There are two graphs used to calculate the fuel required to reach an alternate at FL100. The first is with one engine inoperative (4.7.1a below), the second with both engines operating. These are used to calculate whether additional fuel is required (see the section on fueling for the requirements of additional fuel). The calculation would be made from the most critical point in a flight a long way from a suitable alternate. In principle both graphs should be consulted and the more restrictive figure, the higher one, used as minimum fuel to have on board at the most critical

point. In practice the aircraft uses more fuel with both engines operating unless there is a strong headwind, so the second graph almost always gives the correct figure.

Start at the bottom with the distance to the diversion from the Critical Point, or PET. Move to the reference line then parallel the fan lines to intersect with the wind component. Then move vertically to the aircraft mass line, and horizontally right to read the fuel required.

IN-FLIGHT DIVERSION DISTANCE

At all times a twin-engined performance-class A aircraft must be within 60 minutes flight time in still air of a suitable alternate with one engine operating. If the aircraft, crew and operator are certified for extended-range twin operations (ETOPS) that time can be extended to a figure given by that certification, up to 180 minutes.

Figure 4.7.2 is used to determine the maximum distance that the aircraft can be flown from a suitable alternate either for the non-ETOPS case or for any given ETOPS time. Hence the table gives time from 60 minutes.

We can calculate the maximum distance from a suitable alternate considering an aircraft at 48,000 kg to be flown at Mach 0.74 then 310 kts after transition, for both the non-ETOPS case and for an ETOPS certification for 130 minutes. The easiest error to make is to look at the lines for the wrong speeds. In this case the figures seem to be about 413 nm for a 60-minute diversion time, without ETOPS, and about 868 nm for 130-minute ETOPS.

A simplified flight-planning graph for planning after an engine failure is then given in figure 4.7.3.

FUEL TANKERING

If fuel is more expensive at the destination and the aircraft is not already at maximum take-off weight it might be worth carrying more fuel than strictly necessary, to avoid spending too much money.

To find out whether it is worth tankering, two graphs are used. The first determines how much of the extra fuel will be burnt just to carry that fuel, and the second determines from that figure and the fuel prices at each end whether it is cost-effective. It does this by calculating the break-even price at the destination, i.e. the price at which it costs as much to carry fuel as the extra price to buy it. If the destination price is higher, it is financially worth tankering, and vice versa.

On a 1900 nm trip at Mach 0.74 and FL350, landing at 45,000 kg, at what destination fuel price is it worth tankering, given a price of $0.90 at the departure point?

Carrying the surplus fuel on that trip will burn 17.2% of that fuel. Use this figure to enter the graph on figure 4.8.2, and move up to the fuel price at departure on the fan lines. Read across to the left-hand scale to give a break-even fuel price at the destination.

In this case it is worth tankering fuel if the price at the destination airport is greater than 109 cents per gallon.